Elementary Statistics

Custom Edition for Chemeketa Community College

Taken from:
Elementary Statistics, 12th Edition
by Mario F. Triola

Statistics: The Art and Science of Learning from Data, 3rd Edition
by Alan Agresti and Christine Franklin

Stats: Data and Models, 3rd Edition
by Richard D. De Veaux, Paul F. Velleman, and David E. Bock

Pearson Learning Solutions, 501 Boylston Street, Suite 900, Boston, MA 02116
A Pearson Education Company
www.pearsoned.com

Printed in the United States of America

1 2 3 4 5 6 7 8 9 10 0BRV 17 16 15 14 13

000200010271849168

CW

ISBN 10: 1-269-60411-2
ISBN 13: 978-1-269-60411-6

About the Author

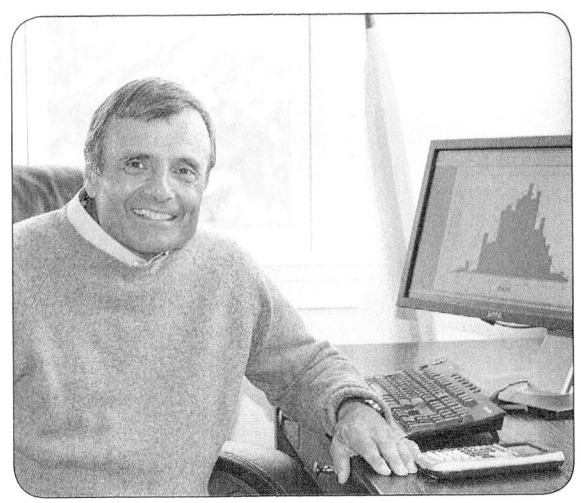

Mario F. Triola is a Professor Emeritus of Mathematics at Dutchess Community College, where he has taught statistics for over 30 years. Marty is the author of *Essentials of Statistics*, 4th edition, *Elementary Statistics Using Excel*, 5th edition, *Elementary Statistics Using the TI-83/84 Plus Calculator*, 3rd edition, and he is a co-author of *Biostatistics for the Biological and Health Sciences, Statistical Reasoning for Everyday Life*, 4th edition, *Business Statistics*, and *Introduction to Technical Mathematics*, 5th edition. *Elementary Statistics* is currently available as an International Edition, and it has been translated into several foreign languages. Marty designed the original STATDISK statistical software, and he has written several manuals and workbooks for technology supporting statistics education. He has been a speaker at many conferences and colleges. Marty's consulting work includes the design of casino slot machines and fishing rods, and he has worked with attorneys in determining probabilities in paternity lawsuits, analyzing data in medical malpractice lawsuits, identifying salary inequities based on gender, and analyzing disputed election results. He has also used statistical methods in analyzing medical school surveys, and analyzing survey results for the New York City Transit Authority. Marty has testified as an expert witness in New York State Supreme Court. The Text and Academic Authors Association has awarded Marty a "Texty" for Excellence for his work on *Elementary Statistics*.

Contents

Taken from: *Elementary Statistics*, 12th Edition, by Mario F. Triola.

Statistics: The Art and Science of Learning from Data, 3rd Edition, by Alan Agresti and Christine Franklin.

Stats: Data and Models, 3rd Edition, by Richard D. DeVeaux, Paul F. Velleman, and David E. Bock.

Preface

This Twelfth Edition was written with several goals:

- To provide an abundance of new and interesting data sets, examples, and exercises.
- To foster personal growth of students through critical thinking, use of technology, collaborative work, and development of communication skills.
- To incorporate the latest and best methods used by professional statisticians.
- To include information personally helpful to students, such as the best job search methods and the importance of avoiding mistakes on résumés.
- To provide the largest and best set of supplements to enhance teaching and learning.

GAISE This book reflects recommendations from the American Statistical Association and its *Guidelines for Assessment and Instruction in Statistics Education* (GAISE). Those guidelines suggest the following objectives and strategies.

1. **Emphasize statistical literacy and develop statistical thinking:** Each section exercise set begins with *Statistical Literacy and Critical Thinking* exercises. Many of the book's exercises are designed to encourage statistical thinking rather than the blind use of mechanical procedures.

2. **Use real data:** 91% of the examples and 89% of the exercises use real data.

3. **Stress conceptual understanding rather than mere knowledge of procedures:** Instead of seeking simple numerical answers, exercises and examples involve conceptual understanding through questions that encourage practical interpretations of results. Also, each chapter includes a *Data to Decision* project.

4. **Foster active learning in the classroom:** Each chapter ends with several *Cooperative Group Activities*.

5. **Use technology for developing conceptual understanding and analyzing data:** Computer software displays are included throughout the book. Special *Using Technology* subsections include instruction for using the software. Each chapter includes a *Technology Project*. When there are discrepancies between answers based on tables and answers based on technology, Appendix D provides *both* answers. The CD-ROM included with the book includes instructions for downloading free text-specific software (STATDISK) and data sets formatted for several different technologies, which are also listed in Appendix B.

6. **Use assessments to improve and evaluate student learning:** Assessment tools include an abundance of section exercises, Chapter Quick Quizzes, Chapter Review Exercises, Cumulative Review Exercises, technology projects, "Data to Decision" projects, and Cooperative Group Activity projects.

Audience/Prerequisites

Elementary Statistics is written for students majoring in any subject. Algebra is used minimally, but students should have completed at least a high school or college elementary algebra course. In many cases, underlying theory is included, but this book does not require the mathematical rigor more suitable for mathematics majors.

Changes in This Edition

As in previous editions, this twelfth edition includes a substantial revision of examples, exercises, and Chapter Problems, as shown in the following table:

	Number	New to This Edition	Use Real Data
Exercises	1851	85% (1582)	89% (1640)
Examples	227	84% (191)	91% (206)
Chapter Problems	14	100% (14)	100% (14)

Organization

New Section Section 15-1: "Ethics in Statistics," discusses ethics in data collection, analysis, and reporting, as well as samples of ethical guidelines that have been established by various organizations.

Combined Sections

- The 11th edition Section 1-2 ("Statistical Thinking") and Section 1-4 ("Critical Thinking") have been combined into one section in this 12th edition:

  Section 1-2 Statistical and Critical Thinking

- The 11th edition Section 2-4 ("Statistical Graphics") and Section 2-5 ("Critical Thinking: Bad Graphs") have been combined into one section in this 12th edition:

  Section 2-4 Graphs That Enlighten and Graphs That Deceive

- The 11th edition Section 7-3 ("Estimating a Population Mean: σ Known") and Section 7-4 ("Estimating a Population Mean: σ Not Known") have been combined into one section in this 12th edition:

  Section 7-3 Estimating a Population Mean

  This change is motivated by two factors: (1) Technology makes use of the t distribution relatively simple, and (2) professional statisticians almost never use the normal distribution when constructing confidence interval estimates of population means.

- The 11th edition Section 8-4 ("Testing a Claim About a Mean: σ Known") and Section 8-5 ("Testing a Claim About a Mean: σ Not Known") have been combined into one section in this 12th edition:

  Section 8-4 Testing a Claim About a Mean

  This change is motivated by two factors: (1) Technology makes use of the t distribution relatively simple, and (2) professional statisticians almost never use the normal distribution when testing claims about a population mean.

- Section 11-4 ("McNemar's Test for Matched Pairs") in the 11th edition has been moved to Part 2 of Section 11-3 in this 12th edition.

Switched Sections Sections 6-6 and 6-7 from the previous edition have been switched so that Section 6-6 is now "Assessing Normality" and Section 6-7 is now "Normal as Approximation to Binomial." This change is motivated by the widespread availability of technology that facilitates methods for assessing normality, while the same technology has diminished the importance of using a normal approximation for a binomial distribution.

Moved to CD Section 4-6 ("Probabilities Through Simulations") in the 11th edition has been moved from the text to the CD that is included with this book. Section 4-7 ("Counting") from the 11th edition now becomes Section 4-6 in this 12th edition.

Exercises

Many exercises require the *interpretation* of results. Great care has been taken to ensure their usefulness, relevance, and accuracy. Exercises are arranged in order of increasing difficulty and by dividing them into two groups: (1) Basic Skills and Concepts and (2) Beyond the Basics. Beyond the Basics exercises address more difficult concepts or require a stronger mathematical background. In a few cases, these exercises introduce a new concept.

Real data

Hundreds of hours have been devoted to finding data that are real, meaningful, and interesting to students. All of the Chapter Problems are based on real data, 91% of the examples are based on real data, and 89% of the exercises are based on real data. Some exercises refer to the 23 large data sets listed in Appendix B, and 10 of those data sets are new to this edition. Exercises requiring use of the Appendix B data sets are located toward the end of each exercise set, where they are clearly identified.

Flexible Syllabus

This book's organization reflects the preferences of most statistics instructors, but there are two common variations:

- **Early coverage of correlation and regression:** Some instructors prefer to cover the basics of correlation and regression early in the course. *Sections 10-2 ("Correlation") and 10-3 ("Regression") can be covered early.* Simply limit coverage to Part 1 ("Basic Concepts") in each of those two sections.

- **Minimum probability:** Some instructors prefer extensive coverage of probability, while others prefer to include only basic concepts. Instructors preferring minimum coverage can include Section 4-2 while skipping the remaining sections of Chapter 4, as they are not essential for the chapters that follow. Many instructors prefer to cover the fundamentals of probability along with the basics of the addition rule and multiplication rule, and those topics can be covered with Sections 4-1 through 4-4.

Hallmark Features

Great care has been taken to ensure that each chapter of *Elementary Statistics* will help students understand the concepts presented. The following features are designed to help meet that objective:

Chapter-opening features:

- A list of chapter sections previews the chapter for the student.
- A chapter-opening problem, using real data, motivates the chapter material. Examples and exercises that further explore the ideas presented in the opening problem are marked with an icon.
- The first section is a brief review of relevant earlier concepts and previews the chapter's objectives.

End-of-chapter features:

A chapter **Review** summarizes the key concepts and topics of the chapter.

A **Chapter Quick Quiz** provides 10 review questions that require brief answers.

Review Exercises offer practice on the chapter concepts and procedures.

Cumulative Review Exercises reinforce earlier material.

A **Technology Project** provides an activity for STATDISK, Minitab, Excel, a TI-83/84 Plus calculator, or StatCrunch.

From Data to Decision is a capstone problem that requires critical thinking and writing.

Cooperative Group Activities encourage active learning in groups.

Other features:

Real Data Sets Appendix B contains printed versions of 23 large data sets referenced throughout the book, including 10 that are new. These data sets are also available on the companion Web site (http://www.pearsonhighered.com/triola), the CD-ROM bound in the back of new copies of the book, and MyStatLab.

Margin Essays Of 117 margin essays, 20% are new and several others have been updated. New topics include *Statistics for Online Dating, DNA Evidence Misused, Bar Code,* and *How Many People Do You Know?*

Flowcharts The text includes 17 flowcharts that simplify and clarify more complex concepts and procedures. Animated versions of the text's flowcharts are available within MyStatLab and MathXL.

Top 20 Topics The most important topics in any introductory statistics course are identified in the text with an icon. Students using MyStatLab have access to additional resources for learning these topics with definitions, animations, and video lessons.

Quick-Reference Endpapers Tables A-2 and A-3 (the normal and *t* distributions) are reproduced on the rear inside cover pages.

Detachable Formula and Table Card This insert, organized by chapter, gives students a quick reference for studying, or for use when taking tests (if allowed by the instructor). It also includes the most commonly used tables.

CD-ROM The CD-ROM was prepared by Mario F. Triola and is bound into the back of every new copy of the book. It contains the data sets from Appendix B available as txt files, Minitab worksheets, SPSS files, SAS files, JMP files, Excel workbooks, and a TI-83/84 Plus application. The CD also includes sections on *Probabilities Through Simulations* and *Bayes' Theorem,* an index of applications, a symbols table, programs for the TI-83/84 Plus graphing calculator, and instructions for obtaining STATDISK Statistical Software (Version 12).

Technology

New: This edition now includes instructions and displays from the StatCrunch technology, and XLSTAT is now used in Excel screenshots.

As in the preceding edition, there are many displays of screens from technology throughout the book, and some exercises are based on displayed results from technology. Where appropriate, sections end with a *Using Technology* subsection that includes instruction for STATDISK, Minitab®, Excel®, StatCrunch, or a TI-83/84 Plus® calculator. (Throughout this text, "TI-83/84 Plus" is used to identify a TI-83 Plus, TI-84 Plus, or TI-Nspire calculator with the TI-84 Plus keypad installed.) The end-of-chapter features include a *Technology Project.*

The STATDISK (Version 12) statistical software package is designed specifically for this textbook. STATDISK is free to users of this book and instructions for downloading it are included on the CD-ROM.

Acknowledgments

I would like to thank the thousands of statistics professors and students who have contributed to the success of this book. I would like to extend special thanks to Mitch Levy, Broward College; Kate Kozak, Coconino Community College; Steve Schwager, Cornell University; Rick Woodmansee, Sacramento City College; Rob Fusco, Broward College; Joe Pick, Palm Beach State College; Richard Weil, Brown College; Donald Burd, Monroe College; James Bryan, Merced College; Richard Herbst, Montgomery County Community College; Diane Hollister, Reading Area Community College; George Jahn, Palm Beach State College; Dan Kumpf, Ventura College; Kim McHale, Heartland Community College; Ken Mulzet, Florida State College at Jacksonville; Sandra Spain, Thomas Nelson Community College; Ellen G. Stutes, Louisiana State University, Eunice; Barbara Ward, Belmont University; Richard Hertz; Chris Vertullo, Marist College; Kelly Smitch, Brevard College; Robert Black, United States Air Force Academy; Michael Huber.

Recent reviewers have included Raid W.Amin, University of West Florida; Keith Carroll, Benedictine University; Monte Cheney, Central Oregon Community College; Christopher Donnelly, Macomb Community College; Billy Edwards, University of Tennessee—Chattanooga; Marcos Enriquez, Moorpark College; Angela Everett, Chattanooga State Technical Community College; Joe Franko, Mount San Antonio College; Sanford Geraci, Broward College; Laura Heath, Palm Beach State College; Laura Hillerbrand, Broward College; Gary King, Ozarks Technical Community College; Mickey Levendusky, Pima County Community College; Tristan Londre, Blue River Community College; Alma Lopez, South Plains College; Carla Monticelli, Camden County Community College; Julia Norton, California State University Hayward; Michael Oriolo, Herkimer Community College; Jeanne Osborne, Middlesex Community College; Ali Saadat, University of California—Riverside; Radha Sankaran, Passaic County Community College; Pradipta Seal, Boston University; Sharon Testone, Onondaga Community College; Dave Wallach, University of Findlay; Cheng Wang, Nova Southeastern University; Gail Wiltse, St. John River Community College; Claire Wladis, Borough of Manhattan Community College; Yong Zeng, University of Missouri at Kansas City; Jim Zimmer, Chattanooga State Technical Community College; Cathleen Zucco-Teveloff, Rowan University; Mark Z. Zuiker, Minnesota State University, Mankato.

This twelfth edition of *Elementary Statistics* is truly a team effort, and I consider myself fortunate to work with the dedication and commitment of the Pearson Arts & Sciences team. I thank Chris Cummings, Deirdre Lynch, Rachel Reeve, Sherry Berg (of Cenveo Publiser Services), Elizabeth Bernardi, Peggy McMahon, Tracy Patruno, Sonia Ashraf, Christina Lepre, Joe Vetere, and Beth Paquin. I extend special thanks to Marc Triola, M.D., New York University, for his outstanding work on the STAT-DISK software, and Scott Triola for his help in creating the new section on ethics.

I thank the following for their help in checking the accuracy of text and answers in this twelfth edition: James Lapp, David Lund, and Kimberley Polly.

M.F. T.
Madison, Connecticut
September 2012

Supplements

For the Student

Student's Solutions Manual, by Michael Butros (Victor Valley College), provides detailed, worked-out solutions to all odd-numbered text exercises.
(ISBN-13: 978-0-321-83792-9; ISBN-10: 0-321-83792-4)

Student Workbook for the Triola Statistics Series, by Anne Landry (Florida Community College at Jacksonville) offers additional examples, concept exercises, and vocabulary exercises for each chapter.
(ISBN- 13: 978-0-321-89196-9; ISBN 10: 0-321-89196-1)

The following technology manuals include instructions, examples from the main text, and interpretations to complement those given in the text.

Excel Student Laboratory Manual and Workbook, by Beverly Dretzke (University of Minnesota).
(ISBN-13: 978-0-321-83799-8; ISBN-10: 0-321-83799-1)

MINITAB Student Laboratory Manual and Workbook, by Mario F. Triola.
(ISBN-13: 978-0-321-83379-2; ISBN-10: 0-321-83379-1)

Graphing Calculator Manual for the TI-83 Plus, TI-84 Plus, TI-89 and TI-Nspire, by Kathleen McLaughlin (University of Connecticut) & Dorothy Wakefield (University of Connecticut Health Center).
(ISBN-13: 978-0-321-83803-2; ISBN 10: 0-321-83803-3)

STATDISK Student Laboratory Manual and Workbook (Download Only), by Mario F. Triola. These files are available to instructors and students through the Triola Statistics Series Web site, www.pearsonhighered.com/triola, and MyStatLab.

SPSS Student Laboratory Manual and Workbook (Download Only), by James J. Ball (Indiana State University). These files are available to instructors and students through the Triola Statistics Series Web site, www.pearsonhighered.com/triola, and MyStatLab.

StatCrunch Manual (Download Only), by Diane Hollister (Reading Area Community College). These files are available to instructors and students through the Triola Statistics Series Web site, www.pearsonhighered.com/triola, and MyStatLab.

For the Instructor

Annotated Instructor's Edition, by Mario F. Triola, contains answers to exercises in the margin, plus recommended assignments, and teaching suggestions.
(ISBN-13: 978-0-321-83378-5; ISBN-10: 0-321-83378-3)

Instructor's Solutions Manual (Download Only), by Michael Butros (Victor Valley College), contains solutions to all the exercises. These files are available to qualified instructors through Pearson Education's online catalog at www.pearsonhighered.com/irc or within MyStatLab.

Insider's Guide to Teaching with the Triola Statistics Series, by Mario F. Triola, contains sample syllabi and tips for incorporating projects, as well as lesson overviews, extra examples, minimum outcome objectives, and recommended assignments for each chapter.
(ISBN-13: 978-0-321-83372-3; ISBN-10: 0-321-83372-4)

Testing System: TestGen® (www.pearsoned.com/testgen), enables instructors to build, edit, print, and administer tests using a computerized bank of questions developed to cover all the objectives of the text. TestGen is algorithmically based, allowing instructors to create multiple but equivalent versions of the same question or test with the click of a button. Instructors can also modify test bank questions or add new questions. The software and testbank are available for download from Pearson Education's online catalog at www.pearsonhighered.com. **Test Forms (Download Only)** are also available from the online catalog.

PowerPoint® Lecture Slides: Free to qualified adopters, this classroom lecture presentation software is geared specifically to the sequence and philosophy of *Elementary Statistics*. Key graphics from the book are included to help bring the statistical concepts alive in the classroom. These files are available to qualified instructors through Pearson Education's online catalog at www.pearsonhighered.com/irc or within MyStatLab.

Active Learning Questions: Prepared in PowerPoint®, these questions are intended for use with classroom response systems. Several multiple-choice questions are available for each section of the book, allowing instructors to quickly assess mastery of material in class. These files are available to qualified instructors through Pearson Education's online catalog at www.pearsonhighered.com/irc or within MyStatLab.

Technology Resources

On the CD-ROM, Triola Statistics Series Web site (http://www.pearsonhighered.com/triola), and MyStatLab

- Appendix B data sets formatted for Minitab, SPSS, SAS, Excel, JMP, and as text files. Additionally, these data sets are available as an APP for the TI-83/84 Plus calculators, and supplemental programs for the TI-83/84 Plus calculator are also available.

- STATDISK statistical software instructions for download. New features include *Normality Assessment, modified boxplots,* and the ability to handle more than nine columns of data.

- Extra data sets, *Probabilities Through Simulations, Bayes' Theorem*, an index of applications, and a symbols table.

Video Resources have been expanded and now supplement most sections in the book, with many topics presented by the author. The videos feature technologies found in the book and the worked-out Chapter Review exercises. This is an excellent resource for students who have missed class or wish to review a topic. It is also an excellent resource for instructors involved with distance learning, individual study, or self-paced learning programs. These Videos also contain optional English and Spanish captioning. All videos are available through the MyStatLab online course.

MyStatLab™ Online Course (access code required) MyStatLab is a course management system that delivers **proven results** in helping individual students succeed.

- MyStatLab can be successfully implemented in any environment—lab-based, hybrid, fully online, traditional—and demonstrates the quantifiable difference that integrated usage has on student retention, subsequent success, and overall achievement.

- MyStatLab's comprehensive online gradebook automatically tracks students' results on tests, quizzes, homework, and in the study plan. Instructors can use the gradebook to provide positive feedback or intervene if students have trouble. Gradebook data can be easily exported to a variety of spreadsheet programs, such as Microsoft Excel. You can determine which points of data you want to export, and then analyze the results to determine success.

MyStatLab provides **engaging experiences** that personalize, stimulate, and measure learning for each student. In addition to the resources below, each course includes a full interactive online version of the accompanying textbook.

- **Tutorial Exercises with Multimedia Learning Aids:** The homework and practice exercises in MyStatLab align with the exercises in the textbook, and they regenerate algorithmically to give students unlimited opportunity for practice and mastery. Exercises offer immediate helpful feedback, guided solutions, sample problems, animations, videos, and eText clips for extra help at point-of-use.

- **StatTalk Videos:** *24 Conceptual Videos to Help You Actually Understand Statistics.* Fun-loving statistician Andrew Vickers takes to the streets of Brooklyn, NY, to demonstrate important statistical concepts through interesting stories and real-life events. These fun and engaging videos will help students actually understand statistical concepts. Available with an instructors user guide and assessment questions.

- **Getting Ready for Statistics:** A library of questions now appears within each MyStatLab course to offer the developmental math topics students need for the course. These can be assigned as a prerequisite to other assignments, if desired.

- **Conceptual Question Library:** In addition to algorithmically regenerated questions that are aligned with your textbook, there is a library of 1000 Conceptual Questions available in the assessment manager that require students to apply their statistical understanding.

- **StatCrunch™:** MyStatLab integrates the Web-based statistical software, StatCrunch, within the online assessment platform so that students can easily analyze data sets from exercises and the text. In addition, MyStatLab includes access to www.StatCrunch.com, a Web site where users can access more than 15,000 shared data sets, conduct online surveys, perform complex analyses using the powerful statistical software, and generate compelling reports.

Statistical Software Support:• Knowing that students often use external statistical software, we make it easy to copy our data sets, both from the ebook and the MyStatLab questions, into software such as StatCrunch, Minitab, Excel, and more. Students have access to a variety of support tools—Technology Tutorial Videos, Technology Study Cards, and Technology Manuals for select titles—to learn how to effectively use statistical software.

Expert Tutoring:• Although many students describe the whole of MyStatLab as "like having your own personal tutor," students also have access to live tutoring from Pearson. Qualified statistics instructors provide tutoring sessions for students via MyStatLab.

And, MyStatLab comes from a **trusted partner** with educational expertise and an eye on the future. Knowing that you are using a Pearson product means knowing that you are using quality content. That means that our eTexts are accurate and our assessment tools work. Whether you are just getting started with MyStatLab, or have a question along the way, we're here to help you learn about our technologies and how to incorporate them into your course.

To learn more about how MyStatLab combines proven learning applications with powerful assessment, visit **www.mystatlab.com** or contact your Pearson representative.

MyStatLab™ Ready to Go Course (access code required)

These new Ready to Go courses provide students with all the same great MyStatLab features but make it easier for instructors to get started. Each course includes preassigned homework and quizzes to make creating a course even simpler. Ask your Pearson representative about the details for this particular course or to see a copy of this course.

MathXL® for Statistics Online Course (access code required)

MathXL® is the homework and assessment engine that runs MyStatLab. (MyStatLab is MathXL plus a learning management system.)

With MathXL for Statistics, instructors can:

- Create, edit, and assign online homework and tests using algorithmically generated exercises correlated at the objective level to the textbook.

- Create and assign their own online exercises and import TestGen tests for added flexibility.

- Maintain records of all student work, tracked in MathXL's online gradebook.

With MathXL for Statistics, students can:

- Take chapter tests in MathXL and receive personalized study plans and/or personalized homework assignments based on their test results.

- Use the study plan and/or the homework to link directly to tutorial exercises for the objectives they need to study.

- Students can also access supplemental animations and video clips directly from selected exercises.

- Knowing that students often use external statistical software, we make it easy to copy our data sets, both from

the ebook and the MyStatLab questions, into software like StatCrunch™, Minitab, Excel, and more.

MathXL for Statistics is available to qualified adopters. For more information, visit our web site at www.mathxl.com, or contact your Pearson representative.

StatCrunch™

StatCrunch is powerful, web-based statistical software that allows users to perform complex analyses, share data sets, and generate compelling reports. A vibrant online community offers more than 15,000 data sets for students to analyze.

- **Collect.** Users can upload their own data to StatCrunch or search a large library of publicly shared data sets, spanning almost any topic of interest. Also, an online survey tool allows users to quickly collect data via web-based surveys.

- **Crunch.** A full range of numerical and graphical methods allow users to analyze and gain insights from any data set. Interactive graphics help users understand statistical concepts and are available for export to enrich reports with visual representations of data.

- **Communicate.** Reporting options help users create a wide variety of visually appealing representations of their data.

Full access to StatCrunch is available with a MyStatLab kit, and StatCrunch is available by itself to qualified adopters. StatCrunch Mobile is now available to access from your mobile device. For more information, visit our Web site at www.StatCrunch.com, or contact your Pearson representative.

The Student Edition of MINITAB is a condensed version of the Professional release of MINITAB statistical software. It offers the full range of statistical methods and graphical capabilities, along with worksheets that can include up to 10,000 data points. Individual copies of the software can be bundled with the text (ISBN-13: 978-0-321-11313-9; ISBN-10: 0-321-11313-6) (CD only).

JMP Student Edition is an easy-to-use, streamlined version of JMP desktop statistical discovery software from SAS Institute, Inc. and is available for bundling with the text (ISBN-13: 978-0-321-89164-8 ISBN-10: 0-321-89164-3).

The following is taken from
Elementary Statistics, Twelfth Edition
by Mario F. Triola

.

1 Introduction to Statistics

Survey: Have you ever been hit with a computer virus?

The world in which we live is now saturated with surveys. Surveys are essential tools used in marketing. Surveys determine what television shows we watch. Surveys guide political candidates. Surveys shape business practices and many other aspects of our lives. Surveys provide us with understanding about the thinking of the rest of the world. Let's consider one particular survey dealing with a topic of great concern to all of us who have embraced the use of computer technology. The survey question and responses are given below, and Figure 1-1 graphically depicts the survey results. (Figure 1-1 was generated using Minitab statistical software.)

"Have you ever been hit by a computer virus?"

- Yes: 106,685
- No: 63,378

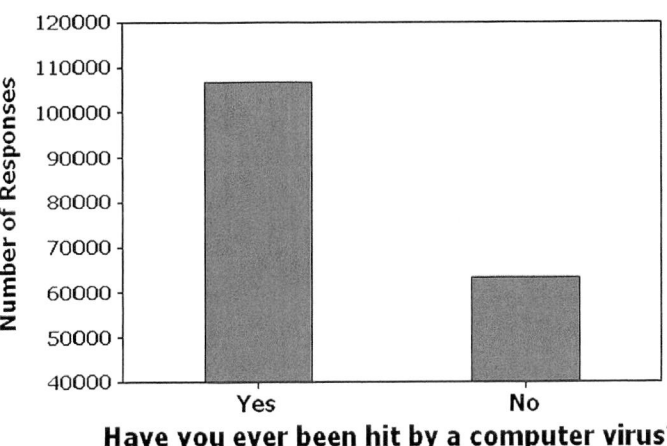

Figure 1-1   Survey Results

The results of the survey appear to be quite dramatic. The total number of respondents is 170,063 adults, and that is a very large number of respondents. Many polls have only about one thousand or two thousand respondents. Also, by looking at the bars in Figure 1-1, we see that roughly three times as many respondents have been hit by computer viruses as have not been hit. One important objective of this text is to encourage the use of critical thinking so that such results are not blindly accepted. We might question whether the survey results are valid. Who conducted the survey? How were respondents selected? Does the graph in Figure 1-1 depict the results in a way that is not misleading?

The survey results presented here have two major flaws. Because these two flaws are among the most common, it is especially important to recognize them. Following are brief descriptions of each of the two major flaws.

3

Flaw 1: Misleading Graph   Figure 1-1 is deceptive. Using a vertical scale that does not start at zero exaggerates the difference between the two numbers of responses. Thus Figure 1-1 makes it appear that the "yes" responses are about three times the number of "no" responses, but examination of the actual response counts shows that the "yes" responses are really about 1.7 times the "no" responses. Deceptive graphs are discussed in more detail in Section 2-4.

Flaw 2: Bad Sampling Method   The survey responses are from a recent America OnLine survey of Internet users. The survey question was posted on the America OnLine Web site and Internet users decided whether to respond. This is an example of a *voluntary response sample*—a sample in which respondents decide themselves whether to participate. With a voluntary response sample, it often happens that those with a strong interest in the topic are more likely to participate, so the results are very questionable. The large number of respondents does not overcome this flaw of having a voluntary response sample. When we want to use sample data to learn something about a population, it is *extremely* important to obtain sample data that are representative of the population from which the data are drawn. As we proceed through this chapter and discuss types of data and sampling methods, we should focus on these key concepts:

- **Sample data must be collected in an appropriate way, such as through a process of *random* selection.**
- **If sample data are not collected in an appropriate way, the data may be so completely useless that no amount of statistical torturing can salvage them.**

It would be easy to accept the preceding survey results and blindly proceed with calculations and statistical analyses, but if we did so, we would miss the critical two flaws described above. We might then develop conclusions that are fundamentally wrong and misleading. Instead, we should develop skills in statistical thinking and critical thinking so we can understand why the survey is so seriously flawed and why we should not rely on it to yield any valid information.

1-1   Review and Preview

The first section of each of Chapter 1 through Chapter 14 begins with a brief review of what preceded the chapter, and a preview of what the chapter includes. This first chapter isn't preceded by much of anything except the Preface, and we won't review that (most people don't even read it). However, we can review and formally define some statistical terms that are commonly used. The Chapter Problem discussed an America OnLine poll that collected sample data. Polls collect data from a small part of a larger group so that we can learn something about the larger group. This is a common and important goal of statistics: Learn about a large group by examining sample data from some of its members. In this context, the terms *sample* and *population* have special meanings. Formal definitions for these and other basic terms are given here.

DEFINITIONS

Data are collections of observations, such as measurements, genders, or survey responses. (A single data value is called a *datum*, a term that does not see very much use.)

Statistics is the science of planning studies and experiments; obtaining data; and then organizing, summarizing, presenting, analyzing, and interpreting those data and then drawing conclusions based on them.

A **population** is the complete collection of *all* measurements or data that are being considered.

A **census** is the collection of data from *every* member of the population.

A **sample** is a *subcollection* of members selected from a population.

Because populations are often very large, a common objective of the use of statistics is to obtain data from a sample and then use those data to form a conclusion about the population. See Example 1.

Example 1   Gallup Poll: Identity Theft

In a poll conducted by the Gallup corporation, 1013 adults in the United States were randomly selected and surveyed about identity theft. Results showed that 66% of the respondents worried about identity theft frequently or occasionally.

Gallup pollsters decided who would be asked to participate in the survey and they used a sound method of randomly selecting adults. The respondents are not a voluntary response sample, and the results are likely to be better than those obtained from the America OnLine survey discussed earlier.

In this case, the population consists of all 241,472,385 adults in the United States, and it is not practical to survey each of them. The sample consists of the 1013 adults who were surveyed. The objective is to use the sample data as a basis for drawing a conclusion about the population of all adults, and methods of statistics are helpful in drawing such conclusions.

Origin of "Statistics"

The word *statistics* is derived from the Latin word *status* (meaning "state"). Early uses of statistics involved compilations of data and graphs describing various aspects of a state or country. In 1662, John Graunt published statistical information about births and deaths. Graunt's work was followed by studies of mortality and disease rates, population sizes, incomes, and unemployment rates. Households, governments, and businesses rely heavily on statistical data for guidance. For example, unemployment rates, inflation rates, consumer indexes, and birth and death rates are carefully compiled on a regular basis, and the resulting data are used by business leaders to make decisions affecting future hiring, production levels, and expansion into new markets.

1-2   Statistical and Critical Thinking

Key Concept This section provides an overview of the process involved in conducting a statistical study. This process consists of "prepare, analyze, and conclude." We begin with a preparation that involves consideration of the context, consideration of the source of data, and consideration of the sampling method. Next, we construct suitable graphs, explore the data, and execute computations required for the statistical method being used. Finally, we form conclusions by determining whether results have statistical significance and practical significance. See Figure 1-2 for a summary of this process.

Figure 1-2 includes key elements in a statistical study. Note that the procedure outlined in Figure 1-2 does not focus on mathematical calculations. Thanks to wonderful developments in technology, we now have tools that effectively do the number crunching so that we can focus on understanding and interpreting results.

Prepare

1. **Context**
   What do the data mean?
   What is the goal of study?
2. **Source of the Data**
   Are the data from a source with a special interest so that there is pressure to obtain results that are favorable to the source?
3. **Sampling Method**
   Were the data collected in a way that is unbiased, or were the data collected in a way that is biased (such as a procedure in which respondents volunteer to participate)?

Analyze

1. **Graph the Data**
2. **Explore the Data**
   Are there any outliers (numbers very far away from almost all of the other data)?
   What important statistics summarize the data (such as the mean and standard deviation described in later)?
   How are the data distributed?
   Are there missing data?
   Did many selected subjects refuse to respond?
3. **Apply Statistical Methods**
   Use technology to obtain results.

Conclude

1. **Statistical Significance**
   Do the results have statistical significance?
   Do the results have practical significance?

Figure 1-2   **Statistical Thinking**

Prepare

Context Let's consider the data in Table 1-1. (The data are from Data Set 6 in Appendix B.) The data in Table 1-1 consist of measured IQ scores and measured brain volumes from 10 different subjects. The data are matched in the sense that each individual "IQ/brain volume" pair of values is from the same subject. The first subject had a measured IQ score of 96 and a brain volume of 1005 cm^3. The format of Table 1-1 suggests the following goal: Determine whether there is a relationship between IQ score and brain volume. This goal suggests a possible hypothesis: People with larger brains tend to have higher IQ scores.

Table 1-1   IQ Scores and Brain Volumes (cm^3)

IQ	96	87	101	103	127	96	88	85	97	124
Brain Volume (cm^3)	1005	1035	1281	1051	1034	1079	1104	1439	1029	1160

Source of the Data The data in Table 1-1 were provided by M. J. Tramo, W. C. Loftus, T. A. Stukel, J. B. Weaver, and M. S. Gazziniga, who discuss the data in the article "Brain Size, Head Size, and IQ in Monozygotic Twins," *Neurology*, Vol. 50. The researchers are from reputable medical schools and hospitals, and they would not gain by putting spin on the results. In contrast, Kiwi Brands, a maker of shoe polish, commissioned a study that resulted in this statement, which was printed in some newspapers: "According to a nationwide survey of 250 hiring professionals, scuffed shoes was the most common reason for a male job seeker's failure to make a good first impression." We should be very wary of such a survey in which the sponsor can somehow profit from the results. When physicians who conduct clinical experiments on the efficacy of drugs receive funding from drug companies they have an incentive to obtain favorable results. Some professional journals, such as the *Journal of the American Medical Association*, now require that physicians report such funding in journal articles. We should be skeptical of studies from sources that may be biased.

Sampling Method The data in Table 1-1 were obtained from subjects who were recruited by researchers, and the subjects were paid for their participation. All subjects were between 24 years and 43 years of age, they all had at least a high school education, and the medical histories of subjects were reviewed in an effort to ensure that no subjects had neurologic or psychiatric disease. In this case, the sampling method appears to be sound.

Sampling methods and the use of randomization will be discussed in Section 1-4, but for now, we simply emphasize that a sound sampling method is absolutely essential for good results in a statistical study. It is generally a bad practice to use voluntary response (or self-selected) samples, even though their use is common.

> **DEFINITION** A **voluntary response sample** (or **self-selected sample**) is one in which the respondents themselves decide whether to be included.

The following types of polls are common examples of voluntary response samples. By their very nature, all are seriously flawed because we should not make conclusions about a population on the basis of such a biased sample:

- Internet polls, in which people online can decide whether to respond

- Mail-in polls, in which subjects can decide whether to reply

- Telephone call-in polls, in which newspaper, radio, or television announcements ask that you voluntarily call a special number to register your opinion

With such voluntary response samples, we can draw valid conclusions only about the specific group of people who chose to participate; nevertheless, such samples are often incorrectly used to assert or imply conclusions about a larger population. From a statistical viewpoint, such a sample is fundamentally flawed and should not be used for making general statements about a larger population. The Chapter Problem involves an America OnLine poll with a voluntary response sample. See also Examples 1 and 2, which follow.

Value of a Statistical Life

The *value of a statistical life* (VSL) is a measure routinely calculated and used for making decisions in fields such as medicine, insurance, environmental health, and transportation safety. As of this writing, the value of a statistical life is $6.9 million.

Many people oppose the concept of putting a value on a human life, but the word *statistical* in the "value of a statistical life" is used to ensure that we don't equate it with the true worth of a human life. Some people legitimately argue that every life is priceless, but others argue that there are conditions in which it is impossible or impractical to save every life, so a value must be somehow assigned to a human life in order that sound and rational decisions can be made. Not far from the author's home, a parkway was modified at a cost of about $3 million to improve safety at a location where car occupants had previously died in traffic crashes. In the cost-benefit analysis that led to this improvement in safety, the value of a statistical life was surely considered.

Publication Bias

There is a "publication bias" in professional journals. It is the tendency to publish positive results (such as showing that some treatment is effective) much more often than negative results

(such as showing that some treatment has no effect). In the article "Registering Clinical Trials" (*Journal of the American Medical Association*, Vol. 290, No. 4), authors Kay Dickersin and Drummond Rennie state that "the result of not knowing who has performed what (clinical trial) is loss and distortion of the evidence, waste and duplication of trials, inability of funding agencies to plan, and a chaotic system from which only certain sponsors might benefit, and is invariably against the interest of those who offered to participate in trials and of patients in general." They support a process in which *all* clinical trials are registered in one central system, so that future researchers have access to all previous studies, not just the studies that were published.

Example 1   Voluntary Response Sample

Literary Digest magazine conducted a poll for the 1936 presidential election by sending out 10 million ballots. The magazine received 2.3 million responses. The poll results suggested incorrectly that Alf Landon would win the presidency. In a much smaller poll of 50,000 people, George Gallup correctly predicted that Franklin D. Roosevelt would win. The lesson here is that it is not necessarily the *size* of the sample that makes it effective, but the *sampling method*. The *Literary Digest* ballots were sent to magazine subscribers as well as to registered car owners and those who used telephones. On the heels of the Great Depression, this group included disproportionately more wealthy people, who were Republicans. But the real flaw in the *Literary Digest* poll is that it resulted in a voluntary response sample. In contrast, Gallup used an approach in which he obtained a representative sample based on demographic factors. (Gallup modified his methods when he made a wrong prediction in the famous 1948 Dewey/Truman election. Gallup stopped polling too soon, and he failed to detect a late surge in support for Truman.) The *Literary Digest* poll is a classic illustration of the flaws inherent in basing conclusions on a voluntary response sample.

Example 2   Voluntary Response Sample

The ABC television show *Nightline* asked viewers to call with their opinion about whether the United Nations headquarters should remain in the United States. Viewers then decided themselves whether to call with their opinions, and 67% of 186,000 respondents said that the United Nations should be *moved out* of the United States. In a separate poll, 500 respondents were randomly selected and 72% of them wanted the United Nations to *stay* in the United States. The two polls produced dramatically different results. Even though the *Nightline* poll involved 186,000 volunteer respondents, the much smaller poll of 500 randomly selected respondents is more likely to provide better results because of the superior sampling method.

Analyze

Graph and Explore After carefully considering context, source of the data, and sampling method, we can proceed with an analysis that should begin with appropriate graphs and explorations of the data. Graphs are discussed in Chapter 2, and important statistics are discussed in Chapter 3.

Apply Statistical Methods Later chapters describe important statistical methods, but application of these methods is often made easy with calculators and/or statistical software packages. A good statistical analysis does not require strong computational skills. A good statistical analysis does require using common sense and paying careful attention to sound statistical methods.

Conclude

Statistical Significance *Statistical significance* is achieved in a study when we get a result that is very unlikely to occur by chance.

- Getting 98 girls in 100 random births is statistically significant because such an extreme event is not likely to be the result of random chance.

- Getting 52 girls in 100 births is not statistically significant, because that event could easily occur with random chance.

Practical Significance It is possible that some treatment or finding is effective, but common sense might suggest that the treatment or finding does not make enough of a difference to justify its use or to be practical, as illustrated in Example 3.

Example 3 Statistical Significance versus Practical Significance

In a test of the Atkins weight loss program, 40 subjects using that program had a mean weight loss of 2.1 kg (or 4.6 pounds) after one year (based on data from "Comparison of the Atkins, Ornish, Weight Watchers, and Zone Diets for Weight Loss and Heart Disease Risk Reduction," by Dansinger et al., *Journal of the American Medical Association*, Vol. 293, No. 1). Using formal methods of statistical analysis, we can conclude that the mean weight loss of 2.1 kg is statistically significant. That is, based on statistical criteria, the diet appears to be effective. However, using common sense, it does not seem very worthwhile to pursue a weight loss program resulting in such relatively insignificant results. Someone starting a weight loss program would probably want to lose considerably more than 2.1 kg. Although the mean weight loss of 2.1 kg is statistically significant, it does not have practical significance. The statistical analysis suggests that the weight loss program is effective, but *practical* considerations suggest that the program is basically ineffective.

Analyzing Data: Potential Pitfalls

Here are a few more items that could cause problems when analyzing data.

Misleading Conclusions When forming a conclusion based on a statistical analysis, we should make statements that are clear even to those who have no understanding of statistics and its terminology. We should carefully avoid making statements not justified by the statistical analysis. For example, Section 10-2 introduces the concept of a *correlation*, or association between two variables, such as smoking and pulse rate. A statistical analysis might justify the statement that there is a correlation between the number of cigarettes smoked and pulse rate, but it would not justify a statement that the number of cigarettes smoked *causes* a person's pulse rate to change. Such a statement about causality can be justified by physical evidence, not by statistical analysis.

Correlation does not imply causation.

Reported Results When collecting data from people, it is better to take measurements yourself instead of asking subjects to report results. Ask people what they weigh and you are likely to get their *desired* weights, not their actual weights. Accurate weights are collected by using a scale to measure weights, not by asking people to report their weights.

Small Samples Conclusions should not be based on samples that are far too small. The Children's Defense Fund published *Children Out of School in America*, in which it was reported that among secondary school students suspended in one region, 67% were suspended at least three times. But that figure is based on a sample of only *three* students! Media reports failed to mention that this sample size was so small.

Loaded Questions If survey questions are not worded carefully, the results of a study can be misleading. Survey questions can be "loaded" or intentionally worded to

---

Detecting Phony Data

A class is given the homework assignment of recording the results when a coin is tossed 500 times. One dishonest student decides to save time by just making up the results instead of actually flipping a coin. Because people generally cannot make up results that are really random, we can often identify such phony data. With 500 tosses of an actual coin, it is extremely likely that at some point, you will get a run of six heads or six tails, but people almost never include such a run when they make up results.

Another way to detect fabricated data is to establish that the results violate Benford's law: For many collections of data, the leading digits are not uniformly distributed. Instead, the leading digits of 1, 2, . . . , 9 occur with rates of 30%, 18%, 12%, 10%, 8%, 7%, 6%, 5%, and 5%, respectively. (See "The Difficulty of Faking Data," by Theodore Hill, *Chance*, Vol. 12, No. 3.)

elicit a desired response. Here are the actual rates of "yes" responses for the two different wordings of a question:

97% yes: "Should the President have the line item veto to eliminate waste?"

57% yes: "Should the President have the line item veto, or not?"

Order of Questions Sometimes survey questions are unintentionally loaded by such factors as the order of the items being considered. See the following two questions from a poll conducted in Germany, along with the very different response rates:

- "Would you say that traffic contributes more or less to air pollution than industry?" (45% blamed traffic; 27% blamed industry.)
- "Would you say that industry contributes more or less to air pollution than traffic?" (24% blamed traffic; 57% blamed industry.)

Nonresponse A *nonresponse* occurs when someone either refuses to respond to a survey question or is unavailable. When people are asked survey questions, some firmly refuse to answer. The refusal rate has been growing in recent years, partly because many persistent telemarketers try to sell goods or services by beginning with a sales pitch that initially sounds like it is part of an opinion poll. (This "selling under the guise" of a poll is now called *sugging*.) In *Lies, Damn Lies, and Statistics,* author Michael Wheeler makes this very important observation:

> People who refuse to talk to pollsters are likely to be different from those who do not. Some may be fearful of strangers and others jealous of their privacy, but their refusal to talk demonstrates that their view of the world around them is markedly different from that of those people who will let poll-takers into their homes.

Missing Data Results can sometimes be dramatically affected by missing data. Sometimes sample data values are missing because of random factors (such as subjects dropping out of a study for reasons unrelated to the study), but some data are missing because of special factors, such as the tendency of people with low incomes to be less likely to report their incomes. It is well known that the U.S. Census suffers from missing people, and the missing people are often from the homeless or low income groups.

Precise Numbers Example 1 in Section 1-1 included a statement that there are 241,472,385 adults in the United States. Because that figure is very precise, many people incorrectly assume that it is also *accurate*. In this case, that number is an estimate, and it would be better to state that the number of adults in the United States is about 240 million.

Percentages Some studies cite misleading or unclear percentages. Keep in mind that 100% of some quantity is *all* of it, but if there are references made to percentages that exceed 100%, such references are often not justified. In referring to lost baggage, Continental Airlines ran ads claiming that this was "an area where we've already improved 100% in the last six months." In an editorial criticizing this statistic, the *New York Times* correctly interpreted the 100% improvement to mean that no baggage is now being lost—an accomplishment that was not achieved by Continental Airlines.

The following list identifies some key principles to apply when dealing with percentages. These principles all use the basic notion that % or "percent" really means "divided by 100." The first principle is used often in this book.

Percentage of: To find a *percentage of* an amount, drop the % symbol and divide the percentage value by 100, then multiply. This example shows that 6% of 1200 is 72:

$$6\% \text{ of } 1200 \text{ responses } = \frac{6}{100} \times 1200 = 72$$

Fraction→Percentage: To *convert from a fraction to a percentage*, divide the denominator into the numerator to get an equivalent decimal number; then multiply by 100 and affix the % symbol. This example shows that the fraction 3/4 is equivalent to 75%:

$$\frac{3}{4} = 0.75 \rightarrow 0.75 \times 100\% = 75\%$$

Decimal→Percentage: To *convert from a decimal to a percentage*, multiply by 100%. This example shows that 0.25 is equivalent to 25%:

$$0.25 \rightarrow 0.25 \times 100\% = 25\%$$

Percentage→Decimal: To *convert from a percentage to a decimal number*, delete the % symbol and divide by 100. This example shows that 85% is equivalent to 0.85:

$$85\% = \frac{85}{100} = 0.85$$

There are many examples of the misuse of statistics. Books such as Darrell Huff's classic *How to Lie with Statistics*, Robert Reichard's *The Figure Finaglers*, and Cynthia Crossen's *Tainted Truth* describe some of those other cases. Understanding these practices will be extremely helpful in evaluating the statistical data encountered in everyday situations.

What Is Statistical Thinking? Statisticians universally agree that statistical thinking is good, but there are different views of what actually constitutes statistical thinking. If you ask the 18,000 members of the American Statistical Association to define statistical thinking, you will probably get 18,001 different definitions. In this section we have described statistical thinking in terms of the ability to see the big picture; to consider such relevant factors as context, source of data, and sampling method; and to form conclusions and identify practical implications. Statistical thinking involves critical thinking and the ability to make sense of results. Statistical thinking might involve determining whether results are statistically significant and practically significant. Statistical thinking demands so much more than the ability to execute complicated calculations. Through numerous examples, exercises, and discussions, this text will help you develop the statistical thinking skills that are so important in today's world.

1-2 Basic Skills and Concepts

Statistical Literacy and Critical Thinking

1. Statistical Significance versus Practical Significance What is the difference between statistical significance and practical significance? Can a statistical study have statistical significance, but not practical significance?

2. Source of Data In conducting a statistical study, why is it important to consider the source of the data?

3. Voluntary Response Sample What is a voluntary response sample, and why is such a sample generally not suitable for a statistical study?

4. Correlation and Causation What is meant by the statement that "correlation does not imply causation"?

Consider the Source.   *In Exercises 5–8, determine whether the given source has the potential to create a bias in a statistical study.*

5. Physicians Committee for Responsible Medicine The Physicians Committee for Responsible Medicine tends to oppose the use of meat and dairy products in our diets, and that organization has received hundreds of thousands of dollars in funding from the Foundation to Support Animal Protection.

6. Body Measurements Data Set 1 in Appendix B includes body measurements obtained by the U.S. Department of Health and Human Services, National Center for Health Statistics.

7. Word Counts Data Set 17 in Appendix B includes word counts obtained by members of the Departments of Psychology at the University of Arizona, Washington University, and the University of Texas at Austin.

8. Chocolate An article in *Journal of Nutrition* (Vol. 130, No. 8) noted that chocolate is rich in flavonoids. The article notes that "regular consumption of foods rich in flavonoids may reduce the risk of coronary heart disease." The study received funding from Mars, Inc., the candy company, and the Chocolate Manufacturers Association.

Sampling Method.   *In Exercises 9–12, determine whether the sampling method appears to be sound or is flawed.*

9. Wi-Fi Security A survey of 721 subjects involved the providing of personal information when using Wi-Fi hotspots. The survey subjects were Internet users who responded to a question that was posted on the electronic edition of *USA Today*.

10. Text Messaging In a survey of 109 subjects, each was asked to indicate how many text messages they send and receive each day. The sample consisted of those who chose to respond to the request posted on the StatCrunch Web site.

11. Applying for a Job In a survey of 514 human resource professionals, each was asked about the importance of the appearance of a job applicant. The survey subjects were randomly selected by Harris Interactive pollsters.

12. Evolution In a survey of beliefs about evolution, Gallup pollsters randomly selected and telephoned 1018 adults in the United States.

Statistical Significance and Practical Significance.   *In Exercises 13–16, determine whether the results appear to have statistical significance, and also determine whether the results have practical significance.*

13. Waite Diet In a study of the Marisa Waite diet, four subjects lost an average of 45 pounds. It is found that there is about a 30% chance of getting such results with a diet that has no effect.

14. Gender Selection In a study of the Gender Aide method of gender selection, 1000 users of the method gave birth to 540 boys and 460 girls. There is about a 1% chance that such extreme results would occur if the method had no effect.

15. Guessing Technique When making random guesses for difficult multiple-choice test questions with possible answers of a, b, c, d, and e, we expect to get about 20% of the answers correct. The Ashton Prep Program claims to have developed a better method of guessing. In a test of that program, guesses were made for 100 answers, and 23 were found to be correct. There is a 23% chance of getting such results if the program has no effect.

16. IQ Scores Most people have IQ scores between 70 and 130. For $32, you can purchase a computer program from Highiqpro.com that is claimed to increase your IQ score by 10 to 20 points. The program claims to be "the only proven IQ increasing software in the brain training market," but the author of your text could find no data supporting that claim, so let's suppose that these results were obtained: In a study of 12 subjects using the program, the average increase in IQ score is 3 IQ points. There is a 25% chance of getting such results if the program has no effect.

In Exercises 17–20, refer to the data in the table below. (The pulse rates are from one sample of randomly selected males and a different sample of randomly selected females listed in Data Set 1 in Appendix B.)

Pulse Rate (beats per minute)					
Male	60	64	60	72	64
Female	68	72	88	60	60

17. Context of the Data Refer to the table of pulse rates. Is there some meaningful way in which each male pulse rate is matched with the corresponding female pulse rate? If the male pulse rates and the female pulse rates are not matched, does it make sense to use the difference between any of the pulse rates that are in the same column?

18. Source of the Data The listed pulse rates were obtained for the Third National Health and Nutrition Examination Survey conducted by the U.S. Department of Health and Human Services, National Center for Health Statistics. Is the source of the data likely to be unbiased?

19. Conclusion Given the data in the table, what issue can be addressed by conducting a statistical analysis of the pulse rates?

20. Conclusion If we use the listed pulse rates with suitable methods of statistics, we conclude that when the 64.0 average (mean) of the pulse rates of the five males is compared to the 69.6 average (mean) of the pulse rates of the five females, there is a 36% chance that the difference can be explained by random results obtained from populations of males and females having the same average (mean) pulse rate. Does this prove that the populations of males and females have the same average (mean) pulse rate? Why or why not? Would better results be obtained with larger samples?

In Exercises 21–24, refer to the data in the table below. The IQ score and brain volume are listed for each of five different subjects. (The values are from Data Set 6 in Appendix B.)

IQ Score and Brain Volume					
Subject	1	2	3	4	5
IQ Score	87	127	101	94	97
Brain Volume (cm³)	1035	1034	1173	1347	1029

21. Context of the Data Refer to the given table of measurements. Is there some meaningful way in which the IQ scores are matched with the corresponding brain volumes? If they are matched, does it make sense to use the difference between each IQ score and the brain volume that is in the same column? Why or why not?

22. Conclusion Given the context of the data in the table, what issue can be addressed by conducting a statistical analysis of the measurements?

23. Source of the Data The data in the table were obtained by members of departments at Harvard Medical School, Massachusetts General Hospital, Dartmouth College, Dartmouth Medical School, and the University of California at Davis. Funding for the study was provided by awards from the National Institutes of Health, which is an agency of the

U.S. Department of Health and Human Services. Does the source of the data appear to be unbiased?

24. Conclusion If we were to use such data and conclude that there is a correlation or association between IQ score and brain volume, does it follow that larger brains are the cause of higher IQ scores?

What's Wrong?   *In Exercises 25–28, identify what is wrong.*

25. Potatoes In a poll sponsored by the Idaho Potato Commission, 1000 adults were asked to select their favorite vegetables, and the favorite choice was potatoes, which were selected by 26% of the respondents.

26. College Major In a *USA Today* online poll, 728 Internet users chose to respond, and 41% of them said that their college majors prepared them for their chosen careers very well.

27. Cell Phones and Pirates In recent years, the numbers of cell phones and the numbers of pirates have both increased, so there is a correlation, or association, between those two variables. Therefore, cell phones cause pirates.

28. Storks and Babies In the years following the end of World War II, it was found that there was a strong correlation, or association, between the number of human births and the stork population. It therefore follows that storks cause babies.

Percentages.   *In Exercises 29–36, answer the given questions, which are related to percentages.*

29. Evolution A Gallup poll of 1018 adults reported that 39% believe in evolution.

a. What is the exact value that is 39% of 1018?

b. Could the result from part (a) be the actual number of adults who said that they believe in evolution? Why or why not?

c. What is the actual number of adults who said that they believe in evolution?

d. Among the 1018 respondents, 255 said that they did not believe in evolution. What percentage of respondents said that they did not believe in evolution?

30. Online Shopping In a *Consumer Reports* Research Center Telephone survey of 427 women, 38% said that they purchased clothing online.

a. What is the exact value that is 38% of 427?

b. Could the result from part (a) be the actual number of women who said that they purchase clothing online? Why or why not?

c. What is the actual number of women who said that they purchase clothing online?

d. Among the 427 respondents, 30 said that they purchase electronics online. What percentage of the women said that they purchase electronics online?

31. Piercings and Tattoos In a Harris poll of 2302 adults, 14% said that they have a tattoo.

a. What is the exact value that is 14% of 2302?

b. Could the result from part (a) be actual number of adults who said that they have a tattoo? Why or why not?

c. What is the actual number of adults who said that they have a tattoo?

d. Among the 2302 respondents, 46 said that they had face piercings only. What percentage of respondents had face piercings only?

32. Dollar for Your Thoughts In a Harris poll of 2513 adults, 76% said that they prefer $1 to be in the form of paper currency.

a. What is the exact value that is 76% of 2513?

b. Could the result from part (a) be the actual number of adults who said that they prefer $1 to be in the form of paper currency? Why or why not?

c. What is the actual number of adults who said that they prefer $1 to be in the form of paper currency?

d. Among the 2513 respondents, 327 said that they prefer $1 to be currency in the form of a coin. What is the percentage of respondents who said that they prefer $1 to be currency in the form of a coin?

33. Percentages in Advertising An ad for Big Skinny wallets included the statement that one of their wallets "reduces your filled wallet size by 50%–200%." What is wrong with this statement?

34. Percentages in Advertising In an ad for the Club, a device used to discourage car thefts, it was stated that "The Club reduces your odds of car theft by 400%." What is wrong with this statement?

35. Percentages in the Media In the *New York Times Magazine,* a report about the decline of Western investment in Kenya included this statement: "After years of daily flights, Lufthansa and Air France had halted passenger service. Foreign investment fell 500 percent during the 1990s." What is wrong with this statement?

36. Percentages in Advertising A *New York Times* editorial criticized a chart caption that described a dental rinse as one that "reduces plaque on teeth by over 300%." What is wrong with this statement?

1-2 Beyond the Basics

37. ATV Accidents The Associated Press provided an article with a headline stating that ATV accidents killed 704 people in the last year. The article noted that this is a new record high and compares it to 617 ATV deaths the year before that. Other data about the frequencies of injuries were included. What important value was not included? Why is it important?

38. Falsifying Data A researcher at the Sloan-Kettering Cancer Research Center was once criticized for falsifying data. Among his data were figures obtained from 6 groups of mice, with 20 individual mice in each group. The following values were given for the percentage of successes in each group: 53%, 58%, 63%, 46%, 48%, 67%. What's wrong with those values?

39. What's Wrong with This Picture? The *Newport Chronicle* ran a survey by asking readers to call in their response to this question: "Do you support the development of atomic weapons that could kill millions of innocent people?" It was reported that 20 readers responded and that 87% said "no," while 13% said "yes." Identify four major flaws in this survey.

1-3 Types of Data

Key Concept A common and important use of statistics involves collecting sample data and using them to make inferences, or conclusions, about the population from which the data were obtained. The terms *sample* and *population* were defined in Section 1-1. We should also know and understand the meanings of the terms *statistic* and *parameter,* as defined below. The terms *statistic* and *parameter* are used to distinguish

Six Degrees of Separation

Social psychologists, historians, political scientists, and communications specialists are interested in "The Small World Problem":

Given any two people in the world, how many intermediate links are necessary to connect the two original people? In the 1950s and 1960s, social psychologist Stanley Milgram conducted an experiment in which subjects tried to contact other target people by mailing an information folder to an acquaintance who they thought would be closer to the target. Among 160 such chains that were initiated, only 44 were completed, so the failure rate was 73%. Among the successes, the number of intermediate acquaintances varied from 2 to 10, with a median of 6 (hence "six degrees of separation"). The experiment has been criticized for its high failure rate and its disproportionate inclusion of subjects with above-average incomes. A more recent study conducted by Microsoft researcher Eric Horvitz and Stanford Assistant Professor Jure Leskovec involved 30 billion instant messages and 240 million people. This study found that for instant messages that used Microsoft, the mean length of a path between two individuals is 6.6, suggesting "seven degrees of separation." Work continues in this important and interesting field.

between cases in which we have data for a sample, and cases in which we have data for an entire population.

We also need to know the difference between the terms *quantitative data* and *categorical data*. Some numbers, such as those on the shirts of basketball players, are not quantities because they don't measure or count anything, and it would not make sense to perform calculations with such numbers. In this section we describe different types of data. The type of data is one of the key factors that determine the statistical methods we use in our analysis.

Parameter/Statistic

> **DEFINITIONS**
>
> A **parameter** is a numerical measurement describing some characteristic of a *population*.
>
> A **statistic** is a numerical measurement describing some characteristic of a *sample*.

HINT The alliteration in "population parameter" and "sample statistic" helps us remember the meaning of these terms.

Using the foregoing definitions and those given in Section 1-1, we see that the term *statistics* has two possible meanings:

1. Statistics are two or more numerical measurements describing characteristics of samples.

2. Statistics is the science of planning studies and experiments; obtaining data; organizing, summarizing, presenting, analyzing, and interpreting those data; and then drawing conclusions based on them.

We can determine which of these two definitions applies by considering the context in which the term *statistics* is used. The following example uses the first meaning of *statistics* as given above.

Example 1   Parameter/Statistic

In a Harris Poll, 2320 adults in the United States were surveyed about body piercings, and 5% of the respondents said that they had a body piercing, but not on the face. Based on the latest available data at the time of this writing, there are 241,472,385 adults in the United States. The results from the survey are a sample drawn from the population of all adults.

1. **Parameter:** The population size of 241,472,385 is a *parameter*, because it is based on the entire population of all adults in the United States.

2. **Statistic:** The sample size of 2320 surveyed adults is a *statistic*, because it is based on a sample, not the entire population of all adults in the United States. The value of 5% is another statistic, because it is also based on the sample, not on the entire population.

Quantitative/Categorical

Some data are numbers representing counts or measurements (such as a height of 60 inches or an IQ of 135), whereas others are attributes (such as eye color of green or brown) that are not counts or measurements. The terms *quantitative data* and *categorical data* distinguish between these types.

> **DEFINITIONS**
>
> **Quantitative** (or **numerical**) **data** consist of *numbers* representing counts or measurements.
>
> **Categorical** (or **qualitative** or **attribute**) **data** consist of names or labels that are not numbers representing counts or measurements.

CAUTION Categorical data are sometimes coded with numbers, but those numbers are actually a different way to express names. Although such numbers might appear to be quantitative, they are actually categorical data. See the third part of Example 2.

Example 2   Quantitative/Categorical

1. **Quantitative Data:** The ages (in years) of survey respondents

2. **Categorical Data as Labels:** The political party affiliations (Democrat, Republican, Independent, other) of survey respondents

3. **Categorical Data as Numbers:** The numbers 12, 74, 77, 76, 73, 78, 88, 19, 9, 23, and 25 were sewn on the jerseys of the starting offense for the New Orleans Saints when they won a recent Super Bowl. Those numbers are substitutes for names. They don't measure or count anything, so they are categorical data.

Include Units of Measurement With quantitative data, it is important to use the appropriate units of measurement, such as dollars, hours, feet, or meters. We should carefully observe information given about the units of measurement, such as "all amounts are in *thousands of dollars*," "all times are in *hundredths of a second*," or "all units are in *kilograms.*" Ignoring such units of measurement can be very costly. NASA lost its $125 million Mars Climate Orbiter when the orbiter crashed because the controlling software had acceleration data in *English* units, but they were incorrectly assumed to be in *metric* units.

Discrete/Continuous

Quantitative data can be further described by distinguishing between *discrete* and *continuous* types.

> **DEFINITIONS**
>
> **Discrete data** result when the data values are quantitative and the number of values is finite or "countable." (If there are infinitely many values, the collection of values is countable if it is possible to count them individually, such as the number of tosses of a coin before getting tails.)
>
> **Continuous (numerical) data** result from infinitely many possible quantitative values, where the collection of values is not countable. (That is, it is impossible to count the individual items because at least some of them are on a continuous scale, such as the lengths from 0 cm to 12 cm.)

CAUTION The concept of *countable* data plays a key role in the preceding definitions, but it is not a particularly easy concept to understand. Carefully study Example 3.

Example 3   Discrete/Continuous

1. **Discrete Data of the Finite Type:** The numbers of eggs that hens lay in one week are *discrete* data because they are finite numbers, such as 5 and 7 that result from a counting process.

2. **Discrete Data of the Infinite Type:** Consider the number of rolls of a die required to get an outcome of 2. It is possible that you could roll a die forever without ever getting a 2, but you can still *count* the number of rolls as you proceed. The collection of rolls is countable, because you can count them, even though you might go on counting forever.

3. **Continuous Data:** During a year, a cow might yield an amount of milk that can be any value between 0 liters and 7000 liters. There are infinitely many values between 0 liters and 7000 liters, but it is impossible to *count* the number of different possible values on such a continuous scale.

When we are describing smaller amounts, correct grammar dictates that we use "fewer" for discrete amounts and "less" for continuous amounts. It is correct to say that we drank *fewer* cans of cola and that, in the process, we drank *less* cola. The numbers of cans of cola are discrete data, whereas the volume amounts of cola are continuous data.

Levels of measurement

Another common way of classifying data is to use four levels of measurement: nominal, ordinal, interval, and ratio. When we are applying statistics to real problems, the level of measurement of the data helps us decide which procedure to use. There will be some references to these levels of measurement in this book, but the important point here is based on common sense: *Don't do computations and don't use statistical methods that are not appropriate for the data.* For example, it would not make sense to compute an average (mean) of Social Security numbers, because those numbers are data that are used for identification, and they don't represent measurements or counts of anything.

DEFINITION The **nominal level of measurement** is characterized by data that consist of names, labels, or categories only. The data cannot be arranged in an ordering scheme (such as low to high).

Example 4 Nominal Level

Here are examples of sample data at the nominal level of measurement.

1. **Yes/No/Undecided:** Survey responses of *yes*, *no*, and *undecided*

2. **Political Party:** The political party affiliations of survey respondents (Democrat, Republican, Independent, other)

3. **Social Security Numbers:** Social Security numbers are just substitutes for names; they do not count or measure anything.

Because nominal data lack any ordering or numerical significance, they should not be used for calculations. Numbers such as 1, 2, 3, and 4 are sometimes assigned to the different categories (especially when data are coded for computers), but these numbers have no real computational significance and any average (mean) calculated from them is meaningless.

DEFINITION Data are at the **ordinal level of measurement** if they can be arranged in some order, but differences (obtained by subtraction) between data values either cannot be determined or are meaningless.

Example 5 Ordinal Level

Here are examples of sample data at the ordinal level of measurement.

1. **Course Grades:** A college professor assigns grades of A, B, C, D, or F. These grades can be arranged in order, but we can't determine differences between the grades. For example, we know that A is higher than B (so there is an ordering), but we cannot subtract B from A (so the difference cannot be found).

2. **Ranks:** *U.S. News & World Report* ranks colleges. As of this writing, Harvard was ranked first and Princeton was ranked second. Those ranks of 1 and 2 determine an ordering, but the difference between those ranks is meaningless. The difference of "second minus first" might suggest $2 - 1 = 1$ but this difference of 1 is meaningless because it is not an exact quantity that can be compared to other such differences. The *difference* between Harvard and Princeton cannot be quantitatively compared to the *difference* between Yale and Columbia, the universities ranked third and fourth, respectively.

Ordinal data provide information about relative comparisons, but not the magnitudes of the differences. Usually, ordinal data should not be used for calculations such as an average, but this guideline is sometimes ignored (such as when we use letter grades to calculate a grade-point average).

DEFINITION Data are at the **interval level of measurement** if they can be arranged in order, and differences between data values can be found and are meaningful. Data at this level do not have a *natural* zero starting point at which *none* of the quantity is present.

Measuring Disobedience

How are data collected about something that doesn't seem to be measurable, such as people's level of disobedience? Psychologist Stanley Milgram devised the following experiment: A researcher instructed a volunteer subject to operate a control board that gave increasingly painful "electrical shocks" to a third person. Actually, no real shocks were given, and the third person was an actor. The volunteer began with 15 volts and was instructed to increase the shocks by increments of 15 volts. The disobedience level was the point at which the subject refused to increase the voltage. Surprisingly, two-thirds of the subjects obeyed orders even when the actor screamed and faked a heart attack.

> **Example 6**   Interval Level
>
> These examples illustrate the interval level of measurement.
>
> 1. **Temperatures:** Outdoor temperatures of 40°F and 90°F are examples of data at this interval level of measurement. Those values are ordered, and we can determine their difference of 50°F. However, there is no natural starting point. The value of 0°F might seem like a starting point, but it is arbitrary and does not represent the total absence of heat.
>
> 2. **Years:** The years 1492 and 1776 can be arranged in order, and the difference of 284 years can be found and is meaningful. However, time did not begin in the year 0, so the year 0 is arbitrary instead of being a natural zero starting point representing "no time."

DEFINITION Data are at the **ratio level of measurement** if they can be arranged in order, differences can be found and are meaningful, and there is a natural zero starting point (where zero indicates that *none* of the quantity is present). For data at this level, differences and ratios are both meaningful.

> **Example 7**   Ratio Level
>
> The following are examples of data at the ratio level of measurement. Note the presence of the natural zero value, and also note the use of meaningful ratios of "twice" and "three times."
>
> 1. **Car Lengths:** Car lengths of 106 in. for a Smart car and 212 in. for a Mercury Grand Marquis (0 in. represents no length, and 212 in. is twice as long as 106 in.)
>
> 2. **Class Times:** The times of 50 min and 100 min for a statistics class (0 min represents no class time, and 100 min is twice as long as 50 min.)

HINT This level of measurement is called the ratio level because the zero starting point makes ratios meaningful, so here is an easy test to determine whether values are at the ratio level: Consider two quantities where one number is twice the other, and ask whether "twice" can be used to correctly describe the quantities. Because a person with a height of 6 ft is *twice* as tall as a person with a height of 3 ft, the heights are at the ratio level of measurement. In contrast, 50° F is *not twice* as hot as 25° F, so Fahrenheit temperatures are *not* at the ratio level. See Table 1-2.

Table 1-2 Levels of Measurement

Level of Measurement	Brief Description	Example
Ratio	There is a natural zero starting point and ratios are meaningful.	Heights, lengths, distances, volumes
Interval	Differences are meaningful, but there is no natural zero starting point and ratios are meaningless.	Body temperatures in degrees Fahrenheit or Celsius
Ordinal	Data can be arranged in order, but differences can't be found or are meaningless.	Ranks of colleges in *U.S. News & World Report*
Nominal	Categories only. Data cannot be arranged in order.	Eye colors

1-3 Basic Skills and Concepts

Statistical Literacy and Critical Thinking

1. Parameter and Statistic What is a parameter, and what is a statistic?

2. Quantitative/Categorical Data How do quantitative data and categorical data differ?

3. Discrete/Continuous Data Which of the following describe discrete data?

a. The numbers of people surveyed in each of the next several Gallup polls

b. The exact heights of individuals in a sample of several statistics students

c. The number of Super Bowl football games that must be played before one of the teams scores exactly 75 points

4. Identifying the Population In a Gallup poll of 1010 adults in the United States, 55% of the respondents said that they used local TV stations daily as a source of news. Is the 1010 value a statistic or a parameter? Is the 55% value a statistic or a parameter? Describe the population.

In Exercises 5–12, determine whether the given value is a statistic or a parameter.

5. Distracted Driving In a AAA Foundation for Traffic Safety survey, 21% of the respondents said that they recently texted or e-mailed while driving.

6. States There are 50 state capitols in the United States.

7. Titanic A study was conducted of all 2223 passengers aboard the *Titanic* when it sank.

8. Late Flights Among the flights included in the sample of flights in Data Set 15 of Appendix B, 21% arrived late.

9. IQ Scores The mean IQ score for subjects taking the Wechsler Adult Intelligence Scale IQ test is 100.

10. Periodic Table The average (mean) atomic weight of all elements in the periodic table is 134.355 unified atomic mass units.

11. Brain Volume The average (mean) volume of the brains included in Data Set 6 of Appendix B is 1126.0 cm^3.

12. HDTV Penetration In a random sample of households, it was found that 47% of the sampled households had high-definition TVs.

In Exercises 13–20, determine whether the given values are from a discrete or continuous data set.

13. Honda Civic Crash Test In Data Set 13 of Appendix B, the measured chest deceleration of a Honda Civic in a crash test is 39 g, where g is a force of gravity.

14. Honda Civic Cylinders The Honda Civic has 4 cylinders.

15. Word Count From Data Set 17 in Appendix B we see that a male spoke 13,825 words in one day.

16. First President George Washington was 188 cm tall.

17. House of Representatives Currently the House of Representatives has 435 members.

18. Crash Test Results Data Set 13 in Appendix B includes crash test results from 21 different cars.

19. Earthquake From Data Set 16 in Appendix B we see that an earthquake had a measurement of 0.70 on the Richter scale.

20. Arm Circumference From Data Set 1 in Appendix B we see that a female had an arm circumference of 27.5 cm.

In Exercises 21–28, determine which of the four levels of measurement (nominal, ordinal, interval, ratio) is most appropriate.

21. Colors of M&Ms (red, orange, yellow, brown, blue, green) listed in Data Set 20 in Appendix B

22. Depths (km) of earthquakes listed in Data Set 16 of Appendix B

23. Years in which U.S. presidents were inaugurated

24. The movie *Avatar* was given a rating of 4 stars on a scale of 5 stars.

25. Volumes (cm^3) of brains listed in Data Set 6 of Appendix B

26. Car models (Chevrolet Aveo, Honda Civic, . . . , Buick Lucerne) used for crash testing, as listed in Data Set 13 of Appendix B

27. Blood lead levels of low, medium, and high used to describe the subjects in Data Set 5 of Appendix B

28. Body temperatures (in degrees Fahrenheit) listed in Data Set 3 of Appendix B

In Exercises 29–32, identify the level of measurement of the data. Also, explain what is wrong with the given calculation.

29. Political Parties In a preelection survey of likely voters, political parties of respondents are identified as 1 for a Democrat, 2 for a Republican, 3 for an Independent, and 4 for anything else. The average (mean) is calculated for 850 respondents and the result is 1.7.

30. Flight Numbers Data Set 15 in Appendix B lists flight numbers of 48 different flights, and the average (mean) of those flight numbers is 11.0.

31. Lead Levels In Data Set 5 in Appendix B, blood lead levels are represented as 1 for low, 2 for medium, and 3 for high. The average (mean) of the 121 blood lead levels is 1.53.

32. World Series Champs As of this writing, the New York Yankees were the last team to win the World Series, and the numbers of the starting lineup are 2, 18, 25, 13, 20, 55, 24, 33, and 53. The average (mean) of those numbers is 27.0.

1-3 Beyond the Basics

33. Countable For each of the following, categorize the nature of the data using one of these three descriptions: (1) Discrete because the number of possible values is finite; (2) discrete because the number of possible values is infinite and countable; (3) continuous because the number of possible values is infinite and not countable.

a. Exact braking distances of cars, measured on a scale from 100 ft to 200 ft

b. Braking distances of cars, measured on a scale from 100 ft to 200 ft and rounded to the nearest foot

c. The numbers of students now in statistics classes

d. The number of attempts required to roll a single die and get an outcome of 7

34. Scale for Rating Food A group of students develops a scale for rating the quality of cafeteria food, with 0 representing "neutral: not good and not bad." Bad meals are given negative numbers and good meals are given positive numbers, with the magnitude of the number corresponding to the degree of badness or goodness. The first three meals are rated as 2, 4, and −5. What is the level of measurement for such ratings? Explain your choice.

35. Interpreting Temperature Increase In the *Born Loser* cartoon strip by Art Sansom, Brutus expresses joy over an increase in temperature from 1° to 2°. When asked what is so good about 2°, he answers that "it's twice as warm as this morning." Explain why Brutus is wrong yet again.

1-4   Collecting Sample Data

Key Concept An absolutely critical concept in applying methods of statistics is consideration of the method used to collect the sample data. Of particular importance is the method of using a *simple random sample*. We will make frequent use of this sampling method throughout the remainder of this book.

As you read this section, remember this:

If sample data are not collected in an appropriate way, the data may be so utterly useless that no amount of statistical torturing can salvage them.

Part 1 of this section introduces the basics of data collection, and Part 2 describes some common ways in which observational studies and experiments are conducted.

Part 1: Basics of Collecting Data

Statistical methods are driven by the data that we collect. We typically obtain data from two distinct sources: *observational studies* and *experiments*.

> **DEFINITIONS**
>
> In an **observational study,** we observe and measure specific characteristics, but we don't attempt to *modify* the subjects being studied.
>
> In an **experiment,** we apply some *treatment* and then proceed to observe its effects on the subjects. (Subjects in experiments are called **experimental units.**)

Experiments are often better than observational studies, because experiments typically reduce the chance of having the results affected by some variable that is not part of a study. (A **lurking variable** is one that affects the variables included in the study, but it is not included in the study.) In one classic example, we could use an observational study to incorrectly conclude that ice cream causes drownings based on data showing that increases in ice cream sales are associated with increases in drownings. Our error is to miss the lurking variable of temperature and thus fail to recognize that warmer months result in both increased ice cream sales and increased drownings. If, instead of using data from an observational study, we conducted an *experiment* with one group treated with ice cream while another group got no ice cream, we would see that ice cream consumption has no effect on drownings.

Example 1   Observational Study and Experiment

Observational Study: The typical survey is a good example of an observational study. For example, the Pew Research Center surveyed 2252 adults in the United States and found that 59% of them go online wirelessly. The respondents were asked questions, but they were not given any treatment, so this is an example of an observational study.

Clinical Trials vs. Observational Studies

In a *New York Times* article about hormone therapy for women, reporter Denise Grady wrote about randomized clinical trials that involve subjects who were randomly assigned to a treatment group and another group not given the treatment. Such randomized clinical trials are often referred to as the "gold standard" for medical research. In contrast, observational studies can involve patients who decide themselves to undergo some treatment. Subjects who decide themselves to undergo treatments are often healthier than other subjects, so the treatment group might appear to be more successful simply because it involves healthier subjects, not necessarily because the treatment is effective. Researchers criticized observational studies of hormone therapy for women by saying that results might appear to make the treatment more effective than it really is.

Experiment: In the largest public health experiment ever conducted, 200,745 children were given a treatment consisting of the Salk vaccine, while 201,229 other children were given a placebo. The Salk vaccine injections constitute a treatment that modified the subjects, so this is an example of an experiment.

Whether one is conducting an observational study or an experiment, it is important to select the sample of subjects in such a way that the sample is likely to be representative of the larger population. In Section 1-2 we saw that in a voluntary response sample, the subjects decide themselves whether to respond. Although voluntary response samples are very common, their results are generally useless for making valid inferences about larger populations. The following defintion refers to one common and effective way to collect sample data.

> **DEFINITION** A **simple random sample** of *n* subjects is selected in such a way that every possible *sample of the same size n* has the same chance of being chosen. (A simple random sample is often called a random sample, but strictly speaking, a random sample has the weaker requirement that all members of the population have the same chance of being selected. That distinction is not so important in this text.)

Throughout, we will use various statistical procedures, and we often have a requirement that we have collected a *simple random sample*, as defined above.

The definition of a simple random sample requires more than selecting subjects in such a way that each has the same chance of being selected. Consider the selection of three students from the class of six students depicted below. If you use a coin toss to select a row, randomness is used and each student has the same chance of being selected, but the result is not a simple random sample. The coin toss will produce only two possible samples; some samples of three students have *no chance* of being selected, such as a sample consisting of a female and two males. This violates the requirement that all samples of the same size have the same chance of being selected. Instead of the coin toss, you could get a simple random sample of three students by writing each of the six different student names on separate index cards, which could then be placed in a bowl and mixed. The selection of three index cards will yield a simple random sample, because every different possible sample of three students now has the same chance of being selected.

Heads: 👩👩👩

Tails: 🧍🧍🧍

With random sampling we expect all components of the population to be (approximately) proportionately represented. Random samples are selected by many different methods, including the use of computers to generate random numbers. Unlike careless or haphazard sampling, random sampling usually requires very careful planning and execution. Wayne Barber of Chemeketa Community College is quite correct when he tells his students that "randomness needs help."

Other Sampling Methods In addition to simple random sampling, here are some other sampling methods commonly used for surveys. Figure 1-3 illustrates these different sampling methods.

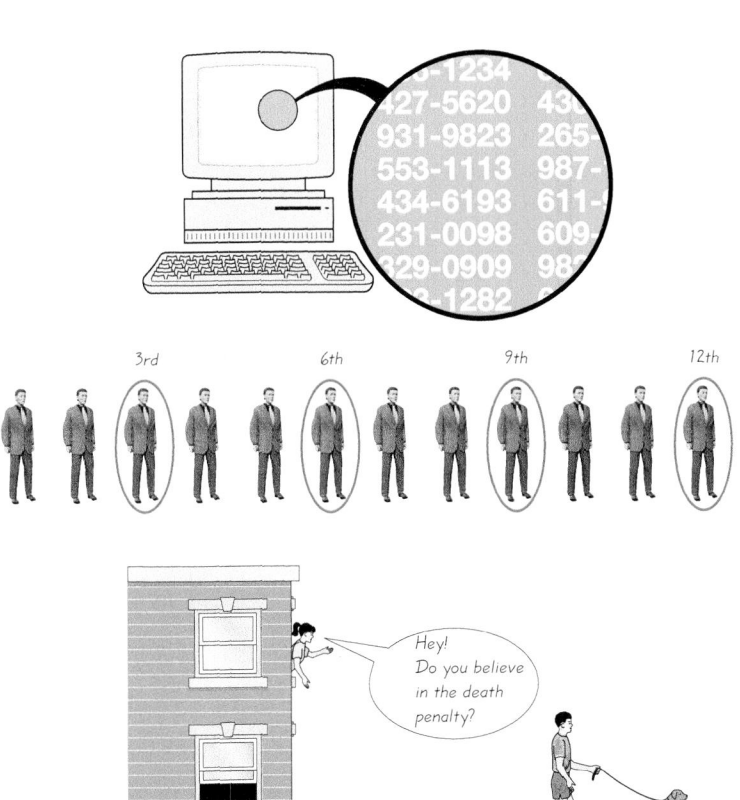

Random Sampling:

Each member of the population has an equal chance of being selected. Computers are often used to generate random telephone numbers.

Simple Random Sampling:

A sample of n subjects is selected in such a way that every possible sample of the same size n has the same chance of being chosen.

Systematic Sampling:

Select some starting point, then select every kth (such as every 50th) element in the population.

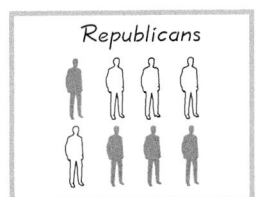

Convenience Sampling:

Use results that are easy to get.

Stratified Sampling:

Subdivide the population into at least two different subgroups (or strata) so that subjects within the same subgroup share the same characteristics (such as gender or age bracket), then draw a sample from each subgroup.

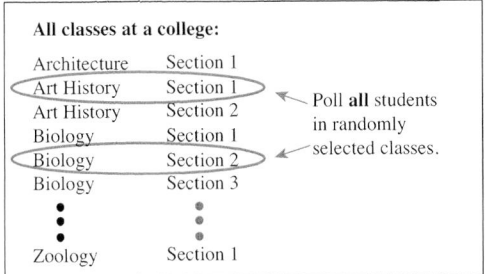

Cluster Sampling:

Divide the population into sections (or clusters), then randomly select some of those clusters, and then choose all members from those selected clusters.

Figure 1-3   Common Sampling Methods

Hawthorne and Experimenter Effects

The well-known placebo effect occurs when an untreated subject incorrectly believes that he or she is receiving a real treatment and reports an improvement in symptoms. The Hawthorne effect occurs when treated subjects somehow respond differently, simply because they are part of an experiment. (This phenomenon was called the "Hawthorne effect" because it was first observed in a study of factory workers at Western Electric's Hawthorne plant.) An experimenter effect (sometimes called a Rosenthal effect) occurs when the researcher or experimenter unintentionally influences subjects through such factors as facial expression, tone of voice, or attitude.

DEFINITIONS

In **systematic sampling,** we select some starting point and then select every kth (such as every 50th) element in the population.

With **convenience sampling,** we simply use results that are very easy to get.

In **stratified sampling,** we subdivide the population into at least two different subgroups (or strata) so that subjects within the same subgroup share the same characteristics (such as age bracket). Then we draw a sample from each subgroup (or stratum).

In **cluster sampling,** we first divide the population area into sections (or clusters). Then we randomly select some of those clusters and choose *all* the members from those selected clusters.

It is easy to confuse stratified sampling and cluster sampling, because they both use subgroups. But cluster sampling uses *all* members from a *sample* of clusters, whereas stratified sampling uses a *sample* of members from *all* strata. An example of cluster sampling is a preelection poll, in which pollsters randomly select 30 election precincts from a large number of precincts and then survey all voters in each of those precincts. This is faster and much less expensive than selecting one voter from each of the many precincts in the population area. Pollsters can adjust or weight the results of stratified or cluster sampling to correct for any disproportionate representation of groups.

For a fixed sample size, if you randomly select subjects from different strata, you are likely to get more consistent (and less variable) results than by simply selecting a random sample from the general population. For that reason, pollsters often use stratified sampling to reduce the variation in the results. Many of the methods discussed later in this book require that sample data be derived from a *simple random sample*, and neither stratified sampling nor cluster sampling satisfies that requirement.

Multistage Sampling Professional pollsters and government researchers often collect data by using some combination of the basic sampling methods. In a **multistage sample design,** pollsters select a sample in different stages, and each stage might use different methods of sampling. For example, one multistage sample design might involve the random selection of clusters, but instead of surveying all members of the chosen clusters, you might randomly select 50 men and 50 women in each selected cluster; thus you begin with cluster sampling and end with stratified sampling. See Example 2 for an actual multistage sample design that is complex, but effective.

Example 2   Multistage Sample Design

The U.S. government's unemployment statistics are based on surveyed households. It is impractical to personally visit each member of a simple random sample, because individual households are spread all over the country. Instead, the U.S. Census Bureau and the Bureau of Labor Statistics collaborate to conduct a survey called the Current Population Survey. This survey obtains data describing such factors as unemployment rates, college enrollments, and weekly earnings amounts. One recent survey incorporates a multistage sample design, roughly following these steps:

1. The entire United States is partitioned into 2025 different regions called *primary sampling units* (PSUs). The primary sampling units are metropolitan areas, large counties, or combinations of smaller counties. These primary sampling units are geographically connected. The 2025 primary sampling units are then grouped into 824 different strata.

2. In each of the 824 different strata, one of the primary sampling units is selected so that the probability of selection is proportional to the size of the population in each primary sampling unit.

3. In each of the 824 selected primary sampling units, census data are used to identify a census *enumeration district,* with each containing about 300 households. Enumeration districts are then randomly selected.

4. In each of the selected enumeration districts, clusters of about four addresses (contiguous whenever possible) are randomly selected.

5. Respondents in the 60,000 selected households are interviewed about the employment status of each household member of age 16 or older.

This multistage sample design includes random, stratified, and cluster sampling at different stages. The end result is a very complicated sampling design, but it is much more practical and less expensive than using a simpler design, such as a simple random sample.

Part 2: Beyond the Basics of Collecting Data

In Part 2 of this section, we refine what we've learned about observational studies and experiments by discussing different types of observational studies and different ways of designing experiments.

There are various types of observational studies in which investigators observe and measure characteristics of subjects. The following definitions identify the standard terminology used in professional journals for different types of observational studies. These definitions are illustrated in Figure 1-4.

Figure 1-4 **Types of Observational Studies**

Prospective National Children's Study

A good example of a prospective study is the National Children's Study begun in 2005. It is tracking 100,000 children from birth to age 21. The children are from 96 different geographic regions.

The objective is to improve the health of children by identifying the effects of environmental factors, such as diet, chemical exposure, vaccinations, movies, and television. The study will address questions such as these: How do genes and the environment interact to promote or prevent violent behavior in teenagers? Are lack of exercise and poor diet the only reasons why many children are overweight? Do infections impact developmental progress, asthma, obesity, and heart disease? How do city and neighborhood planning and construction encourage or discourage injuries?

National Children's Study

The National Children's Study, launched in 2009, is designed to follow 100,000 U.S. children from before birth to age 21. Subjects have been selected from 105 different counties so that it will include a good mix of characteristics. Because children are observed from birth into the future, this is a good example of a prospective study. The cost of the study was originally expected to be $3 billion, but it has grown to almost $7 billion. Data are being collected from such varied sources as breast milk and carpet dust. The general goal is to collect data that will enhance our understanding of the effects of genetics and the environment on children. It is hoped that this understanding will lead to improvements in children's health. The National Children's Study is the largest, most expensive, and most comprehensive study of its type ever undertaken. It is being sponsored by several federal organizations, including the Department of Health and Human Services, the National Institutes of Health, and the Environmental Protection Agency.

> **DEFINITIONS**
>
> In a **cross-sectional study**, data are observed, measured, and collected at one point in time, not over a period of time.
>
> In a **retrospective** (or **case-control**) **study**, data are collected from a past time period by going back in time (through examination of records, interviews, and so on).
>
> In a **prospective** (or **longitudinal** or **cohort**) **study**, data are collected in the future from groups that share common factors (such groups are called *cohorts*).

The sampling done in retrospective studies differs from that in prospective studies. In retrospective studies we go back in time to collect data about the characteristic that is of interest, such as a group of drivers who died in car crashes and another group of drivers who did not die in car crashes. In prospective studies we go forward in time by following a group with a potentially causative factor and a group without it, such as a group of drivers who use cell phones and a group of drivers who do not use cell phones.

Designs of Experiments

We begin with Example 3, which describes the largest public health experiment ever conducted, and which serves as an example of an experiment having a good design. After describing the experiment in more detail, we describe the characteristics of randomization, replication, and blinding that typify a good design in experiments.

Example 3   The Salk Vaccine Experiment

In 1954, a large-scale experiment was designed to test the effectiveness of the Salk vaccine in preventing polio, which had killed or paralyzed thousands of children. In that experiment, 200,745 children were given a treatment consisting of Salk vaccine injections, while a second group of 201,229 children were injected with a placebo that contained no drug. The children being injected did not know whether they were getting the Salk vaccine or the placebo. Children were assigned to the treatment or placebo group through a process of random selection, equivalent to flipping a coin. Among the children given the Salk vaccine, 33 later developed paralytic polio, and among the children given a placebo, 115 later developed paralytic polio.

Randomization is used when subjects are assigned to different groups through a process of random selection. The 401,974 children in the Salk vaccine experiment were assigned to the Salk vaccine treatment group or the placebo group via a process of random selection equivalent to flipping a coin. In this experiment, it would be extremely difficult to directly assign children to two groups having similar characteristics of age, health, sex, weight, height, diet, and so on. There could easily be important variables that we might not think of including. The logic behind randomization is to use chance as a way to create two groups that are similar. Although it might seem that we should not leave anything to chance in experiments, randomization has been found to be an extremely effective method for assigning subjects to groups. However, it is possible for randomization to result in unbalanced samples, especially when very small sample sizes are involved.

Replication is the repetition of an experiment on more than one subject. Samples should be large enough so that the erratic behavior that is characteristic of very small samples will not disguise the true effects of different treatments. Replication is used effectively when we have enough subjects to recognize differences resulting from different treatments. (In another context, *replication* refers to the repetition or duplication of an experiment so that results can be confirmed or verified.) With replication, the large sample sizes increase the chance of recognizing different treatment effects. However, a large sample is not necessarily a good sample. Although it is important to have a sample that is sufficiently large, it is even more important to have a sample in which subjects have been chosen in some appropriate way, such as random selection.

Use a sample size that is large enough to let us see the true nature of any effects, and obtain the sample using an appropriate method, such as one based on *randomness*.

In the experiment designed to test the Salk vaccine, 200,745 children were given the actual Salk vaccine and 201,229 other children were given a placebo. Because the actual experiment used sufficiently large sample sizes, the researchers could observe the effectiveness of the vaccine.

Blinding is in effect when the subject doesn't know whether he or she is receiving a treatment or a placebo. Blinding enables us to determine whether the treatment effect is significantly different from a **placebo effect,** which occurs when an untreated subject reports an improvement in symptoms. (The reported improvement in the placebo group may be real or imagined.) Blinding minimizes the placebo effect or allows investigators to account for it. The polio experiment was **double-blind,** which means that blinding occurred at two levels: (1) The children being injected didn't know whether they were getting the Salk vaccine or a placebo, and (2) the doctors who gave the injections and evaluated the results did not know either. Codes were used so that the researchers could objectively evaluate the effectiveness of the Salk vaccine.

Controlling Effects of Variables Results of experiments are sometimes ruined because of *confounding*.

> **DEFINITION Confounding** occurs in an experiment when the investigators are not able to distinguish among the effects of different factors.
>
> **Try to design the experiment in such a way that confounding does not occur.**

Designs of Experiments See Figure 1-5(a), where confounding can occur when the treatment group of women shows strong positive results. Here the treatment group consists of women and the placebo group consists of men. Confounding has occurred because we cannot determine whether the treatment or the gender of the subjects caused the positive results. It is important to design experiments in such a way as to control and understand the effects of the variables (such as treatments). The Salk vaccine experiment in Example 3 illustrates one method for controlling the effect of the treatment variable: Use a *completely randomized experimental design,* whereby randomness is used to assign subjects to the treatment group and the placebo group. A completely randomized experimental design is one of the following methods that are used to control effects of variables.

Completely Randomized Experimental Design: Assign subjects to different treatment groups through a process of *random selection,* as illustrated in Example 3 and Figure 1-5(b).

Randomized Block Design: A **block** is a group of subjects that are similar, but blocks differ in ways that might affect the outcome of the experiment. Use the following procedure, as illustrated in Figure 1-5(c):

1. Form blocks (or groups) of subjects with similar characteristics.

2. Randomly assign treatments to the subjects within each block.

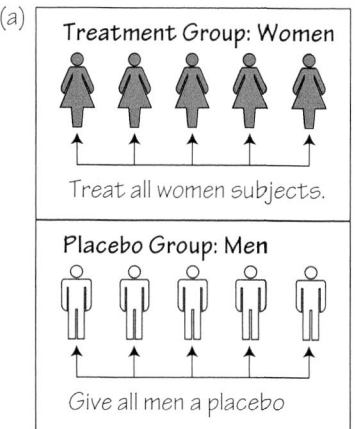

(a)

Bad experimental design:
Treat all women subjects and give the men a placebo.
(Problem: We don't know if effects are due to sex or to treatment.)

(b)

Completely randomized experimental design:
Use randomness to determine who gets the treatment and who gets the placebo.

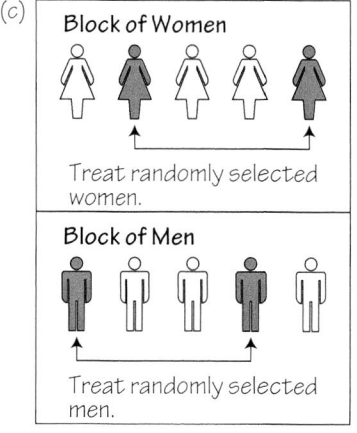

(c)

Randomized block design:
1. Form a block of women and a block of men.
2. Within each block, randomly select subjects to be treated.

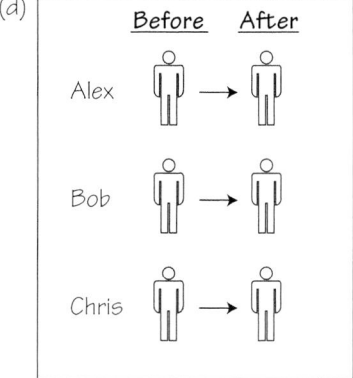

(d)

Matched pairs design:
Get measurements from the same subjects before and after some treatment.

Figure 1-5   Designs of Experiments

For example, in designing an experiment to test the effectiveness of aspirin treatments on heart disease, we might form a block of men and a block of women, because it is known that the hearts of men and women can behave differently. By controlling for gender, this randomized block design eliminates gender as a possible source of confounding.

A randomized block design uses the same basic idea as stratified sampling, but randomized block designs are used when designing experiments, whereas stratified sampling is used for surveys.

Matched Pairs Design: Compare two treatment groups (such as treatment and placebo) by using subjects matched in pairs that are somehow related or have similar characteristics, as in the following cases.

- Before/After: Matched pairs might consist of measurements from subjects before and after some treatment, as illustrated in Figure 1-5(d). Each subject yields a "before" measurement and an "after" measurement, and each before/after pair of measurements is a matched pair.

- Twins: A test of Crest toothpaste used matched pairs of twins, where one twin used Crest and the other used another toothpaste.

Rigorously Controlled Design: Carefully assign subjects to different treatment groups, so that those given each treatment are similar in the ways that are important to the experiment. In an experiment testing the effectiveness of aspirin on heart disease, if the placebo group includes a 27-year-old male smoker who drinks heavily and consumes an abundance of salt and fat, the treatment group should also include a person with these characteristics (such a person would be easy to find). This approach can be extremely difficult to implement, and often we can never be sure that we have accounted for all of the relevant factors.

Sampling Errors In an algebra course, you will get the correct result if you use the correct methods and apply them correctly. In statistics, you could use a good sampling method and do everything correctly, and yet it is possible for the result to be wrong. No matter how well you plan and execute the sample collection process, there is likely to be some error in the results. Suppose that you randomly select 1000 adults, ask them whether they use a cell phone while driving, and record the sample percentage of "yes" responses. If you randomly select another sample of 1000 adults, it is likely that you will obtain a *different* sample percentage. The different types of sampling errors are described here.

> **DEFINITIONS**
>
> A **sampling error** (or **random sampling error**) occurs when the sample has been selected with a random method, but there is a discrepancy between a sample result and the true population result; such an error results from chance sample fluctuations.
>
> A **nonsampling error** is the result of human error, including such factors as wrong data entries, computing errors, questions with biased wording, false data provided by respondents, forming biased conclusions, or applying statistical methods that are not appropriate for the circumstances.
>
> A **nonrandom sampling error** is the result of using a sampling method that is not random, such as using a convenience sample or a voluntary response sample.

If we carefully collect a random sample so that it is representative of the population, we can use methods in this book to analyze the sampling error, but we must exercise great care to minimize nonsampling error.

Experimental design requires much more thought and care than we can describe in this relatively brief section. Taking a complete course in the design of experiments is a good start in learning so much more about this important topic.

Misleading Statistics in Journalism

New York Times reporter Daniel Okrant wrote that although every sentence in his newspaper is copy-edited for clarity and good writing, "numbers, so alien to so many, don't get nearly this respect. The paper requires no specific training to enhance numeracy and [employs] no specialists whose sole job is to foster it." He cites an example of the *New York Times* reporting about an estimate of more than $23 billion that New Yorkers spend for counterfeit goods each year. Okrant writes that "quick arithmetic would have demonstrated that $23 billion would work out to roughly $8000 per city household, a number ludicrous on its face."

1-4 Basic Skills and Concepts

Statistical Literacy and Critical Thinking

1. Simple Random Sample At a national conference of the American Appliances Association, a market researcher plans to conduct a survey of conference attendees. She uses the list of attendee names and selects every 20th name. Is the result a simple random sample? Why or why not? In general, what is a simple random sample?

2. Observational Study and Experiment You want to conduct a study to determine whether fruit consumption leads to reduced weight. Why would an experiment be better than an observational study?

3. Simple Random Convenience Sample A student of the author listed his adult friends, and then he surveyed a simple random sample of them. What is the population from which the simple random sample was selected? Are the results likely to be representative of the general population of adults in the United States? Why or why not?

4. Convenience Sample The author conducted a survey of the students in all of his classes. He asked the students to indicate whether they are left-handed or right-handed. Is this convenience sample likely to provide results that are typical of the population? Are the results likely to be good or bad? Does the quality of the results in this survey reflect the quality of convenience samples in general?

In Exercises 5–8, determine whether the given description corresponds to an observational study or an experiment. In each case, give a brief explanation of your choice.

5. Contentious Survey The Milgram Research Company wants to study reactions to stress, so it administers surveys in which the person asking the questions pretends to become very angry with the survey subject. At one point, the surveyor screams at the subject and asks how anyone could have such "stupid" opinions.

6. Clinical Trial In a clinical trial of the cholesterol drug Lipitor, 188 subjects were given 20-mg doses of the drug, and 3.7% of them experienced nausea (based on data from Pfizer, Inc.).

7. Touch Therapy Nine-year-old Emily Rosa was an author of an article in the *Journal of the American Medical Association* after she tested professional touch therapists. Using a cardboard partition, she held her hand above one of the therapist's hands, and the therapist was asked to identify the hand that Emily chose.

8. Happiness Survey In a study sponsored by Coca-Cola, 12,500 people were asked what contributes most to their happiness, and 77% of the respondents said that it was their family or partner.

In Exercises 9–20, identify which of these types of sampling is used: random, systematic, convenience, stratified, *or* cluster.

9. Harry Potter The author collected sample data by randomly selecting 12 different pages from *Harry Potter and the Sorcerer's Stone* and then finding the number of words in each sentence on each of those pages.

10. Sexuality of Women The sexuality of women was discussed in Shere Hite's book *Women and Love: A Cultural Revolution.* Her conclusions were based on sample data that consisted of 4500 mailed responses from 100,000 questionnaires that were sent to women.

 11. Twitter Poll In a Pew Research Center poll, 1007 adults were called after their telephone numbers were randomly generated by a computer, and 85% of the respondents were able to correctly identify what Twitter is.

12. Ecology When collecting data from different sample locations in a lake, a researcher uses the "line transect method" by stretching a rope across the lake and collecting samples at every interval of 5 meters.

13. CBS News The CBS News station in New York City often obtains opinions by interviewing neighbors of a person who is the focus of a news story.

14. Acupuncture Study In a study of treatments for back pain, 641 subjects were randomly assigned to the four different treatment groups of individualized acupuncture, standardized acupuncture, simulated acupuncture, and usual care (based on data from "A Randomized Trial Comparing Acupuncture, Simulated Acupuncture, and Usual Care for Chronic Low Back Pain," by Cherkin et al., *Archives of Internal Medicine,* Vol. 169, No. 9).

15. Deforestation Rates Satellites are used to collect sample data used to estimate deforestation rates. The Forest Resources Assessment of the UN Food and Agriculture Organization uses a method of selecting a sample of a 10-km-wide square at every 1° intersection of latitude and longitude.

16. Dictionary The author collected sample data by randomly selecting 20 different pages from a printed version of the *Merriam-Webster Dictionary* and then counting the number of defined words on each of those pages.

17. Testing Lipitor In a clinical trial of the cholesterol drug Lipitor, subjects were partitioned into groups given a placebo or Lipitor doses of 10 mg, 20 mg, 40 mg, or 80 mg. The subjects were randomly assigned to the different treatment groups (based on data from Pfizer, Inc.).

18. Exit Polls On the day of the last presidential election, ABC News organized an exit poll in which specific polling stations were randomly selected and all voters were surveyed as they left the premises.

19. Literary Digest Poll In 1936, *Literary Digest* magazine mailed questionnaires to 10 million people and obtained 2,266,566 responses. The responses indicated that Alf Landon would win the presidential election, but Franklin D. Roosevelt actually won the election.

20. Highway Strength The New York State Department of Transportation evaluated the quality of the New York State Throughway by testing core samples collected at regular intervals of one mile.

Simple Random Samples.   *In Exercises 21–26, determine whether the sample is a simple random sample. Give a brief explanation of your choice.*

21. Bayer Aspirin Bayer HealthCare LLC produces low-dose aspirin pills designed to contain 81 mg of aspirin. Because each pill contains other ingredients, including corn starch, talc, and propylene glycol, it is difficult to check whether manufactured pills contain 81 mg of aspirin. A quality control plan is to select every 1000th pill, which is then tested for the correct amount of aspirin.

22. Market Research In order to test for a gender gap in the way that men and women purchase cars, the Grant Survey Company polls exactly 750 adult men and 750 adult women randomly selected from adults in the United States.

23. Post-Election Survey In the last general election, 132,312 adults voted in Dutchess County, New York. You plan to conduct a post-election survey of 500 of those voters. After obtaining a list of those who voted, you number the list from 1 to 132,312, and then you use a computer to randomly generate 500 numbers between 1 and 132,312. Your sample consists of the voters corresponding to the selected numbers.

24. Jury Selection According to the State of New York Unified Court System, names of potential jurors are selected from a variety of different sources. When a trial requires a jury, names from the list are randomly selected in a way that is equivalent to writing the names on slips of paper, mixing them in a bowl, and selecting the required number of potential jurors.

25. Mall Research Mall managers commonly research how customers use the malls. The author was approached by a pollster at the Galleria Mall in Dutchess County, New York. The pollster was obviously selecting subjects who appeared to be approachable.

26. Car Crash Tests The National Highway Traffic Safety Administration (NHTSA) conducts crash tests of cars. One car of each different model is randomly selected for testing.

1-4 Beyond the Basics

In Exercises 27–30, indicate whether the observational study used is cross-sectional, retrospective, *or* prospective.

27. Nurses' Health Study The Nurses' Health Study was started in 1976 with 121,700 female registered nurses who were between the ages of 30 and 55. The subjects were surveyed in 1976 and every two years thereafter. The study is ongoing.

28. Drinking and Driving Study In order to study the seriousness of drinking and driving, a researcher obtains records from past car crashes. Drivers are partitioned into a group that had no alcohol consumption and another group that did have evidence of alcohol consumption at the time of the crash.

29. Smoking Study Researchers from the National Institutes of Health want to determine the current rates of smoking among adult males and adult females. They conduct a survey of 500 adults of each gender.

30. Meat and Mortality Researchers at the National Cancer Institute studied meat consumption and its relationship to mortality. Approximately one-half million people were surveyed, and they were then followed for a period of 10 years.

In Exercises 31–34, identify which of these designs is most appropriate for the given experiment: completely randomized design, randomized block design, *or* matched pairs design.

31. Lisinipril Lisinipril is a drug designed to lower blood pressure. In a clinical trial of Lisinipril, blood pressure levels of subjects are measured before and after they have been treated with the drug.

32. Aspirin A clinical trial of aspirin treatments is being planned to determine whether the rate of myocardial infarctions (heart attacks) is different for men and women.

33. West Nile Vaccine Currently, there is no approved vaccine for the prevention of West Nile virus. A clinical trial of a possible vaccine is being planned to include subjects treated with the vaccine while other subjects are given a placebo.

34. HIV Vaccine The HIV Trials Network is conducting a study to test the effectiveness of two different experimental HIV vaccines. Subjects will consist of 80 pairs of twins. For each pair of twins, one of the subjects will be treated with the DNA vaccine and the other twin will be treated with the adenoviral vector vaccine.

35. Blinding For the study described in Exercise 34, blinding will be used. What is blinding, and why was it important in this experiment?

36. Sample Design Literacy In "Cardiovascular Effects of Intravenous Triiodothyronine in Patients Undergoing Coronary Artery Bypass Graft Surgery" (*Journal of the American Medical Association,* Vol. 275, No. 9), the authors explain that patients were assigned to one of three groups: (1) a group treated with triiodothyronine, (2) a group treated with normal saline bolus and dopamine, and (3) a placebo group given normal saline. The authors summarize the sample design as a "prospective, randomized, double-blind, placebo-controlled trial." Describe the meaning of each of those terms in the context of this study.

Chapter 1   Review

The single most important concept presented in this chapter is to recognize that when one is using methods of statistics with sample data to form conclusions about a population, it is absolutely essential to collect sample data in a way that is appropriate. Using data from a voluntary response (self-selected) sample is a really bad idea, because such a sample could very easily be biased in that it might not be at all representative of the population. One common and effective method for collecting data is to use a *simple random sample*. With a simple random sample of *n* items, all possible samples of *n* items have the same chance of being selected.

Statistical literacy includes a clear understanding of such important terms as *sample, population, statistic, parameter, quantitative data, categorical data, voluntary response sample, observational study, experiment,* and *simple random sample*. Section 1-2 introduced statistical thinking, and Figure 1-2 summarized important issues to consider in preparation for analysis, conducting the analysis, and forming conclusions. Section 1-3 discussed different types of data, and it is crucial to understand the distinction between quantitative data and categorical data. After completing this chapter, you should be able to do the following:

- Distinguish between a population and a sample, and distinguish between a parameter and a statistic.

- Recognize the importance of good sampling methods in general, and recognize the importance of a *simple random sample* in particular. Understand that even though voluntary response samples are common, they should not be used for a statistical analysis.

Chapter Quick Quiz

1. Chicago Bulls The numbers of the current players for the Chicago Bulls basketball team are 1, 2, 3, 5, 6, 9, 11, 13, 16, 20, 22, 26, 32, and 40. Does it make sense to calculate the average (mean) of these numbers?

2. Chicago Bulls Which of the following best describes the level of measurement of the data listed in Exercise 1: nominal, ordinal, interval, ratio?

3. Earthquake Depths Data Set 16 includes depths (km) of the sources of earthquakes. Are these values discrete or continuous?

4. Earthquake Depths Are the earthquake depths described in Exercise 3 quantitative data or categorical data?

5. Earthquake Depths Which of the following best describes the level of measurement of the earthquake depths described in Exercise 3: nominal, ordinal, interval, ratio?

6. Earthquake Depths True or false: If you construct a sample by selecting every sixth earthquake depth from the list given in Data Set 16, the result is a simple random sample.

7. Gallup Poll In a recent Gallup poll, pollsters randomly selected adults and asked them whether they smoke. Because the subjects agreed to respond, is the sample a voluntary response sample?

8. Parameter and Statistic In a recent Gallup poll, pollsters randomly selected adults and asked them whether they smoke. Among the adults who responded to the survey question, 21% said that they did smoke. Is that value of 21% an example of a statistic or an example of a parameter?

9. Observational Study or Experiment Are the data described in Exercise 8 the result of an observational study or an experiment?

10. Statistical Significance and Practical Significance True or false: If data lead to a conclusion with statistical significance, then the results also have practical significance.

Review Exercises

1. Walmart Stores Currently, there are 4227 Walmart stores in the United States and another 3210 stores outside of the United States.

a. Are the numbers of Walmart stores discrete or continuous?

b. What is the level of measurement for the numbers of Walmart stores in different years? (nominal, ordinal, interval, ratio)

c. If a survey is conducted by randomly selecting 10 customers in every Walmart store, what type of sampling is used? (random, systematic, convenience, stratified, cluster)

d. If a survey is conducted by randomly selecting 20 Walmart stores and interviewing all of the employees at the selected stores, what type of sampling is used? (random, systematic, convenience, stratified, cluster)

e. What is wrong with surveying customer satisfaction by mailing questionnaires to 10,000 randomly selected customers?

2. What's Wrong? A survey sponsored by the American Laser Centers included responses from 575 adults, and 24% of the respondents said that the face is their favorite body part (based on data from *USA Today*). What is wrong with this survey?

3. What's Wrong? A survey included 4230 responses from Internet users who decided to respond to a question posted by America OnLine (AOL). Here is the question: How often do you use credit cards for purchases? Among the respondents, 67% said that they used credit cards frequently. What is wrong with this survey?

4. Sampling Seventy-two percent of Americans squeeze their toothpaste tube from the top. This and other not-so-serious findings are included in *The First Really Important Survey of American Habits*. Those results are based on 7000 responses from the 25,000 questionnaires that were mailed.

a. What is wrong with this survey?

b. As stated, the value of 72% refers to all Americans, so is that 72% a statistic or a parameter? Explain.

c. Does the survey constitute an observational study or an experiment?

5. Percentages

a. The labels on U-Turn protein energy bars include the statement that these bars contain "125% less fat than the leading chocolate candy brands" (based on data from *Consumer Reports magazine*). What is wrong with that claim?

b. In a Pew Research Center poll on driving, 58% of the 1182 respondents said that they like to drive. What is the actual number of respondents who said that they like to drive?

c. In a Pew Research Center poll on driving, 331 of the 1182 respondents said that driving is a chore. What percentage of respondents said that driving is a chore?

6. Why the Discrepancy? A Gallup poll was taken two years before a presidential election, and it showed that Hillary Clinton was preferred by about 50% more voters than Barack Obama. The subjects in the Gallup poll were randomly selected and surveyed by telephone. An America OnLine (AOL) poll was conducted at the same time as the Gallup poll, and it showed that Barack Obama was preferred by about twice as many respondents as Hillary Clinton. In the AOL poll, Internet users responded to voting choices that were posted on the AOL site. How can the large discrepancy between the two polls be explained? Which poll is more likely to reflect the true opinions of American voters at the time of the poll?

7. Statistical Significance and Practical Significance The Gengene Research Group has developed a procedure designed to increase the likelihood that a baby will be born a girl. In a clinical trial of their procedure, 112 girls were born to 200 different couples. If the method has no effect, there is about a 4% chance that such extreme results would occur. Does the procedure appear to have statistical significance? Does the procedure appear to have practical significance?

8. Marijuana Survey In a recent Pew poll of 1500 adults, 52% of the respondents said that the use of marijuana should not be made legal. In the same poll, 23% of the respondents said that the use of marijuana for medical purposes should not be legal.

a. The sample of 1500 adults was selected from the population of all adults in the United States. The method used to select the sample was equivalent to placing the names of all adults in a giant bowl, mixing the names, and then drawing 1500 names. What type of sampling is this? (random, systematic, convenience, stratified, cluster)

b. If the sampling method consisted of a random selection of 30 adults from each of the 50 states, what type of sampling would this be? (random, systematic, convenience, stratified, cluster)

c. What is the level of measurement of the responses of yes, no, don't know, and refused to respond?

d. Is the given value of 52% a statistic or a parameter? Why?

e. What would be wrong with conducting the survey by mailing a questionnaire that respondents could complete and mail back?

9. Marijuana Survey Identify the type of sampling (random, systematic, convenience, stratified, cluster) used when a sample of the 1500 survey responses is obtained as described. Then determine whether the sampling scheme is likely to result in a sample that is representative of the population of all adults.

a. A complete list of all 241,472,385 adults in the United States is compiled and every 150,000th name is selected until the sample size of 1500 is reached.

b. A complete list of all 241,472,385 adults in the United States is compiled and 1500 adults are randomly selected from that list.

c. The United States is partitioned into regions with 100 adults in each region. Then 15 of those regions are randomly selected, and all 100 people in each of those regions are surveyed.

d. The United States is partitioned into 150 regions with approximately the same number of adults in each region, then 10 people are randomly selected from each of the 150 regions.

e. A survey is mailed to 10,000 randomly selected adults, and the 1500 responses are used.

10. Marijuana Survey Exercise 8 referred to a Pew poll of 1500 adults, and 52% of the respondents said that the use of marijuana should not be made legal.

a. Among the 1500 adults who responded, what is the number of respondents who said that the use of marijuana should not be made legal?

b. In the same poll of 1500 adults, 345 of the respondents said that the use of marijuana for medical purposes should not be legal. What is the percentage of respondents who said that the use of marijuana for medical purposes should not be legal?

c. In this survey of 1500 adults, 727 are men and 773 are women. Find the percentage of respondents who are men, and then find the percentage of respondents who are women.

d. Does the difference between the two percentages from part (c) appear to have statistical significance?

e. Does the difference between the two percentages from part (c) appear to have practical significance?

Cumulative Review Exercises

For Chapter 2 through Chapter 14, the Cumulative Review Exercises include topics from preceding chapters. For this chapter, we present a few *calculator warm-up exercises*, with expressions similar to those found throughout this book. Use your calculator to find the indicated values.

1. Flights Refer to the flight numbers listed in the first column of Data Set 15 in Appendix B. What value is obtained when those 48 numbers are added and the total is then divided by 48? (This result, called the *mean*, is discussed in Chapter 3.) Does the result have any meaning?

2. IQ Scores Refer to the IQ scores listed in Data Set 6 in Appendix B. What value is obtained when those 20 IQ scores are added and the total is then divided by 20? (This result, called the *mean*, is discussed in Chapter 3.) Is the result reasonably close to 100, which is the mean IQ score for the population?

3. Height of Tallest Man Sultan Kosen is the tallest man, and the expression below converts his height of 247 cm to a standardized score. Find this value and round the result to two decimal places. Such standardized scores are considered to be unusually high if they are greater than 2 or 3. Is the result unusually high?

$$\frac{247 - 176}{6}$$

4. Transportation Safety The given expression is used for determining the likelihood that a water taxi will have a total passenger weight that exceeds the maximum safe weight of 3500 lb. Find the given value and round the result to two decimal places.

$$\frac{175 - 172}{\frac{29}{\sqrt{20}}}$$

5. Determining Sample Size The given expression is used to determine the size of the sample necessary to estimate the proportion of college students who have the profound wisdom to take a statistics course. Find the value and round the result to the nearest whole number.

$$\frac{1.96^2 \cdot 0.25}{0.03^2}$$

6. Testing the Effectiveness of Echinacea The given expression is part of a calculation used to study the effectiveness of Echinacea in treating colds. Round the result to four decimal places.

$$\frac{(88 - 88.570)^2}{88.570}$$

7. Variation in Body Temperatures The given expression is used to compute a measure of the variation (variance) of three IQ scores.

$$\frac{(96 - 100)^2 + (106 - 100)^2 + (98 - 100)^2}{3 - 1}$$

8. Standard Deviation The given expression is used to compute the standard deviation of three IQ scores. (The standard deviation is introduced in Section 3-3.) Round the result to one decimal place.

$$\sqrt{\frac{(96 - 100)^2 + (106 - 100)^2 + (98 - 100)^2}{3 - 1}}$$

Scientific Notation. *In Exercises 9–12, the given expressions are designed to yield results expressed in a form of scientific notation. For example, the calculator-displayed result of 1.23E5 can be expressed as 123,000, and the result of 4.56E-4 can be expressed as 0.000456. Perform the indicated operation and express the result as an ordinary number that is not in scientific notation.*

9. 0.6^{14} **10.** 8^{12} **11.** 7^{14} **12.** 0.3^{10}

Technology Project

Simple Random Sample In this project, we will use technology and randomness to identify a simple random sample. Let's assume that we want to conduct a survey of people randomly selected from a population. Instead of using a very large population, we will refer to Data Set 12 in Appendix B for the list of 38 names of the presidents of the United States. (That list does not include presidents who took office as the result of a resignation or assassination.) We will use a process that results in a simple random sample of five of those names. The basic idea is to consider the list of 38 names to be numbered from 1 through 38. We will use technology to randomly generate five numbers between 1 and 38, and then we will identify the five names corresponding to those five random numbers.

STATDISK: Click on **Data** at the top of the screen, then select **Uniform Generator.** In the window that appears, enter a sample size of 5, enter 1 for the minimum value, enter 38 for the maximum value, and enter 0 for the number of decimal places (because we want whole numbers). Click on **Generate** and you will get five **random numbers** between 1 and 38. If any numbers are duplicates, repeat the process to get five *different* numbers between 1 and 38. Identify the five presidents from Data Set 12 that correspond to the five different random numbers.

Minitab: Click on **Calc,** select **Random Data,** then select **Integer.** In the window that appears, enter 5 for the "Number of rows to generate," enter C1 for the column that will contain the random numbers, enter 1 for the minimum value, enter 38 for the maximum value, then click on **OK.** If any numbers are duplicates, repeat the process to get five *different* numbers between 1 and 38. Identify the five presidents from Data Set 12 that correspond to the five different random numbers.

Excel: Click on the toolbar entry of f_x. Select the "Category" item of **Math & Trig.** Select the "function" of **RANDBETWEEN**. Click **OK.** In the dialog box that appears, enter 1 for the "Bottom" and enter 38 for the "top." Click **OK** and a random number will be generated. Repeat this process until five different random numbers between 1 and 38 are obtained.

TI-83/84 Plus: Press **MATH** and then use the ▷ key to scroll to **PRB.** In the PRB menu, select **randInt** and press **ENTER**. The format of the randInt command is to enter the minimum value, the maximum value, and the number of values to be generated. Those entries should be separated by commas so that the command is **randInt(1, 38, 5)**. Press **ENTER** and you will get five random numbers between 1 and 38 inclusive. If any numbers are duplicates, repeat the process to get five *different* numbers between 1 and 38. Identify the five presidents from Data Set 12 that correspond to the five different random numbers.

StatCrunch Select **Data** from the top menu bar, then select **Simulate data.** Choose the option of **Discrete uniform.** Make the required entries in the dialog box. (For this project, use 5 rows, 1 column, a minimum of 1, and a maximum of 38; store the values in a stacked column; and use a single dynamic seed.) Click on **Simulate.** If any numbers are duplicates, repeat the process to get five *different* numbers between 1 and 38. Identify the five presidents from Data Set 12 that correspond to the five different random numbers.

The preceding procedure results in a simple random sample of five names selected from a list of 38 different names. The same procedure can be used with a much larger population.

Pollsters often use the above procedure to randomly generate telephone numbers. Suppose that you want to randomly generate phone numbers beginning with an area code of 347 and an exchange of 489 (as in the song "Diary" by Alicia Keys). You can use the above procedure to randomly generate numbers between 0 and 9999, and the result will be a complete phone number that could be called for a survey. Now randomly generate 10 such numbers, and combine them with the area code of 347 and the exchange of 489 so that you have a list of 10 people who can be reached at phone numbers with the format of (347) 489–xxxx.

from data TO DECISION

Critical Thinking

The concept of "six degrees of separation" grew from a 1967 study conducted by psychologist Stanley Milgram. His original finding was that two random residents in the United States are connected by an average of six intermediaries. In his first experiment, he sent 60 letters to subjects in Wichita, Kansas, and asked them to forward the letters to a specific woman in Cambridge, Massachusetts. The subjects were instructed to hand-deliver the letters to acquaintances who they believed could reach the target person either directly or through other acquaintances. Of the 60 subjects who were solicited, 50 participated, and three of the letters reached the target. Two subsequent experiments also had low completion rates, but Milgram eventually reached a 35% completion rate, and he found that for completed chains, the mean number of intermediaries was around six. Consequently, Milgram's original data led to the concept referred to as "six degrees of separation."

Analyzing the Results

1. Did Stanley Milgram's original experiment have a good design, or was it flawed? Explain.

2. Do Milgram's original data justify the concept of "six degrees of separation?"

3. Describe a sound experiment for determining whether the concept of six degrees of separation is valid.

Cooperative Group Activities

1. In-class activity From the cafeteria, obtain 18 straws. Cut 6 of them in half, cut 6 of them into quarters, and leave the other 6 as they are. There should now be 42 straws of three different lengths. Put them in a bag, mix them up, then select one straw, find its length, and then replace it. Repeat this until 20 straws have been selected. (*Important:* Select the straws without looking into the bag, and select the first straw that you touch.) Find the average (mean) of the lengths of the sample of 20 straws. Now remove all of the straws and find the mean of the lengths of the population. Did the sample provide an average that was close to the true population average (mean)? Why or why not?

2. In-class activity In mid-December of a recent year, the Internet service provider America OnLine (AOL) ran a survey of its users. This question was asked about Christmas trees: "Which do you prefer?" The response could be "a real tree" or "a fake tree." Among the 7073 responses received by the Internet users, 4650 indicated a real tree, and 2423 indicated a fake tree. We have already noted that because the sample is a voluntary response sample, no conclusions can be made about a population larger than the 7073 people who responded. Identify other problems with this survey question.

3. In-class activity Identify the problems with the following:

- A recent report on *CNN Headline News* included a comment that crime in the United States fell in the 1980s because of the growth of abortions in the 1970s, which resulted in fewer unwanted children.

- *Consumer Reports* magazine mailed an Annual Questionnaire about cars and other consumer products. Also included were a request for a voluntary contribution of money and a ballot for the Board of Directors. Responses were to be mailed back in envelopes that required postage stamps.

4. Out-of-class activity Find a report of a survey that is based on a voluntary response sample. Describe how it is quite possible that the results do not accurately reflect the population.

5. Out-of-class activity Find a professional journal with an article that includes a statistical analysis of an experiment. Describe and comment on the design of the experiment. Identify one particular issue, and determine whether the result was found to be statistically significant. Determine whether that same result has practical significance.

2 Summarizing and Graphing Data

Does exposure to lead affect IQ score?

chapter problem

Data Set 5 in Appendix B includes full IQ scores from three groups of children who lived near a lead smelter. The children in Group 1 had *low* levels of measured lead in their blood (with blood levels less than 40 micrograms/100 mL in each of two years). Group 2 had *medium* levels of measured lead in their blood (with blood levels of at least 40 micrograms/100 mL in exactly one of two years). Group 3 had *high* levels of measured lead in their blood (with blood levels of at least 40 micrograms/100 mL in each of two years).

Let's consider the measured full IQ scores from Group 1 (low lead level) and Group 3 (high lead level), as listed in Table 2-1. It is an exceptionally rare person who can look at both lists of IQ scores and form meaningful conclusions. Almost all of us must work at describing, exploring, and comparing the two sets of data. ("Describing, Exploring, and Comparing Data" would be a great title for a chapter in a statistics book—see Chapter 3.) In this chapter we present methods that focus on summarizing the data and using graphs that enable us to understand important characteristics of the data, especially the *distribution* of the data. These methods will help us compare the two sets of data so that we can determine whether IQ scores of the *low* lead group are somehow different from the IQ scores of the *high* lead group. Such comparisons will be helpful as we try to address this important and key issue: Does exposure to lead have an effect on IQ score?

Table 2-1 Full IQ Scores of Low Lead Group and High Lead Group

Low Lead Level (Group 1)

70	85	86	76	84	96	94	56	115	97	77	128	99	80	118	86
141	88	96	96	107	86	80	107	101	91	125	96	99	99	115	106
105	96	50	99	85	88	120	93	87	98	78	100	105	87	94	89
80	111	104	85	94	75	73	76	107	88	89	96	72	97	76	107
104	85	76	95	86	89	76	96	101	108	102	77	74	92		

High Lead Level (Group 3)

82	93	85	75	85	80	101	89	80	94	88	104	88	88	83	104
96	76	80	79	75											

2-1   Review and Preview

Chapter 1 presented some critically important concepts, including context of data, source of data, sampling method, conclusions, and practical implications. Like the data in Table 2-1, many samples of data are large, so understanding them requires that we organize, summarize, and represent the data in a way that allows us to gain insight. We can organize and summarize data numerically in tables or visually in graphs, as described in this chapter. Of course, our ultimate goal is not the mere generation of tables or graphs; instead, we want to use tables and graphs as keys that unlock the hidden and important characteristics of data. In this chapter we are mainly concerned with the *distribution* of a data set, which is one of the following five characteristics that are typically most important. This chapter focuses mainly on the distribution of data. Chapter 3 presents methods for investigating the other characteristics.

Characteristics of Data

1. **Center:** A representative value that indicates where the middle of the data set is located.

2. **Variation:** A measure of the amount that the data values vary.

3. **Distribution:** The nature or shape of the spread of the data over the range of values (such as bell-shaped).

4. **Outliers:** Sample values that lie very far away from the vast majority of the other sample values.

5. **Time:** Any change in the characteristics of the data over time.

Study Hint: Blind memorization is not effective in remembering information. To remember the above characteristics of data, it may be helpful to use a memory device (or mnemonic) for the first five letters **CVDOT.** Remembering the sentence "Computer Viruses Destroy Or Terminate" is an easy way to help us remember the five key characteristics of data.

Critical Thinking and Interpretation: Going Beyond Formulas and Manual Calculations

In the modern statistics course, it is not so important to memorize formulas or manually perform complex arithmetic calculations. Instead, we get results by using technology (a calculator or computer software), and then we focus on making practical sense of results through critical thinking. This chapter includes detailed steps for important procedures, but it is not necessary to master those steps in all cases. However, we recommend that in each case you perform a few manual calculations before using technology. This will enhance your understanding and help you acquire a better appreciation of the results obtained from the technology.

2-2   Frequency Distributions

Key Concept When one is working with large data sets, a *frequency distribution* (or *frequency table*) is often helpful in organizing and summarizing data. A frequency distribution helps us to understand the nature of the *distribution* of a data set.

> **DEFINITION** A **frequency distribution** (or **frequency table**) shows how data are partitioned among several categories (or *classes*) by listing the categories along with the number (frequency) of data values in each of them.

Consider the IQ scores of the low lead group listed in Table 2-1. Table 2-2 is a frequency distribution summarizing those IQ scores. The **frequency** for a particular class is the number of original values that fall into that class. For example, the first class in Table 2-2 has a frequency of 2, so 2 of the IQ scores are between 50 and 69 inclusive.

The following standard terms are sometimes used in constructing frequency distributions and graphs.

Table 2-2
IQ Scores of Low Lead Group

IQ Score	Frequency
50–69	2
70–89	33
90–109	35
110–129	7
130–149	1

DEFINITIONS

Lower class limits are the smallest numbers that can belong to the different classes. (Table 2-2 has lower class limits of 50, 70, 90, 110, and 130.)

Upper class limits are the largest numbers that can belong to the different classes. (Table 2-2 has upper class limits of 69, 89, 109, 129, and 149.)

Class boundaries are the numbers used to separate the classes, but without the gaps created by class limits. Figure 2-1 shows the gaps created by the class limits from Table 2-2. In Figure 2-1 we see that the values of 69.5, 89.5, 109.5, and 129.5 are in the centers of those gaps, and following the pattern of those class boundaries, we see that the lowest class boundary is 49.5 and the highest class boundary is 149.5. Thus the complete list of class boundaries is 49.5, 69.5, 89.5, 109.5, 129.5, and 149.5.

Class midpoints are the values in the middle of the classes. Table 2-2 has class midpoints of 59.5, 79.5, 99.5, 119.5, and 139.5. Each class midpoint is computed by adding the lower class limit to the upper class limit and dividing the sum by 2.

Class width is the difference between two consecutive lower class limits (or two consecutive lower class boundaries) in a frequency distribution. Table 2-2 uses a class width of 20.

CAUTION Finding the correct class width and class boundaries can be tricky. For class width, don't make the most common mistake of using the difference between a lower class limit and an upper class limit. See Table 2-2 and note that the class width is 20, not 19.

For class boundaries, remember that they split the difference between the end of one class and the beginning of the next class, as shown in Figure 2-1.

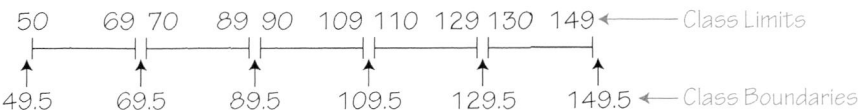

Figure 2-1　Finding Class Boundaries from Class Limits in Table

Procedure for Constructing a Frequency Distribution

We construct frequency distributions (1) so that we can summarize large data sets, (2) so that we can analyze the data to see the distribution and identify outliers, and (3) so that we have a basis for constructing graphs (such as *histograms,* introduced in the next section). Although technology can generate frequency distributions, the steps for manually constructing them are as follows:

1. Select the number of classes, usually between 5 and 20. The number of classes might be affected by the convenience of using round numbers.

Authors Identified

In 1787–88 Alexander Hamilton, John Jay, and James Madison anonymously published the famous *Federalist Papers* in an attempt to convince New Yorkers that they should ratify the Constitution. The identity of most of the papers' authors became known, but the authorship of 12 of the papers was contested. Through statistical analysis of the frequencies of various words, we can now conclude that James Madison is *likely* to have been the author of these 12 papers. For many of the disputed papers, the evidence in favor of Madison's authorship is overwhelming to the degree that we can be almost certain of being correct.

2. Calculate the class width.

$$\text{Class width} \approx \frac{(\text{maximum data value}) - (\text{minimum data value})}{\text{number of classes}}$$

Round this result to get a convenient number. (It's usually best to round *up*.) Using a specific number of classes is not too important, and it's usually wise to change the number of classes so that they use convenient values for the class limits.

3. Choose the value for the first lower class limit by using either the minimum value or a convenient value below the minimum.

4. Using the first lower class limit and the class width, list the other lower class limits. (Add the class width to the first lower class limit to get the second lower class limit. Add the class width to the second lower class limit to get the third lower class limit, and so on.)

5. List the lower class limits in a vertical column and then determine and enter the upper class limits.

6. Take each individual data value and put a tally mark in the appropriate class. Add the tally marks to find the total frequency for each class.

When constructing a frequency distribution, be sure the classes do not overlap. Each of the original values must belong to exactly one class. Include all classes, even those with a frequency of zero. Try to use the same width for all classes, although it is sometimes impossible to avoid open-ended intervals, such as "65 years or older."

Example 1   IQ Scores of Low Lead Group

Using the IQ scores of the low lead group in Table 2-1, follow the above procedure to construct the frequency distribution shown in Table 2-2. Use five classes.

Solution

Step 1: Select 5 as the number of desired classes.

Step 2: Calculate the class width. Note that we round 18.2 up to 20, which is a much more convenient number.

$$\begin{aligned}\text{Class width} &\approx \frac{(\text{maximum data value}) - (\text{minimum data value})}{\text{number of classes}}\\ &= \frac{141 - 50}{5} = 18.2 \approx 20 \text{ (rounded up to a convenient number)}\end{aligned}$$

Step 3: The minimum data value is 50 and it is a convenient starting point, so use 50 as the first lower class limit. (If the minimum value had been 52 or 53, we would have rounded down to the more convenient starting point of 50.)

50–

70–

90–

110–

130–

Step 4: Add the class width of 20 to 50 to get the second lower class limit of 70. Continue to add the class width of 20 until we have five lower class limits. The lower class limits are therefore 50, 70, 90, 110, and 130.

Step 5: List the lower class limits vertically as shown in the margin. From this list, we identify the corresponding upper class limits as 69, 89, 109, 129, and 149.

Step 6: Enter a tally mark for each data value in the appropriate class. Then add the tally marks to find the frequencies shown in Table 2-2.

So far we have discussed frequency distributions using only quantitative data sets, but frequency distributions can also be used to summarize categorical (or qualitative or attribute) data, as illustrated in Example 2.

Example 2 **East Haven Police Department Traffic Tickets**

Table 2-3 summarizes the race/ethnic classifications recorded on traffic tickets issued by Connecticut's East Haven Police Department during a recent nine-month period. Here is an interesting and revealing fact about the data: Table 2-3 shows that 18 of those given tickets were classified by police as being Hispanic, but in fact, 209 of those given tickets had Hispanic names!

Table 2-3 East Haven Traffic Tickets

Race	Frequency
White	329
Black	15
Asian	0
Hispanic	18
White/Hispanic	4
Blank (no indication)	5

Relative Frequency Distribution

A variation of the basic frequency distribution is a **relative frequency distribution** or **percentage frequency distribution,** in which each class frequency is replaced by a relative frequency (or proportion) or a percentage. In this text we use the term "relative frequency distribution" whether we use relative frequencies or percentages. Relative frequencies and percentages are calculated as follows.

$$\text{Relative frequency for a class} = \frac{\text{frequency for a class}}{\text{sum of all frequencies}}$$

$$\text{Percentage for a class} = \frac{\text{frequency for a class}}{\text{sum of all frequencies}} \times 100\%$$

Table 2-4 is an example of a relative frequency distribution. It is a variation of Table 2-2 in which each class frequency is replaced by the corresponding percentage

Table 2-4 Relative Frequency Distribution of IQ Scores of Low Lead Group

IQ Score	Frequency
50–69	2.6%
70–89	42.3%
90–109	44.9%
110–129	9.0%
130–149	1.3%

value. Because there are 78 data values, divide each class frequency by 78, and then multiply by 100%. The first class of Table 2-2 has a frequency of 2, so divide 2 by 78 to get 0.0256, and then multiply by 100% to get 2.56%, which we rounded to 2.6%. The sum of the percentages should be 100%, with a small discrepancy allowed for rounding errors, so a sum such as 99% or 101% is acceptable. The sum of the percentages in Table 2-4 is 100.1%.

The sum of the percentages in a relative frequency distribution must be very close to 100%.

Cumulative Frequency Distribution

Another variation of a frequency distribution is a **cumulative frequency distribution** in which the frequency for each class is the sum of the frequencies for that class and all previous classes. Table 2-5 is a cumulative frequency distribution based on Table 2-2. Using the original frequencies of 2, 33, 35, 7, and 1, we add 2 + 33 to get the second cumulative frequency of 35, then we add 2 + 33 + 35 to get the third, and so on. See Table 2-5, and note that in addition to the use of cumulative frequencies, the class limits are replaced by "less than" expressions that describe the new ranges of values.

Table 2-5 Cumulative Frequency Distribution of IQ Scores of Low Lead Group

IQ Score	Cumulative Frequency
Less than 70	2
Less than 90	35
Less than 110	70
Less than 130	77
Less than 150	78

Critical Thinking: Using Frequency Distributions to Understand Data

Earlier, we noted that a frequency distribution can help us understand the *distribution* of a data set, which is the nature or shape of the spread of the data over the range of values (such as bell-shaped). In statistics we are often interested in determining whether the data have a *normal distribution*. (Normal distributions are discussed extensively in Chapter 6.) Data that have an approximately normal distribution are characterized by a frequency distribution with the following features:

Normal Distribution

1. The frequencies start low, then increase to one or two high frequencies, and then decrease to a low frequency.

2. The distribution is approximately symmetric, with frequencies preceding the maximum being roughly a mirror image of those that follow the maximum.

Table 2-6 satisfies these two conditions. The frequencies start low, increase to the maximum of 56, then decrease to a low frequency. Also, the frequencies of 1 and 10 that precede the maximum are a mirror image of the frequencies 10 and 1 that follow the maximum. Real data sets are usually not so perfect as Table 2-6, and judgment must be used to determine whether the distribution comes "close enough" to satisfying those two conditions.

Table 2-6 Frequency Distribution Showing a Normal Distribution

Score	Frequency	Normal Distribution
50–69	1	← Frequencies start low, . . .
70–89	10	
90–109	56	← Increase to a maximum, . . .
110–129	10	
130–149	1	← Decrease to become low again.

The following examples illustrate how frequency distributions are used to describe, explore, and compare data sets.

Example 3 Describing Data: How Were the Weights Obtained in California?

When collecting weights of people, it's better to actually weigh people than to ask them what they weigh. People often tend to round *way* down, so that a weight of 196 lb might be reported as 170 lb. Table 2-7 summarizes the *last digits* of the weights of 100 people used in the California Health Interview Survey. If people are actually weighed on a scale, the last digits of weights tend to have frequencies that are approximately the same, but Table 2-6 shows that the vast majority of weights have last digits of 0 or 5, and this is strong evidence that people reported their weights and were not physically weighed. (Also, the word "interview" in the title of the California Health Interview Survey reveals that people were interviewed and were not physically measured.)

Table 2-7 Last Digits of Weights from the California Health Interview Survey

Last Digit of Weight	Frequency
0	46
1	1
2	2
3	3
4	3
5	30
6	4
7	0
8	8
9	3

Example 4 Exploring Data: What Does a Gap Tell Us?

Table 2-8 is a frequency distribution of the weights (grams) of randomly selected pennies. Examination of the frequencies reveals a large *gap* between the lightest pennies and the heaviest pennies. This suggests that we have two different populations: Pennies made before 1983 are 95% copper and 5% zinc, but pennies made

Missing Data

Samples are commonly missing some data. Missing data fall into two general categories: (1) missing values that result from random causes unrelated to the data values, and (2) missing values resulting from causes that are not random. Random causes include factors such as the incorrect entry of sample values or lost survey results. Such missing values can often be ignored because they do not systematically hide some characteristic that might significantly affect results. It's trickier to deal with values missing because of factors that are not random. For example, results of an income analysis might be seriously flawed if people with very high incomes refuse to provide those values because they fear income tax audits. Those missing high incomes should not be ignored, and further research would be needed to identify them.

after 1983 are 2.5% copper and 97.5% zinc, which explains the large gap between the lightest pennies and the heaviest pennies in Table 2-8.

Table 2-8 Randomly Selected Pennies

Weight (grams) of Penny	Frequency
2.40–2.49	18
2.50–2.59	19
2.60–2.69	0
2.70–2.79	0
2.80–2.89	0
2.90–2.99	2
3.00–3.09	25
3.10–3.19	8

Gaps Example 4 illustrates this principle:

The presence of gaps can suggest that the data are from two or more different populations.

The converse of this principle is not true, because data from different populations do not necessarily result in gaps.

Example 5   Comparing IQ Scores of the Low Lead Group and the High Lead Group

Table 2-1, which is given with the Chapter Problem at the beginning of this chapter, lists IQ scores from the low lead group and the high lead group. Because the sample sizes of 78 and 21 are so different, a comparison of frequency distributions is not easy, but Table 2-9 shows the relative frequency distributions for those two groups. By comparing those relative frequencies, we see that the majority of children in the low lead group had IQ scores of 90 or higher, but the majority of children in the high lead group had IQ scores below 90. This suggests that perhaps high lead exposure has a detrimental effect on IQ scores.

Table 2-9 IQ Scores from the Low Lead Group and the High Lead Group

IQ Score	Low Lead Group	High Lead Group
50–69	2.6%	
70–89	42.3%	71.4%
90–109	44.9%	28.6%
110–129	9.0%	
130–149	1.3%	

2-2 Basic Skills and Concepts

Statistical Literacy and Critical Thinking

 1. Frequency Distribution Table 2-2 on page 45 is a frequency distribution summarizing the IQ scores of a group of children with low lead exposure. Is it possible to identify the original list of the 78 individual IQ scores from Table 2-2? Why or why not?

2. Relative Frequency Distribution After construction of a relative frequency distribution summarizing the times that males spend each day thinking about females, what should be the sum of the relative frequencies?

3. Do You Believe? In a Harris Interactive survey, 2303 adults were asked whether they believe in five different things, and the accompanying table summarizes the results. Does this table describe a relative frequency distribution? Why or why not?

4. Analyzing a Frequency Distribution The accompanying frequency distribution summarizes the heights of a sample of people in Vassar Road Elementary School. What can you conclude about the people included in the sample?

In Exercises 5–10, identify the class width, class midpoints, and class boundaries for the given frequency distribution. The frequency distributions are based on real data from Appendix B.

Table for Exercise 3

Believe in the devil	60%
Believe in hell	61%
Believe in UFOs	32%
Believe in astrology	26%
Believe in reincarnation	20%

Table for Exercise 4

Height (in.)	Frequency
35–39	6
40–44	31
45–49	67
50–54	21
55–59	0
60–64	0
65–69	6
70–74	10

5.

Age (years) of Best Actress When Oscar Was Won	Frequency
20–29	27
30–39	34
40–49	13
50–59	2
60–69	4
70–79	1
80–89	1

6.

Age (years) of Best Actor When Oscar Was Won	Frequency
20–29	1
30–39	26
40–49	35
50–59	13
60–69	6
70–79	1

7.

Verbal IQ Score of Subject Exposed to Lead	Frequency
50–59	4
60–69	10
70–79	25
80–89	43
90–99	26
100–109	8
110–119	3
120–129	2

8.

Years President Lived after First Inauguration	Frequency
0–4	8
5–9	2
10–14	5
15–19	7
20–24	4
25–29	6
30–34	0
35–39	1

9.

White Blood Cell Count of Males	Frequency
3.0–4.9	8
5.0–6.9	15
7.0–8.9	11
9.0–10.9	5
11.0–12.9	1

10.

White Blood Cell Count of Females	Frequency
3.0–4.9	6
5.0–6.9	16
7.0–8.9	9
9.0–10.9	7
11.0–12.9	0
13.0–14.9	2

Normal Distributions.   *In Exercises 11–14, answer the given questions which are related to normal distributions.*

11. Identifying the Distribution Using a reasonably strict interpretation of the relevant criteria, does the frequency distribution given in Exercise 5 appear to have a normal distribution? Explain.

12. Identifying the Distribution Does the frequency distribution given in Exercise 7 appear to have a normal distribution? Explain.

13. Normal Distribution Refer to the frequency distribution given in Exercise 9 and ignore the given frequencies. Assume that the first two frequencies are 4 and 7, respectively. Assuming that the distribution of the 40 sample values is a normal distribution, identify the remaining three frequencies.

14. Normal Distribution Refer to the frequency distribution given in Exercise 10 and ignore the given frequencies. Assume that the first two frequencies are 2 and 6, respectively. Assuming that the distribution of the 40 sample values is a normal distribution, identify the remaining four frequencies.

Relative Frequencies for Comparisons.   *In Exercises 15 and 16, construct the relative frequencies and answer the given questions.*

15. Oscar Winners Construct one table (similar to Table 2-9 on page 50) that includes relative frequencies based on the frequency distributions from Exercises 5 and 6, and then compare the ages of Oscar-winning actresses and actors. Are there notable differences?

16. White Blood Cell Counts Construct one table (similar to Table 2-9 on page 50) that includes relative frequencies based on the frequency distributions from Exercises 9 and 10, and then compare the white blood cell counts of females and males. Are there notable differences?

Cumulative Frequency Distributions.   *In Exercises 17 and 18, construct the cumulative frequency distribution that corresponds to the frequency distribution in the exercise indicated.*

17. Exercise 5

18. Exercise 6

Constructing Frequency Distributions.   *In Exercises 19–28, use the indicated data and construct the frequency distribution.*

19. Analysis of Last Digits Heights of statistics students were obtained by the author as part of an experiment conducted for class. The last digits of those heights are listed below. Construct a frequency distribution with 10 classes. Based on the distribution, do the heights appear to be reported or actually measured? What do you know about the accuracy of the results?

0 0 0 0 0 0 0 0 1 1 2 3 3 3 4 5 5 5 5 5 5 5 5 5 5 5 5 5 5 6 6 8 8 8 9

20. Analysis of Last Digits Weights of respondents were recorded as part of the California Health Interview Survey. The last digits of weights from 50 randomly selected respondents are listed below. Construct a frequency distribution with 10 classes. Based on the distribution, do the heights appear to be reported or actually measured? What do you know about the accuracy of the results?

5 0 1 0 2 0 5 0 5 0 3 8 5 0 5 0 5 6 0 0 0 0 0 0 8
5 5 0 4 5 0 0 4 0 0 0 0 8 0 9 5 3 0 5 0 0 0 5 8

21. Pulse Rates of Males Refer to Data Set 1 in Appendix B and use the pulse rates (beats per minute) of males. Begin with a lower class limit of 40 and use a class width of 10. Do the pulse rates of males appear to have a normal distribution?

22. Pulse Rates of Females Refer to Data Set 1 in Appendix B and use the pulse rates (beats per minute) of females. Begin with a lower class limit of 50 and use a class width of 10. Compare the frequency distribution to the one found in the preceding exercise. Is there a notable difference between pulse rates of males and females?

23. Earthquake Magnitudes Refer to the earthquake magnitudes listed in Data Set 16 of Appendix B. Begin with a lower class limit of 0.00 and use a class width of 0.50. Using a very strict interpretation of the requirements for a normal distribution, do the magnitudes appear to be normally distributed?

24. Earthquake Depths Refer to the earthquake depths listed in Data Set 16 in Appendix B. Begin with a lower class limit of 1.00 km and use a class width of 4.00 km. Using a very strict interpretation of the requirements for a normal distribution, do the depths appear to be normally distributed?

25. Male Red Blood Cell Counts Refer to Data Set 1 in Appendix B and use the red blood cell counts (million cells/µL) for males. Begin with a lower class limit of 4.00 and use a class width of 0.40. Using a very loose interpretation of the requirements for a normal distribution, do the red blood cell counts appear to be normally distributed?

26. Female Red Blood Cell Counts Refer to Data Set 1 in Appendix B and use the red blood cell counts (million cells/µL) for females. Begin with a lower class limit of 3.60 and use a class width of 0.40. Using a very loose interpretation of the requirements for a normal distribution, do the red blood cell counts appear to be normally distributed?

27. Flight Arrival Times Refer to Data Set 15 in Appendix B and use the times of the arrival delays. Begin with a lower class limit of −60 min and use a class width of 30 min. Based on the result, does it appear that most of the American Airline flights from JFK to LAX are close to arriving in Los Angeles without too much delay?

28. Flight Taxi-Out Times Refer to Data Set 15 in Appendix B and use the times required to taxi out for takeoff. Begin with a lower class limit of 10 min and use a class width of 5 min. Based on the result, does it appear that the time required to taxi out can be predicted with reasonable accuracy?

Categorical Data. *In Exercises 29–32, use the given categorical data to construct the relative frequency distribution.*

29. Titanic Survivors The 2223 people aboard the *Titanic* include 361 male survivors, 1395 males who died, 345 female survivors, and 122 females who died.

30. Train Derailments An analysis of 50 train derailment incidents identified the main causes listed below, where T denotes bad track, E denotes faulty equipment, H denotes human error, and O denotes other causes (based on data from the Federal Railroad Administration).

$$T\,T\,E\,E\,H\,H\,H\,H\,H\,O\,O\,H\,H\,H\,E\,E\,T\,T\,T\,E\,T\,H\,O\,T$$

$$T\,T\,T\,T\,T\,H\,T\,T\,H\,E\,E\,T\,T\,E\,E\,T\,T\,T\,H\,T\,T\,O\,O\,O$$

31. Fatal Plane Crashes Among fatal plane crashes that occurred during the past 60 years, 650 were due to pilot error, 78 were due to other human error, 156 were due to weather, 286 were due to mechanical problems, and 117 were due to sabotage. (These results are based on data from PlaneCrashInfo.com, and they do not include private aircraft, military aircraft, aircraft carrying 10 or fewer people, or helicopters.) What is the most serious threat to aviation safety, and can anything be done about it?

32. California Lottery The digits drawn in one month for the California Daily 4 lottery were recorded. The digits 0 through 9 had these frequencies: 20, 10, 12, 12, 8 11, 9, 10, 9, 19. Do the digits appear to be selected with a process that is functioning correctly? Why are these digits *categorical* data?

2-2 Beyond the Basics

33. Interpreting Effects of Outliers Refer to Data Set 22 in Appendix B for the axial loads of aluminum cans that are 0.0111 in. thick. The load of 504 lb is an *outlier* because it is very far away from all of the other values. Construct a frequency distribution that includes the value of 504 lb, and then construct another frequency distribution with the value of 504 lb excluded. In both cases, start the first class at 200 lb and use a class width of 20 lb. State a generalization about the effect of an outlier on a frequency distribution.

34. Number of Classes According to what is known as Sturges' guideline, the ideal number of classes for a frequency distribution can be approximated by $1 + (\log n)/(\log 2)$ where n is the number of data values. Use this guideline to complete the table in the margin.

Table for Exercise 34

Number of Data Values	Ideal Number of Classes
16–22	5
23–45	6
?	7
?	8
?	9
?	10
?	11
?	12

2-3   Histograms

Key Concept While a frequency distribution is a useful tool for summarizing data and investigating the distribution of data, an even better tool is a *histogram*, which consists of a graph that is easier to interpret than a table of numbers.

> **DEFINITION** A **histogram** is a graph consisting of bars of equal width drawn adjacent to each other (unless there are gaps in the data). The horizontal scale represents classes of quantitative data values and the vertical scale represents frequencies. The heights of the bars correspond to the frequency values.

A histogram is basically a graph of a frequency distribution. For example, Figure 2-2 shows the Minitab-generated histogram corresponding to the frequency distribution given in Table 2-2 on page 45.

Class frequencies should be used for the vertical scale and that scale should be labeled as in Figure 2-2. The bar locations on the horizontal scale are usually labeled with one of the following: (1) class boundaries (as shown in Figure 2-2), (2) class midpoints, or (3) lower class limits. The first and second options are technically correct, while the third option introduces a small error. It is often easier for us mere mortals to use class midpoints for the horizontal scale. Histograms can usually be generated using technology.

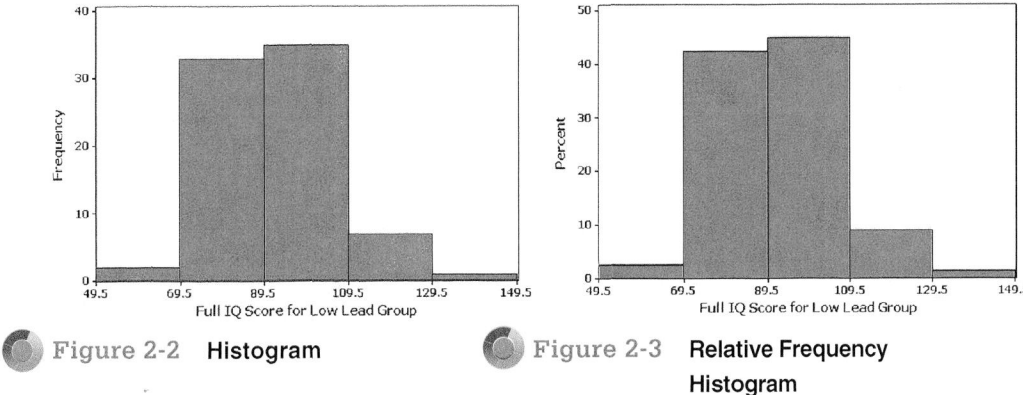

Figure 2-2   **Histogram**   Figure 2-3   **Relative Frequency Histogram**

Relative Frequency Histogram

A **relative frequency histogram** has the same shape and horizontal scale as a histogram, but the vertical scale uses relative frequencies (as percentages or proportions) instead of actual frequencies. Figure 2-3 is the relative frequency histogram corresponding to Figure 2-2.

Critical Thinking: Interpreting Histograms

Even though creating histograms is more fun than human beings should be allowed to have, the ultimate objective is not creating a histogram, but rather *understanding* something about the data. Analyze the histogram to see what can be learned about "CVDOT": the center of the data, the variation (which will be discussed at length in Section 3-3), the distribution, and whether there are any outliers (values far away from the other values). Examining Figure 2-2, we see that the histogram is centered close to 90, the values vary from around 50 to 150, and the distribution is roughly bell-shaped.

Normal Distribution

When graphed as a histogram, a normal distribution has a "bell" shape similar to the one superimposed in Figure 2-4. In a normal distribution, (1) the frequencies increase to a maximum and then decrease, and (2) the graph has symmetry, with the left half of the histogram being roughly a mirror image of the right half. Figure 2-4 shows

Figure 2-4   **Bell-Shaped Distribution**
Because this histogram is roughly bell-shaped, we say that the data have a *normal distribution*.

that the histogram in Figure 2-2 roughly satisfies those two conditions, so we say that the IQ scores are approximately normally distributed. (There are more advanced and less subjective methods for determining whether the distribution is a normal distribution; see Section 6-6.) Many statistical methods require that sample data come from a population having a distribution that is approximately a normal distribution, and we can often use a histogram to determine whether this requirement is satisfied.

Common Distribution Shapes

The histograms shown in Figure 2-5 depict four common distribution shapes. We have already discussed the characteristics of the normal distribution. With a **uniform distribution,** the different possible values occur with approximately the same frequency, so the heights of the bars in the histogram are approximately uniform, as in Figure 2-5(b). Figure 2-5(b) depicts outcomes of digits from state lotteries.

Skewness

A distribution of data is **skewed** if it is not symmetric and extends more to one side than to the other. Data **skewed to the right** (also called *positively skewed*) have a longer right tail, as in Figure 2-5(c), which depicts annual incomes (in thousands of dollars) of adult Americans. Data **skewed to the left** (also called *negatively skewed*) have a longer left tail, as in Figure 2-5(d). Distributions skewed to the right are more common than those skewed to the left because it's often easier to get exceptionally

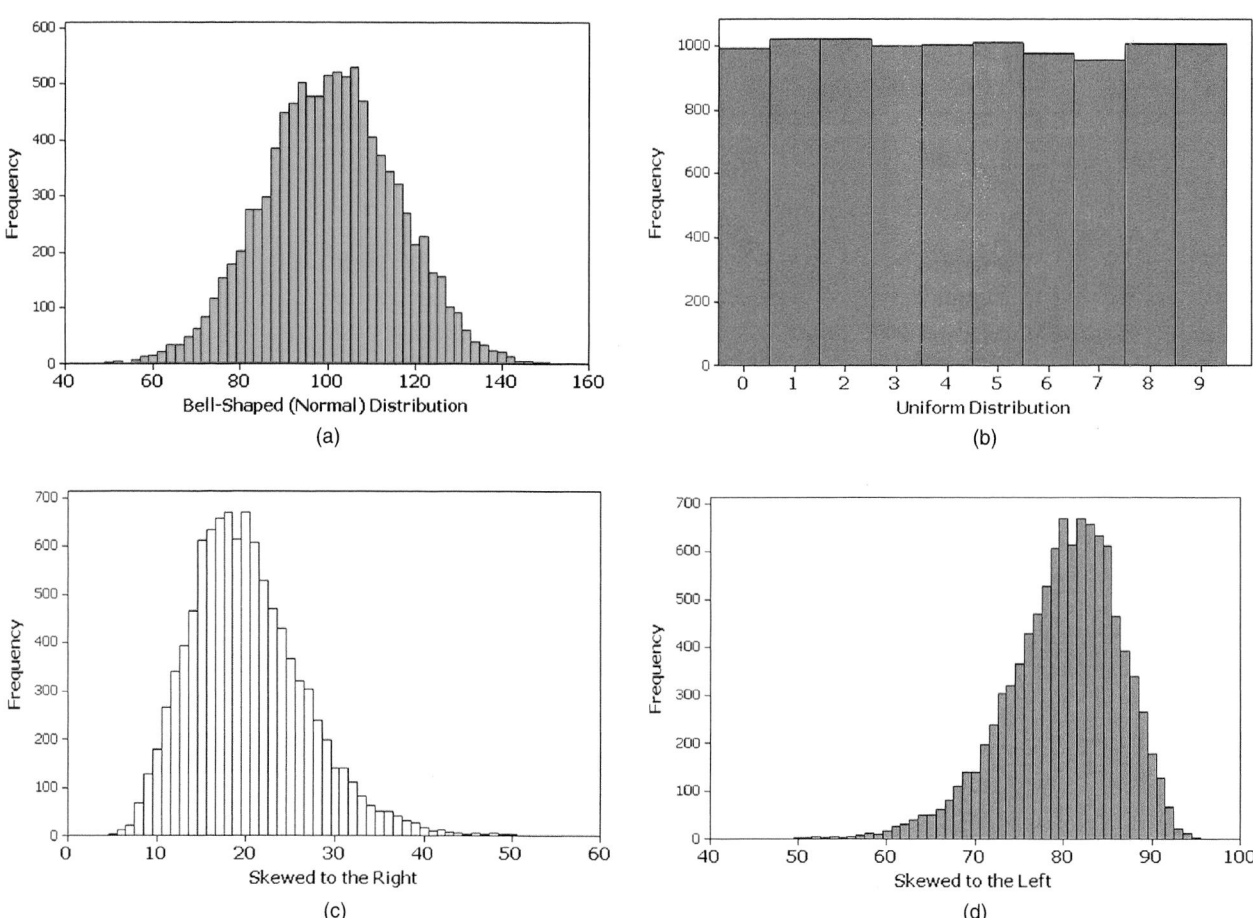

Figure 2-5   Common Distributions

large values than values that are exceptionally small. With annual incomes, for example, it's impossible to get values below zero, but there are a few people who earn millions or billions of dollars in a year. Annual incomes therefore tend to be skewed to the right.

Assessing Normality: Normal Quantile Plot Some really important methods presented in later chapters have a requirement that sample data must be from a population having a normal distribution. We can see that a histogram is often helpful in determining whether the normality requirement is satisfied. However, histograms are not very helpful with small data sets. Section 6-6 discusses methods for *assessing normality*—that is, determining whether the sample data are from a normally distributed population. Section 6-6 includes a procedure for constructing *normal quantile plots*, which involve plotting transformed sample values. Normal quantile plots are easy to generate using technology such as STATDISK, Minitab, XLSTAT, StatCrunch, or a TI-83/84 Plus calculator. Interpretation of a normal quantile plot is based on the following criteria:

Criteria for Assessing Normality with a Normal Quantile Plot

Normal Distribution: The population distribution is normal if the pattern of the points in the normal quantile plot is reasonably close to a straight line, and the points do not show some systematic pattern that is not a straight-line pattern.

Not a Normal Distribution: The population distribution is *not* normal if the normal quantile plot has either or both of these two conditions:

• The points do not lie reasonably close to a straight line.

• The points show some *systematic pattern* that is not a straight-line pattern.

The following are examples of normal quantile plots. Procedures for creating such plots are described in Section 6-6.

Normal Distribution: The points are reasonably close to a straight-line pattern, and there is no other systematic pattern that is not a straight-line pattern.

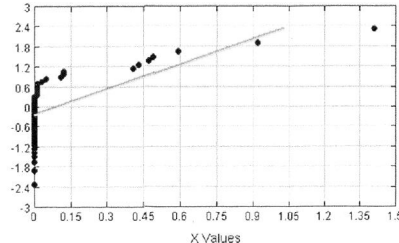
Not a Normal Distribution: The points do not lie reasonably close to a straight line.

Not a Normal Distribution: The points show a systematic pattern that is not a straight-line pattern.

using TECHNOLOGY

Statistical software packages are effective for generating histograms. Throughout this text, we make frequent reference to STATDISK, Minitab, Excel, the TI-83/84 Plus calculator, and StatCrunch, and all of these technologies can generate histograms. The detailed instructions can vary from easy to complex, so we provide some relevant comments below. For detailed instructions, see the STATDISK, Minitab, Excel, SPSS, SAS, and TI-83/84 Plus manuals that are supplements to this book.

STATDISK Enter or open the data in the STATDISK Data Window, click **Data,** click **Histogram,** and then click on the **Plot** button. To use your own class width and starting point, click on the "User defined" button before clicking on Plot. Click on the **Turn labels on** button to see the frequency for each class. (In addition to generating a histogram, this is also an easy way to identify the entries in a frequency distribution.)

continued

MINITAB **Minitab 15 and earlier versions:** Enter or open the data in a column, click on **Graph,** then **Histogram.** Select the "Simple" histogram. Enter the column in the "Graph variables" window and click **OK. Minitab 16:** Click on **Assistant** and select **Graphical Assistant.** Click on **Histogram,** select the column to be used, and then click **OK.**

Minitab uses default settings for the class width and starting point, but those defaults can be changed as follows: Right-click on the horizontal axis and select **Edit X scale,** then use the **Scale** tab to enter the locations of the tick marks (class boundaries or class midpoints), and use the **Binning** tab to enter the midpoints of the classes. See Figures 2-2, 2-3, and 2-4 for examples of Minitab-generated histograms.

TI-83/84 PLUS Enter a list of data in L1 or use a list of values assigned to a name. Select the **STAT PLOT** function by pressing **2ND** **Y=** . Press **ENTER** and use the arrow keys to turn Plot1 to "On" and select the graph with bars. The screen display should be as shown here.

If you want to let the calculator determine the class width and starting point, press **ZOOM** **9** to get a histogram with default settings. (To enter your own class width and class boundaries, press **WINDOW** and enter the maximum and minimum values. The Xscl value will be the class width. Press **GRAPH** to osbtain the graph.)

EXCEL Excel can generate histograms, but it is *extremely* difficult. To generate a histogram easily, use XLSTAT. After loading XLSTAT with Excel included, click on **XLSTAT** at the top. Select **Visualizing Data,** then select **Histograms.** In the Data box, enter the range of cells containing the data, such as A1:A78 for 78 values in column A. Click on the "Sample labels" box only if the first cell contains the name of your data. You can click **OK** to get a histogram with default settings, or you can click on the **Options** tab. One of the options is "User defined," which allows you to enter the range of cells containing your desired class boundaries that you must enter in another column.

STATCRUNCH Click on **Open StatCrunch,** then enter or open a data set. Click on **Graphics,** then click on **Histogram.** Select the column containing the data. Click on **Next** to enter a desired starting point and class width. Click **Create Graph.**

2-3 Basic Skills and Concepts

Statistical Literacy and Critical Thinking

1. Histogram Table 2-2 is a frequency distribution summarizing the IQ scores of the low lead group listed in Table 2-1, and Figure 2-2 is a histogram depicting that same data set. When trying to better understand the IQ data, what is the advantage of examining the histogram instead of the frequency distribution?

2. Voluntary Response Sample The histogram in Figure 2-2 on page 55 is constructed from a *simple random sample* of children. If you construct a histogram with data collected from a *voluntary response sample,* will the distribution depicted in the histogram reflect the true distribution of the population? Why or why not?

3. Small Data NASA provides these duration times (in minutes) of all flights of the space shuttle *Challenger:* 7224, 8784, 8709, 11,476, 10,060, 11,844, 10,089, 11,445, 10,125, 1. Why does it not make sense to construct a histogram for this data set? What is notable about this data set?

4. Normal Distribution When it refers to a normal distribution, does the term "normal" have the same meaning as in ordinary language? What criterion can be used to determine whether the data depicted in a histogram have a distribution that is approximately a normal distribution? Is this criterion totally objective, or does it involve subjective judgment?

Interpreting a Histogram.   *In Exercises 5–8, answer the questions by referring to the following Minitab-generated histogram, which represents the heights (inches) of people randomly selected from those who entered New York City's Museum of Natural History during a recent Friday morning.*

MINITAB

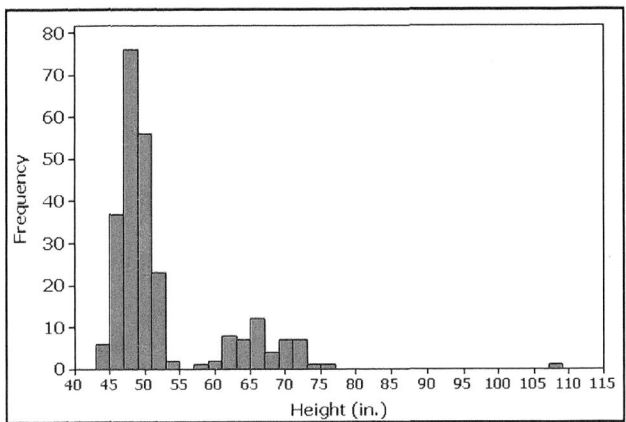

5. Sample Size What is the approximate number of people with heights of 55 in. or less?

6. Class Width and Class Limits What is the class width? What are the approximate lower and upper class limits of the first class?

7. Outlier? What is the height of the tallest person included in the histogram? Where on the histogram is that height depicted? Is that height an outlier? Could that height be an exceptional value that is correct, or is it an error? Explain.

8. Gap What is a reasonable explanation for the gap between the group of people with heights between 43 in. and 55 in., and the group of people with heights between 57 in. and 77 in.?

Constructing Histograms.   *In Exercises 9–18, construct the histograms and answer the given questions.*

9. Analysis of Last Digits Use the frequency distribution from Exercise 19 in Section 2-2 to construct a histogram. What can you conclude from the distribution of the digits? Specifically, do the heights appear to be reported or actually measured?

10. Analysis of Last Digits Use the frequency distribution from Exercise 20 in Section 2-2 to construct a histogram. What can you conclude from the distribution of the digits? Specifically, do the weights appear to be reported or actually measured?

11. Pulse Rates of Males Use the frequency distribution from Exercise 21 in Section 2-2 to construct a histogram. Does the histogram appear to depict data that have a normal distribution? Why or why not?

12. Pulse Rates of Females Use the frequency distribution from Exercise 22 in Section 2-2 to construct a histogram. Does the histogram appear to depict data that have a normal distribution? Why or why not?

13. Earthquake Magnitudes Use the frequency distribution from Exercise 23 in Section 2-2 to construct a histogram. Using a loose interpretation of the requirements for a normal distribution, do the magnitudes appear to be normally distributed? Why or why not?

14. Earthquake Depths Use the frequency distribution from Exercise 24 in Section 2-2 to construct a histogram. Using a strict interpretation of the requirements for a normal distribution, do the depths appear to be normally distributed? Why or why not?

15. Male Red Blood Cell Counts Use the frequency distribution from Exercise 25 in Section 2-2 to construct a histogram. Using a very loose interpretation of the requirements for a normal distribution, do the red blood cell counts appear to be normally distributed? Why or why not?

16. Female Red Blood Cell Counts Use the frequency distribution from Exercise 26 in Section 2-2 to construct a histogram. Using a very loose interpretation of the requirements for a normal distribution, do the red blood cell counts appear to be normally distributed? Why or why not?

17. Flight Arrival Times Use the frequency distribution from Exercise 27 in Section 2-2 to construct a histogram. Which part of the histogram depicts flights that arrived early, and which part depicts flights that arrived late?

18. Flight Taxi-Out Times Use the relative frequency distribution from Exercise 28 in Section 2-2 to construct a histogram. If the quality of air traffic procedures were improved so that the taxi-out times vary much less, would the histogram be affected?

2-3 Beyond the Basics

19. Back-to-Back Relative Frequency Histograms When using histograms to compare two data sets, it is sometimes difficult to make comparisons by looking back and forth between the two histograms. A *back-to-back relative frequency histogram* has a format that makes the comparison much easier. Instead of frequencies, we should use relative frequencies (percentages or proportions) so that the comparisons are not difficult when there are different sample sizes. Use the relative frequency distributions of the ages of Oscar-winning actresses and actors from Exercise 15 in Section 2-2, and complete the back-to-back relative frequency histograms shown below. Then use the result to compare the two data sets.

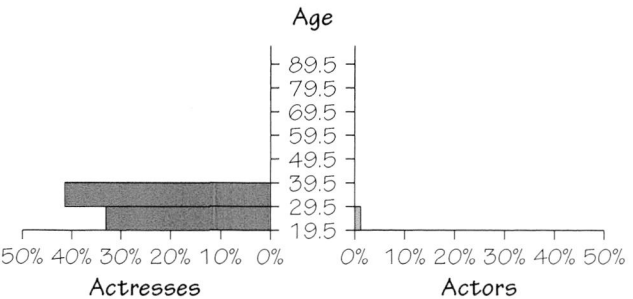

20. Interpreting a Histogram Refer to the histogram given for Exercises 5–8 and answer the following questions:

a. What are the possible values (rounded to the nearest inch) of the largest height included in the histogram? What are those values expressed in feet and inches?

b. Why is it wrong to say that the people with heights between 43 in. and 55 in. are the tallest people because they have the tallest bars in the histogram?

2-4   Graphs That Enlighten and Graphs That Deceive

Key Concept Section 2-3 presented the histogram as a graph that is helpful in learning about the shape of the distribution of data. The histogram is a graph that enlightens in the sense that it gives us better understanding of data. In this section we introduce other commonly used graphs that enlighten. We also discuss some graphs that deceive in the sense that they tend to create impressions about data that are somehow misleading or wrong.

The days of charming and primitive hand-drawn graphs are well behind us, and technology now provides us with powerful tools for generating a wide variety of different graphs. In this section, all figures except Figure 2-19 were generated using technology.

Graphs That Enlighten

Scatterplots

A **scatterplot** (or **scatter diagram**) is a plot of paired (x, y) quantitative data with a horizontal x-axis and a vertical y-axis. The horizontal axis is used for the first (x) variable, and the vertical axis is used for the second variable. The pattern of the plotted points is often helpful in determining whether there is a correlation (or relationship) between the two variables. (This issue is discussed at length when the topic of correlation is considered in Section 10-2.)

> **Example 1** Correlation: Waist and Arm Circumference

Data Set 1 in Appendix B includes the waist circumferences (cm) and arm circumferences (cm) of randomly selected males. Figure 2-6 is a scatterplot of the paired waist/arm measurements. The points show a pattern of increasing values from left to right. This pattern suggests that there is a correlation, or relationship, between waist circumference and arm circumference in males.

> **Example 2** No Correlation: Weight and Pulse Rate

Data Set 1 in Appendix B includes weights (kg) and pulse rates (beats per minute) of randomly selected males. Figure 2-7 is a scatterplot of the paired weight/pulse rate measurements. The points in Figure 2-7 do not show any obvious pattern, and this lack of a pattern suggests that there is no correlation, or relationship, between the weight and pulse rate of males.

Correlation Coefficient Examples 1 and 2 involve making decisions about a correlation based on subjective judgments of scatterplots, but Chapter 10 introduces more objective methods. Those methods involve calculating a value of a *linear correlation coefficient r*, which is a value between -1 and 1. If r is close to -1 or close to 1, there appears to be a correlation, but if r is close to 0, there does not appear to be a correlation. For the data depicted in the scatterplot of Figure 2-6, $r = 0.788$, and the data in the scatterplot of Figure 2-7 result in $r = -0.213$. Section 10-2 describes the calculation and interpretation of a value of r, so that a decision about correlation is much more objective. Even though the methods based on calculations of r are much more objective than the subjective interpretation of a scatterplot, it is always wise to construct a scatterplot first, so that we can see characteristics that cannot be seen by examining the list of paired data values.

The Power of a Graph

With annual sales around $13 billion and with roughly 50 million people using it, Pfizer's prescription drug Lipitor has become the most profitable and most widely used prescription drug ever marketed. In the early stages of its development, Lipitor was compared to other drugs (Zocor, Mevacor, Lescol, and Pravachol) in a process that involved controlled trials. The summary report included a graph showing a Lipitor curve that had a steeper rise than the curves for the other drugs, visually showing that Lipitor was more effective in reducing cholesterol than the other drugs. Pat Kelly, who was then a senior marketing executive for Pfizer, said "I will never forget seeing that chart. . . . It was like 'Aha!' Now I know what this is about. We can communicate this!" The Food and Drug Administration approved Lipitor and allowed Pfizer to include the graph with each prescription. Pfizer sales personnel also distributed the graph to physicians.

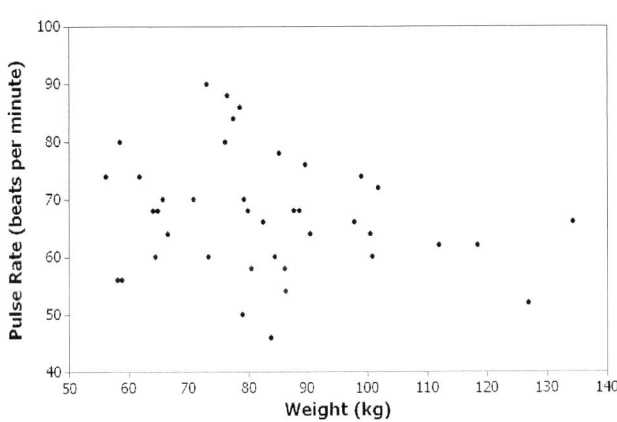

Figure 2-6 Waist Circumference and Arm Circumference in Males

Figure 2-7 Weight and Pulse Rate in Males

Florence Nightingale

Florence Nightingale (1820–1910) is known to many as the founder of the nursing profession, but she also saved thousands of lives by using statistics. When she encountered an unsanitary and undersupplied hospital, she improved those conditions and then used statistics to convince others of the need for more widespread medical reform. She developed original graphs to illustrate that during the Crimean War, more soldiers died as a result of unsanitary conditions than were killed in combat. Florence Nightingale pioneered the use of social statistics as well as graphics techniques.

Example 3   Clusters and a Gap

Consider the scatterplot in Figure 2-8. It consists of paired data consisting of the weight (grams) and year of manufacture for each of 72 pennies. This scatterplot shows two very distinct clusters separated by a gap, which can be explained by the inclusion of two different populations: pre-1983 pennies are 97% copper and 3% zinc, whereas post-1983 pennies are 3% copper and 97% zinc. If we ignored the characteristic of the clusters, we might incorrectly think that there is a relationship between the weight of a penny and the year it was made. If we examine the two groups separately, we see that there does *not* appear to be a relationship between the weights of pennies and the years in which they were produced.

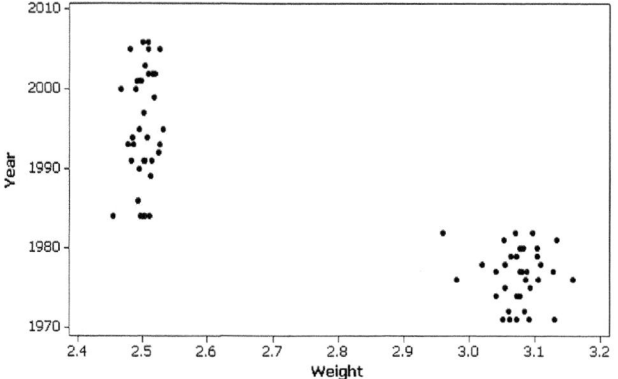

Figure 2-8   Weights (g) of Pennies and Years of Production

Time-Series Graph

A **time-series graph** is a graph of *time-series data,* which are quantitative data that have been collected at different points in time, such as monthly or yearly.

Example 4   Time-Series Graph: Dow Jones Industrial Average

The time-series graph shown in Figure 2-9 depicts the yearly high values of the Dow Jones Industrial Average (DJIA) for the New York Stock Exchange. This graph shows a fairly consistent pattern of increases from 1980 to 1999, but the DJIA high values have been much more erratic in recent years.

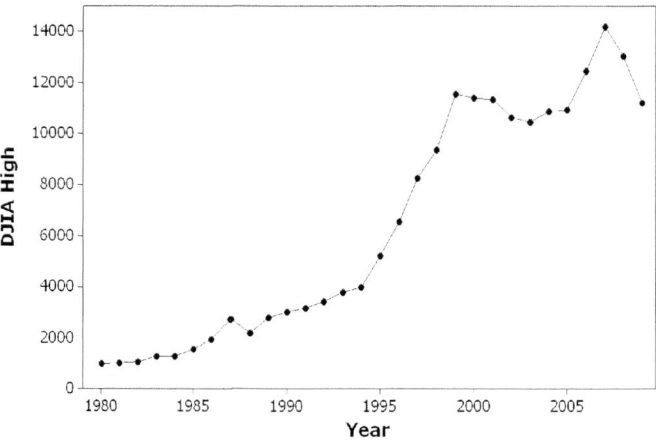

Figure 2-9   Dow Jones Industrial Average

Dotplots

A **dotplot** consists of a graph in which each data value is plotted as a point (or dot) along a horizontal scale of values. Dots representing equal values are stacked.

Go Figure

Among U. S. men between 20 and 40 years of age and taller than 7 feet, 17% of them play basketball in the NBA.

Example 5 Dotplot: IQ Scores of Low Lead Group

Figure 2-10 shows a dotplot of the IQ scores of the low lead group from Table 2-1 included with the Chapter Problem at the beginning of this chapter. The five stacked dots above the position at 76 indicate that five of the IQ scores are 76. There are three dots stacked above 80, so three of the IQ scores are 80. This dotplot reveals the distribution of the IQ scores. It is possible to recreate the original list of data values, because each data value is represented by a single point.

IQ Scores of Low Lead Group

Figure 2-10   Dotplot: IQ Scores of Low Lead Group

Stemplots

A **stemplot** (or **stem-and-leaf plot**) represents quantitative data by separating each value into two parts: the stem (such as the leftmost digit) and the leaf (such as the rightmost digit). Better stemplots are often obtained by first rounding the original data values. Also, stemplots can be *expanded* to include more rows and can be *condensed* to include fewer rows, as in Exercise 26.

One advantage of the stemplot is that we can see the distribution of data while keeping the original data values. Another advantage is that constructing a stemplot is a quick way to *sort* data (arrange them in order), which is required for some statistical procedures (such as finding a median, or finding percentiles as described later in this book).

Example 6 Stemplot: IQ Scores of Low Lead Group

The following stemplot displays the IQ scores of the low lead group in Table 2-1 given with the Chapter Problem. The lowest IQ score of 50 is separated into its stem of 5 and its leaf of 0, and each of the remaining values is separated in a similar way. The stems and leaves are arranged in increasing order, not the order in which they occur in the original list. Note that if you turn the stemplot on its side, you can see distribution of the IQ scores in the same way you would see it in a histogram.

```
 5 | 06  ◄──────────────── Lowest IQ scores are 50 and 56.
 6 |
 7 | 0234566666778
 8 | 00045555666677888999
 9 | 123444566666667789999
10 | 01124455677778
11 | 1558  ◄──────────────── These IQ scores are 111, 115, 115, and 118.,
12 | 058
13 |
14 | 1
```

Bar Graphs

A **bar graph** uses bars of equal width to show frequencies of categories of *categorical* (or qualitative) data. The vertical scale represents frequencies or relative frequencies. The horizontal scale identifies the different categories of qualitative data. The bars may or may not be separated by small gaps. A **multiple bar graph** has two or more sets of bars and is used to compare two or more data sets.

Example 7   Multiple Bar Graph of Income by Gender

See Figure 2-11 for a multiple bar graph of the median incomes of males and females in different years. The data are from the U.S. Census Bureau, and the values for 2010 are projected. From this graph we see that males consistently have much higher median incomes than females, and that both males and females have steadily increasing incomes over time. Comparing the heights of the bars from left to right reveals that the ratios of incomes of males to incomes of females appear to be decreasing, which indicates that the gap between male and female median incomes is gradually becoming smaller.

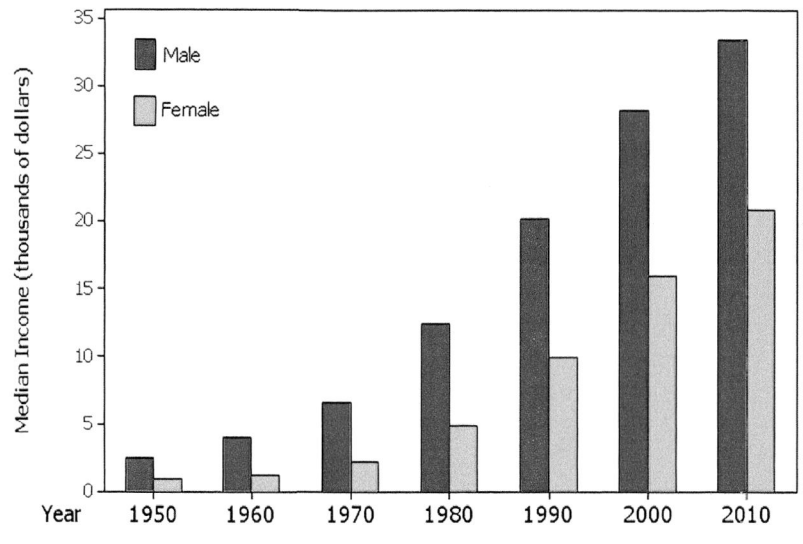

Figure 2-11   **Multiple Bar Graph: Median Income by Gender**

Pareto Charts

When we want a bar graph to draw attention to the more important categories, we can use a **Pareto chart**, which is a bar graph for categorical data, with the added stipulation that the bars are arranged in descending order according to frequencies. The vertical scale in a Pareto chart represents frequencies or relative frequencies. The horizontal scale identifies the different categories of qualitative data. The bars decrease in height from left to right.

Example 8   Pareto Chart: What Contributes Most to Happiness?

In a Coca-Cola survey of 12,500 people, respondents were asked what contributes most to their happiness. Figure 2-12 is a Pareto chart summarizing the results. We see that family or partner is by far the most frequently selected choice.

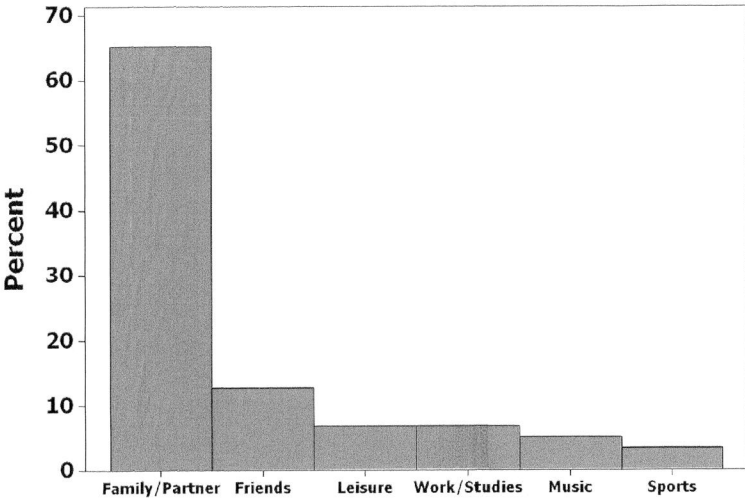

Figure 2-12   Pareto Chart: What Contributes Most to Happiness?

Pie Charts

A **pie chart** is a graph that depicts categorical data as slices of a circle, in which the size of each slice is proportional to the frequency count for the category.

> **Example 9**   Pie Chart: What Contributes Most to Happiness?

Figure 2-13 is a pie chart corresponding to the same data from Example 8. Construction of a pie chart involves slicing up the circle into the proper proportions that represent relative frequencies. For example, the category of friends accounts for 13% of the total, so the slice representing friends should be 13% of the total (with a central angle of $0.13 \times 360° = 47°$).

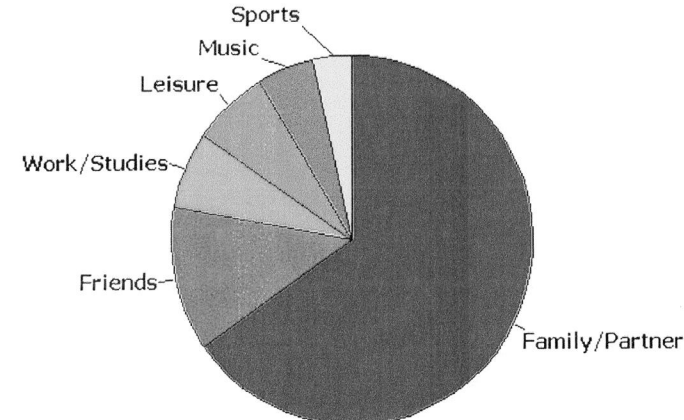

Figure 2-13   Pie Chart: What Contributes Most to Happiness?

The Pareto chart in Figure 2-12 and the pie chart in Figure 2-13 depict the same data in different ways, but the Pareto chart does a better job of showing the relative sizes of the different components. Graphics expert Edwin Tufte makes the following suggestion:

Never use pie charts because they waste ink on components that are not data, and they lack an appropriate scale.

Frequency Polygon

A **frequency polygon** uses line segments connected to points located directly above class midpoint values. A frequency polygon is very similar to a histogram, but a frequency polygon uses line segments instead of bars. We construct a frequency polygon from a frequency distribution as shown in Example 10.

> **Example 10**   Frequency Polygon: IQ Scores of Low Lead Group
>
> See Figure 2-14 for the frequency polygon corresponding to the IQ scores of the low lead group summarized in the frequency distribution of Table 2-2 on page 45. The heights of the points correspond to the class frequencies, and the line segments are extended to the right and left so that the graph begins and ends on the horizontal axis. Just as it is easy to construct a histogram from a frequency distribution table, it is also easy to construct a frequency polygon from a frequency distribution table.

Figure 2-14   **Frequency Polygon: IQ Scores of Low Lead Group**

> A variation of the basic frequency polygon is the **relative frequency polygon,** which uses relative frequencies (proportions or percentages) for the vertical scale. When one is trying to compare two data sets, it is often very helpful to graph two relative frequency polygons on the same axes.

> **Example 11**   Relative Frequency Polygon:
> IQ Scores of Lead Groups
>
> See Figure 2-15, which shows the relative frequency polygons for the IQ scores of the low lead group and the high lead group as listed in Table 2-1 given with the Chapter Problem at the beginning of this chapter. Figure 2-15 shows that the high lead group generally has lower (farther left) IQ scores than the low lead group.

Figure 2-15   **Relative Frequency Polygons: IQ Scores**

It appears that the greater exposure to lead tends to be associated with lower IQ scores. Figure 2-15 enables us to understand data in a way that is not possible with visual examination of the lists of data in Table 2-1.

Ogive

Another type of statistical graph is an **ogive** (pronounced "oh-jive"), which depicts *cumulative* frequencies. Ogives are useful for determining the number of values below some particular value, as illustrated in Example 3. An ogive uses class boundaries along the horizontal scale and uses cumulative frequencies along the vertical scale.

Example 12 Ogive: IQ Scores of Low Lead Group

Figure 2-16 shows an ogive corresponding to the cumulative frequency distribution table (Table 2-5) on page 48. From Figure 2-16, we see that for the low lead group, 35 of the IQ scores are less than 89.5.

Figure 2-16   **Ogive: IQ Scores of Low Lead Group**

Graphs That Deceive

Some graphs deceive because they contain errors, and some deceive because they are technically correct but misleading. It is important to develop the ability to recognize deceptive graphs. Here we present two of the ways in which graphs are commonly used to deceive.

Example 13 Nonzero Axis

Figure 2-17 and Figure 2-18 are based on the same data from Data Set 14 in Appendix B. By using a vertical scale starting at 30 mi/gal instead of at 0 mi/gal, Figure 2-17 exaggerates the differences and creates the false impression that the Honda Civic gets mileage that is substantially better than the mileage ratings found for the Chevrolet Aveo and the Toyota Camry. Figure 2-18 shows that the differences among the three mileage ratings are actually small.

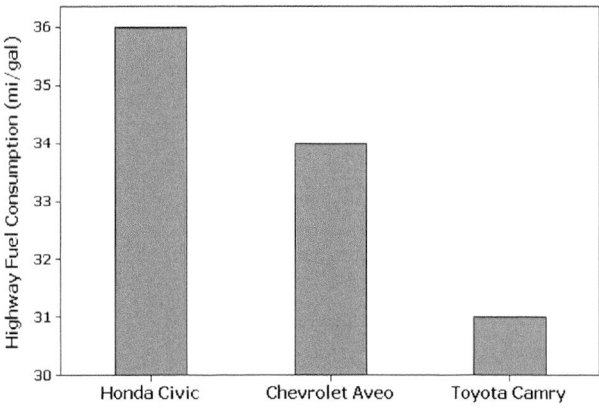

Figure 2-17   **Highway Fuel Consumption with Vertical Scale Not Starting at Zero**

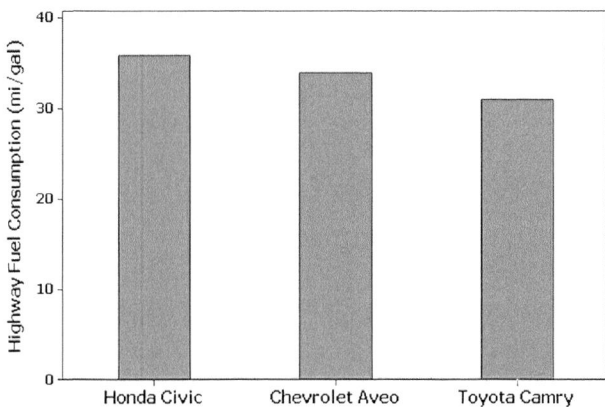

Figure 2-18   **Highway Fuel Consumption with Vertical Scale Starting at Zero**

Pictographs

Drawings of objects, called *pictographs,* are often misleading. Data that are one-dimensional in nature (such as budget amounts) are often depicted with two-dimensional objects (such as dollar bills) or three-dimensional objects (such as stacks of coins, homes, or barrels). By using pictographs, artists can create false impressions that grossly distort differences by using these simple principles of basic geometry: (1) When you double each side of a square, the area doesn't merely double; it increases by a factor of *four.* (2) When you double each side of a cube, the volume doesn't merely double; it increases by a factor of *eight.* See Figure 2-19 in the following example, and note that the larger airliner is twice as long, twice as tall, and twice as deep as the first airliner, so the volume of the larger airliner is eight times that of the smaller airliner.

Example 14   Pictograph of Airline Passengers

In 1984, U.S. airlines carried 345 million passengers, and in 2010 they carried 706 million passengers, so the number of passengers approximately doubled from 1984 to 2010. The pictograph in Figure 2-19 illustrates these data with images of airliners that are objects of volume. Readers can have a variety of perceptions. Some might think that the numbers of passengers are the same in both images, because the same numbers of seats are included. Others might look at the different sizes of the airliners and see objects of volume, the larger aircraft being roughly eight times the size of the smaller one. Even though Figure 2-19 includes attractive images, it does a very poor job of accurately and unambiguously depicting the data. In contrast, Figure 2-20 is a simple bar graph that does a good job of depicting the data accurately.

Passengers in 1984   Passengers in 2010

Figure 2-19   **Revenue Passengers Carried by U.S. Airlines**

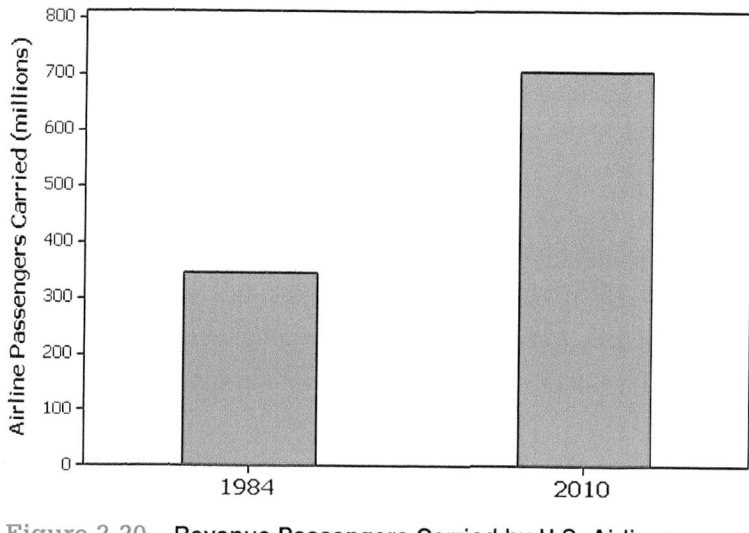

Figure 2-20   Revenue Passengers Carried by U.S. Airlines

Examples 13 and 14 illustrate the following principles related to misleading graphs:

- **Nonzero axis:** Always examine a graph to see whether an axis begins at some point other than zero so that differences are exaggerated.

- **Pictographs:** When examining data depicted with a pictograph, determine whether the graph is misleading because objects of area or volume are used to depict amounts that are actually one-dimensional. (Histograms and bar charts represent one-dimensional data with two-dimensional bars, but they use bars with the same width so that the graph is not misleading.)

Conclusion

In this section we saw that graphs are excellent tools for describing, exploring, and comparing data.

Describing data: In a histogram, for example, consider the distribution, center, variation, and outliers (values that are very far away from almost all of the other data values). What is the approximate value of the center of the distribution, and what is the approximate range of values? Consider the overall shape of the distribution. Are the values evenly distributed? Is the distribution skewed (lopsided) to the right or left? Does the distribution peak in the middle? Is there a large gap, suggesting that the data might come from different populations? Identify any extreme values and any other notable characteristics.

Exploring data: Look for features of the graph that reveal some useful and/or interesting characteristics of the data set. For example, the scatterplot included with Example 1 shows that there appears to be a relationship between the waist circumferences and arm circumferences of males.

Comparing data: Construct similar graphs to compare data sets. For example, Figure 2-14 shows a frequency polygon for the IQ scores of a group with low lead exposure and another frequency polygon for a group with high lead exposure, and both polygons are shown on the same set of axes. Figure 2-14 makes the comparison relatively easy.

In addition to the graphs we have discussed in this section, there are many other useful graphs—some of which have not yet been created. The world desperately needs more people who can create original graphs that enlighten us about the nature of data. For some really helpful information about graphs, see *The Visual Display of Quantitative Information,* second edition, by Edward Tufte (Graphics Press, PO Box 430, Cheshire, CT 06410). Here are just a few of the important principles that Tufte suggests:

- For small data sets of 20 values or fewer, use a table instead of a graph.
- A graph of data should make us focus on the true nature of the data, not on other elements, such as eye-catching but distracting design features.
- Do not distort data; construct a graph to reveal the true nature of the data.
- Almost all of the ink in a graph should be used for the data, not for other design elements.

using TECHNOLOGY

Here we list the graphs that can be generated by various technologies. (Detailed instructions can range from quite simple to extremely complex, so see the individual manuals that are supplements to this book.)

STATDISK Histograms, scatterplots, and pie charts

MINITAB Histograms, frequency polygons, dotplots, stemplots, bar graphs, multiple bar graphs, Pareto charts, pie charts, scatterplots, and time-series graphs

EXCEL Histograms and scatterplots

TI-83/84 PLUS Histograms and scatterplots

STATCRUNCH Histograms, scatterplots, pie charts, bar charts, stemplots, and dotplots

2-4 Basic Skills and Concepts

Statistical Literacy and Critical Thinking

1. Bar Chart and Pareto Chart A bar chart and a Pareto chart both use bars to show frequencies of categories of categorical data. What characteristic distinguishes a Pareto chart from a bar chart, and how does that characteristic help us in understanding the data?

2. Scatterplot What is a scatterplot? What type of data is required for a scatterplot? What characteristic of the data can be better understood by looking at a scatterplot?

3. SAT Scores Listed below are SAT scores from a sample of students (based on data from www.talk.collegeconfidential.com). Why is it that a graph of these data will not be very effective in helping us understand the data?

2400   2200   2150   2040   2230   1890   2100   2090

4. SAT Scores Given that the data in Exercise 3 were obtained from students who made a decision to submit their SAT scores to a Web site, what type of sample is given in that exercise? If we had a much larger sample of that type, would a graph help us understand some characteristics of the population?

Scatterplots.   *In Exercises 5–8, use the given paired data from Appendix B to construct a scatterplot.*

5. President's Heights Refer to Data Set 12 in Appendix B, and use the heights of U.S. presidents and the heights of their main opponents in the election campaign. Does there appear to be a correlation?

6. Brain Volume and IQ Refer to Data Set 6 in Appendix B, and use the brain volumes (cm^3) and IQ scores. A simple hypothesis is that people with larger brains are more intelligent and thus have higher IQ scores. Does the scatterplot support that hypothesis?

7. Bear Chest Size and Weight Refer to Data Set 7 in Appendix B, and use the measured chest sizes and weights of bears. Does there appear to be a correlation between those two variables?

8. Coke Volume and Weight Refer to Data Set 19 in Appendix B, and use the volumes and weights of regular Coke. Does there appear to be a correlation between volume and weight? What else is notable about the arrangement of the points, and how can it be explained?

Time-Series Graphs.   *In Exercises 9 and 10, construct the time-series graph.*

9. Harry Potter Listed below are the gross amounts (in millions of dollars) earned from box office receipts for the movie *Harry Potter and the Half-Blood Prince.* The movie opened on a Wednesday, and the amounts are listed in order for the first 14 days of the movie's release. Suggest an explanation for the fact that the three highest amounts are the first, third, and fourth values listed.

58   22   27   29   21   10   10   8   7   9   11   9   4   4

10. Home Runs Listed below are the numbers of home runs in major league baseball for each year beginning with 1990 (listed in order by row). Is there a trend?

3317   3383   3038   4030   3306   4081   4962   4640   5064   5528

5693   5458   5059   5207   5451   5017   5386   4957   4878   4655

Dotplots.   *In Exercises 11 and 12, construct the dotplot.*

11. Coke Volumes Refer to Data Set 19 in Appendix B, and use the volumes of regular Coke. Does the configuration of the points appear to suggest that the volumes are from a population with a normal distribution? Why or why not? Are there any outliers?

12. Car Pollution Refer to Data Set 14 in Appendix B, and use the greenhouse gas (GHG) emissions from the sample of cars. Does the configuration of the points appear to suggest that the amounts are from a population with a normal distribution? Why or why not?

Stemplots.   *In Exercises 13 and 14, construct the stemplot.*

13. Car Crash Tests Refer to Data Set 13 in Appendix B and use the 21 pelvis (PLVS) deceleration measurements from the car crash tests. Is there strong evidence suggesting that the data are *not* from a population having a normal distribution?

14. Car Braking Distances Refer to Data Set 14 in Appendix B and use the 21 braking distances (ft). Are there any outliers? Is there strong evidence suggesting that the data are *not* from a population having a normal distribution?

Pareto Charts.   *In Exercises 15 and 16, construct the Pareto chart.*

15. Awful Sounds In a survey, 1004 adults were asked to identify the most frustrating sound that they hear in a day. In response 279 chose jackhammers, 388 chose car alarms, 128 chose barking dogs, and 209 chose crying babies (based on data from Kelton Research).

16. School Day Here are weekly instruction times for school children in different countries: 23.8 hours (Japan), 26.9 hours (China), 22.2 hours (U.S.), 24.6 hours (U.K.), 24.8 hours (France). What do these results suggest about education in the United States?

Pie Charts.   *In Exercises 17 and 18, construct the pie chart.*

17. Awful Sounds Use the data from Exercise 15.

18. School Day Use the data from Exercise 16. Does it make sense to use a pie chart for the given data?

Frequency Polygon.   *In Exercises 19 and 20, construct the frequency polygon.*

19. Earthquake Magnitudes Use the frequency distribution from Exercise 23 in Section 2-2 to construct a frequency polygon. Applying a loose interpretation of the requirements for a normal distribution, do the magnitudes appear to be normally distributed? Why or why not?

20. Earthquake Depths Use the frequency distribution from Exercise 24 in Section 2-2 to construct a frequency polygon. Applying a strict interpretation of the requirements for a normal distribution, do the depths appear to be normally distributed? Why or why not?

Deceptive Graphs.   *In Exercises 21–24, identify the characteristic that causes the graph to be deceptive.*

21. Election Results The accompanying graph depicts the numbers of votes (in millions) in the 2008 U.S. presidential election.

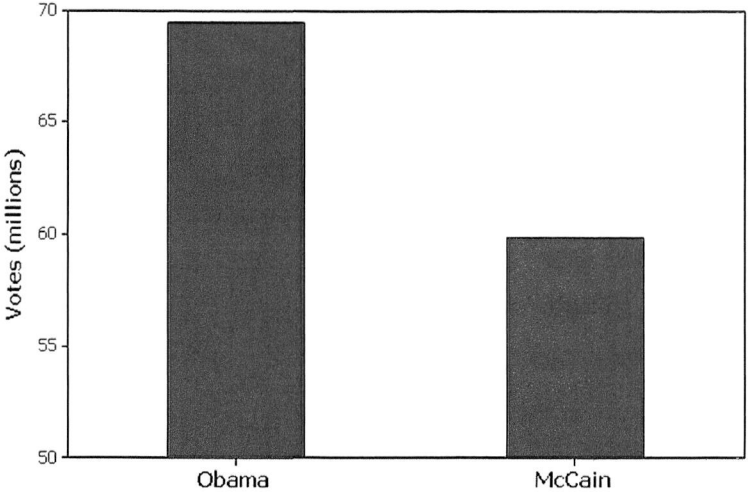

22. Subway Fare In 1986, the New York City subway fare cost $1, and as of this writing, it now costs $2, so the price doubled. In the accompanying graph, the $2 bill is twice as long and twice as tall as the $1 bill.

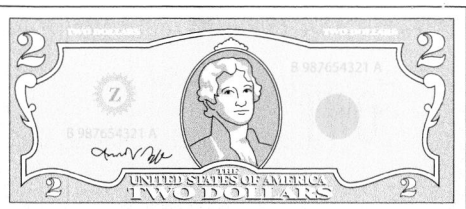

1986 Subway Fare   Current Subway Fare

23. Oil Consumption China currently consumes 7.6 million barrels of oil per day, compared to the United States oil consumption of 20.7 million barrels of oil per day. In the accompanying illustration, the larger barrel is about three times as wide and three times as tall as the smaller barrel.

China   United States

24. Braking Distance Data Set 14 in Appendix B lists braking distances (ft) of different cars, and the braking distances of three of those cars are shown in the accompanying illustration.

2-4 Beyond the Basics

25. Back-to-Back Stemplots Exercise 19 in Section 2-3 used back-to-back relative frequency histograms for the ages of actresses and actors that are listed in Data Set 11 of Appendix B. Use the same method to construct back-to-back stemplots of the ages of actresses and actors, and then use the results to compare the two data sets.

26. Expanded and Condensed Stemplots

a. A stemplot can be *expanded* by subdividing rows into those with leaves having digits of 0 through 4 and those with leaves having digits 5 through 9. Using the body temperatures from 12 AM on Day 2 listed in Data Set 3 of Appendix B, the first three rows of an expanded stemplot have stems of 96 (for leaves between 5 and 9 inclusive), 97 (for leaves between 0 and 4 inclusive), and 97 (for leaves between 5 and 9 inclusive). Construct the complete expanded stemplot for the body temperatures from 12 AM on Day 2 listed in Data Set 3 of Appendix B.

b. A stemplot can be *condensed* by combining adjacent rows. Using the LDL cholesterol measurements from males in Data Set 1 of Appendix B, we obtain the first two rows of the condensed stemplot as shown below. Note that we insert an asterisk to separate digits in the leaves associated with the numbers in each stem. Every row in the condensed plot must include exactly one asterisk so that the shape of the condensed stemplot is not distorted. Complete the condensed stemplot. What is an advantage of using a condensed stemplot instead of one that is not condensed?

```
6-7 | 79*778
8-9 | 45678*049
```

Chapter 2   Review

This chapter presented methods for organizing, summarizing, and graphing data sets. When one is investigating a data set, the characteristics of center, variation, distribution, outliers, and changing pattern over time are generally very important, and this chapter includes a variety of tools for investigating the distribution of the data. After completing this chapter, you should be able to do the following:

- Construct a frequency distribution or relative frequency distribution to summarize data (Section 2-2).

- Construct a histogram or relative frequency histogram to show the distribution of data (Section 2-3).

- Examine a histogram or normal quantile plot to determine whether sample data appear to be from a population having a normal distribution (Section 2-3).

- Construct graphs of data using a scatterplot (for paired data), frequency polygon, dotplot, stemplot, bar graph, multiple bar graph, Pareto chart, pie chart, or time-series graph (Section 2-4).

- Critically analyze a graph to determine whether it objectively depicts data or is somehow misleading or incorrect (Section 2-4).

Chapter Quick Quiz

1. When one is constructing a table representing the frequency distribution of weights (lb) of discarded textile items from Data Set 23 in Appendix B, the first two classes of a frequency distribution are 0.00–0.99 and 1.00–1.99. What is the class width?

2. Using the same first two classes from Exercise 1, identify the class boundaries of the first class.

3. The first class described in Exercise 1 has a frequency of 51. If you know only the class limits given in Exercise 1 and the frequency of 51, can you identify the original 51 data values?

4. A stemplot is created from the intervals (min) between eruptions of the Old Faithful geyser in Yellowstone National Park, and one row of that stemplot is 6 | 1222279. Identify the values represented by that row.

5. In the California Daily 4 lottery, four digits between 0 and 9 inclusive are randomly selected each day. We normally expect that each of the ten different digits will occur about 1/10 of the time, and an analysis of last year's results shows that this did happen. Because the results are what we normally expect, is it correct to say that the distribution of selected digits is a normal distribution?

6. In an investigation of the travel costs of college students, which of the following does not belong: center; variation; distribution; bar graph; outliers; changing patterns over time?

7. In an investigation of the relationship between SAT scores and grade point averages (GPA) of college students, which of the following graphs is most helpful: histogram; pie chart; scatterplot; stemplot; dotplot?

8. As a quality control manager at Sony, you find that defective CDs have various causes, including worn machinery, human error, bad supplies, and packaging mistreatment. Which of the following graphs would be best for describing the causes of defects: histogram; scatterplot; Pareto chart; dotplot; pie chart?

9. What characteristic of a data set can be better understood by constructing a histogram?

10. A histogram is to be constructed from the brain sizes listed in Data Set 6 of Appendix B. Without actually constructing that histogram, simply identify two key features of the histogram that would suggest that the data have a *normal distribution*.

Review Exercises

1. Frequency Distribution of Brain Volumes Construct a frequency distribution of the 20 brain volumes (cm³) listed below. (These volumes are from Data Set 6 of Appendix B.) Use the classes 900–999, 1000–1099, and so on.

1005   963   1035   1027   1281   1272   1051   1079   1034   1070

1173   1079   1067   1104   1347   1439   1029   1100   1204   1160

2. Histogram of Brain Volumes Construct the histogram that corresponds to the frequency distribution from Exercise 1. Applying a very strict interpretation of the requirements for a normal distribution, does the histogram suggest that the data are from a population having a normal distribution? Why or why not?

3. Dotplot of California Lottery In the California Daily 4 lottery, four digits are randomly selected each day. Listed below are the digits that were selected in one recent week. Construct a dotplot. Does the dotplot suggest that the lottery is fair?

5 3 8 9 2 9 1 1 3 0 9 7 3 8 7 4 7 4 8 5 6 8 0 0 4 7 5 3

4. Stemplot of IQ Scores Listed below are the first eight IQ scores from Data Set 6 in Appendix B. Construct a stemplot of these eight values. Is this data set large enough to reveal the true nature of the distribution of IQ scores for the population from which the sample is obtained?

96 89 87 87 101 103 103 96

5. CO Emissions Listed below are the amounts (million metric tons) of carbon monoxide emissions in the United States for each year of a recent ten-year period. The data are listed in order. Construct the graph that is most appropriate for these data. What type of graph is best? What does the graph suggest?

5638 5708 5893 5807 5881 5939 6024 6032 5946 6022

6. CO and NO Emissions Exercise 5 lists the amounts of carbon monoxide emissions, and listed below are the amounts (million metric tons) of nitrous oxide emissions in the United States for the same ten-year period as in Exercise 5. What graph is best for exploring the relationship between carbon monoxide emissions and nitrous oxide emissions? Construct that graph. Does the graph suggest that there is a relationship between carbon monoxide emissions and nitrous oxide emissions?

351 349 345 339 335 335 362 371 376 384

7. Sports Equipment According to *USA Today*, the largest categories of sports equipment sales are as follows: fishing ($2.0 billion); firearms and hunting ($3.1 billion); camping ($1.7 billion); golf ($2.5 billion). Construct the graph that best depicts these different categories and their relative amounts. What type of graph is best?

Cumulative Review Exercises

In Exercises 1–5, refer to the table in the margin, which summarizes results from 641 people who responded to a USA Today survey. Participants responded to this question: "Who do you most like to get compliments from at work?"

Response	Frequency
Co-workers	260
Boss	241
Strangers	82
People who report to me	58

1. Graph Which of the following graphs would be best for visually illustrating the data in the table: histogram; dotplot; scatterplot; Pareto chart; stemplot?

2. Level of Measurement Is the level of measurement of the 641 individual responses nominal, ordinal, interval, or ratio? Why?

3. Sampling The results in the table were obtained by posting the question on a Web site, and readers of *USA Today* could respond to the question if they chose to. What is this type of sampling called? Is this type of sample likely to be representative of the population of all workers? Why or why not?

4. Misleading Graph How is the accompanying graph misleading? How could it be modified so that it would not be misleading? (The graph is on the top of the next page.)

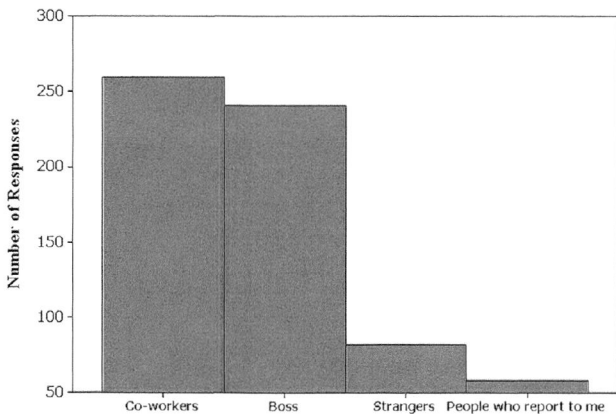

5. Statistic or Parameter? Among the 641 people who responded to the *USA Today* survey, what is the percentage of respondents who chose the category of boss? When considered in the context of the population of all workers, is that percentage a statistic or a parameter? Explain.

6. Grooming Time Listed below are times (minutes) spent on hygiene and grooming in the morning (by randomly selected subjects) (based on data from a Svenska Cellulosa Aktiebolaget survey). Construct a table representing the frequency distribution. Use the classes 0–9, 10–19, and so on.

0 5 12 15 15 20 22 24 25 25 25 27 27 28 30 30 35 35 40 45

7. Histogram of Grooming Times Use the frequency distribution from Exercise 6 to construct a histogram. Based on the result, do the data appear to be from a population with a normal distribution? Explain.

8. Stemplot of Grooming Times Use the data from Exercise 6 to construct a stemplot.

Technology Project

It was noted in this section that the days of charming and primitive hand-drawn graphs are well behind us, and technology now provides us with powerful tools for generating a wide variety of different graphs. The data sets in Appendix B are available as files that can be opened by statistical software packages, such as STATDISK, Minitab, Excel, SPSS, and SAS. Use a statistical software package to open the male and female body measurements from Data Set 1 in Appendix B. Use the statistical software with the methods of this chapter to describe, explore, and compare the blood platelet measurements of males and females. Does there appear to be a gender difference in blood platelet counts? When analyzing blood platelet counts of patients, should physicians take the gender of patients into account? Support your conclusions with printouts of suitable graphs. (Later chapters will present more formal methods for making such comparisons.)

from data TO DECISION

Flight Planning

Data Set 15 in Appendix B includes data about American Airline flights from New York (JFK airport) to Los Angeles (LAX airport). The data are from the Bureau of Transportation.

Critical Thinking

Use the methods from this chapter to address the following questions.

1. Is there a relationship between taxi-out times at JFK and taxi-in times at LAX? Explain.

2. Is there a relationship between departure delay times at JFK and arrival delay times at LAX? Explain.

3. Arrival delay times are important because they can affect the plans of passengers. Explore the arrival delay times by using the methods of this chapter and comment on the results. Is there very small variation among the arrival delay times? Are there any outliers? What is the nature of the distribution of arrival delay times? Based on the results, are arrival delay times very predictable?

Cooperative Group Activities

1. In-class activity Using a package of purchased chocolate chip cookies, each student should be given two or three cookies. Proceed to count the number of chocolate chips in each cookie. Not all of the chocolate chips are visible, so "destructive testing" must be used through a process involving consumption. Record the numbers of chocolate chips for each cookie and combine all results. Construct a frequency distribution, histogram, dotplot, and stemplot of the results. Given that the cookies were made through a process of mass production, we might expect that the numbers of chips per cookie would not vary much. Is that indicated by the results? Explain. (See "Chocolate Chip Cookies as a Teaching Aid" by Herbert K. H. Lee, *American Statistician,* Vol. 61, No. 4.)

2. In-class activity In class, each student should record two pulse rates by counting the number of her or his heartbeats in one minute. The first pulse rate should be measured while seated, and the second pulse rate should be measured while standing. Using the pulse rates measured while seated, construct a frequency distribution and histogram for the pulse rates of males, and then construct another frequency distribution and histogram for the pulse rates of females. Using the pulse rates measured while standing, construct a frequency distribution and histogram for the pulse rates of males, and then construct another frequency distribution and histogram for the pulse rates of females. Compare the results. Do males and females appear to have different pulse rates? Do pulse rates measured while seated appear to be different from pulse rates measured while standing? Use an appropriate graph to determine whether there is a relationship between sitting pulse rate and standing pulse rate.

3. In-class activity Given below are recent measurements from the Old Faithful geyser in Yellowstone National Park. The time intervals between eruptions are matched with the corresponding times of duration of the geyser; thus the interval of 76 min is paired with the duration of 4.53 min, the interval of 84 min is paired with the duration of 3.83 min, and so on. Use the methods of this chapter to summarize and explore each of the two sets of data separately, and then investigate whether there is some relationship between them. Describe the methods used and the conclusions reached.

Intervals (min) between eruptions

        76 84 76 103 92 47 98 54 80 91 69 86 83 75 93

        89 96 65 94 85 94 60 94 86 93 88 61 96 52 98

Durations (min) of eruptions

    4.53 3.83 3.83 4.23 4.70 1.83 4.00 2.00 3.57 4.25 2.75 4.47 3.35 3.27 4.30

    4.25 4.05 2.12 4.63 4.18 4.05 2.13 4.60 4.53 3.70 4.17 1.87 4.68 1.83 4.10

4. Out-of-class activity Search newspapers and magazines to find an example of a graph that is misleading. (See Examples 13 and 14 in Section 2-4.) Describe how the graph is misleading. Redraw the graph so that it depicts the information correctly.

5. Out-of-class activity Obtain a copy of *The Visual Display of Quantitative Information,* second edition, by Edward Tufte (Graphics Press, PO Box 430, Cheshire, CT 06410). Find the graph describing Napoleon's march to Moscow and back, and explain why Tufte says that "it may well be the best graphic ever drawn."

6. Out-of-class activity Obtain a copy of *The Visual Display of Quantitative Information,* second edition, by Edward Tufte (Graphics Press, PO Box 430, Cheshire, CT 06410). Find the graph that appeared in *American Education,* and explain why Tufte says that "this may well be the worst graphic ever to find its way into print." Construct a graph that is effective in depicting the same data.

3 Statistics for Describing, Exploring, and Comparing Data

How many chips are in a chocolate chip cookie?

This edition of *Elementary Statistics* and previous editions have included data obtained from M&M plain candies. This Chapter Problem continues the legacy of using snack foods for statistical purposes, and the choice here is chocolate chip cookies as suggested by the article "Chocolate Chip Cookies as a Teaching Aid," by Herbert Lee (*The American Statistician,* Vol. 61, No. 4).

Table 3-1 lists the numbers of chocolate chips counted in different brands. The counts were obtained by the author, who found that the counting process was not as simple as it might seem. What do you do with loose chocolate chips that were found in each package? Some chocolate chips were stuck together, so they had to be counted with great care. Care also had to be taken to not count nut particles as chocolate chips. There were some small fragments that were not counted after the author made an arbitrary decision about the minimum size required to be counted as an official chocolate chip.

The counts in Table 3-1 do not include weights of the chocolate chips, and the Hannaford brand had many that were substantially larger than any of the chocolate chips in the other brands. Also, there is an issue with the sampling method. The author used all of the cookies in one package from each of the different brands. A better sampling method would involve randomly selecting cookies from different packages obtained throughout the country, and this would have required extensive travel by the author—a prospect with some appeal. In developing this Chapter Problem, the author learned much about chocolate chip cookies, including the observation that a huge pile of crushed chocolate chip cookies has absolutely none of the appeal of a single cookie untouched by human hands.

Table 3-1 Numbers of Chocolate Chips in Different Brands of Cookies

Chips Ahoy (regular)

22	22	26	24	23	27	25	20	24	26	25	25	19	24	20	22	24	25	25	20
23	30	26	20	25	28	19	26	26	23	25	23	23	23	22	26	27	23	28	24

Chips Ahoy (chewy)

21	20	16	17	16	17	20	22	14	20	19	17	20	21	21	18
20	20	21	19	22	20	20	19	16	19	16	15	24	23	14	24

Chips Ahoy (reduced fat)

13	24	18	16	21	20	14	20	18	12	24	23	28	18	18	19	22	21	22	16
13	20	20	23	24	20	17	20	19	21	27	16	24	19	23	25	14	18	15	19

Keebler

29	31	25	32	27	31	30	29	31	26	32	33	32	30	33	29	30
28	32	35	37	31	24	30	30	34	29	27	24	38	37	32	26	30

Hannaford

13	15	16	21	15	14	14	15	13	13	16	11
14	12	13	12	14	12	16	17	14	16	14	15

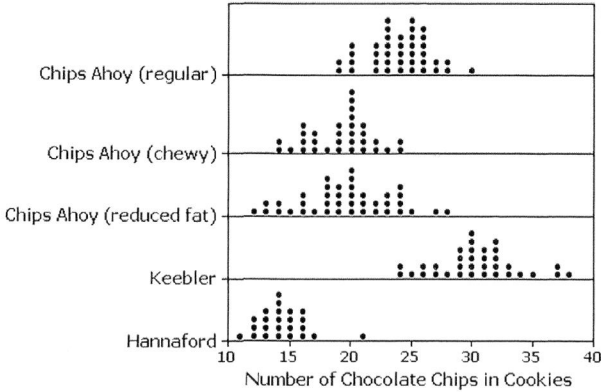

Figure 3-1   **Dotplot of Numbers of Chocolate Chips in Cookies**

Figure 3-1 is a dotplot (described in Section 2-4) that includes all of the cookies from Table 3-1. Figure 3-1 shows some obvious differences. Instead of relying solely on subjective interpretations of a graph like Figure 3-1, this chapter introduces measures that are essential to any study of statistics. The mean, median, standard deviation, and variance are among the most important statistics presented in this chapter, and those statistics will be used in our description, exploration, and comparison of the counts in Table 3-1.

3-1   Review and Preview

Chapter 1 discussed methods of collecting sample data. Chapter 2 presented frequency distributions and a variety of different graphs that help us summarize and visualize data. In Chapter 2 we noted that when describing, exploring, and comparing data sets, these characteristics are usually extremely important: (1) center; (2) variation; (3) distribution; (4) outliers; and (5) changing characteristics of data over time. In this chapter we introduce important statistics, including the mean, median, and standard deviation. Upon completing this chapter, you should be able to find the mean, median, standard deviation, and variance from a data set, and you should be able to clearly understand and interpret such values. It is especially important to understand values of standard deviation by using tools such as the range rule of thumb described in Section 3-3.

Critical Thinking and Interpretation: Beyond Formulas

This chapter includes several formulas used to compute basic statistics. Because many of these statistics can be easily calculated by using technology, it is not so important for us to memorize formulas and manually perform complex calculations. Instead, we should focus on understanding and interpreting the values we obtain from them.

The methods and tools presented in Chapter 2 and in this chapter are often called methods of **descriptive statistics,** because they summarize or describe relevant characteristics of data. Later in this book, we will use **inferential statistics** to make inferences, or generalizations, about a population.

3-2   Measures of Center

Key Concept The focus of this section is the characteristic of center of a data set. In particular, we present measures of center, including *mean* and *median,* as tools for analyzing data. Our objective here is not only to find the value of each measure of center, but also to interpret those values. Part 1 of this section includes core concepts that should be understood before considering Part 2.

Part 1: Basic Concepts of Measures of Center

In this Part 1, we introduce the mean, median, mode, and midrange as different measures of center.

> **DEFINITION** A **measure of center** is a value at the center or middle of a data set.

There are several different ways to determine the center, so we have different definitions of measures of center, including the mean, median, mode, and midrange. We begin with the mean.

Mean

The mean (or arithmetic mean) is generally the most important of all numerical measurements used to describe data, and it is what most people call an *average*.

> **DEFINITION** The **arithmetic mean,** or the **mean,** of a set of data is the measure of center found by adding the data values and dividing the total by the number of data values.

Important Properties of the Mean

• Sample means drawn from the same population tend to vary less than other measures of center.

• The mean of a data set uses every data value.

• A disadvantage of the mean is that just one extreme value (outlier) can change the value of the mean substantially. (Since the mean cannot resist substantial changes caused by extreme values, we say that the mean is not a *resistant* measure of center.)

Calculation and Notation of the Mean

The definition of the mean can be expressed as Formula 3-1, in which the Greek letter Σ (uppercase sigma) indicates that the data values should be added, so Σx represents the sum of all data values. The symbol n denotes the **sample size,** which is the number of data values.

Formula 3-1

$$\text{mean} = \frac{\Sigma x}{n} \quad \begin{matrix} \leftarrow \text{ sum of all data values} \\ \leftarrow \text{ number of data values} \end{matrix}$$

If the data are a *sample* from a population, the mean is denoted by $\bar{x}$ (pronounced "x-bar"); if the data are the entire population, the mean is denoted by μ (lowercase Greek mu). (Sample statistics are usually represented by English letters, such as $\bar{x}$, and population parameters are usually represented by Greek letters, such as μ.)

Average Bob

According to Kevin O'Keefe, author of *The Average American: The Extraordinary Search for the Nation's Most Ordinary Citizen*, Bob Burns is the most average person in the United States. O'Keefe spent 2 years using 140 criteria to identify the single American who is most average. He identified statistics revealing preferences of the majority and applied them to the many people he encountered. Bob Burns is the only person who satisfied all of the 140 criteria. Bob Burns is 5 ft 8 in. tall, weighs 190 pounds, is 54 years of age, married, has three children, wears glasses, works 40 hours per week, drives an eight-year-old car, has an outdoor grill, mows his own lawn, drinks coffee each day, and walks his dog each evening.

Class Size Paradox

There are at least two ways to obtain the mean class size, and they can have very different results. At one college, if we take the

numbers of students in 737 classes, we get a mean of 40 students. But if we were to compile a list of the class sizes for each student and use this list, we would get a mean class size of 147. This large discrepancy is due to the fact that there are many students in large classes, while there are few students in small classes. Without changing the number of classes or faculty, we could reduce the mean class size experienced by students by making all classes about the same size. This would also im-prove attendance, which is better in smaller classes.

Notation

Σ	denotes the *sum* of a set of data values.
x	is the *variable* usually used to represent the individual data values.
n	represents the *number of data values* in a *sample*.
N	represents the *number of data values* in a *population*.

$$\bar{x} = \frac{\Sigma x}{n} \quad \text{is the mean of a set of } sample \text{ values.}$$

$$\mu = \frac{\Sigma x}{N} \quad \text{is the mean of all values in a } population.$$

Example 1   Mean

Table 3-1 includes counts of chocolate chips in different cookies. Find the mean of the first five counts for Chips Ahoy regular cookies: 22 chips, 22 chips, 26 chips, 24 chips, and 23 chips.

Solution

The mean is computed by using Formula 3-1. First add the data values, then divide by the number of data values:

$$\bar{x} = \frac{\Sigma x}{n} = \frac{22 + 22 + 26 + 24 + 23}{5} = \frac{117}{5}$$

$$= 23.4 \text{ chips}$$

The mean of the first five chip counts is 23.4 chips.

Median

The median can be thought of loosely as a "middle value" in the sense that about half of the values in a data set are less than the median and half are greater than the median. The following definition is more precise.

> **DEFINITION** The **median** of a data set is the measure of center that is the *middle value* when the original data values are arranged in order of increasing (or decreasing) magnitude.

Calculation and Notation of the Median The median is often denoted by $\widetilde{x}$ (pronounced "*x*-tilde"). To find the median, first *sort* the values (arrange them in order), and then follow one of these two procedures:

1. If the number of data values is odd, the median is the number located in the exact middle of the sorted list.

2. If the number of data values is even, the median is found by computing the mean of the two middle numbers in the sorted list.

Important Properties of the Median

- The median does not change by large amounts when we include just a few extreme values (so the median is a *resistant* measure of center).
- The median does not use every data value.

Example 2   Median

Find the median of the five sample values used in Example 1: 22 chips, 22 chips, 26 chips, 24 chips, and 23 chips.

Table A-3 *t* Distribution: Critical *t* Values

Degrees of Freedom	Area in One Tail				
	0.005	0.01	0.025	0.05	0.10
	Area in Two Tails				
	0.01	0.02	0.05	0.10	0.20
1	63.657	31.821	12.706	6.314	3.078
2	9.925	6.965	4.303	2.920	1.886
3	5.841	4.541	3.182	2.353	1.638
4	4.604	3.747	2.776	2.132	1.533
5	4.032	3.365	2.571	2.015	1.476
6	3.707	3.143	2.447	1.943	1.440
7	3.499	2.998	2.365	1.895	1.415
8	3.355	2.896	2.306	1.860	1.397
9	3.250	2.821	2.262	1.833	1.383
10	3.169	2.764	2.228	1.812	1.372
11	3.106	2.718	2.201	1.796	1.363
12	3.055	2.681	2.179	1.782	1.356
13	3.012	2.650	2.160	1.771	1.350
14	2.977	2.624	2.145	1.761	1.345
15	2.947	2.602	2.131	1.753	1.341
16	2.921	2.583	2.120	1.746	1.337
17	2.898	2.567	2.110	1.740	1.333
18	2.878	2.552	2.101	1.734	1.330
19	2.861	2.539	2.093	1.729	1.328
20	2.845	2.528	2.086	1.725	1.325
21	2.831	2.518	2.080	1.721	1.323
22	2.819	2.508	2.074	1.717	1.321
23	2.807	2.500	2.069	1.714	1.319
24	2.797	2.492	2.064	1.711	1.318
25	2.787	2.485	2.060	1.708	1.316
26	2.779	2.479	2.056	1.706	1.315
27	2.771	2.473	2.052	1.703	1.314
28	2.763	2.467	2.048	1.701	1.313
29	2.756	2.462	2.045	1.699	1.311
30	2.750	2.457	2.042	1.697	1.310
31	2.744	2.453	2.040	1.696	1.309
32	2.738	2.449	2.037	1.694	1.309
33	2.733	2.445	2.035	1.692	1.308
34	2.728	2.441	2.032	1.691	1.307
35	2.724	2.438	2.030	1.690	1.306
36	2.719	2.434	2.028	1.688	1.306
37	2.715	2.431	2.026	1.687	1.305
38	2.712	2.429	2.024	1.686	1.304
39	2.708	2.426	2.023	1.685	1.304
40	2.704	2.423	2.021	1.684	1.303
45	2.690	2.412	2.014	1.679	1.301
50	2.678	2.403	2.009	1.676	1.299
60	2.660	2.390	2.000	1.671	1.296
70	2.648	2.381	1.994	1.667	1.294
80	2.639	2.374	1.990	1.664	1.292
90	2.632	2.368	1.987	1.662	1.291
100	2.626	2.364	1.984	1.660	1.290
200	2.601	2.345	1.972	1.653	1.286
300	2.592	2.339	1.968	1.650	1.284
400	2.588	2.336	1.966	1.649	1.284
500	2.586	2.334	1.965	1.648	1.283
1000	2.581	2.330	1.962	1.646	1.282
2000	2.578	2.328	1.961	1.646	1.282
Large	2.576	2.326	1.960	1.645	1.282

Formulas and Tables by Mario F. Triola
Copyright 2014 Pearson Education, Inc.

Ch. 8: Test Statistics (one population)

$$z = \frac{\hat{p} - p}{\sqrt{\frac{pq}{n}}} \quad \text{Proportion—one population}$$

$$t = \frac{\bar{x} - \mu}{\frac{s}{\sqrt{n}}} \quad \text{Mean—one population (} \sigma \text{ unknown)}$$

$$z = \frac{\bar{x} - \mu}{\frac{\sigma}{\sqrt{n}}} \quad \text{Mean—one population (} \sigma \text{ known)}$$

$$\chi^2 = \frac{(n-1)s^2}{\sigma^2} \quad \begin{array}{l}\text{Standard deviation or variance—}\\ \text{one population}\end{array}$$

Ch. 9: Test Statistics (two populations)

$$z = \frac{(\hat{p}_1 - \hat{p}_2) - (p_1 - p_2)}{\sqrt{\frac{\bar{p}\,\bar{q}}{n_1} + \frac{\bar{p}\,\bar{q}}{n_2}}} \quad \text{Two proportions} \qquad \bar{p} = \frac{x_1 + x_2}{n_1 + n_2}$$

$$t = \frac{(\bar{x}_1 - \bar{x}_2) - (\mu_1 - \mu_2)}{\sqrt{\frac{s_1^2}{n_1} + \frac{s_2^2}{n_2}}} \quad \begin{array}{l}\text{df = smaller of}\\ n_1 - 1, n_2 - 1\end{array}$$

Two means—independent; σ_1 and σ_2 unknown, and not assumed equal.

$$t = \frac{(\bar{x}_1 - \bar{x}_2) - (\mu_1 - \mu_2)}{\sqrt{\frac{s_p^2}{n_1} + \frac{s_p^2}{n_2}}} \quad (\text{df} = n_1 + n_2 - 2) \qquad s_p^2 = \frac{(n_1 - 1)s_1^2 + (n_2 - 1)s_2^2}{n_1 + n_2 - 2}$$

Two means—independent; σ_1 and σ_2 unknown, but assumed equal.

$$z = \frac{(\bar{x}_1 - \bar{x}_2) - (\mu_1 - \mu_2)}{\sqrt{\frac{\sigma_1^2}{n_1} + \frac{\sigma_2^2}{n_2}}} \quad \begin{array}{l}\text{Two means—independent;}\\ \sigma_1, \sigma_2 \text{ known.}\end{array}$$

$$t = \frac{\bar{d} - \mu_d}{\frac{s_d}{\sqrt{n}}} \quad \text{Two means—matched pairs (df} = n - 1)$$

$$F = \frac{s_1^2}{s_2^2} \quad \begin{array}{l}\text{Standard deviation or variance—}\\ \text{two populations (where } s_1^2 \geq s_2^2)\end{array}$$

Ch. 11: Goodness-of-Fit and Contingency Tables

$$\chi^2 = \sum \frac{(O - E)^2}{E} \quad \text{Goodness-of-fit (df} = k - 1)$$

$$\chi^2 = \sum \frac{(O - E)^2}{E} \quad \text{Contingency table [df} = (r-1)(c-1)]$$

$$\text{where } E = \frac{(\text{row total})(\text{column total})}{(\text{grand total})}$$

$$\chi^2 = \frac{(|b - c| - 1)^2}{b + c} \quad \text{McNemar's test for matched pairs (df} = 1)$$

Ch. 10: Linear Correlation/Regression

$$\text{Correlation } r = \frac{n\Sigma xy - (\Sigma x)(\Sigma y)}{\sqrt{n(\Sigma x^2) - (\Sigma x)^2}\sqrt{n(\Sigma y^2) - (\Sigma y)^2}}$$

$$\text{or } r = \frac{\sum (z_x z_y)}{n - 1} \quad \begin{array}{l}\text{where } z_x = z \text{ score for } x\\ z_y = z \text{ score for } y\end{array}$$

$$\text{Slope:} \qquad b_1 = \frac{n\Sigma xy - (\Sigma x)(\Sigma y)}{n(\Sigma x^2) - (\Sigma x)^2}$$

$$\text{or } b_1 = r\frac{s_y}{s_x}$$

y-Intercept:

$$b_0 = \bar{y} - b_1\bar{x} \text{ or } b_0 = \frac{(\Sigma y)(\Sigma x^2) - (\Sigma x)(\Sigma xy)}{n(\Sigma x^2) - (\Sigma x)^2}$$

$$\hat{y} = b_0 + b_1 x \quad \text{Estimated eq. of regression line}$$

$$r^2 = \frac{\text{explained variation}}{\text{total variation}}$$

$$s_e = \sqrt{\frac{\Sigma(y - \hat{y})^2}{n - 2}} \text{ or } \sqrt{\frac{\Sigma y^2 - b_0\Sigma y - b_1\Sigma xy}{n - 2}}$$

$$\hat{y} - E < y < \hat{y} + E \quad \text{Prediction interval}$$

$$\text{where } E = t_{\alpha/2}s_e \sqrt{1 + \frac{1}{n} + \frac{n(x_0 - \bar{x})^2}{n(\Sigma x^2) - (\Sigma x)^2}}$$

Ch. 12: One-Way Analysis of Variance

Procedure for testing $H_0: \mu_1 = \mu_2 = \mu_3 = \cdots$

1. Use software or calculator to obtain results.
2. Identify the P-value.
3. Form conclusion:

    If P-value $\leq \alpha$, reject the null hypothesis of equal means.
    If P-value $> \alpha$, fail to reject the null hypothesis of equal means.

Ch. 12: Two-Way Analysis of Variance

Procedure:

1. Use software or a calculator to obtain results.
2. Test H_0: There is no interaction between the row factor and column factor.
3. Stop if H_0 from Step 2 is rejected.

    If H_0 from Step 2 is not rejected (so there does not appear to be an interaction effect), proceed with these two tests:
    Test for effects from the row factor.
    Test for effects from the column factor.

Formulas and Tables by Mario F. Triola
Copyright 2014 Pearson Education, Inc.

Table A-4 Chi-Square (χ^2) Distribution

Area to the Right of the Critical Value

Degrees of Freedom	0.995	0.99	0.975	0.95	0.90	0.10	0.05	0.025	0.01	0.005
1	—	—	0.001	0.004	0.016	2.706	3.841	5.024	6.635	7.879
2	0.010	0.020	0.051	0.103	0.211	4.605	5.991	7.378	9.210	10.597
3	0.072	0.115	0.216	0.352	0.584	6.251	7.815	9.348	11.345	12.838
4	0.207	0.297	0.484	0.711	1.064	7.779	9.488	11.143	13.277	14.860
5	0.412	0.554	0.831	1.145	1.610	9.236	11.071	12.833	15.086	16.750
6	0.676	0.872	1.237	1.635	2.204	10.645	12.592	14.449	16.812	18.548
7	0.989	1.239	1.690	2.167	2.833	12.017	14.067	16.013	18.475	20.278
8	1.344	1.646	2.180	2.733	3.490	13.362	15.507	17.535	20.090	21.955
9	1.735	2.088	2.700	3.325	4.168	14.684	16.919	19.023	21.666	23.589
10	2.156	2.558	3.247	3.940	4.865	15.987	18.307	20.483	23.209	25.188
11	2.603	3.053	3.816	4.575	5.578	17.275	19.675	21.920	24.725	26.757
12	3.074	3.571	4.404	5.226	6.304	18.549	21.026	23.337	26.217	28.299
13	3.565	4.107	5.009	5.892	7.042	19.812	22.362	24.736	27.688	29.819
14	4.075	4.660	5.629	6.571	7.790	21.064	23.685	26.119	29.141	31.319
15	4.601	5.229	6.262	7.261	8.547	22.307	24.996	27.488	30.578	32.801
16	5.142	5.812	6.908	7.962	9.312	23.542	26.296	28.845	32.000	34.267
17	5.697	6.408	7.564	8.672	10.085	24.769	27.587	30.191	33.409	35.718
18	6.265	7.015	8.231	9.390	10.865	25.989	28.869	31.526	34.805	37.156
19	6.844	7.633	8.907	10.117	11.651	27.204	30.144	32.852	36.191	38.582
20	7.434	8.260	9.591	10.851	12.443	28.412	31.410	34.170	37.566	39.997
21	8.034	8.897	10.283	11.591	13.240	29.615	32.671	35.479	38.932	41.401
22	8.643	9.542	10.982	12.338	14.042	30.813	33.924	36.781	40.289	42.796
23	9.260	10.196	11.689	13.091	14.848	32.007	35.172	38.076	41.638	44.181
24	9.886	10.856	12.401	13.848	15.659	33.196	36.415	39.364	42.980	45.559
25	10.520	11.524	13.120	14.611	16.473	34.382	37.652	40.646	44.314	46.928
26	11.160	12.198	13.844	15.379	17.292	35.563	38.885	41.923	45.642	48.290
27	11.808	12.879	14.573	16.151	18.114	36.741	40.113	43.194	46.963	49.645
28	12.461	13.565	15.308	16.928	18.939	37.916	41.337	44.461	48.278	50.993
29	13.121	14.257	16.047	17.708	19.768	39.087	42.557	45.722	49.588	52.336
30	13.787	14.954	16.791	18.493	20.599	40.256	43.773	46.979	50.892	53.672
40	20.707	22.164	24.433	26.509	29.051	51.805	55.758	59.342	63.691	66.766
50	27.991	29.707	32.357	34.764	37.689	63.167	67.505	71.420	76.154	79.490
60	35.534	37.485	40.482	43.188	46.459	74.397	79.082	83.298	88.379	91.952
70	43.275	45.442	48.758	51.739	55.329	85.527	90.531	95.023	100.425	104.215
80	51.172	53.540	57.153	60.391	64.278	96.578	101.879	106.629	112.329	116.321
90	59.196	61.754	65.647	69.126	73.291	107.565	113.145	118.136	124.116	128.299
100	67.328	70.065	74.222	77.929	82.358	118.498	124.342	129.561	135.807	140.169

Source: From Donald B. Owen, *Handbook of Statistical Tables.*

Degrees of Freedom

$n-1$	Confidence Interval or Hypothesis Test with a standard deviation or variance
$k-1$	Goodness-of-Fit with k categories
$(r-1)(c-1)$	Contingency Table with r rows and c columns
$k-1$	Kruskal-Wallis test with k samples

Formulas and Tables by Mario F. Triola
Copyright 2014 Pearson Education, Inc.

Ch. 3: Descriptive Statistics

$\bar{x} = \dfrac{\Sigma x}{n}$ Mean

$\bar{x} = \dfrac{\Sigma (f \cdot x)}{\Sigma f}$ Mean (frequency table)

$s = \sqrt{\dfrac{\Sigma (x - \bar{x})^2}{n - 1}}$ Standard deviation

$s = \sqrt{\dfrac{n(\Sigma x^2) - (\Sigma x)^2}{n(n-1)}}$ Standard deviation (shortcut)

$s = \sqrt{\dfrac{n[\Sigma (f \cdot x^2)] - [\Sigma (f \cdot x)]^2}{n(n-1)}}$ Standard deviation (frequency table)

variance $= s^2$

Ch. 4: Probability

$P(A \text{ or } B) = P(A) + P(B)$ if A, B are mutually exclusive

$P(A \text{ or } B) = P(A) + P(B) - P(A \text{ and } B)$
  if A, B are not mutually exclusive

$P(A \text{ and } B) = P(A) \cdot P(B)$ if A, B are independent

$P(A \text{ and } B) = P(A) \cdot P(B|A)$ if A, B are dependent

$P(\bar{A}) = 1 - P(A)$ Rule of complements

$_nP_r = \dfrac{n!}{(n-r)!}$ Permutations (no elements alike)

$\dfrac{n!}{n_1! \, n_2! \, \cdots \, n_k!}$ Permutations (n_1 alike, . . .)

$_nC_r = \dfrac{n!}{(n-r)! \, r!}$ Combinations

Ch. 5: Probability Distributions

$\mu = \Sigma [x \cdot P(x)]$ Mean (prob. dist.)

$\sigma = \sqrt{\Sigma [x^2 \cdot P(x)] - \mu^2}$ Standard deviation (prob. dist.)

$P(x) = \dfrac{n!}{(n-x)! \, x!} \cdot p^x \cdot q^{n-x}$ Binomial probability

$\mu = n \cdot p$ Mean (binomial)

$\sigma^2 = n \cdot p \cdot q$ Variance (binomial)

$\sigma = \sqrt{n \cdot p \cdot q}$ Standard deviation (binomial)

$P(x) = \dfrac{\mu^x \cdot e^{-\mu}}{x!}$ Poisson distribution
  where $e = 2.71828$

Ch. 6: Normal Distribution

$z = \dfrac{x - \mu}{\sigma}$ or $\dfrac{x - \bar{x}}{s}$ Standard score

$\mu_{\bar{x}} = \mu$ Central limit theorem

$\sigma_{\bar{x}} = \dfrac{\sigma}{\sqrt{n}}$ Central limit theorem (Standard error)

Ch. 7: Confidence Intervals (one population)

$\hat{p} - E < p < \hat{p} + E$ Proportion

  where $E = z_{\alpha/2} \sqrt{\dfrac{\hat{p}\hat{q}}{n}}$

$\bar{x} - E < \mu < \bar{x} + E$ Mean

  where $E = t_{\alpha/2} \dfrac{s}{\sqrt{n}}$ (σ unknown)

  or $E = z_{\alpha/2} \dfrac{\sigma}{\sqrt{n}}$ (σ known)

$\dfrac{(n-1)s^2}{\chi_R^2} < \sigma^2 < \dfrac{(n-1)s^2}{\chi_L^2}$ Variance

Ch. 7: Sample Size Determination

$n = \dfrac{[z_{\alpha/2}]^2 0.25}{E^2}$ Proportion

$n = \dfrac{[z_{\alpha/2}]^2 \hat{p}\hat{q}}{E^2}$ Proportion ($\hat{p}$ and $\hat{q}$ are known)

$n = \left[\dfrac{z_{\alpha/2}\sigma}{E} \right]^2$ Mean

Ch. 9: Confidence Intervals (two populations)

$(\hat{p}_1 - \hat{p}_2) - E < (p_1 - p_2) < (\hat{p}_1 - \hat{p}_2) + E$

  where $E = z_{\alpha/2} \sqrt{\dfrac{\hat{p}_1 \hat{q}_1}{n_1} + \dfrac{\hat{p}_2 \hat{q}_2}{n_2}}$

$(\bar{x}_1 - \bar{x}_2) - E < (\mu_1 - \mu_2) < (\bar{x}_1 - \bar{x}_2) + E$ (Indep.)

  where $E = t_{\alpha/2} \sqrt{\dfrac{s_1^2}{n_1} + \dfrac{s_2^2}{n_2}}$ (df = smaller of $n_1 - 1, n_2 - 1$)

(σ_1 and σ_2 unknown and not assumed equal)

  $E = t_{\alpha/2} \sqrt{\dfrac{s_p^2}{n_1} + \dfrac{s_p^2}{n_2}}$ (df $= n_1 + n_2 - 2$)

  $s_p^2 = \dfrac{(n_1 - 1)s_1^2 + (n_2 - 1)s_2^2}{(n_1 - 1) + (n_2 - 1)}$

(σ_1 and σ_2 unknown but assumed equal)

  $E = z_{\alpha/2} \sqrt{\dfrac{\sigma_1^2}{n_1} + \dfrac{\sigma_2^2}{n_2}}$

  (σ_1, σ_2 known)

$\bar{d} - E < \mu_d < \bar{d} + E$ (Matched pairs)

  where $E = t_{\alpha/2} \dfrac{s_d}{\sqrt{n}}$ (df $= n - 1$)

NEGATIVE z Scores

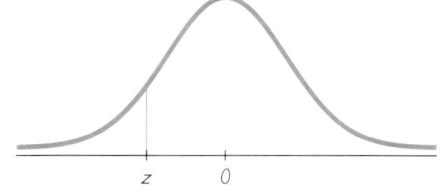

Table A-2 Standard Normal (z) Distribution: Cumulative Area from the LEFT

z	.00	.01	.02	.03	.04	.05	.06	.07	.08	.09
−3.50 and lower	.0001									
−3.4	.0003	.0003	.0003	.0003	.0003	.0003	.0003	.0003	.0003	.0002
−3.3	.0005	.0005	.0005	.0004	.0004	.0004	.0004	.0004	.0004	.0003
−3.2	.0007	.0007	.0006	.0006	.0006	.0006	.0006	.0005	.0005	.0005
−3.1	.0010	.0009	.0009	.0009	.0008	.0008	.0008	.0008	.0007	.0007
−3.0	.0013	.0013	.0013	.0012	.0012	.0011	.0011	.0011	.0010	.0010
−2.9	.0019	.0018	.0018	.0017	.0016	.0016	.0015	.0015	.0014	.0014
−2.8	.0026	.0025	.0024	.0023	.0023	.0022	.0021	.0021	.0020	.0019
−2.7	.0035	.0034	.0033	.0032	.0031	.0030	.0029	.0028	.0027	.0026
−2.6	.0047	.0045	.0044	.0043	.0041	.0040	.0039	.0038	.0037	.0036
−2.5	.0062	.0060	.0059	.0057	.0055	.0054	.0052	.0051*	.0049	.0048
−2.4	.0082	.0080	.0078	.0075	.0073	.0071	.0069	.0068	.0066	.0064
−2.3	.0107	.0104	.0102	.0099	.0096	.0094	.0091	.0089	.0087	.0084
−2.2	.0139	.0136	.0132	.0129	.0125	.0122	.0119	.0116	.0113	.0110
−2.1	.0179	.0174	.0170	.0166	.0162	.0158	.0154	.0150	.0146	.0143
−2.0	.0228	.0222	.0217	.0212	.0207	.0202	.0197	.0192	.0188	.0183
−1.9	.0287	.0281	.0274	.0268	.0262	.0256	.0250	.0244	.0239	.0233
−1.8	.0359	.0351	.0344	.0336	.0329	.0322	.0314	.0307	.0301	.0294
−1.7	.0446	.0436	.0427	.0418	.0409	.0401	.0392	.0384	.0375	.0367
−1.6	.0548	.0537	.0526	.0516	.0505*	.0495	.0485	.0475	.0465	.0455
−1.5	.0668	.0655	.0643	.0630	.0618	.0606	.0594	.0582	.0571	.0559
−1.4	.0808	.0793	.0778	.0764	.0749	.0735	.0721	.0708	.0694	.0681
−1.3	.0968	.0951	.0934	.0918	.0901	.0885	.0869	.0853	.0838	.0823
−1.2	.1151	.1131	.1112	.1093	.1075	.1056	.1038	.1020	.1003	.0985
−1.1	.1357	.1335	.1314	.1292	.1271	.1251	.1230	.1210	.1190	.1170
−1.0	.1587	.1562	.1539	.1515	.1492	.1469	.1446	.1423	.1401	.1379
−0.9	.1841	.1814	.1788	.1762	.1736	.1711	.1685	.1660	.1635	.1611
−0.8	.2119	.2090	.2061	.2033	.2005	.1977	.1949	.1922	.1894	.1867
−0.7	.2420	.2389	.2358	.2327	.2296	.2266	.2236	.2206	.2177	.2148
−0.6	.2743	.2709	.2676	.2643	.2611	.2578	.2546	.2514	.2483	.2451
−0.5	.3085	.3050	.3015	.2981	.2946	.2912	.2877	.2843	.2810	.2776
−0.4	.3446	.3409	.3372	.3336	.3300	.3264	.3228	.3192	.3156	.3121
−0.3	.3821	.3783	.3745	.3707	.3669	.3632	.3594	.3557	.3520	.3483
−0.2	.4207	.4168	.4129	.4090	.4052	.4013	.3974	.3936	.3897	.3859
−0.1	.4602	.4562	.4522	.4483	.4443	.4404	.4364	.4325	.4286	.4247
−0.0	.5000	.4960	.4920	.4880	.4840	.4801	.4761	.4721	.4681	.4641

NOTE: For values of z below −3.49, use 0.0001 for the area.
*Use these common values that result from interpolation:

z score	Area
−1.645	0.0500
−2.575	0.0050

Overview of Statistical Methods

Prepare

1. Context
What do the data mean?
What is the goal of study?

2. Source of the Data
Are the data from a source with a special interest so that there is pressure to obtain results that are favorable to the source?

3. Sampling Method
Were the data collected in a way that is unbiased, or were the data collected in a way that is biased (such as a procedure in which respondents volunteer to participate)?

Analyze

1. Graph the Data

2. Explore the Data
Are there any outliers (numbers very far away from almost all of the other data)?
What important statistics summarize the data (such as the mean and standard deviation)?
How are the data distributed?
Are there missing data?
Did many selected subjects refuse to respond?

3. Apply Statistical Methods
Use technology to obtain results.

Conclude

1. Statistical Significance
Do the results have statistical significance?
Do the results have practical significance?

Finding *P*-Values

Inferences about μ: choosing between t and normal distributions		
t distribution:	or	σ not known and normally distributed population σ not known and $n > 30$
Normal distribution:	or	σ known and normally distributed population σ known and $n > 30$
Nonparametric method or bootstrapping: Population not normally distributed and $n \leq 30$		

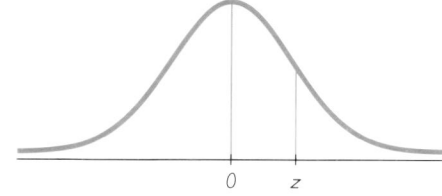

POSITIVE z Scores

Table A-2 (*continued*) Cumulative Area from the LEFT

z	.00	.01	.02	.03	.04	.05	.06	.07	.08	.09
0.0	.5000	.5040	.5080	.5120	.5160	.5199	.5239	.5279	.5319	.5359
0.1	.5398	.5438	.5478	.5517	.5557	.5596	.5636	.5675	.5714	.5753
0.2	.5793	.5832	.5871	.5910	.5948	.5987	.6026	.6064	.6103	.6141
0.3	.6179	.6217	.6255	.6293	.6331	.6368	.6406	.6443	.6480	.6517
0.4	.6554	.6591	.6628	.6664	.6700	.6736	.6772	.6808	.6844	.6879
0.5	.6915	.6950	.6985	.7019	.7054	.7088	.7123	.7157	.7190	.7224
0.6	.7257	.7291	.7324	.7357	.7389	.7422	.7454	.7486	.7517	.7549
0.7	.7580	.7611	.7642	.7673	.7704	.7734	.7764	.7794	.7823	.7852
0.8	.7881	.7910	.7939	.7967	.7995	.8023	.8051	.8078	.8106	.8133
0.9	.8159	.8186	.8212	.8238	.8264	.8289	.8315	.8340	.8365	.8389
1.0	.8413	.8438	.8461	.8485	.8508	.8531	.8554	.8577	.8599	.8621
1.1	.8643	.8665	.8686	.8708	.8729	.8749	.8770	.8790	.8810	.8830
1.2	.8849	.8869	.8888	.8907	.8925	.8944	.8962	.8980	.8997	.9015
1.3	.9032	.9049	.9066	.9082	.9099	.9115	.9131	.9147	.9162	.9177
1.4	.9192	.9207	.9222	.9236	.9251	.9265	.9279	.9292	.9306	.9319
1.5	.9332	.9345	.9357	.9370	.9382	.9394	.9406	.9418	.9429	.9441
1.6	.9452	.9463	.9474	.9484	.9495 *	.9505	.9515	.9525	.9535	.9545
1.7	.9554	.9564	.9573	.9582	.9591	.9599	.9608	.9616	.9625	.9633
1.8	.9641	.9649	.9656	.9664	.9671	.9678	.9686	.9693	.9699	.9706
1.9	.9713	.9719	.9726	.9732	.9738	.9744	.9750	.9756	.9761	.9767
2.0	.9772	.9778	.9783	.9788	.9793	.9798	.9803	.9808	.9812	.9817
2.1	.9821	.9826	.9830	.9834	.9838	.9842	.9846	.9850	.9854	.9857
2.2	.9861	.9864	.9868	.9871	.9875	.9878	.9881	.9884	.9887	.9890
2.3	.9893	.9896	.9898	.9901	.9904	.9906	.9909	.9911	.9913	.9916
2.4	.9918	.9920	.9922	.9925	.9927	.9929	.9931	.9932	.9934	.9936
2.5	.9938	.9940	.9941	.9943	.9945	.9946	.9948	.9949 *	.9951	.9952
2.6	.9953	.9955	.9956	.9957	.9959	.9960	.9961	.9962	.9963	.9964
2.7	.9965	.9966	.9967	.9968	.9969	.9970	.9971	.9972	.9973	.9974
2.8	.9974	.9975	.9976	.9977	.9977	.9978	.9979	.9979	.9980	.9981
2.9	.9981	.9982	.9982	.9983	.9984	.9984	.9985	.9985	.9986	.9986
3.0	.9987	.9987	.9987	.9988	.9988	.9989	.9989	.9989	.9990	.9990
3.1	.9990	.9991	.9991	.9991	.9992	.9992	.9992	.9992	.9993	.9993
3.2	.9993	.9993	.9994	.9994	.9994	.9994	.9994	.9995	.9995	.9995
3.3	.9995	.9995	.9995	.9996	.9996	.9996	.9996	.9996	.9996	.9997
3.4	.9997	.9997	.9997	.9997	.9997	.9997	.9997	.9997	.9997	.9998
3.50 and up	.9999									

NOTE: For values of z above 3.49, use 0.9999 for the area.
*Use these common values that result from interpolation:

z score	Area
1.645	0.9500
2.575	0.9950

Common Critical Values

Confidence Level	Critical Value
0.90	1.645
0.95	1.96
0.99	2.575

Ch. 13: Nonparametric Tests

$$z = \frac{(x + 0.5) - (n/2)}{\frac{\sqrt{n}}{2}}$$ Sign test for $n > 25$

$$z = \frac{T - n(n + 1)/4}{\sqrt{\frac{n(n + 1)(2n + 1)}{24}}}$$ Wilcoxon signed ranks (matched pairs and $n > 30$)

$$z = \frac{R - \mu_R}{\sigma_R} = \frac{R - \frac{n_1(n_1 + n_2 + 1)}{2}}{\sqrt{\frac{n_1 n_2(n_1 + n_2 + 1)}{12}}}$$ Wilcoxon rank-sum (two independent samples)

$$H = \frac{12}{N(N + 1)}\left(\frac{R_1^2}{n_1} + \frac{R_2^2}{n_2} + \cdots + \frac{R_k^2}{n_k}\right) - 3(N + 1)$$

Kruskal-Wallis (chi-square df $= k - 1$)

$$r_s = 1 - \frac{6\Sigma d^2}{n(n^2 - 1)}$$ Rank correlation

$$\left(\text{critical values for } n > 30: \frac{\pm z}{\sqrt{n - 1}}\right)$$

$$z = \frac{G - \mu_G}{\sigma_G} = \frac{G - \left(\frac{2n_1 n_2}{n_1 + n_2} + 1\right)}{\sqrt{\frac{(2n_1 n_2)(2n_1 n_2 - n_1 - n_2)}{(n_1 + n_2)^2(n_1 + n_2 - 1)}}}$$ Runs test for $n > 20$

Ch. 14: Control Charts

R chart: Plot sample ranges

UCL: $D_4 \overline{R}$

Centerline: $\overline{R}$

LCL: $D_3 \overline{R}$

$\overline{x}$ chart: Plot sample means

UCL: $\overline{\overline{x}} + A_2 \overline{R}$

Centerline: $\overline{\overline{x}}$

LCL: $\overline{\overline{x}} - A_2 \overline{R}$

p chart: Plot sample proportions

UCL: $\overline{p} + 3\sqrt{\frac{\overline{p}\,\overline{q}}{n}}$

Centerline: $\overline{p}$

LCL: $\overline{p} - 3\sqrt{\frac{\overline{p}\,\overline{q}}{n}}$

Table A-6 Critical Values of the Pearson Correlation Coefficient r

n	$\alpha = .05$	$\alpha = .01$
4	.950	.990
5	.878	.959
6	.811	.917
7	.754	.875
8	.707	.834
9	.666	.798
10	.632	.765
11	.602	.735
12	.576	.708
13	.553	.684
14	.532	.661
15	.514	.641
16	.497	.623
17	.482	.606
18	.468	.590
19	.456	.575
20	.444	.561
25	.396	.505
30	.361	.463
35	.335	.430
40	.312	.402
45	.294	.378
50	.279	.361
60	.254	.330
70	.236	.305
80	.220	.286
90	.207	.269
100	.196	.256

NOTE: To test H_0: $\rho = 0$ against H_1: $\rho \neq 0$, reject H_0 if the absolute value of r is greater than the critical value in the table.

Control Chart Constants

Subgroup Size n	D_3	D_4	A_2
2	0.000	3.267	1.880
3	0.000	2.574	1.023
4	0.000	2.282	0.729
5	0.000	2.114	0.577
6	0.000	2.004	0.483
7	0.076	1.924	0.419

Solution

First sort the data values by arranging them in order, as shown below:

22   22   **23**   24   26

Because the number of data values is an odd number (5), the median is the number located in the exact middle of the sorted list, which is 23. The median is therefore 23 chips. Note that the median of 23 chips is different from the mean of 23.4 chips found in Example 1.

Example 3   Median

Repeat Example 2 after including the sixth count of 27 chips. That is, find the median of these counts: 22 chips, 22 chips, 26 chips, 24 chips, 23 chips, and 27 chips.

Solution

First arrange the values in order:

22   22   **23**   **24**   26   27

Because the number of data values is an even number (6), the median is found by computing the mean of the two middle numbers, which are 23 and 24.

$$\text{Median} = \frac{23 + 24}{2} = \frac{47}{2} = 23.5$$

The median is 23.5 chips.

CAUTION Never use the term *average* when referring to a measure of center. The word *average* is often used for the mean, but it is sometimes used for other measures of center. To avoid any confusion, we use the correct and specific term, such as *mean* or *median*; *average* is not used by statisticians and it will not be used throughout the remainder of this book when referring to a specific measure of center.

Mode

The mode is another measure of center.

DEFINITION The **mode** of a data set is the value that occurs with the greatest frequency.

Finding the Mode: A data set can have one mode, more than one mode, or no mode.

- When two data values occur with the same greatest frequency, each one is a mode and the data set is **bimodal.**
- When more than two data values occur with the same greatest frequency, each is a mode and the data set is said to be **multimodal.**
- When no data value is repeated, we say that there is **no mode.**

Example 4 Mode

Find the mode of these same values used in Example 1: 22 chips, 22 chips, 26 chips, 24 chips, and 23 chips.

Solution

The mode is 22 chips, because it is the data value with the greatest frequency.

In Example 4 the mode is a single value. Here are two other possible circumstances:

Two modes: The values of 22, 22, 22, 23, 23, 23, 24, 24, 26, and 27 have two modes: 22 and 23.

No mode: The values of 22, 23, 24, 26, and 27 have no mode because no value is repeated.

In reality, the mode isn't used much with numerical data. However, the mode is the only measure of center that can be used with data at the nominal level of measurement. (Remember, the nominal level of measurement applies to data that consist of names, labels, or categories only.)

Midrange

Another measure of center is the midrange.

> **DEFINITION** The **midrange** of a data set is the measure of center that is the value midway between the maximum and minimum values in the original data set. It is found by adding the maximum data value to the minimum data value and then dividing the sum by 2, as in the following formula:

$$\text{midrange} = \frac{\text{maximum data value} + \text{minimum data value}}{2}$$

Important Properties of the Midrange

- Because the midrange uses only the maximum and minimum values, it is very sensitive to those extremes.

- In practice, the midrange is rarely used, but it has three redeeming features:

  1. The midrange is very easy to compute.

  2. The midrange helps reinforce the very important point that there are several different ways to define the center of a data set.

  3. The value of the midrange is sometimes used incorrectly for the median, so confusion can be reduced by clearly defining the midrange along with the median.

 Example 5 Midrange

Find the midrange of these values from Example 1: 22 chips, 22 chips, 26 chips, 24 chips, and 23 chips.

Solution

The midrange is found as follows:

$$\text{Midrange} = \frac{\text{maximum data value} + \text{minimum data value}}{2}$$

$$= \frac{26 + 22}{2} = 24$$

The midrange is 24.0 chips.

When calculating measures of center, we often need to round the result. We use the following rule.

Round-Off Rules:

For the mean, median, and midrange, carry one more decimal place than is present in the original set of values.

For the mode, leave the value as is without rounding (because values of the mode are the same as some of the original data values).

When applying this rule, round only the final answer, *not intermediate values that occur during calculations.* For example, the mean of 2, 3, and 5 is 3.333333 . . . , which is rounded to 3.3, which has one more decimal place than the original values of 2, 3, and 5. As another example, the mean of 80.4 and 80.6 is 80.50 (one more decimal place than was used for the original values). Because the mode is one or more of the original data values, we do not round values of the mode; we simply use the same original values.

Critical Thinking

Although we can calculate measures of center for a set of sample data, we should always think about whether the results are reasonable. In Section 1-3 we noted that it does not make sense to do numerical calculations with data at the nominal level of measurement, because those data consist of names, labels, or categories only, so statistics such as the mean and median are meaningless. We should also think about the sampling method used to collect the data. If the sampling method is not sound, the statistics we obtain may be very misleading.

Example 6 Critical Thinking and Measures of Center

For each of the following, identify a major reason why the mean and median are *not* meaningful statistics.

   a. Zip codes of the author, White House, Air Force division of the Pentagon, Empire State Building, and Statue of Liberty: 12590, 20500, 20330, 10118, 10004.

   b. Rank (by sales) of selected statistics textbooks: 1, 4, 5, 3, 2, 15.

   c. Numbers on the jerseys of the starting offense for the New Orleans Saints when they won the last Super Bowl (as of this writing): 12, 74, 77, 76, 73, 78, 88, 19, 9, 23, 25.

> **Solution**
>
> **a.** The zip codes don't measure or count anything. The numbers are actually labels for geographic locations.
>
> **b.** The ranks reflect an ordering, but they don't measure or count anything. The rank of 1 is from a book with sales substantially greater then the book with rank of 2, so the different numbers don't correspond to the magnitudes of the sales.
>
> **c.** The numbers on the football jerseys don't measure or count anything. Those numbers are simply substitutes for names.

Example 6 involves data that do not justify the use of statistics such as the mean or median. Example 7 involves a more subtle issue.

> **Example 7**   Class Size
>
> It is well known that smaller classes are generally more effective. According to the National Center for Education Statistics, California has a mean of 20.9 students per teacher, and Alaska has a mean of 16.8 students per teacher. (These values are based on elementary and secondary schools only.) If we combine the two states, we might find the mean number of students per teacher to be 18.85, as in the calculation shown below, but is this result correct? Why or why not?
>
> $$\bar{x} = \frac{20.9 + 16.8}{2} = 18.85$$

> **Solution**
>
> The combined states of California and Alaska do *not* have a mean of 18.85 students per teacher. The issue here is that California has substantially more students and teachers than Alaska, and those different numbers should be taken into account. Combining California and Alaska, we get a total of 6,539,429 students and 315,013 teachers, so the student/teacher ratio is 6,539,429/315,013 = 20.8 (not the value of 18.85 from the above calculation). When using values from different sample sizes, consider whether those sample sizes should be taken into account.

As another illustration of the principle in Example 7, if you have a list of the 50 state per capita income amounts and you find the mean of those 50 values, the result is not the mean per capita income for the entire United States. The population sizes of the 50 different states must be taken into account. (See the *weighted mean* in the following subsection.)

Part 2: Beyond the Basics of Measures of Center

Calculating the Mean From a Frequency Distribution

The first two columns of Table 3-2 shown here are the same as the frequency distribution of Table 2-2 from Chapter 2. When working with data summarized in a frequency distribution, we don't know the exact values falling in a particular class, so we make calculations possible by pretending that all sample values in each class are equal to the class midpoint. For example, consider the first class interval of 50–69 with a

Table 3-2 IQ Scores of Low Lead Group

IQ Score	Frequency f	Class Midpoint x	f · x
50–69	2	59.5	119.0
70–89	33	79.5	2623.5
90–109	35	99.5	3482.5
110–129	7	119.5	836.5
130–149	1	139.5	139.5
Totals:	Σf = 78		Σ(f·x) = 7201.0

frequency of 2. We pretend that each of the two IQ scores is 59.5 (the class midpoint). With the IQ score of 59.5 repeated twice, we have a total of $59.5 \cdot 2 = 119$ as shown in the last column of Table 3-2. We can then add such products to find the total of all sample values, which we then divide by the sum of the frequencies, Σf. Formula 3-2 is used to compute the mean when the sample data are summarized in a frequency distribution. Formula 3-2 is not really a new concept; it is simply a variation of Formula 3-1.

Formula 3-2

First multiply each frequency and class midpoint; then add the products.
↓

Mean from frequency distribution:
$$\bar{x} = \frac{\Sigma(f \cdot x)}{\Sigma f}$$
↑
Sum of frequencies

The following example illustrates the procedure for finding the mean from a frequency distribution.

Example 8 Computing Mean from a Frequency Distribution

The first two columns of Table 3-2 constitute a frequency distribution summarizing the full IQ scores of the low lead group in Data Set 5 from Appendix B. Use that frequency distribution to find the mean.

Solution

Table 3-2 illustrates the procedure for using Formula 3-2 when calculating a mean from data summarized in a frequency distribution. The class midpoint values are shown in the third column, and the products $f \cdot x$ are shown in the last column. The bottom row of Table 3-2 shows the two components we need for the calculation of the mean (as in Formula 3-2): $\Sigma f = 78$ and $\Sigma(f \cdot x) = 7201.0$. The calculation using Formula 3-2 is as follows:

$$\bar{x} = \frac{\Sigma(f \cdot x)}{\Sigma f} = \frac{7201.0}{78} = 92.3$$

The result of $\bar{x} = 92.3$ is an approximation because it is based on the use of class midpoint values instead of the original list of full IQ scores. The mean of 92.9 found by using all of the original full IQ scores is a better result.

Calculating a Weighted Mean

When different x data values are assigned different weights w, we can compute a **weighted mean.** Formula 3-3 can be used to compute the weighted mean.

Formula 3-3

$$\text{weighted mean: } \bar{x} = \frac{\Sigma (w \cdot x)}{\Sigma w}$$

Formula 3-3 tells us to first multiply each weight w by the corresponding value x, then to add the products, and then finally to divide that total by the sum of the weights, Σw.

Example 9   Computing Grade Point Average

In her first semester of college, a student of the author took five courses. Her final grades along with the number of credits for each course were A (3 credits), A (4 credits), B (3 credits), C (3 credits), and F (1 credit). The grading system assigns quality points to letter grades as follows: A = 4; B = 3; C = 2; D = 1; F = 0. Compute her grade point average.

Solution

Use the numbers of credits as weights: $w = 3, 4, 3, 3, 1$. Replace the letter grades of A, A, B, C, and F with the corresponding quality points: $x = 4, 4, 3, 2, 0$. We now use Formula 3-3 as shown below. The result is a first-semester grade point average of 3.07. (Using the preceding round-off rule, the result should be rounded to 3.1, but it is common to round grade point averages to two decimal places.)

$$\bar{x} = \frac{\Sigma (w \cdot x)}{\Sigma w}$$

$$= \frac{(3 \times 4) + (4 \times 4) + (3 \times 3) + (3 \times 2) + (1 \times 0)}{3 + 4 + 3 + 3 + 1}$$

$$= \frac{43}{14} = 3.07$$

using TECHNOLOGY

The calculations of this section are fairly simple, but some of the calculations in the following sections are not so simple. Many computer software programs allow you to enter a data set and use one operation to get several different sample statistics, referred to as *descriptive statistics*. Here are some of the procedures for obtaining such displays. (The accompanying displays are based on the numbers of chocolate chips in Chips Ahoy regular cookies, as listed in Table 3-1.)

STATDISK   Enter the data in the Data Window or open an existing data set. Click on **Data,** select **Descriptive Statistics,** and enter the column number for the desired data set. Now click on **Evaluate** to get the various descriptive statistics, including the mean, median, midrange, and other statistics to be discussed in the following sections. (Click on **Data** and use the **Explore Data** option to display descriptive statistics along with a histogram and other items discussed later.)

STATDISK

```
Descriptive Statistics
Column 1

Sample Size, n:  40
Mean:            23.95
Median:          24
Midrange:        24.5
RMS:             24.08215
Variance, s^2:   6.510256
St Dev, s:       2.55152
Mean Abs Dev:    2.0075
Range:           11
Coeff. Of Var.   10.65%

Minimum:         19
1st Quartile:    22.5
2nd Quartile:    24
3rd Quartile:    26
Maximum:         30

Sum:             958
Sum Sq:          23198
```

MINITAB Enter the data in the column with the heading C1 (or open an existing data set). Click on **Stat,** select **Basic Statistics,** then select **Descriptive Statistics.** Double-click on C1 or another column so that it appears in the box labeled "Variables." (Optional: Click on the box labeled "Statistics" to check or uncheck the statistics that you want.) Click **OK.** The results will include the mean and median as well as other statistics.

MINITAB

```
Descriptive Statistics: Chips

Variable   N    Mean  StDev  Minimum      Q1  Median      Q3  Maximum
Chips     40  23.950  2.552   19.000  22.250  24.000  26.000   30.000
```

EXCEL **XLSTAT:** If XLSTAT is available, click on **XL-STAT** at the top, select **Describing Data,** then select **Descriptive Statistics.** Enter the range of cells (such as A1:A40) in the "Quantitative Data" box. Check the "Sample labels" box only if the first cell contains the name of the data set. Click **OK** to continue. The result will be a list of 33 different statistics, including the mean and median. The accompanying display shows some of the more important results.

XLSTAT

Minimum	19.0000
Maximum	30.0000
Freq. of minimum	2
Freq. of maximum	1
Range	11.0000
1st Quartile	22.7500
Median	24.0000
3rd Quartile	26.0000
Sum	958.0000
Mean	23.9500
Variance (n)	6.3475
Variance (n-1)	6.5103
Standard deviation (n)	2.5194
Standard deviation (n-1)	2.5515

DATA ANALYSIS: If XLSTAT is not available, the Data Analysis add-in must be installed. (If the Data Analysis add-in is not yet installed, install it using the **Help** feature: Search for "Data Analysis," select "Load the Analysis Tool Pak," and follow the instructions.) In Excel 2003, select **Tools,** then **Data Analysis,** then select **Descriptive Statistics** and click **OK.** In Excel 2013, 2010, or 2007, click on **Data,** select **Data Analysis,** then select **Descriptive Statistics** in the pop-up window, and click **OK.** In the dialog box, enter the input range (such as A1:A40 for 40 values in column A), click on **Summary Statistics,** then click **OK.**

If it is necessary to widen the columns to see all of the results, select **Format,** then select the **AutoFit Column Width** option. (In Excel 2003, use **Format, Column, AutoFit Selection**).

Caution: If Excel finds more than one mode, it provides only the first one that it finds, so there may be modes other than the one identified by Excel.

EXCEL (DATA ANALYSIS ADD-IN)

Column1	
Mean	23.95
Standard Error	0.4034308
Median	24
Mode	23
Standard Deviation	2.551520411
Sample Variance	6.51025641
Kurtosis	-0.138051213
Skewness	-0.08759594
Range	11
Minimum	19
Maximum	30
Sum	958
Count	40

TI-83/84 PLUS Enter a list of data in L1 or use a list of values already assigned to a name. (To enter data, press **STAT**, then select **Edit** and press the **ENTER** key.) After the data values have been entered or opened, press **STAT** and select **CALC,** then select **1-Var Stats** and press **ENTER** twice. The display will include the mean $\bar{x}$, the median, the minimum value, and the maximum value. Press the down-arrow key ⌄ to view the results that don't fit on the initial display.

TI-83/84 PLUS

STATCRUNCH Click on **Open StatCrunch,** then enter or open a data set. Click on **Stats,** then click on **Summary Stats,** then **Columns.** Select the column containing the data. Click on **Next** to select the desired statistics, then click on **Calculate.**

STATCRUNCH

Summary statistics:										
Column	n	Mean	Variance	Std. Dev.	Std. Err.	Median	Range	Min	Max	Q1	Q3
var1	40	23.95	6.5102563	2.5515203	0.4034308	24	11	19	30	22.5	26

Other Technologies

To see results from some other technologies, the displays from SPSS and JMP are shown in the following displays.

continued

SPSS

	N	Range	Minimum	Maximum	Mean	Std. Deviation	Variance
Chips	40	11.00	19.00	30.00	23.9500	2.55152	6.510
Valid N (listwise)	40						

JMP

Mean	23.95
Std Dev	2.5515204
Std Err Mean	0.4034308
Upper 95% Mean	24.766016
Lower 95% Mean	23.133984

3-2 Basic Skills and Concepts

Statistical Literacy and Critical Thinking

1. Employment Data Listed below are results from the National Health and Nutrition Examination.

$$1 \quad 3 \quad 3 \quad 2 \quad 1 \quad 1 \quad 1 \quad 7 \quad 9 \quad 1 \quad 1 \quad 1 \quad 4 \quad 4$$

These results indicate the working status of the person being surveyed, and the listed values represent these responses: 1 = Working; 2 = With a job but not at work; 3 = Looking for work; 4 = Not working; 7 = Refused to answer; 9 = Don't know. Does it make sense to calculate the mean of these numbers? Why or why not?

2. Average The web site IncomeTaxList.com lists the "average" annual income for California as $44,400. What is the role of the term *average* in statistics? Should another term be used in place of *average*?

3. Median In an editorial, the *Poughkeepsie Journal* printed this statement: "The median price—the price exactly in between the highest and lowest— . . . ." Does that statement correctly describe the median? Why or why not?

4. Measures of Center In what sense are the mean, median, mode, and midrange measures of "center"?

In Exercises 5–20, find the (a) **mean,** *(b)* **median,** *(c)* **mode,** *and (d)* **midrange** *for the given sample data. Express answers with the appropriate units of measurement. Then answer the given questions.*

5. Top 10 Celebrity Incomes Listed below are the earnings (in millions of dollars) of the celebrities with the 10 highest incomes in a recent year. The celebrities in order are Steven Spielberg, Howard Stern, George Lucas, Oprah Winfrey, Jerry Seinfeld, Tiger Woods, Dan Brown, Jerry Bruckheimer, J. K. Rowling, and Tom Cruise. Can this "Top 10" list be used to learn anything about the mean annual earnings of all celebrities?

$$332 \quad 302 \quad 235 \quad 225 \quad 100 \quad 90 \quad 88 \quad 84 \quad 75 \quad 67$$

6. Top 10 Most Expensive Colleges Listed below are the annual tuition amounts of the 10 most expensive colleges in the United States for a recent year. The colleges listed in order are Sarah Lawrence, NYU, George Washington, Bates, Skidmore, Johns Hopkins, Georgetown, Connecticut College, Harvey Mudd, and Vassar. What does this "Top 10" list tell us about the population of all U.S. college tuitions?

$$\$54,410 \quad \$51,991 \quad \$51,730 \quad \$51,300 \quad \$51,196$$
$$\$51,190 \quad \$51,122 \quad \$51,115 \quad \$51,037 \quad \$50,875$$

7. Car Crash Test Measurements Listed below are head injury measurements from small cars that were tested in crashes. The measurements are in "hic," which is a measurement of a standard "head injury criterion." The data are from Data Set 13 in Appendix B, which is based on data from the National Highway Traffic Safety Administration. The listed values correspond to these cars: Chevrolet Aveo, Honda Civic, Volvo S40, VW Jetta, Hyundai Elantra,

Kia Rio, and Kia Spectra. Which car appears to be safest? Based on these limited results, do small cars appear to have about the same risk of head injury in a crash?

$$371 \quad 356 \quad 393 \quad 544 \quad 326 \quad 520 \quad 501$$

8. Tests of Child Booster Seats The National Highway Traffic Safety Administration conducted crash tests of child booster seats for cars. Listed below are results from those tests, with the measurements given in "hic," which is a measurement of a standard "head injury criterion." According to the safety requirement, the hic measurement should be less than 1000 hic. Do the results suggest that all child booster seats meet the specified requirement?

$$774 \quad 649 \quad 1210 \quad 546 \quad 431 \quad 612$$

9. Harry Potter Listed below are the gross amounts (in millions of dollars) earned in box office receipts for the movie *Harry Potter and the Half-Blood Prince.* The movie opened on a Wednesday, and the amounts are listed in order for the first 14 days of the movie's release. What important feature of the data is not revealed through the different measures of center? What is an explanation for the fact that the three highest amounts are the first, third, and fourth values listed?

$$58 \quad 22 \quad 27 \quad 29 \quad 21 \quad 10 \quad 10 \quad 8 \quad 7 \quad 9 \quad 11 \quad 9 \quad 4 \quad 4$$

10. Florida Manatee Deaths Listed below are the numbers of manatee deaths caused each year by collisions with watercraft. Manatees, also called "sea cows," are large mammals that live underwater, often in or near waterways. The data are listed in order for each year of the past decade. The data are from the Florida Fish and Wildlife Conservation Commission. What important feature of the data is not revealed through the different measures of center?

$$78 \quad 81 \quad 95 \quad 73 \quad 69 \quad 79 \quad 92 \quad 73 \quad 90 \quad 97$$

11. Ghost Prices Listed below are the prices listed for Norton Ghost 14.0 software from these vendors: Newegg, Dell, Buycheapsoftware.com, PC Connection, Walmart, and Overstock.com. For this collection of data values, are any of the measures of center the most important statistic? Is there a different statistic that is most relevant here? If so, which one?

$$\$55.99 \quad \$69.99 \quad \$48.95 \quad \$48.92 \quad \$71.77 \quad \$59.68$$

12. CEO Compensation Listed below are recent annual compensation amounts for these chief executive officers: Mulally (Ford), Jobs (Apple), Kent (Coca-Cola), Otellini (Intel), and McNerney (Boeing). The data are from the Associated Press. What is particularly notable about these compensation amounts?

$$\$17,688,241 \quad \$1 \quad \$19,628,585 \quad \$12,407,800 \quad \$14,765,410$$

13. Lead in Medicine Listed below are the lead concentrations (in $\mu g/g$) measured in different Ayurveda medicines. Ayurveda is a traditional medical system commonly used in India. The lead concentrations listed here are from medicines manufactured in the United States. The data are based on the article "Lead, Mercury, and Arsenic in US and Indian Manufactured Ayurvedic Medicines Sold via the Internet," by Saper et al., *Journal of the American Medical Association,* Vol. 300, No. 8. What do the results suggest about the safety of these medicines? What do the decimal values of the listed amounts suggest about the precision of the measurements?

$$3.0 \quad 6.5 \quad 6.0 \quad 5.5 \quad 20.5 \quad 7.5 \quad 12.0 \quad 20.5 \quad 11.5 \quad 17.5$$

14. Mercury in Sushi Listed below are the amounts of mercury (in parts per million, or ppm) found in tuna sushi sampled at different stores in New York City. The study was sponsored by the *New York Times* and the stores (in order) are D'Agostino, Eli's Manhattan, Fairway, Food Emporium, Gourmet Garage, Grace's Marketplace, and Whole Foods. Which store has the healthiest tuna? Does it appear that the different stores get their tuna from the same supplier?

$$0.56 \quad 0.75 \quad 0.10 \quad 0.95 \quad 1.25 \quad 0.54 \quad 0.88$$

15. Years to Earn Bachelor's Degree Listed below are the lengths of time (in years) it took for a random sample of college students to earn bachelor's degrees (based on data from the National Center for Education Statistics). Based on these results, does it appear that it is common to earn a bachelor's degree in 4 years?

4   4   4   4   4   4   4.5   4.5   4.5   4.5   4.5   4.5   6   6   8   9   9   13   13   15

16. Cell Phone Radiation Listed below are the measured radiation emissions (in W/kg) corresponding to these cell phones: Samsung SGH-tss9, Blackberry Storm, Blackberry Curve, Motorola Moto, T-Mobile Sidekick, Sanyo Katana Eclipse, Palm Pre, Sony Ericsson, Nokia 6085, Apple iPhone 3G S, and Kyocero Neo E1100. The data are from the Environmental Working Group. The media often present reports about the dangers of cell phone radiation as a cause of cancer. The Federal Communications Commission has a standard that cell phone radiation must be 1.6 W/kg or less. If you are planning to purchase a cell phone, are any of the measures of center the most important statistic? Is there another statistic that is most relevant? If so, which one?

0.38   0.55   1.54   1.55   0.50   0.60   0.92   0.96   1.00   0.86   1.46

17. JFK to LAX Flight Delays Listed below are the arrival delay times (in minutes) of randomly selected American Airline flights from New York's JFK airport to Los Angeles (LAX). Negative values correspond to flights that arrived early before the scheduled arrival time, and positive values represent lengths of delays. Based on these very limited results, what do you conclude about the on-time performance of American Airlines? (The data are from the Bureau of Transportation, and more data are listed in Data Set 15 in Appendix B.)

−15   −18   −32   −21   −9   −32   11   2

18. Freshman 15 According to the "freshman 15" legend, college freshmen gain 15 pounds (or 6.8 kilograms) during their freshman year. Listed below are the amounts of weight change (in kilograms) for a simple random sample of freshmen included in a study ("Changes in Body Weight and Fat Mass of Men and Women in the First Year of College: A Study of the 'Freshman 15'" by Hoffman, Policastro, Quick, and Lee, *Journal of American College Health,* Vol. 55, No. 1). Positive values correspond to students who gained weight and negative values correspond to students who lost weight. Do these values appear to support the legend that college students gain 15 pounds (or 6.8 kilograms) during their freshman year? Why or why not?

11   3   0   −2   3   −2   −2   5   −2   7   2   4   1   8   1   0   −5   2

19. Saints in Super Bowl Listed below are the numbers on the jerseys of the starting lineup for the New Orleans Saints when they recently won their first Super Bowl football game. What do the measures of center tell us about the team? Does it make sense to compute the measures of center for these data?

9   23   25   88   12   19   74   77   76   73   78

20. Phenotypes of Peas Biologists conducted experiments to determine whether a deficiency of carbon dioxide in the soil affects the phenotypes of peas. Listed below are the phenotype codes, where 1 = smooth-yellow, 2 = smooth-green, 3 = wrinkled-yellow, and 4 = wrinkled-green. Can the measures of center be obtained for these values? Do the results make sense?

2   1   1   1   1   1   1   4   1   2   2   1   2   3   3   2   3   1   3   1   3   1   3   2   2

In Exercises 21–24, find the **mean** *and* **median** *for each of the two samples; then compare the two sets of results.*

21. Speeding and Race Listed below are speeds (in mi/h) of cars on the New Jersey Turnpike. All cars are going in the same direction, and all of the cars are from New Jersey. The speeds were measured with a radar gun and the researchers observed the races of the drivers.

The data are from Statlib and the authors are Joseph Kadane and John Lamberth. Does it appear that drivers of either race speed more than drivers of the other race?

White drivers: 74 77 69 71 77 69 72 75 74 72

African American drivers: 79 70 71 76 76 74 71 75 74 74

22. Parking Meter Theft Listed below are amounts (in millions of dollars) collected from parking meters by Brinks and others in New York City during similar time periods. A larger data set was used to convict five Brinks employees of grand larceny. The data were provided by the attorney for New York City, and they are listed on the DASL web site. Do the limited data listed here show evidence of stealing by Brinks employees?

Collection contractor was Brinks: 1.3 1.5 1.3 1.5 1.4 1.7 1.8 1.7 1.7 1.6

Collection contractor was not Brinks: 2.2 1.9 1.5 1.6 1.5 1.7 1.9 1.6 1.6 1.8

23. Political Contributions Listed below are contributions (in dollars) made to the two presidential candidates in a recent election. All contributions are from the same Zip code as the author, and the data are from the *Huffington Post*. Do the contributions appear to favor either candidate? What do you conclude after learning that there were 66 contributions to Obama and 20 contributions to McCain?

Obama: $275 $452 $300 $1000 $1000 $500 $100 $1061

$1200 $235 $875 $2000 $350 $210 $250

McCain: $50 $75 $240 $302 $250 $700 $350 $500

$1250 $1500 $500 $500 $40 $221 $400

24. Customer Waiting Times Waiting times (in minutes) of customers at the Jefferson Valley Bank (where all customers enter a single waiting line) and the Bank of Providence (where customers wait in individual lines at three different teller windows) are listed below. Determine whether there is a difference between the two data sets that is not apparent from a comparison of the measures of center. If so, what is it?

Jefferson Valley (single line): 6.5 6.6 6.7 6.8 7.1 7.3 7.4 7.7 7.7 7.7

Providence (individual lines): 4.2 5.4 5.8 6.2 6.7 7.7 7.7 8.5 9.3 10.0

Large Data Sets from Appendix B. *In Exercises 25–28, refer to the indicated data set in Appendix B. Use computer software or a calculator to find the* **means** *and* **medians.**

25. Earthquakes Use the magnitudes (Richter scale) of the earthquakes listed in Data Set 16 in Appendix B. In 1989, the San Francisco Bay Area was struck with an earthquake that measured 7.0 on the Richter scale. That earthquake occurred during the warm-up period for the third game of the baseball World Series. Is the magnitude of that World Series earthquake an *outlier* (data value that is very far away from the others) when considered in the context of the sample data given in Data Set 16? Explain.

26. Flight Data Refer to Data Set 15 in Appendix B and use the times required to taxi out for takeoff. For American Airlines, how is it helpful to find the mean?

27. Presidential Longevity Refer to Data Set 12 in Appendix B and use the numbers of years that U.S. presidents have lived after their first inauguration. What is the value of finding the mean of those numbers?

28. IQ Scores Refer to Data Set 6 in Appendix B and use the listed IQ scores. IQ tests are designed so that the mean IQ of the population is 100. Does the sample mean suggest that the sample is consistent with the population?

In Exercises 29–32, find the mean *of the data summarized in the given frequency distribution. Also, compare the* computed means *to the* actual means *obtained by using the original list of data values, which are as follows: (Exercise 29) 35.9 years; (Exercise 30) 44.1 years; (Exercise 31) 84.4; (Exercise 32) 15.0 years.*

29.

Age of Best Actress When Oscar Was Won	Frequency
20–29	27
30–39	34
40–49	13
50–59	2
60–69	4
70–79	1
80–89	1

30.

Age of Best Actor When Oscar Was Won	Frequency
20–29	1
30–39	26
40–49	35
50–59	13
60–69	6
70–79	1

31.

Verbal IQ Score of Subject Exposed to Lead	Frequency
50–59	4
60–69	10
70–79	25
80–89	43
90–99	26
100–109	8
110–119	3
120–129	2

32.

Years President Lived After First Inauguration	Frequency
0–4	8
5–9	2
10–14	5
15–19	7
20–24	4
25–29	6
30–34	0
35–39	1

3-2 Beyond the Basics

33. Degrees of Freedom Carbon monoxide is measured in San Francisco on five different days, and the mean of those five values is 0.62 parts per million. Four of the values (in parts per million) are 0.3, 0.4, 1.1, and 0.7. (The data are from the California Environmental Protection Agency.)

a. Find the missing value.

b. We need to create a list of n values that have a specific known mean. We are free to select any values we desire for some of the n values. How many of the n values can be freely assigned before the remaining values are determined? (The result is referred to as the *number of degrees of freedom*.)

34. Censored Data Data Set 12 in Appendix B lists the numbers of years that U.S. presidents lived after their first inauguration. As of this writing, five of the presidents are still alive and after their first inauguration they have lived 33 years, 21 years, 17 years, 9 years, and 1 year so far. We might use the values of 33+, 21+, 17+, 9+, and 1+, where the plus signs indicate that the actual value is equal to or greater than the current value. (These values were said to be *censored* at the time that this list was compiled.) If you use the values in Data Set 12 and ignore the presidents who are still alive, what is the mean? If you use the values given in Data Set 12 along with the additional values of 33+, 21+, 17+, 9+, and 1+, what do we know about the mean? Do the two results differ by much?

35. Trimmed Mean Because the mean is very sensitive to extreme values, we say that it is not a *resistant* measure of center. By deleting some low values and high values, the **trimmed mean** is more resistant. To find the 10% trimmed mean for a data set, first arrange the data in order, then delete the bottom 10% of the values and delete the top 10% of the values, and then calculate the mean of the remaining values. Refer to the BMI values for females in Data Set 1 in Appendix B, and change the highest value from 47.24 to 472.4, so the value of 472.4 is an outlier. Find (a) the mean; (b) the 10% trimmed mean; (c) the 20% trimmed mean. How do the results compare?

36. Harmonic Mean The **harmonic mean** is often used as a measure of center for data sets consisting of rates of change, such as speeds. It is found by dividing the number of values n by the sum of the *reciprocals* of all values, expressed as

$$\frac{n}{\Sigma \frac{1}{x}}$$

(No value can be zero.) The author drove 1163 miles to a conference in Orlando, Florida. For the trip to the conference, the author stopped overnight, and the mean speed from start to finish was 38 mi/h. For the return trip, the author stopped only for food and fuel, and the mean speed from start to finish was 56 mi/h. Is the actual "average" speed for the round-trip the mean of 38 mi/h and 56 mi/h? Why or why not? What is the harmonic mean of 38 mi/h and 56 mi/h, and does this represent the true "average" speed?

37. Geometric Mean The **geometric mean** is often used in business and economics for finding average rates of change, average rates of growth, or average ratios. Given n values (all of which are positive), the geometric mean is the nth root of their product. Find the *average growth factor* for money deposited in annual certificates of deposit for the past 5 years (as of this writing) with annual interest rates of 1.7%, 3.7%, 5.2%, 5.1%, and 2.7% by computing the geometric mean of 1.017, 1.037, 1.052, 1.051, and 1.027. What single percentage growth rate would be the same as having the five given successive growth rates? Is that result the same as the mean of the five annual interest rates?

38. Quadratic Mean The **quadratic mean** (or **root mean square**, or **R.M.S.**) is usually used in physical applications. In power distribution systems, for example, voltages and currents are usually referred to in terms of their R.M.S. values. The quadratic mean of a set of values is obtained by squaring each value, adding those squares, dividing the sum by the number of values n, and then taking the square root of that result, as indicated below:

$$\text{Quadratic mean} = \sqrt{\frac{\Sigma x^2}{n}}$$

Find the R.M.S. of these voltages measured from household current: 0, 100, 162, 162, 100, 0, −100, −162, −162, −100, 0. How does the result compare to the mean?

39. Median When data are summarized in a frequency distribution, the median can be found by first identifying the *median class,* which is the class that contains the median. We then assume that the values in that class are evenly distributed and we interpolate. Letting n denote the sum of all class frequencies, and letting m denote the sum of the class frequencies that *precede* the median class, the median can be estimated as shown here:

$$(\text{lower limit of median class}) \ + \ (\text{class width})\left(\frac{\left(\frac{n+1}{2}\right) - (m+1)}{\text{frequency of median class}}\right)$$

Use this procedure to find the median of the frequency distribution given in Exercise 29. How does the result compare to the median found from the original list of data, which is 33.0 years? Which value of the median is better: the value computed using the frequency table or the value of 33.0 years?

3-3   Measures of Variation

Key Concept The topic of variation discussed in this section is the single most important topic in statistics. This section presents three important measures of variation: *range, standard deviation,* and *variance*. Being measures of variation, these statistics result in numbers, but it is essential to know that our focus is not only finding numerical values but developing the ability to *interpret* and *understand* the numbers that we get. This section is not really about arithmetic; it is about conceptual understanding, and the concept is one of paramount importance.

Study Hint: Part 1 of this section presents basic concepts of variation and Part 2 presents additional concepts related to the standard deviation. Although both parts contain several formulas for computation, do not spend too much time memorizing those formulas and doing arithmetic calculations. Instead, make it a priority to *understand* and *interpret* values of standard deviation.

Part 1: Basic Concepts of Variation

To visualize the effect of variation, see Figure 3-2 and verify this important observation: The numbers of chocolate chips in Chips Ahoy cookies (top dotplot) have more *variation* than those in the Triola cookies (bottom dotplot). The top dotplot shows more spread than the bottom dotplot. Although both brands have the same mean (24.0), the Chips Ahoy cookies vary from 19 chocolate chips to 30, but the Triola cookies only vary from 23 chocolate chips to 25. This characteristic of spread, or variation, or dispersion, is so important that we measure it with numbers. (*Note:* The Chips Ahoy data are real and they are listed in Table 3-1, but the Triola cookie data are fabricated. The author doesn't actually produce chocolate chip cookies, but if the writing job doesn't work out, you never know.)

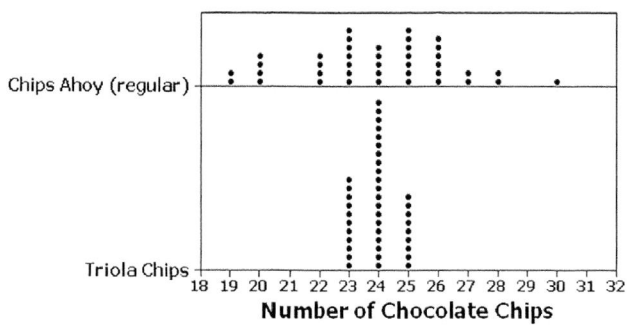

Figure 3-2   Dotplots of Numbers of Chocolate Chips in Cookies

Range

We noted that this section includes these measures of variation: (1) range; (2) standard deviation; (3) variance. We begin with the range because it is so easy to compute, even though it is not as important as the other measures of variation.

> **DEFINITION** The **range** of a set of data values is the difference between the maximum data value and the minimum data value.
>
> **Range = (maximum data value) − (minimum data value)**

Because the range uses only the maximum and the minimum data values, it is very sensitive to extreme values and isn't as useful as other measures of variation that use every data value, such as the standard deviation. To keep our round-off rules as consistent and as simple as possible, we will round the range using the same round-off rule for all measures of variation discussed in this section.

Round-Off Rule for Measures of Variation

When rounding the value of a measure of variation, carry one more decimal place than is present in the original set of data.

Example 1   Range

Find the range of these numbers of chocolate chips: 22, 22, 26, 24. (These are the first four chip counts for the Chips Ahoy cookies.)

Solution

The range is found by subtracting the lowest value from the largest value, so we get

$$\text{range} = (\text{maximum value}) - (\text{minimum value}) = 26 - 22 = 4.0$$

The result is shown with one more decimal place than is present in the original data values. We conclude that the range is 4.0 chocolate chips.

Standard Deviation of a Sample

The *standard deviation* is the measure of variation most commonly used in statistics.

DEFINITION The **standard deviation** of a set of sample values, denoted by s, is a measure of how much data values deviate away from the mean. It is calculated by using Formula 3-4 or 3-5. Formula 3-5 is just a different version of Formula 3-4, so both formulas are algebraically the same.

Formula 3-4

$$s = \sqrt{\frac{\Sigma (x - \bar{x})^2}{n - 1}} \qquad \text{sample standard deviation}$$

Formula 3-5

$$s = \sqrt{\frac{n(\Sigma x^2) - (\Sigma x)^2}{n(n - 1)}} \qquad \text{shortcut formula for sample standard deviation (formula used by calculators and computer programs)}$$

Later in this section we describe the reasoning behind these formulas, but for now we recommend that you use Formula 3-4 for an example or two, and then learn how to find standard deviation values using your calculator and by using a software program. (Most scientific calculators are designed so that you can enter a list of values and automatically get the standard deviation.) The following properties are consequences of the way in which the standard deviation is defined.

Important Properties of Standard Deviation

• The standard deviation is a measure of how much data values deviate away from the *mean*.

What the Median Is Not

Harvard biologist Stephen Jay Gould wrote, "The Median Isn't the Message." In it, he describes how he learned that he had abdominal mesothelioma, a form of cancer. He went to the library to learn more, and he was shocked to find that mesothelioma was incurable, with a median survival time of only *eight months* after it was discovered. Gould wrote this: "I suspect that most people, without training in statistics, would read such a statement as 'I will probably be dead in eight months' the very conclusion that must be avoided, since it isn't so, and since attitude (in fighting the cancer) matters so much." Gould went on to carefully interpret the value of the median. He knew that his chance of living longer than the median was good because he was young, his cancer was diagnosed early, and he would get the best medical treatment. He also reasoned that some could live much longer than eight months, and he saw no reason why he could not be in that group. Armed with this thoughtful interpretation of the median and a strong positive attitude, Gould lived for *20 years* after his diagnosis. He died of another cancer not related to the mesothelioma.

- The value of the standard deviation s is usually positive. It is zero only when all of the data values are the same number. (It is never negative.) Also, larger values of s indicate greater amounts of variation.

- The value of the standard deviation s can increase dramatically with the inclusion of one or more outliers (data values that are very far away from all of the others).

- The units of the standard deviation s (such as minutes, feet, pounds, and so on) are the same as the units of the original data values.

- The sample standard deviation s is a **biased estimator** of the population standard deviation σ, as described in Part 2 of this section.

If our goal was to develop skills for manually calculating values of standard deviations, we would focus on Formula 3-5, which simplifies the calculations. However, we prefer to show a calculation using Formula 3-4, because that formula better illustrates that the standard deviation is based on deviations of sample values away from the mean.

Example 2   Calculating Standard Deviation with Formula 3-4

Use Formula 3-4 to find the standard deviation of these numbers of chocolate chips: 22, 22, 26, 24. (These are the first four chip counts for the Chips Ahoy cookies. Here we use only four values so that we can illustrate calculations with a relatively simple example.)

Solution

The left column of Table 3-2 summarizes the general procedure for finding the standard deviation using Formula 3-4, and the right column illustrates that procedure for the sample values 22, 22, 26, and 24. The result shown in Table 3-2 is 1.9 chips, which is rounded to one more decimal place than is present in the original list of sample values (22, 22, 26, 24). Also, the units for the standard deviation are the same as the units of the original data. Because the original data are actually 22 chips, 22 chips, 26 chips, and 24 chips, the standard deviation is 1.9 chips.

Table 3-2

General Procedure for Finding Standard Deviation with Formula 3-4	Specific Example Using These Sample Values: 22, 22, 26, 24
Step 1: Compute the mean $\overline{x}$.	The sum of 22, 22, 26, and 24 is 94, so $$\overline{x} = \frac{\Sigma x}{n} = \frac{22 + 22 + 26 + 24}{4} = \frac{94}{4} = 23.5$$
Step 2: Subtract the mean from each individual sample value. (The result is a list of deviations of the form $(x - \overline{x})$.)	Subtract the mean of 23.5 from each sample value to get these deviations away from the mean: $-1.5, -1.5, 2.5, 0.5$.
Step 3: Square each of the deviations obtained from Step 2. (This produces numbers of the form $(x - \overline{x})^2$.)	The squares of the deviations from Step 2 are: 2.25, 2.25, 6.25, 0.25.
Step 4: Add all of the squares obtained from Step 3. The result is $\Sigma(x - \overline{x})^2$.	The sum of the squares from Step 3 is $2.25 + 2.25 + 6.25 + 0.25 = 11$.
Step 5: Divide the total from Step 4 by the number $n - 1$, which is 1 less than the total number of sample values present.	With $n = 4$ data values, $n - 1 = 3$, so we divide 11 by 3 to get this result: $\frac{11}{3} = 3.6667$
Step 6: Find the square root of the result of Step 5. The result is the standard deviation, denoted by s.	The standard deviation is $\sqrt{3.6667} = 1.9149$. Rounding the result, we get $s = 1.9$ chips.

Example 3 Calculating Standard Deviation with Formula 3-5

Use Formula 3-5 to find the standard deviation of the sample values 22, 22, 26, and 24 from Example 1.

Solution

Shown below is the computation of the standard deviation of 22, 22, 26, and 24 using Formula: 3-5.

$n = 4$ (because there are 4 values in the sample)

$\Sigma x = 94$ (found by adding the sample values:
                  $22 + 22 + 26 + 24 = 94$)

$\Sigma x^2 = 2220$ (found by adding the squares of the sample values, as in
                  $22^2 + 22^2 + 26^2 + 24^2 = 2220$)

Using Formula 3-5, we get

$$s = \sqrt{\frac{n(\Sigma x^2) - (\Sigma x)^2}{n(n-1)}} = \sqrt{\frac{4(2220) - (94)^2}{4(4-1)}} = \sqrt{\frac{44}{12}} = 1.9 \text{ chips}$$

The result of $s = 1.9$ chips is the same as the result in Example 2.

Comparing Variation in Different Samples Examples 1, 2, and 3 used only four values (22, 22, 26, 24) so that calculations are relatively simple. If we use all 80 chocolate chip counts depicted in Figure 3-2, we get the measures of center and measures of variation listed in Table 3-3. From the table we see that the range for Chips Ahoy cookies is much larger than the range for Triola cookies. Table 3-3 also shows that the standard deviation for Chips Ahoy is much larger than the standard deviation for Triola cookies, but *it's a good practice to compare two sample standard deviations only when the sample means are approximately the same.* When comparing variation in samples with very different means, it is better to use the coefficient of variation, which is defined later in this section. We also use the coefficient of variation when we want to compare variation from two samples with different scales or units of values, such as the comparison of variation of heights of men and weights of men. (See Example 8, which involves numbers of chocolate chips and weights of cola.)

Table 3-3   Comparison of Chocolate Chips in Cookies from Figure 3-2

	Chips Ahoy (regular)	Triola Chips
Number	40	40
Mean	24.0	24.0
Range	11.0	2.0
Standard Deviation	2.6	0.7

CAUTION *Compare two sample standard deviations only when the sample means are approximately the same.* When comparing variation in samples with very different means, it is better to use the coefficient of variation, which is defined later in this section.

Where Are the 0.400 Hitters?

The last baseball player to hit above 0.400 was Ted Williams, who hit 0.406 in 1941. There were averages above 0.400 in 1876, 1879, 1887, 1894, 1895, 1896, 1897, 1899, 1901, 1911, 1920, 1922, 1924, 1925, and 1930, but none since 1941. Are there no longer great hitters? The late Stephen Jay Gould of Harvard University noted that the mean batting average has been steady at 0.260 for about 100 years, but the standard deviation has been decreasing from 0.049 in the 1870s to 0.031, where it is now. He argued that today's stars are as good as those from the past, but consistently better pitchers now keep averages below 0.400.

Range Rule of Thumb for Understanding Standard Deviation

Three different concepts that can help us understand and interpret values of standard deviations are (1) the range rule of thumb, (2) the empirical rule, and (3) Chebyshev's theorem. Here we discuss the range rule of thumb. The empirical rule and Chebyshev's theorem will be discussed in Part 2 of this section.

The *range rule of thumb* is a crude but simple tool for understanding and interpreting standard deviation. It is based on the principle that for many data sets, the vast majority (such as 95%) of sample values lie within 2 standard deviations of the mean. We could improve the accuracy of this rule by taking into account such factors as the size of the sample and the distribution, but here we sacrifice accuracy for the sake of simplicity.

Range Rule of Thumb

Interpreting a Known Value of the Standard Deviation If the standard deviation of a collection of data is a known value, use it to find rough estimates of the minimum and maximum *usual* sample values as follows:

$$\text{minimum "usual" value} = (\text{mean}) - 2 \times (\text{standard deviation})$$

$$\text{maximum "usual" value} = (\text{mean}) + 2 \times (\text{standard deviation})$$

Estimating a Value of the Standard Deviation s To roughly estimate the standard deviation from a collection of known sample data, use

$$s \approx \frac{\text{range}}{4}$$

where range = (maximum data value) − (minimum data value).

 Example 4   Range Rule of Thumb for Interpreting s

Using the 40 chocolate chip counts for the Chips Ahoy (regular) cookies in Table 3-1, the mean is 24.0 chocolate chips and the standard deviation is 2.6 chocolate chips. Use the range rule of thumb to find the minimum and maximum "usual" numbers of chocolate chips; then determine whether the cookie with 30 chocolate chips is "unusual."

Solution

With a mean of 24.0 and a standard deviation of 2.6, we use the range rule of thumb to find the minimum and maximum usual numbers of chocolate chips as follows:

$$\text{minimum "usual" value} = (\text{mean}) - 2 \times (\text{standard deviation})$$
$$= 24.0 - 2(2.6) = 18.8$$
$$\text{maximum "usual" value} = (\text{mean}) + 2 \times (\text{standard deviation})$$
$$= 24.0 + 2(2.6) = 29.2$$

Interpretation

Based on these results, we expect that typical Chips Ahoy (regular) cookies have between 18.8 chocolate chips and 29.2 chocolate chips. Because 30 falls above the maximum "usual" value, we can consider it to be a cookie with an unusually high number of chocolate chips.

Example 5 Range Rule of Thumb for Estimating s

Use the range rule of thumb to estimate the standard deviation of the sample of 40 chocolate chip counts for the Chips Ahoy (regular) cookies as listed in Table 3-1. Those 40 values have a minimum of 19 and a maximum of 30.

Solution

The range rule of thumb indicates that we can estimate the standard deviation by finding the range and dividing it by 4. With a minimum of 19 and a maximum of 30, the range rule of thumb can be used to estimate the standard deviation s as follows:

$$s \approx \frac{\text{range}}{4} = \frac{30 - 19}{4} = 2.75 \text{ chips}$$

Interpretation

The actual value of the standard deviation is $s = 2.6$ chips, so the estimate of 2.75 chips is quite close. Because this estimate is based on only the minimum and maximum values, it is generally a rough estimate that might be off by a considerable amount.

Standard Deviation of a Population

The definition of standard deviation and Formulas 3-4 and 3-5 apply to the standard deviation of *sample* data. A slightly different formula is used to calculate the standard deviation σ (lowercase sigma) of a *population:* Instead of dividing by $n - 1$, we divide by the population size N, as shown here:

$$\text{population standard deviation} \quad \sigma = \sqrt{\frac{\Sigma (x - \mu)^2}{N}}$$

Because we generally deal with sample data, we will usually use Formula 3-4, in which we divide by $n - 1$. Many calculators give both the sample standard deviation and the population standard deviation, but they use a variety of different notations.

CAUTION When using a calculator to find standard deviation, identify the notation used by your particular calculator so that you get the *sample* standard deviation, not the population standard deviation.

Variance of a Sample and a Population

So far, we have used the term *variation* as a general description of the amount that values vary among themselves. (The terms *dispersion* and *spread* are sometimes used instead of *variation.*) The term *variance* has a specific meaning.

DEFINITIONS

The **variance** of a set of values is a measure of variation equal to the square of the standard deviation.

Sample variance: s^2 = square of the standard deviation s.

Population variance: σ^2 = square of the population standard deviation σ.

More Stocks, Less Risk

In their book *Investments*, authors Zvi Bodie, Alex Kane, and Alan Marcus state that "the average standard deviation for returns of portfolios composed of only one stock was 0.554. The average portfolio risk fell rapidly as the number of stocks included in the portfolio increased." They note that with 32 stocks, the standard deviation is 0.325, indicating much less variation and risk. They make the point that with only a few stocks, a portfolio has a high degree of "firm-specific" risk, meaning that the risk is attributable to the few stocks involved. With more than 30 stocks, there is very little firm-specific risk; instead, almost all of the risk is "market risk," attributable to the stock market as a whole. They note that these principles are "just an application of the well-known law of averages."

Notation Here is a summary of notation for the standard deviation and variance:

s = *sample* standard deviation
s^2 = *sample* variance
σ = *population* standard deviation
σ^2 = *population* variance

Note: Articles in professional journals and reports often use SD for standard deviation and VAR for variance.

Important Properties of Variance

- The units of the variance are the *squares* of the units of the original data values. (If the original data values are in feet, the variance will have units of ft^2; if the original data values are in seconds, the variance will have units of sec^2.)

- The value of the variance can increase dramatically with the inclusion of one or more outliers (data values that are very far away from all of the others).

- The value of the variance is usually positive. It is zero only when all of the data values are the same number. (It is never negative.)

- The sample variance s^2 is an **unbiased estimator** of the population variance σ^2, as described in Part 2 of this section.

The variance is a statistic used in some statistical methods, but for our present purposes, the variance has the serious disadvantage of using units that are *different than the units of the original data set.* This makes it difficult to understand variance as it relates to the original data set. Because of this property, it is better to focus on the standard deviation when trying to develop an understanding of variation, as we do in this section.

Part 2: Beyond the Basics of Variation

In this subsection we focus on making sense of the standard deviation so that it is not some mysterious number devoid of any practical significance. We begin by addressing common questions that relate to the standard deviation.

Why is Standard Deviation Defined as in Formula 3-4?

Why do we measure variation using Formula 3-4? In measuring variation in a set of sample data, it makes sense to begin with the individual amounts by which values deviate from the mean. For a particular data value x, the amount of **deviation** is $x - \bar{x}$, which is the difference between the individual x value and the mean. It makes sense to somehow combine those deviations into one number that can serve as a measure of the variation. Simply adding the deviations doesn't work, because the sum will always be zero. To get a statistic that measures variation (instead of always being zero), we need to avoid the canceling out of negative and positive numbers. One simple and natural approach is to add absolute values, as in $\Sigma |x - \bar{x}|$. If we find the mean of that sum, we get the **mean absolute deviation** (or **MAD**), which is the mean distance of the data from the mean:

$$\text{mean absolute deviation} = \frac{\Sigma |x - \bar{x}|}{n}$$

Why Not Use the Mean Absolute Deviation Instead of the Standard Deviation? Computation of the mean absolute deviation uses absolute values, so it uses an operation that is not "algebraic." (The algebraic operations include addition, multiplication, extracting roots, and raising to powers that are integers or fractions, but absolute value is not included among the algebraic operations.) Although the use of absolute values would be simple and easy, it would create algebraic difficulties in inferential methods of statistics discussed in later chapters. For example, Section 9-3 presents a method for making inferences about the means of two populations, and that method is built around an additive property of variances, but the mean absolute deviation has no such additive property. (Here is a simplified version of the additive property of variances: If you have two independent populations and you randomly select one value from each population and add them, such sums will have a variance equal to the sum of the variances of the two populations.) Also, the mean absolute deviation is a *biased* estimator, meaning that when you find mean absolute deviations of samples, you do not tend to target the mean absolute deviation of the population. The standard deviation has the advantage of using only algebraic operations. Because it is based on the square root of a sum of squares, the standard deviation closely parallels distance formulas found in algebra. There are many instances where a statistical procedure is based on a similar sum of squares. Therefore, instead of using absolute values, we square all deviations $(x - \bar{x})$ so that they are nonnegative. This approach leads to the standard deviation. For these reasons, scientific calculators typically include a standard deviation function, but they almost never include the mean absolute deviation.

Why Divide by $n - 1$? After finding all of the individual values of $(x - \bar{x})^2$, we combine them by finding their sum. We then divide by $n - 1$ because there are only $n - 1$ independent values. With a given mean, only $n - 1$ values can be freely assigned any number before the last value is determined. Exercise 45 illustrates that division by $n - 1$ yields a better result than division by n. That exercise shows how division by $n - 1$ causes the sample variance s^2 to target the value of the population variance σ^2, whereas division by n causes the sample variance s^2 to underestimate the value of the population variance σ^2.

How Do We Make Sense of a Value of Standard Deviation? Part 1 of this section included the range rule of thumb for interpreting a known value of a standard deviation or estimating a value of a standard deviation. (See Examples 4 and 5.) We now discuss two other approaches for interpreting standard deviation: the empirical rule and Chebyshev's theorem.

Empirical (or 68–95–99.7) Rule for Data with a Bell-Shaped Distribution

A concept helpful in interpreting the value of a standard deviation is the **empirical rule.** This rule states that *for data sets having a distribution that is approximately bell-shaped,* the following properties apply. (See Figure 3-3 on the next page.)

- About 68% of all values fall within 1 standard deviation of the mean.
- About 95% of all values fall within 2 standard deviations of the mean.
- About 99.7% of all values fall within 3 standard deviations of the mean.

Example 6   The Empirical Rule

IQ scores have a bell-shaped distribution with a mean of 100 and a standard deviation of 15. What percentage of IQ scores are between 70 and 130?

Solution

The key to solving this problem is to recognize that 70 and 130 are each exactly 2 standard deviations away from the mean of 100, as shown below:.

$$2 \text{ standard deviations} = 2s = 2(15) = 30$$

Therefore, 2 standard deviations from the mean is

$$100 - 30 = 70$$
$$\text{or}\quad 100 + 30 = 130$$

The empirical rule tells us that about 95% of all values are within 2 standard deviations of the mean, so about 95% of all IQ scores are between 70 and 130.

Figure 3-3

The Empirical Rule

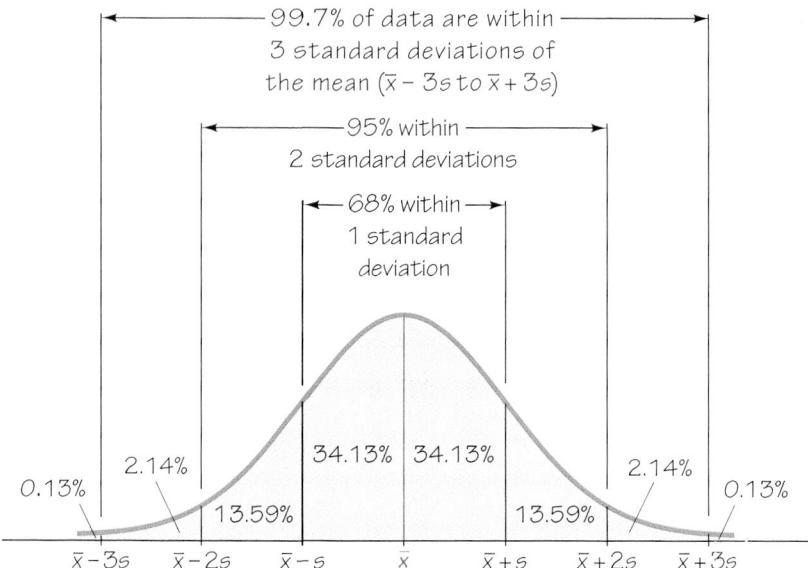

Another concept helpful in understanding or interpreting a value of a standard deviation is **Chebyshev's theorem.** The empirical rule applies only to data sets with bell-shaped distributions, but Chebyshev's theorem applies to *any* data set. Unfortunately, results from Chebyshev's theorem are only approximate. Because the results are lower limits ("at least"), Chebyshev's theorem has limited usefulness.

Chebyshev's Theorem

The proportion (or fraction) of any set of data lying within K standard deviations of the mean is always *at least* $1 - 1/K^2$, where K is any positive number greater than 1. For $K = 2$ and $K = 3$, we get the following statements:

- At least $3/4$ (or 75%) of all values lie within 2 standard deviations of the mean.
- At least $8/9$ (or 89%) of all values lie within 3 standard deviations of the mean.

Example 7   Chebyshev's Theorem

IQ scores have a mean of 100 and a standard deviation of 15. What can we conclude from Chebyshev's theorem?

Solution

Applying Chebyshev's theorem with a mean of 100 and a standard deviation of 15, we can reach the following conclusions:.

- At least $3/4$ (or 75%) of IQ scores are within 2 standard deviations of the mean (between 70 and 130).
- At least $8/9$ (or 89%) of all IQ scores are within 3 standard deviations of the mean (between 55 and 145).

Comparing Variation in Different Populations

In Part 1 of this section, we noted that when comparing variation in two different sets of data, the standard deviations should be compared only if the two sets of data use the same scale and units and have approximately the same mean. If the means are substantially different, or if the samples use different scales or measurement units, we can use the *coefficient of variation,* defined as follows.

> **DEFINITION** The **coefficient of variation** (or **CV**) for a set of nonnegative sample or population data, expressed as a percent, describes the standard deviation relative to the mean, and is given by the following:
>
> | Sample | Population |
> |---|---|
> | $CV = \dfrac{s}{\bar{x}} \cdot 100\%$ | $CV = \dfrac{\sigma}{\mu} \cdot 100\%$ |

Round-Off Rule for the Coefficient of Variation

Round the coefficient of variation to one decimal place (such as 18.3%).

Example 8 Chocolate Chip Cookies and Coke

Compare the variation in the numbers of chocolate chips in Chips Ahoy (regular) cookies (listed in Table 3-1) and the weights of regular Coke listed in Data Set 19 of Appendix B. Using the sample data, we have these results: Cookies have $\bar{x} = 24.0$ chips and $s = 2.6$ chips; Coke has $\bar{x} = 0.81682$ lb and $s = 0.00751$ lb. Note that we want to compare variation among *numbers of chocolate chips* to variation among *weights of Coke.*

Solution

We can compare the standard deviations if the same scales and units are used and the two means are approximately equal, but here we have different scales (numbers of chocolate chips and weights of Coke) and different units of measurement (numbers and pounds), so we use the coefficients of variation:

Numbers of chocolate chips: $\quad CV = \dfrac{s}{\bar{x}} \cdot 100\% = \dfrac{2.6 \text{ chocolate chips}}{24.0 \text{ chocolate chips}} \cdot 100\% = 10.8\%$

Weights of Coke: $\quad CV = \dfrac{s}{\bar{x}} \cdot 100\% = \dfrac{0.00751 \text{ lb}}{0.81682 \text{ lb}} \cdot 100\% = 0.9\%$

Although the standard deviation of 2.6 chocolate chips cannot be compared to the standard deviation of 0.00751 lb, we can compare the coefficients of variation, which have no units. We can see that the numbers of chocolate chips (with $CV = 10.8\%$) vary considerably more than weights of Coke (with $CV = 0.9\%$). This makes intuitive sense, because variation among the numbers of chocolate chips is not a big deal, but if some cans of Coke were underfilled or overfilled by large amounts, the result would be angry consumers.

Biased and Unbiased Estimators

The sample standard deviation s is a **biased estimator** of the population standard deviation σ. This means that values of the sample standard deviation s do *not* target the value of the population standard deviation σ. Although individual values of s can equal or exceed the value of σ, values of s generally tend to *underestimate* the value of σ. For example, consider an IQ test designed so that the population standard deviation is 15. If you repeat the process of randomly selecting 100 subjects, giving them IQ tests, and calculating the sample standard deviation s in each case, the sample standard deviations that you obtain will tend to be less than 15, which is the population standard deviation. There is no correction that allows us to fix the bias for all distributions of data. There is a correction that allows us to fix the bias for normally distributed populations, but it is rarely used because it is too complex and makes relatively minor corrections.

The sample variance s^2 is an **unbiased estimator** of the population variance σ^2, which means that values of s^2 tend to target the value of σ^2 instead of systematically tending to overestimate or underestimate σ^2. Consider an IQ test designed so that the population variance is 225. If you repeat the process of randomly selecting 100 subjects, giving them IQ tests, and calculating the sample variance s^2 in each case, the sample variances that you obtain will tend to center around 225, which is the population variance.

The concepts of biased estimators and unbiased estimators will be discussed more in Section 6-4.

using TECHNOLOGY

STATDISK, Minitab, Excel, the TI-83/84 Plus calculator, and StatCrunch can be used for the important calculations of this section. Use the same procedures given at the end of Section 3-2.

3-3 Basic Skills and Concepts

Statistical Literacy and Critical Thinking

1. Comparing Variation Which do you think has less variation: the IQ scores of students in your statistics class or the IQ scores of a simple random sample taken from the general population? Why?

2. Correct Statements? Which of the following statements are true?

a. If each of 25 sample values is equal to 20 min, the standard deviation of the sample is 0 min.

b. For any set of sample values, the standard deviation can *never* be a negative value.

c. If the standard deviation of a sample is 3 kg, then the variance is 9 kg.

d. If the variance of a sample is 16 sec^2, then the standard deviation is 4 sec.

e. If the standard deviation of a sample is 25 cm, then the variance is 5 cm^2.

3. Variation and Variance In statistics, how do the terms *variation* and *variance* differ?

4. Symbols Identify the symbols used for each of the following: (a) sample standard deviation; (b) population standard deviation; (c) sample variance; (d) population variance.

In Exercises 5–20, find the range, variance, *and* standard deviation *for the given sample data. Include appropriate units (such as "minutes") in your results. (The same data were used in Section 3-2 where we found measures of center. Here we find measures of variation.) Then answer the given questions.*

5. Top 10 Celebrity Incomes Listed below are the earnings (in millions of dollars) of the celebrities with the 10 highest incomes in a recent year. The celebrities in order are Steven Spielberg, Howard Stern, George Lucas, Oprah Winfrey, Jerry Seinfeld, Tiger Woods, Dan Brown, Jerry Bruckheimer, J. K. Rowling, and Tom Cruise. Can this "Top 10" list be used to learn anything about the standard deviation of the annual earnings of all celebrities?

332   302   235   225   100   90   88   84   75   67

6. Top 10 Most Expensive Colleges Listed below are the annual tuition amounts of the 10 most expensive colleges in the United States for a recent year. The colleges listed in order are Sarah Lawrence, NYU, George Washington, Bates, Skidmore, Johns Hopkins, Georgetown, Connecticut College, Harvey Mudd, and Vassar. Can this "Top 10" list tell us anything about the standard deviation of the population of all U.S. college tuitions?

$54,410 $51,991 $51,730 $51,300 $51,196
$51,190 $51,122 $51,115 $51,037 $50,875

7. Car Crash Test Measurements Listed below are head injury measurements from small cars that were tested in crashes. The measurements are in "hic," which is a measurement of a standard "head injury criterion." The data are from Data Set 13 in Appendix B, which is based on data from the National Highway Traffic Safety Administration. The listed values correspond to these cars: Chevrolet Aveo, Honda Civic, Volvo S40, VW Jetta, Hyundai Elantra, Kia Rio, and Kia Spectra. Given that all of the cars are small, does it appear that the head injury measurements are about the same for all small cars?

371   356   393   544   326   520   501

8. Tests of Child Booster Seats The National Highway Traffic Safety Administration conducted crash tests of child booster seats for cars. Listed below are results from those tests, with the measurements given in "hic," which is a measurement of a standard "head injury criterion." According to the safety requirement, the hic measurement should be less than 1000 hic. Do the different child booster seats have much variation among their crash test measurements?

774   649   1210   546   431   612

9. Harry Potter Listed below are the gross amounts (in millions of dollars) earned in box office receipts for the movie *Harry Potter and the Half-Blood Prince.* The movie opened on a Wednesday, and the amounts are listed in order for the first 14 days of the movie's release. If you invested in this movie, what characteristic of the data set would you care about most, and is it a measure of center or variation?

58   22   27   29   21   10   10   8   7   9   11   9   4   4

10. Florida Manatee Deaths Listed below are the numbers of manatee deaths caused each year by collisions with watercraft. Manatees, also called "sea cows," are large mammals that live underwater, often in or near waterways. The data are listed in order for each year of the past decade. The data are from the Florida Fish and Wildlife Conservation Commission. What important feature of the data is not revealed through the different measures of variation?

78   81   95   73   69   79   92   73   90   97

11. Ghost Prices Listed below are the prices listed for Norton Ghost 14.0 software from these vendors: Newegg, Dell, Buycheapsoftware.com, PC Connection, Walmart, and Overstock.com. When trying to find the best deal, how helpful are the measures of variation?

$55.99 $69.99 $48.95 $48.92 $71.77 $59.68

12. CEO Compensation Listed below are the recent annual compensation amounts for these chief executive officers: Mulally (Ford), Jobs (Apple), Kent (Coca-Cola), Otellini (Intel), and McNerney (Boeing). The data are from the Associated Press. What is particularly notable about these compensation amounts?

$$\$17,688,241 \quad \$1 \quad \$19,628,585 \quad \$12,407,800 \quad \$14,765,410$$

13. Lead in Medicine Listed below are the lead concentrations (in $\mu g/g$) measured in different Ayurveda medicines. Ayurveda is a traditional medical system commonly used in India. The lead concentrations listed here are from medicines manufactured in the United States. The data are based on the article "Lead, Mercury, and Arsenic in US and Indian Manufactured Ayurvedic Medicines Sold via the Internet," by Saper et al., *Journal of the American Medical Association,* Vol. 300, No. 8. What would be the values of the measures of variation if the medicines contained no lead?

$$3.0 \quad 6.5 \quad 6.0 \quad 5.5 \quad 20.5 \quad 7.5 \quad 12.0 \quad 20.5 \quad 11.5 \quad 17.5$$

14. Mercury in Sushi Listed below are the amounts of mercury (in parts per million, or ppm) found in tuna sushi sampled at different stores in New York City. The study was sponsored by the *New York Times,* and the stores (in order) are D'Agostino, Eli's Manhattan, Fairway, Food Emporium, Gourmet Garage, Grace's Marketplace, and Whole Foods. What would be the values of the measures of variation if the tuna sushi contained no mercury?

$$0.56 \quad 0.75 \quad 0.10 \quad 0.95 \quad 1.25 \quad 0.54 \quad 0.88$$

15. Years to Earn Bachelor's Degree Listed below are the lengths of time (in years) it took for a random sample of college students to earn bachelor's degrees (based on data from the National Center for Education Statistics). Based on these results, is it *unusual* for someone to earn a bachelor's degree in 12 years?

$$4 \quad 4 \quad 4 \quad 4 \quad 4 \quad 4 \quad 4.5 \quad 4.5 \quad 4.5 \quad 4.5 \quad 4.5 \quad 4.5 \quad 6 \quad 6 \quad 8 \quad 9 \quad 9 \quad 13 \quad 13 \quad 15$$

16. Cell Phone Radiation Listed below are the measured radiation emissions (in W/kg) corresponding to these cell phones: Samsung SGH-tss9, Blackberry Storm, Blackberry Curve, Motorola Moto, T-Mobile Sidekick, Sanyo Katana Eclipse, Palm Pre, Sony Ericsson, Nokia 6085, Apple iPhone 3G S, and Kyocero Neo E1100. The data are from the Environmental Working Group. If one of each model of cell phone is measured for radiation and the results are used to find the standard deviation, is that standard deviation equal to the standard deviation of the population of all cell phones that are in use? Why or why not?

$$0.38 \quad 0.55 \quad 1.54 \quad 1.55 \quad 0.50 \quad 0.60 \quad 0.92 \quad 0.96 \quad 1.00 \quad 0.86 \quad 1.46$$

17. JFK to LAX Flight Delays Listed below are the arrival delay times (in minutes) of randomly selected American Airline flights from New York's JFK airport to Los Angeles (LAX). Negative values correspond to flights that arrived early before the scheduled arrival time, and positive values represent lengths of delays. (The data are from the Bureau of Transportation, and more data are listed in Data Set 15 in Appendix B.) Some of the sample values are negative, but can the standard deviation ever be negative?

$$-15 \quad -18 \quad -32 \quad -21 \quad -9 \quad -32 \quad 11 \quad 2$$

18. Freshman 15 According to the "freshman 15" legend, college freshmen gain 15 pounds (or 6.8 kilograms) during their freshman year. Listed below are the amounts of weight change (in kilograms) for a simple random sample of freshmen included in a study ("Changes in Body Weight and Fat Mass of Men and Women in the First Year of College: A Study of the 'Freshman 15'" by Hoffman, Policastro, Quick, and Lee, *Journal of American College Health,* Vol. 55, No. 1). Positive values correspond to students who gained weight and negative values correspond to students who lost weight. Is a weight gain of 15 pounds (or 6.8 kg) *unusual?* Why or why not? If 15 pounds (or 6.8 kg) is not unusual, does that support the legend of the "freshman 15"?

$$11 \quad 3 \quad 0 \quad -2 \quad 3 \quad -2 \quad -2 \quad 5 \quad -2 \quad 7 \quad 2 \quad 4 \quad 1 \quad 8 \quad 1 \quad 0 \quad -5 \quad 2$$

19. Saints in Super Bowl Listed below are the numbers on the jerseys of the starting lineup for the New Orleans Saints when they recently won their first Super Bowl football game. What do the measures of variation tell us about the team? Does it make sense to compute the measures of variation for these data?

$$9 \quad 23 \quad 25 \quad 88 \quad 12 \quad 19 \quad 74 \quad 77 \quad 76 \quad 73 \quad 78$$

20. Phenotypes of Peas Biologists conducted experiments to determine whether a deficiency of carbon dioxide in the soil affects the phenotypes of peas. Listed below are the phenotype codes, where 1 = smooth-yellow, 2 = smooth-green, 3 = wrinkled-yellow, and 4 = wrinkled-green. Can the measures of center be obtained for these values? Do the results make sense?

$$2 \quad 1 \quad 1 \quad 1 \quad 1 \quad 1 \quad 1 \quad 4 \quad 1 \quad 2 \quad 2 \quad 1 \quad 2 \quad 3 \quad 3 \quad 2 \quad 3 \quad 1 \quad 3 \quad 1 \quad 3 \quad 1 \quad 3 \quad 2 \quad 2$$

In Exercises 21–24, find the **coefficient of variation** *for each of the two samples; then compare the variation. (The same data were used in Section 3-2.)*

21. Speeding and Race Listed below are speeds (in mi/h) of cars on the New Jersey Turnpike by race of the driver. All cars are going in the same direction, and all of the cars are from New Jersey. The data are from Statlib and the authors are Joseph Kadane and John Lamberth.

| White drivers: | 74 | 77 | 69 | 71 | 77 | 69 | 72 | 75 | 74 | 72 |

| African American drivers: | 79 | 70 | 71 | 76 | 76 | 74 | 71 | 75 | 74 | 74 |

22. Parking Meter Theft Listed below are amounts (in millions of dollars) collected from parking meters by Brinks and others in New York City during similar time periods. A larger data set was used to convict five Brinks employees of grand larceny. The data were provided by the attorney for New York City, and they are listed on the DASL web site. Do the limited data listed here show evidence of stealing by Brinks employees?

Collection contractor was Brinks: 1.3 1.5 1.3 1.5 1.4 1.7 1.8 1.7 1.7 1.6

Collection contractor was not Brinks: 2.2 1.9 1.5 1.6 1.5 1.7 1.9 1.6 1.6 1.8

23. Political Contributions Listed below are contributions (in dollars) made to the two presidential candidates in the most recent election. All contributions are from the same Zip code as the author, and the data are from the *Huffington Post*.

Obama: $275 $452 $300 $1000 $1000 $500 $100 $1061

$1200 $235 $875 $2000 $350 $210 $250

McCain: $50 $75 $240 $302 $250 $700 $350 $500

$1250 $1500 $500 $500 $40 $221 $400

24. Customer Waiting Times Waiting times (in minutes) of customers at the Jefferson Valley Bank (where all customers enter a single waiting line) and the Bank of Providence (where customers wait in individual lines at three different teller windows) are listed below.

Jefferson Valley (single line):   6.5   6.6   6.7   6.8   7.1   7.3   7.4   7.7   7.7   7.7

Providence (individual lines):   4.2   5.4   5.8   6.2   6.7   7.7   7.7   8.5   9.3   10.0

Large Data Sets from Appendix B.   *In Exercises 25–28, refer to the indicated data set in Appendix B. Use computer software or a calculator to find the range, variance, and standard deviation. Express answers using appropriate units, such as "minutes."*

25. Earthquakes Use the magnitudes (Richter scale) of the earthquakes listed in Data Set 16 in Appendix B.

26. Flight Data Refer to Data Set 15 in Appendix B and use the times required to taxi out for takeoff.

27. Presidential Longevity Refer to Data Set 12 in Appendix B and use the numbers of years that U.S. presidents have lived after their first inauguration.

28. IQ Scores Refer to Data Set 6 in Appendix B and use the listed IQ scores.

Estimating Standard Deviation with the Range Rule of Thumb. *In Exercises 29–32, refer to the data in the indicated exercise. After finding the range of the data, use the range rule of thumb to estimate the value of the standard deviation. Compare the result to the standard deviation computed with all of the data.*

29. Exercise 25   **30.** Exercise 26

31. Exercise 27   **32.** Exercise 28

Identifying Unusual Values with the Range Rule of Thumb. *In Exercises 33–36, use the range rule of thumb to determine whether a value is* unusual.

33. Pulse Rates of Females Based on Data Set 1 in Appendix B, females have pulse rates with a mean of 77.5 beats per minute and a standard deviation of 11.6 beats per minute. Is it unusual for a female to have a pulse rate of 99 beats per minute? (All of these pulse rates are measured at rest.) Explain.

34. Pulse Rates of Males Based on Data Set 1 in Appendix B, males have pulse rates with a mean of 67.3 beats per minute and a standard deviation of 10.3 beats per minute. Is it unusual for a male to have a pulse rate of 45 beats per minute? (All of these pulse rates are measured at rest.) Explain.

35. Volumes of Coke Based on Data Set 19 in Appendix B, cans of regular Coke have volumes with a mean of 12.19 oz and a standard deviation of 0.11 oz. Is it unusual for a can to contain 11.9 oz of Coke? Explain.

36. Weights of Pepsi Based on Data Set 19 in Appendix B, cans of regular Pepsi have weights with a mean of 0.82410 lb and a standard deviation of 0.00570 lb. Is it unusual for a can to contain 0.8133 lb of Pepsi? Explain.

Finding Standard Deviation from a Frequency Distribution. *In Exercises 37–40, find the standard deviation of sample data summarized in a frequency distribution table by using the formula below, where x represents the class midpoint, f represents the class frequency, and n represents the total number of sample values. Also, compare the computed standard deviations to these standard deviations obtained by using Formula 3-4 with the original list of data values: (Exercise 37) 11.1 years; (Exercise 38) 9.0 years; (Exercise 39) 13.4; (Exercise 40) 9.7 years.*

$$s = \sqrt{\frac{n\left[\Sigma\left(f \cdot x^2\right)\right] - \left[\Sigma\left(f \cdot x\right)\right]^2}{n(n-1)}}$$ Standard deviation for frequency distribution

37.

Age of Best Actress When Oscar Was Won	Frequency
20–29	27
30–39	34
40–49	13
50–59	2
60–69	4
70–79	1
80–89	1

38.

Age of Best Actor When Oscar Was Won	Frequency
20–29	1
30–39	26
40–49	35
50–59	13
60–69	6
70–79	1

39.

Verbal IQ Score of Subject Exposed to Lead	Frequency
50–59	4
60–69	10
70–79	25
80–89	43
90–99	26
100–109	8
110–119	3
120–129	2

40.

Years President Lived After First Inauguration	Frequency
0–4	8
5–9	2
10–14	5
15–19	7
20–24	4
25–29	6
30–34	0
35–39	1

41. The Empirical Rule Based on Data Set 1 in Appendix B, blood platelet counts of women have a bell-shaped distribution with a mean of 280 and a standard deviation of 65. (All units are 1000 cells/μL.) Using the empirical rule, what is the approximate percentage of women with platelet counts

a. within 2 standard deviations of the mean, or between 150 and 410?

b. between 215 and 345?

42. The Empirical Rule Based on Data Set 3 in Appendix B, body temperatures of healthy adults have a bell-shaped distribution with a mean of 98.20°F and a standard deviation of 0.62°F. Using the empirical rule, what is the approximate percentage of healthy adults with body temperatures

a. within 1 standard deviation of the mean, or between 97.58°F and 98.82°F?

b. between 96.34°F and 100.06°F?

43. Chebyshev's Theorem Based on Data Set 1 in Appendix B, blood platelet counts of women have a bell-shaped distribution with a mean of 280 and a standard deviation of 65. (All units are 1000 cells/μL.) Using Chebyshev's theorem, what do we know about the percentage of women with platelet counts that are within 2 standard deviations of the mean? What are the minimum and maximum platelet counts that are within 2 standard deviations of the mean?

44. Chebyshev's Theorem Based on Data Set 3 in Appendix B, body temperatures of healthy adults have a bell-shaped distribution with a mean of 98.20°F and a standard deviation of 0.62°F. Using Chebyshev's theorem, what do we know about the percentage of healthy adults with body temperatures that are within 3 standard deviations of the mean? What are the minimum and maximum body temperatures that are within 3 standard deviations of the mean?

3-3 Beyond the Basics

45. Why Divide by $n - 1$? Let a *population* consist of the values 2 min, 3 min, 8 min. (These are departure delay times taken from American Airlines flights from New York's JFK airport to Los Angeles. See Data Set 15 in Appendix B.) Assume that samples of two values are randomly selected *with replacement* from this population. (That is, a selected value is replaced before the second selection is made.)

a. Find the variance σ^2 of the population {2 min, 3 min, 8 min}.

b. After listing the nine different possible samples of two values selected with replacement, find the sample variance s^2 (which includes division by $n - 1$) for each of them; then find the mean of the nine sample variances s^2.

c. For each of the nine different possible samples of two values selected with replacement, find the variance by treating each sample as if it is a population (using the formula for population variance, which includes division by n), then find the mean of those nine population variances.

d. Which approach results in values that are better estimates of σ^2: part (b) or part (c)? Why? When computing variances of samples, should you use division by n or $n - 1$?

e. The preceding parts show that s^2 is an unbiased estimator of σ^2. Is s an unbiased estimator of σ? Explain.

46. Mean Absolute Deviation Use the same population of {2 min, 3 min, 8 min} from Exercise 45. Show that when samples of size 2 are randomly selected with replacement, the samples have mean absolute deviations that do not center about the value of the mean absolute deviation of the population. What does this indicate about a sample mean absolute deviation being used as an estimator of the mean absolute deviation of a population?

3-4   Measures of Relative Standing and Boxplots

Key Concept This section introduces measures of relative standing, which are numbers showing the location of data values relative to the other values within the same data set. The most important concept in this section is the z score, which will be used often in following chapters. We also discuss percentiles and quartiles, which are common statistics, as well as a new statistical graph called a boxplot.

Part 1: Basics of z Scores, Percentiles, Quartiles, and Boxplots

z Scores

A z score (or standardized value) is found by converting a value to a standardized scale, as given in the following definition. This definition shows that a z score is the number of standard deviations that a data value is away from the mean. We will use z scores extensively in Chapter 6 and later chapters.

> **DEFINITION** A **z score** (or **standardized value**) is the number of standard deviations that a given value x is above or below the mean. The z score is calculated by using one of the following:
>
> | Sample | Population |
> |:---:|:---:|
> | $z = \dfrac{x - \bar{x}}{s}$ | or $\quad z = \dfrac{x - \mu}{\sigma}$ |

Round-Off Rule for z Scores

Round z scores to two decimal places (such as 2.31).

This round-off rule is motivated by the format of standard tables in which z scores are expressed with two decimal places. See Table A-2 in Appendix A, which is a typical table of z scores, and notice that Table A-2 has z scores expressed with two decimal places. Example 1 illustrates how z scores can be used to compare values, even if they come from different populations.

 Example 1   Comparing a Count and a Weight

Example 8 in Section 3-3 used the coefficient of variation to compare the variation among numbers of chocolate chips in cookies to the variation among weights of regular Coke in cans. We now consider a comparison of two *individual* data values with this question: Which of the following two data values is more extreme?

- The Chips Ahoy (regular) cookie with 30 chocolate chips (among 40 cookies with a mean of 24.0 chocolate chips and a standard deviation of 2.6 chocolate chips)

- The can of regular Coke with a weight of 0.8295 lb (among 36 cans of regular Coke with a mean weight of 0.81682 lb and a standard deviation of 0.00751 lb)

Both of the above data values are the largest values in their respective data sets, but which of them is more extreme relative to the data sets from which they came?

Solution

The two given data values are measured on different scales with different units of measurement, but we can standardize the data values by converting them to z scores. Note that in the following calculations, the individual scores are substituted for the variable x.

Chips Ahoy cookie with 30 chocolate chips:

$$z = \frac{x - \bar{x}}{s} = \frac{30 \text{ chocolate chips} - 24.0 \text{ chocolate chips}}{2.6 \text{ chocolate chips}} = 2.31$$

can of Coke with weight of 0.8295 lb:

$$z = \frac{x - \bar{x}}{s} = \frac{0.8295 \text{ lb} - 0.81682 \text{ lb}}{0.00751 \text{ lb}} = 1.69$$

Interpretation

The results show that the cookie is 2.31 standard deviations above the mean, and the can of Coke is 1.69 standard deviations above the mean. Because the cookie is more standard deviations above the mean, it is the more extreme value. A cookie with 30 chocolate chips is more extreme than a can of Coke weighing 0.8295 lb.

Using z Scores to Identify Unusual Values In Section 3-3 we used the range rule of thumb to conclude that a value is "unusual" if it is more than 2 standard deviations away from the mean. It follows that unusual values have z scores less than -2 or greater than $+2$, as illustrated in Figure 3-4. Using this criterion with the two individual values used in Example 1 above, we see that the cookie with 30 chocolate chips is unusual (because its z score is 2.31, which is greater than 2), but the can of Coke weighing 0.8295 lb is not unusual (because its z score is 1.69, which is between -2 and $+2$).

Usual values: $-2 \leq z \text{ score } \leq 2$

Unusual values: $z \text{ score } < -2 \ or \ z \text{ score } > 2$

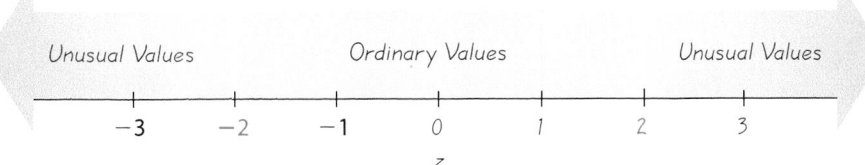

Unusual Values   Ordinary Values   Unusual Values

$-3 \quad -2 \quad -1 \quad 0 \quad 1 \quad 2 \quad 3$

z

Changing Populations

Included among the five important data set characteristics listed in Chapter 2 is the changing pattern of data over time. Some populations change, and their important statistics change as well. Car seat belt standards haven't changed in 40 years, even though the weights of Americans have increased considerably since then. In 1960, 12.8% of adult Americans were considered obese, compared to 22.6% in 1994.

According to the National Highway Traffic Safety Administration, seat belts must fit a standard crash dummy (designed according to 1960 data) placed in the most forward position, with 4 in. to spare. In theory, 95% of men and 99% of women should fit into seat belts, but those percentages are now lower because of the increases in weight over the last half-century. Some car companies provide seat belt extenders, but some do not.

Figure 3-4

Interpreting z Scores

Unusual values are those with z scores less than −2.00 or greater than 2.00.

Example 2   Is a Pulse Rate of 48 Unusual?

As the author was creating this example, he measured his pulse rate to be 48 beats per minute. (The author has too much time on his hands.) Is that pulse rate unusual? (Based on the pulse rates of males from Data Set 1 in Appendix B, assume that a large sample of adult males has pulse rates with a mean of 67.3 beats per minute and a standard deviation of 10.3 beats per minute.)

Solution

The author's pulse rate of 48 beats per minute is converted to a z score as shown below:

Pulse rate of 48:

$$z = \frac{x - \bar{x}}{s} = \frac{48 \text{ beats per minute} - 67.3 \text{ beats per minute}}{10.3 \text{ beats per minute}} = -1.87$$

Interpretation

The result shows that the author's pulse rate of 48 beats per minute is converted to the z score of -1.87. Refer to Figure 3-4 to see that $z = -1.87$ is between -2 and $+2$, so it is not unusual.

In Example 2, the pulse rate of 48 beats per minute resulted in a *negative z* score because that pulse rate is *less than* the mean of 67.3 beats per minute. Also, the units of "beats per minute" all canceled out, and the resulting z score has no units associated with it. These observations are included in the following summary describing z scores.

Properties of z Scores

1. A z score is the number of standard deviations that a given value x is above or below the mean.

2. z scores are expressed as numbers with no units of measurement.

3. A data value is unusual if its z score is less than -2 or greater than $+2$.

4. If an individual data value is less than the mean, its z score is a negative number.

A z score is a measure of position, in the sense that it describes the location of a value (in terms of standard deviations) relative to the mean. Quartiles and percentiles are other measures of position useful for comparing values within the same data set or between different sets of data.

Percentiles

Percentiles are one type of *quantiles*—or *fractiles*—which partition data into groups with roughly the same number of values in each group.

> **DEFINITION** **Percentiles** are measures of location, denoted $P_1, P_2, \ldots, P_{99}$, which divide a set of data into 100 groups with about 1% of the values in each group.

For example, the 50th percentile, denoted P_{50}, has about 50% of the data values below it and about 50% of the data values above it. So the 50th percentile is the same as the median. There is not universal agreement on a single procedure for calculating percentiles, but we will describe two relatively simple procedures for (1) finding the percentile of a data value and (2) converting a percentile to its corresponding data value. We begin with the first procedure.

Finding the Percentile of a Data Value The process of finding the percentile that corresponds to a particular data value x is given by the following (round the result to the nearest whole number):

$$\text{Percentile of value } x = \frac{\text{number of values less than } x}{\text{total number of values}} \cdot 100$$

Example 3   Finding a Percentile

Table 3-4 lists the same counts of chocolate chips in 40 Chips Ahoy regular cookies listed in Table 3-1, but in Table 3-4 those counts are arranged in increasing order. Find the percentile for a cookie with 23 chocolate chips.

Table 3-4 *Sorted* Counts of Chocolate Chips in Chips Ahoy (Regular) Cookies

19	19	20	20	20	20	22	22	22	22
23	23	23	23	23	23	23	24	24	24
24	24	25	25	25	25	25	25	25	26
26	26	26	26	26	27	27	28	28	30

Solution

From the sorted list of chocolate chip counts in Table 3-4, we see that there are 10 cookies with fewer than 23 chocolate chips, so

$$\text{Percentile of } 23 = \frac{10}{40} \cdot 100 = 25$$

Interpretation

A cookie with 23 chocolate chips is in the 25th percentile. This can be interpreted loosely as: A cookie with 23 chocolate chips separates the lowest 25% of cookies from the highest 75%.

Example 3 shows how to convert from a given sample value to the corresponding percentile. There are several different methods for the reverse procedure of converting a given percentile to the corresponding value in the data set. The procedure we will use is summarized in Figure 3-5, which uses the following notation.

Notation

n total number of values in the data set

k percentile being used (Example: For the 25th percentile, $k = 25$.)

L locator that gives the *position* of a value (Example: For the 12th value in the sorted list, $L = 12$.)

P_k kth percentile (Example: P_{25} is the 25th percentile.)

Example 4   Converting a Percentile to a Data Value

Refer to the sorted chocolate chip counts in Table 3-4 and use the procedure in Figure 3-5 to find the value of the 18th percentile, P_{18}.

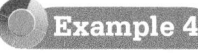

Figure 3-5

Converting from the *k*th percentile to the corresponding data value

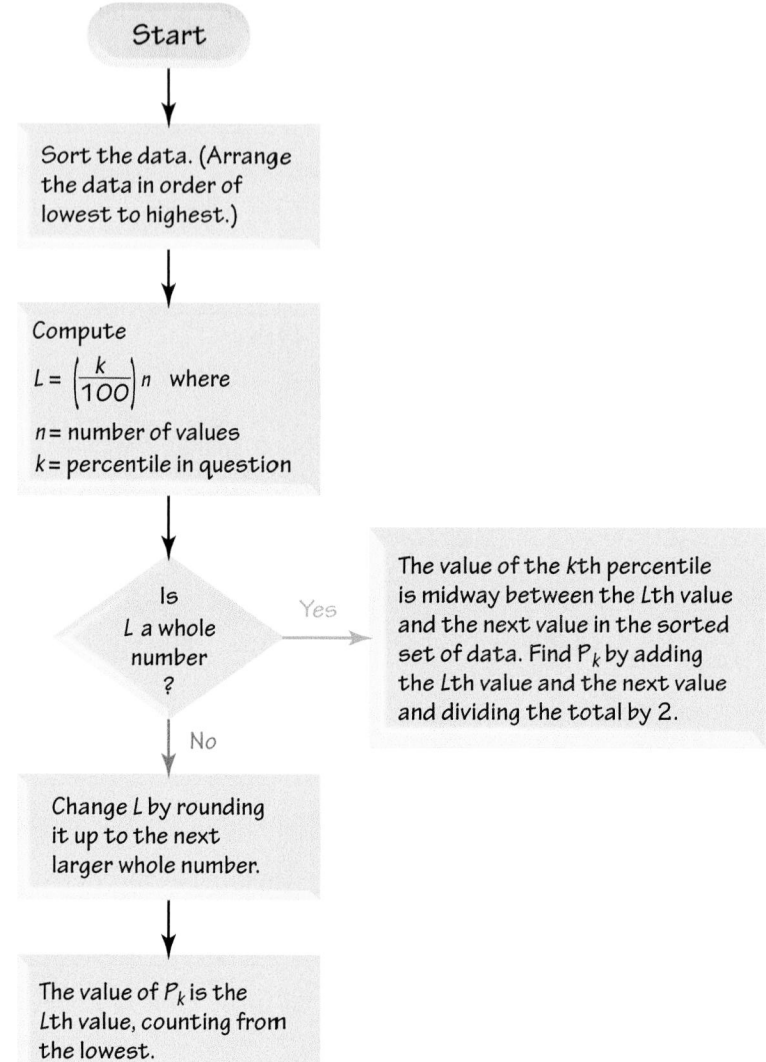

Solution

From Figure 3-5, we see that the sample data are already sorted, so we can proceed to find the value of the locator L. In this computation we use $k = 18$ because we are trying to find the value of the 18th percentile. We use $n = 40$ because there are 40 data values.

$$L = \frac{k}{100} \cdot n = \frac{18}{100} \cdot 40 = 7.2$$

Since $L = 7.2$ is not a whole number, we proceed to the next lower box where we change L by rounding it up from 7.2 to 8. (In this book we typically round off the usual way, but this is one of two cases where we round *up* instead of rounding *off*.) From the last box we see that the value of P_{18} is the 8th value, counting from the lowest. In Table 3-4, the 8th value is 22. That is, $P_{18} = 22$ chocolate chips. Roughly speaking, about 18% of the cookies have fewer than 22 chocolate chips and 82% of the cookies have more than 22 chocolate chips.

Example 5   Converting a Percentile to a Data Value

Refer to the sorted chocolate chip counts in Table 3-4. Use Figure 3-5 to find the 25th percentile, denoted by P_{25}.

Solution

Referring to Figure 3-5, we see that the sample data are already sorted, so we can proceed to compute the value of the locator L. In this computation, we use $k = 25$ because we are attempting to find the value of the 25th percentile, and we use $n = 40$ because there are 40 data values.

$$L = \frac{k}{100} \cdot n = \frac{25}{100} \cdot 40 = 10$$

Since $L = 10$ is a whole number, we proceed to the box located at the right. We now see that the value of the 10th percentile is midway between the Lth (10th) value and the next value in the original set of data. That is, the value of the 10th percentile is midway between the 10th value and the 11th value. The 10th value in Table 3-4 is 22 and the 11th value is 23, so the value midway between them is 22.5 chocolate chips. We conclude that the 25th percentile is $P_{25} = 22.5$ chocolate chips.

Quartiles

Just as there are 99 percentiles that divide the data into 100 groups, there are three quartiles that divide the data into four groups.

> **DEFINITION Quartiles** are measures of location, denoted Q_1, Q_2, and Q_3, which divide a set of data into four groups with about 25% of the values in each group.

Here are descriptions of quartiles that are more accurate than those given in the preceding definition:

Q_1 **(First quartile):**   Same value as P_{25}. It separates the bottom 25% of the sorted values from the top 75%. (To be more precise, at least 25% of the sorted values are less than or equal to Q_1, and at least 75% of the values are greater than or equal to Q_1.)

Q_2 **(Second quartile):**   Same as P_{50} and same as the median. It separates the bottom 50% of the sorted values from the top 50%.

Q_3 **(Third quartile):**   Same as P_{75}. It separates the bottom 75% of the sorted values from the top 25%. (To be more precise, at least 75% of the sorted values are less than or equal to Q_3, and at least 25% of the values are greater than or equal to Q_3.)

Finding values of quartiles can be accomplished with the same procedure used for finding percentiles. Simply use the relationships shown in the margin.

$$Q_1 = P_{25}$$
$$Q_2 = P_{50}$$
$$Q_3 = P_{75}$$

Example 6   Finding a Quartile

Refer to the chocolate chip counts listed in Table 3-4. Find the value of the first quartile Q_1.

Solution

Finding Q_1 is really the same as finding P_{25}. See Example 5 above for the procedure used to find this result: $P_{25} = 22.5$ chocolate chips.

Nielsen Ratings for College Students

The Nielsen ratings are one of the most important measures of television viewing, and they affect

billions of dollars in television advertising. In the past, the television viewing habits of college students were ignored, with the result that a large segment of the important young viewing audience was ignored. Nielsen Media Research is now including college students who do not live at home.

Some television shows have large appeal to viewers in the 18–24 age bracket, and the ratings of such shows have increased substantially with the inclusion of college students. For males, NBC's *Sunday Night Football* broadcast had an increase of 20% after male college students were included. For females, the TV show *Grey's Anatomy* had an increase of 54% after female college students were included. Those increased ratings ultimately translate into greater profits from charges to commercial sponsors. These ratings also give college students recognition that affects the programming they receive.

Just as there is not universal agreement on a procedure for finding percentiles, there is not universal agreement on a single procedure for calculating quartiles, and different computer programs often yield different results. If you use a calculator or computer software for exercises involving quartiles, you may get results that differ somewhat from the answers obtained by using the procedures described here.

CAUTION There is not universal agreement on procedures for finding quartiles, and different technologies may yield different quartile values.

In earlier sections of this chapter we described several statistics, including the mean, median, mode, range, and standard deviation. Some other statistics are defined using quartiles and percentiles, as in the following:

$$\text{Interquartile range (or IQR)} = Q_3 - Q_1$$

$$\text{Semi-interquartile range} = \frac{Q_3 - Q_1}{2}$$

$$\text{Midquartile} = \frac{Q_3 + Q_1}{2}$$

$$\text{10–90 percentile range} = P_{90} - P_{10}$$

5-Number Summary and Boxplot

The values of the three quartiles (Q_1, Q_2, Q_3) are used for the 5-number summary and the construction of boxplot graphs.

DEFINITION For a set of data, the **5-number summary** consists of these five values:

1. Minimum
2. First quartile, Q_1
3. Second quartile, Q_2 (same as the median)
4. Third quartile, Q_3
5. Maximum

A **boxplot** (or **box-and-whisker diagram**) is a graph of a data set that consists of a line extending from the minimum value to the maximum value, and a box with lines drawn at the first quartile Q_1, the median, and the third quartile Q_3. (See Figure 3-6.)

Example 7   Finding a 5-Number Summary

Use the chocolate chip counts listed in Table 3-4 to find the 5-number summary.

Solution

Because the chocolate chip counts in Table 3-4 are sorted, it is easy to see that the minimum is 19 and the maximum is 30. The value of the first quartile is $Q_1 = 22.5$, as was found in Examples 5 and 6. Also, $Q_3 = 26.0$ can be found by using the same procedure for finding P_{75} (as summarized in Figure 3-5). The 5-number summary is 19, 22.5, 24.0, 26.0, and 30.

The 5-number summary is used to construct a boxplot, as in the following procedure.

Procedure for Constructing a Boxplot

1. Find the 5-number summary (minimum value, Q_1, Q_2, Q_3, maximum value).

2. Construct a scale with values that include the minimum and maximum data values.

3. Construct a box (rectangle) extending from Q_1 to Q_3, and draw a line in the box at the value of Q_2 (median).

4. Draw lines extending outward from the box to the minimum and maximum data values.

CAUTION Because there is not universal agreement on procedures for finding quartiles, and because boxplots are based on quartiles, different technologies may yield different boxplots.

Example 8 Constructing a Boxplot

Use the chocolate chip counts listed in Table 3-4 to construct a boxplot.

Solution

The boxplot uses the 5-number summary found in Example 7: 19, 22.5, 24.0, 26.0, and 30. Figure 3-6 is the boxplot representing the chocolate chip counts listed in Table 3-4.

Figure 3-6   Boxplot of Chocolate Chip Counts in Regular Chips Ahoy Cookies

Boxplots give us some information about the spread of the data. Shown below is a boxplot from a data set with a normal (bell-shaped) distribution and a boxplot from a data set with a distribution that is skewed to the right (based on data from *USA Today*).

Normal Distribution: Heights from a simple random sample of women

Skewed Distribution: Salaries (in thousands of dollars) of NCAA football coaches

Because the shape of a boxplot is determined by the five values from the 5-number summary, a boxplot is not a graph of the distribution of the data, and it doesn't show as much detailed information as a histogram or stemplot. However, boxplots are often great for comparing two or more data sets. When using two or more boxplots for comparing different data sets, graph the boxplots on the same scale so that comparisons can be easily made.

 Example 9   Do the Different Brands of Cookies Have Different Chocolate Chip Counts?

The Chapter Problem includes Table 3-1, which lists counts of chocolate chips in cookies from different brands. Use the same scale to construct the five corresponding boxplots; then compare the results.

Solution

The STATDISK-generated boxplots shown in Figure 3-7 suggest that the numbers of chocolate chips in the different brands of cookies are very different. In particular, the counts from the Keebler and Hannaford cookies appear to be very different; the boxplots show that there isn't any overlap, and all of the Hannaford cookies have lower counts than any of the Keebler cookies. It might seem that the Hannaford brand is stingy with its chocolate chips, but the Hannaford brand had many chips that were substantially larger than those in any of the other brands.

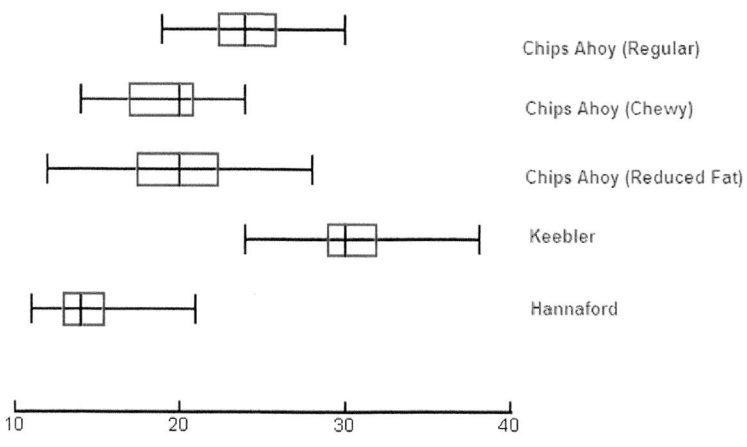

Figure 3-7   Boxplots of Counts of Chocolate Chips in Cookies

Methods discussed later in this book allow us to analyze this issue more formally. It is always wise to construct suitable graphs, such as histograms, dotplots, and boxplots, but we should not rely solely on subjective judgments based on graphs.

 Outliers

When analyzing data, it is important to identify and consider outliers because they can strongly affect values of some important statistics (such as the mean and standard deviation), and they can also strongly affect important methods discussed later in this book. In Section 2-1 we described outliers as sample values that lie very far away from the vast majority of the other values in a set of data, but that description is vague and it does not provide specific objective criteria. Part 2 of this section includes a description of *modified boxplots* along with a specific definition of outliers used in the context of creating modified boxplots.

CAUTION When analyzing data, always identify outliers and consider their effects, which can be substantial.

Part 2: Outliers and Modified Boxplots

Outliers

We noted that the description of outliers is somewhat vague, but for the purposes of constructing *modified boxplots*, we can consider outliers to be data values meeting specific criteria based on quartiles and the interquartile range. (The interquartile range is often denoted by IQR, and IQR $= Q_3 - Q_1$.)

1. Find the quartiles Q_1, Q_2, and Q_3.

2. Find the interquartile range (IQR), where IQR $= Q_3 - Q_1$.

3. Evaluate $1.5 \times$ IQR.

4. **In a modified boxplot, a data value is an *outlier* if it is**

   above Q_3, by an amount greater than 1.5 $\times$ IQR

   or   below Q_1, by an amount greater than 1.5 $\times$ IQR

Modified Boxplots

The boxplots described earlier are called **skeletal** (or **regular**) **boxplots,** but some statistical software packages provide modified boxplots, which represent outliers as special points. A **modified boxplot** is a regular boxplot constructed with these modifications: (1) A special symbol (such as an asterisk or point) is used to identify outliers as defined above, and (2) the solid horizontal line extends only as far as the minimum data value that is not an outlier and the maximum data value that is not an outlier. (*Note: Exercises involving modified boxplots are found in the "Beyond the Basics" exercises only.*)

 Example 10   Modified Boxplot

Use the Hannaford chocolate chip counts from Table 3-1 to construct a modified boxplot.

Solution

Let's begin with the above four steps for identifying outliers in a modified boxplot.

1. Using the Hannaford chocolate chip counts from Table 3-1, the three quartiles are $Q_1 = 13.0$, $Q_2 = 14.0$, and $Q_3 = 15.5$.

2. The interquartile range is IQR $= Q_3 - Q_1 = 15.5 - 13.0 = 2.5$.

3. $1.5 \times$ IQR $= 1.5 \times 2.5 = 3.75$.

4. Any outliers are above $Q_3 = 15.5$ by more than 3.75, or below $Q_1 = 13.0$ by more than 3.75. This means that any outliers are greater than 19.25 or less than 9.25.

We can now examine the original Hannaford chocolate chip counts to see that 21 is the only value greater than 19.25, and there are no values less than 9.25. Therefore, 21 is the only outlier.

We can now construct the modified boxplot shown in Figure 3-8. In Figure 3-8, the outlier is identified as a special point, the three quartiles are shown as in a regular

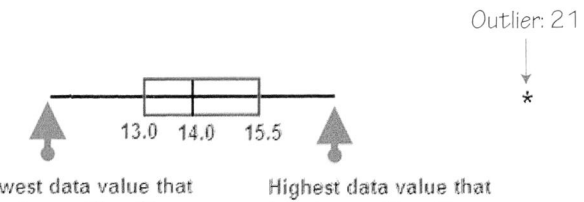

Figure 3-8
Modified Boxplots of Hannaford Chocolate Chip Counts

boxplot, and the horizontal line extends from the lowest data value that is not an outlier (11) to the highest data value that is not an outlier (17).

CAUTION Because there is not universal agreement on procedures for finding quartiles, and because modified boxplots are based on quartiles, different technologies may yield different modified boxplots.

Putting It All Together

We have discussed several basic tools commonly used in statistics. When designing an experiment, analyzing data, reading an article in a professional journal, or doing anything else with data, it is important to consider certain key factors, such as:

- Context of the data
- Source of the data
- Sampling method
- Measures of center
- Measures of variation
- Distribution
- Outliers
- Changing patterns over time
- Conclusions
- Practical implications

This is an excellent checklist, but it should not replace *thinking* about any other relevant factors. It is very possible that some application of statistics requires factors not included in the above list, and it is also possible that some of the factors in the list are not relevant for certain applications.

using TECHNOLOGY

Boxplots

STATDISK Enter or open the data in the Data Window, then click on **Data**, then **Boxplot**. Click on the columns that you want to include, then click on either **BoxpPlot** or **Modified Boxplot.**

MINITAB Enter or open the data in columns. With Minitab 16, click on **Assistant,** then select **Graphical Assistant,** then click on the image of a boxplot. With earlier versions of Minitab, select **Graph,** then select **Boxplot.** Select the "Simple" option for one boxplot or the "Simple" option for multiple boxplots. Enter the column names in the Variables box, then click **OK.** Minitab provides modified boxplots as described in Part 2 of this section.

EXCEL Although Excel is not designed to generate boxplots, they can be generated using XLSTAT. First enter the data in column A. Click on **XLSTAT** at the top, select **Describing Data,** then select **Descriptive Statistics.** Enter the range of cells (such as

A1:A40) in the "Quantitative Data" box. Check the "Sample labels" box only if the first cell contains the name of the data set. Click on the **Charts** tab, then check the box labelled **Boxplots.** Click **OK** to continue. The result will include descriptive statistics as well as a boxplot.

TI-83/84 PLUS Enter the sample data in list L1 (or enter the data and assign them to a list with a name). Now select **STAT PLOT** by pressing **2ND** **Y=** . Press **ENTER**, then select the option of **ON** . For a simple boxplot as described in Part 1 of this section, select the boxplot type that is positioned in the middle of the second row; for a modified boxplot as described in Part 2 of this section, select the boxplot that is positioned at the far left of the second row. The Xlist should indicate L1 (or the assigned list name) and the Freq value should be 1. Now press **ZOOM** and select option 9 for **ZoomStat.** Press **ENTER** and the boxplot should be displayed. You can use the arrow keys to move right or left so that values can be read from the horizontal scale.

STATCRUNCH Click on **Open StatCrunch,** then enter or open a data set. Click on **Graphics,** then select **Boxplot.** Select the column containing the data. Click on **Create Graph.**

5-Number Summary

STATDISK, Minitab, and the TI-83/84 Plus calculator provide the values of the 5-number summary. Use the same procedure given at the end of Section 3-2. Excel provides the minimum, maximum, and median, and the quartiles can be obtained by clicking on *fx*, selecting the function category of Statistical, and selecting QUARTILE. (In Excel 2010, select QUARTILE.INC, which is the same as QUARTILE in Excel 2003 and Excel 2007, or select the new function QUARTILE.EXC, which is supposed to be "consistent with industry best practices.")

Outliers

To identify outliers, sort the data in order from the minimum to the maximum, then examine the minimum and maximum values to determine whether they are far away from the other data values. Here are instructions for sorting data:

STATDISK Click on **Data** and select the menu item of **Sort Data.** Click on **Sort** after making the desired choices.

MINITAB Click on **Data** and select **Sort.** Enter the column in the "Sort column(s)" box and enter that same column in the "By column" box.

EXCEL In Excel 2003, click on the "sort ascending" icon, which has the letter A stacked above the letter Z and a downward arrow. In Excel 2013, 2010, or 2007, click on **Data,** then click on the "sort ascending" icon, which has the letter A stacked above the letter Z and a downward arrow.

TI-83/84 PLUS Press **STAT** and select **SortA** (for sort in ascending order). Press **ENTER**. Enter the list to be sorted, such as L1 or a named list, then press **ENTER**.

STATCRUNCH Click on **Open StatCrunch.** Enter or open a data set. Click on **Data,** then select the menu item of **Sort columns.** Click on the column to be sorted, then click on **Sort columns.**

3-4 Basic Skills and Concepts

Statistical Literacy and Critical Thinking

1. z Scores James Madison, the fourth President of the United States, was 163 cm tall. His height converts to the z score of -2.28 when included among the heights of all presidents. Is his height above or below the mean? How many standard deviations is Madison's height away from the mean?

2. z Scores If your score on your next statistics test is converted to a z score, which of these z scores would you prefer: -2.00, -1.00, 0, 1.00, 2.00? Why?

3. Boxplots Shown below is a STATDISK-generated boxplot of the amounts of money (in millions of dollars) that movies grossed (based on data from the Motion Picture Association of America). What do the displayed values of 5, 47, 104, 121, and 380 tell us?

4. Measures of Location The values of P_{50}, Q_2, and the median are found for the net incomes reported on all individual 1040 tax forms filed last year. What do those values have in common?

z Scores.   *In Exercises 5–8, express all z scores with two decimal places.*

5. Obama's Net Worth As of this writing, Barack Obama is President of the United States and he has a net worth of $3,670,505. The 17 members of the Executive Branch have a mean net worth of $4,939,455 with a standard deviation of $7,775,948 (based on data from opensecrets.org).

a. What is the difference between President Obama's net worth and the mean net worth of all members of the Executive Branch?

b. How many standard deviations is that (the difference found in part (a))?

c. Convert President Obama's net worth to a z score.

d. If we consider "usual" amounts of net worth to be those that convert to z scores between -2 and 2, is President Obama's net worth usual or unusual?

6. Earthquakes Data Set 16 in Appendix B lists 50 magnitudes (Richter scale) of 50 earthquakes, and those earthquakes have magnitudes with a mean of 1.184 with a standard deviation of 0.587. The strongest of those earthquakes had a magnitude of 2.95.

a. What is the difference between the magnitude of the strongest earthquake and the mean magnitude?

b. How many standard deviations is that (the difference found in part (a))?

c. Convert the magnitude of the strongest earthquake to a z score.

d. If we consider "usual" magnitudes to be those that convert to z scores between -2 and 2, is the magnitude of the strongest earthquake usual or unusual?

7. Jobs' Job When Steve Jobs was Chief Executive Officer (CEO) of Apple, he earned an annual salary of \$1. The CEOs of the 50 largest U. S. companies had a mean salary of \$1,449,779 and a standard deviation of \$527,651 (based on data from USA Today).

a. What is the difference between Jobs' salary and the mean CEO salary?

b. How many standard deviations is that (the difference found in part (a))?

c. Convert Steve Jobs' salary to a z score.

d. If we consider "usual" salaries to be those that convert to z scores between -2 and 2, is Steve Jobs' salary usual or unusual?

8. Student's Pulse Rate A male student of the author has a measured pulse rate of 52 beats per minute. Based on Data Set 1 in Appendix B, males have a mean pulse rate of 67.3 beats per minute and a standard deviation of 10.3 beats per minute.

a. What is the difference between the student's pulse rate and the mean pulse rate of males?

b. How many standard deviations is that (the difference found in part (a))?

c. Convert the student's pulse rate to a z score.

d. If we consider "usual" pulse rates to be those that convert to z scores between -2 and 2, is the student's pulse rate usual or unusual?

Usual and Unusual Values.   *In Exercises 9–12, consider a value to be* unusual *if its z score is less than -2 or greater than 2.*

9. IQ Scores The Wechsler Adult Intelligence Scale measures IQ scores with a test designed so that the mean is 100 and the standard deviation is 15. Consider the group of IQ scores that are unusual. What are the z scores that separate the unusual IQ scores from those that are usual? What are the IQ scores that separate the unusual IQ scores from those that are usual?

10. Designing Aircraft Seats In the process of designing aircraft seats, it was found that men have hip breadths with a mean of 36.6 cm and a standard deviation of 2.5 in. (based on anthropometric survey data from Gordon, Clauser, et al.). Consider the values of hip breadths of men that are unusual. What are the z scores that separate the unusual hip breadths from those that are usual? What are the hip breadths that separate the unusual hip breadths from those that are usual?

11. Earthquakes The Southern California Earthquake Data Center recorded magnitudes (Richter scale) of 10,594 earthquakes in a recent year. The mean is 1.240 and the standard deviation is 0.578. Consider the magnitudes that are unusual. What are the magnitudes that separate the unusual earthquakes from those that are usual?

12. Female Voice Based on data from Data Set 17 in Appendix B, the words spoken in a day by women have a mean of 16,215 words and a standard deviation of 7301 words. Consider the women with an unusual word count in a day. What are the numbers of words that separate the unusual word counts from those that are usual?

Comparing Values. *In Exercises 13–16, use z scores to compare the given values.*

13. Tallest Man and Woman As of this writing, the tallest living man is Sultan Kosen, who has a height of 247 cm. The tallest living woman is De-Fen Yao, who is 236 cm tall. Heights of men have a mean of 175 cm and a standard deviation of 7 cm. Heights of women have a mean of 162 cm and a standard deviation of 6 cm. Relative to the population of the same gender, who is taller? Explain.

14. Oscars As of this writing, Sandra Bullock was the last woman to win an Oscar for Best Actress and Jeff Bridges was the last man to win for Best Actor. At the time of the awards ceremony, Sandra Bullock was 45 years of age and Jeff Bridges was 60 years of age. Based on Data Set 11 in Appendix B, the Best Actresses have a mean age of 35.9 years and a standard deviation of 11.1 years. The Best Actors have a mean age of 44.1 years and a standard deviation of 9.0 years. (All ages are determined at the time of the awards ceremony.) Relative to their genders, who was younger when winning the Oscar: Sandra Bullock or Jeff Bridges? Explain.

15. Comparing Test Scores Scores on the SAT test have a mean of 1518 and a standard deviation of 325. Scores on the ACT test have a mean of 21.1 and a standard deviation of 4.8. Which is relatively better: a score of 1490 on the SAT test or a score of 17.0 on the ACT test? Why?

16. Red Blood Cell Counts Based on Data Set 1 in Appendix B, males have red blood cell counts with a mean of 5.072 and a standard deviation of 0.395, while females have red blood cell counts with a mean of 4.577 and a standard deviation of 0.382. Who has the higher count relative to the sample from which it came: A male with a count of 4.91 or a female with a count of 4.32? Explain.

Percentiles. *In Exercises 17–20, use the following duration times (seconds) of 24 eruptions of the Old Faithful geyser in Yellowstone National Park. The duration times are sorted from lowest to highest. Find the percentile corresponding to the given time.*

| 110 | 120 | 178 | 213 | 234 | 234 | 235 | 237 | 240 | 243 | 245 | 245 |
| 250 | 250 | 251 | 252 | 254 | 255 | 255 | 259 | 260 | 266 | 269 | 273 |

17. 213 sec   **18.** 240 sec   **19.** 250 sec   **20.** 260 sec

In Exercises 21–28, use the same list of 24 sorted Old Faithful eruption duration times given for Exercises 17–20. Find the indicated percentile or quartile.

21. P_{60} **22.** Q_1

23. Q_3 **24.** P_{40}

25. P_{50} **26.** P_{75}

27. P_{25} **28.** P_{85}

Boxplots. *In Exercises 29–32, use the given data to construct a boxplot and identify the 5-number summary.*

29. *Challenger* Flights The following are the duration times (minutes) of all missions flown by the space shuttle *Challenger*.

1   7224   8709   8784   10,060   10,089   10,125   11,445   11,476   11,844

30. Old Faithful The following are the interval times (minutes) between eruptions of the Old Faithful geyser in Yellowstone National Park (based on data from the U.S. National Park Service).

81   81   86   87   89   92   93   94   95   96   97   98   98   101   101   106

31. Grooming Times The following are amounts of time (minutes) spent on hygiene and grooming in the morning by survey respondents (based on data from an SCA survey).

4   6   7   9   14   15   15   16   18   18   25   26   30   32   41   45   55   63

32. Speeds The following are speeds (mi/h) of cars measured with a radar gun on the New Jersey Turnpike (based on data from Statlib and authors Joseph Kadane and John Lamberth).

70   70   71   72   72   73   73   74   76   77   78   78   78   79   79

Boxplots from Larger Data Sets in Appendix B. *In Exercises 33–36, use the given data sets from Appendix B.*

33. Pulse Rates Use the same scale to construct boxplots for the pulse rates of males and females from Data Set 1 in Appendix B. Use the boxplots to compare the two data sets.

34. Ages of Oscar Winners Use the same scale to construct boxplots for the ages of the best actresses and best actors from Data Set 11 in Appendix B. Use the boxplots to compare the two data sets.

35. Weights of Regular Coke and Diet Coke Use the same scale to construct boxplots for the weights of regular Coke and diet Coke from Data Set 19 in Appendix B. Use the boxplots to compare the two data sets.

36. Lead and IQ Use the same scale to construct boxplots for the full IQ scores (IQF) for the low lead level group and the high lead level group in Data Set 5 of Appendix B.

3-4 Beyond the Basics

37. Outliers and Modified Boxplots Repeat Exercise 34 using modified boxplots. Identify any outliers as defined in Part 2 of this section. What do the modified boxplots show that the regular boxplots do not show?

38. Interpolation When finding percentiles using Figure 3-5, if the locator L is not a whole number, we round it up to the next larger whole number. An alternative to this procedure is to *interpolate*. For example, using interpolation with a locator of $L = 23.75$ leads to a value that is 0.75 (or 3/4) of the way between the 23rd and 24th values. Use this method of interpolation to find P_{17} for the chocolate chip counts in Table 3-4. How does the result compare to the value that would be found by using Figure 3-5 without interpolation?

Chapter 3   Review

This chapter presented fundamentally and critically important measures that are essential for effectively describing, exploring, and comparing data. Here are key skills that should be mastered upon completion of this chapter:

• Calculate measures of center by finding the mean and median (Section 3-2).

• Calculate measures of variation by finding the standard deviation, variance, and range (Section 3-3).

• *Understand* and *interpret* the standard deviation by using tools such as the range rule of thumb (Section 3-3).

• Compare data values by using *z* scores, quartiles, or percentiles (Section 3-4).

• Investigate the spread of data by constructing a boxplot.

Chapter Quick Quiz

1. Find the mean of these times that American Airlines flights used to taxi to the Los Angeles terminal after landing from a flight: 12 min, 8 min, 21 min, 17 min, 12 min. (Data are from Data Set 15 in Appendix B.)

2. What is the median of the sample values listed in Exercise 1?

3. What is the mode of the sample values listed in Exercise 1?

4. The standard deviation of the sample values in Exercise 1 is 5.0 min. What is the variance (including units)?

5. The taxi-in times for 48 flights that landed in Los Angeles have a mean of 11.4 min and a standard deviation of 7.0 min. What is the *z* score for a taxi-in time of 6 min?

6. You plan to investigate the variation of taxi-in times for flights that have landed in Los Angeles. Name at least two measures of variation for those data.

7. Consider a sample taken from the population of all taxi-in times for all flights that land in Los Angeles. Identify the symbols used for the sample mean and the population mean.

8. Consider a sample taken from the population of all taxi-in times for all flights that land in Los Angeles. Identify the symbols used for the sample standard deviation, the population standard deviation, the sample variance, and the population variance.

9. Approximately what percentage of taxi-in times is less than the 75th percentile?

10. For a sample of motorcycle speeds, name the values that constitute the 5-number summary.

Review Exercises

1. Ergonomics When designing an eye-recognition security device, engineers must consider the eye heights of standing women. (It's easy for men to bend lower, but it's more difficult for women to rise higher.) Listed below are the eye heights (in millimeters) obtained from a simple random sample of standing adult women (based on anthropometric survey data from Gordon, Churchill, et al.). Use the given eye heights to find the (a) mean; (b) median; (c) mode; (d) midrange; (e) range; (f) standard deviation; (g) variance; (h) Q_1; (i) Q_3.

1550   1642   1538   1497   1571

2. z Score Using the sample data from Exercise 1, find the *z* score corresponding to the eye height of 1642 mm. Is that eye height unusual? Why or why not?

3. Boxplot Using the same standing heights listed in Exercise 1, construct a boxplot and include the values of the 5-number summary. Does the boxplot indicate that the data are from a population with a normal (bell-shaped) distribution? Explain.

4. ZIP Codes An article in the *New York Times* noted that these new ZIP codes were created in New York City: 10065, 10021, 10075. Find the mean of these three numbers. What is fundamentally wrong with this result?

5. Comparing BMI The body mass indices (BMI) of a sample of males have a mean of 26.601 and a standard deviation of 5.359. The body mass indices of a sample of females have a mean of 28.441 and a standard deviation of 7.394 (based on Data Set 1 in Appendix B). When considered among members of the same gender, who has the relatively larger BMI: a male with a BMI of 28.00 or a female with a BMI of 29.00? Why?

6. Movies: Estimating Mean and Standard Deviation Consider the prices of regular movie tickets (not 3-D, and not discounted for children or seniors).

a. Estimate the mean price.

b. Use the range rule of thumb to make a rough estimate of the standard deviation of the prices.

7. Professors: Estimating Mean and Standard Deviation Use the range rule of thumb to estimate the standard deviation of ages of all teachers at your college.

8. Aircraft Design Engineers designing overhead bin storage in an aircraft must consider the sitting heights of male passengers. Sitting heights of adult males have a mean of 914 mm and a standard deviation of 36 mm (based on anthropometric survey data from Gordon, Churchill, et al.). Use the range rule of thumb to identify the minimum "usual" sitting height and the maximum "usual" sitting height. Which of those two values is more relevant in this situation? Why?

9. Interpreting a Boxplot Shown below is a boxplot of a sample of 20 brain volumes (cm^3). What do the numbers in the boxplot represent?

10. Mean or Median? A statistics class with 40 students consists of 30 students with no income, 10 students with small incomes from part-time jobs, and a professor with a very large income that is well deserved. Which is better for describing the income of a typical person in this class: mean or median? Explain.

Cumulative Review Exercises

Please be aware that some of the following problems may require knowledge of concepts presented in previous chapters.

1. Designing Gloves An engineer is designing a machine to manufacture gloves and she obtains the following sample of hand lengths (mm) of randomly selected adult males (based on anthropometric survey data from Gordon, Churchill, et al.):

173   179   207   158   196   195   214   199

a. Are exact hand lengths from a population that is discrete or continuous?

b. What is the level of measurement of the hand lengths? (nominal, ordinal, interval, ratio)

2. Frequency Distribution Use the hand lengths in Exercise 1 to construct a frequency distribution. Use a class width of 10 mm, and use 150 mm as the lower class limit of the first class.

3. Histogram Use the frequency distribution from Exercise 2 to construct a histogram.

4. Stemplot Use the hand lengths from Exercise 1 to construct a stemplot.

5. Descriptive Statistics Use the hand lengths in Exercise 1 and find the following: (a) mean; (b) median; (c) standard deviation; (d) variance; (e) range. Include the appropriate units of measurement.

6. Normal Distribution Instead of using the hand lengths in Exercise 1, a much larger sample of hand lengths is used and a frequency distribution is created. The frequencies listed in order are 1, 8, 56, 237, 382, 228, 48, 4, 1. Does it appear that the sample is from a population having a normal distribution? Explain.

7. Sampling Shortly after the World Trade Center towers were destroyed, America Online ran a poll of its Internet subscribers and asked this question: "Should the World Trade Center towers be rebuilt?" Among the 1,304,240 responses, 768,731 answered "yes," 286,756 answered "no," and 248,753 said that it was "too soon to decide." Given that this sample is extremely large, can the responses be considered to be representative of the population of the United States? Explain.

8. Histogram The accompanying histogram depicts outcomes of digits from the California Daily 4 lottery. What is the major flaw in this histogram?

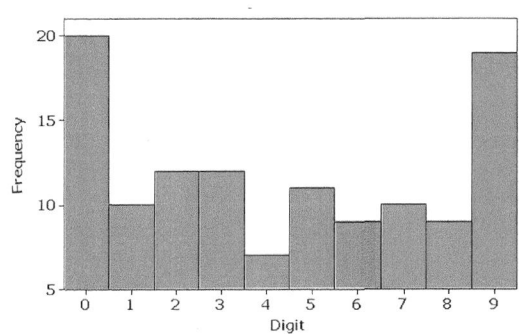

Technology Project

When dealing with large data sets, manual entry of data can become quite tedious and time-consuming. There are better things to do with your time, such as rotating the tires on your car or folding laundry. Refer to Data Set 1 in Appendix B, which includes a variety of real body measurements from randomly selected males and females. Instead of manually entering the data, use a TI-83/84 Plus calculator or STATDISK, Minitab, Excel, StatCrunch, or any other statistics software package. Load the data sets, which are available on the CD included with this book. Identify a variable to be used as a basis for comparison between the two genders. Proceed to generate histograms, any other suitable graphs, and find appropriate statistics that allow you to compare the two sets of data. Are there any outliers? Do both data sets have properties that are basically the same? Are there any significant differences? What would be a consequence of having significant differences? Write a brief report including your conclusions and supporting graphs.

from data TO DECISION

Flight Planning

The *From Data to Decision* project at the end of Chapter 2 involved data from American Airline flights from New York (JFK airport) to Los Angeles (LAX airport), and the data are listed in Data Set 15 in Appendix B.

Critical Thinking

Use the methods from this chapter to explore the arrival delay times at LAX. Those times are important because they can affect passenger plans. Are there any outliers? Based on the results, should you somehow modify the scheduled arrival times? If so, how? Write a brief report of your conclusions, and provide supporting statistical evidence.

Cooperative Group Activities

1. Out-of-class activity The Chapter Problem involves counts of chocolate chips in five different brands of cookies. Obtain your own sample of chocolate chip cookies and proceed to count the number of chocolate chips in each cookie. Use the data to generate a histogram and any other suitable graphs. Find the descriptive statistics. Compare your chocolate chip counts to those given in Table 3-1. Are there any differences? Explain.

2. In-class activity In class, each student should record two pulse rates by counting the number of heartbeats in one minute. The first pulse rate should be measured while seated, and the second pulse rate should be measured while standing. Use the methods of this chapter to compare results. Do males and females appear to have different pulse rates? Do pulse rates measured while seated appear to be different from pulse rates measured while standing?

3. Out-of-class activity In the article "Weighing Anchors" in *Omni* magazine, author John Rubin observed that when people estimate a value, their estimate is often "anchored" to (or influenced by) a preceding number, even if that preceding number is totally unrelated to the quantity being estimated. To demonstrate this, he asked people to give a quick estimate of the value of $8 \times 7 \times 6 \times 5 \times 4 \times 3 \times 2 \times 1$. The mean of the answers given was 2250, but when the order of the numbers was reversed, the mean became 512. Rubin explained that when we begin calculations with larger numbers (as in $8 \times 7 \times 6$), our estimates tend to be larger. He noted that both 2250 and 512 are far below the correct product, 40,320. The article suggests that irrelevant numbers can play a role in influencing real estate appraisals, estimates of car values, and estimates of the likelihood of nuclear war.

Conduct an experiment to test this theory. Select some subjects and ask them to quickly estimate the value of

$$8 \times 7 \times 6 \times 5 \times 4 \times 3 \times 2 \times 1$$

Then select other subjects and ask them to quickly estimate the value of

$$1 \times 2 \times 3 \times 4 \times 5 \times 6 \times 7 \times 8$$

Record the estimates along with the particular order used. Carefully design the experiment so that conditions are uniform and the two sample groups are selected in a way that minimizes any bias. Don't describe the theory to subjects until after they have provided their estimates. Compare the two sets of sample results by using the methods of this chapter. Provide a printed report that includes the data collected, the detailed methods used, the method of analysis, any relevant graphs and/or statistics, and a statement of conclusions. Include a critique of the experiment, with reasons why the results might not be correct, and describe ways in which the experiment could be improved.

4. Out-of-class activity In each group of three or four students, collect an original data set of values at the interval or ratio level of measurement. Provide the following: (1) a list of sample values, (2) printed computer results of descriptive statistics and graphs, and (3) a written description of the nature of the data, the method of collection, and important characteristics.

5. Out-of-class activity Appendix B includes many real and interesting data sets. In each group of three or four students, select a data set from Appendix B and analyze it using the methods discussed so far in this book. Write a brief report summarizing key conclusions.

6. Out-of-class activity Record the service times of randomly selected customers at a drive-up window of a bank or fast-food restaurant, and describe important characteristics of those times.

7. Out-of-class activity Record the times that cars are parked at a gas pump, and describe important characteristics of those times.

4 Probability

Pre-employment drug screening

80% of companies in the United States now test employees and/or job applicants for drug use. One common approach to pre-employment drug screening is to require an initial urine test, such as the EMIT (enzyme multiplied immunoassay technique) test, which is a "five panel" test for the presence of any of five drugs: marijuana, cocaine, amphetamines, opiates, or phencyclidine. The EMIT test is one of the least expensive and most common tests used by employers. Most companies require that positive test results be confirmed by a more reliable GC-MS (gas chromotography mass spectometry) test.

Drug testing is typically a process with some degree of inaccuracy, and results are sometimes wrong. Wrong results are of two types: (1) false positive results and (2) false negative results. These terms are included among several terms commonly used in references to drug testing. A subject getting a false positive result is in the very undesirable position of appearing to be a drug user when that person is not actually a drug user.

Analyzing the Results

Table 4-1 includes results from 1000 adults in the United States. If one of the 1000 subjects from Table 4-1 is randomly selected, what is the probability that the subject will test positive if this person is not a drug user? If one of the subjects from Table 4-1 is randomly selected, what is the probability that the subject will get a correct result? We will address such questions in this chapter.

- **False positive:** *Wrong* result in which the test incorrectly indicates the presence of a condition when the subject does not actually have that condition.
- **False negative:** *Wrong* result in which the test incorrectly indicates that the subject does *not* have a condition when the subject actually does have that condition.
- **True positive:** *Correct* result in which the test correctly indicates that a condition is present when it really is present.
- **True negative:** *Correct* result in which the test correctly indicates that a condition is not present when it really is not present.

- **Test sensitivity:** The probability of a true positive, given that the subject actually has the condition being tested.
- **Test specificity:** The probability of a true negative, given that the subject does not have the condition being tested.
- **Positive predictive value:** Probability that a subject is a true positive, given that the test yields a positive result (indicating that the condition is present).
- **Negative predictive value:** Probability that the subject is a true negative, given that the test yields a negative result (indicating that the condition is not present).
- **Prevalence:** Proportion of subjects having some condition.

Table 4-1 Pre-Employment Drug Screening Results

	Positive Test Result (Drug Use Is Indicated)	Negative Test Result (Drug Use Is Not Indicated)
Subject Uses Drugs	44 (True Positive)	6 (False Negative)
Subject Is Not a Drug User	90 (False Positive)	860 (True Negative)

4-1   Review and Preview

The preceding chapters have presented some critically important concepts in the study and application of statistics. We have discussed the importance of sound sampling methods. We have discussed common measures of characteristics of data, including the mean and standard deviation. The main objective of this chapter is to develop a sound understanding of probability values, because those values constitute the underlying foundation on which methods of inferential statistics are built. Statisticians use the following *rare event rule for inferential statistics.*

Rare Event Rule for Inferential Statistics

If, under a given assumption, the probability of a particular observed event is extremely small, we conclude that the assumption is probably not correct.

Example 1   Rare Event Rule for Inferential Statistics

The Genetics & IVF Institute has developed a method of gender selection so that couples could increase the likelihood of having a baby girl. Instead of using some of their real results, let's use a more obvious example. Suppose that 100 couples use the procedure for trying to have a baby girl, and results consist of 98 girls and only 2 boys. We have two possible explanations for these results:

1. *Chance:* The gender-selection technique is not effective and the result of 98 girls and 2 boys occurred by random chance.

2. *Not Chance:* The results did not occur by chance, so it appears that the gender-selection technique is effective.

When choosing between the above two possible explanations, the *probability* of getting 98 girls and 2 boys is the deciding factor. Without calculating that probability, it is safe to say that it is *extremely* small. The probability of 98 girls and 2 boys is so small that the first explanation of chance would be rejected as being reasonable. Instead, it would be generally recognized that the results provide strong support for the claim that the gender-selection technique is effective. This is exactly how statisticians think: They reject explanations based on very low probabilities.

If you follow the thought process in Example 1, you understand a fundamental way of statistical thinking. Example 1 did not provide an actual probability value, and the main objective of this chapter is to develop a sound understanding of probability values that will be used in later chapters of this book. A secondary objective is to develop the basic skills necessary to determine probability values in a variety of important circumstances.

4-2 Basic Concepts of Probability

Key Concept Although this section presents three different approaches to finding the *probability* of an event, the most important objective of this section is to learn how to *interpret* probability values, which are expressed as values between 0 and 1. We should know that a small probability, such as 0.001, corresponds to an event that rarely occurs. In Part 2 of this section we discuss expressions of *odds* and how probability is used to determine the odds of an event occurring. The concepts related to odds are not needed for topics that follow, but odds are often used in some everyday situations, especially those that involve lotteries and gambling.

Part 1: Basics of Probability

In considering probability, we deal with procedures (such as answering a multiple-choice test question or undergoing a test for drug use) that produce outcomes.

> **DEFINITIONS**
>
> An **event** is any collection of results or outcomes of a procedure.
>
> A **simple event** is an outcome or an event that cannot be further broken down into simpler components.
>
> The **sample space** for a procedure consists of all possible *simple* events. That is, the sample space consists of all outcomes that cannot be broken down any further.

Example 1 illustrates the concepts defined above.

Example 1

In the following display, we use "b" to denote a baby boy and "g" to denote a baby girl.

Procedure	Example of Event	Sample Space (List of Simple Events)
Single birth	1 girl (simple event)	{b, g}
3 births	2 boys and 1 girl (bbg, bgb, and gbb are all simple events resulting in 2 boys and 1 girl)	{bbb, bbg, bgb, bgg, gbb, gbg, ggb, ggg}

With one birth, the result of 1 female is a *simple event* because it cannot be broken down any further. With three births, the event of "2 girls and 1 boy" is *not a simple event* because it can be broken down into simpler events, such as ggb, gbg, or bgg. With three births, the *sample space* consists of the eight simple events listed above. With three births, the outcome of ggb is considered a simple event, because it is an outcome that cannot be broken down any further. We might incorrectly think that ggb can be further broken down into the individual results of g, g, and b, but g, g, and b are not individual outcomes from three births. With three births, there are exactly eight outcomes that are simple events: bbb, bbg, bgb, bgg, gbb, gbg, ggb, and ggg.

We first list some basic notation, then we present three different approaches to finding the probability of an event.

Notation for Probabilities

P denotes a probability.

A, B, and *C* denote specific events.

$P(A)$ denotes the probability of event A occurring.

1. **Relative Frequency Approximation of Probability** Conduct (or observe) a procedure, and count the number of times that event *A* actually occurs. Based on these actual results, $P(A)$ is *approximated* as follows:

$$P(A) = \frac{\text{number of times } A \text{ occurred}}{\text{number of times the procedure was repeated}}$$

2. **Classical Approach to Probability (Requires Equally Likely Outcomes)** Assume that a given procedure has *n* different simple events and that *each of those simple events has an equal chance of occurring.* If event *A* can occur in *s* of these *n* ways, then

$$P(A) = \frac{\text{number of ways } A \text{ occur}}{\text{number of different simple events}} = \frac{s}{n}$$

CAUTION When using the classical approach, always verify that the outcomes are *equally likely*.

3. **Subjective Probabilities** $P(A)$, the probability of event *A,* is *estimated* by using knowledge of the relevant circumstances.

Note that the classical approach requires *equally likely outcomes.* If the outcomes are not equally likely, we must use the relative frequency approximation or we must rely on our knowledge of the circumstances to make an *educated guess.* Figure 4-1 illustrates the three approaches.

(a)

(b)

(c)

Figure 4-1   Three Approaches to Finding a Probability

(a) **Relative Frequency Approach:** When trying to determine the probability that an individual car crashes in a year, we must examine past results to determine the number of cars in use in a year and the number of them that crashed; then we find the ratio of the number of cars that crashed to the total number of cars. For a recent year, the result is a probability of 0.0480. (See Example 2.)

(b) **Classical Approach:** When trying to determine the probability of winning the grand prize in a lottery by selecting six numbers between 1 and 60, each combination has an equal chance of occurring. The probability of winning is 0.0000000200, which can be found by using methods presented in Section 4-6.

(c) **Subjective Probability:** When trying to estimate the probability of a passenger dying in a plane crash, we know that there are thousands of flights every day, but fatal plane crashes are quite rare, so the probability is very small. A good guess would be about 1 in 10 million, or 0.0000001.

When finding probabilities with the relative frequency approach, we obtain an *approximation* instead of an exact value. As the total number of observations increases, the corresponding approximations tend to get closer to the actual probability. This property is stated as a theorem commonly referred to as the *law of large numbers.*

Law of Large Numbers

As a procedure is repeated again and again, the relative frequency probability of an event tends to approach the actual probability.

The law of large numbers tells us that relative frequency approximations tend to get better with more observations. This law reflects a simple notion supported by common sense: A probability estimate based on only a few trials can be off by a substantial amount, but with a very large number of trials, the estimate tends to be much more accurate.

CAUTION The law of large numbers applies to behavior over a large number of trials, and it does not apply to one outcome. Don't make the foolish mistake of losing large sums of money by incorrectly thinking that a string of losses increases the chances of a win on the next bet.

Probability and Outcomes That Are Not Equally Likely One common mistake is to incorrectly assume that outcomes are equally likely just because we know nothing about the likelihood of each outcome. When we know nothing about the likelihood of different possible outcomes, we cannot necessarily assume that they are equally likely. For example, we should not conclude that the probability of passing the next statistics test is $1/2$, or 0.5 (because we either pass the test or do not). The actual probability depends on factors such as the amount of preparation and the difficulty of the test.

Example 2   Relative Frequency Probability: Smoking

A recent Harris Interactive survey of 1010 adults in the United States showed that 202 of them smoke. Find the probability that a randomly selected adult in the United States is a smoker.

Solution

We use the relative frequency approach as follows:

$$P(\text{smoker}) = \frac{\text{number of smokers}}{\text{total number of people surveyed}} = \frac{202}{1010} = 0.200$$

Note that the classical approach cannot be used since the two outcomes (smoker, not a smoker) are not equally likely.

Example 3   Classical Probability: Positive Test Result

Refer to Table 4-1 included with the Chapter Problem. Assuming that one of the 1000 subjects included in Table 4-1 is randomly selected, find the probability that the selected subject got a positive test result.

Solution

The sample space consists of results from 1000 subjects listed in Table 4-1. Among the 1000 results, 134 of them are positive test results (found from 44 + 90). Because

Winning the Lottery

In the New York State Lottery Mega Millions game, you select five numbers from 1 to 56, then you select another "Mega Ball" number from 1 to 46. To win, you must get the correct five numbers *and* the correct Mega Ball number. The chance of winning this lottery with one ticket is 1/175,711,536, even though commercials for this lottery state that "all you need is a little bit of luck." The probability of 1/175,711,536 is not easily perceived by many people, so let's consider a helpful analogy developed by Brother Donald Kelly of Marist College. A stack of 175,711,536 dimes is about 154 miles high. Commercial jets typically fly about 7 miles high, so this stack of dimes is about 22 times taller than the height of a commercial jet when it is at cruising altitude. The chance of winning the Mega Millions lottery game is equivalent to the chance of randomly selecting *one* specific dime from that pile of dimes that is 154 miles high. Any of us who spend money on this lottery should understand that the chance of winning the grand prize is very, very, very close to zero.

How Probable?

How do we interpret such terms as *probable, improbable,* or *extremely improbable*? The FAA interprets these terms as follows.

- *Probable:* A probability on the order of 0.00001 or greater for each hour of flight. Such events are expected to occur several times during the operational life of each airplane.

- *Improbable:* A probability on the order of 0.00001 or less. Such events are not expected to occur during the total operational life of a single airplane of a particular type, but may occur during the total operational life of all airplanes of a particular type.

- *Extremely improbable:* A probability on the order of 0.000000001 or less. Such events are so unlikely that they need not be considered to ever occur.

the subject is randomly selected, each test result is equally likely, so we can apply the classical approach as follows:

$$P(\text{positive test result from Table 4-1}) = \frac{\text{number of positive test results}}{\text{total number of results}}$$

$$= \frac{134}{1000} = 0.134$$

Example 4   Classical Probability: Three Children of the Same Gender

When three children are born, the sample space of genders is as shown in Example 1: {bbb, bbg, bgb, bgg, gbb, gbg, ggb, ggg}. If boys and girls are equally likely, then the eight simple events are equally likely. Assuming that boys and girls are equally likely, find the probability of getting three children all of the same gender when three children are born. (In reality, a boy is slightly more likely than a girl.)

Solution

The sample space {bbb, bbg, bgb, bgg, gbb, gbg, ggb, ggg} in this case includes equally likely outcomes. Among the eight outcomes, there are exactly two in which the three children are of the same gender: bbb and ggg. We can use the classical approach to get

$$P(\text{three children of the same gender}) = \frac{2}{8} = 0.25$$

Example 5   Subjective Probability: Professorial Attire

Find the probability that in your next statistics class, the professor wears a hat with a huge feather protruding from the top.

Solution

The sample space consists of two simple events: Your professor wears a hat with a huge feather protruding from the top, or does not. We can't use the relative frequency approach because we lack data on past results. We can't use the classical approach because the two possible outcomes are events that are not equally likely. We are left with making a subjective estimate. The event is possible, but highly unlikely, so we can estimate its probability as something like 0.000001.

Example 6   Subjective Probability: Stuck in an Elevator

What is the probability that you will get stuck in the next elevator that you ride?

Solution

In the absence of historical data on elevator failures, we cannot use the relative frequency approach. There are two possible outcomes (becoming stuck or not becoming stuck), but they are not equally likely, so we cannot use the classical approach. That leaves us with a subjective estimate. In this case, experience suggests that the probability is quite small. Let's estimate it to be, say, 0.0001 (equivalent to 1 chance in 10,000). That subjective estimate, based on our general knowledge, is likely to be in the general ballpark of the true probability.

CAUTION Don't make the mistake of finding a probability value by mindlessly dividing a smaller number by a larger number. Instead, think carefully about the numbers involved and what they represent. Be especially careful when determining the total number of items being considered, as in the following example.

Example 7 **Tainted Currency**

In a study of U.S. paper currency, bills from 17 large cities were analyzed for the presence of cocaine. Here are the results: 23 of the bills were not tainted by cocaine and 211 were tainted by cocaine. Based on these results, if a bill is randomly selected, find the probability that it is tainted by cocaine.

Solution

Hint: Instead of trying to determine an answer directly from the printed statement, begin by first summarizing the given information in a format that allows you to clearly understand the information. For example, use this format:

$$
\begin{array}{ll}
23 & \text{bills not tainted by cocaine} \\
\underline{211} & \underline{\text{bills tainted by cocaine}} \\
234 & \text{total number of bills analyzed}
\end{array}
$$

We can now use the relative frequency approach as follows:

$$
P(\text{bill tainted by cocaine}) = \frac{\text{number of bills tainted by cocaine}}{\text{total number of bills analyzed}} = \frac{211}{234}
$$
$$
= 0.902
$$

Interpretation

There is a 0.902 probability that if a U.S. bill is randomly selected, it is tainted by cocaine.

Simulations The statements of the three approaches for finding probabilities and the preceding examples might seem to suggest that we should always use the classical approach when a procedure has equally likely outcomes, but many situations are so complicated that the classical approach is impractical. In the game of solitaire, for example, the outcomes (hands dealt) are all equally likely, but it is extremely difficult to try to use the classical approach to find the probability of winning. In such cases we can more easily get good estimates by using the relative frequency approach, and simulations are often helpful when using this approach. A *simulation* of a procedure is a process that behaves in the same ways as the procedure itself so that similar results are produced. (See the Technology Project near the end of this chapter.) For example, it's much easier to use the relative frequency approach for approximating the probability of winning at solitaire—that is, to play the game many times (or to run a computer simulation)—than to perform the complex calculations required with the classical approach.

Example 8 **Thanksgiving Day**

If a year is selected at random, find the probability that Thanksgiving Day in the United States will be (a) on a Wednesday or (b) on a Thursday.

Simulations in Baseball

Simulations are being used to identify the most effective strategies in a variety of circumstances that occur in baseball. On this topic, *New York Times* reporter Alan Schwarz quoted Harvard University statistician Carl Morris as saying that "computer simulations work pretty well in baseball for two reasons. In general, they allow you to study fairly complicated processes that you can't really get at with pure mathematics. But also, sports are great for simulations—you can play 10,000 seasons overnight." Many baseball teams now use simulations to help them decide which players should be traded.

Here are some strategies suggested by computer simulations of baseball:

- It is not wise to intentionally walk a player.
- The sacrifice bunt should be used very rarely.

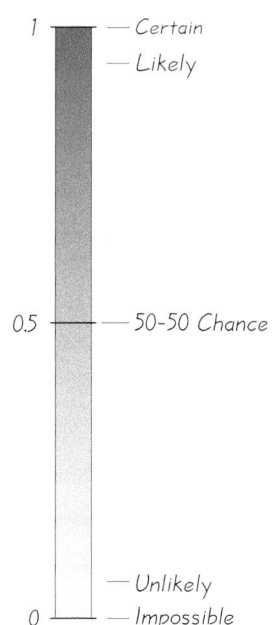

> **Solution**
>
> **a.** In the United States, Thanksgiving Day always falls on the fourth Thursday in November. It is therefore impossible for Thanksgiving to be on a Wednesday. When an event is impossible, we say that its probability is 0.
>
> **b.** It is certain that Thanksgiving will be on a Thursday. When an event is certain to occur, we say that its probability is 1.
>
> Because any event imaginable is impossible, certain, or somewhere in between, it follows that the mathematical probability of any event A is 0, 1, or a number between 0 and 1 (see Figure 4-2). That is, $0 \leq P(A) \leq 1$.

Figure 4-2 shows the possible values of probabilities and the more familiar and common expressions of likelihood.

1 — Certain
— Likely

0.5 — 50-50 Chance

— Unlikely
0 — Impossible

Figure 4-2 Possible Values for Probabilities

Complementary Events

Sometimes we need to find the probability that an event A does *not* occur.

> **DEFINITION** The **complement** of event A, denoted by $\overline{A}$, consists of all outcomes in which event A does *not* occur.

Example 9   Complement of Smoker

Results from Example 2 show that if we randomly select an adult in the United States, the probability of selecting a smoker is 0.200. Find the probability of randomly selecting an adult in the United States and getting someone who does *not* smoke.

> **Solution**
>
> Because 202 of the 1010 surveyed adults in the United States are smokers, it follows that the other 808 are not smokers, so
>
> $$P(\text{not a smoker}) = \frac{808}{1010} = 0.800$$

> **Interpretation**
>
> The probability of randomly selecting an adult in the United States and getting someone who is *not* a smoker is 0.800.

Although it is difficult to develop a universal rule for rounding off probabilities, the following guide will apply to most problems in this text.

Rounding Off Probabilities

When expressing the value of a probability, either give the *exact* fraction or decimal or round off final decimal results to three significant digits. (*Suggestion:* When a probability is not a simple fraction such as 2/3 or 5/9, express it as a decimal so that the number can be better understood.) All digits in a number are significant except for the zeros that are included for proper placement of the decimal point.

Example 10 Rounding Probabilities

- The probability of 0.9017094017 (from Example 7) has ten significant digits (9017094017), and it can be rounded to three significant digits as 0.902.

- The probability of 1/3 can be left as a fraction or rounded to 0.333. (Do *not* round to 0.3.)

- The probability of 2/8 (from Example 4) can be expressed as 1/4 or 0.25; because 0.25 is exact, there's no need to express it with three significant digits as 0.250.

The mathematical expression of probability as a number between 0 and 1 is fundamental and common in statistical procedures, and we will use it throughout the remainder of this text. A typical computer output, for example, may include a "*P*-value" expression such as "significance less than 0.001." We will discuss the meaning of *P*-values later, but they are essentially probabilities of the type discussed in this section. For now, you should recognize that a probability of 0.001 (equivalent to 1/1000) corresponds to an event so rare that it occurs an average of only once in a thousand trials. Example 12 involves the interpretation of such a small probability value.

Interpreting Probabilities: *Unlikely* Events and *Unusual* Events

We can consider an event with a small probability (such as 0.05 or less) to be *unlikely*. But we often need to determine when an event consists of an *unusually high* number of outcomes of a particular type or an *unusually low* number of such outcomes. An event has a number of particular outcomes that is unusually low or unusually high if that number is *extreme* in the sense that it is far from the number that we typically expect. The following definitions are not standard with universal use, but they are very helpful in interpreting probability values and developing concepts used extensively in later chapters.

> **DEFINITIONS** An event is **unlikely** if its probability is very small, such as 0.05 or less. (See Figure 4-2.) An event has an **unusually low number** of outcomes of a particular type or an **unusually high number** of those outcomes if that number is far from what we typically expect.

Unlikely: Small probability (such as 0.05 or less)

Unusual: Extreme result (number of outcomes of a particular type is far below or far above the typical values)

By associating "unusual" with *extreme* outcomes, we are consistent with the range rule of thumb (Section 3-3) and the use of *z* scores for identifying unusual values (Section 3-4).

Example 11 Unlikely/Unlikely

a. When a fair coin is tossed 1000 times, the result consists of exactly 500 heads. The probability of getting exactly 500 heads in 1000 tosses is 0.0252. Is this result unlikely? Is 500 heads unusually low or unusually high?

b. When a fair coin is tossed 1000 times, the result consists of 10 heads. Is this result unlikely? Is 10 heads unusually low or unusually high?

How Many Shuffles?

After conducting extensive research, Harvard mathematician Persi Diaconis found that it takes seven shuffles of a deck of cards to get a complete mixture. The mixture is complete in the sense that all possible arrangements are equally likely. More than seven shuffles will not have a significant effect, and fewer than seven are not enough. Casino dealers rarely shuffle as often as seven times, so the decks are not completely mixed. Some expert card players have been able to take advantage of the incomplete mixtures that result from fewer than seven shuffles.

Gambling to Win

In the typical state lottery, the "house" has a 65% to 70% advantage, since only 30% to 35% of the money bet is returned as prizes. The house advantage at race-tracks is usually around 15%. In casinos, the house advantage is 5.26% for roulette, 1.4% for craps, and 3% to 22% for slot machines.

The house advantage is 5.9% for blackjack, but some professional gamblers can systematically win with a 1% player advantage by using complicated card-counting techniques that require many hours of practice. If a card-counting player were to suddenly change from small bets to large bets, the dealer would recognize the card counting and the player would be ejected. Card counters try to beat this policy by working with a team. When the count is high enough, the player signals an accomplice who enters the game with large bets. A group of MIT students supposedly won millions of dollars by counting cards in blackjack.

Solution

a. Because the probability of exactly 500 heads in 1000 tosses is 0.0252, that result is *unlikely*. However, we usually get around 500 heads, so this outcome is neither unusually low nor unusually high.

b. Without actually finding the exact probability value, it is reasonable to conclude that there is a very low probability of getting 10 heads in 1000 tosses of a fair coin, so this event is unlikely. Also, the outcome of 10 heads is so far below the number of heads we typically expect (around 500), we conclude that this is an unusually low number of heads.

Example 11 considers the result of 500 heads in 1000 tosses and the result of 10 heads in 1000 tosses. Figure 4-3 is a graph of the probabilities for all possible numbers of heads in 1000 tosses. (Such a graph of outcomes and their probabilities is called a *probability histogram,* and it is formally defined in Section 5-2.) From Figure 4-3 we see that every individual number of heads is *unlikely,* because its probability is small (0.0252 or less). The red shaded regions show those outcomes that are *unusually low* or *unusually high,* because they are so far away from the outcomes that we typically expect (around 500). In Chapter 5 we will develop methods for finding the cumulative probabilities corresponding to such unusually low and unusually high numbers of outcomes. For the results shown in Figure 4-3, the probability of getting any number of heads that is unusually low or unusually high is less than 0.05.

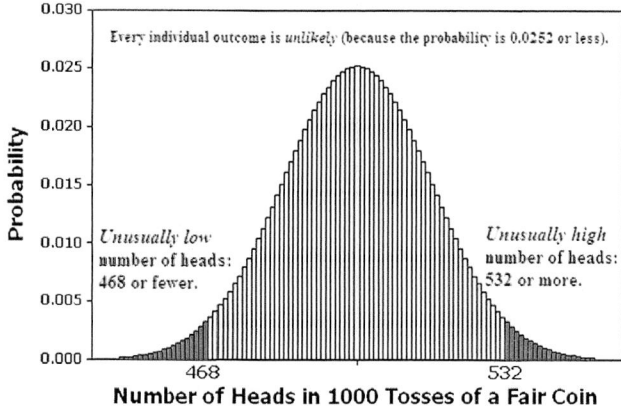

Figure 4-3   Graph of Outcomes and Their Probabilities

Section 4-1 introduced the rare event rule, and that rule is the focus of the next example.

Example 12   Rare Event Rule

In a clinical experiment of the Salk vaccine for polio, 200,745 children were given a placebo and 201,229 other children were treated with the Salk vaccine. There were 115 cases of polio among those in the placebo group and 33 cases of polio in the treatment group. If we assume that the vaccine has no effect, the probability of getting such test results is found to be "less than 0.001." What does that probability imply about the effectiveness of the vaccine?

Solution

A probability value less than 0.001 is very small. It indicates that the event will occur fewer than once in a thousand times, so it is very unlikely that the event will occur by chance, assuming that the vaccine has no effect. We have two possible explanations for the results of this clinical experiment: (1) The vaccine has no effect and the results occurred by chance; (2) the vaccine has an effect, which explains why the treatment group had a much lower incidence of polio. Because the probability is so small (less than 0.001), the second explanation is more reasonable. We conclude that the vaccine appears to be effective.

The preceding example illustrates the "rare event rule for inferential statistics" given in Section 4-1. Under the assumption of a vaccine with no effect, we find that the probability of the results is extremely small (less than 0.001), so we conclude that the assumption is probably not correct. The preceding example also illustrates the role of probability in making important conclusions about clinical experiments. For now, we should understand that when a probability is small, such as less than 0.001, it indicates that the event is very unlikely to occur.

The following list summarizes some key notation and principles discussed so far in this section.

Important Principles and Notation for Probability

- **The probability of an event is a fraction or decimal number between 0 and 1 inclusive.**
- **The probability of an impossible event is 0.**
- **The probability of an event that is certain to occur is 1.**
- **Notation: The probability of event A is denoted by $P(A)$.**
- **Notation: The probability that event A does *not* occur is denoted by $P(\overline{A})$.**

Part 2: Beyond the Basics of Probability: Odds

Expressions of likelihood are often given as *odds*, such as 50:1 (or "50 to 1"). Because the use of odds makes many calculations difficult, statisticians, mathematicians, and scientists prefer to use probabilities. The advantage of odds is that they make it easier to deal with money transfers associated with gambling, so they tend to be used in casinos, lotteries, and racetracks. Note that in the three definitions that follow, the *actual odds against* and the *actual odds in favor* are calculated with the actual likelihood of some event, but the *payoff odds* describe the relationship between the bet and the amount of the payoff. The actual odds correspond to actual probabilities of outcomes, but the payoff odds are set by racetrack and casino operators. Racetracks and casinos are in business to make a profit, so the payoff odds will not be the same as the actual odds.

DEFINITIONS

The **actual odds against** event A occurring are the ratio $P(\overline{A})/P(A)$, usually expressed in the form of $a{:}b$ (or "a to b"), where a and b are integers having no common factors.

The **actual odds in favor** of event A occurring are the ratio $P(A)/P(\overline{A})$, which is the reciprocal of the actual odds against that event. If the odds against A are $a{:}b$, then the odds in favor of A are $b{:}a$.

The **payoff odds** against event A occurring are the ratio of net profit (if you win) to the amount bet:

$$\text{payoff odds against event } A = (\text{net profit}){:}(\text{amount bet})$$

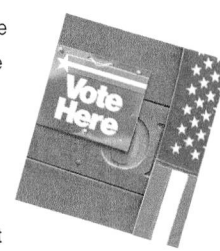

Probability of an Event That Has Never Occurred

Some events are possible, but are so unlikely that they have never occurred. Here is one such problem of great interest to political scientists: Estimate the probability that your single vote will determine the winner in a U.S. Presidential election. Andrew Gelman, Gary King, and John Boscardin write in the *Journal of the American Statistical Association* (Vol. 93, No. 441) that "the exact value of this probability is of only minor interest, but the number has important implications for understanding the optimal allocation of campaign resources, whether states and voter groups receive their fair share of attention from prospective presidents, and how formal 'rational choice' models of voter behavior might be able to explain why people vote at all." The authors show how the probability value of 1 in 10 million is obtained for close elections.

The Random Secretary

One classical problem of probability goes like this: A secretary addresses 50 different letters and envelopes to 50 different people, but the letters are randomly mixed before being put into envelopes. What is the probability that at least one letter gets into the correct envelope? Although the probability might seem like it should be small, it's actually 0.632. Even with a million letters and a million envelopes, the probability is 0.632. The solution is beyond the scope of this text—way beyond.

Example 13

If you bet $5 on the number 13 in roulette, your probability of winning is $1/38$ and the payoff odds are given by the casino as 35:1.

a. Find the actual odds against the outcome of 13.

b. How much net profit would you make if you win by betting on 13?

c. If the casino was not operating for profit and the payoff odds were changed to match the actual odds against 13, how much would you win if the outcome were 13?

Solution

a. With $P(13) = 1/38$ and $P(\text{not } 13) = 37/38$, we get

$$\text{actual odds against } 13 = \frac{P(\text{not } 13)}{P(13)} = \frac{37/38}{1/38} = \frac{37}{1} \text{ or } 37{:}1$$

b. Because the payoff odds against 13 are 35:1, we have

$$35{:}1 = (\text{net profit}){:}(\text{amount bet})$$

So there is a $35 profit for each $1 bet. For a $5 bet, the net profit is $175. The winning bettor would collect $175 plus the original $5 bet. After winning, the total amount collected would be $180, for a net profit of $175.

c. If the casino were not operating for profit, the payoff odds would be changed to 37:1, which are the actual odds against the outcome of 13. With payoff odds of 37:1, there is a net profit of $37 for each $1 bet. For a $5 bet the net profit would be $185. (The casino makes its profit by paying only $175 instead of the $185 that would be paid with a roulette game that is fair instead of favoring the casino.)

4-2 Basic Skills and Concepts

Statistical Literacy and Critical Thinking

1. Florida Lottery Let A denote the event of placing a $1 straight bet on the Florida Play 4 lottery and winning. The chance of event A occurring is 1 in 10,000. What is the value of $P(A)$? What is the value of $P(\overline{A})$?

2. Probability Given that the following statement is incorrect, rewrite it correctly: "The probability of a baby being born a boy is 50–50."

3. Interpreting Weather While this exercise was being created, Weather.com indicated that there was a 20% chance of rain for the author's home region. Based on that report, which of the following is the most reasonable interpretation?

a. 1/5 of the author's region will get rain today.

b. In the author's region, it will rain for 1/5 of the day.

c. In the author's region, there is a 1/5 probability that it will rain at some point during the day.

4. Subjective Probability Estimate the probability that the next time you ride in a car, you will *not* be delayed because of some car crash blocking the road.

5. Identifying Probability Values Which of the following values are *not* probabilities?

5:2   3/7   7/3   −0.9   0.123   123/456   456/123   0   1

6. U.S. President "Who was the 14th president of the United States: Taylor, Fillmore, Pierce, or Buchanan?" If you make a random guess for the answer to that question, what is the probability that your answer is the correct answer of Pierce?

7. Digits of Pi "Which of the following is the mean of the first 100 digits of pi after the decimal point: 4.4, 4.5, 4.6, 4.7, or 4.8?" If you make a random guess for the answer to that question, what is the probability that your answer is the correct answer of 4.8?

8. The Die Is Cast When rolling a single die, what is the probability that the outcome is 7?

In Exercises 9–12, assume that 400 births are randomly selected. Use subjective judgment to determine whether the given outcome is unlikely, and also determine whether it is unusual in the sense that the result is far from what is typically expected.

9. Exactly 205 girls.   **10.** Exactly 380 girls.

11. Exactly 111 girls.   **12.** Exactly 197 girls.

In Exercises 13–20, express the indicated degree of likelihood as a probability value between 0 and 1.

13. Traffic Light When arriving at the traffic light closest to the author's home, there is a 25% chance that the light will be red.

14. Weather While this exercise was being created, Weather.com indicated that there is a 20% chance of rain for the author's home region.

15. Testing If you make a random guess for the answer to a true/false test question, there is a 50–50 chance of being correct.

16. Pierced Ears Based on a Harris poll, there is a 50–50 chance that a randomly selected adult has pierced ears.

17. SAT Test When guessing the answer to a multiple-choice question on an SAT test, the chance of guessing correctly is 1 in 5.

18. Dice When rolling a pair of dice at the Bellagio Casino in Las Vegas, there is 1 chance in 36 that the outcome is a 12.

19. Statistics Test It is impossible to pass a statistics test without studying.

20. Death and Taxes Benjamin Franklin said that death is a certainty of life.

 In Exercises 21–24, refer to the sample data in Table 4-1, which is included with the Chapter Problem. Assume that one of the subjects included in Table 4-1 is randomly selected.

21. Pre-Employment Drug Screening Find the probability of selecting someone who got a result that is a false negative. Who would suffer from a false negative result? Why?

22. Pre-Employment Drug Screening Find the probability of selecting someone who got a result that is a false positive. Who would suffer from a false positive result? Why?

23. Pre-Employment Drug Screening Find the probability of selecting someone who uses drugs. Is the result close to the probability of 0.134 for a positive test result?

24. Pre-Employment Drug Screening Find the probability of selecting someone who does not use drugs. Is the result close to the probability of 0.866 for a negative test result?

25. XSORT Gender Selection MicroSort's XSORT gender-selection technique is designed to increase the likelihood that a baby will be a girl. In updated results (as of this writing) of the XSORT gender-selection technique, 945 births consisted of 879 baby girls and 66 baby boys (based on data from the Genetics & IVF Institute). Based on these results, what is the probability of a girl born to a couple using MicroSort's XSORT method? Does it appear that the technique is effective in increasing the likelihood that a baby will be a girl?

26. YSORT Gender Selection MicroSort's YSORT gender-selection technique is designed to increase the likelihood that a baby will be a boy. In updated results (as of this writing) from a test of MicroSort's YSORT gender-selection technique, 291 births consisted of 239 baby boys and 52 baby girls (based on data from the Genetics & IVF Institute). Based on these results, what is the probability of a boy born to a couple using MicroSort's YSORT method? Does it appear that the technique is effective in increasing the likelihood that a baby will be a boy?

27. Struck by Lightning In a recent year, 304 of the approximately 300,000,000 people in the United States were struck by lightning. Estimate the probability that a randomly selected person in the United States will be struck by lightning this year. Is a golfer reasoning correctly if he or she is caught out in a thunderstorm and does not seek shelter from lightning because the probability of being struck is so small?

28. Mendelian Genetics When Mendel conducted his famous genetics experiments with peas, one sample of offspring consisted of 428 green peas and 152 yellow peas. Based on those results, estimate the probability of getting an offspring pea that is green. Is the result reasonably close to the expected value of 3/4, as claimed by Mendel?

Using Probability to Identify Unlikely Events. *In Exercises 29–36, consider an event to be "unlikely" if its probability is less than or equal to 0.05. (This is equivalent to the same criterion commonly used in inferential statistics, but the value of 0.05 is not absolutely rigid, and other values such as 0.01 are sometimes used instead.)*

29. Guessing Birthdays On their first date, Kelly asks Mike to guess the date of her birth, not including the year.

a. What is the probability that Mike will guess correctly? (Ignore leap years.)

b. Would it be unlikely for him to guess correctly on his first try?

c. If you were Kelly, and Mike did guess correctly on his first try, would you believe his claim that he made a lucky guess, or would you be convinced that he already knew when you were born?

d. If Kelly asks Mike to guess her age, and Mike's guess is too high by 15 years, what is the probability that Mike and Kelly will have a second date?

30. Credit Card Purchases In a survey, 169 respondents say that they never use a credit card, 1227 say that they use it sometimes, and 2834 say that they use it frequently. What is the probability that a randomly selected person uses a credit card frequently? Is it unlikely for someone to use a credit card frequently? How are all of these results affected by the fact that the responses were obtained by those who decided to respond to the survey posted on the Internet by America OnLine?

31. Car Crashes In a recent year, among 135,933,000 registered passenger cars in the United States, there were 10,427,000 crashes. Find the probability that a randomly selected passenger car in the United States will crash this year. Is it unlikely for a car to crash in a given year? What does this suggest about driving?

32. Air Travel Fatalities One measure of air travel safety is this: There are 117 fatalities per billion passenger flights. Express that measure as a probability. Is it unlikely for an air passenger to be a fatality? How does air travel compare to the car fatality rate of 40 fatalities per billion trips? Is this comparison fair?

33. Texting While Driving In a *New York Times*/CBS News poll, respondents were asked if it should be legal or illegal to send a text message while driving. Eight said that it should be legal and 804 said that it should be illegal. What is the probability of randomly selecting someone who believes it should be legal to text while driving? Is it unlikely to randomly select someone with that belief?

34. Cell Phones While Driving In a *New York Times*/CBS News poll, respondents were asked if it should be legal or illegal to use hand-held cell phones while driving. One hundred forty-one said that it should be legal, and 663 said that it should be illegal. What is the probability of randomly selecting someone who believes it should be legal to use a hand-held cell phone while driving? Is it unlikely to randomly select someone with that belief?

35. Favorite Seat on a Plane Among respondents asked which is their favorite seat on a plane, 492 chose the window seat, 8 chose the middle seat, and 306 chose the aisle seat (based on data from *USA Today*). What is the probability that a passenger prefers the middle seat? Is is unlikely for a passenger to prefer the middle seat? If so, why do you think the middle seat is so unpopular?

36. At the End of the Day In a Marist poll, respondents chose the most annoying phrases used in conversation. Nineteen chose "at the end of the day," 441 chose "whatever," 235 chose "you know," 103 chose "it is what it is," 66 chose "anyway," and 75 were unsure. Based on these results, what is the probability of selecting someone who considers "at the end of the day" to be the most annoying phrase? At the end of the day, is it unlikely to select someone with that choice?

Probability from a Sample Space. *In Exercises 37–42, use the given sample space or construct the required sample space to find the indicated probability.*

37. Three Children Use this sample space listing the eight simple events that are possible when a couple has three children (as in Example 1): {bbb, bbg, bgb, bgg, gbb, gbg, ggb, ggg}. Assume that boys and girls are equally likely, so that the eight simple events are equally likely. Find the probability that when a couple has three children, there is exactly one girl.

38. Three Children Using the same sample space and assumption from Exercise 37, find the probability that when a couple has three children, there are exactly two girls.

39. Two Children Exercise 37 lists the sample space for a couple having three children. First identify the sample space for a couple having two children, then find the probability of getting one child of each gender. Again assume that boys and girls are equally likely.

40. Four Children Exercise 37 lists the sample space for a couple having three children. First identify the sample space for a couple having four children, then find the probability of getting three girls and one boy (in any order).

41. Genetics: Eye Color Each of two parents has the genotype brown/blue, which consists of the pair of alleles that determine eye color, and each parent contributes one of those alleles to a child. Assume that if the child has at least one brown allele, that color will dominate and the eyes will be brown. (The actual determination of eye color is somewhat more complicated.)

a. List the different possible outcomes. Assume that these outcomes are equally likely.

b. What is the probability that a child of these parents will have the blue/blue genotype?

c. What is the probability that the child will have brown eyes?

42. X-Linked Genetic Disease Men have XY (or YX) chromosomes and women have XX chromosomes. X-linked recessive genetic diseases (such as juvenile retinoschisis) occur when there is a defective X chromosome that occurs *without* a paired X chromosome that is good. In the following, represent a defective X chromosome with lowercase x, so a child with the xY or Yx pair of chromosomes will have the disease and a child with XX or XY or YX or xX or Xx will not have the disease. Each parent contributes one of the chromosomes to the child.

a. If a father has the defective x chromosome and the mother has good XX chromosomes, what is the probability that a son will inherit the disease?

b. If a father has the defective x chromosome and the mother has good XX chromosomes, what is the probability that a daughter will inherit the disease?

c. If a mother has one defective x chromosome and one good X chromosome and the father has good XY chromosomes, what is the probability that a son will inherit the disease?

d. If a mother has one defective x chromosome and one good X chromosome and the father has good XY chromosomes, what is the probability that a daughter will inherit the disease?

4-2 Beyond the Basics

Odds. *In Exercises 43–46, answer the given questions that involve odds.*

43. Texas Pick 3 In the Texas Pick 3 lottery, you can bet $1 by selecting the exact order of three digits between 0 and 9 inclusive, so the probability of winning is 1/1000. If the same three numbers are drawn in the same order, you collect $500, so your net profit is $499.

a. Find the actual odds against winning.

b. Find the payoff odds.

c. The web site www.txlottery.org indicates "Odds 1:1000" for this bet. Is that description accurate?

44. Finding Odds in Roulette A roulette wheel has 38 slots. One slot is 0, another is 00, and the others are numbered 1 through 36, respectively. You place a bet that the outcome is an odd number.

a. What is your probability of winning?

b. What are the actual odds against winning?

c. When you bet that the outcome is an odd number, the payoff odds are 1:1. How much profit do you make if you bet $18 and win?

d. How much profit would you make on the $18 bet if you could somehow convince the casino to change its payoff odds so that they are the same as the actual odds against winning? (*Recommendation:* Don't actually try to convince any casino of this; their sense of humor is remarkably absent when it comes to things of this sort.)

45. Kentucky Derby Odds When the horse Super Saver won the 136th Kentucky Derby, a $2 bet that Super Saver would win resulted in a return of $18.

a. How much net profit was made from a $2 win bet on Super Saver?

b. What were the payoff odds against a Super Saver win?

c. Based on preliminary wagering before the race, bettors collectively believed that Super Saver had a 0.093 probability of winning. Assuming that 0.093 was the true probability of a Super Saver victory, what were the actual odds against his winning?

d. If the payoff odds were the actual odds found in part (c), how much would a $2 win ticket be worth after the Super Saver win?

46. Finding Probability from Odds If the actual odds against event A are $a{:}b$, then $P(A) = b/(a + b)$. Find the probability of the horse Make Music for Me winning the 136th Kentucky Derby, given that the actual odds against his winning that race were 36:1.

47. Relative Risk and Odds Ratio In a clinical trial of 2103 subjects treated with Nasonex, 26 reported headaches. In a control group of 1671 subjects given a placebo, 22 reported headaches. Denoting the proportion of headaches in the treatment group by p_t and denoting the proportion of headaches in the control (placebo) group by p_c, the *relative risk* is p_t/p_c. The relative risk is a measure of the strength of the effect of the Nasonex treatment. Another such measure is the *odds ratio,* which is the ratio of the odds in favor of a headache for the treatment group to the odds in favor of a headache for the control (placebo) group, found by evaluating the following:

$$\frac{p_t/(1 - p_t)}{p_c/(1 - p_c)}$$

The relative risk and odds ratios are commonly used in medicine and epidemiological studies. Find the relative risk and odds ratio for the headache data. What do the results suggest about the risk of a headache from the Nasonex treatment?

48. Flies on an Orange If two flies land on an orange, find the probability that they are on points that are within the same hemisphere.

49. Points on a Stick Two points along a straight stick are randomly selected. The stick is then broken at those two points. Find the probability that the three resulting pieces can be arranged to form a triangle. (This is possibly the most difficult exercise in this book.)

4-3 Addition Rule

Key Concept In this section we present the *addition rule* as a tool for finding $P(A \text{ or } B)$, which is the probability that either event A occurs or event B occurs (or they both occur) as the single outcome of a procedure. To find the probability of event A occurring or event B occurring, we begin by adding the number of ways that A can occur and the number of ways that B can occur, but we add without double counting. That is, we do not count any outcomes more than once. The key word in this section is *or*, which generally indicates *addition* of probabilities. Throughout this text we use the *inclusive or,* which means either one or the other or both. (Except for Exercise 41, we do not consider the *exclusive or,* which means either one or the other but not both.)

In Section 4-2 we presented the basics of probability and considered events categorized as *simple* events. In this and the following section we consider *compound events.*

> **DEFINITION** A **compound event** is any event combining two or more simple events.

Notation for Addition Rule

$P(A \text{ or } B) = P(\text{in a single trial, event } A \text{ occurs or event } B \text{ occurs or they both occur})$

In Section 4-2 we considered simple events, such as the probability of getting a false positive when 1 test result is randomly selected from the 1000 test results listed in Table 4-1, reproduced on the next page for the convenience and pleasure of the reading audience. In Example 1 we consider $P(\text{positive test result } or \text{ a subject uses drugs})$ when 1 of the 1000 test results is randomly selected. Follow the reasoning used in Example 1 and you will have a basic understanding of the addition rule that is the focus of this section.

Coincidences?

John Adams and Thomas Jefferson (the second and third presidents) both died on July 4, 1826. President Lincoln was assassinated in Ford's Theater; President Kennedy was assassinated in a Lincoln car made by the Ford Motor Company. Lincoln and Kennedy were both succeeded by vice presidents named Johnson. Fourteen years *before* the sinking of the *Titanic,* a novel described the sinking of the *Titan,* a ship that hit an iceberg; see Martin Gardner's *The Wreck of the Titanic Foretold?* Gardner states, "In most cases of startling coincidences, it is impossible to make even a rough estimate of their probability."

Table 4-1 Pre-Employment Drug Screening Results*		
	Positive Test Result (Drug Use Is Indicated)	Negative Test Result (Drug Use Is Not Indicated)
Subject Uses Drugs	**44** (True Positive)	6 (False Negative)
Subject Is Not a Drug User	**90** (False Positive)	860 (True Negative)

Numbers in bold correspond to positive test results or subjects who use drugs, and the total of those numbers is 140.

Example 1 Pre-Employment Drug Screening

Refer to Table 4-1. If 1 subject is randomly selected from the 1000 subjects given a drug test, find the probability of selecting a subject who had a positive test result or uses drugs. This probability is denoted by P(positive test result or subject uses drugs).

Solution

Refer to Table 4-1 and carefully count the number of subjects who tested positive (first column) or use drugs (first row), but be careful to count subjects once, not twice. *When adding the frequencies from the first column and the first row, include the frequency of 44 only once.* In Table 4-1, there are 140 subjects who had positive test results or use drugs. We get this result:

$$P(\text{positive test result or subject uses drugs}) = 140/1000 = 0.140$$

In Example 1, there are several ways to count the subjects who tested positive or use drugs. Any of the following would work:

• Color the cells representing subjects who tested positive or use drugs; then add the numbers in those colored cells, being careful to add each number only once. This approach yields

$$44 + 90 + 6 = 140$$

• Add the 134 subjects who tested positive to the 50 subjects who use drugs, but the total of 184 involves double counting of 44 subjects, so compensate for the double counting by subtracting the overlap consisting of the 44 subjects who were counted twice. This approach yields a result of

$$134 + 50 - 44 = 140$$

• Start with the total of 134 subjects who tested positive, then add those subjects who use drugs and were not yet included in that total to get a result of

$$134 + 6 = 140$$

Example 1 illustrates that when finding the probability of an event A or event B, use of the word *or* suggests addition, and the addition must be done without double counting.

The preceding example suggests a general rule whereby we add the number of outcomes corresponding to each of the events in question:

When finding the probability that event *A* occurs or event *B* occurs, find the total of the number of ways *A* can occur and the number of ways *B* can occur, but *find that total in such a way that no outcome is counted more than once.*

One way to formalize the rule is to add the probability of event *A* and the probability of event *B* and, if there is any overlap, compensate by subtracting the probability of outcomes that are included twice, as in the following rule.

Formal Addition Rule

$P(A \text{ or } B) = P(A) + P(B) - P(A \text{ and } B)$

where $P(A \text{ and } B)$ denotes the probability that *A* and *B* both occur at the same time as an outcome in a trial of a procedure.

Although the formal addition rule is presented as a formula, blind use of formulas is not recommended. It is generally better to *understand* the spirit of the rule and use that understanding, as follows.

Intuitive Addition Rule

To find $P(A \text{ or } B)$, find the sum of the number of ways event *A* can occur and the number of ways event *B* can occur, *adding in such a way that every outcome is counted only once.* $P(A \text{ or } B)$ is equal to that sum, divided by the total number of outcomes in the sample space.

The addition rule is simplified when the events are *disjoint*.

DEFINITION Events *A* and *B* are **disjoint** (or **mutually exclusive**) if they cannot occur at the same time. (That is, disjoint events do not overlap.)

Example 2   Disjoint Events

Example of disjoint events:

Randomly selecting someone who is a registered Democrat

Randomly selecting someone who is a registered Republican

(The selected person *cannot* be both.)

Example of events that are *not* disjoint:

Randomly selecting someone taking a statistics course

Randomly selecting someone who is a female

(The selected person *can* be both.)

Figure 4-4 shows a Venn diagram that provides a visual illustration of the formal addition rule. Figure 4-4 shows that the probability of *A* or *B* equals the probability of *A* (left circle) plus the probability of *B* (right circle) minus the probability of *A* and *B* (football-shaped middle region). This figure shows that the addition of the areas of the two circles will cause double counting of the football-shaped middle region. This is the basic concept that underlies the addition rule. Because of the relationship between the addition rule and the Venn diagram shown in Figure 4-4, the notation $P(A \cup B)$ is sometimes used in place of $P(A \text{ or } B)$. Similarly, the

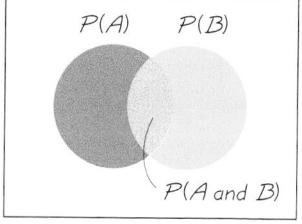

Total Area = 1

Figure 4-4   Venn Diagram for Events That Are Not Disjoint

Total Area = 1

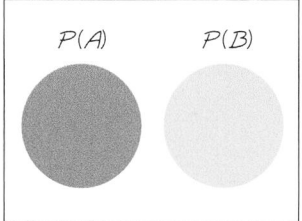

Figure 4-5   Venn Diagram for Disjoint Events

notation $P(A \cap B)$ is sometimes used in place of $P(A \text{ and } B)$, so the formal addition rule can be expressed as

$$P(A \cup B) = P(A) + P(B) - P(A \cap B)$$

Whenever A and B are disjoint, $P(A \text{ and } B)$ becomes zero in the addition rule. Figure 4-5 illustrates that when A and B are disjoint, we have $P(A \text{ or } B) = P(A) + P(B)$.

Here is a summary of the key points of this section:

1. To find $P(A \text{ or } B)$, begin by associating use of the word *or* with addition.

2. Consider whether events A and B are disjoint; that is, can they happen at the same time? If they are not disjoint (that is, they can happen at the same time), be sure to avoid (or compensate for) double counting when adding the relevant probabilities. If you understand the importance of not double counting when you find $P(A \text{ or } B)$, you don't necessarily have to calculate the value of $P(A) + P(B) - P(A \text{ and } B)$.

CAUTION Errors made when applying the addition rule often involve double counting; that is, events that are not disjoint are treated as if they were. One indication of such an error is a total probability that exceeds 1; however, errors involving the addition rule do not always cause the total probability to exceed 1.

Complementary Events and the Addition Rule

In Section 4-2 we used $\overline{A}$ to indicate that A does not occur. Common sense dictates this principle: We are certain (with probability 1) that either an event A occurs *or* it does not occur, so it follows that $P(A \text{ or } \overline{A}) = 1$. Because events A and $\overline{A}$ must be disjoint, we can use the addition rule to express that commonsense principle as follows:

$$P(A \text{ or } \overline{A}) = P(A) + P(\overline{A}) = 1$$

This result of the addition rule leads to the following three expressions that are equivalent in the sense that they are different forms of the same principle.

Total Area = 1

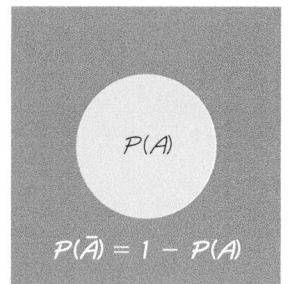

$P(A)$

$P(\overline{A}) = 1 - P(A)$

Figure 4-6   Venn Diagram for the Complement of Event A

Rule of Complementary Events

$$P(A) + P(\overline{A}) = 1 \qquad P(\overline{A}) = 1 - P(A) \qquad P(A) = 1 - P(\overline{A})$$

Figure 4-6 visually displays this relationship between $P(A)$ and $P(\overline{A})$.

Example 3   Devilish Belief

Based on data from a Harris Interactive poll, the probability of randomly selecting someone who believes in the devil is 0.6, so $P(\text{believes in the devil}) = 0.6$. If a person is randomly selected, find the probability of getting someone who does *not* believe in the devil.

Solution

Using the rule of complementary events, we get

$$P(\text{does } not \text{ believe in the devil}) = 1 - P(\text{believes in the devil}) = 1 - 0.6 = 0.4$$

The probability of randomly selecting someone who does not believe in the devil is 0.4.

A major advantage of the *rule of complementary events* is that it simplifies certain probability problems, as we illustrate in Section 4-5.

4-3 Basic Skills and Concepts

Statistical Literacy and Critical Thinking

1. Complements What is wrong with the expression $P(A) + P(\overline{A}) = 0.5$?

2. Casino Craps A gambler plans to play the casino dice game called craps, and he plans to place a bet on the "pass line." Let A be the event of winning. Based on the rules used in almost all casinos, $P(A) = 244/495$. Describe the event $\overline{A}$ and find the value of $P(\overline{A})$.

3. Disjoint Events For a Gallup poll, M is the event of randomly selecting a male, and R is the event of randomly selecting a Republican. Are events M and R disjoint? Why or why not?

4. Rule of Complements One form of the rule of complements is this: $P(A \text{ or } \overline{A}) = 1$. Write a sentence describing the message that this rule represents.

Determining Whether Events Are Disjoint. *For Exercises 5–12, determine whether the two events are disjoint for a single trial.* (**Hint: Consider "disjoint" to be equivalent to "separate" or "not overlapping."**)

5. Arriving late for your next statistics class.

Arriving early for your next statistics class.

6. Asking for a date through a Twitter post.

Asking for a date in French, the romance language.

7. Randomly selecting a survey respondent and getting someone who believes in UFOs.

Randomly selecting a survey respondent and getting someone who believes in the devil.

8. Randomly selecting a statistics student and getting one who uses a TI calculator in class.

Randomly selecting a statistics student and getting one who uses the STATDISK computer program.

9. Randomly selecting a drug screening result and getting one that is a false negative.

Randomly selecting a drug screening result and getting one from someone who is not a drug user.

10. Randomly selecting a drug screening result and getting one that is a false positive.

Randomly selecting a drug screening result and getting one from someone who uses drugs.

11. Randomly selecting a drug screening result and getting one that is a false positive.

Randomly selecting a drug screening result and getting one from someone who does not use drugs.

12. Randomly selecting a drug screening result and getting one that is a false positive.

Randomly selecting a drug screening result and getting one that is a false negative.

Finding Complements. *In Exercises 13–16, find the indicated complements.*

13. Whatever A Marist poll survey showed that 47% of respondents chose "whatever" as the most annoying phrase used in conversation. What is the probability of randomly selecting someone choosing something different from "whatever" as the most annoying phrase in conversation?

14. Online Courses According to the National Association for College Admissions Counseling and *USA Today,* 19.8% of college students take at least one class online. What is the probability of randomly selecting a college student who does not take any college courses online?

15. Flirting Survey In a Microsoft Instant Messaging survey, respondents were asked to choose the most fun way to flirt, and it found that $P(D) = 0.550$, where D is directly in person. If someone is randomly selected, what does $P(\overline{D})$ represent, and what is its value?

16. Sobriety Checkpoint When the author observed a sobriety checkpoint conducted by the Dutchess County Sheriff Department, he saw that 676 drivers were screened and 6 were arrested for driving while intoxicated. Based on those results, we can estimate that $P(I) = 0.00888$, where I denotes the event of screening a driver and getting someone who is intoxicated. What does $P(\overline{I})$ denote, and what is its value?

 In Exercises 17–20, use the drug screening data given in Table 4-1, which is included with the Chapter Problem.

17. Drug Screening If one of the test subjects is randomly selected, find the probability that the subject had a positive test result or a negative test result.

18. Drug Screening If one of the test subjects is randomly selected, find the probability that the subject had a positive test result or does not use drugs.

19. Drug Screening If one of the subjects is randomly selected, find the probability that the subject had a negative test result or does not use drugs.

20. Drug Screening If one of the subjects is randomly selected, find the probability that the subject had a negative test result or uses drugs.

Dosage Calculations. *In Exercises 21–26, use the data in the accompanying table, which lists the numbers of correct and wrong dosage amounts calculated by physicians. In a research experiment, one group of physicians was given bottles of epinephrine labeled with a concentration of "1 milligram in 1 milliliter solution," and another group of physicians was given bottles labeled with a ratio of "1 milliliter of a 1:1000 solution." The two labels describe the exact same amount, and the physicians were instructed to administer 0.12 milligrams of epinephrine. The results were reported in The New York Times.*

	Correct Dosage Calculation	Wrong Dosage Calculation
Concentration Label ("1 milligram in 1 milliliter solution")	11	3
Ratio Label ("1 milliliter of a 1:1000 solution")	2	12

21. Correct Dosage If one of the physicians is randomly selected, what is the probability of getting one who calculated the dose correctly? Is that probability as high as it should be?

22. Wrong Dosage If one of the physicians is randomly selected, what is the probability of getting one who calculated the dose incorrectly? Is that probability as low as it should be?

23. Correct or Concentration If one of the physicians is randomly selected, find the probability of getting one who made a correct dosage calculation or was given the bottle with a concentration label.

24. Wrong Dosage or Ratio If one of the physicians is randomly selected, find the probability of getting one who made a wrong dosage calculation or was given the bottle with a ratio label.

25. Which Group Did Better?

a. For the physicians given the bottles labeled with a concentration, find the percentage of correct dosage calculations, then express it as a probability.

b. For the physicians given the bottles labeled with a ratio, find the percentage of correct dosage calculations; then express it as a probability.

c. Does it appear that either group did better? What does the result suggest about drug labels?

26. Which Group Did Worse?

a. For the physicians given the bottles labeled with a concentration, find the percentage of wrong dosage calculations; then express it as a probability.

b. For the physicians given the bottles labeled with a ratio, find the percentage of wrong dosage calculations; then express it as a probability.

c. Does it appear that either group did worse? What does the result suggest about drug labels?

Survey Refusals. *In Exercises 27–32, refer to the following table summarizing results from a study of people who refused to answer survey questions (based on data from* "*I Hear You Knocking but You Can't Come In," by Fitzgerald and Fuller,* Sociological Methods and Research, *Vol. 11, No. 1). In each case, assume that one of the subjects is randomly selected.*

	Age					
	18–21	22–29	30–39	40–49	50–59	60 and over
Responded	73	255	245	136	138	202
Refused	11	20	33	16	27	49

27. Survey Refusals What is the probability that the selected person refused to answer? Does that probability value suggest that refusals are a problem for pollsters? Why or why not?

28. Survey Refusals A pharmaceutical company is interested in opinions of the elderly, because they are either receiving Medicare or will receive it soon. What is the probability that the selected subject is someone 60 and over who responded?

29. Survey Refusals What is the probability that the selected person responded or is in the 18–21 age bracket?

30. Survey Refusals What is the probability that the selected person refused to respond or is over 59 years of age?

31. Survey Refusals A market researcher is interested in responses, especially from those between the ages of 22 and 39, because they are the people more likely to make purchases. Find the probability that a selected subject responds or is between the ages of 22 and 39.

32. Survey Refusals A market researcher is not interested in refusals or subjects below 22 years of age or over 59. Find the probability that the selected person refused to answer or is below 22 or is older than 59.

In Exercises 33–38, use these results from the "1-Panel-THC" test for marijuana use, which is provided by the company Drug Test Success: Among 143 subjects with positive test results, there are 24 false positive results; among 157 negative results, there are 3 false negative results. (Hint: Construct a table similar to Table 4-1, which is included with the Chapter Problem.)

33. Screening for Marijuana Use

a. How many subjects are included in the study?

b. How many subjects did not use marijuana?

c. What is the probability that a randomly selected subject did not use marijuana?

34. Screening for Marijuana Use If one of the test subjects is randomly selected, find the probability that the subject tested positive or used marijuana.

35. Screening for Marijuana Use If one of the test subjects is randomly selected, find the probability that the subject tested negative or did not use marijuana.

36. Screening for Marijuana Use If one of the test subjects is randomly selected, find the probability that the subject actually used marijuana. Do you think that the result reflects the marijuana use rate in the general population?

37. Screening for Marijuana Use Find the probability of a false positive or false negative. What does the result suggest about the test's accuracy?

38. Screening for Marijuana Use Find the probability of a correct result by finding the probability of a true positive or a true negative. How does this result relate to the result from Exercise 37?

4-3 Beyond the Basics

39. Gender Selection When analyzing results from a test of the MicroSort gender-selection technique developed by the Genetics IVF Institute, a researcher wants to compare the results to those obtained from a coin toss. Assume that boys and girls are equally likely and find $P(G \text{ or } H)$, which is the probability of getting a baby girl *or* getting heads from a coin toss.

40. Disjoint Events If events A and B are disjoint and events B and C are disjoint, must events A and C be disjoint? Give an example supporting your answer.

41. Exclusive Or The formal addition rule expressed the probability of A or B as follows: $P(A \text{ or } B) = P(A) + (B) - P(A \text{ and } B)$. The *exclusive or* means either one or the other events occurs, but not both. Rewrite the expression for $P(A \text{ or } B)$ assuming that the addition rule uses the *exclusive or* instead of the *inclusive or*. (*Hint:* Draw a Venn diagram.)

42. Extending the Addition Rule Extend the formal addition rule to develop an expression for $P(A \text{ or } B \text{ or } C)$. (*Hint:* Draw a Venn diagram.)

43. Complements and the Addition Rule

a. Develop a formula for the probability of not getting either A or B on a single trial. That is, find an expression for $P(\overline{A \text{ or } B})$.

b. Develop a formula for the probability of not getting A or not getting B on a single trial. That is, find an expression for $P(\overline{A} \text{ or } \overline{B})$.

c. Compare the results from parts (a) and (b). Does $P(\overline{A \text{ or } B}) = P(\overline{A} \text{ or } \overline{B})$?

4-4   Multiplication Rule: Basics

Key Concept This section presents the basic multiplication rule used for finding $P(A \text{ and } B)$, which is the probability that event A occurs and event B occurs. If the outcome of event A somehow affects the probability of event B, it is important to adjust the probability of B to reflect the occurrence of event A. The rule for finding $P(A \text{ and } B)$ is called the *multiplication rule* because it involves the multiplication of the probability of event A and the probability of event B (where, if necessary, the probability of event B is adjusted because of the outcome of event A). In Section 4-3 we associated use of the word *or* with addition; in this section we associate use of the word *and* with multiplication.

We begin with basic notation followed by the multiplication rule. We strongly suggest that you focus on the *intuitive* multiplication rule, because it is based on understanding instead of blind use of a formula.

Notation

$P(A \text{ and } B) = P(\text{event } A \text{ occurs in a first trial and event } B \text{ occurs in a second trial})$

$P(B|A)$ represents the probability of event B occurring after it is assumed that event A has already occurred. (Interpret $B|A$ as "event B occurring after event A has already occurred.")

Formal Multiplication Rule

$P(A \text{ and } B) = P(A) \cdot P(B|A)$

Intuitive Multiplication Rule

To find the probability that event A occurs in one trial and event B occurs in another trial, multiply the probability of event A by the probability of event B, but *be sure that the probability of event B takes into account the previous occurrence of event A.*

When applying the multiplication rule and considering whether event B must be adjusted to account for the previous occurrence of event A, we are focusing on whether events A and B are *independent.*

DEFINITIONS Two events A and B are **independent** if the occurrence of one does not affect the *probability* of the occurrence of the other. (Several events are similarly independent if the occurrence of any does not affect the probabilities of the occurrence of the others.) If A and B are not independent, they are said to be **dependent.**

CAUTION Don't think that *dependence* of two events means that one is the direct *cause* of the other. Having a working TV in your room and having working lights in your room are dependent events (because they have the same power source), even though neither has a direct effect on the other.

In the wonderful world of statistics, sampling methods are critically important, and the following relationships hold:
- Sampling *with replacement: Selections are independent* events.
- Sampling *without replacement: Selections are dependent* events.

Exception: Treating Dependent Events as Independent

Some cumbersome calculations can be greatly simplified by using the common practice of treating events as independent when *small samples* are drawn from *large populations.* In such cases, it is rare to select the same item twice.

Here is a common guideline routinely used with applications such as analyses of survey results:

Independent Jet Engines

Soon after departing from Miami, Eastern Airlines Flight 855 had

one engine shut down because of a low oil pressure warning light. As the L-1011 jet turned to Miami for landing, the low pressure warning lights for the other two engines also flashed. Then an engine failed, followed by the failure of the last working engine. The jet descended without power from 13,000 ft to 4000 ft when the crew was able to restart one engine, and the 172 people on board landed safely. With independent jet engines, the probability of all three failing is only 0.0001^3, or about one chance in a trillion. The FAA found that the same mechanic who replaced the oil in all three engines failed to replace the oil plug sealing rings. The use of a single mechanic caused the operation of the engines to become dependent, a situation corrected by requiring that the engines be serviced by different mechanics.

Treating Dependent Events as Independent: 5% Guideline for Cumbersome Calculations

When calculations with sampling are very cumbersome and the sample size is no more than 5% of the size of the population., treat the selections as being *independent* (even if they are actually dependent).

Example 1 illustrates the basic multiplication rule, with independent events in part (a) and dependent events in part (b). Example 2 is another illustration of the multiplication rule, and part (c) of Example 2 illustrates use of the above 5% guideline for cumbersome calculations.

Example 1 Drug Screening

Let's use only the 50 test results from the subjects who use drugs (from Table 4-1), as shown below:

Positive Test Results:	44
Negative Test Results:	6
Total Results:	50

a. If 2 of the 50 subjects are randomly selected *with replacement*, find the probability that the first selected person had a positive test result and the second selected person had a negative test result.

b. Repeat part (a) by assuming that the two subjects are selected *without* replacement.

Solution

a. *With Replacement:* First selection (with 44 positive results among 50 total results):

$$P(\text{positive test result}) = \frac{44}{50}$$

Second selection (with 6 negative test results among the same 50 total results):

$$P(\text{negative test result}) = \frac{6}{50}$$

We now apply the multiplication rule as follows:

$$P(\text{1st selection is positive and 2nd is negative}) = \frac{44}{50} \cdot \frac{6}{50} = 0.106$$

b. *Without Replacement:* Without replacement of the first subject, the calculations are the same as in part (a), except that the second probability must be adjusted to reflect the fact that the first selection was positive and is not available for the second selection. After the first positive result is selected, we have 49 test results remaining, and 6 of them are negative. The second probability is therefore 6/49, as shown in the calculation below:

$$P(\text{1st selection is positive and 2nd is negative}) = \frac{44}{50} \cdot \frac{6}{49} = 0.108$$

The key point of part (b) in Example 1 is this: *We must adjust the probability of the second event to reflect the outcome of the first event.* Because selection of the second subject is made *without* replacement of the first subject, the second probability must take into account the fact that the first selection removed a subject who tested positive, so only 49 subjects are available for the second selection, and 6 of them had a negative test result.

In Example 2, we consider three situations: (a) The items are selected *with* replacement; (b) the items are selected *without* replacement, but the required calculations are not too cumbersome; (c) the items are selected *without* replacement, but the required calculations are cumbersome and the "5% guideline for cumbersome calculations" can be used.

Example 2   Airport Baggage Scales

Airport baggage scales can show that bags are overweight and high additional fees can be imposed. The New York City Department of Consumer Affairs checked all 810 scales at JFK and LaGuardia, and 102 scales were found to be defective and ordered out of use (based on data reported in *The New York Times*).

a. If 2 of the 810 scales are randomly selected *with replacement*, find the probability that they are both defective.

b. If 2 of the 810 scales are randomly selected *without replacement*, find the probability that they are both defective.

c. A larger population of 10,000 scales includes exactly 1259 defective scales. If 5 scales are randomly selected from this larger population without replacement, find the probability that all 5 are defective.

Solution

a. *With Replacement:* If the 2 scales are randomly selected *with replacement*, the two selections are independent because the second event is not affected by the first outcome. In each of the two selections there are 102 defective scales among the 810 scales available, so we get

$$P(\text{both scales are defective}) = P(\text{first is defective } and \text{ second is defective})$$

$$= P(\text{first is defective}) \cdot P(\text{second is defective})$$

$$= \frac{102}{810} \cdot \frac{102}{810} = 0.0159$$

b. *Without Replacement:* If the 2 scales are randomly selected *without replacement*, the two selections are dependent because the probability of the second event is affected by the first outcome. Being careful to adjust the second probability to reflect the result of a defect on the first selection, we get

$$P(\text{both scales are defective}) = P(\text{first is defective } and \text{ second is defective})$$

$$= P(\text{first is defective}) \cdot P(\text{second is defective})$$

$$= \frac{102}{810} \cdot \frac{101}{809} = 0.0157$$

c. With 1259 defective scales among 10,000, the exact calculation for getting 5 defective scales when 5 scales are randomly selected without replacement is cumbersome, as shown here:

$$\frac{1259}{10,000} \cdot \frac{1258}{9999} \cdot \frac{1257}{9998} \cdot \frac{1256}{9997} \cdot \frac{1255}{9996} = 0.0000314 \text{ (yuck!)}$$

Convicted by Probability

A witness described a Los Angeles robber as a Caucasian woman with blond hair in a ponytail who escaped in a yellow car driven by an African-American male with a mustache and beard. Janet and Malcolm Collins fit this description, and they were convicted based on testimony that there is only about 1 chance in 12 million that any couple would have these characteristics. It was estimated that the probability of a yellow car is 1/10, and the other probabilities were estimated to be 1/10, 1/3, 1/10, and 1/1000. The convictions were later overturned when it was noted that no evidence was presented to support the estimated probabilities or the independence of the events. However, because the couple was not randomly selected, a serious error was made in not considering the probability of *other* couples being in the same region with the same characteristics.

Instead, we can use the 5% guideline for cumbersome calculations. The sample size of 5 is less than 5% of the population of 10,000, so we can treat the events as independent, even though they are actually dependent. We get this much easier (although not quite as accurate) calculation:

$$\frac{1259}{10,000} \cdot \frac{1259}{10,000} \cdot \frac{1259}{10,000} \cdot \frac{1259}{10,000} \cdot \frac{1259}{10,000} = \left(\frac{1259}{10,000}\right)^5 = 0.0000316$$

For Example 2, the following comments are important:

• In part (b) we adjust the second probability to take into account the selection of a defective scale in the first outcome.

• In part (c) we applied the 5% guideline for cumbersome calculations.

• While parts (a) and (b) apply to two events, part (c) illustrates that the multipli-cation rule extends quite easily to more than two events.

If you're thinking that the exact calculation in part (c) of Example 2 is not all that bad, consider a pollster who randomly selects 1000 survey subjects from the 230,118,473 adults in the United States. Pollsters sample without replacement, so the selections are dependent. Instead of doing exact calculations with some *really* messy numbers, they typically treat the selections as being independent, even though they are actually dependent. The world then becomes a much better place in which to live. Apart from trying to avoid messy calculations, in statistics we have a special interest in sampling with replacement, and this will be discussed in Section 6-4.

CAUTION In any probability calculation, it is extremely important to carefully identify the event being considered. See Example 3 where parts (a) and (b) might seem quite similar, but their solutions are very different.

Example 3   **Birthdays**

When two different people are randomly selected from those in your class, find the indicated probability by assuming that birthdays occur on the days of the week with equal frequencies.

a. Find the probability that the two people are born on the *same day of the week*.

b. Find the probability that the two people are both born on *Monday*.

Solution

a. Because no particular day of the week is specified, the first person can be born on any one of the seven weekdays. The probability that the second per-son is born on the same day as the first person is 1/7. The probability that two people are born on the same day of the week is therefore 1/7.

b. The probability that the first person is born on Monday is 1/7 and the probabil-ity that the second person is also born on Monday is 1/7. Because the two events are independent, the probability that both people are born on Monday is

$$\frac{1}{7} \cdot \frac{1}{7} = \frac{1}{49}$$

Important Applications of the Multiplication Rule

The following two examples illustrate practical applications of the multiplication rule. Example 4 gives us some insight into *hypothesis testing* (which is introduced in Chapter 8), and Example 5 illustrates the principle of *redundancy*, which is used to increase the reliability of many mechanical and electrical systems.

Example 4 *Hypothesis Testing:*
Effectiveness of Gender Selection

MicroSort's XSORT gender-selection technique is designed to increase the likelihood that a baby will be a girl.

a. Assume that in a preliminary test of the XSORT technique, 20 couples gave birth to 20 babies, and all 20 babies were girl. If we were to assume that the XSORT method has no effect, what is the probability of getting 20 girl in 20 births by random chance? What does the result suggest?

b. Here are actual results of the XSORT gender-selection technique: Among 945 babies born, 879 were girls (based on data from the Genetics & IVF Institute). The probability of these results occurring by random chance with no effect from the XSORT method is calculated to be 0+, where 0+ denotes a positive probability that is so close to 0 that we can consider it to be 0 for all practical purposes. Does the probability of 0+ provide strong evidence to support a claim that the XSORT method is effective in increasing the likelihood that a baby will be a girl?

Solution

a. We want to find P(all 20 babies are girls) with the assumption that the XSORT method has no effect so that the probability of any individual offspring being a girl is 0.5. Because separate couples were used, we treat the events as being independent. We get this result:

P(all 20 babies are girls)

$= P($1st is girl and 2nd is girl and 3rd is girl $\cdots$ and 20th is girl$)$

$= P(\text{girl}) \cdot P(\text{girl}) \cdot \cdots \cdot P(\text{girl})$

$= 0.5 \cdot 0.5 \cdot \cdots \cdot 0.5$

$= 0.5^{20} = 0.000000954$

Because the probability of 0.000000954 is so small, it appears that random chance is a poor explanation. The more reasonable explanation is that use of the XSORT technique makes babies more likely to be girls.

b. The probability of getting 879 girls in 945 births is 0+, which is a small positive number that is almost 0. This shows that these results are nearly impossible if boys and girls are equally likely. These results do provide strong evidence to support a claim that the XSORT method is effective in increasing the likelihood that a baby will be a girl.

Redundancy

Reliability of systems can be greatly improved with redundancy of critical components. Race cars in the NASCAR Winston Cup series have two ignition systems so that if one fails, the other will keep the car running. Airplanes have two independent electrical systems, and aircraft used for instrument flight typically have two separate radios. The following is from a *Popular Science* article about stealth aircraft: "One plane built largely of carbon fiber was the Lear Fan 2100 which had to carry two radar transponders. That's because if a single transponder failed, the plane was nearly invisible to radar." Such redundancy is an application of the multiplication rule in probability theory. If one component has a 0.001 probability of failure, the probability of two independent components both failing is only 0.000001.

To Win, Bet Boldly

The New York Times published an article by Andrew Pollack in which he reported lower than expected earnings for the Mirage casino in Las Vegas. He wrote that "winnings for Mirage can be particularly volatile, because it caters to high rollers, gamblers who might bet $100,000 or more on a hand of cards. The law of averages does not work as consistently for a few large bets as it does for thousands of smaller ones . . ." This reflects the most fundamental principle of gambling: To win, place one big bet instead of many small bets! With the right game, such as craps, you have just under a 50% chance of doubling your money if you place one big bet. With many small bets, your chance of doubling your money drops substantially.

Example 5   Airbus 310: *Redundancy* for Better Safety

Modern aircraft are now highly reliable, and one design feature contributing to that reliability is the use of *redundancy*, whereby critical components are duplicated so that if one fails, the other will work. For example, the Airbus 310 twin-engine airliner has three independent hydraulic systems, so if any one system fails, full flight control is maintained with another functioning system. For this example, we will assume that for a typical flight, the probability of a hydraulic system failure is 0.002.

   a. If the Airbus 310 were to have one hydraulic system, what is the probability that it would work for a flight?

   b. Given that the Airbus 310 actually has three independent hydraulic systems, what is the probability that on a typical flight, control can be maintained with a working hydraulic system?

Solution

   a. The probability of a hydraulic system failure is 0.002, so the probability that it does *not* fail is 0.998. That is, the probability that flight control can be maintained is as follows:

$$P(1 \text{ hydraulic system } does \text{ } not \text{ } fail)$$
$$= 1 - P(\text{failure}) = 1 - 0.002 = 0.998$$

   b. With three independent hydraulic systems, flight control will be maintained provided that the three systems do not all fail. The probability of all three hydraulic systems failing is $0.002 \cdot 0.002 \cdot 0.002 = 0.000000008$. It follows that the probability of maintaining flight control is as follows:

$$P(\text{it does } not \text{ happen that all three hydraulic systems fail})$$
$$= 1 - 0.000000008 = 0.999999992$$

Interpretation

With only one hydraulic system we have a 0.002 probability of failure, but with three independent hydraulic systems, there is only a 0.000000008 probability that flight control cannot be maintained because all three systems failed. By using three hydraulic systems instead of only one, risk of failure is decreased not by a factor of $1/3$, but by a factor of $1/250,000$. By using three independent hydraulic systems, risk is dramatically decreased and safety is dramatically increased.

Rationale for the Multiplication Rule

To see the reasoning that underlies the multiplication rule, consider a pop quiz consisting of (1) a true/false question and (2) a multiple-choice question with five possible answers (a, b, c, d, e). We will use the following two questions:

   1. True or false: A pound of feathers is heavier than a pound of gold.

   2. Who said that "By a small sample, we may judge of the whole piece"?
       (a) Judge Judy; (b) Judge Dredd; (c) Miguel de Cervantes;
       (d) George Gallup; (e) Gandhi

   The answer key is T (for "true") and c. (The first answer is true, because weights of feathers are given in avoirdupois units, but weights of gold and other precious metals are given in troy units. An avoirdupois pound is 453.59 g, which is greater than the 373.24 g in a troy pound. The second answer is Cervantes, and the quote is from his famous novel *Don Quixote*.)

One way to find the probability that if someone makes random guesses for both answers, the first answer will be correct *and* the second answer will be correct, is to list the sample space as follows:

Ta   Tb   Tc   Td   Te   Fa   Fb   Fc   Fd   Fe

If the two answers are random guesses, then the above 10 possible outcomes are equally likely, so

$$P(\text{both correct}) = P(T \text{ and } c) = \frac{1}{10} = 0.1$$

With $P(T \text{ and } c) = 1/10$, $P(T) = 1/2$, and $P(c) = 1/5$, we see that

$$\frac{1}{10} = \frac{1}{2} \cdot \frac{1}{5}$$

A *tree diagram* is a picture of the possible outcomes of a procedure, shown as line segments emanating from one starting point. These diagrams are sometimes helpful in determining the number of possible outcomes in a sample space, if the number of possibilities is not too large. The tree diagram shown in Figure 4-7 summarizes the outcomes of the true/false and multiple-choice questions. From Figure 4-7 we see that if both answers are random guesses, all 10 branches are equally likely and the probability of getting the correct pair (T,c) is $1/10$. For each response to the first question, there are 5 responses to the second. *The total number of outcomes is 5 taken 2 times, or 10.* The tree diagram in Figure 4-7 therefore provides a visual illustration for using multiplication.

Probability Rules! We can summarize the addition rule from Section 4-3 and the multiplication rule from this section as follows:

Addition Rule for $P(A \text{ or } B)$: The word *or* suggests addition, and when adding $P(A)$ and $P(B)$, we must be careful to add in such a way that every outcome is counted only once.

Multiplication Rule for $P(A \text{ and } B)$: The word *and* suggests multiplication, and when multiplying $P(A)$ and $P(B)$, we must be careful to be sure that the probability of event B takes into account the previous occurrence of event A. Figure 4-8 summarizes the multiplication rule and shows the role of independence in applying it.

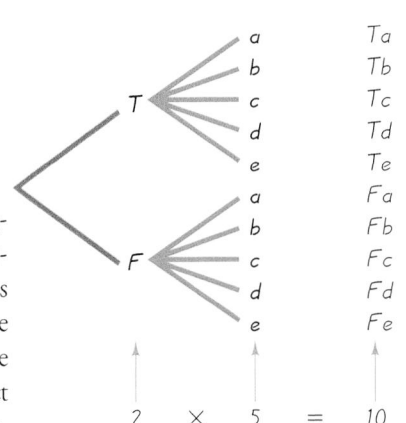

Figure 4-7   Tree Diagram of Test Answers

Figure 4-8   Applying the Multiplication Rule

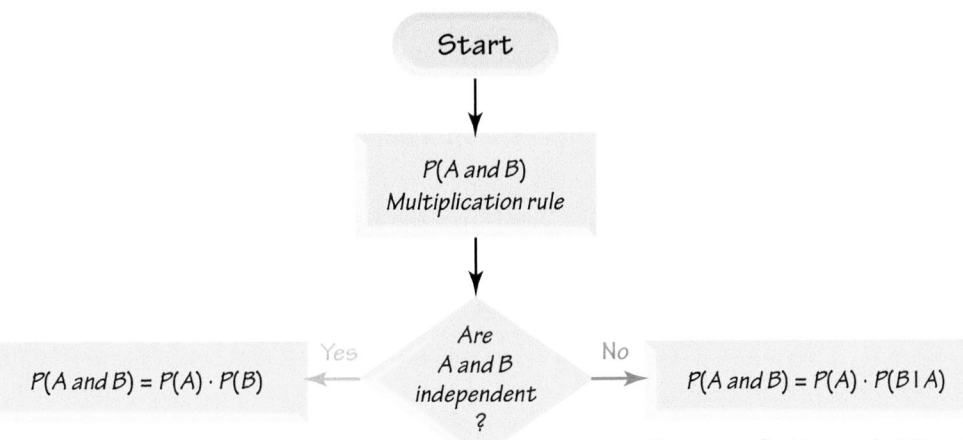

4-4 Basic Skills and Concepts

Statistical Literacy and Critical Thinking

1. Notation Let R be the event of randomly selecting a senator and getting a Republican, and let D represent the event of randomly selecting a second *different* senator and getting a Democrat. Use words to describe what the notation $P(D \mid R)$ represents.

2. Independent and Dependent Events Are events R and D from Exercise 1 independent or dependent? Explain.

3. Independent and Dependent Events True or false: The event of finding that your car's radio works and the event of finding that your car's air conditioner works are independent events because they work separately from each other. Explain.

4. Sample for a Poll There are currently 28,741,346 adults in California, and they are all included in one large numbered list. The Gallup organization uses a computer to randomly select 1068 *different* numbers between 1 and 28,741,346 and then contacts the corresponding adults for a survey. Are the events of selecting the adults actually independent or dependent? If the events are dependent, can they be treated as being independent for the purposes of calculations?

Independent and Dependent Events. *In Exercises 5–12, (a) determine whether events* A *and* B *are independent or dependent, and (b) find* P(A *and* B), *the probability that events* A *and* B *both occur.*

5. *A:* When a month is randomly selected and ripped from a calendar and destroyed, it is July.

   B: When a different month is randomly selected and ripped from a calendar, it is November.

6. *A:* When a baby is born, it is a girl.

   B: When a second baby is born into a different family, it is also a girl.

7. *A:* When a baby is born, it is a girl.

   B: When a single die is rolled, the outcome is 6.

8. *A:* When a day of the week is randomly selected, it is a Saturday.

   B: When a second *different* day of the week is randomly selected, it is a Monday.

9. *A:* When one of the 222 coins listed in Data Set 21 is randomly selected, it is one of the 5 Indian pennies.

   B: When another one of the 222 coins listed in Data Set 21 is randomly selected, it is also one of the 5 Indian pennies.

10. *A:* When the first digit (0 through 9) of a four-digit lottery number is chosen by someone buying a ticket, it is the same first digit that is later drawn in the official lottery.

   B: When the second digit of a four-digit lottery number is chosen by someone buying a ticket, it is the same second digit that is later drawn in the official lottery.

11. *A:* When a survey subject is randomly selected from the 100 senators in the 111th Congress, it is one of the 58 Democrats.

   B: When a second *different* senator is randomly selected, it is the one senator who is an Independent.

12. *A:* When an M&M is randomly selected from the 100 M&Ms listed in Data Set 20, it is one of the 8 yellow M&Ms.

   B: When a second *different* M&M is randomly selected from those listed in Data Set 20, it is also a yellow M&M.

Pre-Employment Drug Screening. *In Exercises 13–16, use the test results summarized in Table 4-1, reproduced here. Consider an event to be "unlikely" if its probability is 0.05 or less.*

Table 4-1 Pre-Employment Drug Screening Results		
	Positive Test Result (Drug Use Is Indicated)	**Negative Test Result** (Drug Use Is Not Indicated)
Subject Uses Drugs	44 (True Positive)	6 (False Negative)
Subject Is Not a Drug User	90 (False Positive)	860 (True Negative)

13. Pre-Employment Drug Screening If 2 of the 1000 test subjects are randomly selected, find the probability that they both had false positive results. Is it unlikely to randomly select 2 subjects and get 2 results that are both false positive results?

a. Assume that the 2 selections are made with replacement.

b. Assume that the 2 selections are made without replacement.

14. Pre-Employment Drug Screening If 3 of the 1000 test subjects are randomly selected, find the probability that they all had false negative results. Is it unlikely to randomly select 3 subjects and get 3 results that are all false negative results?

a. Assume that the 3 selections are made with replacement.

b. Assume that the 3 selections are made without replacement.

15. Pre-Employment Drug Screening If 3 of the 1000 test subjects are randomly selected, find the probability that they all had correct test results (either true positive or true negative). Is such an event unlikely?

a. Assume that the 3 selections are made with replacement.

b. Assume that the 3 selections are made without replacement.

16. Pre-Employment Drug Screening If 4 of the 1000 test subjects are randomly selected, find the probability that they all had true negative test results. Is such an event unlikely?

a. Assume that the 4 selections are made with replacement.

b. Assume that the 4 selections are made without replacement.

17. Acceptance Sampling With one method of a procedure called *acceptance sampling,* a sample of items is randomly selected without replacement and the entire batch is accepted if every item in the sample is okay. Among 8834 cases of heart pacemaker malfunctions, 504 were found to be caused by firmware, which is software programmed into the device (based on data from "Pacemaker and ICD Generator Malfunctions," by Maisel et al., *Journal of the American Medical Association,* Vol. 295, No. 16). If the firmware is tested in three *different* pacemakers randomly selected from this batch of 8834, what is the probability that the firmware in the entire batch will be accepted? Does this procedure suggest that the entire batch consists of good pacemakers? Why or why not?

18. Acceptance Sampling With one method of a procedure called *acceptance sampling,* a sample of items is randomly selected without replacement and the entire batch is accepted if every item in the sample is okay. Among 810 airport baggage scales, 102 are defective (based on data from the New York City Department of Consumer Affairs). If four of the scales are randomly selected and tested, what is the probability that the entire batch will be accepted? Is this scheme likely to detect the large number of defects?

19. Redundancy in Computer Hard Drives It is generally recognized that it is wise to back up computer data. Assume that there is a 2% rate of disk drive failure in a year (based on data from various sources, including "Failure Trends in Large Disk Drive Population," by Pinhero et al. of Google, Inc.).

a. If you store all of your computer data on a single hard disk drive, what is the probability that the drive will fail during a year?

b. If all of your computer data is stored on a hard disk drive with a copy stored on a second hard disk drive, what is the probability that both drives will fail during a year?

c. If copies of all of your computer data are stored on three independent hard disk drives, what is the probability that all three will fail during a year?

d. Describe the improved reliability that is gained with backup drives.

20. Redundancy in Aircraft Radios The FAA requires that commercial aircraft used for flying in instrument conditions must have two independent radios instead of one. Assume that for a typical flight, the probability of a radio failure is 0.0035. What is the probability that a particular flight will be threatened with the failure of both radios? Describe how the second independent radio increases safety in this case.

21. Born on the 4th of July For the following, ignore leap years and assume that births on the 365 different days of the year are equally likely.

a. What is the probability that a randomly selected person was born on July 4?

b. What is the probability that two randomly selected people were both born on July 4?

c. What is the probability that two randomly selected people were born on the same day?

22. Hiring Employees Assume that Google, Inc. hires employees on the different business days of the week (Monday through Friday) with equal likelihood.

a. If two different employees are randomly selected, what is the probability that they were both hired on a Monday?

b. If two different employees are randomly selected, what is the probability that they were both hired on the same day of the week?

c. What is the probability that 10 people in the same department were all hired on the same day of the week? Is such an event unlikely?

*In Exercises 23–26, use these results from the "1-Panel-THC" test for marijuana use, which is provided by the company Drug Test Success: Among 143 subjects with positive test results, there are 24 false positive results; among 157 negative results, there are 3 false negative results. (**Hint:** Construct a table similar to Table 4-1, which is included with the Chapter Problem.)*

23. Screening for Marijuana Use If 2 of the subjects are randomly selected without replacement, what is the probability that they both had correct test results (either true positive or true negative)? Is such an event unlikely?

24. Screening for Marijuana Use If 2 of the subjects are randomly selected without replacement, what is the probability that they both had incorrect test results (either false positive or false negative)? Is such an event unlikely?

25. Screening for Marijuana Use If 3 of the subjects are randomly selected without replacement, what is the probability that they all had false positive test results? Is such an event unlikely?

26. Screening for Marijuana Use If 3 of the subjects are randomly selected without replacement, what is the probability that they all had true negative test results? Is such an event unlikely?

In Exercises 27–30, find the probabilities and indicate when the "5% guideline for cumbersome calculations" is used.

27. Road Rage In a Prince Market Research survey of 2518 motorists, 252 said that they made an obscene gesture in the previous month.

a. If 1 of the surveyed motorists is randomly selected, what is the probability that this motorist did *not* make an obscene gesture in the previous month?

b. If 50 of the surveyed motorists are randomly selected without replacement, what is the probability that none of them made an obscene gesture in the previous month?

28. Flirting In a Microsoft Instant Messaging survey, 1021 adults were asked to identify the most fun way to flirt, and 61 of them chose e-mail.

a. If 1 of the surveyed adults is randomly selected, what is the probability that this person chose something other than e-mail?

b. If 40 of the different subjects are randomly selected without replacement, what is the probability that each of them chose something other than e-mail?

29. Online Shopping Survey 427 different adult women were randomly selected and asked what they purchase online, and 162 of the women said that they purchase clothes online (based on a survey by the *Consumer Reports* Research Center).

a. If 2 of the surveyed women are randomly selected without replacement, what is the probability that they both chose the category of clothing?

b. If 10 different surveyed women are randomly selected without replacement, what is the probability that *none* of them chose the category of clothing?

30. Airline Survey Among respondents asked which is their favorite seat on a plane, 492 chose the window seat, 8 chose the middle seat, and 306 chose the aisle seat (based on data from *USA Today*).

a. What is the probability of randomly selecting 1 of the surveyed people and getting one who did not choose the middle seat?

b. If 2 of the surveyed people are randomly selected without replacement, what is the probability that neither of them chose the middle seat?

c. If 25 different surveyed people are randomly selected without replacement, what is the probability that none of them chose the middle seat?

4-4 Beyond the Basics

31. System Reliability Refer to the figure at the top of the next page in which surge protectors p and q are used to protect an expensive 3D HDTV. If there is a surge in the voltage, the surge protector reduces it to a safe level. Assume that each surge protector has a 0.99 probability of working correctly when a voltage surge occurs.

a. If the two surge protectors are arranged in series, what is the probability that a voltage surge will not damage the television? (Do not round the answer.)

b. If the two surge protectors are arranged in parallel, what is the probability that a voltage surge will not damage the television? (Do not round the answer.)

c. Which arrangement should be used for the better protection?

Series Configuration   *Parallel Configuration*

32. Same Birthdays If 25 people are randomly selected, find the probability that no 2 of them have the same birthday. Ignore leap years.

4-5   Multiplication Rule: Complements and Conditional Probability

Key Concept Section 4-4 presented the basic concept of the multiplication rule, and in this section we extend the use of the multiplication rule to include the following two special applications:

1. **Probability of "at least one":** Find the probability that among several trials, we get *at least one* of some specified event.

2. **Conditional probability:** Find the probability of an event occurring when we have additional information that some other event has already occurred.

We begin with situations in which we want to find the probability that among several trials, *at least one* will result in some specified outcome.

Complements: The Probability of "At Least One"

When finding the probability of some event occurring at least once, it is usually best to solve the problem "backwards" by working directly with the complementary event. In this context, the meaning of language must be clearly understood. In particular, the following principle should be well known:

In multiple trials, if *at least one* of some event occurs, then the complement (opposite) is that the event does not occur at all. If you don't get at least one occurrence of event *A*, then event *A* does not happen at all.

- "At least one" has the same meaning as "one or more."

- The *complement* of getting at least one particular event is that you get *no* occurrences of that event.

For example, not getting at least 1 defective DVD in a lot of 50 DVDs is the same as getting no defective DVDs, which is also the same as getting 50 good DVDs. The following steps describe the details of this backward method of finding the probability of getting at least one of some event:

Finding the probability of getting *at least one* of some event:

1. Let A = getting *at least one* of some event

2. Then $\overline{A}$ = getting ***none*** **of the event being considered.**

3. **Find** $P(\overline{A})$ = **probability that event** ***A*** **does not occur.** (This should be relatively easy with the multiplication rule.)

4. **Subtract the result from 1. That is, evaluate this expression:**

$$P(\textit{at least one} \text{ occurrence of event } A)$$

$$= 1 - P(\textit{no} \text{ occurrences of event } A)$$

Example 1   At Least One Defective DVD

Topford Development, Ltd., supplies X-Data DVDs in lots of 50, and they have a reported defect rate of 0.5%, so the probability of an individual disk being defective is 0.005. It follows that the probability of a disk being good is 0.995. If a quality control engineer wants to carefully analyze a defective disk, what is the probability of her getting at least one defective disk in a lot of 50? Is the probability high enough that the engineer can be reasonably sure of getting a defective disk that can be used for her analysis?

Solution

Step 1: Let A = at least 1 of the 50 disks is defective.

Step 2: Identify the event that is the complement of A.

$$\overline{A} = \textit{not} \text{ getting at least 1 defective disk among 50}$$
$$= \text{all 50 disks are good}$$

Step 3: Find the probability of the complement by evaluating $P(\overline{A})$.

$$P(\overline{A}) = P(\text{all 50 disks are good})$$
$$= 0.995 \cdot 0.995 \cdot \ \cdots \ \cdot 0.995$$
$$= 0.995^{50} = 0.778$$

Step 4: Find $P(A)$ by evaluating $1 - P(\overline{A})$.

$$P(A) = 1 - P(\overline{A}) = 1 - 0.778 = 0.222$$

Interpretation

In a lot of 50 DVDs, the engineer has a 0.222 probability of getting at least 1 defective DVD. This probability is not very high, so if a defective DVD is required for analysis, the engineer should start with more than one lot consisting of 50 DVDs.

Conditional Probability

We now consider the second application of this section, which is based on the principle that the probability of an event is often affected by knowledge that some other event has occurred. For example, the probability of a golfer making a hole in one is $1/12{,}000$ (based on past results), but if you have the additional knowledge that the selected golfer is a touring professional, the probability changes to $1/2375$ (based on data from *USA Today*). In general, a *conditional probability* of an event is used when the probability is calculated with the knowledge that some other event has occurred.

> **DEFINITION** A **conditional probability** of an event is a probability obtained with the additional information that some other event has already occurred. $P(B\,|\,A)$ denotes the conditional probability of event B occurring, given that event A has already occurred. $P(B\,|\,A)$ can be found by dividing the probability of events A and B both occurring by the probability of event A:
>
> $$P(B\,|\,A) = \frac{P(A \text{ and } B)}{P(A)}$$

Prosecutor's Fallacy

The *prosecutor's fallacy* is misunderstanding or confusion of two different conditional probabilities: (1) the probability that a defendant is innocent, given that forensic evidence shows a match; (2) the probability that forensics shows a match, given that a person is innocent. The prosecutor's fallacy has led to wrong convictions and imprisonment of some innocent people.

Lucia de Berk was a nurse who was convicted of murder and sentenced to prison in the Netherlands. Hospital administrators observed suspicious deaths that occurred in hospital wards where de Berk had been present. An expert testified that there was only 1 chance in 342 million that her presence was a coincidence. However, mathematician Richard Gill calculated the probability to be closer to $1/150$, or possibly as low as $1/5$. The court used the probability that the suspicious deaths could have occurred with de Berk present, given that she was innocent. The court should have considered the probability that de Berk is innocent, given that the suspicious deaths occurred when she was present. This error of the prosecutor's fallacy is subtle and can be very difficult to understand and recognize, yet it can lead to the imprisonment of innocent people.

The preceding formula is a formal expression of conditional probability, but blind use of formulas is not recommended. Instead, we recommend the following intuitive approach.

Intuitive Approach to Conditional Probability

Finding $P(B|A)$ The conditional probability of B occurring given that A has occurred can be found by assuming that event A has occurred and then calculating the probability that event B will occur.

Example 2 Pre-Employment Drug Screening

Refer to Table 4-1 to find the following:

a. If 1 of the 1000 test subjects is randomly selected, find the probability that the subject had a positive test result, given that the subject actually uses drugs. That is, find P(positive test result | subject uses drugs).

b. If 1 of the 1000 test subjects is randomly selected, find the probability that the subject actually uses drugs, given that he or she had a positive test result. That is, find P(subject uses drugs | positive test result).

Table 4-1 Pre-Employment Drug Screening Results

	Positive Test Result (Drug Use Is Indicated)	Negative Test Result (Drug Use Is Not Indicated)
Subject Uses Drugs	44 (True Positive)	6 (False Negative)
Subject Is Not a Drug User	90 (False Positive)	860 (True Negative)

Solution

a. *Intuitive Approach to Conditional Probability:* We want P(positive test result | subject uses drugs), the probability of getting someone with a positive test result, *given that the selected subject uses drugs.* Here is the key point: If we assume that the selected subject actually uses drugs, we are dealing only with the 50 subjects in the first row of Table 4-1. Among those 50 subjects, 44 had positive test results, so we get this result:

$$P(\text{positive test result} \mid \text{subject uses drugs}) = \frac{44}{50} = 0.88$$

Using the Formula for Conditional Probability: The same result can be found by using the formula for $P(B|A)$ given with the definition of conditional probability. We use the following notation.

$$P(B|A) = P(\text{positive test result} \mid \text{subject uses drugs})$$

where B = positive test result and A = subject uses drugs.

In the following calculation, we use P(subject uses drugs and had a positive test result) = $44/1000$ and P(subject uses drugs) = $50/1000$ to get the following results:

$$P(B \mid A) = \frac{P(A \text{ and } B)}{P(A)}$$

becomes

$P(\text{positive test result} \mid \text{subject uses drugs})$

$$= \frac{P(\text{subject uses drugs and had a positive test result})}{P(\text{subject uses drugs})}$$

$$= \frac{44/1000}{50/1000} = 0.88$$

By comparing the intuitive approach to the use of the formula, it should be clear that the intuitive approach is much easier to use, and it is also less likely to result in errors. The intuitive approach is based on an *understanding* of conditional probability, instead of manipulation of a formula, and understanding is so much better.

b. Here we want $P(\text{subject uses drugs} \mid \text{positive test result})$. This is the probability that the selected subject uses drugs, *given that the subject had a positive test result*. If we assume that the subject had a positive test result, we are dealing with the 134 subjects in the first column of Table 4-1. Among those 134 subjects, 44 use drugs, so

$$P(\text{subject uses drugs} \mid \text{positive test result}) = \frac{44}{134} = 0.328$$

Again, the same result can be found by applying the formula for conditional probability, but we will leave that for those with a special fondness for manipulations with formulas.

Interpretation

The first result of $P(\text{positive test result} \mid \text{subject uses drugs}) = 0.88$ indicates that a subject who uses drugs has a 0.88 probability of getting a positive test result. The second result of $P(\text{subject uses drugs} \mid \text{positive test result}) = 0.328$ indicates that for a subject who gets a positive test result, there is a 0.328 probability that this subject actually uses drugs.

Confusion of the Inverse

Note that in Example 2, $P(\text{positive test result} \mid \text{subject uses drugs}) \neq P(\text{subject uses drugs} \mid \text{positive test result})$. This example proves that in general, $P(B \mid A) \neq P(A \mid B)$. (There could be individual cases where $P(A \mid B)$ and $P(B \mid A)$ are equal, but they are generally not equal.) To incorrectly think that $P(B \mid A)$ and $P(A \mid B)$ are equal or to incorrectly use one value for the other is called *confusion of the inverse*.

Example 3 Confusion of the Inverse

Consider the probability that it is dark outdoors, given that it is midnight: $P(\text{dark} \mid \text{midnight}) = 1$. (We conveniently ignore the Alaskan winter and other such anomalies.) But the probability that it is midnight, given that it is dark outdoors, is almost zero. Because $P(\text{dark} \mid \text{midnight}) = 1$ but $P(\text{midnight} \mid \text{dark})$ is almost zero, we can clearly see that in this case, $P(B \mid A) \neq P(A \mid B)$. Confusion of the inverse occurs when we incorrectly switch those probability values or think that they are equal.

One study showed that physicians often give very misleading information when they confuse the inverse. They tended to confuse $P(\text{cancer} \mid \text{positive test result})$ with $P(\text{positive test result} \mid \text{cancer})$. About 95% of physicians estimated $P(\text{cancer} \mid \text{positive test result})$ to be about 10 times too high, with the result that patients were given diagnoses that were very misleading, and patients were unnecessarily distressed by the incorrect information. See Exercise 35.

DNA Evidence Misused

Micheal Bobelian wrote "DNA's Dirty Little Secret" that was published in *Washington Monthly*. He describes the use of DNA in the conviction of John Puckett for the murder of a young nurse. Thirty years after the murder, police used DNA found on the victim to identify John Puckett as the assailant, and the jury was told that there was only one chance in 1.1 million that a random person's DNA would match the DNA found on the victim. Although the DNA was degraded, this was the only physical evidence linking Puckett to the crime. Michael Bobelian wrote that when old and degraded DNA is used in a search through a large database, the "odds are exponentially higher" of getting a match with someone who is not actually guilty. He wrote that "in Puckett's case the actual chance of a false match is a staggering one in three, according to the formula endorsed by the FBI's DNA advisory board and the National Research Council." Yet Puckett's attorneys were not allowed to mention that. A serious consequence of this process is that the use of DNA evidence in similar cases might result in the conviction of innocent people. Puckett was convicted and sentenced to life in prison, but is he actually guilty?

4-5 Basic Skills and Concepts

Statistical Literacy and Critical Thinking

1. Subjective Probability

a. Estimate the probability that on the next test in a randomly selected statistics class, at least one student earns a grade of A.

b. Answer part (a) with the additional knowledge that the selected class is a special section for honors students with very high grade point averages.

2. Conditional Probability What is a conditional probability?

3. Notation Let event A = subject is telling the truth and event B = polygraph test indicates that the subject is lying. Use your own words to translate the notation $P(B|A)$ into a verbal statement.

4. Confusion of the Inverse Using the same events A and B described in Exercise 3, what is confusion of the inverse? (Express the answer in both words and symbols.)

Describing Complements. *In Exercises 5–8, provide a written description of the complement of the given event, then find the probability of the complement of the given event.*

5. Five Girls When a couple has five children, all five are girls. (Assume that boys and girls are equally likely.)

6. No Girls When a couple has five children, none of the five is a girl. (Assume that boys and girls are equally likely.)

7. At Least One Zero When four digits (between 0 and 9 inclusive) are randomly selected with replacement for a lottery ticket, at least one of the digits is 0.

8. No 7s When four digits (between 0 and 9 inclusive) are randomly selected with replacement for a lottery ticket, none of the digits is a 7.

9. At Least One Correct Answer If you make random guesses for 10 multiple-choice test questions (each with five possible answers), what is the probability of getting at least 1 correct? If a very lenient instructor says that passing the test occurs if there is at least one correct answer, can you reasonably expect to pass by guessing?

10. At Least One Working Calculator A statistics student plans to use a TI-84 Plus calculator on her final exam. From past experience, she estimates that there is 0.92 probability that the calculator will work on any given day. Because the final exam is so important, she plans to use redundancy by bringing in two TI-84 Plus calculators. What is the probability that she will be able to complete her exam with a working calculator? Does she really gain much by bringing in the backup calculator? Explain.

11. Probability of a Girl Assuming that boys and girls are equally likely, find the probability of a couple having at least one boy after their fifth child is born, given that the first four children were all girls.

12. At Least One Correct Answer If you make random guesses for 10 multiple-choice test questions (each with five possible answers), what is the probability of getting at least one answer correct, given that the first nine answers are all wrong?

13. Births in the United States In the United States, the true probability of a baby being a boy is 0.512 (based on the data available at this writing). Among the next five randomly selected births in the United States, what is the probability that at least one of them is a girl?

14. Births in China In China, the probability of a baby being a boy is 0.545. Many couples are allowed to have only one child. Among the next five randomly selected births in China, what is the probability that at least one of them is a girl? Can this system continue to work indefinitely?

15. Car Crashes The probability of a randomly selected car crashing during a year is 0.0423 (based on data from the *Statistical Abstract of the United States*). If a family has three cars, find the probability that at least one of them has a crash during the year. Is there any reason why this probability might be wrong?

16. Cleared Burglaries According to FBI data, 12.4% of burglaries are cleared with arrests. A new detective is assigned to five different burglaries.

a. What is the probability that at least one of them is cleared with an arrest?

b. What is the probability that the detective clears five burglaries with arrests?

c. What should we conclude if the detective clears all five burglaries with arrests?

17. Wi-Fi Based on a poll conducted through the e-edition of *USA Today*, 67% of Internet users are more careful about personal information when using a public Wi-Fi hotspot. What is the probability that among four randomly selected Internet users, at least one is more careful about personal information when using a public Wi-Fi hotspot? How is the result affected by the additional information that the survey subjects volunteered to respond?

18. Compliments at Work Based on a poll conducted through e-mail by *USA Today*, 41% of survey respondents most liked to get compliments at work from their co-workers. Among 12 randomly selected workers, what is the probability of getting at least 1 who most likes to get compliments from co-workers? How is the result affected by the additional information that the survey subjects volunteered to respond?

In Exercises 19–24, refer to Table 4-1, included with the Chapter Problem. In each case, assume that 1 of the 1000 test subjects is randomly selected.

19. False Positive Find the probability of selecting a subject with a positive test result, given that the subject does not use drugs. Why is this particular case problematic for test subjects?

20. False Negative Find the probability of selecting a subject with a negative test result, given that the subject uses drugs. Who would suffer from this type of error?

21. Inverse Probabilities Find P(subject uses drugs | negative test result). Compare this result to the result found in Exercise 20. Are P(subject uses drugs | negative test result) *and* P(negative test result | subject uses drugs) equal?

22. Inverse Probabilities

a. Find P(negative test result | subject does not use drugs).

b. Find P(subject does not use drugs | negative test result).

c. Compare the results from parts (a) and (b). Are they equal?

23. Positive Predictive Value Find the positive predictive value for the test. That is, find the probability that a subject uses drugs, given that the test yields a positive result.

24. Negative Predictive Value Find the negative predictive value for the test. That is, find the probability that a subject does not use drugs, given that the test yields a negative result.

Identical and Fraternal Twins. *In Exercises 25–28, use the data in the following table. Instead of summarizing observed results, the entries reflect the actual probabilities based on births of twins (based on data from the Northern California Twin Registry and the article "Bayesians, Frequentists, and Scientists" by Bradley Efron,* **Journal of the American Statistical Association,** *Vol. 100, No. 469). Identical twins come from a single egg that* *splits into two embryos, and fraternal twins are from separate fertilized eggs. The table entries reflect the principle that among sets of twins, 1/3 are identical and 2/3 are fraternal. Also, identical twins must be of the same sex and the sexes are equally likely (approximately), and sexes of fraternal twins are equally likely.*

	Sexes of Twins			
	boy/boy	boy/girl	girl/boy	girl/girl
Identical Twins	5	0	0	5
Fraternal Twins	5	5	5	5

25. Identical Twins

a. After having a sonogram, a pregnant woman learns that she will have twins. What is the probability that she will have identical twins?

b. After studying the sonogram more closely, the physician tells the pregnant woman that she will give birth to twin boys. What is the probability that she will have identical twins? That is, find the probability of identical twins given that the twins consist of two boys.

26. Fraternal Twins

a. After having a sonogram, a pregnant woman learns that she will have twins. What is the probability that she will have fraternal twins?

b. After studying the sonogram more closely, the physician tells the pregnant woman that she will give birth to twins consisting of one boy and one girl. What is the probability that she will have fraternal twins?

27. Fraternal Twins If a pregnant woman is told that she will give birth to fraternal twins, what is the probability that she will have one child of each sex?

28. Fraternal Twins If a pregnant woman is told that she will give birth to fraternal twins, what is the probability that she will give birth to two girls?

29. Redundancy in Computer Hard Drives Assume that there is a 2% rate of disk drive failure in a year (based on data from various sources, including "Failure Trends in Large Disk Drive Population," by Pinhero et al. of Google, Inc.).

a. If all of your computer data is stored on a hard disk drive with a copy stored on a second hard disk drive, what is the probability that during a year, you can avoid catastrophe with at least one working drive?

b. If copies of all of your computer data are stored on three independent hard disk drives, what is the probability that during a year, you can avoid catastrophe with at least one working drive?

30. Redundancy in Aircraft Radios The FAA requires that commercial aircraft used for flying in instrument conditions must have two independent radios instead of one. Assume that for a typical flight, the probability of a radio failure is 0.0035. What is the probability that a particular flight will be safe with at least one working radio? Why does the usual rounding rule of three significant digits not work here? Is this probability high enough to ensure flight safety?

31. Composite Drug Screening Based on the data in Table 4-1, assume that the probability of a randomly selected person testing positive for drug use is 0.134. If drug screening samples are collected from 8 random subjects and combined, find the probability that the combined sample will reveal a positive result. Is that probability low enough so that further testing of the individual samples is rarely necessary?

32. Composite Water Samples The Fairfield County Department of Public Health tests water for contamination due to the presence of *E. coli* (*Escherichia coli*) bacteria. To reduce laboratory costs, water samples from five public swimming areas are combined for one test, and further testing is done only if the combined sample tests positive. Based on past results, there is a 0.005 probability of finding *E. coli* bacteria in a public swimming area. Find the probability that a combined sample from five public swimming areas will reveal the presence of *E. coli* bacteria. Is that probability low enough so that further testing of the individual samples is rarely necessary?

4-5 Beyond the Basics

33. Shared Birthdays Find the probability that of 25 randomly selected people,

a. no 2 share the same birthday.

b. at least 2 share the same birthday.

34. Unseen Coins A statistics professor tosses two coins that cannot be seen by any students. One student asks this question: "Did one of the coins turn up heads?" Given that the professor's response is "yes," find the probability that both coins turned up heads.

35. Confusion of the Inverse In one study, physicians were asked to estimate the probability of a malignant cancer given that a test showed a positive result. They were told that the cancer had a prevalence rate of 1%, the test has a false positive rate of 10%, and the test is 80% accurate in correctly identifying a malignancy when the subject actually has the cancer. (See *Probabilistic Reasoning in Clinical Medicine* by David Eddy, Cambridge University Press.)

a. Find $P(\text{malignant} \mid \text{positive test result})$. (*Hint:* Assume that the study involves 1000 subjects and use the given information to construct a table with the same format as Table 4-1.)

b. Find $P(\text{positive test result} \mid \text{malignant})$. (*Hint:* Assume that the study involves 1000 subjects and construct a table with the same format as Table 4-1.)

c. Out of 100 physicians, 95 estimated $P(\text{malignant} \mid \text{positive test result})$ to be about 75%. Were those estimates reasonably accurate, or did they exhibit confusion of the inverse? What would be a consequence of confusion of the inverse in this situation?

4-6 Counting

Key Concept Probability problems typically require that we know the total number of simple events, but finding that number often requires one of the five rules presented in this section. With the addition rule, multiplication rule, and conditional probability, we stressed intuitive rules based on understanding and we discouraged blind use of formulas, but this section requires much greater use of formulas as we consider different methods for counting the number of possible outcomes in a variety of different situations.

Permutations and Combinations: Does *Order* Count?

When using different counting methods, it is essential to know whether different arrangements of the same items are counted only once or are counted separately. The terms *permutations* and *combinations* are standard in this context, and they are defined as follows:

> **DEFINITIONS**
>
> **Permutations** of items are arrangements in which different sequences of the same items are counted separately. For example, with the letters {a, b, c}, the arrangements of abc, acb, bac, bca, cab, and cba are all counted separately as six different permutations.
>
> **Combinations** of items are arrangements in which different sequences of the same items are *not* counted separately. For example, with the letters {a, b, c}, the arrangements of abc, acb, bac, bca, cab, and cba are all considered to be same combination.

Group Testing

During World War II, the U.S. Army tested for syphilis by giving each soldier an individual blood test that was analyzed separately. One researcher suggested mixing pairs of blood samples. After the mixed pairs were tested, those with syphilis could be identified by retesting the few blood samples that were in the pairs that tested positive. Since the total number of analyses was reduced by pairing blood specimens, why not combine them in groups of three or four or more? This technique of combining samples in groups and retesting only those groups that test positive is known as *group testing* or *pooled testing,* or *composite testing.* University of Nebraska statistician Christopher Bilder wrote an article about this topic in *Chance* magazine, and he cited some real applications. He noted that the American Red Cross uses group testing to screen for specific diseases, such as hepatitis, and

 group testing is used by veterinarians when cattle are tested for the bovine viral diarrhea virus.

Mnemonics When trying to remember which of the two preceding terms involves order, think of **p**ermutations **p**osition, where the alliteration reminds us that with permutations, the positions of the items makes a difference. You might also use the alliteration in **c**ombinations **c**ommittee, where those words remind us that with members of a committee, rearrangements of the same members result in the same committee, so order does not count.

This section includes the following notation and counting rules. Illustrative examples follow.

Notation

The **factorial symbol** (!) denotes the product of decreasing positive whole numbers. For example, $4! = 4 \cdot 3 \cdot 2 \cdot 1 = 24$. By special definition, $0! = 1$.

Counting Rules

1. Fundamental Counting Rule

$m \cdot n =$ Number of ways that two events can occur, given that the first event can occur m ways and the second event can occur n ways. (This rule extends easily to situations with more than two events.) *Example:* For a two-character code consisting of a letter followed by a digit, the number of different possible codes is $26 \cdot 10 = 260$.

2. Factorial Rule

$n! =$ Number of different *permutations* (order counts) of n different items when all n of them are selected. (This rule reflects the fact that the first item may be selected n different ways, the second item may be selected $n - 1$ ways, and so on.) *Example:* The number of ways that the five letters {a, b, c, d, e} can be arranged is as follows:

$$5! = 5 \cdot 4 \cdot 3 \cdot 2 \cdot 1 = 120$$

3. Permutations Rule (When All of the Items Are Different)

$${}_nP_r = \frac{n!}{(n-r)!} =$$ Number of different *permutations* (order counts) when n different

items are available, but only r of them are selected *without replacement*. (Rearrangements of the same items are counted as being different.) *Example:* If the five letters {a, b, c, d, e} are available and three of them are to be selected without replacement, the number of different permutations is as follows:

$${}_nP_r = \frac{n!}{(n-r)!} = \frac{5!}{(5-3)!} = 60$$

4. Permutations Rule (When Some Items Are Identical to Others)

$$\frac{n!}{n_1!n_2! \cdots n_k!} =$$ Number of different *permutations* (order counts) when n items are

available and all n are selected *without replacement,* but some of the items are identical to others: n_1 are alike, n_2 are alike, . . . , and n_k are alike. *Example:* If the 10 letters {a, a, a, a, b, b, c, c, d, e} are available and all 10 of them are to be selected without replacement, the number of different permutations is as follows:

$$\frac{n!}{n_1!n_2! \cdots n_k!} = \frac{10!}{4!2!2!} = \frac{3{,}628{,}800}{24 \cdot 2 \cdot 2} = 37{,}800$$

5. Combinations Rule

$${}_nC_r = \frac{n!}{(n-r)!r!} =$$ Number of different combinations (order does not count) when

n different items are available, but only r of them are selected *without replacement.* (Note that rearrangements of the same items are counted as being the same.) *Example:* If the five letters {a, b, c, d, e} are available and three of them are to be selected without replacement, the number of different combinations is as follows:

$${}_nC_r = \frac{n!}{(n-r)!r!} = \frac{5!}{(5-3)!3!} = \frac{120}{2 \cdot 6} = 10$$

Example 1   Fundamental Counting Rule: Computer Design

Computers are typically designed so that the most basic unit of information is a *bit* (or binary digit), which represents either a 0 or a 1. Letters, digits, and punctuation symbols are represented as a *byte,* which is a sequence of eight bits in a particular order. For example, the ASCII coding system represents the letter *A* as 01000001 and the number 7 is represented as 00110111. How many different characters are possible if they are all to be represented as bytes?

Solution

The byte is a sequence of eight numbers, and there are only two possible numbers (0 or 1) for each of them. By applying the fundamental counting rule, the number of different possible bytes is

$$2 \cdot 2 \cdot 2 \cdot 2 \cdot 2 \cdot 2 \cdot 2 \cdot 2 = 2^8 = 256$$

Interpretation

There are 256 different characters (letters, digits, punctuations) that can be represented with different bytes. The author's keyboard has 47 keys for characters, and each of those keys is used for two different characters, so the byte system is more than adequate for such keyboards.

Example 2   Factorial Rule: Chronological Order of Presidents

A history pop quiz has one question in which students are asked to arrange the following presidents in chronological order: Hayes, Taft, Polk, Taylor, Grant, Pierce. If an unprepared student makes random guesses, what is the probability of selecting the correct chronological order?

Solution

The factorial rule tells us that six different items have 6! different possible rearrangements.

$$6! = 6 \cdot 5 \cdot 4 \cdot 3 \cdot 2 \cdot 1 = 720$$

Interpretation

Because only one of the 720 possible arrangements is correct, the probability of getting the correct chronological order with random guessing is 1/720, or 0.00139. With such a low probability, it is highly unlikely that a student will get the correct answer with random guessing. (The correct chronological order can be found from Data Set 12 in Appendix B.)

Example 3   Permutations Rule (with Different Items): Exacta Bet

In horse racing, a bet on an *exacta* in a race is won by correctly selecting the horses that finish first and second, and you must select those two horses in the correct order. The 136th running of the Kentucky Derby had a field of 20 horses. If a bettor randomly selects two of those horses for an exacta bet, what is the probability of

Choosing Personal Security Codes

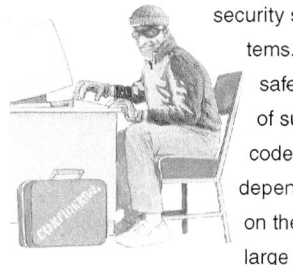

All of us use personal security codes for ATM machines, computer Internet accounts, and home security systems. The safety of such codes depends on the large number of different possibilities, but hackers now have sophisticated tools that can largely overcome that obstacle. Researchers found that by using variations of the user's first and last names along with 1800 other first names, they could identify 10% to 20% of the passwords on typical computer systems. When choosing a password, *do not* use a variation of any name, a word found in a dictionary, a password shorter than seven characters, telephone numbers, or social security numbers. Do include nonalphabetic characters, such as digits or punctuation marks.

Go Figure

43,252,003,274,489,856,000: Number of possible positions on a Rubik's cube.

How to Choose Lottery Numbers

Many books and suppliers of computer programs claim to be helpful in predicting winning lottery numbers. Some use the theory that particular numbers are "due" (and should be selected) because they haven't been coming up often; others use the theory that some numbers are "cold" (and should be avoided) because they haven't been coming up often; and still others use astrology, numerology, or dreams. Because selections of winning lottery number combinations are independent events, such theories are worthless. A valid approach is to choose numbers that are "rare" in the sense that they are not selected by other people, so that if you win, you will not need to share your jackpot with many others. The combination of 1, 2, 3, 4, 5, 6 is a poor choice because many people tend to select it. In a Florida lottery with a $105 million prize, 52,000 tickets had 1, 2, 3, 4, 5, 6; if that combination had won, the prize would have been only $1000. It's wise to pick combinations not selected by many others. Avoid combinations that form a pattern on the entry card.

winning by selecting Super Saver to win and Ice Box to finish second (as they did)? Do all of the different possible exacta bets have the same chance of winning?

Solution

We have $n = 20$ horses available, and we must select $r = 2$ of them without replacement. The number of different sequences of arrangements is found as shown:

$$_nP_r = \frac{n!}{(n-r)!} = \frac{20!}{(20-2)!} = 380$$

There are 380 different possible arrangements of 2 horses selected from the 20 that are available. If one of those arrangements is randomly selected, there is a probability of $1/380$ that the winning arrangement is selected. There are 380 different possible exacta bets, but not all of them have the same chance of winning, because some horses tend to be faster than others. (A correct $2 exacta bet in this race won $152.40.)

Example 4   Permutations Rule (with Some Identical Items): Designing Surveys

Here are two tricks that pollsters use when designing surveys: (1) Give different subjects rearrangements of the questions so that order does not have an effect; (2) as a check to see if a subject is thoughtlessly spewing answers just to finish the survey, repeat a question with some rewording and check to see if the answers are consistent. For one particular survey with 10 questions, 2 of the questions are the same, and 3 other questions are also identical. For this survey, how many different arrangements are possible? Is it practical to survey enough subjects so that every different possible arrangement is used?

Solution

We have 10 questions with 2 that are alike and 3 others that are alike, and we want the number of permutations. Using the rule for permutations with some items identical to others, we get

$$\frac{n!}{n_1!n_2! \cdots n_k!} = \frac{10!}{2!3!} = \frac{3,628,800}{2 \cdot 6} = 302,400$$

Interpretation

There are 302,400 different possible arrangements of the 10 questions. For typical surveys, the number of subjects is around 1000. For the vast majority of typical surveys, it is not practical to use 302,400 subjects; that is far too many.

Example 5   Combinations Rule: Lottery

In the Pennsylvania Match 6 Lotto, winning the jackpot requires that you select six different numbers from 1 to 49, and the same six numbers must be drawn in the lottery. The winning numbers can be drawn in any order, so order does not make a difference. Find the probability of winning the jackpot when one ticket is purchased.

Solution

We have 49 different numbers and we must select 6 without replacement (because the selected numbers must be different). Because order does not count, we need to find the number of different possible *combinations*. With $n = 49$ numbers available and $r = 6$ numbers selected, the number of combinations is as shown below:

$$_nC_r = \frac{n!}{(n-r)!r!} = \frac{49!}{(49-6)!6!} = \frac{49!}{43! \cdot 6!} = 13,983,816$$

Interpretation

If you select one 6-number combination, your probability of winning is $1/13,983,816$. Typical lotteries rely on the fact that people rarely know the value of this probability and have no realistic sense for how small that probability is. This is why the lottery is sometimes called a "tax on people who are bad at math."

Because choosing between permutations and combinations can often be tricky, we provide the following example that emphasizes the difference between them.

Example 6 Permutations and Combinations: Corporate Officials and Committees

The Teknomite Corporation must appoint a president, chief executive officer (CEO), and chief operating officer (COO). It must also appoint a Planning Committee with three different members. There are eight qualified candidates, and officers can also serve on the committee.

a. How many different ways can the officers be appointed?

b. How many different ways can the committee be appointed?

Solution

Note that in part (a), order is important because the officers have very different functions. However, in part (b), the order of selection is irrelevant because the committee members serve the same function.

a. Because order does count, we want the number of *permutations* of $r = 3$ people selected from the $n = 8$ available people. We get

$$_nP_r = \frac{n!}{(n-r)!} = \frac{8!}{(8-3)!} = 336$$

b. Because order does *not* count, we want the number of *combinations* of $r = 3$ people selected from the $n = 8$ available people. We get

$$_nC_r = \frac{n!}{(n-r)!r!} = \frac{8!}{(8-3)!3!} = 56$$

With order taken into account, there are 336 different ways that the officers can be appointed, but without order taken into account, there are 56 different possible committees.

This section presented five different counting rules summarized near the beginning of the section. Not all counting problems can be solved with these five rules, but

Bar Codes

In 1974, the first bar code was scanned on a pack of Juicy Fruit gum that cost 67¢. Now, bar codes or "Universal Product Codes" are scanned about 10 billion times each day. When used for numbers, the bar code consists of black lines that represent a sequence of 12 digits, so the total number of different bar code sequences can be found by applying the fundamental counting rule. The number of difference bar code sequences is $10 \times 10 \times 10 \times 10 \times 10 \times 10 \times 10 \times 10 \times 10 \times 10 \times 10 \times 10 = 10^{12} = 1,000,000,000,000$. The effectiveness of bar codes depends on the large number of different possible products that can be identified with unique numbers.

When a bar code is scanned, the detected number is not price; it is a number that identifies the particular product. The scanner uses that identifying number to look up the price in a central computer. Shown below is the bar code representing the author's name, so that letters are used instead of digits. There will be no price corresponding to the bar code below, because this person is priceless—at least according to most members of his immediate family.

Go Figure

10^{80} is the number of particles in the observable universe. The probability of a monkey randomly hitting keys and typing Shakespeare's *Hamlet* is $10^{-216,159}$.

they do provide a strong foundation for the most common rules that can be used in a wide variety of real applications.

4-6 Basic Skills and Concepts

Statistical Literacy and Critical Thinking

1. Notation What does the symbol ! represent? Four different people can stand in a line 4! different ways. What is the actual number of ways that four people can stand in a line?

2. California Fantasy The winning numbers for the current California Fantasy 5 lottery are 13, 18, 22, 24, and 32 in any order. Do calculations for winning this lottery involve permutations or combinations? Why?

3. California Daily 4 The winning numbers for the current California Daily 4 lottery are 5, 0, 0, and 4 in that exact order. Because order counts, do calculations for this lottery involve either of the two permutation rules presented in this section? Why or why not? If not, what rule does apply?

4. Selections with Replacement When randomly selecting items, if successive selections are made *with replacement* of previously selected items, which of the five rules of this section apply: (1) fundamental couting rule; (2) factorial rule; (3) permutations rule (when all items are different); (4) permutations rule (when some items are identical to others); (5) combinations rule?

In Exercises 5–36, express all probabilities as fractions.

5. ATM Pin Numbers A thief steals an ATM card and must randomly guess the correct pin code that consists of four digits (0 through 9) that must be entered in the correct order. Repetition of digits is allowed. What is the probability of a correct guess on the first try?

6. Social Security Numbers A Social Security number consists of nine digits in a particular order, and repetition of digits is allowed. If randomly selecting digits for one Social Security number, what is the probability that you get the Social Security number of the president?

7. Baseball Batting Order If you know the names of the starting batters for a baseball team, what is the probability of randomly selecting a batting order and getting the order that is used in the beginning of the game?

8. Harry Potter Books There are seven books in the Harry Potter series. If the books are read in a randomly selected order, what is the probability that they are read in the order that they were written?

9. Lady Antebellum Songs A fan of Lady Antebellum music plans to make a custom CD with 12 of her 27 songs. How many different combinations of 12 songs are possible? Is it practical to make a different CD for each possible combination?

10. Blackjack In the game of blackjack played with one deck, a player is initially dealt 2 different cards from the 52 different cards in the deck. Find the probability of getting a 2-card initial hand consisting of the ace of clubs and the ace of spades in any order.

11. Scheduling Routes A presidential candidate plans to begin her campaign by visiting the capitals in 4 of the 50 states. What is the probability that she selects the route of Sacramento, Albany, Juneau, and Hartford? Is it practical to list all of the different possible routes in order to select the one that is best?

12. FedEx Deliveries With a short time remaining in the day, a FedEx driver has time to make deliveries at three locations among the eight locations remaining. How many different routes are possible?

13. Classic Counting Problem A classic counting problem is to determine the number of different ways that the letters of "Mississippi" can be arranged. Find that number.

14. Statistics Count How many different ways can the letters of "statistics" be arranged?

15. Connecticut Lottery Winning the jackpot in the Connecticut Classic Lotto requires that you choose six different numbers from 1 to 44, and your numbers must match the same six numbers that are later drawn. The order of the selected numbers does not matter. If you buy one ticket, what is the probability of winning the jackpot?

16. Florida Lottery Winning the jackpot in the Florida Lotto requires that you choose six different numbers from 1 to 53, and your numbers must match the same six numbers that are later drawn. The order of the selected numbers does not matter. If you buy one ticket, what is the probability of winning the jackpot?

17. Teed Off When four golfers are about to begin a game, they often toss a tee to randomly select the order in which they tee off. What is the probability that they tee off in alphabetical order?

18. Stacking Books The author currently has seven different books in print. If those seven books are stacked in a random order, what is the probability that they are arranged in alphabetical order from top to bottom?

19. Maine Lottery

a. In the Maine Megabucks game, you win the jackpot by selecting five different whole numbers from 1 through 41 and getting the same five numbers (in any order) that are later drawn. What is the probability of winning a jackpot in this game?

b. In the Maine Pick 4 game, you win a straight bet by selecting four digits (with repetition allowed) and getting the same four digits in the exact same order they are later drawn. What is the probability of winning this game?

c. The Maine Pick 4 game returns $5000 for a winning $1 ticket. What should be the return if Maine were to run this game for no profit?

20. Illinois Lottery

a. In the Illinois Little Lotto game, you win the jackpot by selecting five different whole numbers from 1 through 39 and getting the same five numbers (in any order) that are later drawn. What is the probability of winning a jackpot in this game?

b. In the Illinois Pick 3 game, you win a bet by selecting three digits (with repetition allowed) and getting the same three digits in the exact same order as they are later drawn. What is the probability of winning this game?

c. The Illinois Pick 3 game returns $500 for a winning $1 ticket. What should be the return if Illinois were to run this game for no profit?

21. Corporate Officials and Committees The Teknomill Corporation must appoint a president, chief executive officer (CEO), chief operating officer (COO), and chief financial officer (CFO). It must also appoint a Planning Committee with four different members. There are 12 qualified candidates, and officers can also serve on the committee.

a. How many different ways can the officers be appointed?

b. How many different ways can the committee be appointed?

c. What is the probability of randomly selecting the committee members and getting the 4 youngest of the qualified candidates?

22. Phase I of a Clinical Trial A clinical test on humans of a new drug is normally done in three phases. Phase I is conducted with a relatively small number of healthy volunteers. For example, a phase I test of bexarotene involved only 14 subjects. Assume that we want to treat 14 healthy humans with this new drug and we have 16 suitable volunteers available.

a. If the subjects are selected and treated *in sequence*, so that the trial is discontinued if anyone displays adverse effects, how many different sequential arrangements are possible if 14 people are selected from the 16 that are available?

b. If 14 subjects are selected from the 16 that are available, and the 14 selected subjects are all treated at the same time, how many different treatment groups are possible?

c. If 14 subjects are randomly selected and treated at the same time, what is the probability of selecting the 14 youngest subjects?

23. Combination Lock The typical combination lock uses three numbers between 0 and 49, and they must be selected in the correct sequence. How many different "combinations" are possible? Which of the five rules of this section is used to find that number? Is the name of "combination lock" appropriate? If not, what other name would be better?

24. Safety with Numbers The author owns a safe in which he stores all of his great ideas for the next edition of this book. The safe "combination" consists of four numbers between 0 and 99, and the safe is designed so that numbers can be repeated. If another author breaks in and tries to steal these ideas, what is the probability that he or she will get the correct combination on the first attempt? Assume that the numbers are randomly selected. Given the number of possibilities, does it seem feasible to try opening the safe by making random guesses for the combination?

25. Jumble Puzzle Many newspapers carry "Jumble," a puzzle in which the reader must unscramble letters to form words. The letters MYAIT were included in newspapers on the day this exercise was written. How many ways can those letters be arranged? Identify the correct unscrambling; then determine the probability of getting that result by randomly selecting one arrangement of the given letters.

26. Jumble Puzzle Repeat the preceding exercise using these letters: RAWHOR.

27. Counting with Fingers How many different ways can you touch two or more fingers to each other on one hand?

28. Identity Theft with Credit Cards Credit card numbers typically have 16 digits, but not all of them are random. Answer the following and express probabilities as fractions.

a. What is the probability of randomly generating 16 digits and getting *your* MasterCard number?

b. Receipts often show the last four digits of a credit card number. If those last four digits are known, what is the probability of randomly generating the other digits of your MasterCard number?

c. Discover cards begin with the digits 6011. If you also know the last four digits of a Discover card, what is the probability of randomly generating the other digits and getting all of them correct? Is this something to worry about?

29. Electricity When testing for current in a cable with five color-coded wires, the author used a meter to test two wires at a time. How many different tests are required for every possible pairing of two wires?

30. ATM You want to obtain cash by using an ATM machine, but it's dark and you can't see your card when you insert it. The card must be inserted with the front side up and the printing configured so that the beginning of your name enters first.

a. What is the probability of selecting a random position and inserting the card with the result that the card is inserted correctly?

b. What is the probability of randomly selecting the card's position and finding that it is incorrectly inserted on the first attempt, but it is correctly inserted on the second attempt?

c. How many random selections are required to be absolutely sure that the card works because it is inserted correctly?

31. DNA Nucleotides DNA (deoxyribonucleic acid) is made of nucleotides. Each nucleotide can contain any one of these nitrogenous bases: A (adenine), G (guanine), C (cytosine), T (thymine). If one of those four bases (A, G, C, T) must be selected three times to form a linear triplet, how many different triplets are possible? All four bases can be selected for each of the three components of the triplet.

32. World Cup Soccer Tournament Every four years, 32 soccer teams compete in a world tournament.

a. How many games are required to get one championship team from the field of 32 teams?

b. If you make random guesses for each game of the tournament, find the probability of picking the winner in every game.

33. Powerball As of this writing, the Powerball lottery is run in 42 states. Winning the jackpot requires that you select the correct five numbers between 1 and 59 and, in a separate drawing, you must also select the correct single number between 1 and 39. Find the probability of winning the jackpot.

34. Mega Millions As of this writing, the Mega Millions lottery is run in 42 states. Winning the jackpot requires that you select the correct five numbers between 1 and 56 and, in a separate drawing, you must also select the correct single number between 1 and 46. Find the probability of winning the jackpot.

35. Designing Experiment Clinical trials of Nasonex involved a group given placebos and another group given treatments of Nasonex. Assume that a preliminary phase I trial is to be conducted with 10 subjects, including 5 men and 5 women. If 5 of the 10 subjects are randomly selected for the treatment group, find the probability of getting 5 subjects of the same sex. Would there be a problem with having members of the treatment group all of the same sex?

36. Area Codes *USA Today* reporter Paul Wiseman described the old rules for the three-digit telephone area codes by writing about "possible area codes with 1 or 0 in the second digit. (Excluded: codes ending in 00 or 11, for toll-free calls, emergency services, and other special uses.)" Codes beginning with 0 or 1 should also be excluded. How many different area codes were possible under these old rules?

4-6 Beyond the Basics

37. Computer Variable Names A common computer programming rule is that names of variables must be between one and eight characters long. The first character can be any of the 26 letters, while successive characters can be any of the 26 letters or any of the 10 digits. For example, allowable variable names are A, BBB, and M3477K. How many different variable names are possible?

38. Handshakes

a. Five managers gather for a meeting. If each manager shakes hands with each other manager exactly once, what is the total number of handshakes?

b. If n managers shake hands with each other exactly once, what is the total number of handshakes?

c. How many different ways can five managers be seated at a round table? (Assume that if everyone moves to the right, the seating arrangement is the same.)

d. How many different ways can n managers be seated at a round table?

39. Change for a Quarter How many different ways can you make change for a quarter? (Different arrangements of the same coins are not counted separately.)

40. Oldie but Goodie A secretary types 10 different letters and addresses 10 corresponding envelopes. If he is in a hurry and randomly inserts the letters into the envelopes, what is the probability that exactly 9 of the letters are in the correct envelopes? (Based on *Mathematics Magazine*, Vol. 23, No. 4, 1950)

4-7   Probabilities Through Simulations (on CD-ROM)

The CD-ROM included with this book includes another section that discusses the use of simulation methods for finding probabilities. Simulations are also discussed in the Technology Project near the end of this chapter.

4-8   Bayes' Theorem (on CD-ROM)

The CD-ROM included with this book includes another section dealing with conditional probability. This additional section discusses applications of *Bayes' theorem* (or *Bayes' rule*), which we use for revising a probability value based on additional information that is later obtained. See the CD-ROM for the discussion, examples, and exercises describing applications of Bayes' theorem.

Chapter 4   Review

The single most important concept presented in this chapter is the *rare event rule for inferential statistics*, because it forms the basis for *hypothesis testing* introduced in Chapter 8.

Rare Event Rule for Inferential Statistics

If, under a given assumption, the probability of a particular observed event is extremely small, we conclude that the assumption is probably not correct.

In Section 4-2 we presented the basic definitions and notation associated with probability. We should know that a probability value, which is expressed as a number between 0 and 1, reflects the likelihood of some event. We introduced the following important principles and notation.

Important Principles and Notation for Probability

- The probability of an event is a fraction or decimal number between 0 and 1 inclusive.
- The probability of an impossible event is 0.
- The probability of an event that is certain to occur is 1.
- Notation: The probability of event A is denoted by $P(A)$.
- Notation: The probability that event A does *not* occur is denoted by $P(\overline{A})$.

We gave three approaches to finding probabilities:

$$P(A) = \frac{\text{number of times that A occurred}}{\text{number of times trial was repeated}}$$ (relative frequency)

$$P(A) = \frac{\text{number of ways A can occur}}{\text{number of different simple events}} = \frac{s}{n}$$ (for equally likely outcomes)

$P(A)$ is *estimated* by using knowledge of the relevant circumstances. (subjective probability)

In Sections 4-3, 4-4, and 4-5 we considered compound events, which are events combining two or more simple events. We associated the word *or* with the addition rule and the word *and* with the multiplication rule.

Addition Rule for $P(A \text{ or } B)$

- $P(A \text{ or } B)$ denotes the probability that for a single trial, the outcome is event A or event B or both.

- The word *or* suggests addition, and when adding $P(A)$ and $P(B)$, we must be careful to add in such a way that every outcome is counted only once.

Multiplication Rule for $P(A \text{ and } B)$

- $P(A \text{ and } B)$ denotes the probability that event A occurs in one trial *and* event B occurs in another trial.

- The word *and* suggests multiplication, and when multiplying $P(A)$ and $P(B)$, we must be careful to ensure that the probability of event B takes into account the previous occurrence of event A.

- $P(B \mid A)$ denotes the conditional probability of event B occurring, given that event A has already occurred.

- $P(\textit{at least one} \text{ occurrence of event } A) = 1 - P(\textit{no} \text{ occurrences of event } A)$

Section 4-6 was devoted to the following five counting techniques, which are used to determine the total number of outcomes in probability problems:

Counting Rules

1. Fundamental Counting Rule

  $m \cdot n =$ Number of ways that two events can occur, given that the first event can occur m ways and the second event can occur n ways.

2. Factorial Rule

  $n! =$ Number of different *permutations* (order counts) of n different items when all n of them are selected.

3. Permutations Rule (When All of the Items Are Different)

  $_nP_r = \dfrac{n!}{(n-r)!} =$ Number of different *permutations* (order counts) when n different items are available, but only r of them are selected *without replacement*.

4. Permutations Rule (When Some Items Are Identical to Others)

  $\dfrac{n!}{n_1! n_2! \cdots n_k!} =$ Number of different *permutations* (order counts) when n items are available and all n are selected *without replacement* but some of the items are identical to others: n_1 are alike, n_2 are alike, . . . , and n_k are alike.

5. Combinations Rule

$$_nC_r = \frac{n!}{(n-r)!r!} = \text{Number of different combinations (order does not count)}$$

when n different items are available, but only r of them are selected *without replacement*.

Chapter Quick Quiz

1. A multiple-choice question on a statistics quiz has possible correct answers of a, b, c, d, e. What is the probability that "false" is the correct answer?

2. As the author is creating this exercise, a weather reporter stated that there are 3 chances in 10 of rain today. What is the probability of no rain today?

3. If a day of the week is randomly selected, what is the probability that it is a day containing the letter *y*?

4. Based on a Harris poll, 20% of adults smoke. If two adults are randomly selected, what is the probability that they both smoke?

5. Estimate the probability that a randomly selected prime-time television show will be interrupted with a news bulletin.

In Exercises 6–10, use the following results from the 839 player challenges to referee calls in the first U.S. Open tennis tournament to use the Hawk-Eye electronic instant replay system.

	Player Challenge Was Accepted	Player Challenge Was Rejected
Male Player	201	288
Female Player	126	224

6. If 1 of the 839 challenges is randomly selected, find the probability of getting a challenge that was rejected.

7. If 1 of the 839 challenges is randomly selected, find the probability of getting a challenge that was made by a male player or was rejected.

8. Find the probability of randomly selecting 1 of the 839 challenges and getting a challenge that was accepted and was made by a female player.

9. Find the probability of randomly selecting 2 different challenges and finding that they were both accepted challenges made by female players.

10. Find the probability of randomly selecting 1 of the 839 challenges and getting a challenge that was accepted, given that it was made by a female player.

Review Exercises

Prison and Plea.   *In Exercises 1–10, use the data in the accompanying table (based on data from "Does It Pay to Plead Guilty? Differential Sentencing and the Functioning of the Criminal Courts," by Brereton and Casper,* **Law and Society Review,** *Vol. 16, No. 1). Express all probabilities as decimal numbers.*

	Guilty Plea	Plea of Not Guilty
Sentenced to Prison	392	58
Not Sentenced to Prison	564	14

1. Prison and Plea If 1 of the 1028 subjects is randomly selected, find the probability of selecting someone sentenced to prison.

2. Prison and Plea Find the probability of being sentenced to prison, given that the subject entered a plea of guilty.

3. Prison and Plea Find the probability of being sentenced to prison, given that the subject entered a plea of not guilty.

4. Prison and Plea After comparing the results from Exercises 2 and 3, what do you conclude about the wisdom of entering a guilty plea?

5. Prison and Plea If 1 of the subjects is randomly selected, find the probability of selecting someone who was sentenced to prison or entered a plea of guilty.

6. Prison and Plea If 2 different study subjects are randomly selected, find the probability that they both were sentenced to prison.

7. Prison and Plea If 2 different study subjects are randomly selected, find the probability that they both entered pleas of not guilty.

8. Prison and Plea If 1 of the subjects is randomly selected, find the probability of selecting someone who entered a plea of not guilty or was not sentenced to prison.

9. Prison and Plea If 1 of the 1028 subjects is randomly selected, find the probability of selecting someone who was sentenced to prison and entered a guilty plea.

10. Prison and Plea If 1 of the subjects is randomly selected, find the probability of selecting someone who was not sentenced to prison and did not enter a plea of guilty.

11. Red Cars Use subjective probability to estimate the probability of randomly selecting a car and getting one that is red.

12. Blue Eyes About 35% of the population has blue eyes (based on a study by Dr. P. Sorita Soni at Indiana University).

a. If someone is randomly selected, what is the probability that he or she does not have blue eyes?

b. If four different people are randomly selected, what is the probability that they all have blue eyes?

c. Would it be unlikely to randomly select four people and find that they all have blue eyes? Why or why not?

13. National Statistics Day

a. If a person is randomly selected, find the probability that his or her birthday is October 18, which is National Statistics Day in Japan. Ignore leap years.

b. If a person is randomly selected, find the probability that his or her birthday is in October. Ignore leap years.

c. Estimate a subjective probability for the event of randomly selecting an adult American and getting someone who knows that October 18 is National Statistics Day in Japan.

d. Is it unlikely to randomly select an adult American and get someone who knows that October 18 is National Statistics Day in Japan?

14. Composite Sampling for STDs Currently, the rate for sexually transmitted diseases (STDs) is 213 per 100,000 (based on data from the Centers for Disease Control and Prevention). When testing for the presence of STDs, the Acton Medical Testing Company saves money by combining blood samples for tests. The combined sample tests positive if at least one person is infected. If the combined sample tests positive, then the individual blood tests are performed. In a test for STDs, blood samples from 10 randomly selected people are combined.

Find the probability that the combined sample tests positive with at least 1 of the 10 people infected. Is it likely that such combined samples test positive?

15. Georgia Win for Life In the Georgia Win for Life lottery, winning the top prize of $1000 a week for life requires that you select the correct six numbers between 1 and 42 (in any order). What is the probability of winning the top prize? Express the answer as a fraction.

16. Georgia Fantasy 5 In the Georgia Fantasy 5 lottery, winning the top prize requires that you select the correct five numbers between 1 and 39 (in any order). What is the probability of winning the top prize? Express the answer as a fraction.

17. Numbers Game Before the proliferation of legal lotteries, illegal numbers games were commonly run by members of organized crime groups. In the typical numbers game, bettors would win by selecting the same three digits that were later drawn in the same order. A common payoff was $600 for a winning $1 bet. Find the probability of winning with a bet in such a numbers game.

18. Trifecta In horse racing, a trifecta is a bet that the first three finishers in a race are selected in the correct order. In a race with 12 horses, how many different trifecta bets are possible? If you randomly guess the order of the first three finishers in a race with 12 horses, what is the probability of winning?

Cumulative Review Exercises

Please be aware that some of the following problems may require knowledge of concepts presented in previous chapters.

1. Oscar Winners Listed below are the differences (in years) between the ages of actresses and actors when they won Oscars. The differences are found by subtracting the age of the male winner from the age of the female winner: (actress age) − (actor age). The differences are found using results from the last 12 years (as listed in Data Set 11 in Appendix B).

$$-20 \quad -15 \quad -3 \quad -12 \quad 6 \quad -15 \quad -7 \quad -9 \quad 16 \quad -18 \quad -15 \quad -15$$

a. Find the mean. Compare the result to the value of the mean that would be expected if there is no gender discrepancy between the ages of Oscar-winning actresses and actors.

b. Find the median. Compare the result to the value of the median that would be expected if there is no gender discrepancy between the ages of Oscar-winning actresses and actors.

c. Find the standard deviation.

d. Find the variance. Be sure to include the units of measurement.

e. Find the value of the first quartile, Q_1.

f. Find the value of the third quartile, Q_3.

g. Construct a boxplot. What does the boxplot suggest about the distribution of the data?

2. Unusual/Unlikely Events

a. The mean pulse rate for adult women is 77.5 beats per minute, with a standard deviation of 11.6 beats per minute (based on Data Set 1 in Appendix B). Using the range rule of thumb, would a pulse rate of 100 beats per minute be considered unusual? Explain.

b. For the pulse rates of adult women described in part (a), is a pulse rate of 50 beats per minute unusual? Explain.

c. For a couple having eight children, is it unlikely to have all girls? Explain.

d. For a couple having three children, is it unlikely to have all girls? Explain.

3. Organ Donors *USA Today* provided information about a survey of 5100 adult Internet users. Of the respondents, 2346 said they are willing to donate organs after death. In this survey conducted for Donate Life America, 100 adults were surveyed in each state and the District of Columbia, and results were weighted to account for the different state population sizes.

a. What percentage of respondents said that they are willing to donate organs after death?

b. Based on the poll results, what is the probability of randomly selecting an adult who is willing to donate organs after death?

c. What term is used to describe the sampling method of randomly selecting 100 adults from each state and the District of Columbia?

4. Driving Survey In a survey of Americans age 16 years or older, respondents were asked if they texted or e-mailed while driving during the previous 30 days. The results are summarized in the accompanying graph (based on data from AAA Foundation for Traffic Safety). What is wrong with this graph?

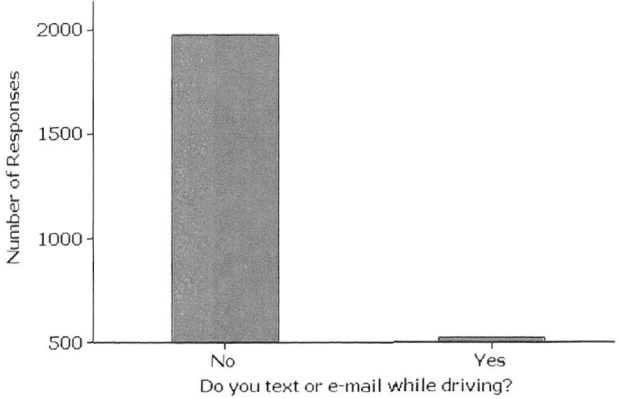

5. Sampling Eye Color Based on a study by Dr. P. Sorita Soni at Indiana University, we know that eye colors in the United States are distributed as follows: 40% brown, 35% blue, 12% green, 7% gray, 6% hazel.

a. A statistics instructor collects eye color data from her students. What is the name for this type of sample?

b. Identify one factor that might make this particular sample biased and not representative of the general population of people in the United States.

c. If one person is randomly selected, what is the probability that this person will have brown or blue eyes?

d. If two people are randomly selected, what is the probability that at least one of them has brown eyes?

6. Scatterplot of Bear Chest Sizes and Weights Given below are the chest sizes (inches) and weights (pounds) of 10 bears taken from Data Set 7 in Appendix B. Construct a scatterplot. Based on the scatterplot, does there appear to be a correlation between the chest sizes of bears and their weights?

Chest Size (in.)	26	45	54	49	35	41	41	49	38	31
Weight (lb)	80	344	416	348	166	220	262	360	204	144

7. Vermont Hot Lotto Winning the jackpot in the Vermont Hot Lotto game requires that you select five numbers between 1 and 39 and another number between 1 and 19. The first five numbers must match (in any order) the same five numbers that are later drawn, and the sixth number must also match the sixth number that is later drawn.

a. What is the probability that the first five selected numbers match the five numbers that are later drawn?

b. What is the probability that the sixth selected number matches the sixth number that is later drawn?

c. What is the probability of winning the jackpot?

Technology Project

Simulations

Calculating probabilities can often be painfully difficult, but *simulations* provide us with a very practical alternative to calculations based on formal rules. A **simulation** of a procedure is a process that behaves the same way as the procedure so that similar results are produced. Instead of calculating the probability of getting exactly 5 boys in 10 births, you could repeatedly toss 10 coins and count the number of times that 5 heads (or simulated "boys") occur. Better yet, you could do the simulation with a random number generator on a computer or calculator to randomly generate 1s (or simulated "boys") and 0s (or simulated "girls").

Let's consider this probability exercise:

Classic Birthday Problem

Find the probability that among 25 randomly selected people, at least 2 have the same birthday.

For the above classic birthday problem, a simulation begins by representing birthdays by integers from 1 through 365, where 1 represents a birthday of January 1, and 2 represents January 2, and so on. We can simulate 25 birthdays by using a calculator or computer to generate 25 random numbers (with repetition allowed) between 1 and 365. Those numbers can then be sorted, so it becomes easy to examine the list to determine whether any 2 of the simulated birth dates are the same. (After sorting, equal numbers are adjacent.) We can repeat the process as many times as we like, until we are satisfied that we have a good estimate of the probability. There are several ways of obtaining randomly generated numbers from 1 through 365, including the following:

STATDISK: Select **Data**, then select **Uniform Generator.** Enter a sample size of 25, a minimum of 1, and a maximum of 365, and enter 0 for the number of decimal places. The resulting STATDISK display will consist of 25 simulated birthdays. Use copy/paste to copy the data set to the **Sample Editor,** where the values can be sorted. To sort a column of data, click on Data, then select the first menu item of Sort Data. Make selections at the top and click on Sort.

Minitab: Click on **Calc**, select **Random Data,** then select **Integer.** In the dialog box, enter 25 for the number of rows, store the results in column C1, and enter a minimum of 1 and a maximum of 365. To sort the 25 simulated birthdays, click on **Data** and select **Sort** to arrange the data in increasing order.

Excel: Click on cell A1 (in the upper left corner), then click on the function icon *fx.* Select **Math & Trig,** then select **RANDBETWEEN.** In the dialog box, enter 1 for "bottom," and enter 365 for "top." After getting the random number in the first cell, click and hold down the mouse button to drag the lower right corner of this first cell, and pull it down the column until 25 cells are highlighted. When you release the mouse button, all 25 random numbers should be present.

TI-83/84 Plus: Press **MATH**, select **PRB,** then choose **randInt.** Enter the minimum of 1, the maximum of 365, and 25 for the number of values, all separated by commas, as in **randInt(1, 365, 25).** Press **ENTER**. You can store the results in list L1, then you can sort list L1 by pressing **STAT** and selecting **SortA** (sort in ascending order).

StatCrunch: Click on **Open StatCrunch,** then click on **Data** and select the menu item of **Simulate data.** Among the options available, select **Discrete Uniform.** In the dialog box that appears, enter 25 for the number of rows and enter 20 for the number of columns (as required for the following simulation). Enter 1 for the minimum and enter 365 for the maximum, then click on **Simulate.** You can sort columns by clicking on **Data,** then selecting the menu item of **Sort columns.** The sorted columns will appear to the right of the original columns.

Applying Simulation Methods

1. Use the above simulation method to randomly generate 20 different groups of 25 birthdays. Use the results to estimate the probability that among 25 randomly selected people, at least 2 have the same birthday.

2. One of the author's favorite class activities is to give this assignment: All students take out a coin and flip it. Students getting heads go home and actually flip a coin 200 times and record the results. Students getting tails make up their own results for 200 coin flips. In the next class, the author could select any student's results and quickly determine whether the results are real or fabricated by using this criterion: If there is a run of six heads or six tails, the results are real, but if there is no such run, the results are fabricated. This is based on the principle that when fabricating results, people almost never include a run of six or more heads or tails, but with 200 actual coin flips, there is a very high probability of getting such a run of at least six heads or tails. The calculation for the probability of getting a run of at least six heads or six tails is *extremely* difficult. Fortunately, simulations can let us know whether such runs are likely in 200 coin flips. Simulate 200 actual coin flips, repeat the simulation 20 times, then estimate the probability of getting a run of at least six heads or six tails when 200 coins are tossed. *Caution:* Do not sort generated numbers, because the probability should be based on the original sequence of coin tosses.

from data **TO DECISION**

Critical Thinking: Interpreting medical test results

All of us undergo medical tests at various times in our lives. Some of us are tested for drug use when we apply for jobs, some of us are tested for disease when we exhibit fever or other symptoms, some of us are tested for a variety of disorders when we undergo routine physical examinations, and some of us undergo tests for pregnancy. Because such tests typically provide some wrong results, it is important that we, along with our physicians, understand how to correctly interpret results. We should know that a positive test result does not necessarily mean that a condition is present, and we should know that a negative test result does not necessarily mean that the condition is not present.

West Nile Virus (WNV) is potentially serious and is sometimes fatal. Humans commonly acquire this virus through a mosquito bite. The table below includes results based on tests given to subjects in Queens, New York (based on data from the Centers for Disease Control and Prevention).

West Nile Virus Test

	Positive Test Result (West Nile Virus Is Indicated)	Negative Test Result (West Nile Virus Is Not Indicated)
Subject Is Infected	17 (True Positive)	6 (False Negative)
Subject Is Not Infected	2 (False Positive)	652 (True Negative)

Analyzing the Results

1. **False Positive** Based on the results in the table, find the probability that a subject is not infected, given that the test result is positive. That is, find P(false positive).

2. **True Positive** Based on the results in the table, find the probability that a subject is infected, given that the test result is positive. That is, find P(true positive).

3. **False Negative** Based on the results in the table, find the probability that a subject is infected, given that the test result is negative. That is, find P(false negative).

4. **True Negative** Based on the results in the table, find the probability that a subject is not infected, given that the test result is negative. That is, find P(true negative).

5. **Sensitivity** Find the *sensitivity* of the test by finding the probability of a true positive, given that the subject is actually infected.

6. **Specificity** Find the *specificity* of the test by finding the probability of a true negative, given that the subject is not infected.

7. **Positive Predictive Value** Find the *positive predictive value* of the test by finding the probability of a true positive, given that the test yields a positive result.

8. **Negative Predictive Value** Find the *negative predictive value* of the test by finding the probability of a true negative, given that the test yields a negative result.

9. **Confusion of the Inverse** Find the following values, then compare them. In this case, what is confusion of the inverse?

   - P(subject is infected | positive test result)

   - P(positive test result | subject is infected)

Cooperative Group Activities

1. Out-of-class activity Divide into groups of three or four and create a new carnival game. Determine the probability of winning. Determine how much money the operator of the game can expect to take in each time the game is played.

2. In-class activity Divide into groups of three or four and use coin flipping to develop a simulation that emulates the kingdom that abides by this decree: After a mother gives birth to a son, she will not have any other children. If this decree is followed, does the proportion of girls increase?

3. In-class activity Divide into groups of three or four and use actual thumbtacks to estimate the probability that when dropped, a thumbtack will land with the point up. How many trials are necessary to get a result that appears to be reasonably accurate when rounded to the first decimal place?

4. In-class activity Divide into groups of three or four and use Hershey's Kiss candies to estimate the probability that when dropped, they land with the flat part lying on the floor. How many trials are necessary to get a result that appears to be reasonably accurate when rounded to the first decimal place?

5. In-class activity Divide into groups of three or four and use a paper cup to estimate the probability that when dropped, the cup will land upside down, with the opening on the floor. How many trials are necessary to get a result that appears to be reasonably accurate when rounded to the first decimal place?

6. Out-of-class activity Marine biologists often use the *capture-recapture method* as a way to estimate the size of a population, such as the number of fish in a lake. This method involves capturing a sample from the population, tagging each member in the sample, then returning them to the population. A second sample is later captured, and the tagged members are counted along with the total size of this second sample. The results can be used to estimate the size of the population.

Instead of capturing real fish, simulate the procedure using some uniform collection of items such as BBs, colored beads, M&Ms, Fruit Loop cereal pieces, or index cards. Start with a large collection of such items. Collect a sample of 50 and use a magic marker to "tag" each one. Replace the tagged items, mix the whole population, then select a second sample and proceed to estimate the population size. Compare the result to the actual population size obtained by counting all of the items.

7. Out-of-class activity Divide into groups of three or four. First, use subjective estimates for the probability of randomly selecting a car and getting each of these car colors: black, white, blue, red, silver, other. Then design a sampling plan for obtaining car colors through observation. Execute the sampling plan and obtain revised probabilities based on the observed results. Write a brief report of the results.

8. In-class activity The manufacturing process for a new computer integrated circuit has a yield of 1/6, meaning that 1/6 of the circuits are good and the other 5/6 are defective. Use a die to simulate this manufacturing process, and consider an outcome of 1 to be a good circuit, while outcomes of 2, 3, 4, 5, or 6 represent defective circuits. Find the mean number of circuits that must be manufactured to get one that is good.

9. In-class activity The *Monty Hall problem* is based on the old television game show *Let's Make a Deal,* hosted by Monty Hall. Suppose you are a contestant who has selected one of three doors after being told that two of them conceal nothing, but that a new red Corvette is behind one of the three. Next, the host opens one of the doors you didn't select and shows that there is nothing behind it. He then offers you the choice of *sticking* with your first selection or *switching* to the other unopened door. Should you stick with your first choice or should you switch? Divide into groups of two and simulate this game to determine whether you should stick or switch. (According to *Chance* magazine, business schools at such institutions as Harvard and Stanford use this problem to help students deal with decision making.)

5 Discrete Probability Distributions

Is the XSORT gender-selection method effective?

We live in a time with incredible advances in technology, medicine, and health care. Cloning is no longer science fiction. We have iPods, iPads, iPhones, and 3-D televisions. We carry calculators that can instantly execute many complex statistical calculations. Heart pacemakers have defibrillators capable of shocking and restarting stopped hearts. Couples use procedures that are claimed to greatly increase the chance of having a baby with a desired gender.

Some people argue that gender-selection methods should be banned, regardless of the reason, while others enthusiastically support the use of such methods. Lisa Belkin asked in the *New York Times Magazine,* "If we allow parents to choose the sex of their child today, how long will it be before they order up eye color, hair color, personality traits, and IQ?" There are some convincing arguments in favor of at least limited use of gender selection. One such argument involves couples carrying X-linked recessive genes. For some of those couples, any male children have a 50% chance of inheriting a serious disorder, but none of the female children will inherit the disorder. Those couples may want to use gender selection as a way to ensure that they have baby girls, thereby guaranteeing that a serious disorder will not be inherited by any of their children.

The Genetics and IVF Institute in Fairfax, Virginia developed a technique called MicroSort that it claims increases the chances of a couple having a baby with a desired gender. The MicroSort XSORT method is claimed to increase the chances of a couple having a baby girl, and the MicroSort YSORT method is claimed to increase the chances of a baby boy. Current results for the XSORT method consist of 945 couples who wanted to have baby girls. After using the XSORT technique, 879 of those couples had baby girls. (See Figure 5-1 for a bar graph illustrating these results.) We usually expect that in 945 births, the number of girls should be somewhere around 472 or 473. Given that 879 out of 945 couples had girls, can we conclude that the XSORT technique is effective, or might we explain the outcome as just a chance sample result? In answering that question, we will use principles of probability to determine whether the observed birth results differ significantly from results that we would expect from random chance. This is a common goal of inferential statistics: Determine whether results can be reasonably explained by random chance or whether random chance doesn't appear to be a feasible explanation, so that other factors are influencing results. In

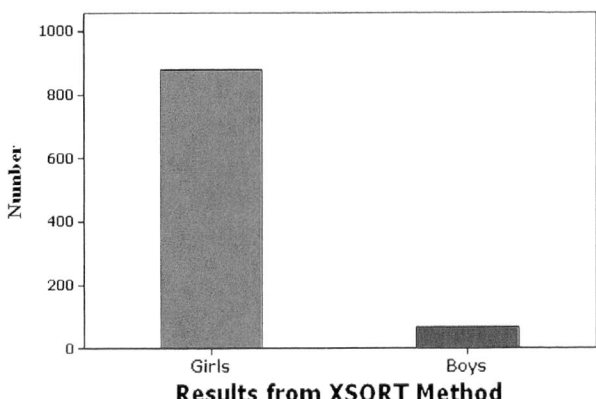

Figure 5-1 Current Results from the XSORT Method of Gender Selection

this chapter we present methods that allow us to find the probabilities we need for determining whether the XSORT results are significant, suggesting that the method is effective.

5-1   Review and Preview

Figure 5-2 provides a visual illustration of what this chapter accomplishes. When investigating the numbers of girls in families with exactly two children, we can use the following two different approaches:

- **Use real sample data:** The approach of Chapters 2 and 3 is to collect sample data from actual families, then summarize the results in a table representing the frequency distribution, and then find statistics, such as the sample mean $\bar{x}$ and the sample standard deviation s.

- **Use probabilities to find the results that are expected:** Using principles of probability from Chapter 4, we can find the probability for each possible number of girls. Then we could summarize the results in a table representing a probability distribution.

In this chapter we merge the above two approaches as we create a table describing what we expect to happen, then proceed to find parameters such as the population mean μ and population standard deviation σ. (These values are population parameters because they describe the behavior of the population of all families with two children, not an actual sample of a limited number of such families.) The table at the extreme right in Figure 5-2 represents a *probability distribution,* because it describes the distribution using probabilities instead of frequency counts from actual families. The remainder of this book and the very core of inferential statistics are based on some knowledge of probability distributions. In this chapter we focus on *discrete* probability distributions. *Continuous* probability distributions are discussed in Chapter 6.

Figure 5-2

5-2   Probability Distributions

Key Concept In this section we introduce the concept of a *random variable* and the concept of a *probability distribution.* We illustrate how a *probability histogram* is a graph that visually depicts a probability distribution. We show how to find the important parameters of mean, standard deviation, and variance for a probability distribution. Most importantly, we describe how to determine whether outcomes are *unlikely* to occur by chance. We begin with the related concepts of *random variable* and *probability distribution.*

Part 1: Basic Concepts of a Probability Distribution

> **DEFINITIONS**
>
> A **random variable** is a variable (typically represented by x) that has a single numerical value, determined by chance, for each outcome of a procedure.
>
> A **probability distribution** is a description that gives the probability for each value of the random variable. It is often expressed in the format of a table, formula, or graph.

In Section 1-3 we made a distinction between discrete and continuous data. Random variables may also be discrete or continuous, and the following two definitions are consistent with those given in Section 1-3.

> **DEFINITIONS**
>
> A **discrete random variable** has a collection of values that is finite or countable. (If there are infinitely many values, the number of values is countable if it is possible to count them individually, such as the number of tosses of a coin before getting tails.)
>
> A **continuous random variable** has infinitely many values, and the collection of values is not countable. (That is, it is impossible to count the individual items because at least some of them are on a continuous scale.)

This chapter deals exclusively with discrete random variables, but the following chapters will deal with continuous random variables.

Every probability distribution must satisfy each of the following three requirements.

Probability Distribution: Requirements

1. There is a numerical random variable x and its values are associated with corresponding probabilities.

2. $\Sigma P(x) = 1$ where x assumes all possible values. (The sum of all probabilities must be 1, but sums such as 0.999 or 1.001 are acceptable because they result from rounding errors.)

3. $0 \leq P(x) \leq 1$ for every individual value of the random variable x. (That is, each probability value must be between 0 and 1 inclusive.)

The second requirement comes from the simple fact that the random variable x represents all possible events in the entire sample space, so we are certain (with probability 1) that one of the events will occur. The third requirement comes from the basic principle that any probability value must be 0 or 1 or a value between 0 and 1.

Example 1 Genetics

Although the Chapter Problem involves 945 births, let's consider a simpler example that involves only two births with the following random variable:

$$x = \text{number of girls in two births}$$

The above x is a random variable because its numerical values depend on chance. With two births, the number of girls can be 0, 1, or 2, and Table 5-1 is a probability distribution because it gives the probability for each value of the random variable x and it satisfies the three requirements listed earlier:

1. The variable x is a numerical random variable and its values are associated with probabilities, as in Table 5-1.

2. $\Sigma P(x) = 0.25 + 0.50 + 0.25 = 1$

3. Each value of $P(x)$ is between 0 and 1. (Specifically, 0.25 and 0.50 and 0.25 are each between 0 and 1 inclusive.)

The random variable x in Table 5-1 is a *discrete* random variable, because it has three possible values (0, 1, 2), and 3 is a finite number, so this satisfies the requirement of being finite or countable.

Table 5-1 Probability Distribution for the Number of Girls in Two Births

Number of Girls x	P(x)
0	0.25
1	0.50
2	0.25

Notation

In tables such as Table 5-1 or the Binomial Probabilities in Table A-1 in Appendix A, we sometimes use 0+ to represent a probability value that is positive but very small, such as 0.000000123. (When rounding a probability value for inclusion in such a table, a rounded value of 0 would be misleading because it incorrectly suggests that the event is impossible.)

Probability Distribution: Graph

There are various ways to graph a probability distribution, but we will consider only the **probability histogram.** Figure 5-3 is a probability histogram corresponding to Table 5-1. Notice that it is similar to a relative frequency histogram (described in Section 2-3), but the vertical scale shows *probabilities* instead of relative frequencies based on actual sample results.

In Figure 5-3, we see that the values of 0, 1, 2 along the horizontal axis are located at the centers of the rectangles. This implies that the rectangles are each 1 unit wide, so the areas of the rectangles are 0.25, 0.50, and 0.25. The *areas*

Figure 5-3

Probability Histogram for Number of Girls in Two Births

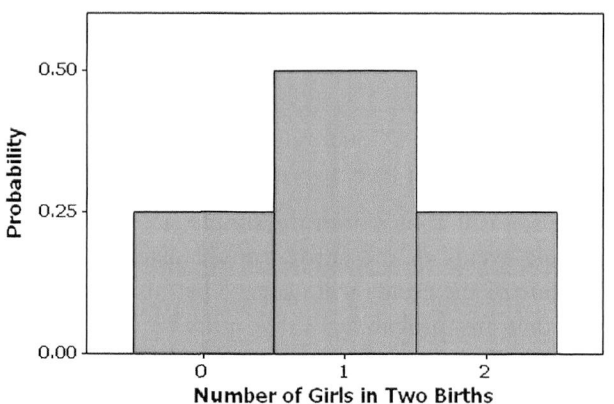

of these rectangles are the same as the *probabilities* in Table 5-1. We will see in Chapter 6 and future chapters that such a correspondence between area and probability is very useful.

Example 2 Marijuana Survey

In a Pew Research Center poll, subjects were asked if the use of marijuana should be made legal, and the results from that poll have been used to create Table 5-2. Does Table 5-2 describe a probability distribution?

Solution

Consider the three requirements listed earlier.

1. The responses (yes, no, don't know) are not numerical, so we do not have a numerical random variable. The first requirement is violated, so Table 5-2 does not describe a probability distribution.

2. The sum of the probabilities is 1.

3. Each probability is between 0 and 1 inclusive.

Because one of the three requirements is not met, Table 5-2 does not describe a probability distribution.

Table 5-2 Should Marijuana Use Be Legal?

Response	$P(x)$
Yes	0.41
No	0.52
Don't know	0.07

Example 3 When to Discuss Salary

Senior executives were asked when job applicants should discuss salary, and Table 5-3 is based on their responses (based on data from an Accountemps survey). Does Table 5-3 describe a probability distribution?

Solution

To be a probability distribution, we must have a numerical random variable x such that $P(x)$ must satisfy the preceding three requirements.

1. The variable x is a numerical random variable and its values are associated with probabilities, as in Table 5-3.

2. $\Sigma P(x) = P(1) + P(2) + P(3)$
   $= 0.30 + 0.26 + 0.10$
   $= 0.66$ [showing that $\Sigma P(x) \neq 1$]

3. Each value of $P(x)$ is between 0 and 1 inclusive.

Because the second requirement is not satisfied, we conclude that Table 5-3 does *not* describe a probability distribution.

Table 5-3 When to Discuss Salary

Number of Interviews x	$P(x)$
1	0.30
2	0.26
3	0.10

Example 4

Does $P(x) = \dfrac{x}{3}$ (where x can be 0, 1, or 2) determine a probability distribution?

Solution

To be a probability distribution, we must have a numerical random variable x such that $P(x)$ must satisfy the preceding three requirements. From the given formula we find that $P(0) = 0/3$ and $P(1) = 1/3$ and $P(2) = 2/3$.

1. The variable x is a numerical random variable and its values (0, 1, 2) are associated with probabilities, as determined by the given formula.

2. $\Sigma P(x) = P(0) + P(1) + P(2) = \dfrac{0}{3} + \dfrac{1}{3} + \dfrac{2}{3} = 1$

3. Each value of $P(x)$ is between 0 and 1 inclusive.

Because the three requirements are satisfied, we conclude that the given formula does describe a probability distribution.

Parameters of a Probability Distribution: Mean, Variance, and Standard Deviation

Remember that with a probability distribution, we have a description of a *population* instead of a sample, so the values of the mean, standard deviation, and variance are *parameters* instead of statistics. The mean is the central or "average" value of the random variable. The variance and standard deviation measure the variation of the random variable. These parameters can be found with the following formulas:

Formula 5-1 $\mu = \Sigma [x \cdot P(x)]$

Mean for a probability distribution

Formula 5-2 $\sigma^2 = \Sigma [(x - \mu)^2 \cdot P(x)]$

Variance for a probability distribution (This format is easier to understand.)

Formula 5-3 $\sigma^2 = \Sigma [x^2 \cdot P(x)] - \mu^2$

Variance for a probability distribution (This format is easier for manual computations.)

Formula 5-4 $\sigma = \sqrt{\Sigma [x^2 \cdot P(x)] - \mu^2}$

Standard deviation for a probability distribution

When applying Formulas 5-1 through 5-4, use the following rule for rounding results.

Round-off Rule for μ, σ, and σ^2 from a Probability Distribution

Round results by carrying one more decimal place than the number of decimal places used for the random variable x. If the values of x are integers, round μ, σ, and σ^2 to one decimal place.

It is sometimes necessary to use a different rounding rule because of special circumstances, such as results that require more decimal places to be meaningful. For example, with four-engine jets the mean number of jet engines working successfully throughout a flight is 3.999714286, which becomes 4.0 when rounded to one more decimal place than the original data. Here, 4.0 would be misleading because it suggests that all jet engines always work successfully. We need more precision to correctly reflect the true mean, such as the precision in the number 3.999714.

Expected Value

The mean of a discrete random variable x is the theoretical mean outcome for infinitely many trials. We can think of that mean as the *expected value* in the sense that it is the average value that we would expect to get if the trials could continue indefinitely. The uses of expected value (also called *expectation,* or *mathematical expectation*) are extensive and varied, and they play an important role in *decision theory.* (See Example 8 in Part 2 of this section.)

> **DEFINITION** The **expected value** of a discrete random variable x is denoted by E, and it is the mean value of the outcomes, so $E = \mu$ and E can also be found by evaluating $\Sigma [x \cdot P(x)]$, as in Formula 5-1.

CAUTION An expected value need not be a whole number, even if the different possible values of x might all be whole numbers. We say that the expected number of girls in five births is 2.5, even though five specific births can never result in 2.5 girls. If we were to survey many couples with five children, we *expect* that the mean number of girls will be 2.5.

Example 5 Finding the Mean, Variance, and Standard Deviation

Table 5-1 describes the probability distribution for the number of girls in two births. Find the mean, variance, and standard deviation for the probability distribution described in Table 5-1 from Example 1.

Solution

In Table 5-4, the two columns at the left describe the probability distribution given earlier in Table 5-1; we create the three columns at the right for the purposes of the calculations required.

Using Formulas 5-1 and 5-2 and the table results, we get

Mean: $\mu = \Sigma [x \cdot P(x)] = 1.0$

Variance: $\sigma^2 = \Sigma [(x - \mu)^2 \cdot P(x)] = 0.5$

The standard deviation is the square root of the variance, so

Standard deviation: $\sigma = \sqrt{0.5} = 0.707107 = 0.7$ (rounded)

Table 5-4 Calculating μ and σ for a Probability Distribution

x	$P(x)$	$x \cdot P(x)$	$(x - \mu)^2 \cdot P(x)$
0	0.25	$0 \cdot 0.25 = 0.00$	$(0 - 1)^2 \cdot 0.25 = 0.25$
1	0.50	$1 \cdot 0.50 = 0.50$	$(1 - 1)^2 \cdot 0.50 = 0.00$
2	0.25	$2 \cdot 0.25 = 0.50$	$(2 - 1)^2 \cdot 0.25 = 0.25$
Total		1.00	0.50
		↑	↑
		$\mu = \Sigma [x \cdot P(x)]$	$\sigma^2 = \Sigma [(x - \mu)^2 \cdot P(x)]$

Interpretation

The mean number of girls in two births is 1.0 girl, the variance is 0.50 "girls squared," and the standard deviation is 0.7 girl. Also, the expected value for the number of girls in two births is 1.0 girl, which is the same value as the mean. If we were to collect data on a large number of couples with two children, we expect to get a mean of 1.0 girl.

Making Sense of Results: Identifying Unusual Values

We present the following two different approaches for determining whether a value of a random variable x is unusually low or unusually high.

Identifying Unusual Results with the Range Rule of Thumb

The range rule of thumb (introduced in Section 3-3) may be helpful in interpreting the value of a standard deviation. According to the range rule of thumb, the vast majority of values should lie within 2 standard deviations of the mean, so we can consider a value to be unusual if it is more than 2 standard deviations away from the mean. (The use of 2 standard deviations is not an absolutely rigid value, and other values such as 3 could be used instead.) We can therefore identify "unusual" values by determining that they lie outside of these limits:

Range Rule of Thumb

$$\text{maximum usual value} = \mu + 2\sigma$$
$$\text{minimum usual value} = \mu - 2\sigma$$

CAUTION Know that the use of the number 2 in the range rule of thumb is somewhat arbitrary, and this rule is a guideline, not an absolutely rigid rule.

Example 6   Identifying Unusual Results with the Range Rule of Thumb

In Example 5 we found that for families with two children, the mean number of girls is 1.0 and the standard deviation is 0.7 girl. Use those results and the range rule of thumb to find the maximum and minimum usual values for the number of girls. Based on the results, if a couple has two children, is 2 girls an unusually high number of girls?

Solution

Using the range rule of thumb, we can find the maximum and minimum usual values as follows:

maximum usual value: $\mu + 2\sigma = 1.0 + 2(0.7) = 2.4$

minimum usual value: $\mu - 2\sigma = 1.0 - 2(0.7) = -0.4$

Interpretation

Based on these results, we conclude that for families with two children, the number of girls should usually fall between -0.4 and 2.4, so 2 girls is not an unusually high number of girls (because 2 falls between -0.4 and 2.4). (In this case, the minimum usual value is actually 0, because that is the lowest possible number of girls, and the maximum usual value is 2 because that is the highest possible number of girls.)

Identifying Unusual Results with Probabilities: The Rare Event Rule for Inferential Statistics

If, under a given assumption (such as the assumption that boys and girls have the same chance of being born), the probability of a particular observed event (such as 879 girls in 945 births) is extremely small, we conclude that the assumption is probably not correct.

Probabilities can be used to apply the rare event rule as follows:

Using Probabilities to Determine When Results Are Unusual

- **Unusually *high* number of successes:** x successes among n trials is an *unusually high* number of successes if the probability of x or more successes is unlikely with a probability of 0.05 or less. This criterion can be expressed as follows: $P(x \text{ or more}) \le 0.05$.*

- **Unusually *low* number of successes:** x successes among n trials is an *unusually low* number of successes if the probability of x or fewer successes is unlikely with a probability of 0.05 or less. That is, x is an unusually low number of successes if $P(x \text{ or fewer}) \le 0.05$.*

*The value 0.05 is not absolutely rigid. Other values, such as 0.01, could be used to distinguish between results that can easily occur by chance and events that are very unlikely to occur by chance.

CAUTION The above criteria are not exactly equivalent to those used for the range rule of thumb. Chapter 8 introduces more formal and exact methods that will replace the above criteria and the range rule of thumb.

Unusually High or Unusually Low Number of Successes: Not *Exactly,* but "At Least as Extreme"

In Section 4-2 we stated that a number of successes is unusually low or unusually high if that number is far from what we typically expect. We will now refine that description by using a probability value to judge whether a particular number of successes among n trials is unusually high or unusually low. Use the probability of getting x *or any other values that are more extreme;* do *not* use only the probability of *exactly* x successes. For example, suppose you were tossing a coin to determine whether it favors heads, and suppose 1000 tosses resulted in 501 heads. We can use methods from Section 5-3 to find the following two probabilities:

- $P(exactly \text{ 501 heads in 1000 tosses}) = 0.0252$ (so exactly 501 heads is *unlikely*)

- $P(501 \text{ } or \text{ } more \text{ heads in 1000 tosses}) = 0.487$ (so 501 heads is *not unusually high*)

We use the second of the preceding two probabilities for determining whether 501 heads in 1000 tosses is an unusually high number of heads. (We do not base our answer on the probability of *exactly* 501 heads, which is the small value of 0.0252. In this situation, any specific number of heads will have a very low probability.) Based on the 0.487 probability of getting 501 heads or more, we conclude that 501 heads in 1000 tosses of a fair coin is not an unusually high number of heads. (See Example 11 in Section 4-2.)

 Example 7   Identifying Unusual Results with Probabilities

The Chapter Problem includes results consisting of 879 girls in 945 births. Is 879 girls in 945 births an unusually high number of girls? What does it suggest about the effectiveness of the XSORT method of gender selection?

Solution

The result of 879 girls in 945 births is more than we expect under normal circumstances, so we want to determine whether 879 girls is *unusually high.* Here, the relevant probability is the probability of getting *879 or more* girls in 945 births. Using methods covered later in Section 5-3, we can find that P(879 or more girls in 945 births) $= 0.000$ when rounded to three decimal places. (We can denote such a probability as $0+$.) Because the probability of getting 879 or more girls is less than or equal to 0.05, we conclude that 879 girls in 945 births is an unusually high number of girls.

Interpretation

Because it is so unlikely that we would get 879 or more girls in 945 births by chance, these results suggest that the XSORT method of gender selection is effective in increasing the likelihood that a baby will be a girl. (However, this does not *prove* that the XSORT method is responsible for the large number of girls.)

Part 2: Expected Value in Decision Theory and Rationale for Formulas 5-1 through 5-4

Expected Value in Decision Theory

In Part 1 of this section we noted that the expected value of a random variable x is equal to the mean μ. We can therefore find the expected value by computing $\Sigma \left[x \cdot P(x) \right]$, just as we do for finding the value of μ. We also noted that the concept of expected value is used in *decision theory*. In Example 8 we illustrate this use of expected value with a situation in which we must choose between two different bets. Example 8 involves a real and practical decision.

Example 8   Be a Better Bettor

You have $5 to place on a bet in the Golden Nugget casino in Las Vegas. You have narrowed your choice to one of two bets:

Roulette: Bet on the number 7 in roulette.

Craps: Bet on the "pass line" in the dice game of craps.

a. If you bet $5 on the number 7 in roulette, the probability of losing $5 is 37/38 and the probability of making a net gain of $175 is 1/38. (The prize is $180, including your $5 bet, so the net gain is $175.) Find your expected value if you bet $5 on the number 7 in roulette.

b. If you bet $5 on the pass line in the dice game of craps, the probability of losing $5 is 251/495 and the probability of making a net gain of $5 is 244/495. (If you bet $5 on the pass line and win, you are given $10 that includes your bet, so the net gain is $5.) Find your expected value if you bet $5 on the pass line.

Which of the preceding two bets is better? Why?

Solution

a. Roulette The probabilities and payoffs for betting $5 on the number 7 in roulette are summarized in Table 5-5. Table 5-5 also shows that the expected value is $\Sigma\left[x \cdot P(x)\right] = -26¢$. That is, for every $5 bet on the number 7, you can expect to *lose* an average of 26¢.

Table 5-5 Roulette

Event	x	P(x)	x · P(x)
Lose	−$5	37/38	−$4.868421
Win (net gain)	$175	1/38	$4.605263
Total			−$0.26 (rounded) (or −26¢)

b. Dice The probabilities and payoffs for betting $5 on the pass line in craps are summarized in Table 5-6. Table 5-6 also shows that the expected value is $\Sigma\left[x \cdot P(x)\right] = -7¢$. That is, for every $5 bet on the pass line, you can expect to lose an average of 7¢.

Table 5-6 Dice

Event	x	P(x)	x · P(x)
Lose	−$5	251/495	−$2.535353
Win (net gain)	$5	244/495	$2.464646
Total			−$0.07 (rounded) (or −7¢)

Interpretation

The $5 bet in roulette results in an expected value of −26¢ and the $5 bet in craps results in an expected value of −7¢. Because you are better off losing 7¢ instead of losing 26¢, the craps game is better in the long run, even though the roulette game provides an opportunity for a larger payoff.

Rationale for Formulas 5-1 through 5-4

Instead of blindly accepting and using formulas, it is much better to have some under-standing of why they work. When computing the mean from a frequency distribu-tion, f represents class frequency and N represents population size. In the expression below, we rewrite the formula for the mean of a frequency table so that it applies to a population. In the fraction f/N, the value of f is the frequency with which the value x occurs and N is the population size, so f/N is the probability for the value of x. When we replace f/N with $P(x)$, we make the transition from relative frequency based on a limited number of observations to probability based on infinitely many trials. This result shows why Formula 5-1 is as given earlier in this section.

$$\mu = \frac{\Sigma(f \cdot x)}{N} = \Sigma\left[\frac{f \cdot x}{N}\right] = \Sigma\left[x \cdot \frac{f}{N}\right] = \Sigma[x \cdot P(x)]$$

Similar reasoning enables us to take the variance formula from Chapter 3 and apply it to a random variable for a probability distribution; the result is Formula 5-2. Formula 5-3 is a shortcut version that will always produce the same result as Formula 5-2. Although Formula 5-3 is usually easier to work with, Formula 5-2 is easier to understand directly. Based on Formula 5-2, we can express the standard deviation as

$$\sigma = \sqrt{\Sigma[(x - \mu)^2 \cdot P(x)]}$$

or as the equivalent form given in Formula 5-4.

5-2 Basic Skills and Concepts

Statistical Literacy and Critical Thinking

1. Random Variable Table 5-7 lists probabilities for the corresponding numbers of girls in three births. What is the random variable, what are its possible values, and are its values numerical?

2. Discrete or Continuous? Is the random variable given in Table 5-7 discrete or continuous? Explain.

3. Probability Distribution Does Table 5-7 describe a probability distribution? Show how the requirements are satisfied or are not satisfied.

4. Unusual For 200 births, the probability of exactly 90 girls is 0.0208 and the probability of 90 or fewer girls is 0.089.

a. Is exactly 90 girls in 200 births unlikely?

b. Among 200 births, is 90 girls an unusually low number of girls?

Table 5-7 Number of Girls in Three Births

Number of Girls x	P(x)
0	0.125
1	0.375
2	0.375
3	0.125

Identifying Discrete and Continuous Random Variables. *In Exercises 5 and 6, identify the given values as a* **discrete random variable, continuous random variable,** *or* **not a random variable.**

5. a. Exact weights of quarters now in circulation in the United States

b. Numbers of tosses of quarters required to get heads

c. Responses to the survey question "Did you smoke at least one cigarette in the last week?"

d. Numbers of spins of roulette wheels required to get the number 7

e. Exact foot lengths of humans

f. Shoe sizes (such as 8 or 8½) of humans

6. a. Eye colors of humans on commercial aircraft flights

b. Weights of humans on commercial aircraft flights

c. Numbers of passengers on commercial aircraft flights

d. Numbers of randomly generated digits before getting the digit 3

e. Political party affiliations of adults in the United States

f. Exact costs of presidential campaigns

Identifying Probability Distributions. *In Exercises 7–14, determine whether a probability distribution is given. If a probability distribution is given, find its mean and standard deviation. If a probability distribution is not given, identify the requirements that are not satisfied.*

7. Genetic Disorder Four males with an X-linked genetic disorder have one child each. The random variable x is the number of children among the four who inherit the X-linked genetic disorder.

x	P(x)
0	0.0625
1	0.2500
2	0.3750
3	0.2500
4	0.0625

8. Male Color Blindness When conducting research on color blindness in males, a researcher forms random groups with five males in each group. The random variable x is the number of males in the group who have a form of color blindness (based on data from the National Institutes of Health).

x	P(x)
0	0.659
1	0.287
2	0.050
3	0.004
4	0.001
5	0+

9. Pickup Line Ted is not particularly creative. He uses this pickup line "If I could rearrange the alphabet, I'd put U and I together." The random variable x is the number of girls Ted approaches before encountering one who reacts positively.

x	P(x)
1	0.001
2	0.020
3	0.105
4	0.233
5	0.242

10. Fun Ways to Flirt In a Microsoft Instant Messaging survey, respondents were asked to choose the most fun way to flirt, and the accompanying table is based on the results.

	P(x)
E-mail	0.06
In person	0.55
Instant message	0.24
Text message	0.15

11. Fun Ways to Flirt A sociologist randomly selects single adults for different groups of four, and the random variable x is the number in the group who say that the most fun way to flirt is in person (based on a Microsoft Instant Messaging survey).

x	P(x)
0	0.041
1	0.200
2	0.367
3	0.299
4	0.092

12. Happiness Groups of people aged 15–65 are randomly selected and arranged in groups of six. The random variable x is the number in the group who say that their family and/or partner contribute most to their happiness (based on a Coca-Cola survey).

x	P(x)
0	0+
1	0.003
2	0.025
3	0.111
4	0.279
5	0.373
6	0.208

13. Happiness In a survey sponsored by Coca-Cola, subjects aged 15–65 were asked what contributes most to their happiness, and the table is based on their responses.

	P(x)
Family/partner	0.77
Friends	0.15
Work/studies	0.08
Leisure	0.08
Music	0.06
Sports	0.04

14. Casino Games When betting on the pass line in the dice game of craps at the Mohegan Sun casino in Connecticut, the table lists the probabilities for the number of bets that must be placed in order to have a win.

x	P(x)
1	0.493
2	0.250
3	0.127
4	0.064
5	0.033

Genetics. *In Exercises 15–18, refer to the accompanying table, which describes results from groups of 10 births from 10 different sets of parents. The random variable x represents the number of girls among 10 children.*

Number of Girls x	P(x)
0	0.001
1	0.010
2	0.044
3	0.117
4	0.205
5	0.246
6	0.205
7	0.117
8	0.044
9	0.010
10	0.001

15. Mean and Standard Deviation Find the mean and standard deviation for the numbers of girls in 10 births.

16. Range Rule of Thumb for Unusual Events Use the range rule of thumb to identify a range of values containing the usual numbers of girls in 10 births. Based on the result, is 1 girl in 10 births an unusually low number of girls? Explain.

17. Using Probabilities for Unusual Events

a. Find the probability of getting exactly 8 girls in 10 births.

b. Find the probability of getting 8 or more girls in 10 births.

c. Which probability is relevant for determining whether 8 is an unusually high number of girls in 10 births: the result from part (a) or part (b)?

d. Is 8 an unusually high number of girls in 10 births? Why or why not?

18. Using Probabilities for Unusual Events

a. Find the probability of getting exactly 1 girl in 10 births.

b. Find the probability of getting 1 or fewer girls in 10 births.

c. Which probability is relevant for determining whether 1 is an unusually low number of girls in 10 births: the result from part (a) or part (b)?

d. Is 1 an unusually low number of girls in 10 births? Why or why not?

Car Failures.   *In Exercises 19–22, refer to the accompanying table, which describes results of roadworthiness tests of Ford Focus cars that are 3 years old (based on data from the Department of Transportation). The random variable x represents the number of cars that failed among six that were tested for roadworthiness.*

x	P(x)
0	0.377
1	0.399
2	0.176
3	0.041
4	0.005
5	0+
6	0+

19. Mean and Standard Deviation Find the mean and standard deviation for the numbers of cars that failed among the six cars that are tested.

20. Range Rule of Thumb for Unusual Events Use the range rule of thumb with the results from Exercise 19 to identify a range of values containing the usual numbers of car failures among six cars tested. Based on the result, is three an unusually high number of failures among six cars tested? Explain.

21. Using Probabilities for Unusual Events

a. Find the probability of getting exactly three cars that fail among six cars tested.

b. Find the probability of getting three or more cars that fail among six cars tested.

c. Which probability is relevant for determining whether three is an unusually high number of failures among six cars tested: the result from part (a) or part (b)?

d. Is three an unusually high number of failures? Why or why not?

22. Using Probabilities for Unusual Events

a. Find the probability of getting exactly one car that fails among six cars tested.

b. Find the probability of getting one or fewer cars that fail among six cars tested.

c. Which probability is relevant for determining whether one is an unusually low number of cars that fail among six cars tested: the result from part (a) or part (b)?

d. Is one an unusually low number of cars that fail among six cars tested? Why or why not?

5-2 Beyond the Basics

23. Expected Value for the Texas Pick 3 Game In the Texas Pick 3 lottery, you can bet $1 by selecting three digits, each between 0 and 9 inclusive. If the same three numbers are drawn in the same order, you win and collect $500.

a. How many different selections are possible?

b. What is the probability of winning?

c. If you win, what is your net profit?

d. Find the expected value.

e. If you bet $1 on the pass line in the casino dice game of craps, the expected value is −1.4¢. Which bet is better: a $1 bet in the Texas Pick 3 game or a $1 bet on the pass line in craps? Explain.

24. Expected Value in Maine's Pick 4 Game In Maine's Pick 4 lottery game, you can pay $1 to select a sequence of four digits, such as 1332. If you select the same sequence of four digits that are drawn, you win and collect $5000.

a. How many different selections are possible?

b. What is the probability of winning?

c. If you win, what is your net profit?   **d.** Find the expected value.

e. If you bet $1 in Maine's Pick 3 game, the expected value is −50¢. Which bet is better: A $1 bet in the Maine Pick 3 game or a $1 bet in the Maine Pick 4 game? Explain.

25. Expected Value in Roulette When playing roulette at the Venetian casino in Las Vegas, a gambler is trying to decide whether to bet $5 on the number 27 or to bet $5 that the outcome is any one of these five possibilities: 0, 00, 1, 2, 3. From Example 8, we know that the expected value of the $5 bet for a single number is −26¢. For the $5 bet that the outcome is 0, 00, 1, 2, or 3, there is a probability of 5/38 of making a net profit of $30 and a 33/38 probability of losing $5.

a. Find the expected value for the $5 bet that the outcome is 0, 00, 1, 2, or 3.

b. Which bet is better: a $5 bet on the number 27 or a $5 bet that the outcome is 0, 00, 1, 2, or 3? Why?

26. Expected Value for *Deal or No Deal* The television game show *Deal or No Deal* begins with individual suitcases containing the amounts of 1¢, $1, $5, $10, $25, $50, $75, $100, $200, $300, $400, $500, $750, $1000, $5000, $10,000, $25,000, $50,000, $75,000, $100,000, $200,000, $300,000, $400,000, $500,000, $750,000, and $1,000,000. If a player adopts the strategy of choosing the option of "no deal" until one suitcase remains, the payoff is one of the amounts listed, and they are all equally likely.

a. Find the expected value for this strategy.   **b.** Find the value of the standard deviation.

c. Use the range rule of thumb to identify the range of usual outcomes.

d. Based on the preceding results, is a result of $750,000 or $1,000,000 unusually high? Why or why not?

5-3   Binomial Probability Distributions

Key Concept Section 5-2 introduced the important concept of a discrete probability distribution. Among all of the different types of discrete probability distributions that exist, there are a few that are particularly important, and the focus of this section is the type that we call *binomial* probability distributions. We begin with a basic definition of a binomial probability distribution, along with notation and methods for finding probability values. As in other sections, we stress the importance of *interpreting* probability values to determine whether events are unlikely (with a low probability, such as 0.05 or less) or unusually high or low.

Binomial probability distributions allow us to deal with circumstances in which the outcomes belong to *two* relevant categories, such as acceptable/defective or survived/died. Other requirements are given in the following definition.

> **DEFINITION** A **binomial probability distribution** results from a procedure that meets all the following requirements:
>
> **1.** The procedure has a *fixed number of trials*. (A trial is a single observation.)
>
> **2.** The trials must be *independent*. (The outcome of any individual trial doesn't affect the probabilities in the other trials.)
>
> **3.** Each trial must have all outcomes classified into *two categories* (commonly referred to as *success* and *failure*).
>
> **4.** The probability of a success remains the same in all trials.

Independence Requirement

When selecting a sample (such as survey subjects) for some statistical analysis, we usually sample without replacement. Sampling without replacement involves dependent events, which violates the second requirement in the definition above. However, we can often assume independence by applying the following 5% guideline introduced in Section 4-4:

Treating Dependent Events as Independent:
The 5% Guideline for Cumbersome Calculations

If calculations are cumbersome and if a sample size is no more than 5% of the size of the population, treat the selections as being *independent* (even if the selections are made without replacement, so that they are actually dependent).

If a procedure satisfies the four requirements above, the distribution of the random variable x (number of successes in n trials) is called a *binomial probability distribution* (or *binomial distribution*). The following notation is commonly used.

Notation for Binomial Probability Distributions

S and F (success and failure) denote the two possible categories of all outcomes.

$P(S) = p$	(p = probability of a success)
$P(F) = 1 - p = q$	(q = probability of a failure)
n	denotes the fixed number of trials.
x	denotes a specific number of successes in n trials, so x can be any whole number between 0 and n, inclusive.
p	denotes the probability of *success* in one of the n trials.
q	denotes the probability of *failure* in one of the n trials.
$P(x)$	denotes the probability of getting exactly x successes among the n trials.

The word *success* as used here is arbitrary and does not necessarily represent something good. Either of the two possible categories may be called the success S as long as its probability is identified as p. (The value of q can always be found by subtracting p from 1: If $p = 0.95$, then $q = 1 - 0.95 = 0.05$.)

CAUTION When using a binomial probability distribution, always be sure that x and p are consistent in the sense that they both refer to the *same* category being called a success.

Example 1 Twitter

When an adult is randomly selected (with replacement), there is a 0.85 probability that this person knows what Twitter is (based on results from a Pew Research Center survey). Suppose that we want to find the probability that exactly three of five random adults know what Twitter is.

  a. Does this procedure result in a binomial distribution?

  b. If this procedure does result in a binomial distribution, identify the values of n, x, p, and q.

> **Solution**
>
> **a.** This procedure does satisfy the requirements for a binomial distribution, as shown below.
>
>   **1.** The number of trials (5) is fixed.
>
>   **2.** The 5 trials are independent, because the probability of any adult knowing Twitter is not affected by results from other selected adults.
>
>   **3.** Each of the 5 trials has two categories of outcomes: The selected person knows what Twitter is or that person does not know what Twitter is.
>
>   **4.** For each randomly selected adult, there is a 0.85 probability that this person knows what Twitter is, and that probability remains the same for each of the five selected people.
>
> **b.** Having concluded that the given procedure does result in a binomial distribution, we now proceed to identify the values of n, x, p, and q.
>
>   **1.** With five randomly selected adults, we have $n = 5$.
>
>   **2.** We want the probability of exactly three who know what Twitter is, so $x = 3$.
>
>   **3.** The probability of success (getting a person who knows what Twitter is) for one selection is 0.85, so $p = 0.85$.
>
>   **4.** The probability of failure (not getting someone who knows what Twitter is) is 0.15, so $q = 0.15$.
>
> Again, it is very important to be sure that x and p both refer to the same concept of "success." In this example, we use x to count the number of people who know what Twitter is, so p must be the probability that the selected person knows what Twitter is. Therefore, x and p do use the same concept of success: knowing what Twitter is.

We now discuss three methods for finding the probabilities corresponding to the random variable x in a binomial distribution. The first method involves calculations using the *binomial probability formula* and is the basis for the other two methods. The second method involves the use of computer software or a calculator, and the third method involves the use of the Binomial Probabilities table in the Appendix Table A-1. (With technology so widespread, such tables are becoming obsolete.) If you are using computer software or a calculator that automatically produces binomial probabilities, we recommend that you solve one or two exercises using Method 1 to better understand the basis for the calculations. Understanding is always infinitely better than blind application of formulas.

Method 1: Using the Binomial Probability Formula In a binomial probability distribution, probabilities can be calculated by using Formula 5-5.

Formula 5-5   Binomial Probability Formula

$$P(x) = \frac{n!}{(n - x)!x!} \cdot p^x \cdot q^{n-x} \qquad \text{for } x = 0, 1, 2, \ldots, n$$

where

$n =$ number of trials

$x =$ number of successes among n trials

$p =$ probability of success in any one trial

$q =$ probability of failure in any one trial ($q = 1 - p$)

The factorial symbol !, introduced in Section 4-6, denotes the product of decreasing factors. Two examples of factorials are $3! = 3 \cdot 2 \cdot 1 = 6$ and $0! = 1$ (by definition).

Example 2   Twitter

Given that there is a 0.85 probability that a randomly selected adult knows what Twitter is, use the binomial probability formula to find the probability of getting exactly three adults who know what Twitter is when five adults are randomly selected. That is, apply Formula 5-5 to find $P(3)$ given that $n = 5$, $x = 3$, $p = 0.85$, and $q = 0.15$.

Solution

Using the given values of n, x, p, and q in the binomial probability formula (Formula 5-5), we get

$$P(3) = \frac{5!}{(5-3)!3!} \cdot 0.85^3 \cdot 0.15^{5-3}$$

$$= \frac{5!}{2!3!} \cdot 0.614125 \cdot 0.0225$$

$$= (10)(0.614125)(0.0225) = 0.138178$$

$$= 0.138 \text{ (rounded)}$$

The probability of getting exactly three adults who know Twitter among five randomly selected adults is 0.138.

Calculation hint: When computing a probability with the binomial probability formula, it's helpful to get a single number for $n!/[(n-x)!x!]$, a single number for p^x, and a single number for q^{n-x}, then simply multiply the three factors together as shown in the third line of the calculation in the preceding example. Don't round too much when you find those three factors; round only at the end.

Method 2: Using Technology STATDISK, Minitab, Excel, StatCrunch, SPSS, SAS, and the TI-83/84 Plus calculator are all technologies that can be used to find binomial probabilities. (Instead of directly providing probabilities for individual values of x, SPSS and SAS are more difficult to use because they provide *cumulative*

STATDISK

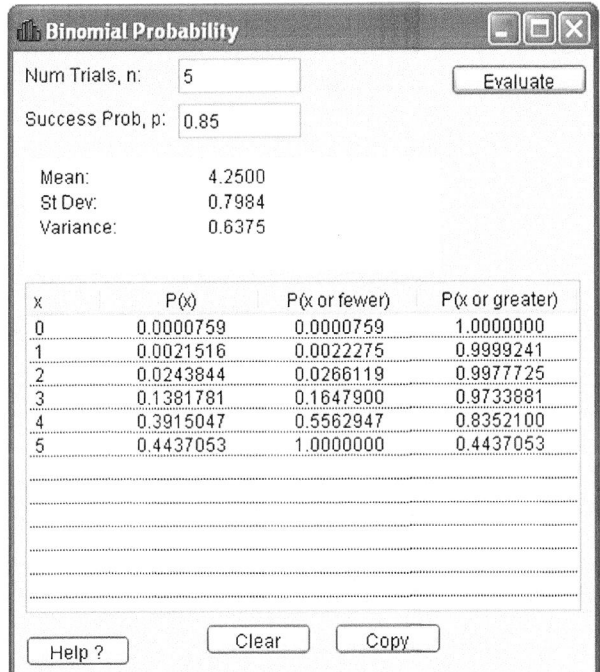

MINITAB

x	P(x)
0	0.000076
1	0.002152
2	0.024384
3	0.138178
4	0.391505
5	0.443705

EXCEL

	A	B
1	0	7.594E-05
2	1	0.0021516
3	2	0.0243844
4	3	0.1381781
5	4	0.3915047
6	5	0.4437053

TI-83/84 PLUS

L1	L2	L3 2
0	7.6E-5	------
1	.00215	
2	.02438	
3	.13818	
4	.3915	
5	.44371	

L2(7) =

probabilities of x or fewer successes.) The screen displays list binomial probabilities for $n = 5$ and $p = 0.85$, as in Example 2. Notice that in each display, the probability distribution is given as a table. The Excel and TI-83/84 Plus display the first probability in scientific notation. (The Excel probability of 7.594E-05 is another way of expressing 7.594×10^{-5}, which can be expressed in a standard format as 0.00007594.)

 Example 3   XSORT Method of Gender Selection

In the Chapter Problem, we noted that each of 945 couples gave birth to a child, and 879 of those children were girls. In order to determine whether such results can be explained by chance, we need to find the probability of getting 879 girls or a result at least as extreme as that. Find the probability of at least 879 girls in 945 births, assuming that boys and girls are equally likely.

Solution

Using the notation for binomial probabilities, we have $n = 945, p = 0.5, q = 0.5$, and we want to find the sum of all probabilities for each value of x from 879 through 945. The formula is not practical here, because we would need to apply it 67 times—that's not the way to go. Table A-1 (Binomial Probabilities) doesn't apply because $n = 945$, which is way beyond the scope of that table. Instead, we wisely choose to use technology.

The accompanying STATDISK display shows that the probability of 879 or more girls in 945 births is 0.0000000 when rounded to seven decimal places. This shows that it is *very* unlikely that we would get 879 girls in 945 births by chance. If we effectively rule out chance, we are left with the more reasonable explanation that the XSORT method appears to be effective in increasing the likelihood that a baby will be born a girl.

STATDISK

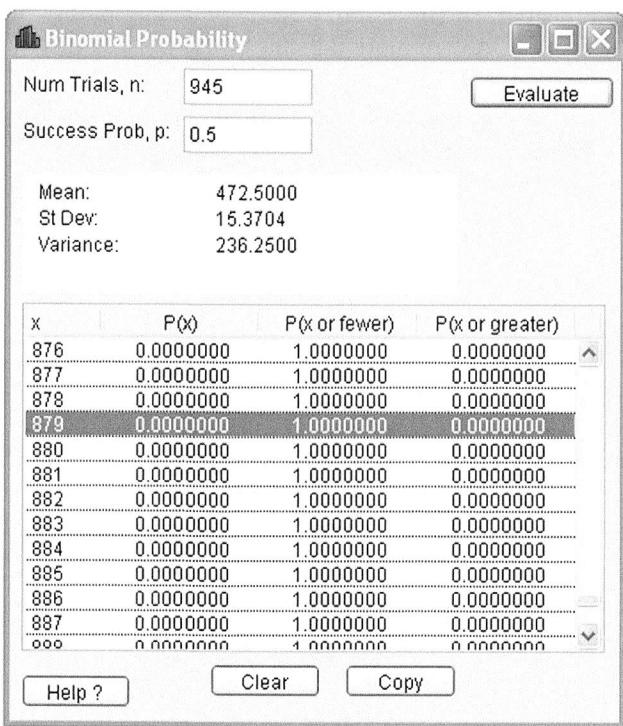

Example 3 illustrates well the power and ease of using technology. Example 3 also illustrates the rare event rule of statistical thinking: If under a given assumption (such as the assumption that the XSORT method has no effect), the probability of a particular observed event (such as 879 girls in 945 births) is extremely small (such as 0.05 or less), we conclude that the assumption is probably not correct.

Method 3: Using Table A-1 in Appendix A Table A-1 in Appendix A lists binomial probabilities for select values of n and p. It cannot be used for Example 2 because the probability of $p = 0.85$ is not one of the probabilities included. Example 3 illustrates the use of the table.

To use the table of binomial probabilities, we must first locate n and the desired corresponding value of x. At this stage, one row of numbers should be isolated. Now align that row with the desired probability of p by using the column across the top. The isolated number represents the desired probability. A very small probability, such as 0.000064, is indicated by 0+.

Example 4 Devil of a Problem

Based on a recent Harris poll, 60% of adults believe in the devil. Assuming that we randomly select five adults, use Table A-1 to find the following:

a. The probability that exactly three of the five adults believe in the devil

b. The probability that the number of adults who believe in the devil is at least two

Solution

a. The following excerpt from the table shows that when $n = 5$ and $p = 0.6$, the probability for $x = 3$ is given by $P(3) = 0.346$.

TABLE A-1			Binomial Probabilities				x	P(x)
					p			
n	x	.01	.50	.60	.70			
5	0	.951	.031	.010	.002		0	0.010
	1	.048	.156	.077	.028		1	0.077
	2	.001	.312	.230	.132		2	0.230
	3	0+	.312	.346	.309		3	0.346
	4	0+	.156	.259	.360		4	0.259
	5	0+	.031	.078	.168		5	0.078

b. The phrase "at least two" successes means that the number of successes is 2 or 3 or 4 or 5.

$$P(\text{at least 2 believe in the devil}) = P(2 \text{ or } 3 \text{ or } 4 \text{ or } 5)$$
$$= P(2) + P(3) + P(4) + P(5)$$
$$= 0.230 + 0.346 + 0.259 + 0.078$$
$$= 0.913$$

If we wanted to use the binomial probability formula to find $P(\text{at least 2})$, as in part (b) of Example 3, we would need to apply the formula four times to compute four different probabilities, which would then be added. Given this choice between the formula and the table, it makes sense to use the table. However, given a choice that includes the formula, table, and technology, the use of technology is the way to go. Here is an effective and efficient strategy for choosing a method for finding binomial probabilities:

1. Use computer software or a T1-83/84 Plus calculator, if available.

2. If neither computer software nor a T1-83/84 Plus calculator is available, use Table A-1(Binomial Probabilities) if possible.

3. If neither computer software nor the T1-83/84 Plus calculator is available and the probabilities can't be found using Table A-1, use the binomial probability formula.

Rationale for the Binomial Probability Formula

The binomial probability formula is the basis for all three methods presented in this section. Instead of accepting and using that formula blindly, let's see why it works.

In Example 2, we used the binomial probability formula to find the probability of getting exactly three adults who know Twitter when five adults are randomly selected. With $P(\text{knows Twitter}) = 0.85$, we can use the multiplication rule from Section 4-4 to find the probability that the first three adults know Twitter while the last two adults do not know Twitter. We get the following result:

$P(3$ adults know Twitter followed by 2 adults who do not know Twitter$)$
$$= 0.85 \cdot 0.85 \cdot 0.85 \cdot 0.15 \cdot 0.15$$
$$= 0.85^3 \cdot 0.15^2$$
$$= 0.0138$$

This result gives a probability of randomly selecting five adults and finding that the first three know Twitter and the last two do not. However, the probability of 0.0138 is not the probability of getting exactly three adults who know Twitter because it assumes a particular sequence for three people who know Twitter and two who do not. Other different sequences are possible.

In Section 4-6 we saw that with three subjects identical to each other (such as adults who know Twitter) and two other subjects identical to each other (such as adults who do not know Twitter), the total number of arrangements, or permutations, is $5!/[(5 - 3)!3!]$ or 10. Each of those 10 different arrangements has a probability of $0.85^3 \cdot 0.15^2$, so the total probability is as follows:

$$P(3 \text{ adults know Twitter among 5}) = \frac{5!}{(5 - 3)!3!} \cdot 0.85^3 \cdot 0.15^2 = 0.138$$

This particular result can be generalized as the binomial probability formula (Formula 5-5). That is, the binomial probability formula is a combination of the multiplication rule of probability and the counting rule for the number of arrangements of n items when x of them are identical to each other and the other $n - x$ are identical to each other. (See Exercises 13 and 14.)

The number of outcomes with   The probability of x successes among
exactly x successes among n trials n trials for any one particular order

$$P(x) = \frac{n!}{(n - x)!x!} \cdot p^x \cdot q^{n-x}$$

using TECHNOLOGY

STATDISK Select **Analysis** from the main menu, select **Probability Distributions,** then select the **Binomial Probabilities** option. Enter the requested values for n and p, then click on **Evaluate** and the entire probability distribution will be displayed (or you have the option of entering a single value of x to get a single probability). Other columns represent cumulative probabilities that are obtained by adding the values of $P(x)$ as you go down or up the column.

MINITAB First enter a column C1 of the x values for which you want probabilities (such as 0, 1, 2, 3, 4, 5), then select **Calc** from the main menu. Select the submenu items of **Probability Distributions** and **Binomial.** Select **Probabilities,** and enter the number of trials, the probability of success, and C1 for the input column. Click **OK.**

EXCEL List the values of x in column A (such as 0, 1, 2, 3, 4, 5). Click on cell B1, then click on **ƒx** from the toolbar. Select the function category **Statistical** and then the function name **BINOMDIST** (or **BINOM.DIST**). In the dialog box, enter A1 for the entry indicated by **Number_s** (number of successes), enter the number of trials (the value of n), enter the probability, and enter 0 for the cell indicated by **Cumulative** (instead of 1 for the cumulative binomial distribution). A value should appear in cell B1. Click and drag the lower right corner of

cell B1 down the column to match the entries in column A, then release the mouse button. The probabilities should all appear in column B.

TI-83/84 PLUS Press **2ND** **VARS** (to get **DISTR,** which denotes "distributions"), then select the option identified as **binompdf(.** Complete the entry of **binompdf(n, p, x)** with specific values for n, p, and x, then press **ENTER**. The result will be the probability of getting x successes among n trials.

You could also enter **binompdf(n, p)** to get a list of *all* of the probabilities corresponding to $x = 0, 1, 2, \ldots, n$. You could store this list in L2 by pressing **STO)** **L2**. You could then manually enter the values of $0, 1, 2, \ldots, n$ in list L1, which would allow you to calculate statistics (by pressing **STAT**, selecting **CALC,** pressing **ENTER**, then entering **L1, L2**), or view the distribution in a table format (by pressing **STAT**, then selecting **EDIT**).

The command **binomcdf** yields *cumulative* probabilities from a binomial distribution. The command **binomcdf(n, p, x)** provides the sum of all probabilities from $x = 0$ through the specific value entered for x.

STATCRUNCH Click on **Open StatCrunch,** then click on **Stat.** Select **Calculators,** then select **Binomial.**

5-3 Basic Skills and Concepts

Statistical Literacy and Critical Thinking

1. Calculating Probabilities Based on a Saint Index survey, assume that when adults are asked to identify the most unpopular projects for their hometown, 54% include Wal-Mart among their choices. Suppose we want to find the probability that when five adults are randomly selected, exactly two of them include Wal-Mart. What is wrong with using the multiplication rule to find the probability of getting two adults who include Wal-Mart followed by three people who do not include Wal-Mart, as in this calculation: (0.54)(0.54)(0.46)(0.46)(0.46)?

2. Consistent Notation If we use the binomial probability formula (Formula 5-5) for finding the probability described in Exercise 1, what is wrong with letting p denote the probability of getting an adult who includes Wal-Mart while x counts the number of adults who do not include Wal-Mart?

3. Independent Events Based on a Saint Index survey, when 1000 adults were asked to identify the most unpopular projects for their hometown, 54% included Wal-Mart among their choices. Consider the probability that among 30 different adults randomly selected from the 1000 who were surveyed, there are at least 18 who include Wal-Mart. Given that the subjects surveyed were selected without replacement, are the 30 selections independent? Can they be treated as being independent? Can the probability be found by using the binomial probability formula? Explain.

4. Notation of 0+ Using the same survey from Exercise 3, the probability of randomly selecting 30 of the 1000 adults and getting exactly 28 who include Wal-Mart is represented as 0+. What does 0+ indicate? Does 0+ indicate that it is it impossible to get exactly 28 adults who include Wal-Mart?

Identifying Binomial Distributions.   *In Exercises 5–12, determine whether the given procedure results in a binomial distribution (or a distribution that can be treated as binomial). For those that are not binomial, identify at least one requirement that is not satisfied.*

5. Clinical Trial of YSORT The YSORT method of gender selection, developed by the Genetics & IVF Institute, is designed to increase the likelihood that a baby will be a boy. When 291 couples use the YSORT method and give birth to 291 babies, the weights of the babies are recorded.

6. Clinical Trial of YSORT The YSORT method of gender selection, developed by the Genetics & IVF Institute, is designed to increase the likelihood that a baby will be a boy. When 291 couples use the YSORT method and give birth to 291 babies, the genders of the babies are recorded.

7. Veggie Survey In an Idaho Potato Commission survey of 1000 adults, subjects are asked to select their favorite vegetables, and each response was recorded as "potatoes" or "other."

8. Veggie Survey In an Idaho Potato Commission survey of 1000 adults, subjects are asked to select their favorite vegetables, and responses of potatoes, corn, broccoli, tomatoes, or "other" were recorded.

9. Surveying Senators The current Senate consists of 83 males and 17 females. Forty different senators are randomly selected without replacement, and the gender of each selected senator is recorded.

10. Surveying Senators Ten different senators are randomly selected without replacement, and the numbers of terms that they have served are recorded.

11. Smartphone Survey In a RingCentral survey, 380 different smartphone users are randomly selected without replacement. Respondents were asked to identify the only thing that they can't live without. Responses consist of whether a smartphone was identified.

12. Online Shopping In a *Consumer Reports* survey, 427 different women are randomly selected without replacement, and each woman is asked what she purchases online. Responses consist of whether clothing was identified.

13. Guessing Answers The math portion of the ACT test consists of 60 multiple-choice questions, each with five possible answers (a, b, c, d, e), one of which is correct. Assume that you guess the answers to the first three questions.

a. Use the multiplication rule to find the probability that the first two guesses are wrong and the third is correct. That is, find $P(\text{WWC})$, where C denotes a correct answer and W denotes a wrong answer.

b. Beginning with WWC, make a complete list of the different possible arrangements of two wrong answers and one correct answer, then find the probability for each entry in the list.

c. Based on the preceding results, what is the probability of getting exactly one correct answer when three guesses are made?

14. Win 4 Lottery In the New York State Win 4 lottery, you place a bet by selecting four digits. Repetition is allowed, and winning requires that your sequence of four digits matches the four digits that are later drawn. Assume that you place one bet with a sequence of four digits.

a. Use the multiplication rule to find the probability that your first two digits match those drawn and your last two digits do not match those drawn. That is, find $P(\text{MMXX})$, where M denotes a match and X denotes a digit that does not match the winning number.

b. Beginning with MMXX, make a complete list of the different possible arrangements of two matching digits and two digits that do not match, then find the probability for each entry in the list.

c. Based on the preceding results, what is the probability of getting exactly two matching digits when you select four digits for the Win 4 lottery game?

Using the Binomial Probability Table. *In Exercises 15–20, assume that random guesses are made for five multiple-choice questions on an ACT test, so that there are n = 5 trials, each with probability of success (correct) given by p = 0.20. Use the Binomial Probability table(Table A-1) to find the indicated probability for the number of correct answers.*

15. Find the probability that the number x of correct answers is exactly 3.

16. Find the probability that the number x of correct answers is at least 3.

17. Find the probability that the number x of correct answers is more than 2.

18. Find the probability that the number x of correct answers is fewer than 3.

19. Find the probability of no correct answers.

20. Find the probability that all answers are correct.

Using Technology or the Binomial Probability Formula. *In Exercises 21–24, assume that when blood donors are randomly selected, 45% of them have blood that is Group O (based on data from the Greater New York Blood Program).*

21. If the number of blood donors is $n = 8$, find the probability that the number with Group O blood is $x = 3$.

22. If the number of blood donors is $n = 16$, find the probability that the number with Group O blood is $x = 6$.

23. If the number of blood donors is $n = 20$, find the probability that the number with Group O blood is $x = 16$.

24. If the number of blood donors is $n = 11$, find the probability that the number with Group O blood is $x = 9$.

Using Computer Results. *In Exercises 25–28, refer to the accompanying Excel display. (In one of Mendel's hybridization experiments with peas, the probability of offspring peas having green pods is ¾, or 0.75.) The display lists the probabilities obtained by entering the values of n = 6 and p = 0.75. Those probabilities correspond to the numbers of peas with green pods in a group of six offspring peas.*

EXCEL Peas with Green Pods	
X	P(x)
0	0.000
1	0.004
2	0.033
3	0.132
4	0.297
5	0.356
6	0.178

25. Genetics Find the probability that at least two of the six offspring peas have green pods. If at least two offspring peas with green pods are required for further experimentation, is it reasonable to expect that at least two will be obtained?

26. Genetics Find the probability that at most five of the six offspring peas have green pods.

27. Genetics Find the probability that at most two of the six offspring peas have green pods. Is two an unusually low number of peas with green pods (among six)? Why or why not?

28. Genetics Find the probability that five or more of the six offspring peas will have green pods. Is five an unusually high number of offspring peas with green pods? Why or why not?

In Exercises 29–32, use either technology or the Binomial Probability table (Table A-1).

29. See You Later Based on a Harris Interactive poll, 20% of adults believe in reincarnation. Assume that six adults are randomly selected, and find the indicated probability.

a. What is the probability that exactly five of the selected adults believe in reincarnation?

b. What is the probability that all of the selected adults believe in reincarnation?

c. What is the probability that at least five of the selected adults believe in reincarnation?

d. If six adults are randomly selected, is five an unusually high number who believe in reincarnation?

30. Live TV Based on a Comcast survey, there is a 0.8 probability that a randomly selected adult will watch prime-time TV live, instead of online, on DVR, etc. Assume that seven adults are randomly selected, and find the indicated probability.

a. Find the probability that exactly two of the selected adults watch prime-time TV live.

b. Find the probability that exactly one of the selected adults watches prime-time TV live.

c. Find the probability that fewer than three of the selected adults watch prime-time TV live.

d. If we randomly select seven adults, is two an unusually low number for those who watch prime-time TV live?

31. Too Young to Tat Based on a Harris poll, among adults who regret getting tattoos, 20% say that they were too young when they got their tattoos. Assume that five adults who regret getting tattoos are randomly selected, and find the indicated probability.

a. Find the probability that none of the selected adults say that they were too young to get tattoos.

b. Find the probability that exactly one of the selected adults says that he or she was too young to get tattoos.

c. Find the probability that the number of selected adults saying they were too young is 0 or 1.

d. If we randomly select five adults, is one an unusually low number who say that they were too young to get tattoos?

32. Tainted Currency Based on the American Chemical Society, there is a 0.9 probability that in the United States, a randomly selected dollar bill is tainted with traces of cocaine. Assume that eight dollar bills are randomly selected.

a. Find the probability that all of them have traces of cocaine.

b. Find the probability that exactly seven of them have traces of cocaine.

c. Find the probability that the number of dollar bills with traces of cocaine is seven or more.

d. If we randomly select eight dollar bills, is seven an unusually high number for those with traces of cocaine?

33. Death of Taxes Based on a Bellowes survey of adults, there is a 0.48 probability that a randomly selected adult uses a tax preparer to file taxes. Find the probability that among 20 randomly selected adults, exactly 12 use tax preparers to file their taxes. Among 20 random adults, is 12 an unusually high number for those who use tax preparers to file their taxes?

34. Career Choice Based on a Ridgid survey of high school students, 25% of high school students plan to choose a career in information technology. Find the probability that among 24 randomly selected high school students, exactly 6 plan to choose a career in information technology. Is it unlikely to find that among the 24 selected high school students, exactly 25% plan to choose a career in information technology?

35. On-Time Flights The U.S. Department of Transportation recently reported that 80.5% of U.S. airline flights arrived on time. Find the probability that among 12 randomly selected flights, exactly 10 arrive on time. Does that probability apply to the author, who must make 12 flights originating in New York?

36. Online Banking Based on data from a *USA Today* Snapshot, 72% of adults have security concerns about online banking. Find the probability that among 30 randomly selected adults, exactly 20 have security concerns. Among 30 random adults, is 20 an unusually low number for those who have security concerns?

37. Nielsen Rating CBS televised a recent Super Bowl football game between the New Orleans Saints and the Indianapolis Colts. That game received a rating of 45, indicating that among all U.S. households, 45% were tuned to the game (based on data from Nielsen Media Research). An advertiser wants to obtain a second opinion by conducting its own survey, and a pilot survey begins with 12 randomly selected households.

a. Find the probability that none of the households is tuned to the Saints/Colts game.

b. Find the probability that at least one household is tuned to the Saints/Colts game.

c. Find the probability that at most one household is tuned to the Saints/Colts game.

d. If at most one household is tuned to the Saints/Colts game, does it appear that the 45 share value is wrong? Why or why not?

38. Overbooking Flights When someone buys a ticket for an airline flight, there is a 0.0995 probability that the person will not show up for the flight (based on data from an IBM research paper by Lawrence, Hong, and Cherrier). The Beechcraft 1900C jet can seat 19 passengers. Is it wise to book 21 passengers for a flight on the Beechcraft 1900C? Explain.

39. XSORT Method of Gender Selection When testing a method of gender selection, we assume that the rate of female births is 50%, and we reject that assumption if we get results that are unusual in the sense that they are very unlikely to occur with the 50% rate. In a preliminary test of the XSORT method of gender selection, 14 births included 13 girls.

a. Assuming a 50% rate of female births, find the probability that in 14 births, the number of girls is 13.

b. Assuming a 50% rate of female births, find the probability that in 14 births, the number of girls is 14.

c. Assuming a 50% rate of female births, find the probability that in 14 births, the number of girls is 13 or more.

d. Do these preliminary results suggest that the XSORT method is effective in increasing the likelihood of a baby being a girl? Explain.

40. Challenged Calls in Tennis In a recent U.S. Open tennis tournament, among 20 of the calls challenged by players, 8 were overturned after a review using the Hawk-Eye electronic system. Assume that when players challenge calls, they are successful in having them overturned 50% of the time.

a. Find the probability that among 20 challenges, exactly 8 are successfully overturned.

b. The probability that among 20 challenges, 8 or fewer are overturned is 0.252. Does this result suggest that the success rate is less than 50%? Why or why not?

Composite Sampling. *Exercises 41 and 42 involve the method of composite sampling, whereby a medical testing laboratory saves time and money by combining blood samples for tests so that only one test is conducted for several people. A combined sample tests positive if at least one person has the disease. If a combined sample tests positive, then individual blood tests are used to identify the individual with the disease.*

41. HIV The probability of a randomly selected adult in the United States being infected with the human immunodeficiency virus (HIV) is 0.006 (based on data from the Kaiser Family Foundation). In tests for HIV, blood samples from 24 people are combined. What is the probability that the combined sample tests positive for HIV? Is it unlikely for such a combined sample to test positive?

42. STD Based on data from the Centers for Disease Control, the probability of a randomly selected person having gonorrhea is 0.00114. In tests for gonorrhea, blood samples from

16 people are combined. What is the probability that the combined sample tests positive for gonorrhea? Is it unlikely for such a combined sample to test positive?

Acceptance Sampling. *Exercises 43 and 44 involve the method of acceptance sampling, whereby a shipment of a large number of items is accepted if tests of a sample of those items result in only one or none that are defective.*

43. Aspirin The Medassist Pharmaceutical Company receives large shipments of aspirin tablets and uses this acceptance sampling plan: Randomly select and test 40 tablets, then accept the whole batch if there is only one or none that doesn't meet the required specifications. If one shipment of 5000 aspirin tablets actually has a 3% rate of defects, what is the probability that this whole shipment will be accepted? Will almost all such shipments be accepted, or will many be rejected?

44. Chocolate Chip Cookies The Killington Market chain uses this acceptance sampling plan for large shipments of packages of its generic chocolate chip cookies: Randomly select 30 packages and determine whether each is within specifications (not too many broken cookies, acceptable taste, distribution of chocolate chips, and so on). The entire shipment is accepted if at most 2 packages do not meet specifications. A shipment contains 1200 packages of chocolate chips, and 2% of those packages do not meet specifications. What is the probability that this whole shipment will be accepted? Will almost all such shipments be accepted, or will many be rejected?

5-3 Beyond the Basics

45. Geometric Distribution If a procedure meets all the conditions of a binomial distribution except that the number of trials is not fixed, then the **geometric distribution** can be used. The probability of getting the first success on the xth trial is given by $P(x) = p(1 - p)^{x-1}$, where p is the probability of success on any one trial. Subjects are randomly selected for the National Health and Nutrition Examination Survey conducted by the National Center for Health Statistics, Centers for Disease Control. Find the probability that the first subject to be a universal blood donor (with group O and type Rh$^-$ blood) is the fifth person selected. The probability that someone is a universal donor is 0.06.

46. Multinomial Distribution The binomial distribution applies only to cases involving two types of outcomes, whereas the **multinomial distribution** involves more than two categories. Suppose we have three types of mutually exclusive outcomes denoted by A, B, and C. Let $P(A) = p_1$, $P(B) = p_2$, and $P(C) = p_3$. In n independent trials, the probability of x_1 outcomes of type A, x_2 outcomes of type B, and x_3 outcomes of type C is given by

$$\frac{n!}{(x_1)!(x_2)!(x_3)!} \cdot p_1^{x_1} \cdot p_2^{x_2} \cdot p_3^{x_3}$$

A roulette wheel in the Hard Rock casino in Las Vegas has 18 red slots, 18 black slots, and 2 green slots. If roulette is played 12 times, find the probability of getting 5 red outcomes, 4 black outcomes, and 3 green outcomes.

47. Hypergeometric Distribution If we sample from a small finite population without replacement, the binomial distribution should not be used because the events are not independent. If sampling is done without replacement and the outcomes belong to one of two types, we can use the **hypergeometric distribution.** If a population has A objects of one type (such as lottery numbers matching the ones you selected), while the remaining B objects are of the other type (such as lottery numbers different from the ones you selected), and if n objects are sampled without replacement (such as six drawn lottery numbers), then the probability of getting x objects of type A and $n - x$ objects of type B is

$$P(x) = \frac{A!}{(A - x)!x!} \cdot \frac{B!}{(B - n + x)!(n - x)!} \div \frac{(A + B)!}{(A + B - n)!n!}$$

In Pennsylvania's Match 6 Lotto game, a bettor selects six numbers from 1 to 49 (without repetition), and a winning six-number combination is later randomly selected. Find the probabilities of the following events and express them in decimal form.

a. You purchase one ticket with a six-number combination and you get exactly four winning numbers. (*Hint:* Use $A = 6$, $B = 43$, $n = 6$, and $x = 4$.)

b. You purchase one ticket with a six-number combination and you get all six of the winning numbers.

c. You purchase one ticket with a six-number combination and you get none of the winning numbers.

5-4 Parameters for Binomial Distributions

Key Concept Section 5-2 introduced the general concept of a probability distribution, and Section 5-3 focused on binomial probability distributions, which constitute a specific type of discrete probability distribution. This section continues with binomial distributions as these two goals are addressed:

1. Provide an easy method for finding the parameters of the mean and standard deviation from a binomial distribution. (Because a binomial distribution describes a *population*, the mean and standard deviation are *parameters*, not statistics.)

2. Use the range rule of thumb for determining whether events are *unusual*.

Section 5-2 included Formulas 5-1, 5-3, and 5-4 for finding the mean, variance, and standard deviation from *any* discrete probability distribution. Because a binomial distribution is a particular type of discrete probability distribution, we could use those same formulas, but if we know the values of n and p, it is much easier to use these formulas:

For Binomial Distributions

Formula 5-6	Mean:	$\mu = np$
Formula 5-7	Variance:	$\sigma^2 = npq$
Formula 5-8	Standard Deviation:	$\sigma = \sqrt{npq}$

As in earlier sections, finding values for μ and σ can be great fun, but it is especially important to *interpret* and *understand* those values, so the range rule of thumb can be very helpful. Here is a brief summary of the range rule of thumb: Values are unusually high or unusually low if they differ from the mean by more than 2 standard deviations, as described by the following:

Range Rule of Thumb

maximum usual value: $\mu + 2\sigma$

minimum usual value: $\mu - 2\sigma$

Example 1 Parameters

The brand name of McDonald's has a 95% recognition rate (based on data from Retail Marketing Group and Harris Interactive). A special focus group consists of 12 randomly selected adults to be used for extensive market testing. For such random groups of 12 people, find the mean and standard deviation for the number of people who recognize the brand name of McDonald's.

Solution

We have $n = 12$, which is the sample size. We have $p = 0.95$ (from 95%), and we have $q = 0.05$ (from $q = 1 - p$). Using $n = 12$, $p = 0.95$, and $q = 0.05$, Formulas 5-6 and 5-8 can be applied as follows:

$$\mu = np = (12)(0.95) = 11.4$$

$$\sigma = \sqrt{npq} = \sqrt{(12)(0.95)(0.05)} = 0.754983 = 0.8 \text{ (rounded)}$$

For random groups of 12 adults, the mean number of people who recognize the brand name of McDonald's is 11.4 people, and the standard deviation is 0.8 people.

Example 2   Unusual Outcomes

From Example 1 we see that for groups of 12 randomly selected people, the mean number of people who recognize the brand name of McDonald's is $\mu = 11.4$ people, and the standard deviation is $\sigma = 0.8$ people.

a. For groups of 12 randomly selected people, use the range rule of thumb to find the minimum usual number and the maximum usual number of people who recognize the brand name of McDonald's.

b. In one particular randomly selected group of 12 people, is 12 an unusually high number of people who recognize the brand name of McDonald's?

Solution

a. With $\mu = 11.4$ people and $\sigma = 0.8$ people, we use the range rule of thumb as follows:

maximum usual value: $\mu + 2\sigma = 11.4 + 2(0.8) = 13$ people

minimum usual value: $\mu - 2\sigma = 11.4 - 2(0.8) = 9.8$ people

For groups of 12 randomly selected people, the number who recognize the brand name of McDonald's should usually fall between 9.8 and 13. (Actually, with 12 people selected, the maximum usual value cannot exceed 12, so the range of usual values is between 9.8 and 12.)

b. Because 12 falls within the range of usual values (from 9.8 to 13), we conclude that 12 is *not an unusually high number* of people who recognize the brand name of McDonald's (assuming that the recognition rate is 95%).

Example 3   XSORT Method of Gender Selection

The Chapter Problem includes results from the XSORT method of gender selection. Among 945 births, there were 879 girls born to parents using the XSORT method.

a. Assuming that boys and girls are equally likely, use Formulas 5-6 and 5-8 to find the mean and standard deviation for the numbers of girls born in groups of 945 babies (as in the Chapter Problem).

b. Use the range rule of thumb to find the minimum usual number and the maximum usual number of girls born in groups of 945 births, assuming that boys and girls are equally likely.

c. The Chapter Problem described the XSORT method of gender selection that resulted in 879 girls born in a group of 945 babies. Is 879 girls unusually high?

Solution

a. Using the values $n = 945$, $p = 0.5$, and $q = 0.5$, Formulas 5-6 and 5-8 can be applied as follows:

$$\mu = np = (945)(0.5) = 472.5 \text{ girls}$$

$$\sigma = \sqrt{npq} = \sqrt{(945)(0.5)(0.5)} = 15.4 \text{ girls (rounded)}$$

b. With $\mu = 472.5$ girls and $\sigma = 15.4$ girls, we use the range rule of thumb as follows:

minimum usual value: $\mu - 2\sigma = 472.5 - 2(15.4) = 441.7$ girls

maximum usual value: $\mu + 2\sigma = 472.5 + 2(15.4) = 503.3$ girls

For groups of 945 births, the number of girls should usually fall between 441.7 girls and 503.3 girls (assuming that boys and girls are equally likely).

c. Because the result of 879 girls falls above the range of usual values (from 441.7 girls to 503.3 girls), we consider the result of 879 girls to be an unusually high number of girls.

Interpretation

The result of 879 girls in 945 births is unusually high, so it is not a result we expect to occur by chance. Because chance does not seem to be a reasonable explanation, because 879 girls is so much higher than we expect with chance, and because the 945 couples used the XSORT method of gender selection, it appears that the XSORT method is effective in increasing the likelihood that a baby is born a girl. (However, this does not *prove* that the XSORT method is the cause of the increased number of girls; such proof must be based on direct physical evidence.)

In this section we presented easy procedures for finding the parameters of μ (population mean) and σ (population standard deviation) from a binomial probability distribution. However, it is really important to be able to *interpret* those values by using such devices as the range rule of thumb for identifying a range of usual values.

5-4 Basic Skills and Concepts

Statistical Literacy and Critical Thinking

1. Notation In a clinical trial of the cholesterol drug Lipitor, 270 subjects were given a placebo, and 7% of them developed headaches. For such randomly selected groups of 270 subjects given a placebo, identify the values of n, p, and q that would be used for finding the mean and standard deviation for the number of subjects who develop headaches.

2. Standard Deviation For the binomial distribution described by the conditions in Exercise 1, find the standard deviation by evaluating $\sqrt{npq}$. Some books use the expression $\sqrt{np(1 - p)}$ for the standard deviation. Will that expression always yield the same result?

3. Variance An Office Team survey of 150 executives found that 93.3% of them said that they would be concerned about gaps in a résumé of a job applicant. Based on these results, such randomly selected groups of 150 executives have a mean of 140.0 executives and a standard deviation of 3.1 executives. Find the variance, and express it with the appropriate units.

4. Why a Parameter? Given the results described in Exercise 3, is the mean of 140.0 executives expressed with μ or $\bar{x}$? Explain why the mean of 140.0 executives is a parameter instead of a statistic.

Finding μ, σ, and Unusual Values.   In Exercises 5–8, assume that a procedure yields a binomial distribution with n trials and the probability of success for one trial is p. Use the given values of n and p to find the mean μ and standard deviation σ. Also, use the range rule of thumb to find the minimum usual value $\mu - 2\sigma$ and the maximum usual value $\mu - 2\sigma$.

5. Guessing on ACT Random guesses are made for the 60 multiple-choice questions on the math portion of the ACT test, so $n = 60$ and $p = 1/5$ (because each question has possible answers of a, b, c, d, e, and only one of them is correct).

6. Gender Selection In an analysis of preliminary test results from the XSORT gender-selection method, 14 babies are born and it is assumed that 50% of babies are girls, so $n = 14$ and $p = 0.5$.

7. Identity Theft In a Gallup poll of 1013 randomly selected adults, 66% said that they worry about identity theft, so $n = 1013$ and $p = 0.66$.

8. Clinical Trial In a clinical trial of the cholesterol drug Lipitor, 94 subjects were treated with 80 mg of Lipitor, and 6.4% of them developed headaches, so $n = 94$ and $p = 0.064$.

9. Gender Selection In a test of the YSORT method of gender selection, 291 babies are born to couples trying to have baby boys, and 239 of those babies are boys (based on data from the Genetics & IVF Institute).

a. If the gender-selection method has no effect and boys and girls are equally likely, find the mean and standard deviation for the numbers of boys born in groups of 291.

b. Is the result of 239 boys unusually high? Does it suggest that the YSORT gender-selection method appears to be effective?

10. Mendelian Genetics When Mendel conducted his famous genetics experiments with peas, one sample of offspring consisted of 580 peas, and Mendel theorized that 25% of them would be yellow peas.

a. If Mendel's theory is correct, find the mean and standard deviation for the numbers of yellow peas in such groups of 580 offspring peas.

b. The actual results consisted of 152 yellow peas. Is that result unusually high? What does this result suggest about Mendel's theory?

11. Are 20% of M&M Candies Orange? Mars, Inc. claims that 20% of its M&M plain candies are orange, and a sample of 100 such candies is randomly selected.

a. Find the mean and standard deviation for the number of orange candies in such groups of 100.

b. Data Set 20 in Appendix B consists of a random sample of 100 M&Ms, including 25 that are orange. Is this result unusually high? Does it seem that the claimed rate of 20% is wrong?

12. Are 14% of M&M Candies Yellow? Mars, Inc. claims that 14% of its M&M plain candies are yellow, and a sample of 100 such candies is randomly selected.

a. Find the mean and standard deviation for the number of yellow candies in such groups of 100.

b. Data Set 20 in Appendix B consists of a random sample of 100 M&Ms, including 8 that are yellow. Is this result unusually low? Does it seem that the claimed rate of 14% is wrong?

13. Cell Phones and Brain Cancer In a study of 420,095 cell phone users in Denmark, it was found that 135 developed cancer of the brain or nervous system. If we assume that the use of cell phones has no effect on developing such cancer, then the probability of a person having such a cancer is 0.000340.

a. Assuming that cell phones have no effect on developing cancer, find the mean and standard deviation for the numbers of people in groups of 420,095 that can be expected to have cancer of the brain or nervous system.

b. Based on the results from part (a), is 135 cases of cancer of the brain or nervous system unusually low or high?

c. What do these results suggest about the publicized concern that cell phones are a health danger because they increase the risk of cancer of the brain or nervous system?

14. Test of Touch Therapy Nine-year-old Emily Rosa conducted this test: A professional touch therapist put both hands through a cardboard partition and Emily would use a coin flip to randomly select one of the hands. Emily would place her hand just above the hand of the therapist, who was then asked to identify the hand that Emily had selected. Touch therapists believed that they could sense the energy field and identify the hand that Emily had selected. The trial was repeated 280 times. (Based on data from "A Close Look at Therapeutic Touch," by Rosa et al., *Journal of the American Medical Association,* Vol. 279, No. 13.)

a. Assuming that the touch therapists have no special powers and made random guesses, find the mean and standard deviation for the numbers of correct responses in groups of 280 trials.

b. The professional touch therapists identified the correct hand 123 times in the 280 trials. Is that result unusually low or high? What does the result suggest about the ability of touch therapists to select the correct hand by sensing an energy field?

15. Deciphering Messages The Central Intelligence Agency has specialists who analyze the frequencies of letters of the alphabet in an attempt to decipher intercepted messages that are sent as ciphered text. In standard English text, the letter *r* is used at a rate of 6%.

a. Find the mean and standard deviation for the number of times the letter *r* will be found on a typical page of 2600 characters.

b. In an intercepted ciphered message sent to Iran, a page of 2600 characters is found to have the letter *r* occurring 178 times. Is this unusually low or high?

16. Deciphering Messages The Central Intelligence Agency has specialists who analyze the frequencies of letters of the alphabet in an attempt to decipher intercepted messages that are sent as ciphered text. In standard English text, the letter *e* is used at a rate of 12.7%.

a. Find the mean and standard deviation for the number of times the letter *e* will be found on a typical page of 2600 characters.

b. In an intercepted ciphered message sent to France, a page of 2600 characters is found to have the letter *e* occurring 290 times. Is 290 unusually low or unusually high?

17. Too Young to Tat Based on a Harris poll of 370 adults who regret getting tattoos, 20% say that they were too young when they got their tattoos.

a. For randomly selected groups of 370 adults who regret getting tattoos, find the mean and standard deviation for the number who say that they were too young when they got their tattoos.

b. For a randomly selected group of 370 adults who regret getting tattoos, would 90 be an unusually low or high number who say that they were too young when they got their tattoos?

18. Roulette If you place a bet on the number 7 in roulette, you have a 1/38 probability of winning.

a. Find the mean and standard deviation for the number of wins for people who bet on the number 7 fifty times.

b. Would 0 wins in 50 bets be an unusually low number of wins?

19. Born on the 4th of July For the following questions, ignore leap years.

a. For classes of 30 students, find the mean and standard deviation for the number born on the 4th of July. Express results using seven decimal places.

b. For a class of 30 students, would 2 be an unusually high number who were born on the 4th of July?

20. Powerball Lottery As of this writing, the Powerball lottery is run in 42 states. If you buy one ticket, the probability of winning is 1/195,249,054. If you buy one ticket each week for 50 years, you play this lottery 2600 times.

a. Find the mean and standard deviation for the number of wins for people who buy a ticket each week for 50 years. Express the results using six decimal places.

b. Would it be unusual for someone to win this lottery at least once if they buy a ticket each week for 50 years?

5-4 Beyond the Basics

21. Finding *n*, *p*, *q* In a survey of randomly selected adults, subjects were asked if they could identify at least one current member of the Supreme Court. After obtaining the results, the range rule of thumb was used to find that for randomly selected groups of the same size, the minimum usual number who could identify at least one member of the Supreme Court is 48.0 and the maximum number is 72.0. Find the sample size *n*, the percentage of surveyed subjects who could identify at least one member of the Supreme Court, and the percentage of subjects who could not identify at least one member of the Supreme Court.

22. Acceptable/Defective Products A new integrated circuit board is being developed for use in computers. In the early stages of development, a lack of quality control results in a 0.2 probability that a manufactured integrated circuit board has no defects. Engineers need 24 integrated circuit boards for further testing. What is the minimum number of integrated circuit boards that must be manufactured in order to be at least 98% sure that there are at least 24 that have no defects?

23. Hypergeometric Distribution A statistics class consists of 10 females and 30 males, and each day, 12 of the students are randomly selected without replacement. Because the sampling is from a small finite population without replacement, the hypergeometric distribution applies. (See Exercise 47 in Section 5-3.) Using the hypergeometric distribution, find the mean and standard deviation for the numbers of females that are selected on the different days.

5-5   Poisson Probability Distributions

Key Concept This chapter began by considering discrete probability distributions in general. Sections 5-3 and 5-4 were devoted to binomial probability distributions, which is one particular category of discrete probability distributions. In this section we introduce *Poisson distributions,* which constitute another category of discrete probability distributions. Poisson distributions are often used for describing the behavior of rare events (with small probabilities).

Poisson distributions are used for describing behavior such as radioactive decay, arrivals of people in a line, eagles nesting in a region, patients arriving at an emergency room, crashes on the Massachusetts Turnpike, and Internet users logging onto a web site. For example, suppose your local hospital experiences a mean of 2.3 patients arriving at the emergency room on Fridays between 10:00 P.M. and 11:00 P.M. We can use a Poisson distribution to find the probability that for a randomly selected Friday, exactly four patients arrive at the ER between 10:00 P.M. and 11:00 P.M.

DEFINITION A **Poisson distribution** is a discrete probability distribution that applies to occurrences of some event *over a specified interval*. The random variable x is the number of occurrences of the event in an interval. The interval can be time, distance, area, volume, or some similar unit. The probability of the event occurring x times over an interval is given by Formula 5-9.

Formula 5-9   Poisson Probability Distribution

$$P(x) = \frac{\mu^x \cdot e^{-\mu}}{x!}$$

where $e \approx 2.71828$

        $\mu =$ mean number of occurrences of the event over the intervals

Requirements for the Poisson Distribution

1. The random variable x is the number of occurrences of an event *over some interval.*

2. The occurrences must be *random.*

3. The occurrences must be *independent* of each other.

4. The occurrences must be *uniformly distributed* over the interval being used.

Parameters of the Poisson Distribution

- The mean is μ.
- The standard deviation is $\sigma = \sqrt{\mu}$.

A Poisson distribution differs from a binomial distribution in these fundamental ways:

1. A particular binomial distribution is determined by the sample size n and the probability p, but a Poisson distribution is determined only by the mean μ.

2. In a binomial distribution, the possible values of the random variable x are 0, 1, . . . , n, but a Poisson distribution has possible x values of 0, 1, 2, . . . , with no upper limit.

Example 1   Hurricanes

For a recent period of 100 years, there were 530 Atlantic hurricanes (based on data from the University of Maryland Department of Geography and Environmental Systems). Assume that the Poisson distribution is a suitable model.   *continued*

a. Find μ, the mean number of hurricanes per year.

b. If $P(x)$ is the probability of x Atlantic hurricanes in a randomly selected year, find $P(0)$, $P(2)$, and $P(9)$.

c. There were actually 2 years with no Atlantic hurricanes, 5 years with two Atlantic hurricanes, and 4 years with nine Atlantic hurricanes. How do these actual results compare to the probabilities found in part (b)? Does the Poisson distribution appear to be a good model in this case?

Solution

a. The Poisson distribution applies because we are dealing with the occurrences of an event (hurricanes) over some interval (a year). The mean number of hurricanes per year is

$$\mu = \frac{\text{number of hurricanes}}{\text{number of years}} = \frac{530}{100} = 5.3$$

b. Using Formula 5-9, the calculation for $x = 0$ hurricanes in a year is as follows (with μ replaced by 5.3 and e replaced by 2.71828):

$$P(0) = \frac{\mu^x \cdot e^{-\mu}}{x!} = \frac{5.3^0 \cdot 2.71828^{-5.3}}{0!} = \frac{1 \cdot 0.00499}{1} = 0.00499$$

The probability of exactly 0 hurricanes in a year is $P(0) = 0.00499$. We can use the same procedure to find that $P(2) = 0.0701$ and $P(9) = 0.0454$, as shown below.

$$P(2) = \frac{\mu^x \cdot e^{-\mu}}{x!} = \frac{5.3^2 \cdot 2.71828^{-5.3}}{2!} = \frac{28.09 \cdot 0.00499}{2} = 0.0701$$

$$P(9) = \frac{\mu^x \cdot e^{-\mu}}{x!} = \frac{5.3^9 \cdot 2.71828^{-5.3}}{9!} = \frac{3{,}299{,}763.592 \cdot 0.00499}{362{,}880} = 0.0454$$

c. The probability of $P(0) = 0.00499$ from part (b) is the likelihood of getting 0 Atlantic hurricanes in one year. So in 100 years, the expected number of years with 0 Atlantic hurricanes is $100 \times 0.00499 = 0.499$ years. The other expected values are included here:

Hurricanes in a Year	Actual Number of Years	Expected Number of Years (Using Poisson)
0	2	0.499
2	5	7.01
9	4	4.54

These expected frequencies don't differ dramatically from the actual frequencies, indicating that for these values of x, the Poisson distribution does a reasonably good job of describing the frequencies of Atlantic hurricanes. Instead of relying on a subjective judgment about the closeness of actual frequencies and expected frequencies, we can use more advanced methods to determine whether the Poisson distribution is a good model in this case. For example, we could use the method for testing "goodness-of-fit" in Section 11-2.

Poisson Distribution as an Approximation to the Binomial Distribution

The Poisson distribution is sometimes used to approximate the binomial distribution when n is large and p is small. One rule of thumb is to use such an approximation when the following two requirements are both satisfied.

Requirements for Using the Poisson Distribution as an Approximation to the Binomial

1. $n \geq 100$

2. $np \leq 10$

If both requirements are satisfied and we want to use the Poisson distribution as an approximation to the binomial distribution, we need a value for μ. That value can be calculated by using Formula 5-6 (first presented in Section 5-4):

Formula 5-6   Mean for Poisson Distribution as an Approximation to the Binomial

$$\mu = np$$

Example 2   Maine Pick 4

In the Maine Pick 4 game, you pay 50¢ to select a sequence of four digits, such as 2449. If you play this game once every day, find the probability of winning at least once in a year with 365 days.

Solution

Because the time interval is 365 days, $n = 365$. Because there is one winning set of numbers among the 10,000 that are possible (from 0000 to 9999), $p = 1/10,000$. With $n = 365$ and $p = 1/10,000$, the conditions $n \geq 100$ and $np \leq 10$ are both satisfied, so we can use the Poisson distribution as an approximation to the binomial distribution. We first need the value of μ, which is found as follows:

$$\mu = np = 365 \cdot \frac{1}{10,000} = 0.0365$$

Having found the value of μ, we can proceed to find the probability for specific values of x. Because we want the probability that x is "at least 1," we will use the clever strategy of first finding $P(0)$, the probability of no wins in 365 days. The probability of at least one win can then be found by subtracting that result from 1. We find $P(0)$ by using $x = 0$, $\mu = 0.0365$, and $e = 2.71828$, as shown here:

$$P(0) = \frac{\mu^x \cdot e^{-\mu}}{x!} = \frac{0.0365^0 \cdot 2.71828^{-0.0365}}{0!} = \frac{1 \cdot 0.9642}{1} = 0.9642$$

Using the Poisson distribution as an approximation to the binomial distribution, we find that there is a 0.9642 probability of no wins, so the probability of at least one win is $1 - 0.9642 = 0.0358$. If we use the binomial distribution, we get a probability of 0.0358, so the Poisson approximation is quite good here.

using TECHNOLOGY

STATDISK   Select **Analysis** from the main menu bar, select **Probability Distributions,** then select **Poisson Distribution.** Enter the value of the mean. Click **Evaluate** and scroll for values that do not fit in the initial window. See the accompanying STATDISK display using the mean of 5.3 from Example 1 in this section.

STATDISK

MINITAB   First enter the desired value of x in column C1. Now select Calc from the main menu bar, then select **Probability Distributions,** then **Poisson.** Enter the value of the mean and enter C1 for the input column.

EXCEL   Click on *fx* on the main menu bar, then select the function category of **Statistical.** Select **POISSON** (or **POISSON .DIST**). Click **OK.** In the dialog box, enter the values for x and the mean, and enter 0 for "Cumulative." (Entering 1 for "Cumulative" results in the probability for values up to and including the entered value of x.)

TI-83/84 PLUS   Press **2ND** **VARS** (to get **DISTR**), then select **poissonpdf(.** Now press **ENTER**, then proceed to enter x, μ (including the comma). For μ, enter the value of the mean; for x, enter the desired number of occurrences over an interval.

STATCRUNCH   Click on **Open StatCrunch,** then click on **Stat.** Select **Calculators,** then select **Poisson.**

5-5 Basic Skills and Concepts

Statistical Literacy and Critical Thinking

1. Notation In analyzing hits by V-1 buzz bombs in World War II, South London was partitioned into 576 regions, each with an area of 0.25 km². A total of 535 bombs hit the combined area of 576 regions. Assume that we want to find the probability that a randomly selected region had exactly two hits. In applying Formula 5-9, identify the values of μ, x, and e. Also, briefly describe what each of those symbols represents.

2. Tornadoes During a recent 46-year period, New York State had a total of 194 tornadoes that measured 1 or greater on the Fujita scale. Let the random variable x represent the number of such tornadoes to hit New York State in one year, and assume that it has a Poisson distribution. What is the mean number of such New York tornadoes in one year? What is the standard deviation? What is the variance?

3. Poisson Approximation to Binomial Assume that we want to find the probability of getting at least one win when playing the Texas Pick 3 lottery 50 times. For one bet, there is a 1/1000 probability of winning. If we want to use the Poisson distribution as an approximation to the binomial, are the requirements satisfied? Why or why not?

4. Poisson Approximation to Binomial Assume that we plan to play the Texas Pick 3 lottery 100 times. For one bet, there is a 1/1000 probability of winning. If we want to use the Poisson distribution as an approximation to the binomial, are the requirements satisfied? If we use the Poisson distribution to find the probability of 101 wins, we get an extremely small positive number, so is it correct to conclude that the probability of 101 wins is possible, but highly unlikely?

Aircraft Accidents. *In Exercises 5–8, assume that the Poisson distribution applies, assume that the mean number of aircraft accidents in the United States is 8.5 per month (based on data from the National Transportation and Safety Board), and proceed to find the indicated probability.*

5. Find $P(0)$, the probability that in a month, there will be no aircraft accidents. Is it unlikely to have a month with no aircraft accidents?

6. Find $P(6)$, the probability that in a month, there will be 6 aircraft accidents. Is it unlikely to have a month with exactly 6 aircraft accidents?

7. Find $P(10)$, the probability that in a month, there will be 10 aircraft accidents. Is it unlikely to have a month with exactly 10 aircraft accidents?

8. Find $P(12)$, the probability that in a month, there will be 12 aircraft accidents. Is it unlikely to have a month with exactly 12 aircraft accidents?

In Exercises 9–16, use the Poisson distribution to find the indicated probabilities.

9. Earthquakes in the United States Various sources provide different earthquake data, but assume that for a recent 41-year period in the United States, there were 268 earthquakes measured at 6.0 or higher on the Richter scale (based on U.S. Geological Survey data).

a. Find the mean number of earthquakes per year.

b. Find the probability that in a given year, there is at least one earthquake in the United States that measures 6.0 or higher on the Richter scale.

c. Is it unlikely to have a year without any earthquakes that measure 6.0 or higher on the Richter scale? Why or why not?

10. Earthquakes in the World Various sources provide different earthquake data, but assume that for a recent 41-year period in the world, there were 5469 earthquakes measured at 6.0 or higher on the Richter scale (based on U.S. Geological Survey data).

a. Find the mean number of earthquakes per year.

b. Find the probability that in a given year, there are exactly 133 earthquakes that measures 6.0 or higher on the Richter scale.

c. If, in a particular year, there are exactly 133 earthquakes that measure 6.0 or higher on the Richter scale, would it make sense to report that this is a year with an unusual number of earthquakes? Why or why not?

11. Radioactive Decay Radioactive atoms are unstable because they have too much energy. When they release their extra energy, they are said to decay. When studying cesium-137, a nuclear engineer found that over 365 days, 1,000,000 radioactive atoms decayed to 977,287 radioactive atoms, so 22,713 atoms decayed during 365 days.

a. Find the mean number of radioactive atoms that decayed in a day.

b. Find the probability that on a given day, 50 radioactive atoms decayed.

12. Deaths from Horse Kicks A classical example of the Poisson distribution involves the number of deaths caused by horse kicks to men in the Prussian Army between 1875 and 1894. Data for 14 corps were combined for the 20-year period, and the 280 corps-years included a total of 196 deaths. After finding the mean number of deaths per corps-year, find the probability that a randomly selected corps-year has the following numbers of deaths: (**a**) 0, (**b**) 1, (**c**) 2, (**d**) 3, (**e**) 4.

continued

The actual results consisted of these frequencies: 0 deaths (in 144 corps-years);1 death (in 91 corps-years); 2 deaths (in 32 corps-years); 3 deaths (in 11 corps-years); 4 deaths (in 2 corps-years). Compare the actual results to those expected by using the Poisson probabilities. Does the Poisson distribution serve as a good tool for predicting the actual results?

13. World War II Bombs In Exercise 1 we noted that in analyzing hits by V-1 buzz bombs in World War II, South London was partitioned into 576 regions, each with an area of 0.25 km^2. A total of 535 bombs hit the combined area of 576 regions.

a. Find the probability that a randomly selected region had exactly 2 hits.

b. Among the 576 regions, find the expected number of regions with exactly 2 hits.

c. How does the result from part (b) compare to this actual result: There were 93 regions that had exactly 2 hits?

14. Disease Cluster Neuroblastoma, a rare form of malignant tumor, occurs in 11 children in a million, so its probability is 0.000011. Four cases of neuroblastoma occurred in Oak Park, Illinois, which had 12,429 children.

a. Assuming that neuroblastoma occurs as usual, find the mean number of cases in groups of 12,429 children.

b. Using the unrounded mean from part (a), find the probability that the number of neuroblastoma cases in a group of 12,429 children is 0 or 1.

c. What is the probability of more than one case of neuroblastoma?

d. Does the cluster of four cases appear to be attributable to random chance? Why or why not?

15. Chocolate Chip Cookies In the production of chocolate chip cookies, we can consider each cookie to be the specified interval unit required for a Poisson distribution, and we can consider the variable x to be the number of chocolate chips in a cookie. Table 3-1 is included with the Chapter Problem for Chapter 3, and it includes the numbers of chocolate chips in 34 different Keebler cookies. The Poisson distribution requires a value for μ, so use 30.4, which is the mean number of chocolate chips in the 34 Keebler cookies. Assume that the Poisson distribution applies.

a. Find the probability that a cookie will have 26 chocolate chips, then find the expected number of cookies with 26 chocolate chips among 34 different Keebler cookies, then compare the result to the actual number of Keebler cookies with 26 chocolate chips.

b. Find the probability that a cookie will have 30 chocolate chips, then find the expected number of cookies with 30 chocolate chips among 34 different Keebler cookies, then compare the result to the actual number of Keebler cookies with 30 chocolate chips.

16. Chocolate Chip Cookies Consider an individual chocolate chip cookie to be the specified interval unit required for a Poisson distribution, and consider the variable x to be the number of chocolate chips in a cookie. Table 3-1 is included with the Chapter Problem for Chapter 3, and it includes the numbers of chocolate chips in 40 different reduced fat Chips Ahoy cookies. The Poisson distribution requires a value for μ, so use 19.6, which is the mean number of chocolate chips in the 40 reduced fat Chips Ahoy cookies. Assume that the Poisson distribution applies.

a. Find the probability that a cookie will have 18 chocolate chips, then find the expected number of cookies with 18 chocolate chips among 40 different reduced fat Chips Ahoy cookies, then compare the result to the actual number of reduced fat Chips Ahoy cookies with 18 chocolate chips.

b. Find the probability that a cookie will have 21 chocolate chips, then find the expected number of cookies with 21 chocolate chips among 40 different reduced fat Chips Ahoy cookies, then compare the result to the actual number of reduced fat Chips Ahoy cookies with 21 chocolate chips.

5-5 Beyond the Basics

17. Poisson Approximation to Binomial Distribution An experiment consists of rolling a single die 12 times and the variable x is the number of times that the outcome is 6.

a. Can the Poisson distribution be used to find the probability that the outcome of 6 occurs exactly 3 times? Why or why not?

b. If the Poisson distribution is used, is the result OK? Why or why not?

Chapter 5   Review

This chapter introduced the important concept of a probability distribution, which describes the probability for each value of a random variable. This chapter includes only discrete probability distributions, but the following chapters will include continuous probability distributions.

In Section 5-2 we introduced probability distributions and the following definitions.

• A *random variable* has values that are determined by chance.

• A *probability distribution* consists of all values of a random variable, along with their corresponding probabilities. A probability distribution must satisfy three requirements: there is a numerical random variable x and its values are associated with corresponding probabilities, the sum of all of the probabilities for values of the random variable must be 1, and each probability value must be between 0 and 1 inclusive. The second and third requirements are expressed as $\sum P(x) = 1$ and, for each value of x, $0 \leq P(x) \leq 1$.

• Important characteristics of a *probability distribution* can be explored by constructing a probability histogram and by computing its mean and standard deviation using these formulas:

$$\mu = \sum [x \cdot P(x)]$$
$$\sigma = \sqrt{\sum [x^2 \cdot P(x)] - \mu^2}$$

• In Section 5-3, we introduced *binomial distributions,* which have two categories of outcomes and a fixed number of independent trials with a constant probability. The probability of x successes among n trials can be found by using the binomial probability formula, or Table A-1 (the Binomial Probability table), or computer software (such as STATDISK, Minitab, Excel, or StatCrunch), or a TI-83/84 Plus calculator.

• In Section 5-4 we noted that for a binomial distribution, the parameters of the mean and standard deviation are described by $\mu = np$ and $\sigma = \sqrt{npq}$.

• In Section 5-5 we introduced *Poisson probability distributions,* which apply to occurrences of some event over a specific interval. Probabilities for a Poisson distribution can be computed with Formula 5-9.

• *Unusual Outcomes:* In this chapter, we saw that we could determine when an outcome has an unusually low or unusually high number of successes. We used two different criteria: (1) the range rule of thumb, and (2) the use of probabilities, described as follows.

Using the range rule of thumb to identify unusual values:

$$\text{maximum usual value} = \mu + 2\sigma$$

$$\text{minimum usual value} = \mu - 2\sigma$$

Using probabilities to identify unusual values:

Unusually high number of successes: x successes among n trials is an unusually high number of successes if $P(x \text{ or more}) \leq 0.05.$*

Unusually low number of successes: x successes among n trials is an unusually low number of successes if $P(x \text{ or fewer}) \leq 0.05.$*

*The value of 0.05 is commonly used but is not absolutely rigid. Other values, such as 0.01, could be used to distinguish between events that can easily occur by chance and events that are very unlikely to occur by chance.

Chapter Quick Quiz

1. Is a probability distribution defined if the only possible values of a random variable are 0, 1, 2, 3, and $P(0) = P(1) = P(2) = P(3) = 0.25$?

2. There are 100 questions from an SAT test, and they are all multiple choice with possible answers of a, b, c, d, e. For each question, only one answer is correct. Find the mean number of correct answers for those who make random guesses for all 100 questions.

3. Using the same SAT questions described in Exercise 2, find the standard deviation for the numbers of correct answers for those who make random guesses for all 100 questions.

4. If boys and girls are equally likely, groups of 400 births have a mean of 200 girls and a standard deviation of 10 girls. Is 232 girls in 400 births an unusually high number of girls?

5. If boys and girls are equally likely, groups of 400 births have a mean of 200 girls and a standard deviation of 10 girls. Is 185 girls in 400 births an unusually low number of girls?

x	P(x)
0	0+
1	0.006
2	0.048
3	0.198
4	0.409
5	0.338

In Exercises 6–10, use the following: Five U.S. domestic flights are randomly selected, and the table in the margin lists the probabilities for the number that arrive on time (based on data from the Department of Transportation). Assume that five flights are randomly selected.

6. Does the table describe a probability distribution?

7. What does the probability of 0+ indicate? Does it indicate that among five randomly selected flights, it is impossible that none of them arrives on time?

8. What is the probability that at least three of the five flights arrive on time?

9. Is 0 an unusually low number of flights arriving on time?

10. Is 5 an unusually high number of flights arriving on time?

Review Exercises

In Exercises 1–4, assume that 40% of the population has brown eyes (based on data from Dr. P. Sorita at Indiana University).

1. **Brown Eyes** If six people are randomly selected, find the probability that none of them has brown eyes.

2. **Brown Eyes** Find the probability that among six randomly selected people, exactly four of them have brown eyes.

3. Brown Eyes Groups of 600 people are randomly selected. Find the mean and standard deviation for the numbers of people with brown eyes in such groups, then use the range rule of thumb to identify the range of usual values for those with brown eyes. For such a group of 600 randomly selected people, is 200 with brown eyes unusually low or high?

4. Brown Eyes When randomly selecting 600 people, the probability of exactly 239 people with brown eyes is $P(239) = 0.0331$. Also, $P(239$ or fewer$) = 0.484$. Which of those two probabilities is relevant for determining whether 239 is an unusually low number of people with brown eyes? Is 239 an unusually low number of people with brown eyes?

In Exercises 5 and 6, refer to the table in the margin. The random variable x is the number of males with tinnitus (ringing ears) among four randomly selected males (based on data from "Prevalence and Characteristics of Tinnitus among US Adults" by Shargorodsky et al., American Journal of Medicine, *Vol. 123, No. 8).*

x	P(x)
0	0.674
1	0.280
2	0.044
3	0.003
4	0+

5. Tinnitus Does the table describe a probability distribution? Why or why not?

6. Tinnitus Find the mean and standard deviation for the random variable x. Use the range rule of thumb to identify the range of usual values for the number of males with tinnitus among four randomly selected males. Is it unusual to get three males with tinnitus among four randomly selected males?

7. Brand Recognition In a study of brand recognition of the Kindle eReader, four consumers are interviewed. If x is the number of consumers in the group who recognize the Kindle brand name, then x can be 0, 1, 2, 3, or 4. If the corresponding probabilities are 0.026, 0.154, 0.346, 0.246, and 0.130, does the given information describe a probability distribution? Why or why not?

8. Expected Value for *Deal or No Deal* In the television game show *Deal or No Deal,* contestant Elna Hindler had to choose between acceptance of an offer of $193,000 or continuing the game. If she continued to refuse all further offers, she would have won one of these five equally likely prizes: $75, $300, $75,000, $500,000, and $1,000,000. Find her expected value if she continued the game and refused all further offers. Based on the result, should she accept the offer of $193,000, or should she continue?

9. Expected Value for a Magazine Sweepstakes *Reader's Digest* ran a sweepstakes in which prizes were listed along with the chances of winning: $1,000,000 (1 chance in 90,000,000), $100,000 (1 chance in 110,000,000), $25,000 (1 chance in 110,000,000), $5,000 (1 chance in 36,667,000), and $2,500 (1 chance in 27,500,000).

a. Assuming that there is no cost of entering the sweepstakes, find the expected value of the amount won for one entry.

b. Find the expected value if the cost of entering this sweepstakes is the cost of a postage stamp. Is it worth entering this contest?

10. Phone Calls In the month preceding the creation of this exercise, the author made 18 phone calls in 30 days. No calls were made on 19 days, 1 call was made on 8 days, and 2 calls were made on 5 days.

a. Find the mean number of calls per day.

b. Use the Poisson distribution to find the probability of no calls in a day.

c. Based on the probability in part (b), how many of the 30 days are expected to have no calls?

d. There were actually 18 days with no calls. How does this actual result compare to the expected value from part (c)?

Cumulative Review Exercises

Please be aware that some of the following problems may require knowledge of concepts presented in previous chapters.

1. Weekly Instruction Time The Organization for Economic Cooperation and Development provided the following mean weekly instruction times (hours) for elementary and high school students in various countries: 22.2 (United States); 24.8 (France); 24.2 (Mexico); 26.9 (China); 23.8 (Japan). Use the five given times for the following.

a. Find the mean.

b. Find the median.

c. Find the range.

d. Find the standard deviation.

e. Find the variance.

f. Use the range rule of thumb to identify the range of usual values.

g. Based on the result from part (f), are any of the times unusual? Why or why not?

h. What is the level of measurement of the data: nominal, ordinal, interval, or ratio?

i. Are the data discrete or continuous?

j. There is something fundamentally wrong with using the given times to find statistics such as the mean. What is wrong?

2. Ohio Pick 4 In Ohio's Pick 4 game, you pay \$1 to select a sequence of four digits, such as 7709. If you buy only one ticket and win, your prize is \$5000 and your net gain is \$4999.

a. If you buy one ticket, what is the probability of winning?

b. Construct a table describing the probability distribution corresponding to the purchase of one Pick 4 ticket.

c. If you play this game once every day, find the mean number of wins in years with exactly 365 days.

d. If you play this game once every day, find the probability of winning exactly once in 365 days.

e. Find the expected value for the purchase of one ticket.

3. Tennis Challenge In the last U.S. Open tennis tournament, there were 611 challenges made by singles players, and 172 of them resulted in referee calls that were overturned. The accompanying table lists the results by gender.

	Challenge Upheld with Overturned Call	Challenge Rejected with No Change
Challenges by Men	121	279
Challenges by Women	51	160

a. If one of the 611 challenges is randomly selected, what is the probability that it resulted in an overturned call?

b. If one of the challenges made by the men is randomly selected, what is the probability that it resulted in an overturned call?

c. If one of the challenges made by the women is randomly selected, what is the probability that it resulted in an overturned call?

d. If one of the overturned calls is randomly selected, what is the probability that the challenge was made by a woman?

e. If two different challenges are randomly selected with replacement, find the probability that they both resulted in an overturned call.

f. If one of the 611 challenges is randomly selected, find the probability that it was made by a man or was upheld with an overturned call.

g. If one of the challenged calls is randomly selected, find the probability that it was made by a man given that the call was upheld with an overturned call.

4. Gender Gap In recent years, the discrepancy between incomes of women and men has been shrinking, but it continues to exist. The accompanying graph illustrates the current gap. The graph shows that for every $100 earned by men, women earn $82.80 (based on data from the Bureau of Labor Statistics). Identify what is wrong with the graph, then redraw it so that it is not deceptive.

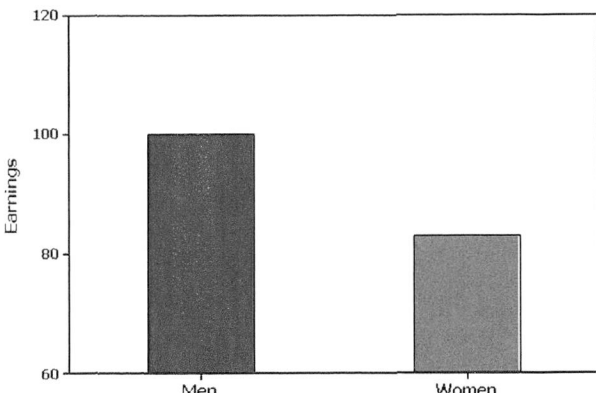

5. Random Digits The digits 0, 1, 2, 3, 4, 5, 6, 7, 8, and 9 are randomly selected for applications including the selection of lottery numbers and the selection of telephone numbers to be called as part of a survey. In the following tables, the table at the left summarizes actual results from 100 randomly selected digits, and the table at the right summarizes the probabilities of the different digits.

Digit	Frequency
0	9
1	7
2	12
3	10
4	10
5	11
6	8
7	8
8	14
9	11

Digit x	P(x)
0	0.1
1	0.1
2	0.1
3	0.1
4	0.1
5	0.1
6	0.1
7	0.1
8	0.1
9	0.1

a. What is the table at the left called?   **b.** What is the table at the right called?

c. Use the table at the left to find the mean. Is the result a statistic or a parameter?

d. Use the table at the right to find the mean. Is the result a statistic or a parameter?

e. If you were to randomly generate 1000 such digits, would you expect the mean of these 1000 digits to be close to the result from part (c) or part (d)? Why?

6. Investing in College Based on a *USA Today* poll, assume that 10% of the population believes that college is no longer a good investment.

a. Find the probability that among 16 randomly selected people, exactly 4 believe that college is no longer a good investment.

b. Find the probability that among 16 randomly selected people, at least 1 believes that college is no longer a good investment.

c. The poll results were obtained by Internet users logged on to the *USA Today* web site, and the Internet users decided whether to ignore the posted survey or respond. What type of sample is this? What does it suggest about the validity of the results?

Technology Project

Overbooking Flights American Airlines Flight 201 from New York's JFK airport to LAX airport in Los Angeles uses a Boeing 767-200 with 168 seats available for passengers. Because some people with reservations don't show up, American can overbook by accepting more than 168 reservations. If the flight is not overbooked, the airline will lose revenue due to empty seats, but if too many seats are sold and some passengers are denied seats, the airline loses money from the compensation that must be given to the bumped passengers. Assume that there is a 0.0995 probability that a passenger with a reservation will not show up for the flight (based on data from the IBM research paper "Passenger-Based Predictive Modeling of Airline No-Show Rates," by Lawrence, Hong, and Cherrier). Also assume that the airline accepts 182 reservations for the 168 seats that are available.

Find the probability that when 182 reservations are accepted for American Airlines Flight 201, there are more passengers showing up than there are seats available. Table A-1 (the Binomial Probabilities table) cannot be used and calculations with the binomial probability formula would be extremely time-consuming and tedious. The best approach is to use statistics software or a TI-83/84 Plus calculator. (See Section 5-3 for instructions describing the use of STATDISK, Minitab, Excel, StatCrunch, or a TI-83/84 Plus calculator.) Is the probability of overbooking small enough so that it does not happen very often, or does it seem too high so that changes must be made to make it lower? Now use trial and error to find the maximum number of reservations that could be accepted so that the probability of having more passengers than seats is 0.05 or less.

from data TO DECISION

Critical Thinking: Did Mendel's results from plant hybridization experiments contradict his theory?

Gregor Mendel conducted original experiments to study the genetic traits of pea plants. In 1865 he wrote "Experiments in Plant Hybridization," which was published in *Proceedings of the Natural History Society.* Mendel presented a theory that when there are two inheritable traits, one of them will be dominant and the other will be recessive. Each parent contributes one gene to an offspring and, depending on the

combination of genes, that offspring could inherit the dominant trait or the recessive trait. Mendel conducted an experiment using pea plants. The pods of pea plants can be green or yellow. When one pea carrying a dominant green gene and a recessive yellow gene is crossed with another pea carrying the same green/yellow genes, the offspring can inherit any one of these four combinations of genes: (1) green/green; (2) green/yellow; (3) yellow/green; (4) yellow/yellow. Because green is dominant and yellow is recessive, the

offspring pod will be green if either of the two inherited genes is green. The offspring can have a yellow pod only if it inherits the yellow gene from each of the two parents. Given these conditions, we expect that 3/4 of the offspring peas should have green pods; that is, *P*(green pod) = 3/4.

When Mendel conducted his famous hybridization experiments using parent pea plants with the green/yellow combination of genes, he obtained 580 offspring. According to Mendel's theory, 3/4 of the offspring should have green pods, but the actual number of plants with green pods was 428. So the proportion of offspring with green pods to the total number of offspring is 428/580 = 0.738. Mendel *expected* a proportion of 3/4 or 0.75, but his *actual result* is a proportion of 0.738.

a. Assuming that P(green pod) = 3/4, find the probability that among 580 offspring, the number

of peas with green pods is *exactly* 428.

b. Assuming that P(green pod) = 3/4, find the probability that among 580 offspring, the number of peas with green pods is 428 *or fewer.*

c. Which of the two preceding probabilities should be used for

determining whether 428 is an unusually low number of peas with green pods?

d. Use probabilities to determine whether 428 peas with green pods is an unusually low number. (*Hint:* See "Using Probabilities to Determine When Results Are Unusual" in Section 5-2.)

Cooperative Group Activities

1. In-class activity Win $1,000,000! The James Randi Educational Foundation offers a $1,000,000 prize to anyone who can show "under proper observing conditions, evidence of any paranormal, supernatural, or occult power or event." Divide into groups of three. Select one person who will be tested for extrasensory perception (ESP) by trying to correctly identify a digit randomly selected by another member of the group. Another group member should record the randomly selected digit, the digit guessed by the subject, and whether the guess was correct or wrong. Construct the table for the probability distribution of randomly generated digits, construct the relative frequency table for the random digits that were actually obtained, and construct a relative frequency table for the guesses that were made. After comparing the three tables, what do you conclude? What proportion of guesses are correct? Does it seem that the subject has the ability to select the correct digit significantly more often than would be expected by chance?

2. In-class activity See the preceding activity and *design an experiment* that would be effective in testing someone's claim that they have the ability to identify the color of a card selected from a standard deck of playing cards. Describe the experiment with great detail. Because the prize of $1,000,000 is at stake, we want to be careful to avoid the serious mistake of concluding that the person has a paranormal power when that power is not actually present. There will likely be some chance that the subject could make random guesses and be correct every time, so identify a probability that is reasonable for the event of the subject passing the test with random guesses. Be sure that the test is designed so that this probability is equal to or less than the probability value selected.

3. In-class activity Suppose we want to identify the probability distribution for the number of children born to randomly selected couples. For each student in the class, find the number of brothers and sisters and record the total number of children (including the student) in each family. Construct the relative frequency table for the result obtained. (The values of the random variable *x* will be 1, 2, 3, ...) What is wrong with using this relative frequency table as an estimate of the probability distribution for the number of children born to randomly selected couples?

4. Out-of-class activity The analysis of the last digits of data can sometimes reveal whether the data have been collected through actual measurements or reported by the subjects. Refer to an almanac or the Internet and find a collection of data (such as lengths of rivers in the world), then analyze the distribution of last digits to determine whether the values were obtained through actual measurements.

5. Out-of-class activity In the past, leading digits of the amounts on checks have been analyzed for fraud. For checks not involving fraud, the leading digit of 1 is expected about 30.1% of the time. Obtain a random sample of actual check amounts and record the leading digits. Compare the actual number of checks with amounts that have a leading digit of 1 to the 30.1% rate expected. Do the actual checks conform to the expected rate, or is there a substantial discrepancy? Explain.

6 Normal Probability Distributions

Reaching new heights

Ergonomics is the study of people fitting into their environments, and heights are extremely important in many applica-
tions. Section 4.4.2 of the Americans with Disabilities Act relates to height clearances with this
statement: "Walks, halls, corridors, passageways, aisles, or other circulation spaces shall have
80 in. (2030 mm) minimum clear head room." A CBS News report identified many low-hanging
signs in New York City subway walkways that violated that requirement with height clearances
less than 80 in. Even when that 80 in. minimum height clearance is maintained, not all people
can walk through without bending.

Due to aircraft cabin designs and other considerations, British Airways and many other
carriers have a cabin crew height requirement between 5 ft 2 in. and 6 ft 1 in. For aesthetic
reasons, Rockette dancers at New York's Radio City Music Hall must be between 66.5 in. and
71.5 in. tall. For practical reasons, the U.S. Army requires that women must be between 58 in.
and 80 in. tall. For social reasons, Tall Clubs International requires that male members must be
at least 6 ft 2 in. tall, and women members must be at least 5 ft 10 in. tall.

Given that heights are so important in so many different circumstances, what do we know
about heights? Based on preceding chapters, we know that an investigation of heights should
involve much more than simply finding a mean. We should consider the "CVDOT" elements
of center, variation, distribution, outliers, and changes over time. We might use the mean as a
measure of center, the standard deviation as a measure of variation, and the histogram as a
tool for visualizing the distribution of the data, and we should determine whether outliers are
present. We should also consider whether we are dealing with a static population or one that
is changing over time. For heights of adults, we might refer to Data Set 1 in Appendix B to
estimate that heights of adult males have a mean of 69.5 in. and a standard deviation of 2.4 in.,
while heights of adult females have a mean of 63.8 in. and a standard deviation of 2.6 in. (These
values are very close to the values that would be obtained by using a much larger sample.)
For distributions of heights, we might examine histograms, such as those shown here (based
on Data Set 1 in Appendix B). Note that the histograms appear to be roughly bell-shaped,
suggesting that the heights are from populations having normal distributions (as described in
Section 2-3). For outliers, we might examine the histograms and note that there is one male
with a height that is somewhat, but not dramatically, different from the others. Also, we know
that heights are changing over time, so our studies will focus on current heights, not heights
from past or future centuries.

6-1 Review and Preview

6-2 The Standard Normal
Distribution

6-3 Applications of Normal
Distributions

6-4 Sampling Distributions
and Estimators

6-5 Central Limit Theorem

6-6 Assessing Normality

6-7 Normal as
Approximation to
Binomial

This chapter introduces the statistical tools that are basic to good ergonomic design. After completing this chapter, we will be able to solve problems in a wide variety of different disciplines as well. We will be able to answer questions such as these:

- What percentages of men and women can easily navigate in an area with the height clearance of 80 in. that is stipulated in the Americans with Disabilities Act?
- What percentages of men and women satisfy the flight cabin crew requirement of having a height between 5 ft 2 in. and 6 ft 1 in.?
- What percentage of women are eligible for membership in Tall Clubs International because they are at least 5 ft 10 in. tall?
- Current doorways are typically 6 ft 8 in. tall, but if we were to redesign doorways to accommodate 99% of the population, what should the height be?

6-1   Review and Preview

The preceding chapters introduced some extremely important characteristics of data. In Chapter 2 we considered the distribution of data, and in Chapter 3 we considered some important measures of data sets, including measures of center (such as the mean) and measures of variation (such as the standard deviation). In Chapter 4 we discussed basic principles of probability, and in Chapter 5 we presented the concept of a probability distribution. In Chapter 5 we considered only *discrete* probability distributions, but in this chapter we introduce *continuous* probability distributions. To illustrate the correspondence between area and probability, we begin with a *uniform distribution*, but most of this chapter focuses on *normal distributions*. Normal distributions occur often in real applications, and they play an important role in methods of inferential statistics. Here we present concepts of normal distributions that will be used often in the remaining chapters. Several of the statistical methods discussed in later chapters are based on concepts related to the central limit theorem discussed in Section 6-5. Many other sections require normally distributed populations, and Section 6-6 presents methods for analyzing sample data to determine whether the sample appears to be from a normally distributed population.

> **DEFINITION** If a continuous random variable has a distribution with a graph that is symmetric and bell-shaped, as in Figure 6-1, and it can be described by the equation given as Formula 6-1, we say that it has a **normal distribution.**

Curve is bell-shaped and symmetric

μ

Value

Figure 6-1
The Normal Distribution

Formula 6-1

$$y = \frac{e^{-\frac{1}{2}\left(\frac{x-\mu}{\sigma}\right)^2}}{\sigma\sqrt{2\pi}}$$

We won't actually use Formula 6-1, and we include it only to illustrate that any particular normal distribution is determined by two parameters: the mean, μ, and standard deviation, σ. In that formula, the letter π represents the constant value 3.14159 . . . and e represents the constant value 2.71828 . . . . The symbols μ and σ represent fixed values for the mean and standard deviation, respectively. Once specific values are selected for μ and σ, we can graph Formula 6-1 and the result will look like Figure 6-1. From Formula 6-1 we see that a normal distribution is determined by the fixed values of the mean μ and standard deviation σ. Fortunately, that's all we need to know about that formula.

<table>
<tr><td>**6-2**</td><td>## The Standard Normal Distribution</td></tr>
</table>

Key Concept In this section we present the *standard normal distribution,* which has these three properties:

1. The graph of the standard normal distribution is bell-shaped (as in Figure 6-1).

2. The standard normal distribution has a mean equal to 0 (that is, $\mu = 0$).

3. The standard normal distribution has a standard deviation equal to 1 (that is, $\sigma = 1$).

In this section we develop the skill to find areas (or probabilities or relative frequencies) corresponding to various regions under the graph of the standard normal distribution. In addition, we find z scores that correspond to areas under the graph. These skills become important as we study nonstandard normal distributions and all of the real and important applications that they involve.

Uniform Distributions

The focus of this chapter is the concept of a normal probability distribution, but we begin with a *uniform distribution.* The uniform distribution allows us to see the following two very important properties:

1. The area under the graph of a probability distribution is equal to 1.

2. There is a correspondence between area and probability (or relative frequency), so some probabilities can be found by identifying the corresponding areas in the graph.

Chapter 5 considered only discrete probability distributions, but we now consider continuous probability distributions, beginning with the *uniform distribution.*

> **DEFINITION** A continuous random variable has a **uniform distribution** if its values are spread *evenly* over the range of possibilities. The graph of a uniform distribution results in a rectangular shape.

Example 1 Subway to Mets Game

For New York City weekday late-afternoon subway travel from Times Square to the Mets stadium, you can take the #7 train that leaves Times Square every 5 minutes. Given the subway departure schedule and the arrival of a passenger, the waiting time x is between 0 min and 5 min, as described by the uniform distribution depicted in Figure 6-2. Note that in Figure 6-2, waiting times can be *any* value between 0 min and 5 min, so it is possible to have a waiting time of 2.33457 min. Note also that all of the different possible waiting times are equally likely.

The graph of a continuous probability distribution, such as in Figure 6-2, is called a **density curve.** A density curve must satisfy the following two requirements.

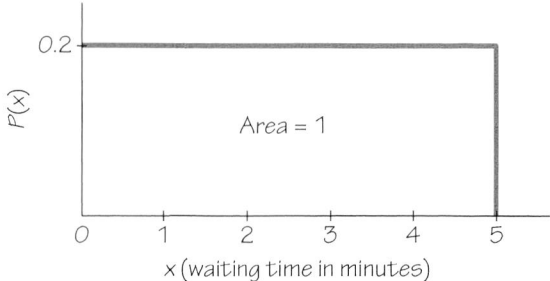

Figure 6-2   **Uniform Distribution of Waiting Time**

Requirements for a Density Curve

1. The total area under the curve must equal 1.

2. Every point on the curve must have a vertical height that is 0 or greater. (That is, the curve cannot fall below the x-axis.)

By setting the height of the rectangle in Figure 6-2 to be 0.2, we force the enclosed area to be $0.2 \times 5 = 1$, as required. (In general, the area of the rectangle becomes 1 when we make its height equal to the value of $1/\text{range}$.) The requirement that the area must equal 1 simplifies probability problems, so the following statement is important:

Because the total area under the density curve is equal to 1, there is a correspondence between *area* and *probability*.

Example 2   Subway Waiting Time

Given the uniform distribution illustrated in Figure 6-2, find the probability that a randomly selected passenger has a waiting time greater than 2 minutes.

Solution

The shaded area in Figure 6-3 represents waiting times greater than 2 minutes. Because the total area under the density curve is equal to 1, there is a correspondence between area and probability. We can find the desired probability by using areas as follows:

$$P(\text{wait time greater than 2 min}) = \text{area of shaded region in Figure 6-3}$$
$$= 0.2 \times 3$$
$$= 0.6$$

Figure 6-3   **Using Area to Find Probability**

Interpretation

The probability of randomly selecting a passenger with a waiting time greater than 2 minutes is 0.6.

Standard Normal Distribution

The density curve of a uniform distribution is a horizontal straight line, so we can find the area of any rectangular region by applying this formula: Area = height × width. Because the density curve of a normal distribution has a complicated bell shape as shown in Figure 6-1, it is more difficult to find areas. However, the basic principle is the same: *There is a correspondence between area and probability.* In Figure 6-4 we show that for a standard normal distribution, the area under the density curve is equal to 1.

> **DEFINITION** The **standard normal distribution** is a normal distribution with the parameters of $\mu = 0$ and $\sigma = 1$. The total area under its density curve is equal to 1 (as in Figure 6-4).

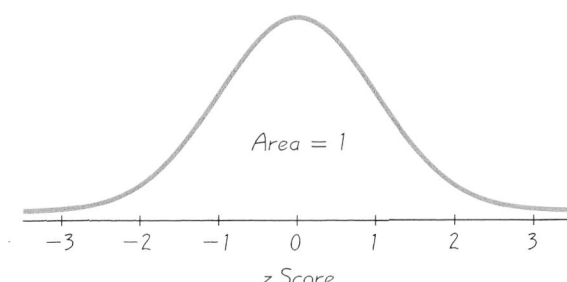

Area = 1

z Score

Figure 6-4   Standard Normal Distribution

It is not easy to manually find areas in Figure 6-4, but we have two other relatively easy ways of finding those areas: (1) Use technology; (2) use Table A-2 in Appendix A (the Standard Normal Distribution table in the Appendix).

Finding Probabilities when Given *z* Scores

We can find areas (or probabilities) for many different regions in Figure 6-4 by using a TI-83/84 Plus calculator or computer software such as STATDISK, Minitab, Excel, or StatCrunch, or we can also use Table A-2 (in Appendix A and the *Formulas and Tables* insert card). Key features of the different methods are summarized in Table 6-1 that follows. Because calculators or computer software generally give more accurate results than Table A-2, we strongly recommend using technology. (When there are discrepancies, answers in Appendix D will generally include results based on Table A-2 as well as answers based on technology.)

If using Table A-2, it is essential to understand these points:

1. Table A-2 is designed only for the *standard* normal distribution, which has a mean of 0 and a standard deviation of 1.

2. Table A-2 is on two pages, with the left page for *negative z* scores and the right page for *positive z* scores.

3. Each value in the body of the table is a *cumulative area from the left* up to a vertical boundary above a specific *z* score.

4. When working with a graph, avoid confusion between *z* scores and areas.

> *z* score: *Distance* **along the horizontal scale of the standard normal distribution; refer to the leftmost column and top row of Table A-2.**
>
> Area: *Region* **under the curve; refer to the values in the** *body* **of Table A-2.**

5. The part of the *z* score denoting hundredths is found across the top row of Table A-2.

CAUTION When working with a normal distribution, be careful to avoid confusion between *z* scores and areas.

Table 6-1 Methods for Finding Normal Distribution Areas

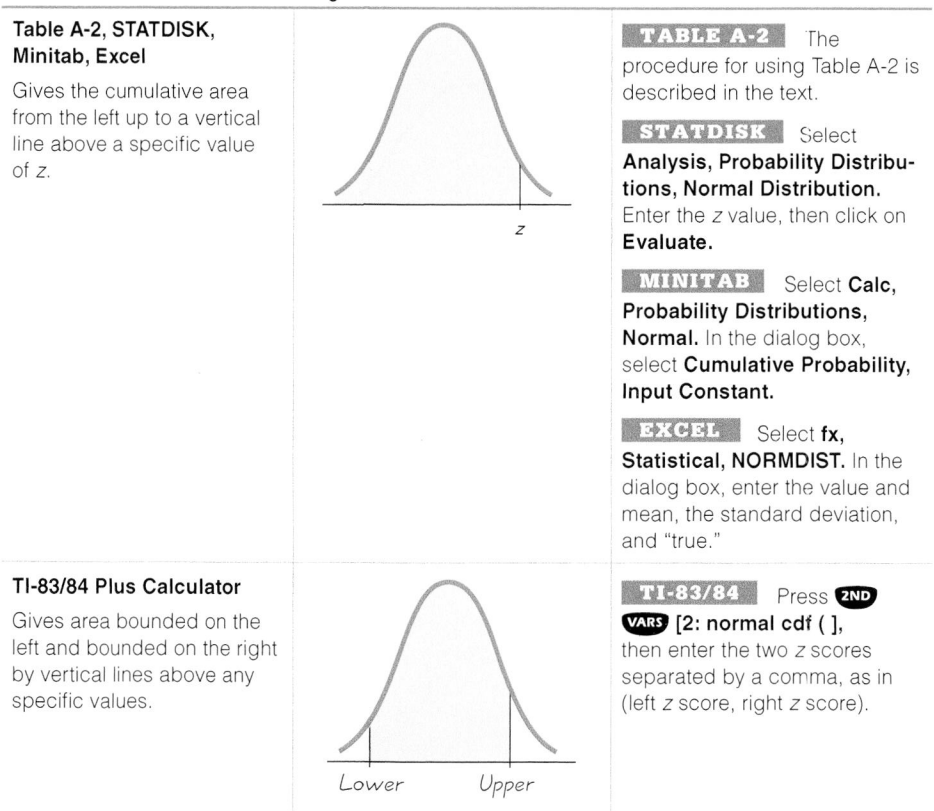

Table A-2, STATDISK, Minitab, Excel

Gives the cumulative area from the left up to a vertical line above a specific value of *z*.

TABLE A-2 The procedure for using Table A-2 is described in the text.

STATDISK Select **Analysis, Probability Distributions, Normal Distribution.** Enter the *z* value, then click on **Evaluate.**

MINITAB Select **Calc, Probability Distributions, Normal.** In the dialog box, select **Cumulative Probability, Input Constant.**

EXCEL Select **fx, Statistical, NORMDIST.** In the dialog box, enter the value and mean, the standard deviation, and "true."

TI-83/84 Plus Calculator

Gives area bounded on the left and bounded on the right by vertical lines above any specific values.

TI-83/84 Press **2ND** **VARS** [2: normal cdf ( ], then enter the two *z* scores separated by a comma, as in (left *z* score, right *z* score).

The following examples illustrate procedures that can be used with real and important applications introduced in the following sections.

Example 3 Bone Density Test

A bone mineral density test can be helpful in identifying the presence or likelihood of osteoporosis, a disease causing bones to become more fragile and more likely to break. The result of a bone density test is commonly measured as a *z* score. The population of z scores is normally distributed with a mean of 0 and a standard deviation of 1, so these test results meet the requirements of a standard normal distribution; Figure 6-4 is a graph of these test results.

A randomly selected adult undergoes a bone density test. Find the probability that the result is a reading less than 1.27.

Solution

We need to find the area in Figure 6-5 below z = 1.27. The *area* below z = 1.27 is equal to the *probability* of randomly selecting a person with a bone density test result that is less than 1.27. If using technology, see the instructions included at the end of this section. If using Table A-2, begin with the z score of 1.27 by locating 1.2 in the left column; next find the value in the adjoining row of probabilities that is directly below 0.07, as shown in the accompanying excerpt. Table A-2 shows that there is an area of 0.8980 corresponding to z = 1.27. We want the area *below* 1.27, and Table A-2 gives the cumulative area from the left, so the desired area is 0.8980. Because we have a correspondence between area and probability, we know that the probability of a z score below 1.27 is 0.8980.

Figure 6-5
Finding Area below z = 1.27

TABLE A-2	(continued) Cumulative Area from the LEFT									
z	.00	.01	.02	.03	.04	.05	.06	.07	.08	.09
0.0	.5000	.5040	.5080	.5120	.5160	.5199	.5239	.5279	.5319	.5359
0.1	.5398	.5438	.5478	.5517	.5557	.5596	.5636	.5675	.5714	.5753
0.2	.5793	.5832	.5871	.5910	.5948	.5987	.6026	.6064	.6103	.6141
1.0	.8413	.8438	.8461	.8485	.8508	.8531	.8554	.8577	.8599	.8621
1.1	.8643	.8665	.8686	.8708	.8729	.8749	.8770	.8790	.8810	.8830
1.2	.8849	.8869	.8888	.8907	.8925	.8944	.8962	.8980	.8997	.9015
1.3	.9032	.9049	.9066	.9082	.9099	.9115	.9131	.9147	.9162	.9177
1.4	.9192	.9207	.9222	.9236	.9251	.9265	.9279	.9292	.9306	.9319

Interpretation

The *probability* that a randomly selected person has a bone density test result below 1.27 is 0.8980, as shown as the shaded region in Figure 6-5. Another way to interpret this result is to conclude that 89.80% of people have bone density levels below 1.27.

Example 4   Bone Density Test

Using the same bone density test from Example 3, find the probability that a randomly selected person has a result above −1.00. A value above −1.00 is considered to be in the "normal" range of bone density readings.

Solution

We again find the desired *probability* by finding a corresponding *area*. We are looking for the area of the region to the right of $z = -1.00$ that is shaded in Figure 6-6. The accompanying STATDISK display shows that the area to the right of $z = -1.00$ is 0.841345.

If we use Table A-2, we should know that it is designed to apply only to cumulative areas from the *left*. Referring to the page with *negative z* scores, we find that the cumulative area from the left up to $z = -1.00$ is 0.1587 as shown in Figure 6-6. Because the total area under the curve is 1, we can find the shaded area by subtracting 0.1587 from 1. The result is 0.8413. Even though Table A-2 is designed only for cumulative areas from the left, we can use it to find cumulative areas from the right, as shown in Figure 6-6.

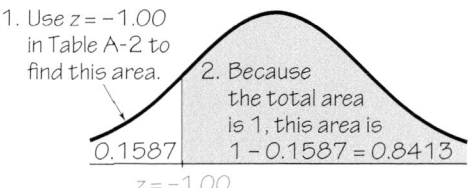

1. Use $z = -1.00$ in Table A-2 to find this area.

2. Because the total area is 1, this area is $1 - 0.1587 = 0.8413$

0.1587

$z = -1.00$

Figure 6-6   Finding the Area above z

STATDISK

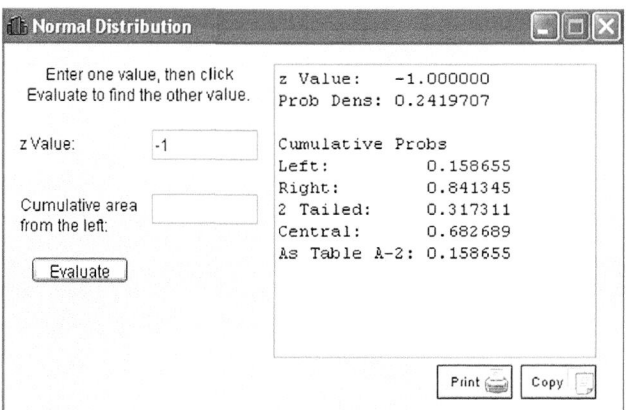

Interpretation

Because of the correspondence between probability and area, we conclude that the *probability* of randomly selecting someone with a bone density reading above −1 is 0.8413 (which is the *area* to the right of $z = -1.00$). We might also say that 84.13% of people have bone density levels above −1.00.

Example 4 illustrates a way that Table A-2 can be used indirectly to find a cumulative area from the right. The following example illustrates another way that we can find an area indirectly by using Table A-2.

Example 5 Bone Density Test

A bone density test reading between −1.00 and −2.50 indicates that the subject has osteopenia, which is some bone loss. Find the probability that a randomly selected subject has a reading between −1.00 and −2.50.

Solution

We are again dealing with normally distributed values having a mean of 0 and a standard deviation of 1. The values between −1.00 and −2.50 correspond to the shaded region at the far right in Figure 6-7. Table A-2 cannot be used to find that area directly, but we can use it to find the following:

1. The area to the left of $z = -2.50$ is 0.0062.

2. The area to the left of $z = -1.00$ is 0.1587.

3. The area *between* $z = -2.50$ and $z = -1.00$ (the shaded area at the far right in Figure 6-7) is the difference between the areas found in the preceding two steps:

$$0.1587 - 0.0062 = 0.1525$$

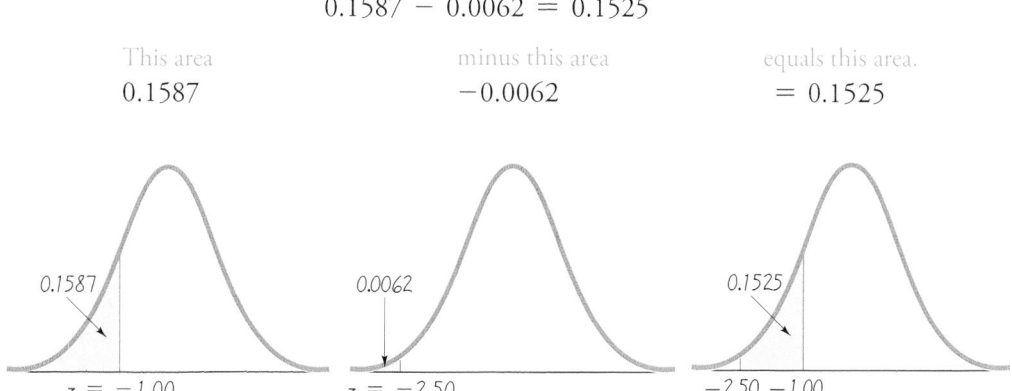

| This area | minus this area | equals this area. |
| 0.1587 | −0.0062 | = 0.1525 |

Figure 6-7 Finding the Area between Two z Scores

Interpretation

Using the correspondence between probability and area, we conclude that there is a probability of 0.1525 that a randomly selected subject has a bone density reading between −1.00 and −2.50. Another way to interpret this result is to state that 15.25% of people have osteopenia, with bone density readings between −1.00 and −2.50.

Example 5 can be generalized as the following rule: **The area corresponding to the region *between* two z scores can be found by finding the difference between the two areas found in Table A-2.** Figure 6-8 illustrates this general rule. The shaded region *B* can be found by calculating the *difference* between two areas found from Table A-2.

Learning hint: Don't try to memorize a rule or formula for this case. Focus on *understanding* that Table A-2 gives cumulative areas from the left only. Draw a graph, shade the desired area, then think of a way to find the desired area given the condition that Table A-2 provides only cumulative areas from the left.

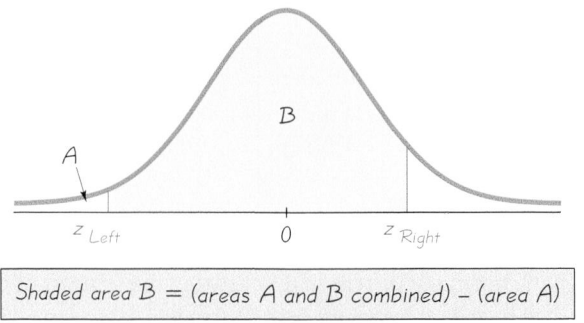

Figure 6-8   **Finding the Area between Two z Scores**

Probabilities such as those in the preceding examples can also be expressed with the following notation.

Notation

$P(a < z < b)$ denotes the probability that the *z* score is between *a* and *b*.

$P(z > a)$ denotes the probability that the *z* score is greater than *a*.

$P(z < a)$ denotes the probability that the *z* score is less than *a*.

Using this notation, $P(-2.50 < z < -1.00) = 0.1525$, states in symbols that the probability of a *z* score falling between -2.50 and -1.00 is 0.1525 (as in Example 5).

Finding z Scores from Known Areas

Examples 3, 4, and 5 all involved the standard normal distribution, and they were all examples with this same format: Given *z* scores, find areas (or probabilities). In many cases, we need a method for reversing the format: Given a known area (or probability), find the corresponding *z* score. In such cases, it is really important to avoid confusion between *z* scores and areas. Remember, *z* scores are *distances* along the horizontal scale, but areas (or probabilities) are regions under the curve. (Table A-2 lists *z*-scores in the left column and across the top row, but areas are found in the *body* of the table.) We should also remember that *z* scores positioned in the left half of the curve are always negative. If we already know a probability and want to find the corresponding *z* score, we use the following procedure.

Procedure for Finding a z Score from a Known Area

1. Draw a bell-shaped curve and identify the region under the curve that corresponds to the given probability. If that region is not a cumulative region from the left, work instead with a known region that is a cumulative region from the left.

2. Use technology or Table A-2 to find the *z* score. With Table A-2, use the cumulative area from the left, locate the closest probability in the *body* of the table, and identify the corresponding *z* score.

Example 6   **Bone Density Test**

Use the same bone density test scores described in Example 3. Those scores are normally distributed with a mean of 0 and a standard deviation of 1, so they meet the requirements of a standard normal distribution. Find the bone density score corresponding to P_{95}, the 95th percentile. That is, find the bone density score that separates the bottom 95% from the top 5%. See Figure 6-9.

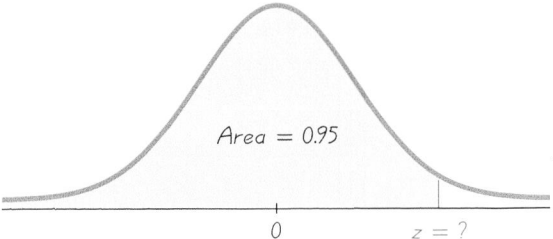

Figure 6-9   Finding the 95th Percentile

Solution

Figure 6-9 shows the z score that is the 95th percentile, with 95% of the area (or 0.95) below it. We could find the z score using technology. The accompanying Excel display shows that the z score with an area of 0.95 to its left is $z = 1.644853627$, or 1.645 when rounded.

If using Table A-2, search for the area of 0.95 *in the body* of the table and then find the corresponding z score. In Table A-2 we find the areas of 0.9495 and 0.9505, but there's an asterisk with a special note indicating that 0.9500 corresponds to a z score of 1.645. We can now conclude that the z score in Figure 6-9 is 1.645, so the 95th percentile is $z = 1.645$.

EXCEL

Function Arguments			?X
NORM.INV			
Probability	0.95	[⊞]	= 0.95
Mean	0	[⊞]	= 0
Standard_dev	1	[⊞]	= 1
			= 1.644853627

Returns the inverse of the normal cumulative distribution for the specified mean and standard deviation.

  Standard_dev is the standard deviation of the distribution, a positive number.

Formula result = 1.644853627

Help on this function   OK   Cancel

Interpretation

For bone density test scores, 95% of the scores are less than or equal to 1.645, and 5% of them are greater than or equal to 1.645.

Special Cases In the solution to Example 6, Table A-2 led to a z score of 1.645, which is midway between 1.64 and 1.65. When using Table A-2, we can usually avoid interpolation by simply selecting the closest value. The accompanying table lists special cases that are often used in a wide variety of applications. (For one of those special cases, the value of $z = 2.576$ gives an area slightly closer to the area of 0.9950, but $z = 2.575$ has the advantage of being the value midway between $z = 2.57$ and $z = 2.58$.) Except in these special cases, we can usually select the closest value in the table. (If a desired value is midway between two table values, select the larger value.) For z scores above 3.49, we can use 0.9999 as an approximation of the cumulative area from the left; for z scores below -3.49, we can use 0.0001 as an approximation of the cumulative area from the left.

Table A-2 Special Cases Table

z Score	Cumulative Area from the Left
1.645	0.9500
−1.645	0.0500
2.575	0.9950
−2.575	0.0050
Above 3.49	0.9999
Below −3.49	0.0001

Example 7   Bone Density Test

Using the same bone density test described in Example 3, we have a standard normal distribution with a mean of 0 and a standard deviation of 1. Find the bone density test score that separates the bottom 2.5% and find the score that separates the top 2.5%.

Solution

The required z scores are shown in Figure 6-10. Those z scores can be found using technology. If using Table A-2 to find the z score located to the left, we search the *body of the table* for an area of 0.025. The result is $z = -1.96$. To find the z score located to the right, we search *the body of Table A-2* for an area of 0.975. (Remember that Table A-2 always gives cumulative areas from the *left*.) The result is $z = 1.96$. The values of $z = -1.96$ and $z = 1.96$ separate the bottom 2.5% and the top 2.5%, as shown in Figure 6-10.

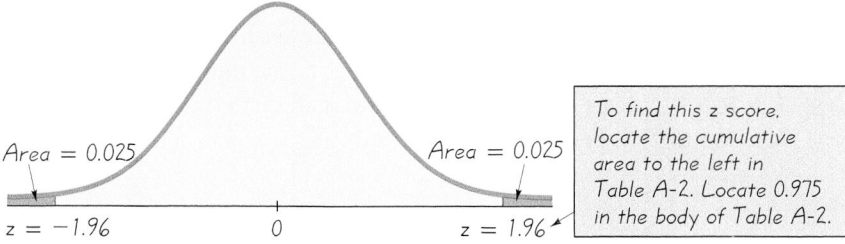

Figure 6-10   **Finding z Scores**

Interpretation

For the population of bone density test scores, 2.5% of the scores are equal to or less than -1.96 and 2.5% of the scores are equal to or greater than 1.96. Another interpretation is that 95% of all bone density test scores are between -1.96 and 1.96.

Critical Values For a normal distribution, a *critical value* is a z score on the borderline separating the z scores that are *likely* to occur from those that are unlikely. Common critical values are $z = -1.96$ and $z = 1.96$, and they are obtained as shown in Example 7. In Example 7, the values below $z = -1.96$ are unlikely, because only 2.5% of the population have scores below -1.96, and the values above $z = 1.96$ are unlikely because only 2.5% of the population have scores above 1.96. The reference to *critical values* is not so important in this chapter, but will become extremely important in following chapters. The following notation is used for critical z values found by using the standard normal distribution.

DEFINITION For the standard normal distribution, a **critical value** is a z score separating unlikely values from those that are likely to occur.

Notation

The expression z_α denotes the z score with an area of α to its right. (α is the Greek letter alpha.)

Example 8 Finding z_{α}

In the expression z_{α}, let $\alpha = 0.025$ and find the value of $z_{0.025}$.

Solution

The notation of $z_{0.025}$ is used to represent the z score with an area of 0.025 to its right. Refer to Figure 6-10 and note that the value of $z = 1.96$ has an area of 0.025 to its right, so $z_{0.025} = 1.96$.

CAUTION When using Table A-2 for finding a value of z_{α} for a particular value of α, note that α is the area to the *right* of z_{α}, but Table A-2 lists cumulative areas to the *left* of a given z score. To find the value of z_{α} by using the table, resolve that conflict by using the value of $1 - \alpha$. In Example 8, the value of $z_{0.025}$ can be found by locating the area of 0.9750 in the body of the table.

Examples 3 through 7 in this section are based on the real application of the bone density test, with scores that are normally distributed with a mean of 0 and standard deviation of 1, so that these scores have a standard normal distribution. Apart from the bone density test scores, it is rare to find such convenient parameters, because typical normal distributions involve means different from 0 and standard deviations different from 1. In the next section we present methods for working with such normal distributions.

using TECHNOLOGY

When working with the standard normal distribution, a technology can be used to find z scores or areas instead of Table A-2. The following instructions describe how to find such z scores or areas with technology.

STATDISK Select **Analysis, Probability Distributions, Normal Distribution.** Either enter the z score to find corresponding areas, or enter the cumulative area from the left to find the z score. After entering a value, click on the **Evaluate** button. See the STATDISK display included with Example 4.

MINITAB

- To find the cumulative area to the left of a z score (as in Table A-2), select **Calc, Probability Distributions, Normal, Cumulative probabilities.** Then enter the mean of 0 and standard deviation of 1. Click on the **Input Constant** button and enter the z score.

- To find a z score corresponding to a known probability, select **Calc, Probability Distributions, Normal.** Then select **Inverse cumulative probabilities** and the option **Input constant.** For the input constant, enter the total area to the left of the given value.

EXCEL

- To find the cumulative area to the left of a z score (as in Table A-2), click on *fx*, then select **Statistical, NORMSDIST (or NORMS.DIST).** Enter the z score.

- To find a z score corresponding to a known probability, select *fx*, **Statistical, NORMSINV (or NORMS.INV).** Enter the total area to the left of the given value.

TI-83/84 PLUS Unlike most other technologies, the TI-83/84 Plus calculator does not base areas on cumulative regions from the left. Instead, the areas correspond to the z score that is a left boundary and another z score that is a right boundary. Press **2ND** **VARS** and select **normalcdf.** Proceed to enter the two z scores separated by a comma, as in (left z score, right z score). Example 5 could be solved with the command of **normalcdf(-2.50, -1.00),** which yields a probability of 0.1524 (rounded) as shown in the accompanying screen.

TI-83/84 PLUS

To find a z score corresponding to a known probability, press **2ND** **VARS** and select **invNorm.** Proceed to enter the total area to the left of the z score. For example, the command of **invNorm(0.975)** yields a z score of 1.959963986, which is rounded to 1.96, as in Example 8.

STATCRUNCH Click on **Open StatCrunch,** then click on **Stat.** Select **Calculators,** then select **Normal.** You can either enter a probability or a value of x. Click on **Compute.**

6-2 Basic Skills and Concepts

Statistical Literacy and Critical Thinking

1. Normal Distribution When we refer to a "normal" distribution, does the word *normal* have the same meaning as in ordinary language, or does it have a special meaning in statistics? What exactly is a normal distribution?

2. Normal Distribution A normal distribution is informally described as a probability distribution that is "bell-shaped" when graphed. Draw a rough sketch of a curve having the bell shape that is characteristic of a normal distribution.

3. Standard Normal Distribution Identify the requirements necessary for a normal distribution to be a *standard* normal distribution.

4. Notation What does the notation z_α indicate?

Continuous Uniform Distribution. *In Exercises 5–8, refer to the continuous uniform distribution depicted in Figure 6-2 and described in Example 1. Assume that a subway passenger is randomly selected, and find the probability that the waiting time is within the given range.*

5. Greater than 1.25 minutes

6. Less than 0.75 minutes

7. Between 1 minute and 3 minutes

8. Between 1.5 minutes and 4.5 minutes

Standard Normal Distribution. *In Exercises 9–12, find the area of the shaded region. The graph depicts the standard normal distribution of bone density scores with mean 0 and standard deviation 1.*

9.

$z = 0.44$

10.

$z = -1.04$

11.
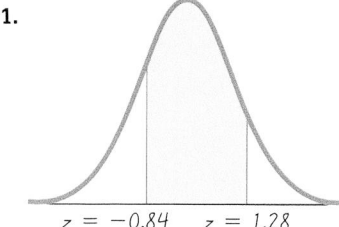
$z = -0.84$ $z = 1.28$

12.
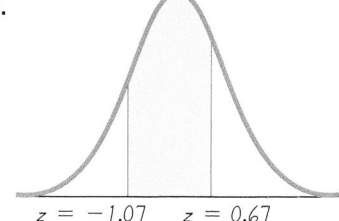
$z = -1.07$ $z = 0.67$

Standard Normal Distribution. *In Exercises 13–16, find the indicated z score. The graph depicts the standard normal distribution of bone density scores with mean 0 and standard deviation 1.*

13.

0.8907
0 z

14.
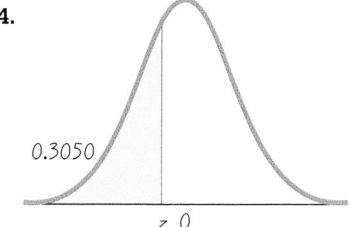
0.3050
z 0

15.

0.9265

z 0

16.

0.2061

0 z

Standard Normal Distribution. *In Exercises 17–36, assume that a randomly selected subject is given a bone density test. Those test scores are normally distributed with a mean of 0 and a standard deviation of 1. In each case, draw a graph and find the probability of the given scores. If using technology instead of Table A-2, round answers to four decimal places.*

17. Less than -2.04

18. Less than -0.19

19. Less than 2.33

20. Less than 1.96

21. Greater than 0.82

22. Greater than 1.82

23. Greater than -1.50

24. Greater than -0.84

25. Between 0.25 and 1.25

26. Between 1.23 and 2.37

27. Between and -2.75 and -2.00

28. Between -1.93 and -0.45

29. Between -2.20 and 2.50

30. Between -0.62 and 1.78

31. Between -2.11 and 4.00

32. Between -3.90 and 2.00

33. Less than 3.65

34. Greater than -3.80

35. Greater than 0

36. Less than 0

Finding Bone Density Scores. *In Exercises 37–40 assume that a randomly selected subject is given a bone density test. Bone density test scores are normally distributed with a mean of 0 and a standard deviation of 1. In each case, draw a graph, then find the bone density test score corresponding to the given information.*

37. Find P_{90}, the 90th percentile. This is the bone density score separating the bottom 90% from the top 10%.

38. Find P_5, the 5th percentile. This is the bone density score separating the bottom 5% from the top 95%.

39. If bone density scores in the bottom 2.5% and the top 2.5% are used as cutoff points for levels that are too low or too high, find the two readings that are cutoff values.

40. Find the bone density scores that can be used as cutoff values separating the most extreme 1% of all scores.

Finding Critical Values. *In Exercises 41–44, find the indicated critical value.*

41. $z_{0.025}$

42. $z_{0.01}$

43. $z_{0.05}$

44. $z_{0.03}$

Basis for the Range Rule of Thumb and the Empirical Rule. *In Exercises 45–48, find the indicated area under the curve of the standard normal distribution, then convert it to a percentage and fill in the blank. The results form the basis for the range rule of thumb and the empirical rule introduced in Section 3-3.*

45. About _____% of the area is between $z = -1$ and $z = 1$ (or within 1 standard deviation of the mean).

46. About _____% of the area is between $z = -2$ and $z = 2$ (or within 2 standard deviations of the mean).

47. About _____% of the area is between $z = -3$ and $z = 3$ (or within 3 standard deviations of the mean).

48. About _____% of the area is between $z = -3.5$ and $z = 3.5$ (or within 3.5 standard deviations of the mean).

6-2 Beyond the Basics

49. For bone density scores that are normally distributed with a mean of 0 and a standard deviation of 1, find the *percentage* of scores that are

a. within 1 standard deviation of the mean.

b. more than 2 standard deviations away from the mean.

c. within 1.96 standard deviations of the mean.

d. between $\mu - 2\sigma$ and $\mu + 2\sigma$.

e. more than 3 standard deviations away from the mean.

50. In a continuous uniform distribution,

$$\mu = \frac{\text{minimum} + \text{maximum}}{2} \qquad \text{and} \qquad \sigma = \frac{\text{range}}{\sqrt{12}}$$

a. Find the mean and standard deviation for the distribution of the subway waiting times represented in Figure 6-2.

b. For a continuous uniform distribution with $\mu = 0$ and $\sigma = 1$, the minimum is $-\sqrt{3}$ and the maximum is $\sqrt{3}$. For this continuous uniform distribution, find the probability of randomly selecting a value between -1 and 1, and compare it to the value that would be obtained by incorrectly treating the distribution as a standard normal distribution. Does the distribution affect the results very much?

 ## 6-3 Applications of Normal Distributions

Key Concept The objective of this section is to extend the methods of the previous section so that we can work with normal distributions having any mean and any standard deviation, instead of being limited to the standard normal distribution with mean 0 and standard deviation 1. The key element of this section is a simple conversion (Formula 6-2) that allows us to standardize any normal distribution so that the methods of the preceding section can be used with real and meaningful applications. Specifically, given some nonstandard normal distribution, we should be able to find probabilities corresponding to values of the variable x, and given some probability value, we should be able to find the corresponding value of the variable x.

> **When working with a normal distribution that is nonstandard (with a mean different from 0 and/or a standard deviation different from 1), we use Formula 6-2 to transform a value x to a z score, then we proceed with the same methods from Section 6-2.**

Formula 6-2

$$z = \frac{x - \mu}{\sigma} \qquad \text{(round } z \text{ scores to 2 decimal places)}$$

Some calculators and computer software programs do not require the above conversion to z scores because probabilities can be found directly. However, if you use Table A-2 to find probabilities, you **must** first convert values to standard z scores. Whether using technology or Table A-2, it is important to clearly understand the above conversion principle, because it is an important foundation for concepts introduced in the following chapters.

Figure 6-11 illustrates the conversion from a nonstandard to a standard normal distribution. The area in any normal distribution bounded by some score x (as in Figure 6-11(a)) is the same as the area bounded by the equivalent z score in the standard normal distribution (as in Figure 6-11(b)). This shows that when working with a nonstandard normal distribution, you can use Table A-2 the same way it was used in Section 6-2, provided that you first convert the values to z scores.

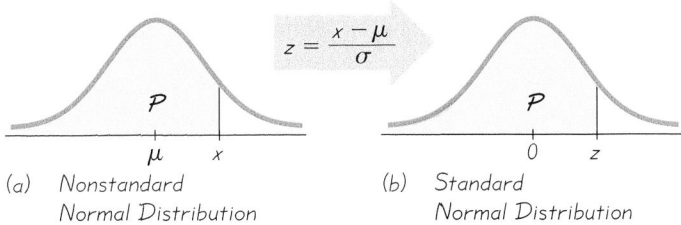

(a) Nonstandard   (b) Standard
     Normal Distribution   Normal Distribution

Figure 6-11   Converting Distributions

When finding areas with a nonstandard normal distribution, use the following procedure.

Procedure for Finding Areas with a Nonstandard Normal Distribution

1. Sketch a normal curve, label the mean and any specific x values, then *shade* the region representing the desired probability.

2. For each relevant value x that is a boundary for the shaded region, use Formula 6-2 to convert that value to the equivalent z score.

3. Use computer software or a calculator or Table A-2 to find the area of the shaded region. This area is the desired probability.

The following example applies these three steps to illustrate the relationship between a typical nonstandard normal distribution and the standard normal distribution.

Example 1   **What Proportion of Women Are Eligible for Tall Clubs International?**

The social organization Tall Clubs International has a requirement that women must be at least 70 in. tall. Given that women have normally distributed heights with a mean of 63.8 in. and a standard deviation of 2.6 in., find the percentage of women who satisfy that height requirement.

Solution

Step 1: See Figure 6-12, which incorporates this information: Women have heights that are normally distributed with a mean of 63.8 in. and a standard deviation of 2.6 in. The shaded region represents the women who satisfy the height requirement by being at least 70 in. tall.

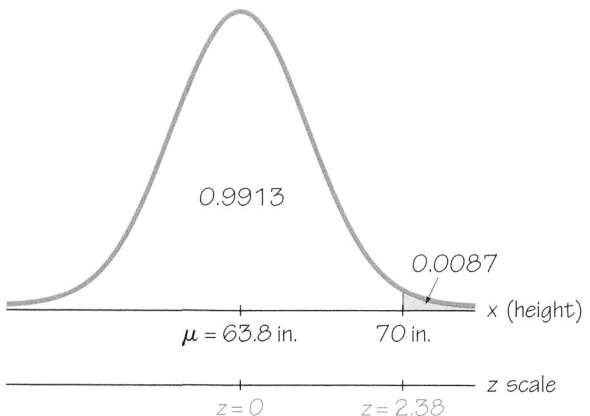

Figure 6-12   Heights of Women

Step 2: We can convert the height of 70 in. to a z score by using Formula 6-2 as follows:

$$z = \frac{x - \mu}{\sigma} = \frac{70 - 63.8}{2.6} = 2.38$$

Step 3: To use technology, refer to the instructions at the end of this section. Shown here is the STATDISK display that results from an entry of $z = 2.38$; it shows that the area to the right of $z = 2.38$ is 0.008656 (or 0.0087 rounded) and that is the shaded area in Figure 6-12.

STATDISK

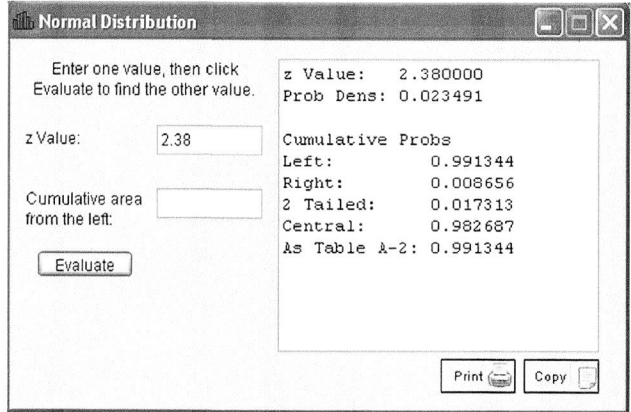

To use Table A-2, refer to that table with $z = 2.38$ and find that the cumulative area to the *left* of $z = 2.38$ is 0.9913. (Remember, Table A-2 is designed so that all areas are cumulative areas from the *left*.) Because the total area under the curve is 1, it follows that the shaded area in Figure 6-12 is $1 - 0.9913 = 0.0087$.

Interpretation

The proportion of women taller than 70 in. is 0.0087, or 0.87%. That is, just under 1% of women meet the minimum height requirement of 70 in. Tall Clubs International allows only the tallest of women.

Example 2 Airline Flight Crew Requirement

The Chapter Problem stated that British Airways and many other airlines have a requirement that a member of the cabin crew must have a height between 62 in. and 73 in. (or between 5 ft 2 in. and 6 ft 1 in.). Given that men have normally distributed heights with a mean of 69.5 in. and a standard deviation of 2.4 in., find the percentage of men who satisfy that height requirement.

Solution

Figure 6-13 shows the shaded region representing heights of men between 62 in. and 73 in.

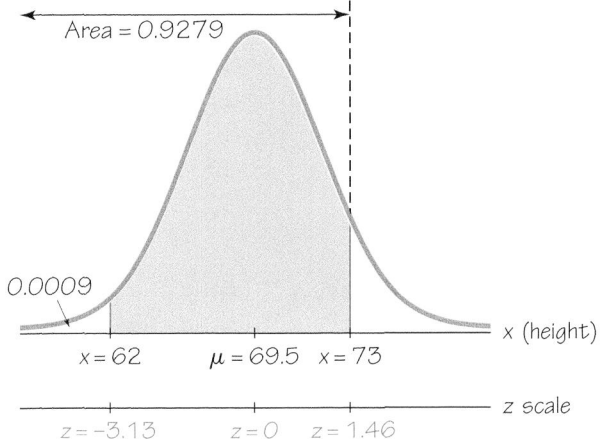

Figure 6-13   Heights of Men

Step 1: See Figure 6-13, which incorporates this information: Men have heights that are normally distributed with a mean of 69.5 in. and a standard deviation of 2.4 in. The shaded region represents the men who satisfy the height requirement by having a height between 62 in. and 73 in.

Step 2: To use technology, refer to the instructions at the end of this section. Technology will show that the shaded area in Figure 6-13 is 0.9267.

If using Table A-2, we cannot find the shaded area directly, but we can find it indirectly by using the same procedures from Section 6-2, as follows: (1) Find the cumulative area from the left up to 73 in. (or $z = 1.46$); (2) find the cumulative area from the left up to 62 in. (or $z = -3.13$); (3) find the difference between those two areas. The heights of 73 in. and 62 in. are converted to z scores by using Formula 6-2 as follows:

For $x = 73$ in.: $z = \dfrac{x - \mu}{\sigma} = \dfrac{73 - 69.5}{2.4} = 1.46$ ($z = 1.46$ yields an area of 0.9279.)

For $x = 62$ in.: $z = \dfrac{x - \mu}{\sigma} = \dfrac{62 - 69.5}{2.4} = -3.13$ ($z = -3.13$ yields an area of 0.0009.)

Step 3: If using Table A-2, refer to that table with $z = 1.46$ and find that the cumulative area to the *left* of $z = 1.46$ is 0.9279. (Remember, Table A-2 is designed so that all areas are cumulative areas from the *left*.) Table A-2 also shows that $z = -3.13$ corresponds to an area of 0.0009.

Because the areas of 0.9279 and 0.0009 are *cumulative areas from the left*, we find the shaded area in Figure 6-13 as follows:

$$\text{Shaded area in Figure 6-13} = 0.9279 - 0.0009 = 0.9270$$

There is a small discrepancy between the area of 0.9267 obtained using technology and the area of 0.9270 obtained using Table A-2. The area obtained from technology is more accurate because it is based on unrounded z scores of 1.4583333 and −3.125, whereas Table A-2 requires z scores rounded to two decimal places.

Interpretation

Expressing the result as a percentage, we conclude that about 93% of men satisfy the height requirement between 62 in. and 73 in. About 7% of men do not meet that requirement and they are not eligible to work as cabin crew members. Figure 6-13 shows that most of the ineligible men are those who are very tall, and this makes sense when we consider that some jets have low cabin heights that would cause problems for the tallest men. For example, the Embraer 145 jet has a cabin ceiling height of 71.7 in., so men taller than 71.7 in. would need to bend the entire time that they are standing.

Finding Values from Known Areas

Here are helpful hints for those cases in which the area (or probability or percentage) is known and we must find the relevant value(s):

1. *Don't confuse z scores and areas.* Remember, z scores are *distances* along the horizontal scale, but areas are *regions* under the normal curve. Table A-2 lists z scores in the left columns and across the top row, but areas are found in the body of the table.

2. *Choose the correct (right / left) side of the graph.* A value separating the *top* 10% from the others will be located on the right side of the graph, but a value separating the *bottom* 10% will be located on the left side of the graph.

3. A z score must be *negative* whenever it is located in the *left* half of the normal distribution.

4. Areas (or probabilities) are positive or zero values, but they are never negative.

Graphs are extremely helpful in visualizing, understanding, and successfully working with normal probability distributions, so they should be used whenever possible.

Procedure for Finding Values from Known Areas or Probabilities

1. Sketch a normal distribution curve, enter the given probability or percentage in the appropriate region of the graph, and identify the x value(s) being sought.

2. If using technology, refer to the instructions at the end of this section. If using Table A-2, refer to the *body* of Table A-2 to find the area to the left of x, then identify the z score corresponding to that area.

3. If you know z and must convert to the equivalent x value, use Formula 6-2 by entering the values for μ, σ, and the z score found in Step 2, then solve for x. Based on Formula 6-2, we can solve for x as follows:

$$x = \mu + (z \cdot \sigma)$$ (another form of Formula 6-2)

(If z is located to the left of the mean, be sure that it is a negative number.)

4. Refer to the sketch of the curve to verify that the solution makes sense in the context of the graph and in the context of the problem.

The following example uses this procedure for finding a value from a known area.

Example 3   Designing Aircraft Cabins

When designing an environment, one common criterion is to use a design that accommodates 95% of the population. What aircraft ceiling height will allow 95% of men to stand without bumping their heads? That is, find the 95th percentile of heights of men. Assume that heights of men are normally distributed with a mean of 69.5 in. and a standard deviation of 2.4 in.

Solution

Step 1: Figure 6-14 shows the normal distribution with the height x that we want to identify. The shaded area represents the 95% of men with heights that would allow them to stand without bumping their heads on the aircraft ceiling.

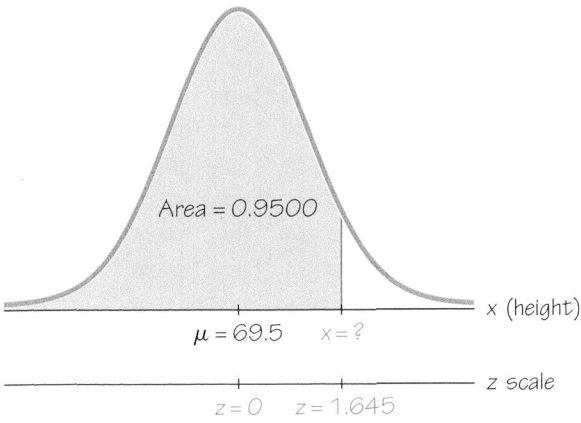

Figure 6-14   Finding the 95th Percentile

Step 2: To use technology, refer to the instructions at the end of this section. Technology will provide the value of x in Figure 6-14. For example, see the accompanying Excel display showing that $x = 73.4476487$, or 73.4 when rounded.

EXCEL

NORM.INV

Probability	0.95		= 0.95
Mean	69.5		= 69.5
Standard_dev	2.4		= 2.4
			= 73.4476487

continued

If using Table A-2, search for an area of 0.9500 *in the body* of the table. (The area of 0.9500 shown in Figure 6-14 is a cumulative area from the left, and that is exactly the type of area listed in Table A-2.) The area of 0.9500 is between the Table A-2 areas of 0.9495 and 0.9505, but there is an asterisk and footnote indicating that an area of 0.9500 corresponds to $z = 1.645$.

Step 3: With $z = 1.645$, $\mu = 69.5$ in., and $\sigma = 2.4$ in., we can solve for x by using Formula 6-2:

$$z = \frac{x - \mu}{\sigma} \quad \text{becomes} \quad 1.645 = \frac{x - 69.5}{2.4}$$

The result of $x = 73.448$ in. can be found directly or by using the following version of Formula 6-2:

$$x = \mu + (z \cdot \sigma) = 69.5 + (1.645 \cdot 2.4) = 73.448 \text{ in.}$$

Step 4: The solution of $x = 73.4$ in. (rounded) in Figure 6-14 is reasonable because it is greater than the mean of 69.5 in.

Interpretation

An aircraft cabin height of 73.4 in. (or 6 ft 1.4 in.) would allow 95% of men to fit without bumping their heads. It follows that 5% of men would *not* fit without bending. The safety and comfort of passengers are factors suggesting that it might be wise to use a design with a higher ceiling.

Example 4   Ability Grouping

Some educators argue that all students are served better if they are separated into groups according to their abilities. Assume that students are to be separated into a group with IQ scores in the bottom 30%, a second group with IQ scores in the middle 40%, and a third group with IQ scores in the top 30%. The Wechsler Adult Intelligence Scale yields an IQ score obtained through a test, and the scores are normally distributed with a mean of 100 and a standard deviation of 15. Find the Wechsler IQ scores that separate the three groups.

Solution

Step 1: We begin with the graph shown in Figure 6-15. We have entered the mean of 100, and we have identified the x values separating the lowest 30% and the highest 30%.

Step 2: To use technology, refer to the instructions at the end of this section. Technology will show that the values of x in Figure 6-15 are 92.1 and 107.9 when rounded.

If using Table A-2, we must work with cumulative areas from the left. For the leftmost value of x, the cumulative area from the left is 0.3, so search for an area of 0.3000 *in the body* of the table to get $z = -0.52$ (which corresponds to the closest area of 0.3015). For the rightmost value of x, the cumulative area from the left is 0.7, so search for an area of 0.7000 *in the body* of the table to get $z = 0.52$ (which corresponds to the closest area of 0.6985). Having found the two z scores, we now proceed to convert them to IQ scores.

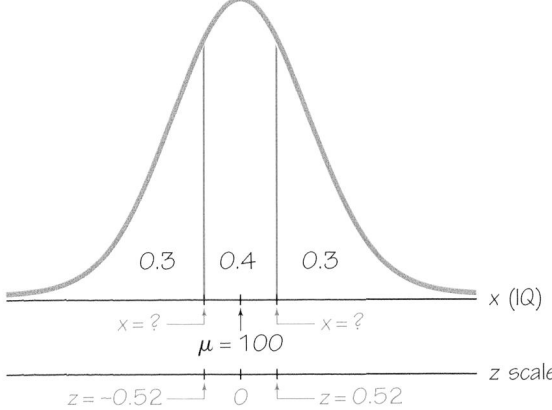

Figure 6-15   IQ Scores for Ability Grouping

Step 3: We now solve for the two values of x by using Formula 6-2 directly or by using the following version of Formula 6-2:

Leftmost value of x: $x = \mu + (z \cdot \sigma) = 100 + (-0.52 \cdot 15) = 92.2$

Rightmost value of x: $x = \mu + (z \cdot \sigma) = 100 + (0.52 \cdot 15) = 107.8$

Step 4: Referring to Figure 6-15, we see that the leftmost value of $x = 92.2$ is reasonable because it is less than the mean of 100. Also, the rightmost value of 107.8 is reasonable because it is above the mean of 100.

There is a small discrepancy between the results from technology and the results from Table A-2, and that discrepancy is due to the fact that Table A-2 requires that we first round z scores to two decimal places. The results from technology are more accurate.

Interpretation

The Wechsler IQ scores of 92.2 and 107.8 can be used as cutoff values separating the three groups. Those in the lowest group have IQ scores below 92.2, those in the middle group have IQ scores between 92.2 and 107.8, and those in the highest group have IQ scores above 107.8.

For the methods of this section, we should carefully consider the following:

- We should *always* draw a graph to visualize the information.

- We should determine whether we want to find an area or a value of x.

- Regardless of the situation, we must usually work with a cumulative area from the *left*.

- We should know that a z score and x value are *distances* along horizontal scales, but percentages or probabilities correspond to *areas* under a curve.

using TECHNOLOGY

When working with a nonstandard normal distribution, a technology can be used to find areas or values of the relevant variable, so technology can be used instead of Table A-2. The following instructions describe the use of technology.

STATDISK   Select **Analysis, Probability Distributions, Normal Distribution.** Either enter the z score to find corresponding areas or enter the cumulative area from the left to find the

continued

z score. After entering a value, click on the **Evaluate** button. (See the STATDISK display in Example 1.)

MINITAB

- *Finding Area:* To find the cumulative area to the left of a z score (as in Table A-2), select **Calc, Probability Distributions, Normal, Cumulative probabilities.** Enter the mean and standard deviation, then click on the **Input Constant** button and enter the value.

- *Finding x Value:* To find a value corresponding to a known area, select **Calc, Probability Distributions, Normal,** then select **Inverse cumulative probabilities.** Enter the mean and standard deviation. Select the option **Input constant,** and enter the total area to the left of the given value.

EXCEL

- *Finding Area:* To find the cumulative area to the left of a value (as in Table A-2), click on *fx,* then select **Statistical, NORMDIST** (or **NORM.DIST**). In the dialog box, enter the value for *x,* enter the mean and standard deviation, and enter 1 in the "cumulative" space.

- *Finding x Value:* To find a value corresponding to a known area, select *fx,* **Statistical, NORMINV** (or **NORM.INV**) and proceed to make the entries in the dialog box. When entering the probability value, enter the total area to the left of the given value. (See the Excel display in Example 3.)

TI-83/84 PLUS

- *Finding Area:* To find the area between two values, press **2ND**, then press **VARS** to get to the **DISTR** (distribution) menu. Select **normalcdf.** Enter the two values, the mean, and the standard

deviation, all separated by commas, as in this format: (left value, right value, mean, standard deviation).

Hint: If there is no left value, enter the left value as −999999, and if there is no right value, enter the right value as 999999. In Example 1 we want the area to the right of $x = 70$ in. and we have a normal distribution with mean 63.8 in. and standard deviation 2.6 in., so use the command **normalcdf (70, 999999, 63.8, 2.6)** as shown in the accompanying screen display. Because Example 1 uses a rounded z score, the result of 0.0085 (rounded) shown here is more accurate than the result of 0.0087 found in Example 1.

TI-83/83 PLUS

- *Finding x Value:* To find a value corresponding to a known area, press **2ND**, then press **VARS** to get to the **DISTR** (distribution) menu. Select **invNorm,** and proceed to enter the total area to the left of the value, the mean, and the standard deviation in the format of (total area to the left, mean, standard deviation) with the commas included. For Example 3, the command of **invNorm(0.95, 69.5, 2.4)** will yield the result of 73.4476487, which is 73.4 when rounded.

STATCRUNCH   Click on **Open StatCrunch,** then click on **Stat.** Select **Calculators,** then select **Normal.** You can either enter a probability or a value of *x.* Click on **Compute.**

6-3 Basic Skills and Concepts

Statistical Literacy and Critical Thinking

1. Pulse Rates Pulse rates of women are normally distributed with a mean of 77.5 beats per minute and a standard deviation of 11.6 beats per minute (based on Data Set 1 in Appendix B).

a. What are the values of the mean and standard deviation after converting all pulse rates of women to z scores using $z = (x - \mu)/\sigma$?

b. The original pulse rates are measured with units of "beats per minute." What are the units of the corresponding z scores?

2. IQ Scores The Wechsler Adult Intelligence Scale is an IQ score obtained through a test, and the scores are normally distributed with a mean of 100 and a standard deviation of 15. A bell-shaped graph is drawn to represent this distribution.

a. For the bell-shaped graph, what is the area under the curve?

b. What is the value of the median?

c. What is the value of the mode?

d. What is the value of the variance?

3. Normal Distributions What is the difference between a standard normal distribution and a nonstandard normal distribution?

4. Random Digits Computers are commonly used to randomly generate digits of telephone numbers to be called when conducting a survey. Can the methods of this section be used to find the probability that when one digit is randomly generated, it is less than 3? Why or why not? What is the probability of getting a digit less than 3?

IQ Scores.   In Exercises 5–8, find the area of the shaded region. The graphs depict IQ scores of adults, and those scores are normally distributed with a mean of 100 and a standard deviation of 15 (as on the Wechsler test).

5.

118

6.

91

7.

79   133

8.
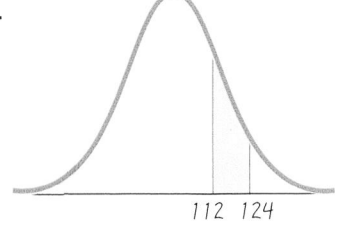
112 124

IQ Scores.   In Exercises 9–12, find the indicated IQ score, and round to the nearest whole number. The graphs depict IQ scores of adults, and those scores are normally distributed with a mean of 100 and a standard deviation of 15 (as on the Wechsler test).

9.

0.9918
x

10.

0.1587
x

11.

0.9798
x

12.
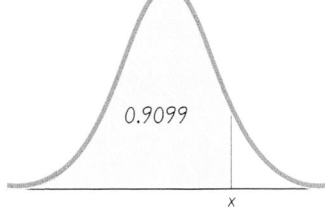
0.9099
x

IQ Scores.   In Exercises 13–20, assume that adults have IQ scores that are normally distributed with a mean of 100 and a standard deviation of 15 (as on the Wechsler test). For a randomly selected adult, find the indicated probability or IQ score. Round IQ scores to the nearest whole number. (Hint: Draw a graph in each case.)

13. Find the probability of an IQ less than 85.

14. Find the probability of an IQ greater than 70 (the requirement for being a statistics textbook author).

15. Find the probability that a randomly selected adult has an IQ between 90 and 110 (referred to as the *normal* range).

16. Find the probability that a randomly selected adult has an IQ between 110 and 120 (referred to as *bright normal*).

17. Find P_{90}, which is the IQ score separating the bottom 90% from the top 10%.

18. Find the first quartile Q_1, which is the IQ score separating the bottom 25% from the top 75%.

19. Find the third quartile Q_3, which is the IQ score separating the top 25% from the others.

20. Mensa Mensa International calls itself "the international high IQ society." and it has more than 100,000 members. Mensa states that "candidates for membership of Mensa must achieve a score at or above the 98th percentile on a standard test of intelligence (a score that is greater than that achieved by 98 percent of the general population taking the test)." Find the 98th percentile for the population of Wechsler IQ scores. This is the lowest score meeting the requirement for Mensa membership.

 In Exercises 21–24, use these parameters (based on Data Set 1 in Appendix B):

- *Men's heights are normally distributed with mean 69.5 in. and standard deviation 2.4 in.*

- *Women's heights are normally distributed with mean 63.8 in. and standard deviation 2.6 in.*

21. Navy Pilots The U.S. Navy requires that fighter pilots have heights between 62 in. and 78 in.

a. Find the percentage of women meeting the height requirement. Are many women not qualified because they are too short or too tall?

b. Find the percentage of men meeting the height requirement. Are many men not qualified because they are too short or too tall?

c. If the Navy changes the height requirements so that all women are eligible except the shortest 2% and the tallest 2%, what are the new height requirements for women?

d. If the Navy changes the height requirements so that all men are eligible except the shortest 1% and the tallest 1%, what are the new height requirements for men?

22. Air Force Pilots The U.S. Air Force requires that pilots have heights between 64 in. and 77 in.

a. Find the percentage of women meeting the height requirement.

b. Find the percentage of men meeting the height requirement.

c. If the Air Force height requirements are changed to exclude only the tallest 3% of men and the shortest 3% of women, what are the new height requirements?

23. Disney Characters Most of the live characters at Disney World have height requirements with a minimum of 4 ft 8 in. and a maximum of 6 ft 3 in.

a. Find the percentage of women meeting the height requirement.

b. Find the percentage of men meeting the height requirement.

c. If the height requirements are changed to exclude only the tallest 5% of men and the shortest 5% of women, what are the new height requirements?

24. Executive Jet Doorway The Gulfstream 100 is an executive jet that seats six, and it has a doorway height of 51.6 in.

a. What percentage of adult men can fit through the door without bending?

b. What percentage of adult women can fit through the door without bending?

c. Does the door design with a height of 51.6 in. appear to be adequate? Why didn't the engineers design a larger door?

d. What doorway height would allow 60% of men to fit without bending?

25. **Water Taxi Safety** When a water taxi sank in Baltimore's Inner Harbor, an investigation revealed that the safe passenger load for the water taxi was 3500 lb. It was also noted that the mean weight of a passenger was assumed to be 140 lb. Assume a "worst-case" scenario in which all of the passengers are adult men. (This could easily occur in a city that hosts conventions in which people of the same gender often travel in groups.) Assume that weights of men are normally distributed with a mean of 182.9 lb and a standard deviation of 40.8 lb (based on Data Set 1 in Appendix B).

a. If one man is randomly selected, find the probability that he weighs less than 174 lb (the new value suggested by the National Transportation and Safety Board).

b. With a load limit of 3500 lb, how many male passengers are allowed if we assume a mean weight of 140 lb?

c. With a load limit of 3500 lb, how many male passengers are allowed if we use a new mean weight of 182.9 lb?

d. Why is it necessary to periodically review and revise the number of passengers that are allowed to board?

26. **Designing a Work Station** A common design requirement is that an environment must fit the range of people who fall between the 5th percentile for women and the 95th percentile for men. In designing an assembly work table, we must consider *sitting knee height,* which is the distance from the bottom of the feet to the top of the knee. Males have sitting knee heights that are normallly distributed with a mean of 21.4 in. and a standard deviation of 1.2 in.; females have sitting knee heights that are normally distributed with a mean of 19.6 in. and a standard deviation of 1.1 in. (based on data from the Department of Transportation).

a. What is the minimum table clearance required to satisfy the requirement of fitting 95% of men? Why is the 5th percentile for women ignored in this case?

b. The author is writing this exercise at a table with a clearance of 23.5 in. above the floor. What percentage of men fit this table, and what percentage of women fit this table? Does the table appear to be made to fit almost everyone?

27. **Lengths of Pregnancies** The lengths of pregnancies are normally distributed with a mean of 268 days and a standard deviation of 15 days.

a. One classical use of the normal distribution is inspired by a letter to "Dear Abby" in which a wife claimed to have given birth 308 days after a brief visit from her husband, who was serving in the Navy. Given this information, find the probability of a pregnancy lasting 308 days or longer. What does the result suggest?

b. If we stipulate that a baby is *premature* if the length of pregnancy is in the lowest 3%, find the length that separates premature babies from those who are not premature. Premature babies often require special care, and this result could be helpful to hospital administrators in planning for that care.

28. **Body Temperatures** Based on the sample results in Data Set 3 in Appendix B, assume that human body temperatures are normally distributed with a mean of 98.20°F and a standard deviation of 0.62°F.

a. Bellevue Hospital in New York City uses 100.6°F as the lowest temperature considered to be a fever. What percentage of normal and healthy persons would be considered to have a fever? Does this percentage suggest that a cutoff of 100.6°F is appropriate?

b. Physicians want to select a minimum temperature for requiring further medical tests. What should that temperature be, if we want only 5.0% of healthy people to exceed it? (Such a result is a *false positive*, meaning that the test result is positive, but the subject is not really sick.)

29. Earthquakes Based on Data Set 16 in Appendix B, assume that Richter scale magnitudes of earthquakes are normally distributed with a mean of 1.184 and a standard deviation of 0.587.

a. Earthquakes with magnitudes less than 2.000 are considered "microearthquakes" that are not felt. What percentage of earthquakes fall into this category?

b. Earthquakes above 4.0 will cause indoor items to shake. What percentage of earthquakes fall into this category?

c. Find the 95th percentile. Will all earthquakes above the 95th percentile cause indoor items to shake?

 30. Aircraft Seat Width Engineers want to design seats in commercial aircraft so that they are wide enough to fit 99% of all males. (Accommodating 100% of males would require very wide seats that would be much too expensive.) Men have hip breadths that are normally distributed with a mean of 14.4 in. and a standard deviation of 1.0 in. (based on anthropometric survey data from Gordon, Clauser, et al.). Find P_{99}. That is, find the hip breadth for men that separates the smallest 99% from the largest 1%.

31. Chocolate Chip Cookies The Chapter Problem for Chapter 3 includes Table 3-1, which lists the numbers of chocolate chips in Chips Ahoy regular cookies. Those numbers have a distribution that is approximately normal with a mean of 24.0 chocolate chips and a standard deviation of 2.6 chocolate chips. Find P_1 and P_{99}. How might those values be helpful to the producer of Chips Ahoy regular cookies?

32. Quarters After 1964, quarters were manufactured so that the weights had a mean of 5.67 g and a standard deviation of 0.06 g. Some vending machines are designed so that you can adjust the weights of quarters that are accepted. If many counterfeit coins are found, you can narrow the range of acceptable weights with the effect that most counterfeit coins are rejected along with some legitimate quarters.

a. If you adjust vending machines to accept weights between 5.64 g and 5.70 g, what percentage of legal quarters are rejected? Is that percentage too high?

b. If you adjust vending machines to accept all legal quarters except those with weights in the top 2.5% and the bottom 2.5%, what are the limits of the weights that are accepted?

Large Data Sets.   *In Exercises 33 and 34, refer to the data sets in Appendix B and use computer software or a calculator.*

33. Appendix B Data Set: Pulse Rates of Males Refer to Data Set 1 in Appendix B and use the pulse rates of males.

a. Find the mean and standard deviation, and verify that the pulse rates have a distribution that is roughly normal.

b. Treating the unrounded values of the mean and standard deviation as parameters, and assuming that male pulse rates are normally distributed, find the pulse rate separating the lowest 2.5% and the pulse rate separating the highest 2.5%. These values could be helpful when physicians try to determine whether pulse rates are unusually low or unusually high.

34. Appendix B Data Set: Weights of Diet Pepsi Refer to Data Set 19 in Appendix B and use the weights (pounds) of Diet Pepsi.

a. Find the mean and standard deviation, and verify that the data have a distribution that is roughly normal.

b. Treating the unrounded values of the mean and standard deviation as parameters, and assuming that the weights are normally distributed, find the weight separating the lowest 0.5% and the weight separating the highest 0.5%. These values could be helpful when quality control specialists try to control the manufacturing process so that underweight or overweight cans are rejected.

6-3 Beyond the Basics

35. Curving Test Scores A statistics professor gives a test and finds that the scores are normally distributed with a mean of 40 and a standard deviation of 10. She plans to curve the scores.

a. If she curves by adding 35 to each grade, what is the new mean? What is the new standard deviation?

b. Is it fair to curve by adding 35 to each grade? Why or why not?

c. If the grades are curved so that grades of B are given to scores above the bottom 70% and below the top 10%, find the numerical limits for a grade of B.

d. Which method of curving the grades is fairer: Adding 35 to each original score or using a scheme like the one given in part (c)? Explain.

36. Using Continuity Correction There are many situations in which a normal distribution can be used as a good approximation to a random variable that has only *discrete* values. In such cases, we can use this *continuity correction:* Represent each whole number by the interval extending from 0.5 below the number to 0.5 above it. The Chapter Problem for Chapter 3 includes Table 3-1, which lists the numbers of chocolate chips in Chips Ahoy regular cookies. Those numbers have a distribution that is approximately normal with a mean of 24.0 chocolate chips and a standard deviation of 2.6 chocolate chips. Find the percentage of such cookies having between 20 and 30 chocolate chips inclusive.

a. Find the result without using the continuity correction.

b. Find the result using the continuity correction.

c. Does the use of the continuity correction make much of a difference in this case?

37. Outliers For the purposes of constructing modified boxplots as described in Section 3-4, outliers defined as data values that are above Q_3 by an amount greater than $1.5 \times$ IQR or below Q_1 by an amount greater than $1.5 \times$ IQR, where IQR is the interquartile range. Using this definition of outliers, find the probability that when a value is randomly selected from a normal distribution, it is an outlier.

38. SAT and ACT Tests Based on recent results, scores on the SAT test are normally distributed with a mean of 1511 and a standard deviation of 312. Scores on the ACT test are normally distributed with a mean of 21.1 and a standard deviation of 5.1. Assume that the two tests use different scales to measure the same aptitude.

a. If someone gets an SAT score that is in the 95th percentile, find the actual SAT score and the equivalent ACT score.

b. If someone gets an SAT score of 2100, find the equivalent ACT score.

6.4   Sampling Distributions and Estimators

Key Concept In this section we consider the concept of a *sampling distribution of a statistic*. Instead of focusing on the original population, we want to focus on the values of *statistics* (such as sample means or sample proportions) obtained from the population. (The population is like parents, and sample statistics are like children; we all know how parents behave, and now we want to study the behavior of their children.) For example, if pollsters each randomly selected 50 people from the population, obtained their incomes, then computed the mean of each sample of 50 values, what do we know about the sample means that are obtained? How are those sample means distributed? What is the mean of those sample means? Table 6-2 tells us the key points that we need to know, so try really, really hard to understand the story that Table 6-2 tells.

The Story of Table 6-2 To understand Table 6-2, let's start with the top section that describes means. Beginning at the left, imagine a population having a mean μ,

Table 6-2 General Behavior of Sampling Distributions

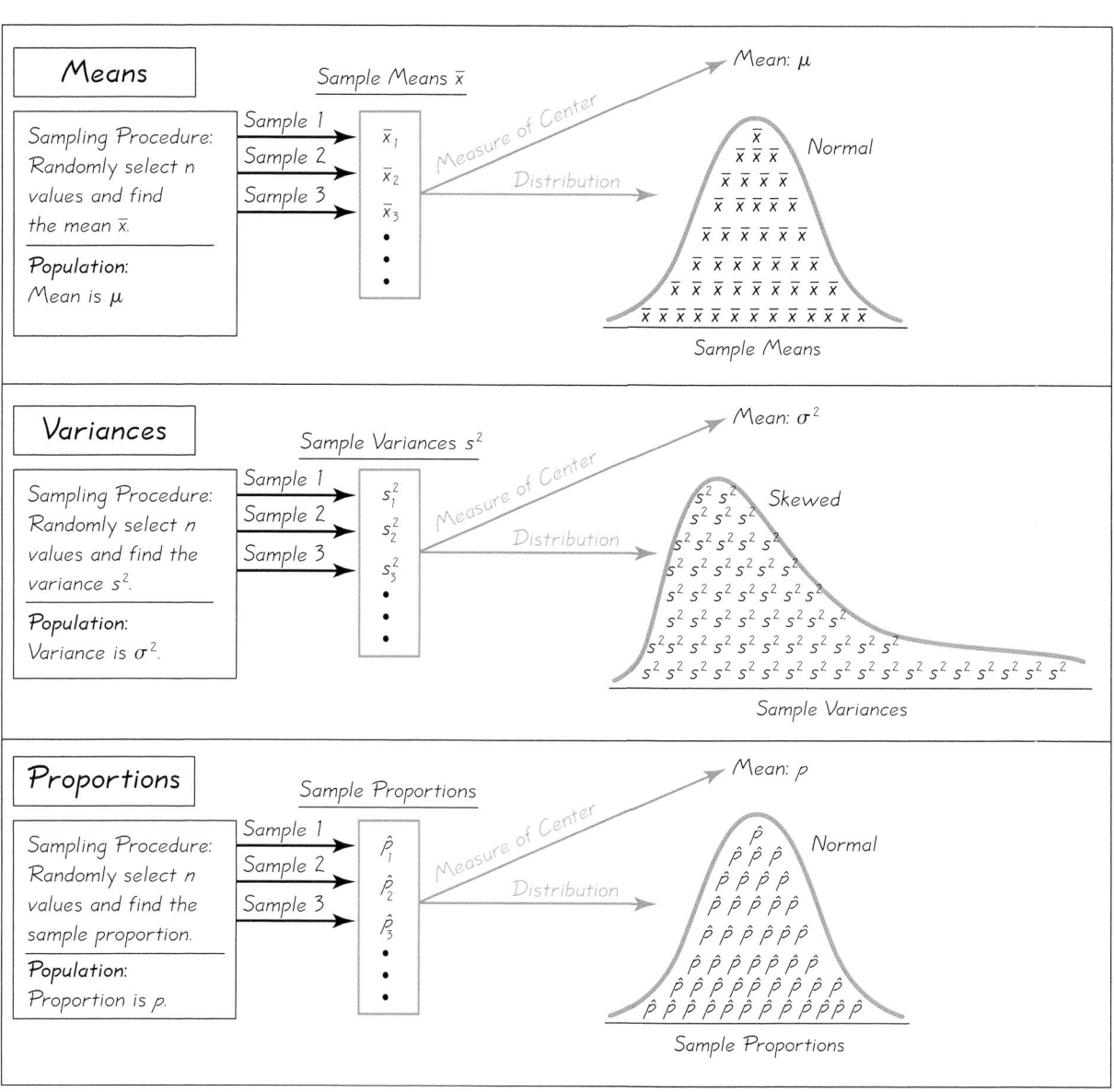

such as the population of adult incomes in the United States. Now imagine pollsters, each randomly selecting 50 people. Each pollster computes the mean of the 50 incomes, so we get a collection of sample means, which we denote as $\bar{x}_1$, $\bar{x}_2$, $\bar{x}_3$, and so on. These sample means are shown in the green box near the top of Table 6-2. What do we know about this collection of sample means? As we move farther to the right in Table 6-2, we see that the sample means tend to have a *normal* distribution (even if the original population is not normally distributed). We might write an ending to this story by saying that "the sampling distribution of the sample mean is a normal distribution." Now there's a happy ending. Let's now formally define a general definition of a sampling distribution of a statistic.

> **DEFINITION** The **sampling distribution of a statistic** (such as a sample mean or sample proportion) is the distribution of all values of the statistic when all possible samples of the same size n are taken from the same population. (The sampling distribution of a statistic is typically represented as a probability distribution in the format of a table, probability histogram, or formula.)

Sampling Distribution of the Sample Mean

The preceding definition is general, so let's consider the specific sampling distribution of the sample mean.

> **DEFINITION** The **sampling distribution of the sample mean** is the distribution of all possible sample means (or the distribution of the variable $\bar{x}$), with all samples having the same sample size n taken from the same population. (The sampling distribution of the sample mean is typically represented as a probability distribution in the format of a table, probability histogram, or formula.)

These concepts are very abstract, so let's deal with a concrete application so that we can gain better understanding.

Example 1 Sampling Distribution of the Sample Mean

A friend of the author has three children with ages of 4, 5, and 9. Let's consider the population consisting of {4, 5, 9}. (We don't usually know all values in a population, and we don't usually work with such a small population, but it works well for the purposes of this example.) If two ages are randomly selected with replacement from the population {4, 5, 9}, identify the sampling distribution of the sample mean by creating a table representing the probability distribution of the sample mean. Do the values of the sample mean target the value of the population mean?

Solution

If two values are randomly selected with replacement from the population {4, 5, 9}, the leftmost column of Table 6-3 lists the nine different possible samples. Because we want to identify the sampling distribution of the sample mean, we compute the mean of each of the nine samples, and those sample means are listed in the second column of Table 6-3. The nine samples are equally likely with a probability of 1/9 (as shown in the third column of Table 6-3). We saw in Section 5-2 that a probability distribution is a description that gives the probability for each value of a random variable, as in the second and third columns of Table 6-3. The second and

Push Polling

In a recent campaign for mayor of New York City, Anthony Weiner was considering a run against incumbent Michael Bloomberg. In one survey, people were asked questions such as these: "Are you registered to vote? Do you plan to vote in the mayoral election? Would you vote for Anthony Weiner if you knew that he has an association with European models?" Some survey questions were routine, but some questions were clearly designed to discredit candidate Weiner. This is an example of *push polling*, which is the practice of political campaigning under the guise of a poll. Its name is derived from its objective of pushing voters away from opposition candidates by asking loaded questions designed to discredit them. This survey question was used in another campaign: "Please tell me if you would be more likely or less likely to vote for Roy Romer if you knew that Gov. Romer appoints a parole board which has granted early release to an average of four convicted felons per day every day since Romer took office." The National Council on Public Polls says that push polls are unethical, and reputable pollsters do not approve of push polling.

third columns of Table 6-3 constitute a probability distribution for the random variable representing sample means, so those two columns represent the sampling distribution of the sample mean. In Table 6-3, some of the sample mean values are repeated, so we combined equal sample mean values in Table 6-4.

Table 6-3 Sampling Distribution of Mean

Sample	Sample Mean $\bar{x}$	Probability
4, 4	4.0	1/9
4, 5	4.5	1/9
4, 9	6.5	1/9
5, 4	4.5	1/9
5, 5	5.0	1/9
5, 9	7.0	1/9
9, 4	6.5	1/9
9, 5	7.0	1/9
9, 9	9.0	1/9

$\longleftrightarrow$

Table 6-4 Sampling Distribution of Mean (Condensed)

Sample Mean $\bar{x}$	Probability
4.0	1/9
4.5	2/9
5.0	1/9
6.5	2/9
7.0	2/9
9.0	1/9

Interpretation

Because Table 6-4 lists the possible values of the sample mean along with their corresponding probabilities, Table 6-4 is an example of a sampling distribution of a sample mean.

The value of the mean of the population {4, 5, 9} is $\mu = 6.0$. Using either Table 6-3 or 6-4, we could calculate the mean of the sample values; we get 6.0. Because the mean of the sample means (6.0) is equal to the mean of the population (6.0), we conclude that the values of the sample mean do *target* the value of the population mean. (The top of Table 6-2 also shows that the values of the sample mean have a measure of center equal to μ.) It's unfortunate that this sounds so much like doublespeak, but this illustrates that *the mean of the sample means is equal to the population mean μ.* Read that last sentence a few times until it makes sense.

If we were to create a probability histogram from Table 6-4, it would not have the bell shape that is characteristic of a normal distribution (as suggested by the top of Table 6-2), but that is because we are working with such small samples. If the population of {4, 5, 9} were much larger and if we were selecting samples much larger than $n = 2$ as in this example, we would get a probability histogram that is much closer to being bell-shaped, indicating a normal distribution, as in Example 2.

Example 2   Sampling Distribution of the Sample Mean

Consider repeating this process: Roll a die 5 times to randomly select 5 values from the population {1, 2, 3, 4, 5, 6}, then find the mean $\bar{x}$ of the results. What do we know about the behavior of all sample means that are generated as this process continues indefinitely?

Solution

The top portion of Table 6-5 illustrates a process of rolling a die 5 times and finding the mean of the results. Table 6-5 shows results from repeating this process 10,000 times, but the true sampling distribution of the mean involves repeating the process indefinitely. Because the values of 1, 2, 3, 4, 5, 6 are all equally likely, the population has a mean of $\mu = 3.5$, and Table 6-5 shows that the 10,000 sample means have a mean of 3.49. If the process is continued indefinitely, the mean of the sample means will be 3.5. Also, Table 6-5 shows that the distribution of the sample means is approximately a normal distribution.

Interpretation

Based on the actual sample results shown in the top portion of Table 6-5, we can describe the sampling distribution of the mean by the histogram at the top of Table 6-5. The actual sampling distribution would be described by a histogram based on all possible samples, not only the 10,000 samples included in the histogram, but the number of trials is large enough to suggest that the true sampling distribution of means is approximately a normal distribution with its characteristic bell shape.

Table 6-5 Specific Results from 10,000 Trials

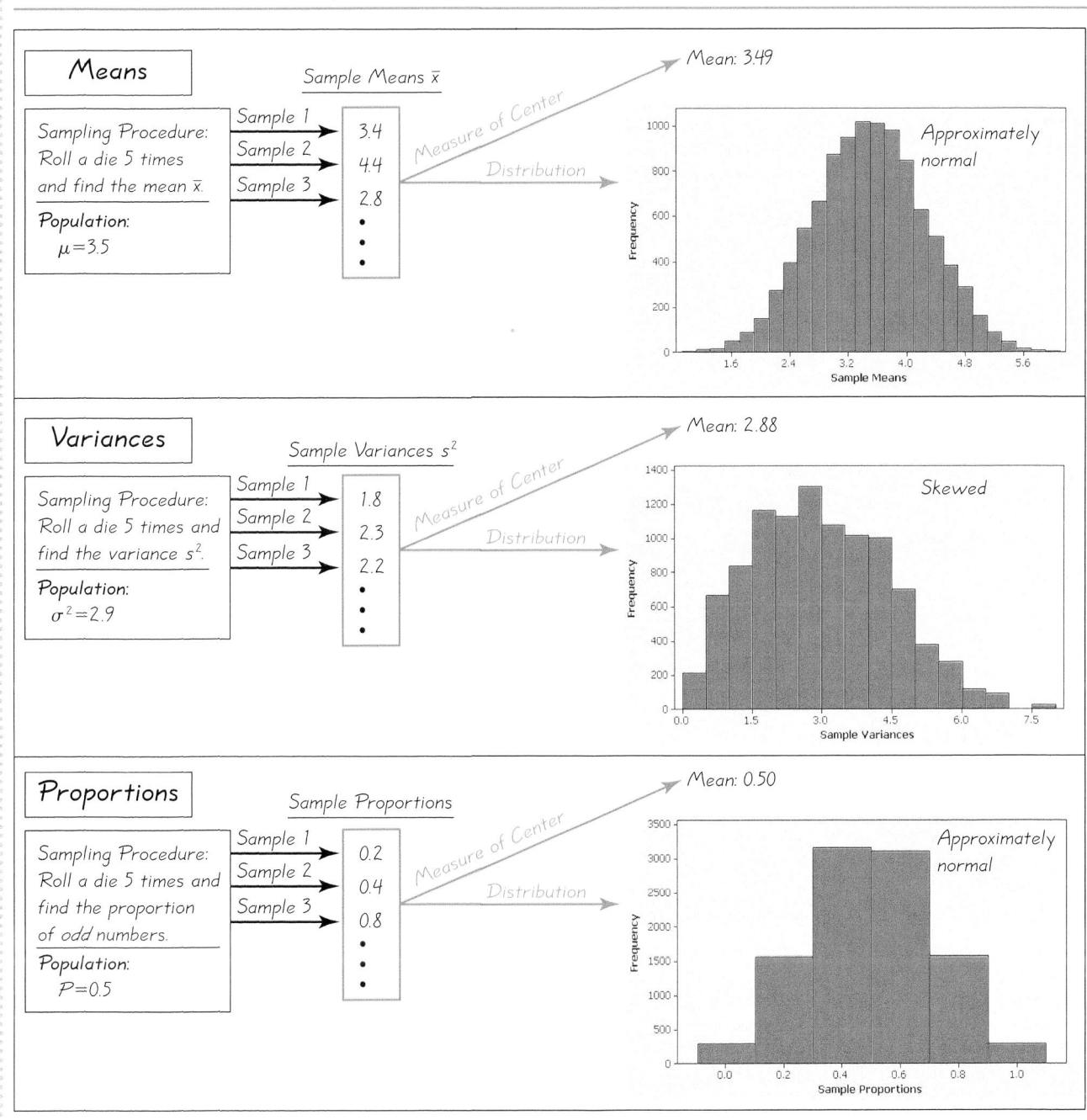

The results of Example 2 allow us to observe the following two important properties of the sampling distribution of the sample mean.

Behavior of Sample Means

1. The sample means *target* the value of the population mean. (That is, the mean of the sample means is the population mean. The expected value of the sample mean is equal to the population mean.)

2. The distribution of sample means tends to be a normal distribution. (This will be discussed further in the following section, but the distribution tends to become closer to a normal distribution as the sample size increases.)

Sampling Distribution of the Sample Variance

Let's now consider the sampling distribution of sample variances.

> **DEFINITION** The **sampling distribution of the sample variance** is the distribution of sample variances, with all samples having the same sample size n taken from the same population. (The sampling distribution of the sample variance is typically represented as a probability distribution in the format of a table, probability histogram, or formula.)

> **CAUTION** When working with population standard deviations or variances, be sure to evaluate them correctly. In Section 3-3 we saw that the computations for *population* standard deviations or variances involve division by the population size N (not the value of $n - 1$), as shown here.

$$\text{Population standard deviation:} \qquad \sigma = \sqrt{\frac{\Sigma(x - \mu)^2}{N}}$$

$$\text{Population variance:} \qquad \sigma^2 = \frac{\Sigma(x - \mu)^2}{N}$$

Because the calculations are typically performed with computer software or calculators, be careful to correctly distinguish between the standard deviation of a sample and the standard deviation of a population. Also be careful to distinguish between the variance of a sample and the variance of a population.

Example 3   Sampling Distribution of the Sample Variance

Consider repeating this process: Roll a die 5 times and find the variance s^2 of the results. What do we know about the behavior of all sample variances that are generated as this process continues indefinitely?

Solution

The middle portion of Table 6-5 illustrates a process of rolling a die 5 times and finding the variance of the results. Table 6-5 shows results from repeating this process 10,000 times, but the true sampling distribution of the sample variance involves repeating the process indefinitely. Because the values of 1, 2, 3, 4, 5, 6 are all equally likely, the population has a variance of $\sigma^2 = 2.9$, and Table 6-5 shows that the 10,000 sample variances have a mean of 2.88. If the process is continued indefinitely, the mean of the sample variances will be 2.9. Also, the middle portion of Table 6-5 shows that the distribution of the sample variances is a skewed distribution, not a normal distribution with its characteristic bell shape.

Interpretation

Based on the actual sample results shown in the middle portion of Table 6-5, we can describe the sampling distribution of the sample variance by the histogram in the middle of Table 6-5. The actual sampling distribution would be described by a histogram based on all possible samples, not the 10,000 samples included in the histogram, but the number of trials is large enough to suggest that the true sampling distribution of sample variances is a distribution skewed to the right.

The results of Example 3 allow us to observe the following two important properties of the sampling distribution of the sample variance.

Behavior of Sample Variances

1. The sample variances *target* the value of the population variance. (That is, the mean of the sample variances is the population variance. The expected value of the sample variance is equal to the population variance.)

2. The distribution of sample variances tends to be a distribution skewed to the right.

Sampling Distribution of Sample Proportion

We now consider the sampling distribution of a sample proportion.

> **DEFINITION** The **sampling distribution of the sample proportion** is the distribution of sample proportions, with all samples having the same sample size n taken from the same population.

We need to distinguish between a population proportion p and some sample proportion, so the following notation is commonly used.

Notation for Proportions

p = *population* proportion

$\hat{p}$ = *sample* proportion

Example 4   Sampling Distribution of the Sample Proportion

Consider repeating this process: Roll a die 5 times and find the proportion of *odd* numbers. What do we know about the behavior of all sample proportions that are generated as this process continues indefinitely?

Solution

The bottom portion of Table 6-5 illustrates a process of rolling a die 5 times and finding the proportion of odd numbers. Table 6-5 shows results from repeating this process 10,000 times, but the true sampling distribution of the sample proportion involves repeating the process indefinitely. Because the values of 1, 2, 3, 4, 5, 6 are all equally likely, the proportion of odd numbers in the population is 0.5, and Table 6-5 shows that the 10,000 sample proportions have a mean of 0.50.   *continued*

If the process is continued indefinitely, the mean of the sample proportions will be 0.5. Also, the bottom portion of Table 6-5 shows that the distribution of the sample proportions is approximately a normal distribution.

Interpretation

Based on the actual sample results shown in the bottom portion of Table 6-5, we can describe the sampling distribution of the sample proportion by the histogram at the bottom of Table 6-5. The actual sampling distribution would be described by a histogram based on all possible samples, not the 10,000 samples included in the histogram, but the number of trials is large enough to suggest that the true sampling distribution of sample proportions is approximately a normal distribution.

The results of Example 4 allow us to observe the following two important properties of the sampling distribution of the proportion.

Behavior of Sample Proportions

1. Sample proportions *target* the value of the population proportion. (That is, the mean of the sample proportions is the population proportion. The expected value of the sample proportion is equal to the population proportion.)

2. The distribution of sample proportions tends to approximate a normal distribution.

Estimators: Unbiased and Biased

The preceding examples show that sample means, variances, and proportions tend to *target* the corresponding population parameters. More formally, we say that sample means, variances, and proportions are *unbiased estimators*. See the following two definitions.

> **DEFINITIONS**
>
> An **estimator** is a statistic used to infer (estimate) the value of a population parameter.
>
> An **unbiased estimator** is a statistic that targets the value of the population parameter in the sense that the sampling distribution of the statistic has a mean that is equal to the mean of the corresponding parameter.

Unbiased Estimators These statistics are unbiased estimators. That is, they each target the value of the corresponding population parameter:

- Mean $\bar{x}$
- Variance s^2
- Proportion $\hat{p}$

Biased Estimators These statistics are biased estimators. That is, they do *not* target the value of the corresponding population parameter:

- Median
- Range
- Standard deviation s*

*Important Note: The sample standard deviations do not target the population standard deviation σ, but the bias is relatively small in large samples, so **s is often used to estimate** σ even though s is a biased estimator of σ.

Example 5 Sampling Distribution of the Sample Range

As in Example 1, consider samples of size $n = 2$ randomly selected from the population {4, 5, 9}.

a. List the different possible samples along with the probability of each sample, then find the range for each sample.

b. Describe the sampling distribution of the sample range in the format of a table summarizing the probability distribution.

c. Based on the results, do the sample ranges target the population range, which is $9 - 4 = 5$?

d. What do these results indicate about the sample range as an estimator of the population range?

Solution

a. In Table 6-6 we list the nine different possible samples of size $n = 2$ selected with replacement from the population {4, 5, 9}. The nine samples are equally likely, so each has probability 1/9. Table 6-6 also shows the range for each of the nine samples.

Table 6-6 Sampling Distribution of Range

Sample	Sample Range	Probability
4, 4	0	1/9
4, 5	1	1/9
4, 9	5	1/9
5, 4	1	1/9
5, 5	0	1/9
5, 9	4	1/9
9, 4	5	1/9
9, 5	4	1/9
9, 9	0	1/9

b. The last two columns of Table 6-6 list the values of the range along with the corresponding probabilities, so the last two columns constitute a table summarizing the probability distribution. Table 6-6 therefore describes the *sampling distribution* of the sample range.

c. The mean of the sample ranges in Table 6-6 is 20/9, or 2.2. The range of the population {4, 5, 9} is $9 - 4 = 5$. Because the mean of the sample ranges (2.2) is not equal to the population range (5), the sample ranges do *not* target the value of the population range.

d. Because the sample ranges do not target the population range, the sample range is a *biased estimator* of the population range.

Interpretation

We conclude that the sample range is a biased estimator of the population range. This shows that, in general, a sample range should not be used to estimate the value of the population range.

Why Sample *with* Replacement? All of the examples in this section involved sampling *with replacement*. Sampling *without replacement* would have the very practical advantage of avoiding wasteful duplication whenever the same item is selected more than once. However, we are particularly interested in sampling *with replacement* for these two very important reasons:

1. When selecting a relatively small sample from a large population, it makes no significant difference whether we sample with replacement or without replacement.

2. Sampling with replacement results in independent events that are unaffected by previous outcomes, and independent events are easier to analyze and result in simpler calculations and formulas.

For the reasons above, we focus on the behavior of samples that are randomly selected *with replacement*. Many of the statistical procedures discussed in the following chapters are based on the assumption that sampling is conducted with replacement.

The key point of this section is to introduce the concept of a sampling distribution of a statistic. Consider the goal of trying to find the mean body temperature of all adults. Because that population is so large, it is not practical to measure the temperature of every adult. Instead, we obtain a sample of body temperatures and use it to estimate the population mean. Data Set 3 in Appendix B includes a sample of 106 such body temperatures. The mean for that sample is $\bar{x} = 98.20°F$. Conclusions that we make about the population mean temperature of all adults require that we understand the behavior of the sampling distribution of all such sample means. Even though it is not practical to obtain every possible sample and we are stuck with just one sample, we can form some very meaningful conclusions about the population of all body temperatures. A major goal of the following sections and chapters is to learn how we can effectively use a sample to form inferences or conclusions about a population. In Section 6-5 we consider more details about the sampling distribution of sample means, and in Section 6-7 we consider more details about the sampling distribution of sample proportions.

> **CAUTION** Many methods of statistics require a *simple random sample*. Some samples, such as voluntary response samples or convenience samples, could easily result in very wrong results.

6-4 Basic Skills and Concepts

Statistical Literacy and Critical Thinking

1. Minting Quarters In a recent year, the U.S. Mint in Denver manufactured 270 million quarters. Assume that on each day of production, a sample of 50 quarters is randomly selected, and the mean weight is obtained.

a. Given that the population of quarters has a mean weight of 5.67 g, what do you know about the mean of the sample means?

b. What do you know about the shape of the distribution of the sample means?

c. The population of quarters has a mean of 5.67 g, but the weights of individual quarters vary. For each sample of 50 quarters, consider the proportion of quarters that weigh less than 5.67 g. What do you know about the shape of the distribution of the sample proportions?

2. Sampling with Replacement In a recent year, the U.S. Mint in Denver manufactured 270 million quarters. As part of the mint's quality control program, samples of quarters are randomly selected each day for detailed inspection to confirm that they meet all required specifications.

a. Do you think the quarters are randomly selected with replacement or without replacement?

b. Give two reasons why statistical methods tend to be based on the assumption that sampling is conducted *with* replacement, instead of without replacement.

3. Unbiased Estimators Data Set 1 in Appendix B includes a sample of 40 pulse rates of women. If we compute the values of sample statistics from that sample, which of the following statistics are *unbiased* estimators of the corresponding population parameters: sample mean; sample median; sample range; sample variance; sample standard deviation; sample proportion?

4. Sampling Distribution Data Set 20 in Appendix B includes a sample of weights of 100 M&M candies. If we explore this sample of 100 weights by constructing a histogram and finding the mean and standard deviation, do those results describe the sampling distribution of the mean? Why or why not?

5. Good Sample? For the population of all college students currently taking a statistics course, you want to estimate the proportion who are women. You obtain a simple random sample of statistics students at Broward College in Florida. Is the resulting sample proportion a good estimator of the population proportion of all college statistics students? Why or why not?

6. Lottery Results Many states have a Pick 3 lottery in which three digits are randomly selected each day. Winning requires that you select the same three digits in the same order that they are drawn. Assume that you compute the mean of each set of three selected digits.

a. What is the approximate shape of the distribution of the sample means (uniform, normal, skewed, other)?

b. What value do the sample means target? That is, what is the mean of all such sample means?

c. For each set of three digits that is selected, if you find the proportion of odd numbers, what is the mean of those proportions?

In Exercises 7–10, use the same population of {4, 5, 9} that was used in Examples 1 and 5. As in Examples 1 and 5, assume that samples of size n = 2 are randomly selected with replacement.

7. Sampling Distribution of the Sample Variance

a. Find the value of the population variance σ^2.

b. Table 6-3 describes the sampling distribution of the sample mean. Construct a similar table representing the sampling distribution of the sample variance s^2. Then combine values of s^2 that are the same, as in Table 6-4. (*Hint:* See Example 1 for Tables 6-3 and 6-4 that describe the sampling distribution of the sample mean.)

c. Find the mean of the sampling distribution of the sample variance.

d. Based on the preceding results, is the sample variance an unbiased estimator of the population variance? Why or why not?

8. Sampling Distribution of the Sample Standard Deviation For the following, round results to three decimal places.

a. Find the value of the population standard deviation σ.

b. Table 6-3 describes the sampling distribution of the sample mean. Construct a similar table representing the sampling distribution of the sample standard deviation s. Then combine values of s that are the same, as in Table 6-4. (*Hint:* See Example 1 for Tables 6-3 and 6-4 that describe the sampling distribution of the sample mean.)

c. Find the mean of the sampling distribution of the sample standard deviation.

d. Based on the preceding results, is the sample standard deviation an unbiased estimator of the population standard deviation? Why or why not?

9. Sampling Distribution of the Sample Median

a. Find the value of the population median.

b. Table 6-3 describes the sampling distribution of the sample mean. Construct a similar table representing the sampling distribution of the sample median. Then combine values of the median that are the same, as in Table 6-4. (*Hint:* See Example 1 for Tables 6-3 and 6-4 that describe the sampling distribution of the sample mean.)

c. Find the mean of the sampling distribution of the sample median.

d. Based on the preceding results, is the sample median an unbiased estimator of the population median? Why or why not?

10. Sampling Distribution of the Sample Proportion

a. For the population, find the proportion of odd numbers.

b. Table 6-3 describes the sampling distribution of the sample mean. Construct a similar table representing the sampling distribution of the sample proportion of odd numbers. Then combine values of the sample proportion that are the same, as in Table 6-4. (*Hint:* See Example 1 for Tables 6-3 and 6-4 that describe the sampling distribution of the sample mean.)

c. Find the mean of the sampling distribution of the sample proportion of odd numbers.

d. Based on the preceding results, is the sample proportion an unbiased estimator of the population proportion? Why or why not?

In Exercises 11–14, use the population of ages {56, 49, 58, 46} of the four U.S. presidents (Lincoln, Garfield, McKinley, Kennedy) when they were assassinated in office. Assume that random samples of size n = 2 are selected with replacement.

11. Sampling Distribution of the Sample Mean

a. After identifying the 16 different possible samples, find the mean of each sample, then construct a table representing the sampling distribution of the sample mean. In the table, combine values of the sample mean that are the same. (*Hint:* See Table 6-4 in Example 1.)

b. Compare the mean of the population {56, 49, 58, 46} to the mean of the sampling distribution of the sample mean.

c. Do the sample means target the value of the population mean? In general, do sample means make good estimators of population means? Why or why not?

12. Sampling Distribution of the Median Repeat Exercise 11 using medians instead of means.

13. Sampling Distribution of the Range Repeat Exercise 11 using ranges instead of means.

14. Sampling Distribution of the Variance Repeat Exercise 11 using variances instead of means.

15. Births: Sampling Distribution of Sample Proportion When two births are randomly selected, the sample space for genders is bb, bg, gb, and gg. Assume that those four outcomes are equally likely. Construct a table that describes the sampling distribution of the sample proportion of girls from two births. Does the mean of the sample proportions equal the proportion of girls in two births? Does the result suggest that a sample proportion is an unbiased estimator of a population proportion?

16. Births: Sampling Distribution of Sample Proportion When three births are randomly selected, the sample space for genders is bbb, bbg, bgb, bgg, gbb, gbg, ggb, and ggg. Assume that those eight outcomes are equally likely. Construct a table that describes the sampling distribution of the sample proportion of girls from three births. Does the mean of the sample proportions equal the proportion of girls in three births?

17. SAT and ACT Tests Because they enable efficient procedures for evaluating answers, multiple-choice questions are commonly used on standardized tests, such as the SAT or ACT. Such questions typically have five choices, one of which is correct. Assume that you must make random guesses for two such questions. Assume that both questions have correct answers of "a."

a. After listing the 25 different possible samples, find the proportion of correct answers in each sample, then construct a table that describes the sampling distribution of the sample proportions of correct responses.

b. Find the mean of the sampling distribution of the sample proportion.

c. Is the mean of the sampling distribution (from part (b)) equal to the population proportion of correct responses? Does the mean of the sampling distribution of proportions *always* equal the population proportion?

18. Quality Control After constructing a new manufacturing machine, five prototype integrated circuit chips are produced and it is found that two are defective (D) and three are acceptable (A). Assume that two of the chips are randomly selected *with replacement* from this population.

a. After identifying the 25 different possible samples, find the proportion of defects in each of them, then use a table to describe the sampling distribution of the proportions of defects.

b. Find the mean of the sampling distribution.

c. Is the mean of the sampling distribution (from part (b)) equal to the population proportion of defects? Does the mean of the sampling distribution of proportions *always* equal the population proportion?

6-4 Beyond the Basics

19. Using a Formula to Describe a Sampling Distribution Exercise 15 requires the construction of a table that describes the sampling distribution of the proportions of girls from two births. Consider the formula shown here, and evaluate that formula using sample proportions x of 0, 0.5, and 1. Based on the results, does the formula describe the sampling distribution? Why or why not?

$$P(x) = \frac{1}{2(2 - 2x)!(2x)!} \quad \text{where } x = 0, 0.5, 1$$

20. Mean Absolute Deviation Is the mean absolute deviation of a sample a good statistic for estimating the mean absolute deviation of the population? Why or why not? (*Hint:* See Example 5.)

6-5 The Central Limit Theorem

Key Concept In Section 6-4 we saw that the sampling distribution of sample means tends to be a normal distribution as the sample size increases. In this section we use the sampling distribution of sample means as we introduce and apply the *central limit theorem* that allows us to use a normal distribution for some very meaningful applications.

Central Limit Theorem

For all samples of the same size n with $n > 30$, the sampling distribution of $\bar{x}$ can be approximated by a normal distribution with mean μ and standard deviation $\sigma/\sqrt{n}$.

According to the central limit theorem, the original population can have *any* distribution (uniform, skewed, and so on), but the distribution of sample means $\bar{x}$ can be approximated by a normal distribution when $n > 30$. (There are some special cases of very nonnormal distributions for which the requirement of $n > 30$ isn't quite enough, so the number 30 must be higher, but those cases are relatively rare.)

Example 1   Normal, Uniform, and U-Shaped Distributions

Table 6-7 illustrates the central limit theorem at work. The top dotplots in Table 6-7 show an approximately normal distribution, a uniform distribution, and a distribution with a shape resembling the letter *U*. In each column, the second dotplot shows the distribution of sample means for samples of size $n = 10$, and the bottom dotplot shows the distribution of sample means for samples of size $n = 50$. As we proceed down each column of Table 6-7, we can see that the distribution of sample means is approaching the shape of a normal distribution. That characteristic is included among the following observations that we can make from Table 6-7.

- As the sample size increases, the sampling distribution of sample means tends to approach a normal distribution.

Table 6-7 Sampling Distributions

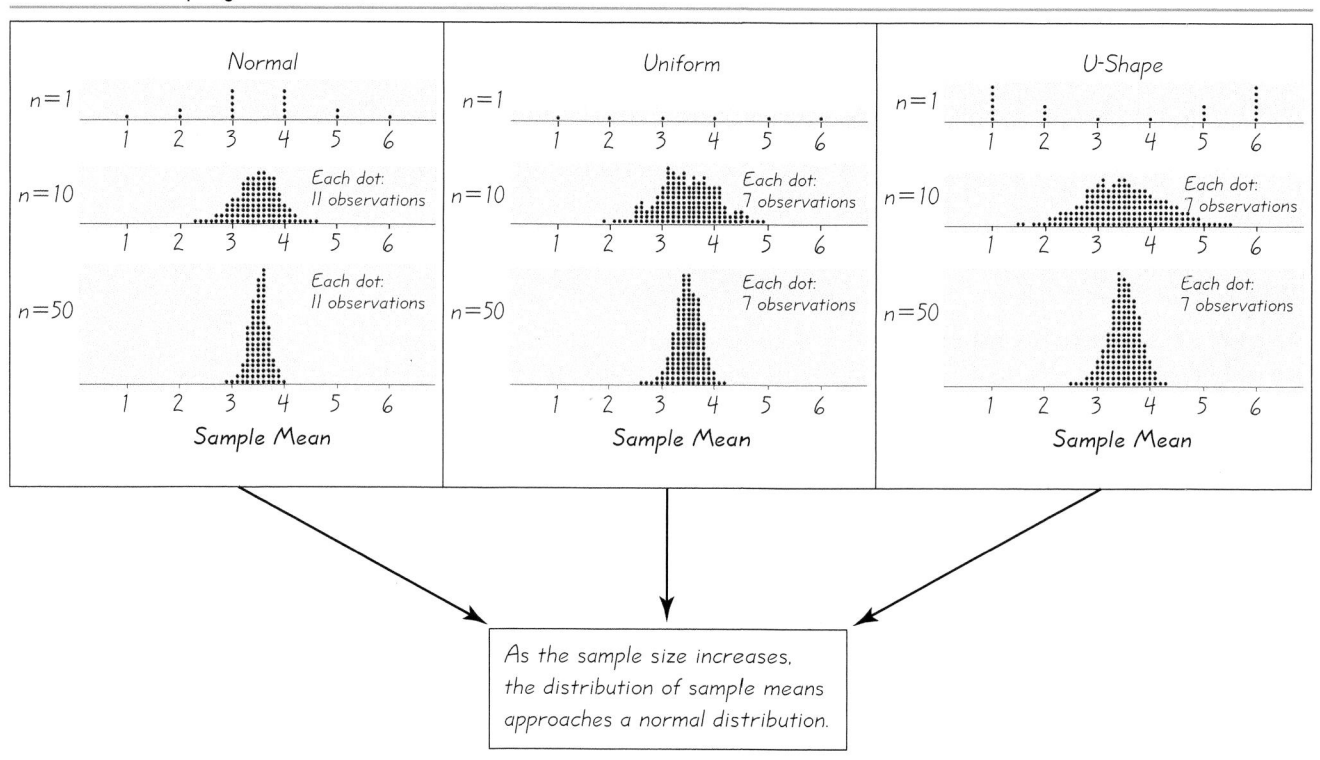

As the sample size increases, the distribution of sample means approaches a normal distribution.

- The mean of all sample means is equal to the mean of the original population.

- As the sample size increases, the spans of the dotplots become narrower, showing that the standard deviations of sample means become smaller as the sample size increases.

The following key points form the foundation for estimating population parameters and hypothesis testing—topics discussed at length in the following chapters.

The Central Limit Theorem and the Sampling Distribution of $\bar{x}$

Given

1. The original population has mean μ and standard deviation σ.

2. Simple random samples of the same size n are selected from the population.

Practical Rules for Real Applications Involving a Sample Mean $\bar{x}$

Case 1: Original population *is* normally distributed.

For *any* sample size *n*: The distribution of $\bar{x}$ is a normal distribution with these parameters:

Mean of all values of $\bar{x}$: $\quad\quad\quad \mu_{\bar{x}} = \mu$

Standard deviation of all values of $\bar{x}$: $\quad \sigma_{\bar{x}} = \dfrac{\sigma}{\sqrt{n}}$

z score conversion of $\bar{x}$: $\quad\quad\quad z = \dfrac{\bar{x} - \mu}{\dfrac{\sigma}{\sqrt{n}}}$

Distribution of Original Population	Distribution of Sample Means
Normal	Normal (for *any* sample size *n*)
Not normal and $n > 30$	Normal (approximately)
Not normal and $n \leq 30$	*Not normal*

Case 2: Original population is *not* normally distributed.

For $n > 30$: The distribution of $\bar{x}$ is approximately a normal distribution with these parameters:

Mean of all values of $\bar{x}$: $\quad\quad\quad \mu_{\bar{x}} = \mu$

Standard deviation of all values of $\bar{x}$: $\quad \sigma_{\bar{x}} = \dfrac{\sigma}{\sqrt{n}}$

z score conversion of $\bar{x}$: $\quad\quad\quad z = \dfrac{\bar{x} - \mu}{\dfrac{\sigma}{\sqrt{n}}}$

For $n \leq 30$: The distribution of $\bar{x}$ cannot be approximated well by a normal distribution and the methods of this section do not apply. Use other methods, such as nonparametric methods or bootstrapping methods. (See the Technology Project for Chapter 7.)

Considerations for Practical Problem Solving

1. **Check Requirements:** When working with the mean from a sample, verify that the normal distribution can be used by confirming that the original population has a normal distribution or $n > 30$.

2. **Individual Value or Mean from a Sample?** Determine whether you are using a normal distribution with a single value x or the mean $\bar{x}$ from a sample of n values. See the following.

- **Individual value:** When working with an *individual* value from a normally distributed population, use the methods of Section 6-3 with $z = \frac{x - \mu}{\sigma}$.

- **Mean from a sample of values:** When working with a mean for some *sample* of n values, be sure to use the value of $\sigma/\sqrt{n}$ for the standard deviation of the sample means, so use $z = \frac{\bar{x} - \mu}{\sigma/\sqrt{n}}$.

The central limit theorem involves two different distributions: (1) the distribution of the *original population* and (2) the distribution of values of $\bar{x}$. As in previous chapters, we use the symbols μ and σ to denote the mean and standard deviation of the original population, but we use the following new notation for the mean and standard deviation of the distribution of $\bar{x}$.

Notation for the Sampling Distribution of $\bar{x}$

If all possible simple random samples of size n are selected from a population with mean μ and standard deviation σ, the mean of the sample means is denoted by $\mu_{\bar{x}}$ and the standard deviation of all sample means is denoted by $\sigma_{\bar{x}}$. ($\sigma_{\bar{x}}$ is called the standard error of the mean.)

Mean of all values of $\bar{x}$: $\qquad \mu_{\bar{x}} = \mu$

Standard deviation of all values of $\bar{x}$: $\qquad \sigma_{\bar{x}} = \dfrac{\sigma}{\sqrt{n}}$

It's very important to know when the normal distribution can be used and when it cannot be used. See Case 1 and Case 2 in the box on the preceding page.

Applying the Central Limit Theorem

Many practical problems can be solved with the central limit theorem. Example 2 is a good illustration of the central limit theorem because we can see the difference between working with an *individual* value in part (a) and working with the *mean* for a sample in part (b). Study Example 2 carefully to understand the fundamental difference between the procedures used in parts (a) and (b). In particular, note that when working with an *individual* value, we use $z = \frac{x - \mu}{\sigma}$, but when working with the mean $\bar{x}$ for a group of *sample* values, we use $z = \frac{\bar{x} - \mu}{\sigma / \sqrt{n}}$.

Example 2   Designing Elevators

When designing elevators, an obviously important consideration is the weight capacity. An Ohio college student died when he tried to escape from a dormitory elevator that was overloaded with 24 passengers. The elevator was rated for a capacity of 16 passengers with a total weight of 2500 lb. Weights of adults are changing over time, and Table 6-8 shows values of recent parameters (based on Data Set 1 in Appendix B). For the following, we assume a worst-case scenario in which all of the passengers are males (which could easily happen in a dormitory setting). If an elevator is loaded to a capacity of 2500 lb with 16 males, the mean weight of a passenger is 156.25 lb.

Table 6-8 Weights of Adults

	Males	Females
μ	182.9 lb	165.0 lb
σ	40.8 lb	45.6 lb
Distribution	Normal	Normal

a. Find the probability that 1 randomly selected adult male has a weight greater than 156.25 lb.

b. Find the probability that a sample of 16 randomly selected adult males has a mean weight greater than 156.25 lb (so that the total weight exceeds the maximum capacity of 2500 lb).

Solution

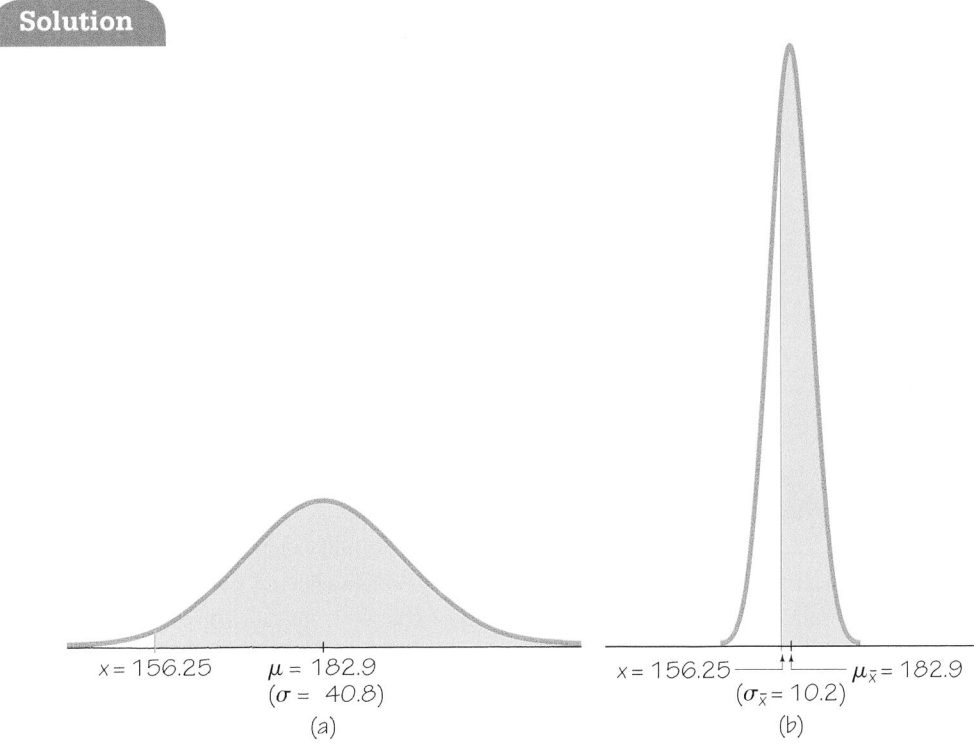

Figure 6-16   Elevator Weights

a. *Approach Used for an Individual Value: Use the methods presented in Section 6-3* (because we are dealing with an *individual* value from a normally distributed population). We seek the area of the green-shaded region in Figure 6-16(a). If using technology (as described at the end of Section 6-3), we find that the green-shaded area is 0.7432. If using Table A-2, we convert the weight of $x = 156.25$ lb to the corresponding z score of $z = -0.65$ as shown here:

$$z = \frac{x - \mu}{\sigma} = \frac{156.25 - 182.9}{40.8} = -0.65$$

We refer to Table A-2 to find that the cumulative area to the *left* of $z = -0.65$ is 0.2578, so the green-shaded area in Figure 6-16 (a) is $1 - 0.2578 = 0.7422$. (The result of 0.7432 from technology is more accurate than the result found from Table A-2.)

b. *Approach Used for the Mean of Sample Values: Use the central limit theorem* (because we are dealing with the *mean of a sample* of 16 males, not an individual male).

Requirement check We can use the normal distribution if the original population is normally distributed or $n > 30$. The sample size is not greater than 30, but the original population of weights of males has a normal distribution, so samples of *any* size will yield means that are normally distributed.

Because we are now dealing with a distribution of sample means, we must use the parameters $\mu_{\bar{x}}$ and $\sigma_{\bar{x}}$, which are evaluated as follows:

$$\mu_{\bar{x}} = \mu = 182.9$$

$$\sigma_{\bar{x}} = \frac{\sigma}{\sqrt{n}} = \frac{40.8}{\sqrt{16}} = 10.2$$

We want to find the green-shaded area shown in Figure 6-16(b). If using technology, the green-shaded area in Figure 6-16(b) is 0.9955. If using Table A-2, we convert the value of $\bar{x} = 156.25$ lb to the corresponding z score of $z = -2.61$ as shown here:

$$z = \frac{\bar{x} - \mu_{\bar{x}}}{\sigma_{\bar{x}}} = \frac{156.25 - 182.9}{\dfrac{40.8}{\sqrt{16}}} = \frac{-26.65}{10.2} = -2.61$$

From Table A-2 we find that the cumulative area to the *left* of $z = -2.61$ is 0.0045, so the green-shaded area if Figure 6-16(b) is $1 - 0.0045 = 0.9955$ (which happens to be the same result obtained using technology). The probability that 16 randomly selected males have a mean weight greater than 156.25 lb is 0.9955.

Interpretation

There is a 0.7432 probability that an individual male will weigh more than 156.25 lb, and there is a 0.9955 probability that 16 randomly selected males will have a mean weight of more than 156.25 lb. Given that the safe capacity of the elevator is 2500 lb, there is a very good chance (with probability 0.9955) that it will be overweight if is filled with 16 randomly selected males. Given that the elevator was crammed with 24 passengers, it is very likely that the safe weight capacity was exceeded.

The calculations used here are exactly the type of calculations used by engineers when they design ski lifts, escalators, airplanes, boats, amusement park rides, and other devices that carry people.

Example 3   Designing Desks for Kindergarten Children

You need to obtain new desks for an incoming class of 25 kindergarten students who are all 5 years of age. An important characteristic of the desks is that they must accommodate the sitting heights of those students. (The sitting height is the height of a seated student from the bottom of the feet to the top of the knee.) Table 6-9 lists the parameters for sitting heights of 5-year-old children (based on data from "Nationwide Age References for Sitting Height, Leg Length, and Sitting Height/Height Ratio, and Their Diagnostic Value for Disproportionate Growth Disorders," by Fredriks et al., *Archives of Disease in Childhood,* Vol. 90, No. 8).

a. What sitting height will accommodate 95% of the boys?

b. What sitting height is greater than 95% of the means of sitting heights from random samples of 25 boys?

c. Based on the preceding results, what single value should be the minimum sitting height accommodated by the desks? Why are the sitting heights of girls not included in the calculations?

Table 6-9 Sitting Heights of 5-Year-Old Children

	Boys	Girls
μ	61.8 cm	61.2 cm
σ	2.9 cm	3.1 cm
Distribution	Normal	Normal

Solution

Requirement check We can use the normal distribution if the original population is normally distributed or $n > 30$. In parts (a) and (b), the original population is normally distributed, so the normal distribution can be used. ✓

a. If the sitting height accommodates 95% of the boys, it accommodates the *lowest* 95%. Only the boys with sitting heights in the top 5% would not fit. We therefore want the sitting height that separates the lowest 95% from the top 5%, and this corresponds to the sitting height with a cumulative left area of 0.95 under the normal distribution curve. See Figure 6-17(a). Because we are working with individual students, we use the methods of Section 6-3. If using technology, we find that the shaded area in Figure 6-17(a) is bounded by the sitting height of 66.6 cm. If using Table A-2, we refer to that table to find that $z = 1.645$ corresponds to a cumulative left area of 0.95. Using $z = (x - \mu)/\sigma$, we substitute $z = 1.645$, $\mu = 61.8$, and $\sigma = 2.9$, then we solve to get $x = 66.6$ cm.

b. Because we are now working with means from samples of 25 boys, we must use these parameters:

$$\mu_{\bar{x}} = \mu = 61.8$$

$$\sigma_{\bar{x}} = \frac{\sigma}{\sqrt{n}} = \frac{2.9}{\sqrt{25}} = 0.58$$

Figure 6-17(b) shows the shaded area corresponding to the lowest 95% of the means of sitting heights. We can find the sitting height that is at the rightmost boundary for that shaded area by using the same procedures developed in Section 6-3. If using technology, we find that the sitting height is 62.8 cm. If using Table A-2, we refer to the table to find that $z = 1.645$ corresponds to a cumulative left area of 0.95, and we get the following:

$$z = \frac{\bar{x} - \mu_{\bar{x}}}{\sigma_{\bar{x}}} \text{ becomes } 1.645 = \frac{\bar{x} - 61.8}{0.58}$$

Solving for $\bar{x}$ in the equation above results in $\bar{x} = 62.8$ cm.

c. See the following interpretation of the results.

Interpretation

Parts (a) and (b) provide us with two different sitting heights: 66.6 cm and 62.8 cm. We now temporarily leave the world of statistical calculations and enter the world of common sense. A critical consideration is that we really don't care about the means from part (b). Each desk will be occupied by one individual child, not a group of 25 children, so we are concerned with the distribution of sitting heights of individuals, as in part (a). Next, Table 6-9 shows that boys have greater sitting heights than girls, so if we accommodate 95% of the boys, more than 95% of the girls will also be accommodated. We should therefore use desks designed to accommodate a sitting height of 66.6 cm.

The Fuzzy Central Limit Theorem

In *The Cartoon Guide to Statistics*, by Gonick and Smith, the authors describe the Fuzzy Central Limit Theorem as follows: "Data that are influenced by many small and unrelated random effects are approximately normally distributed. This explains why the normal is everywhere: stock market fluctuations, student weights, yearly temperature averages, SAT scores: All are the result of many different effects." People's heights, for example, are the results of hereditary factors, environmental factors, nutrition, health care, geographic region, and other influences which, when combined, produce normally distributed values.

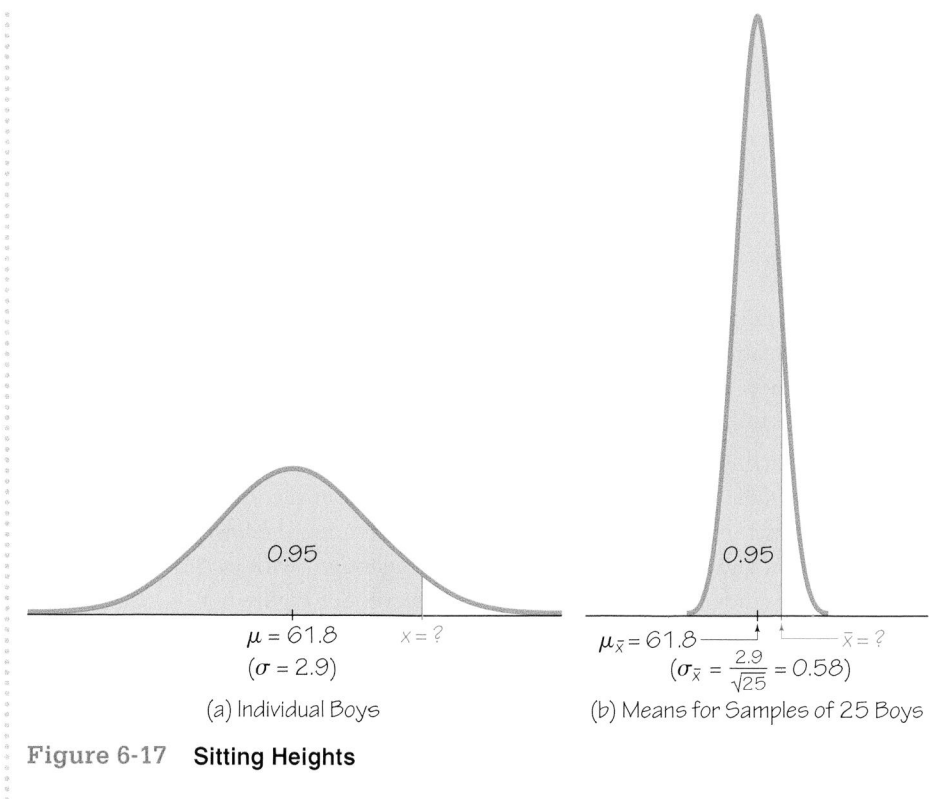

Figure 6-17   Sitting Heights

In Example 2, we were concerned with the *mean* weight of elevator passengers, but in Example 3, the most relevant consideration involves the distribution of *individual* sitting heights. It is important to use sound *critical thinking* in determining what is most relevant.

Introduction to Hypothesis Testing

Carefully examine the conclusions that are reached in the next example illustrating the type of thinking that is the basis for the important procedure of hypothesis testing (discussed in Chapter 8). Example 4 uses the rare event rule for inferential statistics, first presented in Section 4-1.

Rare Event Rule for Inferential Statistics

If, under a given assumption, the probability of a particular observed event is extremely small (such as less than 0.05), we conclude that the assumption is probably not correct.

Example 4   Filling Coke Cans

Cans of regular Coke are labeled to indicate that they contain 12 oz. Data Set 19 in Appendix B lists measured amounts for a sample of Coke cans. The corresponding sample statistics are $n = 36$ and $\bar{x} = 12.19$ oz. Assuming that the Coke cans are filled so that $\mu = 12$ oz (as labeled) and the population standard deviation is $\sigma = 0.11$ oz (based on the sample results), find the probability that a sample of 36 cans will have a mean of 12.19 oz or greater. Do these results suggest that the Coke cans are filled with an amount greater than 12.00 oz?

Solution

Requirement check We can use the normal distribution if the original population is normally distributed or $n > 30$. The sample size of $n = 36$ is greater than 30, so we can approximate the sampling distribution of $\bar{x}$ with a normal distribution. ✅

The parameters of this normal distribution are as follows:

$$\mu_{\bar{x}} = \mu = 12.00 \text{ (by assumption)}$$

$$\sigma_{\bar{x}} = \frac{\sigma}{\sqrt{n}} = \frac{0.11}{\sqrt{36}} = 0.018333$$

Figure 6-18 shows the shaded area (see the small region in the right tail of the graph) corresponding to the probability we seek. Having already found the parameters that apply to the distribution shown in Figure 6-18, we can now find the shaded area by using the same procedures developed in Section 6-3.

If using technology, the shaded area in Figure 6-18 is 0.0000 when rounded to four decimal places. If using Table A-2, we first find the z score as shown here:

$$z = \frac{\bar{x} - \mu_{\bar{x}}}{\sigma_{\bar{x}}} = \frac{12.19 - 12.00}{0.018333} = 10.36$$

Referring to Table A-2, we find that $z = 10.36$ is off the chart, but for values of z above 3.49, we use 0.9999 for the cumulative left area. We therefore conclude that the shaded region in Figure 6-18 is 0.0001.

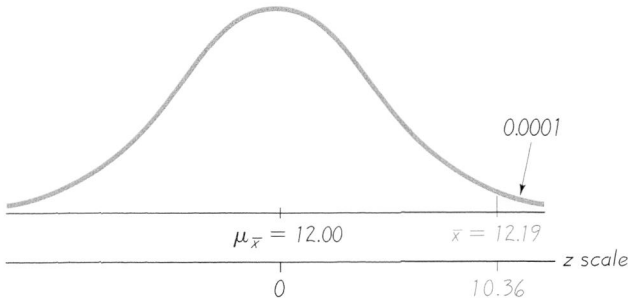

0.0001

$\mu_{\bar{x}} = 12.00$ $\bar{x} = 12.19$

z scale

0 10.36

Figure 6-18 **Distribution of Amounts of Coke**

Interpretation

The result shows that if the mean amount in Coke cans is really 12.00 oz, then there is an extremely small probability of getting a sample mean of 12.19 oz or greater when 36 cans are randomly selected. Because we did obtain such a sample mean, there are two possible explanations: (1) Either the population mean really is 12.00 oz and the sample represents a chance event that is extremely rare; or (2) the population mean is actually greater than 12.00 oz. Because the probability is so close to 0, it seems more reasonable to conclude that the population mean is greater than 12.00 oz. It appears that Coke cans are being filled with more than 12.00 oz. However, the sample mean of 12.19 oz suggests that the mean amount of overfill is very small. It appears that the Coca-Cola company has found a way to ensure that very few cans have less than 12 oz while not wasting very much of their product.

Correction for a Finite Population

In applying the central limit theorem, our use of $\sigma_{\bar{x}} = \sigma/\sqrt{n}$ assumes that the population has infinitely many members. When we sample with replacement (that is, put back each selected item before making the next selection), the population is effectively infinite. Yet many realistic applications involve sampling without replacement, so successive samples depend on previous outcomes. In manufacturing, quality control inspectors typically sample items from a finite production run without replacing them. For such a finite population, we may need to adjust $\sigma_{\bar{x}}$. Here is a common rule of thumb:

> **When sampling without replacement and the sample size n is greater than 5% of the finite population size N (that is, $n > 0.05N$), adjust the standard deviation of sample means $\sigma_{\bar{x}}$ by multiplying it by the *finite population correction factor*:**

$$\sqrt{\frac{N-n}{N-1}}$$

Except for Exercises 23, 24, and 25 the examples and exercises in this section assume that the finite population correction factor does *not* apply, because we are sampling with replacement, or the population is infinite, or the sample size doesn't exceed 5% of the population size.

6-5 Basic Skills and Concepts

Statistical Literacy and Critical Thinking

1. Standard Error of the Mean The population of current statistics students has ages with mean μ and standard deviation σ. Samples of statistics students are randomly selected so that there are exactly 40 students in each sample. For each sample, the mean age is computed. What does the central limit theorem tell us about the distribution of those mean ages?

2. Small Sample Heights of adult females are normally distributed. Samples of heights of adult females, each of size $n = 3$, are randomly collected and the sample means are found. Is it correct to conclude that the sample means cannot be treated as a normal distribution because the sample size is too small? Explain.

3. Notation The population of distances that adult females can reach forward is normally distributed with a mean of 60.5 cm and a standard deviation of 6.6 cm (from the Federal Aviation Administration). If samples of 36 adult females are randomly selected, what do $\mu_{\bar{x}}$ and $\sigma_{\bar{x}}$ represent, and what are their values?

4. Lottery Numbers In each drawing for the Texas Pick 3 lottery, three digits between 0 and 9 inclusive are randomly selected. What is the distribution of the selected digits? If the mean is calculated for each drawing, can the distribution of the sample means be treated as a normal distribution?

 Using the Central Limit Theorem. *In Exercises 5–10, use this information about the overhead reach distances of adult females: $\mu = 205.5$ cm, $\sigma = 8.6$ cm, and overhead reach distances are normally distributed (based on data from the Federal Aviation Administration). The overhead reach distances are used in planning assembly work stations.*

5. a. If 1 adult female is randomly selected, find the probability that her overhead reach is less than 222.7 cm.

b. If 49 adult females are randomly selected, find the probability that they have a mean overhead reach less than 207.0 cm.

6. a. If 1 adult female is randomly selected, find the probability that her overhead reach is less than 196.9 cm.

b. If 36 adult females are randomly selected, find the probability that they have a mean overhead reach less than 205.0 cm.

7. a. If 1 adult female is randomly selected, find the probability that her overhead reach is greater than 218.4 cm.

b. If 9 adult females are randomly selected, find the probability that they have a mean overhead reach greater than 204.0 cm.

c. Why can the normal distribution be used in part (b), even though the sample size does not exceed 30?

8. a. If 1 adult female is randomly selected, find the probability that her overhead reach is greater than 195.0 cm.

b. If 25 adult females are randomly selected, find the probability that they have a mean overhead reach greater than 203.0 cm.

c. Why can the normal distribution be used in part (b), even though the sample size does not exceed 30?

9. a. If 1 adult female is randomly selected, find the probability that her overhead reach is between 179.7 cm and 231.3 cm.

b. If 40 adult females are randomly selected, find the probability that they have a mean overhead reach between 204.0 cm and 206.0 cm.

10. a. If 1 adult female is randomly selected, find the probability that her overhead reach is between 180.0 cm and 200.0 cm.

b. If 50 adult females are randomly selected, find the probability that they have a mean overhead reach between 198.0 cm and 206.0 cm.

11. Elevator Safety Example 2 referred to an Ohio elevator with a maximum capacity of 2500 lb. When rating elevators, it is common to use a 25% safety factor, so the elevator should actually be able to carry a load that is 25% greater than the stated limit. The maximum capacity of 2500 lb becomes 3125 lb after it is increased by 25%, so 16 male passengers can have a mean weight of up to 195.3 lb. If the elevator is loaded with 16 male passengers, find the probability that it is overloaded because they have a mean weight greater than 195.3 lb. (As in Example 2, assume that weights of males are normally distributed with a mean of 182.9 lb and a standard deviation of 40.8 lb.) Does this elevator appear to be safe?

12. Elevator Safety Exercise 11 uses μ182.9 lb, which is based on Data Set 1 in Appendix B. Repeat Exercise 11 using μ174 lb (instead of 182.9 lb), which is the assumed mean weight that was commonly used just a few years ago. Assuming that the mean weight of males is now 182.9 lb, not the value of 174 lb that was used just a few years ago, what do you conclude about the effect of using an outdated mean that is substantially lower than it should be?

13. Designing Hats Women have head circumferences that are normally distributed with a mean of 22.65 in. and a standard deviation of 0.80 in. (based on data from the National Health and Nutrition Examination Survey).

a. If the Hats by Leko company produces women's hats so that they fit head circumferences between 21.00 in. and 25.00 in., what percentage of women can fit into these hats?

b. If the company wants to produce hats to fit all women except for those with the smallest 2.5% and the largest 2.5% head circumferences, what head circumferences should be accommodated?   *continued*

c. If 64 women are randomly selected, what is the probability that their mean head circumference is between 22.00 in. and 23.00 in.? If this probability is high, does it suggest that an order for 64 hats will very likely fit each of 64 randomly selected women? Why or why not?

 14. Designing Manholes According to the web site www.torchmate.com, "manhole covers must be a minimum of 22 in. in diameter, but can be as much as 60 in. in diameter." Assume that a manhole is constructed to have a circular opening with a diameter of 22 in. Men have shoulder breadths that are normally distributed with a mean of 18.2 in. and a standard deviation of 1.0 in. (based on data from the National Health and Nutrition Examination Survey).

a. What percentage of men will fit into the manhole?

b. Assume that the Connecticut Light and Power company employs 36 men who work in manholes. If 36 men are randomly selected, what is the probability that their mean shoulder breadth is less than 18.5 in.? Does this result suggest that money can be saved by making smaller manholes with a diameter of 18.5 in.? Why or why not?

 15. Water Taxi Safety Passengers died when a water taxi sank in Baltimore's Inner Harbor. Men are typically heavier than women and children, so when loading a water taxi, assume a worst-case scenario in which all passengers are men. Assume that weights of men are normally distributed with a mean of 182.9 lb and a standard deviation of 40.8 lb (based on Data Set 1 in Appendix B). The water taxi that sank had a stated capacity of 25 passengers, and the boat was rated for a load limit of 3500 lb.

a. Given that the water taxi that sank was rated for a load limit of 3500 lb, what is the mean weight of the passengers if the boat is filled to the stated capacity of 25 passengers?

b. If the water taxi is filled with 25 randomly selected men, what is the probability that their mean weight exceeds the value from part (a)?

c. After the water taxi sank, the weight assumptions were revised so that the new capacity became 20 passengers. If the water taxi is filled with 20 randomly selected men, what is the probability that their mean weight exceeds 175 lb, which is the maximum mean weight that does not cause the total load to exceed 3500 lb?

d. Is the new capacity of 20 passengers safe?

16. Loading M&M Packages M&M plain candies have a mean weight of 0.8565 g and a standard deviation of 0.0518 g (based on Data Set 20 in Appendix B). The M&M candies used in Data Set 20 came from a package containing 465 candies, and the package label stated that the net weight is 396.9 g. (If every package has 465 candies, the mean weight of the candies must exceed 396.9/465 = 0.8535 g for the net contents to weigh at least 396.9 g.)

a. If 1 M&M plain candy is randomly selected, find the probability that it weighs more than 0.8535 g.

b. If 465 M&M plain candies are randomly selected, find the probability that their mean weight is at least 0.8535 g.

c. Given these results, does it seem that the Mars Company is providing M&M consumers with the amount claimed on the label?

 17. Gondola Safety A ski gondola in Vail, Colorado, carries skiers to the top of a mountain. It bears a plaque stating that the maximum capacity is 12 people or 2004 lb. That capacity will be exceeded if 12 people have weights with a mean greater than 2004/12 = 167 lb. Because men tend to weigh more than women, a worst-case scenario involves 12 passengers who are all men. Assume that weights of men are normally distributed with a mean of 182.9 lb and a standard deviation of 40.8 lb (based on Data Set 1 in Appendix B).

a. Find the probability that if an individual man is randomly selected, his weight will be greater than 167 lb.

b. Find the probability that 12 randomly selected men will have a mean weight that is greater than 167 lb (so that their total weight is greater than the gondola maximum capacity of 2004 lb).

c. Does the gondola appear to have the correct weight limit? Why or why not?

18. Pulse Rates of Women Women have pulse rates that are normally distributed with a mean of 77.5 beats per minute and a standard deviation of 11.6 beats per minute (based on Data Set 1 in Appendix B).

a. Find the percentiles P_1 and P_{99}.

b. Dr. Puretz sees exactly 25 female patients each day. Find the probability that 25 randomly selected women have a mean pulse rate between 70 beats per minute and 85 beats per minute.

c. If Dr. Puretz wants to select pulse rates to be used as cutoff values for determining when further tests should be required, which pulse rates are better to use: the results from part (a) or the pulse rates of 70 beats per minute and 85 beats per minute from part (b)? Why?

19. Redesign of Ejection Seats When women were allowed to become pilots of fighter jets, engineers needed to redesign the ejection seats because they had been originally designed for men only. The ACES-II ejection seats were designed for men weighing between 140 lb and 211 lb. Weights of women are now normally distributed with a mean of 165.0 lb and a standard deviation of 45.6 lb (based on Data Set 1 in Appendix B).

a. If 1 woman is randomly selected, find the probability that her weight is between 140 lb and 211 lb.

b. If 36 different women are randomly selected, find the probability that their mean weight is between 140 lb and 211 lb.

c. When redesigning the fighter jet ejection seats to better accommodate women, which probability is more relevant: the result from part (a) or the result from part (b)? Why?

20. Loading a Tour Boat The Ethan Allen tour boat capsized and sank in Lake George, New York, and 20 of the 47 passengers drowned. Based on a 1960 assumption of a mean weight of 140 lb for passengers, the boat was rated to carry 50 passengers. After the boat sank, New York State changed the assumed mean weight from 140 lb to 174 lb.

a. Given that the boat was rated for 50 passengers with an assumed mean of 140 lb, the boat had a passenger load limit of 7000 lb. Assume that the boat is loaded with 50 male passengers, and assume that weights of men are normally distributed with a mean of 182.9 lb and a standard deviation of 40.8 lb (based on Data Set 1 in Appendix B). Find the probability that the boat is overloaded because the 50 male passengers have a mean weight greater than 140 lb.

b. The boat was later rated to carry only 14 passengers, and the load limit was changed to 2436 lb. If 14 passengers are all males, find the probability that the boat is overloaded because their mean weight is greater than 174 lb (so that their total weight is greater than the maximum capacity of 2436 lb). Do the new ratings appear to be safe when the boat is loaded with 14 male passengers?

21. Doorway Height The Boeing 757-200 ER airliner carries 200 passengers and has doors with a height of 72 in. Heights of men are normally distributed with a mean of 69.5 in. and a standard deviation of 2.4 in. (based on Data Set 1 in Appendix B).

a. If a male passenger is randomly selected, find the probability that he can fit through the doorway without bending.

b. If half of the 200 passengers are men, find the probability that the mean height of the 100 men is less than 72 in.

c. When considering the comfort and safety of passengers, which result is more relevant: the probability from part (a) or the probability from part (b)? Why?

d. When considering the comfort and safety of passengers, why are women ignored in this case?

22. Loading Aircraft Before every flight, the pilot must verify that the total weight of the load is less than the maximum allowable load for the aircraft. The Bombardier Dash 8 aircraft can carry 37 passengers, and a flight has fuel and baggage that allows for a total passenger load of 6200 lb. The pilot sees that the plane is full and all passengers are men. The aircraft will be overloaded if the mean weight of the passengers is greater than 6200 lb/37 = 167.6 lb. What is the probability that the aircraft is overloaded? Should the pilot take any action to correct for an overloaded aircraft? Assume that weights of men are normally distributed with a mean of 182.9 lb and a standard deviation of 40.8 lb (based on Data Set 1 in Appendix B).

6-5 Beyond the Basics

23. Correcting for a Finite Population In a study of babies born with very low birth weights, 275 children were given IQ tests at age 8, and their scores approximated a normal distribution with $\mu = 95.5$ and $\sigma = 16.0$ (based on data from "Neurobehavioral Outcomes of School-age Children Born Extremely Low Birth Weight or Very Preterm," by Anderson et al., *Journal of the American Medical Association*, Vol. 289, No. 24). Fifty of those children are to be randomly selected for a follow-up study.

a. When considering the distribution of the mean IQ scores for samples of 50 children, should $\sigma_{\bar{x}}$ be corrected by using the finite population correction factor? Why or why not? What is the value of $\sigma_{\bar{x}}$?

b. Find the probability that the mean IQ score of the follow-up sample is between 95 and 105.

24. Correcting for a Finite Population The Orange County Spa began with 300 members. Those members had weights with a distribution that is approximately normal with a mean of 177 lb and a standard deviation of 40 lb. The facility includes an elevator that can hold up to 16 passengers.

a. When considering the distribution of sample means from weights of samples of 16 passengers, should $\sigma_{\bar{x}}$ be corrected by using the finite population correction factor? Why or why not? What is the value of $\sigma_{\bar{x}}$?

b. If the elevator is designed to safely carry a load of up to 3000 lb, what is the maximum safe mean weight of passengers when the elevator is loaded with 16 passengers?

c. If the elevator is filled with 16 randomly selected club members, what is the probability that the total load exceeds the safe limit of 3000 lb? Is this probability low enough?

d. What is the maximum number of passengers that should be allowed if we want at least a 0.999 probability that the elevator will not be overloaded when it is filled with randomly selected club members?

25. Population Parameters Use the same population of {4, 5, 9} from Example 1 in Section 6-4. Assume that samples of size $n = 2$ are randomly selected *without* replacement.

a. Find μ and σ for the population.

b. After finding all samples of size $n = 2$ that can be obtained *without* replacement, find the population of all values of $\bar{x}$ by finding the mean of each sample of size $n = 2$.

c. Find the mean $\mu_{\bar{x}}$ and standard deviation $\sigma_{\bar{x}}$ for the population of sample means found in part (b).

d. Verify that

$$\mu_{\bar{x}} = \mu \quad \text{and} \quad \sigma_{\bar{x}} = \frac{\sigma}{\sqrt{n}}\sqrt{\frac{N-n}{N-1}}$$

6-6 Assessing Normality

Key Concept The following chapters include several important statistical methods requiring that sample data are a simple random sample from a population having a *normal* distribution. In this section we present criteria for determining whether the requirement of a normal distribution is satisfied. The criteria involve (1) visual inspection of a histogram to see if it is roughly bell-shaped; (2) identifying any outliers; and (3) constructing a graph called a *normal quantile plot*.

Part 1: Basic Concepts of Assessing Normality

When trying to determine whether a collection of data has a distribution that is approximately normal, we can visually inspect a histogram to see if it is approximately bell-shaped (as discussed in Section 2-3), we can identify outliers, and we can also use a *normal quantile plot* (discussed briefly in Section 2-3).

> **DEFINITION** A **normal quantile plot** (or **normal probability plot**) is a graph of points (*x*, *y*) where each *x* value is from the original set of sample data, and each *y* value is the corresponding *z* score that is a quantile value expected from the standard normal distribution.

Procedure for Determining Whether It Is Reasonable to Assume That Sample Data Are from a Population Having a Normal Distribution

1. *Histogram:* Construct a histogram. If the histogram departs dramatically from a bell shape, conclude that the data do not have a normal distribution.

2. *Outliers:* Identify outliers. If there is more than one outlier present, conclude that the data do not have a normal distribution. (Just one outlier could be an error or the result of chance variation, but be careful, because even a single outlier can have a dramatic effect on results.)

3. *Normal quantile plot:* If the histogram is basically symmetric and the number of outliers is 0 or 1, use technology to generate a *normal quantile plot*. Apply the following criteria to determine whether or not the distribution is normal. (These criteria can be used loosely for small samples, but they should be used more strictly for large samples.)

   Normal Distribution: The population distribution is normal if the pattern of the points is reasonably close to a straight line and the points do not show some systematic pattern that is not a straight-line pattern.

   Not a Normal Distribution: The population distribution is *not* normal if either or both of these two conditions applies:
   - The points do not lie reasonably close to a straight line.
   - The points show some *systematic pattern* that is not a straight-line pattern.

Later in this section we will describe the actual process of constructing a normal quantile plot, but for now we focus on interpreting such a plot.

Example 1 Determining Normality

The accompanying displays show histograms of data along with the corresponding normal quantile plots.

continued

Normal: The first case shows a histogram of IQ scores that is close to being bell-shaped, so the histogram suggests that the IQ scores are from a normal distribution. The corresponding normal quantile plot shows points that are reasonably close to a straight-line pattern, and the points do not show any other systematic pattern that is not a straight line. It is safe to assume that these IQ scores are from a population that has a normal distribution.

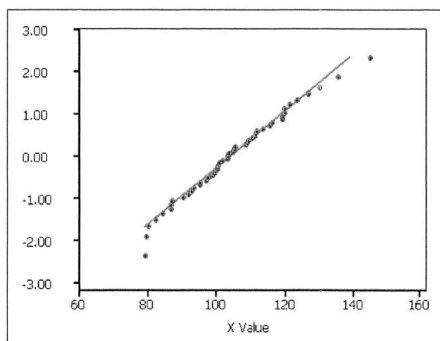

Uniform: The second case shows a histogram of data having a uniform distribution. The corresponding normal quantile plot suggests that the points are not normally distributed. Although the pattern of points is reasonably close to a straight-line pattern, *there is another systematic pattern that is not a straight-line pattern*. We conclude that these sample values are from a population having a distribution that is not normal.

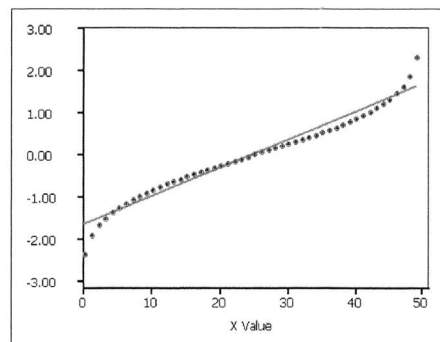

Skewed: The third case shows a histogram of the amounts of rainfall (in inches) in Boston for every Monday during one year. The shape of the histogram is skewed, not bell-shaped. The corresponding normal quantile plot shows points that are not at all close to a straight-line pattern. These rainfall amounts are from a population having a distribution that is not normal.

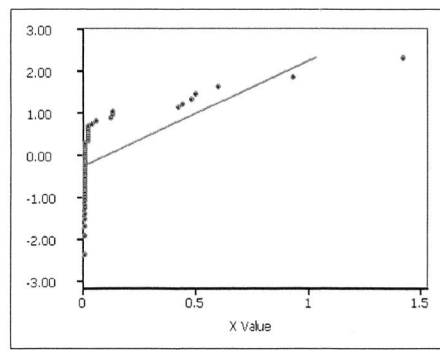

Here are some important comments about procedures for determining whether data are from a normally distributed population:

- If the requirement of a normal distribution is not too strict, simply look at a histogram and find the number of outliers. If the histogram is roughly bell-shaped and the number of outliers is 0 or 1, treat the population as if it has a normal distribution.

- Normal quantile plots can be difficult to construct on your own, but they can be generated with a TI-83/84 Plus calculator or suitable computer software, such as STATDISK, SPSS, SAS, Minitab, Excel, or StatCrunch.

- In addition to the procedures discussed in this section, there are other, more advanced procedures for assessing normality, such as the chi-square goodness-of-fit test, the Kolmogorov-Smirnov test, the Lilliefors test, the Anderson-Darling test, and the Ryan-Joiner test (discussed briefly in Part 2).

Part 2: Beyond the Basics of Assessing Normality

The following is a relatively simple procedure for manually constructing a normal quantile plot, and it is the same procedure used by STATDISK and the TI-83/84 Plus calculator. Some statistical packages use various other approaches, but the interpretation of the graph is basically the same.

Manual Construction of a Normal Quantile Plot

Step 1: First sort the data by arranging the values in order from lowest to highest.

Step 2: With a sample of size n, each value represents a proportion of $1/n$ of the sample. Using the known sample size n, identify the areas of $\frac{1}{2n}, \frac{3}{2n}, \frac{5}{2n}$, and so on. These are the cumulative areas to the left of the corresponding sample values.

Step 3: Use the standard normal distribution (software or a calculator or Table A-2) to find the z scores corresponding to the cumulative left areas found in Step 2. (These are the z scores that are expected from a normally distributed sample.)

Step 4: Match the original sorted data values with their corresponding z scores found in Step 3, then plot the points (x, y), where each x is an original sample value and y is the corresponding z score.

Step 5: Examine the normal quantile plot and conclude that the population has a normal distribution if the pattern of the points is reasonably close to a straight line and the points do not show some systematic pattern that is not a straight-line pattern.

Example 2 Earthquake Magnitudes

Data Set 16 in Appendix B includes Richter-scale magnitudes of earthquakes. Let's consider this sample of five magnitudes: 0.70, 2.20, 1.64, 1.01, 1.62. With only five values, a histogram will not be very helpful in revealing the distribution of the data. Instead, construct a normal quantile plot for these five values and determine whether they appear to come from a population that is normally distributed.

Solution

The following steps correspond to those listed in the procedure above for constructing a normal quantile plot.   *continued*

Step 1: First, sort the data by arranging them in order. We get 0.70, 1.01, 1.62, 1.64, 2.20.

Step 2: With a sample of size $n = 5$, each value represents a proportion of $1/5$ of the sample, so we proceed to identify the cumulative areas to the left of the corresponding sample values. The cumulative left areas, which are expressed in general as $\frac{1}{2n}, \frac{3}{2n}, \frac{5}{2n}$, and so on, become these specific areas for this example with $n = 5$: $\frac{1}{10}, \frac{3}{10}, \frac{5}{10}, \frac{7}{10}$, and $\frac{9}{10}$. The cumulative left areas expressed in decimal form are 0.1, 0.3, 0.5, 0.7, and 0.9.

Step 3: We now use technology (or Table A-2) with the cumulative left areas of 0.1000, 0.3000, 0.5000, 0.7000, and 0.9000 to find these corresponding z scores: $-1.28, -0.52, 0, 0.52$, and 1.28.

Step 4: We now pair the original sorted earthquake magnitudes with their corresponding z scores. We get these (x, y) coordinates, which are plotted in the accompanying STATDISK display: $(0.70, -1.28), (1.01, -0.52), (1.62, 0), (1.64, 0.52), (2.20, 1.28)$.

STATDISK

Interpretation

We examine the normal quantile plot in the STATDISK display. Because the points appear to lie reasonably close to a straight line and there does not appear to be a systematic pattern that is not a straight-line pattern, we conclude that the sample of five earthquake magnitudes appears to come from a normally distributed population.

Ryan-Joiner Test The Ryan-Joiner test is one of several formal tests of normality, each having their own advantages and disadvantages. STATDISK has a feature of **Normality Assessment** that displays a histogram, normal quantile plot, the number of potential outliers, and results from the Ryan-Joiner test. Information about the Ryan-Joiner test is readily available on the Internet.

Example 3   Earthquake Magnitudes

Example 2 used only the first five earthquake magnitudes listed in Data Set 16 from Appendix B. If we include all 50 magnitudes, we can use the **Normality Assessment** feature of STATDISK to get the accompanying display.

STATDISK

Let's use the display with the three criteria for assessing normality.

1. *Histogram:* We can see that the histogram is approximately bell-shaped.

2. *Outliers:* There are two possible outliers, but after sorting the data, we see that the five highest magnitudes are 1.98, 2.20, 2.24, 2.50, 2.95, so the possible outliers of 2.50 and 2.95 aren't too far away from the other data values.

3. *Normal quantile plot:* The points in the normal quantile plot are not far from a straight-line pattern, and there is no other pattern that is not a straight-line pattern. It is reasonable to conclude that the 50 earthquake magnitudes are from a population with a normal distribution.

Data Transformations Many data sets have a distribution that is not normal, but we can *transform* the data so that the modified values have a normal distribution. One common transformation is to transform each value of x by taking its logarithm. (You can use natural logarithms or logarithms with base 10. If any original values are 0, take logarithms of values of $x + 1$). If the distribution of the logarithms of the values is a normal distribution, the distribution of the original values is called a **lognormal distribution.** (See Exercises 22 and 23.) In addition to transformations with logarithms, there are other transformations, such as replacing each x value with $\sqrt{x}$, or $1/x$, or x^2. In addition to getting a required normal distribution when the original data values are not normally distributed, such transformations can be used to correct deficiencies, such as a requirement (found in later chapters) that different data sets have the same variance.

using **TECHNOLOGY**

STATDISK STATDISK can be used to generate a normal quantile plot, and the result is consistent with the procedure described in this section. Enter the data in a column of the Sample Editor window or open a data set. Next, select **Data** from the main menu bar at the top. Select **Normal Quantile Plot** to generate the graph. Better yet, select **Normality Assessment** to obtain the normal quantile plot included in the same display with other results helpful in assessing normality. Proceed to enter the column number for the data, then click **Evaluate.**

continued

MINITAB Minitab can generate a graph similar to the normal quantile plot described in this section. Minitab's procedure is somewhat different, but the graph can be interpreted by using the same criteria given in this section. That is, normally distributed data should lie reasonably close to a straight line, and points should not reveal a pattern that is not a straight-line pattern. First enter the values in column C1 or open a data set, then select **Stat, Basic Statistics,** and **Normality Test.** Enter **C1** for the variable, then click on **OK.**

Minitab can also generate a graph that includes boundaries. If the points all lie within the boundaries, conclude that the values are normally distributed. If points lie beyond the boundaries, conclude that the values are not normally distributed. To generate the graph that includes the boundaries, first enter the values in column C1, select the main menu item of **Graph,** select **Probability Plot,** then select the option of **Simple.** Proceed to enter **C1** for the variable, then click **OK.** The accompanying Minitab display is based on the 50 earthquake *depths* (km) listed in Data Set 16 from Appendix B, and it includes the boundaries. See that there are points lying outside of the boundaries, suggesting that the data are not from a population having a normal distribution.

MINITAB

EXCEL Use XLSTAT. Click on **XLSTAT,** then click on **Describing Data,** then select **Normality Tests.** In the Data box, enter the range of data, such as A1:A50. Put a check in the "Sample labels" box only if the first cell includes a name for the data. Click on the **Charts** tab and be sure that there is a checkmark next to the "Normal Q-Q Plot" box. Click **OK** and proceed to get the graph.

TI-83/84 PLUS The TI-83/84 Plus calculator can be used to generate a normal quantile plot, and the result is consistent with the procedure described in this section. First enter the sample data in list L1. Press **2ND** **Y=** (for **STAT PLOT**), then press **ENTER**. Select **ON,** select the "type" item, which is the last item in the second row of options, and enter **L1** for the data list. The screen should appear as shown here. After making all selections, press **ZOOM**, then **9,** and the points in the normal quantile plot will be displayed.

TI-83/84 PLUS

STATCRUNCH Click on **Open StatCrunch,** then enter or open a column of sample data. Click on **Graphics,** then select the menu item of **QQPlot.** In the dialog box that appears, select the column to be used, then click on **Create Graph.** The result will be similar to the normal quantile plot described in this section, but the axes will be switched. The interpretation will be the same as described in this section.

6-6 Basic Skills and Concepts

Statistical Literacy and Critical Thinking

1. Normal Quantile Plot Data Set 1 in Appendix B includes the heights of 40 randomly selected women. If you were to construct a histogram of those heights, what shape do you expect the histogram to have? If you were to construct a normal quantile plot of those heights, what pattern would you expect to see in the graph?

2. Normal Quantile Plot After constructing a histogram of the ages of the 40 women included in Data Set 1 in Appendix B, you see that the histogram is far from being bell-shaped. What do you now know about the normal quantile plot?

3. Small Sample An article includes elapsed times (hours) to lumbar puncture for 19 patients who entered emergency rooms with sudden and severe "thunderclap" headaches (based on data from "Thunderclap Headache and Normal Computed Tomographic Results: Value of Cerebrospinal Fluid Analysis," by DuPont et al., *Mayo Clinic Proceedings,* Vol. 83, No. 12). Given that the sample size is less than 30, what requirement must be met in order to treat the sample mean as a value from a normally distributed population? Identify three ways of verifying that requirement.

4. Assessing Normality The accompany histogram is constructed from the platelet counts of the 40 women included in Data Set 1 in Appendix B. If you plan to conduct further statistical tests and there is a loose requirement of a normally distributed population, what do you conclude about the population distribution based on this histogram?

MINITAB

Interpreting Normal Quantile Plots. In Exercises 5–8, examine the normal quantile plot and determine whether the sample data appear to be from a population with a normal distribution.

5. Ages of Oscar-Winning Actresses The normal quantile plot represents the ages of actresses when they won Oscars. The data are from Data Set 11 in Appendix B.

6. Body Temperatures The normal quantile plot represents body temperatures of adults from Data Set 3 in Appendix B.

7. White Blood Cell Counts The normal quantile plot represents white blood cell counts of males from Data Set 1 in Appendix B.

8. Flight Departure Delays The normal quantile plot represents flight departure delay times (minutes) from Data Set 15 in Appendix B.

Determining Normality.   *In Exercises 9–12, refer to the indicated sample data and determine whether they appear to be from a population with a normal distribution. Assume that this requirement is loose in the sense that the population distribution need not be exactly normal, but it must be a distribution that is roughly bell-shaped.*

9. Flight Arrival Delays The arrival delay times (minutes) as listed in Data Set 15 in Appendix B.

10. Heights of Presidents The heights (cm) of the presidents of the United States as listed in Data Set 12 in Appendix B.

11. Blood Pressure The systolic blood pressure measurements of males as listed in Data Set 1 in Appendix B.

12. Secondhand Smoke The cotinine measurements of nonsmokers who were exposed to tobacco smoke at home or work, as listed in Data Set 9 in Appendix B.

Using Technology to Generate Normal Quantile Plots.   *In Exercises 13–16, use the data from the indicated exercise in this section. Use computer software (such as STATDISK, Minitab, Excel, or StatCrunch) or a TI-83/84 Plus calculator to generate a normal quantile plot. Then determine whether the data come from a normally distributed population.*

13. Exercise 9   **14.** Exercise 10

15. Exercise 11   **16.** Exercise 12

Constructing Normal Quantile Plots.   *In Exercises 17–20, use the given data values to identify the corresponding z scores that are used for a normal quantile plot, then identify the coordinates of each point in the normal quantile plot. Construct the normal quantile plot, then determine whether the data appear to be from a population with a normal distribution.*

17. Braking Distances A sample of braking distances (in feet) measured under standard conditions for a sample of large cars from Data Set 14 in Appendix B: 139, 134, 145, 143, 131.

18. Taxi Out Times A sample of flights is selected, and the times (minutes) required to taxi out for takeoff are 37, 13, 14, 15, 31, 15 (from Data Set 15 in Appendix B).

19. Brain Volumes A sample of human brain volumes (cm^3) is obtained from those listed in Data Set 6 from Appendix B: 1272, 1051, 1079, 1034, 1070, 1173, 1079, 1067.

20. M&M Weights A sample of weights (g) of M&Ms is obtained from those listed in Data Set 20 from Appendix B: 0.864, 0.825, 0.855, 0.942, 0.825, 0.869, 0.912, 0.887, 0.886.

6-6 Beyond the Basics

21. Transformations The heights (in inches) of men listed in Data Set 1 in Appendix B have a distribution that is approximately normal, so it appears that those heights are from a normally distributed population.

a. If 2 inches is added to each height, are the new heights also normally distributed?

b. If each height is converted from inches to centimeters, are the heights in centimeters also normally distributed?

c. Are the logarithms of normally distributed heights also normally distributed?

22. Earthquake Magnitudes Richter scale earthquake magnitudes are listed in Data Set 16 of Appendix B.

a. Determine whether those magnitudes are from a population with a normal distribution.

b. For the Richter scale, assume that the magnitude of the energy from an earthquake is first measured, then the logarithm (base 10) of the value is computed. Based on this description of the Richter scale and the result from part (a), what is the distribution of the original measurements before their logarithms are computed?

c. Given that the magnitudes in Data Set 16 result from computing logarithms (base 10), construct the normal quantile plot of the original magnitudes before logarithms are applied. Do the original values appear to be from a population with a normal distribution?

23. Lognormal Distribution The following are the values of net worth (in thousands of dollars) of the members of the executive branch of the current U.S. government. Test these values for normality, then take the logarithm of each value and test for normality. What do you conclude?

82490	27650	26652	21454	11494	10463	7291	5613	3784	3671	3466	3435	3395
3044	2287	1332	1305	878	872	783	556	463	397	145	27	

6-7   Normal as Approximation to Binomial

Key Concept This section presents a method for using a normal distribution as an approximation to a binomial probability distribution, so that some problems involving proportions can be solved by using a normal distribution. Here are the two main points of this section:

- For a proportion p, if the conditions $np \geq 5$ and $nq \geq 5$ are both satisfied, then probabilities from a binomial probability distribution can be approximated reasonably well by using a normal distribution with these parameters: $\mu = np$ and $\sigma = \sqrt{npq}$.

- Because a binomial probability distribution typically uses only whole numbers for the random variable x, but the normal approximation is continuous, we use a "continuity correction" with a whole number x represented by the interval from $x - 0.5$ to $x + 0.5$.

Brief Review In Section 5-3 we noted that a *binomial probability distribution* has (1) a fixed number of trials; (2) trials that are independent; (3) trials that are each classified into two categories commonly referred to as *success* and *failure*; (4) trials with the property that the probability of success remains constant. Section 5-3 also introduced the following notation.

Notation

$n =$ the fixed number of trials

$x =$ the specific number of successes in n trials

$p =$ probability of *success* in *one* of the n trials

$q =$ probability of *failure* in *one* of the n trials (so $q = 1 - p$)

Rationale for Using Normal Approximation Instead of providing a theoretical derivation proving that a normal distribution can approximate a binomial distribution, we simply demonstrate it with an illustration involving this situation: In 431 professional football games that went to overtime, the teams that won the coin toss went on to win 235 games (based on data from "The Overtime Rule in the National Football League: Fair or Unfair?" by Gorgievski et al., *MathAMATYC Educator*, Vol. 2, No. 1). If we assume that the coin toss is fair, the probability of winning the game after winning the coin toss should be 0.5. With $p = 0.5$ and $n = 431$ games, we get a binomial probability distribution that is graphed in the accompanying Minitab display. The graph shows the probability for each number of wins from 180 to 250. (The other possible numbers of wins have probabilities that are very close to 0.) See how the graph of the binomial probabilities is close to being a normal distribution. This graph suggests that we can use a normal distribution to approximate the binomial distribution.

MINITAB

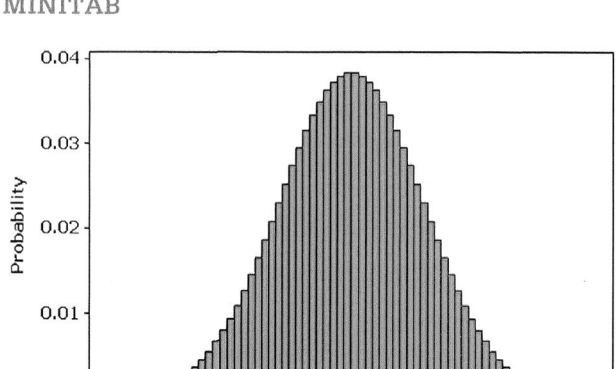

Number of Wins In 431 Games

Normal Distribution as an Approximation to the Binomial Distribution

Requirements

1. The sample is a simple random sample of size n from a population in which the proportion of successes is p, or the sample is the result of conducting n independent trials of a binomial experiment in which the probability of success is p.

2. $np \geq 5$ and $nq \geq 5$.

Normal Approximation

If the above requirements are satisfied, then the probability distribution of the random variable x can be approximated by a normal distribution with these parameters:

- $\mu = np$
- $\sigma = \sqrt{npq}$

Continuity Correction

When using the normal approximation, adjust the discrete whole number x by using a *continuity correction* so that x is represented by the interval from $x - 0.5$ to $x + 0.5$.

Note that the requirements include verification of $np \geq 5$ and $nq \geq 5$. The minimum value of 5 is common, but it isn't an absolutely rigid value, and a few textbooks use 10 instead. This requirement is included in the following procedure for using a normal approximation to a binomial distribution.

Procedure for Using a Normal Distribution to Approximate a Binomial Distribution

1. Verify the two preceding requirements. (If these requirements are not both satisfied, then you must use computer software, or a calculator, or Table A-1, or calculations using the binomial probability formula.)

2. The normal distribution requires values for μ and σ, so find those values by calculating $\mu = np$ and $\sigma = \sqrt{npq}$.

3. Identify the discrete whole number x that is relevant to the binomial probability problem being considered.

   Example: If you're trying to find the probability of getting at least 235 successes among 431 trials (as in Example 1), the discrete whole number of concern is $x = 235$. First focus on the value of 235 itself, and temporarily ignore whether you want at least 235, more than 235, fewer than 235, at most 235, or exactly 235.

4. Draw a normal distribution centered about the value of μ, then draw a *vertical strip area* centered over x. Mark the left side of the strip at $x - 0.5$, and mark the right side at $x + 0.5$.

   Example: For $x = 235$, draw a strip from 234.5 to 235.5 and *consider the entire area of the entire strip to represent the probability of the discrete whole number 235.*

5. Determine whether the value of x itself should be included in the probability you want. Shade the area to the right or left of the strip from Step 4, as appropriate; shade the *interior* of the strip *if and only if x itself* is to be included. This total shaded region corresponds to the probability being sought.

   Example: The phrase "at least 235" *does* include 235 itself, but "more than 235" *does not* include 235 itself.

6. Using either $x - 0.5$ or $x + 0.5$ in place of x itself, find the area of the shaded region from Step 5 as follows:

   i. Find the z score: $z = (x - \mu)/\sigma$ (replacing x with either $x + 0.5$ or $x - 0.5$).

   ii. Use that z score to find the cumulative area to the left of the adjusted value of x.

   iii. The cumulative left area can now be used to identify the shaded area corresponding to the desired probability.

Example 1 Is the NFL Coin Toss Fair?

In 431 NFL football games that went to overtime, the teams that won the coin toss went on to win 235 of those games. If the coin-toss method is fair, we expect that the teams winning the coin toss would win about 50% of the games, so we expect about 215.5 wins in 431 overtime games. Assuming that there is a 0.5 probability of winning a game after winning the coin toss, find the probability of getting at least 235 winning games among the 431 teams that won the coin toss. That is, given $n = 431$ and $p = 0.5$, find P(at least 235 wins).

Solution

The given problem involves a binomial distribution with $n = 431$ independent trials. When a team wins the coin toss in overtime, there are two categories for each outcome: The team goes on to win the game or does not win. The assumed probability of winning ($p = 0.5$) presumably remains constant from game to game. Calculations with the binomial probability formula are not practical, because we would have to apply it 197 times, once for each value of x from 235 to 431 inclusive. Software and calculators can be used to find that the probability is 0.0335, but we will proceed to show how the normal approximation method can be used. We use the preceding six-step procedure.

Step 1: Requirement check: The 431 overtime NFL games are from recent years, but we will proceed under the assumption that we have a simple random sample. We must also verify that $np \geq 5$ and $nq \geq 5$. With $n = 431$ and $p = 0.5$ and $q = 0.5$, those requirements are both satisfied with $np = 215.5$ and $nq = 215.5$.

Step 2: We now proceed to find μ and σ needed for the normal distribution. We get the following:

$$\mu = np = 431 \cdot 0.5 = 215.5$$

$$\sigma = \sqrt{npq} = \sqrt{431 \cdot 0.5 \cdot 0.5} = 10.380270$$

Step 3: We want the probability of at least 235 wins, so the discrete whole number relevant to this example is $x = 235$.

Step 4: See Figure 6-19, which shows the normal distribution and the vertical strip from 234.5 to 235.5.

Step 5: We want to find the probability of getting *at least* 235 *wins,* so we want to shade the vertical strip representing 235 as well as the area to its right. The desired area is shaded in Figure 6-19.

Step 6: We want the area to the right of 234.5 in Figure 6-19. If using technology, we find that the shaded area in Figure 6-19 is 0.0336. If using Table A-2, we must first find the z score using $x = 234.5$, $\mu = 215.5$, and $\sigma = 10.380270$ as follows:

$$z = \frac{x - \mu}{\sigma} = \frac{234.5 - 215.5}{10.380270} = 1.83$$

Using Table A-2, we find that $z = 1.83$ corresponds to cumulative left area of 0.9664, so the shaded region in Figure 6-19 is $1 - 0.9664 = 0.0336$.

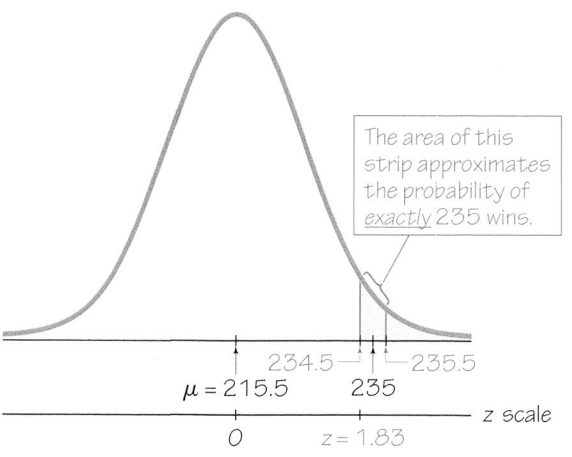

The area of this strip approximates the probability of *exactly* 235 wins.

234.5   235.5

$\mu = 215.5$ 235

z scale

0    $z = 1.83$

Figure 6-19   Probability of 235 Wins

Interpretation

If we assume that the overtime coin toss does not favor either team, then among 431 teams that won the overtime coin toss, there is a 0.0336 probability of at least 235 wins. This probability is low enough to suggest that the team winning the coin toss has an advantage over the team losing the coin toss. Given that winning the overtime coin toss provides an unfair advantage, it appears that overtime rules should be modified to reduce or eliminate that unfair advantage.

Continuity Correction

The procedure for using a normal distribution to approximate a binomial distribution includes a *continuity correction,* defined as follows.

> **DEFINITION** When we use the normal distribution (which is a *continuous* probability distribution) as an approximation to the binomial distribution (which is *discrete*), a **continuity correction** is made to a discrete whole number x in the binomial distribution by representing the discrete whole number x by the *interval* from $x - 0.5$ to $x + 0.5$ (that is, adding and subtracting 0.5).

In the preceding six-step procedure for using a normal distribution to approximate a binomial distribution, Steps 3 and 4 incorporate the continuity correction. (See Steps 3 and 4 in the solutions to Examples 1 and 2.)

To see examples of continuity corrections, examine the common cases illustrated in Figure 6-20. Those cases correspond to the statements in the following list:

Statement	Area
At least 235 (includes 235 and above)	To the *right* of 234.5
More than 235 (doesn't include 235)	To the *right* of 235.5
At most 235 (includes 235 and below)	To the *left* of 235.5
Fewer than 235 (doesn't include 235)	To the *left* of 234.5
Exactly 235	Between 234.5 and 235.5

Example 2   **Exactly 235 Wins**

Using the same information from Example 1, find the probability of *exactly* 235 wins by the 431 teams that won the coin toss in overtime. That is, given $n = 431$ and assuming that $p = 0.5$, find $P(\text{exactly } 235 \text{ wins})$. Is this result useful for determining whether the overtime coin toss is fair?

Solution

Using the same six-step procedure given earlier, Steps 1, 2, and 3 are the same as in Example 1.

Step 4: See Figure 6-21, which shows the normal distribution with $\mu = 215.5$ and $\sigma = 10.380270$. Also, the shaded area represents the probability of *exactly* 235 wins. That region is the vertical strip between 234.5 and 235.5, as shown.

Step 5: Because we want the probability of *exactly* 235 wins, we want only the shaded area shown in Figure 6-21.

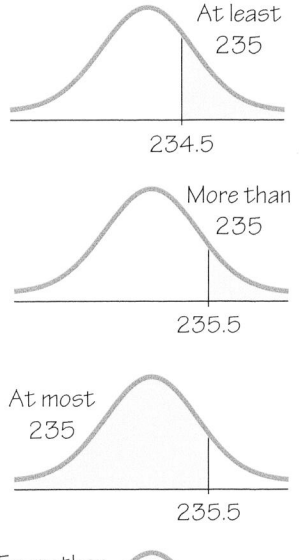

Figure 6-20
Using Continuity Corrections

continued

Step 6: If using technology to find the shaded region in Figure 6-21, we get 0.0066. If using Table A-2 to find the shaded area in Figure 6-21, we find the two z scores corresponding to 234.5 and 235.5. We use those two z scores to find the cumulative area to the left of 234.5 and the cumulative area to the left of 235.5, then we find the *difference* between those two areas. Let's begin with the total area to the left of 235.5. If using Table A-2, we must first find the z score corresponding to 235.5. We get

$$z = \frac{235.5 - 215.5}{10.380270} = 1.93$$

We use Table A-2 to find that $z = 1.93$ has a cumulative left area of 0.9732. Now we find the area to the left of 234.5 by first finding its corresponding z score:

$$z = \frac{234.5 - 215.5}{10.380270} = 1.83$$

We use Table A-2 to find that $z = 1.83$ corresponds to a cumulative left area of 0.9664. Using Table A-2 the shaded area of Figure 6-21 is $0.9732 - 0.9664 = 0.0068$.

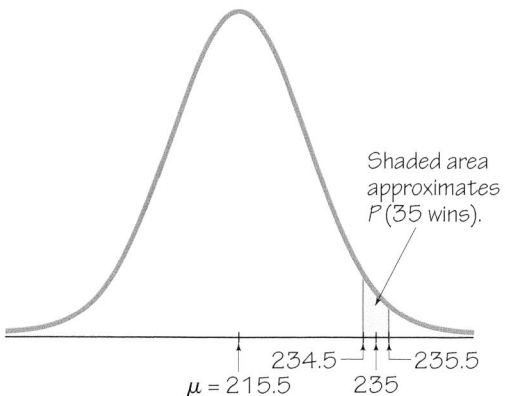

Figure 6-21   Probability of Exactly 235 Wins

Interpretation

If we assume that the overtime coin toss does not favor either team, then among 431 teams that won the overtime coin toss, the probability of *exactly* 235 wins is 0.0068. This result is not very helpful in determining whether the overtime coin toss is fair. If the coin toss gives no advantage, we expect that in 431 overtime games, the team winning the coin toss would win about 215.5 times (about half of the time). But we see that there are 235 wins, which is more than 215.5. The relevant result is the probability of getting a result *at least as extreme* as the one obtained, so the relevant result is the probability of *at least* 235 wins (as in Example 1), not the probability of exactly 235 wins (as in this example). See the following comments about interpreting results, and see Section 5-2 for the comments under the heading of "Unusually High or Unusually Low Number of Successes: Not *Exactly,* but At Least as Extreme."

Interpreting Results

When we use a normal distribution as an approximation to a binomial distribution, our ultimate goal is not simply to find a probability number. We often need to make some *judgment* based on the probability value. The following criterion (from Section 5-2) describes the use of probabilities to determine whether results could easily occur by chance.

Using Probabilities to Determine When Results Are Unusual

- **Unusually *high* number of successes:** x successes among n trials is an *unusually high* number of successes if the probability of x or more successes is unlikely with a probability of 0.05 or less. This criterion can be expressed as follows: $P(x \text{ or more}) \leq 0.05$.*

- **Unusually *low* number of successes:** x successes among n trials is an *unusually low* number of successes if the probability of x or fewer successes is unlikely with a probability of 0.05 or less. This criterion can be expressed as follows: $P(x \text{ or fewer}) \leq 0.05$.*

---

* The value 0.05 is not absolutely rigid. Other values, such as 0.01, could be used to distinguish between results that can easily occur by chance and events that are very unlikely to occur by chance.

6-7 Basic Skills and Concepts

Statistical Literacy and Critical Thinking

1. Exact Value and Approximation Refer to Figure 6-21 in Example 2, and refer to the Minitab display near the beginning of this section. Figure 6-21 shows the shaded region representing exactly 235 wins among 431 games. What is the shape of the corresponding region in the Minitab display? If we use technology without an approximation, the probability of exactly 235 wins is found to be 0.0066. If we use the normal approximation to the binomial distribution, the probability of exactly 235 wins is found from Table A-2 to be 0.0068. Which result is better? Is the approximation off by much?

2. Continuity Correction In a preliminary test of the MicroSort method of gender selection, 14 couples were treated and 13 of them had baby girls. If we plan to use the normal approximation to the binomial distribution for finding the probability of exactly 13 girls (assuming that the probability of a girl is 0.5), what is the continuity correction, and how would it be applied in finding that probability?

3. Notation The SAT test uses multiple-choice test questions, each with possible answers of a, b, c, d, e, and each question has only one correct answer. For people who make random guesses for answers to a block of 25 questions, identify the values of p, q, μ, and σ. What do μ and σ measure?

4. Checking Requirement The SAT test uses multiple-choice test questions, each with possible answers of a, b, c, d, e, and each question has only one correct answer. We want to find the probability of getting exactly 10 correct answers for someone who makes random guesses for answers to a block of 25 questions. If we plan to use the methods of this section with a normal distribution used to approximate a binomial distribution, are the necessary requirements satisfied? Explain.

Using Normal Approximation. *In Exercises 5–8, do the following: If the requirements of $np \geq 5$ and $nq \geq 5$ are both satisfied, estimate the indicated probability by using the normal distribution as an approximation to the binomial distribution; if $np < 5$ or $nq < 5$, then state that the normal approximation should not be used.*

5. With $n = 13$ and $p = 0.4$, find $P(\text{fewer than } 3)$.

6. With $n = 12$ and $p = 0.7$, find $P(\text{fewer than } 8)$.

7. With $n = 20$ and $p = 0.8$, find $P(\text{more than } 11)$.

8. With $n = 25$ and $p = 0.4$, find $P(\text{more than } 9)$.

Voters.   *In Exercises 9–12, use a normal approximation to find the probability of the indicated number of voters. In each case, assume that 100 eligible voters aged 18–24 are randomly selected. The most recent Census Bureau results show that among eligible voters aged 18–24, 22% of them voted.*

9. Probability that fewer than 20 voted

10. Probability that at least 25 voted

11. Probability of exactly 23 voters

12. Probability of exactly 19 voters

13. Tennis Replay In the year that this exercise was written, there were 611 challenges made to referee calls in professional tennis singles play. Among those challenges, 172 were upheld with the call overturned. Assume that 30% of the challenges are successfully upheld with the call overturned.

a. Find the probability that among the 611 challenges, the number of overturned calls is exactly 172.

b. Of the 611 challenges, the number of 172 overturned calls is fewer than 30%. Find the probability that among the 611 challenges, the number of overturned calls is 172 or fewer. If the 30% rate is correct, is 172 overturned calls for 611 challenges an unusually low number?

c. Which result is useful for determining whether the 30% rate is correct: part (a) or part (b)? Explain.

d. Is there strong evidence to suggest that the rate of overturned calls is not 30%?

14. Tennis Replay Repeat the preceding exercise after changing the assumed rate of overturned calls from 30% to 33%.

15. Mendelian Genetics When Mendel conducted his famous genetics experiments with peas, one sample of offspring consisted of 580 peas, with 428 of them having green pods. If we assume, as Mendel did, that under these circumstances, there is a 3/4 probability that a pea will have a green pod, we would expect that 435 of the peas would have green pods, so the result of 428 peas with green pods is fewer than expected. For the following, assume that the probability of a pea having a green pod is 3/4.

a. Find the probability that among the 580 offspring peas, exactly 428 of them have green pods.

b. The result of 428 peas with green pods is fewer than 3/4 of 580. Find the probability that among the 580 offspring peas, 428 or fewer have green pods. Is the result of 428 peas with green pods unusually low?

c. Which result is useful for determining whether Mendel's claimed rate of 75% is incorrect: part (a) or part (b)? Explain.

d. Is there strong evidence to suggest that Mendel's probability of 3/4 is wrong?

16. Dream Job In a Marist College poll of 1004 adults, 291 chose professional athlete as their dream job. Assume that 25% of adults consider being a professional athlete their dream job.

a. The result of 291 is more than 25% of 1004, so find the probability that among 1004 random adults, 291 or more consider being a professional athlete their dream job.

b. If the value of 25% is correct, is the result of 291 unusually high?

c. Does the result suggest that the rate is greater than 25%?

17. XSORT Gender Selection MicroSort's XSORT gender-selection technique is designed to increase the likelihood that a baby will be a girl. In updated results (as of this writing) of the XSORT gender-selection technique, 945 births consisted of 879 baby girls and 66 baby boys (based on data from the Genetics & IVF Institute). In analyzing these results, assume that the XSORT method has no effect so that boys and girls are equally likely.

a. Find the probability of getting exactly 879 girls in 945 births.

b. Find the probability of getting 879 or more girls in 945 births. If boys and girls are equally likely, is 879 girls in 945 births unusually high?

c. Which probability is relevant for trying to determine whether the XSORT method is effective: the result from part (a) or the result from part (b)?

d. Based on the results, does it appear that the XSORT method is effective? Why or why not?

18. Washing Hands Based on *observed* males using public restrooms, 85% of adult males wash their hands in a public restroom (based on data from the American Society for Microbiology and the American Cleaning Institute). In a survey of 523 adult males, 518 *reported* that they wash their hands in a public restroom. Assuming that the 85% observed rate is correct, find the probability that among 523 randomly selected adult males, 518 or more wash their hands in a public restroom. What do you conclude?

19. Voters Lying? In a survey of 1002 people, 701 said that they voted in a recent presidential election (based on data from ICR Research Group). Voting records show that 61% of eligible voters actually did vote. Given that 61% of eligible voters actually did vote, find the probability that among 1002 randomly selected eligible voters, at least 701 actually did vote. What does the result suggest?

20. Cell Phones and Brain Cancer In a study of 420,095 cell phone users in Denmark, it was found that 135 developed cancer of the brain or nervous system. Assuming that the use of cell phones has no effect on developing such cancers, there is a 0.000340 probability of a person developing cancer of the brain or nervous system. We therefore expect about 143 cases of such cancers in a group of 420,095 randomly selected people. Estimate the probability of 135 or fewer cases of such cancers in a group of 420,095 people. What do these results suggest about media reports that cell phones cause cancer of the brain or nervous system?

21. Smoking Based on a recent Harris Interactive survey, 20% of adults in the United States smoke. In a survey of 50 statistics students, it is found that 6 of them smoke. Find the probability that should be used for determining whether the 20% rate is correct for statistics students. What do you conclude?

22. Smoking Repeat the preceding exercise after changing the results so that among 50 statistics students, it is found that 3 smoke.

23. Online TV In a Comcast survey of 1000 adults, 17% said that they watch prime-time TV online. If we assume that 20% of adults watch prime-time TV online, find the probability that should be used to determine whether the 20% rate is correct or whether it should be lower than 20%? What do you conclude?

24. Internet Access Of U.S. households, 67% have Internet access (based on data from the Census Bureau). In a random sample of 250 households, 70% are found to have Internet access. Find the probability that should be used to determine whether the 67% rate is too low. What do you conclude?

6-7 Beyond the Basics

25. Decision Theory Marc Taylor plans to place 200 bets of $5 each on a game at the Mirage casino in Las Vegas.

a. One strategy is to bet on the number 7 at roulette. A win pays off with odds of 35:1 and, on any one spin, there is a probability of 1/38 that 7 will be the winning number. Among the

200 bets, what is the minimum number of wins needed for Marc to make a profit? Find the probability that Marc will make a profit.

b. Another strategy is to bet on the pass line in the dice game of craps. A win pays off with odds of 1:1 and, on any one game, there is a probability of 244/495 that he will win. Among the 200 bets, what is the minimum number of wins needed for Marc to make a profit? Find the probability that Marc will make a profit.

c. Based on the preceding results, which game is the better "investment": the roulette game from part (a) or the craps game from part (b)? Why?

26. Overbooking a Boeing 767-300 A Boeing 767-300 aircraft has 213 seats. When someone buys a ticket for a flight, there is a 0.0995 probability that the person will not show up for the flight (based on data from an IBM research paper by Lawrence, Hong, and Cherrier). How many reservations could be accepted for a Boeing 767-300 for there to be at least a 0.95 probability that all reservation holders who show will be accommodated?

Chapter 6   Review

In this chapter we introduced the normal probability distribution—the most important distribution in the study of statistics.

Section 6-2 Section 6-2 introduced the standard normal distribution, which is a normal distribution with these parameters: $\mu = 0$ and $\sigma = 1$. Two extremely important basic procedures are presented in Section 6-2:

1. Given some z score, find an area under the curve representing the graph of the standard normal distribution.

2. Given some area under the curve representing the standard normal distribution, find the corresponding z score.

Section 6-3 In Section 6-3 we extended the methods from Section 6-2 so that we could work with any normal distribution, not just the standard normal distribution. A key element of Section 6-3 is the formula $z = (x - \mu)/\sigma$ that allows us to convert from a nonstandard normal distribution to the standard normal distribution so that we can solve problems such as these:

1. Given that IQ scores are normally distributed with $\mu = 100$ and $\sigma = 15$, find the probability of randomly selecting someone with an IQ above 90.

2. Given that IQ scores are normally distributed with $\mu = 100$ and $\sigma = 15$, find the IQ score separating the bottom 85% from the top 15%.

Section 6-4 In Section 6-4 we introduced the concept of a sampling distribution of a statistic. The sampling distribution of the sample mean is the probability distribution of sample means, with all samples having the same sample size n. The sampling distribution of the sample proportion is the probability distribution of sample proportions, with all samples having the same sample size n. In general, the sampling distribution of any statistic is the probability distribution of that statistic.

Section 6-5 In Section 6-5 we presented the following so that we could address many important problems involving sample means:

1. The distribution of sample means $\bar{x}$ will, as the sample size n increases, approach a normal distribution.

2. The mean of the sample means is the population mean μ.

3. The standard deviation of the sample means is $\sigma/\sqrt{n}$.

Section 6-6   In Section 6-6 we presented procedures for determining whether sample data appear to come from a population that has a normal distribution. Some of the statistical methods covered later in this book have a loose requirement of a normally distributed population. In such cases, examination of a histogram and outliers might be all that is needed. In other cases, normal quantile plots might be necessary because of factors such as a small sample or a very strict requirement that the population must have a normal distribution.

Section 6-7   In Section 6-7 we noted that a normal distribution can sometimes approximate a binomial probability distribution. Consequently, when working with probabilities or proportions or percentages, we can often use a normal distribution. If both $np \geq 5$ and $nq \geq 5$, the binomial random variable x is approximately normally distributed with the mean and standard deviation given as $\mu = np$ and $\sigma = \sqrt{npq}$. Because the binomial probability distribution deals with discrete data and the normal distribution deals with continuous data, we apply the continuity correction, with the interval from $x - 0.5$ to $x + 0.5$ representing the discrete value of x.

Chapter Quick Quiz

1. Identify the values of μ and σ for the standard normal distribution.

Bone Density Test.   *In Exercises 2–5, assume that scores on a bone mineral density test are normally distributed with a mean of 0 and a standard deviation of 1.*

2. Sketch a graph showing the shape of the distribution of bone density test scores.

3. Find the score separating the lowest 98% of scores from the highest 2%.

4. For a randomly selected subject, find the probability of a score greater than -1.

5. For a randomly selected subject, find the probability of a score between 1.37 and 2.42.

In Exercises 6–10, assume that red blood cell counts of women are normally distributed with a mean of 4.577 and a standard deviation of 0.382.

6. Find the probability that a randomly selected woman has a red blood cell count below the normal range of 4.2 to 5.4.

7. Find the probability that a randomly selected woman has a red blood cell count above the normal range of 4.2 to 5.4.

8. Find P_{80}, the 80th percentile for the red blood cell counts of women.

9. If 25 women are randomly selected, find the probability that the mean of their red blood cell counts is less than 4.444.

10. What percentage of women have red blood cell counts in the normal range from 4.2 to 5.4?

Review Exercises

1. Bone Density Test A bone mineral density test is used to identify a bone disease. The result of a bone density test is commonly measured as a z score, and the population of z scores is normally distributed with a mean of 0 and a standard deviation of 1.

a. For a randomly selected subject, find the probability of a bone density test score less than 2.93.

b. For a randomly selected subject, find the probability of a bone density test score greater than -1.53.

c. For a randomly selected subject, find the probability of a bone density test score between -1.07 and 2.07.

d. Find P_{30}, the bone density test score separating the bottom 30% from the top 70%.

e. If the mean bone density test score is found for 16 randomly selected subjects, find the probability that the mean is greater than 0.27.

 2. Door Peephole Standing eye heights of women are normally distributed with a mean of 1516 mm and a standard deviation of 63 mm (based on anthropometric survey data from Gordon, Churchill, et al.).

a. A door peephole is placed at a height that is uncomfortable for women with standing eye heights greater than 1605 mm. What percentage of women will find that height uncomfortable?

b. In selecting the height of a door peephole, the architect wants its height to be suitable for the highest 99% of standing eye heights of women. What standing eye height of women separates the highest 99% of standing eye heights from the lowest 1%?

 3. Window Placement Standing eye heights of men are normally distributed with a mean of 1634 mm and a standard deviation of 66 mm (based on anthropometric survey data from Gordon, Churchill, et al.).

a. If a window is positioned so that it is comfortable for men with standing eye heights greater than 1500 mm, what percentage of men will find that height comfortable?

b. A window is positioned to be comfortable for the lowest 95% of eye heights of men. What standing eye height of men separates the lowest 95% from the highest 5%?

4. Sampling Distributions Scores on the ACT test have a distribution that is approximately normal with mean 21.1 and standard deviation 5.1. A sample of 80 ACT scores is randomly selected and the sample mean is computed.

a. Describe the distribution of such sample means.

b. What is the mean of all such sample means?

c. What is the standard deviation of all such sample means?

5. Unbiased Estimators

a. What is an unbiased estimator?

b. For the following statistics, identify those that are unbiased estimators: mean, median, range, variance, proportion.

c. Determine whether the following statement is true or false: "The sample standard deviation is a biased estimator, but the bias is relatively small in large samples, so s is often used to estimate σ."

 6. Monorail and Airliner Doors The Mark VI monorail used at Disney World has doors with a height of 72 in. Heights of men are normally distributed with a mean of 69.5 in. and a standard deviation of 2.4 in. (based on Data Set 1 in Appendix B).

a. What percentage of adult men can fit through the doors without bending? Does the door design with a height of 72 in. appear to be adequate? Explain.

b. What doorway height would allow 99% of adult men to fit without bending?

 7. Aircraft Safety Standards Under older Federal Aviation Administration rules, airlines were required to estimate the weight of a passenger as 185 lb. (That amount is for an adult traveling in winter, and it includes 20 lb of carry-on baggage.) Rules were revised to use an estimate of 195 lb. Men now have weights that are normally distributed with a mean of 182.9 lb and a standard deviation of 40.9 lb (based on Data Set 1 in Appendix B).

a. If 1 adult male is randomly selected and is assumed to have 20 lb of carry-on baggage, find the probability that his total weight is greater than 195 lb.

b. If a Boeing 767-300 aircraft is full of 213 adult male passengers and each is assumed to have 20 lb of carry-on baggage, find the probability that the mean passenger weight (including carry-on baggage) is greater than 195 lb. Based on that probability, does a pilot have to be concerned about exceeding this weight limit?

8. Assessing Normality Listed below are the current salaries (in thousands of dollars) of players on the New York Yankees baseball team.

a. Do these salaries appear to come from a population that has a normal distribution? Why or why not?

b. Can the mean of this sample be treated as a value from a population having a normal distribution? Why or why not?

403	1250	16500	1400	6000	433	403	13000	414	21600	3750	13000	2125
6550	400	5500	13100	422	455	15000	33000	15286	5400	20625	433	5000

9. Genetics Experiment In one of Mendel's experiments with plants, 1064 offspring consisted of 787 plants with long stems. According to Mendel's theory, 3/4 of the offspring plants should have long stems. Assuming that Mendel's proportion of 3/4 is correct, find the probability of getting 787 or fewer plants with long stems among 1064 offspring plants. Based on the result, is 787 offspring plants with long stems unusually low? What does the result imply about Mendel's claimed proportion of 3/4?

10. Job Applicant Background Check There is an 80% chance that a prospective employer will check the educational background of a job applicant (based on data from the Bureau of National Affairs, Inc.). Sixty-four job applications are randomly selected.

a. Find the probability that at least 50 of the applicants have their educational backgrounds checked.

b. Find the probability that exactly 50 of the applicants have their educational backgrounds checked.

Cumulative Review Exercises

Please be aware that some of the following problems may require knowledge of concepts presented in previous chapters.

1. Miami Heat The following are current annual salaries (in thousands of dollars) for the starting players on the Miami Heat basketball team: 14,500, 14,500, 14,000, 5000, 3500.

a. Find the mean $\bar{x}$ and express the result in dollars instead of thousands of dollars.

b. Find the median and express the result in dollars instead of thousands of dollars.

c. Find the standard deviation s and express the result in dollars instead of thousands of dollars.

d. Find the variance s^2 and express the result in appropriate units.

e. Convert the first salary of $14,500,000 to a z score.

f. What level of measurement (nominal, ordinal, interval, ratio) describes this data set?

g. Are the salaries discrete data or continuous data?

h. Do the given salaries appear to be representative of all players for the Miami Heat team? Why or why not?

2. College as an Investment Assume that 10% of us believe that college is not a good investment (based on a survey in *USA Today*).

a. Let *A* denote the event of selecting someone who believes that college is not a good investment. What does the event $\overline{A}$ denote?

b. Find the value of $P(\overline{A})$.

c. Find the probability of randomly selecting three different people and finding that each of them has the belief that college is not a good investment.

d. The given rate of 10% is based on results from Internet users who chose to respond to a question posted on the *USA Today* web site. What is this type of sample called? What does this suggest about the accuracy of the 10% rate?

3. Birth Weights Birth weights in the United States have a distribution that is approximately normal with a mean of 3369 g and a standard deviation of 567 g (based on data from "Comparison of Birth Weight Distributions between Chinese and Caucasian Infants," by Wen, Kramer, Usher, *American Journal of Epidemiology*, Vol. 172, No. 10).

a. One definition of a premature baby is that the birth weight is below 2500 g. If a baby is randomly selected, find the probability of a birth weight below 2500 g.

b. Another definition of a premature baby is that the birth weight is in the bottom 10%. Find the birth weight that is the cutoff between the bottom 10% and the top 90%.

c. A definition of a "very low birth weight" is one that is less than 1500 g. If a baby is randomly selected, find the probability of a "very low birth weight."

d. If 25 babies are randomly selected, find the probability that their mean birth weight is greater than 3400 g.

4. POTUS The accompanying graph is a histogram of ages of U.S. presidents at the time they were inaugurated (from Data Set 12 in Appendix B).

a. Identify two features of the vertical scale that cause the graph to be somewhat misleading.

b. Does the histogram appear to show data from a population having a normal distribution? Explain.

c. From the graph, identify the lowest and highest possible ages, then use the range rule of thumb to estimate the standard deviation of the ages. How does the result compare to the standard deviation of 6.6 years calculated from the original list of sample values?

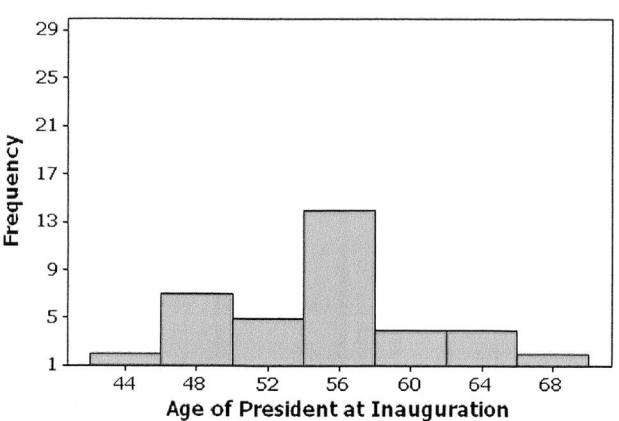

5. Left-Handedness According to data from the American Medical Association, 10% of us are left-handed.

a. If three people are randomly selected, find the probability that they are all left-handed.

b. If three people are randomly selected, find the probability that at least one of them is left-handed.

c. Why can't we solve the problem in part (b) by using the normal approximation to the binomial distribution?

d. If groups of 50 people are randomly selected, what is the mean number of left-handed people in such groups?

e. If groups of 50 people are randomly selected, what is the standard deviation for the numbers of left-handed people in such groups?

f. Use the range rule of thumb to determine whether it would be unusual to get 8 left-handed people in a randomly selected group of 50 people.

Technology Projects

Some methods in this chapter are easy with technology but very difficult without it. The two projects that follow illustrate how easy it is to use technology for assessing normality and finding binomial probabilities.

1. Assessing Normality It is often necessary to determine whether sample data appear to be from a normally distributed population, and that determination is helped with the construction of a histogram and normal quantile plot. Construction of a histogram is relatively simple but time-consuming, and construction of a normal quantile plot can be a real challenge without technology. This first project shows how easy it is to get those graphs by using STATDISK. With just a few clicks of a mouse, you can painlessly and quickly generate a histogram and normal quantile plot together. If STATDISK has not yet been used, it can be downloaded from www.statdisk.org.

The data sets in Appendix B are available by clicking on **Datasets** on the top menu bar, then selecting the textbook you are using. STATDISK can be used to assess normality of a sample by clicking on **Data** and selecting the menu item of **Normality Assessment.** Use the Normality Assessment feature with the female body measurements in Data Set 1 of Appendix B. For each of the 14 columns of data, determine whether the data appear to be from a normally distributed population.

2. Binomial Probabilities Section 6-7 described a method for using a normal distribution to approximate a binomial distribution. STATDISK, Minitab, Excel, StatCrunch, and the TI-83/84 Plus calculator are all capable of generating probabilities for a binomial distribution. Instructions for these different technologies are found in the Using Technology subsection at the end of Section 5-3. Instead of using a normal approximation to a binomial distribution, use technology to find the exact binomial probabilities in Exercises 9–12 of Section 6-7.

from data TO DECISION

Critical Thinking: Designing aircraft seats

When designing seats for aircraft, we want to have sufficient room so that passengers are comfortable and safe, but we don't want too much room, because fewer seats could be installed and profits would drop. It has been estimated that removing one row of seats would cost around $8 million over the life of an aircraft.

Figure 6-22(a) shows an important human consideration: The buttock-to-knee length. The accompanying table includes relevant buttock-to-knee length parameters obtained from studies of large numbers of people. Figure 6-22(b) shows a traditional aircraft seat, and Figure 6-22(c) shows the new SkyRider seat design by the Italian company Aviointeriors. The SkyRider seat is dramatically different from traditional aircraft seats. The seats are like saddles, and they are higher

so that passenger legs slant downward with weight on the legs. The most dramatic difference is that SkyRider seats have much less legroom. The distance of 23 in. shown in Figure 6-22(c) is a distance of 30 in. to 32 in. for most current economy seats. As of this writing, the SkyRider seats have not yet been approved by the Federal Aviation Administration, but approval would allow a new class of seating with very low fares.

When designing aircraft seats, we must make some hard choices. If we are to accommodate *everyone* in the population, we will have a sitting distance that is so costly in terms of reduced seating that it might not be economically feasible. Some questions we must address are: (1) What percentage of the population are we willing to exclude? (2) How much extra room do we want to provide for passenger comfort and safety?

1. A common design criterion is to accommodate people falling between the 5th percentile and the 95th percentile. Find those values for the buttock-to-knee lengths of men and women.

2. Of the four values found in Exercise 1, which single value is most important? Explain.

3. Why do the values found in Exercise 1 not apply to the SkyRider seat?

4. Apart from the drastically reduced leg room, identify at least one other disadvantage of the SkyRider seat.

5. Seat pitch is defined to be the distance between the same point on two successive seats. In addition to buttock-to-knee length, what other important factor affects the choice of seat pitch?

6. Based on the preceding results, what would you tell an engineer who is designing and configuring seats for an aircraft?

Buttock-to-Knee Length (inches)

	Mean	St. Dev.	Distribution
Males	23.5 in.	1.1 in.	Normal
Females	22.7 in.	1.0 in.	Normal

• *Distance from the seat back cushion to the seat in front*
• *Buttock-to-knee length plus any additional distance to provide comfort*

(a)

Buttock-to-knee length

(b)

23"

(c)

Figure 6-22   Distances Used in the Design of Aircraft Seats

Cooperative Group Activities

1. Out-of-class activity Bring a tape measure to a movie theater, car, bus, train, or subway, and measure the distance between the front of your vertical seat cushion and the back of the seat in front. See the Data to Decision Project for the relevant lengths and parameters. Analyze the seating design and write a brief report of the results.

2. Out-of-class activity Use the Internet to find Pick 4 lottery results for 50 different drawings. Find the 50 different means. Graph a histogram of the original 400 digits that were selected, and graph a histogram of the 50 sample means. What important principle do you observe?

3. In-class activity Divide into groups of three or four students and address these issues affecting the design of manhole covers.

• Which of the following is most relevant for determining whether a manhole cover diameter of 24 in. is large enough: weights of men, weights of women, heights of men, heights of women, hip breadths of men, hip breadths of women, shoulder breadths of men, shoulder breadths of women?

• Why are manhole covers usually round? (This was once a popular interview question asked of applicants at IBM, and there are at least three good answers. One good answer is sufficient here.)

4. Out-of-class activity Divide into groups of three or four students. In each group, develop an original procedure to illustrate the central limit theorem. The main objective is to show that when you randomly select samples from a population, the means of those samples tend to be *normally* distributed, regardless of the nature of the population distribution. For this illustration, begin with some population of values that does not have a normal distribution.

5. In-class activity Divide into groups of three or four students. Using a coin to simulate births, each individual group member should simulate 25 births and record the number of simulated girls. Combine all results from the group and record $n =$ total number of births and $x =$ number of girls. Given batches of n births, compute the mean and standard deviation for the number of girls. Is the simulated result unusual? Why or why not?

6. In-class activity Divide into groups of three or four students. Select a set of data from Appendix B (excluding Data Sets 1, 3, 6, 9, 10, 12, 14, 15, 16, and 20, which were used in examples or exercises in Section 6-6). Use the methods of Section 6-6 to construct a histogram and normal quantile plot, then determine whether the data set appears to come from a normally distributed population.

7 Estimates and Sample Sizes

chapter problem

Poll: Do you know what Twitter is?

The Pew Research Center recently conducted a survey of 1007 U.S. adults and found that 85% of those surveyed know what Twitter is. Based on the results of that poll, media reports suggested that 85% of the adult population know what Twitter is. How do they know that? Did they somehow obtain survey results from the population of *all* adults in the U.S.? No. Those media reports are *estimates* based on the results from the poll.

Currently, there are 241,472,385 adults in the United States. Because the Twitter poll involved only 1007 respondents, we see that only 0.0004% of the population was polled. It is natural to question the accuracy of results based on a sample that is so small when compared to the ginormous size of the population. Statistics to the rescue! Using methods presented in this chapter, we can answer questions such as these:

- How do we actually use sample results to estimate values of population parameters? Specifically, if a sample of 1007 adults is polled and it is found that 85% of them know what Twitter is, what does that sample percentage tell us about the percentage for the whole population of adults?

- How accurate is the sample result of 85% likely to be?

- Given that only 1007 people were polled in the population of 241,472,385 adults, is the sample size too small to be meaningful?

- Does the *method* of selecting the sample units have much of an effect on the results?

We can answer the last question based on the sound sampling methods discussed in Chapter 1. The method of selecting the people or households to be surveyed most definitely has an effect on the results. The results are likely to be poor if a convenience sample or some other nonrandom sampling method is used. If the sample is a simple random sample, the results are likely to be good. Because the Pew Research Center uses sophisticated sampling methods that are very carefully planned, its results are generally quite good. The Pew Research Center is a reputable polling company that uses sound sampling methods, so it is reasonable to treat the sample of 1007 adults as a simple random sample.

Our ability to understand polls and surveys and to interpret the results is crucial for our role as citizens. As we consider the topics of this chapter, we will learn much about polls and surveys and how to correctly interpret and present results.

7-1   Review and Preview

In Chapters 2 and 3 we used *descriptive statistics* when we summarized data using tools such as graphs and statistics such as the mean and standard deviation. This and following chapters present methods of *inferential statistics* that involve the use of sample data to form generalizations or inferences about a population. See the following two major activities.

Major Activities of Inferential Statistics

1. Use sample data to estimate values of population parameters (such as a population proportion or population mean).

2. Test hypotheses (or claims) made about population parameters.

In this chapter we begin working with the true core of inferential statistics as we use sample data to estimate values of population parameters. For example, the Chapter Problem refers to a survey of 1007 adults, and we see that 85% of them know what Twitter is. Based on the sample statistic of 85%, we will estimate the percentage of *all* U.S. adults who know what Twitter is. In so doing, we are using sample results to make an inference about the population.

This chapter focuses on the use of sample data to estimate a population parameter, and Chapter 8 will introduce the basic methods for testing claims (or hypotheses) that have been made about a population parameter.

Brief Review Because Sections 7-2 and 7-3 use *critical values,* it is helpful to review this notation introduced in Section 6-2: z_α denotes the z score with an area of α to its right. (α is the Greek letter alpha.) See Example 8 in Section 6-2, where it is shown that if $\alpha = 0.025$, the critical value is $z_{0.025} = 1.96$. That is, for the standard normal distribution, the critical value of $z_{0.025} = 1.96$ has an area of 0.025 to its right.

7-2   Estimating a Population Proportion

Key Concept This section presents methods for using a sample proportion to make an inference about the value of the corresponding population proportion. Here are the three main concepts included in this section:

- **Point Estimate:** The sample proportion (denoted by $\hat{p}$) is the best *point estimate* (or single value estimate) of the population proportion p.

- **Confidence Interval:** We can use a sample proportion to construct a *confidence interval* estimate of the true value of a population proportion, and we should know how to construct and interpret such confidence intervals.

- **Sample Size:** We should know how to find the sample size necessary to estimate a population proportion.

The concepts presented in this section are used in the following sections and chapters, so it is important to understand this section quite well.

Proportion, Probability, and Percent Although this section focuses on the population proportion p, we can also work with probabilities or percentages. When working with percentages, we will perform calculations with the equivalent proportion value.

In the Chapter Problem, for example, it was noted that 85% of 1007 surveyed adults know what Twitter is. The sample statistic of 85% can be expressed in decimal form as 0.85, so we will work with the sample proportion of $\hat{p} = 0.85$.

Point Estimate If we want to estimate a population proportion with a single value, the best estimate is the sample proportion $\hat{p}$. Because $\hat{p}$ consists of a single value, it is called a *point estimate*.

> **DEFINITION** A **point estimate** is a single value (or point) used to approximate a population parameter.

The sample proportion $\hat{p}$ is the best *point estimate* of the population proportion p.

We use $\hat{p}$ as the point estimate of p because it is unbiased and it is the most consistent of the estimators that could be used. (Unbiased estimators are discussed in Section 6-4.) The sample proportion $\hat{p}$ is the most consistent estimator of p in the sense that the standard deviation of sample proportions tends to be smaller than the standard deviation of other unbiased estimators of p.

Example 1   Twitter Poll

The Pew Research Center conducted a survey of 1007 adults and found that 85% of them know what Twitter is. Based on that result, find the best point estimate of the proportion of *all* adults who know what Twitter is.

Solution

Because the sample proportion is the best point estimate of the population proportion, we conclude that the best point estimate of p is 0.85. (If using the sample results to estimate the *percentage* of all adults who know what Twitter is, the best estimate is 85%.)

Why do We Need Confidence Intervals?

In Example 1 we saw that 0.85 was our *best* point estimate of the population proportion p, but a point estimate is a single value that gives us no indication of how *good* that best estimate is. Statisticians have cleverly developed the *confidence interval* or *interval estimate,* which consists of a range (or an interval) of values instead of just a single value. A confidence interval gives us a much better sense of how good an estimate is.

> **DEFINITION** A **confidence interval** (or **interval estimate**) is a range (or an interval) of values used to estimate the true value of a population parameter. A confidence interval is sometimes abbreviated as CI.

> **DEFINITION** The **confidence level** is the probability $1 - \alpha$ (such as 0.95, or 95%) that the confidence interval actually does contain the population parameter, assuming that the estimation process is repeated a large number of times. (The confidence level is also called the **degree of confidence,** or the **confidence coefficient.**)

Curbstoning

The glossary for the Census defines *curbstoning as* "the practice by which a census enumerator fabricates a questionnaire for a residence without actually visiting it." Curbstoning occurs when a census enumerator sits on a curbstone (or anywhere else) and fills out survey forms by making up responses. Because data from curbstoning are not real, they can affect the validity of the Census. The extent of curbstoning has been investigated in several studies, and one study showed that about 4% of Census enumerators practiced curbstoning at least some of the time.

The methods of Section 7-2 assume that the sample data have been collected in an appropriate way, so if much of the sample data have been obtained through curbstoning, then the resulting confidence interval estimates might be very flawed.

A confidence interval is associated with a specific confidence level, such as 0.95 (or 95%). The confidence level gives us the *success rate of the procedure* used to construct the confidence interval. See the following and notice the relationship between the confidence level and the corresponding value of α.

Most Common Confidence Levels	Corresponding Values of α
90% (or 0.90) confidence level:	$\alpha = 0.10$
95% (or 0.95) confidence level:	$\alpha = 0.05$
99% (or 0.99) confidence level:	$\alpha = 0.01$

The confidence level of 95% is most common because it provides a good balance between precision (as reflected in the width of the confidence interval) and reliability (as expressed by the confidence level).

Here's an example of a confidence interval found later (in Example 3), which is based on the sample data of 1007 adults polled, with 85% of them knowing what Twitter is:

The 0.95 (or 95%) confidence interval estimate of the population proportion p is $0.828 < p < 0.872$.

Interpreting a Confidence Interval

We must be careful to interpret confidence intervals correctly. There is a correct interpretation and many different and creative incorrect interpretations of the confidence interval $0.828 < p < 0.872$.

Correct: "We are 95% confident that the interval from 0.828 to 0.872 actually does contain the true value of the population proportion p." This means that if we were to select many different samples of size 1007 and construct the corresponding confidence intervals, 95% of them would actually contain the value of the population proportion p. (In this correct interpretation, the confidence level of 95% refers to the *success rate of the process* used to estimate the population proportion.)

Incorrect: "There is a 95% chance that the true value of p will fall between 0.828 and 0.872."

Incorrect: "95% of sample proportions will fall between 0.828 and 0.872."

CAUTION Know the correct interpretation of a confidence interval, as given above.

At any specific time, a population has a fixed and constant value of the proportion p, and a confidence interval constructed from a sample either includes p or does not. Similarly, if a baby has just been born and the doctor is about to announce its gender, it's incorrect to say that there is a probability of 0.5 that the baby is a girl; the baby is a girl or is not, and there's no probability involved. A population proportion p is like the baby that has been born—the value of p is fixed, so the confidence interval limits either contain p or do not, and that is why it's incorrect to say that there is a 95% chance that p will fall between values such as 0.828 and 0.872.

A confidence level of 95% tells us that the *process* we are using will, in the long run, result in confidence interval limits that contain the true population proportion 95% of the time. Suppose that the proportion of $p = 0.90$ is the true population proportion of all adults who know what Twitter is. Then the confidence interval obtained from the Pew Research Center poll does not contain the population proportion, because $p = 0.90$ is not between 0.828 and 0.872. Figure 7-1 illustrates this, and it also shows that 19 out of 20 (or 95%) different confidence intervals contain the assumed value of $p = 0.90$. Figure 7-1 is trying to tell the story that with a 95% confidence level, we expect about 19 out of 20 confidence intervals (or 95%) to contain the true value of p.

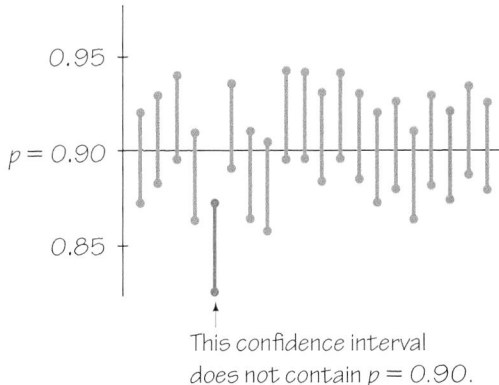

This confidence interval does not contain $p = 0.90$.

Figure 7-1   **Confidence Intervals from 20 Different Samples**

CAUTION Confidence intervals can be used informally to compare different data sets, but *the overlapping of confidence intervals should not be used for making formal and final conclusions about equality of proportions.* (See "On Judging the Significance of Differences by Examining the Overlap Between Confidence Intervals," by Schenker and Gentleman, *American Statistician,* Vol. 55, No. 3.)

Using Confidence Intervals for Hypothesis Tests

A confidence interval can be used to *test some claim* made about a population proportion p. Formal methods of hypothesis testing are introduced in Chapter 8, and those methods might require adjustments to confidence intervals that are not described in this chapter.

Some examples and exercises in this chapter require that we address some claim, but in this chapter we do not yet use a formal method of hypothesis testing, so we simply generate a confidence interval and make an *informal judgment* based on the result. For example, if sample results consist of 70 heads in 100 tosses of a coin, the resulting 95% confidence interval of $0.610 < p < 0.790$ can be used to *informally* support a claim that the proportion of heads is *greater than* 50%. (A one-sided claim is a statement that p is *greater than* some value or is *less than* some value, and a formal hypothesis test might require that we construct a one-sided confidence interval, as in Exercise 43, or adjust the confidence level by using 90% instead of 95%.)

BMI a Bad Measure?

The body mass index (BMI) of a person is calculated by finding their weight in kilograms and dividing it by the square of their height in meters. The Centers for Disease Control (CDC) publishes recommendations, including one stating that someone is obese if their BMI is 30.0 or higher. Keith Devlin wrote "Top 10 Reasons Why the BMI is Bogus" for *Your Health*, a podcast by NPR. He argues that, although it is commonly used, the BMI is not a valid measure of fat or obesity. He says that it makes no sense to square a person's height. Also, the BMI makes no adjustment for people with strong bones or good muscle tone. He says that a person with high body fat will have a high BMI, but a person with a high BMI will not necessarily have high body fat. He also says that using the BMI causes us to neglect using more reliable measures of obesity.

CAUTION Know that in this chapter, when we use a confidence interval to address a claim about a population proportion p, we simply make an *informal judgment* (that may or may not be consistent with formal methods of hypothesis testing introduced in Chapter 8).

Critical Values

The methods of this section (and many of the other statistical methods found in the following chapters) include reference to a standard z score that can be used to distinguish between sample statistics that are likely to occur and those that are unlikely. Such a z score is called a *critical value*. (Critical values were first presented in Section 6-2, and they are formally defined below.) Critical values are based on the following observations:

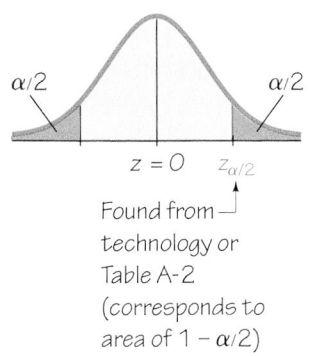

1. Under certain conditions, the sampling distribution of sample proportions can be approximated by a normal distribution, as shown in Figure 7-2.

2. A z score associated with a sample proportion has a probability of $\alpha/2$ of falling in the right tail of Figure 7-2.

3. The z score separating the right-tail region is commonly denoted by $z_{\alpha/2}$ and is referred to as a *critical value* because it is on the borderline separating z scores from sample proportions that are likely to occur from those that are unlikely.

$\alpha/2$ $\alpha/2$

$z = 0$ $z_{\alpha/2}$

Found from technology or Table A-2 (corresponds to area of $1 - \alpha/2$)

Figure 7-2
Critical Value $z_{\alpha/2}$ in the Standard Normal Distribution

DEFINITION A **critical value** is the number on the borderline separating sample statistics that are likely to occur from those that are unlikely. The number $z_{\alpha/2}$ is a critical value that is a z score with the property that it separates an area of $\alpha/2$ in the right tail of the standard normal distribution (as in Figure 7-2).

Example 2   Finding a Critical Value

Find the critical value $z_{\alpha/2}$ corresponding to a 95% confidence level.

Solution

A 95% confidence level corresponds to $\alpha/2 = 0.025$. Figure 7-3 shows that the area in each of the red-shaded tails is $\alpha/2 = 0.025$. We find $z_{\alpha/2} = 1.96$ by noting that the cumulative area to its left must be $1 - 0.025$, or 0.975. We can use technology or refer to Table A-2 to find that the cumulative left area of 0.9750 (found *in the body* of the table) corresponds to $z = 1.96$. For a 95% confidence level, the critical value is therefore $z_{\alpha/2} = 1.96$. To find the critical z score for a 95% confidence level, use a cumulative left area of 0.9750 (*not* 0.95).

Note: Many technologies can be used to find critical values. STATDISK, Excel, Minitab, StatCrunch, and the TI-83/84 Plus calculator all provide critical values for the normal distribution.

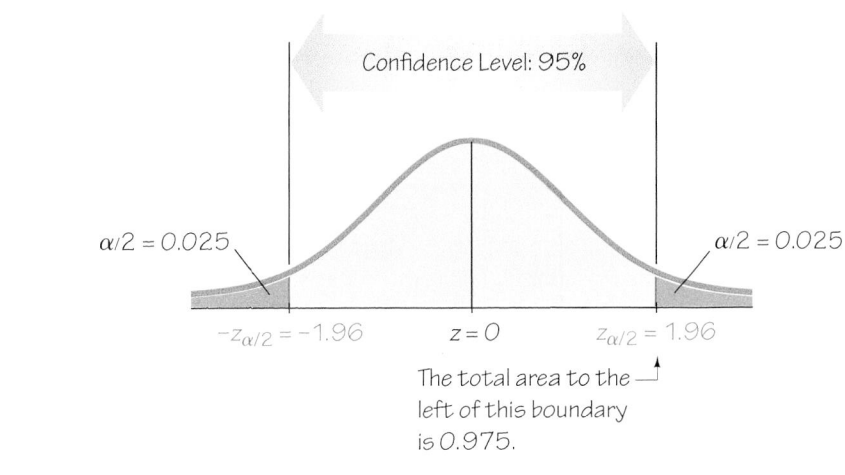

Figure 7-3 Finding $z_{\alpha/2}$ for a 95% Confidence Level

Example 2 showed that a 95% confidence level results in a critical value of $z_{\alpha/2} = 1.96$. This is the most common critical value, and it is listed with two other common values in the table that follows.

Confidence Level	α	Critical Value, $z_{\alpha/2}$
90%	0.10	1.645
95%	0.05	1.96
99%	0.01	2.575

Margin of Error

When we collect sample data that result in a sample proportion, such as the Pew Research Center poll given in Example 1, we can identify the sample proportion $\hat{p}$. Because of random variation in samples, the sample proportion $\hat{p}$ is typically different from the population proportion p. The difference between the sample proportion and the population proportion can be thought of as an error. We now define the *margin of error E* as follows.

> **DEFINITION** When data from a simple random sample are used to estimate a population proportion p, the **margin of error,** denoted by **E,** is the maximum likely difference (with probability $1 - \alpha$, such as 0.95) between the observed sample proportion $\hat{p}$ and the true value of the population proportion p. The margin of error E is also called the *maximum error of the estimate* and can be found by multiplying the critical value and the standard deviation of sample proportions, as shown in Formula 7-1.

Formula 7-1 $$E = z_{\alpha/2}\sqrt{\frac{\hat{p}\hat{q}}{n}} \qquad \text{margin of error for proportions}$$

For a 95% confidence level, $\alpha = 0.05$, so there is a probability of 0.05 that the sample proportion will be in error by more than E. This property is generalized in the following box.

Confidence Interval for Estimating a Population Proportion *p*

Objective

Construct a confidence interval used to estimate a population proportion *p*.

Notation

p = population proportion

$\hat{p}$ = sample proportion

n = number of sample values

E = margin of error

$z_{\alpha/2}$ = *z* score separating an area of $\alpha/2$ in the right tail of the standard normal distribution

(*Note:* The symbol π is sometimes used to denote the population proportion. Because π is so closely associated with the value of 3.14159..., this text uses *p* to denote the population proportion.)

Requirements

1. The sample is a simple random sample. (*Caution:* If the sample data have been obtained in a way that is not suitable, the estimate of the population proportion may be very wrong.)

2. The conditions for the binomial distribution are satisfied. That is, there is a fixed number of trials, the trials are independent, there are two categories of outcomes, and the probabilities remain constant for each trial. (See Section 5-3.)

3. There are at least 5 successes and at least 5 failures. (With the population proportions *p* and *q* unknown, we estimate their values using the sample proportion, so this requirement is a way of verifying that $np \geq 5$ and $nq \geq 5$ are both satisfied, so the normal distribution is a suitable approximation to the binomial distribution. There are procedures for dealing with situations in which the normal distribution is not a suitable approximation, as in Exercise 40.)

Confidence Interval

$$\hat{p} - E < p < \hat{p} + E \quad \text{where} \quad E = z_{\alpha/2}\sqrt{\frac{\hat{p}\hat{q}}{n}}$$

The confidence interval is often expressed in the following equivalent formats:

$$\hat{p} \pm E$$

or

$$(\hat{p} - E, \hat{p} + E)$$

Round-Off Rule for Confidence Interval Estimates of *p*

Round the confidence interval limits for *p* to three significant digits.

Confidence intervals can be easily created by using technology or Table A-2 with the following procedure:

Procedure for Constructing a Confidence Interval for *p*

1. Verify that the requirements in the preceding box are satisfied.

2. Use technology or Table A-2 to find the critical value $z_{\alpha/2}$ that corresponds to the desired confidence level.

3. Evaluate the margin of error $E = z_{\alpha/2}\sqrt{\hat{p}\hat{q}/n}$.

4. Using the value of the calculated margin of error E and the value of the sample proportion $\hat{p}$, find the values of the *confidence interval limits* $\hat{p} - E$ and $\hat{p} + E$. Substitute those values in the general format for the confidence interval:

$$\hat{p} - E < p < \hat{p} + E$$

or

$$\hat{p} \pm E$$

or

$$(\hat{p} - E, \hat{p} + E)$$

5. Round the resulting confidence interval limits to three significant digits.

Example 3 **Constructing a Confidence Interval: Poll Results**

In the Chapter Problem we noted that a Pew Research Center poll of 1007 randomly selected U.S. adults showed that 85% of the respondents know what Twitter is. The sample results are $n = 1007$ and $\hat{p} = 0.85$.

  a. Find the margin of error E that corresponds to a 95% confidence level.

  b. Find the 95% confidence interval estimate of the population proportion p.

  c. Based on the results, can we safely conclude that more than 75% of adults know what Twitter is?

  d. Assuming that you are a newspaper reporter, write a brief statement that accurately describes the results and includes all of the relevant information.

Solution

Requirement check We first verify that the necessary requirements are satisfied. (1) The polling methods used by the Pew Research Center result in samples that can be considered to be simple random samples. (2) The conditions for a binomial experiment are satisfied, because there is a fixed number of trials (1007), the trials are independent (because the response from one person doesn't affect the probability of the response from another person), there are two categories of outcome (subject knows what Twitter is or does not), and the probability remains constant. (3) With 85% of the respondents knowing what Twitter is, the number who know is 856 (or 85% of 1007). If 856 of the 1007 subjects know what Twitter is, the other 151 do not know, so the number of successes (856) and the number of failures (151) are both at least 5. The check of requirements has been successfully completed. ✓

Technology The confidence interval and margin of error can be easily found using technology. From the STATDISK display on the next page we can see the required entries on the left and the results displayed on the right. Like most technologies, STATDISK requires a value for the number of successes, so we simply find 85% of 1007 and round the result of 855.95 to the whole number of 856. The results show that the margin of error is $E = 0.022$ (rounded) and the confidence interval is $0.828 < p < 0.872$ (rounded). (The Wilson Score confidence interval is discussed near the end of this section.)

STATDISK

We will now proceed to show how the results for parts (a) and (b) can be obtained with manual calculations.

a. The margin of error is found by using Formula 7-1 with $z_{\alpha/2} = 1.96$ (as found in Example 2), $\hat{p} = 0.85$, $\hat{q} = 0.15$, and $n = 1007$.

$$E = z_{\alpha/2}\sqrt{\frac{\hat{p}\hat{q}}{n}} = 1.96\sqrt{\frac{(0.85)(0.15)}{1007}} = 0.0220545$$

b. Constructing the confidence interval is quite easy now that we know the values of $\hat{p}$ and E. We simply substitute those values to obtain this result:

$$\hat{p} - E < p < \hat{p} + E$$
$$0.85 - 0.0220545 < p < 0.85 + 0.0220545$$
$$0.828 < p < 0.872 \quad \text{(rounded to three significant digits)}$$

This same result could be expressed in the format of 0.85 ± 0.022 or $(0.828, 0.872)$. If we want the 95% confidence interval for the true population *percentage,* we could express the result as $82.8\% < p < 87.2\%$.

c. Based on the confidence interval obtained in part (b), it does appear that more than 75% of adults know what Twitter is. Because the limits of 0.828 and 0.872 are likely to contain the true population proportion, it appears that the population proportion is a value greater than 0.75. (See also Exercise 43.)

d. Here is one statement that summarizes the results: 85% of U.S. adults know what Twitter is. That percentage is based on a Pew Research Center poll of 1007 randomly selected adults in the United States. In theory, in 95% of such polls, the percentage should differ by no more than 2.2 percentage points in either direction from the percentage that would be found by interviewing all adults in the United States.

Analyzing Polls Example 3 deals with a typical poll. When analyzing results from polls, we should consider the following.

1. The sample should be a simple random sample, not an inappropriate sample (such as a voluntary response sample).

2. The confidence level should be provided. (It is often 95%, but media reports often neglect to identify it.)

3. The sample size should be provided. (It is often provided by the media, but not always.)

4. Except for relatively rare cases, the quality of the poll results depends on the sampling method and the size of the sample, but the size of the population is usually not a factor.

CAUTION Never have the common misconception that poll results are unreliable if the sample size is a small percentage of the population size. The population size is usually not a factor in determining the reliability of a poll.

Determining Sample Size

If we plan to collect sample data in order to estimate some population proportion, how do we know *how many* sample units must be obtained? If we solve the formula for the margin of error E (Formula 7-1) for the sample size n, we get Formula 7-2 below. Formula 7-2 requires $\hat{p}$ as an estimate of the population proportion p, but if no such estimate is known (as is often the case), we replace $\hat{p}$ by 0.5 and replace $\hat{q}$ by 0.5, with the result given in Formula 7-3.

Finding the Sample Size Required to Estimate a Population Proportion

Objective

Determine how large the sample n should be in order to estimate the population proportion p.

Notation

p = population proportion

$\hat{p}$ = sample proportion

n = number of sample values

E = desired margin of error

$z_{\alpha/2}$ = z score separating an area of $\alpha/2$ in the right tail of the standard normal distribution

Requirements

The sample must be a simple random sample of independent sample units.

When an estimate $\hat{p}$ is known: **Formula 7-2** $n = \dfrac{[z_{\alpha/2}]^2 \hat{p}\hat{q}}{E^2}$

When no estimate $\hat{p}$ is known: **Formula 7-3** $n = \dfrac{[z_{\alpha/2}]^2 0.25}{E^2}$

Round-Off Rule for Determining Sample Size

If the computed sample size n is not a whole number, round the value of n up to the next *larger* whole number.

If reasonable estimates of $\hat{p}$ can be made by using previous samples, a pilot study, or someone's expert knowledge, use Formula 7-2. If nothing is known about the value of $\hat{p}$, use Formula 7-3.

Role of the Population Size N Formulas 7-2 and 7-3 are remarkable because they show that the sample size does not depend on the size (N) of the population; the sample size depends on the desired confidence level, the desired margin of error, and sometimes the known estimate of $\hat{p}$. (See Exercise 39 for dealing with cases in which a relatively large sample is selected without replacement from a finite population, so the sample size n does depend on the population size N.)

Example 4   What Percentage of Adults Buy Clothing Online?

Gap, Banana Republic, J. Crew, Yahoo, and America Online are just a few of the many companies interested in knowing the percentage of adults who buy clothing online. How many adults must be surveyed in order to be 95% confident that the sample percentage is in error by no more than three percentage points?

   a. Use this recent result from the Census Bureau: 66% of adults buy clothing online.

   b. Assume that we have no prior information suggesting a possible value of the proportion.

Solution

   a. The prior study suggests that $\hat{p} = 0.66$, so $\hat{q} = 0.34$ (found from $\hat{q} = 1 - 0.66$). With a 95% confidence level, we have $\alpha = 0.05$, so $z_{\alpha/2} = 1.96$. Also, the margin of error is $E = 0.03$ (the decimal equivalent of "three percentage points"). Because we have an estimated value of $\hat{p}$, we use Formula 7-2 as follows:

$$n = \frac{[z_{\alpha/2}]^2\hat{p}\hat{q}}{E^2} = \frac{[1.96]^2(0.66)(0.34)}{0.03^2}$$

$$= 957.839 = 958 \qquad \text{(rounded up)}$$

   We must obtain a simple random sample that includes at least 958 adults.

   b. As in part (a), we again use $z_{\alpha/2} = 1.96$ and $E = 0.03$, but with no prior knowledge of $\hat{p}$ (or $\hat{q}$), we use Formula 7-3 as follows:

$$n = \frac{[z_{\alpha/2}]^2 \cdot 0.25}{E^2} = \frac{[1.96]^2 \cdot 0.25}{0.03^2}$$

$$= 1067.11 = 1068 \qquad \text{(rounded up)}$$

Interpretation

To be 95% confident that our sample percentage is within three percentage points of the true percentage for all adults, we should obtain a simple random sample of 1068 adults. By comparing this result to the sample size of 958 found in part (a), we can see that if we have no knowledge of a prior study, a larger sample is required to achieve the same results as when the value of $\hat{p}$ can be estimated.

CAUTION Try to avoid these two common errors when calculating sample size:

   1. Don't make the mistake of using $E = 3$ as the margin of error corresponding to "three percentage points." If the margin of error is three percentage points, use $E = 0.03$.

   2. Be sure to substitute the critical z score for $z_{\alpha/2}$. For example, if you are working with 95% confidence, be sure to replace $z_{\alpha/2}$ with 1.96. Don't make the mistake of replacing $z_{\alpha/2}$ with 0.95 or 0.05.

Finding the Point Estimate and E from a Confidence Interval

Sometimes we want to better understand a confidence interval that might have been obtained from a journal article or technology. If we already know the confidence interval limits, the sample proportion (or the best point estimate) $\hat{p}$ and the margin of error E can be found as follows:

Point estimate of p:

$$\hat{p} = \frac{(\text{upper confidence interval limit}) \ + \ (\text{lower confidence interval limit})}{2}$$

Margin of error:

$$E = \frac{(\text{upper confidence interval limit}) \ - \ (\text{lower confidence interval limit})}{2}$$

Example 5

The article "High-Dose Nicotine Patch Therapy," by Dale, Hurt, et al. (*Journal of the American Medical Association,* Vol. 274, No. 17) includes this statement: "Of the 71 subjects, 70% were abstinent from smoking at 8 weeks (95% confidence interval [CI], 58% to 81%)." Use that statement to find the point estimate $\hat{p}$ and the margin of error E.

Solution

We get the 95% confidence interval of $0.58 < p < 0.81$ from the given statement. The point estimate $\hat{p}$ is the value midway between the upper and lower confidence interval limits, so we get

$$\hat{p} = \frac{(\text{upper confidence limit}) \ + \ (\text{lower confidence limit})}{2}$$

$$= \frac{0.81 + 0.58}{2} = 0.695$$

The margin of error can be found as follows:

$$E = \frac{(\text{upper confidence limit}) \ - \ (\text{lower confidence limit})}{2}$$

$$= \frac{0.81 - 0.58}{2} = 0.115$$

Better-Performing Confidence Intervals

Important note: The exercises for this section are based on the method for constructing a confidence interval as described above, not the confidence intervals described in the following discussion.

Adjusted Wald CI The confidence interval described in this section has the format typically presented in introductory statistics courses, but it does not perform as well as some other confidence intervals. The *adjusted Wald confidence interval* performs better in the sense that its probability of containing the true population proportion p is closer to the confidence level that is used. The adjusted Wald confidence interval uses this simple procedure: Add 2 to the number of successes x, add 2 to the number of failures (so that the number of trials n is increased by 4), then find the confidence interval as described in this section. For example, if we use the methods of this section with $x = 10$ and $n = 20$, we get this 95% confidence interval: $0.281 < p < 0.719$. With $x = 10$ and $n = 20$ we use the adjusted Wald confidence interval by letting $x = 12$ and $n = 24$ to get this confidence interval: $0.300 < p < 0.700$. The chance that the confidence interval $0.300 < p < 0.700$ contains p is closer to 95% than the chance that $0.281 < p < 0.719$ contains p.

Wilson Score CI Another confidence interval that performs better than the one described in this section and the adjusted Wald confidence interval is the *Wilson score confidence interval:*

$$\frac{\hat{p} + \dfrac{z_{\alpha/2}^2}{2n} \pm z_{\alpha/2}\sqrt{\dfrac{\hat{p}\hat{q} + \dfrac{z_{\alpha/2}^2}{4n}}{n}}}{1 + \dfrac{z_{\alpha/2}^2}{n}}$$

It is easy to see why this approach is not used much in introductory courses. The complexity of the above expression can be overcome by using some technologies, such as STATDISK, that provide Wilson score confidence interval results. Using $x = 10$ and $n = 20$, the 95% Wilson score confidence interval is $0.299 < p < 0.701$.

For a discussion of these and other confidence intervals for p, see "Approximation Is Better than 'Exact' for Interval Estimation of Binomial Proportions," by Agresti and Coull, *American Statistician*, Vol. 52, No. 2.

using TECHNOLOGY

Confidence Intervals

STATDISK Select **Analysis,** then **Confidence Intervals,** then **Proportion One Sample,** and proceed to enter the requested items. The confidence interval will be displayed, as in the STATDISK results included with Example 3.

MINITAB Select **Stat, Basic Statistics,** then **1 Proportion.** In the dialog box, click on the button for **Summarized Data.** Also click on the **Options** button, and enter the desired confidence level (the default is 95%). Instead of using a normal approximation, Minitab's default procedure is to determine the confidence interval limits by using an exact method. To use the normal approximation method presented in this section, click on the **Options** button and then click on the box with this statement: "Use test and interval based on normal distribution."

EXCEL Use XLSTAT. Click on **XLSTAT** at the top, click on **Parametric Tests,** then select **Tests for one proportion.** Start in the lower left corner of the dialog box by selecting **Frequency** (if you know the number of successes x) or **Proportion** (if you know the sample proportion $\hat{p}$). Enter the frequency (number of successes) or the sample proportion, enter the sample size in the "Sample size" box, and enter 0.5 in the **Test Proportion** box. Be sure that the box next to "z test" is checked. For the "Range" box, enter A1 so that the results will start at cell A1. Click on the **Options**

tab, to enter the desired "Significance level (%)." Enter 5 for a 95% confidence interval. For the "Variance (confidence interval)" options, select **Sample** (so that the sample proportion is used in the computation of the confidence interval). There are four options for the type of confidence interval; accept the default of **Wald.** Click **OK.** After the results are displayed, look for "confidence interval on the proportion (Wald)."

TI-83/84 PLUS Press **STAT**, select **TESTS,** then select **1-PropZInt** and enter the required items. The accompanying display shows the result for Example 3. Like many technologies, the TI-83/84 Plus calculator requires entry of the number of successes, so 856 (which is 85% of the 1007 people polled) was entered for the value of x. Also like many technologies, the confidence interval limits are expressed in the format shown on the second line of the display.

TI-83/84 PLUS

```
1-PropZInt
(.828,.8721)
p̂=.8500496524
n=1007
```

STATCRUNCH Click on **Open StatCrunch,** then enter or open a data set. Click on **Stat,** then select **Proportion.** Select **One sample,** then select **with summary.** Proceed to enter the number of successes and the number of observations, click on **Next,** then select **Confidence Interval** and use the **Standard-Wald** option.

Sample Size Determination

STATDISK Select **Analysis,** then **Sample Size Determination,** then **Estimate Proportion.** Enter the required items in the dialog box.

MINITAB 16 Minitab Release 16 has a procedure for determining sample size using the binomial distribution, not the normal approximation to the binomial distribution, so results will not agree with those found by using the methods of this section. For Minitab's procedure, select **Stat, Power and Sample Size,** then select **Sample Size for Estimation** and choose the menu item of **Proportion (Binomial).** Complete the dialog box and click **OK.**

Sample size determination is not available as a built-in function with Excel or StatCrunch or the TI-83/84 Plus calculator.

7-2 Basic Skills and Concepts

Statistical Literacy and Critical Thinking

1. Poll Results in the Media *USA Today* provided a "snapshot" illustrating poll results from 1910 professionals who interview job applicants. The illustration showed that 26% of them said the biggest interview turnoff is that the applicant did not make an effort to learn about the job or the company. The margin of error was given as ± 3 percentage points. What important feature of the poll was omitted?

2. Margin of Error For the poll described in Exercise 1, describe what is meant by the statement that "the margin of error is ± 3 percentage points."

3. Notation For the poll described in Exercise 1, what do $\hat{p}$, $\hat{q}$, n, E, and p represent? If the confidence level is 95%, what is the value of α?

4. Confidence Levels Given specific sample data, such as the data given in Exercise 1, which confidence interval is wider: the 95% confidence interval or the 80% confidence interval? Why is it wider?

Finding Critical Values. *In Exercises 5–8, find the indicated critical z value.*

5. Find the critical value $z_{\alpha/2}$ that corresponds to a confidence level of 80%.

6. Find the critical value $z_{\alpha/2}$ that corresponds to a 99% confidence level.

7. Find $z_{\alpha/2}$ for $\alpha = 0.10$.

8. Find $z_{\alpha/2}$ for $\alpha = 0.04$.

Formats of Confidence Intervals. *In Exercises 9–12, express the confidence interval using the indicated format. (The confidence intervals are based on the proportions of red, orange, yellow, and blue M&Ms in Data Set 20 from Appendix B.)*

9. Express the confidence interval $0.0641 < p < 0.186$ in the form of $\hat{p} \pm E$.

10. Express the confidence interval $0.165 < p < 0.335$ in the form of $\hat{p} \pm E$.

11. Express the confidence interval $(0.0268, 0.133)$ in the form of $\hat{p} - E < p < \hat{p} + E$.

12. Express the confidence interval 0.270 ± 0.087 in the form of $\hat{p} - E < p < \hat{p} + E$.

Constructing and Interpreting Confidence Intervals. *In Exercises 13–16, use the given sample data and confidence level. In each case, (a) find the best point estimate of the population proportion p; (b) identify the value of the margin of error E; (c) construct the confidence interval; (d) write a statement that correctly interprets the confidence interval.*

13. From a KRC Research poll in which respondents were asked if they felt vulnerable to identify theft: $n = 1002$, $x = 531$ who said "yes." Use a 95% confidence level.

14. From a 3M Privacy Filters poll in which respondents were asked to identify their favorite seat when they fly: $n = 806$, $x = 492$ who chose the window seat. Use a 99% confidence level.

15. From a Prince Market Research poll in which respondents were asked if they acted to annoy a bad driver: $n = 2518$, $x = 1083$ who said that they honked. Use a 90% confidence level.

16. From an Angus Reid Public Opinion poll in which respondents were asked if they felt that U.S. nuclear weapons made them feel safer: $n = 1005$, $x = 543$ who said "yes." Use a confidence level of 80%.

17. Gender Selection The Genetics and IVF Institute conducted a clinical trial of the XSORT method designed to increase the probability of conceiving a girl. As of this writing, 945 babies were born to parents using the XSORT method, and 879 of them were girls.

a. What is the best point estimate of the population proportion of girls born to parents using the XSORT method?

b. Use the sample data to construct a 95% confidence interval estimate of the proportion of girls born to parents using the XSORT method.

c. Based on the results, does the XSORT method appear to be effective? Why or why not?

18. Gender Selection The Genetics and IVF Institute conducted a clinical trial of the YSORT method designed to increase the probability of conceiving a boy. As of this writing, 291 babies were born to parents using the YSORT method, and 239 of them were boys.

a. What is the best point estimate of the population proportion of boys born to parents using the YSORT method?

b. Use the sample data to construct a 99% confidence interval estimate of the proportion of boys born to parents using the YSORT method.

c. Based on the results, does the YSORT method appear to be effective? Why or why not?

19. Touch Therapy When she was 9 years of age, Emily Rosa did a science fair experiment in which she tested professional touch therapists to see if they could sense her energy field. She flipped a coin to select either her right hand or her left hand, then she asked the therapists to identify the selected hand by placing their hand just under Emily's hand without seeing it and without touching it. Among 280 trials, the touch therapists were correct 123 times (based on data in "A Close Look at Therapeutic Touch," *Journal of the American Medical Association,* Vol. 279, No. 13).

a. Given that Emily used a coin toss to select either her right hand or her left hand, what proportion of correct responses would be expected if the touch therapists made random guesses?

b. Using Emily's sample results, what is the best point estimate of the therapist's success rate?

c. Using Emily's sample results, construct a 99% confidence interval estimate of the proportion of correct responses made by touch therapists.

d. What do the results suggest about the ability of touch therapists to select the correct hand by sensing an energy field?

20. Mendelian Genetics When Mendel conducted his famous genetics experiments with peas, one sample of offspring consisted of 428 green peas and 152 yellow peas.

a. Find a 95% confidence interval estimate of the percentage of yellow peas.

b. Based on his theory of genetics, Mendel expected that 25% of the offspring peas would be yellow. Given that the percentage of offspring yellow peas is not 25%, do the results contradict Mendel's theory? Why or why not?

21. Online Books A *Consumer Reports* Research Center survey of 427 women showed that 29.0% of them purchase books online.

a. Among the 427 women who were surveyed, what is the number of women who said that they purchase books online?

b. Find a 95% confidence interval estimate of the *percentage* of all women who purchase books online.

c. Can we safely conclude that less than 50% of all women purchase books online? Why or why not?

d. Can we safely conclude that at least 25% of all women purchase books online? Why or why not?

e. What do the results tell us about the percentage of *men* who purchase books online?

22. Want Boss's Job? In a *USA Today* survey, 20.8% of 144 respondents said that they aspired to have their boss's job. Construct a 95% confidence interval estimate of the *percentage* of all workers who aspire to have their boss's job. How are the results affected by the additional knowledge that the respondents chose to answer an online question posted on the *USA Today* web site?

23. Job Interviews In a Harris poll of 514 human resource professionals, 45.9% said that body piercings and tattoos were big grooming red flags.

a. Among the 514 human resource professionals who were surveyed, how many of them said that body piercings and tattoos were big grooming red flags?

b. Construct a 99% confidence interval estimate of the proportion of all human resource professionals believing that body piercings and tattoos are big grooming red flags.

c. Repeat part (b) using a confidence level of 80%.

d. Compare the confidence intervals from parts (b) and (c) and identify the interval that is wider. Why is it wider?

24. Job Interviews In a Harris poll of 514 human resource professionals, 90% said that the appearance of a job applicant is most important for a good first impression.

a. Among the 514 human resource professionals who were surveyed, how many of them said that the appearance of a job applicant is most important for a good first impression?

b. Construct a 99% confidence interval estimate of the proportion of all human resource professionals believing that the appearance of a job applicant is most important for a good first impression.

c. Repeat part (b) using a confidence level of 80%.

d. Compare the confidence intervals from parts (b) and (c) and identify the interval that is wider. Why is it wider?

25. M&Ms The Mars candy company claims that 13% of its M&M candies are brown, but Data Set 20 in Appendix B lists data from 100 M&Ms, and 8% of them are brown. Use the sample data to construct a 98% confidence interval estimate of the proportion of brown M&Ms. Does it appear that the claimed rate of 13% rate is wrong? Why or why not?

26. Misleading Survey Responses In a survey of 1002 people, 70% said that they voted in a recent presidential election (based on data from ICR Research Group). Voting records show that 61% of eligible voters actually did vote.

a. Find a 98% confidence interval estimate of the proportion of people who say that they voted.

b. Are the survey results consistent with the actual voter turnout of 61%? Why or why not?

27. Cell Phones and Cancer A study of 420,095 Danish cell phone users found that 0.0321% of them developed cancer of the brain or nervous system. Prior to this study of cell phone use, the rate of such cancer was found to be 0.0340% for those not using cell phones. The data are from the *Journal of the National Cancer Institute.*

a. Use the sample data to construct a 90% confidence interval estimate of the *percentage* of cell phone users who develop cancer of the brain or nervous system.

b. Do cell phone users appear to have a rate of cancer of the brain or nervous system that is different from the rate of such cancer among those not using cell phones? Why or why not?

28. Medication Usage In a survey of 3005 adults aged 57 through 85 years, it was found that 81.7% of them used at least one prescription medication (based on data from "Use of Prescription and Over-the-Counter Medications and Dietary Supplements Among Older Adults in the United States," by Qato et al., *Journal of the American Medical Association,* Vol. 300, No. 24).

a. How many of the 3005 subjects used at least one prescription medication?

b. Construct a 90% confidence interval estimate of the *percentage* of adults aged 57 through 85 years who use at least one prescription medication.

c. What do the results tell us about the proportion of college students who use at least one prescription medication?

Determining Sample Size.   *In Exercises 29–36, use the given data to find the minimum sample size required to estimate a population proportion or percentage.*

29. Republicans Find the sample size needed to estimate the percentage of Republicans among registered voters in California. Use a 0.03 margin of error, use a confidence level of 90%, and assume that $\hat{p}$ and $\hat{q}$ are unknown.

30. Robberies Find the sample size needed to estimate the percentage of robberies in Texas that result in arrests. Use a 0.04 margin of error, use a confidence level of 80%, and assume that $\hat{p}$ and $\hat{q}$ are unknown.

31. Tattooed Democrats Find the sample size needed to estimate the percentage of Democrats who have tattoos. Use a 0.05 margin of error, use a confidence level of 99%, and use results from a prior Harris poll suggesting that 15% of Democrats have tattoos.

32. Fortune Tellers Find the sample size needed to estimate the percentage of adults who have consulted fortune tellers. Use a 0.03 margin of error, use a confidence level of 98%, and use results from a prior Pew Research Center poll suggesting that 15% of adults have consulted fortune tellers.

33. Airline Seating You are the operations manager for American Airlines and you are considering a higher fare level for passengers in aisle seats. You want to estimate the percentage of passengers who now prefer aisle seats. How many randomly selected air passengers must you survey? Assume that you want to be 95% confident that the sample percentage is within 2.5 percentage points of the true population percentage.

a. Assume that nothing is known about the percentage of passengers who prefer aisle seats.

b. Assume that a recent survey suggests that about 38% of air passengers prefer an aisle seat (based on a 3M Privacy Filters survey).

34. Windows Penetration You plan to develop a new software system that you believe will surpass the success of Google and Facebook combined. In planning for the operating system that you will use, you need to estimate the percentage of computers that use Windows. How many computers must be surveyed in order to be 99% confident that your estimate is in error by no more than one percentage point?

a. Assume that nothing is known about the percentage of computers with Windows operating systems.

b. Assume that a recent survey suggests that about 90% of computers use Windows operating systems (based on data from Net Applications).

c. Does the additional survey information from part (b) have much of an effect on the sample size that is required?

35. Twitter As manager for an advertising company, you must plan a campaign designed to increase Twitter usage. You want to first determine the percentage of adults who know what Twitter is. How many adults must you survey in order to be 90% confident that your estimate is within five percentage points of the true population percentage?

a. Assume that nothing is known about the percentage of adults who know what Twitter is.

b. Assume that a recent survey suggests that about 85% of adults know what Twitter is (based on a Pew Research Center survey).

c. Given that the required sample size is relatively small, could you simply survey the adults at the nearest college?

36. On-time Rate You have been given the task of estimating the percentage of Southwest flights that arrive on time, which is no later than 15 minutes after the scheduled arrival time. How many flights must you survey in order to be 80% confident that your estimate is within three percentage points of the true population percentage?

a. Assume that nothing is known about the percentage of on-time Southwest flights.

b. Assume that for a recent year, 84% of Southwest flights were on time (based on data from the Bureau of Transportation Statistics).

c. Given that the sample size is relatively small, can you select Southwest flights between New York (LaGuardia) and San Francisco?

Using Appendix B Data Sets. *In Exercises 37 and 38, use the indicated data set from Appendix B.*

37. Heights of Presidents Refer to Data Set 12 in Appendix B. Treat the data as a sample and find the proportion of presidents who were taller than their opponents. Use that result to construct a 95% confidence interval estimate of the population percentage. Based on the result, does it appear that greater height is an advantage for presidential candidates? Why or why not?

38. Arrival Delays Refer to Data Set 15 in Appendix B. A flight is considered on time if it arrives no later than 15 minutes after the scheduled arrival time. The last column of Data Set 15 lists arrival delays, so on-time flights correspond to values in that column that are 15 or less. Use the data to construct a 90% confidence interval estimate of the population percentage of on-time flights. Does the confidence interval describe the percentage of on-time flights for all American Airlines flights? Why or why not?

7-2 Beyond the Basics

39. Finite Population Correction Factor For Formulas 7-2 and 7-3 we assume that the population is infinite or very large and that we are sampling with replacement. When we have a relatively small population with size N and sample without replacement, we modify E to include the *finite population correction factor* shown here, and we can solve for n to obtain the result given here. Use this result to repeat Exercise 33, assuming that we limit our population to 200 particular passengers on a Boeing 757-200 ER aircraft.

$$E = z_{\alpha/2} \sqrt{\frac{\hat{p}\hat{q}}{n}} \sqrt{\frac{N - n}{N - 1}} \qquad n = \frac{N\hat{p}\hat{q}[z_{\alpha/2}]^2}{\hat{p}\hat{q}[z_{\alpha/2}]^2 + (N - 1)E^2}$$

40. Confidence Interval from Small Sample Special tables are available for finding confidence intervals for proportions involving small numbers of cases, where the normal distribution approximation cannot be used. For example, given $x = 3$ successes among $n = 8$ trials, the 95% confidence interval found in *Standard Probability and Statistics Tables and Formulae* (CRC Press) is $0.085 < p < 0.755$. Find the confidence interval that would result if you were to incorrectly use the normal distribution as an approximation to the binomial distribution. Are the results reasonably close?

41. Interpreting Confidence Interval Limits Repeat Exercise 38 using a 99% confidence level. What is unusual about the result? Does common sense suggest a modification of the result?

42. Coping with No Success According to the *Rule of Three*, when we have a sample size n with $x = 0$ successes, we have 95% confidence that the true population proportion has an upper bound of $3/n$. (See "A Look at the Rule of Three," by Jovanovic and Levy, *American Statistician*, Vol. 51, No. 2.)

a. If n independent trials result in no successes, why can't we find confidence interval limits by using the methods described in this section?

b. If 40 couples use a method of gender selection and each couple has a baby girl, what is the 95% upper bound for p, the proportion of all babies who are boys?

43. One-Sided Confidence Interval A one-sided claim about a population proportion is a claim that the proportion is less than (or greater than) some specific value. Such a claim can be formally addressed using a *one-sided confidence interval* for p, which can be expressed as $p < \hat{p} + E$ or $p > \hat{p} - E$, where the margin of error E is modified by replacing $z_{\alpha/2}$ with z_α. (Instead of dividing α between two tails of the standard normal distribution, put all of it in one tail.) Repeat part (c) of Example 3 by constructing an appropriate one-sided 95% confidence interval.

7-3 Estimating a Population Mean

Key Concept This section presents methods for using a sample mean $\bar{x}$ to make an inference about the value of the corresponding population mean μ. Here are the three main concepts included in this section:

- **Point Estimate:** The sample mean $\bar{x}$ is the best *point estimate* (or single value estimate) of the population mean μ.

- **Confidence Interval:** We can use a sample mean to construct a *confidence interval* estimate of the true value of a population mean, and we should know how to construct and interpret such confidence intervals.

- **Sample Size:** We should know how to find the sample size necessary to estimate a population mean.

Part 1 of this section deals with the very realistic and commonly used case in which the population standard deviation σ is not known. Part 2 includes a brief discussion of the procedure used when σ is known, which is very rare.

Part 1: Estimating a Population Mean When σ Is Not Known

It's rare that we want to estimate the unknown value of a population mean but we somehow know the value of the population standard deviation σ. The realistic situation is that σ is not known. When σ is not known, we construct the confidence interval by using the Student t distribution instead of the standard normal distribution.

Point Estimate The sample mean $\bar{x}$ is an *unbiased estimator* of the population mean μ, and for many populations, sample means tend to vary less than other measures of center, so the sample mean $\bar{x}$ is usually the best point estimate of the population mean μ.

The sample mean $\bar{x}$ is the best *point estimate* of the population mean μ.

Although the sample mean $\bar{x}$ is usually the *best* point estimate of the population mean μ, it does not give us any indication of just how *good* our best estimate is, so we construct a *confidence interval* (or *interval estimate*), which consists of a range (or an interval) of values instead of just a single value.

Requirement of Normality or $n > 30$ The procedure we use has a requirement that the population is normally distributed or the sample size is greater than 30. This procedure is *robust* against a departure from normality, meaning that it works reasonably well if the departure from normality is not too extreme. Verify that there are no outliers and that the histogram or dotplot has a shape that is not very far from a normal distribution.

If the original population is not itself normally distributed, we use the condition $n > 30$ for justifying use of the normal distribution, but there is no exact specific minimum sample size that works for all cases. Sample sizes of 15 to 30 are sufficient if the population has a distribution that is not far from normal, but some other populations have distributions that are extremely far from normal and sample sizes greater than 30 might be necessary. We use the simplified criterion of $n > 30$ as justification for treating the distribution of sample means as a normal distribution, regardless of how far the distribution departs from a normal distribution.

Confidence Level The confidence interval is associated with a confidence level, such as 0.95 (or 95%). The confidence level gives us the *success rate of the procedure*

Confidence Interval for Estimating a Population Mean with σ Not Known

Objective

Construct a confidence interval used to estimate a population mean.

Notation

μ = population mean

$\bar{x}$ = sample mean

n = number of sample values

E = margin of error

Requirements

1. The sample is a simple random sample.

2. Either or both of these conditions is satisfied: The population is normally distributed or $n > 30$.

Confidence Interval

$$\bar{x} - E < \mu < \bar{x} + E$$

or

$$\bar{x} \pm E$$

or

$$(\bar{x} - E, \bar{x} + E)$$

where the margin of error E is found from the following:

$$E = t_{\alpha/2} \cdot \frac{s}{\sqrt{n}} \qquad (\text{Use df} = n - 1.)$$

where $t_{\alpha/2}$ = critical t value separating an area of $\alpha/2$ in the right tail of the Student t distribution, and df = $n - 1$ is the number of degrees of freedom. (Find $t_{\alpha/2}$ using technology or Table A-3.)

Round-Off Rule

1. When constructing a confidence interval from the *original set of data* values, round the confidence interval limits to one more decimal place than is used for the original set of data.

2. When constructing a confidence interval from *summary statistics* (n and $\bar{x}$ and s), round the confidence interval limits to the same number of decimal places used for the sample mean.

used to construct the confidence interval. As in Section 7-2, α is the complement of the confidence level. For a 0.95 (or 95%) confidence level, $\alpha = 0.05$.

Student t Distribution

If σ is not known, but the relevant requirements are satisfied, we use a *Student t distribution* (instead of a normal distribution), as developed by William Gosset (1876–1937). Gosset was a Guinness Brewery employee who needed a distribution that could be used with small samples. The Irish brewery where he worked did not allow the publication of research results, so Gosset published under the pseudonym "Student." (In the interest of research and better serving his readers, the author visited the Guinness Brewery and sampled some of the product. This is true author dedication.) Gosset first referred to his distribution as a z distribution, but it was modified and he later called it a t distribution. Here are some key points about the Student t distribution:

- **Student t Distribution** If a population has a normal distribution, then the distribution of

$$t = \frac{\bar{x} - \mu}{\frac{s}{\sqrt{n}}}$$

is a **Student t distribution** for all samples of size n. A Student t distribution is commonly referred to simply as a **t distribution.**

- **Degrees of Freedom** Finding a critical value $t_{\alpha/2}$ requires a value for the **degrees of freedom** (or **df**). In general, the number of degrees of freedom for a collection of sample data is the number of sample values that can vary after certain restrictions have been imposed on all data values. (*Example:* If 10 test scores have the restriction that their mean is 80, then their sum must be 800, and we can freely assign values to the first 9 scores, but the 10th score would then be determined, so in this case there are 9 degrees of freedom.) For the methods of this section, the number of degrees of freedom is the sample size minus 1.

$$\text{degrees of freedom} = n - 1$$

- **Finding Critical Value $t_{\alpha/2}$** A critical value $t_{\alpha/2}$ can be found using technology or Table A-3. Technology can be used with any number of degrees of freedom, but a t distribution table can be used for select numbers of degrees of freedom only.

- **Using Table A-3 when a Number of Degrees of Freedom Is Not Included** If using Table A-3 to find a critical value of $t_{\alpha/2}$, but the table does not include the number of degrees of freedom, you could use the closest value, or you could be conservative by using the next lower number of degrees of freedom found in the table, or you could interpolate.

Example 1 Finding a Critical t Value

A sample of size $n = 12$ is a simple random sample selected from a normally distributed population (as in Example 2 that follows). Find the critical value $t_{\alpha/2}$ corresponding to a 95% confidence level.

Solution

Because $n = 12$, the number of degrees of freedom is given by $n - 1 = 11$. The 95% confidence level corresponds to $\alpha = 0.05$, so there is an area of 0.025 in each of the two tails of the t distribution, as shown in Figure 7-4 on the next page. Technology or a t distribution table can be used to find that for 11 degrees of freedom and an area of 0.025 in each tail, the critical value is $t_{\alpha/2} = 2.201$. We could also express this as $t_{0.025} = 2.201$.

To find $t_{\alpha/2} = 2.201$ using Table A-3, locate the 11th row (because df $= 11$) by referring to the column at the extreme left, then use the column with 0.05 for the "Area in Two Tails" (or use the same column with 0.025 for the "Area in One Tail").

Largest Inauguration Ever?

When Barack Obama was inaugurated as the first African American president, a huge crowd filled the region from the Capitol building to the Lincoln Memorial. The National Park Service estimated that 1.8 million people attended the inauguration. Instead of making somewhat casual estimates of the size of a crowd, aerial photographs can be used to develop reasonably good estimates based on crowd density. Allison Puccioni, an analyst for IHS Jane's, studied a satellite photograph, and she estimated that the crowd size was between 1.031 million and 1.411 million people—about 22% less than the estimate made by the National Park Service.

In another case, a celebration parade for the Boston Red Sox was attended by 3.2 million fans (according to Boston city officials), or 1 million fans (according to Boston police), or at most 400,000 fans (according to Boston University Professor Farouk El-Baz, who analyzed photos). MIT physicist Bill Donnelly said that "it's a serious thing if people are just putting out any number. It means other things aren't being vetted that carefully."

Figure 7-4   Critical Value $t_{\alpha/2}$

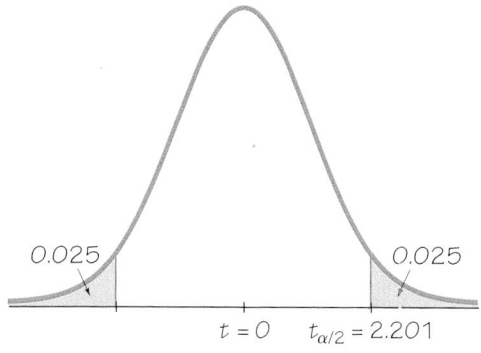

0.025 0.025

$t = 0$ $t_{\alpha/2} = 2.201$

Confidence intervals can be easily constructed with technology or they can be manually constructed by using the following procedure.

Procedure for Constructing a Confidence Interval for μ

1. Verify that the two requirements in the preceding box are satisfied.
2. With σ unknown (as is usually the case), use $n - 1$ degrees of freedom and use technology or a t distribution table to find the critical value $t_{\alpha/2}$ that corresponds to the desired confidence level (as in the preceding Example 1).
3. Evaluate the margin of error using $E = t_{\alpha/2} \cdot s/\sqrt{n}$.
4. Using the value of the calculated margin of error E and the value of the sample mean $\bar{x}$, find the values of the confidence interval limits: $\bar{x} - E$ and $\bar{x} + E$. Substitute those values in one of these three general formats for the confidence interval:

$$\bar{x} - E < \mu < \bar{x} + E$$

or

$$\bar{x} \pm E$$

or

$$(\bar{x} - E, \bar{x} + E)$$

5. Round the resulting confidence interval limits using the round-off rule given in the preceding box.

Interpreting a Confidence Interval Be careful to interpret confidence intervals correctly. If we obtain a 95% confidence interval such as $58.1 < \mu < 63.3$, there is a correct interpretation and many incorrect interpretations.

Correct: "We are 95% confident that the interval from 58.1 to 63.3 actually does contain the true value of μ." This means that if we were to select many different samples of the same size and construct the corresponding confidence intervals, in the long run 95% of them would actually contain the value of μ. (This correct interpretation refers to the *success rate of the process* being used to estimate the population mean.)

Incorrect: Because μ is a fixed constant, it would be incorrect to say "there is a 95% chance that μ will fall between 58.1 and 63.3." It would also be incorrect to say that "95% of all data values are between 58.1 and 63.3," or that "95% of sample means fall between 58.1 and 63.3." Other possible incorrect interpretations are limited only by the imagination of the reader.

Using Confidence Intervals for Hypothesis Tests

A confidence interval can be used to *test some claim* made about a population mean μ. Formal methods of hypothesis testing are introduced in Chapter 8, and those methods might require adjustments to confidence intervals that are not described in this chapter. (We might need to construct a one-sided confidence interval or adjust the confidence level by using 90% instead of 95%.)

> **CAUTION** Know that in this chapter, when we use a confidence interval to address a claim about a population mean μ, we are making an *informal judgment* (that may or may not be consistent with formal methods of hypothesis testing introduced in Chapter 8).

Example 2   Constructing a Confidence Interval: Highway Speeds

Listed below are speeds (mi/h) measured from southbound traffic on I-280 near Cupertino, California (based on data from SigAlert). This simple random sample was obtained at 3:30 P.M. on a weekday. The speed limit for this road is 65 mi/h. Use the sample data to construct a 95% confidence interval for the mean speed. What does the confidence interval suggest about the speed limit?

62   61   61   57   61   54   59   58   59   69   60   67

Solution

Requirement check We must first verify that the requirements are satisfied. (1) The sample is a simple random sample. (2) The accompanying dotplot shows that the speeds have a distribution that is not dramatically different from a normal distribution, so the requirement that "the population is normally distributed or $n > 30$" is satisfied. ✓

Using Technology Technology can be used to automatically construct the confidence interval. (See instructions near the end of this section.) Shown here is the Minitab display resulting from the list of 12 sample highway speeds. The confidence interval is expressed in the format of (58.08, 63.26).

MINITAB

```
One-Sample T: Speeds

Variable   N   Mean   StDev   SE Mean     95% CI
Speeds     12  60.67  4.08    1.18     (58.08, 63.26)
```

Using a t Distribution Table Using the listed sample values, we find that $n = 12$, $\bar{x} = 60.7$ mi/h, and $s = 4.1$ mi/h. For a confidence level of 95% and 11 degrees of freedom, the critical value is $t_{0.025} = 2.201$ as shown in Example 1. We now find the margin of error E as shown here:

$$E = t_{\alpha/2} \frac{s}{\sqrt{n}} = 2.201 \cdot \frac{4.1}{\sqrt{12}} = 2.60503$$

Estimating Wildlife Population Sizes

The National Forest Management Act protects endangered species, including the northern spotted owl, with the result that the forestry industry was not allowed to cut vast regions of trees in the Pacific Northwest. Biologists and statisticians were asked to analyze the problem, and they concluded that survival rates and population sizes were decreasing for the female owls, known to play an important role in species survival. Biologists and statisticians also studied salmon in the Snake and Columbia Rivers in Washington State, and penguins in New Zealand. In the article "Sampling Wildlife Populations" (*Chance*, Vol. 9, No. 2), authors Bryan Manly and Lyman McDonald comment that in such studies, "biologists gain through the use of modeling skills that are the hallmark of good statistics. Statisticians gain by being introduced to the reality of problems by biologists who know what the crucial issues are."

Estimating Sugar in Oranges

In Florida, members of the citrus industry make extensive use of statistical methods. One particular application involves the way in which growers are paid for oranges used to make orange juice. An arriving truckload of oranges is first weighed at the receiving plant, then a sample of about a dozen oranges is randomly selected. The sample is weighed and then squeezed, and the amount of sugar in the juice is measured. Based on the sample results, an estimate is made of the total amount of sugar in the entire truckload. Payment for the load of oranges is based on the estimate of the amount of sugar because sweeter oranges are more valuable than those less sweet, even though the amounts of juice may be the same.

With $\bar{x} = 60.7$ and $E = 2.60503$, we construct the confidence interval as follows:

$$\bar{x} - E < \mu < \bar{x} + E$$

$$60.7 - 2.60503 < \mu < 60.7 + 2.60503$$

$$58.1 < \mu < 63.3 \quad \text{(rounded to one decimal place more than the original sample values)}$$

Interpretation

This result could also be expressed in the format of (58.1, 63.3) or the format of 60.7 ± 2.6. We are 95% confident that the limits of 58.1 mi/h and 63.3 mi/h actually do contain the value of the population mean μ. It appears that the mean speed is below the speed limit of 65 mi/h.

Because σ is rarely known, confidence interval estimates of a population mean μ almost always use the Student t distribution instead of the standard normal distribution. Here are some important properties of the Student t distribution.

Important Properties of the Student t Distribution

1. The Student t distribution is different for different sample sizes. (See Figure 7-5 for the cases $n = 3$ and $n = 12$.)

2. The Student t distribution has the same general symmetric bell shape as the standard normal distribution, but has more variability (with wider distributions) as we expect with small samples.

3. The Student t distribution has a mean of $t = 0$ (just as the standard normal distribution has a mean of $z = 0$).

4. The standard deviation of the Student t distribution varies with the sample size, but it is greater than 1 (unlike the standard normal distribution, which has $\sigma = 1$).

5. As the sample size n gets larger, the Student t distribution gets closer to the standard normal distribution.

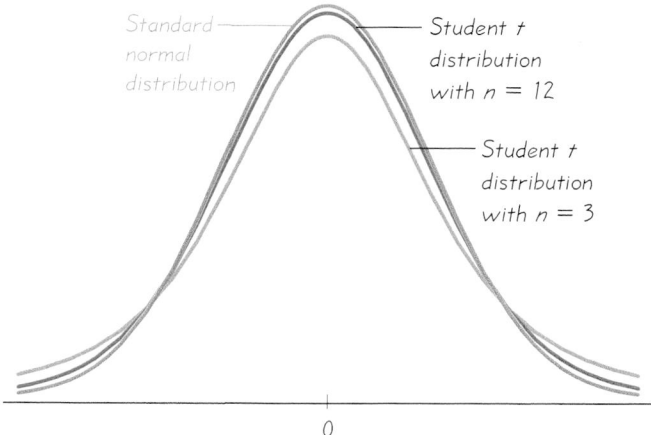

Figure 7-5   **Student *t* Distributions for *n* = 3 and *n* = 12**
The Student *t* distribution has the same general shape and symmetry as the standard normal distribution, but it reflects the greater variability that is expected with small samples.

Example 3 Confidence Interval for Alcohol Use in Video Games

Twelve different video games showing substance use were observed. The duration times (in seconds) of alcohol use were recorded, with the times listed below (based on data from "Content and Ratings of Teen-Rated Video Games," by Haninger and Thompson, *Journal of the American Medical Association,* Vol. 291, No. 7). The design of the study justifies the assumption that the sample can be treated as a simple random sample. Use the sample data to construct a 95% confidence interval estimate of μ, the mean duration time that the video showed the use of alcohol.

$$84 \quad 14 \quad 583 \quad 50 \quad 0 \quad 57 \quad 207 \quad 43 \quad 178 \quad 0 \quad 2 \quad 57$$

Solution

Requirement check We must first verify that the requirements are satisfied. (1) We can consider the sample to be a simple random sample. (2) When checking the requirement that "the population is normally distributed or $n > 30$," we see that the sample size is $n = 12$, so we must determine whether the data appear to be from a population with a normal distribution. Shown below are a Minitab-generated histogram and a STATDISK-generated normal quantile plot. The histogram does not appear to be bell-shaped, and the points in the normal quantile plot are not reasonably close to a straight-line pattern, so it appears that the times are not from a population having a normal distribution. The requirements are not satisfied. If we were to proceed with the construction of the confidence interval, we would get 1.8 sec $< \mu <$ 210.7 sec, but this result is questionable because it assumes incorrectly that the requirements are satisfied. ✓

Captured Tank Serial Numbers Reveal Population Size

During World War II, Allied intelligence specialists wanted to determine the number of tanks Germany was producing. Traditional spy techniques provided unreliable results, but statisticians obtained accurate estimates by analyzing serial numbers on captured tanks. As one example, records show that Germany actually produced 271 tanks in June 1941. The estimate based on serial numbers was 244, but traditional intelligence methods resulted in the extreme estimate of 1550. (See "An Empirical Approach to Economic Intelligence in World War II," by Ruggles and Brodie, *Journal of the American Statistical Association,* Vol. 42.)

STATDISK

MINITAB

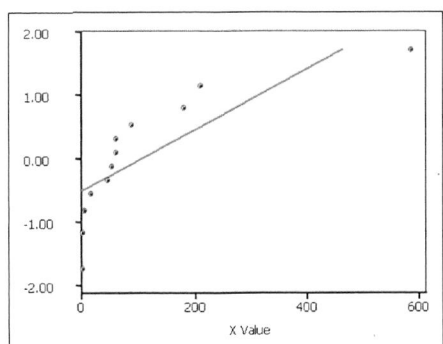

Interpretation

Because the requirement that "the population is normally distributed or $n > 30$" is not satisfied, we do not have 95% confidence that the limits of 1.8 sec and 210.7 sec actually do contain the value of the population mean. We should use some other approach for finding the confidence interval limits. For example, we could use the bootstrap resampling method described in the Technology Project at the end of this chapter.

Finding a Point Estimate and E from a Confidence Interval

When using technology to create a confidence interval, the result is often expressed in a format such as (18.128, 20.060). The sample mean $\bar{x}$ is the value midway between those limits, and the margin of error E is one-half the difference between those limits (because the upper limit is $\bar{x} + E$ and the lower limit is $\bar{x} - E$, the distance separating them is $2E$).

$$\text{Point estimate of } \mu: \quad \bar{x} = \frac{(\text{upper confidence limit}) + (\text{lower confidence limit})}{2}$$

$$\text{Margin of error:} \quad E = \frac{(\text{upper confidence limit}) - (\text{lower confidence limit})}{2}$$

Example 4   Chocolate Chips

The accompanying TI-83/84 Plus calculator screen displays results from counts of chocolate chips in a sample of 32 Chips Ahoy chewy cookies. The display shows the confidence interval limits for a 95% confidence level. Use the displayed confidence interval to find the values of the best point estimate $\bar{x}$ and the margin of error E.

Solution

The following results show that for the population of Chips Ahoy chewy cookies, the mean number of chocolate chips per cookie is estimated to be 19.1 (rounded) and the margin of error is 1.0 (rounded).

TI-83/84 PLUS

$$\bar{x} = \frac{(\text{upper confidence limit}) + (\text{lower confidence limit})}{2}$$

$$= \frac{20.06 + 18.128}{2} = 19.094 \text{ chocolate chips}$$

$$E = \frac{(\text{upper confidence limit}) - (\text{lower confidence limit})}{2}$$

$$= \frac{20.06 - 18.128}{2} = 0.966 \text{ chocolate chips}$$

Using Confidence Intervals to Describe, Explore, or Compare Data

In some cases, we might use a confidence interval to achieve an ultimate goal of estimating the value of a population parameter. In other cases, confidence intervals might be among the different tools used to describe, explore, or compare data sets.

Example 5   Second-Hand Smoke

Figure 7-6 shows graphs of confidence interval estimates of the mean cotinine level in each of three samples: (1) people who smoke; (2) people who don't smoke but are exposed to tobacco smoke at home or work; (3) people who don't smoke and are not exposed to smoke. (The sample data are listed in Data Set 9 in Appendix B.) Because cotinine is produced by the body when nicotine is absorbed, cotinine is a good indication of nicotine intake. Figure 7-6 helps us see the effects of second-hand smoke. In Figure 7-6, we see that the confidence interval for smokers does not overlap the other confidence intervals, so it appears that the mean cotinine level of smokers is different from that of the other two groups. The two nonsmoking groups have confidence intervals that do overlap, so it is possible that they have the same mean cotinine level. It is helpful to compare confidence intervals or their graphs, but such comparisons should not be used for making formal and final conclusions about equality of means. Chapters 9 and 12 introduce better methods for formal comparisons of means.

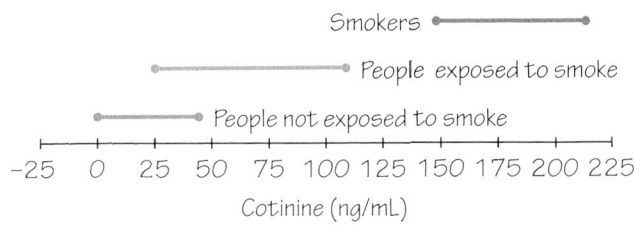

Figure 7-6   Comparing Confidence Intervals

CAUTION As in Sections 7-2 and 7-3, confidence intervals can be used *informally* to compare different data sets, but *the overlapping of confidence intervals should not be used for making formal and final conclusions about equality of means.*

Determining Sample Size If we want to collect a sample to be used for estimating a population mean μ, *how many* sample values do we need? When determining the sample size needed to estimate a population mean, we must have an estimated or known value of the population standard deviation σ, so that we can use Formula 7-4 shown in the accompanying box.

Finding the Sample Size Required to Estimate a Population Mean

Objective

Determine the sample size n required to estimate the value of a population mean μ.

Notation

μ = population mean

σ = population standard deviation

$\bar{x}$ = sample mean

E = desired margin of error

$z_{\alpha/2}$ = z score separating an area of $\alpha/2$ in the right tail of the standard normal distribution

Requirement

The sample must be a simple random sample.

Sample Size

The required sample size is found by using Formula 7-4.

Formula 7-4
$$n = \left[\frac{z_{\alpha/2}\sigma}{E} \right]^2$$

Round-Off Rule

If the computed sample size n is not a whole number, round the value of n up to the next *larger* whole number.

Population Size Formula 7-4 does not depend on the size (N) of the population (except for cases in which a relatively large sample is selected without replacement from a finite population).

Rounding The sample size must be a whole number because it is the number of sample values that must be found, but Formula 7-4 usually gives a result that is not a whole number. The round-off rule is based on the principle that when rounding is necessary, the required sample size should be rounded *upward* so that it is at least adequately large instead of being slightly too small.

Dealing with Unknown σ When Finding Sample Size Formula 7-4 requires that we substitute a known value for the population standard deviation σ, but in reality, it is usually unknown. When determining a required sample size (not constructing a confidence interval), here are some ways that we can work around the problem of not knowing the value of σ:

1. Use the range rule of thumb (see Section 3-3) to estimate the standard deviation as follows: $\sigma \approx \text{range}/4$. (With a sample of 87 or more values randomly selected from a normally distributed population, range/4 will yield a value that is greater than or equal to σ at least 95% of the time. See "Using the Sample Range as a Basis for Calculating Sample Size in Power Calculations," by Richard Browne, *American Statistician,* Vol. 55, No. 4.)

2. Start the sample collection process without knowing σ and, using the first several values, calculate the sample standard deviation s and use it in place of σ. The estimated value of σ can then be improved as more sample data are obtained, and the required sample size can be adjusted as you collect more sample data.

3. Estimate the value of σ by using the results of some other earlier study.

In addition, we can sometimes be creative in our use of other known results. For example, IQ tests are typically designed so that the mean is 100 and the standard deviation is 15. Statistics students have IQ scores with a mean greater than 100 and a standard deviation less than 15 (because they are a more homogeneous group than people randomly selected from the general population). We do not know the specific value of σ for statistics students, but we can play it safe by using $\sigma = 15$. Using a value for σ that is larger than the true value will make the sample size larger than necessary, but using a value for σ that is too small would result in a sample size that is inadequate. *When calculating the sample size n, any errors should always be conservative in the sense that they make n too large instead of too small.*

Example 6   IQ Scores of Statistics Students

Assume that we want to estimate the mean IQ score for the population of statistics students. How many statistics students must be randomly selected for IQ tests if we want 95% confidence that the sample mean is within 3 IQ points of the population mean?

Solution

For a 95% confidence interval, we have $\alpha = 0.05$, so $z_{\alpha/2} = 1.96$. Because we want the sample mean to be within 3 IQ points of μ, the margin of error is $E = 3$.

Also, we can assume that $\sigma = 15$ (see the discussion that immediately precedes this example). Using Formula 7-4, we get

$$n = \left[\frac{z_{\alpha/2}\sigma}{E}\right]^2 = \left[\frac{1.96 \cdot 15}{3}\right]^2 = 96.04 = 97 \quad (\text{rounded } up)$$

Interpretation

Among the thousands of statistics students, we need to obtain a simple random sample of at least 97 of their IQ scores. With a simple random sample of only 97 statistics students, we will be 95% confident that the sample mean $\bar{x}$ is within 3 IQ points of the true population mean μ.

Part 2: Estimating a Population Mean When σ is Known

In the real world of professional statisticians and professional journals and reports, it is extremely rare that we want to estimate an unknown value of a population mean but we somehow know the value of the population standard deviation σ. If we somehow do know the value of σ, the confidence interval is constructed using the standard normal distribution instead of the Student t distribution, as shown in the following box.

Confidence Interval for Estimating a Population Mean with σ Known

Requirements

1. The sample is a simple random sample.

2. Either or both of these conditions is satisfied: The population is normally distributed or $n > 30$.

Confidence Interval

$$\bar{x} - E < \mu < \bar{x} + E$$

or

$$\bar{x} \pm E$$

or

$$(\bar{x} - E, \bar{x} + E)$$

where the margin of error E is found from the following:

$$E = z_{\alpha/2} \cdot \frac{\sigma}{\sqrt{n}}$$

where $z_{\alpha/2}$ = critical z score separating an area of $\alpha/2$ in the right tail of the standard normal distribution. (Find $z_{\alpha/2}$ using technology or Table A-2.)

Example 7   Confidence Interval Estimate of μ with Known σ

Use the same sample of 12 highway speeds given in Example 2 and construct a 95% confidence interval estimate of the population mean by assuming that σ is known to be 4.1.

Solution

Requirement check The requirements were checked with the help of a dotplot in Example 2. The requirements are satisfied. ✓   *continued*

Power of Small Samples

The Environmental Protection Agency (EPA) had discovered that Chryslers had malfunctioning carburetors, with the result that carbon monoxide emissions were too high. Chryslers with 360- and 400-cubic-inch displacements and two-barrel carburetors were involved. The EPA ordered Chrysler to fix the problem, but Chrysler refused, and the case of *Chrysler Corporation vs. The Environmental Protection Agency* followed. That case led to the conclusion that there was "substantial evidence" that the Chryslers produced excessive levels of carbon monoxide. The EPA won the case and Chrysler was forced to recall and repair 208,000 vehicles. In discussing this case in an article in *AMSTAT News,* Chief Statistician for the EPA Barry Nussbaum wrote this: "Sampling is expensive, and environmental sampling is usually quite expensive. At the EPA, we have to do the best we can with small samples or develop models. . . . What was the sample size required to affect such a recall (of the 208,000 Chryslers)? The answer is a mere 10. It is both an affirmation of the power of inferential statistics and a challenge to explain how such a (small) sample could possibly suffice."

We can proceed with the construction of the confidence interval by first finding the critical value $z_{\alpha/2}$. With a 95% confidence level, we have $\alpha = 0.5$, and we get $z_{\alpha/2} = 1.96$ (as shown in Example 2 from Section 7-2). Using $z_{\alpha/2} = 1.96$, $\sigma = 4.1$, and $n = 12$, we find the value of the margin of error E:

$$E = z_{\alpha/2} \cdot \frac{\sigma}{\sqrt{n}}$$

$$= 1.96 \cdot \frac{4.1}{\sqrt{12}} = 2.31979$$

Using the 12 sample values listed in Example 2, we find that $\bar{x} = 60.7$. With $\bar{x} = 60.7$ and $E = 2.31979$, we find the 95% confidence interval as follows:

$$\bar{x} - E < \mu < \bar{x} + E$$

$$60.7 - 2.31979 < \mu < 60.7 + 2.31979$$

$$58.4 < \mu < 63.0 \quad \text{(rounded to one decimal place more than the original sample values)}$$

Remember, this example illustrates the situation in which the population standard deviation σ is known, which is rare. The more realistic situation with σ unknown is considered in Part 1 of this section.

Choosing the Appropriate Distribution

When constructing a confidence interval estimate of the population mean μ, it is important to use the correct distribution. Table 7-1 summarizes the key points to consider. Table 7-1 shows that when we have a small sample ($n < 30$) drawn from a distribution that differs dramatically from a normal distribution, we can't use the methods of this chapter. In such cases, we might use nonparametric methods (see Chapter 13) or bootstrap resampling methods. (The bootstrap method is described in the Technology Project at the end of this chapter.) Remember that in reality, σ is rarely known, so estimates of μ typically involve the Student t distribution, provided that its requirements are met.

Table 7-1 Choosing between Student t and z (Normal) Distributions

Conditions	Method
σ not known and normally distributed population *or* σ not known and $n > 30$	Use Student t distribution.
σ known and normally distributed population *or* σ known and $n > 30$ (In reality, σ is rarely known.)	Use normal (z) distribution.
Population is not normally distributed and $n \le 30$.	Use a nonparametric method or the bootstrapping method.

Notes: 1. **Criteria for deciding whether the population is normally distributed:** The normality requirement is loose, so the distribution should appear to be somewhat symmetric with one mode and no outliers.

2. **Sample size $n > 30$:** This is a common guideline, but sample sizes of 15 to 30 are adequate if the population appears to have a distribution that is not far from being normal and there are no outliers. For some population distributions that are extremely far from normal, the sample size might need to be larger than 30.

using TECHNOLOGY

Confidence Intervals

STATDISK You must first find the sample size n, the sample mean $\bar{x}$, and the sample standard deviation s. (Find those statistics using the STATDISK procedure described in Section 3-2.) Select **Analysis** from the main menu bar, select **Confidence Intervals,** then select **Population Mean.** Enter the items in the dialog box, then click the **Evaluate** button. The confidence interval will be displayed. STATDISK will automatically choose between the normal and t distributions, depending on whether a value for the population standard deviation is entered.

MINITAB Minitab allows you to use either the summary statistics n, $\bar{x}$, and s or a list of the original sample values. Select **Stat** and **Basic Statistics.** If σ is not known, select **1-sample t** and enter the summary statistics or enter **C1** in the box located at the top right. (If σ is known, select **1-sample Z** and enter the summary statistics or enter **C1** in the box located at the top right. Also enter the value of σ in the "Standard Deviation" or "Sigma" box.) Use the **Options** button to enter the confidence level, such as 95.0.

EXCEL Use XLSTAT. Click on **XLSTAT** at the top, click on **Parametric tests,** then select **One sample t test and z test.** In the screen that appears, for the "Data" box enter the range of data, such as A1:A12 for 12 data values in column A. For "Data Format" select **One sample.** Click on the "Student's t test" box (or click on the "z test" box if σ is known). Click on the **Options** tab to enter the desired "Significance level (%)." Enter 5 for a 95% confidence interval. Select the format of "Mean 1 $\neq$ Theoretical mean" and enter any value for the theoretical mean. Click **OK.** After the results are displayed, look for "confidence interval on the mean." (The use of Excel's **CONFIDENCE** tool is not recommended, for a variety of reasons.)

TI-83/84 PLUS The TI-83/84 Plus calculator can be used to generate confidence intervals for original sample values stored in a list, or you can use the summary statistics n, $\bar{x}$, and s. Either enter the data in list L1 or have the summary statistics available, then press **STAT**. Now select **TESTS** and choose **TInterval** if σ is not known. (Choose **ZInterval** if σ is known.) After making the required entries, the calculator display will include the confidence interval in the format of $(\bar{x} - E, \bar{x} + E)$. For example, see the TI-83/84 Plus display that accompanies Example 4 in this section.

STATCRUNCH Click on **Open StatCrunch.** Click on **Stat,** then select **T statistics.** Select **One sample,** then select **with data** (for a list of sample data) or **with summary** (for summary statistics). Click on **Next,** then select **Confidence Interval** and click on **Calculate.**

Sample Size Determination

STATDISK Select **Analysis** from the main menu bar at the top, then select **Sample Size Determination,** followed by **Estimate Mean.** Enter the confidence level (such as 0.95) and the margin of error E. You can also enter the population standard deviation σ if it is known. There is also an option that allows you to enter a known population size N, assuming that you are sampling without replacement from a finite population.

MINITAB Using Minitab 16 or later, select **Stat** from the main menu, select **Power and Sample Size,** then select **Sample Size for Estimation.** Choose the parameter of **Mean (Normal).** Complete the dialog box and click **OK.**

Sample size determination is not available as a built-in function with Excel or StatCrunch or the TI-83/84 Plus calculator.

7-3 Basic Skills and Concepts

Statistical Literacy and Critical Thinking

In Exercises 1–3, refer to the accompanying screen display that results from a sample of 40 duration times (seconds) of eruptions of the Old Faithful geyser in Yellowstone National Park.

1. Confidence Interval Refer to the accompanying screen display.

a. Express the confidence interval in the format that uses the "less than" symbol.

b. Identify the best point estimate of μ and the margin of error.

TI-83/84 Plus

```
TInterval
 (233.4,256.65)
 x̄=245.025
 Sx=36.35754604
 n=40
```

2. Degrees of Freedom For the accompanying screen display, a simple random sample of size $n = 40$ was obtained from the population of duration times (seconds) of eruptions of the Old Faithful geyser.

a. What is the number of degrees of freedom that should be used for finding the critical value $t_{\alpha/2}$?

b. Find the critical value $t_{\alpha/2}$ corresponding to $n = 40$ and a 95% confidence level.

c. Give a brief general description of the number of degrees of freedom.

3. Interpreting a Confidence Interval The results in the screen display are based on a 95% confidence level. Write a statement that correctly interprets the confidence interval.

4. Normality Requirement What does it mean when we say that the confidence interval methods of this section are *robust* against departures from normality? Does the dotplot below appear to satisfy the requirement of this section? Why or why not?

Chocolate Chips in Chips Ahoy Reduced Fat Cookies

Using Correct Distribution. *In Exercises 5–8, assume that we want to construct a confidence interval. Do one of the following, as appropriate: (a) Find the critical value $t_{\alpha/2}$, (b) find the critical value $z_{\alpha/2}$, (c) state that neither the normal distribution nor the t distribution applies.*

5. Confidence level is 95%, σ is known to be $4,385,000, and the dotplot of a sample of Red Sox baseball player salaries is as shown below.

Salary (thousands of dollars)

6. Confidence level is 90%, σ is not known, and the dotplot of IQ scores of 20 randomly selected statistics instructors is as shown below.

IQ

7. Confidence level is 99%, σ is not known, and the dotplot of a sample of 40 values of professional baseball player salaries is as shown below.

Salary (thousands of dollars)

8. Confidence level is 99%, σ is known to be $4,385,000, and the dotplot of 40 sample values of professional baseball players is as shown in Exercise 7.

Confidence Intervals. *In Exercises 9–24, construct the confidence interval.*

9. Earthquake Depths Data Set 16 in Appendix B lists the depths (km) of a sample of 50 earthquakes. Those 50 depths have a mean of 9.808 km and a standard deviation of 5.013 km. Construct a 98% confidence interval estimate of the mean of all such depths. Is the confidence interval affected by the fact that the data appear to be from a population that is not normally distributed? (*Hint:* If using Table A-3 to find the critical value $t_{\alpha/2}$, that table does not include 49 degrees of freedom, so use the closest value for 50 degrees of freedom.)

10. Mercury in Sushi Listed below are the amounts of mercury (in parts per million, or ppm) found in tuna sushi sampled at different stores in New York City. The study was sponsored by the *New York Times,* and the stores (in order) are D'Agostino, Eli's Manhattan, Fairway, Food Emporium, Gourmet Garage, Grace's Marketplace, and Whole Foods. The sample mean is 0.719 ppm and the standard deviation is 0.366 ppm. Construct a 90% confidence interval estimate of the mean amount of mercury in the population.

0.56   0.75   0.10   0.95   1.25   0.54   0.88

11. CEO Compensation Listed below are the recent annual compensation amounts (in thousands of dollars) for a random sample of chief executive officers (Mulally from Ford, Jobs from Apple, Kent from Coca-Cola, Otellini from Intel, and McNerney from Boeing). The mean of the sample is 12,898 (thousand dollars) and the standard deviation is 7719 (thousand dollars). Construct a 95% confidence interval estimate of the mean of the population of all such chief executive officers. Is there anything notable about the sample data that might have an effect on the result?

17,688   0.001   19,629   12,408   14,765

12. Chocolate Chip Cookies The Chapter Problem for Chapter 3 includes the numbers of chocolate chips in a sample of 40 Chips Ahoy regular cookies. The mean is 23.95 chocolate chips and the standard deviation is 2.55 chocolate chips. Construct a 99% confidence interval estimate of the mean number of chocolate chips in all such cookies. How does the confidence interval not contradict the fact that most of the original values do not fall between the confidence interval limits?

13. Mean Body Temperature Data Set 3 in Appendix B includes a sample of 106 body temperatures having a mean of 98.20°F and a standard deviation of 0.62°F. Construct a 95% confidence interval estimate of the mean body temperature for the entire population. What does the result suggest about the common belief that 98.6°F is the mean body temperature?

14. Atkins Weight Loss Program In a test of weight loss programs, 40 adults used the Atkins weight loss program. After 12 months, their mean weight *loss* was found to be 2.1 lb, with a standard deviation of 4.8 lb. Construct a 90% confidence interval estimate of the mean weight loss for all such subjects. Does the Atkins program appear to be effective? Does it appear to be practical?

15. Garlic for Reducing Cholesterol In a test of the effectiveness of garlic for lowering cholesterol, 49 subjects were treated with raw garlic. Cholesterol levels were measured before and after the treatment. The changes (before minus after) in their levels of LDL cholesterol (in mg/dL) had a mean of 0.4 and a standard deviation of 21.0 (based on data from "Effect of Raw Garlic vs Commercial Garlic Supplements on Plasma Lipid Concentrations in Adults with Moderate Hypercholesterolemia," by Gardner et al., *Archives of Internal Medicine,* Vol. 167). Construct a 98% confidence interval estimate of the mean net change in LDL cholesterol after the garlic treatment. What does the confidence interval suggest about the effectiveness of garlic in reducing LDL cholesterol?

16. Insomnia Treatment A clinical trial was conducted to test the effectiveness of the drug zopiclone for treating insomnia in older subjects. Before treatment with zopiclone, 16 subjects had a mean wake time of 102.8 min. After treatment with zoplicone, the

16 subjects had a mean wake time of 98.9 min and a standard deviation of 42.3 min (based on data from "Cognitive Behavioral Therapy vs Zopiclone for Treatment of Chronic Primary Insomnia in Older Adults," by Siversten et al., *Journal of the American Medical Association*, Vol. 295, No. 24). Assume that the 16 sample values appear to be from a normally distributed population and construct a 98% confidence interval estimate of the mean wake time for a population with zopiclone treatments. What does the result suggest about the mean wake time of 102.8 min before the treatment? Does zopiclone appear to be effective?

17. Harry Potter Listed below are the gross amounts (in millions of dollars) earned from box office receipts for the movie *Harry Potter and the Half-Blood Prince.* The movie opened on a Wednesday, and the amounts are listed in order for the first 14 days of the movie's release. Use the sample values to construct a 99% confidence interval estimate of the population mean. What is the population? Identify at least one major problem with this data set.

58   22   27   29   21   10   10   8   7   9   11   9   4   4

18. Years in College Listed below are the numbers of years it took for a random sample of college students to earn bachelor's degrees (based on data from the National Center for Education Statistics). Construct a 90% confidence interval estimate of the mean time required for all college students to earn bachelor's degrees. Does the confidence interval contain the value of 4 years? Is there anything about the data that would suggest that the confidence interval might not be a good result?

4   4   4   4   4   4   4.5   4.5   4.5   4.5   4.5   4.5   6   6   8   9   9   13   13   15

19. Cell Phone Radiation Listed below are the measured radiation emissions (in W/kg) corresponding to these cell phones: Samsung SGH-tss9, Blackberry Storm, Blackberry Curve, Motorola Moto, T-Mobile Sidekick, Sanyo Katana Eclipse, Palm Pre, Sony Ericsson, Nokia 6085, Apple iPhone 3G S, Kyocero Neo E1100. The data are from the Environmental Working Group. The media often present reports about the dangers of cell phone radiation as a cause of cancer. Construct a 90% confidence interval estimate of the population mean. What does the result suggest about the Federal Communications Commission standard that cell phone radiation must be 1.6 W/kg or less?

0.38   0.55   1.54   1.55   0.50   0.60   0.92   0.96   1.00   0.86   1.46

20. Ages of Race Car Drivers Listed below are the ages (years) of randomly selected race car drivers (based on data reported in *USA Today*). Construct a 98% confidence interval estimate of the mean age of all race car drivers.

32   32   33   33   41   29   38   32   33   23   27   45   52   29   25

21. Lead in Medicine Listed below are the lead concentrations (in $\mu g/g$) measured in different Ayurveda medicines. Ayurveda is a traditional medical system commonly used in India. The lead concentrations listed here are from medicines manufactured in the United States. The data are based on the article "Lead, Mercury, and Arsenic in US and Indian Manufactured Ayurvedic Medicines Sold via the Internet," by Saper et al., *Journal of the American Medical Association*, Vol. 300, No. 8. Use the sample data to construct a 95% confidence interval estimate of the mean of the lead concentrations for the population of all such medicines. If a safety standard requires lead concentrations less than 7 $\mu g/g$, does it appear that the population mean is less than that level?

3.0   6.5   6.0   5.5   20.5   7.5   12.0   20.5   11.5   17.5

22. Brain Volume Listed below are brain volumes (cm^3) of unrelated subjects used in a study. (See Data Set 6 in Appendix B.) Use the sample data to construct a 99% confidence interval estimate of the mean of the brain volume of the population. Given that typical brain volumes are between 950 cm^3 and 1800 cm^3, do these values appear to be typical?

963   1027   1272   1079   1070   1173   1067   1347   1100   1204

23. Age Discrimination? The accompanying stemplots depict ages of applicants who were unsuccessful in winning promotion and ages of applicants who were successful in winning promotion (based on data from "Debating the Use of Statistical Evidence in Allegations of Age Discrimination" by Barry and Boland, *American Statistician*, Vol. 58, No. 2). Assume that the samples are simple random samples and use a 95% confidence level to construct the two confidence interval estimates of the two population means. Compare the results. What do you conclude?

Ages of Unsuccessful Applicants	Ages of Successful Applicants
3 | 4778	3 | 367889
4 | 12344555689	4 | 2233444555566778899
5 | 3344567	5 | 1124
6 | 0	

24. Interbreeding of Cultures Changes in head sizes over time suggest interbreeding with people from other regions. Use the data depicted in the accompanying dotplots and construct 95% confidence intervals to determine whether skull breadths (mm) appear to have changed from 4000 B.C. to 150 A.D. Explain your conclusion.

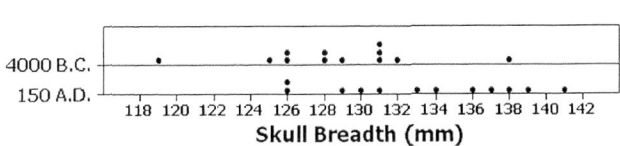

Skull Breadth (mm)

Sample Size. *In Exercises 25–32, find the sample size required to estimate the population mean.*

25. Mean IQ of Professional Pilots The Wechsler IQ test is designed so that the mean is 100 and the standard deviation is 15 for the population of normal adults. Find the sample size necessary to estimate the mean IQ score of professional pilots. We want to be 90% confident that our sample mean is within 3 IQ points of the true mean. The mean for this population is clearly greater than 100. The standard deviation for this population is probably less than 15 because it is a group with less variation than a group randomly selected from the general population; therefore, if we use $\sigma = 15$ we are being conservative by using a value that will make the sample size at least as large as necessary. Assume then that $\sigma = 15$ and determine the required sample size. Does the sample size appear to be reasonable?

26. Mean Grade Point Average As part of a study of grade inflation, you want to estimate the mean grade point average of all current college students in the United States. All grade point averages are to be standardized for a scale between 0 and 4. How many grade point averages must be obtained so that the sample mean is within 0.2 of the population mean? Assume that a 99% confidence level is desired. Also assume that a pilot study showed that the population standard deviation is estimated to be 0.79. Does it make sense to collect the entire sample at your college?

27. Buying a Corvette Research of selling prices for used two-year-old Corvettes reveals that they have a standard deviation of $2157 (based on data from Edmunds.com). How many selling prices must you obtain in order to estimate the mean selling price of these cars? Assume that you want 98% confidence that your sample mean is within $250 of the population mean. Is it likely that you will find that many two-year-old used Corvettes in your region?

28. Facebook Time You want to estimate the mean amount of time Internet users spend on Facebook each month. How many Internet users must be surveyed in order to be 95% confident that your sample mean is within 15 minutes of the population mean? Based on results from a prior Nielsen survey, assume that the standard deviation of the population of monthly times spent on Facebook is 210 min. What is a major obstacle to getting a good estimate of the population mean?

29. Sample Size Using Range Rule of Thumb You want to estimate the mean SAT score of all college applicants. First use the range rule of thumb to make a rough estimate of the standard deviation of those scores. Possible SAT scores range from 600 to 2400. Use the estimated standard deviation to determine the sample size corresponding to a 98% confidence level and a margin of error of 100 points. What isn't quite right with this exercise?

30. Sample Size Using Range Rule of Thumb You want to estimate the mean amount of annual tuition being paid by current full-time college students in the United States. First use the range rule of thumb to make a rough estimate of the standard deviation of the amounts spent. It is reasonable to assume that tuition amounts range from $0 to about $45,000. Then use that estimated standard deviation to determine the sample size corresponding to 99% confidence and a $100 margin of error. Does the resulting sample size seem practical?

31. Sample Size Using Sample Data Refer to Data Set 1 in Appendix B and find the maximum and minimum pulse rates for males, then use those values with the range rule of thumb to estimate σ. How many adult males must you randomly select and test if you want to be 95% confident that the sample mean pulse rate is within 2 beats (per minute) of the true population mean μ. The standard deviation of the 40 pulse rates of males in Data Set 1 is 10.3 beats per minute. If, instead of using the range rule of thumb, the standard deviation of the sample is used as an estimate of σ, is the required sample size very different? Which result is likely to be closer to the correct sample size?

32. Sample Size Using Sample Data Refer to Data Set 16 in Appendix B and find the maximum and minimum earthquake magnitudes, then use those values with the range rule of thumb to estimate σ. How many earthquakes must you randomly select if you want to be 95% confident that the sample mean magnitude is within 0.2 of the true population mean μ? The standard deviation of the 50 earthquake magnitudes in Data Set 16 is 0.587. Find the required sample size by using the standard deviation of the sample as an estimate of σ. Which of the two results is likely to be better?

Appendix B Data Sets. *In Exercises 33 and 34, use the data sets from Appendix B.*

33. Earthquake Magnitudes Use the earthquake magnitudes listed in Data Set 16 from Appendix B and construct a 99% confidence interval estimate of the mean of all such magnitudes.

34. Second-Hand Smoke Figure 7-6 from Example 5 shows a graph of three different confidence intervals. Use the cotinine levels of smokers listed in Data Set 9 from Appendix B and construct the 95% confidence interval estimate of the population mean μ.

7-3 Beyond the Basics

Confidence Interval with Known σ. *In Exercises 35–38, find the confidence interval using the known value of σ.*

35. Construct the confidence interval for Exercise 9 assuming that σ is known to be 5.013 km.

36. Construct the confidence interval for Exercise 10 assuming that σ is known to be 0.366 ppm.

37. Construct the confidence interval for Exercise 11 assuming that σ is known to be 7718.8 thousand dollars.

38. Construct the confidence interval for Exercise 12 assuming that σ is known to be 2.55 chocolate chips.

39. Outlier Effect If the first value of 3.0 in Exercise 21 is changed to 300, it becomes an outlier. Does this outlier have much of an effect on the confidence interval? How should you handle outliers when they are found in sample data sets that will be used for the construction of confidence intervals?

40. Finite Population Correction Factor If a simple random sample of size n is selected without replacement from a finite population of size N, and the sample size is more than 5% of the population size ($n > 0.05N$), better results can be obtained by using the finite population correction factor, which involves multiplying the margin of error E by $\sqrt{(N - n)/(N - 1)}$. For the sample of 100 weights of M&M candies in Data Set 20 from Appendix B, we get $\bar{x} = 0.8565$ g and $s = 0.0518$ g. First construct a 95% confidence interval estimate of μ assuming that the population is large, then construct a 95% confidence interval estimate of the mean weight of M&Ms in the full bag from which the sample was taken. The full bag has 465 M&Ms. Compare the results.

41. Confidence Interval for Sample of Size $n = 1$ Based on the article "An Effective Confidence Interval for the Mean with Samples of Size One and Two," by Wall, Boen, and Tweedie (*American Statistician,* Vol. 55, No. 2), a 95% confidence interval for μ can be found (using methods not discussed in this book) for a sample of size $n = 1$ randomly selected from a normally distributed population, and it can be expressed as $x \pm 9.68|x|$. Use this result to construct a 95% confidence interval using only the first sample value listed in Exercise 21. How does it compare to the result found in Exercise 21 when all of the sample values are used?

7-4 Estimating a Population Standard Deviation or Variance

Key Concept This section presents methods for using a sample standard deviation s (or a sample variance s^2) to estimate the value of the corresponding population standard deviation σ (or population variance σ^2). The methods of this section require that we use a *chi-square distribution*. (The Greek letter chi is pronounced "kigh.") Here are the main concepts included in this section:

- **Point Estimate:** The sample variance s^2 is the best *point estimate* (or single value estimate) of the population variance σ^2. The sample standard deviation s is commonly used as a point estimate of σ (even though it is a biased estimator). (Section 6-4 showed that s^2 is an unbiased estimator of σ^2, but s is a biased estimator of σ.)

- **Confidence Interval:** When constructing a *confidence interval* estimate of a population standard deviation (or population variance), we construct the confidence interval using the χ^2 (*chi-square*) *distribution*.

- **Chi-Square Distribution:** We should know how to find critical values of χ^2.

Here are some key points about the chi-square distribution:

Chi-Square Distribution: In a normally distributed population with variance σ^2, if we randomly select independent samples of size n and, for each sample, compute the sample variance s^2 (which is the square of the sample standard deviation s), the sample statistic $\chi^2 = (n - 1)s^2/\sigma^2$ has a sampling distribution called the **chi-square distribution,** so Formula 7-5 shows the format of the sample statistic.

Formula 7-5
$$\chi^2 = \frac{(n - 1)s^2}{\sigma^2}$$

- **Finding Critical Values of X^2** We denote a right-tailed critical value by X_R^2 and we denote a left-tailed critical value by X_L^2. Those critical values can be found by using technology or Table A-4, and they require that we first determine a value for the number of *degrees of freedom.*

- **Degrees of Freedom** In general, the number of **degrees of freedom** (or **df**) for a collection of sample data is the number of sample values that can vary after certain restrictions have been imposed on all data values. For the methods of this section, the number of degrees of freedom is the sample size minus 1.

$$\text{degrees of freedom: df} = n - 1$$

CAUTION In later chapters we will encounter situations in which the degrees of freedom are not $n - 1$, so it is wrong to make the incorrect generalization that the number of degrees of freedom is always $n - 1$.

Properties of the Chi-Square Distribution

1. The chi-square distribution is not symmetric, unlike the normal and Student t distributions (see Figure 7-7). (As the number of degrees of freedom increases, the distribution becomes more symmetric, as Figure 7-8 illustrates.)

2. The values of chi-square can be zero or positive, but they cannot be negative (as shown in Figure 7-7).

3. The chi-square distribution is different for each number of degrees of freedom (as illustrated in Figure 7-8). As the number of degrees of freedom increases, the chi-square distribution approaches a normal distribution.

Figure 7-7   Chi-Square Distribution

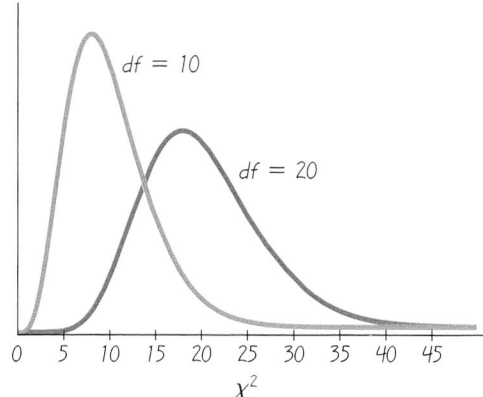

Figure 7-8   Chi-Square Distribution for df = 10 and df = 20

Because the chi-square distribution is not symmetric, a confidence interval for σ^2 does not fit a format of $s^2 - E < \sigma^2 < s^2 + E$, so we must do separate calculations for the upper and lower confidence interval limits. If using Table A-4 for finding critical values, note the following design feature of that table:

In Table A-4, each critical value of X^2 in the body of the table corresponds to an area given in the top row of the table, and each area in that top row is a *cumulative area to the right* of the critical value.

Example 1 Finding Critical Values of X^2

A simple random sample of 22 IQ scores is obtained (as in Example 2 which follows). Construction of a confidence interval for the population standard deviation σ requires the left and right critical values of X^2 corresponding to a confidence level of 95% and a sample size of $n = 22$. Find the critical value of X^2 separating an area of 0.025 in the left tail, and find the critical value of X^2 separating an area of 0.025 in the right tail.

Solution

With a sample size of $n = 22$, the number of degrees of freedom is df $= n - 1 = 21$. See Figure 7-9.

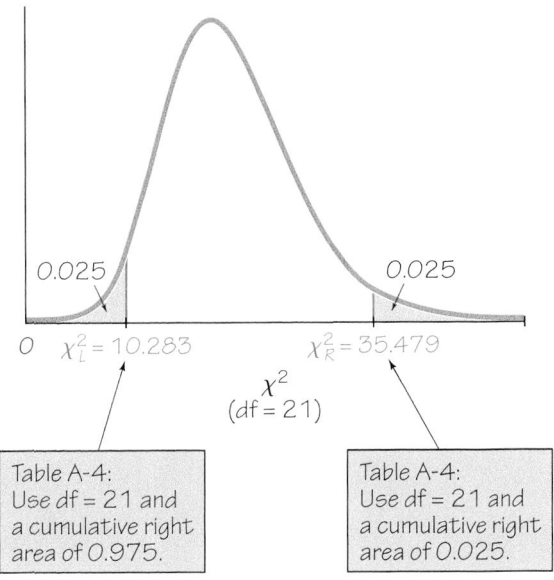

Figure 7-9 Finding Critical Values of χ_2

The critical value to the right ($X_R^2 = 35.479$) is obtained in a straightforward manner by locating 21 in the degrees-of-freedom column at the left and 0.025 across the top row. The leftmost critical value of $X_L^2 = 10.283$ also corresponds to 21 in the degrees-of-freedom column, but we must locate 0.975 (found by subtracting 0.025 from 1) across the top row because the values in the top row are always *areas to the right* of the critical value. Refer to Figure 7-9 and see that the total area to the right of $X_L^2 = 10.283$ is 0.975. Figure 7-9 shows that, for a sample of 22 values taken from a normally distributed population, the chi-square statistic $(n - 1)s^2/\sigma^2$ has a 0.95 probability of falling between the chi-square critical values of 10.283 and 35.479.

Instead of using Table A-4, technology (such as STATDISK, Excel, Minitab, and StatCrunch) can be used to find critical values of X^2. A major advantage of technology is that it can be used for any number of degrees of freedom and any confidence level, not just the limited choices included in Table A-4. Another major advantage of technology is that you can often generate the confidence interval without going through the steps of finding the critical values and manually calculating the confidence interval limits.

How Many People Do You Know?

Although the typical person cannot identify the number of people that he or she knows, methods of statistics can be used to estimate that number. The simple approach of simply asking someone how many people are known has been found to work poorly, due in large part to the same problems associated with voluntary response samples. Some other past approaches are based on the use of diaries and phonebooks. With one method, subjects are asked how many people they know in specific sub-populations. For example, subjects might be asked how many people they know who are named Adam, or how many people they know who have a twin brother or sister. Responses to such questions could be used to project the total number of people that are known. According to one estimate, the mean number of people known is 611, and the median is 472 (based on "How Many People Do You Know?: Efficiently Estimating Personal Network Size," by McCormick, Salganik, and Zheng, *Journal of the American Statistical Association*, Vol. 105, No. 489).

When obtaining critical values of X^2 from Table A-4, the numbers of degrees of freedom are consecutive integers from 1 to 30, followed by 40, 50, 60, 70, 80, 90, and 100. If a number of degrees of freedom (such as 52) is not found in the table, you can be conservative by using the next lower number of degrees of freedom, or you can use the closest critical value in the table, or you can get an approximate result with interpolation. For numbers of degrees of freedom greater than 100, use the equation given in Exercise 23, or use a more extensive table, or use technology.

Although s^2 is the best point estimate of σ^2, there is no indication of how good it actually is. To compensate for that deficiency, we develop an interval estimate (or confidence interval) that gives us a range of values associated with a confidence level.

Confidence Interval for Estimating a Population Standard Deviation or Variance

Objective

Construct a confidence interval used to estimate a population standard deviation or variance.

Notation

σ = population standard deviation σ^2 = population variance

s = sample standard deviation s^2 = sample variance

n = number of sample values E = margin of error

X_L^2 = left-tailed critical value of X^2 X_R^2 = right-tailed critical value of X^2

Requirements

1. The sample is a simple random sample.

2. The population must have normally distributed values (even if the sample is large). The requirement of a normal distribution is much stricter here than in earlier sections, so departures from normal distributions can result in large errors.

Confidence Interval for the Population Variance σ^2

$$\frac{(n-1)s^2}{X_R^2} < \sigma^2 < \frac{(n-1)s^2}{X_L^2}$$

Confidence Interval for the Population Standard Deviation σ

$$\sqrt{\frac{(n-1)s^2}{X_R^2}} < \sigma < \sqrt{\frac{(n-1)s^2}{X_L^2}}$$

Round-Off Rule

1. When using the *original set of data* values to construct a confidence interval, round the confidence interval limits to one more decimal place than is used for the original set of data.

2. When using the *summary statistics* (n, s) for constructing a confidence interval, round the confidence interval limits to the same number of decimal places used for the sample standard deviation.

Confidence intervals can be easily constructed with technology or they can be constructed by using Table A-4 with the following procedure.

Procedure for Constructing a Confidence Interval for σ or σ^2

1. Verify that the two requirements in the preceding box are satisfied.

2. Using $n - 1$ degrees of freedom, use technology or refer to Table A-4 to find the critical values χ^2_R and χ^2_L that correspond to the desired confidence level (as in Example 1).

3. Evaluate the upper and lower confidence interval limits using this format of the confidence interval:

$$\frac{(n - 1)s^2}{\chi^2_R} < \sigma^2 < \frac{(n - 1)s^2}{\chi^2_L}$$

4. If a confidence interval estimate of σ is desired, take the square root of the upper and lower confidence interval limits and change σ^2 to σ.

5. Round the resulting confidence interval limits using the round-off rule given in the preceding box.

CAUTION Confidence intervals can be used *informally* to compare the variation in different data sets, but *the overlapping of confidence intervals should not be used for making formal and final conclusions about equality of variances or standard deviations.*

Using Confidence Intervals for Hypothesis Tests

A confidence interval can be used to *test some claim* made about σ or σ^2. Formal methods of hypothesis testing are introduced in Chapter 8, and those methods might require adjustments to confidence intervals that are not described in this chapter. (We might need to construct a one-sided confidence interval or adjust the confidence level by using 90% instead of 95%.)

CAUTION Know that in this chapter, when we use a confidence interval to address a claim about σ or σ^2, we are making an *informal judgment* (that may or may not be consistent with formal methods of hypothesis testing introduced in Chapter 8).

Example 2 Confidence Interval for Estimating σ of IQ Scores

Data Set 5 in Appendix B lists IQ scores for subjects in three different lead exposure groups. The 22 full IQ scores for the group with medium exposure to lead (Group 2) have a standard deviation of 14.3. Consider the sample to be a simple random sample and construct a 95% confidence interval estimate of σ, the standard deviation of the population from which the sample was obtained.

Solution

Requirement check

Step 1: We first verify that the requirements are satisfied. (1) The sample can be treated as a simple random sample. (2) The following display shows a Minitab-generated histogram. Except for one low score, the shape of the histogram is very close to the bell shape of a normal distribution, so the requirement of normality is satisfied. (It would be wise to find the confidence interval with the low score excluded so we can see its effect.) This check of requirements is Step 1 in the process of finding a confidence interval of σ, so we proceed with Step 2. ✓

MINITAB

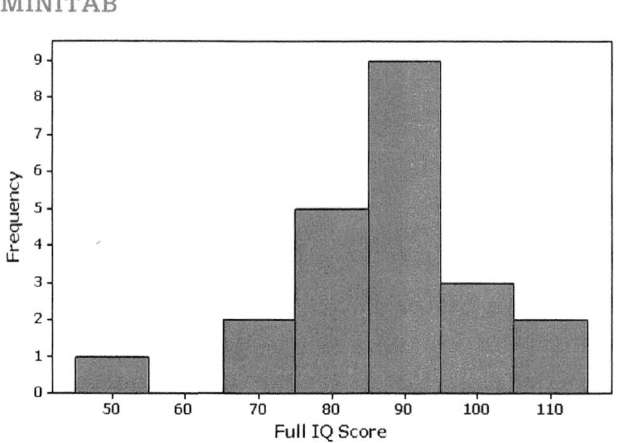

Step 2: The confidence interval can be found using technology. If using Table A-4, we first use the sample size of $n = 22$ to determine that the number of degrees of freedom is given by df $= n - 1 = 21$. If we use Table A-4, we refer to the row corresponding to 21 degrees of freedom, and we refer to the columns with areas of 0.975 and 0.025. (For a 95% confidence level, we divide $\alpha = 0.05$ equally between the two tails of the chi-square distribution, and we refer to the values of 0.975 and 0.025 across the top row of Table A-4.) The critical values are $\chi_L^2 = 10.283$ and $\chi_R^2 = 35.479$ (as shown in Example 1).

Step 3: Using the critical values of 10.283 and 35.479, the sample standard deviation of $s = 14.3$, and the sample size of $n = 22$, we construct the 95% confidence interval by evaluating the following:

$$\frac{(n-1)s^2}{\chi_R^2} < \sigma^2 < \frac{(n-1)s^2}{\chi_L^2}$$

$$\frac{(22-1)(14.3)^2}{35.479} < \sigma^2 < \frac{(22-1)(14.3)^2}{10.283}$$

Step 4: Evaluating the expression above results in $121.0 < \sigma^2 < 417.6$. Finding the square root of each part (before rounding), then rounding to one decimal place, yields this 95% confidence interval estimate of the population standard deviation: $11.0 < \sigma < 20.4$.

Interpretation

Based on this result, we have 95% confidence that the limits of 11.0 and 20.4 contain the true value of σ. The confidence interval can also be expressed as (11.0, 20.4).

The IQ test was designed so that the population of IQ scores would have a standard deviation of 16, and the value of 16 is contained within the confidence interval, so the variation of the IQ scores does not appear to be unusual.

Rationale for the Confidence Interval If we obtain simple random samples of size n from a normally distributed population with variance σ^2, there is a probability of $1 - \alpha$ that the statistic $(n - 1)s^2/\sigma^2$ will fall between the critical values of χ_L^2 and χ_R^2. (In Figure 7-9, the confidence level of 95% corresponds to $\alpha = 0.05$, and there is a 0.95 probability that the χ^2 test statistic falls between χ_L^2 and χ_R^2.) It follows that there is a $1 - \alpha$ probability that both of the following are true:

$$\frac{(n-1)s^2}{\sigma^2} < \chi_R^2 \quad \text{and} \quad \frac{(n-1)s^2}{\sigma^2} > \chi_L^2$$

If we multiply both of the preceding inequalities by σ^2 and divide each inequality by the appropriate critical value of χ^2, the two preceding inequalities can be expressed in these equivalent forms:

$$\frac{(n-1)s^2}{\chi_R^2} < \sigma^2 \quad \text{and} \quad \frac{(n-1)s^2}{\chi_L^2} > \sigma^2$$

The two preceding inequalities can be combined into one inequality to get the format of the confidence interval used in this section:

$$\frac{(n-1)s^2}{\chi_R^2} < \sigma^2 < \frac{(n-1)s^2}{\chi_L^2}$$

Determining Sample Size The procedures for finding the sample size necessary to estimate σ^2 are much more complex than the procedures given earlier for means and proportions. Instead of using very complicated procedures, we will use Table 7-2.

Table 7-2 Finding Sample Size

σ		σ^2	
To be 95% confident that s is within	of the value of σ, the sample size n should be at least	To be 95% confident that s^2 is within	of the value of σ^2, the sample size n should be at least
1%	19,205	1%	77,208
5%	768	5%	3,149
10%	192	10%	806
20%	48	20%	211
30%	21	30%	98
40%	12	40%	57
50%	8	50%	38
To be 99% confident that s is within	of the value of σ, the sample size n should be at least	To be 99% confident that s^2 is within	of the value of σ^2 the sample size n should be at least
1%	33,218	1%	133,449
5%	1,336	5%	5,458
10%	336	10%	1,402
20%	85	20%	369
30%	38	30%	172
40%	22	40%	101
50%	14	50%	68

STATDISK also provides sample sizes. With STATDISK, select **Analysis, Sample Size Determination,** and then **Estimate St Dev.** If using Minitab Release 16 or later, select **Stat,** then **Power and Sample Size.** Excel, StatCrunch, and the TI-83/84 Plus calculator do not provide such sample sizes.

Example 3   Finding Sample Size for Estimating σ

We want to estimate the standard deviation σ of all IQ scores of people with exposure to lead. We want to be 95% confident that our estimate is within 10% of the true value of σ. How large should the sample be? Assume that the population is normally distributed.

Solution

From Table 7-2, we can see that 95% confidence and an error of 10% for σ correspond to a sample of size 192. We should obtain a simple random sample of 192 IQ scores from the population of subjects exposed to lead.

using TECHNOLOGY

For Confidence Intervals

STATDISK   First obtain the descriptive statistics and verify that the distribution is normal by using a histogram or normal quantile plot. Next, select **Analysis** from the main menu, then select **Confidence Intervals,** and **Population StDev.** Enter the required data.

MINITAB   Click on **Stat,** click on **Basic Statistics,** and select 1 **Variance.** In the Data box, select the option of using a column containing the list of sample data or enter the value of the sample standard deviation or sample variance. Click on the **Options** button and enter the confidence level, such as 95.0. Click **OK** twice. The results will include a confidence interval for the standard deviation and a confidence interval for the variance.

EXCEL   Neither Excel nor XLSTAT has a function for generating a confidence interval estimate of standard deviation or variance.

TI-83/84 PLUS   The TI-83/84 Plus calculator does not provide confidence intervals for σ or σ^2 directly, but the program **S2INT** can be used. That program was written by Michael Lloyd of Henderson State University, and it is on the CD included with this book, or it can be downloaded from www.aw.com/triola. The program S2INT uses the program ZZINEWT, so that program must also be installed. After storing the programs on the calculator, press **PRGM**, select **S2INT,** and enter the sample variance s^2, the sample size n, and the confidence level (such as 0.95). Press **ENTER**, and wait a while for the display of the confidence interval limits for σ^2. Find the square root of the confidence interval limits if an estimate of σ is desired.

STATCRUNCH   Click on **Open StatCrunch.** Click on **Stat,** then select **Variance.** Select **One sample,** then select **with data** (for a list of sample data) or **with summary** (for summary statistics). Click on **Next,** then select **Confidence Interval** and click on **Calculate.**

7-4 Basic Skills and Concepts

Statistical Literacy and Critical Thinking

1. LDL Cholesterol Using the 40 LDL cholesterol levels of women listed in Data Set 1, we get this 95% confidence interval estimate: $916.591 < \sigma^2 < 2252.119$, and the units of measurement are $(\text{mg/dL})^2$. Identify the corresponding confidence interval estimate of σ and include the appropriate units. Given that the original values are whole numbers, round the limits using the round-off rule given in this section. Write a statement that correctly interprets the confidence interval estimate of σ.

2. Expressing Confidence Intervals Example 2 showed how the statistics of $n = 22$ and $s = 14.3$ result in this 95% confidence interval estimate of σ: $11.0 < \sigma < 20.4$. That confidence interval can also be expressed as (11.0, 20.4), but it cannot be expressed as 15.7 ± 4.7. Given that 15.7 ± 4.7 results in values of 11.0 and 20.4, why can't we express the confidence interval as 15.7 ± 4.7?

3. Pick 4 Lottery The dotplot below depicts individual digits selected in the Pick 4 lottery from different states. Can the original list of individual sample digits be identified? Can the sample data be used to construct a 95% confidence interval estimate of the population standard deviation for all such digits? Why or why not?

4. Normality Requirement What is different about the normality requirement for a confidence interval estimate of σ and the normality requirement for a confidence interval estimate of μ?

Finding Critical Values and Confidence Intervals. In Exercises 5–8, use the given information to find the number of degrees of freedom, the critical values χ_L^2 and χ_R^2, and the confidence interval estimate of σ. The samples are from Appendix B and it is reasonable to assume that a simple random sample has been selected from a population with a normal distribution.

5. Nicotine in Menthol Cigarettes 99% confidence; $n = 25$, $s = 0.24$ mg.

6. Weights of Dollar Coins 99% confidence; $n = 20$, $s = 0.04111$ g.

7. Platelet Counts of Women 95% confidence; $n = 40$, $s = 65.2$.

8. Earthquake Magnitudes 95% confidence; $n = 50$, $s = 0.587$.

Finding Confidence Intervals. In Exercises 9–16, assume that each sample is a simple random sample obtained from a population with a normal distribution.

9. Mean Body Temperature Data Set 3 in Appendix B includes a sample of 106 body temperatures having a mean of 98.20°F and a standard deviation of 0.62°F. Construct a 90% confidence interval estimate of the standard deviation of the body temperatures for the entire population.

10. Chocolate Chip Cookies The Chapter Problem for Chapter 3 includes the numbers of chocolate chips in a sample of 40 Chips Ahoy regular cookies. The mean is 23.95 and the standard deviation is 2.55. Construct a 90% confidence interval estimate of the standard deviation of the numbers of chocolate chips in all such cookies.

11. Antifreeze A container of car antifreeze is supposed to hold 3785 mL of the liquid. Realizing that fluctuations are inevitable, the quality-control manager of the Taconic Chemical Company wants to be quite sure that the standard deviation is less than 30 mL. Otherwise, some containers would overflow while others would not have enough of the coolant. She selects a simple random sample of 24 containers and finds that the mean is 3789 mL and the standard deviation is 42.8 mL. Use these sample results to construct the 99% confidence interval for the true value of σ. Does this confidence interval suggest that the variation is at an acceptable level?

12. Pulse Rates of Men and Women Data Set 1 in Appendix B includes 40 pulse rates of men, and those pulse rates have a mean of 67.3 beats per minute and a standard deviation of 10.3 beats per minute. That data set also includes 40 pulse rates of women, and those pulse rates have a mean of 77.5 beats per minute and a standard deviation of 11.6 beats per minute.

a. Construct a 99% confidence interval estimate of the standard deviation of the pulse rates of men.

b. Construct a 99% confidence interval estimate of the standard deviation of the pulse rates of women.

c. Compare the variation of the pulse rates of men and women. Does there appear to be a difference?

13. Mercury in Sushi Listed below are the amounts of mercury (in parts per million, or ppm) found in tuna sushi sampled at different stores in New York City. The study was sponsored by the *New York Times,* and the stores (in order) are D'Agostino, Eli's Manhattan, Fairway, Food Emporium, Gourmet Garage, Grace's Marketplace, and Whole Foods. Construct a 90% confidence interval estimate of the standard deviation of the amounts of mercury in the population.

0.56   0.75   0.10   0.95   1.25   0.54   0.88

14. Highway Speeds Listed below are speeds (mi/h) measured from southbound traffic on I-280 near Cupertino, California (based on data from SigAlert). This simple random sample was obtained at 3:30 P.M. on a weekday. Use the sample data to construct a 95% confidence interval estimate of the population standard deviation. Does the confidence interval describe the standard deviation for all times during the week?

62   61   61   57   61   54   59   58   59   69   60   67

15. Promotion and Age Listed below are ages of applicants who were unsuccessful in winning promotion and ages of applicants who were successful in winning promotion (based on data from "Debating the Use of Statistical Evidence in Allegations of Age Discrimination" by Barry and Boland, *American Statistician*, Vol. 58, No. 2). Construct 99% confidence interval estimates of the standard deviations of the two populations from which the samples were obtained. Compare the results. What do you conclude?

Ages of Unsuccessful Applicants:	34	37	37	38	41	42	43	44	44
	45	45	45	46	48	49	53	53	54
	54	55	56	57	60				

Ages of Successful Applicants:	33	36	37	38	38	39	42	42	43	43
	44	44	44	45	45	45	45	46	46	47
	47	48	48	49	49	51	51	52	54	

16. a. Comparing Waiting Lines The values listed below are waiting times (in minutes) of customers at the Jefferson Valley Bank, where customers enter a single waiting line that feeds three teller windows. Construct a 95% confidence interval for the population standard deviation σ.

6.5   6.6   6.7   6.8   7.1   7.3   7.4   7.7   7.7   7.7

b. The values listed below are waiting times (in minutes) of customers at the Bank of Providence, where customers may enter any one of three different lines that have formed at three teller windows. Construct a 95% confidence interval for the population standard deviation σ.

4.2   5.4   5.8   6.2   6.7   7.7   7.7   8.5   9.3   10.0

c. Interpret the results found in parts (a) and (b). Do the confidence intervals suggest a difference in the variation among waiting times? Which arrangement seems better: the single-line system or the multiple-line system?

Using Large Data Sets from Appendix B. *In Exercises 17 and 18, use the data set from Appendix B. Assume that each sample is a simple random sample obtained from a population with a normal distribution.*

17. Penny Weights Refer to Data Set 21 in Appendix B and use the weights of the post-1983 pennies to construct a 98% confidence interval estimate of the standard deviation of the weights of all post-1983 pennies.

18. Ages of Presidents Refer to Data Set 12 in Appendix B and use the ages (years) of the presidents at the times of their inaugurations. Treating the data as a sample, construct a 98% confidence interval estimate of the standard deviation of the population of all such ages.

Determining Sample Size. *In Exercises 19–22, assume that each sample is a simple random sample obtained from a normally distributed population. Use Table 7-2 to find the indicated sample size.*

19. IQ of Statistics Professors You want to estimate σ for the population of IQ scores of statistics professors. Find the minimum sample size needed to be 99% confident that the sample standard deviation s is within 1% of σ. Is this sample size practical?

20. McDonald's Waiting Times You want to estimate σ for the population of waiting times at McDonald's drive-up windows, and you want to be 95% confident that the sample standard deviation is within 20% of σ. Find the minimum sample size. Is this sample size practical?

21. Flight Delays You want to estimate the standard deviation of arrival delays for American Airlines flights from Chicago to Miami. Find the minimum sample size needed to be 95% confident that the sample standard deviation is within 5% of the population standard deviation. A histogram of a sample of those arrival delays suggests that the distribution is skewed, not normal. How does the distribution affect the sample size?

22. U.S. Incomes You want to estimate the standard deviation of the population of current annual incomes of adults in the United States. Find the minimum sample size needed to be 99% confident that the sample standard deviation is within 5% of the population standard deviation. Does the population of incomes have a normal distribution, and how is the sample size affected by the distribution?

7-4 Beyond the Basics

23. Finding Critical Values In constructing confidence intervals for σ or σ^2, Table A-4 can be used to find the critical values χ_L^2 and χ_R^2 only for select values of n up to 101, so the number of degrees of freedom is 100 or smaller. For larger numbers of degrees of freedom, we can approximate χ_L^2 and χ_R^2 by using

$$\chi^2 = \frac{1}{2}[\pm z_{\alpha/2} + \sqrt{2k - 1}]^2$$

where k is the number of degrees of freedom and $z_{\alpha/2}$ is the critical z score described in Section 7-2. Use this approximation to find the critical values χ_L^2 and χ_R^2 for Exercise 9. How do the results compare to the actual critical values of 82.354 and 129.918?

Chapter 7   Review

This chapter begins the presentation of methods for using sample data to make inferences about a population. Specifically, we use sample data to find *estimates* of population proportions, population means, and population variances (or standard deviations). This chapter included procedures for finding each of the following:

- point estimate of a population proportion, mean, standard deviation, or variance
- confidence interval estimate of a population proportion, mean, standard deviation, or variance
- sample size required to estimate a population proportion, mean, standard deviation, or variance

Because point estimates consist of single values, they have the serious disadvantage of not revealing how close to the population parameter that they are likely to be, so confidence intervals (or interval estimates) are commonly used as more informative and useful estimates. We also considered ways of determining the sample sizes necessary to estimate parameters to within given margins of error. This chapter also introduced the Student t and chi-square distributions. We must be careful to use the correct probability distribution for each set of circumstances. The following table summarizes some key elements of this chapter.

Parameter	Point Estimate	Confidence Interval
Proportion p	$\hat{p}$	$\hat{p} - E < p < \hat{p} + E$ where $E = z_{\alpha/2} \sqrt{\dfrac{\hat{p}\hat{q}}{n}}$
Mean μ	$\bar{x}$	$\bar{x} - E < \mu < \bar{x} + E$ where $E = t_{\alpha/2} \dfrac{s}{\sqrt{n}}$ or $E = z_{\alpha/2} \cdot \dfrac{\sigma}{\sqrt{n}}$
Standard deviation σ	s (commonly used)	$\sqrt{\dfrac{(n-1)s^2}{\chi_R^2}} < \sigma < \sqrt{\dfrac{(n-1)s^2}{\chi_L^2}}$
Variance σ^2	s^2	$\dfrac{(n-1)s^2}{\chi_R^2} < \sigma^2 < \dfrac{(n-1)s^2}{\chi_L^2}$

For the confidence interval and sample size procedures in this chapter, it is very important to verify that the requirements are satisfied. If they are not, then we cannot use the methods of this chapter and we may need to use other methods, such as the bootstrap method described in the Technology Project at the end of this chapter, or nonparametric methods, such as those discussed in Chapter 13.

Chapter Quick Quiz

1. *USA Today* reported that 40% of people surveyed planned to use accumulated loose change for paying bills. The margin of error was given as ± 3.1 percentage points. Identify the confidence interval that corresponds to that information.

2. Here is a 95% confidence interval estimate of the proportion of female medical school students: $0.449 < p < 0.511$ (based on data from the *Journal of the American Medical Association*). What is the best point estimate of the proportion of females in the population of medical school students?

3. Write a brief statement that correctly interprets the confidence interval given in Exercise 2.

4. In a survey of 1023 high school students, 102 chose education for their career choice (based on results from a KeyStat Marketing survey). Find the critical value that would be used for constructing a 90% confidence interval estimate of the population proportion.

5. Find the sample size required to estimate the percentage of college students who own a car. Assume that we want 90% confidence that the proportion from the sample is within three percentage points of the true population percentage.

6. Find the sample size required to estimate the mean IQ of students currently taking a statistics course. Assume that we want 99% confidence that the mean from the sample is within two IQ points of the true population mean. Also assume that $\sigma = 15$.

7. Six human skulls from around 4000 B.C. were measured, and the lengths have a mean of 94.2 mm and a standard deviation of 4.9 mm. If you want to construct a 95% confidence interval estimate of the mean length of all such skulls, what requirements must be satisfied?

8. In general, what does "degrees of freedom" refer to? For the sample data described in Exercise 7, find the number of degrees of freedom, assuming that you want to construct a confidence interval estimate of μ.

9. Refer to Exercise 7 and assume that the requirements are satisfied. Find the critical value that would be used for constructing a 95% confidence interval estimate of μ.

10. Refer to Exercise 7 and assume that the requirements are satisfied. Find the critical values that would be used to construct a 95% confidence interval estimate of σ.

Review Exercises

1. Overpaid In a Gallup poll of 557 randomly selected adults, 284 said that they were underpaid.

a. Identify the best point estimate of the *percentage* of all adults who say that they are underpaid.

b. Construct a 95% confidence interval estimate of the *percentage* of all adults who say that they are underpaid.

c. Can we safely conclude that the majority of adults say that they are underpaid?

2. Lefties The author had difficulty finding the percentage of people who write with their left hand. If we want to estimate that percentage based on survey results, how many people must we survey in order to be 99% confident that we are within two percentage points of the population percentage? Assume that we know nothing about the percentage of the population that writes with the left hand.

3. Lefties Yet Again There have been several studies conducted in an attempt to identify ways in which left-handed people are different from those who are right handed. Assume that you want to estimate the mean IQ of all left-handed adults. How many random left-handed adults must be tested in order to be 98% confident that the mean IQ of the sample group is within three IQ points of the mean IQ of all left-handed adults? Assume that σ is known to be 16.

4. Distributions Identify the distribution (normal, Student t, chi-square) that applies to each of the following situations. (If none of the three distributions is appropriate, then so state.)

a. In constructing a confidence interval of μ, you have 50 sample values and they appear to be from a population with a skewed distribution. The population standard deviation is not known.

b. In constructing a confidence interval estimate of μ, you have 50 sample values and they appear to be from a population with a skewed distribution. The population standard deviation is known to be 18.2 cm.

c. In constructing a confidence interval estimate of σ, you have 50 sample values and they appear to be from a population with a skewed distribution.

d. In constructing a confidence interval estimate of σ, you have 50 sample values and they appear to be from a population with a normal distribution.

e. In constructing a confidence interval estimate of p, you have 850 survey responses and 10% of them answered "yes" to the first question.

5. Sample Size You have been hired by a college foundation to conduct a survey of graduates.

a. If you want to estimate the percentage of graduates who have made a donation to the college after graduation, how many graduates must you survey if you want 98% confidence that your percentage has a margin of error of five percentage points?

b. If you want to estimate the mean amount of all charitable contributions made by graduates, how many graduates must you survey if you want 98% confidence that your sample mean is in error by no more than $50? (Based on results from a pilot study, assume that the standard deviation of donations by graduates is $337.)

c. If you plan to obtain the estimates described in parts (a) and (b) with a single survey having several questions, how many graduates must be surveyed?

6. Alcohol Consumption In a Gallup poll, 1011 adults were asked if they consume alcoholic beverages, and 64% of them said that they did. Construct a 90% confidence interval estimate of the proportion of all adults who consume alcoholic beverages. Can we safely conclude that the majority of adults consume alcoholic beverages?

7. Wristwatch Accuracy Students of the author collected data measuring the accuracy of wristwatches. The times (sec) below show the discrepancy between the real time and the time indicated on the wristwatch. Negative values correspond to watches that are running ahead of the actual time. The data satisfy a loose requirement of appearing to come from a normally distributed population. Construct a 95% confidence interval estimate of the mean discrepancy for the population of wristwatches.

$$-85 \quad 325 \quad 20 \quad 305 \quad -93 \quad 15 \quad 282 \quad 27 \quad 555 \quad 570 \quad -241 \quad 36$$

8. White Blood Cell Counts Data Set 1 in Appendix B lists the white blood cell counts (1000 cells/μL) of 40 randomly selected women. The mean of those 40 values is 7.15 and the standard deviation is 2.28. Construct a 90% confidence interval estimate of the mean white blood cell count for the population of women. Does the confidence interval also serve as an estimate of the mean white blood cell count of men?

9. Car Crash Tests Data Set 13 in Appendix B includes crash test measurements for small cars. The seven chest deceleration measurements have a mean of 42.7 g and a standard deviation of 5.6 g, where g is a force of gravity. Use the sample data to construct a 95% confidence interval estimate of the mean chest deceleration measurement for the population of all small cars. (Assume that the sample is a simple random sample and the measurements satisfy the loose requirement of being from a normally distributed population.) Write a brief statement that interprets the confidence interval.

10. Car Crash Tests Refer to the sample data described in Exercise 9 and construct a 95% confidence interval estimate of the population standard deviation.

Cumulative Review Exercises

Please be aware that some of the following problems may require knowledge of concepts presented in previous chapters.

Campus Aggravated Assaults. *Colleges sometimes downplay occurrences of crimes on campus so that future applications are not affected. Listed below are the numbers of aggravated assaults on six college campuses. The listed values are randomly selected from the 56 largest urban campuses with residence halls, and the counts are for a recent year. In Exercises 1–5, use these values.*

6   4   2   7   2   12

1. Find the mean, median, and standard deviation.

2. Use the results from Exercise 1 with the range rule of thumb to find the range of usual values.

3. What is the level of measurement of these data (nominal, ordinal, interval, ratio)? Are the data continuous or discrete?

4. Find the sample size necessary to estimate the mean number of aggravated assaults on all college campuses so that there is 95% confidence that the sample mean is in error by no more than 2. Assume that a pilot study suggests that the numbers of aggravated assaults at all colleges have a standard deviation of 5.8.

5. Campus Assaults The numbers of aggravated assaults on 40 large urban campuses with residence halls have a mean of 5.5 and a standard deviation of 5.8. Construct a 95% confidence interval estimate of the population mean. In this situation, what is the population?

6. Normality Assessment Data Set 15 in Appendix B includes the times required for flights to taxi out for takeoff. All of the flights are American Airlines flights from New York (JFK) to Los Angeles and they all occurred in January of a recent year. The 48 taxi-out times are depicted in the histogram and normal quantile plot shown below. Based on those graphs, does it appear that the taxi-out times are from a population having a normal distribution? Give an explanation for the distribution shown. Do the taxi-out times appear to satisfy the requirements necessary for construction of a confidence interval estimate of the standard deviation of the population of all such times?

7. Purell Survey In a survey of 1003 people, 59% said that they have never hesitated to give a handshake because they had a fear of germs. The survey results were reported in *USA Today,* and the survey was conducted by Wakefield Research for Purell, a supplier of hand sanitizer products.

a. Construct a 95% confidence interval estimate of the proportion of people in the population who have never hesitated to give a handshake because of a fear of germs.

b. Is there anything about the survey that might make the results questionable?

c. If an independent pollster wanted to conduct another survey to confirm or refute the results, how many people must be surveyed? Assume that we want 90% confidence that the sample percentage is within 2.5 percentage points of the true population proportion.

8. Cholesterol Listed below are HDL and LDL cholesterol measurements (all in mg/dL) from 10 randomly selected women (based on Data Set 1 in Appendix B). Also shown is a scatterplot of the paired data. Based on the scatterplot does there appear to be a correlation between HDL cholesterol levels and LDL cholesterol levels in women?

HDL	42	81	44	60	52	50	69	41	55	23
LDL	111	59	192	107	122	130	123	104	158	115

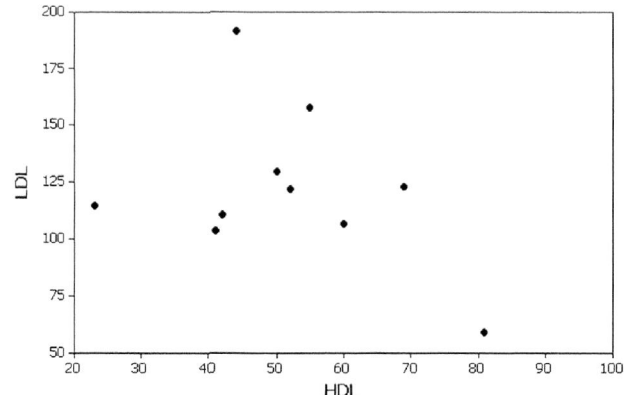

9. Designing Gloves In designing gloves for women, it is found that the lengths of their hands are normally distributed with a mean of 175 mm and a standard deviation of 9 mm (based on anthropometric survey data from Gordon, Churchill, et al.).

a. What percentage of women have hands longer than 185 mm? If no gloves are made to fit hands longer than 185 mm, would a large percentage of the market be lost?

b. Find the 5th percentile and 95th percentile for the lengths of women's hands.

10. Pick 3 Lottery Ohio and several other states have a Pick 3 lottery in which you select three digits, each between 0 and 9. Winning requires that you get the same three digits that are drawn, and they must be in the same order.

a. What is the probability of winning a Pick 3 lottery if you buy a single three-digit ticket?

b. What is the probability of *not* winning a Pick 3 lottery if you buy a single three-digit ticket?

c. What is the probability of not winning on each of 10 different tickets if each ticket has a single three-digit selection?

Technology Project

Bootstrap Resampling The *bootstrap resampling method* can be used to construct confidence intervals when the sample data suggest that the requirement of a normally distributed population is not satisfied. Listed below are 10 values randomly selected from a population with a distribution that is very far from normal. First, use technology to generate a normal quantile plot and write a brief statement interpreting that graph.

14   29   36   36   47   48   180   513   676   5642

Because methods requiring a normal distribution cannot be used, we will use **bootstrap resampling,** which has no requirements about the distribution of the population. This method typically requires a computer to repeatedly sample with replacement from the original sample. In this way, we pull the original sample up "by its own bootstraps" to simulate the original population. Using the sample data given above, construct a 95% confidence interval estimate of the population mean μ by using the following procedure.

Procedure Various technologies can be used for this bootstrap procedure. The STATDISK statistical software program is very easy to use. Enter the listed sample values in column 1 of the Data Window, then select the main menu item of **Analysis,** and select the menu item of **Bootstrap Resampling.**

a. In STATDISK, enter 500 for the number of resamplings and click on **Resample.** This will create 500 new samples, each of size 10, by selecting 10 values with replacement from the original 10 sample values given above.

b. Find the mean of each of the 500 bootstrap samples generated in part (a). In STATDISK, the means will be automatically listed in the second column of the Data Window.

c. Sort the 500 means (arrange them in order). In STATDISK, click on the main menu item of **Data,** then select **Sort Data.** Proceed to sort the means in column 2.

d. Find the percentiles $P_{2.5}$ and $P_{97.5}$ for the sorted means that result from the preceding step. ($P_{2.5}$ is the mean of the 12th and 13th values in the sorted list of means; $P_{97.5}$ is the mean of the 487th and 488th values in the sorted list of means.) Identify the resulting confidence interval by substituting the values for $P_{2.5}$ and $P_{97.5}$ in $P_{2.5} < \mu < P_{97.5}$.

Now use the same bootstrap resampling method to find a 95% confidence interval estimate of the population standard deviation σ. Use the same steps given above, but use the standard deviations of the samples. (In STATDISK, the standard deviations are automatically listed in the third column of the data window, so sort that third column and then find $P_{2.5}$ and $P_{97.5}$ for the sorted standard deviations.)

Interpretation Does the confidence interval for μ contain 1480, which is the true value of the population mean? Does the confidence interval for σ contain 2321, which is the true value of σ?

from data **TO DECISION**

Critical Thinking: What does the survey tell us?

Surveys have become an integral part of our lives. They directly affect us in so many ways, including public policy, the television shows we watch, the products we buy, and the political leaders we elect. Because it is so important that every citizen has the ability to interpret survey results, surveys are the focus of this project.

In a recent Pew Research Center poll, 1501 adults were randomly selected and asked this question: "From what you've read and heard, is there solid evidence that the average temperature on earth has been increasing over the past few decades, or not?" Seventy percent of the 1501 respondents answered "yes."

Analyzing the Data

1. Use the survey results to construct a 95% confidence interval estimate of the *percentage* of all adults who believe that there is solid evidence of increasing temperatures.

2. Identify the margin of error for this survey.

3. Explain why it would or would not be okay for a newspaper to make this statement: "Based on results from a recent survey, the majority of adults believe that there is solid evidence of global warming."

4. Assume that you are a newspaper reporter. Write a description of the survey results for your newspaper.

5. A common criticism of surveys is that they poll only a very small percentage of the population and therefore cannot be accurate. Is a sample of only 1501 adults taken from a population of 241,472,385 adults a sample size that is too small? Write a brief explanation of why the sample size of 1501 is or is not too small.

6. In reference to another survey, the president of a company wrote to the Associated Press about a nationwide survey of 1223 subjects. Here is what he wrote:

> When you or anyone else attempts to tell me and my associates that 1223 persons account for our opinions and tastes here in America, I get mad as hell! How dare you! When you or anyone else tells me that 1223 people represent America, it is astounding and unfair and should be outlawed.

The writer of that letter then proceeds to claim that because the sample size of 1223 people represents 120 million people, his single letter represents 98,000 (120 million divided by 1223) who share the same views. Do you agree or disagree with this claim? Write a response that either supports or refutes this claim.

Cooperative Group Activities

1. Out-of-class activity Collect sample data, and use the methods of this chapter to construct confidence interval estimates of population parameters. Here are some suggestions for parameters:

• Proportion of students at your college who can raise one eyebrow without raising the other eyebrow.

• Mean age of cars driven by statistics students and/or the mean age of cars driven by faculty.

• Mean length of words in *New York Times* editorials and mean length of words in editorials found in your local newspaper.

• Mean lengths of words in a major magazine, such as *Time*.

• Proportion of students at your college who can correctly identify the president, vice president, and secretary of state.

• Proportion of students at your college who are over the age of 18 and are registered to vote.

• Mean age of full-time students at your college.

• Proportion of motor vehicles in your region that are cars.

• Mean number of hours that students at your college study each week.

• Proportion of student cars that are painted white.

2. In-class activity Without using any measuring device, each student should draw a line believed to be 3 in. long and another line believed to be 3 cm long. Then use rulers to measure and record the lengths of the lines drawn. Find the means and standard deviations of the two sets of lengths. Use the sample data to construct a confidence interval for the length of the line estimated to be 3 in., then do the same for the length of the line estimated to be 3 cm. Do the confidence interval limits actually contain the correct length? Compare the results. Do the estimates of the 3-in. line appear to be more accurate than those for the 3-cm line?

3. In-class activity Assume that a method of gender selection can affect the probability of a baby being a girl, so that the probability becomes 1/4. Each student should simulate 20 births by drawing 20 cards from a shuffled deck. Replace each card after it has been drawn, then reshuffle. Consider the hearts to be girls and consider all other cards to be boys. After making 20 selections and recording the "genders" of the babies, construct a confidence interval estimate of the proportion of girls. Does the result appear to be effective in identifying the true value of the population proportion? (If decks of cards are not available, use some other way to simulate the births, such as using the random number generator on a calculator or using digits from phone numbers or Social Security numbers.)

4. Out-of-class activity Groups of three or four students should go to the library and collect a sample consisting of the ages of books (based on copyright dates). Plan and describe the sampling procedure, execute the sampling procedure, then use the results to construct a confidence interval estimate of the mean age of all books in the library.

5. In-class activity Each student should write an estimate of the age of the current president of the United States. All estimates should be collected and the sample mean and standard deviation should be calculated. Then use the sample results to construct a confidence interval. Do the confidence interval limits contain the correct age of the president?

6. In-class activity A class project should be designed to conduct a test in which each student is given a taste of Coke and a taste of Pepsi. The student is then asked to identify which sample is Coke. After all of the results are collected, analyze the claim that the success rate is better than the rate that would be expected with random guesses.

7. In-class activity Each student should estimate the length of the classroom. The values should be based on visual estimates, with no actual measurements being taken. After the estimates have been collected, construct a confidence interval, then measure the length of the room. Does the confidence interval contain the actual length of the classroom? Is there a "collective wisdom," whereby the class mean is approximately equal to the actual room length?

8. In-class activity Divide into groups of three or four. Examine a sample of different issues from a current magazine and find the proportion of pages that include advertising. Based on the results, construct a 95% confidence interval estimate of the percentage of all such pages that have advertising. Compare results with other groups.

9. In-class activity Divide into groups of two. First find the sample size required to estimate the proportion of times that a coin turns up heads when tossed, assuming that you want 80% confidence that the sample proportion is within 0.08 of the true population proportion. Then toss a coin the required number of times and record your results. What percentage of such confidence intervals should actually contain the true value of the population proportion, which we know is $p = 0.5$? Verify this last result by comparing your confidence interval with the confidence intervals found in other groups.

10. Out-of-class activity Identify a topic of general interest and coordinate with all members of the class to conduct a survey. Instead of conducting a "scientific" survey using sound principles of random selection, use a convenience sample consisting of respondents who are readily available, such as friends, relatives, and other students. Analyze and interpret the results. Identify the population. Identify the shortcomings of using a convenience sample, and try to identify how a sample of subjects randomly selected from the population might be different.

11. Out-of-class activity Each student should find an article in a professional journal that includes a confidence interval of the type discussed in this chapter. Write a brief report describing the confidence interval and its role in the context of the article.

8 Hypothesis Testing

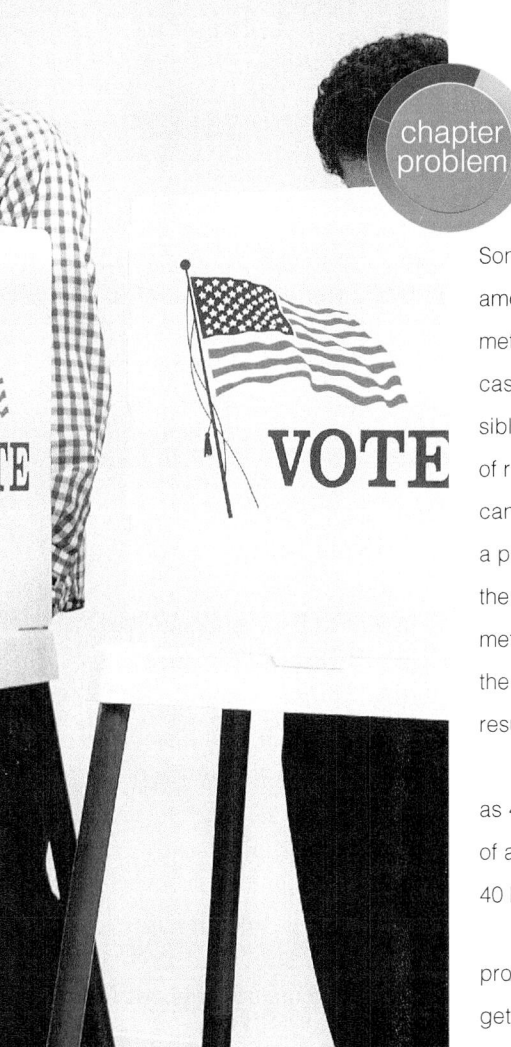

Forensic Statistics:
Did the county clerk
cheat on election ballots?

Some people wrongly believe that the legal profession is among those that do not require any knowledge of statistical methods. In fact, statistics often plays a central role in resolving legal disputes. Consider the case of Nicholas Caputo, the county clerk in Essex County, New Jersey. The clerk was responsible for arranging names for ballot lines used in elections. He was supposed to use a method of random selection for determining the order of the names. This was important, because a candidate can have an advantage if listed first on the ballot. Caputo made his selections using a procedure that was not observed by witnesses. Among 41 different ballots, Democrats won the first line 40 times. Republicans filed a lawsuit and made the claim that instead of using a method of random selection, Caputo was using a method that favored Democrats. Although the results appear to be lopsided and nonrandom, Caputo denied that he was rigging the results to favor Democratic candidates.

A central and key question is this: How likely is it that anyone would get results as extreme as 40 Democrats in 41 selections, assuming that each election involves the random selection of a Democrat or a Republican? This is the same likelihood as getting results as extreme as 40 heads when tossing a coin 41 times.

We must take into account this subtle but important interpretation: Instead of finding the probability of getting *exactly* 40 Democrats in 41 random selections, we need the probability of getting 40 Democrats *or any result that is more extreme*—so we need to find the probability of getting *at least* 40 Democrats in 41 random selections. (See "Identifying *Unusual* Results with Probabilities" in Section 5-2.)

This situation can be addressed by using the method of *hypothesis testing* that is presented in this chapter. We have the Republican claim that $p > 0.5$, which is the symbolic form of the verbal claim that the clerk used a selection process that favored Democrats so that Democrats have more than a 0.5 probability of being selected. We have the clerk's defense that $p = 0.5$, so that his probability of selecting a Democrat is 0.5. This chapter will present the standard methods for testing such claims.

8-1   Review and Preview

By providing methods for estimating values of population parameters using confidence intervals, Chapter 7 introduced one of the two main activities of inferential statistics. This chapter introduces the second major activity of inferential statistics: Testing claims made about population parameters.

The main objective of this chapter is to develop the ability to conduct hypothesis tests for claims made about a population proportion p, a population mean μ, or a population standard deviation σ. Here are examples of hypotheses that can be tested by the procedures in this chapter:

- **Law:** Republicans claimed in a lawsuit that a New Jersey county clerk did not use a required method of random selection when he chose a Democratic candidate to be first on the ballot in 40 out of 41 elections.
- **Genetics:** The Genetics & IVF Institute claims that its XSORT method allows couples to increase the probability of having a baby girl, and sample evidence consists of 879 girls among 945 couples treated with the XSORT method.
- **Health:** It is often claimed that the mean body temperature is 98.6°F, and we can test that claim using Data Set 3 in Appendix B, which includes a sample of 106 body temperatures with a mean of 98.2°F.
- **Business:** A newspaper cites a PriceGrabber.com survey of 1631 subjects and claims that the majority of consumers have heard of the Kindle as an e-book reader.
- **Quality Control:** When new equipment is used to manufacture aircraft altimeters, the new altimeters are better because the variation in the errors is reduced so that the readings are more consistent. (In many industries, the quality of goods and services can often be improved by reducing variation.)

8-2   Basics of Hypothesis Testing

Key Concept In this section we present the general components of a formal hypothesis test. In Part 1 we discuss the basic concepts of hypothesis testing. Because these concepts are used in the following sections and chapters, we should be able to do the following:

- Identify the null hypothesis and alternative hypothesis from a given claim, and express both in symbolic form.
- Calculate the value of the test statistic, given a claim and sample data.
- Choose the sampling distribution that is relevant.
- Either find the P-value or identify the critical value(s).
- State the conclusion about a claim in simple and nontechnical terms.

In Part 2 we describe the *power* of a hypothesis test.

Part 1: Basic Concepts of Hypothesis Testing

Because hypothesis testing is the main focus of this chapter, we begin with two very basic definitions.

> **DEFINITIONS**
>
> In statistics, a **hypothesis** is a claim or statement about a property of a population.
>
> A **hypothesis test** (or **test of significance**) is a procedure for testing a claim about a property of a population.

The "property" referred to in the preceding definitions is often the value of a population parameter, so here are some examples of typical hypotheses (or claims):

- $\mu < 98.6°F$ The mean body temperature of humans is less than 98.6°F.
- $p > 0.5$ The XSORT method of gender selection increases the probability that a baby will be born a girl, so the probability of a girl is greater than 0.5.
- $\sigma = 15$ The population of college students has IQ scores with a standard deviation equal to 15.

Example 1 **Testing the Claim That the XSORT Gender-Selection Method Is Effective**

Assume that 100 babies are born to 100 couples treated with the XSORT method of gender selection that is claimed to make girls more likely. If 58 of the 100 babies are girls, test the claim that "with the XSORT method, the proportion of girls is greater than the proportion of 0.5 that occurs without any treatment." Using p to denote the proportion of girls born with the XSORT method, the claim is that $p > 0.5$.

The big picture In Example 1 we see that getting 58 girls in 100 births is more than the 50 girls that we would expect with no treatment or an ineffective treatment. But is 58 girls high enough to justify the conclusion that the XSORT method is effective? The method of hypothesis testing allows us to answer that question. We will see that without an effective treatment, there is a 0.0548 probability of getting 58 *or more* girls. Because that probability is not small, such as 0.05 or less, we will conclude that it is easy to get 58 girls in 100 births by random chance, so 58 girls is not quite high enough to justify the conclusion that the XSORT method is effective. (The actual XSORT results are more extreme, so in reality it does appear that the XSORT method is effective.)

Using technology It is easy to obtain hypothesis-testing results using technology. The accompanying screen displays show results from four different technologies, so we can use computers or calculators to do all of the computational heavy lifting. Examining the four screen displays, we see some common elements. They all display a "test statistic" of $z = 1.60$, and they all include a "*P*-value" of 0.055 (rounded). These two results are important, but *understanding* the hypothesis-testing procedure is critically important. Focus on *understanding* how the hypothesis-testing procedure

Aspirin Not Helpful for Geminis and Libras

Physician Richard Peto submitted an article to *Lancet*, a British medical journal. The article showed that patients had a better chance of surviving a heart attack if they were treated with aspirin within a few hours of their heart attacks. *Lancet* editors asked Peto to break down his results into subgroups to see if recovery worked better or worse for different groups, such as males or females. Peto believed that he was being asked to use too many subgroups, but the editors insisted. Peto then agreed, but he supported his objections by showing that when his patients were categorized by signs of the zodiac, aspirin was useless for Gemini and Libra heart-attack patients, but aspirin is a lifesaver for those born under any other sign. This shows that when conducting multiple hypothesis tests with many different subgroups, there is a very large chance of getting some wrong results.

STATDISK

Claim: p > p(hyp)

Sample proportion: 0.58
Test Statistic, z: 1.6000
Critical z: 1.6449
P-Value: 0.0548

MINITAB

Test of p = 0.5 vs p > 0.5

Sample	X	N	Sample p	95% Lower Bound	Z-Value	P-Value
1	58	100	0.580000	0.498817	1.60	0.055

TI-83/84 PLUS

```
1-PropZTest
prop>.5
z=1.6
p=.0547992894
p̂=.58
n=100
```

STATCRUNCH

Hypothesis test results:
p : proportion of successes for population
H_0 : p = 0.5
H_A : p > 0.5

Proportion	Count	Total	Sample Prop.	Std. Err.	Z-Stat	P-value
p	58	100	0.58	0.05	1.6	0.0548

works and learn the associated terminology. Only then will results from technology make sense.

The basic idea underlying the hypothesis-testing procedure is based on the rare event rule first presented in Section 4-1. Let's review that rule before proceeding.

Rare Event Rule for Inferential Statistics

If, under a given assumption, the probability of a particular observed event is extremely small, we conclude that the assumption is probably not correct.

Following this rule, we test a claim by analyzing sample data in an attempt to choose between the following two explanations:

1. The sample results could easily occur by chance.

   Example: In testing the XSORT gender-selection method that is supposed to make babies more likely to be girls, the result of 52 girls in 100 births is greater than 50%, but 52 girls could easily occur by chance, so there is not sufficient evidence to conclude that the XSORT method is effective.

2. The sample results are not likely to occur by chance.

   Example: In testing the XSORT gender-selection method that is supposed to make babies more likely to be girls, the result of 95 girls in 100 births is greater than 50%, and 95 girls is so extreme that it could *not* easily occur by chance, so there is sufficient evidence to conclude that the XSORT method is effective.

Figures 8-1 and 8-2 summarize the procedures used in two slightly different methods for conducting a formal hypothesis test. We will proceed to conduct a formal test of the claim from Example 1 that $p > 0.5$. In testing that claim, we will use the sample data consisting of 58 girls in 100 births.

Steps 1, 2, 3: Use the Claim to Create a Null Hypothesis and an Alternative Hypothesis

Objective

Identify the *null hypothesis* and *alternative hypothesis* so that the formal hypothesis test includes these standard components that are used often in many different disciplines.

Null Hypothesis (denoted by H_0)

Statement that the value of a population parameter (such as proportion, mean, or standard deviation) is *equal to* some claimed value. (The term *null* is used to indicate *no* change or no effect or no difference.) We test the null hypothesis directly in the sense that we assume (or pretend) it is true and reach a conclusion to either reject it or fail to reject it.

Example: Here is an example of a null hypothesis involving a proportion: H_0: $p = 0.5$.

Alternative Hypothesis (denoted by H_1 or H_a or H_A)

Statement that the parameter has a value that somehow differs from the null hypothesis. For the methods of this chapter, the symbolic form of the alternative hypothesis must use one of these symbols: $<, >, \neq$.

Example: Here are different examples of alternative hypotheses involving proportions:

$$H_1: p > 0.5 \quad H_1: p < 0.5 \quad H_1: p \neq 0.5$$

The *original claim* could become the null hypothesis (as in a claim that $p = 0.5$), it could become the alternative hypothesis (as in the claim that $p > 0.5$), or it might not be either the null hypothesis or the alternative hypothesis (as in the claim that $p \geq 0.5$).

Figure 8-1   *P*-Value Method

P-Value Method

Start

1 Identify the specific claim or hypothesis to be tested, and put in symbolic form.

2 Give the symbolic form that must be true when the original claim is false.

3 Of the two symbolic expressions obtained so far, let the alternative hypothesis H_1 be the one not containing equality, so that H_1 uses the symbol > or < or ≠. Let the null hypothesis H_0 be the symbolic expression that the parameter equals the fixed value being considered.

4 Select the significance level α based on the seriousness of a type 1 error. Make α small if the consequences of rejecting a true H_0 are severe. The values of 0.05 and 0.01 are very common.

5 Identify the statistic that is relevant to this test and determine its sampling distribution (such as normal, t, chi-square).

6 Find the test statistic and find the *P*-value (see Figure 8-5). Draw a graph and show the test statistic and *P*-value.

7 Reject H_0 if the *P*-value is less than or equal to the significance level α. Fail to reject H_0 if the *P*-value is greater than α.

8 Restate this previous decision in simple, nontechnical terms, and address the original claim.

Stop

Figure 8-2   **Critical Value Method**

Critical Value Method

Start

1 Identify the specific claim or hypothesis to be tested, and put it in symbolic form.

2 Give the symbolic form that must be true when the original claim is false.

3 Of the two symbolic expressions obtained so far, let the alternative hypothesis H_1 be the one not containing equality, so that H_1 uses the symbol > or < or ≠. Let the null hypothesis H_0 be the symbolic expression that the parameter equals the fixed value being considered.

4 Select the significance level α based on the seriousness of a type 1 error. Make α small if the consequences of rejecting a true H_0 are severe. The values of 0.05 and 0.01 are very common.

5 Identify the statistic that is relevant to this test and determine its sampling distribution (such as normal, t, chi-square).

6 Find the test statistic, the critical values, and the critical region. Draw a graph and include the test statistic, critical value(s), and critical region.

7 Reject H_0 if the test statistic is in the critical region. Fail to reject H_0 if the test statistic is not in the critical region.

8 Restate this previous decision in simple, nontechnical terms, and address the original claim.

Stop

Confidence Interval Method

Construct a confidence interval with a confidence level selected as in Table 8-1.

Because a confidence interval estimate of a population parameter contains the likely values of that parameter, reject a claim that the population parameter has a value that is not included in the confidence interval.

Table 8-1   Confidence Level for Confidence Interval

		Two-Tailed Test	One-Tailed Test
Significance	0.01	99%	98%
Level for	0.05	95%	90%
Hypothesis	0.10	90%	80%
Test			

Given the claim from Example 1 that "with the XSORT method, the proportion of girls is greater than the proportion of 0.5 that occurs without any treatment," we apply Steps 1, 2, and 3 in Figures 8-1 and 8-2 as follows.

Step 1:   Identify the claim to be tested and express it in symbolic form. The claim is that "with the XSORT method, the proportion of girls is greater than the proportion of 0.5 that occurs without any treatment." Using p to denote the probability of getting a girl with the XSORT method, we express that claim in symbolic form as $p > 0.5$ (so that p is greater than 0.5, where 0.5 is the assumed probability of a girl when no XSORT treatment is used).

Step 2:   Give the symbolic form that must be true when the original claim is false. If the original claim of $p > 0.5$ is false, then $p \le 0.5$ must be true.

Step 3:   This step is in two parts: Identify the alternative hypothesis H_1 and identify the null hypothesis H_0.

- Identify H_1: Using the two symbolic expressions $p > 0.5$ and $p \le 0.5$, the alternative hypothesis H_1 is the one that does not contain equality. Of those two expressions, $p > 0.5$ does not contain equality, so we get

$$H_1: p > 0.5$$

- Identify H_0: The null hypothesis H_0 is the symbolic expression that the parameter *equals* the fixed value being considered, so we get

$$H_0: p = 0.5$$

The result of the first three steps is the identification of the null and alternative hypothesis:

$$H_0: p = 0.5 \text{ (null hypothesis)}$$

$$H_1: p > 0.5 \text{ (alternative hypothesis)}$$

Note About Always Using the Equals Symbol in H_0: The symbols $\le$ and $\ge$ were sometimes used in the null hypothesis H_0, but that practice has become obsolete. Professional statisticians and professional journals now use only the equals symbol for equality. We conduct the hypothesis test by assuming that the proportion, mean, or standard deviation is *equal to* some specified value so that we can work with a single distribution having a specific value, so the null hypothesis is the statement that we assume true for the purpose of conducting the test.

Note About Forming Your Own Claims (Hypotheses): If you are conducting a study and want to use a hypothesis test to *support* your claim, the claim must be worded so that it becomes the alternative hypothesis (and can be expressed using only the symbols $<$, $>$, or $\ne$). You can never support a claim that some parameter is *equal to* a specified value.

Step 4: Select the Significance Level α

Objective

Identify the value of the significance level α so that we have a specific criterion for distinguishing between sample results that could easily occur by chance and sample results that are unlikely to occur by chance.

The **significance level** α is the probability of making the mistake of rejecting the null hypothesis when it is true. This is the same α introduced in Section 7-2, where we defined the confidence level for a confidence interval to be the probability $1 - \alpha$. Common choices for α are 0.05, 0.01, and 0.10, with 0.05 being most common.

Step 5: Identify the Statistic Relevant to the Test and Determine Its Sampling Distribution (such as normal, t, or χ^2)

Objective

Based on the sample statistic that is relevant to the claim being tested, identify the sampling distribution of the statistic (such as normal, Student t, or χ^2) so that the correct sampling distribution can be used in Step 6.

For this chapter, verify that any requirements are satisfied, then use Table 8-2 to choose the correct sampling distribution.

Example: The claim $p > 0.5$ is a claim about the population proportion p, so use the normal distribution provided that the requirements are satisfied. (With $n = 100$, $p = 0.5$, and $q = 0.5$ as in Example 1, $np \geq 5$ and $nq \geq 5$ are both true.)

Table 8-2

Parameter	Sampling Distribution	Requirements	Test Statistic
Proportion p	Normal (z)	$np \geq 5$ and $nq \geq 5$	$z = \dfrac{\hat{p} - p}{\sqrt{\frac{pq}{n}}}$
Mean μ	t	σ not known and normally distributed population *or* σ not known and $n > 30$	$t = \dfrac{\bar{x} - \mu}{\frac{s}{\sqrt{n}}}$
Mean μ	Normal (z)	σ known and normally distributed population *or* σ known and $n > 30$	$z = \dfrac{\bar{x} - \mu}{\frac{\sigma}{\sqrt{n}}}$
St. dev. σ or variance σ^2	χ^2	Strict requirement: normally distributed population	$\chi^2 = \dfrac{(n - 1)s^2}{\sigma^2}$

Step 6: Find the Value of the Test Statistic, Then Find Either the *P*-Value or the Critical Value(s)

Objective

First transform the relevant sample statistic to a standardized score called the *test statistic*. Then find the *P-value* that can be used to make a decision about the null hypothesis, or find *critical values* that can be used with the test statistic in making a decision about the null hypothesis.

The **test statistic** is a value used in making a decision about the null hypothesis. It is found by converting the sample statistic (such as the sample proportion $\hat{p}$, the sample mean $\bar{x}$, or the sample standard deviation s) to a score (such as z, t, or χ^2) with the assumption that the null hypothesis is true. In this chapter we use the test statistics in the last column of Table 8-2.

Example: From Example 1 we have a claim made about the population proportion p, we have $n = 100$ and $x = 58$,

so $\hat{p} = x/n = 0.58$. Because we also have the null hypothesis of H_0: $p = 0.5$, we are working with the assumption that $p = 0.5$, and it follows that $q = 0.5$. Using $n = 100$, $\hat{p} = 0.58$, $p = 0.5$, and $q = 0.5$, we can evaluate the test statistic as shown below. (See that the result of $z = 1.60$ is included in each of the previous displays from technology, so technology can do this calculation for us.)

$$z = \frac{\hat{p} - p}{\sqrt{\frac{pq}{n}}} = \frac{0.58 - 0.5}{\sqrt{\frac{(0.5)(0.5)}{100}}} = 1.60$$

Types of Hypothesis Tests: Two-Tailed, Left-Tailed, Right-Tailed

The test statistic alone usually does not give us enough information to make a decision about the claim being tested. For that decision, we can use either the *P*-value approach summarized in Figure 8-1 or the critical value approach summarized in Figure 8-2. Both approaches require that we first determine whether our hypothesis test is two-tailed, left-tailed, or right-tailed.

The **critical region** (or **rejection region**) corresponds to the values of the test statistic that cause us to reject the null hypothesis. Depending on the claim being tested, the critical region could be in the two extreme tails, it could be in the left tail, or it could be in the right tail.

Sign used in H_1: ≠
Two-tailed test

Sign used in H_1: <
Left-tailed test

- **Two-tailed test:** The critical region is in the two extreme regions (tails) under the curve (as in the top graph in Figure 8-3).

- **Left-tailed test:** The critical region is in the extreme left region (tail) under the curve (as in the middle graph in Figure 8-3).

- **Right-tailed test:** The critical region is in the extreme right region (tail) under the curve (as in the bottom graph in Figure 8-3).

Sign used in H_1: >
Right-tailed test

Figure 8-3 **Critical Region in Two-Tailed, Left-Tailed, and Right-Tailed Tests**

HINT To determine whether a test is two-tailed, left-tailed, or right-tailed, look at the alternative hypothesis and identify the region that supports that alternative hypothesis and conflicts with the null hypothesis. A useful check is summarized in Figure 8-3. *See that the inequality sign in H_1 points in the direction of the critical region.* The symbol ≠ is sometimes expressed in programming languages as <>, and this reminds us that an alternative hypothesis such as $p \neq 0.5$ corresponds to a two-tailed test.

Example: With H_0: $p = 0.5$ and H_1: $p > 0.5$, we reject the null hypothesis and support the alternative hypothesis only if the sample proportion is greater than 0.5 by a significant amount, so the hypothesis test in this case is *right-tailed*.

Interpreting the Test Statistic: Using the *P*-Value or Critical Value

After determining whether the hypothesis test is two-tailed, left-tailed, or right-tailed, we can proceed with either the *P*-value approach (summarized in Figure 8-1) or the critical value approach (summarized in Figure 8-2). Because technology typically provides a *P*-value in a hypothesis test, the *P*-value method is now much more common than the method based on critical values.

P-Value (or *p*-Value or Probability Value) Method   Find the *P*-value, which is the probability of getting a value of the test statistic that is *at least as extreme* as the one representing the sample data, assuming that the null hypothesis is true. To find the *P*-value, first find the area beyond the test statistic, then use the procedure given in Figure 8-4. That procedure can be summarized as follows:

Critical region in the left tail: *P*-value = area to the *left* of the test statistic
Critical region in the right tail: *P*-value = area to the *right* of the test statistic
Critical region in two tails: *P*-value = *twice* the area in the tail beyond the test statistic

EXAMPLE The test statistic of $z = 1.60$ has an area of 0.0548 to its right, so a right-tailed test with test statistic $z = 1.60$ has a *P*-value of 0.0548. (See the different technology

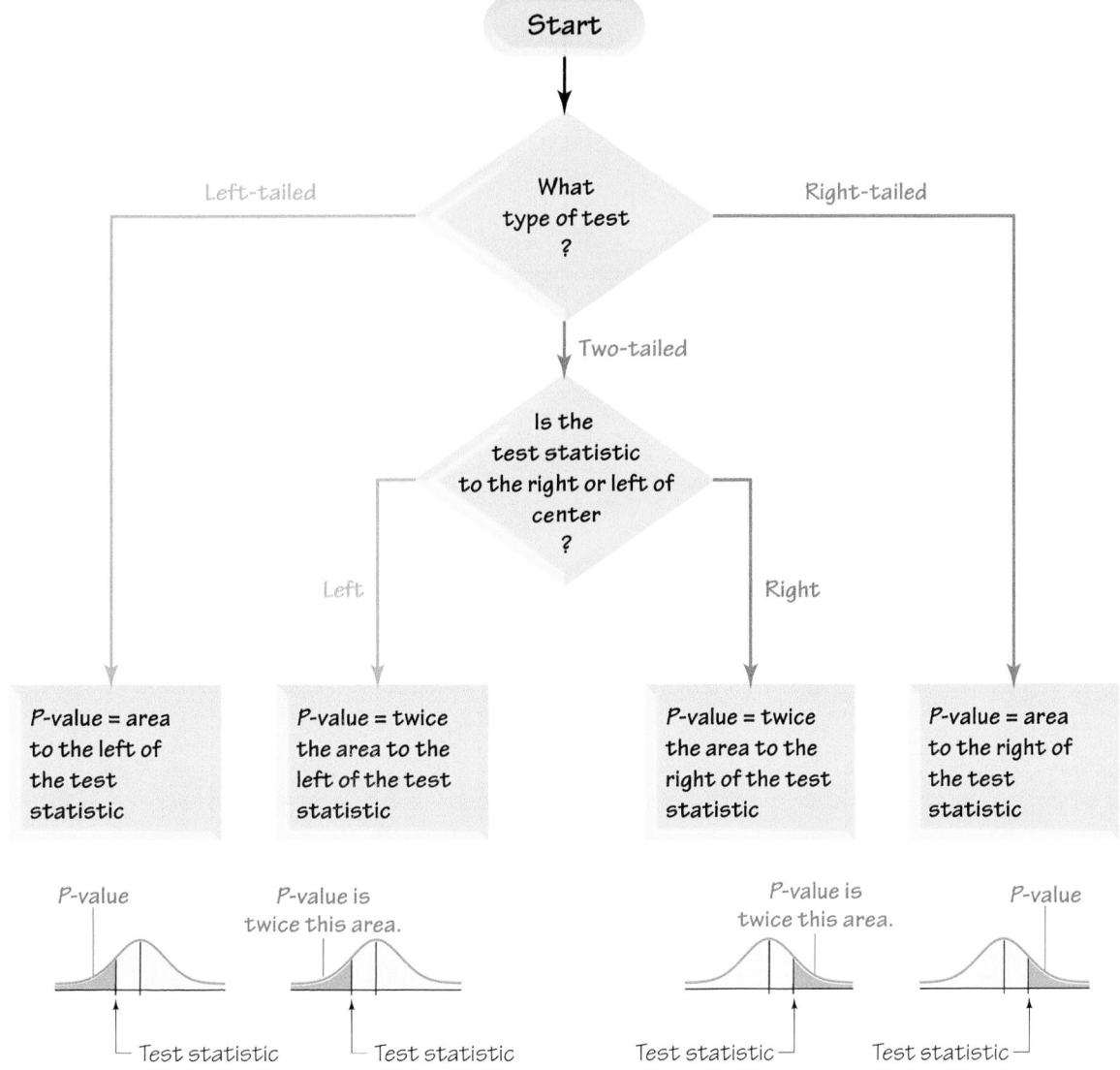

Figure 8-4 Procedure for Finding *P*-Values

displays given earlier, and note that each of them provides the same *P*-value of 0.055 after rounding.)

CAUTION Don't confuse a *P*-value with a proportion *p*. Know this distinction:

P-value = probability of a test statistic at least as extreme as the one obtained

p = population proportion

Critical Value Method With the critical value method (or **traditional method**), we find the **critical value(s),** which separates the critical region (where we reject the null hypothesis) from the values of the test statistic that do not lead to rejection of the null hypothesis. Critical values depend on the nature of the null hypothesis, the sampling distribution, and the significance level α.

EXAMPLE The critical region in Figure 8-5 is shaded in red. Figure 8-5 shows that with $\alpha = 0.05$, the critical value is $z = 1.645$.

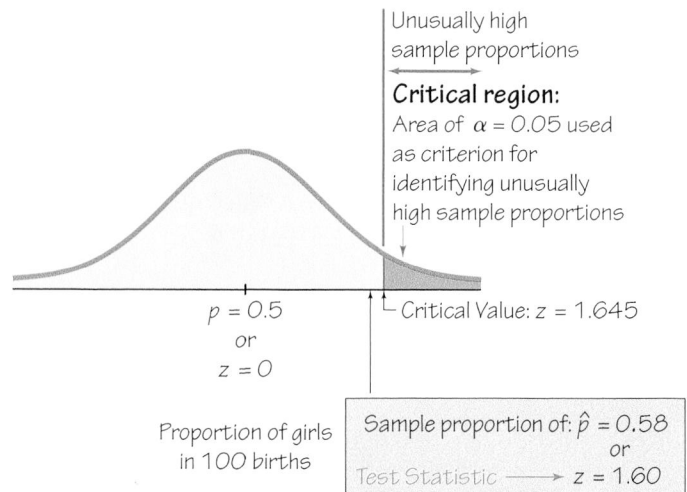

Figure 8-5   **Critical Region, Critical Value, and Test Statistic**

Step 7: Make a Decision: Reject H_0 or Fail to Reject H_0

Objective

Form an initial conclusion that will always be one of the following:

1. Reject the null hypothesis H_0.

2. Fail to reject the null hypothesis H_0.

Decision Criteria for Rejecting H_0

P-value Method:

- If *P*-value $\leq \alpha$, reject H_0.

- If *P*-value $> \alpha$, fail to reject H_0.

Example: With significance level $\alpha = 0.05$ and *P*-value = 0.0548, we have *P*-value $> \alpha$, so fail to reject H_0.

Critical Value Method:

- If the test statistic is in the critical region, reject H_0.

- If the test statistic in not in the critical region, fail to reject H_0.

Example: With test statistic $z = 1.60$ and the critical region from $z = 1.645$ to infinity, the test statistic does not fall within the critical region, so fail to reject H_0.

Step 8: Restate the Decision Using Simple and Nontechnical Terms

Objective

Without using technical terms not understood by most people, state a final conclusion that addresses the original claim with wording that can be understood by those without knowledge of statistical procedures.

Example: There is not sufficient evidence to support the claim that the XSORT method is effective in increasing the probability that a baby will be born a girl.

Wording the Final Conclusion For help in wording the final conclusion, refer to Table 8-3, which lists the four possible circumstances and their corresponding conclusions. Note that only the first case leads to wording indicating *support* for the original conclusion. If you want to support some claim, state it in such a way that it becomes the alternative hypothesis, and then hope that the null hypothesis gets rejected.

Table 8-3 Wording of the Final Conclusion

Condition	Conclusion
Original claim does not include equality, and you reject H_0.	"There is sufficient evidence to *support* the claim that . . . (original claim)."
Original claim does not include equality, and you fail to reject H_0.	"There is not sufficient evidence to support the claim that . . . (original claim)."
Original claim includes equality, and you reject H_0.	"There is sufficient evidence to warrant *rejection* of the claim that . . . (original claim)."
Original claim includes equality, and you fail to reject H_0.	"There is not sufficient evidence to warrant rejection of the claim that . . . (original claim)."

Accept/Fail to Reject A few textbooks continue to say "accept the null hypothesis" instead of "fail to reject the null hypothesis." The term *accept* is misleading, because it implies incorrectly that the null hypothesis has been proved, but we can never prove a null hypothesis. The phrase *fail to reject* says more correctly that the available evidence isn't strong enough to warrant rejection of the null hypothesis. In this text we use the terminology *fail to reject the null hypothesis,* instead of *accept the null hypothesis.*

Multiple Negatives When stating the final conclusion in nontechnical terms, it is possible to get correct statements with up to three negative terms. (*Example:* "There is *not* sufficient evidence to warrant *rejection* of the claim of *no* difference between 0.5 and the population proportion.") Such conclusions are confusing, so it is good to restate them in a way that makes them understandable, but be careful to not change the meaning. For example, instead of saying that "there is not sufficient evidence to warrant rejection of the claim of no difference between 0.5 and the population proportion," better statements would be these:

- Fail to reject the claim that the population proportion is equal to 0.5.

- Unless stronger evidence is obtained, continue to assume that the population proportion is equal to 0.5.

CAUTION Never conclude a hypothesis test with a statement of "reject the null hypothesis" or "fail to reject the null hypothesis." Always make sense of the conclusion with a statement that uses simple nontechnical wording that addresses the original claim.

The Big Picture Revisited Example 1 describes a clinical trial that resulted in 58 girls in 100 births. Try to follow this line of reasoning:

- If we assume that $p = 0.5$ (as in the null hypothesis), the probability of getting 58 or more girls is 0.0548.

- Because the probability of 0.0548 is not small (such as 0.05 or less), we see that random chance is a reasonable explanation for getting 58 (or more) girls in 100 births.

- Because 58 girls in 100 births can easily occur by chance, we don't have sufficient evidence to conclude that the XSORT method is effective.

The hypothesis test procedure basically formalizes the reasoning process above, and it provides a common structure and terminology recognizable by professionals in a wide variety of disciplines, not just statistics.

Errors in Hypothesis Tests

When testing a null hypothesis, we arrive at a conclusion of rejecting it or failing to reject it. Such conclusions are sometimes correct and sometimes wrong (even if we apply all procedures correctly). Table 8-4 summarizes the two different types of errors that can be made, along with the two different types of correct decisions. We distinguish between the two types of errors by calling them type I and type II errors.

- **Type I error:** The mistake of rejecting the null hypothesis when it is actually true. The symbol α (alpha) is used to represent the probability of a type I error.
- **Type II error:** The mistake of failing to reject the null hypothesis when it is actually false. The symbol β (beta) is used to represent the probability of a type II error.

MEMORY HINT Because it is difficult to remember which error is type I and which is type II, we recommend this mnemonic device: Remember "routine for fun," and using only the consonants from those words (**R**ou**T**i**N**e **F**o**R** **F**u**N**), we can easily remember that a type I error is RTN: Reject True Null (hypothesis), and a type II error is FRFN: Fail to Reject a False Null (hypothesis).

Notation

α (alpha) = probability of a type I error (the probability of rejecting the null hypothesis when it is true)

β (beta) = probability of a type II error (the probability of failing to reject a null hypothesis when it is false)

Table 8-4 Type I and Type II Errors

		True State of Nature	
		The null hypothesis is true	The null hypothesis is false
Decision	We decide to reject the null hypothesis	Type I error (rejecting a true null hypothesis) P(type I error) = α	Correct decision
	We fail to reject the null hypothesis	Correct decision	Type II error (failing to reject a false null hypothesis) P(type II error) = β

Example 2   Identifying Type I and Type II Errors

Consider the claim that a method of gender selection increases the likelihood of a baby girl, so that the probability of a baby girl is $p > 0.5$. Here are the null and alternative hypotheses:

$$H_0: p = 0.5$$

$$H_1: p > 0.5 \text{ (original claim that is addressed in the final conclusion)}$$

Identify the following: **a.** Type I error; **b.** Type II error.

Solution

HINT Descriptions of a type I error and a type II error refer to the *null hypothesis* being true or false, but when wording a statement representing a type I error or a type II error, be sure that the conclusion addresses the *original claim* (which may or may not be the null hypothesis). In this example, the claim is that $p > 0.5$, so the following interpretations address the claim of $p > 0.5$.

a. Type I Error: A type I error is the mistake of rejecting a true null hypothesis, so the following is a type I error: In reality $p = 0.5$, but sample evidence leads us to conclude that $p > 0.5$. (In this case, a type I error is to conclude that the gender-selection method is effective when in reality it has no effect.)

b. Type II Error: A type II error is the mistake of failing to reject the null hypothesis when it is false, so the following is a type II error: In reality $p > 0.5$, but we fail to support that conclusion. (In this case, a type II error is to conclude that the gender-selection method has no effect, when it really is effective in increasing the likelihood of a baby girl.)

Controlling Type I and Type II Errors Step 4 in our standard procedure for testing hypotheses is to select a significance level α (such as 0.05), which is the probability of a type I error. The values of α, β, and the sample size n are all related, so if you choose any two of them, the third is automatically determined (although β can't be determined until an alternative value of the population parameter has been specified along with α and n). One common practice is to select the significance level α, then select a sample size that is practical, so the value of β is determined. Generally, try to use the largest α that you can tolerate, but for type I errors with more serious consequences, select smaller values of α. Then choose a sample size n as large as is reasonable, based on considerations of time, cost, and other relevant factors. Another common practice is to select α and β so the required sample size n is automatically determined. (See Example 4 in Part 2 of this section.)

Comprehensive Hypothesis Test

In this section we described the individual components used in a hypothesis test, but the following sections will combine those components in comprehensive procedures. We can test claims about population parameters by using the *P*-value method summarized in Figure 8-1 or the critical value method summarized in Figure 8-2, or we can use confidence intervals, as follows.

Confidence Interval Method for Hypothesis Testing A confidence interval estimate of a population parameter contains the likely values of that parameter. If a confidence interval does not include a claimed value of a population parameter, reject that claim. For two-tailed hypothesis tests, construct a confidence interval with a confidence level of $1 - \alpha$, but for a one-tailed hypothesis test with significance level α, construct a confidence interval with a confidence level of $1 - 2\alpha$. (See Table 8-1 for common cases.) (For a left-tailed test or a right-tailed test, we could also use a one-sided confidence interval. See Exercise 43 in Section 7-2.) After constructing the confidence interval, use this criterion:

A confidence interval estimate of a population parameter contains the likely values of that parameter. We should therefore reject a claim that the population parameter has a value that is not included in the confidence interval.

Cheating Detected

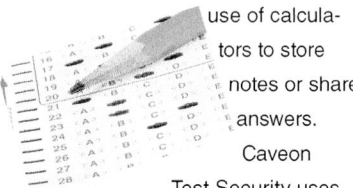

Methods for cheating on tests include the use of cell phones to text answers to friends and the use of calculators to store notes or share answers. Caveon Test Security uses statistical methods to identify when cheating has occurred. That company searches for unlikely patterns, such as identical wrong answers by different students. The company even analyzes erasures on answer sheets to determine whether tests have been compromised by dishonest teachers or administrators who can gain from the appearance of higher test scores. The company also searches the Internet looking for questions or answers that were posted or discussed by previous test subjects.

Statistics plays an important role in the analyses conducted by Caveon Test Security. Unusual patterns are identified and the probabilities of those patterns are computed. If the probability of a pattern is very small, such as less than one chance in a million, the answer sheets are turned over to school administrators.

CAUTION In some cases, a conclusion based on a confidence interval may be different from a conclusion based on a hypothesis test. The P-value method and critical value method are equivalent in the sense that they always lead to the same conclusion. The following table shows that for the methods included in this chapter, a confidence interval estimate of a proportion might lead to a conclusion different from that of a hypothesis test.

Parameter	Is a confidence interval equivalent to a hypothesis test in the sense that they always lead to the same conclusion?
Proportion	No
Mean	Yes
Standard Deviation or Variance	Yes

Part 2: Beyond the Basics of Hypothesis Testing: The Power of a Test

We use β to denote the probability of failing to reject a false null hypothesis, so $P(\text{type II error}) = \beta$. It follows that $1 - \beta$ is the probability of rejecting a false null hypothesis; statisticians refer to this probability as the *power* of a test, and they often use it to gauge the effectiveness of a hypothesis test in allowing us to recognize that a null hypothesis is false.

> **DEFINITION** The **power** of a hypothesis test is the probability $1 - \beta$ of rejecting a false null hypothesis. The value of the power is computed by using a particular significance level α and a *particular* value of the population parameter that is an alternative to the value assumed true in the null hypothesis.

Note that in the definition above, determination of power requires a particular value that is an alternative to the value assumed in the null hypothesis. Consequently, a hypothesis test can have many different values of power, depending on the particular values of the population parameter chosen as alternatives to the null hypothesis.

Example 3   Power of a Hypothesis Test

Consider these preliminary results from the XSORT method of gender selection: There were 13 girls among the 14 babies born to couples using the XSORT method. If we want to test the claim that girls are more likely ($p > 0.5$) with the XSORT method, we have the following null and alternative hypotheses:

$$H_0: p = 0.5 \qquad H_1: p > 0.5$$

Let's use a significance level of $\alpha = 0.05$. In addition to all of the given test components, finding power requires that we select a particular value of p that is an alternative to the value assumed in the null hypothesis $H_0: p = 0.5$. Find the values of power corresponding to these alternative values of p: 0.6, 0.7, 0.8, and 0.9.

Solution

The values of power in the following table were found by using Minitab, and exact calculations are used instead of a normal approximation to the binomial distribution.

Specific Alternative Value of p	β	Power of Test $(1 - \beta)$
0.6	0.820	0.180
0.7	0.564	0.436
0.8	0.227	0.773
0.9	0.012	0.988

Interpretation

Based on the list of power values above, we see that this hypothesis test has power of 0.180 (or 18.0%) of rejecting H_0: $p = 0.5$ when the population proportion p is actually 0.6. That is, if the true population proportion is actually equal to 0.6, there is an 18.0% chance of making the correct conclusion of rejecting the false null hypothesis that $p = 0.5$. That low power of 18.0% is not good.

There is a 0.564 probability of rejecting $p = 0.5$ when the true value of p is actually 0.7. It makes sense that this test is more effective in rejecting the claim of $p = 0.5$ when the population proportion is actually 0.7 than when the population proportion is actually 0.6. (When identifying animals assumed to be horses, there's a better chance of rejecting an elephant as a horse—because of the greater difference—than rejecting a mule as a horse.) In general, increasing the difference between the assumed parameter value and the actual parameter value results in an increase in power, as shown in the table above.

Because the calculations of power are quite complicated, the use of technology is strongly recommended. (In this section, only Exercises 35 and 36 involve power.)

Power and the Design of Experiments

Just as 0.05 is a common choice for a significance level, a power of at least 0.80 is a common requirement for determining that a hypothesis test is effective. (Some statisticians argue that the power should be higher, such as 0.85 or 0.90.) When designing an experiment, we might consider how much of a difference between the claimed value of a parameter and its true value is an important amount of difference. If testing the effectiveness of the XSORT gender-selection method, a change in the proportion of girls from 0.5 to 0.501 is not very important. A change in the proportion of girls from 0.5 to 0.9 would be very important. Such magnitudes of differences affect power. When designing an experiment, a goal of having a power value of at least 0.80 can often be used to determine the minimum required sample size, as in the following example.

Example 4   Finding the Sample Size Required to Achieve 80% Power

Here is a statement similar to one in an article from the *Journal of the American Medical Association:* "The trial design assumed that with a 0.05 significance level, 153 randomly selected subjects would be needed to achieve 80% power to detect a reduction in the coronary heart disease rate from 0.5 to 0.4." Before conducting the experiment, the researchers selected a significance level of 0.05 and a power of at least 0.80. They also decided that a reduction in the proportion of coronary heart disease from 0.5 to 0.4 is an important difference that they wanted to detect (by correctly rejecting the false null hypothesis). Using a significance level of 0.05, power of 0.80, and the alternative proportion of 0.4, technology such as Minitab is used to find that the required minimum sample size is 153. The researchers can then proceed by obtaining a sample of at least 153 randomly selected subjects. Due to factors such as dropout rates, the researchers are likely to need somewhat more than 153 subjects. (See Exercise 37.)

8-2 Basic Skills and Concepts

Statistical Literacy and Critical Thinking

1. M&Ms and Aspirin A package label includes a claim that the mean weight of the M&Ms is 0.8535 g, and another package label includes the claim that the mean amount of aspirin in Bayer tablets is 325 mg. Which has more serious implications: rejection of the M&M claim or rejection of the aspirin claim? Is it wise to use the same significance level for hypothesis tests of both claims?

2. Estimates and Hypothesis Tests Data Set 20 in Appendix B includes sample weights of the M&Ms referenced in Exercise 1. We could use methods of Chapter 7 for making an estimate, or we could use those values to test some claim. What is the difference between estimating and hypothesis testing?

3. Mean Body Temperature A formal hypothesis test is to be conducted using the claim that the mean body temperature is equal to 98.6°F.

a. What is the null hypothesis, and how is it denoted?

b. What is the alternative hypothesis, and how is it denoted?

c. What are the possible conclusions that can be made about the null hypothesis?

d. Is it possible to conclude that "there is sufficient evidence to support the claim that the mean body temperature is equal to 98.6°F"?

4. Interpreting _P_-value When the clinical trial of the XSORT method of gender selection is completed, a formal hypothesis test will be conducted with the alternative hypothesis of $p > 0.5$, which corresponds to the claim that the XSORT method increases the likelihood of having a girl, so that the proportion of girls is greater than 0.5. If you are responsible for developing the XSORT method and you want to show its effectiveness, which of the following _P_-values would you prefer: 0.999, 0.5, 0.95, 0.05, 0.01, 0.001? Why?

Stating Conclusions About Claims.   _In Exercises 5–8, do the following:_

a. Express the original claim in symbolic form.

b. Identify the null and alternative hypotheses.

5. Claim: 20% of adults smoke. A recent Gallup survey of 1016 randomly selected adults showed that 21% of the respondents smoke.

6. Claim: When parents use the XSORT method of gender selection, the proportion of baby girls is greater than 0.5. The latest actual results show that among 945 babies born to couples using the XSORT method of gender selection, 879 were girls.

7. Claim: The mean pulse rate (in beats per minute) of adult females is 76 or lower. For the random sample of adult females in Data Set 1 from Appendix B, the mean pulse rate is 77.5.

8. Claim: The standard deviation of pulse rates of adult women is at least 50. For the random sample of adult females in Data Set 1 from Appendix B, the pulse rates have a standard deviation of 11.6.

Forming Conclusions. *In Exercises 9–12, refer to the exercise identified. Using only the rare event rule, make subjective estimates to determine whether results are likely, then state a conclusion about the original claim. For example, if the claim is that a coin favors heads and sample results consist of 11 heads in 20 flips, conclude that there is not sufficient evidence to support the claim that the coin favors heads (because it is easy to get 11 heads in 20 flips by chance with a fair coin).*

9. Exercise 5   **10.** Exercise 6

11. Exercise 7   **12.** Exercise 8

Finding Test Statistics. *In Exercises 13–16, find the value of the test statistic. (Refer to Table 8-2 to select the correct expression for evaluating the test statistic.)*

13. Community Involvement Claim: Three-fourths of all adults believe that it is important to be involved in their communities. Based on a *USA Today*/Gallup poll of 1021 randomly selected adults, 89% believe that it is important to be involved in their communities.

14. Tax Returns Claim: Among those who file tax returns, less than one-half file them through an accountant or other tax professional. A Fellowes survey of 1002 people who file tax returns showed that 48% of them file through an accountant or other tax professional.

15. White Blood Cell Count Claim: For adult females, the standard deviation of their white blood cell counts is equal to 5.00. The random sample of 40 adult females in Data Set 1 from Appendix B has white blood cell counts with a standard deviation of 2.28.

16. White Blood Cell Count Claim: For adult females, the mean of their white blood cell counts is equal to 8.00. The random sample of 40 adult females in Data Set 1 from Appendix B has white blood cell counts with a mean of 7.15 and a standard deviation of 2.28. (The population standard deviation σ is not known.)

Finding *P*-Values and Critical Values. *In Exercises 17–24, assume that the significance level is $\alpha = 0.05$; use the given statement and find the P-value and critical values. (See Figure 8-4.)*

17. The test statistic of $z = 2.00$ is obtained when testing the claim that $p > 0.5$.

18. The test statistic of $z = -2.00$ is obtained when testing the claim that $p < 0.5$.

19. The test statistic of $z = -1.75$ is obtained when testing the claim that $p = 1/3$.

20. The test statistic of $z = 1.50$ is obtained when testing the claim that $p \neq 0.25$.

21. With $H_1: p \neq 0.25$, the test statistic is $z = -1.23$.

22. With $H_1: p \neq 2/3$, the test statistic is $z = 2.50$.

23. With $H_1: p < 0.6$, the test statistic is $z = -3.00$.

24. With $H_1: p > 7/8$, the test statistic is $z = 2.88$.

Stating Conclusions.   *In Exercises 25–28, assume a significance level of* $\alpha = 0.05$ *and use the given information for the following:*

a. State a conclusion about the null hypothesis. (Reject H_0 or fail to reject H_0.)

b. Without using technical terms, state a final conclusion that addresses the original claim.

25. Original claim: The percentage of blue M&Ms is greater than 5%. The hypothesis test results in a *P*-value of 0.0010.

26. Original claim: Fewer than 20% of M&M candies are green. The hypothesis test results in a *P*-value of 0.0721.

27. Original claim: Women have heights with a mean equal to 160.00 cm. The hypothesis test results in a *P*-value of 0.0614.

28. Original claim: Women have heights with a standard deviation equal to 5.00 cm. The hypothesis test results in a *P*-value of 0.0055.

Terminology.   *In Exercises 29 and 30, use the given information to answer the following:*

a. Identify the null hypothesis and the alternative hypothesis.

b. What is the value of α?

c. What is the sampling distribution of the sample statistic?

d. Is the test two-tailed, left-tailed, or right-tailed?

e. What is the value of the test statistic?

f. What is the *P*-value?

g. What is the critical value?

h. What is the area of the critical region?

29. Gender Selection A 0.01 significance level is used for a hypothesis test of the claim that when parents use the XSORT method of gender selection, the proportion of baby girls is *greater* than 0.5. Assume that sample data consist of 55 girls born in 100 births, so the sample statistic of 0.55 results in a *z* score that is 1.00 standard deviation above 0.

30. Gender Selection A 0.05 significance level is used for a hypothesis test of the claim that when parents use the XSORT method of gender selection, the proportion of baby girls is *different* from 0.5. Assume that sample data consist of 55 girls born in 100 births, so the sample statistic of 0.55 results in a *z* score that is 1.00 standard deviation above 0.

Type I and Type II Errors.   *In Exercises 31–34, identify expressions that identify the type I error and the type II error that correspond to the given claim. (Although conclusions are usually expressed in verbal form, the answers here can be expressed with statements that include symbolic expressions such as* $p = 0.1$.)

31. The proportion of people who write with their left hand is equal to 0.1.

32. The proportion of gamblers who consistently win in casinos is equal to 0.001.

33. The proportion of female statistics students is greater than 0.5.

34. The proportion of husbands taller than their wives is less than 0.9.

8-2 Beyond the Basics

35. Interpreting Power Chantix tablets are used as an aid to help people stop smoking. In a clinical trial, 129 subjects were treated with Chantix twice a day for 12 weeks, and 16 subjects experienced abdominal pain (based on data from Pfizer, Inc.). If someone claims that more than 8% of Chantix users experience abdominal pain, that claim is supported with a hypothesis test conducted with a 0.05 significance level. Using 0.18 as an alternative value of p, the power of the test is 0.96. Interpret this value of the power of the test.

36. Calculating Power Consider a hypothesis test of the claim that the MicroSort method of gender selection is effective in increasing the likelihood of having a baby girl, so that the claim is $p > 0.5$. Assume that a significance level of $\alpha = 0.05$ is used, and the sample is a simple random sample of size $n = 64$.

a. Assuming that the true population proportion is 0.65, find the power of the test, which is the probability of rejecting the null hypothesis when it is false. (*Hint:* With a 0.05 significance level, the critical value is $z = 1.645$, so any test statistic in the right tail of the accompanying top graph is in the rejection region where the claim is supported. Find the sample proportion $\hat{p}$ in the top graph, and use it to find the power shown in the bottom graph.)

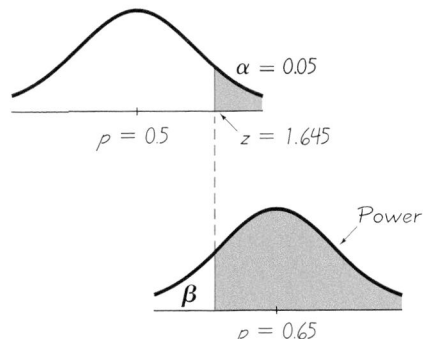

b. Explain why the red-shaded region of the bottom graph represents the power of the test.

37. Finding Sample Size to Achieve Power Researchers plan to conduct a test of a gender-selection method. They plan to use the alternative hypothesis of $H_1: p > 0.5$ and a significance level of $\alpha = 0.05$. Find the sample size required to achieve at least 80% power in detecting an increase in p from 0.5 to 0.55. (This is a very difficult exercise. *Hint:* See Exercise 36.)

8-3 Testing a Claim About a Proportion

Key Concept Section 8-2 presented individual components of a hypothesis test, and this section presents complete procedures for testing a hypothesis (or claim) made about a population proportion p. We illustrate hypothesis testing with the *P*-value method, the critical value method, and the use of confidence intervals. The methods of this section can be used with claims about population proportions, and the same methods can be used for testing claims about probabilities or the decimal equivalents of percents.

Two different approaches for testing a claim about a population proportion are (1) to use a normal distribution as an approximation to the binomial distribution, and (2) to use an exact method based on the binomial probability distribution. Part 1 of this section uses the approximation method with the normal distribution, and Part 2 of this section briefly describes the exact method.

Part 1: Basic Methods of Testing Claims About a Population Proportion p

The following box includes the key elements used for testing a claim about a population proportion.

Testing a Claim About a Population Proportion

Objective

Conduct a formal hypothesis test of a claim about a population proportion p.

Notation

n = sample size or number of trials

$\hat{p} = \dfrac{x}{n}$ (*sample* proportion)

p = population proportion (p is the value used in the statement of the null hypothesis)

$q = 1 - p$

Requirements

1. The sample observations are a simple random sample.

2. The conditions for a *binomial distribution* are satisfied. (There is a fixed number of independent trials having constant probabilities, and each trial has two outcome categories of "success" and "failure.")

3. The conditions $np \geq 5$ and $nq \geq 5$ are both satisfied, so **the binomial distribution of sample proportions can be approximated by a normal distribution with** $\mu = np$ and $\sigma = \sqrt{npq}$ (as described in Section 6-7). Note that p used here is the *assumed* proportion used in the claim, not the sample proportion $\hat{p}$.

Test Statistic for Testing a Claim About a Proportion

$$z = \frac{\hat{p} - p}{\sqrt{\dfrac{pq}{n}}}$$

P-values: *P*-values are automatically provided by technology. If technology is not available, use the standard normal distribution (Table A-2) and refer to Figure 8-1.

Critical values: Use the standard normal distribution (Table A-2).

CAUTION

Reminder: Don't confuse a *P*-value with a proportion p.

- *P*-value = probability of getting a test statistic at least as extreme as the one representing the sample data, assuming that the null hypothesis H_0 is true

- p = population proportion

The test statistic above does not include a correction for continuity (as described in Section 6-7), because its effect tends to be very small with large samples.

Example 1   Reality Check

Based on information from the National Cyber Security Alliance, 93% of computer owners believe that they have antivirus programs installed on their computers. In a random sample of 400 scanned computers, it is found that 380 of them (or 95%) actually have antivirus programs. Use the sample data from the scanned computers to test the claim that 93% of computers have antivirus programs.

Requirement check We first check the three requirements.

1. The 400 computers are randomly selected.

2. There is a fixed number (400) of independent trials with two categories (computer has an antivirus program or does not).

3. The requirements $np \geq 5$ and $nq \geq 5$ are both satisfied with $n = 400$, $p = 0.93$, and $q = 0.07$. (The value of $p = 0.93$ comes from the claim. We get $np = (400)(0.93) = 372$, which is greater than or equal to 5, and we get $nq = (400)(0.07) = 28$, which is also greater than or equal to 5.)

The three requirements are satisfied.

P-Value Method

Technology Computer programs and calculators usually provide a *P*-value, so the *P*-value method is used. See the accompanying TI-83/84 Plus calculator results showing the alternative hypothesis of "prop $\neq$ 0.93," the test statistic of $z = 1.57$ (rounded), and the *P*-value of 0.1169 (rounded).

TI-83/84 PLUS

```
1-PropZTest
 prop≠.93
 z=1.567723603
 P=.1169456657
 p̂=.95
 n=400
```

If technology is not available, Figure 8-1 in the preceding section lists the steps for using the *P*-value method. Using those steps from Figure 8-1, we can test the claim in Example 1 as follows.

Step 1: The original claim is that 93% of computers have antivirus programs, and that claim can be expressed in symbolic form as $p = 0.93$.

Step 2: The opposite of the original claim is $p \neq 0.93$.

Step 3: Of the preceding two symbolic expressions, the expression $p \neq 0.93$ does not contain equality, so it becomes the alternative hypothesis. The null hypothesis is the statement that p equals the fixed value of 0.93. We can therefore express H_0 and H_1 as follows:

$$H_0: p = 0.93 \quad \text{(original claim)}$$
$$H_1: p \neq 0.93$$

Step 4: For the significance level, we select $\alpha = 0.05$, which is a very common choice.

Step 5: Because we are testing a claim about a population proportion p, the sample statistic $\hat{p}$ is relevant to this test. The sampling distribution of sample proportions $\hat{p}$ can be approximated by a normal distribution in this case.

Step 6: The test statistic $z = 1.57$ can be calculated by using $\hat{p} = 380/400$ (sample proportion), $n = 400$ (sample size), $p = 0.93$ (assumed in the null hypothesis), and $q = 1 - 0.93 = 0.07$.

$$z = \frac{\hat{p} - p}{\sqrt{\frac{pq}{n}}} = \frac{\frac{380}{400} - 0.93}{\sqrt{\frac{(0.93)(0.07)}{400}}} = 1.57$$

We now find the *P*-value by using the following procedure, which is shown in Figure 8-4:

Left-tailed test: *P*-value = area to left of test statistic *z*

Right-tailed test: *P*-value = area to right of test statistic *z*

Two-tailed test: *P*-value = *twice* the area of the extreme region bounded by the test statistic *z*

Because the hypothesis test we are considering is two-tailed with a test statistic of $z = 1.57$, the *P*-value is twice the area to the right of $z = 1.57$. Referring to Table A-2, we see that the cumulative area to the *left* of $z = 1.57$ is 0.9418, so the area to the right of that test statistic is $1 - 0.9418 = 0.0582$. The *P*-value is twice 0.0582, so we get *P*-value $= 0.1164$. (If using technology with the unrounded *z* score, the *P*-value is found to be 0.1169, as shown in the TI-83/84 Plus calculator display.) Figure 8-6 shows the test statistic and *P*-value for this example.

Step 7:   Because the *P*-value of 0.1164 is greater than the significance level of $\alpha = 0.05$, we fail to reject the null hypothesis.

Step 8:   Because we fail to reject H_0: $p = 0.93$, we fail to reject the claim that 93% of computers have antivirus programs. We conclude that there is not sufficient sample evidence to warrant rejection of the claim that 93% of computers have antivirus programs. (See Table 8-3 for help with wording this final conclusion.)

Figure 8-6   *P*-Value Method

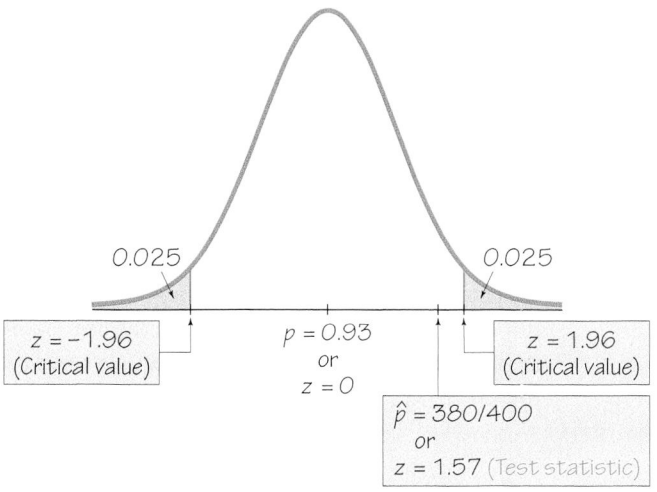

Figure 8-7   **Critical Value Method**

Critical Value Method

The critical value method of testing hypotheses is summarized in Figure 8-2 in Section 8-2. When using the critical value method with the claim given in Example 1, Steps 1 through 5 are the same as in Steps 1 through 5 for the *P*-value method, as shown above. We continue with Step 6 of the critical value method.

Step 6:   The test statistic is computed to be $z = 1.57$ as shown for the preceding *P*-value method. With the critical value method, we now find the critical values (instead of the *P*-value). This is a two-tailed test, so the area of the critical region is an area of $\alpha = 0.05$, which is divided equally between the two tails. Referring to Table A-2 and applying the methods of Section 6-2, we find that the critical values of $z = -1.96$ and $z = 1.96$ are at the boundaries of the critical region, as shown in Figure 8-7.

Step 7: Because the test statistic does not fall within the critical region, we fail to reject the null hypothesis.

Step 8: Because we fail to reject H_0: $p = 0.93$, we fail to reject the claim that 93% of computers have antivirus programs. We conclude that there is not sufficient sample evidence to warrant rejection of the claim that 93% of computers have antivirus programs. (See Table 8-3 for help with wording this final conclusion.)

Confidence Interval Method

The claim of $p = 0.93$ can be tested with a 0.05 significance level by constructing a 95% confidence interval (as shown in Table 8-1 in Section 8-2). (In general, for *two-tailed* hypothesis tests construct a confidence interval with a confidence level corresponding to the significance level, as in Table 8-1.)

The 95% confidence interval estimate of the population proportion p is found using the sample data consisting of $n = 400$ and $\hat{p} = 380/400$. Using the methods of Section 7-2 we get: $0.929 < p < 0.971$. That interval contains the claimed value of 0.93. Because we are 95% confident that the limits of 0.929 and 0.971 contain the true value of p, we do not have sufficient evidence to warrant rejection of the claim that that 93% of computers have antivirus programs. In this case, the conclusion is the same as with the *P*-value method and the critical value method.

CAUTION When testing claims about a population proportion, the critical value method and the *P*-value method are equivalent in the sense that they always yield the same results, but the confidence interval method is not equivalent to them and may result in a different conclusion. (Both the critical value method and *P*-value method use the same standard deviation based on the *claimed proportion p*, but the confidence interval uses an estimated standard deviation based on the *sample proportion*.) Here is a good strategy: Use a confidence interval to *estimate* a population proportion, but use the *P*-value method or critical value method for *testing a claim* about a proportion. See Exercise 36.

Finding the Number of Successes x

Computer software and calculators designed for hypothesis tests of proportions usually require input consisting of the sample size n and the number of successes x, but the sample proportion is often given instead of x. The number of successes x can be found as illustrated in Example 2. Note that in Example 2, the result of 462.6 people must be rounded to the nearest whole number.

Example 2 Finding the Number of Successes x

A Harris Interactive survey conducted for Gillette showed that among 514 human resource professionals polled, 90% said that appearance of a job applicant is most important for a good first impression. What is the actual number of respondents who said that appearance of a job applicant is most important for a good first impression?

Solution

The number of respondents who said that appearance of a job applicant is most important for a good first impression is 90% of 514, or $0.90 \times 514 = 462.6$, but the result must be a whole number, so we round the product to the nearest whole number of 463.

Although a media report about this study used "90%," the more precise percentage of 90.0778% is obtained by using the actual number of respondents who said that appearance of a job applicant is most important for a good first impression ($x = 463$) and the sample size ($n = 514$). When conducting the hypothesis test, better results can be obtained by using the sample proportion of 0.900778 (instead of 0.90).

Example 3   Did the County Clerk Cheat?

The Chapter Problem includes data showing that when the county clerk in Essex County, New Jersey, selected candidates for positions on election ballots, Democrats were selected first in 40 of 41 ballots. Because he was supposed to use a method of random selection, Republicans claimed that instead of using randomness, he used a method that favored Democrats. Use a 0.05 significance level to test the claim that the method favored Democrats.

Solution

Requirement check (1) For the purpose of conducting the hypothesis test, we assume that the county clerk used a process of random selection. (2) There is a fixed number (41) of independent trials with two categories (the Democrat won the top line on the ballot or did not). (3) The requirements $np \geq 5$ and $nq \geq 5$ are both satisfied with $n = 41$ and $p = 0.5$. (We get $np = (41)(0.5) = 20.5$, which is greater than or equal to 5, and we also get $nq = (41)(0.5) = 20.5$, which is greater than or equal to 5.) The three requirements are all satisfied.

If using technology, the test statistic and the P-value will be provided. See the accompanying results from StatCrunch showing that the test statistic is $z = 6.09$ (rounded) and the indication that the P-value is less than 0.0001. The low P-value suggests that we reject the null hypothesis and support the alternative hypothesis that $p > 0.5$, so it appears that the county clerk did use a procedure that favored Democrats for the top position on the election ballots.

STATCRUNCH

Hypothesis test results:
p : proportion of successes for population
$H_0 : p = 0.5$
$H_A : p > 0.5$

Proportion	Count	Total	Sample Prop.	Std. Err.	Z-Stat	P-value
p	40	41	0.9756098	0.07808688	6.090777	<0.0001

If technology is not available, proceed as follows to conduct the hypothesis test using the P-value method summarized in Figure 8-1 from Section 8-2.

Step 1: The original claim is that the clerk used a method that favored Democrats. We express this in symbolic form as $p > 0.5$.

Step 2: The opposite of the original claim is $p \leq 0.5$.

Step 3: Because $p > 0.5$ does not contain equality, it becomes H_1. We get

$H_0: p = 0.50$ (null hypothesis)

$H_1: p > 0.50$ (alternative hypothesis and original claim)

Step 4: The significance level is $\alpha = 0.05$.

Step 5: Because the claim involves the proportion p, the statistic relevant to this test is the sample proportion $\hat{p}$ and the sampling distribution of sample proportions can be approximated by the normal distribution.

Step 6: The test statistic $z = 6.09$ is calculated as follows:

$$z = \frac{\hat{p} - p}{\sqrt{\frac{pq}{n}}} = \frac{\frac{40}{41} - 0.50}{\sqrt{\frac{(0.5)(0.5)}{41}}} = 6.09$$

Refer to Figure 8-4 for the procedure for finding the P-value. Figure 8-4 shows that for this right-tailed test, the P-value is the area to the right of the test statistic. Using Table A-2, we see that $z = 6.09$ is off the chart, so the area to the right of $z = 6.09$ is 0.0001. (Technology provides a more accurate P-value of 0.000000000564.)

Step 7: Because the P-value is less than or equal to the significance level of 0.05, we reject the null hypothesis.

Interpretation

Because we reject the null hypothesis, we support the alternative hypothesis. We therefore conclude that there is sufficient evidence to support the Republican claim that the county clerk used a method that favored Democrats. The county clerk lost his job.

Critical Value Method

If we were to repeat Example 3 using the critical value method of testing hypotheses, we would see that in Step 6 the critical value is $z = 1.645$. In Step 7 we would reject the null hypothesis because the test statistic of $z = 6.09$ would fall within the critical region bounded by $z = 1.645$. We would then reach the same conclusion given in Example 3.

Confidence Interval method

If we were to repeat Example 3 using the confidence interval method, we would use a 90% confidence level because we have a right-tailed test. (See Table 8-1.) We get this 90% confidence interval: $0.936 < p < 1.015$. Because the confidence interval limits do not contain the value of 0.5, it is very unlikely that the success rate is actually 50%, so there is sufficient evidence to reject the 50% rate. In this case, the P-value method, critical value method, and confidence interval method all lead to the same conclusion.

Part 2: Exact Methods for Testing Claims About a Population Proportion p

Instead of using the normal distribution as an *approximation* to the binomial distribution, we can get *exact* results by using the binomial probability distribution itself. Binomial probabilities are a nuisance to calculate manually, but technology makes this approach quite simple. Also, this exact approach does not require that $np \geq 5$ and $nq \geq 5$, so we have a method that applies when that requirement is not satisfied. To test hypotheses using the exact binomial distribution, use the binomial probability distribution with the P-value method, use the value of p assumed in the null hypothesis, and find P-values as follows:

Lefties Die Sooner?

A study by psychologists Diane Halpern and Stanley Coren received considerable media attention and generated considerable interest when it concluded that left-handed people don't live as long as right-handed people. Based on their study, it appeared that left-handed people live an average of nine years less than righties. The Halpern/Coren study has been criticized for using flawed data. They used second-hand data by surveying relatives about people who had recently died. The myth of lefties dying younger became folklore that has survived many years. However, more recent studies show that left-handed people do *not* have shorter lives than those who are right-handed.

Left-tailed test: *P*-value is the probability of *x* or fewer successes among *n* trials.

Right-tailed test: *P*-value is the probability of *x* or more successes among *n* trials.

Two-tailed test: The two-tailed test can be treated with different approaches, some of which are quite complex. For example, Minitab uses a "likelihood ratio test" that is different from the following relatively simple approach:

If $\hat{p} > p$, the *P*-value is twice the probability of *x* or more successes.

If $\hat{p} < p$, the *P*-value is twice the probability of *x* or fewer successes.

Example 4   Using the Exact Method

In testing a method of gender selection, 10 randomly selected couples are treated with the method, they each have a baby, and 9 of the babies are girls. Use a 0.05 significance level to test the claim that with this method, the probability of a baby being a girl is greater than 0.75.

Solution

Requirement check The normal approximation method described in Part 1 of this section requires that $np \geq 5$ and $nq \geq 5$, but $nq = (10)(0.25) = 2.5$, so the requirement is violated. The exact method has only the first two requirements listed near the beginning of this section, and those two requirements are satisfied. Here are the null and alternative hypotheses:

H_0: $p = 0.75$ (null hypothesis)

H_1: $p > 0.75$ (alternative hypothesis and original claim)

Instead of using the normal distribution, we use technology to find probabilities in a binomial distribution with $p = 0.75$. Because this is a right-tailed test, the *P*-value is the probability of 9 or more successes among 10 trials, assuming that $p = 0.75$. See the accompanying STATDISK display of exact probabilities from the binomial distribution. This STATDISK display shows that the probability of 9 or more successes is 0.2440252 when rounded to seven decimal places, so the *P*-value is 0.2440252. The *P*-value is high (greater than 0.05), so we fail to reject the null hypothesis. There is not sufficient evidence to support the claim that with the gender selection method, the probability of a girl is greater than 0.75.

STATDISK

Num Trials, n:	10		Evaluate
Success Prob, p:	0.75		

Mean:	7.5000
St Dev:	1.3693
Variance:	1.8750

x	P(x)	P(x or fewer)	P(x or greater)
0	0.0000010	0.0000010	1.0000000
1	0.0000286	0.0000296	0.9999990
2	0.0003862	0.0004158	0.9999704
3	0.0030899	0.0035057	0.9995842
4	0.0162220	0.0197277	0.9964943
5	0.0583992	0.0781269	0.9802723
6	0.1459980	0.2241249	0.9218731
7	0.2502823	0.4744072	0.7758751
8	0.2815676	0.7559748	0.5255928
9	0.1877117	0.9436865	0.2440252
10	0.0563135	1.0000000	0.0563135

using TECHNOLOGY

STATDISK Select **Analysis, Hypothesis Testing, Proportion-One Sample,** then enter the data in the dialog box.

MINITAB Select **Stat, Basic Statistics, 1 Proportion,** then click on the button for "Summarized data." Enter the sample size and number of successes, then click on **Options** and enter the data in the dialog box. For the confidence level, enter the complement of the significance level. (Enter 95.0 for a significance level of 0.05.) For the "test proportion" value, enter the proportion used in the null hypothesis. For "alternative," select the format used for the alternative hypothesis. Instead of using a normal approximation, Minitab's default procedure is to determine the P-value by using an exact method that is often the same as the one described in Part 2 of this section. (If the test is two-tailed and the assumed value of p is not 0.5, Minitab's exact method is different from the one described in Part 2 of this section.) To use the normal approximation method presented in Part 1 of this section, click on the **Options** button and then click on the box with this statement: "Use test and interval based on normal distribution."

EXCEL Use XLSTAT. Click on **XLSTAT** at the top, click on **Parametric Tests,** then select **Tests for one proportion.** In the screen that appears, enter the sample proportion in the "Proportion" box, enter the sample size in the "Sample size" box, and enter

the claimed value of the population proportion in the "Test proportion" box. (This is the same proportion used in the null hypothesis.) Select the "Data Format" of **Proportion,** and be sure that the box next to "z test" is checked. For the "Range" box, enter A1 so that the results will be displayed in a position starting at cell A1. Click on the **Options** tab to select the type of test; select the option including $\neq$ for a two-tailed test, select the option including $<$ for a left-tailed test, or select the option including $>$ for a right-tailed test. Enter the desired "Significance level (%)." For example, enter 5 for a 0.05 significance level. Click **OK.** After the results are displayed, look for the test statistic identified as "z (Observed value)" and the P-value. Critical values will also be displayed.

T1-83/84 PLUS Press **STAT**, select **TESTS,** and then select **1-PropZTest.** Enter the claimed value of the population proportion for p0, then enter the values for x and n, and then select the type of test. Highlight **Calculate,** then press **ENTER**.

STATCRUNCH Click on **Open StatCrunch.** Click on **Stat,** then select **Proportion.** Select **One sample,** then select **with summary.** Proceed to enter the number of successes and the number of observations, click on **Next,** then select **Hypothesis Test.** Enter the claimed value of the population proportion and select the form of the test, then click on **Calculate.**

8-3 Basic Skills and Concepts

Statistical Literacy and Critical Thinking

1. Hypothesis Tests and Confidence Intervals We can test a claim about a population proportion using the P-value method of hypothesis testing or the critical value method of hypothesis testing, or we could base our conclusion on a confidence interval. Assuming that all three methods are based on the same significance level, which two of the three methods always yield the same conclusion?

2. Sample Proportion In a Wakefield Research survey, respondents were asked if they ever hesitated to give a handshake because of a fear of germs. Of the respondents, 411 answered "yes" and 592 said "no." What is the sample proportion of *yes* responses, and what notation is used to represent it?

3. *P*-Value Using the sample data from Exercise 2, we can test the claim that $p < 0.5$, where p denotes the proportion of "yes" responses for the population. Some technologies provide results that include a P-value of 5.50E—9. Write that number using ordinary notation. What does the P-value suggest about the claim?

4. Notation and *P*-Value

a. Refer to Exercise 2 and distinguish between the value of p and the P-value.

b. It was stated that we can easily remember how to interpret P-values with this: "If the P is low, the null must go." What does this mean?

c. Another memory trick commonly used is this: "If the P is high, the null will fly." Given that a hypothesis test never results in a conclusion of proving or supporting a null hypothesis, how is this memory trick misleading?

In Exercises 5–8, identify the indicated values or interpret the given display. Use the normal distribution as an approximation to the binomial distribution (as described in Part 1 of this section). Assume a 0.05 significance level and answer the following:

a. Is the test two-tailed, left-tailed, or right-tailed?

b. What is the test statistic?

c. What is the *P*-value?

d. What is the null hypothesis, and what do you conclude about it?

e. What is the final conclusion?

TI-83/84 PLUS

```
1-PropZTest
 prop<.1
 z=-1.942721717
 P=.0260248259
 p=.0649819495
 n=277
```

5. Adverse Reactions to Drug The drug Symbicort is used to treat asthma. In a clinical trial of Symbicort, 18 of 277 treated subjects experienced headaches (based on data from AstraZeneca). The accompanying TI-83/84 Plus calculator display shows results from a test of the claim that less than 10% of treated subjects experienced headaches.

6. Guns in the Home In a Gallup poll of 1003 randomly selected subjects, 373 said that they have a gun in their home. The accompanying Minitab display shows results from a test of the claim that 35% of homes have guns in them.

MINITAB

```
Test of p = 0.35 vs p not = 0.35

Variable    X    N Sample p       95% CI        Z-Value P-Value
Guns      373 1003 0.371884 (0.341974, 0.401795)   1.45   0.146
```

7. Brand Recognition A PriceGrabber.com survey of 1631 randomly selected adults showed that 555 of them have heard of the Sony Reader. The following STATDISK display results from a test of the claim that 35% of adults have heard of the Sony Reader.

STATDISK

Sample proportion:	0.340282
Test Statistic, z:	−0.8228
Critical z:	±1.9600
P-Value:	0.4106

8. Public Speaking A TNS poll of 1000 randomly selected adults showed that 460 of them say that public speaking is an activity that they dread most. Shown next is the StatCrunch display resulting from a test of the claim that fewer than half of adults say that public speaking is the activity that they dread most.

STATCRUNCH

Hypothesis test results:
p : proportion of successes for population
H_0 : p = 0.5
H_A : p < 0.5

Proportion	Count	Total	Sample Prop.	Std. Err.	Z-Stat	P-value
p	460	1000	0.46	0.015811387	−2.529822	0.0057

Testing Claims About Proportions. *In Exercises 9–32, test the given claim. Identify the null hypothesis, alternative hypothesis, test statistic, P-value or critical value(s), conclusion about the null hypothesis, and final conclusion that addresses the original claim. Use the P-value method unless your instructor specifies otherwise. Use the normal distribution as an approximation to the binomial distribution (as described in Part 1 of this section).*

9. Mendelian Genetics When Mendel conducted his famous genetics experiments with peas, one sample of offspring consisted of 428 green peas and 152 yellow peas. Use a 0.01

significance level to test Mendel's claim that under the same circumstances, 25% of offspring peas will be yellow.

10. M&Ms Data Set 20 in Appendix B lists data from 100 M&Ms, and 8% of them are brown. Use a 0.05 significance level to test the claim of the Mars candy company that the percentage of brown M&Ms is equal to 13%.

11. Identify Theft In a KRC Research poll, 1002 adults were asked if they felt vulnerable to identify theft, and 531 of them said "yes." Use a 0.05 significance level to test the claim that the majority of adults feel vulnerable to identity theft.

12. Plane Seats In a 3M Privacy Filters poll, 806 adults were asked to identify their favorite seat when they fly, and 492 of them chose a window seat. Use a 0.01 significance level to test the claim that the majority of adults prefer window seats when they fly.

13. Gender Selection The Genetics and IVF Institute conducted a clinical trial of the XSORT method designed to increase the probability of conceiving a girl. As of this writing, 945 babies were born to parents using the XSORT method, and 879 of them were girls. Use a 0.01 significance level to test the claim that the XSORT method is effective in increasing the likelihood that a baby will be a girl.

14. Gender Selection The Genetics and IVF Institute conducted a clinical trial of the YSORT method designed to increase the probability of conceiving a boy. As of this writing, 291 babies were born to parents using the YSORT method, and 239 of them were boys. Use a 0.01 significance level to test the claim that the YSORT method is effective in increasing the likelihood that a baby will be a boy.

15. Touch Therapy When she was 9 years of age, Emily Rosa did a science fair experiment in which she tested professional touch therapists to see if they could sense her energy field. She flipped a coin to select either her right hand or her left hand, then she asked the therapists to identify the selected hand by placing their hand just under Emily's hand without seeing it and without touching it. Among 280 trials, the touch therapists were correct 123 times (based on data in "A Close Look at Therapeutic Touch," *Journal of the American Medical Association,* Vol. 279, No. 13). Use a 0.10 significance level to test the claim that touch therapists use a method equivalent to random guesses. Do the results suggest that touch therapists are effective?

16. Touch Therapy Repeat the preceding exercise using a 0.01 significance level. Does the conclusion change?

17. Tennis Instant Replay The Hawk-Eye electronic system is used in tennis for displaying an instant replay that shows whether a ball is in bounds or out of bounds so players can challenge calls made by referees. In the most recent U.S. Open (as of this writing), singles players made 611 challenges and 172 of them were successful with the call overturned. Use a 0.01 significance level to test the claim that fewer than 1/3 of the challenges are successful. What do the results suggest about the ability of players to see calls better than referees?

18. Perception and Reality In a presidential election, 308 out of 611 voters surveyed said that they voted for the candidate who won (based on data from ICR Survey Research Group). Use a 0.10 significance level to test the claim that among all voters, the percentage who believe that they voted for the winning candidate is equal to 43%, which is the actual percentage of votes for the winning candidate. What does the result suggest about voter perceptions?

19. Cell Phones and Cancer In a study of 420,095 Danish cell phone users, 135 subjects developed cancer of the brain or nervous system (based on data from the *Journal of the National Cancer Institute* as reported in *USA Today*). Test the claim of a somewhat common belief that such cancers are affected by cell phone use. That is, test the claim that cell phone users develop cancer of the brain or nervous system at a rate that is different from the rate of 0.0340% for people who do not use cell phones. Because this issue has such great importance, use a 0.005 significance level. Based on these results, should cell phone users be concerned about cancer of the brain or nervous system?

20. Twitter Poll The Pew Research Center conducted a survey of 1007 adults and found that 856 of them know what Twitter is. Use a 0.01 significance level to test the claim that more than 75% of adults know what Twitter is.

21. Overtime Rule in Football In "The Overtime Rule in the National Football League: Fair or Unfair?" by Gorgievski et al., *MathAMATYC Educator*, Vol. 2, No. 1, the authors report that among 414 football games won in overtime, 235 were won by the team that won the coin toss at the beginning of overtime. Using a 0.05 significance level, test the claim that the coin toss is fair in the sense that neither team has an advantage by winning it.

22. Testing Effectiveness of Nicotine Patches In one study of smokers who tried to quit smoking with nicotine patch therapy, 39 were smoking one year after the treatment and 32 were not smoking one year after the treatment (based on data from "High-Dose Nicotine Patch Therapy," by Dale et al., *Journal of the American Medical Association*, Vol. 274, No. 17). Use a 0.05 significance level to test the claim that among smokers who try to quit with nicotine patch therapy, the majority are smoking a year after the treatment. What do these results suggest about the effectiveness of nicotine patch therapy for those trying to quit smoking?

23. Smartphone Users A RingCentral survey of 380 smartphone users showed that 152 of them said that their smartphone is the only thing they could not live without. Use a 0.01 significance level to test the claim that fewer than half of smartphone users identify the smartphone as the only thing they could not live without. Do these results apply to the general population?

24. Postponing Death An interesting and popular hypothesis is that individuals can temporarily postpone death to survive a major holiday or important event such as a birthday. In a study of this phenomenon, it was found that there were 6062 deaths in the week before Thanksgiving, and 5938 deaths the week after Thanksgiving (based on data from "Holidays, Birthdays, and Postponement of Cancer Death," by Young and Hade, *Journal of the American Medical Association*, Vol. 292, No. 24). If people can postpone death until after Thanksgiving, then the proportion of deaths in the week before should be less than 0.5. Use a 0.05 significance level to test the claim that the proportion of deaths in the week before Thanksgiving is less than 0.5. Based on the result, does there appear to be any indication that people can temporarily postpone death to survive the Thanksgiving holiday?

25. Online Books A *Consumer Reports* Research Center survey of 427 women showed that 29.0% of them purchase books online. Test the claim that more than 25% of women purchase books online.

26. Job Interviews In a Harris poll of 514 human resource professionals, 45.9% said that body piercings and tattoos were big grooming red flags. Use a 0.01 significance level to test the claim that less than half of all human resource professionals say that body piercings are big grooming red flags.

27. Job Interviews In a Harris poll of 514 human resource professionals, 90% said that the appearance of a job applicant is most important for a good first impression. Use a 0.01 significance level to test the claim that more than 3/4 of all human resource professionals say that the appearance of a job applicant is most important for a good first impression.

28. Misleading Survey Responses Voting records show that 61% of eligible voters actually did vote in a recent presidential election. In a survey of 1002 people, 70% said that they voted in that election (based on data from ICR Research Group). Use the survey results to test the claim that the percentage of all voters who say that they voted is equal to 61%. What do the results suggest?

29. Bias in Jury Selection In the case of *Casteneda v. Partida*, it was found that during a period of 11 years in Hidalgo County, Texas, 870 people were selected for grand jury duty and 39% of them were Americans of Mexican ancestry. Among the people eligible for grand jury duty, 79.1% were Americans of Mexican ancestry. Use a 0.01 significance level to test the claim that the selection process is biased against Americans of Mexican ancestry. Does the jury selection system appear to be fair?

30. Finding a Job Through Networking In a survey of 703 randomly selected workers, 61% got their jobs through networking (based on data from Taylor Nelson Sofres Research). Use the sample data with a 0.05 significance level to test the claim that most (more than 50%) workers get their jobs through networking. What does the result suggest about the strategy for finding a job after graduation?

31. Nielsen Ratings A recent Super Bowl football game between the New Orleans Saints and the Indianapolis Colts set a record for the number of television viewers. According to the Nielsen company, that game had a share of 77%, meaning that among the television sets in use at the time of the game, 77% were tuned to the game. Nielsen's sample size is 25,000 households. Use a 0.01 significance level to test the claim of a media report that more than 75% of television sets in use were tuned to the Super Bowl.

32. HDTV Penetration In a survey of 1500 households, it is found that 47% of them have a high-definition television (based on data from the Consumer Electronics Association). Use a 0.01 significance level to test the claim that fewer than half of all households have a high-definition television. Is the result from a few years ago likely to be valid today?

Large Data Sets. *In Exercises 33 and 34, use the data set from Appendix B to test the given claim.*

33. M&Ms Refer to Data Set 20 in Appendix B and find the sample proportion of M&Ms that are green. Use that result to test the claim of Mars, Inc., that 16% of its plain M&M candies are green.

34. On-Time Flights Consider a flight to be on time if it arrives no later than 15 minutes after the scheduled arrival time. Refer to Data Set 15 in Appendix B, and use the sample data to test the claim made by CNN that 79.5% of flights are on time. Use a 0.05 significance level.

8-3 Beyond the Basics

35. Binomial Distribution We want to use a 0.05 significance level to test the claim that a coin favors heads, and sample data consist of 7 heads in 8 tosses. We can't use the normal approximation method because we violate the requirement that $np \geq 5$ and $nq \geq 5$. Use the binomial probability distribution to test the claim.

36. Using Confidence Intervals to Test Hypotheses When analyzing the last digits of telephone numbers in Port Jefferson, it is found that among 1000 randomly selected digits, 119 are zeros. If the digits are randomly selected, the proportion of zeros should be 0.1.

a. Use the critical value method with a 0.05 significance level to test the claim that the proportion of zeros equals 0.1.

b. Use the *P*-value method with a 0.05 significance level to test the claim that the proportion of zeros equals 0.1.

c. Use the sample data to construct a 95% confidence interval estimate of the proportion of zeros. What does the confidence interval suggest about the claim that the proportion of zeros equals 0.1?

d. Compare the results from the critical value method, the *P*-value method, and the confidence interval method. Do they all lead to the same conclusion?

37. Power For a hypothesis test with a specified significance level α, the probability of a type I error is α, whereas the probability β of a type II error depends on the particular value of p that is used as an alternative to the null hypothesis.

continued

a. Using an alternative hypothesis of $p < 0.4$, a sample size of $n = 50$, and assuming that the true value of p is 0.25, find the power of the test. See Exercise 36 in Section 8-2. (*Hint:* Use the values $p = 0.25$ and $pq/n = (0.25)(0.75)/50$.)

b. Find the value of β, the probability of making a type II error.

c. Given the conditions cited in part (a), what do the results indicate about the effectiveness of the hypothesis test?

 8-4   # Testing a Claim About a Mean

Key Concept Because this section presents methods for testing a claim about a population mean, it is one of the most important sections in this book. Part 1 of this section deals with the very realistic and commonly used case in which the population standard deviation σ is not known. Part 2 includes a brief discussion of the procedure used when σ is known, which is very rare.

Part 1: Testing a Claim About a Population Mean When σ Is Not Known

In reality, it is very rare that we test a claim about an unknown value of a population mean but we somehow know the value of the population standard deviation σ. The realistic situation is that we test a claim about a population mean and the value of the population standard deviation σ is not known. When σ is not known, we use a "t test" that incorporates the Student t distribution. The requirements, test statistic, P-value, and critical values are summarized as follows.

Testing Claims About a Population Mean (with σ Not Known)

Use the formal method of hypothesis testing to test a claim about a population mean.

Notation

n = sample size

$\bar{x}$ = *sample* mean

$\mu_{\bar{x}}$ = *population* mean (this value is taken from the claim and is used in the statement of the null hypothesis)

Requirements

1. The sample is a simple random sample.

2. Either or both of these conditions is satisfied: The population is normally distributed or $n > 30$.

Test Statistic for Testing a Claim About a Mean

$$t = \frac{\bar{x} - \mu_{\bar{x}}}{\dfrac{s}{\sqrt{n}}}$$ (Round t to three decimal places, as in Table A-3.)

P-values: Use technology or use the Student t distribution (Table A-3) with degrees of freedom given by df = $n - 1$. (Figure 8-4 in Section 8-2 summarizes the procedure for finding P-values.)

Critical values: Use the Student t distribution (Table A-3) with degrees of freedom given by df = $n - 1$. (If using Table A-3 to find a critical value of t, but the table does not include the number of degrees of freedom, you could be conservative by using the next lower number of degrees of freedom found in the table, or you could use the closest number of degrees of freedom in the table, or you could interpolate.)

Requirement of Normality or $n > 30$ This t test is *robust* against a departure from normality, meaning that the test works reasonably well if the departure from normality is not too extreme. Verify that there are no outliers and that the histogram or dotplot has a shape that is not very far from a normal distribution.

If the original population is not itself normally distributed, we use the condition $n > 30$ for justifying use of the normal distribution, but there is no exact specific minimum sample size that works for all cases. Sample sizes of 15 to 30 are sufficient if the population has a distribution that is not far from normal, but some other populations have distributions that are extremely far from normal, and sample sizes greater than 30 might be necessary. In this text we use the simplified criterion of $n > 30$ as justification for treating the distribution of sample means as a normal distribution, regardless of how far the distribution departs from a normal distribution.

Here is a brief review of important properties of the Student t distribution first presented in Section 7-3:

Important Properties of the Student t Distribution

1. The Student t distribution is different for different sample sizes (see Figure 7-5 in Section 7-3).

2. The Student t distribution has the same general bell shape as the standard normal distribution; its wider shape reflects the greater variability that is expected when s is used to estimate σ.

3. The Student t distribution has a mean of $t = 0$ (just as the standard normal distribution has a mean of $z = 0$).

4. The standard deviation of the Student t distribution varies with the sample size and is greater than 1 (unlike the standard normal distribution, which has $\sigma = 1$).

5. As the sample size n gets larger, the Student t distribution gets closer to the standard normal distribution.

Example 1   Cell Phone Radiation: *P*-Value Method

Listed below are the measured radiation emissions (in W/kg) corresponding to a sample of these cell phones: Samsung SGH-tss9, Blackberry Storm, Blackberry Curve, Motorola Moto, T-Mobile Sidekick, Sanyo Katana Eclipse, Palm Pre, Sony Ericsson, Nokia 6085, Apple iPhone 3G S, and Kyocero Neo E1100 (based on data are from the Environmental Working Group). Use a 0.05 significance level to test the claim that cell phones have a mean radiation level that is less than 1.00 W/kg.

   0.38   0.55   1.54   1.55   0.50   0.60   0.92   0.96   1.00   0.86   1.46

Solution

Requirement check (1) For the purposes of this test, we will assume that the sample is a simple random sample, but it appears that one cell phone of each brand was measured, so this is not a simple random sample of the cell phones in use. This will be discussed further in the interpretation that follows. (2) The sample size is $n = 11$, which is not greater than 30, so we must determine whether the sample appears to be from a population having a normal distribution. With only 11 sample values, a histogram isn't very helpful, but there are no outliers and the accompanying normal quantile plot shows that the points are reasonably close to a straight-line pattern and there is no other pattern that is not a straight line. We conclude that the sample data appear to be from a normally distributed population. The requirements are satisfied. ✔

Normal Quantile Plot (n=11)

Technology We could use technology to obtain the *P*-value. Shown here are the TI-83/84 Plus calculator results for this hypothesis test, and we can see that the *P*-value is 0.3191 (rounded). Because the *P*-value is high (greater than the significance level of $\alpha = 0.05$), we fail to reject the null hypothesis and conclude that there is not sufficient evidence to support the claim that cell phones have a mean radiation level less than 1.00 W/kg.

TI-83/84 PLUS

If technology is not available, we can proceed to use the *P*-value approach summarized in Figure 8-1 or the critical value approach summarized in Figure 8-2. Because of the format of Table A-3, *P*-values can be somewhat difficult to find using that table, so the critical value approach is easier. We will proceed using the critical value approach.

Step 1: The claim that cell phones have a mean radiation level less than 1.00 W/kg is expressed in symbolic form as $\mu < 1.00$ W/kg.

Step 2: The alternative (in symbolic form) to the original claim is $\mu \geq 1.00$ W/kg.

Step 3: Because the statement $\mu < 1.00$ W/kg does not contain the condition of equality, it becomes the alternative hypothesis H_1. The null hypothesis H_0 is the statement that $\mu = 1.00$ W/kg.

$H_0: \mu = 1.00$ W/kg   (null hypothesis)

$H_1: \mu < 1.00$ W/kg   (alternative hypothesis and original claim)

Step 4: As specified in the statement of the problem, the significance level is $\alpha = 0.05$.

Step 5: Because the claim is made about the *population mean* μ, the sample statistic most relevant to this test is the *sample mean* $\bar{x}$. We use the *t* distribution as indicated in the preceding summary box.

Step 6: The sample statistics of $n = 11$ and $\bar{x} = 0.938$ W/kg and the value of $s = 0.423$ W/kg are used to calculate the test statistic as follows:

$$t = \frac{\bar{x} - \mu_{\bar{x}}}{\dfrac{s}{\sqrt{n}}} = \frac{0.938 - 1.00}{\dfrac{0.423}{\sqrt{11}}} = -0.486$$

Using this test statistic of $t = -0.486$, we now proceed to find the critical value from Table A-3. With df $= n - 1 = 10$, refer to Table A-3 and use the column corresponding to an area of 0.05 in one tail to find that the critical value is $t = -1.812$, which is shown in Figure 8-8.

Step 7: Because the test statistic of $t = -0.486$ does not fall in the critical region bounded by the critical value of $t = -1.812$ as shown in Figure 8-8, fail to reject the null hypothesis.

Interpretation

Because we fail to reject the null hypothesis, we conclude that there is not sufficient evidence to support the claim that cell phones have a mean radiation level that is less than 1.00 W/kg.

The validity of this conclusion depends on a sound sampling method. We can see from the given list of cell phone models that one phone was measured for each of 11 different models, so it is possible that we do not have a simple random sample of cell phones selected from the population of cell phones in use. It would be wise to further investigate whether this affects our results.

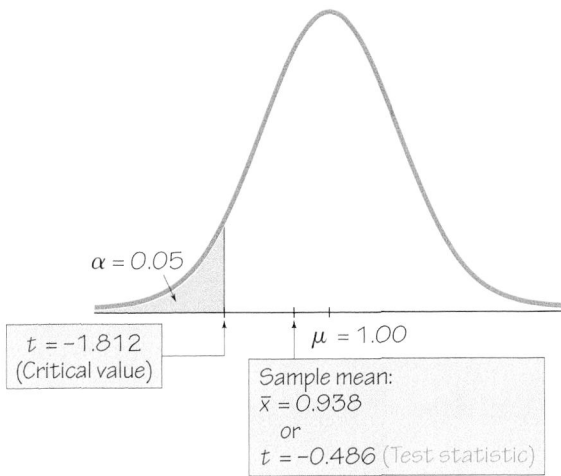

Figure 8-8 *t*-Test: Critical Value Method

Finding *P*-Values with the Student *t* Distribution

Example 1 used the critical value approach to hypothesis testing, but STATDISK, Minitab, XLSTAT, StatCrunch, the TI-83/84 Plus calculator, and many articles in professional journals will display *P*-values. For the preceding example, STATDISK, Minitab, XLSTAT, StatCrunch, and the TI-83/84 Plus calculator display a *P*-value of 0.3191. (Minitab displays the rounded value of 0.319.) With a significance level of 0.05 and a *P*-value greater than 0.05, we fail to reject the null hypothesis, as we did using the critical value method in Example 1. If computer software or a TI-83/84

Plus calculator is not available, we can use Table A-3 to identify a *range of values* containing the *P*-value. We recommend this strategy for finding *P*-values using the *t* distribution:

1. Use software or a TI-83/84 Plus calculator. (STATDISK, Minitab, XLSTAT, StatCrunch, the TI-83/84 Plus calculator, SPSS, and SAS all provide *P*-values for *t* tests.)

2. If technology is not available, use Table A-3 to identify a range of *P*-values as follows: Use the number of degrees of freedom to locate the relevant row of Table A-3, then determine where the test statistic lies relative to the *t* values in that row. Based on a comparison of the *t* test statistic and the *t* values in the row of Table A-3, identify a range of values by referring to the area values given at the top of Table A-3.

Example 2   Finding the *P*-Value

Assuming that neither computer software nor a TI-83/84 Plus calculator is available, use Table A-3 to find a range of values for the *P*-value corresponding to the test statistic of $t = -0.486$ from Example 1.

Solution

Requirement check   The requirements have already been verified in Example 1.

Example 1 involves a left-tailed test, so the *P*-value is the area to the left of the test statistic $t = -0.486$. Because the sample size is $n = 11$, refer to Table A-3 and locate the row corresponding to 10 degrees of freedom (df $= 11 - 1 = 10$). The test statistic of $t = 0.486$ is less than every value in the row for df $= 10$, so the "area in one tail" (to the right of the test statistic) is greater than 0.10. If the area to the right of $t = 0.486$ is greater than 0.10, it follows from symmetry that the area to the left of $t = -0.486$ is also greater than 0.10. Although we can't find the exact *P*-value from Table A-3, we can conclude that the *P*-value is greater than 0.10. When creating a professional report, definitely use technology to find an exact *P*-value instead of a range of *P*-values found from Table A-3.

Because the *P*-value is greater than the significance level of 0.05, we again fail to reject the null hypothesis. There is not sufficient evidence to support the claim that cell phones have a mean radiation level that is less than 1.00 W/kg.

Example 3   Finding the *P*-Value

When using the 40 red blood cell counts for males as listed in Data Set 1 in Appendix B, we get the test statistic $t = 1.956$ when testing the claim that $\mu = 4.950$. Assuming that neither computer software nor a TI-83/84 Plus calculator is available, use Table A-3 to find a range of values for the *P*-value.

Solution

Because the sample size is 40, refer to Table A-3 and locate the row corresponding to 39 degrees of freedom (df $= n - 1$). In the 39th row, the test statistic $t = 1.956$ falls between 2.023 and 1.685, so the area in two tails is between 0.05 and 0.10. (Be sure to use the "Area in Two Tails" whenever the test is two-tailed.) Although we can't find the exact *P*-value, we can conclude that the *P*-value is greater than 0.05 and less than 0.10. (Computer software and the TI-83/84 Plus calculator provide the exact *P*-value of 0.0576.)

Remember, *P*-values can be easily found using computer software or a TI-83/84 Plus calculator. Also, this difficulty in finding *P*-values can be avoided by using the critical value method of testing hypotheses instead of the *P*-value method.

Confidence Interval Method

We can use a confidence interval for testing a claim about μ. For a two-tailed hypothesis test with a 0.05 significance level, we construct a 95% confidence interval, but for a one-tailed hypothesis test with a 0.05 significance level, we construct a 90% confidence interval (as described in Table 8-1 in Section 8-2).

In Section 8-3 we saw that when testing a claim about a population *proportion*, the critical value method and *P*-value method are equivalent, but the confidence interval method is somewhat different. When testing a claim about a population mean, there is no such difference, and all three methods are equivalent.

Example 4 Confidence Interval Method

Use the sample data from Example 1 to construct a confidence interval that can be used to test the claim that $\mu < 1.00$ W/kg, assuming a 0.05 significance level.

Solution

Requirement check The requirements have already been verified in Example 1. ✅

We note that a left-tailed hypothesis test conducted with a 0.05 significance level corresponds to a confidence interval with a 90% confidence level. (See Table 8-1 in Section 8-2.) Using the methods described in Section 7-4, we construct this 90% confidence interval estimate of the population mean:

$$0.707 \text{ W/kg} < \mu < 1.169 \text{ W/kg}$$

Because the assumed value of $\mu = 1.00$ W/kg is contained within the confidence interval, we cannot reject the null hypothesis that $\mu = 1.00$ W/kg. Based on the 11 sample values given in Example 1, we do not have sufficient evidence to support the claim that the mean radiation level is less than 1.00 W/kg.

Example 5 Fatal Overloading

When a plane crashed in Charlotte, North Carolina, 21 passengers were killed. In Lake George, New York, 20 passengers died when the *Ethan Allen* tour boat capsized. In Baltimore's Inner Harbor, 5 passengers died when a water taxi sank. In all of these fatal incidents, overloading was thought to be a contributing factor. Loading capacities were based on old estimates of the mean weight of men, but that mean has increased in recent years with the effect that some boats and airplanes have been overloaded and unsafe. Using the weights of the simple random sample of men from Data Set 1 in Appendix B, we obtain these sample statistics: $n = 40$, $\bar{x} = 182.9$ lb, and $s = 40.8$ lb. (The original weights are in kilograms, and they are converted to pounds before computing these statistics.) Use these results to test the claim that men have a mean weight greater than 166.3 lb, which was the weight in the National Transportation and Safety Board's recommendation M-04-04. Use a 0.05 significance level.

Solution

Requirement check (1) The sample is a simple random sample. (2) Because the sample size of $n = 40$ is greater than 30, we satisfy the requirement that "the population is normally distributed or $n > 30$." The necessary requirements are satisfied. ✅

    The *t* test results are shown in the accompanying screen displays. STATDISK and the TI-83/84 Plus calculator both provide a *P*-value of 0.0070 (rounded). SPSS provides only a two-tailed *P*-value of 0.014, so that value should be halved because this test is right-tailed. Using the rule that "if the *P*-value is low, the null must go," we reject the null hypothesis because the *P*-value of 0.0070 is less than the significance level of 0.05. We conclude that there is sufficient evidence to support the claim that men have a mean weight greater than the mean of 166.3 lb as was assumed by the National Transportation and Safety Board.

    The use of technology makes the *t* test quite easy, but it is essential to understand the procedure along with the requirements and interpretations. Blind and thoughtless use of technology could easily lead to serious errors.

STATDISK

```
t Test
Test Statistic, t: 2.5747
Critical t:        1.6849
P-Value:           0.0070

90% Confidence interval:
172.0467 < μ < 193.8104
```

TI-83/84 PLUS

```
T-Test
μ>166.3
t=2.574655673
p=.0069720329
x̄=182.92856
Sx=40.8475
n=40
```

SPSS

	Test Value = 166.3					
					95% Confidence Interval of the Difference	
	t	df	Sig. (2-tailed)	Mean Difference	Lower	Upper
Weight	2.575	39	.014	16.62862	3.5650	29.6923

Part 2: Testing a Claim About a Population Mean When σ Is Known

In reality, it is very rare to test a claim about an unknown population mean while the population standard deviation is somehow known. For this case, the procedure is essentially the same as in Part 1 of this section, but the test statistic, *P*-value, and critical values are found as follows:

Test Statistic for Testing a Claim About a Mean (When σ Is Known)

$$z = \frac{\bar{x} - \mu_{\bar{x}}}{\frac{\sigma}{\sqrt{n}}}$$

P-Value

Provided by technology, or use the standard normal distribution (Table A-2) with the procedure summarized in Figure 8-4 from Section 8-2.

Critical Values

Use the standard normal distribution (Table A-2).

If we repeat Example 1 with the assumption that the value of $\sigma = 0.480$ W/kg is known, the test statistic is

$$z = \frac{\bar{x} - \mu_{\bar{x}}}{\frac{\sigma}{\sqrt{n}}} = \frac{0.938 - 1.00}{\frac{0.480}{\sqrt{11}}} = -0.43$$

Using this test statistic of $z = -0.43$, we can proceed to find the P-value. (See Figure 8-4 for the flowchart summarizing the procedure for finding P-values.) Example 1 refers to a left-tailed test, so the P-value is the area to the *left* of $z = -0.43$, which is 0.3336 (found from Table A-2). Because the P-value of 0.3336 is greater than the significance level of $\alpha = 0.05$, we fail to reject the null hypothesis, as we did in Example 1. As in Example 1, we conclude that there is not sufficient evidence to support a claim that the population mean is less than 1.00 W/kg.

using TECHNOLOGY

STATDISK   If working with a list of the original sample values, first find the sample size, sample mean, and sample standard deviation by using the STATDISK procedure described in Section 3-2. After finding the values of n, $\bar{x}$, and s, select **Analysis** from the main menu, then select **Hypothesis Testing**, followed by **Mean-One Sample.**

MINITAB   Minitab allows you to use either the summary statistics or a list of the original sample values. Select the menu items **Stat, Basic Statistics,** and **1-Sample t.** (For σ known, select 1-Sample z.) Enter the summary statistics or enter the column containing the list of original sample values. Use the **Options** button to change the format of the alternative hypothesis or the significance level from the default.

EXCEL   Use XLSTAT. First enter the list of original sample values in a list. Click on **XLSTAT** at the top, click on **Parametric tests,** then select **One sample t test and z test.** In the screen that appears, for the "Data" box enter the range of data, such as A1:A11 for 11 data values in column A. For "Data Format" select **One sample.** Click on the "Student's t test" box (or click on the "z test" box if σ is known). Click on the **Options** tab to select the type of test; select the option including $\neq$ for a two-tailed test, select the

option including $<$ for a left-tailed test, or select the option including $>$ for a right-tailed test. For the "Theoretical mean" box, enter the claimed value of the population mean, which is the same value used in the statement of the null hypothesis. Enter the desired "Significance level (%)." For example, enter 5 for a 0.05 significance level. Click **OK.** After the results are displayed, look for the test statistic identified as "t (Observed value)" or "z (Observed value)." The P-value and critical value(s) will also be displayed.

TI-83/84 PLUS   If using a TI-83/84 Plus calculator, press **STAT**, then select **TESTS** and choose the menu item of **T-Test.** (For σ known, select Z-Test.) You can use the original data (**Data**) or the summary statistics (**Stats**) by providing the entries indicated in the window display. The first three items of the TI-83/84 Plus calculator results will include the alternative hypothesis, the test statistic, and the P-value.

STATCRUNCH   Click on **Open StatCrunch.** Click on **Stat,** then select **T statistics.** Select **One sample,** then select **with data** (for a list of sample data) or **with summary** (for summary statistics). Click on **Next,** then select **Hypothesis Test.** Enter the claimed value of the population mean and enter the form of the alternative hypothesis. Click on **Calculate.**

8-4 Basic Skills and Concepts

Statistical Literacy and Critical Thinking

1. Requirements Twelve different video games showing alcohol use were observed. The duration times of alcohol use were recorded, with the times (seconds) listed below (based on data from "Content and Ratings of Teen-Rated Video Games," by Haninger and Thompson, *Journal of the American Medical Association*, Vol. 291, No. 7). What requirements must be satisfied to test the claim that the sample is from a population with a mean greater than 90 sec? Are the requirements all satisfied?

84   14   583   50   0   57   207   43   178   0   2   57

2. df If we are using the sample data from Exercise 1 in a *t* test of the claim that the population mean is greater than 90 sec, what does df denote, and what is its value?

3. *t* Test Exercise 2 refers to a *t* test. What is a *t* test? Why are the *t* test methods of Part 1 in this section so much more likely to be used than the *z* test methods in Part 2?

4. Confidence Interval Assume that we will use the sample data from Exercise 1 with a 0.05 significance level in a test of the claim that the population mean is greater than 90 sec. If we want to construct a confidence interval to be used for testing that claim, what confidence level should be used for the confidence interval? If the confidence interval is found to be 21.1 sec $< \mu <$ 191.4 sec, what should we conclude about the claim?

Finding *P*-values.   *In Exercises 5–8, either use technology to find the P-value or use Table A-3 to find a range of values for the P-value.*

5. Cigarette Nicotine The claim is that for the nicotine amounts in king-size cigarettes, $\mu > 1.10$ mg. The sample size is $n = 25$ and the test statistic is $t = 3.349$.

6. Cigarette Tar The claim is that for the tar amounts in king-size cigarettes, $\mu > 20.0$ mg. The sample size is $n = 25$ and the test statistic is $t = 1.733$.

7. Car Crash Tests The claim is that for measurements of standard head injury criteria in car crash tests, $\mu = 475$ HIC. The sample size is $n = 21$ and the test statistic is $t = -2.242$.

8. Pulse Rates The claim is that for pulse rates of women, $\mu = 73$. The sample size is $n = 40$ and the test statistic is $t = 2.463$.

Testing Hypotheses.   *In Exercises 9–24, assume that a simple random sample has been selected and test the given claim. Unless specified by your instructor, use either the P-value method or the critical value method for testing hypotheses. Identify the null and alternative hypotheses, test statistic, P-value (or range of P-values), critical value(s), and state the final conclusion that addresses the original claim.*

9. Chocolate Chip Cookies The Chapter Problem for Chapter 3 includes the sample mean of the numbers of chocolate chips in 40 Chips Ahoy reduced fat cookies. The sample mean is $\bar{x} = 19.6$ chocolate chips and the sample standard deviation is 3.8 chocolate chips. Use a 0.05 significance level to test the claim that Chips Ahoy reduced-fat cookies have less fat because they have a mean number of chocolate chips that is less than the mean of 24 for regular Chips Ahoy cookies. See the accompanying TI-83/84 Plus display that results from this hypothesis test.

TI-83/84 PLUS

```
T-Test
 μ<24
 t=-7.323169318
 P=3.87325E-9
 x̄=19.6
 Sx=3.8
 n=40
```

10. Earthquake Depths Data Set 16 in Appendix B lists earthquake depths, and the summary statistics are $n = 50$, $\bar{x} = 9.81$ km, and $s = 5.01$ km. Use a 0.01 significance level to test the claim of a seismologist that these earthquakes are from a population with a mean depth equal to 10 km. See the accompanying Minitab display that results from this hypothesis test.

MINITAB

Test of mu = 10 vs not = 10						
N	Mean	StDev	SE Mean	95% CI	T	P
50	9.810	5.010	0.709	(8.386, 11.234)	-0.27	0.790

11. Oscar-Winning Actresses Data Set 11 in Appendix B lists ages of actresses when they won Oscars, and the summary statistics are $n = 82$, $\bar{x} = 35.9$ years, and $s = 11.1$ years. Use a 0.01 significance level to test the claim that the mean age of actresses when they win Oscars is 33 years.

12. Discarded Plastic The weights (lb) of discarded plastic from a sample of households is listed in Data Set 23 in Appendix B, and the summary statistics are $n = 62$, $\bar{x} = 1.911$ lb, and $s = 1.065$ lb. Use a 0.05 significance level to test the claim that the mean weight of discarded plastic from the population of households is greater than 1.800 lb.

13. M&M Weights A simple random sample of the weights of 19 green M&Ms has a mean of 0.8635 g and a standard deviation of 0.0570 g (as in Data Set 20 in Appendix B). Use a 0.05 significance level to test the claim that the mean weight of all green M&Ms is equal to 0.8535 g, which is the mean weight required so that M&Ms have the weight printed on the package label. Do green M&Ms appear to have weights consistent with the package label?

14. Human Body Temperature Data Set 3 in Appendix B includes a sample of 106 body temperatures with a mean of 98.20°F and a standard deviation of 0.62°F. Use a 0.05 significance level to test the claim that the mean body temperature of the population is equal to 98.6°F, as is commonly believed. Is there sufficient evidence to conclude that the common belief is wrong?

15. Is the Diet Practical? When 40 people used the Weight Watchers diet for one year, their mean weight loss was 3.0 lb and the standard deviation was 4.9 lb (based on data from "Comparison of the Atkins, Ornish, Weight Watchers, and Zone Diets for Weight Loss and Heart Disease Reduction," by Dansinger, et al., *Journal of the American Medical Association,* Vol. 293, No. 1). Use a 0.01 significance level to test the claim that the mean weight loss is greater than 0. Based on these results, does the diet appear to be effective? Does the diet appear to have practical significance?

16. Flight Delays Data Set 15 in Appendix B lists 48 different departure delay times (minutes) for American Airlines flights from New York (JFK) to Los Angeles. Negative departure delay times correspond to flights that departed early. The mean of the 48 times is 10.5 min and the standard deviation is 30.8 min. Use a 0.01 significance level to test the claim that the mean departure delay time for all such flights is less than 12.0 min. Is a flight operations manager justified in reporting that the mean departure time is less than 12.0 min?

17. Garlic for Reducing Cholesterol In a test of the effectiveness of garlic for lowering cholesterol, 49 subjects were treated with raw garlic. Cholesterol levels were measured before and after the treatment. The changes (before minus after) in their levels of LDL cholesterol (in mg/dL) have a mean of 0.4 and a standard deviation of 21.0 (based on data from "Effect of Raw Garlic vs Commercial Garlic Supplements on Plasma Lipid Concentrations in Adults with Moderate Hypercholesterolemia," by Gardner et al., *Archives of Internal Medicine,* Vol. 167). Test the claim that with garlic treatment, the mean change in LDL cholesterol is greater than 0. What do the results suggest about the effectiveness of the garlic treatment?

18. Insomnia Treatment A clinical trial was conducted to test the effectiveness of the drug Zopiclone for treating insomnia in older subjects. Before treatment with Zopiclone, 16 subjects had a mean wake time of 102.8 min. After treatment with Zopiclone, the 16 subjects had a mean wake time of 98.9 min and a standard deviation of 42.3 min (based on data from "Cognitive Behavioral Therapy vs Zopiclone for Treatment of Chronic Primary Insomnia in Older Adults," by Siversten, et al., *Journal of the American Medical Association,* Vol. 295, No. 24). Assume that the 16 sample values appear to be from a normally distributed population, and test the claim that after treatment with Zopiclone, subjects have a mean wake time of less than 102.8 min. Does Zopiclone appear to be effective?

19. Years in College Listed below are the numbers of years it took for a random sample of college students to earn bachelor's degrees (based on data from the National Center for Education Statistics). Use a 0.01 significance level to test the claim that for all college students, the mean time required to earn a bachelor's degree is greater than 4.0 years. Is there anything about the data that would suggest that the conclusion might not be valid?

4 4 4 4 4 4 4.5 4.5 4.5 4.5 4.5 4.5 6 6 8 9 9 13 13 15

20. Ages of Race Car Drivers Listed below are the ages (years) of randomly selected race car drivers (based on data reported in *USA Today*). Use a 0.05 significance level to test the claim that the mean age of all race car drivers is greater than 30 years.

32 32 33 33 41 29 38 32 33 23 27 45 52 29 25

21. Lead in Medicine Listed below are the lead concentrations (in μg/g) measured in different Ayurveda medicines. Ayurveda is a traditional medical system commonly used in India. The lead concentrations listed here are from medicines manufactured in the United States. The data are based on the article "Lead, Mercury, and Arsenic in US and Indian Manufactured Ayurvedic Medicines Sold via the Internet," by Saper, et al., *Journal of the American Medical Association,* Vol. 300, No. 8. Use a 0.05 significance level to test the claim that the mean lead concentration for all such medicines is less than 14 μg/g.

3.0 6.5 6.0 5.5 20.5 7.5 12.0 20.5 11.5 17.5

22. Brain Volume Listed below are brain volumes (cm^3) of unrelated subjects used in a study. (See Data Set 6 in Appendix B.) Use a 0.01 significance level to test the claim that the population of brain volumes has a mean equal to 1100.0 cm^3.

963 1027 1272 1079 1070 1173 1067 1347 1100 1204

23. Heights of Supermodels Listed below are the heights (inches) for the simple random sample of supermodels Lima, Bundchen, Ambrosio, Ebanks, Iman, Rubik, Kurkova, Kerr, Kroes, and Swanepoel. Use a 0.01 significance level to test the claim that supermodels have heights with a mean that is greater than the mean height of 63.8 in. for women in the general population. Given that there are only 10 heights represented, can we really conclude that supermodels are taller than the typical woman?

70 71 69.25 68.5 69 70 71 70 70 69.5

24. Highway Speeds Listed below are speeds (mi/h) measured from southbound traffic on I-280 near Cupertino, California (based on data from SigAlert). This simple random sample was obtained at 3:30 P.M. on a weekday. Use a 0.05 significance level to test the claim that the sample is from a population with a mean that is less than the speed limit of 65 mi/h.

62 61 61 57 61 54 59 58 59 69 60 67

Large Data Sets from Appendix B.   *In Exercises 25–28, use the data set from Appendix B to test the given claim. Identify the null hypothesis, alternative hypothesis, test statistic, P-value or critical value(s), conclusion about the null hypothesis, and final conclusion that addresses the original claim. Use the P-value method unless your instructor specifies otherwise.*

25. Earthquake Magnitudes Use the earthquake magnitudes listed in Data Set 16 in Appendix B and test the claim that the population of earthquakes has a mean magnitude greater than 1.00. Use a 0.05 significance level.

26. Blood Pressure Use the systolic blood pressure measurements for females listed in Data Set 1 in Appendix B and test the claim that the female population has a mean systolic blood pressure level less than 120.0 mm Hg. Use a 0.05 significance level.

27. College Weights Use the September weights of males in Data Set 4 from Appendix B and test the claim that male college students have a mean weight that is less than the 83 kg mean weight of males in the general population. Use a 0.01 significance level.

28. Power Supply Data Set 18 in Appendix B lists measured voltage amounts supplied directly to the author's home. The Central Hudson power supply company states that it has a target power supply of 120 volts. Using those home voltage amounts, test the claim that the mean is 120 volts. Use a 0.01 significance level.

8-4 Beyond the Basics

Hypothesis Tests with Known σ. *In Exercises 29–32, conduct the hypothesis test using a known value of the population standard deviation σ.*

29. Repeat Exercise 9 assuming that the population standard deviation σ is known to be 3.8 chocolate chips.

30. Repeat Exercise 10 assuming that the population standard deviation σ is known to be 5.01 km.

31. Repeat Exercise 11 assuming that the population standard deviation σ is known to be 11.1 years.

32. Repeat Exercise 12 assuming that the population standard deviation σ is known to be 1.065 lb.

33. Finding Critical t Values When finding critical values, we sometimes need significance levels other than those available in Table A-3. Some computer programs approximate critical t values by calculating

$$t = \sqrt{df \cdot (e^{A^2/df} - 1)}$$

where $df = n - 1$, $e = 2.718$, $A = z(8 \cdot df + 3)/(8 \cdot df + 1)$ and z is the critical z score. Use this approximation to find the critical t score corresponding to $n = 150$ and a significance level of 0.05 in a right-tailed case. Compare the results to the critical t value of 1.655 found from STATDISK, Minitab, or a TI-83/84 Plus calculator.

34. Using the Wrong Distribution When testing a claim about a population mean with a simple random sample selected from a normally distributed population with unknown σ, the Student t distribution should be used for finding critical values and/or a P-value. If the standard normal distribution is incorrectly used instead, does that mistake make you more or less likely to reject the null hypothesis, or does it not make a difference? Explain.

35. Interpreting Power For Example 1 in this section, the hypothesis test has power of 0.4274 of supporting the claim that $\mu < 1.00$ W/kg when the actual population mean is 0.80 W/kg.

a. Interpret the given value of the power.

b. Identify the value of β and interpret that value.

8-5 Testing a Claim About a Standard Deviation or Variance

Key Concept This section presents methods for conducting a formal hypothesis test of a claim made about a population standard deviation σ or population variance σ^2. The methods of this section use the chi-square distribution that was first introduced in Section 7-4. The assumptions, test statistic, P-value, and critical values are summarized as follows.

Testing Claims About σ or σ^2

Objective

Conduct a hypothesis test of a claim made about a population standard deviation σ or population variance σ^2.

Notation

$n =$ sample size	$\sigma = $ *claimed* value of the *population* standard deviation
$s = $ *sample* standard deviation	$\sigma^2 = $ claimed value of the *population* variance
$s^2 = $ *sample* variance	

Requirements

1. The sample is a simple random sample.

2. The population has a normal distribution. (Instead of being a loose requirement, this test has a fairly strict requirement of a normal distribution.)

Test Statistic for Testing a Claim About σ or σ^2

$$\chi^2 = \frac{(n-1)s^2}{\sigma^2}$$ (round to three decimal places, as in Table A-4)

P-values: Use technology or use Table A-4 with degrees of freedom given by df $= n - 1$. (Table A-4 is based on *cumulative areas from the right.*)

Critical values: Use Table A-4 with degrees of freedom given by df $= n - 1$. (Table A-4 is based on *cumulative areas from the right.*)

CAUTION The χ^2 (chi-square) test of this section is not *robust* against a departure from normality, meaning that the test does not work well if the population has a distribution that is far from normal. The condition of a normally distributed population is therefore a much stricter requirement when testing claims about σ or σ^2 than tests of claims about a population mean μ (Section 8-4).

The chi-square distribution was introduced in Section 7-4, where we noted the following important properties.

Properties of the Chi-Square Distribution

1. All values of χ^2 are nonnegative, and the distribution is not symmetric (see Figure 8-9).

2. There is a different χ^2 distribution for each number of degrees of freedom (see Figure 8-10).

3. The critical values are found in Table A-4 using

$$\text{degrees of freedom} = n - 1$$

If using Table A-4 for finding critical values, note the following design feature of that table:

In Table A-4, each critical value of χ^2 in the body of the table corresponds to an area given in the top row of the table, and each area in that top row is a *cumulative area to the right* of the critical value.

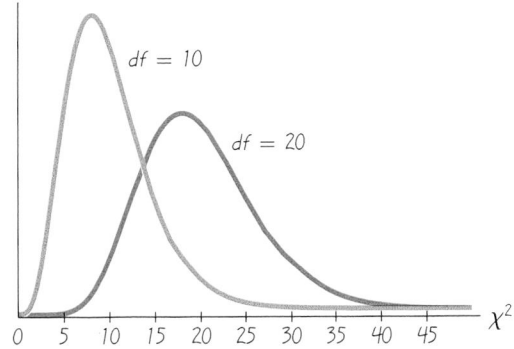

Figure 8-9 **Properties of the Chi-Square Distribution**   **Figure 8-10** **Chi-Square Distribution for df = 10 and df = 20**

CAUTION Table A-2 for the standard normal distribution provides cumulative areas from the *left*, but Table A-4 for the chi-square distribution uses cumulative areas from the *right*. See Example 1 in Section 7-4.

Example 1   Supermodel Heights

Listed below are the heights (inches) for the simple random sample of supermodels Lima, Bundchen, Ambrosio, Ebanks, Iman, Rubik, Kurkova, Kerr, Kroes, and Swanepoel. Consider the claim that supermodels have heights that have much less variation than heights of women in the general population. We will use a 0.01 significance level to test the claim that supermodels have heights with a standard deviation that is less than 2.6 in. for the population of women.

$$70 \quad 71 \quad 69.25 \quad 68.5 \quad 69 \quad 70 \quad 71 \quad 70 \quad 70 \quad 69.5$$

Solution

Requirement check (1) The sample is a simple random sample. (2) In checking for normality, we see that the sample has no outliers, the accompanying normal quantile plot shows points that are reasonably close to a straight-line pattern, and there is no other pattern that is not a straight line. Both requirements are satisfied. ✓

Technology A test of the claim that $\sigma < 2.6$ in. is equivalent to a test of the claim that $\sigma^2 < 6.76$ in.^{2} (because $2.6^2 = 6.76$). Technology capable of conducting this test will typically display the *P*-value. The TI-83/84 Plus calculator can be used as described at the end of this section, and the result will be as shown in the accompanying display. The third line of the display shows that the test statistic is $\chi^2 = 0.851516185$, the last line shows that the *P*-value is 0.0002897435436 when expressed in standard form, and after rounding we have *P*-value = 0.0003.

STATDISK

TI-83/84 PLUS

Because this *P*-value is less than the significance level of 0.01, we reject the null hypothesis and support the claim that supermodels have heights with a standard deviation that is less than 2.6 in. for the population of women.

If technology is not available, the *P*-value method of testing hypotheses is a little challenging because Table A-4 allows us to find only a range of values for the *P*-value. Let's proceed instead with the critical value method of testing hypotheses as outlined in Figure 8-2 from Section 8-2.

Step 1: The claim that "the standard deviation is less than 2.6 in." is expressed in symbolic form as $\sigma < 2.6$ in.

Step 2: If the original claim is false, then $\sigma \geq 2.6$ in.

Step 3: The expression $\sigma < 2.6$ in. does not contain equality, so it becomes the alternative hypothesis. The null hypothesis is the statement that $\sigma = 2.6$ in.

$$H_0: \sigma = 2.6 \text{ in.}$$
$$H_1: \sigma < 2.6 \text{ in.}   \text{(original claim)}$$

Step 4: The significance level is $\alpha = 0.01$.

Step 5: Because the claim is made about σ, we use the χ^2 (chi-square) distribution.

Step 6: The test statistic is calculated by using $\sigma = 2.6$ in. (as assumed in the above null hypothesis), $n = 10$, and $s = 0.7997395$ in., which is the unrounded standard deviation computed from the original list of 10 heights. We get this result:

$$\chi^2 = \frac{(n-1)s^2}{\sigma^2} = \frac{(10-1)(0.7997395)^2}{2.6^2} = 0.852$$

The critical value of $\chi^2 = 2.088$ is found from Table A-4, and it corresponds to 9 degrees of freedom and an "area to the right" of 0.99 (based on the significance level of 0.01 for a left-tailed test). See Figure 8-11.

Step 7: Because the test statistic is in the critical region, we reject the null hypothesis.

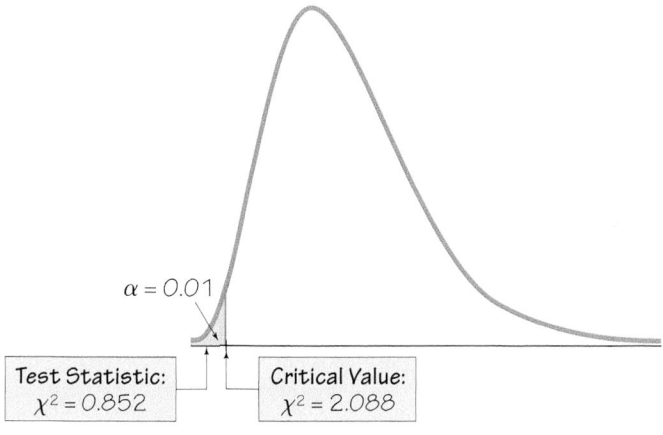

Figure 8-11   Testing the Claim that $\sigma < 2.6$ in.

Interpretation

There is sufficient evidence to support the claim that supermodels have heights with a standard deviation that is less than 2.6 in. for the population of women. Heights of supermodels have much less variation than heights of women in the general population.

P-Value Method

Example 1 can also be solved with the *P*-value method of testing hypotheses as outlined in Figure 8-1. *P*-values are typically provided by technology, but Table A-4 must be used if technology is not available. When using Table A-4, we usually cannot find *exact* *P*-values because the chi-square distribution table includes only selected values of α and selected numbers of degrees of freedom. See Example 2.

Example 2 Supermodel Heights: *P*-Value Method

Repeat Example 1 using the *P*-value method of testing hypotheses.

Solution

In Example 1 we noted that technology provides a *P*-value of 0.0003. Because this *P*-value is less than the significance level of 0.01, we reject the null hypothesis and support the claim that supermodels have heights with a standard deviation that is less than 2.6 in. for the population of women.

   If technology is not available, refer to Table A-4 and use it as follows:

1. Locate the row for 9 degrees of freedom. (Because $n = 10$, we have df $= n - 1 = 9$.)

2. Use the test statistic of $\chi^2 = 0.852$ and see that in the 9th row of Table A-4, the test statistic of 0.852 is less than the lowest table entry of 1.735, so the area to the *right* of the test statistic is greater than 0.995, which means that the area to the *left* of the test statistic is less than $1 - 0.995 = 0.005$.

3. In this left-tailed test, the *P*-value is the area to the left of the test statistic, so we know that "*P*-value < 0.005." (This agrees with our *P*-value of 0.0003 found from technology.)

Using technology we find that *P*-value $= 0.0003$, and using Table A-4 we find that *P*-value < 0.005.

Confidence Interval Method

When testing claims about σ or σ^2, the *P*-value method, critical value method, and the confidence interval method are all equivalent in the sense that they will always lead to the same conclusion. See Example 3.

Example 3 Supermodel Heights: Confidence Interval Method

Repeat the hypothesis test in Example 1 by constructing a suitable confidence interval.

Solution

First, we should be careful to select the correct confidence level. Because the hypothesis test is left-tailed and the significance level is 0.01, we should use a confidence level of 98%, or 0.98. (See Table 8-1 from Section 8-2 for help in selecting the correct confidence level.)

   Using the methods described in Section 7-4, we can use the sample data listed in Example 1 to construct a 98% confidence interval estimate of σ. We use $n = 10$, $s = 0.7997395$ in., $\chi_L^2 = 2.088$, and $\chi_R^2 = 21.666$. (The critical values χ_L^2 and χ_R^2 are found in Table A-4. Use the row with df $= n - 1 = 9$.

Human Lie Detectors

Researchers tested 13,000 people for their ability to determine when someone is lying. They found 31 people with exceptional skills at identifying lies. These human lie detectors had accuracy rates around 90%. They also found that federal officers and sheriffs were quite good at detecting lies, with accuracy rates around 80%. Psychology Professor Maureen O'Sullivan questioned those who were adept at identifying lies, and she said that "all of them pay attention to nonverbal cues and the nuances of word usages and apply them differently to different people. They could tell you eight things about someone after watching a two-second tape. It's scary, the things these people notice." Methods of statistics can be used to distinguish between people unable to detect lying and those with that ability.

The 0.98 confidence level indicates that $\alpha = 0.02$, and we divide that area of 0.02 equally between the two tails so that the areas to the *right* of the critical values are 0.99 and 0.01. Refer to Table A-4 and use the columns with areas of 0.99 and 0.01 and use the 9th row.)

$$\sqrt{\frac{(n-1)s^2}{\chi_R^2}} < \sigma < \sqrt{\frac{(n-1)s^2}{\chi_L^2}}$$

$$\sqrt{\frac{(10-1)(0.7997395^2)}{21.666}} < \sigma < \sqrt{\frac{(10-1)(0.7997395^2)}{2.088}}$$

$$0.5 \text{ in.} < \sigma < 1.7 \text{ in.}$$

Based on this confidence interval, we can support the claim that $\sigma < 2.6$ in. (because all values of the confidence interval are less than 2.6 in.). We reach the same conclusion found with the *P*-value method and the critical value method.

using TECHNOLOGY

STATDISK Select **Analysis**, then **Hypothesis Testing**, then **StDev-One Sample**. Provide the required entries in the dialog box, then click on **Evaluate**. STATDISK will display the test statistic, critical values, *P*-value, and confidence interval.

MINITAB For Minitab Release 15 and later, select **Stat**, then **Basic Statistics**, then select the menu item of σ^2 **1 Variance**. Click on the **Summarized Data** box and enter the sample size and sample standard deviation. Click on the box labeled **Perform hypothesis test** and enter the assumed value of σ from the null hypothesis. Click on the **Options** button and select the correct form of the alternative hypothesis. Click on the **OK** button twice and the *P*-value will be displayed.

In **Minitab 16**, you can use the **Stat** menu as described above, or you could also click on **Assistant**, then **Hypothesis Tests**, then select the case for **1-Sample Standard Deviation**. Fill out the dialog box, then click **OK** to get three windows of results that include the *P*-value and much other helpful information.

EXCEL Neither Excel nor XLSTAT have a function for conducting a hypothesis test of a claim about a standard deviation

or variance. Excel does have a function (CHISQ.INV or CHIINV or CHISQ.INV.RT) that could be used to find critical values.

T1-83/84 PLUS The TI-83/84 Plus calculator does not test hypotheses about σ or σ^2 directly, but the program **S2TEST** can be used. That program was written by Michael Lloyd of Henderson State University, and it can be downloaded from the CD included with this book, or www.aw.com/Triola. The program S2TEST uses the program ZZINEWT, so that program must also be installed. After storing the programs on the calculator, press **PRGM**, select **S2TEST**, and enter the claimed variance σ^2, the sample variance s^2, and the sample size n. Select the format used for the alternative hypothesis and press **ENTER**. The *P*-value will be displayed.

STATCRUNCH Click on **Open StatCrunch**. Click on **Stat**, then select **Variance**. Select **One sample**, then select **with data** (for a list of sample data) or **with summary** (for summary statistics). Click on **Next**, then select **Hypothesis Test** and enter the claimed value of the population variance and select the form of the alternative hypothesis. Click on **Calculate.**

8-5 Basic Skills and Concepts

Statistical Literacy and Critical Thinking

1. Waiting in Line The Jefferson Valley Bank once had a separate customer waiting line at each teller window, but it now has a single waiting line that feeds the teller windows as vacancies occur. The standard deviation of customer waiting times with the old multiple-line configuration was 1.8 min. Listed below is a simple random sample of waiting times (minutes) with the single waiting line. The 10 sample values have a standard deviation of 0.5 min.

a. When the bank changed from multiple waiting lines to a single line, how was the mean waiting time affected?

6.5   6.6   6.7   6.8   7.1   7.3   7.4   7.7   7.7   7.7

b. When the bank changed from multiple waiting lines to a single line, how was the variation among waiting times affected?

c. What improvement occurred with the change from multiple waiting lines to a single line?

d. What procedure can be used to determine that the single waiting line is better?

2. Requirements If we want to use the sample data from Exercise 1 to test the claim that the sample is from a population with a standard deviation less than 1.8 min, we must satisfy the requirements of having a simple random sample and a normally distributed population. In Exercise 1 it was stated that the sample is a simple random sample.

a. In general, how does the normality requirement for a hypothesis test of a claim about a standard deviation differ from the normality requirement for a hypothesis test of a claim about a mean?

b. What methods can be used to determine whether the normality requirement is satisfied?

3. Confidence Interval Method of Hypothesis Testing Assume that we want to use the sample data from Exercise 1 to test the claim that the sample is from a population with a standard deviation less than 1.8 min; we will use a 0.05 significance level to test that claim. If we want to use the confidence interval method of testing hypotheses, what level of confidence should be used for the confidence interval? Will the conclusion based on the confidence interval be the same as the conclusion based on a hypothesis test that uses the P-value method or the critical value method?

4. Hypothesis Test For the sample data from Exercise 1, we have $s = 0.5$ and we want to use that sample to test the claim that the sample is from a population with a standard deviation less than 1.8 min (as it was in the past with multiple waiting lines).

a. Identify the null and alternative hypotheses.

b. Find the value of the test statistic.

c. Using technology, the P-value is found to be 0.0001. What should we conclude about the null hypothesis?

d. Given that the P-value is 0.0001, what should we conclude about the original claim?

e. What does the conclusion suggest about the effectiveness of the change from multiple waiting lines to a single line?

Testing Claims About Variation.   *In Exercises 5–16, test the given claim. Identify the null hypothesis, alternative hypothesis, test statistic, P-value or critical value(s), conclusion about the null hypothesis, and final conclusion that addresses the original claim. Assume that a simple random sample is selected from a normally distributed population.*

5. Cans of Coke Data Set 19 in Appendix B includes volumes (oz) of a simple random sample of 36 cans of regular Coke. Those volumes have a mean of 12.19 oz and a standard deviation of 0.11 oz, and they appear to be from a normally distributed population. If we want the filling process to work so that almost all cans have volumes between 11.8 oz and 12.4 oz, the range rule of thumb can be used to estimate that the standard deviation should be less than 0.15 oz. Use the sample data to test the claim that the population of volumes has a standard deviation less than 0.15 oz. Use a 0.05 significance level.

6. Cans of Pepsi Repeat the preceding exercise using these statistics from a simple random sample of cans of regular Pepsi: $n = 36$, $\bar{x} = 12.29$ oz, $s = 0.09$ oz.

7. Weights of Pennies Data Set 21 in Appendix B includes a simple random sample of 37 weights of post-1983 pennies. Those 37 weights have a mean of 2.49910 g and a standard deviation of 0.01648 g. U.S. Mint specifications require that pennies be manufactured so that the mean weight is 2.500 g. A hypothesis test will verify that the sample appears to come from a population with a mean of 2.500 g as required, but use a 0.05 significance level to test the claim that the population of weights has a *standard deviation* less than the specification of 0.0230 g.

8. Weights of Pennies The preceding exercise involved the claim that *post*-1983 pennies have weights with a standard deviation less than 0.0230 g. Data Set 21 in Appendix B includes the weights of a simple random sample of 35 *pre*-1983 pennies, and that sample has a standard deviation of 0.03910 g. Use a 0.05 significance level to test the claim that pre-1983 pennies have weights with a standard deviation greater than 0.0230 g. Does it appear that weights of pre-1983 pennies vary more than those of post-1983 pennies?

9. Pulse Rates of Men A simple random sample of 40 men results in a standard deviation of 10.3 beats per minute (based on Data Set 1 in Appendix B). The normal range of pulse rates of adults is typically given as 60 to 100 beats per minute. If the range rule of thumb is applied to that normal range, the result is a standard deviation of 10 beats per minute. Use the sample results with a 0.05 significance level to test the claim that pulse rates of men have a standard deviation equal to 10 beats per minute.

10. Pulse Rates of Women Repeat the preceding exercise using the pulse rates of women listed in Data Set 1 of Appendix B. For this sample, $n = 40$ and $s = 11.6$ beats per minute.

11. Cigarette Tar A simple random sample of 25 filtered 100-mm cigarettes is obtained, and the tar content of each cigarette is measured. The sample has a standard deviation of 3.7 mg (based on Data Set 10 in Appendix B). Use a 0.05 significance level to test the claim that the tar content of filtered 100-mm cigarettes has a standard deviation different from 3.2 mg, which is the standard deviation for unfiltered king-size cigarettes.

12. Analysis of Pennies In an analysis investigating the usefulness of pennies, the cents portions of 100 randomly selected credit card charges from the author are recorded, and they have a mean of 47.6 cents and a standard deviation of 33.5 cents. If the amounts from 0 cents to 99 cents are all equally likely, the mean is expected to be 49.5 cents and the population standard deviation is expected to be 28.866 cents. Use a 0.01 significance level to test the claim that the sample is from a population with a standard deviation equal to 28.866 cents. If the amounts from 0 cents to 99 cents are all equally likely, is the requirement of a normal distribution satisfied? If not, how does that affect the conclusion?

13. Ages of Race Car Drivers Listed below are the ages (years) of randomly selected race car drivers (based on data reported in *USA Today*). Most people in the general population have ages that vary between 0 and 90 years, so use of the range rule of thumb suggests that ages in the general population have a standard deviation of 22.5 years. Use a 0.01 significance level to test the claim that the standard deviation of ages of all race car drivers is less than 22.5 years.

32   32   33   33   41   29   38   32   33   23   27   45   52   29   25

14. Highway Speeds Listed below are speeds (mi/h) measured from southbound traffic on I-280 near Cupertino, California (based on data from SigAlert). This simple random sample was obtained at 3:30 P.M. on a weekday. Use a 0.05 significance level to test the claim of the highway engineer that the standard deviation of speeds is equal to 5.0 mi/h.

62   61   61   57   61   54   59   58   59   69   60   67

15. Aircraft Altimeters The Skytek Avionics company uses a new production method to manufacture aircraft altimeters. A simple random sample of new altimeters resulted in the errors listed below. Use a 0.05 level of significance to test the claim that the new production method has errors with a standard deviation greater than 32.2 ft, which was the standard deviation for the old production method. If it appears that the standard deviation is greater, does the new production method appear to be better or worse than the old method? Should the company take any action?

$$-42 \quad 78 \quad -22 \quad -72 \quad -45 \quad 15 \quad 17 \quad 51 \quad -5 \quad -53 \quad -9 \quad -109$$

16. IQ of Professional Pilots The Wechsler IQ test is designed so that the mean is 100 and the standard deviation is 15 for the population of normal adults. Listed below are IQ scores of randomly selected professional pilots. It is claimed that because professional pilots are a more homogeneous group than the general population, they have IQ scores with a standard deviation less than 15. Test that claim using a 0.05 significance level.

$$121 \quad 116 \quad 115 \quad 121 \quad 116 \quad 107 \quad 127 \quad 98 \quad 116 \quad 101 \quad 130 \quad 114$$

Large Data Sets from Appendix B. *In Exercises 17 and 18, use the data set from Appendix B to test the given claim. Identify the null hypothesis, alternative hypothesis, test statistic, P-value or critical value(s), conclusion about the null hypothesis, and final conclusion that addresses the original claim.*

17. Cans of Diet Coke Repeat Exercise 5 using the volumes (oz) of cans of diet Coke.

18. Weights of Pennies Data Set 21 in Appendix B includes a simple random sample of "wheat" pennies. U.S. Mint specifications now use a standard deviation of 0.0230 g for weights of pennies. Use a 0.01 significance level to test the claim that wheat pennies were manufactured so that their weights have a standard deviation equal to 0.0230 g.

8-5 Beyond the Basics

19. Finding Critical Values of χ^2 For large numbers of degrees of freedom, we can approximate critical values of χ^2 as follows:

$$\chi^2 = \frac{1}{2}(z + \sqrt{2k - 1})^2$$

Here k is the number of degrees of freedom and z is the critical value(s) found from technology or Table A-2. In Exercise 5 we have df = 35, so Table A-4 does not list an exact critical value. If we want to approximate a critical value of χ^2 in the left-tailed hypothesis test with $\alpha = 0.05$ and a sample size of 36, we let $k = 35$ with $z = -1.645$. Use this approximation to estimate the critical value of χ^2 for Exercise 5. How close is it to the value of $\chi^2 = 22.465$ obtained by using STATDISK and Minitab?

20. Finding Critical Values of χ^2 Repeat Exercise 19 using this approximation (with k and z as described in Exercise 19):

$$\chi^2 = k\left(1 - \frac{2}{9k} + z\sqrt{\frac{2}{9k}}\right)^3$$

Chapter 8 Review

The major topics in an introductory statistics course include methods of descriptive statistics (mean, standard deviation, histogram, etc.) and the two major activities of inferential statistics: estimating population parameters (as with confidence intervals) and hypothesis testing. In this chapter we introduced basic methods for testing claims about a population proportion, population mean, or population standard deviation (or variance).

In Section 8-2 we presented the basic components of a hypothesis test: null hypothesis, alternative hypothesis, test statistic, critical region, significance level, critical value, *P*-value, type I error, and type II error. We also discussed two-tailed tests, left-tailed tests, right-tailed tests, and the statement of conclusions. We used those components in identifying three different methods for testing hypotheses:

1. The *P*-value method (summarized in Figure 8-1)

2. The critical value method (or traditional method) summarized in Figure 8-2

3. Confidence intervals (Chapter 7)

In Sections 8-3 through 8-5 we discussed specific methods for dealing with different parameters. Because it is so important to select the correct distribution and test statistic, we provide Table 8-4, which summarizes some key elements of the hypothesis-testing procedures of this chapter.

Table 8-4 Hypothesis Tests

Parameter	Requirements: Simple Random Sample and . . .	Distribution and Test Statistic	Critical and *P*-values
Proportion	$np \geq 5$ and $nq \geq 5$	Normal: $z = \dfrac{\hat{p} - p}{\sqrt{\dfrac{pq}{n}}}$	Table A-2
Mean	σ not known and normally distributed population or σ not known and $n > 30$	Student *t*: $t = \dfrac{\bar{x} - \mu_{\bar{x}}}{\dfrac{s}{\sqrt{n}}}$	Table A-3
	σ known and normally distributed population or σ known and $n > 30$	Normal: $z = \dfrac{\bar{x} - \mu_{\bar{x}}}{\dfrac{\sigma}{\sqrt{n}}}$	Table A-2
	Population not normally distributed and $n \leq 30$	Use a nonparametric method or bootstrapping.	
Standard Deviation or Variance	Population normally distributed	Chi- square: $\chi^2 = \dfrac{(n - 1)s^2}{\sigma^2}$	Table A-4

Chapter Quick Quiz

1. Wristwatch Accuracy Students of the author collected a simple random sample of times (sec) of wristwatch errors, and a few of those times are listed below. Negative values correspond to watches that are running ahead of the actual time. Assuming that we want to use a 0.05 significance level to test the claim that the sample is from a population with a mean equal to 0 sec, identify the null hypothesis and the alternative hypothesis.

$$140 \quad -85 \quad 325 \quad 20 \quad 305 \quad 205 \quad 20 \quad -93$$

2. Type of Test Refer to the hypothesis test described in Exercise 1.

a. Is the hypothesis test left-tailed, right-tailed, or two-tailed?

b. If the requirements are satisfied, what distribution should be used for the hypothesis test: normal, Student *t*, chi-square, binomial?

3. *P*-Value If we use technology to conduct the hypothesis test described in Exercise 1, we get a *P*-value of 0.1150.

a. What should we conclude about the null hypothesis?

b. What is the final conclusion that addresses the original claim?

4. Normality For the hypothesis test in Exercise 1, what does it mean when we say that the test is *robust* against departures from normality?

5. Death Penalty Poll In a recent Gallup poll of 511 adults, 64% said that they were in favor of the death penalty for a person convicted of murder. We want to use a 0.01 significance level to test the claim that the majority of adults are in favor of the death penalty for a person convicted of murder.

a. Identify the null and alternative hypotheses.

b. Find the value of the test statistic.

c. Technology is used to find this *P*-value: $1.263996E^{-}10$. Express the *P*-value in ordinary notation, then determine what we should conclude about the original claim.

6. *P*-Value Find the *P*-value in a test of the claim that the mean IQ score of acupuncturists is equal to 100, given that the test statistic is $z = -2.00$.

7. Equivalent Methods Which of the following statements are true?

a. When testing a claim about μ, the *P*-value method, critical value method, and confidence interval method are all equivalent.

b. When testing a claim about a population proportion p, the *P*-value method, critical value method, and confidence interval method are all equivalent.

c. When testing a claim about any population parameter, the *P*-value method, critical value method, and confidence interval method are all equivalent.

8. Chi-Square Test In a test of the claim that $\sigma = 15$ for the population of IQ scores of Facebook friends, we find the the rightmost critical value is $\chi^2 = 71.420$. Is the leftmost critical χ^2 value equal to -71.420?

9. Conclusions True or false: In hypothesis testing, it is *never* valid to form a conclusion of supporting the null hypothesis.

10. Reliability True or false: If correct methods of hypothesis testing are used with a large simple random sample, the conclusion will always be true.

Review Exercises

1. True/False Characterize each of the following statements as being true or false.

a. In a hypothesis test, a very high *P*-value indicates strong support of the alternative hypothesis.

b. The Student t distribution can be used to test a claim about a population mean whenever the sample data are randomly selected from a normally distributed population.

c. When using a χ^2 distribution to test a claim about a population standard deviation, there is a very loose requirement that the sample data be from a population having a normal distribution.

d. When conducting a hypothesis test about the claimed proportion of adults who have current passports, the problems with a convenience sample can be overcome by using a larger sample size.

e. When repeating the same hypothesis test with different random samples of the same size, the conclusions will all be the same.

2. Leisure Time In a Gallup poll, 1010 adults were randomly selected and asked if they were satisfied or dissatisfied with the amount of leisure time that they had. Of this sample 657 said that they were satisfied and 353 said that they were dissatisfied. Use a 0.01 significance level to test the claim that $2/3$ of adults are satisfied with the amount of leisure time that they have.

3. Risky Behavior In a *USA Today* poll of 737 respondents, 92% said that they do not open unfamiliar e-mail and instant-message links. Use a 0.01 significance level to test the claim that more than 75% of us do not open unfamiliar e-mail and instant-message links. How is the validity of the results affected by the knowledge that *USA Today* posted a question on its web site, and 737 people chose to respond?

4. Birth Weight A simple random sample of 1862 births of Chinese babies resulted in a mean birth weight of 3171 g and a standard deviation of 428 g (based on "Comparison of Birth Weight Distributions between Chinese and Caucasian Infants," by Wen et al., *American Journal of Epidemiology*, Vol. 172, No 10). Use a 0.01 significance level to test the claim that the mean birth weight of Chinese babies is less than the mean birth weight of 3369 g for Caucasian babies.

5. Birth Weights A simple random sample of 81 births of Chinese babies resulted in a mean birth weight of 3245 g and a standard deviation of 466 g. Test the claim that the standard deviation of birth weights of Chinese babies is equal to 567 g, which is the standard deviation of birth weights of Caucasian babies. Use a 0.01 significance level and assume that the birth weights are normally distributed.

6. Monitoring Lead in Air Listed below are measured amounts of lead (in micrograms per cubic meter, or $\mu g/m^3$, in the air. The Environmental Protection Agency has established an air quality standard for lead of 1.5 $\mu g/m^3$. The measurements shown below constitute a simple random sample of measurements recorded at Building 5 of the World Trade Center site on different days immediately following the destruction caused by the terrorist attacks of September 11, 2001. After the collapse of the two World Trade Center buildings, there was considerable concern about the quality of the air. Use a 0.05 significance level to test the claim that the sample is from a population with a mean greater than the EPA standard of 1.5 $\mu g/m^3$.

$$5.40 \quad 1.10 \quad 0.42 \quad 0.73 \quad 0.48 \quad 1.10$$

7. Pennsylvania Lottery In the Pennsylvania Match 6 lottery, six numbers between 1 and 49 are randomly drawn. To simulate the number selection process, a TI-83/84 Plus calculator was used to randomly generate 100 numbers between 1 and 49 inclusive. The sample has a mean of 24.2 and a standard deviation of 14.1. Use a 0.01 significance level to test the claim that the sample is selected from a population with a mean equal to 25, which is the mean of the population of all drawn numbers.

8. Type I Error and Type II Error

a. In general, what is a type I error? In general, what is a type II error?

b. For the hypothesis test in Exercise 7, write a statement that would constitute a type I error, and write another statement that would be a type II error.

9. Pennsylvania Lottery and χ^2 Test Assume that we want to use the same sample data from Exercise 7 to test the claim that the standard deviation of all drawn numbers is less than 15.0. Why can't we use a χ^2 test with the methods described in Section 8-4?

10. Tests of Child Booster Seats The National Highway Traffic Safety Administration conducted crash tests of child booster seats for cars. Listed below are results from those tests, with the measurements given in HIC (standard *head injury condition* units). The safety requirement is that the HIC measurement should be less than 1000 HIC. Use a 0.01 significance level to test the claim that the sample is from a population with a mean less than 1000 HIC. Do the results suggest that all of the child booster seats meet the specified requirement?

$$602 \quad 696 \quad 762 \quad 572 \quad 637$$

Cumulative Review Exercises

Please be aware that some of the following problems may require knowledge of concepts presented in previous chapters.

1. Dictionary Words A simple random sample of pages from *Merriam-Webster's Collegiate Dictionary*, 11th edition, is obtained. Listed below are the numbers of words defined on those pages. Find the values of the indicated statistics.

$$51 \quad 63 \quad 36 \quad 43 \quad 34 \quad 62 \quad 73 \quad 39 \quad 53 \quad 79$$

a. Mean   **b.** Median   **c.** Standard deviation   **d.** Variance   **e.** Range

2. Dictionary Words Refer to the sample data in Exercise 1.

a. What is the level of measurement of the data (nominal, ordinal, interval, ratio)?

b. Are the values discrete or continuous?

c. What does it mean to state that the sample is a simple random sample?

3. Confidence Interval for Dictionary Words Use the sample values given in Exercise 1 to construct a 95% confidence interval estimate of the population mean. Assume that the population has a normal distribution.

4. Hypothesis Test for Dictionary Words Refer to the sample data given in Exercise 1. Given that the dictionary has 1459 pages with defined words, the claim that there are more than 70,000 defined words is the same as the claim that the mean number of defined words on a page is greater than 48.0. Use a 0.05 significance level to test the claim that the mean number of defined words on a page is greater than 48.0. What does the result suggest about the claim that there are more than 70,000 defined words in the dictionary?

5. Designing Cars The sitting height (from seat to top of head) of drivers must be considered in the design of a new car model. Men have sitting heights that are normally distributed with a mean of 36.0 in. and a standard deviation of 1.4 in. (based on anthropometric survey data from Gordon, Churchill, et al.).

a. One car is designed to accommodate sitting heights of 38.8 in. or less. Find the percentage of men with sitting heights greater than 38.8 in.

b. If the sitting height is to be changed so that 98% of men will be accommodated, what is the new sitting height?

c. If a car is occupied by four men, find the probability that they have a mean sitting height less than 37.0 in.

6. Left-Handedness Among Americans, 9.7% of males are left-handed and 12.5% of females are left-handed.

a. If three females are randomly selected, find the probability that they are all left-handed. When randomly selecting three females, is it unlikely that all of them are left-handed? Why or why not?

b. If one male is randomly selected and one female is randomly selected, find the probability that they are both left-handed.

c. If five females are randomly selected, find the probability that at least one of them is left-handed.

7. Normal Rainfall The following histogram is obtained from the daily rainfall amounts (in.) in Boston for a year. If we want to conduct a hypothesis test of a claim about the mean, there is a requirement that the population of rainfall amounts must have a normal distribution.

Based on the histogram, does it appear that the population satisfies the requirement of a normal distribution? Why or why not?

8. Analyzing Graph The accompanying graph depicts results from a recent year in which there were 8878 male graduates and 8203 female graduates from medical schools in the United States. Does the graph depict the data in a way that is fair and objective, or is it somehow deceptive? Explain.

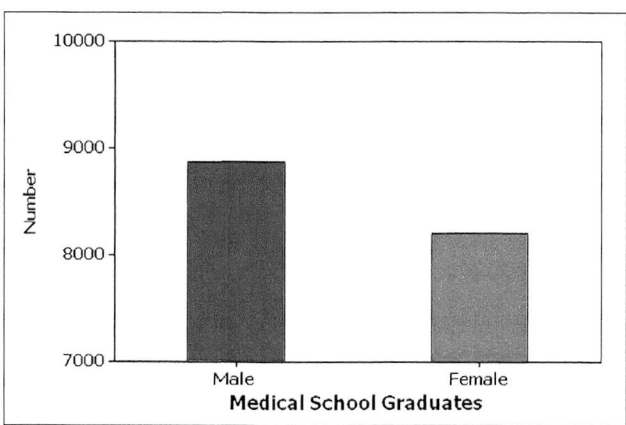

9. Gun Survey In a recent Gallup poll, 1003 randomly selected adults in the United States were asked if they have a gun in their home, and 37.2% of them answered "yes."

a. What is the number of respondents who answered "yes"?

b. Construct a 95% confidence interval estimate of the percentage of all adults who would answer "yes" when asked if they have a gun in their home.

c. Based on a hypothesis test, can we safely conclude that less than 50% of adults answer "yes" when asked if they have a gun in their home? Why or why not?

d. What is a sensible response to the criticism that the Gallup poll cannot provide good results because the sample size is only 1003 adults selected from a large population of 241,472,385 adults in the United States?

10. Hypothesis Test for Gun Survey Refer to the survey results from Exercise 9 and use a 0.01 significance level to test the claim that fewer than 50% of Americans say that they have a gun in their home.

Technology Project

Simulation for the Chapter Problem The Chapter Problem describes a situation in which a county clerk was supposed to use a method of random selection for determining whether the Democrat or Republican would get the top line on each of 41 different election ballots. His procedure resulted in the Democrat being selected 40 times in the 41 trials. Section 8-3 discussed the formal hypothesis test of his claim that he used a random method. This project involves a different approach consisting of simulations. The basic idea is to assume that randomness is used with a 0.5 probability of selecting a Democrat, then making the random selection 41 times. After repeating that simulation 100 times, we will see how often the results are as extreme as 40 or 41 Democrats selected in the 41 trials. We will then understand how unlikely it is to get 40 Democrats in 41 trials. The simulation is basically the same as repeatedly tossing 41 coins and seeing how often the result is 40 heads or 41 heads.

Use STATDISK, Minitab, Excel, StatCrunch, the TI-83/84 Plus calculator, or any other technology that can randomly generate data from a binomial distribution. Conduct 100 simulations of the process of randomly selecting a Democrat or Republican for the top line on each of 41 different election ballots. Examine the results and write a brief statement explaining how they either support or refute the claim that the county clerk did not really use a method of random selection.

Here are instructions for different technologies.

STATDISK: Click on **Data,** then click on **Binomial Generator.** In the dialog box, enter 100 for the sample size (because we want to repeat the selection process 100 times), enter 0.5 for the success probability (so that there is a 0.5 probability of selecting a Democrat), and enter 41 for the number of trials (to simulate the 41 election ballots). Click on **Generate.** Scroll through the results and count the number of times that you got 40 Democrats or 41 Democrats using a process of random selection.

Minitab: Click on the main menu item of **Calc,** then click on **Random Data,** then **Binomial.** In the dialog box, enter 100 for the sample size (because we want to repeat the selection process 100 times), enter C1 as the column to store the results, enter 41 for the number of trials (to simulate 41 election ballots), and enter 0.5 for the event probability (so that there is a 0.5 probability of selecting a Democrat). Click on **OK.** Scroll through the list of results and count the number of times that you got 40 Democrats or 41 Democrats using a process of random selection.

Excel: Click on *fx* just below the tool bar. Select the category of **Math & Trig,** then select **RANDBETWEEN.** Click on **OK.** Proceed to enter 0 for "bottom" and enter 1 for "top." Click on **OK.** Excel will randomly select either 0 or 1 and the result will appear in cell A1. Click on the lower right corner of cell A1 and, while holding the mouse button down, drag the mouse downward until 41 rows are highlighted. When the mouse button is released, column A should include 41 values, each of which is 0 or 1. Now click on cell A41 and, while holding the mouse button down, drag the mouse to the right until reaching column DV, so that 100 columns are highlighted. When the mouse is released, you will have 100 columns of simulated election ballots. In cell A42, enter the expression **=SUM(A1:A41)** so that the sum of the entries in column A will be shown. This is the number of times a Democrate was selected in 41 trials. Click on the lower right corner of cell

A42 and, while holding down the mouse button, drag it to the right until reaching column DV. Row 42 will show the numbers of times a Democrat was selected in 41 ballots. Scroll across row 42 and see how often you get 40 Democrats or 41 Democrats when using a process of random selection.

TI-83/84 Plus: Press **MATH**, then select **PRB** and select the menu item of **randBin.** Make the entries to get **randBin(41, 0.5, 100).** That command causes 100 simulations of the process of randomly selecting Democrats in each of 41 election ballots. Store the results in list L1 by pressing **STO▸** L1. Press **ENTER**. Now press **STAT** and select **Edit,** then scroll through list L1 to see how often you get 40 Democrats or 41 Democrats when using a process of random selection.

StatCrunch: Click on **Data,** then click on **Simulate Data,** then select the menu item of **Binomial.** In the dialog box, enter 100 for the number of rows, enter 1 for the number of columns, enter 41 for n, and enter 0.5 for p. Click on **Simulate.** Scroll through the list of results and count the number of times that you got 40 Democrats or 41 Democrats using a process of random selection.

from data TO DECISION

Critical Thinking: Designing an aircraft cockpit
In designing a cockpit for a Boeing aircraft, the overhead grip reach of a seated pilot is being considered as an important factor for placement of landing light switches to be located directly above the pilot. Listed below are the measured overhead grip reaches (cm) of a simple random sample of

women (based on anthropometric data from Gordon, Churchill, et al.). Use a 0.01 significance level to test the claim that the mean overhead grip reach of women is less than the value of 123 cm that is being planned for an aircraft.

120 115 130 123 118 118 116
121 119 131 125 119 124 122
121 129 125 126 115 122

Analyzing the Results
a. It is not too difficult to conduct the hypothesis test, but is that hypothesis test the best tool for determining whether the value of 123 cm is suitable? If not, determine whether 123 cm is suitable, and if it is not suitable, find a value that is suitable.

b. In this application, why does it make sense to ignore the overhead grip reach of men?

Cooperative Group Activities

1. In-class activity Without using any measuring device, each student should draw a line believed to be 3 in. long and another line believed to be 3 cm long. Then use rulers to measure and record the lengths of the lines drawn. Find the means and standard deviations of the two sets of lengths. Test the claim that the lines estimated to be 3 in. have a mean length that is equal to 3 in. Test the claim that the lines estimated to be 3 cm have a mean length that is equal to 3 cm. Compare the results. Do the estimates of the 3-in. line appear to be more accurate than those for the 3-cm line? Do an Internet search to identify the countries that do not yet use the metric system. What do these results suggest?

2. In-class activity Assume that a method of gender selection can affect the probability of a baby being a girl so that the probability becomes 1/4. Each student should simulate 20 births by drawing 20 cards from a shuffled deck. Replace each card after it has been drawn, then reshuffle. Consider the hearts to be girls and consider all other cards to be boys. After making 20 selections and recording the "genders" of the babies, use a 0.10 significance level to test the claim that the proportion of girls is equal to 1/4. How many students are expected to get results leading to the wrong conclusion that the proportion is not 1/4? How does that relate to the probability of a type I error? Does this procedure appear to be effective in identifying the effectiveness of the gender-selection method? (If decks of cards are not available, use some other way to simulate the births, such as using the random number generator on a calculator or using digits from phone numbers or Social Security numbers.)

3. Out-of-class activity Groups of three or four students should go to the library and collect a sample consisting of the ages of books (based on copyright dates). Plan and describe the sampling plan, execute the sampling procedure, then use the results to test the claim that the mean age of books in the library is greater than 15 years.

4. In-class activity Each student should write an estimate of the age of the current president of the United States. All estimates should be collected and the sample mean and standard deviation should be calculated. Then test the hypothesis that the mean of all such estimates is equal to the actual current age of the president.

5. In-class activity A class project should be designed to conduct a test in which each student is given a taste of Coke and a taste of Pepsi. The student is then asked to identify which sample is Coke. After all of the results are collected, test the claim that the success rate is better than the rate that would be expected with random guesses.

6. In-class activity Each student should estimate the length of the classroom. The values should be based on visual estimates, with no actual measurements being taken. After the estimates have been collected, measure the length of the room, then test the claim that the sample mean is equal to the actual length of the classroom. Is there a "collective wisdom," whereby the class mean is approximately equal to the actual room length?

7. Out-of-class activity Using a wristwatch that is reasonably accurate, set the time to be exact. Use a radio station or telephone time report which states that "at the tone, the time is . . . ." If you cannot set the time to the nearest second, record the error for the watch you are using. Now compare the time on your watch to the time on others. Record the errors with negative signs for watches that are ahead of the actual time and positive signs for those watches that are behind the actual time. Use the data to test the claim that the mean error of all wristwatches is equal to 0. Do we collectively run on time, or are we early or late? Also test the claim that the standard deviation of errors is less than 1 min. What are the practical implications of a standard deviation that is excessively large?

8. In-class activity In a group of three or four people, conduct an ESP experiment by selecting one of the group members as the subject. Draw a circle on one small piece of paper and draw a square on another sheet of the same size. Repeat this experiment 20 times: Randomly select the circle or the square and place it in the subject's hand behind his or her back so that it cannot be seen, then ask the subject to identify the shape (without seeing it); record whether the response is correct. Test the claim that the subject has ESP because the proportion of correct responses is greater than 0.5.

9. In-class activity After dividing into groups of between 10 and 20 people, each group member should record the number of heartbeats in a minute. After calculating the sample mean and standard deviation, each group should proceed to test the claim that the mean is greater than 48, which is the author's result. (When people exercise, they tend to have lower pulse rates, and the author runs 5 miles a few times each week. What a guy!)

10. Out-of-class activity In groups of three or four, collect data to determine whether subjects have a Facebook page, then combine the results and test the claim that more than 1/4 of students have a Facebook page.

11. Out-of-class activity Each student should find an article in a professional journal that includes a hypothesis test of the type discussed in this chapter. Write a brief report describing the hypothesis test and its role in the context of the article.

9 Inferences from Two Samples

chapter problem

Using colors for creativity and accuracy

Some studies are quite intriguing as they reveal various facets of human behavior. One such study is reported in the article "Blue or Red? Exploring the Effect of Color on Cognitive Task Performances," by Mehta and Zhu, *Science Express,* DOI: 10.1126. The researchers from the University of British Columbia conducted studies to investigate the effects of color on creativity and cognitive tasks.

To investigate the effects of color on creativity, subjects with a red background were asked to think of creative uses for a brick, while other subjects with a blue background were given the same task. Both groups were allowed one minute. Responses were scored by a panel of judges and results from scores of creativity were as follows:

Creativity Scores

Red Background:	$n = 35$, $\bar{x} = 3.39$, $s = 0.97$
Blue Background:	$n = 36$, $\bar{x} = 3.97$, $s = 0.63$

In other trials, subjects were given detail-oriented tasks consisting of words displayed on a computer screen with background colors of red and blue. The subjects studied 36 words for 2 minutes, then they were asked to recall as many of the words as they could after waiting 20 minutes. Results from scores on the word recall test are given below.

Accuracy Scores

Red Background:	$n = 35$, $\bar{x} = 15.89$, $s = 5.90$
Blue Background:	$n = 36$, $\bar{x} = 12.31$, $s = 5.48$

Examining the above results, we can see that creativity scores were higher for those having a blue background. It's obvious that the mean of 3.97 is greater than the mean of 3.39, but is the difference *significant*? We can also see that the accuracy scores were higher for those having a red background. The mean of 15.89 is greater than the mean of 12.31, but is the difference *significant*? This is an ideal situation for the use of hypothesis tests. Unlike the hypothesis tests of Chapter 8, this situation involves *two* populations instead of just one. Section 9-3 will present methods for testing claims about *two* population means, and we will consider the test results above in that section. We will then be able to determine whether it appears that the color blue fosters creativity while red fosters accuracy in detail-oriented tasks.

9-1   Review and Preview

Inferential statistics involves forming conclusions (or inferences) about a population parameter. Two major activities of inferential statistics are (1) estimating values of population parameters using confidence intervals, and (2) testing claims made about population parameters. Chapter 7 introduced methods for constructing confidence interval estimates of a population proportion, population mean, or a population standard deviation or variance. Chapter 8 introduced methods for testing claims about a population proportion, population mean, or population standard deviation or variance. Chapters 7 and 8 both involved methods for dealing with a sample from *one* population. The objective of this chapter is to extend the methods for *estimating* values of population parameters and the methods for *testing hypotheses* to situations involving *two* populations. The following are examples typical of those found in this chapter.

- Test the claim that when people in one group are each given four quarters while people in another group are each given a $1 bill, the group given the $1 bill is less likely to spend the money.

- Test the claim that the proportion of children who contract polio is less for children given the Salk vaccine than for children given a placebo.

- Test the claim that the mean body temperature of men is different from the mean body temperature of women.

Because there are so many studies involving a comparison of *two* samples, the methods of this chapter are very important because they apply to a wide variety of real applications.

9-2   Two Proportions

Key Concept In this section we present methods for (1) testing a claim made about two population proportions and (2) constructing a confidence interval estimate of the difference between two population proportions. Although the focus of this section is proportions, we can use the same methods for dealing with probabilities or the decimal equivalents of percentages.

Objectives

(1) Test a claim about two population proportions or (2) construct a confidence interval estimate of the difference between two population proportions.

Notation for Two Proportions

For population 1 we let

p_1 = *population* proportion

n_1 = size of the sample

x_1 = number of successes in the sample

$$\hat{p}_1 = \frac{x_1}{n_1} \text{ (sample proportion)}$$

$$\hat{q}_1 = 1 - \hat{p}_1 \text{ (complement of } \hat{p}_1)$$

The corresponding notations p_2, n_2, x_2, $\hat{p}_2$, and $\hat{q}_2$ apply to population 2.

Pooled Sample Proportion

The **pooled sample proportion** is denoted by $\bar{p}$ and is given by

$$\bar{p} = \frac{x_1 + x_2}{n_1 + n_2}$$
$$\bar{q} = 1 - \bar{p}$$

Requirements

1. The sample proportions are from two simple random samples that are *independent*. (Samples are *independent* if the sample values selected from one population are not related to or somehow naturally paired or matched with the sample values selected from the other population.)

2. For each of the two samples, there are at least 5 successes and at least 5 failures.

   (That is, $n\hat{p} \geq 5$ and $n\hat{q} \geq 5$ for each of the two samples).

Test Statistic for Two Proportions (with $H_0: p_1 = p_2$)

$$z = \frac{(\hat{p}_1 - \hat{p}_2) - (p_1 - p_2)}{\sqrt{\dfrac{\bar{p}\,\bar{q}}{n_1} + \dfrac{\bar{p}\,\bar{q}}{n_2}}}$$ where $p_1 - p_2 = 0$ (assumed in the null hypothesis)

$$\hat{p}_1 = \frac{x_1}{n_1} \quad \text{and} \quad \hat{p}_2 = \frac{x_2}{n_2} \quad \text{(sample proportions)}$$

$$\bar{p} = \frac{x_1 + x_2}{n_1 + n_2} \quad \text{(\textit{pooled} sample proportion)} \quad \text{and} \quad \bar{q} = 1 - \bar{p}$$

P-value: P-values are automatically provided by technology. If technology is not available, use the computed value of the test statistic with the standard normal distribution (Table A-2) and find the P-value by following the procedure summarized in Figure 8-4 in Section 8-2.

Critical values: Use Table A-2. (Based on the significance level α, find critical values by using the same procedures introduced in Section 8-2.)

Confidence Interval Estimate of $p_1 - p_2$

The confidence interval estimate of the difference $p_1 - p_2$ is

$$(\hat{p}_1 - \hat{p}_2) - E < (p_1 - p_2) < (\hat{p}_1 - \hat{p}_2) + E$$

where the margin of error E is given by $E = z_{\alpha/2}\sqrt{\dfrac{\hat{p}_1\hat{q}_1}{n_1} + \dfrac{\hat{p}_2\hat{q}_2}{n_2}}$

Rounding: Round the confidence interval limits to three significant digits.

Hypothesis Tests

For tests of hypotheses made about two population proportions, we consider only tests having a null hypothesis of $p_1 = p_2$ (so the null hypothesis is given as $H_0: p_1 = p_2$). The following example will help clarify the roles of x_1, n_1, $\hat{p}_1$, $\bar{p}$, and so on. Note that with the assumption of equal proportions, the best estimate of the common proportion is obtained by pooling both samples into one big sample, so that $\bar{p}$ is the estimator of the common population proportion.

The Lead Margin of Error

Authors Stephen Ansolabehere and Thomas Belin wrote in their article "Poll Faulting" (*Chance* magazine) that

"our greatest criticism of the reporting of poll results is with the margin of error of a single proportion (usually ±3%) when media attention is clearly drawn to the *lead* of one candidate." They point out that the lead is really the *difference* between two proportions ($p_1 - p_2$) and go on to explain how they developed the following rule of thumb: The lead is approximately $\sqrt{3}$ times larger than the margin of error for any one proportion. For a typical pre-election poll, a reported ±3% margin of error translates to about ±5% for the lead of one candidate over the other. They write that the margin of error for the lead should be reported.

In the article "The Denomination Effect" by Priya Raghubir and Joydeep Srivastava, *Journal of Consumer Research,* Vol. 36, researchers reported results from studies conducted to determine whether people have different spending characteristics when they have larger bills, such as a $20 bill, instead of smaller bills, such as twenty $1 bills. In one of the trials that they conducted, 89 undergraduate business students from two different colleges were randomly assigned to two different groups. In the "dollar bill" group, 46 subjects were given dollar bills; the "quarter" group consisted of 43 subjects given quarters. All subjects from both groups were given a choice of keeping the money or buying gum or mints. The article includes the claim that "money in a large denomination is less likely to be spent relative to an equivalent amount in many smaller denominations." Let's test that claim using a 0.05 significance level with the following sample data from the study.

	Group 1	Group 2
	Subjects Given $1 Bill	Subjects Given 4 Quarters
Spent the money	$x_1 = 12$	$x_2 = 27$
Subjects in group	$n_1 = 46$	$n_2 = 43$

Solution

Requirement check We first verify that the two necessary requirements are satisfied. (1) Because the 89 subjects were randomly assigned to the two groups, we will consider the two samples to be simple random samples (but see the interpretation at the end of this example for more comments). The two samples are independent because subjects are not matched or paired in any way. (2) The subjects given $1 bills include 12 who spent the money and 34 who did not, so the number of successes is at least 5 and the number of failures is at least 5. The subjects given four quarters include 27 who spent the money and 16 who did not, so the number of successes is at least 5 and the number of failures is at least 5. The requirements are satisfied.

Technology Computer programs and calculators usually provide a *P*-value, so the *P*-value method is typically used. See the accompanying StatCrunch results showing the null and alternative hypotheses, the test statistic of $z = -3.49$ (rounded), and the *P*-value of 0.0002.

STATCRUNCH

If technology is not available, see Figure 8-1 in Section 8-2 for the *P*-value method; we will now proceed with that method.

Step 1: The claim that "money in a large denomination is less likely to be spent relative to an equivalent amount in many smaller denominations" can be expressed as $p_1 < p_2$.

Step 2: If $p_1 < p_2$ is false, then $p_1 \geq p_2$.

Step 3: Because the claim of $p_1 < p_2$ does not contain equality, it becomes the alternative hypothesis. The null hypothesis is the statement of equality, so we have

$$H_0: p_1 = p_2 \quad H_1: p_1 < p_2 \text{ (original claim)}$$

Step 4: The significance level is $\alpha = 0.05$.

Step 5: We will use the normal distribution (with the test statistic given earlier in this section) as an approximation to the binomial distribution. We estimate the common value of p_1 and p_2 with the pooled sample estimate $\bar{p}$ calculated as shown below, with extra decimal places used to minimize rounding errors in later calculations.

$$\bar{p} = \frac{x_1 + x_2}{n_1 + n_2} = \frac{12 + 27}{46 + 43} = 0.438202$$

With $\bar{p} = 0.438202$, it follows that $\bar{q} = 1 - 0.438202 = 0.561798$.

Step 6: Because we assume in the null hypothesis that $p_1 = p_2$, the value of $p_1 - p_2$ is 0 in the following calculation of the test statistic:

$$z = \frac{(\hat{p}_1 - \hat{p}_2) - (p_1 - p_2)}{\sqrt{\dfrac{\bar{p}\,\bar{q}}{n_1} + \dfrac{\bar{p}\,\bar{q}}{n_2}}}$$

$$= \frac{\left(\dfrac{12}{46} - \dfrac{27}{43}\right) - 0}{\sqrt{\dfrac{(0.438202)(0.561798)}{46} + \dfrac{(0.438202)(0.561798)}{43}}}$$

$$= -3.49$$

This is a left-tailed test, so the P-value is the area to the left of the test statistic $z = -3.49$ (as indicated by Figure 8-4). Refer to Table A-2 and find that the area to the left of the test statistic $z = -3.49$ is 0.0002, so the P-value is 0.0002. The test statistic and P-value are shown in Figure 9-1(a).

Step 7: Because the P-value of 0.0002 is less than the significance level of $\alpha = 0.05$, we reject the null hypothesis of $p_1 = p_2$.

P-value = 0.0002

$\alpha = 0.05$

$p_1 - p_2 = 0$
or
$z = 0$

$z = -1.645$ $p_1 - p_2 = 0$
or
$z = 0$

Test Statistic:
$z = -3.49$

Test Statistic:
$z = -3.49$

(a) P-Value Method

(b) Critical Value Method

Figure 9-1   Hypothesis Test with Two Proportions

Polio Experiment

In 1954 an experiment was conducted to test the effectiveness of the Salk vaccine as protection against the devastating effects of polio. Approximately 200,000 children were injected with an ineffective salt solution, and 200,000 other children were injected with the vaccine. The experiment was "double blind" because the children being injected didn't know whether they were given the real vaccine or the placebo, and the doctors giving the injections and evaluating the results didn't know either. Only 33 of the 200,000 vaccinated children later developed paralytic polio, whereas 115 of the 200,000 injected with the salt solution later developed paralytic polio. Statistical analysis of these and other results led to the conclusion that the Salk vaccine was indeed effective against paralytic polio.

Interpretation

We must address the original claim that "money in a large denomination is less likely to be spent relative to an equivalent amount in many smaller denominations." Because we reject the null hypothesis, we conclude that there is sufficient evidence to support the claim that $p_1 < p_2$. That is, there is sufficient evidence to support the claim that people with money in large denominations are less likely to spend relative to people with an equivalent amount of money in smaller denominations. (See Table 8-3 in Section 8-2 for help in wording the final conclusion.) Based on these results, it appears that the original claim is supported.

It should be noted that the study subjects were 89 undergraduate business students from two different colleges. It would be wise to qualify the preceding conclusions by saying that the results do not necessarily apply to the general population.

Critical Value Method of Testing Hypotheses

The critical value method of testing hypotheses can also be used for Example 1. In Step 6, instead of finding the P-value, find the critical value. With a significance level of $\alpha = 0.05$ in a left-tailed test based on the normal distribution, we refer to Table A-2 and find that an area of $\alpha = 0.05$ in the left tail corresponds to the critical value of $z = -1.645$. In Figure 9-1(b) we can see that the test statistic of $z = -3.49$ falls within the critical region bounded by the critical value of $z = -1.645$. We again reject the null hypothesis. The conclusions are the same as in Example 1.

Confidence Intervals

Using the format given earlier in this section, we can construct a confidence interval estimate of the difference between population proportions $(p_1 - p_2)$. If a confidence interval estimate of $p_1 - p_2$ does not include 0, we have evidence suggesting that p_1 and p_2 have different values. The confidence interval uses a standard deviation based on estimated values of the population proportions, whereas a hypothesis test uses a standard deviation based on the assumption that the two population proportions are equal. Consequently, a conclusion based on a confidence interval might be different from a conclusion based on a hypothesis test. See the following cautions.

CAUTIONS

1. When testing a claim about two population proportions, the P-value method and the critical value method are equivalent, but they are *not* equivalent to the confidence interval method. If you want to test a claim about two population proportions, use the P-value method or critical value method; if you want to estimate the difference between two population proportions, use a confidence interval.

2. Don't test for equality of two population proportions by determining whether there is an overlap between two individual confidence interval estimates of the two individual population proportions. When compared to the confidence interval estimate of $p_1 - p_2$, the analysis of overlap between two individual confidence intervals is more conservative (by rejecting equality less often), and it has less power (because it is less likely to reject $p_1 - p_2$ when in reality $p_1 \neq p_2$). (See "On Judging the Significance of Differences by Examining the Overlap Between Confidence Intervals," by Schenker and Gentleman, *American Statistician,* Vol. 55, No. 3.) See Exercise 19.

Example 2 Confidence Interval for Claim About Denominations

Use the sample data given in Example 1 to construct a 90% confidence interval estimate of the difference between the two population proportions. (As shown in Table 8-1 in Section 8-2, a one-tailed hypothesis test with significance level $\alpha = 0.05$ requires a confidence level of 90%.) What does the result suggest about the claim that "money in a large denomination is less likely to be spent relative to an equivalent amount in many smaller denominations"?

Solution

Requirement check We are using the same data from Example 1, and the same requirement check applies here, so the requirements are satisfied. ✅

With a 90% confidence level, $z_{\alpha/2} = 1.645$ (from Table A-2). We first calculate the value of the margin of error E as shown here.

$$E = z_{\alpha/2}\sqrt{\frac{\hat{p}_1\hat{q}_1}{n_1} + \frac{\hat{p}_2\hat{q}_2}{n_2}} = 1.645\sqrt{\frac{\left(\frac{12}{46}\right)\left(\frac{34}{46}\right)}{46} + \frac{\left(\frac{27}{43}\right)\left(\frac{16}{43}\right)}{43}}$$

$$= 0.161387$$

With $\hat{p}_1 = 12/46 = 0.260870$ and $\hat{p}_2 = 27/43 = 0.627907$, $\hat{p}_1 - \hat{p}_2 = -0.367037$. With $\hat{p}_1 - \hat{p}_2 = -0.367037$ and $E = 0.161387$, the confidence interval is evaluated as follows, with the confidence interval limits rounded to three significant digits:

$$(\hat{p}_1 - \hat{p}_2) - E < (p_1 - p_2) < (\hat{p}_1 - \hat{p}_2) + E$$

$$-0.367037 - 0.161387 < (p_1 - p_2) < -0.367037 + 0.161387$$

$$-0.528 < (p_1 - p_2) < -0.206$$

Interpretation

The confidence interval limits do not contain 0, implying that there is a significant difference between the two proportions. The confidence interval suggests that the value of p_1 is less than the value of p_2, so there does appear to be sufficient evidence to support the claim that "money in a large denomination is less likely to be spent relative to an equivalent amount in many smaller denominations."

Rationale: Why Do the Procedures of This Section Work? The test statistic given for hypothesis tests is justified by the following reasoning.

With $n_1\hat{p}_1 \geq 5$ and $n_1\hat{q}_1 \geq 5$, the distribution of $\hat{p}_1$ can be approximated by a normal distribution with mean p_1, standard deviation $\sqrt{p_1q_1/n_1}$, and variance p_1q_1/n_1 (based on Sections 6-7 and 7-2). They also apply to the second sample. Because the distributions of $\hat{p}_1$ and $\hat{p}_2$ are each approximated by a normal distribution, the difference $\hat{p}_1 - \hat{p}_2$ will also be approximated by a normal distribution with mean $p_1 - p_2$ and variance

$$\sigma^2_{(\hat{p}_1 - \hat{p}_2)} = \sigma^2_{\hat{p}_1} + \sigma^2_{\hat{p}_2} = \frac{p_1q_1}{n_1} + \frac{p_2q_2}{n_2}$$

(The result above is based on this property: The variance of the *differences* between two independent random variables is the *sum* of their individual variances.) The pooled estimate of the common value of p_1 and p_2 is $\bar{p} = (x_1 + x_2)/(n_1 + n_2)$. If we

 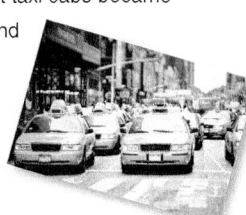

replace p_1 and p_2 by $\bar{p}$ and replace q_1 and q_2 by $\bar{q} = 1 - \bar{p}$, the variance above leads to the following standard deviation:

$$\sigma_{(\hat{p}_1 - \hat{p}_2)} = \sqrt{\frac{\bar{p}\,\bar{q}}{n_1} + \frac{\bar{p}\,\bar{q}}{n_2}}$$

We now know that the distribution of $p_1 - p_2$ is approximately normal, with mean $p_1 - p_2$ and standard deviation as shown above, so the z test statistic has the form given earlier.

The form of the confidence interval requires an expression for the variance different from the one given above. When constructing a confidence interval estimate of the difference between two proportions, we don't assume that the two proportions are equal, and we estimate the standard deviation as

$$\sqrt{\frac{\hat{p}_1\hat{q}_1}{n_1} + \frac{\hat{p}_2\hat{q}_2}{n_2}}$$

In the test statistic

$$z = \frac{(\hat{p}_1 - \hat{p}_2) - (p_1 - p_2)}{\sqrt{\frac{\hat{p}_1\hat{q}_1}{n_1} + \frac{\hat{p}_2\hat{q}_2}{n_2}}}$$

use the positive and negative values of z (for two tails) and solve for $p_1 - p_2$. The results are the limits of the confidence interval given in the box near the beginning of this section.

using TECHNOLOGY

STATDISK Select **Analysis** from the main menu bar, then select either **Hypothesis Testing** or **Confidence Intervals.**

```
Claim:  p1 < p2

Pooled proportion: 0.4382022
Test Statistic,      z: -3.4874
Critical z:            -1.6449
P-Value:              0.0002

90% Confidence interval:
-0.5284103 < p1-p2 < -0.2056645
```

Select the menu item of **Proportion-Two Samples.** Enter the required items in the dialog box, then click on the **Evaluate** button. The accompanying display is from Example 1 in this section.

MINITAB Select **Stat** from the main menu bar, then select **Basic Statistics,** then **2 Proportions.** Click on the button for **Summarized data** and enter the sample values. Click on the **Options** bar and enter the desired confidence level. (Enter 95 for a hypothesis test with a 0.05 significance level.) If testing a hypothesis, enter 0 for the claimed value of $p_1 - p_2$, then select the format for the alternative hypothesis, and click on the box to use the pooled estimate of p for the test. Click **OK** twice.

In **Minitab 16,** you can also click on **Assistant,** then **Hypothesis Tests,** then select the case for **2-Sample % Defective.** Fill out the dialog box, then click **OK** to get three windows of results that include the *P*-value and much other helpful information.

EXCEL Hypothesis Test: Use XLSTAT. Click on **XLSTAT** at the top. Click on **Parametric tests,** then select **Test for two proportions.** In the dialog box that appears, enter the frequency and sample size for each of the two samples. For the "Data format" options, select **Frequencies.** Be sure that there is a checkmark in the box next to "z test." Click on the **Options** tab and select the type of test; for a two-tailed test, select the case including the symbol $\ne$, for a left-tailed test, select the case including $<$; and for a right-tailed test, select the case including $>$. Enter a value in the "Significance level (%)" box. For example, enter 5 for a 0.05 significance level. For the options listed under "Variance," select pq(1/n1 + 1/n2). Click **OK** to get results that include the test statistic and *P*-value.

Confidence Interval: Use XLSTAT. Click on **XLSTAT** at the top. Click on **Parametric tests,** then select **Test for two proportions.** In the dialog box that appears, enter the frequency and sample size for each of the two samples. For the "Data format" options, select **Frequencies.** Be sure that there is a checkmark in the box next to "z test." Click on the **Options** tab. For the alternative hypothesis, select the format of a two-tailed test. Enter a value in the "Significance level (%)" box. For example, enter 5 for a 95% confidence interval. For the options listed under "Variance," select p1q1/n1 + p2q2/n2. Click **OK** to get results that include the confidence interval.

TI-83/84 PLUS The TI-83/84 Plus calculator can be used for hypothesis tests and confidence intervals. Press **STAT** and select **TESTS.** Then choose the option of **2-PropZTest** (for a hypothesis test) or **2-PropZInt** (for a confidence interval). When testing hypotheses, the TI-83/84 Plus calculator will display a *P*-value instead of critical values, so the *P*-value method of testing hypotheses is used.

STATCRUNCH Click on **Open StatCrunch.** Click on **Stat,** then select **Proportions.** Select **Two sample,** then select **with**

summary. Proceed to enter the numbers of successes and the numbers of observations, click on **Next,** then select either **Hypothesis Test** or **Confidence Interval.** Enter the required values, then click on **Calculate.**

9-2 Basic Skills and Concepts

Statistical Literacy and Critical Thinking

1. Verifying Requirements In the largest clinical trial ever conducted, 401,974 children were randomly assigned to two groups. The treatment group consisted of 201,229 children given the Salk vaccine for polio, and the other 200,745 children were given a placebo. Among those in the treatment group, 33 developed polio, and among those in the placebo group, 115 developed polio. If we want to use the methods of this section to test the claim that the rate of polio is less for children given the Salk vaccine, are the requirements for a hypothesis test satisfied? Explain.

2. Notation For the sample data given in Exercise 1, consider the Salk vaccine treatment group to be the first sample. Identify the values of $n_1, \hat{p}_1, \hat{q}_1, n_2, \hat{p}_2, \hat{q}_2, \bar{p}$, and $\bar{q}$. Round all values so that they have six significant digits.

3. Hypotheses and Conclusions Refer to the hypothesis test described in Exercise 1.

a. Identify the null hypothesis and the alternative hypothesis.

b. If the *P*-value for the test is reported as "less than 0.001," what should we conclude about the original claim?

4. Using Confidence Intervals

a. Assume that we want to use a 0.05 significance level to test the claim that $p_1 < p_2$. If we want to test that claim by using a confidence interval, what confidence level should we use?

b. If we test the claim in part (a) using the sample data in Exercise 1, we get this confidence interval: $-0.000508 < p_1 - p_2 < -0.000309$. What does this confidence interval suggest about the claim?

c. In general, when dealing with inferences for two population proportions, which two of the following are equivalent: confidence interval method; *P*-value method; critical value method?

Interpreting Displays. *In Exercises 5 and 6, use the results from the given displays.*

5. Flu Vaccine A *USA Today* article about an experimental nasal spray vaccine for children stated, "In a trial involving 1602 children only 14 (1%) of the 1070 who received the vaccine developed the flu, compared with 95 (18%) of the 532 who got a placebo." The accompanying TI-83/84 Plus calculator display results from a test of the claim that the vaccine had no effect. Identify the test statistic and *P*-value. What should you conclude about the claim?

6. E-mail Privacy Among 436 workers surveyed in a Gallup poll, 192 said that it was seriously unethical to monitor employee e-mail. Among 121 senior-level managers, 40 said that it was seriously unethical to monitor employee e-mail. Consider the claim that for those saying that monitoring e-mail is seriously unethical, the proportion of workers is the same as

TI-83/84 PLUS

the proportion of managers. Identify the test statistic and *P*-value. If using a 0.01 significance level, what should you conclude about the claim?

MINITAB
```
Difference = p (1) - p (2)
Estimate for difference:  0.109788
95% CI for difference:  (0.0138876, 0.205689)
Test for difference = 0 (vs not = 0):  Z = 2.17  P-Value = 0.030
```

Testing Claims About Proportions. *In Exercises 7–18, test the given claim. Identify the null hypothesis, alternative hypothesis, test statistic, P-value or critical value(s), conclusion about the null hypothesis, and final conclusion that addresses the original claim.*

7. Dreaming in Black and White A study was conducted to determine the proportion of people who dream in black and white instead of color. Among 306 people over the age of 55, 68 dream in black and white, and among 298 people under the age of 25, 13 dream in black and white (based on data from "Do We Dream in Color?" by Eva Murzyn, *Consciousness and Cognition*, Vol. 17, No. 4). We want to use a 0.01 significance level to test the claim that the proportion of people over 55 who dream in black and white is greater than the proportion for those under 25.

a. Test the claim using a hypothesis test.

b. Test the claim by constructing an appropriate confidence interval.

c. An explanation given for the results is that those over the age of 55 grew up exposed to media that was mostly displayed in black and white. Can the results from parts (a) and (b) be used to verify that explanation?

8. Ginkgo for Dementia The herb ginkgo biloba is commonly used as a treatment to prevent dementia. In a study of the effectiveness of this treatment, 1545 elderly subjects were given ginkgo and 1524 elderly subjects were given a placebo. Among those in the ginkgo treatment group, 246 later developed dementia, and among those in the placebo group, 277 later developed dementia (based on data from "Ginkgo Biloba for Prevention of Dementia," by DeKosky et al., *Journal of the American Medical Association,* Vol. 300, No. 19). We want to use a 0.01 significance level to test the claim that ginkgo is effective in preventing dementia.

a. Test the claim using a hypothesis test.

b. Test the claim by constructing an appropriate confidence interval.

c. Based on the results, is ginkgo effective in preventing dementia?

9. Are Seat Belts Effective? A simple random sample of front-seat occupants involved in car crashes is obtained. Among 2823 occupants not wearing seat belts, 31 were killed. Among 7765 occupants wearing seat belts, 16 were killed (based on data from "Who Wants Airbags?" by Meyer and Finney, *Chance,* Vol. 18, No. 2). We want to use a 0.05 significance level to test the claim that seat belts are effective in reducing fatalities.

a. Test the claim using a hypothesis test.

b. Test the claim by constructing an appropriate confidence interval.

c. What does the result suggest about the effectiveness of seat belts?

10. Cardiac Arrest at Day and Night A study investigated survival rates for in-hospital patients who suffered cardiac arrest. Among 58,593 patients who had cardiac arrest during the day, 11,604 survived and were discharged. Among 28,155 patients who suffered cardiac arrest at night, 4139 survived and were discharged (based on data from "Survival from

In-Hospital Cardiac Arrest During Nights and Weekends," by Peberdy et al., *Journal of the American Medical Association*, Vol. 299, No. 7). We want to use a 0.01 significance level to test the claim that the survival rates are the same for day and night.

a. Test the claim using a hypothesis test.

b. Test the claim by constructing an appropriate confidence interval.

c. Based on the results, does it appear that for in-hospital patients who suffer cardiac arrest, the survival rate is the same for day and night?

11. Is Echinacea Effective for Colds? Rhino viruses typically cause common colds. In a test of the effectiveness of echinacea, 40 of the 45 subjects treated with echinacea developed rhinovirus infections. In a placebo group, 88 of the 103 subjects developed rhinovirus infections (based on data from "An Evaluation of Echinacea Angustifolia in Experimental Rhinovirus Infections," by Turner, et al., *New England Journal of Medicine*, Vol. 353, No. 4). We want to use a 0.05 significance level to test the claim that echinacea has an effect on rhinovirus infections.

a. Test the claim using a hypothesis test.

b. Test the claim by constructing an appropriate confidence interval.

c. Based on the results, does echinacea appear to have any effect on the infection rate?

12. Bednets to Reduce Malaria In a randomized controlled trial in Kenya, insecticide-treated bednets were tested as a way to reduce malaria. Among 343 infants using bednets, 15 developed malaria. Among 294 infants not using bednets, 27 developed malaria (based on data from "Sustainability of Reductions in Malaria Transmission and Infant Mortality in Western Kenya with Use of Insecticide-Treated Bednets," by Lindblade, et al., *Journal of the American Medical Association*, Vol. 291, No. 21). We want to use a 0.01 significance level to test the claim that the incidence of malaria is lower for infants using bednets.

a. Test the claim using a hypothesis test.

b. Test the claim by constructing an appropriate confidence interval.

c. Based on the results, do the bednets appear to be effective?

13. Tennis Challenges Since the Hawk-Eye instant replay system for tennis was introduced at the U.S. Open in 2006, men challenged 1412 referee calls, with the result that 421 of the calls were overturned. Women challenged 759 referee calls, and 220 of the calls were overturned. We want to use a 0.05 significance level to test the claim that men and women have equal success in challenging calls.

a. Test the claim using a hypothesis test.

b. Test the claim by constructing an appropriate confidence interval.

c. Based on the results, does it appear that men and women have equal success in challenging calls?

14. Police Gunfire In a study of police gunfire reports during a recent year, it was found that among 540 shots fired by New York City police, 182 hit their targets; and among 283 shots fired by Los Angeles police, 77 hit their targets (based on data from the *New York Times*). We want to use a 0.05 significance level to test the claim that New York City police and Los Angeles police have the same proportion of hits.

a. Test the claim using a hypothesis test.

b. Test the claim by constructing an appropriate confidence interval. *continued*

c. Based on the results, does there appear to be a difference between the hit rates of New York City police and Los Angeles police?

15. Headache Treatment In a study of treatments for very painful "cluster" headaches, 150 patients were treated with oxygen and 148 other patients were given a placebo consisting of ordinary air. Among the 150 patients in the oxygen treatment group, 116 were free from headaches 15 minutes after treatment. Among the 148 patients given the placebo, 29 were free from headaches 15 minutes after treatment (based on data from "High-Flow Oxygen for Treatment of Cluster Headache," by Cohen, Burns, and Goadsby, *Journal of the American Medical Association,* Vol. 302, No. 22). We want to use a 0.01 significance level to test the claim that the oxygen treatment is effective.

a. Test the claim using a hypothesis test.

b. Test the claim by constructing an appropriate confidence interval.

c. Based on the results, is the oxygen treatment effective?

16. Spending Large and Small Bills In the same study cited in Example 1, another trial was conducted with 75 women in China given a 100-Yuan bill, while another 75 women in China were given 100 Yuan in the form of smaller bills (a 50-Yuan bill plus two 20-Yuan bills plus two 5-Yuan bills). Among those given the single bill, 60 spent some or all of the money. Among those given the smaller bills, 68 spent some or all of the money. We want to use a 0.05 significance level to test the claim that when given a single large bill, a smaller proportion of women in China spend some or all of the money when compared to the proportion of women in China given the same amount in smaller bills.

a. Test the claim using a hypothesis test.

b. Test the claim by constructing an appropriate confidence interval.

c. If the significance level is changed to 0.01, does the conclusion change?

17. Lefties In a random sample of males, it was found that 23 write with their left hands and 217 do not. In a random sample of females, it was found that 65 write with their left hands and 455 do not (based on data from "The Left-Handed: Their Sinister History," by Elaine Fowler Costas, Education Resources Information Center, Paper 399519). We want to use a 0.01 significance level to test the claim that the rate of left-handedness among males is less than that among females.

a. Test the claim using a hypothesis test.

b. Test the claim by constructing an appropriate confidence interval.

c. Based on the results, is the rate of left-handedness among males less than the rate of left-handedness among females?

18. Marathon Finishers In a recent New York City marathon, 25,221 men finished and 253 dropped out. Also, 12,883 women finished and 163 dropped out (based on data from the *New York Times*). We want to use a 0.01 significance level to test the claim that the rate of those who finish is the same for men and women.

a. Test the claim using a hypothesis test.

b. Test the claim by constructing an appropriate confidence interval.

c. Based on the results, do men and women finish the New York City marathon at the same rate?

9-2 Beyond the Basics

19. Interpreting Overlap of Confidence Intervals In the article "On Judging the Significance of Differences by Examining the Overlap Between Confidence Intervals," by Schenker and Gentleman (*American Statistician,* Vol. 55, No. 3), the authors consider sample data in this statement: "Independent simple random samples, each of size 200, have been drawn, and 112 people in the first sample have the attribute, whereas 88 people in the second sample have the attribute."

a. Use the methods of this section to construct a 95% confidence interval estimate of the difference $p_1 - p_2$. What does the result suggest about the equality of p_1 and p_2?

b. Use the methods of Section 7-2 to construct individual 95% confidence interval estimates for each of the two population proportions. After comparing the overlap between the two confidence intervals, what do you conclude about the equality of p_1 and p_2?

c. Use a 0.05 significance level to test the claim that the two population proportions are equal. What do you conclude?

d. Based on the preceding results, what should you conclude about the equality of p_1 and p_2? Which of the three preceding methods is least effective in testing for the equality of p_1 and p_2?

20. Equivalence of Hypothesis Test and Confidence Interval Two different simple random samples are drawn from two different populations. The first sample consists of 20 people with 10 having a common attribute. The second sample consists of 2000 people with 1404 of them having the same common attribute. Compare the results from a hypothesis test of $p_1 = p_2$ (with a 0.05 significance level) and a 95% confidence interval estimate of $p_1 - p_2$.

21. Determining Sample Size The sample size needed to estimate the difference between two population proportions to within a margin of error E with a confidence level of $1 - \alpha$ can be found by using the following expression:

$$E = z_{\alpha/2}\sqrt{\frac{p_1 q_1}{n_1} + \frac{p_2 q_2}{n_2}}$$

Replace n_1 and n_2 by n in the formula above (assuming that both samples have the same size) and replace each of p_1, q_1, p_2, and q_2 by 0.5 (because their values are not known). Solving for n results in this expression:

$$n = \frac{z_{\alpha/2}^2}{2E^2}$$

Use this expression to find the size of each sample if you want to estimate the difference between the proportions of adult men and women who are college graduates. Assume that you want 90% confidence that your error is no more than 0.02.

9-3 Two Means: Independent Samples

Key Concept This section presents methods for using sample data from two independent samples to test hypotheses made about two population means or to construct confidence interval estimates of the difference between two population means. In Part 1 we discuss situations in which the standard deviations of the two populations are unknown and are not assumed to be equal. In Part 2 we discuss two other situations: (1) The two population standard deviations are both known; (2) the two population standard deviations are unknown but are assumed to be equal.

Using Statistics to Identify Thieves

Methods of statistics can be used to determine that an employee is stealing, and they can also be used to estimate the amount stolen. The following are some of the indicators that have been used. For comparable time periods, samples of sales have means that are significantly different. The mean sale amount decreases significantly. There is a significant increase in the proportion of "no sale" register openings. There is a significant decrease in the ratio of cash receipts to checks. Methods of hypothesis testing can be used to identify such indicators. (See "How to Catch a Thief," by Manly and Thomson, *Chance*, Vol. 11, No. 4.)

Part 1: Independent Samples with σ_1 and σ_2 Unknown and Not Assumed Equal

This section involves two *independent* samples, and the following section deals with samples that are *dependent*. It is important to know the difference between independent samples and dependent samples.

> **DEFINITIONS**
>
> Two samples are **independent** if the sample values from one population are not related to or somehow naturally paired or matched with the sample values from the other population.
>
> Two samples are **dependent** (or consist of **matched pairs**) if the sample values are somehow matched, where the matching is based on some inherent relationship. (That is, each pair of sample values consists of two measurements from the same subject—such as before/after data—or each pair of sample values consists of matched pairs—such as husband/wife data—where the matching is based on some meaningful relationship.)

Example 1

Independent Samples: **Proctored Tests and Nonproctored Tests in Online Courses** Researchers Michael Flesch and Elliot Ostler investigated the reliability of test assessment. One group consisted of 30 students who took proctored tests. A second group consisted of 32 students who took tests online without a proctor. The two samples are independent, because the subjects were not paired or matched in any way.

Independent Samples: **Weights of M&Ms** Data Set 20 in Appendix B includes the following weights (grams) of a sample of yellow M&Ms and a sample of brown M&Ms. The yellow and brown weights might appear to be paired because of the way that they are listed, but they are not matched according to some inherent relationship. They are actually two independent samples that just happen to be listed in a way that might cause us to incorrectly think that they are matched.

Yellow	0.883	0.769	0.859	0.784	0.824	0.858	0.848	0.851
Brown	0.696	0.876	0.855	0.806	0.840	0.868	0.859	0.982

Dependent Samples: **Heights of Husbands and Wives** Students of the author collected data consisting of the heights (cm) of husbands and the heights (cm) of their wives. Five of those pairs of heights are listed below. These two samples are dependent, because the height of each husband is matched with the height of his wife.

Height of Husband	175	180	173	176	178
Height of Wife	160	165	163	162	166

For inferences about means from two independent populations, the following box summarizes key elements of a hypothesis test and a confidence interval estimate of the difference between the population means.

Objectives

1. Conduct a hypothesis test of a claim about two independent population means, or

2. Construct a confidence interval estimate of the difference between two independent population means.

Notation

For population 1 we let

$\mu_1 = population$ mean

$\sigma_1 = population$ standard deviation

$n_1 = $ size of the first sample

$\bar{x}_1 = sample$ mean

$s_1 = sample$ standard deviation

The corresponding notations μ_2, σ_2, $\bar{x}_2$, s_2, and n_2 apply to population 2.

Requirements

1. The values of σ_1 and σ_2 are unknown and we do not assume that they are equal.

2. The two samples are *independent.*

3. Both samples are *simple random samples.*

4. Either or both of these conditions is satisfied: The two sample sizes are both *large* (with $n_1 > 30$ and $n_2 > 30$) or both samples come from populations having normal distributions. (The methods used here are *robust* against departures from normality, so for small samples, the normality requirement is loose in the sense that the procedures perform well as long as there are no outliers and departures from normality are not too extreme.)

Hypothesis Test Statistic for Two Means: Independent Samples

$$t = \frac{(\bar{x}_1 - \bar{x}_2) - (\mu_1 - \mu_2)}{\sqrt{\dfrac{s_1^2}{n_1} + \dfrac{s_2^2}{n_2}}} \quad \text{(where } \mu_1 - \mu_2 \text{ is often assumed to be 0)}$$

Degrees of freedom: When finding critical values or *P*-values, use the following for determining the number of degrees of freedom, denoted by df. (Although these two methods typically result in different numbers of degrees of freedom, the conclusion of a hypothesis test is rarely affected by the choice.)

1. In this book we use this simple and conservative estimate:

$$\text{df} = \textbf{smaller of } n_1 - 1 \textbf{ and } n_2 - 1$$

2. Statistical software packages typically use the more accurate but more difficult estimate given in Formula 9-1. (We will not use Formula 9-1 for the examples and exercises in this book.)

Formula 9-1

$$\text{df} = \frac{(A + B)^2}{\dfrac{A^2}{n_1 - 1} + \dfrac{B^2}{n_2 - 1}}$$

where $A = \dfrac{s_1^2}{n_1}$ and $B = \dfrac{s_2^2}{n_2}$

***P*-values:**   *P*-values are automatically provided by technology. If technology is not available, refer to the *t* distribution in Table A-3. Use the procedure summarized in Figure 8-4 from Section 8-2.

Critical values: Refer to the *t* distribution in Table A-3.   *continued*

Confidence Interval Estimate of $\mu_1 - \mu_2$: Independent Samples

The confidence interval estimate of the difference $\mu_1 - \mu_2$ is

$$(\bar{x}_1 - \bar{x}_2) - E < (\mu_1 - \mu_2) < (\bar{x}_1 - \bar{x}_2) + E$$

where

$$E = t_{\alpha/2}\sqrt{\frac{s_1^2}{n_1} + \frac{s_2^2}{n_2}}$$

and the number of degrees of freedom df is as described above for hypothesis tests. (In this book, we use df = smaller of $n_1 - 1$ and $n_2 - 1$.)

CAUTION Before conducting a hypothesis test, consider the context of the data, the source of the data, and the sampling method, and explore the data with graphs and descriptive statistics. Be sure to verify that the requirements are satisfied.

Equivalent Methods

The *P*-value method of hypothesis testing, the critical value method of hypothesis testing, and confidence intervals all use the same distribution and standard error, so they are all equivalent in the sense that they result in the same conclusions.

Example 2   **Are We More Creative with Blue?**

In the Chapter Problem, we noted that researchers from the University of British Columbia conducted trials to investigate the effects of color on creativity. Subjects with a red background were asked to think of creative uses for a brick; other subjects with a blue background were given the same task. Responses were scored by a panel of judges and results from scores of creativity are given below. The researchers make the claim that "blue enhances performance on a creative task." Test that claim using a 0.01 significance level.

Creativity Scores

Red Background:	$n = 35$, $\bar{x} = 3.39$, $s = 0.97$
Blue Background:	$n = 36$, $\bar{x} = 3.97$, $s = 0.63$

Solution

Requirement check (1) The values of the two population standard deviations are not known and we are not making an assumption that they are equal. (2) The two samples are independent because different subjects were used for the two different color groups. (3) The samples are simple random samples because subjects were randomly assigned to each of the two different color groups. (4) Both samples are large (greater than 30), so we satisfy the requirement that "the two sample sizes are both *large* (with $n_1 > 30$ and $n_2 > 30$) or both samples come from populations having normal distributions." The requirements are all satisfied. ✅

Technology Computer programs and calculators usually provide a *P*-value, so the *P*-value method is used. See the accompanying TI-83/84 Plus calculator results showing the alternative hypothesis of $\mu_1 < \mu_2$ (from the claim that the second

TI-83/84 PLUS

```
2-SampTTest
 μ1<μ2
 t=-2.978951111
 p=.0021077236
 df=58.11153827
 x̄1=3.39
↓x̄2=3.97
```

group of blue has a higher mean), the test statistic of $t = -2.979$ (rounded), and the P-value of 0.0021 (rounded). Because the P-value of 0.0021 is less than the significance level of $\alpha = 0.01$, we reject the null hypothesis. See the interpretation at the end of this example.

We can test the claim using the critical value method as follows.

Step 1: The claim that "blue enhances performance on a creative task" can be restated as the claim that people with a blue background have a higher mean creativity score than those in the first group with a red background. The first group of red background subjects therefore has a lower mean creativity score than the second blue group, and this can be expressed as $\mu_1 < \mu_2$.

Step 2: If the original claim is false, then $\mu_1 \geq \mu_2$.

Step 3: The alternative hypothesis is the expression not containing equality, and the null hypothesis is an expression of equality, so we have

$$H_0: \mu_1 = \mu_2 \qquad H_1: \mu_1 < \mu_2 \text{ (original claim)}$$

We now proceed with the assumption that $\mu_1 = \mu_2$, or $\mu_1 - \mu_2 = 0$.

Step 4: The significance level is $\alpha = 0.01$.

Step 5: Because we have two independent samples and we are testing a claim about the two population means, we use a t distribution with the test statistic given earlier in this section.

Step 6: The test statistic is calculated as follows:

$$t = \frac{(\bar{x}_1 - \bar{x}_2) - (\mu_1 - \mu_2)}{\sqrt{\frac{s_1^2}{n_1} + \frac{s_2^2}{n_2}}} = \frac{(3.39 - 3.97) - 0}{\sqrt{\frac{0.97^2}{35} + \frac{0.63^2}{36}}} = -2.979$$

Critical Values Because we are using a t distribution, the critical value of $t = -2.441$ is found from Table A-3. With an area of 0.01 in the left tail, we want the t value corresponding to 34 degrees of freedom, which is the smaller of $n_1 - 1$ and $n_2 - 1$ (or the smaller of 34 and 35). The test statistic, critical values, and critical region are shown in Figure 9-2.

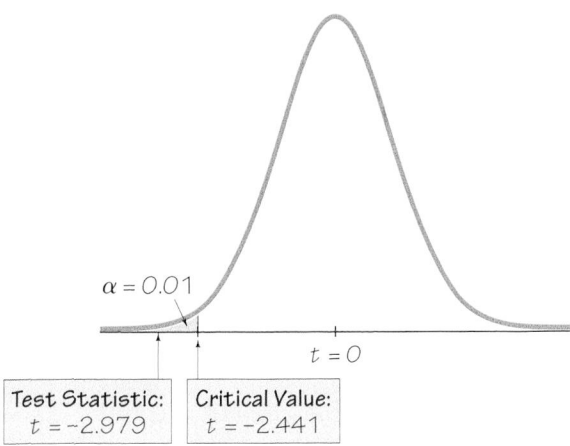

$\alpha = 0.01$

$t = 0$

| Test Statistic: | Critical Value: |
| $t = -2.979$ | $t = -2.441$ |

Figure 9-2 Hypothesis Test of Means from Two Independent Populations

Step 7. Because the test statistic does fall within the critical region, we reject the null hypothesis $\mu_1 = \mu_2$ (or $\mu_1 - \mu_2 = 0$).

Do Real Estate Agents Get You the Best Price?

When a real estate agent sells a home, does he or she get the best price for the seller? This question was addressed by Steven Levitt and Stephen Dubner in *Freakonomics*. They collected data from thousands of homes near Chicago, including homes owned by the agents themselves. Here is what they write: "There's one way to find out: measure the difference between the sales data for houses that belong to real-estate agents themselves and the houses they sold on behalf of clients. Using the data from the sales of those 100,000 Chicago homes, and controlling for any number of variables—location, age and quality of the house, aesthetics, and so on—it turns out that a real-estate agent keeps her own home on the market an average of ten days longer and sells it for an extra 3-plus percent, or $10,000 on a $300,000 house." A conclusion such as this can be obtained by using the methods of this section.

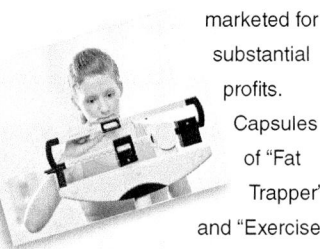

Interpretation

There is sufficient evidence to support the claim that the red background group has a lower mean creativity score than the blue background group. This supports the conclusion that higher creativity scores were achieved by the subjects with the blue background, but the results do not justify the conclusion that the blue background is the *cause* of the higher creativity scores.

Example 3   Confidence Interval for Creativity Scores

Using the sample data given in Example 2, construct a 98% confidence interval estimate of the difference between the mean creativity score for those with a red background and the mean creativity score for those with a blue background.

Solution

Requirement check Because we are using the same data from Example 2, the same requirement check applies here, so the requirements are satisfied. ⊘

We first find the value of the margin of error E. We use the same critical value of $t_{\alpha/2} = 2.441$ found in Example 2. (A more accurate critical value is 2.392.)

$$E = t_{\alpha/2}\sqrt{\frac{s_1^2}{n_1} + \frac{s_2^2}{n_2}} = 2.441\sqrt{\frac{0.97^2}{35} + \frac{0.63^2}{36}} = 0.475261$$

Using $E = 0.475261$, $\bar{x}_1 = 3.39$, and $\bar{x}_2 = 3.97$, we can now find the confidence interval as follows:

$$(\bar{x}_1 - \bar{x}_2) - E < (\mu_1 - \mu_2) < (\bar{x}_1 - \bar{x}_2) + E$$
$$-1.06 < (\mu_1 - \mu_2) < -0.10$$

If we use technology to obtain more accurate results, we get the confidence interval of $-1.05 < (\mu_1 - \mu_2) < -0.11$, so we can see that the confidence interval above is quite good, even though we used a simplified method for finding the number of degrees of freedom (instead of getting more accurate results by using Formula 9-1 to compute the number of degrees of freedom).

Interpretation

We are 98% confident that the limits of -1.05 and -0.11 actually do contain the difference between the two population means. Because those limits do not contain 0, this confidence interval suggests that there is a significant difference between the two means. (We used a 98% confidence level, so the one-sided hypothesis test has a corresponding significance level of 0.01.) Also, because the confidence interval consists entirely of negative values, there is sufficient evidence to support the claim that the red background group has a lower mean creativity score than the blue background group. This supports the claim that "blue enhances performance on a creative task" as claimed by the researchers, but we should be careful to avoid a statement that the blue background is the *cause* of the higher creativity scores.

Rationale for the Test Statistic and Confidence Interval

If the given assumptions are satisfied, the sampling distribution of $\bar{x}_1 - \bar{x}_2$ can be approximated by a t distribution with mean equal to $\mu_1 - \mu_2$ and standard deviation equal to $\sqrt{s_1^2/n_1 + s_2^2/n_2}$. This last expression for the standard deviation is based on the property that the variance of the *differences* between two independent random variables equals the variance of the first random variable *plus* the variance of the second random variable.

Part 2: Alternative Methods

Part 1 of this section dealt with situations in which the two population standard deviations are unknown and are not assumed to be equal. In Part 2 we address two other situations:

1. The two population standard deviations are both known.

2. The two population standard deviations are unknown but are assumed to be equal.

Alternative Method Used When σ_1 and σ_2 are Known

In reality, the population standard deviations σ_1 and σ_2 are almost never known, but if they are somehow known, the test statistic and confidence interval are based on the normal distribution instead of the t distribution. See the summary box below.

Inferences About Means of Two Independent Populations, with σ_1 and σ_2 Known

Requirements

1. The two population standard deviations σ_1 and σ_2 are both known.

2. The two samples are *independent.*

3. Both samples are *simple random samples.*

4. Either or both of these conditions is satisfied: The two sample sizes are both *large* (with $n_1 > 30$ and $n_2 > 30$) or both samples come from populations having normal distributions. (For small samples, the normality requirement is loose in the sense that the procedures perform well as long as there are no outliers and departures from normality are not too extreme.)

Hypothesis Test

Test statistic:

$$z = \frac{(\bar{x}_1 - \bar{x}_2) - (\mu_1 - \mu_2)}{\sqrt{\dfrac{\sigma_1^2}{n_1} + \dfrac{\sigma_2^2}{n_2}}}$$

P-values: *P*-values are automatically provided by technology. If technology is not available, refer to the normal distribution in Table A-2. Use the procedure summarized in Figure 8-4 from Section 8-2.

Critical values: Refer to Table A-2.

Confidence Interval Estimate of $\mu_1 - \mu_2$

$$(\bar{x}_1 - \bar{x}_2) - E < (\mu_1 - \mu_2) < (\bar{x}_1 - \bar{x}_2) + E$$

where

$$E = z_{\alpha/2}\sqrt{\frac{\sigma_1^2}{n_1} + \frac{\sigma_2^2}{n_2}}$$

Alternative Method: Assume That $\sigma_1 = \sigma_2$ and *Pool* the Sample Variances

Even when the specific values of σ_1 and σ_2 are not known, if it can be assumed that they have the *same* value, the sample variances s_1^2 and s_2^2 can be *pooled* to obtain an estimate of the common population variance σ^2. The **pooled estimate of** $\boldsymbol{\sigma^2}$ is denoted by s_p^2 and is a weighted average of s_1^2 and s_2^2, which is described in the following box.

Inferences About Means of Two Independent Populations, Assuming That $\sigma_1 = \sigma_2$

Requirements

1. The two population standard deviations are not known, but they are assumed to be equal. That is, $\sigma_1 = \sigma_2$.

2. The two samples are *independent.*

3. Both samples are *simple random samples.*

4. Either or both of these conditions is satisfied: The two sample sizes are both *large* (with $n_1 > 30$ and

$n_2 > 30$) or both samples come from populations having normal distributions. (For small samples, the normality requirement is loose in the sense that the procedures perform well as long as there are no outliers and departures from normality are not too extreme.)

Hypothesis Test

Test statistic:

$$t = \frac{(\bar{x}_1 - \bar{x}_2) - (\mu_1 - \mu_2)}{\sqrt{\dfrac{s_p^2}{n_1} + \dfrac{s_p^2}{n_2}}}$$

where

$$s_p^2 = \frac{(n_1 - 1)s_1^2 + (n_2 - 1)s_2^2}{(n_1 - 1) + (n_2 - 1)} \quad \text{(pooled sample variance)}$$

and the number of degrees of freedom is df $= n_1 + n_2 - 2$.

Confidence Interval Estimate of $\mu_1 - \mu_2$

$$(\bar{x}_1 - \bar{x}_2) - E < (\mu_1 - \mu_2) < (\bar{x}_1 - \bar{x}_2) + E$$

where

$$E = t_{\alpha/2}\sqrt{\frac{s_p^2}{n_1} + \frac{s_p^2}{n_2}}$$

and s_p^2 is as given in the test statistic above, and df $= n_1 + n_2 - 2$.

If we want to use this method based on equal population standard deviations, how do we determine that $\sigma_1 = \sigma_2$? One approach is to use a hypothesis test of the null hypothesis $\sigma_1 = \sigma_2$, as given in Section 9-5, but that approach is not recommended and we will not use the preliminary test of $\sigma_1 = \sigma_2$. In the article "Homogeneity of Variance in the Two-Sample Means Test" (by Moser and Stevens, *American Statistician*, Vol. 46, No. 1), the authors note that we rarely know that $\sigma_1 = \sigma_2$. They analyze the performance of the different tests by considering sample sizes and powers of the tests. They conclude that more effort should be spent learning the method given in Part 1, and less emphasis should be placed on the method based on the assumption of $\sigma_1 = \sigma_2$. Unless instructed otherwise, we use the following strategy, which is consistent with the recommendations in the article by Moser and Stevens:

> **Assume that σ_1 and σ_2 are unknown, do *not* assume that $\sigma_1 = \sigma_2$, and use the test statistic and confidence interval given in Part 1 of this section.**

Figure 9-3 summarizes the methods for inferences about two independent population means.

Why Not Eliminate the Method of Pooling Sample Variances?

If we use randomness to assign subjects to treatment and placebo groups, we know that the samples are drawn from the same population. So if we conduct a hypothesis test assuming that two population means are equal, it is not unreasonable to also assume that the samples are from populations with the same standard deviations (but we should still check that assumption). The advantage of this alternative method of

Inferences About Two Independent Means

Start

Are σ_1 and σ_2 known?

— Yes → Use normal distribution with standard error.
$$\sqrt{\frac{\sigma_1^2}{n_1} + \frac{\sigma_2^2}{n_2}}$$
This case almost never occurs in reality.

No ↓

Can it be assumed that $\sigma_1 = \sigma_2$?

— Yes → Use *t* distribution with POOLED standard error.
Some statisticians recommend against this approach.

No ↓

Approximate method: Use *t* distribution with standard error.
$$\sqrt{\frac{s_1^2}{n_1} + \frac{s_2^2}{n_2}}$$
Use this method unless instructed otherwise.

Figure 9-3   **Methods for Inferences About Two Independent Means**

Super Bowls

Students were invited to a Super Bowl game and half of them were given large 4-liter snack bowls while the other half were given smaller 2-liter bowls. Those using the large bowls consumed 56% more than those using the smaller bowls. (See "Super Bowls: Serving Bowl Size and Food Consumption," by Wansink and Cheney, *Journal of the American Medical Association,* Vol. 293, No. 14.)

A separate study showed that there is "a significant increase in fatal motor vehicle crashes during the hours following the Super Bowl telecast in the United States." Researchers analyzed 20,377 deaths on 27 Super Bowl Sundays and 54 other Sundays used as controls. They found a 41% increase in fatalities after Super Bowl games. (See "Do Fatal Crashes Increase Following a Super Bowl Telecast?" by Redelmeier and Stewart, *Chance,* Vol. 18, No. 1.)

pooling sample variances is that the number of degrees of freedom is a little higher, so hypothesis tests have more power and confidence intervals are a little narrower. Consequently, statisticians sometimes use this method of pooling, and that is why we include it in this subsection.

using TECHNOLOGY

STATDISK Select the menu item of **Analysis.** Select either **Hypothesis Testing** or **Confidence Intervals,** then select **Mean-Two Independent Samples.** Enter the required values in the dialog box. You have the options of "Not Eq vars: NO POOL," "Eq vars: POOL," or "Prelim F Test." The option of **Not Eq vars: NO POOL** is consistent with the methods described in Part 1 of this section, and this method is recommended. (The F test is described in Section 9-5.)

MINITAB Minitab allows the use of summary statistics or original lists of sample data. If the original sample values are known, enter them in columns C1 and C2. Select the options **Stat, Basic Statistics,** and **2-Sample t.** Make the required entries in the window that pops up. Use the **Options** button to select a confidence level, enter a claimed value of the difference, or select a format for the alternative hypothesis. The Minitab display also includes the confidence interval limits.

If the two population variances appear to be equal, Minitab does allow use of a pooled estimate of the common variance. There will be a box next to **Assume equal variances,** so click on that box only if you want to assume that the two populations have equal variances, but this approach is not recommended.

In **Minitab 16,** you can also click on **Assistant,** then **Hypothesis Tests,** then select the case for **2-Sample t.** Fill out the dialog box, then click **OK** to get three windows of results that include the P-value and much other helpful information.

EXCEL Excel requires entry of the original lists of sample data. Enter the data for the two samples in columns A and B and use either XLSTAT or Excel's Data Analysis add-in.

XLSTAT for Hypothesis Test: Click on **XLSTAT** at the top. Click on **Parametric tests,** then select **Two sample t test and z test.** In the dialog box that appears, enter the range of values for the first sample (such as A1:A13) and enter the range of values for the second sample. For "Data format," select the option of **One column per sample.** For the "Column labels" box, include a checkmark only if the first row of the sample data consists of names or labels. Put a checkmark next to "Student's t test" (use z test if σ is known). Click on the **Options** tab and select the type of test; for a two-tailed test, select the case including the symbol $\neq$, for a left-tailed test select the case including $<$, and for a right-tailed test, select the case including $>$. Enter a value in the "Significance level (%)" box. For example, enter 5 for a 0.05 significance level. Put a checkmark next to "Cochran-Cox" so that the variances are not assumed to be equal. Click **OK** to get results that include the test statistic and P-value.

XLSTAT for Confidence Interval: Click on **XLSTAT** at the top. Click on **Parametric tests,** then select **Two sample t test and z test.** In the dialog box that appears, enter the range of values for the first sample (such as A1:A13) and enter the range of values for the second sample. For "Data format," select the option of **One column per sample.** For the "Column labels" box, include a checkmark only if the first row of the sample data consists of names or labels. Put a checkmark next to "Student's t test" (use z test if σ is known). Click on the **Options** tab. For the alternative hypothesis, select the format of a two-tailed test. Enter a value in the "Significance level (%)" box. For example, enter 5 for a 95% confidence interval. Put a checkmark next to "Cochran-Cox" so that the variances are not assumed to be equal. Click **OK** to get results that include the confidence interval.

Data Analysis Add-in: If using Excel 2013, 2010, or 2007, click on **Data,** then **Data Analysis;** if using Excel 2003, click on **Tools** and select **Data Analysis.** Select one of the following two items (we recommend the assumption of *unequal variances*):

   t-test: Two-Sample Assuming Equal Variances

   t-test: Two-Sample Assuming Unequal Variances

Enter the range for the values of the first sample (such as A1:A50) and then enter the range of values for the second sample. Enter a value for the claimed difference between the two population means, which will often be 0. Enter the significance level in the Alpha box and click on **OK.** (Excel does not provide a confidence interval.)

TI-83/84 PLUS To conduct tests of the type found in this section, press **STAT**, then select **TESTS** and choose **2-SampTTest** (for a hypothesis test) or **2-SampTInt** (for a confidence interval). The TI-83/84 Plus calculator does give you the option of using "pooled" variances (if you believe that $\sigma_1^2 = \sigma_2^2$) or not pooling the variances, but we recommend that the variances not be pooled, so we recommend selecting **No** for the line labeled "Pooled."

STATCRUNCH Click on **Open StatCrunch.** Click on **Stat,** then select **T statistics.** Select **Two sample,** then select **with data** (for lists of sample data) or **with summary** (for entering known summary statistics). Click on **Next,** then select **Hypothesis Test** or **Confidence Interval.** There is a box with a check indicating that variances be pooled, but it is recommended that variances should not be pooled. Click on **Next,** then make the required entries. Click on **Calculate.**

9-3 Basic Skills and Concepts

Statistical Literacy and Critical Thinking

1. Independent and Dependent Samples Which of the following involve independent samples?

a. To test the effectiveness of the Atkins diet, 36 randomly selected subjects are weighed before the diet and six months after treatment with the diet. The two samples consist of the before/after weights.

b. To determine whether smoking affects memory, 50 randomly selected smokers are given a test of word recall and 50 randomly selected nonsmokers are given the same test. Sample data consist of the scores from the two groups.

c. IQ scores are obtained from a random sample of 75 wives and IQ scores are obtained from their husbands.

d. Annual incomes are obtained from a random sample of 1200 residents of Alaska and from another random sample of 1200 residents of Hawaii.

e. Scores from a standard test of mathematical reasoning are obtained from a random sample of statistics students and another random sample of sociology students.

2. Interpreting Confidence Intervals If the heights of men and women from Data Set 1 in Appendix B are used to construct a 95% confidence interval for the difference between the two population means, the result is 11.61 cm $< \mu_1 - \mu_2 <$ 17.32 cm, where heights of men correspond to population 1 and heights of women correspond to population 2. Express the confidence interval with heights of women being population 1 and heights of men being population 2.

3. Interpreting Confidence Intervals What does the confidence interval in Exercise 2 suggest about the heights of men and women?

4. Hypothesis Tests and Confidence Intervals

a. In general, if you conduct a hypothesis test using the methods of Part 1 of this section, will the P-value method, the critical value method, and the confidence interval method result in the same conclusion?

b. Assume that you want to use a 0.05 significance level to test the claim that the mean height of men is greater than the mean height of women. What *confidence level* should be used if you want to test that claim using a confidence interval?

In Exercises 5–20, assume that the two samples are independent simple random samples selected from normally distributed populations, and do not assume that the population standard deviations are equal. Do the following:

a. *Test the given claim using the P-value method or critical value method.*
b. *Construct a confidence interval suitable for testing the given claim.*

5. Color and Creativity Repeat Example 2 with these changes: Use a 0.05 significance level, and test the claim that the two samples are from populations with the same mean.

6. Color and Cognition In the Chapter Problem, it was noted that researchers conducted a study to investigate the effects of color on cognitive tasks. Words were displayed on a computer screen with background colors of red and blue. Results from scores on a test of word recall are given below. Use a 0.05 significance level to test the claim that the samples are from populations with the same mean. Does the background color appear to have an effect on word recall scores? If so, which color appears to be associated with higher word memory recall scores?

$$\text{Red Background:} \quad n = 35, \bar{x} = 15.89, s = 5.90$$
$$\text{Blue Background:} \quad n = 36, \bar{x} = 12.31, s = 5.48$$

7. Magnet Treatment of Pain People spend around $5 billion annually for the purchase of magnets used to treat a wide variety of pains. Researchers conducted a study to determine whether magnets are effective in treating back pain. Pain was measured using the visual analog scale, and the results given below are among the results obtained in the study (based on data from "Bipolar Permanent Magnets for the Treatment of Chronic Lower Back Pain: A Pilot Study," by Collacott, Zimmerman, White, and Rindone, *Journal of the American Medical Association,* Vol. 283, No. 10). Use a 0.05 significance level to test the claim that those treated with magnets have a greater mean reduction in pain than those given a sham treatment (similar to a placebo). Does it appear that magnets are effective in treating back pain? Is it valid to argue that magnets might appear to be effective if the sample sizes are larger?

$$\text{Reduction in Pain Level After Magnet Treatment:} \quad n = 20, \bar{x} = 0.49, s = 0.96$$
$$\text{Reduction in Pain Level After Sham Treatment:} \quad n = 20, \bar{x} = 0.44, s = 1.4$$

8. Do Men Talk Less Than Women? The accompanying table gives results from a study of the words spoken in a day by men and women, and the original data are in Data Set 17 in Appendix B (based on "Are Women Really More Talkative Than Men?" by Mehl, et al., *Science,* Vol. 317, No. 5834). Use a 0.01 significance level to test the claim that the mean number of words spoken in a day by men is less than that for women.

9. Do Men Have a Higher Mean Body Temperature? If we use the body temperatures from 8 A.M. on Day 2 as listed in Data Set 3 in Appendix B, we get the statistics given in the accompanying table. Use these data with a 0.01 significance level to test the claim that men have a higher mean body temperature than women.

10. Do Men and Women Have the Same Mean Body Temperature? Consider the sample of body temperatures (°F) listed in the last column of Data Set 3 in Appendix B. The summary statistics are given in the accompanying table. Use a 0.01 significance level to test the claim that men and women have different mean body temperatures.

11. Skull Measurements from Different Times Researchers measured skulls from different time periods in an attempt to determine whether interbreeding of cultures occurred. Results are given below (based on data from *Ancient Races of the Thebaid,* by Thomson and Randall-Maciver, Oxford University Press). Use a 0.01 significance level to test the claim that the mean maximal skull breadth in 4000 B.C. is less than the mean in A.D. 150.

$$\text{4000 B.C. (Maximal Skull Breadth):} \quad n = 30, \bar{x} = 131.37 \text{ mm}, s = 5.13 \text{ mm}$$
$$\text{A.D. 150 (Maximal Skull Breadth):} \quad n = 30, \bar{x} = 136.17 \text{ mm}, s = 5.35 \text{ mm}$$

12. Flight Arrival Delays Data Set 15 in Appendix B lists arrival delay times (min) for randomly selected flights from New York (JFK) to Los Angeles (LAX). Statistics for times are given below. Use a 0.05 significance level to test the claim that Flight 1 and Flight 3 have the same mean arrival delay time.

$$\text{Flight 1} \quad n = 12, \bar{x} = -20.5 \text{ min}, s = 12.38401 \text{ min}$$
$$\text{Flight 3} \quad n = 12, \bar{x} = -15.08333 \text{ min}, s = 15.62317 \text{ min}$$

13. Proctored and Nonproctored Tests In a study of proctored and nonproctored tests in an online Intermediate Algebra course, researchers obtained the data for test results given below (based on "Analysis of Proctored versus Non-proctored Tests in Online Algebra Courses,"

Table for Exercise 8

Men	Women
$n_1 = 186$	$n_2 = 210$
$\bar{x}_1 = 15{,}668.5$	$\bar{x}_2 = 16{,}215.0$
$s_1 = 8632.5$	$s_2 = 7301.2$

Table for Exercise 9

Men	Women
$n_1 = 11$	$n_2 = 59$
$\bar{x}_1 = 97.69°F$	$\bar{x}_2 = 97.45°F$
$s_1 = 0.89°F$	$s_2 = 0.66°F$

Table for Exercise 10

Men	Women
$n_1 = 15$	$n_2 = 91$
$\bar{x}_1 = 98.38°F$	$\bar{x}_2 = 98.17°F$
$s_1 = 0.45°F$	$s_2 = 0.65°F$

by Flesch and Ostler, *MathAMATYC Educator,* Vol. 2, No. 1). Use a 0.01 significance level to test the claim that students taking nonproctored tests get a higher mean than those taking proctored tests.

Group 1 (Proctored): $n = 30, \bar{x} = 74.30, s = 12.87$

Group 2 (Nonproctored): $n = 32, \bar{x} = 88.62, s = 22.09$

14. Proctored and Nonproctored Tests In the same study described in the preceding exercise, the same groups of students took a nonproctored test; the results are given below. Use a 0.01 significance level to test the claim that the samples are from populations with the same mean.

Group 1 (Nonproctored): $n = 30, \bar{x} = 70.29, s = 22.09$

Group 2 (Nonproctored): $n = 32, \bar{x} = 74.26, s = 18.15$

15. BMI We know that the mean weight of men is greater than the mean weight of women, and the mean height of men is greater than the mean height of women. A person's body mass index (BMI) is computed by dividing weight (kg) by the square of height (m). Given below are the BMI statistics for random samples of males and females from Data Set 1 in Appendix B. Use a 0.05 significance level to test the claim that males and females have the same mean BMI.

Male BMI $\quad n = 40, \bar{x} = 28.44075, s = 7.394076$

Female BMI $\quad n = 40, \bar{x} = 26.6005, s = 5.359442$

16. IQ and Lead Exposure Data Set 5 in Appendix B lists full IQ scores for a random sample of subjects with low lead levels in their blood and another random sample of subjects with high lead levels in their blood. The statistics are summarized below. Use a 0.05 significance level to test the claim that the mean IQ score of people with low lead levels is higher than the mean IQ score of people with high lead levels.

Low Lead Level: $\quad n = 78, \bar{x} = 92.88462, s = 15.34451$

High Lead Level: $\quad n = 21, \bar{x} = 86.90476, s = 8.988352$

17. IQ and Lead Exposure Repeat Exercise 16 after replacing the low lead level group with the following full IQ scores from the medium lead level group.

72 90 92 71 86 79 83 114 100   93 91

98 91 46 85 82 97 91   92   77 111 78

18. Heights of Supermodels Listed below are the heights (inches) for the simple random sample of supermodels Lima, Bundchen, Ambrosio, Ebanks, Iman, Rubik, Kurkova, Kerr, Kroes, and Swanepoel. Data Set 1 in Appendix B includes the heights of a simple random sample of 40 women from the general population, and here are the statistics for those heights: $n = 40, \bar{x} = 63.7815$ in., and $s = 2.59665$ in. Use a 0.01 significance level to test the claim that the supermodels have heights with a mean that is greater than the mean height of women in the general population.

70 71 69.25 68.5 69 70 71 70 70 69.5

19. Longevity Listed below are the numbers of years that popes and British monarchs (since 1690) lived after their election or coronation (based on data from *Computer-Interactive Data Analysis,* by Lunn and McNeil, John Wiley & Sons). Treat the values as simple random samples from a larger population. Use a 0.01 significance level to test the claim that the mean longevity for popes is less than the mean for British monarchs after coronation.

Popes: $\quad$ 2 9 21 3 6 10 18 11 6 25 23 6

$\qquad$ 2 15 32 25 11 8 17 19 5 15 0 26

Kings and Queens: 17 6 13 12 13 33 59 10 7 63 9 25 36 15

20. **Radiation in Baby Teeth** Listed below are amounts of strontium-90 (in millibecquerels, or mBq, per gram of calcium) in a simple random sample of baby teeth obtained from Pennsylvania residents and New York residents born after 1979 (based on data from "An Unexpected Rise in Strontium-90 in U.S. Deciduous Teeth in the 1990s," by Mangano, et al., *Science of the Total Environment*, Vol. 317). Use a 0.05 significance level to test the claim that the mean amount of strontium-90 from Pennsylvania residents is greater than the mean amount from New York residents.

| Pennsylvania: | 155 | 142 | 149 | 130 | 151 | 163 | 151 | 142 | 156 | 133 | 138 | 161 |
| New York: | 133 | 140 | 142 | 131 | 134 | 129 | 128 | 140 | 140 | 140 | 137 | 143 |

Large Data Sets. *In Exercises 21–24, use the indicated Data Sets from Appendix B. Assume that the two samples are independent simple random samples selected from normally distributed populations. Do not assume that the population standard deviations are equal.*

21. **Weights of Quarters** Vending machines reject coins based on weight. Refer to Data Set 21 in Appendix B and use a 0.05 significance level to test the claim that the mean weight of pre-1964 quarters is equal to the mean weight of post-1964 quarters. Given the relatively small sample sizes from the large populations of millions of quarters, can we really conclude that the mean weights are different?

22. **Baseline Characteristics** Reports of results from clinical trials often include statistics about "baseline characteristics," so we can see that different groups have the same basic characteristics. Refer to Data Set 1 in Appendix B and construct a 95% confidence interval estimate of the difference between the mean age of men and the mean age of women. Based on the result, does it appear that the sample of men and the sample of women are from populations with the same mean?

23. **Weights of Pepsi** Refer to Data Set 19 in Appendix B and construct a 95% confidence interval estimate of the difference between the mean weight of the cola in cans of regular Pepsi and the mean weight of cola in cans of Diet Pepsi. Does there appear to be a difference between those two means? If there is a difference in the mean weights, identify the most likely explanation for that difference.

24. **Weights of Coke** Refer to Data Set 19 in Appendix B and use a 0.05 significance level to test the claim that because they contain the same amount of cola, the mean weight of cola in cans of regular Coke is the same as the mean weight of cola in cans of Diet Coke. If there is a difference in the mean weights, identify the most likely explanation for that difference.

9-3 Beyond the Basics

Pooling. *In Exercises 25 and 26, assume that the two samples are independent simple random samples selected from normally distributed populations. Also assume that the population standard deviations are equal ($\sigma_1 = \sigma_2$), so that the standard error of the differences between means is obtained by pooling the sample variances as described in Part 2 of this section.*

25. **Do Men Have a Higher Mean Body Temperature?** Repeat Exercise 9 with the additional assumption that $\sigma_1 = \sigma_2$. How are the results affected by this additional assumption?

26. **Do Men Talk Less Than Women?** Repeat Exercise 8 with the additional assumption that $\sigma_1 = \sigma_2$. How are the results affected by this additional assumption?

27. **No Variation in a Sample** An experiment was conducted to test the effects of alcohol. Researchers measured the breath alcohol levels for a treatment group of people who drank

ethanol and another group given a placebo. The results are given below. Use a 0.05 significance level to test the claim that the two sample groups come from populations with the same mean. The given results are based on data from "Effects of Alcohol Intoxication on Risk Taking, Strategy, and Error Rate in Visuomotor Performance," by Streufert, et al., *Journal of Applied Psychology*, Vol. 77, No. 4.

$$\text{Treatment Group:} \quad n_1 = 22, \bar{x}_1 = 0.049, s_1 = 0.015$$

$$\text{Placebo Group:} \quad n_2 = 22, \bar{x}_2 = 0.000, s_2 = 0.000$$

28. Calculating Degrees of Freedom The confidence interval given in Exercise 2 is based on df $= 39$, which is the "smaller of $n_1 - 1$ and $n_2 - 1$." Use Formula 9-1 to find the number of degrees of freedom. Using the number of degrees of freedom from Formula 9-1 results in this confidence interval: 11.65 cm $< \mu_1 - \mu_2 <$ 17.28 cm. In what sense is "df $=$ smaller of $n_1 - 1$ and $n_2 - 1$" a more conservative estimate of the number of degrees of freedom than the estimate obtained with Formula 9-1?

29. One Standard Deviation Known We sometimes know the value of one population standard deviation from an extensive history of data, but a new procedure or treatment results in sample values with an unknown standard deviation. If σ_1 is known but σ_2 is unknown, use the procedures in Part 1 of this section with these changes: Replace s_1 with the known value of σ_1 and find the number of degrees of freedom using the expression below. (See "The Two-Sample t Test with One Variance Unknown," by Maity and Sherman, *The American Statistician*, Vol. 60, No. 2.) Repeat Exercise 13 by assuming that $\sigma = 15$ for proctored tests.

$$df = \frac{\left(\dfrac{\sigma_1^2}{n_1} + \dfrac{s_2^2}{n_2}\right)^2}{\dfrac{(s_2^2/n_2)^2}{n_2 - 1}}$$

9-4   Two Dependent Samples (Matched Pairs)

Key Concept In this section we present methods for testing hypotheses and constructing confidence intervals involving the mean of the differences of the values from two populations which are dependent in the sense that the data consist of matched pairs. The pairs must be matched according to some relationship, such as before/after measurements from the same subjects or IQ scores of husbands and wives. The following two sets of sample data look similar because they both consist of two samples with five heights each, but the first case has dependent samples because there is a relationship that is a basis for matching the pairs of data. The second case consists of independent samples because there is no relationship that serves as a basis for matching the pairs of data.

Dependent Samples: Matched pairs of heights of U.S. presidents and heights of their main opponents.

Height (cm) of President	189	173	183	180	179
Height (cm) of Main Opponent	170	185	175	180	178

Independent Samples: Heights of males and females that are listed together, but there is no relationship between the males and females.

Height (cm) of Male	178.8	177.5	187.8	172.4	181.7
Height (cm) of Female	163.7	165.5	163.1	166.3	163.6

Good Experimental Design

Suppose we want to conduct an experiment to compare the effectiveness of two different types of fertilizer (one organic and one chemical). The fertilizers are to be used on 20 plots of land with equal area but varying soil quality. To make a fair comparison, we should divide each of the 20 plots in half so that one half is treated with organic fertilizer and the other half is treated with chemical fertilizer. The yields can then be matched by the plots they share, resulting in dependent data. The advantage of using matched pairs is that we reduce extraneous variation, which could occur if each plot were treated with one type of fertilizer rather than both—that is, if the samples were independent. This strategy for designing an experiment can be generalized by the following design principle:

> **When designing an experiment or planning an observational study, using dependent samples with paired data is generally better than using two independent samples.**

t **Test** There are no exact procedures for dealing with dependent samples, but the following approximation methods are commonly used.

Objectives

1. Use the differences from two dependent samples (matched pairs) to test a claim about the mean of the population of all such differences.

2. Use the differences from two dependent samples (matched pairs) to construct a confidence interval estimate of the mean of the population of all such differences.

Notation for Dependent Samples

d = individual difference between the two values in a single matched pair

μ_d = mean value of the differences d for the *population* of all matched pairs of data

$\bar{d}$ = mean value of the differences d for the paired *sample* data

s_d = standard deviation of the differences d for the paired *sample* data

n = number of *pairs* of sample data

Requirements

1. The sample data are dependent (matched pairs).

2. The samples are simple random samples.

3. Either or both of these conditions is satisfied: The number of pairs of sample data is large ($n > 30$) or the pairs of values have differences that are from a

population having a distribution that is approximately normal. (These methods are robust against departures for normality, so for small samples, the normality requirement is loose in the sense that the procedures perform well as long as there are no outliers and departures from normality are not too extreme.)

Hypothesis Test Statistic for Dependent Samples

$$t = \frac{\bar{d} - \mu_d}{\dfrac{s_d}{\sqrt{n}}} \quad \text{(For degrees of freedom use df} = n - 1.)$$

P-values: *P*-values are automatically provided by technology. If technology is not available, refer to the *t* distribution in Table A-3. Use the procedure summarized in Figure 8-4 from Section 8-2.

Critical values: Use Table A-3 (*t* distribution) with degrees of freedom found by df $= n - 1$.

Confidence Intervals for Dependent Samples

$$\bar{d} - E < \mu_d < \bar{d} + E$$

where

$$E = t_{\alpha/2}\frac{s_d}{\sqrt{n}}$$

Critical values of $t_{\alpha/2}$: Use Table A-3 (t distribution) with degrees of freedom df $= n - 1$.

If we compare the components of the preceding box to those used in Part 1 of Section 8-4 for inferences about the mean of a population (with σ not known), we can see that they are very similar. The methods of this section are actually the same as those in Section 8-4, except that here we use the differences.

Procedures for Inferences with Dependent Samples

1. Verify that the sample data consist of dependent samples (or matched pairs), and verify that the preceding requirements are satisfied.

2. Find the difference d for each pair of sample values. (*Caution:* Be sure to subtract in a consistent manner.)

3. Find the mean of the differences (denoted by $\bar{d}$), and find the standard deviation of the differences (denoted by s_d).

4. For hypothesis tests and confidence intervals, use the same t test procedures described in Part 1 of Section 8-5.

Equivalent Methods Because the hypothesis test and confidence interval use the same distribution and standard error, they are *equivalent* in the sense that they result in the same conclusions. Consequently, the null hypothesis that the mean difference equals 0 can be tested by determining whether the confidence interval includes 0.

> **Example 1** **Are Presidents Taller Than Their Main Campaign Opponents?**
> Data Set 12 in Appendix B lists heights of U.S. presidents and their main opponents in the presidential campaigns. We will use only the sample data included in Table 9-1. (We use only a small random selection of the available data so that we can better illustrate the method of hypothesis testing.) Use the sample data in Table 9-1 with a 0.05 significance level to test the claim that for the population of heights of presidents and their main opponents, the differences have a mean greater than 0 cm (so presidents tend to be taller than their opponents).

Table 9-1 Heights (cm) of Presidents and Their Main Opponents

Height (cm) of President	189	173	183	180	179
Height (cm) of Main Opponent	170	185	175	180	178
Difference d	19	−12	8	0	1

Crest and Dependent Samples

In the late 1950s, Procter & Gamble introduced Crest toothpaste as the first such product with fluoride. To test the effectiveness of Crest in reducing cavities, researchers conducted experiments with several sets of twins. One of the twins in each set was given Crest with fluoride, while the other twin continued to use ordinary toothpaste without fluoride. It was believed that each pair of twins would have similar eating, brushing, and genetic characteristics. Results showed that the twins who used Crest had significantly fewer cavities than those who did not. This use of twins as dependent samples allowed the researchers to control many of the different variables affecting cavities.

Solution

Requirement check We address the three requirements listed earlier in this section. (1) The samples are dependent because the values are paired. Each pair consists of the height of the winning president and the height of the main opponent in the same election. (2) The pairs of data are randomly selected from the data available as of this writing. We will consider the data to be a simple random sample. (3) The number of pairs of data in Table 9-1 is $n = 5$, which is not large, so we should check for normality of the differences and we should check for outliers. Inspection of the differences shows that there are no outliers. A histogram isn't too helpful with only five data values, but the accompanying STATDISK display shows the normal quantile plot. Because the points approximate a straight-line pattern with no other pattern, we conclude that the differences satisfy the loose requirement of being from a normally distributed population. All requirements are satisfied. ✓

STATDISK

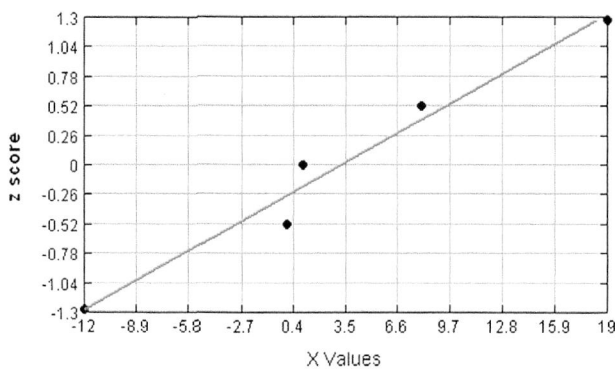

If we use μ_d (where the subscript d denotes "difference") to denote the mean of the differences in height, the claim is that $\mu_d > 0$ cm.

Technology Computer programs and calculators usually provide a P-value, so the P-value method is typically used. See the accompanying SPSS results showing the test statistic of $t = 0.628$. SPSS provides the two-tailed P-value of 0.564, so we halve that value for this right-tailed test to get a P-value of 0.282. Because the P-value of 0.282 is greater than the significance level of 0.05, we fail to reject the null hypothesis and we conclude that there is not sufficient evidence to support the claim that presidents tend to be taller than their opponents.

SPSS

		Paired Differences							
					90% Confidence Interval of the Difference				
		Mean	Std. Deviation	Std. Error Mean	Lower	Upper	t	df	Sig. (2-tailed)
Pair 1	President - Opponent	3.20000	11.38859	5.09313	-7.65778	14.05778	.628	4	.564

If technology is not available, the P-value method, the critical value method, or a confidence interval are all described in Section 8-2. We can test the claim using the critical value method as follows. We will follow the same basic method of hypothesis testing that was introduced in Chapter 8, but we use the test statistic for dependent samples that was given earlier in this section.

Step 1: The claim is that $\mu_d > 0$ cm. (That is, the mean difference is greater than 0 cm.)

Step 2: If the original claim is not true, we have $\mu_d \leq 0$ cm.

Step 3: The null hypothesis must express equality and the alternative hypothesis cannot include equality, so we have

$$H_0: \mu_d = 0 \text{ cm} \quad H_1: \mu_d > 0 \text{ cm (original claim)}$$

Step 4: The significance level is $\alpha = 0.05$.

Step 5: We use the Student t distribution.

Step 6: Before finding the value of the test statistic, we must first find the values of $\overline{d}$ and s_d. Refer to Table 9-1 and use the differences of 19, -12, 8, 0, and 1 to find these sample statistics: $\overline{d} = 3.2$ cm and $s_d = 11.4$ cm. Using these sample statistics and the assumption of the hypothesis test that $\mu_d = 0$ cm, we can now find the value of the test statistic.

$$t = \frac{\overline{d} - \mu_d}{\frac{s_d}{\sqrt{n}}} = \frac{3.2 - 0}{\frac{11.4}{\sqrt{5}}} = 0.628$$

Because we are using a t distribution, we refer to Table A-3 to find the critical value of $t = 2.132$ as follows: Use the column for 0.05 (Area in One Tail), and use the row with degrees of freedom of $n - 1 = 4$. Figure 9-4 shows the test statistic, critical value, and critical region.

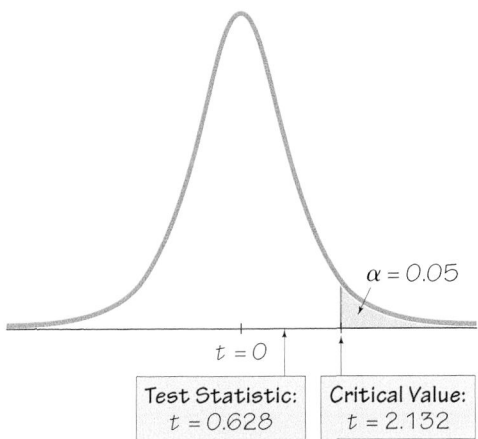

Figure 9-4 **Hypothesis Test with Dependent Samples**

Step 7: Because the test statistic does not fall in the critical region, we fail to reject the null hypothesis.

Interpretation

We conclude that there is not sufficient evidence to support $\mu_d > 0$ cm. That is, there is not sufficient evidence to support the claim that for the population of heights of presidents and their main opponents, the differences have a mean greater than 0 cm. That is, presidents do not appear to be taller than their opponents.

Example 2   Confidence Interval for Estimating the Mean of the Height Differences

Using the same sample data in Table 9-1, construct a 90% confidence interval estimate of μ_d, which is the mean of the differences in height. By using a confidence level of 90%, we get a result that could be used for the hypothesis test in Example 1.

Gender Gap in Drug Testing

A study of the relationship between heart attacks and doses of aspirin involved 22,000 male physicians. This study, like many others, excluded women. The General Accounting Office recently criticized the National Institutes of Health for not including both sexes in many studies because results of medical tests on males do not necessarily apply to females. For example, women's hearts are different from men's in many important ways. When forming conclusions based on sample results, we should be wary of an inference that extends to a population larger than the one from which the sample was drawn.

(Because the hypothesis test is one-tailed with a significance level of $\alpha = 0.05$, the confidence level should be 90%. See Table 8-1.)

Solution

Requirement check The solution for Example 1 includes verification that the requirements are satisfied. ✅

The preceding SPSS display shows the lower and upper confidence interval limits for a 90% confidence interval, but we will show how those values are obtained. We use the values of $\bar{d} = 3.2$ cm, $s_d = 11.4$ cm, and $t_{\alpha/2} = 2.132$ (found from Table A-3 with $n - 1 = 4$ degrees of freedom and an area of 0.10 in two tails). We first find the value of the margin of error E.

$$E = t_{\alpha/2}\frac{s_d}{\sqrt{n}} = 2.132 \cdot \frac{11.4}{\sqrt{5}} = 10.8694$$

We now find the confidence interval.

$$\bar{d} - E < \mu_d < \bar{d} + E$$
$$3.2 - 10.8694 < \mu_d < 3.2 + 10.8694$$
$$-7.7 \text{ cm} < \mu_d < 14.1 \text{ cm}$$

Interpretation

We have 90% confidence that the limits of -7.7 cm and 14.1 cm contain the true value of the mean of the differences in height (president's height − opponent's height). In the long run, 90% of such samples will lead to confidence interval limits that actually do contain the true population mean of the differences. See that the confidence interval includes the value of 0 cm, so it is very possible that the mean of the differences is equal to 0 cm, indicating that there is no significant difference between heights of presidents and heights of their opponents.

using TECHNOLOGY

General Comment: If it appears that your technology does not have a procedure designed specifically for dependent samples, find the differences d and then use technology for conducting a t test of a claim about one population mean, or use the differences to construct a confidence interval estimate of the mean of one population.

STATDISK First enter the matched data in columns of the STATDISK Data Window, then select **Analysis** from the main menu. Select either **Hypothesis Testing** or **Confidence Intervals,** then select **Mean-Matched Pairs.** Complete the entries and make any selections in the dialog box, then click on **Evaluate.**

MINITAB Enter the paired sample data in columns C1 and C2. Click on **Stat,** select **Basic Statistics,** then select **Paired t.** Enter C1 for the first sample, enter C2 for the second sample, then click on the **Options** box so that you can change the confidence level or the form of the alternative hypothesis or to use a value of μ_d different from zero.

EXCEL Enter the paired sample data in columns A and B and proceed to use either XLSTAT or Excel's Data Analysis add-in.

XLSTAT for Hypothesis Test: Click on **XLSTAT** at the top. Click on **Parametric tests,** then select **Two sample t test and z test.** In the dialog box that appears, enter the range of values for the first sample (such as A1:A13) and enter the range of values for the second sample. For "Data format," select the option of **Paired Samples.** For the "Column labels" box, include a checkmark only if the first row of the sample data consists of names or labels. Put a checkmark next to "Student's t test" (use z test if σ_1 and σ_2 are known). Click on the **Options** tab and select the type of test. For a two-tailed test, select the case including the symbol $\neq$, for a left-tailed test, select the case including $<$; and for a right-tailed test, select the case including $>$. Enter a value in the "Significance level (%)" box. For example, enter 5 for a 0.05 significance level. Click **OK** to get results that include the test statistic and *P*-value.

XLSTAT for Confidence Interval: Click on **XLSTAT** at the top. Click on **Parametric tests,** then select **Two sample t test and z test.** In the dialog box that appears, enter the range of values for the first sample (such as A1:A13) and enter the range of values for the second sample. For "Data format," select the option of **Paired samples.** For the "Column labels" box, include a checkmark only if the first row of the sample data consists of names or labels. Put a checkmark next to "Student's t test." Click on the **Options** tab. For the alternative hypothesis, select the format of a two-tailed test. Enter a value in the "Significance level (%)" box. For example, enter 5 for a 95% confidence interval. Click **OK** to get results that include the confidence interval.

Data Analysis Add-in: If using Excel 2013, 2010, or 2007, click on **Data,** then **Data Analysis;** if using Excel 2003, click on **Tools,** found on the main menu bar, then select **Data Analysis,** and proceed to select **t-test Paired Two Sample for Means.** In the dialog box, enter the range of values for each of the two samples, enter the assumed value of the population mean difference (typically 0), and enter the significance level. The displayed

results will include the test statistic, the *P*-values for a one-tailed test and a two-tailed test, and the critical values for a one-tailed test and a two-tailed test.

TI-83/84 PLUS *Caution:* Do not use the menu item **2-SampTTest** because it applies to *independent* samples. Instead, enter the data for the first variable in list L1, enter the data for the second variable in list L2, then clear the screen and enter **L1 − L2** **STO** **L3** so that list L3 will contain the individual differences *d.* Now press **STAT**, then select **TESTS,** and choose the option of **T-Test** (for a hypothesis test) or **TInterval** (for a confidence interval). Use the input option of **Data.** For the list, enter L3. If using **T-Test,** also enter the assumed value of the population mean difference (typically 0) for μ_0. Press **ENTER** when finished.

STATCRUNCH Click on **Open StatCrunch.** Enter the sample data in columns, or open a data set. Click on **Stat,** then select **T statistics.** Select **Paired.** Click on **Next,** then select **Hypothesis Test** or **Confidence Interval.** Make the required entries. Click on **Calculate.**

9-4 Basic Skills and Concepts

Statistical Literacy and Critical Thinking

1. True Statements? For the methods of this section, which of the following statements are true?

a. The requirement of a simple random sample is satisfied if we have matched pairs of voluntary response data.

b. If we have more than 10 matched pairs of sample data, we can consider the sample to be large and there is no need to check for normality.

c. If we have five matched pairs of sample data, there is a loose requirement that the five differences appear to be from a normally distributed population.

d. The methods of this section apply if we have 50 heights of women from Texas and 50 heights of women from Utah.

e. If we want to use a confidence interval to test the claim that $\mu_d > 0$ with a 0.05 significance level, the confidence interval should have a confidence level of 90%.

2. Notation Listed below are combined city–highway fuel consumption ratings (in mi/gal) for five different cars measured under both the old rating system and a new rating system introduced in 2008 (based on data from *USA Today*). The new ratings were implemented in response to complaints that the old ratings were too high. Find the values of $\overline{d}$ and s_d. In general, what does μ_d represent?

| Old Rating (mi/gal) | 16 | 18 | 27 | 17 | 33 |
| New Rating (mi/gal) | 15 | 16 | 24 | 15 | 29 |

3. Units of Measure If the values listed in Exercise 2 are changed so that they are expressed in kilometers per liter (km/L) instead of mi/gal, how is a test statistic affected? How are the confidence interval limits affected?

TI-83/84 PLUS

```
T-Test
 μ>0
 t=.035713579
 P=.4858629522
 x̄=.0588235
 Sx=9.604106
 n=34
```

TI-83/84 PLUS

```
TInterval
 (-2.729,2.8463)
 x̄=.0588235
 Sx=9.604106
 n=34
```

4. Confidence Intervals If we use the sample data in Exercise 2, we get this 95% confidence interval estimate: 1.0 mi/gal $< \mu_d <$ 3.8 mi/gal. Treating the same data as *independent samples* yields -7.8 mi/gal $< \mu_1 - \mu_2 <$ 12.6 mi/gal for a 95% confidence level. What is the difference between interpretations of these two confidence intervals?

5. POTUS Hypothesis Test Example 1 in this section used only five pairs of data from Data Set 12 in Appendix B for a 95% confidence level. Repeat Example 1 using all of the cases with heights for both the president and the main opponent. Results are shown in the accompanying TI-83/84 Plus calculator display.

6. POTUS Confidence Interval Example 2 in this section used only five pairs of data from Data Set 12 in Appendix B. Repeat Example 2 using all of the cases with heights for both the president and the main opponent. The accompanying TI-83/84 Plus calculator display shows results for a 90% confidence interval constructed from the list of differences in height. In this display, $\bar{x}$ is used instead of $\bar{d}$, and Sx is used instead of s_d. What feature of the confidence interval causes us to reach the same conclusion as in Exercise 4?

Calculations with Paired Sample Data. *In Exercises 7 and 8, assume that you want to use a 0.05 significance level to test the claim that paired sample data come from a population for which the mean difference is $\mu_d = 0$. Find (a) $\bar{d}$, (b) s_d, (c) the t test statistic, and (d) the critical values.*

7. Oscars Listed below are ages of actresses and actors at the time that they won Oscars for the categories of Best Actress and Best Actor. The data are from Data Set 11 in Appendix B.

Actress	22	37	28	63	32
Actor	44	41	62	52	41

8. Body Temperatures Listed below are body temperatures of four subjects measured at two different times in a day (from Data Set 3 in Appendix B).

Body Temperature (°F) at 8 A.M. on Day 1	98	97.0	98.6	97.4
Body Temperature (°F) at 12 A.M. on Day 1	98	97.6	98.8	98.0

In Exercises 9–20, assume that the paired sample data are simple random samples and that the differences have a distribution that is approximately normal.

9. Oscars Use the sample data from Exercise 7 to test for a difference between the ages of actresses and actors when they win Oscars. Use a significance level of $\alpha = 0.05$.

10. Body Temperatures Use the sample data from Exercise 8 to test the claim that there is no difference between body temperatures measured at 8 A.M. and at 12 A.M. Use a 0.05 significance level.

11. Flight Operations The table below lists the times (min) required for randomly selected flights to taxi out for takeoff and the corresponding times (min) required to taxi in after landing. (See Data Set 15 in Appendix B.) All flights are Flight 1 of American Airlines from New York (JFK) to Los Angeles (LAX). Construct a 90% confidence interval estimate of the difference between taxi-out times and taxi-in times. What does the confidence interval suggest about the claim of the flight operations manager that for flight delays, more of the blame is attributable to taxi-out times at JFK than taxi-in times at LAX?

Taxi-Out Time	30	19	12	19	18	22	37	13	14	15	31	15
Taxi-In Time	12	13	8	21	17	11	12	12	15	26	9	11

12. Brain Volumes of Twins Listed below are brain volumes (cm³) of twins listed in Data Set 6 of Appendix B. Construct a 99% confidence interval estimate of the mean of the differences between volumes for the first-born and the second-born twins. What does the confidence interval suggest?

| First Born | 1005 | 1035 | 1281 | 1051 | 1034 | 1079 | 1104 | 1439 | 1029 | 1160 |
| Second Born | 963 | 1027 | 1272 | 1079 | 1070 | 1173 | 1067 | 1347 | 1100 | 1204 |

13. Speaking Couples Listed below are the numbers of words spoken in a day by each member of six different couples. The data are randomly selected from the first two columns in Data Set 17 from Appendix B. Use a 0.05 significance level to test the claim that among couples, males speak more words in a day than females.

| Male | 5638 | 21,319 | 17,572 | 26,429 | 46,978 | 25,835 |
| Female | 5198 | 11,661 | 19,624 | 13,397 | 31,553 | 18,667 |

14. Is Blood Pressure the Same for Both Arms? Listed below are systolic blood pressure measurements (mm Hg) taken from the right and left arms of the same woman (based on data from "Consistency of Blood Pressure Differences Between the Left and Right Arms," by Eguchi, et al., *Archives of Internal Medicine,* Vol. 167). Use a 0.01 significance level to test for a difference between the measurements from the two arms. What do you conclude?

| Right arm | 102 | 101 | 94 | 79 | 79 |
| Left arm | 175 | 169 | 182 | 146 | 144 |

15. Is Friday the 13th Unlucky? Researchers collected data on the numbers of hospital admissions resulting from motor vehicle crashes, and results are given below for Fridays on the 6th of a month and Fridays on the following 13th of the same month (based on data from "Is Friday the 13th Bad for Your Health?" by Scanlon, et al., *British Medical Journal,* Vol. 307, as listed in the *Data and Story Line* online resource of data sets). Construct a 95% confidence interval estimate of the mean of the population of differences between hospital admissions on days that are Friday the 6th of a month and days that are Friday the 13th of a month. Use the confidence interval to test the claim that when the 13th day of a month falls on a Friday, the numbers of hospital admissions from motor vehicle crashes are not affected.

| Friday the 6th | 9 | 6 | 11 | 11 | 3 | 5 |
| Friday the 13th | 13 | 12 | 14 | 10 | 4 | 12 |

16. Self-Reported and Measured Male Heights As part of the National Health and Nutrition Examination Survey, the Department of Health and Human Services obtained self-reported heights and measured heights for males aged 12–16. All measurement are in inches. Listed below are sample results. Construct a 99% confidence interval estimate of the mean difference between reported heights and measured heights. Interpret the resulting confidence interval, and comment on the implications of whether the confidence interval limits contain 0.

| Reported Height | 68 | 71 | 63 | 70 | 71 | 60 | 65 | 64 | 54 | 63 | 66 | 72 |
| Measured Height | 67.9 | 69.9 | 64.9 | 68.3 | 70.3 | 60.6 | 64.5 | 67.0 | 55.6 | 74.2 | 65.0 | 70.8 |

17. Harry Potter The Harry Potter books and movies grossed huge sums of money. The table below lists the amounts grossed (in millions of dollars) during the first few days of release of the movies *Harry Potter and the Half-Blood Prince* and *Harry Potter and the Order of the Phoenix.* Use a 0.05 significance level to test the claim that *Harry Potter and the Half-Blood Prince* did better at the box office. Apart from this hypothesis test, what is a better way to judge the validity of the claim?

Day of Release	1	2	3	4	5	6	7	8	9	10
Phoenix	44.2	18.4	25.8	28.3	23.0	10.4	9.1	8.4	7.6	10.2
Prince	58.2	22.0	26.8	29.2	21.8	9.9	9.5	7.5	6.9	9.3

18. Before/After Treatment Results Captopril is a drug designed to lower systolic blood pressure. When subjects were treated with this drug, their systolic blood pressure readings (in mm Hg) were measured before and after the drug was taken. Results are given in the accompanying table (based on data from "Essential Hypertension: Effect of an Oral Inhibitor of Angiotensin-Converting Enzyme," by MacGregor et al., *British Medical Journal,* Vol. 2). Using a 0.01 significance level, is there sufficient evidence to support the claim that Captopril is effective in lowering systolic blood pressure?

Subject	A	B	C	D	E	F	G	H	I	J	K	L
Before	200	174	198	170	179	182	193	209	185	155	169	210
After	191	170	177	167	159	151	176	183	159	145	146	177

19. Hypnotism for Reducing Pain A study was conducted to investigate the effectiveness of hypnotism in reducing pain. Results for randomly selected subjects are given in the accompanying table (based on "An Analysis of Factors That Contribute to the Efficacy of Hypnotic Analgesia," by Price and Barber, *Journal of Abnormal Psychology,* Vol. 96, No. 1). The values are before and after hypnosis; the measurements are in centimeters on a pain scale. Construct a 95% confidence interval for the mean of the "before/after" differences. Does hypnotism appear to be effective in reducing pain?

Subject	A	B	C	D	E	F	G	H
Before	6.6	6.5	9.0	10.3	11.3	8.1	6.3	11.6
After	6.8	2.4	7.4	8.5	8.1	6.1	3.4	2.0

20. Forecast and Actual Temperatures The author recorded actual temperatures (°F) along with the temperatures (°F) that were predicted five days earlier. Results are listed below. Construct a 99% confidence interval estimate of the mean of the population of all "actual/forecast" differences. What does the result suggest about the accuracy of the forecast temperatures?

Date	9/1	9/5	9/12	9/15	9/22	9/23	9/27	9/30
Actual High	80	73	78	73	82	81	74	62
High Forecast Five Days Earlier	80	79	79	78	73	79	70	69

Large Data Sets. *In Exercises 21–24, use the indicated Data Sets from Appendix B. Assume that the paired sample data are simple random samples and the differences have a distribution that is approximately normal.*

21. Oscars Use the sample data from Data Set 11 in Appendix B to test for a difference between the ages of actresses and actors when they win Oscars. Use a significance level of $\alpha = 0.05$.

22. Body Temperatures Use the sample data from 8 A.M. and 12 A.M. on Day 1 as listed in Data Set 3 in Appendix B. Test the claim that there is no difference between body temperatures measured at 8 A.M. and at 12 A.M. Use a 0.05 significance level.

23. Speaking Couples Use the data in the first two columns of Data Set 17 in Appendix B. Those columns list the numbers of words spoken in a day by each member of 56 different couples. Use a 0.05 significance level.

24. Tobacco and Alcohol in Children's Movies Refer to Data Set 8 in Appendix B and use the times (seconds) that animated Disney movies showed the use of tobacco and the times that they showed the use of alcohol. Use a 0.05 significance level to test the claim that the mean of the differences is greater than 0 sec so that more time is devoted to showing tobacco than alcohol. For animated children's movies, how much time should be spent showing the use of tobacco and alcohol?

9-4 Beyond the Basics

25. Freshman 15 The "Freshman 15" refers to the urban legend that is the common belief that students gain an average of 15 lb (or 6.8 kg) during their freshman year. Refer to Data Set 4 in Appendix B and consider the sample values in this format: (April weight) − (September weight). In this format, positive differences represent *gains* in weight, and negative differences represent *losses* of weight. If we use μ_d to denote the mean of the "April − September" differences in weights of college students during their freshman year, the "Freshman 15" is the claim that $\mu_d = 15$ lb or $\mu_d = 6.8$ kg. Test the claim that $\mu_d = 6.8$ kg using a 0.05 significance level with the 67 subjects from Data Set 4 in Appendix B. What do these results suggest about the "Freshman 15"?

9-5 Two Variances or Standard Deviations

Key Concept In this section we present the F test for testing claims made about two population variances (or standard deviations). The F test (named for statistician Sir Ronald Fisher) uses the F distribution introduced in this section. The F test requires that both populations have normal distributions. This test is *very* sensitive to departures from normal distributions, so the normality requirement is quite strict. Part 1 describes the F test procedure for conducting a hypothesis test, and Part 2 gives a brief description of two alternative methods for comparing variation in two samples.

Part 1: *F* Test as a Hypothesis Test with Two Variances or Standard Deviations

The following box includes key elements of a hypothesis test of a claim about two population variances or two population standard deviations. The procedure is based on use of the two sample variances, but the same procedure is used for claims made about two population variances or two population standard deviations.

The actual F test could be two-tailed, left-tailed, or right-tailed, but we can make computations much easier by stipulating that the larger of the two sample variances is denoted by s_1^2. It follows that the smaller sample variance is denoted as s_2^2. This stipulation of denoting the larger sample variance by s_1^2 allows us to avoid the somewhat messy problem of finding a critical value of F for the left tail.

Objective

Conduct a hypothesis test of a claim about two population variances or standard deviations. (Any claim made about two population standard deviations can be restated with an equivalent claim about two population variances, so the same procedure is used for two population standard deviations or two population variances.)

continued

Notation for Hypothesis Tests with Two Variances or Standard Deviations

$s_1^2 = $ *larger* of the two sample variances

$n_1 = $ size of the sample with the *larger* variance

$\sigma_1^2 = $ variance of the population from which the sample with the *larger* variance was drawn

The symbols s_2^2, n_2, and σ_2^2 are used for the other sample and population.

Requirements

1. The two populations are *independent*.

2. The two samples are simple random samples.

3. Each of the two populations must be *normally distributed*, regardless of their sample sizes. This F test is *not robust* against departures from normality, so it performs poorly if one or both of the populations has a distribution that is not normal. The requirement of normal distributions is quite strict for this F test.

Explore the Data! Because the F test requirement of normal distributions is quite strict, be sure to examine the distributions of the two samples using histograms and normal quantile plots, and confirm that there are no outliers. (See "Assessing Normality" in Section 6-6.)

Test Statistic for Hypothesis Tests with Two Variances

$F = \dfrac{s_1^2}{s_2^2}$ (where s_1^2 is the *larger* of the two sample variances)

P-values: *P*-values are automatically provided by technology. If technology is not available, use the computed value of the F test statistic with Table A-5 to find a range for the *P*-value.

Critical values: Use Table A-5 to find critical F values that are determined by the following:

1. The significance level α (Table A-5 includes critical values for $\alpha = 0.025$ and $\alpha = 0.05$.)

2. **Numerator degrees of freedom $= n_1 - 1$** (determines *column* of Table A-5)

3. **Denominator degrees of freedom $= n_2 - 1$** (determines *row* of Table A-5) For significance level

$\alpha = 0.05$, refer to Table A-5 and use the right-tail area of 0.025 or 0.05 depending on the type of test, as shown below:

- *Two-tailed test:* Use Table A-5 with 0.025 in the right tail. (The significance level of 0.05 is divided between the two tails, so the area in the right tail is 0.025.)
- *One-tailed test:* Use Table A-5 with $\alpha = 0.05$ in the right tail.

Find the critical F value for the right tail: Because we are stipulating that the larger sample variance is s_1^2, all one-tailed tests will be right-tailed and all two-tailed tests will require that we find only the critical value located to the right. (We have no need to find the critical value at the left tail, which can be tricky. See Exercise 21.)

F Distribution

For two normally distributed populations with equal variances ($\sigma_1^2 = \sigma_2^2$), the sampling distribution of the test statistic $F = s_1^2/s_2^2$ is the **F distribution** shown in Figure 9-5 (provided that we have not yet imposed the stipulation that the larger sample variance is s_1^2). If you repeat the process of selecting samples from two normally distributed populations with equal variances, the distribution of the ratio s_1^2/s_2^2 is the F distribution.

See Figure 9-5 and note these properties of the F distribution:

- The F distribution is not symmetric.
- Values of the F distribution cannot be negative.
- The exact shape of the F distribution depends on the two different degrees of freedom.

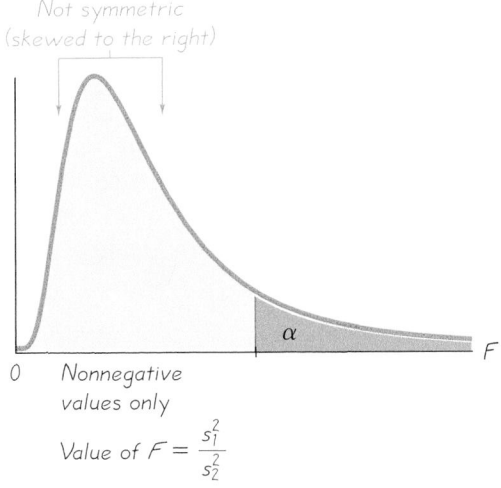

Figure 9-5 *F* Distribution

There is a different *F* distribution for each different pair of degrees of freedom for the numerator and denominator.

Interpreting the *F* Test Statistic

If the two populations really do have equal variances, then the ratio s_1^2/s_2^2 tends to be close to 1 because s_1^2 and s_2^2 tend to be close in value. But if the two populations have radically different variances, s_1^2 and s_2^2 tend to be very different numbers. Because we are stipulating that s_1^2 is the larger sample variance, the ratio s_1^2/s_2^2 will be a large number whenever s_1^2 and s_2^2 are far apart in value. Consequently, a value of *F* near 1 will be evidence suggesting that $\sigma_1^2 = \sigma_2^2$, but a large value of *F* will be evidence against the conclusion of equality of the population variances.

Large **values of *F* are evidence against $\sigma_1^2 = \sigma_2^2$.**

 Example 1 Accurate Red and Creative Blue

In the Chapter Problem, we noted that researchers from the University of British Columbia conducted trials to investigate the effects of color on creativity. Subjects with a red background were asked to think of creative uses for a brick, while other subjects were given the same task with a blue background. Responses were scored by a panel of judges and results from scores of creativity are given below. In Example 2 of Section 9-3 we tested the researchers' claim that "blue enhances performance on a creative task," and we found that there is sufficient evidence to support the claim that subjects with a blue background get higher scores than those with a red background. That hypothesis test involved two independent population means. Let's use the same data to test the claim that those tested with a red background have creativity scores with a standard deviation equal to the standard deviation for those tested with a blue background. Use a 0.05 significance level.

Creativity Scores	
Red Background:	$n = 35, \bar{x} = 3.39, s = 0.97$
Blue Background:	$n = 36, \bar{x} = 3.97, s = 0.63$

Solution

Requirement check (1) The two populations are independent of each other. The two samples are not matched in any way. (2) Given that the design for the study was carefully planned, we assume that the two samples can be treated as simple random samples. (3) The journal article describing the study did not discuss the distributions of the data, so we proceed by assuming that the samples are from normally distributed populations, but we note that the validity of the results depends on that assumption.

TI-83/84 PLUS

```
2-SampFTest.
 σ1≠σ2
 F=2.370622323
 p=.0129276814
 Sx1=.97
 Sx2=.63
↓n1=35
```

Technology Computer programs and calculators usually provide a P-value, so the P-value method is used. See the accompanying TI-83/84 Plus calculator results showing the test statistic of $F = 2.3706$ (rounded), and the P-value of 0.0129 (rounded). Because the P-value of 0.0129 is less than the significance level of $\alpha = 0.05$, we reject the null hypothesis. See the interpretation at the end of this example.

Instead of using the sample standard deviations to test the claim of equal population standard deviations, we use the sample variances to test the claim of equal population variances, but we can state conclusions in terms of standard deviations. Because we stipulate in this section that the larger variance is denoted by s_1^2, we let $s_1^2 = 0.97^2$ and $s_2^2 = 0.63^2$. We now proceed to use the critical value method of testing hypotheses as outlined in Figure 8-2 from Section 8-2.

Step 1: The claim of equal standard deviations is equivalent to a claim of equal variances, which we express symbolically as $\sigma_1^2 = \sigma_2^2$.

Step 2: If the original claim is false, then $\sigma_1^2 \neq \sigma_2^2$.

Step 3: Because the null hypothesis is the statement of equality and because the alternative hypothesis cannot contain equality, we have

$$H_0: \sigma_1^2 = \sigma_2^2 \text{ (original claim)} \quad H_1: \sigma_1^2 \neq \sigma_2^2$$

Step 4: The significance level is $\alpha = 0.05$.

Step 5: Because this test involves two population variances, we use the F distribution.

Step 6: The test statistic is

$$F = \frac{s_1^2}{s_2^2} = \frac{0.97^2}{0.63^2} = 2.3706$$

For the critical values in this two-tailed test, refer to Table A-5 for the area of 0.025 in the right tail. Because we stipulate that the larger variance is placed in the numerator of the F test statistic, we need to find only the right-tailed critical value. The number of degrees of freedom for the numerator is $n_1 - 1 = 34$, and for the denominator we have df $= n_2 - 1 = 35$. From Table A-5 we see that the critical value of F is between 1.8752 and 2.0739. Technology can be used to find that the critical F value is 1.9678.

Step 7: Figure 9-6 shows that the test statistic $F = 2.3706$ does fall within the critical region, so we reject the null hypothesis of equal variances. There is sufficient evidence to warrant rejection of the claim of equal standard deviations.

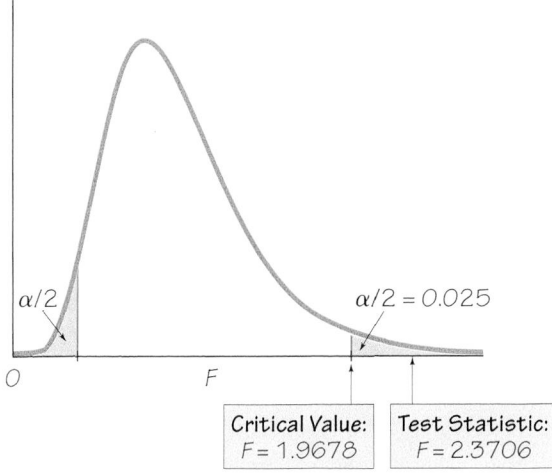

Figure 9-6 **_F_ Test of Equal Standard Deviations**

Interpretation

There is sufficient evidence to warrant rejection of the claim that the two standard deviations are equal. The variation among creativity scores for those with a red background appears to be different from the variation among creativity scores for those with a blue background.

From Example 1 we can see that technology makes the _P_-value method very easy. Without technology, we must use Table A-5 to find a critical value, but the limitations of that table make this approach more difficult.

Part 2: Alternative Methods

Part 1 of this section presents the _F_ test for testing claims made about the standard deviations (or variances) of two independent populations. Because that test is so sensitive to departures from normality, we now briefly describe two alternative methods that are not so sensitive to departures from normality.

Count Five

The _count five_ method is a relatively simple alternative to the _F_ test, and it does not require normally distributed populations. (See "A Quick, Compact, Two-Sample Dispersion Test: Count Five," by McGrath and Yeh, _American Statistician_, Vol. 59, No. 1.) If the two sample sizes are equal, and if one sample has at least five of the largest mean absolute deviations (MAD), then we conclude that its population has a larger variance. See Exercise 19 for the specific procedure.

Levene-Brown-Forsythe Test

The _Levene-Brown-Forsythe test_ (or modified Levene's test) is another alternative to the _F_ test, and it is much more robust against departures from normality. This test begins with a transformation of each set of sample values. Within the first sample, replace each _x_ value with $|x - \text{median}|$, and do the same for the second sample. Using the transformed values, conduct a _t_ test of equality of means for independent samples, as described in Part 1 of Section 9-3. Because the transformed values are now deviations, the t test for equality of means is actually a test comparing variation in the two samples. See Exercise 20.

In addition to the count five test and the Levene-Brown-Forsythe test, there are other alternatives to the F test, as well as adjustments that improve the performance of the F test. See "Fixing the F Test for Equal Variances," by Shoemaker, *American Statistician,* Vol. 57, No. 2.

using TECHNOLOGY

STATDISK   Select **Analysis** from the main menu, then select either **Hypothesis Testing** or **Confidence Intervals,** then **StDev-Two Samples.** Enter the required items in the dialog box and click on the **Evaluate** button.

MINITAB   Either obtain the summary statistics for both samples or enter the individual sample values in two columns. Select **Stat,** then **Basic Statistics,** then **2 Variances.**

In **Minitab 15** or earlier, a dialog box will appear. Either select the option of "Samples in different columns" and enter the column names or select "Summarized data" and enter the summary statistics. Click on the **Options** button and enter the confidence level. (Enter 0.95 for a hypothesis test with a 0.05 significance level.) Click **OK,** then click **OK** in the main dialog box. Minitab will return a P-value for a two-tailed test, so halve it for a one-tailed test.

In **Minitab 16,** a dialog box will appear: Either select the option of "Samples in different columns" and enter the column names or select "Sample standard deviations" or "Sample variances" and enter the summary statistics. Click on the **Options** button and enter the confidence level (enter 0.95 for a hypothesis test with a 0.05 significance level) and select the format of the alternative hypothesis. Click **OK,** then click **OK** in the main dialog box. Minitab will provide the P-value.

In **Minitab 16** you can also click on **Assistant,** then select **Hypothesis Tests,** then select the case for **2-Sample Standard Deviation.** Fill in the dialog box, then click **OK** to get three windows of results that include the P-value and much other helpful information.

EXCEL   Excel requires entry of the original lists of sample data, so enter the data from the first sample in the first column A, then enter the values of the second sample in column B. Proceed to use either XLSTAT or Excel's Data Analysis add-in.

XLSTAT: Click on **XLSTAT** at the top. Click on **Parametric tests,** then select **Two sample comparison of variances.** In the

dialog box that appears, enter the range of values for the first sample (such as A1:A13) and enter the range of values for the second sample. For "Data format," select the option of **One column per sample.** For the "Column labels" box, include a checkmark only if the first row of the sample data consists of names or labels. Put a checkmark next to **Fisher's F test.** Click on the **Options** tab and select the type of test. For a two-tailed test, select the case including the symbol $\neq$; for a left-tailed test, select the case including $<$; and for a right-tailed test, select the case including $>$. Enter a value in the "Significance level (%)" box. For example, enter 5 for a 0.05 significance level. Click **OK** to get results that include the test statistic and P-value.

Data Analysis Add-in: If using Excel 2013, 2010, or 2007, click on **Data,** then **Data Analysis;** if using Excel 2003, click on **Tools** and select **Data Analysis.** Now select **F-Test Two-Sample for Variances.** In the dialog box, enter the range of values for the first sample (such as A1:A40) and the range of values for the second sample. Enter the value of the significance level in the "Alpha" box. Excel will provide the F test statistic, the P-value for the one-tailed case, and the critical F value for the one-tailed case. For a two-tailed test, make two adjustments: (1) Enter the value that is half of the significance level, and (2) double the P-value given by Excel.

TI-83/84 PLUS   Press the **STAT** key, then select **TESTS,** then **2-SampFTEST.** For the Inpt (input) line, you can select **Data** if the data are entered in two lists, or you can select **Stats** if you know the summary statistics.

STATCRUNCH   Click on **Open StatCrunch.** Click on **Stat,** then select **Variance.** Select **Two sample,** then select **with data** (for a list of sample data) or **with summary** (for using known summary statistics). Click on **Next,** then select **Hypothesis Test** or **Confidence Interval.** Make the required entries. Click on **Calculate.**

9-5 Basic Skills and Concepts

Statistical Literacy and Critical Thinking

1. *F* Test Statistic

a. If s_1^2 represents the larger of two sample variances, can the F test statistic ever be less than 1?

b. Can the F test statistic ever be a negative number?

c. If testing the claim that $\sigma_1^2 \neq \sigma_2^2$, what do we know about the two samples if the test statistic is $F = 1$?

2. F Test If using Data Set 1 in Appendix B for a test of the claim that heights of men and heights of women have different variances, we find that $s = 6.60$ cm for women and $s = 6.02$ for men.

a. Find the values of s_1^2 and s_2^2 and express them with appropriate units of measure.

b. What is the null hypothesis?

c. Find the value of the F test statistic and round it to four decimal places.

d. The P-value for this test is 0.2550. What do you conclude about the stated claim?

3. Robust What does it mean when we say that the F test described in this section is *not robust* against departures from normality? Is the F test robust against sampling methods that do not produce simple random samples?

4. Testing Normality Students of the author randomly selected 217 student cars and recorded their ages, and they randomly selected 151 faculty cars and recorded their ages. If using the F test with these data, is it correct to reason that there is no need to check for normality because $n_1 > 30$ and $n_2 > 30$?

Hypothesis Test of Equal Variances. *In Exercises 5 and 6, test the given claim. Use a significance level of $\alpha = 0.05$ and assume that all populations are normally distributed.*

5. Coke Versus Pepsi Data Set 19 in Appendix B includes the weights (in pounds) of samples of regular Coke and regular Pepsi. If we use a TI-83/84 Plus calculator to test the claim that weights of regular Coke and weights of regular Pepsi have different standard deviations, we get the results shown in the accompanying display. Use those results with a 0.05 significance level to test that claim.

TI-83/84 PLUS

```
2-SampFTest
 σ1≠σ2
 F=1.734067094
 p=.1081070292
 Sx1=.007507372
 Sx2=.005701052
↓x1=.8168222222
```

6. Ages of Faculty and Student Cars Students of the author randomly selected 217 student cars and found that they had ages with a mean of 7.89 years and a standard deviation of 3.67 years. They also randomly selected 152 faculty cars and found that they had ages with a mean of 5.99 years and a standard deviation of 3.65 years. Using a significance level of 0.05, is there sufficient evidence to support the claim that ages of student cars vary more than the ages of faculty cars? Use the results from the accompanying StatCrunch display.

STATCRUNCH

Hypothesis test results:
σ_1^2 : variance of population 1
σ_2^2 : variance of population 2
σ_1^2/σ_2^2 : variance ratio
$H_0 : \sigma_1^2/\sigma_2^2 = 1$
$H_A : \sigma_1^2/\sigma_2^2 > 1$

Ratio	n1	n2	Sample Ratio	F-Stat	P-value
σ_1^2/σ_2^2	217	152	1.010989	1.010989	0.4745

Hypothesis Tests of Claims About Variation. *In Exercises 7–16, test the given claim. Assume that both samples are independent simple random samples from populations having normal distributions.*

7. Color and Cognition Example 1 in this section included results from a study of the effects of color on creativity, and the results below were used to study the effects of color on cognition. Words were displayed on a computer screen with background colors of red and blue. Results from scores on a test of word recall are given below. Use a 0.05 significance level to test the claim that the samples are from populations with the same standard deviation. Does the background color appear to have an effect on the variation of word recall scores?

$$\text{Red Background:} \quad n = 35, \bar{x} = 15.89, s = 5.90$$
$$\text{Blue Background:} \quad n = 36, \bar{x} = 12.31, s = 5.48$$

8. Men and Women Talking The accompanying table gives results from a study of the words spoken in a day by men and women, and the original data are in Data Set 17 in Appendix B (based on "Are Women Really More Talkative Than Men?" by Mehl, et al., *Science*, Vol. 317, No. 5834). Use a 0.05 significance level to test the claim that the numbers of words spoken in a day by men vary more than the numbers of words spoken in a day by women.

Number of Words Spoken in a Day

Men	Women
$n_1 = 186$	$n_2 = 210$
$\bar{x}_1 = 15{,}668.5$	$\bar{x}_2 = 16{,}215.0$
$s_1 = 8632.5$	$s_2 = 7301.2$

9. Testing Effects of Alcohol Researchers conducted an experiment to test the effects of alcohol. The errors were recorded in a test of visual and motor skills for a treatment group of 22 people who drank ethanol and another group of 22 people given a placebo. The errors for the treatment group have a standard deviation of 2.20, and the errors for the placebo group have a standard deviation of 0.72 (based on data from "Effects of Alcohol Intoxication on Risk Taking, Strategy, and Error Rate in Visuomotor Performance," by Streufert, et al., *Journal of Applied Psychology*, Vol. 77, No. 4). Use a 0.05 significance level to test the claim that the treatment group has errors that vary more than the errors of the placebo group.

10. Body Temperatures of Men and Women If we use the body temperatures from 8 A.M. on Day 2 as listed in Data Set 3 in Appendix B, we get the statistics given in the accompanying table. Use these data with a 0.05 significance level to test the claim that men have body temperatures that vary more than the body temperatures of women.

Men	Women
$n_1 = 11$	$n_2 = 59$
$\bar{x}_1 = 97.69°F$	$\bar{x}_2 = 97.45°F$
$s_1 = 0.89°F$	$s_2 = 0.66°F$

11. Magnet Treatment of Pain Researchers conducted a study to determine whether magnets are effective in treating back pain, with results given below (based on data from "Bipolar Permanent Magnets for the Treatment of Chronic Lower Back Pain: A Pilot Study," by Collacott, Zimmerman, White, and Rindone, *Journal of the American Medical Association*, Vol. 283, No. 10). The values represent measurements of pain using the visual analog scale. Use a 0.05 significance level to test the claim that those given a sham treatment (similar to a placebo) have pain reductions that vary more than the pain reductions for those treated with magnets.

$$\text{Reduction in Pain Level After Sham Treatment:} \quad n = 20, \bar{x} = 0.44, s = 1.4$$
$$\text{Reduction in Pain Level After Magnet Treatment:} \quad n = 20, \bar{x} = 0.49, s = 0.96$$

12. Skull Measurements from Different Times Researchers measured skulls from different time periods in an attempt to determine whether interbreeding of cultures occurred. Results are given below (based on data from *Ancient Races of the Thebaid*, by Thomson and Randall-Maciver, Oxford University Press). Use a 0.05 significance level to test the claim that the variation of maximal skull breadths in 4000 B.C. is the same as the variation in A.D. 150.

$$\text{4000 B.C. (Maximal Skull Breadth):} \quad n = 30, \bar{x} = 131.37 \text{ mm}, s = 5.13 \text{ mm}$$
$$\text{A.D. 150 (Maximal Skull Breadth):} \quad n = 30, \bar{x} = 136.17 \text{ mm}, s = 5.35 \text{ mm}$$

13. Radiation in Baby Teeth Listed below are amounts of strontium-90 (in millibecquerels, or mBq, per gram of calcium) in a simple random sample of baby teeth obtained from Pennsylvania residents and New York residents born after 1979 (based on data from "An Unexpected Rise in Strontium-90 in U.S. Deciduous Teeth in the 1990s," by Mangano, et al., *Science of the Total Environment*, Vol. 317). Use a 0.05 significance level to test the claim that amounts of strontium-90 from Pennsylvania residents vary more than amounts from New York residents.

Pennsylvania:	155	142	149	130	151	163	151	142	156	133	138	161
New York:	133	140	142	131	134	129	128	140	140	140	137	143

14. Longevity Listed below are the numbers of years that popes and British monarchs (since 1690) lived after their election or coronation (based on data from *Computer-Interactive Data Analysis*, by Lunn and McNeil, John Wiley & Sons). Treat the values as simple random samples from a larger population. Use a 0.05 significance level to test the claim that both populations of longevity times have the same variation.

Popes: 2 9 21 3 6 10 18 11 6 25 23 6 2
15 32 25 11 8 17 19 5 15 0 26

Kings and Queens: 17 6 13 12 13 33 59 10 7 63 9 25 36 15

15. Heights Listed below are heights (cm) of randomly selected females and males taken from Data Set 1 in Appendix B. Use a 0.05 significance level to test the claim that females and males have heights with the same amount of variation.

Female: 163.7 165.5 163.1 166.3 163.6 170.9 153.5 155.7 153.0 157.0
Male: 178.8 177.5 187.8 172.4 181.7 169.0 186.9 183.1 176.4 183.4

16. Weights Listed below are weights (kg) of randomly selected females and males taken from Data Set 1 in Appendix B. Use a 0.05 significance level to test the claim that males have weights with more variation than females.

Female: 59.3 74.5 77.7 97.9 71.7 60.9 60.5 88.2 43.8 47.9
Male: 64.4 61.8 78.5 86.3 73.1 58.5 134.3 79.8 64.8 58.1

Large Data Sets. *In Exercises 17 and 18, use the indicated Data Sets from Appendix B. Assume that both samples are independent simple random samples from populations having normal distributions.*

17. Weights Repeat Exercise 16 using all of the weights listed in Data Set 1 in Appendix B.

18. M&Ms Refer to Data Set 20 in Appendix B and use the weights (g) of the red M&Ms and the orange M&Ms. Use a 0.05 significance level to test the claim that the two samples are from populations with the same amount of variation.

9-5 Beyond the Basics

19. Count Five Test for Comparing Variation in Two Populations Use the original weights of pre-1964 quarters and post-1964 quarters listed in Data Set 21 in Appendix B. Instead of using the F test, use the following procedure for a "count five" test of equal variation. What do you conclude?

a. For the first sample, find the absolute deviation of each value. The absolute deviation of a sample value x is $|x - \bar{x}|$. Sort the absolute deviation values. Do the same for the second sample.

b. Let c_1 be the count of the number of absolute deviation values in the first sample that are greater than the largest absolute deviation value in the other sample. Also, let c_2 be the count of the number of absolute deviation values in the second sample that are greater than the largest absolute deviation value in the other sample. (One of these counts will always be zero.)

c. If the sample sizes are equal ($n_1 = n_2$), use a critical value of 5. If $n_1 \neq n_2$, calculate the critical value shown below.

$$\frac{\log(\alpha/2)}{\log\left(\dfrac{n_1}{n_1 + n_2}\right)}$$

d. If $c_1 \geq$ critical value, then conclude that $\sigma_1^2 > \sigma_2^2$. If $c_2 \geq$ critical value, then conclude that $\sigma_2^2 > \sigma_1^2$. Otherwise, fail to reject the null hypothesis of $\sigma_1^2 = \sigma_2^2$.

20. Levene-Brown-Forsythe Test for Comparing Variation in Two Populations Use the weights (g) of pre-1964 quarters and post-1964 quarters listed in Data Set 21 of Appendix B. Use the Levene-Brown-Forsythe test with a 0.05 significance level to test the claim that weights of pre-1964 quarters and weights of post-1964 quarters are from populations with the same standard deviation.

21. Finding Lower Critical *F* Values For hypothesis tests that were two-tailed, the methods of Part 1 require that we need to find only the upper critical value. Let's denote that value by F_R, where the subscript indicates the critical value for the right tail. The lower critical value F_L (for the left tail) can be found as follows: First interchange the degrees of freedom used for finding F_R, then take the reciprocal of the *F* value found in Table A-5. Using a significance level of 0.05, find the critical values F_L and F_R for a two-tailed hypothesis test with sample sizes of $n_1 = 10$ and $n_2 = 21$.

Chapter 9   Review

In this chapter we considered methods for using two samples for making inferences about two populations. Specifically, we presented methods for testing claims or constructing confidence interval estimates based on the following:

Section 9-2: Proportions from two samples selected from two populations

Section 9-3: Means from samples selected from two independent populations

Section 9-4: Mean of the differences from two dependent samples consisting of matched pairs

Section 9-5: Standard deviations (or variances) from samples selected from two independent populations

Two main activities of inferential statistics are (1) constructing confidence interval estimates of population parameters (as in Chapter 7), and (2) using methods of hypothesis testing to test claims about population parameters (as in Chapter 8). Chapters 7 and 8 considered only cases involving a single population, but in this chapter we considered two samples drawn from two populations.

When using the methods of this chapter, it is important to check the given requirements, including the requirement that the sample data have been collected in an appropriate way. Using data collected with methods that are not appropriate, such as voluntary response samples, could easily provide results that are dramatically wrong.

Chapter Quick Quiz

In Exercises 1–4, use the following survey results: Randomly selected subjects were asked if they agreed with the statement "It is morally wrong for married people to have an affair." Among the 386 women surveyed, 347 agreed with the statement. Among the 359 men surveyed, 305 agreed with the statement (based on data from a Pew Research poll).

1. Identify the null and alternative hypotheses resulting from the claim that the proportion of women who agree with the given statement is equal to the proportion of men who agree.

2. Find the value of the pooled proportion $\bar{p}$ obtained when testing the claim given in Exercise 1.

3. When testing the claim that $p_1 = p_2$, a test statistic of $z = 2.04$ is obtained. Find the *P*-value obtained from this test statistic.

4. When using the given sample data to construct a 95% confidence interval estimate of the difference between the two population proportions, the result of (0.00172, 0.0970) is obtained from technology. Express that confidence interval in a format that uses the symbol $<$.

5. Listed below are the costs (in dollars) of repairing the front ends and rear ends of different cars when they were damaged in controlled low-speed crash tests (based on data from the Insurance Institute for Highway Safety). The cars are Toyota, Mazda, Volvo, Saturn, Subaru, Hyundai, Honda, Volkswagen, and Nissan. Are the data independent or dependent?

Front repair cost	936	978	2252	1032	3911	4312	3469	2598	4535
Rear repair cost	1480	1202	802	3191	1122	739	2769	3375	1787

6. Refer to the sample data given in Exercise 5 and identify the null and alternative hypotheses resulting from the claim that the mean of the differences is greater than zero so that front repair costs are greater than the corresponding rear repair costs. Express those hypotheses in symbolic form.

7. When testing the hypotheses from Exercise 6, we get the test statistic $t = 1.302$ and the *P*-value of 0.2293. What should we conclude?

8. Which distribution is used to test the claim that the standard deviation of the ages of California voters is equal to the standard deviation of voters in Texas (normal, *t*, chi-square, *F*, binomial)?

9. Determine whether the following statement is true or false: When testing the claim that the mean annual income of statistics professors in New York is equal to the mean annual income of statistics professors in Illinois, either the two population standard deviations must be known or both samples must include more than 30 values.

10. Determine whether the following statement is true or false: When using the methods of this chapter to test a claim that two population proportions are equal, each of the two samples must satisfy the requirement that $np \geq 5$ and $nq \geq 5$.

Review Exercises

1. Carpal Tunnel Syndrome Carpal tunnel syndrome is a common wrist complaint resulting from a compressed nerve, and it is often caused by repetitive wrist movements. In a randomized controlled trial, among 73 patients treated with surgery and evaluated one year later, 67 were found to have successful treatments. Among 83 patients treated with splints and evaluated one year later, 60 were found to have successful treatments (based on data from "Splinting vs Surgery in the Treatment of Carpal Tunnel Syndrome," by Gerritsen, et al., *Journal of the American Medical Association,* Vol. 288, No. 10). In a journal article about the trial, authors claimed that "treatment with open carpal tunnel release surgery resulted in better outcomes than treatment with wrist splinting for patients with CTS (carpal tunnel syndrome)." Use a 0.01 significance level to test the stated claim. What treatment strategy is suggested by the results?

2. Carpal Tunnel Syndrome Construct a confidence interval suitable for testing the claim from Exercise 1. What feature of the resulting confidence interval leads to the same conclusion from Exercise 1?

3. Airbags Save Lives In a study of the effectiveness of airbags in cars, 11,541 occupants were observed in car crashes with airbags available, and 41 of them were fatalities. Among 9853 occupants in crashes with airbags not available, 52 were fatalities (based on data from "Who Wants Airbags?" by Meyer and Finney, *Chance*, Vol. 18, No. 2). Use a 0.05 significance level to test the claim that the fatality rate of occupants is lower for those in cars equipped with airbags.

4. Are Flights Cheaper When Scheduled Earlier? Listed below are the costs (in dollars) of flights from New York (JFK) to San Francisco for US Air, Continental, Delta, United,

American, Alaska Airlines, and Northwest. Use a 0.01 significance level to test the claim that flights scheduled one day in advance cost more than flights scheduled 30 days in advance. What strategy appears to be effective in saving money when flying?

Flight scheduled one day in advance	456	614	628	1088	943	567	536
Flight scheduled 30 days in advance	244	260	264	264	278	318	280

5. Self-Reported and Measured Female Heights As part of the National Health and Nutrition Examination Survey conducted by the Department of Health and Human Services, self-reported heights and measured heights were obtained for females aged 12 to 16. Listed below are sample results. Is there sufficient evidence to support the claim that there is a difference between self-reported heights and measured heights of females aged 12 to 16? Use a 0.05 significance level.

Reported height	53	64	61	66	64	65	68	63
Measured height	58.1	62.7	61.1	64.8	63.2	66.4	67.6	63.5

6. Eyewitness Accuracy of Police Does stress affect the recall ability of police eyewitnesses? This issue was studied in an experiment that tested eyewitness memory a week after a nonstressful interrogation of a cooperative suspect and a stressful interrogation of an uncooperative and belligerent suspect. The numbers of details recalled a week after the incident were recorded, and the summary statistics are given below (based on data from "Eyewitness Memory of Police Trainees for Realistic Role Plays," by Yuille et al., *Journal of Applied Psychology*, Vol. 79, No. 6). Use a 0.01 significance level to test the claim in the article that "stress decreases the amount recalled."

$$\text{Nonstress:} \quad n = 40, \bar{x} = 53.3, s = 11.6$$
$$\text{Stress:} \quad n = 40, \bar{x} = 45.3, s = 13.2$$

7. Eyewitness Accuracy of Police Construct a confidence interval suitable for testing the claim from Exercise 6. What feature of the resulting confidence interval leads to the same conclusion from Exercise 6?

8. Effect of Blinding Among 13,200 submitted abstracts that were blindly evaluated (with authors and institutions not identified), 26.7% were accepted for publication. Among 13,433 abstracts that were not blindly evaluated, 29.0% were accepted (based on data from "Effect of Blinded Peer Review on Abstract Acceptance," by Ross, et al., *Journal of the American Medical Association*, Vol. 295, No. 14). Use a 0.01 significance level to test the claim that the acceptance rate is the same with or without blinding. How might the results be explained?

9. Comparing Means The *baseline characteristics* of different treatment groups are often included in journal articles. In one study, 49 subjects treated with raw garlic had LDL cholesterol measurements with a mean of 151 and a standard deviation of 15, while 48 subjects given placebos had LDL cholesterol measurements with a mean of 149 and a standard deviation of 14 (based on data from "Effect of Raw Garlic vs Commercial Garlic Supplements on Plasma Lipid Concentrations in Adults with Moderate Hypercholesterolemia," by Gardner et al., *Archives of Internal Medicine*, Vol. 167). Use a 0.05 significance level to test the claim that there is no difference between the mean LDL cholesterol levels of subjects treated with raw garlic and subjects given placebos. Do both groups appear to be about the same?

10. Comparing Variation Use the sample data from Exercise 9 to test the claim that the two populations have LDL levels with the same standard deviation. Use a 0.05 significance level.

Cumulative Review Exercises

Heights of Mothers and Daughters. *In Exercises 1–5, use the following heights (in.) of mothers, fathers, and their adult daughters. The data are matched so that each column consists of heights from the same family.*

Mother	63	67	62	69	63	64	63	64	60	65
Father	69	70	69	62	66	76	69	68	66	68
Daughter	62.2	67.2	63.4	68.4	62.2	64.7	59.6	61.0	64.0	65.4

1. a. Are the three samples independent or dependent? Why?

b. Find the mean, median, mode, range, standard deviation, and variance of the heights of the daughters. Express results with the appropriate units.

c. What is the level of measurement of the sample data (nominal, ordinal, interval, ratio)?

2. Scatterplot Construct a scatterplot of the paired mother/daughter heights. What does the result suggest?

3. Confidence Interval Construct a 95% confidence interval estimate of the mean height of daughters. Write a brief statement that interprets the confidence interval.

4. Hypothesis Test Use a 0.05 significance level to test the claim that there is no significant difference between the heights of mothers and the heights of their daughters.

5. Assessing Normality Refer to the accompanying normal quantile plot and determine whether the sample of heights of daughters appears to be from a normally distributed population.

6. Dark Survey In a survey of 1032 Americans, respondents were asked what they miss most when electrical power is lost. Of the respondents 134 indicated their computer and/or Internet access (based on results from a Utility Pulse survey). Use the results to construct a 95% confidence interval estimate of the proportion of all Americans who feel that their computer and/or Internet access is missed most when they lose power. Do the results justify the statement that "fewer than 20% of Americans choose their computer and/or Internet access when identifying what they miss most when electrical power is lost"? Explain.

7. Backup Generator The *USA Today* web site posted this question: "Have you considered getting a home generator for backup power?" Among 928 Internet users who chose to respond, 41% answered "yes." If we use those results to construct a 95% confidence interval estimate of the proportion of the population who have considered getting a generator for backup power, we get this: $0.378 < p < 0.441$. Are we 95% confident that the limits of 0.378 and 0.441 contain the true proportion of the population who have considered getting a home generator for backup power? Explain.

8. Juke Survey Late-night talk show host David Lettermen made jokes about the name "Juke" for a Nissan motor vehicle. (It is kind of funny.) If you have been commissioned to conduct a survey of American drivers who see humor in the Juke name, how many American drivers must you survey? Assume that you want 97% confidence that your sample percentage is in error by no more than two percentage points. Is it OK to save money by conducting a telephone survey using only local phone numbers? Why or why not?

9. Normal Distribution Based on the measurements in Data Set 1 of Appendix B, assume that heights of women are normally distributed with a mean of 162.0 cm and a standard deviation of 6.6 cm.

a. If a woman is randomly selected, find the probability that she is taller than 152.1 cm.

b. If four women are randomly selected, find the probability that their mean height is greater than 152.1 cm.

c. Find P_{80}.

10. Mean Income Another (clearly inferior) statistics textbook includes an exercise in which students are given the mean income for each of the 50 states. The students are then asked to compute the mean of those 50 values. Is the result the mean income for the U.S. population? Why or why not?

Technology Project

STATDISK, Minitab, Excel, StatCrunch, the TI 83-84 Plus calculator, and many other statistical software packages are all capable of generating normally distributed data drawn from a population with a specified mean and standard deviation. In Example 3 of Section 6-2, we noted that bone density test scores are measured as z scores having a normal distribution with a mean of 0 and a standard deviation of 1. Generate two sets of sample data that represent simulated bone density scores, as shown below.

> Bone Density Scores of Treatment Group: Generate 10 sample values from a normally distributed population with mean 0 and standard deviation 1.
>
> Bone Density Scores of Placebo Group: Generate 15 sample values from a normally distributed population with mean 0 and standard deviation 1.

STATDISK:	Select **Data,** then select **Normal Generator.**
Minitab:	Select **Calc, Random Data, Normal.**
Excel:	If using Excel 2013, 2010, or 2007, select **Data;** if using Excel 2003, select **Tools.** Select **Data Analysis, Random Number Generator,** and be sure to select **Normal** for the distribution.
TI-83/84 Plus:	Press **MATH**, select **PRB,** then select **randNorm** and enter the mean, standard deviation, and the number of data values in the format of $(\overline{x}, s, n)$.
StatCrunch:	Click on **Data,** then click on **Simulate Data,** then select the menu item of **Normal.** In the dialog box, enter 10 for the number of rows, and enter 1 for the number of columns. Click on **Simulate.** Repeat this process using 15 for the number of rows.

Because each of the two samples consists of random selections from a normally distributed population with a mean of 0 and a standard deviation of 1, the data are generated so that both data sets really come from the same population, so there should be no difference between the two sample means.

a. After generating the two data sets, use a 0.10 significance level to test the claim that the two samples come from populations with the same mean.

b. If this experiment is repeated many times, what is the expected percentage of trials leading to the conclusion that the two population means are different? How does this relate to a type I error?

c. If your generated data should lead to the conclusion that the two population means are different, would this conclusion be correct or incorrect in reality? How do you know?

d. If part (a) is repeated 20 times, what is the probability that none of the hypothesis tests leads to rejection of the null hypothesis?

e. Repeat part (a) 20 times. How often was the null hypothesis of equal means rejected? Is this the result you expected?

from data TO DECISION

Critical Thinking: Ages of workers killed in the Triangle Factory fire
Listed below are the ages (years) of the 146 employees who perished in the Triangle Factory fire that occurred on March 25, 1911 in Manhattan (based on data from the Kheel Center and the *New York Times*). One factor contributing to the large number of deaths is that almost all exits were locked so that employees could be checked for theft when they finished work at the end of the day. That fire revealed grossly poor and unsafe working conditions that led to changes in building codes and labor laws.

Analyzing the Results

1. First *explore* the combined male and female ages using suitable statistics and graphs. What is the mean age? What are the minimum and maximum ages? What is the standard deviation of the ages? Are there any outliers? Describe the distribution of the ages.

2. Examination of the two lists shows that relatively few men perished in the fire. Treat the ages as sample data and determine whether there is sufficient evidence to support the claim that among the workers who perish in such circumstances, the majority are women.

3. Construct a 95% confidence interval estimate of the mean age of males and construct another 95% confidence interval estimate of the mean age of females. Compare the results.

4. Treat the ages as sample data and determine whether there is sufficient evidence to support the claim that female workers have a mean age that is less than that of male workers.

5. Treat the ages as sample data and determine whether there is sufficient evidence to support the claim that ages of males and females have different standard deviations.

6. Based on the preceding results, identify any particularly notable features of the data.

Males

38	19	30	24	23	23	19	18	19	33	17	22	33	25	20	23	22

Females

24	16	25	31	22	18	19	22	16	23	17	15	21	18	17	17	17	31	20	36
18	25	30	16	25	25	21	19	17	18	20	18	26	26	16	18	18	17	22	17
20	22	18	20	16	25	18	40	21	18	19	19	18	18	19	16	19	16	16	21
33	21	14	22	19	19	23	19	18	21	39	20	14	27	22	15	19	16	16	19
18	21	18	19	19	20	18	43	16	20	18	30	21	22	18	21	35	22	21	22
21	22	17	24	25	20	18	32	20	21	19	24	17	18	30	18	16	22	22	17
22	20	15	20	17	21	21	18	17											

Cooperative Group Activities

1. Out-of-class activity Survey married couples and record the number of credit cards each person has. Analyze the paired data to determine whether husbands have more credit cards, wives have more credit cards, or they both have about the same number of credit cards. Try to identify reasons for any discrepancy.

2. Out-of-class activity Measure and record the height of the husband and the height of the wife from each of several different married couples. Estimate the mean of the differences between heights of husbands and the heights of their wives. Compare the result to the difference between the mean height of men and the mean height of women included in Data Set 1 in Appendix B. Do the results suggest that height is a factor when people select marriage partners?

3. Out-of-class activity Are estimates influenced by anchoring numbers? Refer to the related Chapter 3 Cooperative Group Activity. In Chapter 3 we noted that, according to author John Rubin, when people must estimate a value, their estimate is often "anchored" to (or influenced by) a preceding number. In that Chapter 3 activity, some subjects were asked to quickly estimate the value of $8 \times 7 \times 6 \times 5 \times 4 \times 3 \times 2 \times 1$, and others were asked to quickly estimate the value of $1 \times 2 \times 3 \times 4 \times 5 \times 6 \times 7 \times 8$. In Chapter 3, we could compare the two sets of results by using statistics (such as the mean) and graphs (such as boxplots). The methods of Chapter 9 now allow us to compare the results with a formal hypothesis test. Specifically, collect your own sample data and test the claim that when we begin with larger numbers (as in $8 \times 7 \times 6$), our estimates tend to be larger.

4. In-class activity Divide into groups according to gender, with about 10 or 12 students in each group. Each group member should record his or her pulse rate by counting the number of heartbeats in 1 minute, and calculate the group statistics $(n, \bar{x}, s)$. The groups should test the null hypothesis of no difference between their mean pulse rate and the mean of the pulse rates for the population from which subjects of the same gender were selected for Data Set 1 in Appendix B.

5. Out-of-class activity Randomly select a sample of male students and a sample of female students and ask each selected person a yes/no question, such as whether they support a death penalty for people convicted of murder, or whether they believe that the federal government should fund stem cell research. Record the response, the gender of the respondent, and the gender of the person asking the question. Use a formal hypothesis test to determine whether there is a difference between the proportions of *yes* responses from males and females. Also, determine whether the responses appear to be influenced by the gender of the interviewer.

6. Out-of-class activity Use a watch to record the waiting times of a sample of McDonald's customers and the waiting times of a sample of Burger King customers. Use a hypothesis test to determine whether there is a significant difference.

7. Out-of-class activity Construct a short survey of just a few questions, including a question asking the subject to report his or her height. After the subject has completed the survey, measure the subject's height (without shoes) using an accurate measuring system. Record the gender, reported height, and measured height of each subject. Do male subjects appear to exaggerate their heights? Do female subjects appear to exaggerate their heights? Do the errors for males appear to have the same mean as the errors for females?

8. In-class activity Without using any measuring device, ask each student to draw a line believed to be 3 in. long and another line believed to be 3 cm long. Then use rulers to measure and record the lengths of the lines drawn. Record the errors along with the genders of the students making the estimates. Test the claim that when estimating the length of a 3-in. line, the mean error from males is equal to the mean error from females. Also, do the results show that we have a better understanding of the British system of measurement (inches) than the SI system (centimeters)?

9. Out-of-class activity Obtain simple random samples of cars in the student and faculty parking lots, and test the claim that students and faculty have the same proportions of foreign cars.

10. Out-of-class activity Obtain simple random samples of cars in parking lots of a discount store and an upscale department store, and test the claim that cars are newer in the parking lot of the upscale department store.

11. Out-of-class activity Obtain sample data and test the claim that husbands are older than their wives.

12. Out-of-class activity Obtain sample data to test the claim that in the college library, science books have a mean age that is less than the mean age of novels.

13. Out-of-class activity Conduct experiments and collect data to test the claim that there are no differences in taste between ordinary tap water and different brands of bottled water.

14. Out-of-class activity Collect sample data and test the claim that people who exercise tend to have pulse rates that are lower than those who do not exercise.

15. Out-of-class activity Collect sample data and test the claim that the proportion of female students who smoke is equal to the proportion of male students who smoke.

16. Out-of-class activity Collect sample data to test the claim that women carry more pocket change than men.

10 Correlation and Regression

chapter
problem

CSI Statistics: Can we use footprint evidence to estimate a suspect's height?

Police sometimes use footprint evidence to estimate the height of a suspect, and the height is included in a description that becomes part of a BOLO ("be on the lookout"). (Aren't acronyms fun? Wait until you get to ANOVA.) Around 1877, anthropologist Paul Topinard collected foot/height measurements and used them to develop this rule: Estimate a person's height by dividing their foot length by 0.15. (An equivalent calculation is to estimate height by multiplying foot length by 6.67.) Try it yourself by measuring the length of your foot, then divide by 0.15 (or multiply by 6.67) to get your estimated height. Is the result reasonably accurate?

Table 10-1 includes some measurements taken from Data Set 2 in Appendix B. Table 10-1 includes shoe length and height measurements from five males, but Data Set 2 includes more measurements from larger samples of males and females. (The data are from "Estimation of Stature from Foot and Shoe Length: Applications in Forensic Science," by Brenda Rohren M.A., MFS, LIMHP, LADC, MAC. Brenda Rohren was a graduate student at Nebraska Wesleyan University when she conducted the research and wrote the report in Fall 2006. The data are used with her permission.)

Using shoe print measurements, such as those in Table 10-1, can we confirm that there is a relationship between lengths of our shoe prints and our heights? If we do conclude that there is a relationship, how do we use it to develop a formula for estimating height based on the length of a shoe print? Such questions are critically important for many applications, and this chapter provides the tools for answering them.

Table 10-1 Shoe Print Lengths and Heights of Males					
Shoe Print (cm)	29.7	29.7	31.4	31.8	27.6
Height (cm)	175.3	177.8	185.4	175.3	172.7

10-1   Review and Preview

A major focus of this chapter is to analyze *paired* sample data. In Section 9-4 we considered two dependent samples, with each value of one sample somehow paired with a value from the other sample. The goal in Section 9-4 was to describe methods for testing hypotheses and constructing confidence intervals for the *mean of the differences* from the matched pairs. In this chapter we again consider paired sample data, but the objective is fundamentally different from that of Section 9-4. In this chapter we introduce methods for determining whether a *correlation,* or association, between two variables exists and whether the correlation is linear. For linear correlations, we can identify an equation of a straight line that best fits the data, and we can use that equation to predict the value of one variable given the value of the other variable. We also present methods for analyzing differences between predicted values and actual values. In addition, we consider methods for identifying linear equations for correlations among three or more variables. We conclude the chapter with some basic methods for developing a mathematical model that can be used to describe some nonlinear correlations between two variables.

10-2   Correlation

Key Concept In Part 1 of this section we introduce the *linear correlation coefficient r*, which is a number that measures how well paired sample data fit a straight-line pattern when graphed. We use the sample of paired data (sometimes called **bivariate data**) to find the value of *r* (usually using technology), then we use that value to decide whether there is (or is not) a linear correlation between the two variables. In this section we consider only *linear* relationships, which means that when graphed in a scatterplot, the points approximate a straight-line pattern. In Part 2, we discuss methods for conducting a formal hypothesis test that can be used to decide whether there is a linear correlation between two variables.

Part 1: Basic Concepts of Correlation

We begin with the basic definition of *correlation,* a term commonly used in the context of an association between two variables.

> **DEFINITIONS**
>
> A **correlation** exists between two variables when the values of one variable are somehow associated with the values of the other variable.
>
> A **linear correlation** exists between two variables when there is a correlation and the plotted points of paired data result in a pattern that can be approximated by a straight line.

Table 10-1, for example, includes paired sample data consisting of lengths of shoe prints and the corresponding heights of five different males. We will determine whether there is a linear correlation between the variable *x* (length of shoe print) and the variable *y* (height). Instead of blindly jumping into the calculation of the linear correlation coefficient *r*, it is wise to first *explore* the data.

Explore!

Because it is always wise to explore sample data before applying a formal statistical procedure, we should use a scatterplot to explore the paired data visually. Figure 10-1(a) shows the scatterplot of the shoe/height data from Table 10-1. The scatterplot suggests that there might be a pattern, but it isn't very strong. Also, there are no outliers, which are points far away from all the other points. Figure 10-1(b) shows the scatterplot of all 40 pairs of shoe print and height measurements from Data Set 2 in Appendix B. Because Figure 10-1(b) includes more sample data, it gives us a better picture of the relationship between the two variables. Figure 10-1(b) shows that there is a pattern of points tending to rise as they move farther to the right, but the pattern does not appear to be very distinct. Again, there are no outliers.

(a)

(b)

Figure 10-1   Minitab Scatterplots

Interpreting Scatterplots

Figure 10-2 shows four scatterplots with different characteristics. The scatterplot in Figure 10-2(a) shows a distinct straight-line, or linear, pattern. We say that there is a *positive* linear correlation between x and y, since as the x-values increase, the

ActivStats

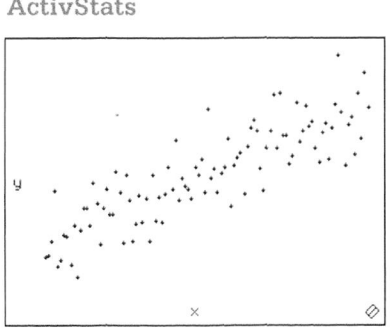

(a) Positive correlation:
   $r = 0.851$

ActivStats

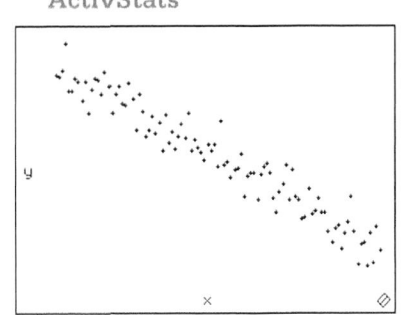

(b) Negative correlation:
   $r = -0.965$

ActivStats

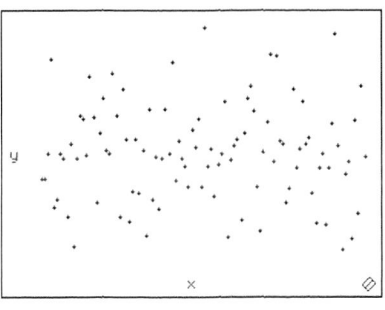

(c) No correlation: $r = 0$

Minitab

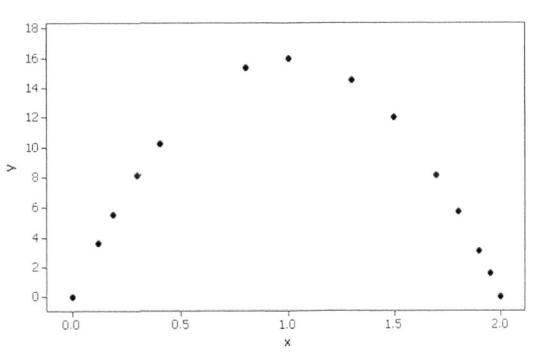

(d) Nonlinear relationship: $r = -0.087$

Figure 10-2   Scatterplots

corresponding *y*-values also increase. The scatterplot in Figure 10-2(b) shows a distinct linear pattern. We say that there is a *negative* linear correlation between *x* and *y*, since as the *x*-values increase, the corresponding *y*-values decrease. The scatterplot in Figure 10-2(c) shows no distinct pattern and suggests that there is no linear correlation between *x* and *y*. The scatterplot in Figure 10-2(d) shows a distinct pattern suggesting a correlation between *x* and *y*, but the pattern is not that of a straight line.

Measure the Strength of the Linear Correlation

Because conclusions based on visual examinations of scatterplots are largely subjective, we need more objective measures. We use the linear correlation coefficient *r*, which is a number that measures the strength of the (linear) association between the two variables.

> **DEFINITION** The **linear correlation coefficient *r*** measures the strength of the linear correlation between the paired quantitative *x*- and *y*-values in a *sample*. (Its value is computed by using Formula 10-1 or Formula 10-2, included in the following box. [The linear correlation coefficient is sometimes referred to as the **Pearson product moment correlation coefficient** in honor of Karl Pearson (1857–1936), who originally developed it.]

Because the linear correlation coefficient *r* is calculated using sample data, it is a sample statistic used to measure the strength of the linear correlation between *x* and *y*. If we had every pair of *x* and *y* values from an entire population, the result of Formula 10-1 or Formula 10-2 would be a population parameter, represented by ρ (Greek letter rho).

Objective

Determine whether there is a linear correlation between two variables.

Notation for the Linear Correlation Coefficient

n	number of pairs of sample data.
Σ	denotes addition of the items indicated.
Σx	sum of all *x*-values.
Σx^2	indicates that each *x*-value should be squared and then those squares added.
$(\Sigma x)^2$	indicates that the *x*-values should be added and the total then squared. Avoid confusing Σx^2 and $(\Sigma x)^2$.
Σxy	indicates that each *x*-value should first be multiplied by its corresponding *y*-value. After obtaining all such products, find their sum.
r	linear correlation coefficient for *sample* data.
ρ	linear correlation coefficient for a *population* of paired data.

Requirements

Given any collection of sample paired quantitative data, the linear correlation coefficient *r* can always be computed, but the following requirements should be satisfied when using the sample data to make a conclusion about correlation in the population.

1. The sample of paired (x, y) data is a simple random sample of quantitative data. (It is important that the sample data have not been collected using some inappropriate method, such as using a voluntary response sample.)

2. Visual examination of the scatterplot must confirm that the points approximate a straight-line pattern.

3. Because results can be strongly affected by the presence of outliers, any outliers must be removed if they are known to be errors. The effects of any other outliers should be considered by calculating r with and without the outliers included.

Note: Requirements 2 and 3 above are simplified attempts at checking this formal requirement: The pairs of (x, y) data must have a **bivariate normal distribution.** Normal distributions are discussed in Chapter 6, but this assumption basically requires that for any fixed value of x, the corresponding values of y have a distribution that is approximately normal, and for any fixed value of y, the values of x have a distribution that is approximately normal. This requirement is usually difficult to check, so for now, we will use Requirements 2 and 3 as listed above.

Formulas for Calculating r

Formula 10-1

$$r = \frac{n(\Sigma xy) - (\Sigma x)(\Sigma y)}{\sqrt{n(\Sigma x^2) - (\Sigma x)^2}\sqrt{n(\Sigma y^2) - (\Sigma y)^2}}$$

Formula 10-1 simplifies manual calculations, but r is usually calculated with computer software or a calculator. Formula 10-2 is better for understanding the reasoning behind r; see the rationale discussed later in this section.

Formula 10-2

$$r = \frac{\Sigma(z_x z_y)}{n - 1}$$

where z_x denotes the z score for an individual sample value x and z_y is the z score for the corresponding sample value y.

Interpreting the Linear Correlation Coefficient r

- *Using Computer Software to Interpret r:* If the P-value computed from r is less than or equal to the significance level, conclude that there is sufficient evidence to support a claim of a linear correlation. Otherwise, there is not sufficient evidence to support a claim of a linear correlation.

- *Using Table A-6 to Interpret r:* Consider critical values from Table A-6 as being both positive and negative, and draw a graph similar to Figure 10-3 that accompanies Example 4.

  Correlation If the computed linear correlation coefficient r lies in the left tail beyond the leftmost critical value or if it lies in the right tail beyond the rightmost critical value, conclude that there is sufficient evidence to support the claim of a linear correlation.

  No Correlation If the computed linear correlation coefficient lies *between* the two critical values, conclude that there is not sufficient evidence to support the claim of a linear correlation.

(Here are equivalent criteria: If the absolute value of r, denoted $|r|$, exceeds the value in Table A-6, conclude that there is a linear correlation. Otherwise, there is not sufficient evidence to support the conclusion of a linear correlation.)

CAUTION Know that the methods of this section apply to a *linear* correlation. If you conclude that there does not appear to be linear correlation, it is possible that there might be some other association that is not linear, as in Figure 10-2(d).

Rounding the Linear Correlation Coefficient r

Round the linear correlation coefficient r to three decimal places (so that its value can be directly compared to critical values in Table A-6). If manually calculating r and other statistics in this chapter, rounding in the middle of a calculation often creates substantial errors, so try to round only the final result.

Properties of the Linear Correlation Coefficient r

1. The value of r is always between -1 and 1 inclusive. That is, $-1 \leq r \leq 1$.

2. *If all values of either variable are converted to a different scale, the value of r does not change.*

3. *The value of r is not affected by the choice of x or y.* Interchange all x- and y-values and the value of r will not change.

4. *r measures the strength of a linear relationship.* It is not designed to measure the strength of a relationship that is not linear (as in Figure 10-2(d)).

5. *r is very sensitive to outliers* in the sense that a single outlier can dramatically affect its value.

Calculating the Linear Correlation Coefficient r

The following three examples illustrate three different methods for finding the value of the linear correlation coefficient r, but you need to use only one method. *The use of computer software or a calculator (as in Example 1) is strongly recommended.* If manual calculations are absolutely necessary, Formula 10-1 is recommended (as in Example 2). If a better understanding of r is desired, Formula 10-2 is recommended (as in Example 3).

Example 1   Finding r Using Computer Software

The paired shoe/height data from five males are listed in Table 10-1. Use computer software or a calculator with these paired sample values to find the value of the linear correlation coefficient r for the paired sample data.

Solution

Requirement check We can always calculate the linear correlation coefficient r from paired quantitative data, but we should check the requirements if we want to use that value for making a conclusion about correlation. (1) The data are a simple random sample of quantitative data. (2) The plotted points in the scatterplot in Figure 10-1(a) appear to roughly approximate a straight-line pattern. (3) The scatterplot in Figure 10-1(a) also shows that there are no outliers. The requirements are satisfied. ✓

If using computer software or a calculator, the value of r will be automatically calculated. For example, see the following Minitab, TI-83/84 Plus calculator, and STATDISK displays showing that $r = 0.591$. Excel and many other computer software packages and calculators provide the same value of $r = 0.591$.

MINITAB

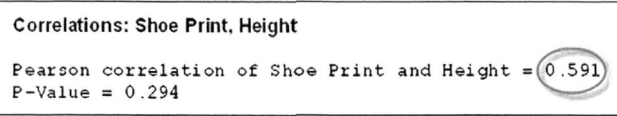

Correlations: Shoe Print, Height

Pearson correlation of Shoe Print and Height = (0.591)
P-Value = 0.294

TI-83/84 PLUS

```
LinRegTTest
y=a+bx
β≠0 and ρ≠0
↑b=1.72745239
s=4.538762333
r²=.3495991312
r=.5912690853
```

STATDISK

```
Correlation Results:
Correlation coeff, r: 0.5912691
Critical r:          ±0.8783393
P-value (two-tailed): 0.29369
```

Example 2 Finding *r* Using Formula 10-1

Use Formula 10-1 to find the value of the linear correlation coefficient *r* for the paired shoe print and height data given in Table 10-1.

Solution

Requirement check See the discussion of the requirement check in Example 1. The same comments apply here. ✓

Using Formula 10-1, the value of *r* is calculated as shown below. Here, the variable *x* is used for the shoe print lengths, and the variable *y* is used for the heights. Because there are five pairs of data, *n* = 5. Other required values are computed in Table 10-2.

Table 10-2 Calculating *r* with Formula 10-1

x (Shoe Print)	y (Height)	x^2	y^2	xy
29.7	175.3	882.09	30730.09	5206.41
29.7	177.8	882.09	31612.84	5280.66
31.4	185.4	985.96	34373.16	5821.56
31.8	175.3	1011.24	30730.09	5574.54
27.6	172.7	761.76	29825.29	4766.52
$\Sigma x = 150.2$	$\Sigma y = 886.5$	$\Sigma x^2 = 4523.14$	$\Sigma y^2 = 157271.47$	$\Sigma xy = 26649.69$

Using Formula 10-1 with the results from Table 10-2, *r* is calculated as follows:

$$r = \frac{n\Sigma xy - (\Sigma x)(\Sigma y)}{\sqrt{n(\Sigma x^2) - (\Sigma x)^2}\sqrt{n(\Sigma y^2) - (\Sigma y)^2}}$$

$$= \frac{5(26649.69) - (150.2)(886.5)}{\sqrt{5(4523.14) - (150.2)^2}\sqrt{5(157271.47) - (886.5)^2}}$$

$$= \frac{96.15}{\sqrt{55.66}\sqrt{475.10}} = 0.591$$

Example 3 Finding *r* Using Formula 10-2

Use Formula 10-2 to find the value of the linear correlation coefficient *r* for the paired shoe print and height data given in Table 10-1.

Solution

Requirement check See the discussion of the requirement check in Example 1. The same comments apply here. ✓

If manual calculations are absolutely necessary, Formula 10-1 is much easier than Formula 10-2, but Formula 10-2 has the advantage of making it easier to *understand* how *r* works. (See the *rationale* for *r* discussed later in this section.) As in Example 2, the variable *x* is used for the shoe print lengths, and the variable *y* is used for the heights. In Formula 10-2, each sample value is replaced by its corresponding

Teacher Evaluations Correlate with Grades

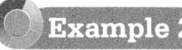

Student evaluations of faculty are often used to measure teaching effectiveness. Many studies reveal a correlation with higher student grades being associated with higher faculty evaluations. One study at Duke University involved student evaluations collected before and after final grades were assigned. The study showed that "grade expectations or received grades caused a change in the way students perceived their teacher and the quality of instruction." It was noted that with student evaluations, "the incentives for faculty to manipulate their grading policies in order to enhance their evaluations increase." It was concluded that "the ultimate consequence of such manipulations is the degradation of the quality of education in the United States." (See "Teacher Course Evaluations and Student Grades: An Academic Tango," by Valen Johnson, Chance, Vol. 15, No. 3.)

z score. For example, the shoe print lengths have a mean of $\bar{x} = 30.04$ cm and a standard deviation of $s_x = 1.66823$ cm, so the first shoe print length of 29.7 cm is converted to a *z* score of -0.20381 as shown here:

$$z_x = \frac{x - \bar{x}}{s_x} = \frac{29.7 - 30.04}{1.66823} = -0.20381$$

Table 10-3 lists the *z* scores for all of the shoe print lengths (see the third column) and the *z* scores for all of the heights (see the fourth column). The last column of Table 10-3 lists the products $z_x \cdot z_y$.

Table 10-3 Calculating *r* with Formula 10-2

x (Shoe Print)	y (Height)	z_x	z_y	$z_x \cdot z_y$
29.7	175.3	−0.20381	−0.41035	0.08363
29.7	177.8	−0.20381	0.10259	−0.02091
31.4	185.4	0.81524	1.66191	1.35485
31.8	175.3	1.05501	−0.41035	−0.43292
27.6	172.7	−1.46263	−0.94380	1.38043
				$\Sigma(z_x \cdot z_y) = 2.36508$

Using $\Sigma(z_x \cdot z_y) = 2.36508$ from Table 10-3, the value of *r* is calculated by using Formula 10-2 as shown below.

$$r = \frac{\Sigma(z_x \cdot z_y)}{n - 1} = \frac{2.36508}{4} = 0.591$$

Is There a Linear Correlation?

We know from the preceding three examples that the value of the linear correlation coefficient is $r = 0.591$ for the sample data in Table 10-1. We now proceed to interpret its meaning, and our goal is to decide whether there appears to be a linear correlation between shoe print lengths and heights of people. Using the criteria given in the preceding box, we can base our interpretation on a *P*-value or a critical value from Table A-6. See the criteria for "Interpreting the Linear Correlation Coefficient *r*" given in the preceding box.

Example 4 Is There a Linear Correlation?

In Examples 1, 2, and 3, we used the sample data from Table 10-1 to find that $r = 0.591$. If we use a significance level of 0.05, is there sufficient evidence to support a claim that there is a linear correlation between shoe print lengths and heights of people?

Solution

Requirement check The requirement check in Example 1 also applies here.

We can base our conclusion about correlation on either the *P*-value obtained from computer software or the critical value found in Table A-6. (See the criteria for "Interpreting the Linear Correlation Coefficient *r*"given in the preceding box.)

- *Using Computer Software to Interpret r:* If the computed *P*-value is less than or equal to the significance level, conclude that there is a linear correlation. Otherwise, there is not sufficient evidence to support the conclusion of a linear correlation. Example 1 includes Minitab, TI-83/84 Plus calculator, and STATDISK displays. Those technologies provide the *P*-value of 0.294. Because that *P*-value is *not* less than or equal to the significance level of 0.05, we conclude that *there is not sufficient evidence to support the conclusion that there is a linear correlation between shoe print lengths and heights of people.*

- *Using Table A-6 to Interpret r:* Consider critical values from Table A-6 as being both positive and negative, and draw a graph like Figure 10-3. For the sample data in Table 10-1, Table A-6 yields $r = 0.878$ (for five pairs of data and a 0.05 significance level). We can now compare the computed value of $r = 0.591$ to the critical values of $r = \pm 0.878$ as shown in Figure 10-3.

- *Correlation* If the computed linear correlation coefficient *r* lies in the left or right tail region beyond the critical value for that tail, conclude that there is sufficient evidence to support the claim of a linear correlation.

- *No Correlation* If the computed linear correlation coefficient lies between the two critical values, conclude that there is not sufficient evidence to support the claim of a linear correlation.

Because Figure 10-3 shows that the computed value of $r = 0.591$ lies between the two critical values, we conclude that *there is not sufficient evidence to support the claim of a linear correlation between shoe print lengths and heights.*

Figure 10-3   Critical Values from Table A-6 and the Computed Value of *r*

Example 5   Larger Data Set

Example 4 used only the shoe lengths and heights from five males. Let's now use the shoe lengths and heights from the 40 subjects listed in Data Set 2 in Appendix B. The scatterplot is shown in Figure 10-1(b). Refer to the following results obtained by using XLSTAT with Excel. See that the value of the linear correlation coefficient is $r = 0.813$ and the *P*-value is less than 0.0001. Is there sufficient evidence to support a claim of a linear correlation between the lengths of shoe prints and heights?

XLSTAT

Correlation matrix (Pearson):

Variables	Shoe Print	Height
Shoe Print	1	0.8129
Height	0.8129	1

Values in bold are different from 0 with a significance level alpha=0.05

p-values:

Variables	Shoe Print	Height
Shoe Print	0	< 0.0001
Height	< 0.0001	0

Values in bold are different from 0 with a significance level alpha=0.05

Solution

Requirement check (1) The sample is a simple random sample of quantitative data. (2) The points in the scatterplot of Figure 10-1(b) roughly approximate a straight-line pattern. (3) There are no outliers that are far away from almost all of the other pairs of data. ✓

Using Software: The P-value obtained from XLSTAT is less than 0.0001. Because the P-value is less than or equal to 0.05, we conclude that there is sufficient evidence to support a claim of a linear correlation between the lengths of shoe prints and heights.

Using Table A-6: If we refer to Table A-6 with $n = 40$ pairs of sample data, we obtain the critical values of -0.312 and 0.312 for $\alpha = 0.05$. Because the computed value of $r = 0.813$ *does* exceed the critical value of 0.312 from Table A-6, the computed value of r lies in the right tail beyond the rightmost critical value of 0.312, so we conclude that there is sufficient evidence to support a claim of a linear correlation between the lengths of shoe prints and heights.

Example 4 used only five pairs of data and we concluded that there is *not* sufficient evidence to support the conclusion that there is a linear correlation between shoe print lengths and heights of people, but this example uses 40 pairs of data and here we conclude that there *is* sufficient evidence to support the conclusion that there is a linear correlation between shoe print lengths and heights of people. This larger data set provided the additional evidence that enabled us to support the presence of a linear correlation. Such is the power of larger data sets.

Interpreting r: Explained Variation

If we conclude that there is a linear correlation between x and y, we can find a linear equation that expresses y in terms of x, and that equation can be used to predict values of y for given values of x. In Section 10-3 we will describe a procedure for finding such equations and show how to predict values of y when given values of x. But a predicted value of y will not necessarily be the exact result that occurs because in addition to x, there are other factors affecting y, such as random variation and other characteristics not included in the study. In Section 10-4 we will present a rationale and more details about this principle:

The value of r^2 is the proportion of the variation in y that is explained by the linear relationship between x and y.

Example 6 Explained Variation

In Example 5 we noted that for the 40 pairs of shoe print lengths and heights listed in Data Set 2 from Appendix B, the linear correlation coefficient is $r = 0.813$. What proportion of the variation in height can be explained by the variation in the length of shoe print?

Solution

With $r = 0.813$, we get $r^2 = 0.661$.

Interpretation

We conclude that 0.661 (or about 66%) of the variation in height can be explained by the linear relationship between lengths of shoe prints and heights. This implies that about 34% of the variation in heights cannot be explained by lengths of shoe prints.

Common Errors Involving Correlation

Here are three of the most common errors made in interpreting results involving correlation:

1. *A common error is to assume that correlation implies causality.* One classic example involves paired data consisting of the stork population in Copenhagen and the number of human births. For several years, the data suggested a linear correlation. *Bulletin:* Storks do not actually cause births, and births do not cause storks. Both variables were affected by some other variable lurking in the background. (A **lurking variable** is one that affects the variables being studied but is not included in the study.)

2. *Another error arises with data based on averages.* Averages suppress individual variation and may inflate the correlation coefficient. One study produced a 0.4 linear correlation coefficient for paired data relating income and education among individuals, but the linear correlation coefficient became 0.7 when regional averages were used.

3. *A third error involves the property of linearity.* If there is no linear correlation, there might be some other correlation that is not linear, as in Figure 10-2(d). (Figure 10-2(d) is a scatterplot that depicts the relationship between distance above ground and time elapsed for an object thrown upward.)

CAUTION Know that *correlation does not imply causality.*

Part 2: Formal Hypothesis Test (Requires Coverage of Chapter 8)

Here in Part 2 we describe formal procedures for conducting hypothesis tests to determine whether there is a significant linear correlation between two variables. The following box contains key elements of the hypothesis test.

Hypothesis Test for Correlation (Using Test Statistic r)

Notation

n = number of pairs of sample data

r = linear correlation coefficient for a *sample* of paired data

ρ = linear correlation coefficient for a *population* of paired data

Requirements

The requirements are the same as those given in the preceding box from Part 1 of this section.

Hypotheses

$$H_0: \rho = 0 \quad \text{(There is no linear correlation.)}$$
$$H_1: \rho \neq 0 \quad \text{(There is a linear correlation.)}$$

Test Statistic: r

Critical values: Refer to Table A-6.

Conclusion

Consider critical values from Table A-6 as being both positive and negative, and draw a graph similar to Figure 10-3.

- **Correlation** If the computed linear correlation coefficient r lies in the left tail beyond the leftmost critical value or if it lies in the right tail beyond the rightmost critical value, reject H_0 and conclude that there is sufficient evidence to support the claim of a linear correlation.

- **No Correlation** If the computed linear correlation coefficient lies *between* the two critical values, fail to reject H_0 and conclude that there is not sufficient evidence to support the claim of a linear correlation.

The following criteria are equivalent to those given above.

- **Correlation** If $|r|$ > critical value from Table A-6, reject H_0 and conclude that there is sufficient evidence to support the claim of a linear correlation.

- **No Correlation** If $|r|$ ≤ critical value, fail to reject H_0 and conclude that there is not sufficient evidence to support the claim of a linear correlation.

Example 7   Hypothesis Test Based on r

Use the paired shoe print lengths and heights in Table 10-1 to conduct a formal hypothesis test of the claim that there is a linear correlation between the two variables. Use a 0.05 significance level.

Solution

Requirement check The solution in Example 1 already includes verification that the requirements are satisfied. ✓

To claim that there is a linear correlation is to claim that the population linear correlation coefficient ρ is different from 0. We therefore have the following hypotheses:

$$H_0: \rho = 0 \quad \text{(There is no linear correlation.)}$$
$$H_1: \rho \neq 0 \quad \text{(There is a linear correlation.)}$$

The test statistic is $r = 0.591$ (from Examples 1, 2, and 3). The critical values of $r = \pm 0.878$ are found in Table A-6 with $n = 5$ and $\alpha = 0.05$. See Example 4 and Figure 10-3. Because the test statistic $r = 0.591$ is between the critical values of -0.878 and 0.878, we fail to reject $H_0: \rho = 0$.

Interpretation

We conclude that there is not sufficient evidence to support the claim of a linear correlation between shoe print lengths and heights.

P-Value Method for a Hypothesis Test for Linear Correlation

The preceding method of hypothesis testing using the test statistic r involves relatively simple calculations. Software packages and the TI-83/84 Plus calculator typically use a P-value method based on a t test. The key components of the t test are as follows.

Hypothesis Test for Correlation (Using P-Value from a t Test)

Hypotheses

$$H_0: \rho = 0 \qquad \text{(There is no linear correlation.)}$$
$$H_1: \rho \neq 0 \qquad \text{(There is a linear correlation.)}$$

Test Statistic

$$t = \frac{r}{\sqrt{\dfrac{1 - r^2}{n - 2}}}$$

P-value: Use software or a TI-83/84 Plus calculator or use Table A-3 with $n - 2$ degrees of freedom to find the P-value corresponding to the test statistic t.

Conclusion

- **Correlation** If the P-value is less than or equal to the significance level, reject H_0 and conclude that there is sufficient evidence to support the claim of a linear correlation.

- **No Correlation** If the P-value is greater than the significance level, fail to reject H_0 and conclude that there is not sufficient evidence to support the claim of a linear correlation.

Example 8   Hypothesis Test Based on P-Value from t Test

Use the paired shoe print lengths and heights in Table 10-1 to conduct a formal hypothesis test of the claim that there is a linear correlation between the two variables. Base the conclusion on a P-value and use a 0.05 significance level.

Solution

Requirement check The solution in Example 1 already includes verification that the requirements are satisfied. ✓

To claim that there is a linear correlation is to claim that the population linear correlation coefficient ρ is different from 0. We therefore have the following hypotheses:

$$H_0: \rho = 0 \quad \text{(There is no linear correlation.)}$$
$$H_1: \rho \neq 0 \quad \text{(There is a linear correlation.)}$$

The linear correlation coefficient is $r = 0.591$ (from Examples 1, 2, and 3) and $n = 5$ (because there are five pairs of sample data), so the test statistic is

$$t = \frac{r}{\sqrt{\dfrac{1 - r^2}{n - 2}}} = \frac{0.591}{\sqrt{\dfrac{1 - 0.591^2}{5 - 2}}} = 1.269$$

Computer software packages use more precision to obtain the more accurate test statistic of $t = 1.270$. With $n - 2 = 3$ degrees of freedom, Table A-3 shows that the test statistic of $t = 1.269$ yields a P-value that is greater than 0.20. Software packages and the TI-83/84 Plus calculator show that the P-value is 0.2937. Because the P-value of 0.2937 is greater than the significance level of 0.05, we fail to reject H_0. ("If the P is low, the null must go." The P-value of 0.2937 is not low.)

Interpretation

We conclude that there is not sufficient evidence to support the claim of a linear correlation between shoe print lengths and heights.

One-Tailed Tests Examples 7 and 8 illustrate a two-tailed hypothesis test. The examples and exercises in this section will generally involve only two-tailed tests, but one-tailed tests can occur with a claim of a positive linear correlation or a claim of a negative linear correlation. In such cases, the hypotheses will be as shown here.

Claim of Negative Correlation (Left-tailed test)	Claim of Positive Correlation (Right-tailed test)
$H_0: \rho = 0$	$H_0: \rho = 0$
$H_1: \rho < 0$	$H_1: \rho > 0$

For these one-tailed tests, the P-value method can be used as in earlier chapters.

Rationale for Methods of This Section We have presented Formulas 10-1 and 10-2 for calculating r and have illustrated their use. Those formulas are given below along with some other formulas that are "equivalent," in the sense that they all produce the same values.

Formula 10-1

$$r = \frac{n\Sigma xy - (\Sigma x)(\Sigma y)}{\sqrt{n(\Sigma x^2) - (\Sigma x)^2}\sqrt{n(\Sigma y^2) - (\Sigma y)^2}}$$

Formula 10-2

$$r = \frac{\Sigma(z_x z_y)}{n - 1}$$

$$r = \frac{\Sigma(x - \bar{x})(y - \bar{y})}{(n - 1)s_x s_y} \qquad r = \frac{\Sigma\left[\dfrac{(x - \bar{x})}{s_x}\dfrac{(y - \bar{y})}{s_y}\right]}{n - 1} \qquad r = \frac{s_{xy}}{\sqrt{s_{xx}}\sqrt{s_{yy}}}$$

We will use Formula 10-2 to help us understand the reasoning that underlies the development of the linear correlation coefficient. Because Formula 10-2 uses z scores, the value of $\Sigma(z_x z_y)$ does not depend on the scale that is used. Figure 10-1(a) shows the scatterplot of the shoe print and height data from Table 10-1, and Figure 10-4 shows the scatterplot of the z scores from the same sample data. Compare Figure 10-1(a) to Figure 10-4 and see that they are essentially the same scatterplots with different scales. The red lines in Figure 10-4 form the same coordinate axes that we have all come to know and love from earlier mathematics courses. The red lines partition Figure 10-4 into four quadrants.

If the points of the scatterplot approximate an uphill line (as in the figure), individual values of the product $z_x \cdot z_y$ tend to be positive (because most of the points are found in the first and third quadrants, where the values of z_x and z_y are either both positive or both negative), so $\Sigma(z_x z_y)$ tends to be positive. If the points of the scatterplot approximate a downhill line, most of the points are in the second and fourth quadrants, where z_x and z_y are opposite in sign, so $\Sigma(z_x z_y)$ tends to be negative. Points that follow no linear pattern tend to be scattered among the four quadrants, so the value of $\Sigma(z_x z_y)$ tends to be close to 0.

We can therefore use $\Sigma(z_x z_y)$ as a measure of how the points are configured among the four quadrants. A large positive sum suggests that the points are predominantly in the first and third quadrants (corresponding to a positive linear correlation), a large negative sum suggests that the points are predominantly in the second and fourth quadrants (corresponding to a negative linear correlation), and a sum near 0 suggests that the points are scattered among the four quadrants (with no linear correlation). We divide $\Sigma(z_x z_y)$ by $n-1$ to get a type of average instead of a statistic that becomes larger simply because there are more data values. (The reasons for dividing by $n-1$ instead of n are essentially the same reasons that relate to the standard deviation.) The end result is Formula 10-2, which can be algebraically manipulated into any of the other expressions for r.

Figure 10-4 **Scatterplot of z Scores from Shoe Print Lengths and Heights in Table 10-1**

using TECHNOLOGY

STATDISK Enter the paired data in columns of the Statdisk Data Window. Select **Analysis** from the main menu bar, then use the option **Correlation and Regression.** Enter a value for the significance level. Select the columns of data to be used, then click on the **Evaluate** button. The STATDISK display will include the value of the linear correlation coefficient along with the critical value of r, the P-value, and other results to be discussed in later sections. A scatterplot can also be obtained by clicking on the **Scatterplot** button. See part of a STATDISK display in Example 1.

continued

MINITAB Enter the paired data in columns C1 and C2, then select **Stat** from the main menu bar, choose **Basic Statistics,** followed by **Correlation,** and enter C1 and C2 for the columns to be used. Minitab will provide the value of the linear correlation coefficient *r* as well as a *P*-value. To obtain a scatterplot, select **Graph, Scatterplot,** then enter C1 and C2 for *X* and *Y*, and click **OK.**

With Minitab 16, you can also click on **Assistant,** then **Regression.** Click on the box with the message **Click to perform analysis.** Fill out the dialog box and select **Linear** for the methods of this section. Click **OK** to get four windows of results that include the value of the linear correlation coefficient *r*, the *P*-value, a scatterplot, and much more helpful information.

EXCEL Excel has a function that calculates the value of the linear correlation coefficient. First enter the paired sample data in columns A and B. Click on the *fx* function key located on the main menu bar. Select the function category **Statistical** and the function name **CORREL,** then click **OK.** In the dialog box, enter the cell range of values for *x*, such as A1:A6. Also enter the cell range of values for *y* such as B1:B6. To obtain a scatterplot, click

on the **Insert** tab, then use the chart type identified as **Scatter.** The style of the scatterplot can be edited by right-clicking on the desired feature.

XLSTAT can also be used. The instructions are included near the end of the following section.

TI-83/84 PLUS Enter the paired data in lists L1 and L2, then press **STAT** and select **TESTS.** Using the option of **LinRegT-Test** will result in several displayed values, including the value of the linear correlation coefficient *r* and a *P*-value.

To obtain a scatterplot, press **2ND**, then **Y=** (for STAT PLOT). Press **ENTER** **ENTER** to turn Plot 1 on, then select the first graph type, which resembles a scatterplot. Set the *X* list and *Y* list labels to L1 and L2 and press **ZOOM**, then select **ZoomStat** and press **ENTER**.

STATCRUNCH Click on **Open StatCrunch.** Enter the columns of data or open a data set. Click on **Stat,** then select **Regression,** then select **Simple Linear.** Enter the columns to be used, then click on **Calculate.**

10-2 Basic Skills and Concepts

Statistical Literacy and Critical Thinking

1. Notation For each of several randomly selected years, the sunspot number and the high value of the Dow Jones Industrial Average are recorded. The sunspot number is a measure of sunspot activity on the sun, and the Dow Jones Industrial Average is one measure of stock market value. For this sample of paired data, what does *r* represent? What does ρ represent? Without doing any research or calculations, estimate the value of *r*.

2. Physics Experiment A physics experiment consists of recording paired data consisting of the time (seconds) elapsed since the beginning of the experiment and the distance (cm) of a robot from its point of origin. Using the paired time/distance data, the value of *r* is calculated to be 0. Is it correct to conclude that there is no relationship between time and distance? Explain.

3. Cause of High Blood Pressure Some studies have shown that there is a correlation between consumption of salt and blood pressure. As more salt is consumed, blood pressure tends to rise. A reporter reads one of these studies and writes the headline "Increased Salt Consumption Causes Blood Pressure to Rise." Is that headline justified? If not, help this reporter by rewriting the headline so that it is correct.

4. Weight Loss and Correlation In a test of the Weight Watchers weight loss program, weights of 40 subjects are recorded before and after the program. Assume that the before/after weights result in $r = 0.876$. Is there sufficient evidence to support a claim of a linear correlation between the before/after weights? Does the value of *r* indicate that the program is effective in reducing weight? Why or why not?

Interpreting *r*. *In Exercises 5–8, use a significance level of* $\alpha = 0.05$.

5. Old Faithful For 40 eruptions of the Old Faithful geyser in Yellowstone National Park, duration times (sec) were recorded along with the time intervals (min) to the next eruption. The paired durations and interval times were used to obtain the results shown in the accompanying

STATDISK display. Is there sufficient evidence to support the claim that there is a linear correlation between the durations of eruptions and the time intervals to the next eruptions? Explain.

STATDISK

```
Correlation Results:
Correlation coeff, r: 0.6869123
Critical r:           ±0.3120061
P-value (two-tailed): 0.000
```

6. Old Faithful For 40 eruptions of the Old Faithful geyser in Yellowstone National Park, duration times (sec) were recorded along with the heights (ft) of the eruptions. The paired duration and height measurements were used to obtain the results shown in the accompanying Excel display. Is there sufficient evidence to support the claim that there is a linear correlation between the durations of eruptions and the heights of the eruptions? Explain.

EXCEL

	A	B	C
		Column 1	Column 2
Column 1		1	
Column 2		0.091648	1

7. Heights of Fathers and Sons The heights (in inches) of a sample of 10 father/son pairs of subjects were measured. Minitab results are shown below (based on data from the National Health Examination Survey). Is there sufficient evidence to support the claim that there is a linear correlation between the heights of fathers and the heights of their sons? Explain.

MINITAB

```
Pearson correlation of FATHER and SON = 0.149
P-Value = 0.681
```

8. Cereal Killers The amounts of sugar (grams of sugar per gram of cereal) and calories (per gram of cereal) were recorded for a sample of 16 different cereals. TI-83/84 Plus calculator results are shown here. Is there sufficient evidence to support the claim that there is a linear correlation between sugar and calories in a gram of cereal? Explain.

TI-83/84 PLUS

Importance of Graphing. *Exercises 9 and 10 provide two data sets from "Graphs in Statistical Analysis," by F. J. Anscombe,* **The American Statistician,** *Vol. 27. For each exercise,*

a. Construct a scatterplot.

b. Find the value of the linear correlation coefficient r, then determine whether there is sufficient evidence to support the claim of a linear correlation between the two variables.

c. Identify the feature of the data that would be missed if part (b) was completed without constructing the scatterplot.

9.

x	10	8	13	9	11	14	6	4	12	7	5
y	9.14	8.14	8.74	8.77	9.26	8.10	6.13	3.10	9.13	7.26	4.74

10.

x	10	8	13	9	11	14	6	4	12	7	5
y	7.46	6.77	12.74	7.11	7.81	8.84	6.08	5.39	8.15	6.42	5.73

11. Effects of an Outlier Refer to the accompanying Minitab-generated scatterplot.

a. Examine the pattern of all 10 points and subjectively determine whether there appears to be a correlation between x and y.

b. After identifying the 10 pairs of coordinates corresponding to the 10 points, find the value of the correlation coefficient r and determine whether there is a linear correlation.

c. Now remove the point with coordinates (10, 10) and repeat parts (a) and (b).

d. What do you conclude about the possible effect from a single pair of values?

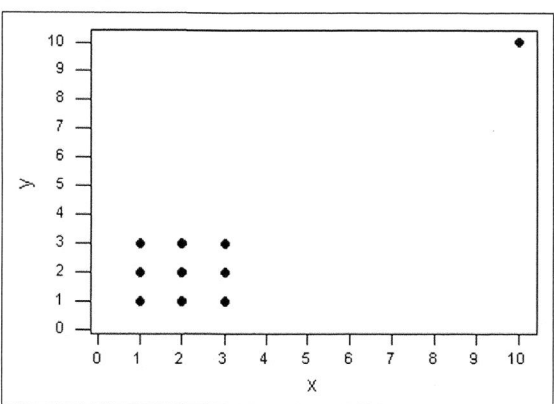

12. Effects of Clusters Refer to the following Minitab-generated scatterplot. The four points in the lower left corner are measurements from women, and the four points in the upper right corner are from men.

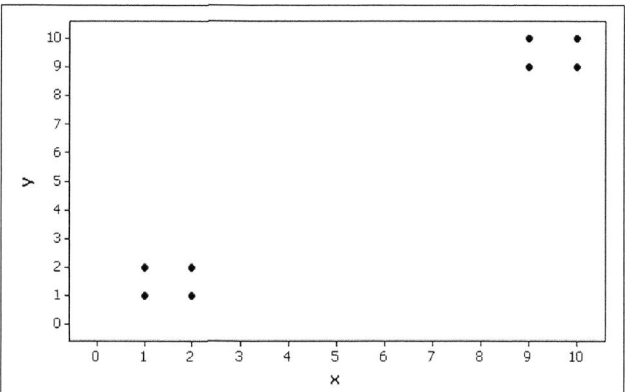

a. Examine the pattern of the four points in the lower left corner (from women) only, and subjectively determine whether there appears to be a correlation between x and y for women.

b. Examine the pattern of the four points in the upper right corner (from men) only, and subjectively determine whether there appears to be a correlation between x and y for men.

c. Find the linear correlation coefficient using only the four points in the lower left corner (for women). Will the four points in the upper left corner (for men) have the same linear correlation coefficient?

d. Find the value of the linear correlation coefficient using all eight points. What does that value suggest about the relationship between x and y?

e. Based on the preceding results, what do you conclude? Should the data from women and the data from men be considered together, or do they appear to represent two different and distinct populations that should be analyzed separately?

Testing for a Linear Correlation. *In Exercises 13–28, construct a scatterplot, and find the value of the linear correlation coefficient r. Also find the P-value or the critical values of r from Table A-6 using α = 0.05. Determine whether there is sufficient evidence to support a claim of a linear correlation between the two variables. (Save your work because the same data sets will be used in Section 10-3 exercises.)*

13. Lemons and Car Crashes Listed below are annual data for various years. The data are weights (metric tons) of lemons imported from Mexico and U.S. car crash fatality rates per 100,000 population [based on data from "The Trouble with QSAR (or How I Learned to Stop Worrying and Embrace Fallacy)" by Stephen Johnson, *Journal of Chemical Information and Modeling,* Vol. 48, No. 1]. Is there sufficient evidence to conclude that there is a linear correlation between weights of lemon imports from Mexico and U.S. car fatality rates? Do the results suggest that imported lemons cause car fatalities?

Lemon Imports	230	265	358	480	530
Crash Fatality Rate	15.9	15.7	15.4	15.3	14.9

14. PSAT and SAT Scores Listed below are PSAT scores and SAT scores from prospective college applicants. The scores were reported by subjects who responded to a request posted by the Web site talk.collegeconfidential.com. Is there sufficient evidence to conclude that there is a linear correlation between PSAT scores and SAT scores? Is there anything about the data that might make the results questionable?

PSAT	183	207	167	206	197	142	193	176
SAT	2200	2040	1890	2380	2290	2070	2370	1980

15. Campus Crime Listed below are numbers of enrolled students (in thousands) and numbers of burglaries for randomly selected large colleges in a recent year (based on data from the *New York Times*). Is there sufficient evidence to conclude that there is a linear correlation between enrollment and burglaries? Do the results change if the actual enrollments are listed as 32,000, 31,000, 53,000, and so on?

Enrollment	32	31	53	28	27	36	42	30	34	46
Burglaries	103	103	86	57	32	131	157	20	27	161

16. Altitude and Temperature Listed below are altitudes (thousands of feet) and outside air temperatures (degrees Fahrenheit) recorded by the author during Delta Flight 1053 from New Orleans to Atlanta. Is there sufficient evidence to conclude that there is a linear correlation between altitude and outside air temperatue? Do the results change if the altitudes are reported in meters and the temperatures are converted to the Celsius scale?

Altitude	3	10	14	22	28	31	33
Temperature	57	37	24	−5	−30	−41	−54

17. Town Courts Listed below are amounts of court fine revenue and salaries paid to the town justices (based on data from the *Poughkeepsie Journal*). All amounts are in thousands of dollars, and all of the towns are in Dutchess County, New York. Is there sufficient evidence to conclude that there is a linear correlation between court incomes and justice salaries? Based on the results, does it appear that justices might profit by levying larger fines?

Court Income	65	404	1567	1131	272	252	111	154	32
Justice Salary	30	44	92	56	46	61	25	26	18

18. Auction Bids The author is a member of the board of directors of a nonprofit organization that held a fund-raising auction. He recorded the opening bids suggested by the auctioneer and the final winning bids for several items. The amounts are listed below. Is there sufficient evidence to conclude that there is a linear correlation between the opening bids suggested by the auctioneer and the final winning bids?

Opening Bid	1500	500	500	400	300
Winning Bid	650	175	125	275	125

19. Galaxy Distances The table below lists measured amounts of redshift and the distances (billions of light-years) to randomly selected clusters of galaxies (based on data from *The Cosmic Perspective* by Bennett et al., Benjamin Cummings). Is there sufficient evidence to conclude that there is a linear correlation between amounts of redshift and distances to clusters of galaxies? What do the results suggest about the relationship between the two variables?

Redshift	0.0233	0.0539	0.0718	0.0395	0.0438	0.0103
Distance	0.32	0.75	1.00	0.55	0.61	0.14

20. Diamond Prices The table below lists weights (carats) and prices (dollars) of randomly selected diamonds. All of the diamonds are round with ratings of "very good" cut, they all have a color rating of F ("slight color"), and a clarity rating of VSI ("very slightly included"). The values are based on data from the retailer Blue Nile. For diamonds of the type described, is there sufficient evidence to conclude that there is a linear correlation between weights and prices? Do the results also apply to other types of diamonds, such as those with different color and clarity ratings?

Weight	0.3	0.4	0.5	0.5	1.0	0.7
Price	510	1151	1343	1410	5669	2277

21. Measuring Seals from Photos Listed below are the overhead widths (in cm) of seals measured from photographs and the weights (in kg) of the seals (based on "Mass Estimation of Weddell Seals Using Techniques of Photogrammetry," by R. Garrott of Montana State University). The purpose of the study was to determine if weights of seals could be determined from overhead photographs. Is there sufficient evidence to conclude that there is a linear correlation between overhead widths of seals from photographs and the weights of the seals?

Overhead Width	7.2	7.4	9.8	9.4	8.8	8.4
Weight	116	154	245	202	200	191

22. Car Repair Costs Listed below are repair costs (in dollars) for cars crashed at 6 mi/h in full-front crash tests and the same cars crashed at 6 mi/h in full-rear crash tests (based on data from the Insurance Institute for Highway Safety). The cars are the Toyota Camry, Mazda 6, Volvo S40, Saturn Aura, Subaru Legacy, Hyundai Sonata, and Honda Accord. Is there sufficient evidence to conclude that there is a linear correlation between the repair costs from full-front crashes and full-rear crashes?

Front	936	978	2252	1032	3911	4312	3469
Rear	1480	1202	802	3191	1122	739	2767

23. Blood Pressure Measurements Listed below are systolic blood pressure measurements (in mm Hg) obtained from the same woman (based on data from "Consistency of Blood Pressure Differences Between the Left and Right Arms," by Eguchi, et al., *Archives of Internal Medicine*, Vol. 167). Is there sufficient evidence to conclude that there is a linear correlation between right and left arm systolic blood pressure measurements?

Right Arm	102	101	94	79	79
Left Arm	175	169	182	146	144

24. Crickets and Temperature One classic application of correlation involves the association between the temperature and the number of times a cricket chirps in a minute. Listed below are the numbers of chirps in 1 min and the corresponding temperatures in °F (based on data from *The Song of Insects* by George W. Pierce, Harvard University Press). Is there sufficient evidence to conclude that there is a linear correlation between the number of chirps in 1 min and the temperature?

Chirps in 1 min	882	1188	1104	864	1200	1032	960	900
Temperature (°F)	69.7	93.3	84.3	76.3	88.6	82.6	71.6	79.6

25. Gas Prices Gas prices have been very volatile in recent years. The table below lists gas prices (dollars per gallon) at randomly selected Connecticut stations at the time of this writing (based on data from AOL Autos). Is there sufficient evidence to conclude that there is a linear correlation between prices of regular gas and prices of premium gas? For the gas stations that sometimes post only the price of regular gas, can you use those prices to get a good sense of the price of premium gas?

Regular	2.77	2.77	2.79	2.81	2.78	2.86	2.75	2.77
Mid-Grade	3.00	2.77	2.89	2.93	2.93	2.96	2.86	2.91
Premium	3.07	3.09	3.00	3.06	3.03	3.06	3.02	3.03

26. Gas Prices Repeat the preceding exercise using the prices of regular gas and the prices of mid-grade gas.

27. Sports Diameters (cm), circumferences (cm), and volumes (cm³) from balls used in different sports are listed in the table below. Is there sufficient evidence to conclude that there is a linear correlation between diameters and circumferences? Does the scatterplot confirm a *linear* association?

	Baseball	Basketball	Golf	Soccer	Tennis	Ping-Pong	Volleyball	Softball
Diameter	7.4	23.9	4.3	21.8	7.0	4.0	20.9	9.7
Circumference	23.2	75.1	13.5	68.5	22.0	12.6	65.7	30.5
Volume	212.2	7148.1	41.6	5424.6	179.6	33.5	4780.1	477.9

28. Sports Repeat the preceding exercise using diameters and volumes.

Large Data Sets.   In Exercises 29–32, use the data from Appendix B to construct a scatterplot, find the value of the linear correlation coefficient r, and find either the P-value or the critical values of r from Table A-6 using $\alpha = 0.05$. Determine whether there is sufficient evidence to support the claim of a linear correlation between the two variables. (Save your work because the same data sets will be used in Section 10-3 exercises.)

29. IQ and Brain Volume Refer to Data Set 6 in Appendix B and use the paired data consisting of brain volume (cm^3) and IQ score.

30. Flight Delays Refer to Data Set 15 in Appendix B and use the departure delay times and the arrival delay times.

31. Word Counts of Men and Women Refer to Data Set 17 in Appendix B and use the word counts measured from men and women in couple relationships listed in the first two columns of Data Set 17.

32. Earthquakes Refer to Data Set 16 in Appendix B and use the magnitudes and depths from the earthquakes.

10-2 Beyond the Basics

33. Transformed Data In addition to testing for a linear correlation between x and y, we can often use *transformations* of data to explore other relationships. For example, we might replace each x value by x^2 and use the methods of this section to determine whether there is a linear correlation between y and x^2. Given the paired data in the accompanying table, construct the scatterplot and then test for a linear correlation between y and each of the following. Which case results in the largest value of r?

a. x **b.** x^2 **c.** $\log x$ **d.** $\sqrt{x}$ **e.** $1/x$

x	2	3	20	50	95
y	0.3	0.5	1.3	1.7	2.0

34. Finding Critical r Values Table A-6 lists critical values of r for selected values of n and α. More generally, critical r values can be found by using the formula

$$r = \frac{t}{\sqrt{t^2 + n - 2}}$$

where the t value is found from the table of critical t values (Table A-3) assuming a two-tailed case with $n - 2$ degrees of freedom. Use the formula for r given here and Table A-3 (with $n - 2$ degrees of freedom) to find the critical r values corresponding to $H_1: \rho \neq 0$, $\alpha = 0.02$, and $n = 27$.

10-3   Regression

Key Concept Suppose that we have a collection of paired data and we use the methods of Section 10-2 to conclude that there is a linear correlation between two variables. This section presents methods for finding the equation of the straight line that best fits a scatterplot of the sample data. That best-fitting straight line is called the *regression line*, and its equation is called the *regression equation*. We can use the regression equation to make predictions for the value of one of the variables given some specific value of the other variable. In Part 2 of this section we discuss marginal change, influential points, and residual plots as tools for analyzing correlation and regression results.

Part 1: Basic Concepts of Regression

In some cases, two variables are related in a *deterministic* way, meaning that given a value for one variable, the value of the other variable is exactly determined without any error, as in the equation $y = 2.54x$ for converting a distance x from inches to centimeters. Such equations are considered in algebra courses, but statistics courses focus on *probabilistic* models, which are equations with a variable that is not determined completely by the other variable. For example, the height of a child cannot be determined completely by the height of the father and/or mother. Sir Francis Galton (1822–1911) studied the phenomenon of heredity and showed that when tall or short couples have children, the heights of those children tend to *regress,* or revert to the more typical mean height for people of the same gender. We continue to use Galton's "regression" terminology, even though our data do not involve the same height phenomena studied by Galton.

DEFINITIONS

Given a collection of paired sample data, the **regression line** (or *line of best fit,* or *least-squares line*) is the straight line that "best" fits the scatterplot of the data. (The specific criterion for the "best-fitting" straight line is the "least-squares" property described later.)

The **regression equation**

$$\hat{y} = b_0 + b_1 x$$

algebraically describes the regression line.

The regression equation expresses a relationship between x (called the **explanatory variable,** or **predictor variable,** or **independent variable**) and $\hat{y}$ (called the **response variable,** or **dependent variable**). The preceding definition shows that in statistics, the typical equation of a straight line $y = mx + b$ is expressed in the form $\hat{y} = b_0 + b_1 x$, where b_0 is the y-intercept and b_1 is the slope.

The values of the slope b_1 and y-intercept b_0 can be easily found by using any one of the many computer programs and calculators designed to provide those values. (See "Using Technology" at the end of this section.)

Objective

Find the equation of a regression line.

Notation for the Equation of a Regression Line

	Population Parameter	Sample Statistic
y-intercept of regression equation	β_0	b_0
Slope of regression equation	β_1	b_1
Equation of the regression line	$y = \beta_0 + \beta_1$	$\hat{y} = b_0 + b_1 x$

Requirements

1. The sample of paired (x, y) data is a *random* sample of quantitative data.

2. Visual examination of the scatterplot shows that the points approximate a straight-line pattern.

3. Outliers can have a strong effect on the regression equation, so remove any outliers if they are known to be errors. Consider the effects of any outliers that are not known errors.

Note: Requirements 2 and 3 above are simplified attempts at checking these formal requirements for regression analysis:

- For each fixed value of x, the corresponding values of y have a normal distribution.

- For the different fixed values of x, the distributions of the corresponding y-values all have the same standard deviation. (This is violated if part of the scatterplot shows points very close to the regression line while another portion of the scatterplot shows points that are much farther away from the regression line. See the discussion of residual plots in Part 2 of this section.)

- For the different fixed values of x, the distributions of the corresponding y-values have means that lie along the same straight line.

The methods of this section are not seriously affected if departures from normal distributions and equal standard deviations are not too extreme.

Formulas for Finding the Slope b_1 and y-Intercept b_0 in the Regression Equation $\hat{y} = b_0 + b_1 x$

Formula 10-3   **Slope:** $b_1 = r\dfrac{s_y}{s_x}$

where r is the linear correlation coefficient, s_y is the standard deviation of the y values, and s_x is the standard deviation of the x values.

Formula 10-4   **y-intercept:** $b_0 = \bar{y} - b_1 \bar{x}$

The slope b_1 and y-intercept b_0 can also be found using the following formulas that are useful for manual calculations or writing computer programs:

$$b_1 = \frac{n(\Sigma xy) - (\Sigma x)(\Sigma y)}{n(\Sigma x^2) - (\Sigma x)^2} \qquad b_0 = \frac{(\Sigma y)(\Sigma x^2) - (\Sigma x)(\Sigma xy)}{n(\Sigma x^2) - (\Sigma x)^2}$$

Rounding the Slope b_1 and the y-Intercept b_0

Round b_1 and b_0 to three significant digits. It's difficult to provide a simple universal rule for rounding values of b_1 and b_0, but this rule will work for most situations in this book. (Depending on how you round, this book's answers to examples and exercises may be slightly different from your answers.)

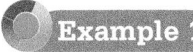 **Example 1** Using Technology to Find the Regression Equation

Refer to the sample data given in Table 10-1 in the Chapter Problem. Use technology to find the equation of the regression line in which the explanatory variable (or x variable) is shoe print length and the response variable (or y variable) is the corresponding height of a person.

Solution

Requirement check (1) The data are assumed to be a simple random sample. (2) Figure 10-1(a) is a scatterplot showing a pattern of points. This pattern is very roughly a straight-line pattern. (3) There are no outliers. The requirements are satisfied.

Using technology: The use of computer software or a calculator is recommended for finding the equation of a regression line. Shown below are the results from STATDISK, Minitab, XLSTAT, the TI-83/84 Plus calculator, SPSS, and JMP. Minitab and XLSTAT provide the actual equation; the other technologies list the values of the y-intercept and the slope. All of these technologies show that the regression equation can be expressed as $\hat{y} = 125 + 1.73x$, where $\hat{y}$ is the predicted height of a person and x is the length of the shoe print.

STATDISK

```
Regression Results:
Y= b0 + b1x:
Y Intercept, b0:       125.4073
Slope, b1:              1.727452
```

EXCEL (XLSTAT)

Equation of the model:		
Height = 125.40733+1.72745*Shoe Print		

MINITAB

```
Regression Analysis: Height versus Shoe Print

The regression equation is
Height = 125 + 1.73 Shoe Print
```

TI-83/84 PLUS

```
LinRegTTest
 y=a+bx
 β≠0 and ρ≠0
↑a=125.4073302
 b=1.72745239
 s=4.538762333
↓r²=.3495991312
```

SPSS

Model		Unstandardized Coefficients		Standardized Coefficients		
		B	Std. Error	Beta	t	Sig.
1	(Constant)	125.407	40.915		3.065	.055
	Shoeprint	1.727	1.360	.591	1.270	.294

JMP

Term	Estimate	Std Error	t Ratio	Prob>|t|
Intercept	125.40733	40.91531	3.07	0.0548
Shoeprint	1.7274524	1.360351	1.27	0.2937

We should know that the regression equation is an *estimate* of the true regression equation for the population of paired data. This estimate is based on one particular set of sample data, but another sample drawn from the same population would probably lead to a slightly different equation.

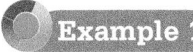 **Example 2** Using Manual Calculations to Find the
                              Regression Equation

Refer to the sample data given in Table 10-1 in the Chapter Problem. Use Formulas 10-3 and 10-4 to find the equation of the regression line in which the explanatory variable (or x variable) is the shoe print length and the response variable (or y variable) is the corresponding height of the person.

Solution

Requirement check The requirements are verified in Example 1.

We begin by finding the slope b_1 with Formula 10-3 as follows (with extra digits included for greater accuracy). Remember, r is the linear correlation coefficient,

s_y is the standard deviation of the sample y values, and s_x is the standard deviation of the sample x values.

$$b_1 = r\frac{s_y}{s_x} = 0.591269 \cdot \frac{4.87391}{1.66823} = 1.72745$$

After finding the slope b_1, we can now use Formula 10-4 to find the y-intercept as follows:

$$b_0 = \bar{y} - b_1\bar{x} = 177.3 - (1.72745)(30.04) = 125.40740$$

After rounding, the slope and y-intercept are $b_1 = 1.73$ and $b_0 = 125$. We can now express the regression equation as $\hat{y} = 125 + 1.73x$, where $\hat{y}$ is the predicted height of a person and x is the length of the shoe print.

Example 3   Graphing the Regression Line

Graph the regression equation $\hat{y} = 125 + 1.73x$ (found in Examples 1 and 2) on the scatterplot of the shoe print and height data from Table 10-1 and examine the graph to subjectively determine how well the regression line fits the data.

Solution

Shown below is the Minitab display of the scatterplot with the graph of the regression line included. We can see that the regression line doesn't fit the data very well.

Using the Regression Equation for Predictions

Regression equations are often useful for *predicting* the value of one variable, given some specific value of the other variable. When making predictions, we should consider the following:

1. Use the regression equation for predictions only if the graph of the regression line on the scatterplot confirms that the regression line fits the points reasonably well.

2. Use the regression equation for predictions only if the linear correlation coefficient r indicates that there is a linear correlation between the two variables (as described in Section 10-2).

3. Use the regression line for predictions only if the data do not go much beyond the scope of the available sample data. (Predicting too far beyond the scope of the available sample data is called *extrapolation,* and it could result in bad predictions.)

4. If the regression equation does not appear to be useful for making predictions, the best predicted value of a variable is its sample mean.

Strategy for Predicting Values of *y*

Is the regression equation a good model?
- **The regression line graphed in the scatterplot shows that the line fits the points well.**
- *r* indicates that there is a linear correlation.
- **The prediction is not much beyond the scope of the available sample data.**

Yes.
The regression equation is a good model.

No.
The regression equation is *not* a good model.

Substitute the given value of *x* into the regression equation $\hat{y} = b_0 + b_1 x$.

Regardless of the value of *x*, the best predicted value of *y* is the value of $\bar{y}$ (the mean of the *y* values).

Figure 10-5   **Recommended Strategy for Predicting Values of *y***

Figure 10-5 summarizes a strategy for predicting values of a variable *y* when given some value of *x*. Figure 10-5 shows that if the regression equation is a good model, then we substitute the value of *x* into the regression equation to find the predicted value of *y*. However, if the regression equation is not a good model, the best predicted value of *y* is simply $\bar{y}$, the mean of the *y* values. Remember, this strategy applies to *linear* patterns of points in a scatterplot. If the scatterplot shows a pattern that is not a straight-line pattern, other methods apply, as described in Section 10-6.

Example 4   Predicting Height

Use the given data to predict the height of someone with a shoe print length of 29 cm.
- **a.** Use the 5 pairs of shoe print lengths and heights from Table 10-1 to predict the height of a person with a shoe print length of 29 cm.
- **b.** Use the 40 pairs of shoe print lengths and heights from Data Set 2 in Appendix B and predict the height of a person with a shoe print length of 29 cm.

Solution

Shown below are key points in the solutions for parts (a) and (b). Note that in part (a), the paired data *do not* result in a good regression model, so the predicted height is $\bar{y}$, the mean of the five heights. However, part (b) shows that the shoe print and height data *do* result in a good regression model, so the predicted height is found by substituting the value of $x = 29$ cm into the regression equation.

(a) Bad Model: Use $\bar{y}$ for Predictions

Use the 5 pairs of sample data from Table 10-1 to predict the height of someone with a shoe print length of 29 cm:

(b) Good Model: Use the Regression Equation for Predictions

Use the 40 pairs of sample data from Data Set 2 in Appendix B to predict the height of someone with a shoe print length of 29 cm:

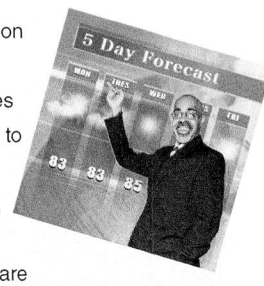

1° Forecast Error = $1 Billion

The prediction of forecast temperatures might seem to be an inexact science, but many companies are working feverishly to obtain more accurate predictions. *USA Today* reporter Del Jones wrote that we could save $1 billion in a year if we could forecast temperatures more accurately by just 1 degree Fahrenheit. Jones reported that for the region served by the Tennessee Valley Authority, forecast temperatures have been off by about 2.35 degrees, and that error is common for forecasts in the United States. He states that reducing the 2.35 degree error to 1.35 degrees would save the TVA an estimated $100,000 every day. Forecast temperatures are used to determine the allocation of power from generators, nuclear plants, hydroelectric plants, coal, natural gas, and wind. Statistical forecasting techniques are now being refined so that we can all benefit from savings of money and natural resources.

(a) Bad Model (*continued*)

The regression line does *not* fit the points well, as shown here.

$r = 0.591$, which suggests that there is *not* a linear correlation between shoe print length and height. (The *P*-value is 0.294.)

The given shoe print length of 29 cm is not beyond the scope of the available data.

Because the regression equation $\hat{y} = 125 + 1.73x$ is *not* a good model, the best predicted height is simply the mean of the sample heights: $\bar{y} = 177.3$ cm (or 69.8 in.).

(b) Good Model (*continued*)

The regression line *does* fit the points well, as shown here. The equation of this regression line can be easily found from technology to be this:

$$\hat{y} = 80.9 + 3.22x$$

$r = 0.813$, which suggests that there *is* a linear correlation between shoe print length and height. (The *P*-value is 0.000.)

The given shoe print length of 29 cm is not beyond the scope of the available data.

Because the regression equation $\hat{y} = 80.9 + 3.22x$ *is* a good model, substitute $x = 29$ cm into this regression equation to get a predicted height of 174.3 cm (or 68.6 in.).

Interpretation

Key point: Use the regression equation for predictions only if it is a good model. If the regression equation is not a good model, use the predicted value of $\bar{y}$.

Part 2: Beyond the Basics of Regression

In Part 2 we consider the concept of marginal change, which is helpful in interpreting a regression equation; then we consider the effects of outliers and special points called *influential points*. We also consider residual plots.

Interpreting the Regression Equation: Marginal Change

We can use the regression equation to see the effect on one variable when the other variable changes by some specific amount.

> **DEFINITION** In working with two variables related by a regression equation, the **marginal change** in a variable is the amount that it changes when the other variable changes by exactly one unit. The slope b_1 in the regression equation represents the marginal change in *y* that occurs when *x* changes by one unit.

Let's consider the 40 pairs of shoe print lengths and heights included in Data Set 2 of Appendix B. Those 40 pairs of values result in this regression equation: $\hat{y} = 80.9 + 3.22x$. The slope of 3.22 tells us that if we increase x (the length of the shoe print) by 1 cm, the predicted height of the person will increase by 3.22 cm. That is, for every additional 1 cm increase in the length of a shoe print, we expect the height to increase by 3.22 cm.

Outliers and Influential Points

A correlation/regression analysis of bivariate (paired) data should include an investigation of *outliers* and *influential points,* defined as follows.

> **DEFINITIONS**
>
> In a scatterplot, an **outlier** is a point lying far away from the other data points.
>
> Paired sample data may include one or more **influential points,** which are points that strongly affect the graph of the regression line.

To determine whether a point is an outlier, examine the scatterplot to see if the point is far away from the others. Here's how to determine whether a point is an influential point: First graph the regression line resulting from the data with the point included, then graph the regression line resulting from the data with the point excluded. If the regression line changes by a considerable amount, the point is influential.

Example 5 Influential Point

Consider the 40 pairs of shoe print lengths and heights from Data Set 2 in Appendix B. The scatterplot located to the left below shows the regression line. If we include this additional pair of data: $x = 35$ cm, $y = 25$ cm (shoe length is 35 cm and height is 25 cm), we get the regression line shown to the right below. The additional point (35 cm, 25 cm) is an influential point because the graph of the regression line did change considerably, as shown by the regression line located to the right below. Compare the two graphs and you will see clearly that the addition of that one pair of values has a very dramatic effect on the regression line, so that additional point is an influential point. The additional point is also an outlier because it is far from the other points.

Original Paired Shoe Print and Height Data

Shoe Print and Height Data with an Additional Point (35 cm, 25 cm)

Residuals and the Least-Squares Property

We stated that the regression equation represents the straight line that "best" fits the data. The criterion to determine the line that is better than all others is based on the vertical distances between the original data points and the regression line. Such distances are called *residuals*.

> **DEFINITION** For a pair of sample x and y values, the **residual** is the difference between the *observed* sample value of y and the y value that is *predicted* by using the regression equation. That is,
>
> $$\text{residual} = \text{observed } y - \text{predicted } y = y - \hat{y}$$

x	1	2	4	5
y	4	24	8	32

The paired data are plotted as blue points in Figure 10-6.

So far, this definition hasn't yet won any prizes for simplicity, but you can easily understand residuals by referring to Figure 10-6, which corresponds to the paired sample data shown in the margin. In Figure 10-6, the residuals are represented by the dashed lines.

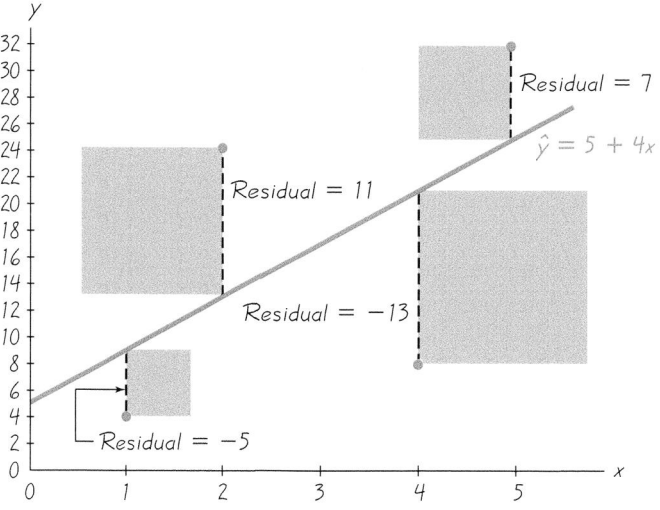

Figure 10-6   Residuals and Squares of Residuals

Consider the sample point with coordinates of (5, 32). If we substitute $x = 5$ into the regression equation $\hat{y} = 5 + 4x$, we get a predicted value of $\hat{y} = 25$. But the actual observed sample value is $y = 32$. The difference $y - \hat{y} = 32 - 25 = 7$ is a residual.

The regression equation represents the line that "best" fits the points according to the following least-squares property.

> **DEFINITION** A straight line satisfies the **least-squares property** if the sum of the squares of the residuals is the smallest sum possible.

From Figure 10-6, we see that the residuals are -5, 11, -13, and 7, so the sum of their squares is

$$(-5)^2 + 11^2 + (-13)^2 + 7^2 = 364$$

We can visualize the least-squares property by referring to Figure 10-6, where the squares of the residuals are represented by the red-square areas. The sum of the red-square areas is 364, which is the smallest sum possible. Use any other straight line, and the red squares will combine to produce an area larger than the combined red area of 364.

Fortunately, we need not deal directly with the least-squares property when we want to find the equation of the regression line. Calculus has been used to build the least-squares property into Formulas 10-3 and 10-4. Because the derivations of these formulas require calculus, we don't include the derivations in this text, and for that, we should be very thankful.

Residual Plots

In this section and the preceding section we listed simplified requirements for the effective analyses of correlation and regression results. We noted that we should always begin with a scatterplot, and we should verify that the pattern of points is approximately a straight-line pattern. We should also consider outliers. A *residual plot* can be another helpful tool for analyzing correlation and regression results and for checking the requirements necessary for making inferences about correlation and regression.

> **DEFINITION** A **residual plot** is a scatterplot of the (x, y) values after each of the y-coordinate values has been replaced by the residual value $y - \hat{y}$ (where $\hat{y}$ denotes the predicted value of y). That is, a residual plot is a graph of the points $(x, y - \hat{y})$.

To construct a residual plot, draw a horizontal reference line through the residual value of 0, then plot the paired values of $(x, y - \hat{y})$. Because the manual construction of residual plots can be tedious, the use of computer software is strongly recommended. When analyzing a residual plot, look for a pattern in the way the points are configured, and use these criteria:

- The residual plot should not have any obvious pattern (not even a straight line pattern). (This confirms that a scatterplot of the sample data is a straight-line pattern and not some other pattern that is not a straight line.)

- The residual plot should not become much wider (or thinner) when viewed from left to right. (This confirms the requirement that for the different fixed values of x, the distributions of the corresponding y values all have the same standard deviation.)

Example 6 Residual Plot

The shoe print and height data from Table 10-1 are used to obtain the accompanying Minitab-generated residual plot. The first sample x value of 29.7 cm is substituted into the regression equation of $\hat{y} = 125 + 1.73x$ (found in Examples 1 and 2). The result is the predicted value of $\hat{y} = 176.4$ cm. For the first x value of 29.7 cm, the actual corresponding y value is 175.3 cm, so the value of the residual is

$$\text{observed } y - \text{predicted } y = y - \hat{y} = 175.3 - 176.4 = -1.1$$

(The result is -1.4 if we use greater precision in the calculations.) Using the x value of 29.7 cm and the residual of -1.1, we get the coordinates of the point $(29.7, -1.1)$, which is one of the points in the residual plot shown on the following page. This residual plot becomes thicker, suggesting that the regression equation might not be a good model.

MINITAB

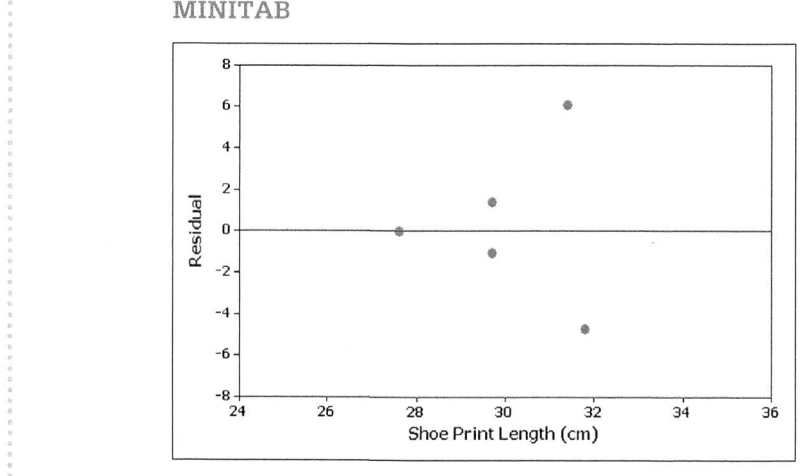

See the three residual plots below. The leftmost residual plot suggests that the regression equation is a good model. The middle residual plot shows a distinct pattern, suggesting that the sample data do not follow a straight-line pattern as required. The rightmost residual plot becomes thicker, which suggests that the requirement of equal standard deviations is violated.

Residual Plot Suggesting That the Regression Equation Is a Good Model	**Residual Plot with an Obvious Pattern, Suggesting That the Regression Equation Is Not a Good Model**	**Residual Plot That Becomes Thicker, Suggesting That the Regression Equation Is Not a Good Model**
		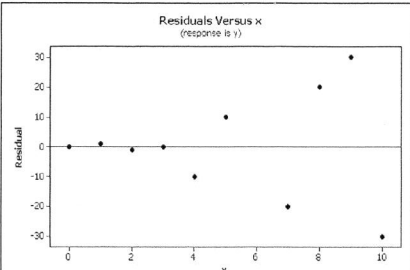

Complete Regression Analysis

In Part 1 of this section, we identified simplified criteria for determining whether a regression equation is a good model. A more complete and thorough analysis can be implemented with the following steps:

1. Construct a scatterplot and verify that the pattern of the points is approximately a straight-line pattern without outliers. (If there are outliers, consider their effects by comparing results that include the outliers to results that exclude the outliers.)

2. Construct a residual plot and verify that there is no pattern and also verify that the residual plot does not become thicker (or thinner).

3. Use a histogram and/or normal quantile plot to confirm that the values of the residuals have a distribution that is approximately normal.

4. Consider any effects of a pattern over time.

using TECHNOLOGY

Because of the messy calculations involved, the linear correlation coefficient r and the slope and y-intercept of the regression line are usually found using a calculator or computer software.

STATDISK First enter the paired data in columns of the Statdisk Data Window. Select **Analysis** from the main menu bar, then use the option **Correlation and Regression.** Enter a value for the significance level and select the columns of data. Click on the **Evaluate** button. The display will include the value of the linear correlation coefficient along with the critical value of r and the P-value, the conclusion about correlation, and the intercept and slope of the regression equation, as well as some other results. Click on **Plot** to get a graph of the scatterplot with the regression line included.

MINITAB First enter the x values in column C1 and enter the y values in column C2 (or use any other columns). In Section 10-2 we saw that we could find the value of the linear correlation coefficient r by selecting **Stat/Basic Statistics/Correlation.** To get the equation of the regression line, select **Stat/Regression/Regression,** and enter C2 for "response" and C1 for "predictor." To get the graph of the scatterplot with the regression line, select **Stat/Regression/Fitted Line Plot,** then enter C2 for the response variable and C1 for the predictor variable. Select the "linear" model.

With Minitab Release 16 or later, you can also click on **Assistant,** then select **Regression.** Click on the icon to perform the analysis, then complete the dialog box that appears. There will be much helpful information displayed.

EXCEL Enter the paired data in columns A and B. Use either XLSTAT or Excel's Data Analysis add-in.

XLSTAT Click on **XLSTAT,** then select **Modeling Data,** then **Linear Regression.** In the dialog box that appears, first enter the range of the sample values for the dependent y variable in the box

identified as "Y/Dependent variable." Next, enter the range of quantitative values for the independent x variable in the box identified as "X/Explanatory variable." Put a checkmark next to the "Variable labels" box only if the first row of each column consists of names or labels. Click **OK.** After the results are displayed, look for the value of the linear correlation coefficient r in the "Correlation matrix" table. The P-value can be found in the last column of the "Analysis of Variance" table. The equation of the regression line is identified as "Equation of the model."

Data Analysis add-in: If using Excel 2103, 2010, or 2007, click on **Data,** then click on **Data Analysis;** if using Excel 2003, click on **Tools,** then click on **Data Analysis.** Select **Regression,** then click on **OK.** Enter the range for the y values, such as B1:B10. Enter the range for the x values, such as A1:A10. Click on the box adjacent to Line Fit Plots, then click **OK.** Among all of the information provided by Excel, the slope and intercept of the regression equation can be found under the table heading "Coefficient." The displayed graph will include a scatterplot of the original sample points along with the points that would be predicted by the regression equation. You can easily get the regression line by connecting the "predicted y" points.

TI-83/84 PLUS Enter the paired data in lists L1 and L2, then press **STAT** and select **TESTS,** then choose the option **LinRegTTest.** The displayed results will include the y-intercept and slope of the regression equation. Instead of b_0 and b_1, the TI-83/84 display represents these values as a and b.

STATCRUNCH Click on **Open StatCrunch.** Enter the columns of data or open a data set. Click on **Stat,** then select **Regression,** then select **Simple Linear.** Enter the columns to be used, then click on **Calculate.** The equation of the regression line will be found in the fourth line of the display.

10-3 Basic Skills and Concepts

Statistical Literacy and Critical Thinking

1. Notation and Terminology If we use the paired height/pulse data for females from Data Set 1 in Appendix B, we get this regression equation: $\hat{y} = 73.9 + 0.0223x$, where x represents height (cm) and the pulse rate is in beats per minute. What does the symbol $\hat{y}$ represent? In this case, what does the predictor variable represent? What does the response variable represent?

2. Best-Fit Line In what sense is the regression line the straight line that "best" fits the points in a scatterplot?

3. Correlation and Slope Formula 10-3 shows that the slope of a regression line can be found by evaluating $r \cdot s_y/s_x$. What do we know about the graph of the regression line if r is a positive value? What do we know about the graph of the regression line if r is a negative value?

4. Notation What is the difference between the regression equation $\hat{y} = b_0 + b_1x$ and the regression equation $y = \beta_0 + \beta_1x$?

Making Predictions.   *In Exercises 5–8, let the predictor variable x be the first variable given. Use the given data to find the regression equation and the best predicted value of the response variable. Be sure to follow the prediction procedure summarized in Figure 10-5.*

5. Old Faithful For 40 eruptions of the Old Faithful geyser in Yellowstone National Park, duration times (sec) were recorded along with the time intervals (min) after the eruptions. The linear correlation coefficient is $r = 0.687$ and the regression equation is $\hat{y} = 47.4 + 0.180x$, where x represents duration time. The mean of the 40 duration times is 245.0 sec and the mean of the 40 interval times is 91.4 min. What is the best predicted interval time following an eruption with a duration time of 120 min?

6. Old Faithful For 40 eruptions of the Old Faithful geyser in Yellowstone National Park, duration times (sec) were recorded along with the heights (ft) of the eruptions. The linear correlation coefficient is $r = 0.0915$ and the regression equation is $\hat{y} = 119 + 0.0331x$, where x represents duration time. The mean of the 40 duration times is 245.0 sec and the mean of the 40 heights is 127.2 ft. What is the best predicted height of an eruption with a duration time of 120 min?

7. Heights of Fathers and Sons The heights (in inches) of a sample of 10 father/son pairs of subjects were measured. The linear correlation coefficient is $r = 0.149$ and the regression equation is $\hat{y} = 66.8 + 0.016x$, where x represents the father's height. The mean of the 10 father heights is 69.7 in. and the mean of the 10 son heights is 68.0 in. What is the best predicted height of a son who has a father with a height of 72.0 in.?

8. Cereal Killers The amounts of sugar (grams of sugar per gram of cereal) and calories (per gram of cereal) were recorded for a sample of 16 different cereals. The linear correlation coefficient is $r = 0.765$ and the regression equation is $\hat{y} = 3.46 + 1.01x$, where x represents the amount of sugar. The mean of the 16 amounts of sugar is 0.295 grams and the mean of the 16 calorie counts is 3.76. What is the best predicted calorie count for a cereal with a measured sugar amount of 0.40 g?

Finding the Equation of the Regression Line.   *In Exercises 9 and 10, use the given data to find the equation of the regression line. Examine the scatterplot and identify a characteristic of the data that is ignored by the regression line.*

9.

x	10	8	13	9	11	14	6	4	12	7	5
y	9.14	8.14	8.74	8.77	9.26	8.10	6.13	3.10	9.13	7.26	4.74

10.

x	10	8	13	9	11	14	6	4	12	7	5
y	7.46	6.77	12.74	7.11	7.81	8.84	6.08	5.39	8.15	6.42	5.73

11. Effects of an Outlier Refer to the Minitab-generated scatterplot given in Exercise 11 of Section 10-2.

a. Using the pairs of values for all 10 points, find the equation of the regression line.

b. After removing the point with coordinates (10, 10), use the pairs of values for the remaining 9 points and find the equation of the regression line.

c. Compare the results from parts (a) and (b).

12. Effects of Clusters Refer to the Minitab-generated scatterplot given in Exercise 12 of Section 10-2.

a. Using the pairs of values for all 8 points, find the equation of the regression line.

b. Using only the pairs of values for the 4 points in the lower left corner, find the equation of the regression line.

c. Using only the pairs of values for the 4 points in the upper right corner, find the equation of the regression line.

d. Compare the results from parts (a), (b), and (c).

Regression and Predictions. *Exercises 13–28 use the same data sets as Exercises 13–28 in Section 10-2. In each case, find the regression equation, letting the first variable be the predictor (x) variable. Find the indicated predicted value by following the prediction procedure summarized in Figure 10-5.*

13. Lemons and Car Crashes Find the best predicted crash fatality rate for a year in which there are 500 metric tons of lemon imports.

Lemon Imports	230	265	358	480	530
Crash Fatality Rate	15.9	15.7	15.4	15.3	14.9

14. PSAT and SAT Scores One subject not included in the given table had a PSAT score of 229. Find the best predicted SAT score for this student. Is the result close to the reported value of 2400? Given that the data are from volunteered responses, are the results valid?

PSAT	183	207	167	206	197	142	193	176
SAT	2200	2040	1890	2380	2290	2070	2370	1980

15. Campus Crime Find the best predicted number of burglaries for Ohio State, which had an enrollment of 51,800 students. Is the predicted value close to 329, which was the actual number of burglaries?

Enrollment	32	31	53	28	27	36	42	30	34	46
Burglaries	103	103	86	57	32	131	157	20	27	161

16. Altitude and Temperature At 6327 ft (or 6.327 thousand feet), the author recorded the temperature. Find the best predicted temperature at that altitude. How does the result compare to the actual recorded value of 48°F?

Altitude	3	10	14	22	28	31	33
Temperature	57	37	24	−5	−30	−41	−54

17. Town Courts The court for the town of Beekman had income of $83,941 (or $83.941 thousand). Find the best predicted salary for the justice. Is the result close to the actual salary of $26,088?

Court Income	65	404	1567	1131	272	252	111	154	32
Justice Salary	30	44	92	56	46	61	25	26	18

18. Auction Bids An item not included in the table is a pair of New York Knicks tickets. The auctioneer started the bidding at $300. Find the best predicted winning bid. Is the result close to the actual winning bid of $250?

Opening Bid	1500	500	500	400	300
Winning Bid	650	175	125	275	125

19. **Galaxy Distances** The cluster Hydra has a measured redshift of 0.0126. Find the best predicted distance to that cluster. Is the result close to the actual distance of 0.18 billion light-years?

Redshift	0.0233	0.0539	0.0718	0.0395	0.0438	0.0103
Distance	0.32	0.75	1.00	0.55	0.61	0.14

20. **Diamond Prices** Not included in the table below is a diamond with a weight of 1.50 carats. Find the best predicted price for this diamond. Is the result close to the actual price of $16,097? What is wrong with predicting the price of a 1.50-carat diamond?

Weight	0.3	0.4	0.5	0.5	1.0	0.7
Price	510	1151	1343	1410	5669	2277

21. **Measuring Seals from Photos** Find the best predicted weight of a seal if the overhead width measured from a photograph is 2 cm. Can the prediction be correct? What is wrong with predicting the weight in this case?

Overhead Width	7.2	7.4	9.8	9.4	8.8	8.4
Weight	116	154	245	202	200	191

22. **Car Repair Costs** Find the best predicted repair costs for a full-rear crash for a Volkswagon Passat, given that its repair cost from a full-front crash is $4594. How does the result compare to the $982 actual repair cost from a full-rear crash?

Front	936	978	2252	1032	3911	4312	3469
Rear	1480	1202	802	3191	1122	739	2767

23. **Blood Pressure Measurements** Find the best predicted systolic blood pressure in the left arm given that the systolic blood pressure in the right arm is 100 mm Hg.

Right Arm	102	101	94	79	79
Left Arm	175	169	182	146	144

24. **Crickets and Temperature** Find the best predicted temperature at a time when a cricket chirps 3000 times in 1 minute. What is wrong with this predicted value?

Chirps in 1 min	882	1188	1104	864	1200	1032	960	900
Temperature (°F)	69.7	93.3	84.3	76.3	88.6	82.6	71.6	79.6

25. **Gas Prices** One gas station not included in the table below had a listed price of $2.78 for regular gas. Find the best predicted price of premium gas at this station. Is the result close to the actual price of $2.93 for premium gas?

Regular	2.77	2.77	2.79	2.81	2.78	2.86	2.75	2.77
Mid-Grade	3.00	2.77	2.89	2.93	2.93	2.96	2.86	2.91
Premium	3.07	3.09	3.00	3.06	3.03	3.06	3.02	3.03

26. Gas Prices Using the data from the preceding exercise, find the best predicted price for mid-grade gas for a station that posted $2.78 as the price of regular gas. Is the result close to the actual price of $2.84 for mid-grade gas?

27. Sports Find the best predicted circumference of a marble with a diameter of 1.50 cm. How does the result compare to the actual circumference of 4.7 cm?

	Baseball	Basketball	Golf	Soccer	Tennis	Ping-Pong	Volleyball	Softball
Diameter	7.4	23.9	4.3	21.8	7.0	4.0	20.9	9.7
Circumference	23.2	75.1	13.5	68.5	22.0	12.6	65.7	30.5
Volume	212.2	7148.1	41.6	5424.6	179.6	33.5	4780.1	477.9

28. Sports Using the data from the preceding exercise, find the best predicted volume of a marble with a diameter of 1.50 cm. How does the result compare to the actual volume of 1.8 cm^3?

Large Data Sets. *Exercises 29–32 use the same Appendix B data sets as Exercises 29–32 in Section 10-2. In each case, find the regression equation, letting the first variable be the predictor (x) variable. Find the indicated predicted values following the prediction procedure summarized in Figure 10-5.*

29. IQ and Brain Volume Refer to Data Set 6 in Appendix B and use the paired data consisting of IQ score and brain volume (cm^3). Find the best predicted IQ score for someone with a brain volume of 1000 cm^3.

30. Flight Delays Refer to Data Set 15 in Appendix B and use the departure delay times and the arrival delay times. Find the best predicted arrival delay time for a flight with no departure delay.

31. Word Counts of Men and Women Refer to Data Set 17 in Appendix B and use the word counts measured from men and women in couple relationships listed in the first two columns of Data Set 17. Find the best predicted word count for a woman who is in a couple relationship with a man having a word count of 10,000.

32. Earthquakes Refer to Data Set 16 in Appendix B and use the magnitudes and depths from the earthquakes. Find the best predicted depth of an earthquake with a magnitude of 1.50.

10-3 Beyond the Basics

33. Equivalent Hypothesis Tests Explain why a test of the null hypothesis $H_0: \rho = 0$ is equivalent to a test of the null hypothesis $H_0: \beta_1 = 0$, where ρ is the linear correlation coefficient for a population of paired data, and β_1 is the slope of the regression line for that same population.

34. Least-Squares Property According to the least-squares property, the regression line minimizes the sum of the squares of the residuals. Refer to the data in Table 10-1.

a. Find the sum of squares of the residuals.

b. Show that the regression equation $\hat{y} = 120 + 2.00x$ results in a larger sum of squares of residuals.

10-4   Prediction Intervals and Variation

Key Concept In Section 10-3 we presented a method for using a regression equation to find a predicted value of y, but it is helpful to have some sense of the accuracy of such predictions. In this section we present a method for constructing a *prediction interval*, which is an interval estimate of a predicted value of y. (Interval estimates of parameters are *confidence intervals*, but interval estimates of variables are called *prediction intervals*.)

In Example 4(b) from the preceding section, we showed that when using the 40 pairs of shoe print lengths and heights from Data Set 2 in Appendix B, the regression equation is $\hat{y} = 80.9 + 3.22x$. Given a shoe print length of 29 cm, the best predicted height is $\hat{y} = 174.3$ cm (which is found by substituting 29 cm for x in the regression equation). For $x = 29$ cm, the best predicted height is $\hat{y} = 174.3$ cm, but we have no sense of the accuracy of that estimated height, so we need an interval estimate. Instead of using a confidence interval (which is used for an estimate of a population parameter), we use a *prediction interval*, which is an interval estimate of a predicted value of the variable y. A prediction interval serves the same role as a confidence interval, except that a prediction interval is used for an estimate of a value of a *variable*, whereas a confidence interval is used for an estimate of a value of a population parameter.

> **DEFINITION** A confidence interval is a range of values used to estimate a population parameter, but a **prediction interval** is a range of values used to estimate a variable, such as a predicted value of y in a regression equation.

A prediction interval estimate of a predicted value $\hat{y}$ can be found using the key elements in the following box. Given the nature of the calculations, the use of technology is highly recommended.

Prediction Interval for an Individual y

Requirement

For each fixed value of x, the corresponding sample values of y are normally distributed about the regression line, and those normal distributions have the same variance.

Given a fixed and known value x_0, the prediction interval for an individual y value is

$$\hat{y} - E < y < \hat{y} + E$$

where the margin of error is

$$E = t_{\alpha/2} s_e \sqrt{1 + \frac{1}{n} + \frac{n(x_0 - \bar{x})^2}{n(\Sigma x^2) - (\Sigma x)^2}}$$

and x_0 represents the given value of x, $t_{\alpha/2}$ has $n - 2$ degrees of freedom, and s_e is the **standard error of estimate** found from Formula 10-5 or Formula 10-6. (The standard error of estimate s_e is a measure of variation of the

residuals, which are the differences between the observed sample y values and the predicted values $\hat{y}$ that are found from the regression equation.)

Formula 10-5

$$s_e = \sqrt{\frac{\Sigma(y - \hat{y})^2}{n - 2}}$$

Formula 10-6

$$s_e = \sqrt{\frac{\Sigma y^2 - b_0 \Sigma y - b_1 \Sigma xy}{n - 2}}$$

(This is an equivalent form of Formula 10-5 that is good for manual calculations or writing computer programs.)

Example 1 Shoe Print and Height: Finding a Prediction Interval

If we use the 40 paired shoe print lengths (cm) and heights (cm) from Data Set 2 in Appendix B, we find that there is sufficient evidence to support the claim of a linear correlation between those two variables. Also, the regression equation is $\hat{y} = 80.9 + 3.22x$. If we measure a suspect's shoe print length and obtain a value of 29.0 cm, we can substitute that value into the regression equation to find the predicted height of 174.3 cm. Construct a 95% prediction interval for the height, given that the shoe print length is 29.0 cm (so that $x = 29.0$ cm).

Solution

The accompanying Minitab display automatically provides the 95% prediction interval, which is 162 cm $< y <$ 186 cm when rounded. The same prediction interval could be manually calculated using these components:

$x_0 = 29.0$ (given)

$s_e = 5.943761$ (provided by many technologies, including STATDISK, Minitab, Excel, and TI-83/84 Plus)

$\hat{y} = 174.3$ (predicted value of y found by substituting $x = 29.0$ into the regression equation)

$t_{\alpha/2} = 2.024$ (from Table A-3 with $df = 38$ and an area of 0.05 in two tails)

$n = 40 \quad \bar{x} = 29.0175 \quad \Sigma x = 1160.7 \quad \Sigma x^2 = 33{,}933.17$

Interpretation

The 95% prediction interval is 162 cm $< y <$ 186 cm. This means that if we measure a shoe print and find a length of 29.0 cm, we have 95% confidence that the limits of 162 cm and 186 cm (or 64 in. and 73 in.) contain the height of the suspect. That is a large range of values, so the single shoe print clue doesn't give us very good information about the suspect's height. The prediction interval would be much narrower and our estimated height would be much better if we were using a much larger set of sample data instead of using only the 40 pairs of values listed in Data Set 2 from Appendix B.

MINITAB

Figure 10-7

Unexplained, Explained, and Total Deviation

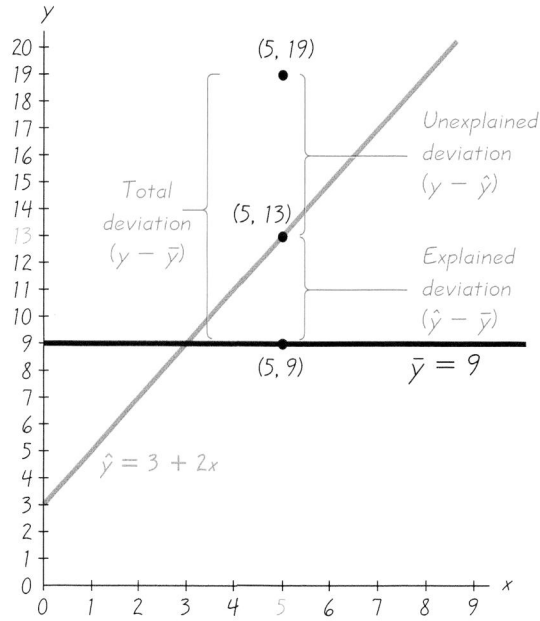

Explained and Unexplained Variation

Assume that we have a sample of paired data having the following properties shown in Figure 10-7:

- There is sufficient evidence to support the claim of a linear correlation between x and y.
- The equation of the regression line is $\hat{y} = 3 + 2x$.
- The mean of the y values is given by $\bar{y} = 9$.
- One of the pairs of sample data is $x = 5$ and $y = 19$.
- The point (5, 13) is one of the points on the regression line, because substituting $x = 5$ into the regression equation of $\hat{y} = 3 + 2x$ yields $\hat{y} = 13$.

Figure 10-7 shows that the point (5, 13) lies on the regression line, but the point (5, 19) from the original data set does not lie on the regression line. If we completely ignore correlation and regression concepts and want to predict a value of y given a value of x and a collection of paired (x, y) data, our best guess would be the mean $\bar{y}$. But in this case there is a linear correlation between x and y, so a better way to predict the value of y when $x = 5$ is to substitute $x = 5$ into the regression equation to get $\hat{y} = 13$. We can explain the discrepancy between $\bar{y} = 9$ and $\hat{y} = 13$ by noting that there is a linear relationship best described by the regression line. Consequently, when $x = 5$, the predicted value of y is 13, not the mean value of 9. For $x = 5$, the predicted value of y is 13, but the observed sample value of y is actually 19. The discrepancy between $\hat{y} = 13$ and $y = 19$ cannot be explained by the regression line, and it is called a *residual* or *unexplained deviation*, which can be expressed in the general format of $y - \hat{y}$.

As in Section 3-3 where we defined the standard deviation, we again consider a *deviation* to be a difference between a value and the mean. (In this case, the mean is $\bar{y} = 9$.) Examine Figure 10-7 carefully and note these specific deviations from $\bar{y} = 9$:

Total deviation (from $\bar{y} = 9$) of the point (5, 19) $= y - \bar{y} = 19 - 9 = 10$

Explained deviation (from $\bar{y} = 9$) of the point (5, 19) $= \hat{y} - \bar{y} = 13 - 9 = 4$

Unexplained deviation (from $\bar{y} = 9$) of the point (5, 19) $= y - \hat{y} = 19 - 13 = 6$

These deviations from the mean are generalized and formally defined as follows.

DEFINITIONS

Assume that we have a collection of paired data containing the sample point (x, y), that $\hat{y}$ is the predicted value of y (obtained by using the regression equation), and that the mean of the sample y values is $\bar{y}$.

The **total deviation** of (x, y) is the vertical distance $y - \bar{y}$, which is the distance between the point (x, y) and the horizontal line passing through the sample mean $\bar{y}$.

The **explained deviation** is the vertical distance $\hat{y} - \bar{y}$, which is the distance between the predicted y value and the horizontal line passing through the sample mean $\bar{y}$.

The **unexplained deviation** is the vertical distance $y - \hat{y}$, which is the vertical distance between the point (x, y) and the regression line. (The distance $y - \hat{y}$ is also called a *residual*, as defined in Section 10-3.)

In Figure 10-7 we can see the following relationship for an individual point (x, y):

$$(\text{total deviation}) = (\text{explained deviation}) + (\text{unexplained deviation})$$
$$(y - \bar{y}) \quad = \quad (\hat{y} - \bar{y}) \quad + \quad (y - \hat{y})$$

The expression above involves deviations away from the mean, and it applies to any one particular point (x, y). If we sum the squares of deviations using all points (x, y), we get amounts of *variation*. The same relationship applies to the sums of squares shown in Formula 10-7, even though the expression above is not algebraically equivalent to Formula 10-7. In Formula 10-7, the **total variation** is the sum of the squares of the total deviation values, the **explained variation** is the sum of the squares of the explained deviation values, and the **unexplained variation** is the sum of the squares of the unexplained deviation values.

Formula 10-7

$$(\text{total variation}) = (\text{explained variation}) + (\text{unexplained variation})$$
$$\text{or} \quad \Sigma(y - \bar{y})^2 \quad = \quad \Sigma(\hat{y} - \bar{y})^2 \quad + \quad \Sigma(y - \hat{y})^2$$

Coefficient of Determination

In Section 10-2 we saw that the linear correlation coefficient r can be used to find the proportion of the total variation in y that can be explained by the linear correlation. This statement was made in Section 10-2:

> **The value of r^2 is the proportion of the variation in y that is explained by the linear relationship between x and y.**

This statement about the explained variation is formalized with the following definition.

DEFINITION The **coefficient of determination** is the proportion of the variation in y that is explained by the regression line. It is computed as

$$r^2 = \frac{\text{explained variation}}{\text{total variation}}$$

We can compute r^2 by using the definition just given with Formula 10-7, or we can simply square the linear correlation coefficient r. Go with squaring r.

Example 2   Shoe Print and Height:
Finding a Coefficient of Determination

If we use the 40 paired shoe print lengths (cm) and heights (cm) from Data Set 2 in Appendix B, we find that the linear correlation coefficient is $r = 0.813$. Find the coefficient of determination. Also, find the percentage of the total variation in y (height) that can be explained by the linear correlation between shoe print length and height.

Solution

With $r = 0.813$, the coefficient of determination is $r^2 = 0.813^2 = 0.661$.

Interpretation

Because r^2 is the proportion of total variation that can be explained, we conclude that 66.1% of the total variation in height can be explained by shoe print length, and the other 33.9% cannot be explained by shoe print length. The other 33.9% might be explained by some other factors and/or random variation.

using TECHNOLOGY

STATDISK   Enter the paired data in columns of the STATDISK Data Window, select **Analysis** from the main menu bar, then select **Correlation and Regression.** Enter a value for the significance level (such as 0.05), and select the two columns of data to be used. Click on **Evaluate.** The STATDISK display will include the linear correlation coefficient r, the coefficient of determination, the regression equation, the value of the standard error of estimate s_e, the total variation, the explained variation, and the unexplained variation.

MINITAB   Minitab can be used to find the regression equation, the standard error of estimate s_e (labeled S), the value of the coefficient of determination (labeled R-sq), and the limits of a prediction interval. Enter the x data in column C1 and the y data in column C2, then select the options **Stat, Regression,** and **Regression.** Enter C2 in the box labeled "Response" and enter C1 in the box labeled "Predictors." If you want a prediction interval for some given value of x, click on the **Options** box and enter the desired value of x_0 in the box labeled "Prediction intervals for new observations."

EXCEL   Excel can be used to find the regression equation, the standard error of estimate s_e, and the coefficient of determination (labeled R square). First enter the paired data in columns A and B and proceed to use either XLSTAT or Excel's Data Analysis add-n.
XLSTAT Use the same procedure given at the end of Section 10-3. See the results in the "Goodness of fit" section, where the value of

s_e is identified as "RMSE" (for root mean square error). The value of r^2 is labeled as R^2.

Data Analysis add-in: If using Excel 2013, 2010, or 2007, click on **Data,** then click on **Data Analysis;** if using Excel 2003, click on **Tools,** then click on **Data Analysis.** Select **Regression,** and then click **OK.** Enter the range for the y values, such as B1:B6. Enter the range for the x values, such as A1:A6. Click **OK.**

TI-83/84 PLUS   The TI-83/84 Plus calculator can be used to find the linear correlation coefficient r, the equation of the regression line, the standard error of estimate s_e, and the coefficient of determination (labeled as r^2). Enter the paired data in lists L1 and L2, then press **STAT** and select **TESTS,** and then choose the option **LinRegTTest.** For Xlist enter L1, for Ylist enter L2, use a Freq (frequency) value of 1, and select $\neq 0$. Scroll down to Calculate, then press **ENTER**.

STATCRUNCH   Click on **Open StatCrunch.** Enter the columns of data or open a data set. Click on **Stat,** then select **Regression,** then select **Simple Linear.** Enter the columns to be used, then click on **Calculate.** Results include the regression equation, the standard error of estimate s_e (identified as "estimate of error standard deviation"), and the value of the coefficient of determination (labeled R-sq). A prediction interval can be obtained by clicking on **Next** and entering a value of x to be used for the prediction.

10-4 Basic Skills and Concepts

Statistical Literacy and Critical Thinking

1. s_e Notation Using Data Set 1 from Appendix B, if we let the predictor variable x represent heights of males and let the response variable y represent weights of males, the sample of

40 heights and weights results in $s_e = 17.5436$ cm. In your own words, describe what that value of s_e represents.

2. Prediction Interval Using the heights and weights described in Exercise 1, a height of 180 cm is used to find that the predicted weight is 88.0 kg, and the 95% prediction interval is displayed by Minitab as (50.7, 123.0). Write a statement that interprets that prediction interval. What is the major advantage of using a prediction interval instead of simply using the predicted weight of 88.0 kg? Why is the terminology of *prediction interval* used instead of *confidence interval*?

3. Coefficient of Determination Using the heights and weights described in Exercise 1, the linear correlation coefficient r is 0.356. Find the value of the coefficient of determination. What practical information does the coefficient of determination provide?

4. Standard Error of Estimate A sample of 12 different statistics textbooks is obtained and their weights are measured in kilograms and in pounds. Using the 12 paired weights (kg, lb), what is the value of s_e? For a Triola textbook that weighs 4.5 lb, the predicted weight in kilograms is 2.04 kg. What is the 95% prediction interval?

Interpreting the Coefficient of Determination. *In Exercises 5–8, use the value of the linear correlation coefficient r to find the coefficient of determination and the percentage of the total variation that can be explained by the linear relationship between the two variables from the Appendix B data sets.*

5. $r = 0.933$ ($x =$ weight of male, $y =$ waist size of male)

6. $r = 0.963$ ($x =$ chest size of a bear, $y =$ weight of a bear)

7. $r = -0.793$ ($x =$ weight of a car, $y =$ highway fuel consumption)

8. $r = 0.751$ ($x =$ weight of discarded plastic, $y =$ household size)

Interpreting a Computer Display. *In Exercises 9–12, refer to the Minitab display obtained by using the paired data consisting of foot lengths (cm) and heights (cm) of the 40 people listed in Data Set 2 of Appendix B. (Unlike the examples in this section, these exercises use foot lengths instead of shoe print lengths.) Along with the paired sample data, Minitab was also given a foot length of 29.0 cm to be used for predicting height.*

MINITAB

```
The regression equation is
Height = 64.1 + 4.29 Foot Length


Predictor      Coef  SE Coef    T      P
Constant      64.13    11.49  5.58  0.000
Foot Length  4.2913   0.4460  9.62  0.000


S = 5.50571   R-Sq = 70.9%   R-Sq(adj) = 70.1%


Predicted Values for New Observations

New Obs     Fit  SE Fit        95% CI              95% PI
      1  188.572   1.718  (185.095, 192.049)  (176.896, 200.247)

Values of Predictors for New Observations

            Foot
New Obs   Length
      1     29.0
```

9. Testing for Correlation Use the information provided in the display to determine the value of the linear correlation coefficient. Given that there are 40 pairs of data, is there sufficient evidence to support a claim of a linear correlation between foot lengths of people and their heights?

10. Identifying Total Variation What percentage of the total variation in height can be explained by the linear correlation between foot length and height?

11. Predicting Height If someone has a foot length of 29.0 cm, what is the single value that is the best predicted height?

12. Finding a Prediction Interval For someone with a foot length of 29.0 cm, identify the 95% prediction interval estimate of their height, and write a statement interpreting that interval.

Finding a Prediction Interval. *In Exercises 13–16, use the paired data consisting of foot lengths (cm) and heights (cm) of the 40 people listed in Data Set 2 of Appendix B. Let x represent foot length and let y represent the corresponding height. Use the given foot length and the given confidence level to construct a prediction interval estimate of height. (Hint: Use the results in the top half of the Minitab display that accompanies Exercises 9–12. Also, $\bar{x} = 25.68$ cm, $\Sigma x = 1027.2$ cm, and $\Sigma x^2 = 26{,}530.92$ cm^2.)*

13. Foot length: 25.0 cm; 95% confidence

14. Foot length: 25.0 cm; 99% confidence

15. Foot length: 22.0 cm; 90% confidence

16. Foot length: 26.0 cm; 95% confidence

Variation and Prediction Intervals. *In Exercises 17–20, find the (a) explained variation, (b) unexplained variation, and (c) indicated prediction interval. In each case, there is sufficient evidence to support a claim of a linear correlation, so it is reasonable to use the regression equation when making predictions.*

17. Altitude and Temperature Listed below are altitudes (thousands of feet) and outside air temperatures (°F) recorded by the author during Delta Flight 1053 from New Orleans to Atlanta. For the prediction interval, use a 95% confidence level with the altitude of 6327 ft (or 6.327 thousand feet).

Altitude	3	10	14	22	28	31	33
Temperature	57	37	24	−5	−30	−41	−54

18. Town Courts Listed below are amounts of court income and salaries paid to the town justices (based on data from the *Poughkeepsie Journal*). All amounts are in thousands of dollars, and all of the towns are in Dutchess County, New York. For the prediction interval, use a 99% confidence level with a court income of $800,000.

Court Income	65	404	1567	1131	272	252	111	154	32
Justice Salary	30	44	92	56	46	61	25	26	18

19. Galaxy Distances The table below lists measured amounts of redshift and the distances (billions of light-years) to randomly selected clusters of galaxies (based on data from *The Cosmic Perspective* by Bennett et al., Benjamin Cummings). For the prediction interval, use a 90% confidence level with a redshift of the cluster Hydra of 0.0126.

Redshift	0.0233	0.0539	0.0718	0.0395	0.0438	0.0103
Distance	0.32	0.75	1.00	0.55	0.61	0.14

20. Diamond Prices The table below lists weights (carats) and prices (dollars) of randomly selected diamonds. For the prediction interval, use a 95% confidence level with a diamond that weighs 0.8 carats.

Weight	0.3	0.4	0.5	0.5	1.0	0.7
Price	510	1151	1343	1410	5669	2277

10-4 Beyond the Basics

21. Confidence Intervals for β_0 and β_1 Confidence intervals for the y-intercept β_0 and slope β_1 for a regression line ($y = \beta_0 + \beta_1 x$) can be found by evaluating the limits in the intervals below.

$$b_0 - E < \beta_0 < b_0 + E$$

where

$$E = t_{\alpha/2} s_e \sqrt{\frac{1}{n} + \frac{\bar{x}^2}{\sum x^2 - \frac{(\sum x)^2}{n}}}$$

$$b_1 - E < \beta_1 < b_1 + E$$

where

$$E = t_{\alpha/2} \cdot \frac{s_e}{\sqrt{\sum x^2 - \frac{(\sum x)^2}{n}}}$$

The y-intercept b_0 and the slope b_1 are found from the sample data and $t_{\alpha/2}$ is found from Table A-3 by using $n - 2$ degrees of freedom. Using the 40 pairs of shoe print lengths (x) and heights (y) from Data Set 2 in Appendix B, find the 95% confidence interval estimates of β_0 and β_1.

22. Confidence Interval for Mean Predicted Value Example 1 in this section illustrated the procedure for finding a prediction interval for an *individual* value of y. When using a specific value x_0 for predicting the *mean* of all values of y, the confidence interval is as follows:

$$\hat{y} - E < \bar{y} < \hat{y} + E$$

where

$$E = t_{\alpha/2} \cdot s_e \sqrt{\frac{1}{n} + \frac{n(x_0 - \bar{x})^2}{n(\sum x^2) - (\sum x)^2}}$$

The critical value $t_{\alpha/2}$ is found with $n - 2$ degrees of freedom. Using the 40 pairs of shoe print lengths (x) and heights (y) from Data Set 2 in Appendix B, find a 95% confidence interval estimate of the mean height given that the shoe print length is 29.0 cm.

10-5 Multiple Regression

Key Concept The preceding sections of this chapter apply to a linear correlation between *two* variables; this section presents methods for analyzing a linear relationship with *more than two* variables. We focus on these key elements: (1) finding the multiple regression equation, and (2) using the value of adjusted R^2 and the P-value as measures of how well the multiple regression equation fits the sample data. Because the required calculations are so difficult, manual calculations are impractical and a threat to mental health, so in this section we emphasize the use and interpretation of results from statistical software or a TI-83/84 Plus calculator.

Part 1: Basic Concepts of a Multiple Regression Equation

As in the preceding sections of this chapter, we will consider *linear* relationships only. The following *multiple regression equation* describes linear relationships involving more than two variables.

> **DEFINITION** A **multiple regression equation** expresses a linear relationship between a response variable y and two or more predictor variables ($x_1, x_2, \ldots, x_k$). The general form of a multiple regression equation obtained from sample data is
>
> $$\hat{y} = b_0 + b_1 x_1 + b_2 x_2 + \ldots + b_k x_k$$

The accompanying box includes the key elements of this section. For notation, the coefficients $b_0, b_1, b_2, \ldots, b_k$ are sample *statistics* used to estimate the corresponding population parameters $\beta_0, \beta_1, \beta_2, \ldots, \beta_k$. Also, note that the multiple regression equation is a natural extension of the format $\hat{y} = b_0 + b_1 x_1$ used in Section 10-3 for regression equations with a single independent variable x_1. In Section 10-3, it would have been reasonable to question why we didn't use the more common format of $y = mx + b$, and we can now see that using $\hat{y} = b_0 + b_1 x_1$ allows us easily to extend that format to include additional predictor variables, as shown below.

Finding a Multiple Regression Equation

Objective

Use sample data from three or more variables to find a multiple regression equation that is useful for predicting values of the response variable y.

Notation

$\hat{y} = b_0 + b_1 x_1 + b_2 x_2 + \ldots + b_k x_k$ (Multiple regression equation found from *sample* data)

$y = \beta_0 + \beta_1 x_1 + \beta_2 x_2 + \ldots + \beta_k x_k$ (Multiple regression equation for the *population* of data)

$\hat{y} =$ predicted value of y (computed using the multiple regression equation)

$k =$ number of *predictor* variables (also called *independent variables* or x variables)

$n =$ sample size (number of values for any one of the variables)

Requirements

For any specific set of x values, the regression equation is associated with a random error often denoted by ε. We assume that such errors are normally distributed with a mean of 0 and a standard deviation of σ and that the random errors are independent. Because these assumptions are difficult to check, we assume throughout this section that the necessary requirements are satisfied.

Procedure for Finding a Multiple Regression Equation

Manual calculations are not practical, so computer software such as STATDISK, Minitab, Excel, StatCrunch, or a TI-83/84 Plus calculator must be used. (See the "Using Technology" instructions at the end of this section.)

Because we use technology to find multiple regression equations, we ignore the actual calculations and focus instead on *interpreting* computer displays.

In 1886, Francis Galton was among the first to study genetics using the methods of regression we are now considering. He wrote the article "Regression Towards Mediocrity in Hereditary Stature" claiming that heights of offspring regress or revert back toward a mean. Example 1 involves that same historical context with more recent data.

Example 1 Heights of Mothers, Fathers, and Daughters

Table 10-4 includes a random sample of heights of mothers, fathers, and their daughters (based on data from the National Health and Nutrition Examination). Find the multiple regression equation in which the response (y) variable is the height of a daughter and the predictor (x) variables are the height of the mother and height of the father.

Solution

Using Minitab with the sample data in Table 10-4, we obtain the results shown in the display.

Table 10-4 Heights (in inches) of Mothers, Fathers, and Their Daughters

Height of Mother	Height of Father	Height of Daughter
63	64	58.6
67	65	64.7
64	67	65.3
60	72	61.0
65	72	65.4
67	72	67.4
59	67	60.9
60	71	63.1
58	66	60.0
72	75	71.1
63	69	62.2
67	70	67.2
62	69	63.4
69	62	68.4
63	66	62.2
64	76	64.7
63	69	59.6
64	68	61.0
60	66	64.0
65	68	65.4

MINITAB

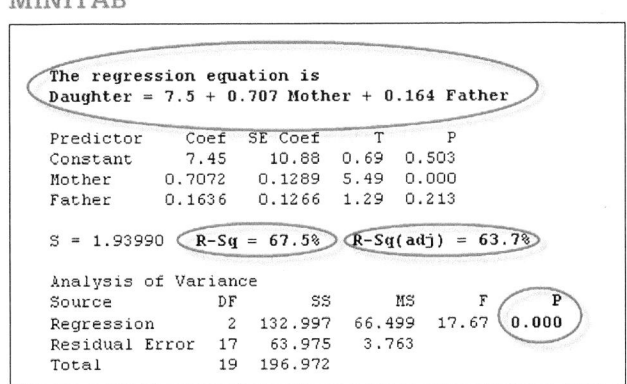

From the display, we see that the multiple regression equation is

$$\text{Daughter} = 7.5 + 0.707\,\text{Mother} + 0.164\,\text{Father}$$

Using our notation presented earlier in this section, we could write this equation as

$$\hat{y} = 7.5 + 0.707x_1 + 0.164x_2$$

where $\hat{y}$ is the predicted height of a daughter, x_1 is the height of the mother, and x_2 is the height of the father.

Predicting Condo Prices

A massive study involved 99,491 sales of condominiums and cooperatives in Manhattan. The study used 41 different variables used to predict the value of the condo or co-op. The variables include condition of the unit, the neighborhood, age, size, and whether there are doormen. Some conclusions: With all factors equal, a condo is worth 15.5% more than a co-op; a fireplace increases the value of a condo 9.69% and it increases the value of a co-op 11.36%; an additional bedroom in a condo increases the value by 7.11% and it increases the value in a co-op by 18.53%. This use of statistical methods allows buyers and sellers to estimate value with much greater accuracy. Methods of multiple regression are used when there is more than one predictor variable, as in this study. (Based on data from "So How Much Is That Worth," by Dennis Hevesi, *New York Times.*)

If a multiple regression equation fits the sample data well, it can be used for predictions. For example, if we determine that the multiple regression equation in Example 1 is suitable for predictions, we can use the heights of a mother and father to predict the height of a daughter. But how do we determine whether the multiple regression equation fits the sample data well? Two very helpful tools are the values of adjusted R^2 and the P-value.

R^2 and Adjusted R^2

R^2 denotes the **multiple coefficient of determination,** which is a measure of how well the multiple regression equation fits the sample data. A perfect fit would result in $R^2 = 1$, and a very good fit results in a value near 1. A very poor fit results in a value of R^2 close to 0. The value of $R^2 = 67.5$ in the Minitab display for Example 1 indicates that 67.5% of the variation in heights of daughters can be explained by the heights of the mothers and fathers. However, the multiple coefficient of determination R^2 has a serious flaw: As more variables are included, R^2 increases. (R^2 could remain the same, but it usually increases.) The largest R^2 is obtained by simply including *all* of the available variables, but the best multiple regression equation does not necessarily use all of the available variables. Because of that flaw, it is better to use the *adjusted coefficient of determination,* which is R^2 adjusted for the number of variables and the sample size.

> **DEFINITION** The **adjusted coefficient of determination** is the multiple coefficient of determination R^2 modified to account for the number of variables and the sample size. It is calculated by using Formula 10-8.

Formula 10-8

$$\text{adjusted } R^2 = 1 - \frac{(n-1)}{[\,n-(k+1)\,]}(1-R^2)$$

where

n = sample size

k = number of predictor (x) variables

The preceding Minitab display for the data shows the adjusted coefficient of determination as R-Sq(adj) = 63.7%. If we use Formula 10-8 with the R^2 value of 0.675, $n = 20$ and $k = 2$, we find that the adjusted R^2 value is 0.637, confirming Minitab's displayed value of 63.7%. When we compare this multiple regression equation to others, it is better to use the adjusted R^2 of 63.7% (or 0.637).

P-Value

The P-value is a measure of the overall significance of the multiple regression equation. The displayed Minitab P-value of 0.000 (rounded to three decimal places) is small, indicating that the multiple regression equation has good overall significance and is usable for predictions. That is, it makes sense to predict heights of daughters based on heights of mothers and fathers. Like the adjusted R^2, this P-value is a good measure of how well the equation fits the sample data. The value of 0.000 results from a test of the null hypothesis that $\beta_1 = \beta_2 = 0$. Rejection of $\beta_1 = \beta_2 = 0$ implies that at least one of β_1 and β_2 is not 0, indicating that this regression equation is effective in predicting heights of daughters. A complete analysis of the Minitab results might include other important elements, such as the significance of the individual coefficients, but we will keeps things simple (!) by limiting our discussion to the three key components—multiple regression equation, adjusted R^2, and P-value.

Finding the Best Multiple Regression Equation

When trying to find the best multiple regression equation, we should not necessarily include all of the available predictor variables. Finding the best multiple regression equation requires abundant use of judgment and common sense, and there is no exact and automatic procedure that can be used to find the best multiple regression equation. *Determination of the best multiple regression equation is often quite difficult and is beyond the scope of this section*, but the following guidelines are helpful.

Guidelines for Finding the Best Multiple Regression Equation

1. *Use common sense and practical considerations to include or exclude variables.* For example, when trying to find a good multiple regression equation for predicting the height of a daughter, we should exclude the height of the physician who delivered the daughter, because that height is obviously irrelevant.

2. *Consider the P-value.* Select an equation having overall significance, as determined by the P-value found in the computer display.

3. *Consider equations with high values of adjusted R^2, and try to include only a few variables.* Instead of including almost every available variable, try to include relatively few predictor (x) variables. Use these guidelines:

   - Select an equation having a value of adjusted R^2 with this property: If an additional predictor variable is included, the value of adjusted R^2 does not increase very much.

   - For a particular number of predictor (x) variables, select the equation with the largest value of adjusted R^2.

   - In excluding predictor (x) variables that don't have much of an effect on the response (y) variable, it might be helpful to find the linear correlation coefficient r for each pair of variables being considered. If two predictor values have a very high linear correlation coefficient, there is no need to include them both, and we should exclude the variable with the lower value of r.

The following example illustrates that common sense and *critical thinking* are essential tools for effective use of methods of statistics.

Example 2 Predicting Height from Footprint Evidence

Data Set 2 in Appendix B includes the age, foot length, shoe print length, shoe size, and height for each of 40 different subjects. Using those sample data, find the regression equation that is best for predicting height. Is the best regression equation a *good* equation for predicting height?

Solution

Using the response variable of height and possible predictor variables of age, foot length, shoe print length, and shoe size, there are 15 different possible combinations of predictor variables. Table 10-5 includes key results from five of those combinations. Blind and thoughtless application of regression methods would suggest that the best regression equation uses all four of the predictor variables, because that combination yields the highest adjusted R^2 value of 0.7585. However, given

Table 10-5 Select Key Results from Data Set 2 in Appendix B

Predictor Variables	Adjusted R^2	P-Value	
Age	0.1772	0.004	← **Not best:** Adjusted R^2 is far less than 0.7014 for Foot Length
Foot Length	**0.7014**	**0.000**	← **Best:** High adjusted R^2 and lowest P-value.
Shoe Print Length	0.6520	0.000	← **Not best:** Adjusted R^2 is less than 0.7014 for Foot Length
Foot Length/Shoe Print Length	0.7484	0.000	← **Not best:** The adjusted R^2 value is not very much higher than 0.7014 for the single variable of Foot Length.
Age/Foot Length/ Shoe Print Length/ Shoe Size	0.7585	0.000	← **Not best:** There are other cases using fewer variables with adjusted R^2 that is not too much smaller.

the objective of using evidence to estimate the height of a suspect, we use *critical thinking* as follows.

1. Delete the variable of age, because criminals rarely leave evidence identifying their ages.

2. Delete the variable of shoe size, because it is really a rounded form of foot length.

3. For the remaining variables of foot length and shoe print length, use only foot length because its adjusted R^2 value of 0.7014 is greater than 0.6520 for shoe print length, and it is not very much less than the adjusted R^2 value of 0.7484 for both foot length and shoe print length. In this case, it is better to use one predictor variable instead of two.

4. Although it appears that the use of the single variable of foot length is best, we also note that criminals usually wear shoes, so shoe print lengths are more likely to be found than foot lengths.

Interpretation

Although blind use of regression methods suggest that when estimating the height of a subject, it is best to use all four predictor variables of age, foot length, shoe print length, and shoe size, other practical considerations suggest that it is best to use the single predictor variable of foot length, so the best regression equation appears to be this: Height = 64.1 + 4.29 (Foot Length). However, given that criminals usually wear shoes, it is best to use the single predictor variable of shoe print length, so the best regression equation appears to be this: Height = 80.9 + 3.22 (Shoe Print Length). The P-value of 0.000 suggests that the regression equation yields a good model for estimating height.

Because the results of this example are based on sample data from only 40 subjects, estimates of heights will not be very accurate. As is usually the case, better results could be obtained by using larger samples.

Tests of Regression Coefficients The preceding guidelines for finding the best multiple regression equation are based on the adjusted R^2 and the P-value, but we could also conduct individual hypothesis tests based on values of the regression coefficients. Consider the regression coefficient of β_1. A test of the null hypothesis

$\beta_1 = 0$ can tell us whether the corresponding predictor variable should be included in the regression equation. Rejection of $\beta_1 = 0$ suggests that β_1 has a nonzero value and is therefore helpful for predicting the value of the response variable. Procedures for such tests are described in Exercise 17.

Part 2: Dummy Variables and Logistic Regression

So far in this section, all variables have been continuous in nature, but many situations involve a **dichotomous variable,** which is a variable with only *two* possible discrete values (such as male/female or dead/alive or cured/not cured). A common procedure is to represent the two possible discrete values by 0 and 1, where 0 represents a "failure" (such as death) and 1 represents a success. A dichotomous variable with the two possible values of 0 and 1 is called a **dummy variable**.

Procedures of analysis differ dramatically, depending on whether the dummy variable is a predictor (x) variable or the response (y) variable. If we include a dummy variable as another *predictor* (x) variable, we can use the methods of this section, as illustrated in Example 3.

Example 3 Using a Dummy Variable

Use the data in Table 10-6 and, for a predictor variable, use the dummy variable of sex (coded as 0 = female, 1 = male). (The data in Table 10-6 are based on data from the National Health and Nutrition Examination.) Given that a mother is 63 in. tall and a father is 69 in. tall, find the multiple regression equation and use it to predict the height of (a) a daughter and (b) a son.

Table 10-6 Heights (in inches) of Mothers, Fathers, and Their Children

Height of Mother	Height of Father	Sex of Child	Height of Child
66	70	M	62.5
66	64	M	69.1
64	68	M	67.1
66	74	M	71.1
64	62	M	67.4
64	67	M	64.9
62	72	M	66.5
62	72	M	66.5
63	71	M	67.5
65	71	M	71.9
63	64	F	58.6
64	67	F	65.3
65	72	F	65.4
59	67	F	60.9
58	66	F	60.0
63	69	F	62.2
62	69	F	63.4
63	66	F	62.2
63	69	F	59.6
60	66	F	64.0

Making Music with Multiple Regression

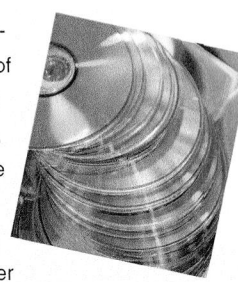

Sony manufactures millions of compact discs in Terre Haute, Indiana. At one step in the manufacturing process, a laser exposes a photographic plate so that a musical signal is transferred into a digital signal coded with 0s and 1s. This process was statistically analyzed to identify the effects of different variables, such as the length of exposure and the thickness of the photographic emulsion. Methods of multiple regression showed that among all of the variables considered, four were most significant. The photographic process was adjusted for optimal results based on the four critical variables. As a result, the percentage of defective discs dropped and the tone quality was maintained. The use of multiple regression methods led to lower production costs and better control of the manufacturing process.

Icing the Kicker

Just as a kicker in football is
about to attempt a field goal, it is

a common
strategy
for the
opposing
coach
to call

a time-out to "ice"
the kicker. The theory is that the
kicker has time to think and become nervous and less confident,
but does the practice actually
work? In "The Cold-Foot Effect"
by Scott M. Berry in *Chance*
magazine, the author wrote about
his statistical analysis of results
from two NFL seasons. He uses
a logistic regression model with
variables such as wind, clouds,
precipitation, temperature, the
pressure of making the kick, and
whether a time-out was called
prior to the kick. He writes that
"the conclusion from the model is
that icing the kicker works—it is
likely icing the kicker reduces the
probability of a successful kick."

Solution

Using the methods of this section and computer software, we get this regression equation:

$$\text{Height of Child} = 25.6 + 0.377\,(\text{Height of Mother}) + 0.195\,(\text{Height of Father}) + 4.15\,(\text{Sex})$$

where the value of the dummy variable of sex is either 0 for a daughter or 1 for a son.

a. To find the predicted height of a *daughter*, we substitute 0 for the sex variable, and we also substitute 63 in. for the mother's height and 69 in. for the father's height. The result is a predicted height of 62.8 in. for a daughter.

b. To find the predicted height of a *son*, we substitute 1 for the sex variable, and we also substitute 63 in. for the mother's height and 69 in. for the father's height. The result is a predicted height of 67.0 in. for a son.

The coefficient of 4.15 in the regression equation shows that when given the height of a mother and the height of a father, a son will have a predicted height that is 4.15 in. more than the height of a daughter.

Logistic Regression In Example 3, we could use the methods of this section because the dummy variable of sex is a *predictor* variable. If the dummy variable is the response (y) variable, we cannot use the methods of this section, and we should use a different method known as **logistic regression.** Example 4 illustrates the method of logistic regression.

Example 4   Logistic Regression

Let a sample data set consist of the heights, weights, waist sizes, and pulse rates of women and men as listed in Data Set 1 in Appendix B. Let the *response y* variable represent gender (0 = female, 1 = male). Using the 80 gender values of y and the combined list of corresponding heights, weights, waist sizes, and pulse rates, we can use logistic regression to obtain this model:

$$\ln\left(\frac{p}{1-p}\right) = -69.3615 + 0.478932(\text{HT}) + 0.0439041(\text{WT}) - 0.0894747(\text{WAIST}) - 0.0947207(\text{PULSE})$$

In the expression above, p is the probability of a male, so $p = 1$ indicates that the child is definitely a male, and $p = 0$ indicates that the child is definitely not a male (or is a female). If we use the model above and substitute a height of 183 cm (or 72.0 in.), a weight of 90 kg (or 198 lb), a waist circumference of 90 cm (or 35.4 in.), and a pulse rate of 85 beats per minute, we can solve for p to get $p = 0.998$, indicating that such a large person is very likely to be a male. In contrast, a small person with a height of 150 cm (or 59.1 in.), a weight of 40 kg (or 90.0 lb), a waist size of 68 cm (or 26.8 in.), and a pulse rate of 85 beats per minute results in a value of $p = 0.0000501$, indicating that such a small person is very unlikely to be a male and so is very likely to be a female.

This section does not include detailed procedures for using logistic regression, but several books are devoted to this topic.

When we discussed regression in Section 10-3, we listed four common errors that should be avoided when using regression equations to make predictions. These same errors should be avoided when using multiple regression equations. Be especially careful about concluding that a cause-effect association exists.

using TECHNOLOGY

STATDISK First enter the sample data in columns of the STATDISK Data Window. Select **Analysis,** then **Multiple Regression.** Select the columns to be included and also identify the column corresponding to the dependent (predictor) y variable. Click on **Evaluate** and you will get the multiple regression equation along with other items, including the multiple coefficient of determination R^2, the adjusted R^2, and the P-value.

MINITAB First enter the values in different columns. To avoid confusion among the different variables, enter a name for each variable in the box atop its column of data. Select the main menu item **Stat,** then select **Regression,** then **Regression** once again. In the dialog box, enter the variable to be used for the response (y) variable, and enter the variables you want included as predictor variables. Click **OK.** The display will include the multiple regression equation, along with other items, including the multiple coefficient of determination R^2, the adjusted R^2, and the P-value.

EXCEL First enter the sample data in columns. Proceed by using either XLSTAT or Excel's Data Analysis add-in.

XLSTAT Click on **XLSTAT,** then select **Modeling Data,** then **Linear Regression.** In the dialog box that appears, first enter the range of the sample values for the dependent y variable in the box identified as "Y/Dependent variable." Next, enter the range of quantitative values for all of the independent x variables in the box identified as "Y/Explanatory variable." For example, enter A1:C:55 for 55 rows of data for the x variables in columns A, B, and C. Put a checkmark next to the "Variable labels" box only if the first row of each *column* consists of names or labels. Click **OK.** A "Factors and interactions" box will appear, and you must put a checkmark next to each x variable that you want to include. After the results are displayed, look for the multiple regression equation ("Equation of the model"), the values of R^2 and adjusted R^2, and the P-value for overall significance (last column of the "Analysis of Variance" table).

Data Analysis add-in: If using Excel 2013, 2010, or 2007, click on **Data,** then click on **Data Analysis;** if using Excel 2003, click on **Tools,** then click on **Data Analysis.** Select **Regression.** In the dialog box, enter the range of values for the dependent Y-variable, then enter the range of values for the independent X-variables, which must be in adjacent columns. (Use Copy/Paste to move columns as desired.) The display will include the multiple coefficient of determination R^2, the adjusted R^2, and a list of the intercept and coefficient values used for the multiple regression equation. The P-value will be shown under the heading of *Significance F.*

TI-83/84 PLUS The TI-83/84 Plus program A2MULREG can be downloaded from the CD-ROM included with this book or from the web site www.aw.com/triola. If using the CD, select the *software* folder, then select the folder with the TI programs. The program must be downloaded to your calculator.

The sample data must first be entered as columns of matrix D, with the first column containing the values of the response (y) variable. To manually enter the data in matrix D, press **2ND** **x⁻¹**, scroll to the right for **EDIT,** scroll down for **[D],** then press **ENTER,** then enter the dimensions of the matrix in the format of rows by columns. For the number of rows enter the number of sample values listed for each variable. For the number of columns enter the total number of x and y variables. Proceed to enter the sample values. If the data are already stored as lists, those lists can be combined and stored in matrix D. Press **2ND** **x⁻¹**, select the top menu item of **MATH,** then select **List → matr,** then enter the list names with the first entry corresponding to the y variable, and also enter the matrix name of [D], all separated by commas. (For example, **List → matr(NICOT, TAR, CO, [D])** creates a matrix D with the values of NICOT in the first column, the values of TAR in the second column, and the values of CO in the third column.)

Now press **PRGM,** select **A2MULREG** and press **ENTER** **ENTER** **ENTER,** then select **MULT REGRESSION** and press **ENTER.** When prompted, enter the number of independent (x) variables, then enter the column numbers of the independent (x) variables that you want to include. The screen will provide a display that includes the P-value and the value of the adjusted R^2. Press **ENTER** to see the values to be used in the multiple regression equation. Press **ENTER** again to get a menu that includes options for generating confidence intervals, prediction intervals, residuals, or quitting. If you want to generate confidence and prediction intervals, use the displayed number of degrees of freedom, go to Table A-3 and look up the corresponding critical t value, enter it, then proceed to enter the values to be used for the predictor (x) variables. Press **ENTER** to select the **QUIT** option.

STATCRUNCH Click on **Open StatCrunch.** Enter the columns of data or open a data set. Click on **Stat,** then select **Regression,** then select **Multiple Linear.** Enter the columns to be used, then click on **Calculate.** The display will include the multiple coefficient of determination R^2 and the adjusted R^2. The intercept and coefficient values used for the multiple regression equation can be found in the second column of the top table. The P-value will be in the last column of the lower table.

10-5 Basic Skills and Concepts

Statistical Literacy and Critical Thinking

1. Terminology Using the lengths (in.), chest sizes (in.), and weights (lb) of bears from Data Set 7 in Appendix B, we get this regression equation: Weight $= -274 + 0.426$ Length $+ 12.1$ Chest Size. Identify the response and predictor variables.

2. Best Multiple Regression Equation For the regression equation given in Exercise 1, the P-value is 0.000 and the adjusted R^2 value is 0.925. If we were to include an additional predictor variable of neck size (in.), the P-value becomes 0.000 and the adjusted R^2 becomes 0.933. Given that the adjusted R^2 value of 0.933 is larger, is it better to use the regression equation with the three predictor variables of length, chest size, and neck size? Explain.

3. Adjusted Coefficient of Determination For Exercise 2, why is it better to use values of adjusted R^2 instead of simply using values of R^2?

4. Interpreting R^2 For the multiple regression equation given in Exercise 1, we get $R^2 = 0.928$. What does that value tell us?

Interpreting a Computer Display.   *In Exercises 5–8, we want to consider the correlation between LDL cholesterol and the predictor variables of weight (WT) and systolic blood pressure (SYS) for females. Refer to the Minitab display and answer the given questions or identify the indicated items. The Minitab display is based on the measured values of LDL cholesterol, weight, and systolic blood pressure amounts for the sample of 40 females from Data Set 1 of Appendix B.*

MINITAB

```
The regression equation is
LDL = 47.4 + 0.085 WT + 0.497 SYS


Predictor     Coef   SE Coef      T      P
Constant     47.44     34.85   1.36  0.182
WT          0.0853    0.2833   0.30  0.765
SYS         0.4968    0.2618   1.90  0.066


S = 36.0398   R-Sq = 9.8%   R-Sq(adj) = 4.9%


Analysis of Variance

Source           DF     SS    MS     F      P
Regression        2   5214  2607  2.01  0.149
Residual Error   37  48058  1299
Total            39  53272
```

5. LDL Cholesterol Identify the multiple regression equation that expresses the level of LDL cholesterol in terms of weight (WT) and diastolic blood pressure (SYS).

6. LDL Cholesterol Identify the following:

a. The P-value corresponding to the overall significance of the multiple regression equation

b. The value of the multiple coefficient of determination R^2

c. The adjusted value of R^2

7. LDL Cholesterol Should the multiple regression equation be used for predicting the LDL cholesterol level based on weight and diastolic blood pressure? Why or why not?

8. LDL Cholesterol A female weighs 59.3 kg and she has a measured systolic blood pressure of 122 mm Hg. Use the multiple regression equation to determine the predicted LDL cholesterol amount. Is the result likely to be a good predicted value? Why or why not?

City Fuel Consumption: Finding the Best Multiple Regression Equation. *In Exercises 9–12, refer to the accompanying table, which was obtained using the data from 21 cars listed in Data Set 14 in Appendix B. The response (y) variable is CITY (fuel consumption in mi/gal). The predictor (x) variables are WT (weight in pounds), DISP (engine displacement in liters), and HWY (highway fuel consumption in mi/gal).*

Predictor (x) Variables	P-value	R^2	Adjusted R^2	Regression Equation
WT/DISP/HWY	0.000	0.943	0.933	CITY = 6.86 − 0.00128 WT − 0.257 DISP + 0.652 HWY
WT/DISP	0.000	0.748	0.720	CITY = 38.0 − 0.00395 WT − 1.29 DISP
WT/HWY	0.000	0.942	0.935	CITY = 6.69 − 0.00159 WT + 0.670 HWY
DISP/HWY	0.000	0.935	0.928	CITY = 1.87 − 0.625 DISP + 0.706 HWY
WT	0.000	0.712	0.697	CITY = 41.8 − 0.00607 WT
DISP	0.000	0.659	0.641	CITY = 29.0 − 2.98 DISP
HWY	0.000	0.924	0.920	CITY = −3.15 + 0.819 HWY

9. If only one predictor (x) variable is used to predict the city fuel consumption, which single variable is best? Why?

10. If exactly two predictor (x) variables are to be used to predict the city fuel consumption, which two variables should be chosen? Why?

11. Which regression equation is best for predicting city fuel consumption? Why?

12. A Honda Civic weighs 2740 lb, it has an engine displacement of 1.8 L, and its highway fuel consumption is 36 mi/gal. What is the best predicted value of the city fuel consumption? Is that predicted value likely to be a good estimate? Is that predicted value likely to be very accurate?

Appendix B Data Sets. *In Exercises 13–16, refer to the indicated data set in Appendix B.*

13. Predicting Nicotine in Cigarettes Refer to Data Set 10 in Appendix B and use the tar, nicotine, and CO amounts for the cigarettes that are 100 mm long, filtered, nonmenthol, and nonlight (the last set of measurements). Find the best regression equation for predicting the amount of nicotine in a cigarette. Why is it best? Is the best regression equation a good regression equation for predicting the nicotine content? Why or why not?

14. Predicting Nicotine in Cigarettes Repeat the preceding exercise using the sample data from the Menthol cigarettes listed in Data Set 10 from Appendix B.

15. Predicting IQ Score Refer to Data Set 6 in Appendix B and find the best regression equation with IQ score as the response (y) variable. Use predictor variables of brain volume and/or body weight. Why is this equation best? Based on these results, can we predict someone's IQ score if we know their brain volume and body weight? Based on these results, does it appear that people with larger brains have higher IQ scores?

16. Full IQ Score Refer to Data Set 5 in Appendix B and find the best regression equation with IQF (full IQ score) as the response (y) variable. Use predictor variables of IQV (verbal IQ score) and IQP (performance IQ score). Why is this equation best? Based on these results, can we predict someone's full IQ score if we know their verbal IQ score and their performance IQ score? Is such a prediction likely to be very accurate?

10-5 Beyond the Basics

17. Testing Hypotheses About Regression Coefficients If the coefficient β_1 has a non-zero value, then it is helpful in predicting the value of the response variable. If $\beta_1 = 0$, it is not helpful in predicting the value of the response variable and can be eliminated from the regression equation. To test the claim that $\beta_1 = 0$ use the test statistic $t = (b_1 - 0)/s_{b_1}$. Critical values or P-values can be found using the t distribution with $n - (k + 1)$ degrees of freedom, where k is the number of predictor (x) variables and n is the number of observations in the sample. The standard error s_{b_1} is often provided by software. For example, the Minitab display in Example 1 shows that $s_{b_1} = 0.1289$ (found in the column with the heading of SE Coeff and the row corresponding to the first predictor variable of the height of the mother). Use the sample data in Table 10-4 and the Minitab display in Example 1 to test the claim that $\beta_1 = 0$. Also test the claim that $\beta_2 = 0$. What do the results imply about the regression equation?

18. Confidence Interval for a Regression Coefficient A confidence interval for the regression coefficient β_1 is expressed as

$$b_1 - E < \beta_1 < b_1 + E$$

where

$$E = t_{\alpha/2}s_{b_1}$$

The critical t score is found using $n - (k + 1)$ degrees of freedom, where k, n, and s_{b_1} are described in Exercise 17. Use the sample data in Table 10-4 and the Minitab display in Example 1 to construct 95% confidence interval estimates of β_1 (the coefficient for the variable representing height of the mother) and β_2 (the coefficient for the variable representing height of the father). Does either confidence interval include 0, suggesting that the variable be eliminated from the regression equation?

19. Dummy Variable Refer to Data Set 7 in Appendix B and use the sex, age, and weight of the bears. For sex, let 0 represent female and let 1 represent male. (In Data Set 7, males are already represented by 1, but for females change the sex values from 2 to 0.) Letting the response (y) variable represent weight, use the variable of age and the dummy variable of sex to find the multiple regression equation. Use the equation to find the predicted weight of a bear with the characteristics given below. Does sex appear to have much of an effect on the weight of a bear?

a. Female bear that is 20 years of age

b. Male bear that is 20 years of age

10-6 Nonlinear Regression

Key Concept Whereas all preceding sections of this chapter deal with *linear* relationships only, this section is a brief introduction to methods for finding some *nonlinear* functions that fit sample data. Much of the value in this section comes with the clear recognition that not all in the world is linear. Because the calculations required for the nonlinear functions of this section are quite complex, we focus on the use of technology for finding a mathematical model (or function) that "fits" or describes real-world data.

Shown on the next page are the five basic generic models considered in this section. (The cubic and quartic models are among the alternatives not included in this section.) Each of the five models is given with a generic formula along with an example of a specific function and its graph.

Linear: $y = a + bx$
Example: $y = 1 + 2x$

Logarithmic: $y = a + b \ln x$
Example: $y = 1 + 2 \ln x$

Power: $y = ax^b$
Example: $y = 3x^{2.5}$

Quadratic: $y = ax^2 + bx + c$
Example: $y = x^2 - 8x + 18$

Exponential: $y = ab^x$
Example: $y = 2^x$

Here are three basic rules for identifying a good mathematical model:

1. *Look for a pattern in the graph.* Use the sample data to construct a graph, such as those shown in the preceding examples. Compare the graph to the examples shown and identify the model that appears to be most similar.

2. *Compare values of R^2.* For each model being considered, use technology to find the value of the coefficient of determination R^2. Choose functions that result in larger values of R^2, because such larger values correspond to functions that better fit the observed sample data.

   - Don't place much importance on small differences, such as the difference between $R^2 = 0.984$ and $R^2 = 0.989$.

   - Unlike Section 10-5, we don't need to use values of adjusted R^2. Because the examples of this section all involve a single predictor variable, it makes sense to compare values of R^2.

   - In addition to R^2, another measure used to assess the quality of a model is the sum of squares of the residuals. See Exercise 18.

3. *Think.* Use common sense. Don't use a model that leads to predicted values that are unrealistic. Use the model to calculate future values, past values, and values for missing data, then determine whether the results are realistic and make sense. Don't go too far beyond the scope of the available sample data.

Example 1 **Finding the Best Population Model**

Table 10-7 lists the population of the United States for different years. Find a mathematical model for the population size, then predict the size of the U.S. population in the year 2020.

Table 10-7 Population (in millions) of the United States

Year	1800	1820	1840	1860	1880	1900	1920	1940	1960	1980	2000
Coded Year	1	2	3	4	5	6	7	8	9	10	11
Population	5	10	17	31	50	76	106	132	179	227	281

TI-83/84 PLUS

Solution

First, we "code" the year values by using 1, 2, 3, . . . , instead of 1800, 1820, 1840, ... The reason for this coding is to use values of x that are much smaller and much less likely to cause computational difficulties.

1. *Look for a pattern in the graph.* Examine the pattern of the data values in the TI-83/84 Plus display (shown in the margin), and compare that pattern to the generic models shown earlier in this section. The pattern of those points is clearly not a straight line, so we rule out a linear model. Good candidates for the model appear to be the quadratic, exponential, and power functions.

2. *Find and compare values of R^2.* The TI-83/84 display for the quadratic model is shown in the margin. For the quadratic model, $R^2 = 0.9992$ (rounded), which is quite high. Table 10-8 includes this result with results from two other potential models. Comparing the values of the coefficient R^2, it appears that the quadratic model is best because it has the highest value of 0.9992. If we select the quadratic function as the best model, we conclude that the equation $y = 2.77x^2 - 6.00x + 10.01$ best describes the relationship between the year x (coded with $x = 1$ representing 1800, $x = 2$ representing 1820, and so on) and the population y (in millions).

   Based on its R^2 value of 0.9992, the quadratic model appears to be best, but the other values of R^2 are also quite high. Our general knowledge of population growth might suggest that the exponential model is most appropriate. (With a constant birth rate and no limiting factors, population will grow exponentially.)

Table 10-8   Models for the Population Data

Model	R^2	Equation
Quadratic	**0.9992**	$y = 2.77x^2 - 6.00x + 10.01$
Exponential	0.9631	$y = 5.24(1.48^x)$
Power	0.9764	$y = 3.35x^{1.77}$

   To predict the U.S. population for the year 2020, first note that the year 2020 is coded as $x = 12$ (see Table 10-7). Substituting $x = 12$ into the quadratic model of $y = 2.77x^2 - 6.00x + 10.01$ results in $y = 337$, which indicates that the U.S. population is estimated to be 337 million in the year 2020.

3. *Think.* The forecast result of 337 million in 2020 seems reasonable. (As of this writing, the latest figures from the U.S. Bureau of the Census use much more sophisticated methods to project that the U.S. population in 2020 will be 325 million.) However, there is considerable danger in making estimates for times that are beyond the scope of the available data. For example, the quadratic model suggests that in 1492, the U.S. population was 671 million, which is a result statisticians refer to as *ridiculous.* The quadratic model appears to be good for the available data (1800–2000), but other models might be better if it is absolutely necessary to make future population estimates.

Example 2 Interpreting R^2

In Example 1, we obtained the value of $R^2 = 0.9992$ for the quadratic model. Interpret that value as it relates to the predictor variable of year and the response variable of population size.

Solution

In the context of the year/population data from Table 10-7, the value of $R^2 = 0.9992$ can be interpreted as follows: 99.92% of the variation in the population size can be explained by the quadratic regression equation (given in Example 1) that relates year and population size.

In "Modeling the U.S. Population" (*AMATYC Review,* Vol. 20, No. 2), Sheldon Gordon makes this important point that applies to all uses of statistical methods:

"The best choice (of a model) depends on the set of data being analyzed and requires an exercise in judgment, not just computation."

using TECHNOLOGY

Any system capable of handling multiple regression can be used to generate some of the models described in this section. For example, STATDISK is not designed to work directly with the quadratic model, but its multiple regression feature can be used with the data in Table 10-7 to generate the quadratic model as follows: First enter the population values in column 1 of the STATDISK Data Window. Enter 1, 2, 3, . . . , 11 in column 2 and enter their squares of 1, 4, 9, . . . , 121 in column 3. Click on **Analysis,** then select **Multiple Regression.** Use columns 1, 2, 3 with column 1 as the dependent variable. After clicking on **Evaluate,** STATDISK generates the equation $y = 10.012 - 6.0028x + 2.7669x^2$ along with $R^2 = 0.99917$, which are the same results obtained from the TI-83/84 Plus calculator.

MINITAB First enter the matched data in columns C1 and C2, then select **Stat, Regression,** and **Fitted Line Plot.** You can choose a linear model, quadratic model, or cubic model. Displayed

results include the equation, the value of R^2, and the sum of squares of the residuals.

TI-83/84 PLUS First turn on the diagnostics feature as follows: Press **2ND** **0** to get to the **CATALOG** menu, then scroll down to **DiagnosticON** and press the **ENTER** key twice. Now enter the matched data in lists L1 and L2. Press **STAT**, select **CALC,** and then select the desired model from the available options. Press **ENTER**, then enter L1, L2 (including the comma), and press **ENTER** again. The display includes the format of the equation along with the coefficients used in the equation; also the value of R^2 is included for many of the models.

STATCRUNCH You can find a model for a polynomial of any order from 1 through 6. Click on **Open StatCrunch.** Enter the columns of data or open a data set. Click on **Stat,** then select **Regression,** then select **Polynomial.** Select the desired order and enter the columns to be used, then click on **Calculate.**

10-6 Basic Skills and Concepts

Statistical Literacy and Critical Thinking

1. Identifying a Model and R^2 A data set is obtained as follows: Squares of different sizes are used, and x represents the length (cm) of a side and y represents the corresponding area (cm^2) of the square. What formula best describes the relationship between x and y? Which of the five models describes this relationship? What should be the value of R^2?

2. Super Bowl and R^2 Let x represent years coded as 1, 2, 3, . . . for years starting in 1980, and let y represent the numbers of points scored in each Super Bowl from 1980. Using the data from 1980 to the last Super Bowl at the time of this writing, we obtain the following values of R^2 for the different models: linear: 0.0185; quadratic: 0.103; logarithmic: 0.000557; exponential: 0.0253; power: 0.00264. Based on these results, which model is best? Is the best model a good model? What do the results suggest about predicting the number of points scored in a future Super Bowl game?

3. Interpreting R^2 In Exercise 2, the quadratic model results in $R^2 = 0.103$. Identify the percentage of the variation in Super Bowl points that can be explained by the quadratic model relating the variable of year and the variable of points scored. (*Hint:* See Example 2.) What does the result suggest about the usefulness of the quadratic model?

4. Interpreting a Graph The accompanying graph plots the numbers of points scored in each Super Bowl from 1980 (coded as year 1) to the last Super Bowl at the time of this writing. The graph also shows the graph of the quadratic equation that best fits the data. What feature of the graph justifies the value of $R^2 = 0.103$ for the quadratic model?

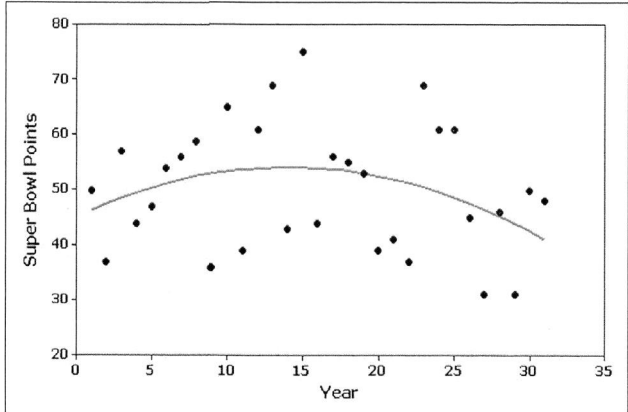

Finding the Best Model. *In Exercises 5–16, construct a scatterplot and identify the mathematical model that best fits the given data. Assume that the model is to be used only for the scope of the given data, and consider only linear, quadratic, logarithmic, exponential, and power models.*

5. Dropped Object The table lists the distance d (meters) above the ground for an object dropped in a vacuum from a height of 300 m. The time t (in sec) is the time after the object has been released.

t	1	2	3	4	5
d	295.1	280.5	256.1	222.0	178.1

6. Landscape Material The table lists the cost y (in dollars) of purchasing a volume of red landscaping mulch from the Red Barn Farm and Nursery in Dutchess County, New York. The mulch is sold by the "yard," which is actually a cubic yard, and the variable x is the length (yd) of each side of a cubic yard.

x	1	1.5	2	2.5	3
Cost	35	118.13	280	546.88	945

7. CD Value The table lists the value y (in dollars) of $100 deposited in a certificate of deposit at Bank of New York.

Year	1	2	3	4	5	20
Value	103	106.09	109.27	112.55	115.93	180.61

8. Sound Intensity The table lists intensities of sounds as multiples of a basic reference sound. A scale similar to the decibel scale is used to measure the sound intensity.

Sound Intensity	316	500	750	2000	5000
Scale Value	25.0	27.0	28.75	33.0	37.0

9. Harry Potter Listed below are the amounts (millions of dollars) grossed during the first three weeks of the movie *Harry Potter and the Half Blood Prince*. Use the best model to predict the gross amount on the 22nd day of the movie's release. Is the result close to the actual amount of $2.2 million? Is there any characteristic of the data not revealed by the model? (*Hint:* The movie opened on a Wednesday.)

58.2 22.0 26.8 29.2 21.8 9.9 9.5 7.5 6.9 9.3

11.2 8.9 4.0 4.0 4.6 3.8 5.4 6.8 5.8 2.5 2.4

10. Deaths from Motor Vehicle Crashes Listed below are the numbers of deaths in the United States resulting from motor vehicle crashes. Use the best model to find the projected number of such deaths for the year 2020.

Year	1975	1980	1985	1990	1995	2000	2005	2010
Deaths	44,525	51,091	43,825	44,599	41,817	41,945	43,443	32,708

11. Richter Scale The table lists different amounts (metric tons) of the explosive TNT and the corresponding value on the Richter scale used for explosions of the TNT.

TNT	2	10	15	50	100	500
Richter Scale	3.4	3.9	4.0	4.4	4.6	5.0

12. Benford's Law According to Benford's law, a variety of different data sets include numbers with leading (first) digits that occur with the proportions listed in the following table.

Leading Digit	1	2	3	4	5	6	7	8	9
Proportion	0.301	0.176	0.125	0.097	0.079	0.067	0.058	0.051	0.046

13. Bacteria Growth In a carefully controlled experiment, bacteria are allowed to grow for a week. The number of bacteria are recorded at the end of each day with these results: 20, 40, 80, 160, 320, 640, 1280.

14. Sunspot Numbers Listed below in order by row are annual sunspot numbers beginning with 1980. Is the best model a good model? Carefully examine the scatterplot and identify the pattern of the points. Which of the models fits that pattern?

154.6 140.5 115.9 66.6 45.9 17.9 13.4 29.2 100.2 157.6

142.6 145.7 94.3 54.6 29.9 17.5 8.6 21.5 64.3 93.3

119.6 123.3 123.3 65.9 40.4 29.8 15.2 7.5 2.9 3.1 16.5

15. Stock Market Listed below in order by row are the annual high values of the Dow Jones Industrial Average for each year beginning with 1990. *Use only the first 10 values* (for 1990–1999) to find the best model and then predict the value for the year 2010. Is the predicted value close to the actual value of 11,655?

3000 3169 3413 3794 3978 5216 6561 8259 9374 11,568
11,401 11,350 10,635 10,454 10,855 10,941 12,464 14,198 13,338 10,606

16. Stock Market Repeat the preceding exercise using all of the data values.

10-6 Beyond the Basics

17. Moore's Law In 1965, Intel cofounder Gordon Moore initiated what has since become known as *Moore's law:* the number of transistors per square inch on integrated circuits will double approximately every 18 months. In the table below, the first row lists different years and the second row lists the number of transistors (in thousands) for different years.

1971	1974	1978	1982	1985	1989	1993	1997	2000	2002	2003	2007	2011
2.3	5	29	120	275	1180	3100	7500	42,000	220,000	410,000	789,000	2,600,000

a. Assuming that Moore's law is correct and transistors per square inch double every 18 months, which mathematical model best describes this law: linear, quadratic, logarithmic, exponential, power? What specific function describes Moore's law?

b. Which mathematical model best fits the listed sample data?

c. Compare the results from parts (a) and (b). Does Moore's law appear to be working reasonably well?

18. Sum of Squares Criterion In addition to the value of R^2, another measurement used to assess the quality of a model is the *sum of squares of the residuals*. Recall from Section 10-3 that a residual is the difference between an observed y value and the value of y predicted from the model, which is denoted as $\hat{y}$. Better models have smaller sums of squares. Refer to the data in Table 10-7.

a. Find $\Sigma(y - \hat{y})^2$, the sum of squares of the residuals resulting from the linear model.

b. Find the sum of squares of residuals resulting from the quadratic model.

c. Verify that according to the sum of squares criterion, the quadratic model is better than the linear model.

Chapter 10   Review

The core content of this chapter focuses on a correlation between two variables, so much of the chapter deals with paired data. Section 9-4 includes methods for forming inferences from two dependent samples, so Section 9-4 also deals with paired data, but this chapter and Section 9-4 have fundamentally different objectives. Consider the table below with the two different scenarios that follow to see the basic difference between them.

x	75	83	66	90	55
y	87	83	69	92	72

Scenario 1: Dependent Samples The data in the table represent measurements of strength. The variable x is the measurement *before* a training program and y is the measurement of the same person *after* a training program. Here, the issue is whether the training program is effective, so we want to test the hypothesis that the sample differences are from a population with a mean that is less than 0, indicating that the posttraining scores are higher than the pretraining scores. The methods of Section 9-4 apply.

Scenario 2: Paired Sample Data The data in the table are measurements from a sample of five subjects. The x values are scores on a test of depth perception, and the y values are the times (sec) required to complete a particular task. Here, the issue is whether there is a correlation between the two variables, and the methods of this chapter apply. The following is a brief review of those methods.

• Section 10-2 includes methods for using scatterplots and the linear correlation coefficient r to determine whether there is sufficient evidence to support a claim of a linear correlation between two variables.

• In Section 10-3 we presented methods for finding the equation of the regression line that best fits a graph of the paired data. When the regression line fits the data reasonably well, the regression equation can be used to predict the value of a variable, given some value of the other variable.

• In Section 10-4 we discussed methods for constructing prediction intervals, which are helpful in judging the accuracy of predicted values. We also introduced the concept of total variation, with components of explained and unexplained variation. The coefficient of determination r^2 gives us the proportion of the variation in the response variable (y) that can be explained by the linear correlation between x and y.

• Section 10-5 includes methods for finding a multiple regression equation, which expresses the relationship of a response variable to two or more predictor variables. We also described methods for finding the value of the multiple coefficient of determination R^2, the adjusted R^2, and a P-value for the overall significance of the equation. Those values are helpful for comparing different multiple regression equations as well as finding the best multiple regression equation. Because of the nature of the calculations involved in this section, the methods are based on the interpretation of results from computer software.

• In Section 10-6 we presented basic methods for finding a mathematical function that can be used to describe a nonlinear relationship between two variables.

Chapter Quick Quiz

The exercises are based on the following sample data obtained from different second-year medical students who took blood pressure measurements of the same person (based on data from Marc Triola, MD).

Systolic	138	130	135	140	120
Diastolic	82	91	100	100	80

1. If you plan to use a 0.05 significance level in a test of a correlation between the systolic and diastolic readings, what are the critical values of r?

2. The linear correlation coefficient r is found to be 0.585. What should you conclude?

3. The sample data result in a linear correlation coeffient of $r = 0.585$ and the regression equation $\hat{y} = -1.99 + 0.698x$. What is the best predicted diastolic reading given a systolic reading of 125, and how was it found?

4. Repeat the preceding exercise assuming that the linear correlation coefficient is $r = 0.989$.

5. Given that the linear correlation coefficient r is found to be 0.585, what is the proportion of the variation in diastolic blood pressure that is explained by the linear relationship between systolic and diastolic blood pressure?

6. True or false: If there is no linear correlation between systolic and diastolic blood pressure, then those two variables are not related in any way.

7. True or false: If the sample data lead us to the conclusion that there is sufficient evidence to support the claim of a linear correlation between systolic and diastolic blood pressure, then we could also conclude that systolic blood pressure causes diastolic blood pressure.

8. If each systolic reading is exactly twice the diastolic reading, what is the value of the linear correlation coefficient r?

9. If you had computed the value of the linear correlation coefficient to be 3.335, what should you conclude?

10. If the sample data were to result in the scatterplot shown here, what is the value of the linear correlation coefficient r?

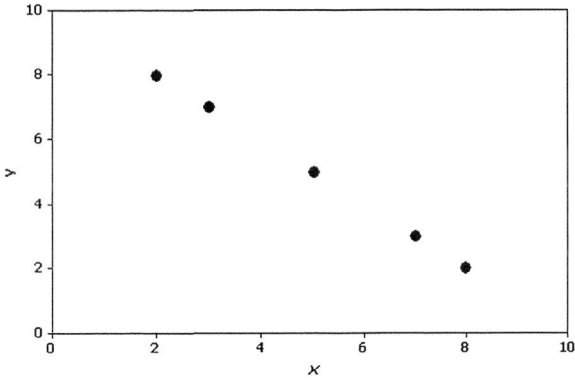

Review Exercises

1. Old Faithful The table below lists measurements from eight different eruptions of the Old Faithful geyser in Yellowstone National Park. The data consist of the duration (sec) of the eruption, height (ft) of the eruption, time interval (min) before the eruption, and time interval (min) after the eruption. Shown below are Minitab results obtained by using the durations and interval-after times.

a. Determine whether there is sufficient evidence to support a claim of a linear correlation between duration and interval-after time for eruptions of the Old Faithful geyser.

b. What percentage of the variation in interval-after times can be explained by the linear correlation between interval-after times and durations?

c. Letting y represent interval-after time and letting x represent duration time, identify the regression equation.

d. If an eruption has a duration of 200 sec, what is the best predicted value for the time interval after the eruption to the next eruption?

Eruptions of the Old Faithful Geyser

Duration	240	120	178	234	235	269	255	220
Height	140	110	125	120	140	120	125	150
Interval Before	98	90	92	98	93	105	81	108
Interval After	92	65	72	94	83	94	101	87

```
Pearson correlation of DURATION and AFTER = 0.926
P-Value = 0.001

The regression equation is
AFTER = 34.8 + 0.234 DURATION
```

2. Old Faithful Refer to the table of data given in Exercise 1 and use the heights and interval-after times.

a. Construct a scatterplot. What does the scatterplot suggest about a linear correlation between heights of eruptions and interval-after times?

b. Find the value of the linear correlation coefficient and determine whether there is sufficient evidence to support a claim of a linear correlation between heights of eruptions and interval-after times.

c. Letting y represent the interval-after time and letting x represent height, find the regression equation.

d. Based on the given sample data, what is the best predicted interval-after time for an eruption with a height of 100 ft?

3. Old Faithful Refer to the table of data given in Exercise 1 and use the durations and heights.

a. Construct a scatterplot. What does the scatterplot suggest about a linear correlation between duration and height?

b. Find the value of the linear correlation coefficient and determine whether there is sufficient evidence to support a claim of a linear correlation between duration and height.

c. Letting y represent height and letting x represent duration, find the regression equation.

d. If an eruption has a duration of 200 sec, what is its best predicted height?

4. Time and Motion In a physics experiment at Doane College, a soccer ball was thrown upward from the bed of a moving truck. The table below lists the time (sec) that has lapsed from the throw and the height (m) of the soccer ball. What do you conclude about the relationship between time and height? What horrible mistake would be easy to make if the analysis is conducted without a scatterplot?

Time (sec)	0.0	0.2	0.4	0.6	0.8	1.0	1.2	1.4	1.6	1.8
Height (m)	0.0	1.7	3.1	3.9	4.5	4.7	4.6	4.1	3.3	2.1

5. Multiple Regression with Old Faithful Refer to the sample data given in Exercise 1 and find the multiple regression equation with the response (y) variable of "interval-after" time and predictor (x) variables of duration and "interval-before" time. Identify the value of the multiple coefficient of determination R^2, the adjusted R^2, and the P-value representing the overall significance of the multiple regression equation. Use a 0.05 significance level and determine whether the regression equation can be used to predict the time interval after an eruption given the duration of the eruption and the time interval before that eruption.

Cumulative Review Exercises

Please be aware that some of the following problems may require knowledge of concepts presented in previous chapters.

Effectiveness of Diet. *Listed below are weights (lb) of subjects before and after the Zone diet. (Data are based on results from "Comparison of the Atkins, Ornish, Weight Watchers, and Zone Diets for Weight Loss and Heart Disease Risk Reduction," by Dansinger et al.,* **Journal of the American Medical Association,** *Vol. 293, No. 1.) Use the data for Exercises 1–5.*

Before	183	212	177	209	155	162	167	170
After	179	198	180	208	159	155	164	166

1. Diet Clinical Trial: Statistics Find the mean and standard deviation of the "before − after" differences.

2. Diet Clinical Trial: z Score Using only the weights before the diet, identify the highest weight and convert it to a z score. In the context of these sample data, is that highest value an "unusual" weight? Why or why not?

3. Diet Clinical Trial: Hypothesis Test Use a 0.05 significance level to test the claim that the diet is effective.

4. Diet Clinical Trial: Confidence Interval Construct a 95% confidence interval estimate of the mean weight of subjects before the diet. Write a brief statement interpreting the confidence interval.

5. Diet Clinical Trial: Correlation Use the before/after weights listed above.

a. Test for a correlation between the before and after weights.

b. If each subject were to weigh exactly the same after the diet as before, what would be the value of the linear correlation coefficient?

c. If all subjects were to lose 5% of their weight from the diet, what would be the value of the linear correlation coefficient found from the before/after weights?

d. What do the preceding results suggest about the suitability of correlation as a tool for testing the effectiveness of the diet?

6. Birth Weights Birth weights in the United States are normally distributed with a mean of 3420 g and a standard deviation of 495 g.

a. What percentage of babies are born with a weight greater than 3500 g?

b. Find P_{10}, which is the 10th percentile.

c. The Rockland Medical Center requires special treatment for babies that are less than 2450 g (unusually underweight) or more than 4390 g (unusually overweight). What is the percentage of babies who require special treatment? Under these conditions, do many babies require special treatment?

7. Honesty In a *USA Today* survey of 456 subjects, 269 answered "yes" to this question: "Is honesty always the best policy?"

a. Use a 0.05 significance level to test the claim that the majority of us say that honesty is always the best policy.

b. The survey results were obtained from Internet users who visited the *USA Today* web site and chose to respond to the question that was posted. What is the term used to describe this type of sample? What does this sampling method suggest about the results given in part (a)?

Congress and Religion. *Based on data from the Pew Forum on Religion and Political Life, the members of Congress have these religious affiliations: Catholic (156), Jewish (39), Protestant (304), Mormon (15), other (15). There were six members of Congress who did not specify a religious affiliation, and the data are current at the time of this writing. Ignore the six unspecified religious affiliations and use these data for Exercises 8–10.*

8. Congress and Religion

a. What is the level of measurement of the religious affiliations (Catholic, Jewish, and so on)?

b. What is the level of measurement of the frequency counts (156, 39, and so on)?

c. Are the frequency counts data that are discrete or continuous?

d. What proportion of the members of Congress are Protestant?

e. Given that the data describe the population of members of Congress, is the result from part (c) a statistic or a parameter?

9. Congress and Religion: Probability

a. If two different members of Congress are randomly selected, what is the probability that they are both Protestant?

b. If a member of Congress is randomly selected, what is the probability that he or she is Catholic or Protestant?

c. If a member of Congress is randomly selected, what is the probability that he or she is not Mormon?

d. What *percentage* of members of Congress are Jewish?

10. Congress and Religion: Graph Construct the graph that is most effective in depicting the religious affiliations of members of Congress.

Technology Project

IQ scores are commonly measured using the Wechsler Adult Intelligence Scale (WAIS). Scores are obtained from tests. WAIS scores are normally distributed with a mean of 100 and a standard deviation of 15.

Much effort is spent studying IQ scores of identical twins that were separated at birth and raised apart in different environments. Identical twins occur when a single fertilized egg splits in two, so both twins share the same genetic makeup. By obtaining IQ scores of identical twins separated at birth, researchers hope to identify the effects of heredity and environment on intelligence.

a. The table below lists IQ scores from 10 sets of twins, but technology was used to simulate the data. Use the methods of Section 10-2 to test for a linear correlation between the IQ scores of the first-born twins and the IQ scores of the second-born twins. Use a significance level of 0.10.

| First-Born Twin | 121 | 113 | 91 | 118 | 81 | 77 | 80 | 90 | 103 | 95 |
| Second-Born Twin | 108 | 110 | 79 | 111 | 138 | 96 | 100 | 80 | 102 | 109 |

b. Many technologies (including STATDISK, Minitab, Excel, StatCrunch, and the TI-83/84 Plus calculator) have a feature that allows you to randomly generate data from a normally distributed population with any mean and standard deviation. Use a technology to randomly generate IQ scores for each of 10 pairs of twins, as in the above table. Using your own simulated IQ scores, test for a linear correlation between the IQ scores of the first-born twin and the IQ scores of the second-born twin. Use a significance level of 0.10.

c. For the test conducted in part (b), a type I error is the mistake of rejecting a true null hypothesis, which, in this case, is to conclude that there is a linear correlation when in reality there is no linear correlation. What proportion of simulated sets of twins should result in a type I error? Repeat part (b) to verify that this proportion is approximately correct.

from data **TO DECISION**

Critical Thinking:
Is replication validation?

The Chapter Problem includes Table 10-1, which lists shoe print lengths and heights for five male subjects. The data in Table 10-1 are from Data Set 2 in Appendix B. Data Set 2 lists a few different measurements from a sample of 19 males and 21 females. Listed below are foot lengths (cm) and heights (cm) for a sample of 50 males used in an anthropometric survey conducted by the U.S. Army. The data are paired according to their corresponding positions. The first male has a foot length of 26.0 cm and a height of 173.5 cm, the second male has a foot length of 29.0 cm and a height of 183.0 cm, and so on.

Foot Length (cm)

26.0	29.0	25.4	27.1	24.0	26.3	26.5	27.2	27.3	27.1
26.8	27.2	26.5	25.1	25.5	25.3	26.9	28.2	26.5	28.1
27.7	25.9	26.0	28.5	27.9	26.9	26.0	24.4	26.4	28.5
25.2	26.0	27.3	27.1	29.7	28.9	29.7	25.7	28.8	25.2
29.0	26.7	26.3	27.8	27.7	27.2	26.7	29.0	28.6	27.1

Height (cm)

173.5	183.0	172.6	178.3	166.9	175.8	178.8	182.9	174.5	164.3
169.8	172.7	173.4	168.4	166.7	168.0	178.5	188.5	184.1	170.2
173.8	173.2	173.9	187.7	172.5	170.4	174.8	164.7	169.9	176.1
167.1	164.4	173.9	174.9	184.5	195.4	184.4	160.1	184.6	167.2
193.4	186.2	169.4	174.0	173.9	171.9	172.2	177.6	189.7	173.0

Analyzing the Results

1. Use the given data to construct a scatterplot, then use the methods of Section 10-2 to test for a linear correlation between foot length and height. Compare the results to those found using the foot lengths and heights of the 19 males listed in Data Set 2 in Appendix B.

2. Use the given data to find the equation of the regression line. Let the response (y) variable be height. Compare the results to those found using the foot lengths and heights of the 19 males listed in Data Set 2 in Appendix B.

3. It was noted in the Chapter Problem that you can estimate a person's height by dividing foot length by 0.15. (An equivalent calculation is to estimate height by multiplying foot length by 6.67.) How does this rule compare to the use of a regression equation?

Cooperative Group Activities

1. In-class activity The Chapter Problem involves the relationship between shoe print length and height. For each student in the class, measure those two variables. Test for a linear correlation and identify the equation of the regression line. Measure the shoe print length of the professor and use it to estimate his or her height. How close is the estimated height to the actual height?

2. In-class activity Divide into groups of 8 to 12 people. For each group member, measure the person's height and also measure his or her navel height, which is the height from the floor to the navel. Is there a correlation between height and navel height? If so, find the regression equation with height expressed in terms of navel height. According to one theory, the average person's ratio of height to navel height is the golden ratio: $(1 + \sqrt{5})/2 \approx 1.6$. Does this theory appear to be reasonably accurate?

3. In-class activity Divide into groups of 8 to 12 people. For each group member, measure height and arm span. For the arm span, the subject should stand with arms extended, like the wings on an airplane. Using the paired sample data, is there a correlation between height and arm span? If so, find the regression equation with height expressed in terms of arm span. Can arm span be used as a reasonably good predictor of height?

4. In-class activity Divide into groups of 8 to 12 people. For each group member, use a string and ruler to measure head circumference and forearm length. Is there a relationship between these two variables? If so, what is it?

5. In-class activity Use a ruler as a device for measuring reaction time. One person should suspend the ruler by holding it at the top while the subject holds his or her thumb and forefinger at the bottom edge ready to catch the ruler when it is released. Record the distance that the ruler falls before it is caught. Convert that distance to the time (in seconds) that it took the subject to react and catch the ruler. (If the distance is measured in inches, use $t = \sqrt{d/192}$. If the distance is measured in centimeters, use $t = \sqrt{d/487.68}$.) Test each subject once with the right hand and once with the left hand, and record the paired data. Test for a correlation. Find the equation of the regression line. Does the equation of the regression line suggest that the dominant hand has a faster reaction time?

6. In-class activity Divide into groups of 8 to 12 people. Record the pulse rate of each group member while seated. Then record the pulse rate of each group member while standing. Is there a relationship between sitting and standing pulse rate? If so, what is it?

7. In-class activity Divide into groups of three or four people. Appendix B includes many data sets not yet included in examples or exercises in this chapter. Search Appendix B for a pair of variables of interest, then investigate correlation and regression. State your conclusions and try to identify practical applications.

8. Out-of-class activity Divide into groups of three or four people. Investigate the relationship between two variables by collecting your own paired sample data and using the methods of this chapter to determine whether there is a significant linear correlation. Also identify the regression equation and describe a procedure for predicting values of one of the variables when given values of the other variable. Suggested topics:

• Is there a relationship between taste and cost of different brands of chocolate chip cookies (or colas)? Taste can be measured on some number scale, such as 1 to 10.

• Is there a relationship between salaries of professional baseball (or basketball, or football) players and their season achievements?

• Is there a relationship between the lengths of men's (or women's) feet and their heights?

• Is there a relationship between student grade point averages and the amount of television watched? If so, what is it?

11 Goodness-of-Fit and Contingency Tables

Are four quarters the same as one dollar?

Are four quarters the same as one dollar? There may be a temptation to answer yes and move on to the next chapter. Using our extensive knowledge base of arithmetic and currency, we do know that in terms of pure purchasing power, four quarters are the same as one dollar. But this Chapter Problem deals more with psychology than basic arithmetic. It involves the *denomination effect,* which refers to the tendency of people to spend money more readily when it is in the form of lower denominations (such as four quarters) instead of higher denominations (such as a $1 bill). This is discussed in "The Denomination Effect" by Priya Raghubir and Joydeep Srivastava, *Journal of Consumer Research*, Vol. 36. In one study of this phenomenon, 43 college students were each given $1 in the form of four quarters, while 46 other college students were each given $1 in the form of a dollar bill. All of the students were then given two choices: (1) Keep the money; (2) spend the money on gum. The results are given in Table 11-1.

Table 11-1 Results from a Study of the Denomination Effect		
	Purchased Gum	**Kept the Money**
Students Given Four Quarters	27	16
Students Given a $1 Bill	12	34

Table 11-1 is called a *two-way table* (because the data are partitioned according to *two* different variables) or a *contingency table* (because we want to determine whether there is a *dependence* between the row and column categories). Similar tables occur often in real applications, so they are extremely important in the study of statistics.

Analyzing the Results

The purpose of the gum/money study is to determine whether the form of the gift (four quarters or $1 bill) appears to affect the decision to purchase gum or keep the money. Table 11-1 has two rows corresponding to the variable of the form of the money, and it has two columns corresponding to the variable of how the subjects chose to use the money. We want to determine whether the row variable has an effect on the column variable. If there is an effect, then people behave differently with money in different denominations, so the "denomination effect" appears to be real. Analyzing the data in Table 11-1, we see that there does appear to be an effect, because 63% of those given four quarters chose to spend the money, but only 26% of those given a $1 bill chose to spend the money. But is that a *significant* difference? That determination can be made using the methods introduced in Section 11-3.

11-1   Review and Preview

By introducing basic concepts of estimating population parameters (with confidence intervals) and methods of hypothesis tests, Chapters 7 and 8 moved us into methods of inferential statistics. Chapters 9 and 10 then involved us with different configurations of data. In this chapter we use statistical methods for analyzing categorical (or qualitative, or attribute) data that can be separated into different cells.

In Section 11-2 we consider hypothesis tests of a claim that observed frequency counts agree with some claimed distribution, so there is a "good fit" of the sample data with the claimed distribution. In Section 11-3 we analyze contingency tables (or two-way frequency tables), which consist of frequency counts arranged in a table with at least two rows and two columns. The objective is to determine whether there appears to be some dependence between the row variable and the column variable.

The methods of this chapter use the same X^2 (chi-square) distribution that was first introduced in Section 7-4. See Section 7-4 for a quick review of properties of the X^2 distribution.

11-2   Goodness-of-Fit

Key Concept By "goodness-of-fit" we mean that sample data consisting of observed frequency counts arranged in a single row or column (called a *one-way frequency table*) agree with some particular distribution being considered. We will use a hypothesis test for the claim that the observed frequency counts agree with some claimed distribution.

> **DEFINITION** A **goodness-of-fit test** is used to test the hypothesis that an observed frequency distribution fits (or conforms to) some claimed distribution.

Objective

Conduct a goodness-of-fit test. That is, conduct a hypothesis test to determine whether a single row (or column) of frequency counts agrees with some specific distribution (such as uniform or normal).

Notation

O represents the *observed frequency* of an outcome, found from the sample data.

E represents the *expected frequency* of an outcome, found by assuming that the distribution is as claimed.

k represents the *number of different categories* or cells.

n represents the total *number of trials* (or observed sample values).

Requirements

1. The data have been randomly selected.

2. The sample data consist of frequency counts for each of the different categories.

3. For each category, the *expected* frequency is at least 5. (The expected frequency for a category is the frequency that would occur if the data actually have the distribution that is being claimed. There is no requirement that the *observed* frequency for each category must be at least 5.)

Null and Alternative Hypotheses

H_0: The frequency counts agree with the claimed distribution.
H_1: The frequency counts do not agree with the claimed distribution.

Test Statistic for Goodness-of-Fit Tests

$$\chi^2 = \sum \frac{(O - E)^2}{E}$$

P-values: P-values are typically provided by technology, or a range of P-values can be found from Table A-4.

Critical values: 1. Critical values are found in Table A-4 by using $k - 1$ degrees of freedom, where k is the number of categories.

   2. Goodness-of-fit hypothesis tests are always *right-tailed.*

Finding Expected Frequencies

Conducting a goodness-of-fit test requires that we identify the observed frequencies, then determine the frequencies expected with the claimed distribution. Table 11-2 (on the next page) includes observed frequencies with a sum of 100, so $n = 100$. If we assume that the 100 digits were obtained from a population in which all digits are equally likely, then we *expect* that each digit should occur in 1/10 of the 100 trials, so each of the 10 expected frequencies is given by $E = 10$. In general, if we are assuming that all of the expected frequencies are equal, each expected frequency is $E = n/k$, where n is the total number of observations and k is the number of categories. In other cases in which the expected frequencies are not all equal, we can often find the expected frequency for each category by multiplying the sum of all observed frequencies and the probability p for the category, so $E = np$. We summarize these two procedures here.

- **Expected frequencies are equal: $E = n/k$.**

- **Expected frequencies are not all equal: $E = np$ for each individual category.**

As good as these two preceding formulas for E might be, it is better to use an informal approach. Just ask, "How can the observed frequencies be split up among the different categories so that there is perfect agreement with the claimed distribution?" Also, note that the *observed* frequencies are all whole numbers because they represent actual counts, but the *expected* frequencies need not be whole numbers. If Table 11-2 had 75 observations instead of 100, each expected frequency would be 7.5.

We know that sample frequencies typically differ somewhat from the values we theoretically expect, so we now present the key question: Are the differences between the actual *observed* frequencies O and the theoretically *expected* frequencies E statistically significant? We need a measure of the discrepancy between the O and E values, so we use the test statistic given in the preceding box. (Later we will explain how this test statistic was developed, but you can see that it has differences of $O - E$ as a key component.)

The χ^2 test statistic is based on differences between the observed and expected values. If the observed and expected values are *close,* the χ^2 test statistic will be small and the P-value will be large. If the observed and expected frequencies are *far apart,* the χ^2 test statistic will be large and the P-value will be small. Figure 11-1 on the next page summarizes this relationship. The hypothesis tests of this section are always

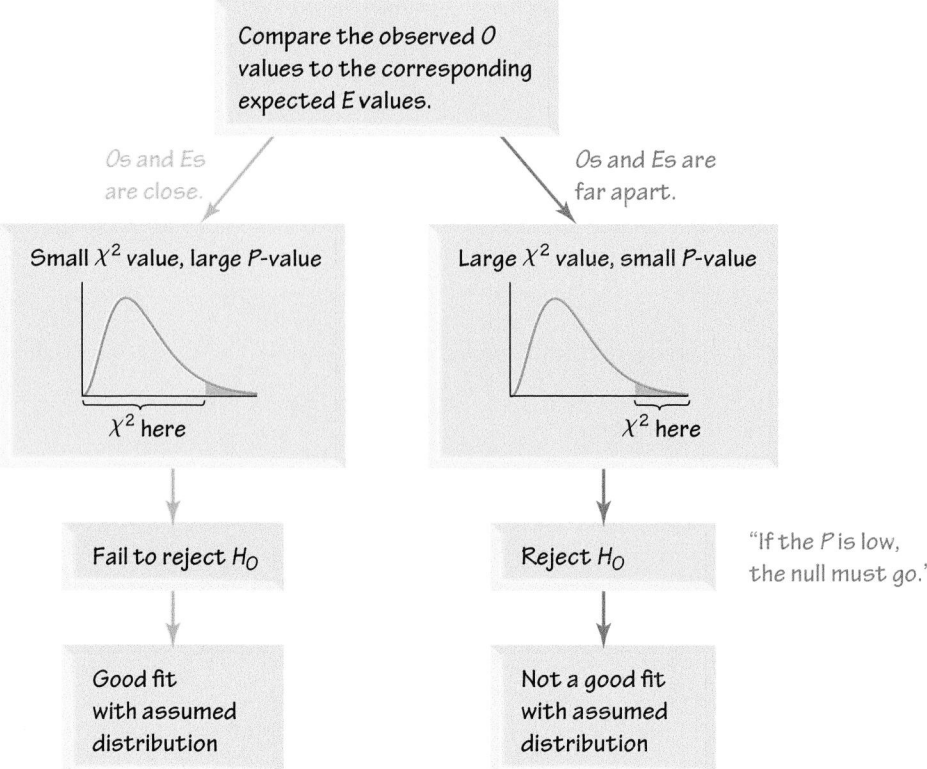

Figure 11-1 Relationships Among the X^2 Test Statistic, *P*-Value, and Goodness-of-Fit

right-tailed, because the critical value and critical region are located at the extreme right of the distribution. If confused, just remember this:

"If the *P* is low, the null must go."

(If the *P*-value is small, reject the null hypothesis that the distribution is as claimed.)

Table 11-2
Last Digits of Weights

Last Digit	Frequency
0	46
1	1
2	2
3	3
4	3
5	30
6	4
7	0
8	8
9	3

Example 1 Last Digits of Weights

A random sample of 100 weights of Californians is obtained, and the last digits of those weights are summarized in Table 11-2 (based on data from the California Department of Public Health). When obtaining weights of subjects, it is extremely important to actually measure their weights instead of asking them to report their weights. By analyzing the *last digits* of weights, researchers can verify that they were obtained through actual measurements instead of being reported. When people report weights, they tend to round, so a weight of 197 lb might be rounded and reported as a more desirable 170 lb. Reported weights tend to have many last digits consisting of 0 or 5. In contrast, if people are actually weighed, the weights tend to have last digits that are uniformly distributed, with 0, 1, 2, . . . , 9 all occurring with roughly the same frequencies.

Test the claim that the sample is from a population of weights in which the last digits do *not* occur with the same frequency. Based on the results, what can we conclude about the procedure used to obtain the weights?

Solution

Requirement check (1) The data come from randomly selected subjects. (2) The data do consist of frequency counts, as shown in Table 11-2. (3) With 100 sample values and 10 categories that are claimed to be equally likely, each expected frequency is 10, so each expected frequency does satisfy the requirement of being a value of at least 5. All of the requirements are satisfied. ✅

The claim that the digits do not occur with the same frequency is equivalent to the claim that the relative frequencies or probabilities of the 10 cells $(p_0, p_1, \ldots, p_9)$ are not all equal. (This is equivalent to testing the claim that the distribution of digits is not a uniform distribution.) We will use the critical value method for testing hypotheses (introduced in Section 8-2).

Step 1: The original claim is that the digits do not occur with the same frequency. That is, at least one of the probabilities $p_0, p_1, \ldots, p_9$ is different from the others.

Step 2: If the original claim is false, then all of the probabilities are the same. That is, $p_0 = p_1 = p_2 = p_3 = p_4 = p_5 = p_6 = p_7 = p_8 = p_9$.

Step 3: The null hypothesis must contain the condition of equality, so we have

H_0: $p_0 = p_1 = p_2 = p_3 = p_4 = p_5 = p_6 = p_7 = p_8 = p_9$

H_1: At least one of the probabilities is different from the others.

Step 4: No significance level was specified, so we select $\alpha = 0.05$.

Step 5: Because we are testing a claim about the distribution of the last digits being a uniform distribution (with all of the digits having the same probability), we use the goodness-of-fit test described in this section. The χ^2 distribution is used with the test statistic given in the preceding box.

Step 6: The observed frequencies O are listed in Table 11-2. Each corresponding expected frequency E is equal to 10 (because the 100 digits would be uniformly distributed among the 10 categories). The Excel add-in XLSTAT is used to obtain the results shown in the accompanying screen display, and Table 11-3 shows the computation of the χ^2 test statistic. The test statistic is $\chi^2 = 212.800$. The critical value is $\chi^2 = 16.919$ (found in Table A-4 with $\alpha = 0.05$ in the right tail and degrees of freedom equal to $k - 1 = 9$). The P-value is less than 0.0001. The test statistic and critical value are shown in Figure 11-2.

XLSTAT

Chi-square (Observed value)	212.8000
Chi-square (Critical value)	16.9190
DF	9
p-value	<0.0001
alpha	0.05

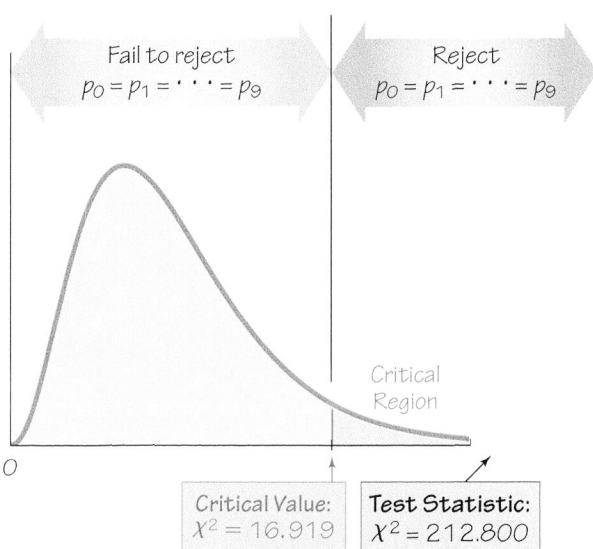

Critical Value: $\chi^2 = 16.919$ Test Statistic: $\chi^2 = 212.800$

Figure 11-2   Test of $p_0 = p_1 = p_2 = p_3 = p_4 = p_5 = p_6 = p_7 = p_8 = p_9$

Which Car Seats Are Safest?

Many people believe that the back seat of a car is the safest place to sit, but is it? University of Buffalo researchers analyzed more than 60,000 fatal car crashes and found that the middle back seat is the safest place to sit in a car. They found that sitting in that seat makes a passenger 86% more likely to survive than those who sit in the front seats, and they are 25% more likely to survive than those sitting in either of the back seats nearest the windows. An analysis of seat belt use showed that when not wearing a seat belt in the back seat, passengers are three times more likely to die in a crash than those wearing seat belts in that same seat. Passengers concerned with safety should sit in the middle back seat wearing a seat belt.

Step 7: If we use the P-value method of testing hypotheses, we see that the P-value is small (less than 0.0001), so we reject the null hypothesis. If we use the critical value method of testing hypotheses, Figure 11-2 shows that the test statistic falls in the critical region, so there is sufficient evidence to reject the null hypothesis.

Step 8: There is sufficient evidence to support the claim that the last digits do not occur with the same relative frequency.

Interpretation

This goodness-of-fit test suggests that the last digits do not provide a good fit with the claimed uniform distribution of equally likely frequencies. Instead of actually weighing the subjects, it appears that the subjects reported their weights. In fact, the weights are from the California Health Interview Survey (CHIS), and the title of that survey indicates that subjects were interviewed, not measured. Because those weights are reported, the reliability of the data is very questionable.

Example 1 involves a situation in which the expected frequencies E for the different categories are all equal. The methods of this section can also be used when the expected frequencies are different, as shown in Example 2.

Table 11-3 Calculating the χ^2 Test Statistic for the Last Digits of Weights

Last Digit	Observed Frequency O	Expected Frequency E	O − E	(O − E)²	$\frac{(O - E)^2}{E}$
0	46	10	36	1296	129.6
1	1	10	−9	81	8.1
2	2	10	−8	64	6.4
3	3	10	−7	49	4.9
4	3	10	−7	49	4.9
5	30	10	20	400	40.0
6	4	10	−6	36	3.6
7	0	10	−10	100	10.0
8	8	10	−2	4	0.4
9	3	10	−7	49	4.9

$$\chi^2 = \sum \frac{(O - E)^2}{E} = 212.8$$

Example 2   Benford's Law: County Populations

According to *Benford's law*, a variety of different data sets includes numbers with leading (first) digits that follow the distribution shown in the first two rows of Table 11-4. The bottom row lists the frequencies of leading digits of the populations of all 120 counties from New York and California combined. Test the claim that those 120 counties have populations with leading digits that follow Benford's law.

Table 11-4 Leading Digits of Populations from NY and CA Counties

Leading Digit	1	2	3	4	5	6	7	8	9
Benford's Law: Distribution of Leading Digits	30.1%	17.6%	12.5%	9.7%	7.9%	6.7%	5.8%	5.1%	4.6%
CA and NY County Populations	33	22	10	15	10	9	5	7	9

Solution

Requirement check (1) The sample data are not randomly selected from a larger population, but we treat them as a random sample for the purpose of determining whether they are typical results that might be obtained from such a random sample. (2) The sample data do consist of frequency counts. (3) Each expected frequency is at least 5, as will be shown later in this solution. All of the requirements are satisfied. ✅

Step 1: The original claim is that the leading digits fit the distribution given as Benford's law. Using subscripts corresponding to the leading digits, we can express this claim as $p_1 = 0.301$ and $p_2 = 0.176$ and $p_3 = 0.125$ and . . . and $p_9 = 0.046$.

Step 2: If the original claim is false, then at least one of the proportions does not have the value as claimed.

Step 3: The null hypothesis must contain the condition of equality, so we have

H_0: $p_1 = 0.301$ and $p_2 = 0.176$ and $p_3 = 0.125$ and . . . and $p_9 = 0.046$.

H_1: At least one of the proportions is not equal to the given claimed value.

Step 4: The significance level is not specified, so we use the common choice of $\alpha = 0.05$.

Step 5: Because we are testing a claim that the distribution of leading digits fits the distribution given by Benford's law, we use the goodness-of-fit test described in this section. The χ^2 distribution is used with the test statistic given earlier.

Step 6: Table 11-5 shows the calculations of the components of the χ^2 test statistic for the leading digits of 1 and 2. If we include all nine leading digits, we get the test statistic of $\chi^2 = 5.958$, as shown in the accompanying TI-84 Plus calculator display. The critical value is $\chi^2 = 15.507$ (found in Table A-4 with $\alpha = 0.05$ in the right tail and degrees of freedom equal to $k - 1 = 8$). The TI-84 Plus calculator display shows the value of the test statistic as well as the P-value of 0.652. (The bottom row of the display shows the expected values, which can be viewed by scrolling to the right. CNTRB is an abbreviated form of "contribution," and the values are the individual contributions to the total value of the χ^2 test statistic.)

Table 11-5 Calculating the χ^2 Test Statistic for Leading Digits in Table 11-4

Leading Digit	Observed Frequency O	Expected Frequency E = np	O − E	(O − E)²	$\frac{(O - E)^2}{E}$
1	33	120 · 0.301 = 36.12	−3.12	9.7344	0.2695
2	22	120 · 0.176 = 21.12	0.88	0.7744	0.0367

Step 7: The P-value of 0.652 is greater than the significance level of 0.05, so there is not sufficient evidence to reject the null hypothesis. (Also, the test statistic of $\chi^2 = 5.958$ does not fall in the critical region bounded by the critical value of 15.507, so there is not sufficient evidence to reject the null hypothesis.)

Step 8: There is not sufficient evidence to warrant rejection of the claim that the 120 counties have populations with leading digits that fit the distribution given by Benford's law.

Safest Seats in a Commercial Jet

A study by aviation writer and researcher David Noland showed that sitting farther back in a commercial jet will increase your chances of surviving in the event of a crash. The study suggests that the chance of surviving is not the same for each seat, so a goodness-of-fit test would lead to rejection of the null hypothesis that every seat has the same probability of surviving. Records from the 20 commercial jet crashes that occurred since 1971 were analyzed. It was found that if you sit in business or first class, you have a 49% chance of surviving a crash, if you sit in coach over the wing or ahead of the wing you have a 56% chance of surviving, and if you sit in the back behind the wing you have a 69% chance of surviving.

In commenting on this study, David Noland stated that he does not seek a rear seat when he flies. He says that because the chance of a crash is so small, he doesn't worry about where he sits, but he prefers a window seat.

TI-84 PLUS

Mendel's Data Falsified?

Because some of Mendel's data from his famous genetics experiments seemed too perfect to be true, statistician R. A. Fisher concluded that the data were probably falsified. He used a chi-square distribution to show that when a test statistic is extremely far to the left and results in a *P*-value very close to 1, the sample data fit the claimed distribution almost perfectly, and this is evidence that the sample data have not been randomly selected. It has been suggested that Mendel's gardener knew what results Mendel's theory predicted, and subsequently adjusted results to fit that theory.

Ira Pilgrim wrote in *The Journal of Heredity* that this use of the chi-square distribution is not appropriate. He notes that the question is not about goodness-of-fit with a particular distribution, but whether the data are from a sample that is truly random. Pilgrim used the binomial probability formula to find the probabilities of the results obtained in Mendel's experiments. Based on his results, Pilgrim concludes that "there is no reason whatever to question Mendel's honesty." It appears that Mendel's results are not too good to be true, and they could have been obtained from a truly random process.

Interpretation

The sample of leading digits does not provide enough evidence to conclude that the Benford distribution is not being followed.

In Figure 11-3 we use a red line to graph the expected proportions given by Benford's law (as in Table 11-4) along with a green line for the observed proportions from Table 11-4. Figure 11-3 allows us to visualize the "goodness-of-fit" between the distribution given by Benford's law and the frequencies that were observed. In Figure 11-3, the red and green lines agree reasonably well, so it appears that the green line for the observed data fits the red line for the expected values reasonably well.

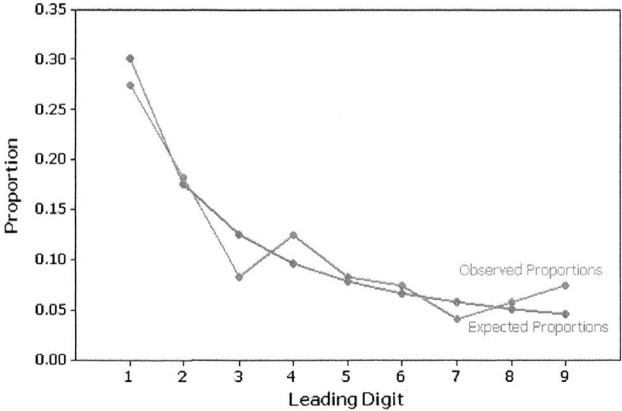

Figure 11-3   **Observed Proportions and Proportions Expected with Benford's Law**

Rationale for the Test Statistic Examples 1 and 2 show that the X^2 test statistic is a measure of the discrepancy between observed and expected frequencies. Simply summing the differences $O - E$ between observed and expected values tells us nothing, because that sum is always 0. Squaring the $O - E$ gives us a better statistic. (The reasons for squaring the $O - E$ values are essentially the same as the reasons for squaring the $x - \bar{x}$ values in the formula for standard deviation.) The value of $\Sigma(O - E)^2$ measures only the magnitude of the differences, but we need to find the magnitude of the differences relative to what was expected. We need a type of average instead of a cumulative total. This relative magnitude is found through division by the expected frequencies, as in the test statistic.

The theoretical distribution of $\Sigma(O - E)^2/E$ is a discrete distribution because the number of possible values is finite. The distribution can be approximated by a chi-square distribution, which is continuous. This approximation is generally considered acceptable, provided that all expected values E are at least 5. (There are ways of circumventing the problem of an expected frequency that is less than 5, such as combining categories so that all expected frequencies are at least 5. Also, there are other methods that can be used when not all expected frequencies are at least 5.)

The number of degrees of freedom reflects the fact that we can freely assign frequencies to $k - 1$ categories before the frequency for every category is determined. (Although we say that we can "freely" assign frequencies to $k - 1$ categories, we cannot have negative frequencies, nor can we have frequencies so large that their sum exceeds the total of the observed frequencies for all categories combined.)

using TECHNOLOGY

STATDISK   First enter the observed frequencies in the first column of the Data Window. If the expected frequencies are not all equal, enter a second column that includes either expected proportions or actual expected frequencies. Select **Analysis** from the main menu bar, then select the option **Goodness-of-Fit.** Choose between "equal expected frequencies" and "unequal expected frequencies" and enter the data in the dialog box, then click on **Evaluate.**

MINITAB   Enter observed frequencies in column C1. If the expected frequencies are not all equal, enter them as proportions in column C2. Select **Stat, Tables,** and **Chi-Square Goodness-of-Fit Test.** Make the entries in the window and click on **OK.**

EXCEL   First enter the observed frequencies in one column, then compute the values of the corresponding expected frequencies and enter them in another column. Proceed by using XLSTAT. Click on **XLSTAT** at the top, then click on **Parametric tests,** then select **Multinomial goodness of fit test.** In the "Frequencies" box enter the range of cells containing the observed frequencies, such as A1: A10. In the "Expected frequencies" box, enter the range of cells containing the expected frequencies. Put a check next to the box identified as "Chi-square." Enter the significance level. For example, enter 5 for a 0.05 significance level. Click **OK** to get the results, which will include the chi-square test statistic and the *P*-value.

TI-83/84 PLUS   Enter the observed frequencies in list L1, then identify the expected frequencies and enter them in list L2. With a TI-84 Plus calculator, press **STAT**, select **TESTS**, select x^2 **GOF-Test,** then enter L1 and L2 and the number of degrees of freedom when prompted. (The number of degrees of freedom is 1 less than the number of categories.) With a TI-83 Plus calculator, use the program X2GOF. Press **PRGM**, select **X2GOF,** then enter L1 and L2 when prompted. Results will include the test statistic and *P*-value.

STATCRUNCH   Click on **Open StatCrunch.** Enter the observed frequencies in one column and enter the expected frequencies in another column. Click on **Stat,** then select **Goodness-of-fit,** then select **Chi-Square test.** Identify the columns to be used, then click on **Calculate.** Results will include the test statistic and *P*-value.

11-2 Basic Skills and Concepts

Statistical Literacy and Critical Thinking

1. Quality Family Time The table below lists days of the week selected by a random sample of 1005 subjects who were asked to identify the day of the week that is best for quality family time (based on results from a Pillsbury survey reported in *USA Today*). Consider the claim that the days of the week are selected with a uniform distribution so that all days have the same chance of being selected. If we test that claim using the goodness-of-fit test described in this section, what is it that we actually test?

Sun	Mon	Tues	Wed	Thurs	Fri	Sat
523	20	9	19	11	41	382

2. Expected Value Exercise 1 includes results from a survey of 1005 randomly selected subjects. Consider the claim that when respondents select days of the week, the seven different days have the same chance of being selected. If that claim is true for the 1005 respondents, what is the expected value for each of the seven days? Identify the values of *O* and *E* for Sunday.

3. χ^2 Value Without performing actual calculations, examine the frequencies in the table given with Exercise 1. Do you expect the value of the χ^2 test statistic to be large or small? Do you expect the *P*-value to be large or small? Explain.

4. Goodness-of-Fit Test For the goodness-of-fit test described in Exercise 1, identify the number of degrees of freedom and the critical value of χ^2, assuming a 0.05 significance level.

In Exercises 5–20, conduct the hypothesis test and provide the test statistic, critical value, and/or P-value, and state the conclusion.

5. Quality Family Time The accompanying STATDISK display shows results from the claim and data given in Exercise 1. Test that claim.

STATDISK

Num Categories:	7
Degrees of freedom:	6
Expected Freq:	143.5714
Test Statistic, X^2:	1934.9791
Critical X^2:	12.59157
P-Value:	0.0000

6. Last Digits of Heights Example 1 in this section involved an analysis of the last digits of weights from a random sample of 100 Californians. Using those same subjects, the last digits of their heights are listed in the table below (based on data from the California Department of Public Health). Use a 0.05 significance level to test the claim that the sample is from a population of heights in which the last digits do *not* occur with the same frequency. The accompanying Minitab display results from the data in the table.

Last Digit	0	1	2	3	4	5	6	7	8	9
Frequency	12	8	14	9	11	9	13	8	11	5

```
MINITAB

  N   DF   Chi-Sq   P-Value
100    9      6.6     0.679
```

7. Testing a Slot Machine The author purchased a slot machine (Bally Model 809) and tested it by playing it 1197 times. There are 10 different categories of outcomes, including no win, win jackpot, win with three bells, and so on. When testing the claim that the observed outcomes agree with the expected frequencies, the author obtained a test statistic of $\chi^2 = 8.185$. Use a 0.05 significance level to test the claim that the actual outcomes agree with the expected frequencies. Does the slot machine appear to be functioning as expected?

8. Flat Tire and Missed Class A classic story involves four carpooling students who missed a test and gave as an excuse a flat tire. On the makeup test, the instructor asked the students to identify the particular tire that went flat. If they really didn't have a flat tire, would they be able to identify the same tire? The author asked 41 other students to identify the tire they would select. The results are listed in the following table (except for one student who selected the spare). Use a 0.05 significance level to test the author's claim that the results fit a uniform distribution. What does the result suggest about the ability of the four students to select the same tire when they really didn't have a flat?

Tire	Left Front	Right Front	Left Rear	Right Rear
Number Selected	11	15	8	6

9. NYC Homicides For a recent year, the following are the numbers of homicides that occurred each month in New York City: 38, 30, 46, 40, 46, 49, 47, 50, 50, 42, 37, 37. Use a 0.05 significance level to test the claim that homicides in New York City are equally likely for each of the 12 months. Is there sufficient evidence to support the police commissioner's claim that homicides occur more often in the summer when the weather is better?

10. Baseball Player Births In his book *Outliers,* author Malcolm Gladwell argues that more baseball players have birthdates in the months immediately following July 31, because that was the cutoff date for nonschool baseball leagues. Here is a sample of frequency counts of months of birthdates of American-born major league baseball players starting with January: 387, 329, 366, 344, 336, 313, 313, 503, 421, 434, 398, 371. Using a 0.05 significance level, is there sufficient evidence to warrant rejection of the claim that American-born major league baseball players are born in different months with the same frequency? Do the sample values appear to support Gladwell's claim?

11. Loaded Die The author drilled a hole in a die and filled it with a lead weight, then proceeded to roll it 200 times. Here are the observed frequencies for the outcomes of 1, 2, 3, 4, 5, and 6, respectively: 27, 31, 42, 40, 28, 32. Use a 0.05 significance level to test the claim that the outcomes are not equally likely. Does it appear that the loaded die behaves differently than a fair die?

12. Births Records of randomly selected births were obtained and categorized according to the day of the week that they occurred (based on data from the National Center for Health Statistics). Because babies are unfamiliar with our schedule of weekdays, a reasonable claim is that births occur on the different days with equal frequency. See the table that follows. Use a 0.01 significance level to test that claim. Can you provide an explanation for the result?

Day	Sun	Mon	Tues	Wed	Thurs	Fri	Sat
Number of Births	77	110	124	122	120	123	97

13. Kentucky Derby The table below lists the frequency of wins for different post positions in the Kentucky Derby horse race (current as of this writing). A post position of 1 is closest to the inside rail, so that horse has the shortest distance to run. (Because the number of horses varies from year to year, only the first 10 post positions are included.) Use a 0.05 significance level to test the claim that the likelihood of winning is the same for the different post positions. Based on the result, should bettors consider the post position of a horse racing in the Kentucky Derby?

Post Position	1	2	3	4	5	6	7	8	9	10
Wins	19	14	11	15	14	7	8	12	5	11

14. Win 4 Lottery The author recorded all digits selected in New York's Win 4 Lottery for two drawings held each day in a recent year. The frequencies of the digits from 0 through 9 are 280, 303, 331, 289, 285, 294, 283, 274, 297, and 284. Use a 0.05 significance level to test the claim of lottery officials that the digits are selected in a way that they are equally likely.

15. Police Calls The police department in Madison, Connecticut released the following numbers of calls for the different days of the week during a recent February that had 28 days: Monday (114); Tuesday (152); Wednesday (160); Thursday (164); Friday (179); Saturday (196); Sunday (130). Use a 0.01 significance level to test the claim that the different days of the week have the same frequencies of police calls. Is there anything notable about the observed frequencies?

16. Police Calls Repeat the preceding exercise using these observed frequencies for police calls received during the month of March: Monday (208); Tuesday (224); Wednesday (246); Thursday (173); Friday (210); Saturday (236); Sunday (154). What is a fundamental error with this analysis?

17. World Series Games The table below lists the numbers of games played in the baseball World Series as of this writing. That table also includes the expected proportions for the numbers of games in a World Series, assuming that in each series, both teams have about the same chance of winning. Use a 0.05 significance level to test the claim that the actual numbers of games fit the distribution indicated by the expected proportions.

Games Played	4	5	6	7
Actual World Series Contests	20	23	23	37
Expected Proportion	2/16	4/16	5/16	5/16

18. American Idol The contestants on the TV show *American Idol* try to win a singing contest. At one point, the web site WhatNotToSing.com listed the actual numbers of eliminations for different orders of singing, and the expected number of eliminations was also listed. The results are in the table below. Use a 0.05 significance level to test the claim that the actual eliminations agree with the expected numbers. Does there appear to be support for the claim that the leadoff singers appear to be at a disadvantage?

Singing Order	1	2	3	4	5	6	7 through 12
Eliminations	20	12	9	8	6	5	9
Expected Eliminations	12.9	12.9	9.9	7.9	6.4	5.5	13.5

19. M&M Candies Mars, Inc. claims that its M&M plain candies are distributed with the following color percentages: 16% green, 20% orange, 14% yellow, 24% blue, 13% red, and 13% brown. Refer to Data Set 20 in Appendix B and use the sample data to test the claim that the color distribution is as claimed by Mars, Inc. Use a 0.05 significance level.

20. Do World War II Bomb Hits Fit a Poisson Distribution? In analyzing hits by V-1 buzz bombs in World War II, South London was subdivided into regions, each with an area of 0.25 km². Shown below is a table of actual frequencies of hits and the frequencies expected with the Poisson distribution. (The Poisson distribution is described in Section 5-5.) Use the values listed and a 0.05 significance level to test the claim that the actual frequencies fit a Poisson distribution.

Number of Bomb Hits	0	1	2	3	4 or more
Actual Number of Regions	229	211	93	35	8
Expected Number of Regions (from Poisson Distribution)	227.5	211.4	97.9	30.5	8.7

Benford's Law. According to Benford's law, a variety of different data sets include numbers with leading (first) digits that follow the distribution shown in the table below. In Exercises 21–24, test for goodness-of-fit with Benford's law.

Leading Digit	1	2	3	4	5	6	7	8	9
Benford's Law: Distribution of Leading Digits	30.1%	17.6%	12.5%	9.7%	7.9%	6.7%	5.8%	5.1%	4.6%

21. Detecting Fraud When working for the Brooklyn district attorney, investigator Robert Burton analyzed the leading digits of the amounts from 784 checks issued by seven suspect companies. The frequencies were found to be 0, 15, 0, 76, 479, 183, 8, 23, and 0, and those digits correspond to the leading digits of 1, 2, 3, 4, 5, 6, 7, 8, and 9, respectively. If the observed frequencies are substantially different from the frequencies expected with Benford's law, the check amounts appear to result from fraud. Use a 0.01 significance level to test for goodness-of-fit with Benford's law. Does it appear that the checks are the result of fraud?

22. Author's Check Amounts Exercise 21 lists the observed frequencies of leading digits from amounts on checks from seven suspect companies. Here are the observed frequencies of the leading digits from the amounts on checks written by the author: 68, 40, 18, 19, 8, 20, 6, 9, 12. (Those observed frequencies correspond to the leading digits of 1, 2, 3, 4, 5, 6, 7, 8, and 9, respectively.) Using a 0.05 significance level, test the claim that these leading digits are from a population of leading digits that conform to Benford's law. Do the author's check amounts appear to be legitimate?

23. Tax Cheating? Frequencies of leading digits from IRS tax files are 152, 89, 63, 48, 39, 40, 28, 25, and 27 (corresponding to the leading digits of 1, 2, 3, 4, 5, 6, 7, 8, and 9 respectively, based on data from Mark Nigrini, who sells software for Benford data analysis). Using a 0.05 significance level, test for goodness-of-fit with Benford's law. Does it appear that the tax entries are legitimate?

24. Author's Computer Files The author recorded the leading digits of the sizes of the files stored on his computer, and the leading digits have frequencies of 45, 32, 18, 12, 9, 3, 13, 9, and 9 (corresponding to the leading digits of 1, 2, 3, 4, 5, 6, 7, 8, and 9, respectively). Using a 0.05 significance level, test for goodness-of-fit with Benford's law.

11-2 Beyond the Basics

25. Testing Goodness-of-Fit with a Normal Distribution Refer to Data Set 1 in Appendix B for the 40 heights of females.

Height (cm)	Less than 155.410	155.410–162.005	162.005–168.601	Greater than 168.601
Frequency				

a. Enter the observed frequencies in the table above.

b. Assuming a normal distribution with mean and standard deviation given by the sample mean and standard deviation, use the methods of Chapter 6 to find the probability of a randomly selected height belonging to each class.

c. Using the probabilities found in part (b), find the expected frequency for each category.

d. Use a 0.01 significance level to test the claim that the heights were randomly selected from a normally distributed population. Does the goodness-of-fit test suggest that the data are from a normally distributed population?

11-3 Contingency Tables

Key Concept This section presents methods for analyzing *contingency tables* (or two-way frequency tables), which include frequency counts for categorical data arranged in a table with at least two rows and at least two columns. In Part 1 of this section, we present a method for conducting a hypothesis test of the null hypothesis that the row and column variables are independent of each other. This test of independence is used in real applications quite often. In Part 2, we will consider three variations of the basic method presented in Part 1: (1) test of homogeneity, (2) Fisher exact test, and (3) McNemar's test for matched pairs.

Part 1: Basic Concepts of Testing for Independence

In this section we use standard statistical methods to analyze frequency counts in a contingency table (or two-way frequency table). We begin with the definition of a contingency table.

> **DEFINITION** A **contingency table** (or **two-way frequency table**) is a table consisting of frequency counts of categorical data corresponding to two different variables. (One variable is used to categorize rows, and a second variable is used to categorize columns.)

Example 1 Contingency Table for Different Treatments

Table 11-6 is a contingency table with four rows and two columns. The cells of the table contain frequency counts. The row variable identifies the treatment used for a stress fracture in a foot bone, and the column variable identifies the outcome as a success or failure (based on data from "Surgery Unfounded for Tarsal Navicular Stress Fracture," by Bruce Jancin, *Internal Medicine News*, Vol. 42, No. 14).

Table 11-6 Study of Success with Different Treatments for Stress Fracture

	Success	Failure
Surgery	54	12
Weight-Bearing Cast	41	51
Non-Weight-Bearing Cast for 6 Weeks	70	3
Non-Weight-Bearing Cast Less Than 6 Weeks	17	5

The word *contingent* has a few different meanings, one of which refers to a *dependence* on some other factor. We use the term *contingency table* because we test for *independence* between the row and column variables. We first define a *test of independence* and we provide key elements of the test in the box that follows.

> **DEFINITION** In a **test of independence,** we test the null hypothesis that in a contingency table, the row and column variables are independent. (That is, there is no dependency between the row variable and the column variable.)

Objective

Conduct a hypothesis test for independence between the row variable and column variable in a contingency table.

Notation

O represents the *observed frequency* in a cell of a contingency table.

E represents the *expected frequency* in a cell, found by assuming that the row and column variables are independent.

r represents the number of rows in a contingency table (not including labels).

c represents the number of columns in a contingency table (not including labels).

Requirements

1. The sample data are randomly selected.

2. The sample data are represented as frequency counts in a two-way table.

3. For every cell in the contingency table, the expected frequency E is at least 5. (There is no requirement that every observed frequency must be at least 5. Also, there is no requirement that the population must have a normal distribution or any other specific distribution.)

Null and Alternative Hypotheses

The null and alternative hypotheses are as follows:

H_0: The row and column variables are independent.

H_1: The row and column variables are dependent.

Test Statistic for a Test of Independence

$$\chi^2 = \sum \frac{(O - E)^2}{E}$$

where O is the observed frequency in a cell and E is the expected frequency found by evaluating

$$E = \frac{(\text{row total})(\text{column total})}{(\text{grand total})}$$

P-Values

P-values are typically provided by technology, or a range of *P*-values can be found from Table A-4.

Critical Values

1. The critical values are found in Table A-4 using

$$\textbf{degrees of freedom} = (r - 1)(c - 1)$$

where r is the number of rows and c is the number of columns.

2. Tests of independence with a contingency table are always *right-tailed*.

The test statistic allows us to measure the amount of disagreement between the frequencies actually observed and those that we would theoretically expect when the two variables are independent. Large values of the χ^2 test statistic are in the rightmost region of the chi-square distribution, and they reflect significant differences between observed and expected frequencies. The distribution of the test statistic χ^2 can be approximated by the chi-square distribution, provided that all expected frequencies are at least 5. The number of degrees of freedom $(r - 1)(c - 1)$ reflects the fact that because we know the total of all frequencies in a contingency table, we can freely assign frequencies to only $r - 1$ rows and $c - 1$ columns before the frequency for every cell is determined. However, we cannot have negative frequencies or frequencies so large that any row (or column) sum exceeds the total of the observed frequencies for that row (or column).

Finding Expected Values E

The test statistic χ^2 is found by using the values of O (observed frequencies) and the values of E (expected frequencies). An individual expected frequency E can be found for a cell by simply multiplying the total of the row frequencies by the total of the column frequencies, then dividing by the grand total of all frequencies, as shown in Example 2.

Example 2   Finding Expected Frequency

Refer to Table 11-6 and find the expected frequency for the first cell, where the observed frequency is 54. (See Table 11-6 on page 577.)

Solution

The first cell lies in the first row (with a total frequency of 66) and the first column (with total frequency of 182). The "grand total" is the sum of all frequencies in the table, which is 253. The expected frequency of the first cell is

$$E = \frac{(\text{row total})\,(\text{column total})}{(\text{grand total})} = \frac{(66)\,(182)}{253} = 47.478$$

Interpretation

We know that the first cell has an observed frequency of $O = 54$ and an expected frequency of $E = 47.478$. We can interpret the expected value by stating that if we assume that success is independent of the treatment, then we expect to find that 47.478 of the subjects would be treated with surgery and that treatment would be successful. There is a discrepancy between $O = 54$ and $E = 47.478$ and such discrepancies are key components of the test statistic that is a collective measure of the overall disagreement between the observed frequencies and the frequencies expected with independence between the row and column variables.

Rationale for Expected Frequencies To better understand expected frequencies, pretend that we know only the row and column totals in Table 11-6. Let's assume that the row and column variables are independent and that one of the 253 study subjects is randomly selected. The probability of getting someone counted in the first cell of Table 11-6 is calculated as follows:

$$P(\text{surgery treatment}) = 66/253 \text{ and } P(\text{success}) = 182/253$$

$$P(\text{surgery treatment } and \text{ success}) = \frac{66}{253} \cdot \frac{182}{253} = 0.187661$$

Polls and Psychologists

Poll results can be dramatically affected by the wording of questions. A phrase such as "over the last few years" is interpreted differently by different people. Over the last few years (actually, since 1980), survey researchers and psychologists have been working together to improve surveys by decreasing bias and increasing accuracy. In one case, psychologists studied the finding that 10 to 15 percent of those surveyed say they voted in the last election when they did not. They experimented with theories of faulty memory, a desire to be viewed as responsible, and a tendency of those who usually vote to say that they voted in the most recent election, even if they did not. Only the last theory was actually found to be part of the problem.

With a probability of 0.187661 for the first cell, we expect that among 253 subjects, there are $253 \cdot 0.187661 = 47.478$ subjects in the first cell. If we generalize these calculations, we get the following:

$$\text{Expected frequency } E = (\text{grand total}) \cdot \frac{(\text{row total})}{(\text{grand total})} \cdot \frac{(\text{column total})}{(\text{grand total})}$$

This expression can be simplified to

$$E = \frac{(\text{row total})(\text{column total})}{(\text{grand total})}$$

We now proceed to conduct a hypothesis test of independence, as in Example 3.

Example 3   Does the Choice of Treatment Affect Success?

If we analyze the data in Table 11-6, it appears that the choice of treatment does affect success. However, we must determine whether those differences are *significant*, and that is the purpose of the test of independence. Use a 0.05 significance level to test the claim that success is independent of the treatment group. What does the result indicate about the increasing trend to use surgery?

Solution

Requirement check (1) Based on the description of the study, we will treat the subjects as being randomly selected and randomly assigned to the different treatment groups. (2) The results are expressed as frequency counts in Table 11-6. (3) The expected frequencies are all at least 5. (The lowest expected frequency is 6.174.) The requirements are satisfied. ✓

The null hypothesis and alternative hypothesis are as follows:

H_0: Success is independent of the treatment.

H_1: Success and the treatment are dependent.

The significance level is $\alpha = 0.05$.

Because the data are in the form of a contingency table, we use the χ^2 distribution with this test statistic:

$$\chi^2 = \sum \frac{(O - E)^2}{E} = \frac{(54 - 47.478)^2}{47.478} + \cdots + \frac{(5 - 6.174)^2}{6.174}$$

$$= 58.393$$

XLSTAT

Chi-square (Observed value)	58.3933
Chi-square (Critical value)	7.8147
DF	3
p-value	< 0.0001
alpha	0.05

***P*-Value** If using technology, results typically include the χ^2 test statistic and the *P*-value. For example, see the accompanying XLSTAT display showing the test statistic is $\chi^2 = 58.393$ and the *P*-value is less than 0.0001. Because the *P*-value is less than the significance level of 0.05, we reject the null hypothesis of independence between success and treatment.

Critical Value If using the critical value method of hypothesis testing, the critical value of $\chi^2 = 7.815$ is found from Table A-4 with $\alpha = 0.05$ in the right tail and the number of degrees of freedom given by $(r - 1)(c - 1) = (4 - 1)(2 - 1) = 3$. The test statistic and critical value are shown in Figure 11-4. Because the test statistic does fall within the critical region, we reject the null hypothesis of independence between success and treatment.

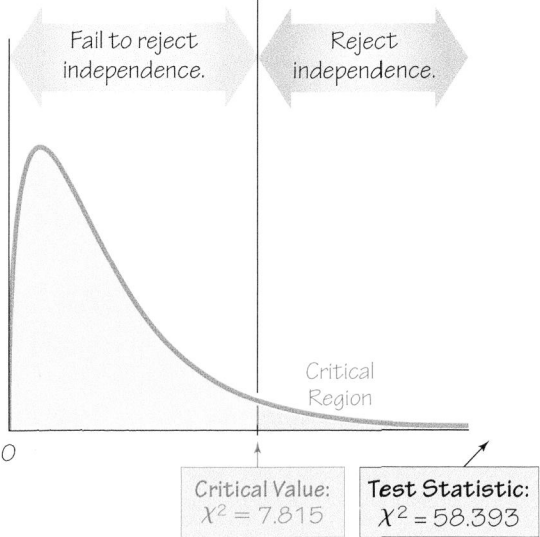

Figure 11-4

Interpretation

It appears that success is dependent on the treatment. Although the results of this test do not tell us which treatment is best, we can see that the success rates of 81.8%, 44.6%, 95.9%, and 77.3% suggest that the best treatment is to use a non-weight-bearing cast for 6 weeks. These results suggest that the increasing use of surgery is a treatment strategy that is not supported by the evidence.

Example 4 Are Four Quarters the Same as One Dollar?

Table 11-1 provided with the Chapter Problem consists of a contingency table with a row variable (whether subject was given four quarters or a one-dollar bill) and a column variable (whether the subject purchased gum or kept the money). Use a 0.05 significance level to test the claim that the row variable is independent of the column variable. What do the results of the test tell us? The table is shown below with results from a TI-83/84 Plus calculator.

Table 11-1 Results from a Study of the Denomination Effect

	Purchased Gum	Kept the Money
Students Given Four Quarters	27	16
Students Given a $1 Bill	12	34

TI-83/84 PLUS

```
X²-Test
 X²=12.1619258
 P=4.877499E-4
 df=1
```

Solution

Requirement check (1) The data in Table 11-1 are from 89 undergraduate business students who were assigned at random to one of two groups. We will treat the data as being random. (2) The sample data are represented as frequency counts in a two-way table. (3) Each expected frequency is at least 5. (The expected frequencies are 18.843, 24.157, 20.157, and 25.843.) The requirements are satisfied.

The null hypothesis and alternative hypothesis are as follows:

H_0: Whether gum was purchased or the money was kept is independent of whether the subject was given four quarters or a one-dollar bill.

H_1: Whether gum was purchased or the money was kept and whether the subject was given four quarters or a one-dollar bill are dependent.

The given TI-83/84 Plus display shows the test statistic of $X^2 = 12.162$ and the P-value of 0.000488 (the rounded P-value expressed in standard form). Because the P-value is less than the significance level of 0.05, reject the null hypothesis of independence. There is sufficient evidence to warrant rejection of independence between the row and column variables.

Interpretation

We reject independence between the row and column variables. It appears that whether the subject purchases gum or keeps the money is dependent on whether the subject is given four quarters or a one-dollar bill. The evidence therefore supports the concept of a "denomination effect."

As in Section 11-2, if observed and expected frequencies are close, the X^2 test statistic will be small and the P-value will be large. If observed and expected frequencies are not close, the X^2 test statistic will be large and the P-value will be small. These relationships are summarized and illustrated in Figure 11-5.

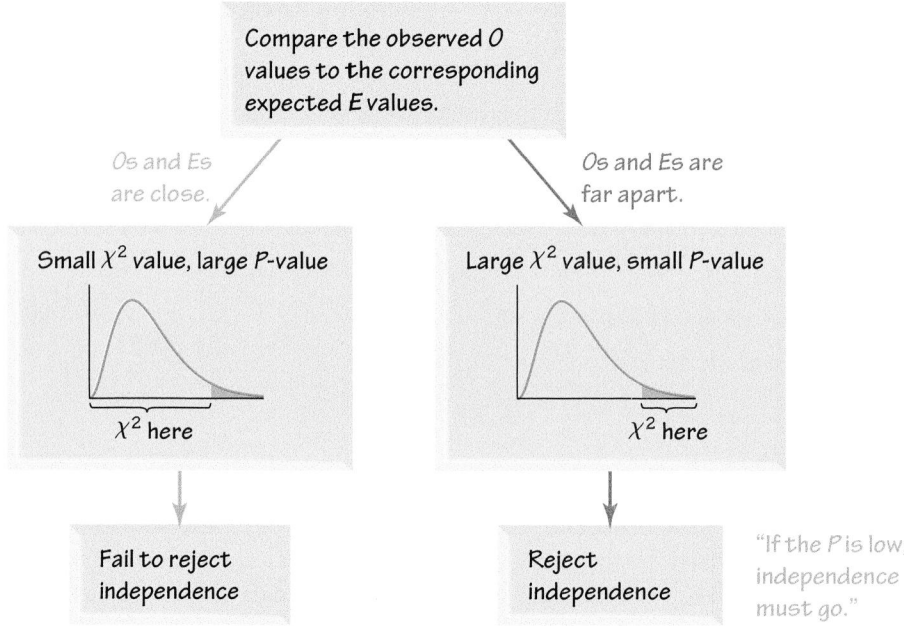

Figure 11-5 **Relationships Among Key Components in Test of Independence**

Part 2: Test of Homogeneity, Fisher Exact Test, and McNemar's Test for Matched Pairs

Test of Homogeneity

In Part 1 of this section, we focused on the test of *independence* between the row and column variables in a contingency table. In Part 1, the sample data are from one population, and individual sample results are categorized with the row and column variables. In a *chi-square test of homogeneity,* we have samples randomly selected from different populations, and we want to determine whether those populations have the same proportions of some characteristic being considered. (The word *homogeneous* means "having the same quality," and in this context, we are testing to determine whether the proportions are the same.) Section 9-2 presented a procedure for testing a claim about *two* populations with categorical data having two possible outcomes, but a chi-square test of homogeneity allows us to use two or more populations with outcomes from several categories.

> **DEFINITION** A **chi-square test of homogeneity** is a test of the claim that *different populations* have the same proportions of some characteristics.

Sampling Plan In a typical test of independence as described in Part 1 of this section, sample subjects are randomly selected from one population (such as people treated for stress fractures in a foot bone) and values of two different variables are observed (such as success/failure for people receiving different treatments). In a typical chi-square test of homogeneity, subjects are randomly selected from the different populations separately.

Procedure In conducting a test of homogeneity, we can use the same notation, requirements, test statistic, critical value, and procedures given in Part 1 of this section, with this exception: Instead of testing the null hypothesis of independence between the row and column variables, we test the null hypothesis that *the different populations have the same proportions of some characteristics.*

> **Example 5** Do the Four Treatment Populations Have the Same Success Rate?
>
> Example 3 used the sample results from Table 11-6 to test for *independence* between treatment and success. If we want to use the same data from Table 11-6 in a test of the null hypothesis that the four populations corresponding to the four different treatment groups have the same proportion of success, we could use the chi-square test of homogeneity. The test statistic, critical value, and *P*-value are the same as those found in Example 3. Based on those values, we should reject the null hypothesis that the four treatment populations have the same success rate.

Fisher Exact Test

The procedures for testing hypotheses with contingency tables have the requirement that every cell must have an expected frequency of at least 5. This requirement is necessary for the χ^2 distribution to be a suitable approximation to the exact distribution of the χ^2 test statistic. The *Fisher exact test* is often used for a 2 $\times$ 2 contingency table with one or more expected frequencies that are below 5. The Fisher exact test provides an *exact P*-value and does not require an approximation technique. Because the calculations are quite complex, it's a good idea to use technology when using the Fisher exact test. STATDISK, Minitab, XLSTAT, and StatCrunch all have the ability to perform the Fisher exact test.

McNemar's Test for Matched Pairs

The methods in Part 1 of this section are based on independent data. For 2×2 tables consisting of frequency counts that result from matched pairs, the frequency counts within each matched pair are not independent and, for such cases, we can use McNemar's test of the null hypothesis that the frequencies from the discordant (different) categories occur in the same proportion.

Table 11-7 shows a general format for summarizing results from data consisting of frequency counts from matched pairs. Table 11-7 refers to two different treatments (such as two different eye drop solutions) applied to two different parts of each subject (such as left eye and right eye). It's a bit difficult to correctly read a table such as Table 11-7. The total number of subjects is $a + b + c + d$, and each of those subjects yields results from each of two parts of a matched pair. If $a = 100$, then 100 subjects were cured with both treatments. If $b = 50$ in Table 11-7, then each of 50 subjects had no cure with treatment X but they were each cured with treatment Y. Remember, the entries in Table 11-7 are frequency counts of subjects, not the total number of individual components in the matched pairs. If 500 people have each eye treated with two different ointments, the value of $a + b + c + d$ is 500 (the number of subjects), not 1000 (the number of treated eyes).

Table 11-7 2 × 2 Table with Frequency Counts from Matched Pairs

		Treatment X	
		Cured	Not Cured
Treatment Y	Cured	a	b
	Not Cured	c	d

McNemar's test requires that for a table such as Table 11-7, the frequencies are such that $b + c \geq 10$. The test is a right-tailed chi-square test with the following test statistic:

$$\chi^2 = \frac{(|b - c| - 1)^2}{b + c}$$

P-values are typically provided by software, and critical values can be found in Table A-4 using 1 degree of freedom. *Caution:* When applying McNemar's test, be careful to use only the two frequency counts from *discordant* (different) pairs, such as the frequency b in Table 11-7 (with different pairs of cured/not cured) and frequency c in Table 11-7 (with different pairs of not cured/cured).

Example 6   Are Hip Protectors Effective?

A randomized controlled trial was designed to test the effectiveness of hip protectors in preventing hip fractures in the elderly. Nursing home residents each wore protection on one hip, but not the other. Results are summarized in Table 11-8 (based on data from "Efficacy of Hip Protector to Prevent Hip Fracture in Nursing Home Residents," by Kiel et al., *Journal of the American Medical Association*, Vol. 298, No. 4). McNemar's test can be used to test the null hypothesis that the following two proportions are the same:

- The proportion of subjects with no hip fracture on the protected hip and a hip fracture on the unprotected hip.

- The proportion of subjects with a hip fracture on the protected hip and no hip fracture on the unprotected hip.

Using the discordant (different) pairs with the general format from Table 11-7, we have $b = 10$ and $c = 15$, so the test statistic is calculated as follows:

$$\chi^2 = \frac{(|b - c| - 1)^2}{b + c} = \frac{(|10 - 15| - 1)^2}{10 + 15} = 0.640$$

With a 0.05 significance level and degrees of freedom given by df $= 1$, we refer to Table A-4 to find the critical value of $\chi^2 = 3.841$ for this right-tailed test. The test statistic of $\chi^2 = 0.640$ does not exceed the critical value of $\chi^2 = 3.841$, so we fail to reject the null hypothesis. (Also, the P-value is 0.424, which is greater than 0.05, indicating that we fail to reject the null hypothesis.) The proportion of hip fractures with the protectors worn is not significantly different from the proportion of hip fractures without the protectors worn. The hip protectors do not appear to be effective in preventing hip fractures.

Table 11-8 Randomized Controlled Trial of Hip Protectors

| | | No Hip Protector Worn | |
		No Hip Fracture	Hip Fracture
Hip Protector Worn	No Hip Fracture	309	10
	Hip Fracture	15	2

using TECHNOLOGY

STATDISK Enter the observed frequencies in the Data Window as they appear in the contingency table. Select **Analysis** from the main menu, then select **Contingency Tables.** Enter a significance level and proceed to identify the columns containing the frequencies. Click on **Evaluate.** The STATDISK results include the test statistic, critical value, and P-value, as shown in the display resulting from Table 11-1.

STATDISK

```
Degrees of freedom: 1

Test Statistic, X^2: 12.1619
Critical X^2:        3.841456
P-Value:             0.0005
```

MINITAB First enter the observed frequencies in columns, then select **Stat** from the main menu bar. Next select the option **Tables,** then select **Chi Square Test (Two-Way Table in Worksheet)** and enter the names of the columns containing the observed frequencies, such as C1 C2 C3 C4. Minitab provides the test statistic and P-value, the expected frequencies, and the individual terms of the χ^2 test statistic.

EXCEL Use XLSTAT. First enter the contingency table in rows and columns. Click on **XLSTAT** at the top. Select **Correlation/Association tests,** then select **Test on contingency table.** In the "Contingency table" box, enter the range of cells containing the frequency counts of the contingency table. For example, enter A1:B4 for a contingency table with two columns (A and B) and four rows. For the "Data format," select the **Contingency Table** option. Click on the **Options** tab, leave a checkmark next to "Chi-square test," and enter a value for "Significance level (%)." For example, enter 5 for a 0.05 significance level. Click **OK** and results including the chi-square test statistic and P-value will be displayed.

TI-83/84 PLUS First enter the contingency table as a matrix by pressing **2ND** **x⁻¹** to get the MATRIX menu (or the MATRIX key on the TI-83). Select **EDIT,** and press **ENTER**. Enter the dimensions of the matrix (rows by columns) and proceed to enter the individual frequencies. When finished, press **STAT**, select **TESTS,** and then select the option χ^2 **-Test.** Be sure that the observed matrix is the one you entered, such as matrix A. The expected frequencies will be automatically calculated and stored in the separate matrix identified as "Expected." Scroll down to **Calculate** and press **ENTER** to get the test statistic, P-value, and number of degrees of freedom.

STATCRUNCH Click on **Open StatCrunch.** Enter the row labels in the first column and enter the cell frequencies in the following columns. Click on **Stat,** select **Tables,** then select **Contingency.** Select the option of **with summary.** Enter the columns to be used, then click on **Calculate.** Results will include the test statistic and P-value.

11-3 Basic Skills and Concepts

Statistical Literacy and Critical Thinking

1. Smoking Cessation The accompanying table summarizes successes and failures when subjects used different methods when trying to stop smoking. The determination of smoking or not smoking was made five months after the treatment was begun, and the data are based on results from the Centers for Disease Control and Prevention. If we test the claim that success is independent of the method used, the TI-83/84 Plus calculator provides a P-value of 0.216 (rounded). What does the P-value tell us about that claim?

	Nicotine Gum	Nicotine Patch	Nicotine Inhaler
Smoking	191	263	95
Not Smoking	59	57	27

2. Terminology The table in Exercise 1 is called a contingency table or two-way table. Why is the term *contingency* used? Why is the terminology of *two-way* table used?

3. Degrees of Freedom and Critical Value For the hypothesis test in Exercise 1, the test statistic is 3.062. Find the number of degrees of freedom used to find the critical value, then find the critical value. Assume a 0.05 significance level.

4. Right-Tailed, Left-Tailed, Two-Tailed Is the hypothesis test in Exercise 1 right-tailed, left-tailed, or two-tailed? Explain your choice.

In Exercises 5–18, test the given claim.

5. Denomination Effect In a study of the "denomination effect" described in the Chapter Problem, 150 women in China were given either a single 100 Yuan bill or a total of 100 Yuan in smaller bills. The value of 100 Yuan is about $15. The women were given the choice of spending the money on specific items or they could keep the money. The results are summarized in the table below, and STATDISK results are provided in the screen display. Use a 0.05 significance level to test the claim that the form of the 100 Yuan is independent of whether the money was spent. What does the result suggest about a denomination effect?

STATDISK

```
Test Statistic, X^2:  3.4091
Critical X^2:         3.841456
P-Value:              0.0648
```

	Spent the Money	Kept the Money
Women Given a Single 100-Yuan Bill	60	15
Women Given 100 Yuan in Smaller Bills	68	7

6. Which Treatment Is Better? A randomized controlled trial was designed to compare the effectiveness of splinting versus surgery in the treatment of carpal tunnel syndrome. Results are given in the table below (based on data from "Splinting vs. Surgery in the Treatment of Carpal Tunnel Syndrome," by Gerritsen et al., *Journal of the American Medical Association*, Vol. 288, No. 10). The results are based on evaluations made one year after the treatment. Minitab results are given below the table. Using a 0.01 significance level, test the claim that success is independent of the type of treatment. What do the results suggest about treating carpal tunnel syndrome?

	Successful Treatment	Unsuccessful Treatment
Splint Treatment	60	23
Surgery Treatment	67	6

MINITAB

```
Chi-Sq = 9.750, DF = 1, P-Value = 0.002
```

7. Testing a Lie Detector The table below includes results from polygraph (lie detector) experiments conducted by researchers Charles R. Honts (Boise State University) and Gordon H. Barland (Department of Defense Polygraph Institute). In each case, it was known if the subject lied or did not lie, so the table indicates when the polygraph test was correct. Use a 0.05 significance level to test the claim that whether a subject lies is independent of the polygraph test indication. Do the results suggest that polygraphs are effective in distinguishing between truths and lies?

	Did the Subject Actually Lie?	
	No (Did Not Lie)	Yes (Lied)
Polygraph test indicated that the subject lied.	15	42
Polygraph test indicated that the subject did not lie.	32	9

8. Discrimination The U.S. Supreme Court considered a case involving the exam for firefighter lieutenant in the city of New Haven, Connecticut. Results from the exam are shown in the table below. Is there sufficient evidence to support the claim that results from the test should be thrown out because they are discriminatory? Use a 0.01 significance level.

	Passed	Failed
White Candidates	17	16
Minority Candidates	9	25

9. Is Sentence Independent of Plea? Many people believe that criminals who plead guilty tend to get lighter sentences than those who are convicted in trials. The accompanying table summarizes randomly selected sample data for San Francisco defendants in burglary cases (based on data from "Does It Pay to Plead Guilty? Differential Sentencing and the Functioning of the Criminal Courts," by Brereton and Casper, *Law and Society Review*, Vol. 16, No. 1). All of the subjects had prior prison sentences. Use a 0.05 significance level to test the claim that the sentence (sent to prison or not sent to prison) is independent of the plea. If you were an attorney defending a guilty defendant, would these results suggest that you should encourage a guilty plea?

	Guilty Plea	Not Guilty Plea
Sent to Prison	392	58
Not Sent to Prison	564	14

10. Nurse a Serial Killer? Alert nurses at the Veteran's Affairs Medical Center in Northampton, Massachusetts, noticed an unusually high number of deaths at times when another nurse, Kristen Gilbert, was working. Those same nurses later noticed missing supplies of the drug epinephrine, which is a synthetic adrenaline that stimulates the heart. Kristen Gilbert was arrested and charged with four counts of murder and two counts of attempted murder. When seeking a grand jury indictment, prosecutors provided a key piece of evidence consisting of the table below. Use a 0.01 significance level to test the defense claim that deaths on shifts are independent of whether Gilbert was working. What does the result suggest about the guilt or innocence of Gilbert?

	Shifts with a Death	Shifts Without a Death
Gilbert Was Working	40	217
Gilbert Was Not Working	34	1350

11. Tennis Challenges The table below shows results since 2006 of challenged referee calls in the U.S. Open. Use a 0.05 significance level to test the claim that the gender of the tennis player is independent of whether the call is overturned.

	Was the Challenge to the Call Successful?	
	Yes	No
Men	421	991
Women	220	539

12. Lefties A random sample of 760 subjects was obtained, and each was tested for left-hand writing. Results are in the table below (based on data from "The Left-Handed: Their Sinister History," by Elaine Fowler Costas, Education Resources Information Center, Paper 399519). Use a 0.05 significance level to test the claim that left-handedness is independent of gender.

	Writes with Left Hand?	
	Yes	No
Male	23	217
Female	65	455

13. Soccer Strategy In soccer, serious fouls result in a penalty kick with one kicker and one defending goalkeeper. The table below summarizes results from 286 kicks during games among top teams (based on data from "Action Bias Among Elite Soccer Goalkeepers: The Case of Penalty Kicks," by Bar-Eli et al., *Journal of Economic Psychology,* Vol. 28, No. 5). In the table, jump direction indicates which way the goalkeeper jumped, where the kick direction is from the perspective of the goalkeeper. Use a 0.05 significance level to test the claim that the direction of the kick is independent of the direction of the goalkeeper jump. Do the results support the theory that because the kicks are so fast, goalkeepers have no time to react, so the directions of their jumps are independent of the directions of the kicks?

	Goalkeeper Jump		
	Left	Center	Right
Kick to Left	54	1	37
Kick to Center	41	10	31
Kick to Right	46	7	59

14. Is Seat Belt Use Independent of Cigarette Smoking? A study of seat belt users and nonusers yielded the randomly selected sample data summarized in the given table (based on data from "What Kinds of People Do Not Use Seat Belts?" by Helsing and Comstock, *American Journal of Public Health,* Vol. 67, No. 11). Test the claim that the amount of smoking is independent of seat belt use. A plausible theory is that people who smoke more are less concerned about their health and safety and are therefore less inclined to wear seat belts. Is this theory supported by the sample data?

	Number of Cigarettes Smoked per Day			
	0	1–14	15–34	35 and over
Wear Seat Belts	175	20	42	6
Don't Wear Seat Belts	149	17	41	9

15. Clinical Trial of Echinacea In a clinical trial of the effectiveness of echinacea for preventing colds, the results in the table below were obtained (based on data from "An Evaluation of *Echinacea Angustifolia* in Experimental Rhinovirus Infections," by Turner et al., *New England Journal of Medicine,* Vol. 353, No. 4). Use a 0.05 significance level to test the claim that getting a cold is independent of the treatment group. What do the results suggest about the effectiveness of echinacea as a prevention against colds?

	Treatment Group		
	Placebo	Echinacea: 20% extract	Echinacea: 60% extract
Got a Cold	88	48	42
Did Not Get a Cold	15	4	10

16. Injuries and Motorcycle Helmet Color A case-control (or retrospective) study was conducted to investigate a relationship between the colors of helmets worn by motorcycle drivers and whether they are injured or killed in a crash. Results are given in the table below (based on data from "Motorcycle Rider Conspicuity and Crash Related Injury: Case-Control Study," by Wells et al., *BMJ USA,* Vol. 4). Test the claim that injuries are independent of helmet color. Should motorcycle drivers choose helmets with a particular color? If so, which color appears best?

	Color of Helmet				
	Black	White	Yellow/Orange	Red	Blue
Controls (not injured)	491	377	31	170	55
Cases (injured or killed)	213	112	8	70	26

17. Survey Refusals A study of people who refused to answer survey questions provided the randomly selected sample data shown in the table below (based on data from "I Hear You Knocking But You Can't Come In," by Fitzgerald and Fuller, *Sociological Methods and Research,* Vol. 11, No. 1). At the 0.01 significance level, test the claim that the cooperation of the subject (response or refusal) is independent of the age category. Does any particular age group appear to be particularly uncooperative?

	Age					
	18–21	22–29	30–39	40–49	50–59	60 and over
Responded	73	255	245	136	138	202
Refused	11	20	33	16	27	49

18. Baseball Player Births In his book *Outliers,* author Malcolm Gladwell argues that more American-born baseball players have birthdates in the months immediately following July 31 because that was the cutoff date for nonschool baseball leagues. The table below lists months of births for a sample of American-born baseball players and foreign-born baseball players. Using a 0.05 significance level, is there sufficient evidence to warrant rejection of the claim that months of births of baseball players are independent of whether they are born in America? Do the data appear to support Gladwell's claim?

	Jan	Feb	March	April	May	June	July	Aug	Sept	Oct	Nov	Dec
Born in America	387	329	366	344	336	313	313	503	421	434	398	371
Foreign Born	101	82	85	82	94	83	59	91	70	100	103	82

19. Clinical Trial of Lipitor Lipitor is the trade name of the drug atorvastatin, which is used to reduce cholesterol in patients. (Until its patent expired in 2011, this was the largest-selling drug in the world, with annual sales of $13 billion.) Adverse reactions have been studied in clinical trials, and the table below summarizes results for infections in patients from different treatment groups (based on data from Parke-Davis). Use a 0.01 significance level to test the claim that getting an infection is independent of the treatment. Does the atorvastatin treatment appear to have an effect on infections?

	Placebo	Atorvastatin 10 mg	Atorvastatin 40 mg	Atorvastatin 80 mg
Infection	27	89	8	7
No Infection	243	774	71	87

20. Genetics and Handedness In a study of left-handedness as a possible inherited trait, the data in the table below were obtained (based on data from "Why Are Some People Left-Handed? An Evolutionary Perspective," by Laurens and Faurie, *Philosophical Transactions*, Vol. 364). Use a 0.01 significance level to test the claim that left-handedness is independent of parental handedness. What do the results suggest about the inheritability of left-handedness?

Parental Handedness	Offspring Left-Handed?	
Father/Mother	Yes	No
Right/Right	5360	50,928
Right/Left	767	2736
Left/Right	741	3667
Left/Left	94	289

11-3 Beyond the Basics

21. Equivalent Tests A X^2 test involving a 2×2 table is equivalent to the test for the difference between two proportions, as described in Section 9-2. Using the claim and table in Example 4, verify that the X^2 test statistic and the z test statistic (found from the test of equality of two proportions) are related as follows: $z^2 = X^2$. Also show that the critical values have that same relationship.

22. Using Yates's Correction for Continuity The chi-square distribution is continuous, whereas the test statistic used in this section is discrete. Some statisticians use *Yates's correction for continuity* in cells with an expected frequency of less than 10 or in all cells of a contingency table with two rows and two columns. With Yates's correction, we replace

$$\sum \frac{(O - E)^2}{E} \quad \text{with} \quad \sum \frac{(|O - E| - 0.5)^2}{E}$$

Given the contingency table in Example 4, find the value of the X^2 test statistic using Yates's correction. What effect does Yates's correction have?

Chapter 11   Review

The two sections of this chapter both involve applications of the X^2 distribution to categorical data consisting of frequency counts. In Section 11-2 we described methods for using frequency counts from different categories for testing goodness-of-fit with some claimed distribution. The test statistic given below is used in a right-tailed test in which the X^2 distribution has $k - 1$ degrees of freedom, where k is the number of categories. This test requires that each of the expected frequencies must be at least 5.

$$\text{Test statistic is } X^2 = \sum \frac{(O - E)^2}{E}.$$

In Section 11-3 we described methods for testing claims involving contingency tables (or two-way frequency tables), which have at least two rows and two columns. Contingency tables have two variables: One variable is used for determining the row that describes a sample value, and the second variable is used for determining the column that describes a sample value. We conduct a test of independence between the row and column variables by using the test statistic given below. This test statistic is used in a right-tailed test in which the X^2 distribution has the number of degrees of freedom given by $(r - 1)(c - 1)$, where r is the number of rows and c is the number of columns. This test requires that each of the expected frequencies must be at least 5.

$$\text{Test statistic is } X^2 = \sum \frac{(O - E)^2}{E}.$$

Chapter Quick Quiz

Questions 1–5 refer to the sample data in the following table (based on data from the Bureau of Labor Statistics). The table lists frequencies for randomly selected nonfatal occupation injuries arranged according to day of the week. Assume that we want to use a 0.05 significance level to test the claim that such injuries occur with equal frequency on different days of the week.

Day	Mon	Tues	Wed	Thurs	Fri
Number	23	23	21	21	19

1. What are the null and alternative hypotheses corresponding to the stated claim?

2. When testing the claim in Question 1, what are the observed and expected frequencies for Monday?

3. Is the hypothesis test left-tailed, right-tailed, or two-tailed?

4. If using a 0.05 significance level to test the stated claim, find the number of degrees of freedom and the critical value.

5. Given that the *P*-value for the hypothesis test is 0.971, what do you conclude?

Questions 6–10 refer to the sample data in the following table (based on data from the Pew Research Center). Randomly selected subjects were asked about the use of marijuana for medical purposes. Assume that we want to use a 0.05 significance level to test the claim that response to the question is independent of gender.

	In Favor	Oppose	Don't Know
Men	538	167	29
Women	557	186	31

6. Identify the null and alternative hypotheses corresponding to the stated claim.

7. What distribution is used to test the stated claim (normal, *t*, *F*, chi-square, uniform)?

8. Is the hypothesis test left-tailed, right-tailed, or two-tailed?

9. Find the number of degrees of freedom and the critical value.

10. Given that the *P*-value for the hypothesis test is 0.836, what do you conclude?

Review Exercises

1. Auto Fatalities The table below lists auto fatalities by day of the week for a recent year (based on data from the Federal Highway Administration). Minitab results are also shown. Use a 0.01 significance level to test the claim that auto fatalities occur on the different days of the week with the same frequency. Can you provide an explanation for the results?

Day	Mon	Tues	Wed	Thurs	Fri	Sat	Sun
Frequency	3797	3615	3724	4004	4867	5786	5004

MINITAB

N	DF	Chi-Sq	P-Value
30797	6	931.347	0.000

2. Measuring Weights When certain quantities are measured, the last digits tend to be uniformly distributed, but if they are estimated or reported, the last digits tend to have disproportionately more 0s or 5s. If we use the last digits (decimal portion) of the 80 weights in Data Set 1 from Appendix B, we get the frequency counts in the table below. Use a 0.05 significance level to test the claim that the last digits of $0, 1, 2, \ldots, 9$ occur with the same frequency. Does it appear that the weights were obtained through measurements?

Last Digit	0	1	2	3	4	5	6	7	8	9
Frequency	6	7	4	11	10	8	5	9	10	10

3. Weather-Related Deaths Listed below are the numbers of weather-related deaths in a recent year (based on data from the National Weather Service). Use a 0.01 significance level to test the claim that weather-related deaths occur in the different months with the same frequency. Can you provide an explanation for the result?

Month	Jan	Feb	March	April	May	June	July	Aug	Sept	Oct	Nov	Dec
Number of Deaths	39	17	20	19	60	79	109	73	28	5	5	35

4. Bicycle Helmets A study was conducted of 531 persons injured in bicycle crashes, and randomly selected sample results are summarized in the accompanying table (based on results from "A Case-Control Study of the Effectiveness of Bicycle Safety Helmets in Preventing Facial Injury," by Thompson et al., *American Journal of Public Health,* Vol. 80, No. 12). The TI-83/84 Plus calculator results also are shown. At the 0.05 significance level, test the claim that wearing a helmet has no effect on whether facial injuries are received. Based on these results, does a helmet seem to be effective in helping to prevent facial injuries in a crash?

	Helmet Worn	No Helmet
Facial Injuries Received	30	182
All Injuries Nonfacial	83	236

TI-83/84 PLUS

5. Flipping and Spinning Pennies Use the data in the table below with a 0.05 significance level to test the claim that when flipping or spinning a penny, the outcome is independent of whether the penny was flipped or spun. (The data are from experimental results given in *Chance News.*) Does the conclusion change if the significance level is changed to 0.01?

	Heads	Tails
Flipping	2048	1992
Spinning	953	1047

6. Home Field Advantage Winning-team data were collected for teams in different sports, with the results given in the accompanying table (based on data from "Predicting Professional Sports Game Outcomes from Intermediate Game Scores," by Copper, DeNeve, and Mosteller, *Chance*, Vol. 5, No. 3–4). Use a 0.05 level of significance to test the claim that home/visitor wins are independent of the sport.

	Basketball	Baseball	Hockey	Football
Home Team Wins	127	53	50	57
Visiting Team Wins	71	47	43	42

Cumulative Review Exercises

Please be aware that some of the following problems may require knowledge of concepts presented in previous chapters.

1. Weather-Related Deaths Review Exercise 3 involved weather-related deaths. Among the 489 deaths included in the table, 325 are males. Use a 0.05 significance level to test the claim that among those who die in weather-related deaths, the percentage of males is equal to 50%.

2. Cigarette Costs In an American Express survey of 1000 adults 18 and older, 62% said that cigarettes should cost more to help offset potential negative health effects. Use the sample data to construct a 95% confidence interval estimate of the percentage of all adults who share that same belief. What can we conclude about a claim that half of all adults share that same belief?

3. ICU Patients Listed below are the ages of randomly selected patients in intensive care units (based on data from "A Multifaceted Intervention for Quality Improvement in a Network of Intensive Care Units," by Scales et al., *Journal of the American Medical Association*, Vol. 305, No. 4). Find the mean, median, and standard deviation. Based on the results, is an age of 16 years *unusual*? Why or why not?

$$38 \quad 64 \quad 35 \quad 67 \quad 42 \quad 29 \quad 68 \quad 62 \quad 74 \quad 58$$

4. ICU Patients Use the sample of ages from Exercise 3 to construct a 95% confidence interval estimate of the mean age of the population of ICU patients. Do the confidence interval limits contain the value of 65.0 years that was found from a sample of 9269 ICU patients?

5. Boats and Manatees The table below lists the numbers of registered pleasure boats (thousands) in Florida and the numbers of watercraft-related manatee deaths for each year of the past decade.

Boats	90	92	94	95	97	99	99	97	95	90
Manatee Deaths	81	95	73	69	79	92	73	90	97	83

a. Test for a linear correlation between the numbers of boats and the numbers of manatee deaths.

b. Find the equation of the regression line. Use the numbers of boats for the independent x variable.

c. What is the best predicted number of manatee deaths for the year preceding those included in the table? For that year, there were 84 (thousand) registered pleasure boats in Florida. How accurate is that predicted value, given that there were actually 78 manatee deaths in that year?

6. Forward Grip Reach and Ergonomics When designing cars and aircraft, we must consider the forward grip reach of women. Women have normally distributed forward grip reaches with a mean of 686 mm and a standard deviation of 34 mm (based on anthropometric survey data from Gordon, Churchill, et al.)

a. If a car dashboard is positioned so that it can be reached by 95% of women, what is the shortest forward grip reach that can access the dashboard?

b. If a car dashboard is positioned so that it can be reached by women with a grip reach greater than 650 mm, what percentage of women cannot reach the dashboard? Is that percentage too high?

c. Find the probability that 16 randomly selected women have forward grip reaches with a mean greater than 680 mm. Does this result have any effect on the design?

7. Honesty Is the Best Policy In a *USA Today* survey of 456 subjects, 269 agreed that honesty is always the best policy. Assume that we plan to use the survey results to estimate the proportion of the population who believe that honesty is always the best policy.

a. Is the sample proportion of 269/456 a statistic or a parameter?

b. Are frequency counts such as 269 categorical data or quantitative data?

c. Are frequency counts such as 269 discrete or continuous?

d. What does it mean for a sample, such as the 456 surveyed subjects, to be a simple random sample?

e. The *USA Today* survey was conducted as follows: A question was posted on the *USA Today* web site and Internet users could choose to respond. In statistics, is this a valid sampling plan?

8. Probability and Honesty Based on the sample described in the preceding exercise, assume that when someone is randomly selected, there is a 0.6 probability that the selected person believes that honesty is always the best policy.

a. If four people are randomly selected, find the probability that they all believe that honesty is always the best policy.

b. If someone is randomly selected, what is the probability that he or she does *not* believe that honesty is always the best policy?

Technology Project

Use STATDISK, Minitab, Excel, StatCrunch, or a TI-83/84 Plus calculator, or any other software package or calculator capable of generating equally likely random digits between 0 and 9 inclusive. Generate 5000 digits and record the results in the accompanying table. Use a 0.05 significance level to test the claim that the sample digits come from a population with a uniform distribution (so that all digits are equally likely). Does the random number generator appear to be working as it should?

Digit	0	1	2	3	4	5	6	7	8	9
Frequency										

from data TO DECISION

Critical Thinking: Was Allstate wrong?

The Allstate insurance company once issued a press release listing revised zodiac signs along with the corresponding numbers of accidents, as shown in the first and last columns in the table below.

In the original press release, Allstate included comments such as one stating that Virgos are worried and shy, and they were involved in 211,650 accidents, making them the worst offenders. Allstate quickly issued another press release saying that the original press release was meant to be a joke.

Zodiac Sign	Dates	Length (days)	Accidents
Capricorn	Jan. 18 – Feb. 15	29	128,005
Aquarius	Feb. 16 – March 11	24	106,878
Pisces	March 12 – April 16	36	172,030
Aries	April 17 – May 13	27	112,402
Taurus	May 14 – June 19	37	177,503
Gemini	June 20 – July 20	31	136,904
Cancer	July 21 – Aug. 9	20	101,539
Leo	Aug. 10 – Sept. 15	37	179,657
Virgo	Sept. 16 – Oct. 30	45	211,650
Libra	Oct. 31 – Nov. 22	23	110,592
Scorpio	Nov. 23 – Nov. 28	6	26,833
Ophiuchus	Nov. 29 – Dec. 17	19	83,234
Sagittarius	Dec. 18 – Jan. 17	31	154,477

Analyzing the Results

The original Allstate press release did not include the lengths (days) of the different zodiac signs. The preceding table lists those lengths in the third column. A reasonable explanation for the different numbers of accidents is that they should be proportional to the lengths of the zodiac signs. For example, people are born under the Capricorn sign on 29 days out of the 365 days in the year, so they should have 29/365 of the total number of accidents. Use the methods of this chapter to determine whether this appears to explain the results in the table. Write a brief report of your findings.

Cooperative Group Activities

1. Out-of-class activity Divide into groups of four or five students. The instructions for Exercises 21–24 in Section 11-2 noted that according to Benford's law, a variety of different data sets include numbers with leading (first) digits that follow the distribution shown in the table below. Collect original data and use the methods of Section 11-2 to support or refute the claim that the data conform reasonably well to Benford's law. Here are some possibilities: (1) leading digits of amounts on the checks that you wrote; (2) leading digits of the prices of stocks; (3) leading digits of the numbers on street addresses; (5) leading digits of the lengths of rivers in the world.

Leading Digit	1	2	3	4	5	6	7	8	9
Benford's Law	30.1%	17.6%	12.5%	9.7%	7.9%	6.7%	5.8%	5.1%	4.6%

2. Out-of-class activity Divide into groups of four or five students and collect past results from a state lottery. Such results are often available on web sites for individual state lotteries. Use the methods of Section 11-2 to test that the numbers are selected in such a way that all possible outcomes are equally likely.

3. Out-of-class activity Divide into groups of four or five students. Each group member should survey at least 15 male students and 15 female students at the same college by asking two questions: (1) Which political party does the subject favor most? (2) If the subject were to make up an absence excuse of a flat tire, which tire would he or she say went flat if the instructor asked? (See Exercise 8 in Section 11-2.) Ask the subject to write the two responses on an index card, and also record the gender of the subject and whether the subject wrote with the right or left hand. Use the methods of this chapter to analyze the data collected. Include these claims:

• The four possible choices for a flat tire are selected with equal frequency.

• The tire identified as being flat is independent of the gender of the subject.

• Political party choice is independent of the gender of the subject.

• Political party choice is independent of whether the subject is right- or left-handed.

• The tire identified as being flat is independent of whether the subject is right- or left-handed.

• Gender is independent of whether the subject is right- or left-handed.

• Political party choice is independent of the tire identified as being flat.

4. Out-of-class activity Divide into groups of four or five students. Each group member should select about 15 other students and first ask them to "randomly" select four digits each. After the four digits have been recorded, ask each subject to write the last four digits of his or her Social Security number. Take the "random" sample results and mix them into one big sample, then mix the Social Security digits into a second big sample. Using the "random" sample set, test the claim that students select digits randomly. Then use the Social Security digits to test the claim that they come from a population of random digits. Compare the results. Does it appear that students can randomly select digits? Are they likely to select any digits more often than others? Are they likely to select any digits less often than others? Do the last digits of Social Security numbers appear to be randomly selected?

5. In-class activity Divide into groups of three or four students. Each group should be given a die along with the instruction that it should be tested for "fairness." Is the die fair or is it biased? Describe the analysis and results.

6. Out-of-class activity Divide into groups of two or three students. The analysis of last digits of data can sometimes reveal whether values are the results of actual measurements or whether they are reported estimates. Refer to an almanac and find the lengths of rivers in the world, then analyze the last digits to determine whether those lengths appear to be actual measurements or whether they appear to be reported estimates.

Instead of lengths of rivers, you could use other variables, such as the following:

• Heights of mountains

• Heights of tallest buildings

• Lengths of bridges

• Heights of roller coasters

13 Nonparametric Statistics

chapter problem

What do we do when requirements are violated?

The statistical methods presented in the preceding chapters typically include requirements, such as these:

Requirement: The population must be normally distributed or the sample must include more than 30 values. (Section 8-4)

Requirement: The two sample sizes are both *large* (with $n_1 > 30$ and $n_2 > 30$) or both samples come from populations having normal distributions. (Section 9-3)

Requirement: The populations have distributions that are approximately normal. (Section 12-2)

When requirements are violated, we can sometimes use different methods not having the same requirements. Let's consider American Airlines Flight 19 and Flight 21 from New York's JFK airport to LAX in Los Angeles. Table 13-1 lists the departure delay times for samples of flights from January of a recent year. The data are included in Data Set 15 from Appendix B, and the times are in minutes.

Table 13-1 Departure Delay Times (min) for American Airlines Flight 19 and Flight 21											
Flight 19	19	−4	−5	−1	−4	73	0	1	13	−1	−8	32
Flight 21	18	60	142	−1	−11	−1	47	13	12	123	1	4

If we want to test the claim that the population of departure delay times for Flight 19 has the same mean as the population of departure delay times for Flight 21, we have this null hypothesis: $H_0: \mu_1 = \mu_2$. Because we want to test for equality of means from two independent populations, we consider using the *t* test method described in Section 9-3, which includes this requirement: "The two sample sizes are both large (with $n_1 > 30$ and $n_2 > 30$) or both samples come from populations having normal distributions." The sample sizes are both $n = 12$, so neither sample is large. Also, both samples have distributions that are very far from normal. See the accompanying normal quantile plot of the Flight 19 departure delay times, which shows points in a pattern that is not close to a straight-line pattern, so the sample data appear to be from a population with a distribution that is not a normal distribution. The Flight 21 departure times have a similar normal quantile plot, so the population of Flight 21 departure delay times does not appear to have a normal distribution. Both samples are small and they both appear to be from populations not having a normal distribution, so the requirement is violated and the *t* test method of Section 9-3 should not be used. This chapter introduces methods that can often be used when methods from the preceding chapters should not be used because the requirements are violated. We will revisit the data in Table 13-1 in Section 13-4 where we present a method that does not have the same requirements for the *t* test method presented in Section 9-3.

STATDISK

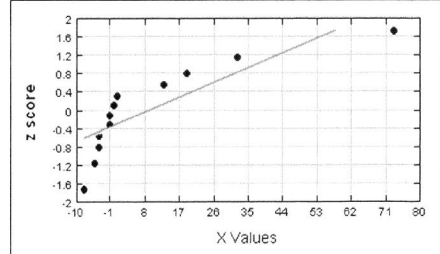

635

13-1   Review and Preview

Many of the statistical methods from the preceding chapters require normally distributed populations and are based on sampling from a population with specific parameters, such as the mean μ, standard deviation σ, or population proportion p. This chapter introduces methods of *nonparametric* statistics, which do not have the stricter requirements of corresponding parametric methods.

> **DEFINITIONS** **Parametric tests** have requirements about the distribution of the populations involved; **nonparametric (or distribution-free) tests** do not require that samples come from populations with normal distributions or any other particular distributions.

Terminology Flaw The term *distribution-free test* correctly indicates that a test does not require a particular distribution. The term *nonparametric tests* is a bit misleading because it suggests that the tests are not based on a parameter, but there are some nonparametric tests that are based on a parameter such as the median. Due to the widespread use of the term *nonparametric test,* we use that terminology, but we define it to be a test that does not require a particular distribution. (The author likes the term *non-distribution test,* but he didn't make it to the front of the line when definitions were being made.)

The following are major advantages and disadvantages of nonparametric tests.

Advantages of Nonparametric Tests

1. Because nonparametric tests have less rigid requirements than parametric tests, they can be applied to a wider variety of situations.

2. Nonparametric tests can be applied to more data types than parametric tests. For example, nonparametric tests can be used with data consisting of ranks, and they can be used with categorical data, such as genders of survey respondents.

Disadvantages of Nonparametric Tests

1. Nonparametric tests tend to waste information because exact numerical data are often reduced to a qualitative form. For example, with the nonparametric sign test (Section 13-2), weight losses by dieters are recorded simply as negative signs, and the actual magnitudes of the weight losses are ignored.

2. Nonparametric tests are not as *efficient* as parametric tests, so a nonparametric test generally needs stronger evidence (such as a larger sample or greater differences) in order to reject a null hypothesis.

Efficiency When the requirements of population distributions are satisfied, nonparametric tests are generally less efficient than their corresponding parametric tests, but the reduced efficiency can be compensated for by an increased sample size. For example, in Section 13-6 we present the concept of *rank correlation,* which has an efficiency rating of 0.91 when compared to linear correlation in Chapter 10. This means that with all other things being equal, nonparametric rank correlation requires 100 sample observations to achieve the same results as 91 sample observations analyzed through parametric linear correlation, assuming the stricter requirements for using the parametric test are met. Table 13-2 lists nonparametric tests along with the corresponding parametric test and **efficiency** rating. Table 13-2 shows that several nonparametric tests have efficiency ratings above 0.90, so the lower efficiency might not be an important factor in choosing between parametric and nonparametric tests. However, because parametric tests do have higher efficiency ratings than their nonparametric counterparts, it's generally better to use the parametric tests when their required assumptions are satisfied.

Table 13-2 Efficiency: Comparison of Parametric and Nonparametric Tests

Application	Parametric Test	Nonparametric Test	Efficiency Rating of Nonparametric Test with Normal Populations
Matched pairs of sample data	t test or z test	Sign test	0.63
		Wilcoxon signed-ranks test	0.95
Two independent samples	t test or z test	Wilcoxon rank-sum test	0.95
Several independent samples	Analysis of variance (F test)	Kruskal-Wallis test	0.95
Correlation	Linear correlation	Rank correlation test	0.91
Randomness	No parametric test	Runs test	No basis for comparison

Ranks

In Sections 13-3 through 13-6 we use methods based on ranks, which are defined below.

> **DEFINITION** Data are *sorted* when they are arranged according to some criterion, such as smallest to largest or best to worst. A **rank** is a number assigned to an individual sample item according to its order in the sorted list. The first item is assigned a rank of 1, the second item is assigned a rank of 2, and so on.

Handling Ties If a tie in ranks occurs, a very common procedure is to find the mean of the ranks involved and then assign this mean rank to each of the tied items, as in the following example.

Example 1 The numbers 4, 5, 5, 5, 10, 11, 12, and 12 are given ranks of 1, 3, 3, 3, 5, 6, 7.5, and 7.5, respectively. The table below illustrates the procedure for handling ties.

Sorted Data	Preliminary Ranking	Rank
4	1	1
5	2 ⎫	3
5	3 ⎬ Mean is 3.	3
5	4 ⎭	3
10	5	5
11	6	6
12	7 ⎫ Mean is 7.5.	7.5
12	8 ⎭	7.5

13-2   Sign Test

Key Concept This section introduces the *sign test*, which involves converting data values to positive and negative signs, then testing to determine whether either sign occurs disproportionately more often.

> **DEFINITION** The **sign test** is a nonparametric (distribution-free) test that uses positive and negative signs to test different claims, including:
>
> **1.** Claims involving matched pairs of sample data
>
> **2.** Claims involving nominal data with two categories
>
> **3.** Claims about the median of a single population

Basic Concept of the Sign Test The basic idea underlying the sign test is to analyze the frequencies of the positive and negative signs to determine whether they are significantly different. For example, consider the results of clinical trials of the Micro-Sort method of gender selection. Among 726 couples who used the XSORT method in trying to have a baby girl, 668 couples did have baby girls. Is 668 girls in 726 births *significant*? Common sense probably suggests that 668 girls in 726 births is significant, but what about 365 girls in 726 births? Or 400 girls in 726 births? The sign test allows us to determine when such results are significant. Figure 13-1 on page 640 summarizes the sign test procedure.

For consistency and simplicity, we will use a test statistic based on the number of times that the *less frequent* sign occurs.

Sign Test

Objective

Use positive and negative signs to test a claim falling into one of the following three categories:

1. Matched Pairs

- Subtract the second value in each pair from the first, record the sign of the difference, and ignore any 0s.

2. Nominal Data with Two Categories

- Represent each member of one category by a positive sign and represent each member of the other category by a negative sign.

3. Median of a Single Population

- Subtract the median from each sample value, record the sign of the difference, and ignore any 0s.

Notation

x = the number of times the *less frequent* sign occurs

n = the total number of positive and negative signs combined

Requirements

The sample data are a simple random sample.

Note: There is *no* requirement that the sample data come from a population with a particular distribution, such as a normal distribution.

Test Statistic

If $n \leq 25$: Test statistic is $x =$ the number of times the less frequent sign occurs.

If $n > 25$: Test statistic is $z = \dfrac{(x + 0.5) - \left(\dfrac{n}{2}\right)}{\dfrac{\sqrt{n}}{2}}$

P-Values

P-values are often provided by technology, or P-values can often be found using the z test statistic.

Critical Values

1. If $n \leq 25$, critical x values are found in Table A-7.

2. If $n > 25$, critical z values are found in Table A-2.

Hint: Because z is based on the *less* frequent sign, all one-sided tests are treated as if they were left-tailed tests.

CAUTION When using the sign test in a one-tailed test, we need to be very careful to avoid making the wrong conclusion when one sign occurs significantly more often than the other but the sample data contradict the alternative hypothesis, as in the following example.

Example 1 Data Contradicting the Alternative Hypothesis

Among 945 couples who used the XSORT method of gender selection, 66 had boys, so the sample proportion of boys is 66/945, or 0.0698 (based on data from the Genetics & IVF Institute). Consider the claim that the XSORT method of gender selection increases the likelihood of baby *boys* so that the probability of a boy is $p > 0.5$. This claim of $p > 0.5$ becomes the alternative hypothesis.

Using common sense, we see that with a sample proportion of boys of 0.0698, we can never support a claim that $p > 0.5$. (We would need a sample proportion of boys *greater* than 0.5 by a significant amount.) The sample proportion of 66/945, or 0.0698, *contradicts* the alternative hypothesis because it is not greater than 0.5.

Interpretation

An alternative hypothesis can never be supported with data that contradict it. We can never support a claim that $p > 0.5$ with a sample proportion of 66/945, or 0.0698, which is *less than* 0.5.

When testing a claim, we should be careful to avoid making the fundamental mistake of thinking that a claim is supported because the sample results are significant; the sample results must be significant *in the same direction* as the alternative hypothesis.

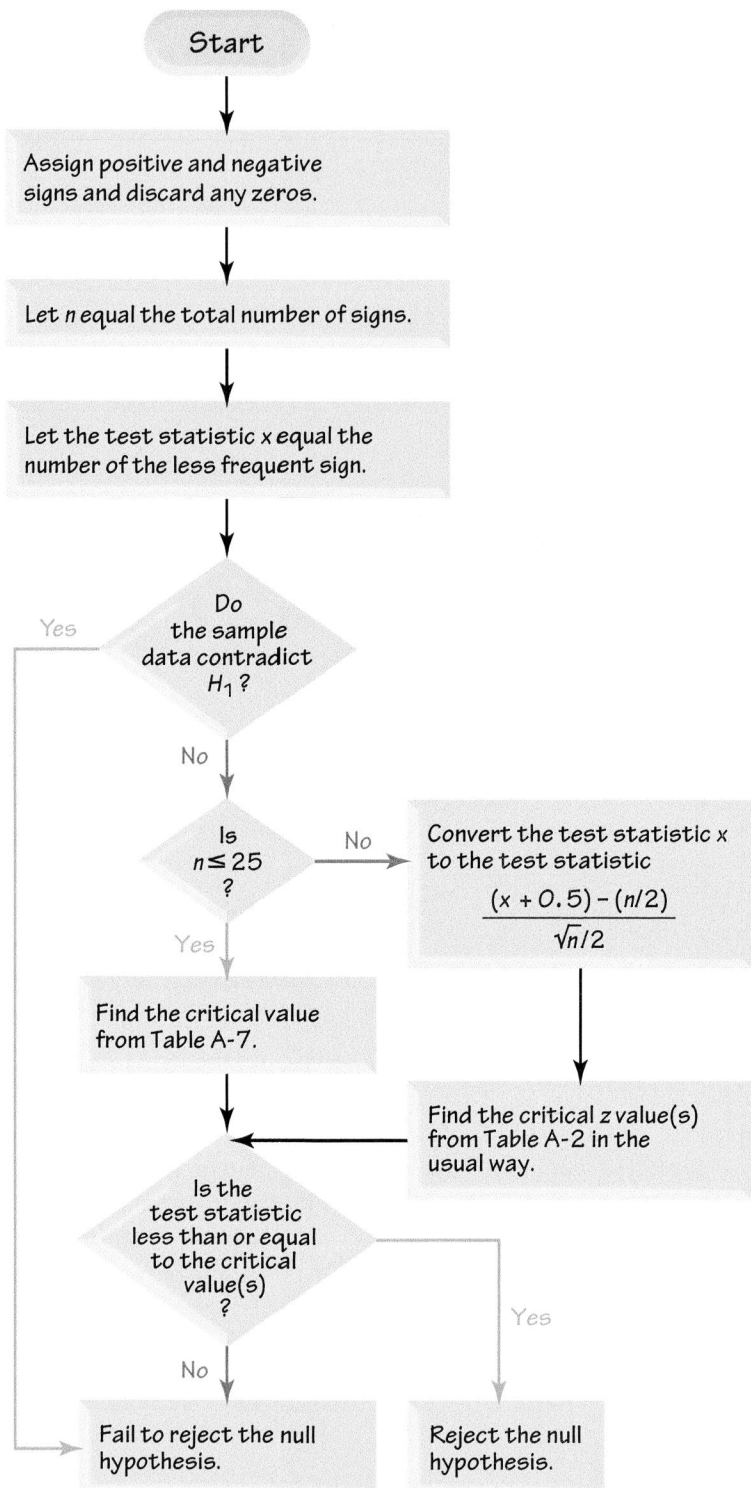

Figure 13-1   **Sign Test Procedure**

Claims about Matched Pairs

When using the sign test with data that are matched pairs, we convert the raw data to positive and negative signs as follows:

1. We subtract each value of the second variable from the corresponding value of the first variable.

2. We record only the *sign* of the difference found in Step 1. We exclude *ties:* that is, we throw out any matched pairs in which both values are equal.

The main concept underlying this use of the sign test is as follows:

If the two sets of data have equal medians, the number of positive signs should be approximately equal to the number of negative signs.

> **Example 2** Flight Data

Table 13-3 includes taxi-out times and taxi-in times for a sample of American Airlines Flight 21 (from Data Set 15 in Appendix B). Use the sign test with the sample data in Table 13-3 to test the claim that there is no difference between taxi-out times and taxi-in times. Use a 0.05 significance level.

Table 13-3 Taxi-Out Times and Taxi-In Times for American Airlines Flight 21

Taxi-out time (min)	13	20	12	17	35	19	22	43	49	45	13	23
Taxi-in time (min)	13	4	6	21	29	5	27	9	12	7	36	12
Sign of difference	0	+	+	−	+	+	−	+	+	+	−	+

> **Solution**

Requirement check The only requirement of the sign test is that the sample data are a simple random sample, and that requirement is satisfied. ✅

If there is no difference between taxi-out times and taxi-in times, the numbers of positive and negative signs should be approximately equal. In Table 13-3 we have 8 positive signs, 3 negative signs, and 1 difference of 0. The sign test tells us whether or not the numbers of positive and negative signs are approximately equal.

The null hypothesis is the claim of no difference between taxi-out times and taxi-in times, and the alternative hypothesis is the claim that there is a difference.

H_0: There is no difference. (The median of the differences is equal to 0.)

H_1: There is a difference. (The median of the differences is not equal to 0.)

Following Figure 13-1, we let $n = 11$ (the total number of positive and negative signs) and we let $x = 3$ (the number of the less frequent sign, or the smaller of 8 and 3).

The sample data do not contradict H_1, because there is a difference between the 8 positive signs and the 3 negative signs. The sample data show a difference, and we need to continue with the test to determine whether that difference is significant.

Figure 13-1 shows that with $n = 11$, we should proceed to find the critical value from Table A-7. We refer to Table A-7 where the critical value of 1 is found for $n = 11$ and $\alpha = 0.05$ in two tails.

Since $n \leq 25$, the test statistic is $x = 3$ (and we do not convert x to a z score). With a test statistic of $x = 3$ and a critical x value of 1, we fail to reject the null hypothesis of no difference. (See Note 2 included with Table A-7: "Reject the null hypothesis if the number of the less frequent sign (x) is less than or equal to the value in the table." Because $x = 3$ is *not* less than or equal to the critical value of 1, we fail to reject the null hypothesis.)

There is not sufficient evidence to warrant rejection of the claim that the median of the differences is equal to 0.

Interpretation

We conclude that there is not sufficient evidence to warrant rejection of the claim of no difference between taxi-out times and taxi-in times. There does not appear to be a difference.

Claims Involving Nominal Data with Two Categories

In Chapter 1 we defined nominal data to be data that consist of names, labels, or categories only. The nature of nominal data limits the calculations that are possible, but we can identify the *proportion* of the sample data that belong to a particular category, and we can test claims about the corresponding population proportion p. The following example uses nominal data consisting of genders (girls/boys). The sign test is used by representing girls with positive (+) signs and boys with negative (−) signs. (Those signs are chosen arbitrarily—honest.)

Example 3   Gender Selection

The Genetics and IVF Institute conducted a clinical trial of its methods for gender selection. As of this writing, 879 of 945 babies born to parents using the XSORT method of gender selection were girls. Use the sign test and a 0.05 significance level to test the claim that this method of gender selection is effective in increasing the likelihood of a baby girl.

Solution

Requirement check The only requirement is that the sample data be a simple random sample. Based on the design of this experiment, we can assume that the sample data are a simple random sample. ✓

Let p denote the population proportion of baby girls. The claim that girls are more likely with the XSORT method can be expressed as $p > 0.5$, so the null and alternative hypotheses are as follows:

H_0: $p = 0.5$ (the proportion of girls is equal to 0.5)

H_1: $p > 0.5$ (girls are more likely)

Denoting girls by positive signs (+) and boys by negative signs (−), we have 879 positive signs and 66 negative signs. Using the sign test procedure summarized in Figure 13-1, we let the test statistic x be the smaller of 879 and 66, so $x = 66$ boys. *Instead of trying to determine whether 879 girls is high enough to be significant, we proceed with the equivalent goal of trying to determine whether 66 boys is low enough to be significant, so we treat the test as a left-tailed test.*

The sample data do not contradict the alternative hypothesis because the sample proportion of girls is $879/945$, or 0.930, which is greater than 0.5, as in the above alternative hypothesis. Continuing with the procedure in Figure 13-1, we note that the value of $n = 945$ is greater than 25, so the test statistic $x = 66$ is converted (using a correction for continuity) to the test statistic z as follows:

$$z = \frac{(x + 0.5) - \left(\frac{n}{2}\right)}{\frac{\sqrt{n}}{2}}$$

$$= \frac{(66 + 0.5) - \left(\frac{945}{2}\right)}{\frac{\sqrt{945}}{2}} = -26.41$$

With $\alpha = 0.05$ in a left-tailed test, the critical value is $z = -1.645$. Figure 13-2 shows that the test statistic $z = -26.41$ is in the critical region bounded by $z = -1.645$, so we reject the null hypothesis that the proportion of girls is equal to 0.5. There is sufficient sample evidence to support the claim that girls are more likely with the XSORT method.

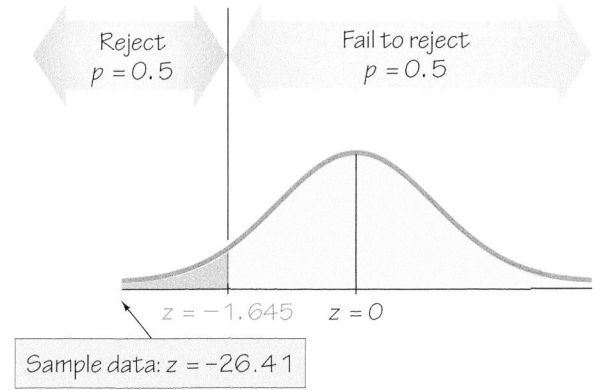

Reject
$p = 0.5$

Fail to reject
$p = 0.5$

$z = -1.645$ $z = 0$

Sample data: $z = -26.41$

Figure 13-2   Testing Effectiveness of the XSORT Gender Selection Method

Interpretation

The XSORT method of gender selection does appear to be associated with an increase in the likelihood of a girl. The XSORT method does appear to be effective in increasing the likelihood of a girl (but this hypothesis test does not prove that the XSORT method is the *cause* of the increase).

Claims about the Median of a Single Population

The next example illustrates the procedure for using the sign test in testing a claim about the median of a single population. See how the negative and positive signs are based on the claimed value of the median.

Example 4   Body Temperatures

Data Set 3 in Appendix B includes measured body temperatures of adults. Use the 106 temperatures listed for 12 A.M. on Day 2 with the sign test to test the claim that the median is less than 98.6°F. Of the 106 subjects, 68 had temperatures below 98.6°F, 23 had temperatures above 98.6°F, and 15 had temperatures equal to 98.6°F.

Solution

Requirement check The only requirement is that the sample data be a simple random sample. Based on the design of this experiment, we assume that the sample data are a simple random sample. ✓

The claim that the median is less than 98.6°F is the alternative hypothesis, while the null hypothesis is the claim that the median is equal to 98.6°F.

H_0: Median is equal to 98.6°F. (median = 98.6°F)

H_1: Median is less than 98.6°F. (median < 98.6°F)

Following the procedure outlined in Figure 13-1, we use a negative sign to represent each temperature below 98.6°F, and we use a positive sign for each temperature above 98.6°F. We discard the 15 data values of 98.6 since they result in differences of zero. We have 68 negative signs and 23 positive signs, so $n = 91$ and $x = 23$ (the number of the less frequent sign). The sample data do not contradict the alternative hypothesis, because most of the 91 temperatures are below 98.6°F. The value of n exceeds 25, so we convert the test statistic x to the test statistic z:

$$z = \frac{(x + 0.5) - \left(\dfrac{n}{2}\right)}{\dfrac{\sqrt{n}}{2}}$$

$$= \frac{(23 + 0.5) - \left(\dfrac{91}{2}\right)}{\dfrac{\sqrt{91}}{2}} = -4.61$$

In this one-tailed test with $\alpha = 0.05$, we use Table A-2 to get the critical z value of -1.645. From Figure 13-3 we can see that the test statistic of $z = -4.61$ does fall within the critical region, so we reject the null hypothesis.

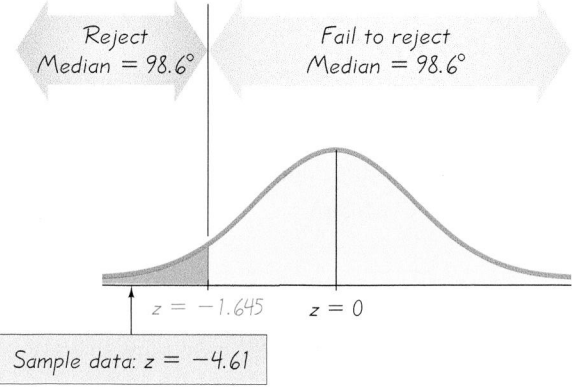

Figure 13-3　**Testing the Claim That the Median Is Less Than 98.6°F**

Interpretation

There is sufficient sample evidence to support the claim that the median body temperature of healthy adults is less than 98.6°F. It is not equal to 98.6, as is commonly believed.

In Example 4, the sign test of the claim that the median is below 98.6°F results in a test statistic of $z = -4.61$ and a P-value of 0.00000202. However, a parametric test of the claim that $\mu < 98.6$°F results in a test statistic of $t = -6.611$ with a P-value of 0.000000000813. Because the P-value from the sign test is not as low as the P-value from the parametric test, we see that the sign test isn't as sensitive as the parametric test. Both tests lead to rejection of the null hypothesis, but the sign test doesn't consider the sample data to be as extreme, partly because the sign test uses only information about the *direction* of the data, ignoring the *magnitudes* of the data values. The next section introduces the Wilcoxon signed-ranks test, which largely overcomes that disadvantage.

Rationale for the Test Statistic Used When $n > 25$ When finding critical values for the sign test, we use Table A-7 only for n up to 25. When $n > 25$, the test statistic z is based on a normal approximation to the binomial probability distribution with $p = q = 1/2$. In Section 6-7 we saw that the normal approximation to the binomial distribution is acceptable when both $np \geq 5$ and $nq \geq 5$. In Section 5-4 we saw that $\mu = np$ and $\sigma = \sqrt{npq}$ for binomial probability distributions. Because this sign test assumes that $p = q = 1/2$, we meet the $np \geq 5$ and $nq \geq 5$ prerequisites whenever $n \geq 10$. Also, with the assumption that $p = q = 1/2$, we get $\mu = np = n/2$ and $\sigma = \sqrt{npq} = \sqrt{n/4} = \sqrt{n}/2$, so the standard z score

$$z = \frac{x - \mu}{\sigma}$$

becomes

$$z = \frac{x - \left(\dfrac{n}{2}\right)}{\dfrac{\sqrt{n}}{2}}$$

We replace x by $x + 0.5$ as a correction for continuity. That is, the values of x are discrete, but since we are using a continuous probability distribution, a discrete value such as 10 is actually represented by the interval from 9.5 to 10.5. Because x represents the less frequent sign, we act conservatively by concerning ourselves only with $x + 0.5$; we get the test statistic z, as given in Figure 13-1.

using TECHNOLOGY

STATDISK Select **Analysis** from the main menu bar, then select **Sign Test.** Select the option **Given Number of Signs** if you know the number of positive and negative signs, or select **Given Pairs of Values** if paired data are in the data window. After making the required entries in the dialog box, the displayed results will include the test statistic, critical value, and conclusion.

MINITAB You must first create a single column of values. For matched pairs, enter a column consisting of the differences. For nominal data in two categories (such as boy/girl), enter a positive sign for each value of one category and enter a negative sign for each value of the other category; use 0 for the claimed value of the median. For a list of individual values to be tested with a claimed median, enter the sample values in a single column.

Select **Stat,** then **Nonparametrics,** then **1-Sample Sign.** Click on the button for **Test Median.** Enter the median value and select the type of test, then click **OK.** Minitab will provide the P-value, so reject the null hypothesis if the P-value is less than or equal to the significance level. Otherwise, fail to reject the null hypothesis.

EXCEL Excel does not have a built-in function dedicated to the sign test, but you can use Excel's BINOMDIST function to find the P-value for a sign test. Click *fx* on the main menu bar, then select the function category **Statistical** and then **BINOMDIST.** (In Excel 2013 or 2010, select **BINOM.DIST.**) In the dialog box, first enter x, then the number of trials n, and then a probability of 0.5. Enter **TRUE** in the box for "cumulative." The resulting

continued

value is the probability of getting *x* or fewer successes among *n* trials. *Double this value for two-tailed tests.* The final result is the *P*-value.

XLSTAT XLSTATcan be used for claims involving matched pairs by selecting **Nonparametric tests**, then **Comparison of two samples.**

TI-83/84 PLUS The TI-83/84 Plus calculator does not have a built-in function dedicated to the sign test, but you can use the binomcdf function to find the *P*-value for a sign test. Press **2ND** **VARS** (to get the **DISTR** menu); then scroll down to select **binomcdf.** Complete the entry of **binomcdf (n, p, x)** with *n* for the total number of plus and minus signs, 0.5 for *p*, and the number of the less frequent sign for *x*. Now press **ENTER**, and the result will be the

probability of getting *x* or fewer successes among *n* trials. *Double this value for two-tailed tests.* The final result is the *P*-value, so reject the null hypothesis if the *P*-value is less than or equal to the significance level. Otherwise, fail to reject the null hypothesis.

STATCRUNCH You can use StatCrunch to test the claim that a single list of values is from a population with a median equal to some specified value. Click **Open StatCrunch.** First enter the column of data or open a data set. Click on **Stat**, select **Nonparametrics**, then select **Sign Test.** Identify the column to be used, click on **Next** and enter the value of the claimed population median. Click on **Calculate** and the display will include the *P*-value.

13-2 Basic Skills and Concepts

Statistical Literacy and Critical Thinking

1. Sign Test for Freshman 15 The table below lists some of the weights from Data Set 4 in Appendix B. Those weights were measured from college students in September and later in April of their freshman year. Assume that we plan to use the sign test to test the claim of no difference between September weights and April weights. What requirements must be satisfied for this test? Is there any requirement that the populations must have a normal distribution or any other specific distribution? In what sense is this sign test a "distribution-free test"?

September weight	67	53	64	74	67	70	55	74	62	57
April weight	66	52	68	77	67	71	60	82	65	58

2. Identifying Signs For the sign test described in Exercise 1, identify the number of positive signs, the number of negative signs, the number of ties, the sample size *n* that is used for the sign test, and the value of the test statistic.

3. Contradicting H_1 An important step in conducting the sign test is to determine whether the sample data contradict the alternative hypothesis H_1. For the sign test described in Exercise 1, identify the null hypothesis and the alternative hypothesis, and explain how the sample data contradict or do not contradict the alternative hypothesis.

4. Efficiency of the Sign Test Refer to Table 13-2 in Section 13-1 and identify the efficiency of the sign test. What does that value tell us about the sign test?

In Exercises 5–8, assume that matched pairs of data result in the given number of signs when the value of the second variable is subtracted from the corresponding value of the first variable. Use the sign test with a 0.05 significance level to test the null hypothesis of no difference.

5. Positive signs: 13; negative signs: 1; ties: 0 (from a preliminary test of the MicroSort method of gender selection)

6. Positive signs: 15; negative signs: 5; ties: 7 (from a class project testing for the difference between reported and measured heights of females)

7. Positive signs: 856; negative signs: 151; ties: 57 (from a Pew Research Center poll of adults who were asked if they know what Twitter is)

8. Positive signs: 172; negative signs: 439; ties: 0 (from challenges to referee calls in the most recent U.S. Open tennis tournament)

In Exercises 9–12, use the sign test for the data consisting of matched pairs.

9. Oscar Winners Listed below are ages of actresses and actors at the times that they won Oscars. These 10 matched pairs are the first 10 from Data Set 11 in Appendix B. The data are paired according to the years that they won. Use a 0.05 significance level to test the claim that there is no difference between the ages of best actresses and the ages of best actors at the time that the awards were presented.

Best Actresses	22	37	28	63	32	26	31	27	27	28
Best Actors	44	41	62	52	41	34	34	52	41	37

10. Oscar Winners Repeat Exercise 9 using all of the 82 pairs of ages in Data Set 11 from Appendix B. For that data set, there are 16 positive signs, 64 negative signs, and 2 ties.

11. Heights of Presidents Refer to Data Set 12 in Appendix B and use the heights of U.S. presidents and their main opponents in the presidential campaigns to test the claim that there is no difference. Use a 0.05 significance level.

12. Flight Data Repeat Example 2 using the following times for American Airlines Flight 19.

Taxi-out time (min)	15	12	19	18	21	20	13	15	43	18	17	19
Taxi-in time (min)	10	10	16	13	9	8	4	3	8	16	9	5

In Exercises 13–16, use the sign test for the claim involving nominal data.

13. Gender Selection The Genetics and IVF Institute conducted a clinical trial of its methods for gender selection. As of this writing, 239 of 291 babies born to parents using the YSORT method were boys. Use a 0.01 significance level to test the claim that the YSORT method has no effect.

14. Predicting Sex of Baby A study addressed the issue of whether women have the ability to predict the sex of their babies. Among 104 recruited subjects, 55% correctly guessed the sex of the baby (based on data from "Are Women Carrying 'Basketballs' Really Having Boys? Testing Pregnancy Folklore," by Perry, DiPietro, and Constigan, *Birth,* Vol. 26, No. 3). Use a 0.05 significance level to test the claim that women do not have the ability to predict the sex of their babies.

15. Touch Therapy At the age of 9, Emily Rosa tested professional touch therapists to see if they could sense her energy field. She flipped a coin to select either her right hand or her left hand, then she asked the therapists to identify the selected hand by placing their hand just under Emily's hand without seeing it and without touching it. Among 280 trials, the touch therapists were correct 123 times and wrong the other times (based on data in "A Close Look at Therapeutic Touch," *Journal of the American Medical Association,* Vol. 279, No. 13). Use a 0.01 significance level to test the claim that the touch therapists make their selections with a method equivalent to random guesses. Based on the results, does it appear that therapists are effective at identifying the correct hand?

16. Football Survey In a *USA Today* poll, people responded to this question "Are today's NFL (football) games too long?" Among the respondents with a definitive answer, 242 answered yes and 396 answered no. Use a 0.05 significance level to test the claim that respondents did not have a strong opinion one way or the other. How are the results affected by the additional information that the responses are from Internet users who chose to answer the question posted on the *USA Today* web site?

Appendix B Data Sets. *In Exercises 17–20, refer to the indicated data set in Appendix B and use the sign test for the claim about the median of a population.*

17. Testing for Median Weight of Quarters Refer to Data Set 21 in Appendix B for the weights (g) of randomly selected quarters that were minted after 1964. The quarters are supposed to have a median weight of 5.670 g. Use a 0.01 significance level to test the claim that the median is equal to 5.670 g. Do quarters appear to be minted according to specifications?

18. Earthquake Magnitudes Refer to Data Set 16 in Appendix B for the earthquake magnitudes. Use a 0.01 significance level to test the claim that the median is equal to 1.00.

19. Coke Contents Refer to Data Set 19 in Appendix B for the amounts (in oz) in cans of regular Coke. The cans are labeled to indicate that the contents are 12 oz of Coke. Use a 0.05 significance level to test the claim that cans of Coke are filled so that the median amount is 12 oz. If the median is not 12 oz, are consumers being cheated?

20. Ages of Best Actresses Refer to Data Set 11 in Appendix B for the ages of actresses at the time that they won Oscars in the category of Best Actress. Use a 0.05 significance level to test the claim that the median age of Oscar-winning actresses is equal to 30 years.

13-2 Beyond the Basics

21. Procedures for Handling Ties In the sign test procedure described in this section, we exclude ties (represented by 0 instead of a sign of $+$ or $-$). A second approach is to treat half of the 0s as positive signs and half as negative signs. (If the number of 0s is odd, exclude one so that they can be divided equally.) With a third approach, in two-tailed tests make half of the 0s positive and half negative; in one-tailed tests make all 0s either positive or negative, whichever supports the null hypothesis. Repeat Example 4 using the second and third approaches to handling ties. Do the different approaches lead to very different results?

22. Finding Critical Values Table A-7 lists critical values for limited choices of α. Use Table A-1 to add a new column in Table A-7 (from $n = 1$ to $n = 8$) that represents a significance level of 0.03 in one tail or 0.06 in two tails. For any particular n, use $p = 0.5$, because the sign test requires the assumption that $P(\text{positive sign}) = P(\text{negative sign}) = 0.5$. The probability of x or fewer like signs is the sum of the probabilities for values up to and including x.

13-3   Wilcoxon Signed-Ranks Test for Matched Pairs

Key Concept This section introduces the *Wilcoxon signed-ranks test,* which involves the conversion of the sample data to ranks. This test can be used for the two different applications described in the following definition.

> **DEFINITION** The **Wilcoxon signed-ranks test** is a nonparametric test that uses ranks for these applications:
>
> **1.** Testing a claim that a population of matched pairs has the property that the matched pairs have differences with a median equal to zero
>
> **2.** Testing a claim that a single population of individual values has a median equal to some claimed value

When testing a claimed value of a median for a population of individual values, we create matched pairs by pairing each sample value with the claimed median, so the same procedure is used for both of the applications above.

Claims Involving Matched Pairs

The sign test (Section 13-2) can be used with matched pairs, but the sign test uses only the signs of the differences. By using ranks instead of signs, the Wilcoxon signed-ranks test takes the magnitudes of the differences into account, so it includes and uses more information than the sign test and therefore tends to yield conclusions that better reflect the true nature of the data.

Wilcoxon Signed-Ranks Test

Objective: Use the Wilcoxon signed-ranks test for the following tests:

- **Matched Pairs:** Test the claim that a population of matched pairs has the property that the matched pairs have differences with a median equal to zero.

- **One Population of Individual Values:** Test the claim that a population has a median equal to some claimed value. (By pairing each sample value with the claimed median, we again work with matched pairs.)

Notation

$T =$ the smaller of the following two sums:

1. The sum of the positive ranks of the nonzero differences d

2. The absolute value of the sum of the negative ranks of the nonzero differences d

(Details for evaluating T are given in the procedure following this box.)

Requirements

1. The data are a simple random sample.

2. The population of differences has a distribution that is approximately *symmetric,* meaning that the left half of its histogram is roughly a mirror image of its right half. (For a sample of matched pairs, obtain differences by subtracting the second value from the first value in each pair; for a sample of individual values, obtain differences by subtracting the value of the claimed median from each sample value.)

Note: There is *no* requirement that the data have a normal distribution.

Test Statistic

If $n \leq 30$, the test statistic is T.

If $n > 30$, the test statistic is $z = \dfrac{T - \dfrac{n(n + 1)}{4}}{\sqrt{\dfrac{n(n + 1)(2n + 1)}{24}}}$

P-Values

P-values are often provided by technology or *P*-values can be found using the z test statistic and Table A-2.

Critical Values

1. If $n \leq 30$, the critical T value is found in Table A-8.   **2.** If $n > 30$, the critical z values are found in Table A-2.

Wilcoxon Signed-Ranks Procedure To see how the following steps are applied, refer to the sample of matched pairs listed in the first two rows of Table 13-4.

Step 1: For each pair of data, find the difference d by subtracting the second value from the first value. Discard any pairs that have a difference of 0.

EXAMPLE: The third row of Table 13-4 lists the differences found by subtracting the taxi-in times from the taxi-out times, and the difference of 0 will be ignored in the following steps.

Step 2: *Ignore the signs of the differences,* then sort the differences from lowest to highest and replace the differences by the corresponding rank value (as described in Section 13-1). When differences have the same numerical value, assign to them the mean of the ranks involved in the tie.

EXAMPLE: The fourth row of Table 13-4 shows the ranks of the values of $|d|$. Ignoring the difference of 0, the smallest value of $|d|$ is 4, so it is assigned the rank of 1. The next smallest value of $|d|$ is 5, so it is assigned a rank of 2. There are two $|d|$ values of 6, so we find the mean of the ranks of 3 and 4, which is 3.5. Each of the $|d|$ values of 6 is assigned a rank of 3.5. The next $|d|$ value is 11, and it is assigned a rank of 5, and so on.

Step 3: Attach to each rank the sign of the difference from which it came. That is, insert the signs that were ignored in Step 2.

EXAMPLE: The bottom row of Table 13-4 lists the same ranks found in the fourth row, but the signs of the differences shown in the third row are inserted.

Step 4: Find the sum of the ranks that are positive. Also find the absolute value of the sum of the negative ranks.

EXAMPLE: The bottom row of Table 13-4 lists the signed ranks. The sum of the positive ranks is $7 + 3.5 + 3.5 + 6 + 9 + 10 + 11 + 5 = 55$. The sum of the negative ranks is $(-1) + (-2) + (-8) = -11$, and the absolute value of this sum is 11. The two rank sums are 55 and 11.

Step 5: Let T be the *smaller* of the two sums found in Step 4. Either sum could be used, but for a simplified procedure we arbitrarily select the smaller of the two sums.

EXAMPLE: The data in Table 13-4 result in the rank sums of 55 and 11, so 11 is the smaller of those two sums.

Step 6: Let n be the number of pairs of data for which the difference d is not 0.

EXAMPLE: The data in Table 13-4 have 11 differences that are not 0, so $n = 11$.

Step 7: Determine the test statistic and critical values based on the sample size, as shown in the preceding box.

EXAMPLE: For the data in Table 13-4 the test statistic is $T = 11$. The sample size is $n = 11$, so the critical value is found in Table A-8. Using a 0.05 significance level with a two-tailed test, the critical value from Table A-8 is 11.

Step 8: When forming the conclusion, reject the null hypothesis if the sample data lead to a test statistic that is in the critical region—that is, the test statistic is less than or equal to the critical value(s). Otherwise, fail to reject the null hypothesis.

EXAMPLE: If the test statistic is T (instead of z), reject the null hypothesis if T is less than or equal to the critical value. Fail to reject the null hypothesis if T is greater than the critical value. For the sample of matched pairs in the first two rows of Table 13-4, $T = 11$ and the critical value is 11, so we reject the null hypothesis.

Table 13-4 Taxi-Out Times and Taxi-In Times for American Airlines Flight 21

Taxi-out time (min)	13	20	12	17	35	19	22	43	49	45	13	23
Taxi-in time (min)	13	4	6	21	29	5	27	9	12	7	36	12
d (difference)	0	16	6	−4	6	14	−5	34	37	38	−23	11
Rank of $\lvert d \rvert$		7	3.5	1	3.5	6	2	9	10	11	8	5
Signed rank		7	3.5	−1	3.5	6	−2	9	10	11	−8	5

Example 1 Flight Data

The first two rows of Table 13-4 include taxi times for a sample of American Airlines Flight 21 from New York to Los Angeles (from Data Set 15 in Appendix B). Use the sample data in the first two rows of Table 13-4 to test the claim that there is no difference between taxi-out times and taxi-in times. Use the Wilcoxon signed-ranks test with a 0.05 significance level.

Solution

Requirement check (1) The data are a simple random sample. (2) The histogram of the differences in the third row of Table 13-4 is shown in the accompanying display. The left side of the graph should be roughly a mirror image of the right side, which does not appear to be the case. But with only 11 differences, the difference between the left and right sides is not too extreme, so we will consider this requirement to be satisfied. ✓

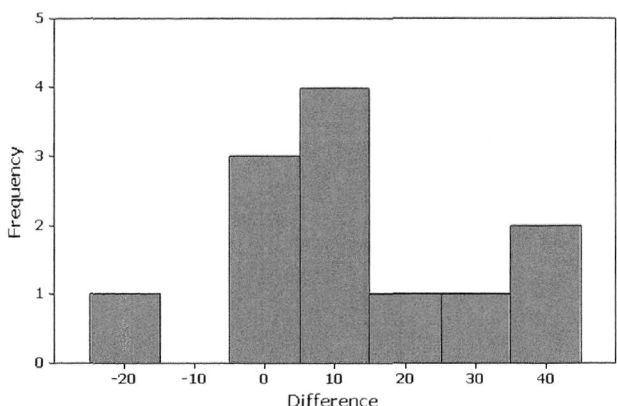

The null hypothesis is the claim of no difference between the taxi-out times and the taxi-in times, and the alternative hypothesis is the claim that there is a difference.

H_0: There is no difference. (The median of the differences is equal to 0.)

H_1: There is a difference. (The median of the differences is not equal to 0.)

Test Statistic: Because we are using the Wilcoxon signed-ranks test, the test statistic is calculated by using the eight-step procedure presented earlier in this section. Those steps include examples illustrating the calculation of the test statistic with the sample data in Table 13-4, and the result is the test statistic of $T = 11$.

Critical Value: The sample size is $n = 11$, so the critical value is found in Table A-8. Using a 0.05 significance level with a two-tailed test, the critical value from Table A-8 is found to be 11.

Conclusion: Table A-8 includes a note stating that we should reject the null hypothesis if the test statistic T is less than or equal to the critical value. Because the test statistic of $T = 11$ is equal to the critical value of 11, we reject the null hypothesis.

Interpretation

We conclude that the taxi-out times and the taxi-in times do *not* appear to be about the same. The large number of positive differences indicates that most flights appear to have longer taxi-out times than taxi-in times.

Claims about the Median of a Single Population

The Wilcoxon signed-ranks test can also be used to test a claim that a single population has some claimed value of the median. The preceding procedures can be used with one simple adjustment:

> **When testing a claim about the median of a single population, create matched pairs by pairing each sample value with the claimed value of the median. The preceding procedure can then be used.**

Example 2   Body Temperatures

Data Set 3 in Appendix B includes measured body temperatures of adults. Use the 106 temperatures listed for 12 A.M. on Day 2 with the Wilcoxon signed-ranks test to test the claim that the median is less than 98.6°F.

Solution

STATDISK

Num Unequal pairs: 91
Using Approximation
Test Statistic, T: 661.0000
Mean, μ: 2093
St Dev: 252.6589
Test Statistic, z: -5.6677
Critical z: ±1.959962

Requirement check (1) By pairing each individual sample value with the median of 98.6°F, we satisfy the requirement of having matched pairs. The design of the experiment that led to the data in Data Set 3 justifies treating the sample as a simple random sample. (2) The requirement of an approximately symmetric distribution of differences is satisfied, because a histogram of those differences is approximately symmetric. ✓

Shown in the margin is the STATDISK display resulting from this hypothesis test. We see that $T = 661$ (which converts to the test statistic $z = -5.67$). The test statistic of $z = -5.67$ falls in the critical region below -1.96, so we reject the null hypothesis that the population of differences between body temperatures and the claimed median of 98.6°F is zero. There is sufficient evidence to support the claim that the median body temperature is less than 98.6°F. This is the same conclusion that results from the sign test, as in Example 4 in Section 13-2.

Rationale: In Example 1, the unsigned ranks of 1 through 11 have a total of 66, so if there are no significant differences, each of the two signed-rank totals should be around 66 ÷ 2, or 33. That is, the negative ranks and positive ranks should split up as 33–33 or something close, such as 32–34. The table of critical values shows that at the 0.05 significance level with 11 pairs of data, a split of 11–55 represents a significant departure from the null hypothesis, and any split that is farther apart (such as 10–56 or 2–64) will also represent a significant departure from the null hypothesis. Conversely, splits like 12–54 do not represent significant departures from a 33–33 split, and they would not justify rejecting the null hypothesis. The Wilcoxon signed-ranks test is based on the lower rank total, so instead of analyzing both numbers constituting the split, we consider only the lower number.

The sum of all the ranks $1 + 2 + 3 + \cdots + n$ is equal to $n(n + 1)/2$. If this rank sum is to be divided equally between two categories (positive and negative), each of the two totals should be near $n(n + 1)/4$, which is half of $n(n + 1)/2$. Recognition of this principle helps us understand the test statistic used when $n > 30$.

using TECHNOLOGY

STATDISK First enter the columns of data in the data window. Select **Analysis** from the main menu bar, then select **Wilcoxon Tests.** Now select **Wilcoxon (Matched Pairs),** and proceed to select the columns of data. Click on **Evaluate.**

MINITAB First create a column C3 consisting of the differences between the matched pairs. Enter the paired data in columns C1 and C2. Click on the Session portion of the screen, then click on **Editor,** then **Enable Command Editor,** and enter the command **LET C3 = C1 − C2.** Press the **Enter** key.

Select the options **Stat, Nonparametrics,** and **1-Sample Wilcoxon.** Enter C3 for the variable and click on the button for **Test Median.** The Minitab display will include the *P*-value.

EXCEL Excel is not programmed for the Wilcoxon signed-ranks test, but XLSTAT can be used by selecting **Nonparametric tests,** then **Comparison of two samples.** Because XLSTAT uses a different procedure than the one described in this section, results may be somewhat different, especially for small samples.

TI-83/84 PLUS The TI-83/84 Plus calculator is not programmed for the Wilcoxon signed-ranks test, but the program SRTEST can be used. The program SRTEST (by Michael Lloyd) is on the CD included with this book, or it can be downloaded

from the site www.addisonwesley.com/triola. First download and install the program. (Also download the program ZZRANK, which is used by the program SRTEST.) Next, create a list of differences between values in the matched pairs. (The first set of values can be entered in list L1, the second set of values can be entered in list L2, then the differences can be stored in list L3 by entering L1 − L2 → L3, where the **STO** key is used for the arrow.) Press **PRGM** and select **SRTEST.** Press **ENTER** **ENTER**. When given the prompt of DATA =, enter the list containing the differences. Press **ENTER** to see the sum of the positive ranks and the sum of the negative ranks. Press **ENTER** again to see the mean and standard deviation, and press **ENTER** once again to see the *z* score. If $n \leq 30$, get the critical *T* value from Table A-8, but if $n > 30$, get the critical *z* values from Table A-2.

STATCRUNCH You can use StatCrunch to test the claim that a single list of values is from a population with a median equal to some specified value. Click on **Open StatCrunch.** First enter the column of data or open a data set. Click on **Stat,** select **Nonparametrics,** then select **Wilcoxon Signed Ranks Test.** Identify the column to be used, click on **Next,** and enter the value of the claimed population median. Click on **Calculate** and the display will include the *P*-value.

13-3 Basic Skills and Concepts

Statistical Literacy and Critical Thinking

1. Wilcoxon Signed-Ranks Test for Freshman 15 The following table lists some of the weights from Data Set 4 in Appendix B. Those weights were measured from college students in September and later in April of their freshman year. Assume that we plan to use the Wilcoxon signed-ranks test to test the claim of no difference between September weights and April weights. What requirements must be satisfied for this test? Is there any requirement that the populations must have a normal distribution or any other specific distribution? In what sense is this Wilcoxon signed-ranks test a "distribution-free test"?

September weight	67	53	64	74	67	70	55	74	62	57
April weight	66	52	68	77	67	71	60	82	65	58

2. Freshman 15 For the matched pairs listed in Exercise 1, identify the following components used in the Wilcoxon signed-ranks test:

a. Differences d

b. The ranks corresponding to the nonzero values of $|d|$

c. The signed ranks

d. The sum of the positive ranks and the sum of the absolute values of the negative ranks

e. The value of T

f. The critical value of T (assuming a 0.05 significance level in a test of no difference between September weights and April weights)

3. Sign Test vs. Wilcoxon Signed-Ranks Test Using the data in Exercise 1, we can test for no difference between September weights and April weights by using the sign test or the Wilcoxon signed-ranks test. In what sense does the Wilcoxon signed-ranks test incorporate and use more information than the sign test?

4. Efficiency of the Wilcoxon Signed-Ranks Test Refer to Table 13-2 in Section 13-1 and identify the efficiency of the Wilcoxon signed-ranks test. What does that value tell us about the test?

Using the Wilcoxon Signed-Ranks Test. *In Exercises 5–8, refer to the sample data for the given exercises in Section 13-2. Use the Wilcoxon signed-ranks test to test the claim that the matched pairs have differences that come from a population with a median equal to zero. Use a 0.05 significance level.*

5. Exercise 9   **6.** Exercise 10

7. Exercise 11   **8.** Exercise 12

Appendix B Data Sets. *In Exercises 9–12, refer to the sample data for the given exercises in Section 13-2. Use the Wilcoxon signed-ranks test for the claim about the median of a population.*

9. Exercise 17   **10.** Exercise 18

11. Exercise 19   **12.** Exercise 20

13-3 Beyond the Basics

13. Rank Sums

a. If we have sample paired data with 75 nonzero differences, what are the smallest and largest possible values of T?

b. If we have sample paired data with 75 nonzero differences, what is the expected value of T if the population consists of matched pairs with differences having a median of 0?

c. If we have sample paired data with 75 nonzero differences and the sum of the positive ranks is 850, find the absolute value of the sum of the negative ranks.

d. If we have sample paired data with n nonzero differences and one of the two rank sums is k, find an expression for the other rank sum.

13-4 Wilcoxon Rank-Sum Test for Two Independent Samples

Key Concept This section describes the *Wilcoxon rank-sum test,* which uses ranks of values from two *independent* samples to test the null hypothesis that the samples are from populations having equal medians. The Wilcoxon rank-sum test is equivalent to the **Mann-Whitney U test** (see Exercise 13), which is included in some other textbooks and technologies (such as Minitab). Here is the basic idea underlying the Wilcoxon rank-sum test: If two samples are drawn from identical populations and the individual values are all ranked as one combined collection of values, then the high and low ranks should fall evenly between the two samples. If the low ranks are found predominantly in one sample and the high ranks are found predominantly in the other sample, we have an indication that the two populations have different medians.

Unlike the parametric *t* tests for two independent samples in Section 9-3, the Wilcoxon rank-sum test does *not* require normally distributed populations and it can be used with data at the ordinal level of measurement, such as data consisting of ranks. In Table 13-2 we noted that the Wilcoxon rank-sum test has a 0.95 efficiency rating when compared to the parametric test. Because this test has such a high efficiency rating and involves easier calculations, it is often preferred over the parametric test, even when the requirement of normality is satisfied.

CAUTION Don't confuse the Wilcoxon rank-sum test for two *independent* samples with the Wilcoxon signed-ranks test for matched pairs. Use Internal Revenue Service as the mnemonic for IRS to remind yourself of "**I**ndependent: **R**ank **S**um."

DEFINITION The **Wilcoxon rank-sum test** is a nonparametric test that uses ranks of sample data from two independent populations to test this null hypothesis: H_0: Two independent samples come from populations with equal medians. (The alternative hypothesis H_1 can be any one of the following three possibilities: The two populations have *different* medians, or the first population has a median *greater than* the median of the second population, or the first population has a median *less than* the median of the second population.)

Wilcoxon Rank-Sum Test

Objective

Use the Wilcoxon rank-sum test with samples from two independent populations for the following null and alternative hypotheses:

H_0: The two samples come from populations with equal medians.

H_1: The median of the first population is different from (or greater than, or less than) the median from the second population.

Notation

n_1 = size of Sample 1

n_2 = size of Sample 2

R_1 = sum of ranks for Sample 1

R_2 = sum of ranks for Sample 2

R = same as R_1 (sum of ranks for Sample 1)

μ_R = mean of the sample R values that is expected when the two populations have equal medians

σ_R = standard deviation of the sample R values that is expected with two populations having equal medians

continued

Requirements

1. There are two independent simple random samples.

2. Each of the two samples has more than 10 values. (For samples with 10 or fewer values, special tables are available in reference books, such as *CRC Standard*

Probability and Statistics Tables and Formulae, published by CRC Press.)

Note: There is *no* requirement that the two populations have a normal distribution or any other particular distribution.

Test Statistic

$$z = \frac{R - \mu_R}{\sigma_R}$$

where

$$\mu_R = \frac{n_1(n_1 + n_2 + 1)}{2}$$

$$\sigma_R = \sqrt{\frac{n_1 n_2(n_1 + n_2 + 1)}{12}}$$

n_1 = size of the sample from which the rank sum R is found

n_2 = size of the other sample

R = sum of ranks of the sample with size n_1

P-Values

P-values can be found from technology or by using the z test statistic and Table A-2.

Critical Values

Critical values can be found in Table A-2 (because the test statistic is based on the normal distribution).

Table 13-5 Pulse Rates (Ranks in parentheses)

Males	Females
60 (**4.5**)	78 (**14**)
74 (**11**)	80 (**17**)
86 (**19**)	68 (**9**)
54 (**1**)	56 (**2.5**)
90 (**20.5**)	76 (**12**)
80 (**17**)	78 (**14**)
66 (**7**)	78 (**14**)
68 (**9**)	90 (**20.5**)
68 (**9**)	96 (**22**)
56 (**2.5**)	60 (**4.5**)
80 (**17**)	98 (**23**)
62 (**6**)	
$n_1 = 12$	$n_2 = 11$
$R_1 = 123.5$	$R_2 = 152.5$

Procedure for Finding the Value of the Test Statistic To see how the following steps are applied, refer to the sample data listed in Table 13-5.

Step 1: Temporarily combine the two samples into one big sample, then replace each sample value with its rank. (The lowest value gets a rank of 1, the next lowest value gets a rank of 2, and so on. If values are tied, assign to them the mean of the ranks involved in the tie. See Section 13-1 for a description of ranks and the procedure for handling ties.)

EXAMPLE: In Table 13-5, the ranks of the 23 sample pulse rates are shown in parentheses. The rank of 1 is assigned to the lowest value of 54. The next lowest values are 56 and 56; because they are tied for the ranks of 2 and 3, we assign the rank of 2.5 to each of them.

Step 2: Find the sum of the ranks for either one of the two samples.

EXAMPLE: In Table 13-5, the sum of the ranks from the first sample is 123.5. (That is, $4.5 + 11 + 19 + \cdots + 6 = 123.5$.)

Step 3: Calculate the value of the z test statistic as shown in the preceding box, where either sample can be used as "Sample 1." (If both sample sizes are greater than 10, then the sampling distribution of R is approximately normal with mean μ_R and standard deviation σ_R, and the test statistic is as shown in the preceding box.)

EXAMPLE: Calculations of μ_R and σ_R and z are shown in Example 1, which follows.

> **Example 1** Pulse Rates of Males and Females

Table 13-5 lists pulse rates of samples of males and females (from Data Set 1 in Appendix B). Use a 0.05 significance level to test the claim that males and females have the same median pulse rate.

> **Solution**

Requirement check (1) The sample data are two independent simple random samples. (2) The sample sizes are 12 and 11, so both sample sizes are greater than 10. The requirements are satisfied. ✓

The null and alternative hypotheses are as follows:

H_0: The median pulse rate of males is equal to the median pulse rate of females.

H_1: The median pulse rate of males is different from the median pulse rate of females.

Rank the combined list of all 23 pulse rates, beginning with a rank of 1 (assigned to the lowest value of 54). The ranks corresponding to the individual sample values are shown in parentheses in Table 13-5. R denotes the sum of the ranks for the sample we choose as Sample 1. If we choose the pulse rates of males as Sample 1, we get

$$R = 4.5 + 11 + 19 + \cdots + 6 = 123.5$$

Because there are pulse rates from 12 males, we have $n_1 = 12$. Also, $n_2 = 11$ because there are pulse rates from 11 females. We can now find the values of μ_R and σ_R and the test statistic z.

$$\mu_R = \frac{n_1(n_1 + n_2 + 1)}{2} = \frac{12(12 + 11 + 1)}{2} = 144$$

$$\sigma_R = \sqrt{\frac{n_1 n_2(n_1 + n_2 + 1)}{12}} = \sqrt{\frac{(12)(11)(12 + 11 + 1)}{12}} = 16.248$$

$$z = \frac{R - \mu_R}{\sigma_R} = \frac{123.5 - 144}{16.248} = -1.26$$

The test is two-tailed because a large positive value of z would indicate that disproportionately more higher ranks are found in Sample 1, and a large negative value of z would indicate that disproportionately more lower ranks are found in Sample 1. In either case, we would have strong evidence against the claim that the two samples come from populations with equal medians.

The significance of the test statistic z can be treated as in previous chapters. We are testing (with $\alpha = 0.05$) the hypothesis that the two populations have equal medians, so we have a two-tailed test with critical values $z = \pm 1.96$. The test statistic of $z = -1.26$ does *not* fall within the critical region, so we fail to reject the null hypothesis that the populations of males and females have the same median.

> **Interpretation**

There is not sufficient evidence to warrant rejection of the claim that males and females have the same median pulse rate. Based on the available sample data, it appears that males and females have pulse rates with the same median.

In Example 1, if we interchange the two sets of sample values and consider the pulse rates of females to be the first sample, then $R = 152.5$, $\mu_R = 132$, $\sigma_R = 16.248$, and $z = 1.26$, so the conclusion is exactly the same.

Example 2   Departure Delay Times

Table 13-1 from the Chapter Problem lists departure delay times (min) for samples from American Airlines Flights 19 and 21. In the Chapter Problem we noted that the parametric t test (Section 9-4) should not be used because the sample data violate this requirement: "The two sample sizes are both large (with $n_1 > 30$ and $n_2 > 30$) or both samples come from populations having normal distributions." Instead of using the t test, we can use the Wilcoxon rank-sum test. The accompanying STATDISK display results from the data in Table 13-1. We can see that the test statistic is $z = -1.44$ (rounded). The test statistic does not fall in the critical region bounded by the critical values of -1.96 and 1.96, so we fail to reject the null hypothesis of equal medians. Using the samples in Table 13-1, we do not have enough evidence to conclude that departure delay times for Flight 19 have a median different from the median of departure delay times for Flight 21.

STATDISK

```
Total Num Values: 24
Rank Sum 1:   125.0000
Rank Sum 2:   175.0000

Mean, μ:        150
St Dev:         17.32051
Test Statistic,  z: -1.4434
Critical z:     ±1.959962

Fail to Reject the Null Hypothesis.
Data do not provide enough evidence to indicate that
the samples come from populations with different medians.
```

using TECHNOLOGY

STATDISK Enter the sample data in columns of the Statdisk data window. Select **Analysis** from the main menu bar, then select **Wilcoxon Tests,** followed by the option **Wilcoxon (Indep. Samples).** Select the columns of data, then click on **Evaluate** to get a display that includes the rank sums, sample size, test statistic, critical value, and conclusion. See the STATDISK display given with Example 2.

MINITAB First enter the two sets of sample data in columns C1 and C2. Then select the options **Stat, Nonparametrics,** and **Mann-Whitney,** and enter C1 for the first sample and C2 for the second sample. The confidence level of 95.0 corresponds to a significance level of $\alpha = 0.05$, and the "alternate: not equal" box refers to the alternative hypothesis, where "not equal" corresponds to a two-tailed hypothesis test. Minitab provides the P-value and conclusion.

EXCEL Excel is not programmed for the Wilcoxon rank-sum test, but XLSTAT can be used by selecting **Nonparametric tests,** then **Comparison of two samples.** Use the Mann-Whitney test, which is equivalent to the Wilcoxon rank-sum test.

TI-83/84 PLUS The TI-83/84 Plus calculator is not programmed for the Wilcoxon rank-sum test, but the program RSTEST can be used. The program RSTEST (by Michael Lloyd) can be downloaded from the CD-ROM included with this book or the web site www.addisonwesley.com/triola. First download and install the program. (Also download the program ZZRANK, which is used by the program RSTEST.) Next, enter the two sets of sample data as lists in L1 and L2. Press **PRGM** and select **RSTEST.** Press **ENTER** **ENTER**. When given the prompt of GROUP A $=$, enter **L1** and press **ENTER**. When given the prompt of GROUP B $=$, enter **L2** and press **ENTER**. The second rank sum will be displayed as the value of R. The mean and standard deviation based on that value of R will also be displayed. Press **ENTER** once again to get the z score based on the second rank sum.

STATCRUNCH Click on **Open StatCrunch.** First enter two columns of data or open a data set. Click on **Stat,** select **Nonparametrics,** then select **Mann-Whitney.** Identify the columns to be used, click on **Next** and enter the value of the claimed difference. Click on **Calculate** and the display will include the P-value.

13-4 Basic Skills and Concepts

Statistical Literacy and Critical Thinking

1. Arrival Delay Times Example 2 in this section used samples of departure delay times from American Airlines Flights 19 and 21, but the table below lists simple random samples of arrival delay times (min) from those same flights. (The data are from Data Set 15 in Appendix B.) Are the requirements for using the Wilcoxon rank-sum test satisfied? Why or why not?

| Flight 19 | −5 | −32 | −13 | −9 | −19 | 49 | −30 | −23 | 14 | −21 | −32 | 11 |
| Flight 21 | −23 | 28 | 103 | −19 | −5 | −46 | 13 | −3 | 13 | 106 | −34 | −24 |

2. Rank Sum After ranking the combined list of 24 arrival delay times, find the sum of the ranks for Flight 19.

3. What Are We Testing? Refer to the sample data in Exercise 1. Assuming that we use the Wilcoxon rank-sum test with those data, identify the null hypothesis and all possible alternative hypotheses.

4. Efficiency Refer to Table 13-2 in Section 13-1 and identify the efficiency of the Wilcoxon rank-sum test. What does that value tell us about the test?

Wilcoxon Rank-Sum Test. *In Exercises 5–8, use the Wilcoxon rank-sum test.*

5. Arrival Delay Times Use the sample data given in Exercise 1 and test the claim that arrival delay times for Flight 19 and Flight 21 have the same median. Use a 0.05 significance level.

6. Taxi-Out Times Listed below are samples of taxi-out times (min) for American Airlines Flights 19 and 21 (from Data Set 15 in Appendix B). Use the sample data to test the claim that taxi-out times for Flight 19 and Flight 21 have the same median. Use a 0.05 significance level.

| Flight 19 | 15 | 12 | 19 | 18 | 21 | 20 | 13 | 15 | 43 | 18 | 17 | 19 |
| Flight 21 | 13 | 20 | 12 | 17 | 35 | 19 | 22 | 43 | 49 | 45 | 13 | 23 |

7. Clinical Trials of Lipitor The sample data below are changes in LDL cholesterol levels in clinical trials of Lipitor (atorvastatin). It was claimed that Lipitor had an effect on LDL cholesterol. (The data are based on results given in a Parke-Davis memo from David G. Orloff, M.D., the medical team leader for clinical trials of Lipitor. Pfizer declined to provide the author with the original data values.) Negative values represent decreases in LDL cholesterol. Use a 0.05 significance level to test the claim that for those treated with 20 mg of atorvastatin and those treated with 80 mg of atorvastatin, changes in LDL cholesterol have the same median. What do the results suggest?

Group treated with 20 mg of atorvastatin:

−28 −32 −29 −39 −31 −35 −25 −36 −35 −26 −29 −34 −30

Group treated with 80 mg of atorvastatin:

−42 −41 −38 −42 −41 −41 −40 −44 −32 −37 −41 −37 −34 −31

8. Radiation in Baby Teeth Listed below are amounts of strontium-90 (in millibecquerels, or mBq, per gram of calcium) in a simple random sample of baby teeth obtained from Pennsylvania residents and New York residents born after 1979 (based on data from "An Unexpected Rise in Strontium-90 in U.S. Deciduous Teeth in the 1990s," by Mangano et al., *Science of the Total Environment*). Use a 0.05 significance level to test the claim that the median amount of strontium-90 from Pennsylvania residents is the same as the median from New York residents.

| Pennsylvania | 155 | 142 | 149 | 130 | 151 | 163 | 151 | 142 | 156 | 133 | 138 | 161 |
| New York | 133 | 140 | 142 | 131 | 134 | 129 | 128 | 140 | 140 | 140 | 137 | 143 |

Appendix B Data Sets.   *In Exercises 9–12, refer to the indicated data set in Appendix B and use the Wilcoxon rank-sum test.*

9. IQ and Lead Exposure Data Set 5 in Appendix B lists full IQ scores for a random sample of subjects with medium lead levels in their blood and another random sample of subjects with high lead levels in their blood. Use a 0.05 significance level to test the claim that subjects with medium lead levels have full IQ scores with a higher median than the median full IQ score for subjects with high lead levels. Does lead level appear to affect full IQ scores?

10. IQ and Lead Exposure Data Set 5 in Appendix B lists performance IQ scores for a random sample of subjects with low lead levels in their blood and another random sample of subjects with high lead levels in their blood. Use a 0.05 significance level to test the claim that subjects with low lead levels have a higher median performance IQ score than those with high lead levels. Does lead exposure appear to have an adverse effect?

11. Weights of Quarters Data Set 21 in Appendix B lists weights (g) of pre-1964 quarters and post-1964 quarters. Use a 0.05 significance level to test the claim that the samples are from populations with the same median. Does it appear that the design of quarters changed in 1964?

12. Weights of Coke Data Set 19 in Appendix B lists weights (lb) of the cola in cans of regular Coke and diet Coke. Use a 0.05 significance level to test the claim that the samples are from populations with the same median. If there appears to be a difference, try to explain it.

13-4 Beyond the Basics

13. Using the Mann-Whitney U Test The Mann-Whitney U test is equivalent to the Wilcoxon rank-sum test for independent samples in the sense that they both apply to the same situations and always lead to the same conclusions. In the Mann-Whitney U test we calculate

$$z = \frac{U - \dfrac{n_1 n_2}{2}}{\sqrt{\dfrac{n_1 n_2 (n_1 + n_2 + 1)}{12}}}$$

where

$$U = n_1 n_2 + \frac{n_1(n_1 + 1)}{2} - R$$

Use the pulse rates listed in Table 13-5 in this section to find the z test statistic for the Mann-Whitney U test. Compare this value to the z test statistic found using the Wilcoxon rank-sum test.

14. Finding Critical Values Assume that we have two treatments (A and B) that produce quantitative results, and we have only two observations for treatment A and two observations for treatment B. We cannot use the test statistic given in this section because both sample sizes do not exceed 10.

	Rank			Rank Sum for Treatment A
1	2	3	4	
A	A	B	B	3

a. Complete the accompanying table by listing the five rows corresponding to the other five cases, and enter the corresponding rank sums for treatment A.

b. List the possible values of R and their corresponding probabilities. (Assume that the rows of the table from part (a) are equally likely.)

c. Is it possible, at the 0.10 significance level, to reject the null hypothesis that there is no difference between treatments A and B? Explain.

13-5 Kruskal-Wallis Test

Key Concept This section introduces the *Kruskal-Wallis test*, which uses ranks of data from three or more independent simple random samples to test the null hypothesis that the samples come from populations with the same median.

In Section 12-2 we used one-way analysis of variance (ANOVA) to test the null hypothesis that three or more populations have the same *mean*, but ANOVA requires that all of the involved populations have normal distributions. The Kruskal-Wallis test for equal *medians* does not require normal distributions.

> **DEFINITION** The **Kruskal-Wallis test** (also called the ***H*** **test**) is a nonparametric test that uses ranks of simple random samples from three or more independent populations to test the null hypothesis that the populations have the same median. (The alternative hypothesis is the claim that the populations have medians that are not all equal.)

In applying the Kruskal-Wallis test, we compute the *test statistic H, which has a distribution that can be approximated by the chi-square distribution as long as each sample has at least five observations.* When we use the chi-square distribution in this context, the number of degrees of freedom is $k - 1$, where k is the number of samples. (For a quick review of the key features of the chi-square distribution, see Section 7-4.)

The H test statistic is basically a measure of the variance of the rank sums $R_1, R_2, \ldots, R_k$. If the ranks are distributed evenly among the sample groups, then H should be a relatively small number. If the samples are very different, then the ranks will be excessively low in some groups and high in others, with the net effect that H will be large. Consequently, only large values of H lead to rejection of the null hypothesis that the samples come from identical populations. *The Kruskal-Wallis test is therefore a right-tailed test.*

Kruskal-Wallis Test

Objective

Use the Kruskal-Wallis test with simple random samples from three or more independent populations for the following null and alternative hypotheses:

H_0: The samples come from populations with the same median.

H_1: The samples come from populations with medians that are not all equal.

Notation

N = total number of observations in all samples combined

k = number of different samples

R_1 = sum of ranks for Sample 1

n_1 = number of observations in Sample 1

For Sample 2, the sum of ranks is R_2 and the number of observations is n_2, and similar notation is used for the other samples.

continued

Requirements

1. We have at least three independent simple random samples.

2. Each sample has at least five observations. (If samples have fewer than five observations, refer to special tables of critical values, such as *CRC Standard*

Probability and Statistics Tables and Formulae, published by CRC Press.)

Note: There is *no* requirement that the populations have a normal distribution or any other particular distribution.

Test Statistic

$$H = \frac{12}{N(N+1)}\left(\frac{R_1^2}{n_1} + \frac{R_2^2}{n_2} + \cdots + \frac{R_k^2}{n_k}\right) - 3(N+1)$$

P-Values

P-values are often provided by technology.

Critical Values

1. The test is *right-tailed* and critical values can be found from technology or from the chi-square distribution in Table A-4.

2. df $= k - 1$ (where df is the number of degrees of freedom and k is the number of different samples)

Procedure for Finding the Value of the H Test Statistic To see how the following steps are applied, refer to the sample data in Table 13-6.

Step 1: Temporarily combine all samples into one big sample and assign a rank to each sample value. (Sort the values from lowest to highest, and in cases of ties, assign to each observation the mean of the ranks involved.)

EXAMPLE: In Table 13-6, the numbers in parentheses are the ranks of the combined data set. The rank of 1 is assigned to the lowest value of 64, the rank of 2 is assigned to the next lowest value of 78, and so on. In the case of ties, each of the tied values is assigned the mean of the ranks involved in the tie.

Step 2: For each sample, find the sum of the ranks and find the sample size.

EXAMPLE: In Table 13-6, the sum of the ranks from the first sample is 86, the sum of the ranks for the second sample is 50.5, and the sum of the ranks for the third sample is 53.5.

Step 3: Calculate H using the results of Step 2 and the notation and test statistic given in the preceding box.

EXAMPLE: The test statistic is computed in Example 1.

Table 13-6 Performance IQ Scores

Low Lead Level	Medium Lead Level	High Lead Level
85 (**6.5**)	78 (**2**)	93 (**10**)
90 (**8.5**)	97 (**12.5**)	100 (**15.5**)
107 (**18.5**)	107 (**18.5**)	97 (**12.5**)
85 (**6.5**)	80 (**4**)	79 (**3**)
100 (**15.5**)	90 (**8.5**)	97 (**12.5**)
97 (**12.5**)	83 (**5**)	
101 (**17**)		
64 (**1**)		
$n_1 = 8$	$n_2 = 6$	$n_3 = 5$
$R_1 = 86$	$R_2 = 50.5$	$R_3 = 53.5$

Example 1 Effect of Lead on IQ Score

Table 13-6 lists performance IQ scores from samples of subjects with low lead exposure, medium lead exposure, and high lead exposure (from Data Set 5 in Appendix B). Use a 0.05 significance level to test the claim that the three samples come from populations with medians that are all equal.

Solution

Requirement check (1) Each of the three samples is a simple random independent sample. (2) Each sample size is at least 5. The requirements are satisfied. ✓
The null and alternative hypotheses are as follows:

H_0: The median performance IQ score is the same for the population of subjects with low lead exposure, the population with medium lead exposure, and the population with high lead exposure.

H_1: The three populations have median performance IQ scores that are not all the same.

Test Statistic In determining the value of the H test statistic, we first rank all of the data, then we find the sum of the ranks for each category. In Table 13-6, ranks are shown in parentheses next to the original sample values. Next we find the sample size (n) and sum of ranks (R) for each sample. Those values are shown at the bottom of Table 13-6. Because the total number of observations is 19, we have $N = 19$. We can now evaluate the test statistic as follows:

$$H = \frac{12}{N(N+1)}\left(\frac{R_1^2}{n_1} + \frac{R_2^2}{n_2} + \cdots + \frac{R_k^2}{n_k}\right) - 3(N+1)$$

$$= \frac{12}{19(19+1)}\left(\frac{86^2}{8} + \frac{50.5^2}{6} + \frac{53.5^2}{5}\right) - 3(19+1)$$

$$= 0.694$$

Critical Value Because each sample has at least five observations, the distribution of H is approximately a chi-square distribution with $k - 1$ degrees of freedom. The number of samples is $k = 3$, so we have $3 - 1 = 2$ degrees of freedom. Refer to Table A-4 to find the critical value of 5.991, which corresponds to 2 degrees of freedom and a 0.05 significance level (with an area of 0.05 in the right tail). Figure 13-4 on the next page shows the test statistic of $H = 0.694$ does not fall within the critical region bounded by 5.991, so we fail to reject the null hypothesis of equal population medians.
Figure 13-4 shows the test statistic of $H = 0.694$ and the critical value of 5.991. (The chi-square distribution has the general shape shown in Figure 13-4 whenever the number of degrees of freedom is 1 or 2.) The test statistic does not fall in the critical region, so we fail to reject the null hypothesis of equal medians.

Interpretation

There is not sufficient evidence to reject the claim that performance IQ scores from subjects with low lead exposure, medium lead exposure, and high lead exposure all have the same median. The population medians do not appear to be different.

Figure 13-4

Chi-Square Distribution for Example 1

Rationale: The Kruskal-Wallis H test statistic is the rank version of the F test statistic used in the analysis of variance discussed in Chapter 12. When we deal with ranks R instead of original values x, many components are predetermined. For example, the sum of all ranks can be expressed as $N(N + 1)/2$, where N is the total number of values in all samples combined. The expression

$$H = \frac{12}{N(N + 1)}\Sigma\, n_i(\overline{R}_i - \overline{\overline{R}})^2$$

where

$$\overline{R}_i = \frac{R_i}{n_i} \qquad \text{and} \qquad \overline{\overline{R}} = \frac{\Sigma\, R_i}{\Sigma\, n_i}$$

combines weighted variances of ranks to produce the H test statistic given here, and this expression for H is algebraically equivalent to the expression for H given earlier as the test statistic.

using TECHNOLOGY

STATDISK   Enter the data in columns of the data window. Select **Analysis** from the main menu bar, then select **Kruskal-Wallis Test** and select the columns of data. STATDISK will display the sum of the ranks for each sample, the H test statistic, the P-value, and the critical value.

MINITAB   Refer to the *Minitab Student Laboratory Manual and Workbook* for the procedure required to use the options **Stat, Nonparametrics,** and **Kruskal-Wallis.** The basic idea is to list all of the sample data in one big column, with another column identifying the sample for the corresponding values. For the data of Table 13-6 in this section, enter the 19 values in Minitab's column C1. In column C2, enter eight 1s followed by six 2s followed by five 3s. Now select **Stat, Nonparametrics,** and **Kruskal-Wallis.** In the dialog box, enter C1 for response, C2 for factor, then click **OK.** The Minitab display includes the H test statistic and the P-value.

EXCEL   Excel is not programmed for the Kruskal-Wallis test, but XLSTAT can be used. First enter the data in separate columns. For example, enter the data in Table 13-6 in three separate columns. Click on **XLSTAT**, select **Nonparametric tests,** then **Comparison of k samples.** For the data in Table 13-6, enter A1:C8 in the data entry box and choose the data format of "One column per sample." Click on the **Options** tab and select **Asymptotic p-value** so that the P-value will be computed using the chi-square distribution.

TI-83/84 PLUS   The TI-83/84 Plus calculator is not programmed for the Kruskal-Wallis test, but the program KWTEST can be used. The program KWTEST (by Michael Lloyd) is included on the CD included with this book or it can be downloaded from the site www.addisonwesley.com/triola. First download and install the program. (Also download the program ZZRANK, which is used by the program KWTEST.) Next, enter the lists of sample data in separate columns of matrix [A]. Press **PRGM**, select **KWTEST,** then press **ENTER**. The value of the test statistic and the number of degrees of freedom will be provided. (*Note:* If the samples have different sizes and one of the data values is zero, add some convenient constant to all of the sample values so that no zeros are present.)

STATCRUNCH Click on **Open StatCrunch.** First enter columns of data or open a data set. Click on **Stat,** select

Nonparametrics, then select **Kruskal-Wallis.** Identify the columns to be used, then click on **Calculate** and the display will include the test statistic and *P*-value.

13-5 Basic Skills and Concepts

Statistical Literacy and Critical Thinking

1. Effect of Lead on IQ Score Listed below are full IQ scores from simple random samples of subjects with low lead exposure, medium lead exposure, and high lead exposure (from Data Set 5 in Appendix B). In using the Kruskal-Wallis test, we must rank all of the data combined, then we must find the sum of the ranks for each sample. Find the sum of the ranks for each of the three samples.

Low Lead Level	Medium Lead Level	High Lead Level
70	72	82
85	90	93
86	92	85
76	71	75
84	86	85
	79	

2. Requirements Assume that we want to use the data from Exercise 1 with the Kruskal-Wallis test. Are the requirements satisfied? Explain.

3. Notation For the data given in Exercise 1, identify the values of n_1, n_2, n_3, and N.

4. Efficiency Refer to Table 13-2 in Section 13-1 and identify the efficiency of the Kruskal-Wallis test. What does that value tell us about the test?

Using the Kruskal-Wallis Test. *In Exercises 5–8, use the Kruskal-Wallis test.*

5. Triathlon Times Jeff Parent is a statistics instructor who participates in triathlons. Listed below are times (in minutes and seconds) he recorded while riding a bicycle for five laps through each mile of a 3-mile loop. Use a 0.05 significance level to test the claim that the samples are from populations with the same median. What do the data suggest?

Mile 1	3:15	3:24	3:23	3:22	3:21
Mile 2	3:19	3:22	3:21	3:17	3:19
Mile 3	3:34	3:31	3:29	3:31	3:29

6. Clancy, Rowling, Tolstoy Readability Pages were randomly selected by the author from *The Bear and the Dragon* by Tom Clancy, *Harry Potter and the Sorcerer's Stone* by J. K. Rowling, and *War and Peace* by Leo Tolstoy. The Flesch Reading Ease scores are listed on the next page. Use a 0.05 significance level to test the claim that the three samples are from populations with the same median. Do the books appear to have different reading levels of difficulty?

Clancy	58.2	73.4	73.1	64.4	72.7	89.2	43.9	76.3	76.4	78.9	69.4	72.9
Rowling	85.3	84.3	79.5	82.5	80.2	84.6	79.2	70.9	78.6	86.2	74.0	83.7
Tolstoy	69.4	64.2	71.4	71.6	68.5	51.9	72.2	74.4	52.8	58.4	65.4	73.6

7. Car Crash Measurements Use the following listed chest deceleration measurements (in g, where g is the force of gravity) from samples of small, midsize, and large cars. (These values are from Data Set 13 in Appendix B.) Use a 0.05 significance level to test the claim that the different size categories have the same median chest deceleration in the standard crash test. Do the data suggest that larger cars are safer?

Small	44	39	37	54	39	44	42
Midsize	36	53	43	42	52	49	41
Large	32	45	41	38	37	38	33

8. Highway Fuel Consumption Listed below are highway fuel consumption amounts (mi/gal) for cars categorized by the sizes of small, midsize, and large (from Data Set 14 in Appendix B). Using a 0.05 significance level, test the claim that the three size categories have the same median highway fuel consumption. Does the size of a car appear to affect highway fuel consumption?

Small	28	26	23	24	26	24	25
Midsize	28	31	26	30	28	29	31
Large	34	36	28	40	33	35	26

Appendix B Data Sets.   *In Exercises 9–12, use the Kruskal-Wallis test with the data set from Appendix B.*

9. IQ and Lead Exposure Data Set 5 in Appendix B lists performance IQ scores for random samples of subjects with blood lead levels categorized as low, medium, and high. Use a 0.01 significance level to test the claim that subjects in those categories have the same median performance IQ score. Does lead exposure appear to have an adverse effect?

10. Passive and Active Smoke Data Set 9 in Appendix B lists measured cotinine levels from a sample of subjects who smoke, another sample of subjects who do not smoke but are exposed to environmental tobacco smoke, and a third sample of subjects who do not smoke and are not exposed to environmental tobacco smoke. Cotinine is produced when the body absorbs nicotine. Use a 0.01 significance level to test the claim that the three samples are from populations with the same median. What do the results suggest about a smoker who argues that he absorbs as much nicotine as people who don't smoke?

11. Nicotine in Cigarettes Refer to Data Set 10 in Appendix B and use the amounts of nicotine (mg per cigarette) in the king-size cigarettes, the 100-mm menthol cigarettes, and the 100-mm nonmenthol cigarettes. The king-size cigarettes are nonfiltered, nonmenthol, and nonlight. The 100-mm menthol cigarettes are filtered and nonlight. The 100-mm nonmenthol cigarettes are filtered and nonlight. Use a 0.05 significance level to test the claim that the three categories of cigarettes yield the same median amount of nicotine. Given that only the king-size cigarettes are not filtered, do the filters appear to make a difference?

12. Car Crash Measurements Refer to Data Set 13 in Appendix B and use the pelvis deceleration measurements for small cars, midsize cars, and large cars. Use a 0.05 significance level to test the claim that the different size categories have the same median pelvis deceleration in the standard crash test. Do the data suggest that larger cars are safer?

13-5 Beyond the Basics

13. Correcting the *H* Test Statistic for Ties In using the Kruskal-Wallis test, there is a correction factor that should be applied whenever there are many ties: Divide *H* by

$$1 - \frac{\Sigma T}{N^3 - N}$$

For each individual group of tied observations in the combined set of all sample data, calculate $T = t^3 - t$, where *t* is the number of observations that are tied within the individual group. Find *t* for each group of tied values, then compute the value of *T* for each group, then add the *T* values to get ΣT. The value of *N* is the total number of observations in all samples combined. Use this procedure to find the corrected value of *H* for Exercise 11. Does the corrected value of *H* differ substantially from the value found in Exercise 11?

13-6 Rank Correlation

Key Concept In this section we describe the nonparametric method of the *rank correlation test,* which uses ranks of paired data to test for an association between two variables. In Chapter 10 we used paired sample data to compute values for the linear correlation coefficient *r*, but in this section we use *ranks* as the basis for computing the rank correlation coefficient r_s. As in Chapter 10, we should begin an analysis of paired data by exploring with a scatterplot so that we can identify any patterns in the data.

> **DEFINITION** The **rank correlation test** (or **Spearman's rank correlation test**) is a nonparametric test that uses ranks of sample data consisting of matched pairs. It is used to test for an association between two variables.

We use the notation r_s for the rank correlation coefficient so that we don't confuse it with the linear correlation coefficient *r*. The subscript *s* does *not* refer to a standard deviation; it is used in honor of Charles Spearman (1863–1945), who originated the rank correlation approach. In fact, r_s is often called **Spearman's rank correlation coefficient.** Key components of the rank correlation test are given in the following box, and the rank correlation procedure is summarized in Figure 13-5.

Rank Correlation

Objective

Compute the rank correlation coefficient r_s and use it to test for an association between two variables. The null and alternative hypotheses are as follows:

$H_0: \rho_s = 0$ (There is no correlation between the two variables.)

$H_1: \rho_s \neq 0$ (There is a correlation between the two variables.)

Notation

r_s = rank correlation coefficient for sample paired data (r_s is a sample statistic)

ρ_s = rank correlation coefficient for all the population data (ρ_s is a population parameter)

n = number of pairs of sample data

d = difference between ranks for the two values within an individual pair

continued

Requirements

The paired data are a simple random sample.

The data are ranks or can be converted to ranks.

Note: Unlike the parametric methods of Section 10-2, there is *no* requirement that the sample pairs of data have a bivariate normal distribution (as described in Section 10-2). There is *no* requirement of a normal distribution for any population.

Test Statistic

Within each sample, first convert the data to *ranks*, then find the exact value of the rank correlation coefficient r_s by using Formula 10-1:

$$r_s = \frac{n\Sigma xy - (\Sigma x)(\Sigma y)}{\sqrt{n(\Sigma x^2) - (\Sigma x)^2}\sqrt{n(\Sigma y^2) - (\Sigma y)^2}}$$

No ties: After converting the data in each sample to ranks, if there are no ties among ranks for the first variable and there are no ties among ranks for the second variable, the exact value of the test statistic can be calculated using Formula 10-1 (at the left) or with this relatively simple formula:

$$r_s = 1 - \frac{6\Sigma d^2}{n(n^2 - 1)}$$

P-Values

P-values are sometimes provided by technology. (*Caution:* When finding r_s, you can convert the sample data to ranks and then use the same technology that was used for the linear correlation coefficient described in Section 10.2, but *do not use P-values from linear correlation for the methods of rank correlation.* Use the *P*-value from technology only if the technology has a procedure designed specifically for rank correlation. See the "Using Technology" instructions given at the end of this section.)

Critical Values

1. If $n \leq 30$, critical values are found in Table A-9.

2. If $n > 30$, critical values of r_s are found using Formula 13-1.

Formula 13-1

$$r_s = \frac{\pm z}{\sqrt{n - 1}} \text{ (critical values when } n > 30\text{)}$$

where the value of z corresponds to the significance level. (For example, if $\alpha = 0.05$, $z = 1.96$.)

CAUTION When working with data having ties among ranks, the rank correlation coefficient r_s can be calculated using Formula 10-1. Technology can be used instead of manual calculations with Formula 10-1, but the displayed *P*-values for linear correlation do not apply to the methods of rank correlation. *Do not use P-values from linear correlation for methods of rank correlation.*

Advantages: Rank correlation has these advantages over the parametric methods discussed in Chapter 10:

    1. Rank correlation can be used with paired data that are ranks or can be converted to ranks. Unlike the parametric methods of Chapter 10, the method of rank correlation does *not* require a normal distribution for any population.

    2. Rank correlation can be used to detect some (not all) relationships that are not linear.

Start

↓

Are the n pairs of data in the form of ranks ? —No→ Convert the data of the first sample to ranks from 1 to n and then do the same for the second sample.

Yes ↓

Does either variable have ties among its ranks ? —No→ Calculate the difference d for each pair of ranks by subtracting the lower rank from the higher rank.

↓

Square each difference d and then find the sum of those squares to get $\Sigma(d^2)$.

Yes ↓

Calculate r_s using Formula 10-1 with the ranks:

$$r_s = \frac{n\Sigma xy - (\Sigma x)(\Sigma y)}{\sqrt{n(\Sigma x^2) - (\Sigma x)^2}\ \sqrt{n(\Sigma y^2) - (\Sigma y)^2}}$$

Complete the computation of
$$r_s = 1 - \frac{6\Sigma d^2}{n(n^2 - 1)}$$
to get the test statistic.

↓

Is $n \leq 30$? —No→ Calculate the critical values
$$r_s = \pm \frac{z}{\sqrt{n - 1}}$$
where z corresponds to the significance level.

Yes ↓

Find the negative and positive critical values of r_s from Table A-9.

↓

- If r_s is between the negative and positive critical values, fail to reject the null hypothesis $\rho_s = 0$ (no correlation).
- If r_s is not between the negative and positive critical values, reject the null hypothesis $\rho_s = 0$ and conclude that there is sufficient evidence to support a claim of a correlation.

Figure 13-5   Rank Correlation Procedure for Testing $H_0: \rho_s = 0$

Direct Link Between Smoking and Cancer

When we find a statistical correlation between two variables, we must be extremely careful to avoid the mistake of concluding that there is a cause-effect link. The tobacco industry has consistently emphasized that correlation does not imply causality as they denied that tobacco products cause cancer. However, Dr. David Sidransky of Johns Hopkins University and other researchers found a direct physical link that involves mutations of a specific gene among smokers. Molecular analysis of genetic changes allows researchers to determine whether cigarette smoking is the cause of a cancer. (See "Association Between Cigarette Smoking and Mutation of the p53 Gene in Squamous-Cell Carcinoma of the Head and Neck," by Brennan, Boyle et al, *New England Journal of Medicine*, Vol 332, No. 11.) Although statistical methods cannot prove that smoking *causes* cancer, statistical methods can be used to identify an association, and physical proof of causation can then be sought by researchers.

Disadvantage: A not very serious disadvantage of rank correlation is its efficiency rating of 0.91, as described in Section 13-1. This efficiency rating shows that with all other circumstances being equal, the nonparametric approach of rank correlation requires 100 pairs of sample data to achieve the same results as only 91 pairs of sample observations analyzed through the parametric approach, assuming that the stricter requirements of the parametric approach are met.

Example 1   Are the Best Televisions the Most Expensive?

Table 13-7 lists quality rankings and prices of 37-inch LCD televisions (based on data from *Consumer Reports*). Find the value of the rank correlation coefficient and use it to determine whether there is a correlation between quality and price. Use a 0.05 significance level. Based on the result, does it appear that you can get better quality by spending more?

Table 13-7 Overall Quality Scores and Prices of LCD Televisions

Quality rank	1	2	3	4	5	6	7
Price (dollars)	1900	1200	1300	2000	1700	1400	2700

Solution

Requirement check The only requirement is that the paired data are a simple random sample. The sample data are a simple random sample from the televisions that were tested. ✓

The quality ranks are consecutive integers and are not from a population that is normally distributed, so we use the rank correlation coefficient to test for a relationship between quality and price. The null and alternative hypotheses are as follows:

$H_0: \rho_s = 0$ (There is *no* correlation between quality and price.)

$H_1: \rho_s \neq 0$ (There is a correlation between quality and price.)

Following the procedure of Figure 13-5, we begin by converting the data in Table 13-7 into their corresponding ranks shown in Table 13-8. The lowest prices of $1200 is assigned a rank of 1, the next lowest price of $1300 is assigned a rank of 2, and so on.

Table 13-8 Ranks of Data from Table 13-7

Quality rank	1	2	3	4	5	6	7
Price rank	5	1	2	6	4	3	7
Difference d	4	1	1	2	1	3	0
d^2	16	1	1	4	1	9	0

Neither of the two variables has ties among ranks, so the exact value of the test statistic can be calculated as shown below. We use $n = 7$ (for 7 pairs of data) and $\Sigma d^2 = 16 + 1 + 1 + 4 + 1 + 9 + 0 = 32$.

$$r_s = 1 - \frac{6 \Sigma d^2}{n(n^2 - 1)} = 1 - \frac{6(32)}{7(7^2 - 1)}$$

$$= 1 - \frac{192}{336} = 0.429$$

Now we refer to Table A-9 to find the critical values of ± 0.786 (based on $\alpha = 0.05$ and $n = 7$). Because the test statistic $r_s = 0.429$ is between the critical values of -0.786 and 0.786, we fail to reject the null hypothesis. There is not sufficient evidence to support a claim of a correlation between quality and price. Based on the given sample data, it appears that you don't necessarily get better quality by paying more.

Example 2   Large Sample Case

Refer to the measured systolic and diastolic blood pressure measurements of 40 randomly selected females in Data Set 1 in Appendix B and use a 0.05 significance level to test the claim that among women, there is a correlation between systolic blood pressure and diastolic blood pressure.

Solution

Requirement check The data are a simple random sample. ✓

Test Statistic The value of the rank correlation coefficient is $r_s = 0.505$, which can be found by using technology.

Critical Values Because there are 40 pairs of data, we have $n = 40$. Because n exceeds 30, we find the critical values from Formula 13-1 instead of Table A-9. With $\alpha = 0.05$ in two tails, we let $z = 1.96$ to get the critical values of -0.314 and 0.314, as shown below.

$$r_s = \frac{\pm 1.96}{\sqrt{40 - 1}} = \pm 0.314$$

The test statistic of $r_s = 0.505$ is not between the critical values of -0.314 and 0.314, so we reject the null hypothesis of $r_s = 0$. There is sufficient evidence to support the claim that among women, there is a correlation between systolic blood pressure and diastolic blood pressure.

Detecting Nonlinear Patterns Rank correlation methods sometimes allow us to detect relationships that we cannot detect with the methods of Chapter 10. See the accompanying scatterplot that shows an S-shaped pattern of points suggesting that there is a correlation between x and y. The methods of Chapter 10 result in the linear correlation coefficient of $r = 0.590$ and critical values of ± 0.632, suggesting that

NONLINEAR PATTERN

there is not a linear correlation between *x* and *y*. But if we use the methods of this section, we get $r_s = 1$ and critical values of ± 0.648, suggesting that there is a correlation between *x* and *y*. *With rank correlation, we can sometimes detect relationships that are not linear.*

using TECHNOLOGY

STATDISK Enter the sample data in columns of the data window. Select **Analysis** from the main menu bar, then select **Rank Correlation.** Select the two columns of data to be included, then click **Evaluate.** The STATDISK results include the exact value of the test statistic r_s and the critical value.

MINITAB Enter the paired data in columns C1 and C2. If the data are not already ranks, select **Data** and **Rank** to convert the data to ranks, then select **Stat,** followed by **Basic Statistics,** followed by **Correlation.** Minitab will display the exact value of the test statistic r_s. Although Minitab identifies it as the Pearson correlation coefficient described in Section 10-2, it is actually the Spearman correlation coefficient described in this section (because it is based on ranks). *Caution:* Ignore the *P*-value, because it is calculated using the methods of Chapter 10, not the methods of this section.

EXCEL Excel does not have a function that calculates the rank correlation coefficient from original sample values, but the exact value of the test statistic r_s can be found as follows. First replace each of the original sample values by its corresponding rank. Enter those ranks in columns A and B. Click on the *fx* function key located on the main menu bar. Select the function category **Statistical** and the function name **CORREL,** then click **OK.** In the dialog box, enter the cell range of values for *x*, such as A1:A10. Also enter the cell

range of values for *y*, such as B1:B10. Excel will display the exact value of the rank correlation coefficient r_s.

XLSTAT XLSTAT can be used by selecting **Correlation/Association tests.** For the type of test, select **Spearman.** The value of r_s will be listed in the table identified as "Correlation matrix (Spearman)," and if the value is displayed in a bold font, we can reject the claim of no correlation.

TI-83/84 PLUS If using a TI-83/84 Plus calculator or any other calculator with 2-variable statistics, you can find the exact value of r_s as follows: (1) Replace each sample value by its corresponding rank, then (2) calculate the value of the linear correlation coefficient *r* with the same procedures used in Section 10-2. Enter the paired ranks in lists L1 and L2, then press **STAT** and select **TESTS.** Using the option **LinRegTTest** will result in several displayed values, including the exact value of the rank correlation coefficient r_s. *Caution:* Ignore the *P*-value, because it is calculated using the methods of Chapter 10, not the methods of this section.

STATCRUNCH Replace each sample value by its corresponding rank, then use the same StatCrunch procedure described in Section 10-2. *Caution:* Ignore the *P*-value, because it is calculated using the methods of Chapter 10, not the methods of this section.

13-6 Basic Skills and Concepts

Statistical Literacy and Critical Thinking

1. Regression If the methods of this section are used with paired sample data, and the conclusion is that there is sufficient evidence to support the claim of a correlation between the two variables, can we use the methods of Section 10-3 to find the regression equation that can be used for predictions? Why or why not?

2. Level of Measurement Which of the levels of measurement (nominal, ordinal, interval, ratio) describe data that cannot be used with the methods of rank correlation? Explain.

3. Notation What do r, r_s, ρ, and ρ_s denote? Why is the subscript *s* used? Does the subscript *s* represent the same standard deviation *s* introduced in Section 3-3?

4. Efficiency Refer to Table 13-2 in Section 13-1 and identify the efficiency of the rank correlation test. What does that value tell us about the test?

In Exercises 5 and 6, use the scatterplot to find the value of the rank correlation coefficient r_s and the critical values corresponding to a 0.05 significance level used to test the null hypothesis of $\rho_s = 0$. Determine whether there is a correlation.

5. Distance/Time Data for a Dropped Object

6. Altitude/Time Data for a Descending Aircraft

Testing for Rank Correlation. *In Exercises 7–12, use the rank correlation coefficient to test for a correlation between the two variables. Use a significance level of $\alpha = 0.05$.*

7. Are the Best Televisions the Most Expensive? The following table lists overall quality scores and prices of 40-inch LCD televisions (based on data from *Consumer Reports*). Do these data suggest that you can get better quality by spending more?

Quality score	74	71	68	65	63	62	57
Price (dollars)	2700	3000	3800	2300	2000	1300	1400

8. Are the Best Paints the Most Expensive? The following table lists overall quality scores and prices for a gallon of exterior paints (based on data from *Consumer Reports*). Do these data suggest that you can get better quality by spending more?

Quality score	90	87	82	78	62	56	23	19
Price (dollars)	27	32	19	15	39	24	15	18

9. Judges of Marching Bands Two judges ranked seven bands in the Texas state finals competition of marching bands (Coppell, Keller, Grapevine, Dickinson, Poteet, Fossil Ridge, Heritage), and their rankings are listed below (based on data from the University Interscholastic League). Test for a correlation between the two judges. Do the judges appear to rank about the same or are they very different?

Band	Cpl	Klr	Grp	Dck	Ptt	FR	Her
First judge	1	3	4	7	5	6	2
Second judge	6	4	5	1	3	2	7

10. Judges of Marching Bands In the same competition described in Exercise 9, a third judge ranked the bands with the results shown below. Test for a correlation between the first and third judges. Do the judges appear to rank about the same or are they very different?

Band	Cpl	Klr	Grp	Dck	Ptt	FR	Her
First judge	1	3	4	7	5	6	2
Third judge	3	4	1	5	7	6	2

11. Measuring Seals from Photos Listed below are the overhead widths (in cm) of seals measured from photographs and the weights of the seals (in kg). The data are based on "Mass Estimation of Weddell Seals Using Techniques of Photogrammetry," by R. Garrott of Montana State University. The purpose of the study was to determine if weights of seals could be determined from overhead photographs. Is there sufficient evidence to conclude that there is a correlation between overhead widths of seals from photographs and the weights of the seals?

Overhead width	7.2	7.4	9.8	9.4	8.8	8.4
Weight	116	154	245	202	200	191

12. Crickets and Temperature The association between the temperature and the number of times a cricket chirps in 1 min was studied. Listed below are the numbers of chirps in 1 min and the corresponding temperatures in degrees Fahrenheit (based on data from *The Song of Insects* by George W. Pierce, Harvard University Press). Is there sufficient evidence to conclude that there is a relationship between the number of chirps in 1 min and the temperature?

Chirps in 1 min	882	1188	1104	864	1200	1032	960	900
Temperature (°F)	69.7	93.3	84.3	76.3	88.6	82.6	71.6	79.6

Appendix B Data Sets.   *In Exercises 13–16, use the data from Appendix B to test for rank correlation with a 0.05 significance level.*

13. Blood Pressure Refer to the measured systolic and diastolic blood pressure measurements of 40 randomly selected males in Data Set 1 in Appendix B and test the claim that among men, there is a correlation between systolic blood pressure and diastolic blood pressure.

14. IQ and Brain Volume Refer to Data Set 6 in Appendix B and use the paired data consisting of brain volume (cm^3) and IQ score.

15. Flight Delays Refer to Data Set 15 in Appendix B and use the departure delay times and the arrival delay times.

16. Earthquakes Refer to Data Set 16 in Appendix B and use the magnitudes and depths from the earthquakes.

13-6 Beyond the Basics

17. Finding Critical Values An alternative to using Table A–9 to find critical values for rank correlation is to compute them using this approximation:

$$r_s = \pm \sqrt{\frac{t^2}{t^2 + n - 2}}$$

Here t is the critical t value from Table A-3 corresponding to the desired significance level and $n - 2$ degrees of freedom. Use this approximation to find critical values of r_s for the following cases. Are the resulting approximations close to the values from Table A-9?

a. $n = 8, \alpha = 0.05$

b. $n = 30, \alpha = 0.01$

13-7 Runs Test for Randomness

Key Concept This section describes the *runs test for randomness*, which can be used to determine whether a sequence of sample data has a random order. This test requires a criterion for categorizing each data value into one of two separate categories, and it analyzes *runs* of those categories to determine whether the runs appear to result from a random process, or whether the runs suggest that the order of the data is not random.

> **DEFINITIONS**
>
> After characterizing each data value as one of two separate categories, a **run** is a sequence of data having the same characteristic; the sequence is preceded and followed by data with a different characteristic or by no data at all.
>
> The **runs test** uses the number of runs in a sequence of sample data to test for randomness in the order of the data.

Fundamental Principle of the Runs Test

The fundamental principle of the runs test can be briefly stated as follows:

Reject randomness if the number of runs is very low or very high.

- Example: The sequence of genders FFFFFMMMMM is not random because it has only 2 runs, so the number of runs is very *low*.

- Example: The sequence of genders FMFMFMFMFM is not random because there are 10 runs, which is very *high*.

CAUTION The runs test for randomness is based on the *order* in which the data occur; it is *not* based on the *frequency* of the data. For example, a sequence of 3 men and 20 women might appear to be random, but the issue of whether 3 men and 20 women constitute a *biased* sample (with disproportionately more women) is *not* addressed by the runs test.

The exact criteria for determining whether a number of runs is very high or low are found in the accompanying box, which summarizes the key elements of the runs test for randomness. The procedure for the runs test for randomness is also summarized in Figure 13-6 on page 677.

Sports Hot Streaks

It is a common belief that athletes often have "hot streaks"—that is, brief periods of extraordinary success. Stanford University psychologist Amos Tversky and other researchers used statistics to analyze the thousands of shots taken by the Philadelphia 76ers for one full season and half of another. They found that the number of "hot streaks" was no different than you would expect from random trials with the outcome of each trial independent of any preceding results. That is, the probability of a hit doesn't depend on the preceding hit or miss.

Runs Test for Randomness

Objective

Apply the runs test for randomness to a *sequence* of sample data to test for randomness in the *order* of the data. Use the following null and alternative hypotheses:

H_0: The data are in a random sequence.
H_1: The data are in a sequence that is not random.

Notation

n_1 = number of elements in the sequence that have one particular characteristic. (The characteristic chosen for n_1 is arbitrary.)
n_2 = number of elements in the sequence that have the other characteristic
G = number of runs

continued

Requirements

1. The sample data are arranged according to some ordering scheme, such as the order in which the sample values were obtained.

2. Each data value can be categorized into one of *two* separate categories (such as male/female).

Test Statistic and Critical Values

For Small Samples and $\alpha = 0.05$: If $n_1 \leq 20$ and $n_2 \leq 20$ and the significance level is $\alpha = 0.05$, the test statistic and critical values are as follows:

Test statistic: G

Critical values: Use Table A-10.

Decision criterion: Reject randomness if the number of runs G is

- less than or equal to the smaller critical value found in Table A-10.

or

- greater than or equal to the larger critical value found in Table A-10.

For Large Samples or $\alpha \neq 0.05$: If $n_1 > 20$ or $n_2 > 20$ or $\alpha \neq 0.05$, the test statistic and critical values are as follows:

Test statistic: $z = \dfrac{G - \mu_G}{\sigma_G}$

where $\mu_G = \dfrac{2n_1 n_2}{n_1 + n_2} + 1$

and $\sigma_G = \sqrt{\dfrac{(2n_1 n_2)(2n_1 n_2 - n_1 - n_2)}{(n_1 + n_2)^2 (n_1 + n_2 - 1)}}$

Critical values of z: Use Table A-2.

Decision criterion: Reject randomness if the test statistic z is

- less than or equal to the negative critical z score (such as -1.96)

or

- greater than or equal to the positive critical z score (such as 1.96).

Example 1   **Small Sample: NBA Champs**

Listed below are the most recent (as of this writing) winners of the NBA basketball championship game. The letter W denotes a winner from the Western Conference, and E denotes a winner from the Eastern Conference. Use a 0.05 significance level to test for randomness in the sequence.

E   E   W   W   W   W   W   E   W   E   W   E   W   W   W

Solution

Requirement check (1) The data are arranged in order. (2) Each data value is categorized into one of two separate categories (Western/Eastern). The requirements are satisfied. ⊘

We will follow the procedure summarized in Figure 13-6. The sequence of two characteristics (Western/Eastern) has been identified. We must now find the values of n_1, n_2, and the number of runs G. The sequence is shown below with spacing used to better identify the separate runs.

E E   W W W W W   E   W   E   W   E   W W W
1st run   2nd run   3rd run 4th run 5th run 6th run 7th run   8th run

continued

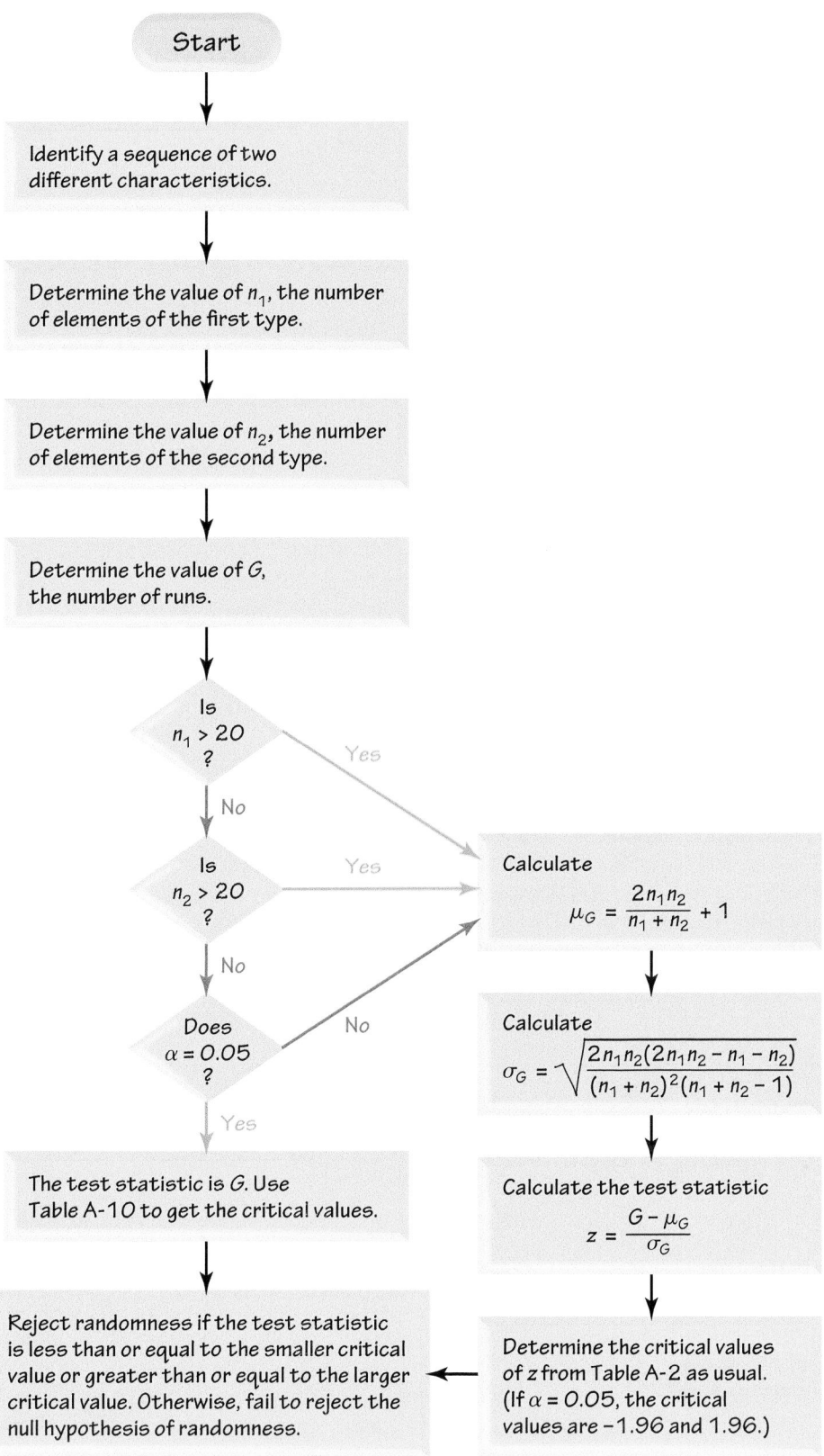

Figure 13-6   **Procedure for Runs Test for Randomness**

Is the iPod Random Shuffle Really Random?

In *The Guardian*, Steven Levy wrote about an interview with Steve Jobs, CEO of Apple, in which he presented Jobs with this dilemma: "I have a situation with my iPod. The shuffle function just doesn't seem random. Some artists come up way too much and some don't come up at all." According to Jeff Robbin, a head of the iTunes development team, "It is absolutely unequivocally random." Mathematician John Allen Paulos said that "[w]e often interpret and impose patterns on events that are random." Levy goes on to state that when we think that the iPod shuffle is not random, the problem is in our perceptions. Our minds perceive patterns and trends that don't really exist. We often hear runs of consecutive songs by the same artist and think that this is not random, but with true randomness, such consecutive runs are much more likely than we would expect.

The incorrect perception of nonrandomness caused Apple to introduce a "smart shuffle" feature in a new version of iTunes. This feature allows users to control multiple consecutive songs by the same artist. With this feature, consecutive runs by the same

artist would be avoided. According to Steve Jobs, "We're making it less random to make it feel more random."

From the display above we can see that there are 5 Eastern Conference winners and 10 Western Conference winners, and the number of runs is 8. We therefore have

$$n_1 = \text{number of Eastern Conference winners} = 5$$
$$n_2 = \text{number of Western Conference winners} = 10$$
$$G = \text{number of runs} = 8$$

Because $n_1 \leq 20$ and $n_2 \leq 20$ and the significance level is $\alpha = 0.05$, the test statistic is $G = 8$ (the number of runs), and we refer to Table A-10 to find the critical values of 3 and 12. Because $G = 8$ is neither less than or equal to the critical value of 3, nor is it greater than or equal to the critical value of 12, *we do not reject randomness.* There is not sufficient evidence to reject randomness in the sequence of winners. Randomness cannot be rejected.

Numerical Data: Randomness Above and Below the Mean or Median In Example 1 we tested for randomness in the sequence of data that clearly fit into two categories. We can also test for randomness in the way numerical data fluctuate above or below a mean or median. To test for randomness above and below the median, for example, use the sample data to find the value of the median, then replace each individual value with the letter A if it is *above* the median and replace it with B if it is *below* the median. Delete any values that are equal to the median. It is helpful to write the A's and B's directly above or below the numbers they represent because this makes checking easier and also reduces the chance of having the wrong number of letters. After finding the sequence of A and B letters, we can proceed to apply the runs test as described earlier. Economists use the runs test for randomness above and below the median to identify trends or cycles. An upward economic trend would contain a predominance of B's at the beginning and A's at the end, so the number of runs would be very small. A downward trend would have A's dominating at the beginning and B's at the end, with a small number of runs. A cyclical pattern would yield a sequence that systematically changes, so the number of runs would tend to be large.

| **Example 2** | Testing Randomness Above and Below the Median |

Listed below are the consecutive annual high values of the Dow Jones Industrial Average for the 1990s. Use a 0.05 significance level to test for randomness above and below the median.

3000	3169	3413	3794	3978	5216	6561	8259	9374	11,568
↓	↓	↓	↓	↓	↓	↓	↓	↓	↓
B	B	B	B	B	A	A	A	A	A

| **Solution** |

Requirement check (1) The data are arranged in order. (2) Each data value is categorized into one of two separate categories (below the median or above the median). The requirements are satisfied. ✓

The median of the listed sample values is 4597.0. We denote a value *below* the median of 4597.0 by B (below) and we denote a value *above* the median by A (above). If there had been any values equal to the median, they would have been deleted. The sequence of B's and A's is shown below the sample values. That sequence has 5 B's, so $n_1 = 5$. The sequence has 5 A's, so $n_2 = 5$. There are 2 runs, so $G = 2$.

Because $n_1 \leq 20$ and $n_2 \leq 20$ and the significance level is $\alpha = 0.05$, the test statistic is $G = 2$ (the number of runs), and we refer to Table A-10 to find the critical values of 2 and 10. Because $G = 2$ is less than or equal to the critical value of 2 (or it is greater than or equal to 10), we *reject the null hypothesis of randomness*. Because all of the values below the median occur in the beginning of the sequence and all values above the median occur at the end, it appears that there is an upward trend in the Dow Jones Industrial Average.

Example 3 Large Sample: Randomness of Study Subjects

Data Set 3 in Appendix B lists data from 107 study subjects. Let's consider the sequence of the listed genders indicated below. (The complete list of 107 genders can be seen in Data Set 3.) Use a 0.05 significance level to test the claim that the sequence is random.

M M M M M M M M M M M M M M M M M M M F F . . . M M M M M

Solution

Requirement check (1) The data are arranged in order. (2) Each data value is categorized into one of two separate categories (male/female). The requirements are satisfied. ✓

The null and alternative hypotheses are as follows:

H_0: The sequence is random.

H_1: The sequence is not random.

Examination of the sequence of 107 genders results in these values:

$$n_1 = \text{number of males} = 92$$
$$n_2 = \text{number of females} = 15$$
$$G = \text{number of runs} = 25$$

Since $n_1 > 20$, we need to calculate the test statistic z. We must first evaluate μ_G and σ_G as follows:

$$\mu_G = \frac{2n_1n_2}{n_1 + n_2} + 1 = \frac{2(92)(15)}{92 + 15} + 1 = 26.7944$$

$$\sigma_G = \sqrt{\frac{(2n_1n_2)(2n_1n_2 - n_1 - n_2)}{(n_1 + n_2)^2(n_1 + n_2 - 1)}}$$

$$= \sqrt{\frac{(2)(92)(15)\left[2(92)(15) - 92 - 15\right]}{(92 + 15)^2(92 + 15 - 1)}} = 2.45633$$

We now find the test statistic:

$$z = \frac{G - \mu_G}{\sigma_G} = \frac{25 - 26.7944}{2.45633} = -0.73$$

Because the significance level is $\alpha = 0.05$ and we have a two-tailed test, the critical values are $z = -1.96$ and $z = 1.96$. The test statistic of $z = -0.73$ does not fall within the critical region, so we fail to reject the null hypothesis of randomness. The given sequence appears to be random.

Interpretation

We can't reject the claim that the sequence of 107 genders listed in Data Set 3 of Appendix B is random. The runs test does not address the issue that there are 92 males and 15 females, so the selection process does not appear to be a random selection of members from the general population.

using TECHNOLOGY

STATDISK First determine the values of n_1, n_2, and the number of runs G. Select **Analysis** from the main menu bar, then select **Runs Test** and enter the required data in the dialog box. The STATDISK display will include the test statistic (G or z as appropriate), and critical values.

MINITAB Minitab will do a runs test with a sequence of numerical data only, but see the *Minitab Student Laboratory Manual and Workbook* for ways to circumvent that constraint. Enter numerical data in column C1, then select **Stat, Nonparametrics,** and **Runs Test.** In the dialog box, enter C1 for the variable, then

choose to test either for randomness above and below the mean or enter a value to be used. Click **OK.** The Minitab results include the number of runs and the P-value.

EXCEL Excel is not programmed for the runs test for randomness.

TI-83/84 PLUS The TI-83/84 plus calculator is not programmed for the runs test for randomness.

STATCRUNCH StatCrunch is not yet programmed for the runs test for randomness.

13-7 Basic Skills and Concepts

Statistical Literacy and Critical Thinking

1. Testing for Bias The last 106 baseball seasons (as of this writing) ended with 62 World Series wins by American League teams and 44 wins by National League teams. Can the runs test be used to show that the American League is better because disproportionately more World Series contests are won by American League teams?

2. Notation Listed below are the most recent (as of this writing) winners of the NBA basketball championship game. The letter W denotes a winner from the Western Conference, and E denotes the winner is from the Eastern Conference. Use that sequence to identify the values of n_1, n_2, and G that would be used in the runs test for randomness.

W W E E E E W W W W W E W E W E W W W

3. Runs Test If we use a 0.05 significance level to test for randomness of the sequence given in Exercise 2, we conclude that there is not sufficient evidence to reject randomness.

a. Rearrange the sequence so that randomness is rejected because the number of runs is very low.

b. Rearrange the sequence so that randomness is rejected because the number of runs is very high.

4. Good Sample? Given a sequence of data, such as the one from Exercise 2, if we fail to reject the claim that the sequence appears to be random, does it follow that the sampling method is suitable for statistical methods? Explain.

Using the Runs Test for Randomness. *In Exercises 5–10, use the runs test with a significance level of $\alpha = 0.05$. (All data are listed in order by row.)*

5. Testing for Randomness of Presidential Election Winners The political parties of the winning candidates for a recent sequence of presidential elections are listed below.

D denotes Democratic party and R denotes Republican party. Does it appear that we elect Democrat and Republican candidates in a sequence that is not random?

R R D R D R R R D D R R R D D D

D D R R D D R R D R R R D D R R D

6. Odd and Even Digits in Pi A *New York Times* article about the calculation of decimal places of π noted that "mathematicians are pretty sure that the digits of π are indistinguishable from any random sequence." Given below are the first 30 decimal places of π. Test for randomness of odd (O) and even (E) digits.

1 4 1 5 9 2 6 5 3 5 8 9 7 9 3 2 3 8 4 6 2 6 4 3 3 8 3 2 7 9

7. Draft Lottery In 1970, a lottery was used to determine who would be drafted into the U.S. Army. The 366 dates in the year were placed in individual capsules, they were mixed, then capsules were selected to identify birth dates of men to be drafted first. The first 30 results are listed below. Test for randomness before and after the middle of the year, which is July 1.

Sept. 14   Apr. 24   Dec. 30   Feb. 14   Oct. 18   Sept. 6   Oct. 26   Sept. 7   Nov. 22
Dec. 6   Aug 31   Dec. 7   July 8   Apr. 11   July 12   Dec. 29   Jan. 15   Sept. 26
Nov. 1   June 4   Aug. 10   June 26   July 24   Oct. 5   Feb. 19   Dec. 14   July 21
June 5   Mar. 2   Mar. 31

8. Newspapers Media experts claim that daily newspapers are declining because of Internet access. Listed below are the numbers of daily newspapers in the United States for a recent sequence of 20 years. Shown below those numbers are letters indicating whether the number is above (A) the median of 1514.5 or below (B) that median. Test for randomness of the numbers above and below the median. What do the results suggest?

1645 1642 1626 1611 1586 1570 1556 1548 1533 1520 1509 1489 1483 1480 1468 1457 1456 1457 1452 1437
↓ ↓ ↓ ↓ ↓ ↓ ↓ ↓ ↓ ↓ ↓ ↓ ↓ ↓ ↓ ↓ ↓ ↓ ↓ ↓
A A A A A A A A A A B B B B B B B B B B

Runs Test with Large Samples. *In Exercises 9–12, use the runs test with a significance level of α = 0.05. (All data are listed in order by row.)*

9. Testing for Randomness of Super Bowl Victories Listed below are the conference designations of teams that won the Super Bowl, where N denotes a team from the NFC and A denotes a team from the AFC. Do the results suggest that either conference is superior?

N N A A A N A A A A A N A A N N A N N N N N N N N N
N N A A N A A N A A A A A N A N N

10. Baseball World Series Victories Test the claim that the sequence of World Series wins by American League and National League teams is random. Given below are recent results (as of this writing), with American League and National League teams represented by A and N, respectively.

A N A N N N A A A A N A A A A N A N N A A N N A
A A A N A N N A A A A A N A N A N A N A A A A A
A A N N A N A N N A A N N N A N A N A N A N A A A N
N A A N N N N A A A N A N A N A A A A N A N A A A
N A N A A N A N A N

11. Stock Market: Testing for Randomness Above and Below the Median Listed below are the annual high values of the Dow Jones Industrial Average for a recent sequence of years (as of this writing). Test for randomness below and above the median. What does the result suggest about the stock market as an investment consideration?

969	995	943	985	969	842	951	1036	1052	892	882	1015
1000	908	898	1000	1024	1071	1287	1287	1553	1956	2722	2184
2791	3000	3169	3413	3794	3978	5216	6561	8259	9374	11568	11401
11350	10635	10454	10855	10941	12464	14198	13279	10580	11625		

12. Global Warming Listed below are global mean temperatures (°C) of the earth for 50 recent and consecutive years (based on data from the Goddard Institute for Space Studies). Test for randomness above and below the mean. What do the results suggest about global warming?

13.98	14.10	14.05	14.03	13.65	13.75	13.93	13.98	13.91	14.00
14.04	13.90	13.95	14.18	13.94	13.98	13.79	14.16	14.07	14.13
14.27	14.40	14.10	14.34	14.16	14.13	14.19	14.35	14.42	14.28
14.49	14.44	14.16	14.18	14.31	14.47	14.36	14.40	14.71	14.44
14.41	14.56	14.70	14.64	14.60	14.77	14.64	14.66	14.68	14.70

13-7 Beyond the Basics

13. Finding Critical Values

a. Using all of the elements A, A, A, B, B, B, B, B, B, list the 84 different possible sequences.

b. Find the number of runs for each of the 84 sequences.

c. Use the results from parts (a) and (b) to find your own critical values for G.

d. Compare your results to those given in Table A-10.

Chapter 13   Review

This chapter introduced six different nonparametric tests, which are also called distribution-free tests because they do not require that the populations have a particular distribution, such as a normal distribution. Nonparametric tests are not as efficient as parametric tests, so we generally need stronger evidence before we reject a null hypothesis.

Table 13-9 lists the nonparametric tests presented in this chapter, along with their functions. The table also lists the corresponding parametric tests.

Table 13-9 Summary of Nonparametric Tests

	Function	Parametric Test
Sign test (Section 13-2)	Test for claimed value of average with one sample	*t* test or *z* test (Section 8-4)
	Test of differences between matched pairs	*t* test (Section 9-4)
	Test for claimed value of a proportion	*z* test (Section 8-3)

continued

	Function	Parametric Test
Wilcoxon signed-ranks test (Section 13-3)	Test of differences between matched pairs	*t* test (Section 9-4)
Wilcoxon rank-sum test (Section 13-4)	Test for difference between two independent samples	*t* test or *z* test (Section 9-3)
Kruskal-Wallis test (Section 13-5)	Test that three or more independent populations have the same average	Analysis of variance (Section 12-2)
Rank correlation (Section 13-6)	Test for correlation between two variables	Linear correlation (Section 10-2)
Runs test (Section 13-7)	Test for randomness of sample data	No parametric test

Chapter Quick Quiz

1. Nonparametric Tests Which of the following terms is sometimes used instead of "non-parametric test": *normality test; abnormality test; distribution-free test; last testament; test of patience?*

2. Presidents Four of the nonparametric methods in this chapter use ranks of data. Find the ranks corresponding to these ages at inauguration of the first five presidents of the United States: 57, 61, 57, 57, 58.

3. Efficiency What does it mean when we say that the rank correlation test has an efficiency rating of 0.91 when compared to the parametric test for linear correlation?

4. Platelets Measures of blood platelet counts are obtained for random samples of females and males, and the results are listed below (based on Data Set 1 in Appendix B). Platelet counts for males and females can be compared by using the Wilcoxon rank-sum test for independent samples. Why is the Wilcoxon rank-sum test called a *distribution-free* test?

Female	317	224	248	309	335	278	312	338	290	236	310
Male	409	187	250	273	278	279	237	200	209	203	206

5. Runs Test Assume that we want to use the runs test to test the claim that the odd and even numbers occur randomly in the platelet counts for females listed in Exercise 4. Find the number of runs *G*.

6. Runs Test and the DJIA When applying the runs test for randomness above and below the median for the 10 annual high values of the Dow Jones Industrial Average, the test statistic is $G = 2$. What does that value tell us about the data?

7. Which Tests? Assume that the platelet counts in Exercise 4 are from 11 pairs of fraternal twins. Which method(s) of this chapter can be used to test the claim that for such pairs of twins, there is no difference in platelet counts?

8. Which Tests? Assume that the platelet counts in Exercise 4 are from 11 pairs of fraternal twins. Which method(s) of this chapter can be used to test the claim that for such pairs of twins, there is a relationship between the female platelet counts and the male platelet counts?

9. Which Tests? Four different judges each rank the quality of 20 different California wines. What method of this chapter can be used to test for agreement among the four judges?

10. Sign Test Identify three different applications of the sign test.

Review Exercises

Using Nonparametric Tests. *In Exercises 1–10, use a 0.05 significance level with the indicated test. If no particular test is specified, use the appropriate nonparametric test from this chapter.*

1. World Series The last 106 baseball seasons (as of this writing) ended with 62 World Series wins by American League teams, compared to 44 wins by National League teams. Use the sign test with a 0.05 significance level to test the claim that in each World Series, the American League team has a 0.5 probability of winning.

2. Airline Fares Listed below are the costs (in dollars) of flights from New York (JFK) to San Francisco for US Air, Virgin America, Delta, American, Continental, United, and Alaska. Use the sign test with a 0.05 significance level to test the claim that there is no difference in cost between flights scheduled 1 day in advance and those scheduled 30 days in advance. What appears to be a wise scheduling strategy?

Flight scheduled one day in advance	475	438	882	474	475	540	2909
Flight scheduled 30 days in advance	236	157	166	182	166	166	240

3. Airline Fares Refer to the same data from Exercise 2. Use a 0.05 significance level with the Wilcoxon signed-ranks test to test the claim that differences between fares for flights scheduled 1 day in advance and those scheduled 30 days in advance have a median equal to 0. What do the results suggest?

4. Randomness Refer to the following ages at inauguration of the elected presidents of the United States (from Data Set 12 in Appendix B). Test for randomness above and below the mean. Do the results suggest an upward trend or a downward trend?

57 61 57 57 58 57 61 54 68 49 64 48 65 52 46 54 49 47
55 54 42 51 56 55 51 54 51 60 62 43 55 56 52 69 64 46
54 47

5. Student and *U.S. News and World Report* Rankings of Colleges Each year, *U.S. News and World Report* publishes rankings of colleges based on statistics such as admission rates, graduation rates, class size, faculty–student ratio, faculty salaries, and peer ratings of administrators. Economists Christopher Avery, Mark Glickman, Caroline Minter Hoxby, and Andrew Metrick took an alternative approach of analyzing the college choices of 3240 high-achieving school seniors. They examined the colleges that offered admission along with the colleges that the students chose to attend. The table below lists rankings for a small sample of colleges. Find the value of the rank correlation coefficient and use it to determine whether there is a correlation between the student rankings and the rankings of the magazine.

Student ranks	1	2	3	4	5	6	7	8
U.S. News and World Report ranks	1	2	5	4	7	6	3	8

6. Accuracy of Weather Forecasts The author conducted a study of the accuracy of weather forecasts by recording the actual high temperatures along with the high temperatures that were forecast 5 days earlier. Differences (actual minus forecast) for 35 days are listed below. Use a 0.05 significance level with the sign test to test the claim that the population of differences has a median of zero. What do the results suggest about the accuracy of the forecasts?

```
  0  -3   2   5  -6  -9   4  -1   6  -2  -2  -1   6  -4  -3   0  -1  -12
-14  -1   3   9   6  -3   3   5   4  -7  -6  -7   1   0  -1  10  -6
```

7. Accuracy of Weather Forecasts Repeat the preceding exercise using the Wilcoxon signed-ranks test.

8. Archeology Listed below are skull breadths obtained from skulls of Egyptian males from three different epochs (based on data from *Ancient Races of the Thebaid,* by Thomson and Randall-Maciver). Use a 0.05 significance level to test the claim that the samples are from populations with the same median. Changes in head shape over time suggest that interbreeding occurred with immigrant populations. Is interbreeding of cultures suggested by the data?

4000 B.C.	125	129	131	132	132	134	135	138	138
1850 B.C.	129	129	134	134	136	137	137	138	136
150 A.D.	128	136	137	137	138	139	141	142	145

9. Archeology Refer to the preceding exercise and use only the skull breadths from 4000 B.C. and 150 A.D. Use the Wilcoxon rank-sum test with a 0.05 significance level to test the claim that the two samples are from populations with the same median.

10. Garbage The table below lists weights (lb) of plastic and food disposed in one week (from Data Set 23 in Appendix B). Use rank correlation with a 0.05 significance level to test for a correlation between weights of plastic and weights of food.

Plastic	0.27	1.41	2.19	2.83	2.19	1.81	0.85	3.05	3.42	2.10	2.93	2.44
Food	1.04	3.68	4.43	2.98	6.30	1.46	8.82	9.62	4.41	2.73	9.31	3.59

Cumulative Review Exercises

Please be aware that some of the following problems may require knowledge of concepts presented in previous chapters.
In Exercises 1–5, use the data listed below. The values are the numbers of credit hours taken in the current semester by full-time students of the author.

15 15 13 16 12 15 18 16 15 14 16 15 17 12 15 15 14 14 12 12

1. Descriptive Statistics Find the mean, median, standard deviation, variance, and range of the sample data. Given that the data are in hours, include the appropriate units in the results.

2. Sampling and Data Type

a. Which of the following best describes the sample: simple random sample, voluntary response sample, convenience sample?

b. Is it likely that the sample is representative of the population of all full-time college students?

c. Are the data discrete or continuous?

d. What is the level of measurement of the data (nominal, ordinal, interval, ratio)?

3. Credit Hours: Hypothesis Test Use the given data to test the claim that the sample is from a population with a mean greater than 14 hours.

4. Credit Hours: Sign Test Use the given data to test the claim that the sample is from a population with a median greater than 14 hours. Use the sign test with a 0.05 significance level.

5. Credit Hours: Confidence Interval Use the data to construct a 95% confidence interval estimate of the number of credit hours taken by the population of full-time students. Write a brief statement that interprets the result.

6. 3D TVs Listed below are prices (dollars), quality scores, and ranks (1 = best) for six different 3D televisions (based on data from *Consumer Reports*). Use a 0.05 significance level to test for a linear correlation between price and quality score. Do you get more quality by paying more?

Price	1350	1900	3600	1800	900	950
Quality score	81	74	74	71	70	69
Rank	1	2	3	4	5	6

7. 3D TVs Refer to the prices and ranks from the preceding exercise. Use a 0.05 significance level to test for a correlation between price and rank.

8. Subway Survey In a study of 740 pay telephones in New York City underground subway stations, it was found the 229 were not functioning (based on data from NYPIRG Straphangers Campaign). Construct a 95% confidence interval estimate of the proportion of all such pay telephones that are not functioning. Based on the result, what can we conclude about a claim that 25% of all such telephones are not functioning?

9. Sample Size Advances in technology are dramatically affecting different aspects of our lives. For example, the number of daily newspapers is decreasing because of easy access to Internet and television news. To help address such issues, we want to estimate the percentage of adults in the United States who use a computer at least once each day. Find the sample size needed to estimate that percentage. Assume that we want 90% confidence that the sample percentage is within two percentage points of the true population percentage.

10. Cell Phones and Crashes: Analyzing Newspaper Report In an article from the Associated Press, it was reported that researchers "randomly selected 100 New York motorists who had been in an accident and 100 who had not been in an accident. Of those in accidents, 13.7 percent owned a cellular phone, while just 10.6 percent of the accident-free drivers had a phone in the car." What is wrong with these results?

Technology Project

Past attempts to identify or contact extraterrestrial intelligent life have involved efforts to send radio messages carrying information about us earthlings. Dr. Frank Drake of Cornell University developed such a radio message that could be transmitted as a series of pulses and gaps. The pulses and gaps can be thought of as 1s and 0s. Listed below is a message consisting of 77 0s and 1s. If we factor 77 into the prime numbers of 7 and 11 and then make an 11 $\times$ 7 grid and put a dot at those positions corresponding to a pulse of 1, we can get a simple picture of something. Assume that the sequence of 77 1s and 0s is sent as a radio message that is intercepted by extraterrestrial life with enough intelligence to have studied this book. If the radio message is tested using the methods of this chapter, will the sequence appear to be "random noise" or will it be identified as a pattern that is not random? Also, construct the image represented by the digits and identify it.

```
0  0  1  1  1  0  0  0  0  1  1  1  0  0  0  0  0  1  0  0  0
1  1  1  1  1  1  1  0  0  1  1  1  0  0  0  0  1  1  1  0  0
0  0  1  1  1  0  0  0  1  0  0  0  1  0  1  0  0  0  0  1  0
1  0  0  0  0  1  0  1  0  0  0  0  1  0
```

from data TO DECISION

Critical Thinking:
Was the draft lottery random?

In 1970, a lottery was used to determine who would be drafted into the U.S. Army. The 366 dates in the year were placed in individual capsules. First, the 31 January capsules were placed in a box; then the 29 February capsules were added and the two months were mixed. Then the 31 March capsules were added and the three months were mixed. This process continued until all months were included. The first capsule selected was September 14, so men born on that date were drafted first. The accompanying list shows the 366 dates in the order of selection.

Analyzing the Results

a. Use the runs test to test the sequence for randomness above and below the median of 183.5.

b. Use the Kruskal-Wallis test to test the claim that the 12 months had priority numbers drawn from the same population.

c. Calculate the 12 monthly means. Then plot those 12 means on a graph.

(The horizontal scale lists the 12 months, and the vertical scale ranges from 100 to 260.) Note any pattern suggesting that the original priority numbers were not randomly selected.

d. Based on the results from parts (a), (b), and (c), decide whether this particular draft lottery was fair. Write a statement explaining why you believe that it was or was not fair. If you decided that this lottery was unfair, describe a process for selecting lottery numbers that would have been fair.

Jan:	305	159	251	215	101	224	306	199	194	325	329	221	318	238	017	121
	235	140	058	280	186	337	118	059	052	092	355	077	349	164	211	
Feb:	086	144	297	210	214	347	091	181	338	216	150	068	152	004	089	212
	189	292	025	302	363	290	057	236	179	365	205	299	285			
Mar:	108	029	267	275	293	139	122	213	317	323	136	300	259	354	169	166
	033	332	200	239	334	265	256	258	343	170	268	223	362	217	030	
Apr:	032	271	083	081	269	253	147	312	219	218	014	346	124	231	273	148
	260	090	336	345	062	316	252	002	351	340	074	262	191	208		
May:	330	298	040	276	364	155	035	321	197	065	037	133	295	178	130	055
	112	278	075	183	250	326	319	031	361	357	296	308	226	103	313	
Jun:	249	228	301	020	028	110	085	366	335	206	134	272	069	356	180	274
	073	341	104	360	060	247	109	358	137	022	064	222	353	209		
Jul:	093	350	115	279	188	327	050	013	277	284	248	015	042	331	322	120
	098	190	227	187	027	153	172	023	067	303	289	088	270	287	193	
Aug:	111	045	261	145	054	114	168	048	106	021	324	142	307	198	102	044
	154	141	311	344	291	339	116	036	286	245	352	167	061	333	011	
Sep:	225	161	049	232	082	006	008	184	263	071	158	242	175	001	113	207
	255	246	177	063	204	160	119	195	149	018	233	257	151	315		
Oct:	359	125	244	202	024	087	234	283	342	220	237	072	138	294	171	254
	288	005	241	192	243	117	201	196	176	007	264	094	229	038	079	
Nov:	019	034	348	266	310	076	051	097	080	282	046	066	126	127	131	107
	143	146	203	185	156	009	182	230	132	309	047	281	099	174		
Dec:	129	328	157	165	056	010	012	105	043	041	039	314	163	026	320	096
	304	128	240	135	070	053	162	095	084	173	078	123	016	003	100	

Cooperative Group Activities

1. Out-of-class activity All students should make up results for 200 coin flips. Then use the runs test to determine whether the results appear to be random.

2. In-class activity Use the existing seating arrangement in your class and apply the runs test to determine whether the students are arranged randomly according to gender. After recording the seating arrangement, analysis can be done in subgroups of three or four students.

3. In-class activity Divide into groups of 8 to 12 people. For each group member, *measure* his or her height and *measure* his or her arm span. For the arm span, the subject should stand with arms extended, like the wings on an airplane. Divide the following tasks among subgroups of three or four people.

a. Use rank correlation with the paired sample data to determine whether there is a correlation between height and arm span.

b. Use the sign test to test for a difference between the two variables.

c. Use the Wilcoxon signed-ranks test to test for a difference between the two variables.

4. In-class activity Do Activity 3 using pulse rate instead of arm span. Measure pulse rates by counting the number of heartbeats in 1 min.

5. Out-of-class activity Divide into groups of three or four students. Investigate the relationship between two variables by collecting your own paired sample data and using the methods of Section 13-6 to determine whether there is a correlation. Suggested topics:

• Is there a correlation between taste and cost of different brands of chocolate chip cookies (or colas)? (Taste can be measured on some number scale, such as 1 to 10.)

• Is there a correlation between salaries of professional baseball (or basketball or football) players and their season achievements (such as batting average or points scored)?

• Rates versus weights: Is there a correlation between car fuel-consumption rates and car weights?

• Is there a correlation between the lengths of men's (or women's) feet and their heights?

• Is there a correlation between student grade point averages and the amount of television watched?

• Is there a correlation between heights of fathers (or mothers) and heights of their first sons (or daughters)?

6. Out-of-class activity See this chapter's "From Data to Decision" project, which involves analysis of the 1970 lottery used for drafting men into the U.S. Army. Because the 1970 results raised concerns about the randomness of selecting draft priority numbers, design a new procedure for generating the 366 priority numbers. Use your procedure to generate the 366 numbers and test your results using the techniques suggested in parts (a), (b), and (c) of the "From Data to Decision" project. How do your results compare to those obtained in 1970? Does your random selection process appear to be better than the one used in 1970? Write a report that clearly describes the process you designed. Also include your analyses and conclusions.

7. Out-of-class activity Divide into groups of three or four. Survey other students by asking them to identify their major and gender. For each surveyed subject, determine the accuracy of the time on his or her wristwatch. First set your own watch to the correct time using an accurate and reliable source ("At the tone, the time is . . ."). For watches that are ahead of the correct time, record negative times. For watches that are behind the correct time, record positive times. Use the sample data to address these questions:

• Do the errors appear to be the same for both genders?

• Do the errors appear to be the same for the different majors?

8. In-class activity Divide into groups of 8 to 12 people. For each group member, measure the person's height and also measure his or her navel height, which is the height from the floor to the navel. Use the rank correlation coefficient to determine whether there is a correlation between height and navel height.

9. In-class activity Divide into groups of three or four people. Appendix B includes many data sets not yet addressed by the methods of this chapter. Search Appendix B for variables of interest, then investigate using appropriate methods of nonparametric statistics. State your conclusions and try to identify practical applications.

10. Out-of-class activity Divide into groups of three or four, with at least one member of each group having an iPod. Establish two categories of songs, such as those by males or females, then test the sequence of iPod songs for randomness.

14 Statistical Process Control

chapter problem

Minting Quarters: Is the manufacturing process of minting quarters out of control?

Congress created the United States Mint when it passed the Coinage Act in 1792, so the Mint has been manufacturing coins for well over 200 years. When the Thomas Adams Gum Company brought vending machines to the United States in 1888, a perfect marriage was formed between coins and various consumer products. Vending machines are designed to reject coins that vary too much from the Mint's target weight of 5.670 g for quarters. This is one of many reasons why it is important to maintain good quality control in the manufacture of quarters.

Principles of statistical process control are routinely used by the Mint and other businesses to monitor the quality of the goods they produce and the services they provide. This Chapter Problem involves the current process of manufacturing quarters. Table 14-1 lists the weight (grams) of quarters selected during each of the first 5 hours of production on each of 20 consecutive days. These quarters are from a new, streamlined production process that is being tested, and we need to determine whether this new process is functioning as it should.

Table 14-1 Weights (grams) of Minted Quarters

Day	Hour 1	Hour 2	Hour 3	Hour 4	Hour 5	$\bar{x}$	s	Range
1	5.543	5.698	5.605	5.653	5.668	5.6334	0.0607	0.155
2	5.585	5.692	5.771	5.718	5.720	5.6972	0.0689	0.186
3	5.752	5.636	5.660	5.680	5.565	5.6586	0.0679	0.187
4	5.697	5.613	5.575	5.615	5.646	5.6292	0.0455	0.122
5	5.630	5.770	5.713	5.649	5.650	5.6824	0.0581	0.140
6	5.807	5.647	5.756	5.677	5.761	5.7296	0.0657	0.160
7	5.686	5.691	5.715	5.748	5.688	5.7056	0.0264	0.062
8	5.681	5.699	5.767	5.736	5.752	5.7270	0.0361	0.086
9	5.552	5.659	5.770	5.594	5.607	5.6364	0.0839	0.218
10	5.818	5.655	5.660	5.662	5.700	5.6990	0.0689	0.163
11	5.693	5.692	5.625	5.750	5.757	5.7034	0.0535	0.132
12	5.637	5.628	5.646	5.667	5.603	5.6362	0.0235	0.064
13	5.634	5.778	5.638	5.689	5.702	5.6882	0.0586	0.144
14	5.664	5.655	5.727	5.637	5.667	5.6700	0.0339	0.090
15	5.664	5.695	5.677	5.689	5.757	5.6964	0.0359	0.093
16	5.707	5.890	5.598	5.724	5.635	5.7108	0.1127	0.292
17	5.697	5.593	5.780	5.745	5.470	5.6570	0.1260	0.310
18	6.002	5.898	5.669	5.957	5.583	5.8218	0.1850	0.419
19	6.017	5.613	5.596	5.534	5.795	5.7110	0.1968	0.483
20	5.671	6.223	5.621	5.783	5.787	5.8170	0.2380	0.602

The last three columns of Table 14-1 list the mean, standard deviation, and range for the five coins selected on each day of production. We will analyze the data in Table 14-1 as we would analyze any process, such as the filling of cans of Coke, repairs of defective iPods, and processing flight passengers through security checkpoints.

Six Sigma at Textron

Textron is a large conglomerate with products that include Cessna jets, Bell helicopters, golf carts, and test instruments. It has annual revenues greater than $14 billion, and has 37,000 employees in 29 countries. Textron recently trained 10,000 employees in Six Sigma methods. The actual reference to Six Sigma suggests 6 standard deviations away from the center of a normal distribution, but the assumption of a perfectly stable process is replaced with the assumption of a process that drifts slightly, so the defect rate is so low that there are no more than three or four defects per million. Implementation of Six Sigma methods started around 1985, and their use has enabled companies to save billions of dollars.

14-1   Review and Preview

In Section 2-1 we noted that an important characteristic of data is a changing pattern over time. Some populations change over time so that values of parameters change. The main objective of this chapter is to learn how to construct and interpret *control charts* that can be used to monitor changing characteristics of data over time. That knowledge will better prepare us for work with businesses trying to maintain or improve the quality of their goods and services.

Minitab, StatCrunch, XLSTAT, and other software packages include programs for automatically generating charts of the type discussed in this chapter, and we will include examples of such displays. Control charts are good examples of visual tools that allow us to *see* and *understand* some properties of data that would be difficult or impossible to understand without graphs. The world needs more people who can construct and interpret graphs, such as the control charts described in this chapter.

14-2   Control Charts for Variation and Mean

Key Concept In this section we introduce run charts, R charts, and $\bar{x}$ charts as tools that enable us to monitor characteristics of data over time. We can use such charts to determine whether a process is statistically stable (or within statistical control).

The following definition formally describes the type of data that will be considered in this chapter.

> **DEFINITION** **Process data** are data arranged according to some time sequence. They are measurements of a characteristic of goods or services that result from some combination of equipment, people, materials, methods, and conditions.

Example 1   Weights of Quarters as Process Data

Table 14-1 includes process data consisting of the weights of manufactured quarters. Because the values in Table 14-1 are arranged according to the time at which they were selected, they are process data.

It is important to know that companies have gone bankrupt because they unknowingly allowed manufacturing processes to deteriorate without constant monitoring. They suffered from a failure to monitor process data. This section introduces three tools commonly used to monitor process data: run charts, R charts, and $\bar{x}$ charts. We begin with run charts.

Run Chart

A run chart is one of a few different tools commonly used to monitor a process to ensure that desired characteristics don't change.

> **DEFINITION** A **run chart** is a sequential plot of *individual* data values over time. One axis (usually the vertical axis) is used for the data values, and the other axis (usually the horizontal axis) is used for the time sequence.

Example 2 Run Chart of Weights of Quarters

Treating the 100 weights of quarters from Table 14-1 as a string of consecutive measurements, construct a run chart using a vertical axis for the weights and a horizontal axis to identify the chronological order of the weights.

Solution

Figure 14-1 is the Minitab-generated run chart for the data in Table 14-1. In Figure 14-1, the horizontal scale identifies the sample number, so the number 1 corresponds to the first coin, the number 2 corresponds to the second coin, and so on. The vertical scale represents the measured weight.

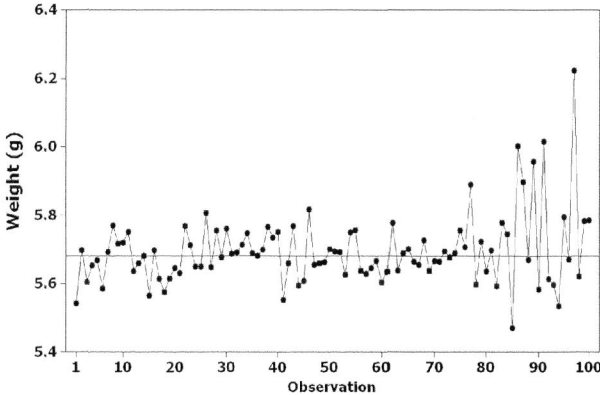

Figure 14-1   Run Chart

Interpretation

Examine Figure 14-1 and try to identify any *patterns*. From Figure 14-1 we see that as time progresses from left to right, the points appear to exhibit *greater variation*. If this pattern continues, some quarters will weigh too much while others will weigh too little. This pattern of increasing variation is a classic issue in quality control, and failure to recognize it has caused companies to go out of business.

> **DEFINITION** A process is **statistically stable** (or **within statistical control**) if it has only natural variation, with no patterns, cycles, or unusual points.

Interpreting Run Charts A run chart with no obvious pattern suggests that the data are from a process that is *statistically stable,* and the data can be treated as if they came from a population with a constant mean, standard deviation, distribution, and other characteristics. Figure 14-1 shows a pattern of increasing variation, and that is one of several criteria for determining that a process is not statistically stable.

- **Increasing Variation:** As the run chart proceeds from left to right, the vertical variation of the points is increasing, so the corresponding data values are experiencing an increase in variation. (See Figure 14-1.) This is a common problem in quality control. The net effect is that products vary more and more until almost all of them are worthless.

- **Upward Trend:** The points are rising from left to right, so the corresponding values are increasing over time.

- **Downward Trend:** The points are falling from left to right, so the corresponding values are decreasing over time.

- **Upward Shift:** The points near the beginning are noticeably lower than those near the end, so the corresponding values have shifted upward.

- **Downward Shift:** The points near the beginning are noticeably higher than those near the end, so the corresponding values have shifted downward.

- **Exceptional Value:** There is a single point that is exceptionally high or low.

- **Cyclical Pattern:** There is a *cyclical pattern* (or repeating cycle).

Many different methods of quality control attempt to *reduce variation* in the product or service. Variation in a process can result from two types of causes.

> **DEFINITIONS**
>
> **Random variation** is due to chance; it is the type of variation inherent in any process that is not capable of producing every good or service exactly the same way every time.
>
> **Assignable variation** results from causes that can be identified (such as defective machinery or untrained employees).

Later in the chapter we will consider ways to distinguish between assignable variation and random variation.

The run chart is one tool for monitoring the stability of a process. We will now consider *control charts,* which are also useful for monitoring the stability of a process.

Control Chart for Monitoring Variation: The *R* Chart

Because control charts were first introduced by Walter Shewhart in 1924, they are sometimes called Shewhart charts. We begin with a basic definition.

> **DEFINITIONS** A **control chart** (or **Shewhart chart** or **process-behavior chart**) of a process characteristic (such as mean or variation) consists of values plotted sequentially over time, and it includes a **centerline** as well as a **lower control limit** (LCL) and an **upper control limit** (UCL). The centerline represents a central value of the characteristic measurements, whereas the control limits are boundaries used to separate and identify any points considered to be *unusual*.

We will assume that the population standard deviation σ is not known as we now consider two of several different types of *control charts:*

1. R charts (or range charts) used to monitor variation

2. $\bar{x}$ charts used to monitor means

When using control charts to monitor a process, it is common to consider R charts and $\bar{x}$ charts together, because a statistically unstable process may be the result of increasing *variation,* changing *means,* or both.

An **R chart** (or **range chart**) is a plot of the sample ranges instead of individual sample values, and it is used to monitor the *variation* in a process. It might make more sense to use standard deviations, but range charts are quite effective for cases in which the size of the samples (or subgroups) is 10 or fewer. If the samples all have a size greater than 10, the use of an s chart is recommended instead of an R chart. (See Exercise 13.) In addition to plotting the values of the ranges, we include a centerline located at $\bar{R}$, which denotes the mean of all sample ranges, as well as another line for the lower control limit and a third line for the upper control limit. The following is a summary of notation and the components of the R chart.

Monitoring Process Variation: Control Chart for R

Objective

Construct a control chart for R (or an "R chart") that can be used to determine whether the *variation* of process data is within statistical control.

Requirements

1. The data are process data consisting of a sequence of samples all of the same size n.

2. The distribution of the process data is essentially normal.

3. The individual sample data values are independent.

Notation

$n =$ size of each sample, or *subgroup*

$\bar{R} =$ mean of the sample ranges (the sum of the sample ranges divided by the number of samples)

Graph

Points plotted: Sample ranges (one point representing the range for each sample or subgroup)

Centerline: $\bar{R}$ (the mean of the sample ranges)

Upper control limit (UCL): $D_4\bar{R}$ (where D_4 is found in Table 14-2)

Lower control limit (LCL): $D_3\bar{R}$ (where D_3 is found in Table 14-2)

Table 14-2 Control Chart Constants

n: Number of Observations in Subgroup	R Chart		$\bar{x}$ Chart		s Chart	
	D_3	D_4	A_2	A_3	B_3	B_4
2	0.000	3.267	1.880	2.659	0.000	3.267
3	0.000	2.574	1.023	1.954	0.000	2.568
4	0.000	2.282	0.729	1.628	0.000	2.266
5	**0.000**	**2.114**	**0.577**	**1.427**	**0.000**	**2.089**
6	0.000	2.004	0.483	1.287	0.030	1.970
7	0.076	1.924	0.419	1.182	0.118	1.882
8	0.136	1.864	0.373	1.099	0.185	1.815
9	0.184	1.816	0.337	1.032	0.239	1.761
10	0.223	1.777	0.308	0.975	0.284	1.716

Source: Adapted from *ASTM Manual on the Presentation of Data and Control Chart Analysis,* © 1976 ASTM, pp. 134–136. Reprinted with permission of American Society for Testing and Materials.

The values of D_4 and D_3 were computed by quality-control experts, and they are intended to simplify calculations. The upper and lower control limits of $D_4\bar{R}$ and $D_3\bar{R}$ are values that are roughly equivalent to 99.7% confidence interval limits. It is therefore highly unlikely that values from a statistically stable process would fall beyond those limits. If a value does fall beyond the control limits, it's very likely that the process is not statistically stable.

Example 3   R Chart of Weights of Quarters

Construct a control chart for R using the weights of quarters listed in Table 14-1. Use the samples of size $n = 5$ for each of the 20 days of production.

Solution

Refer to Table 14-1 to see that the sample ranges are listed in the last column. $\bar{R}$ is the mean of those 20 sample ranges, so its value is found as follows:

$$\bar{R} = \frac{0.155 + 0.186 + \cdots + 0.602}{20} = 0.2054$$

The centerline for our R chart is therefore located at $\bar{R} = 0.2054$. To find the upper and lower control limits, we must first find the values of D_3 and D_4. Referring to Table 14-2 for $n = 5$, we get $D_4 = 2.114$ and $D_3 = 0.000$, so the control limits are as follows:

Upper control limit: $D_4\bar{R} = (2.114)(0.2054) = 0.4342$
Lower control limit: $D_3\bar{R} = (0.000)(0.2054) = 0.0000$

Using a centerline value of $\bar{R} = 0.2054$ and control limits of 0.4342 and 0.0000, we now proceed to plot the 20 sample ranges as 20 individual points. The result is shown in the Minitab display shown on the following page.

R CHART

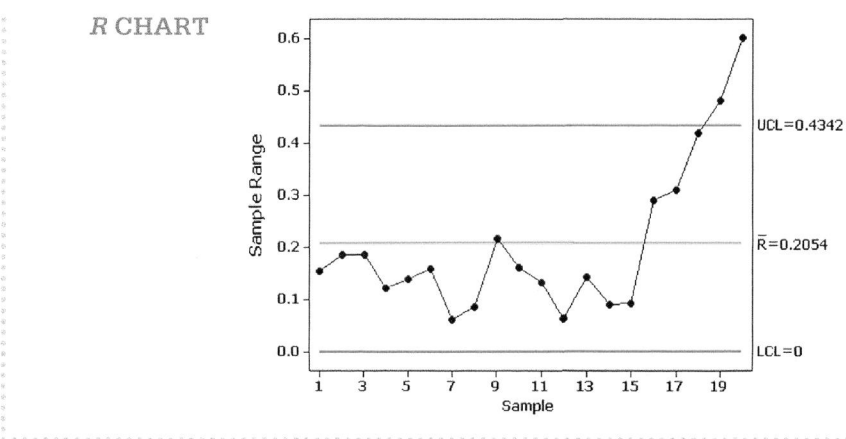

Interpreting Control Charts

When interpreting control charts, the following caution is important:

> **CAUTION** Upper and lower control limits of a control chart are based on the *actual* behavior of the process, not the *desired* behavior. Upper and lower control limits are totally unrelated to any process *specifications* that may have been decreed by the manufacturer.

When investigating the quality of some process, there are typically two key questions that need to be addressed:

1. Based on the current behavior of the process, can we conclude that the process is within statistical control?

2. Do the process goods or services meet design specifications?

The methods of this chapter are intended to address the first question, but not the second. That is, we are focusing on the behavior of the process with the objective of determining whether the process is within statistical control. Also, we should clearly understand the specific criteria for determining whether a process is in statistical control (that is, whether it is statistically stable). See the following criteria.

Criteria for Determining That a Process Is Not Statistically Stable (Out of Statistical Control)

1. There is a pattern, trend, or cycle that is obviously not random.

2. There is at least one point lying outside of the region between the upper and lower control limits. (There is at least one point above the upper control limit or at least one point below the lower control limit.)

3. *Run of 8 Rule:* There are at least eight consecutive points all above or all below the centerline. (With a statistically stable process, there is a 0.5 probability that a point will be above or below the centerline, so it is very unlikely that eight consecutive points will all be above the centerline or all below it.)

In this book we will use only the three out-of-control criteria listed above, but some businesses use additional criteria such as these:

- There are at least six consecutive points all increasing or all decreasing.

- There are at least fourteen consecutive points all alternating between up and down (such as up, down, up, down, and so on).

Costly Assignable Variation

The Mars Climate Orbiter was launched by NASA and sent to Mars, but it was destroyed when it flew too close to Mars. The loss was estimated at $125 million. The cause of the crash was found to be confusion between the use of units used for calculations. Acceleration data were provided in the English units of pounds of force, but the Jet Propulsion Laboratory assumed that those units were in metric "newtons" instead of pounds. The thrusters of the spacecraft subsequently provided wrong amounts of force in adjusting the position of the spacecraft. The errors caused by the discrepancy were fairly small at first, but the cumulative error over months of the spacecraft's journey proved to be fatal to its success.

In 1962, the rocket carrying the Mariner 1 satellite was destroyed by ground controllers when it went off course due to a missing minus sign in a computer program.

Don't Tamper!

Nashua Corp. had trouble with its paper-coating machine and considered spending a million dollars to replace it. The machine was working well with a stable process, but samples were taken every so often and, based on the results, adjustments were made. These overadjustments, called *tampering,* caused shifts away from the distribution that had been good. The effect was an increase in defects. When statistician and quality expert W. Edwards Deming studied the process, he recommended that no adjustments be made unless warranted by a signal that the process had shifted or had become unstable. The company was better off with no adjustments than with the tampering that took place.

- Two out of three consecutive points are beyond control limits that are 2 standard deviations away from the centerline.
- Four out of five consecutive points are beyond control limits that are 1 standard deviation away from the centerline.

Example 4 Interpreting R Chart of Weights of Quarters

Examine the R chart shown in the display for Example 3 and determine whether the process variation is within statistical control.

Solution

We can interpret control charts for R by applying the three out-of-control criteria just listed. Applying the three criteria to the display of the R chart, we conclude that variation in this process is not within statistical control. (1) Because the points at the end appear to show an upward trend, there is an obvious pattern that is not random. (2) The last two points are lying outside of the region between the upper and lower control limits. (3) The first eight points are eight consecutive points all lying below the centerline.

Interpretation

We conclude that the *variation* (not necessarily the mean) of the process is out of statistical control.

Control Chart for Monitoring Means: The $\bar{x}$ Chart

An $\bar{x}$ **chart** is a plot of the sample means, and it is used to monitor the *center* in a process. In addition to plotting the sample means, we include a centerline located at $\bar{\bar{x}}$, which denotes the mean of all sample means (equal to the mean of all sample values combined), as well as another line for the lower control limit and a third line for the upper control limit. Using the approach common in business and industry, the control limits are based on ranges instead of standard deviations. (See Exercise 14 for an $\bar{x}$ chart based on standard deviations.)

Monitoring Process Mean: Control Chart for $\bar{x}$

Objective

Construct a control chart for $\bar{x}$ (or an $\bar{x}$ chart) that can be used to determine whether the *center* of process data is within statistical control.

Requirements

1. The data are process data consisting of a sequence of samples all of the same size n.

2. The distribution of the process data is essentially normal.

3. The individual sample data values are independent.

Notation

n = size of each sample, or *subgroup*

$\bar{\bar{x}}$ = mean of all sample means (equal to the mean of all sample values combined)

Graph

Points plotted: Sample means

Centerline: $\bar{\bar{x}} = $ mean of all sample means

Upper control limit (UCL): $\bar{\bar{x}} + A_2\overline{R}$ (where A_2 is found in Table 14-2)

Lower control limit (LCL): $\bar{\bar{x}} - A_2\overline{R}$ (where A_2 is found in Table 14-2)

Example 5 $\bar{x}$ **Chart of Weights of Quarters**

Using the weights of quarters in Table 14-1 with samples of size $n = 5$ for each of 20 days, construct a control chart for $\bar{x}$. Based on the control chart for $\bar{x}$ only, determine whether the process mean is within statistical control.

Solution

Before plotting the 20 points corresponding to the 20 values of $\bar{x}$, we must first find the values for the centerline and control limits. We get

$$\bar{\bar{x}} = \frac{5.6334 + 5.6972 + \cdots + 5.8170}{20} = 5.6955$$

$$\overline{R} = \frac{0.155 + 0.186 + \cdots + 0.602}{20} = 0.2054$$

Referring to Table 14-2, we find that for $n = 5$, $A_2 = 0.577$. Knowing the values of $\bar{\bar{x}}$, A_2, and $\overline{R}$, we can now evaluate the control limits.

Upper control limit: $\bar{\bar{x}} + A_2\overline{R} = 5.6955 + (0.577)(0.2054) = 5.8140$

Lower control limit: $\bar{\bar{x}} - A_2\overline{R} = 5.6955 - (0.577)(0.2054) = 5.5770$

The resulting control chart for $\bar{x}$ will be as shown in the accompanying Minitab display.

$\bar{x}$ CHART

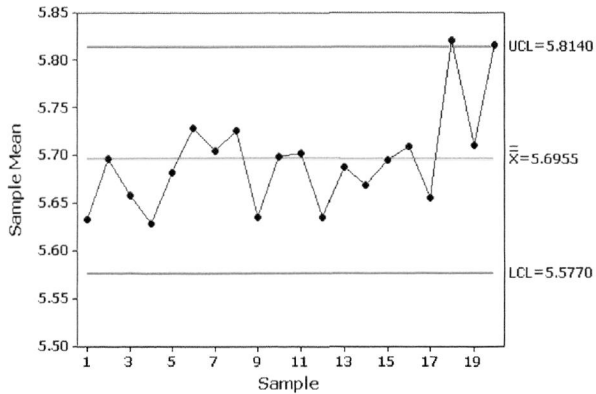

Interpretation

Examination of the $\bar{x}$ chart shows that the process mean is out of statistical control because at least one of the three out-of-control criteria is not satisfied. Specifically, the second criterion is violated because there are points lying beyond the control limits.

Bribery Detected with Control Charts

Control charts were used to help convict a person who bribed Florida jai alai players to lose. (See "Using Control Charts to Corroborate Bribery in Jai Alai," by Charnes and Gitlow, *The American Statistician,* Vol. 49, No. 4.) An auditor for one jai alai facility noticed that abnormally large sums of money were wagered for certain types of bets, and some contestants didn't win as much as expected when those bets were made. *R* charts and $\bar{x}$ charts were used in court as evidence of highly unusual patterns of betting. Examination of the control charts clearly shows points well beyond the upper control limit, indicating that the process of betting was out of statistical control. The statistician was able to identify a date at which assignable variation appeared to stop, and prosecutors knew that it was the date of the suspect's arrest.

By analyzing the weights of quarters in Table 14-1 with a run chart, an R chart, and an $\bar{x}$ chart, we can see that the process is out of statistical control. These values are from a new minting process, so the new procedure needs to be improved before it can be used.

using TECHNOLOGY

STATDISK See the *STATDISK Student Laboratory Manual and Workbook* that is a supplement to this book.

MINITAB **Run Chart:** To construct a run chart, such as the one shown in Figure 14-1, begin by entering all of the sample data in column C1. Select the option **Stat,** then **Quality Tools,** then **Run Chart.** In the indicated boxes, enter C1 for the single column variable, enter 1 for the subgroup size, and then click on **OK.**

R Chart: First enter the individual sample values sequentially in column C1 or enter the sample values in columns and rows as in Table 14-1. Next, select the options **Stat, Control Charts, Variables Charts for Subgroups,** and **R.** Select the format of the data (one column or "observations for each subgroup are in one row of columns") and enter the appropriate column(s) in the data entry box. Click on **R Options,** then **estimate.** Select **Rbar.** (Selection of the R bar estimate causes the variation of the population distribution to be estimated with the sample ranges instead of the sample standard deviations, which is the default.) Click **OK** twice.

$\bar{x}$ Chart: First enter the individual sample values sequentially in column C1 or enter the sample values in columns and rows as in Table 14-1. Next, select the options **Stat, Control Charts,** **Variables Charts for Subgroups,** and **Xbar.** Select the format of the data (one column or "observations for each subgroup are in one row of columns") and enter the appropriate column(s) in the data entry box. Click on **Xbar Options,** then select **estimate** and choose the option of **Rbar.** Click **OK** twice.

EXCEL Use XLSTAT. Enter the data in individual columns, such as the five columns of data in Table 14-1. Click on **XLSTAT,** select **SPC** (for statistical process control), then select **Subgroup charts.** Click on the **General** tab and select the data format of "columns," then enter the range of data in the "Data" box, such as A1:E20. Click on the **Estimation** tab and select **R bar.** Click **OK.** Results will include an R chart and an $\bar{x}$ chart.

Excel's built-in graphics features could be used to create control charts, but the procedure is difficult. See the *Excel Student Laboratory Manual and Workbook* that is a supplement to this book.

STATCRUNCH Click on **Open StatCrunch.** First enter columns of data or open a data set. Click on **Stat,** select **Control Charts,** then select **X-bar, R.** Identify the columns to be used ("Samples in selected columns"), then click on **Calculate.** After the control charts are displayed, click on **Next** to get the values of the upper and lower control limits and the centerlines.

14-2 Basic Skills and Concepts

Statistical Literacy and Critical Thinking

1. Product Specs Table 14-1 lists process data consisting of the weights (g) of quarters, and the United States Mint uses a manufacturing process designed to result in a mean weight equal to 5.670 g. If recent $\bar{x}$ and R control charts show that the process of manufacturing quarters is within statistical control, does that indicate that the quarters have weights that are reasonably close to 5.670 g? Why or why not?

2. Notation and Terminology Consider process data consisting of the amounts of Coke (in oz) in randomly selected cans of regular Coke. The process is to be monitored with $\bar{x}$ and R control charts based on samples of 50 cans randomly selected each day for 20 consecutive days of production. What are $\bar{x}$ and R control charts, and what do $\bar{\bar{x}}$, $\bar{R}$, UCL, and LCL denote?

3. Control Charts When using control charts to monitor a process, why is it necessary to include an $\bar{x}$ chart and an R chart? Why can't we use just one of those control charts?

4. Lake Mead Elevations Shown below are an $\bar{x}$ chart (top) and an R chart (bottom) obtained by using the monthly elevations of Lake Mead at Hoover Dam (based on data from the U.S. Department of the Interior). The elevations are in feet above sea level. The control charts are based on the 12 monthly elevations for each of the 75 consecutive and recent years available as of this writing. What do the control charts tell us about Lake Mead?

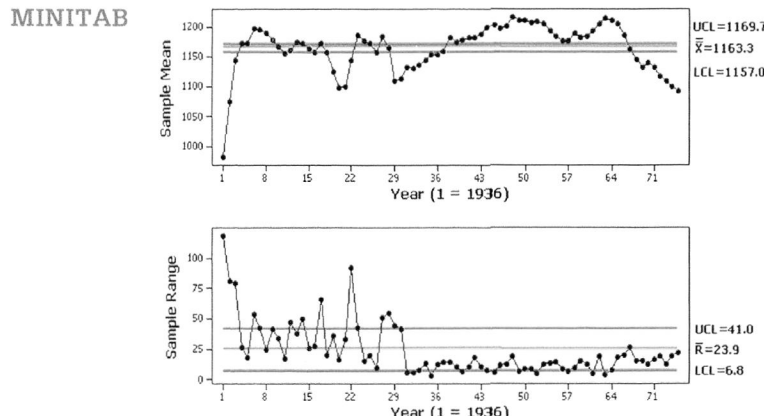

MINITAB

Pepsi Cans.   *In Exercises 5–8, refer to the axial loads (pounds) of aluminum Pepsi cans that are 0.0109 in. thick, as listed in Data Set 22 of Appendix B. An axial load of a can is the maximum weight supported by the side, and it is important to have an axial load high enough so that the can isn't crushed when the top lid is pressed onto the top. There are seven measurements from each of 25 days of production.*

5. Cola Cans: Notation After finding the sample mean and sample range for each of the 25 days, find the values of $\bar{\bar{x}}$ and $\bar{R}$. Also find the values of LCL and UCL for an R chart, then find the values of LCL and UCL for an $\bar{x}$ chart.

6. Cola Cans: Run Chart Treat the 175 axial loads as a string of consecutive measurements and construct a run chart. What does the result suggest?

7. Cola Cans: R Chart Treat the seven measurements from each day as a sample and construct an R chart. What does the result suggest?

8. Cola Cans: $\bar{x}$ Chart Treat the seven measurements from each day as a sample and construct an $\bar{x}$ chart. What does the result suggest?

Global Warming.   *In Exercises 9–12, refer to the following annual temperatures (°C) of the earth for each of the past 50 years. The last two columns list statistics for the five different decades.*

											$\bar{x}$	Range
1960s	13.98	14.10	14.05	14.03	13.65	13.75	13.93	13.98	13.91	14.00	13.938	0.450
1970s	14.04	13.90	13.95	14.18	13.94	13.98	13.79	14.16	14.07	14.13	14.014	0.390
1980s	14.27	14.40	14.10	14.34	14.16	14.13	14.19	14.35	14.42	14.28	14.264	0.320
1990s	14.49	14.44	14.16	14.18	14.31	14.47	14.36	14.40	14.71	14.44	14.396	0.550
2000s	14.41	14.56	14.70	14.64	14.60	14.77	14.64	14.66	14.68	14.70	14.636	0.360

9. Global Warming: Notation Find the values of $\bar{\bar{x}}$ and $\bar{R}$. Also find the values of LCL and UCL for an R chart, then find the values of LCL and UCL for an $\bar{x}$ chart.

10. Global Warming: R Chart Treat the 10 measurements from each decade as a sample and construct an R chart. What does the result suggest?

11. Global Warming: $\bar{x}$ Chart Treat the 10 measurements from each decade as a sample and construct an $\bar{x}$ chart. What does the result suggest?

12. Global Warming: Run Chart Treat the the 50 consecutive measurements from the 50 years as individual values and construct a run chart. What does the result suggest?

14-2 Beyond the Basics

13. *s* Chart In this section we described control charts for R and $\bar{x}$ based on ranges. Control charts for monitoring variation and center (mean) can also be based on standard deviations. An *s chart* for monitoring variation is constructed by plotting sample standard deviations with a centerline at $\bar{s}$ (the mean of the sample standard deviations) and control limits at $B_4\bar{s}$ and $B_3\bar{s}$, where B_4 and B_3 are found in Table 14-2 in this section. Construct an *s* chart for the data of Table 14-1. Compare the result to the R chart given in Example 3.

14. $\bar{x}$ Chart Based on Standard Deviations An $\bar{x}$ chart based on standard deviations (instead of ranges) is made by plotting sample means with a centerline at $\bar{\bar{x}}$ and control limits at $\bar{\bar{x}} + A_3\bar{s}$ and $\bar{\bar{x}} - A_3\bar{s}$, where A_3 is found in Table 14-2 and $\bar{s}$ is the mean of the sample standard deviations. Use the data in Table 14-1 to construct an $\bar{x}$ chart based on standard deviations. Compare the result to the $\bar{x}$ chart based on sample ranges (as in Example 5).

Quality Control at Perstorp

Perstorp Components, Inc., uses a computer that automatically generates control charts to monitor the thicknesses of the floor insulation the company makes for Ford Rangers and Jeep Grand Cherokees. The $20,000 cost of the computer was offset by a first-year savings of $40,000 in labor, which had been used to manually generate control charts to ensure that insulation thicknesses were between the specifications of 2.912 mm and 2.988 mm. Through the use of control charts and other quality-control methods, Perstorp reduced its waste by more than two-thirds.

14-3 Control Charts for Attributes

Key Concept Section 14-2 described methods for constructing control charts used to monitor the variation and mean of process data, but this section presents a method for constructing a control chart to monitor the proportion p for some *attribute*, such as whether a service or manufactured item is defective or nonconforming. (A good or a service is nonconforming if it doesn't meet specifications or requirements. Nonconforming goods are sometimes discarded, repaired, or called "seconds" and sold at reduced prices.) The control chart is interpreted using the same three criteria from Section 14-2 to determine whether the process is statistically stable. As in Section 14-2, we select samples of size n at regular time intervals and plot points in a sequential graph with a centerline and control limits. (There are ways to deal with samples of different sizes, but we don't consider them here.)

> **DEFINITION** A **control chart for p** (or **p chart**) is a graph of proportions of some attribute (such as whether products are defective) plotted sequentially over time, and it includes a centerline, a lower control limit (LCL), and an upper control limit (UCL).

The notation and control chart values are as summarized in the following box. In this box, the attribute of "defective" can be replaced by any other relevant attribute (so that each sample item belongs to one of two distinct categories).

Monitoring a Process Attribute: Control Chart for p

Objective

Construct a control chart for p (or a "p chart") that can be used to determine whether the proportion of some attribute (such as whether products are defective) from process data is within statistical control.

Requirements

1. The data are process data consisting of a sequence of samples all of the same size n.

2. Each sample item belongs to one of two categories (such as defective or not defective).

3. The individual sample data values are independent.

Notation

$\bar{p}$ = estimate of the proportion of defective items in the process

$$= \frac{\text{total number of defects found among all items sampled}}{\text{total number of items sampled}}$$

$\bar{q}$ = estimate of the proportion of process items that are not defective

$= 1 - \bar{p}$

n = size of each sample or subgroup

Graph

Points plotted: Proportions from the individual samples of size n

Centerline: $\bar{p}$

Upper control limit: $\bar{p} + 3\sqrt{\dfrac{\bar{p}\bar{q}}{n}}$ (Use 1 if this result is greater than 1.)

Lower control limit: $\bar{p} - 3\sqrt{\dfrac{\bar{p}\bar{q}}{n}}$ (Use 0 if this result is less than 0.)

CAUTION Upper and lower control limits of a control chart for a proportion p are based on the *actual* behavior of the process, not the *desired* behavior. Upper and lower control limits are totally unrelated to any process *specifications* that may have been decreed by the manufacturer.

We use $\bar{p}$ for the centerline because it is the best estimate of the proportion of defects from the process. The expressions for the control limits correspond to 99.7% confidence interval limits as described in Section 7-2.

Example 1 Defective Quarters

Examples in Section 14-2 involved control charts for variation in the mean weight of quarters manufactured by the United States Mint. Let's now consider the proportion of defective quarters produced by the same new production method used to manufacture the weights listed in Table 14-1. A quarter is designed to weigh 5.670 g and have a diameter of 24.26 mm, a thickness of 1.75 mm, and it should be composed of 8.33% nickel and 91.67% copper, it should have 119 reeds on its edge, and it should be stamped correctly. Large deviations from any of those specifications results in a quarter considered to be defective. Listed below are the numbers of defects in batches of 10,000 quarters randomly selected on each of 20 consecutive days from a new manufacturing process that is being tested. Construct a control chart for the proportion p of defective quarters and determine whether the process is within statistical control. If not, identify which of the three out-of-control criteria apply.

Defects: 8 7 12 9 6 10 10 5 15 14
          12 14 9 6 16 18 20 19 18 24

High Cost of Low Quality

Microsoft announced that it would spend $1.15 billion to repair Xbox 360 game machine consoles. Industry analysts estimate that about one-third of all units were defective and in need of repair. Many users reported that the machine shut down after three flashing red lights appeared on the console.

The Federal Drug Administration recently reached an agreement whereby a pharmaceutical company, the Schering-Plough Corporation, would pay a record $500 million for failure to correct problems in manufacturing drugs. According to a *New York Times* article by Melody Petersen, "Some of the problems relate to the lack of controls that would identify faulty medicines, while others stem from outdated equipment. They involve some 200 medicines, including Claritin, the allergy medicine that is Schering's top-selling product."

Solution

The centerline for the control chart is located by the value of $\bar{p}$:

$$\bar{p} = \frac{\text{total number of defective quarters from all samples combined}}{\text{total number of quarters sampled}}$$

$$= \frac{8 + 7 + 12 + \cdots + 24}{20 \cdot 10,000} = \frac{252}{200,000} = 0.00126$$

Because $\bar{p} = 0.00126$, it follows that $\bar{q} = 1 - \bar{p} = 0.99874$. Using $\bar{p} = 0.00126$, $\bar{q} = 0.99874$, and $n = 10,000$, we find the positions of the centerline and the control limits as follows:

Centerline: $\bar{p} = 0.00126$

Upper control limit:

$$\bar{p} + 3\sqrt{\frac{\bar{p}\bar{q}}{n}} = 0.00126 + 3\sqrt{\frac{(0.00126)(0.99874)}{10,000}} = 0.002324$$

Lower control limit:

$$\bar{p} - 3\sqrt{\frac{\bar{p}\bar{q}}{n}} = 0.00126 - 3\sqrt{\frac{(0.00126)(0.99874)}{10,000}} = 0.000196$$

Having found the values for the centerline and the control limits, we can proceed to plot the proportions of defective quarters. The Minitab control chart for p is shown in the accompanying display.

CONTROL CHART FOR p: DEFECTIVE QUARTERS

Interpretation

We can interpret the control chart for p by considering the three out-of-control criteria listed in Section 14-2. Using those criteria, we conclude that this process is out of statistical control for these reasons: The Run of 8 Rule is violated because there are 8 consecutive points lying below the centerline, and there is a point lying beyond the upper and lower control limits. This is based on a new process that is being tested, and the control chart indicates that this process requires corrective action so that it is brought within statistical control.

using TECHNOLOGY

MINITAB Enter the numbers of defects (or items with any particular attribute) in column C1. Select the option **Stat,** then **Control Charts, Attributes Charts,** then **P.** Enter C1 in the box identified as variable, and enter the size of the samples in the box identified as subgroup size, then click **OK.**

EXCEL Using **XLSTAT:** Begin by entering the numbers of defects or successes in column A. Click on **XLSTAT,** click on **SPC,** then click on **Attribute charts.** Click on the **General** tab and enter the range of data, such as A1:A20. For the "Common subgroup size," enter the sample size that is common to all of the data entries. Place a checkmark next to "Column labels" only if the first cell consists of a name or label. Click **OK** and results will include a p chart.

Using **Excel's Chart Wizard:** Enter the sample proportions in column A. Click on the **Chart Wizard** icon, which looks like a bar graph. For the chart type, select **Line.** For the chart subtype, select the first graph in the second row, then click **Next.** Continue to click **Next,** then **Finish.** The graph can be edited to include labels, delete grid lines, and so on. You can insert the required centerline and upper and lower control limits by editing the graph. Click on the line on the bottom of the screen, then click and drag to position the line correctly.

STATCRUNCH Click on **Open StatCrunch.** First enter a column containing the numbers of "defects." Click on **Stat,** select **Control Charts,** then select **p.** Identify the column to be used and enter the sample size, then click on **Calculate.** After the control chart is displayed, click on **Next** to get the values of the upper and lower control limits and the centerline.

14-3 Basic Skills and Concepts

Statistical Literacy and Critical Thinking

1. Monitoring the Minting of Half Dollars A half dollar is considered to be defective if it deviates substantially from these specifications: The weight is 11.340 g, the diameter is 30.61 mm, the thickness is 2.15 mm, the composition is 8.33% nickel and 91.67% copper, the edge has 150 reeds, and it is stamped correctly. For the same manufacturing process considered in this section, defects are monitored and the accompanying control chart is obtained. Does this process appear to be within statistical control? If not, identify any out-of-control criteria that are violated. Is the manufacturing process deteriorating?

2. Notation The control chart for Exercise 1 shows a value of $\bar{p} = 0.001135$. What does that value denote, and how is it obtained?

3. Control Limits In constructing a control chart for the proportions of defective dimes, it is found that LCL = −0.000025. What does "LCL" represent, and how should that value be adjusted?

4. Interpreting a Control Chart After constructing a control chart for the proportions of defective dimes, it is concluded that the process is within statistical control. Does that imply that almost all of the dimes meet the desired specifications? Explain.

Control Charts for p. *In Exercises 5–12, use the given process data to construct a control chart for p. In each case, use the three out-of-control criteria listed in Section 14-2 and determine whether the process is within statistical control. If it is not, identify which of the three out-of-control criteria apply.*

5. Defective Dimes Consider a process of minting dimes. Listed below are the numbers of defective dimes in successive batches of 10,000 randomly selected on consecutive days of production.

32   21   25   19   35   34   27   30   26   33

6. Defective Dimes Repeat Exercise 5 assuming that the size of each batch is 100 instead of 10,000. Compare the control chart to the one found for Exercise 5. Comment on the general quality of the manufacturing process described in Exercise 5 compared to the manufacturing process described in this exercise.

7. Birth Rate In recent and consecutive years, 100,000 people were randomly selected and the numbers of births they generated were found, with the results given below. (The listed values are based on data from the *CIA World Factbook*, and they are the most recent values available at the time of this writing.)

1422   1410   1414   1415   1413   1414   1414   1416   1418   1382   1383   1383

8. Violent Crimes In each of recent and consecutive years, 100,000 people in the United States were randomly selected and the number who were victims of violent crime was determined, with the results listed below. Does the rate of violent crime appear to exhibit acceptable behavior? (The values are based on data from the U.S. Department of Justice, and they are the most recent values available at the time of this writing.) How does the result affect us?

685   637   611   566   523   507   505   494

476   463   469   474   467   458   429

9. Voting Rate In each of recent and consecutive years of presidential elections, 1000 people of voting age in the United States were randomly selected and the number who voted was determined, with the results listed below. (The data are the latest available as of this writing.) Comment on the voting behavior of the population.

631   619   608   552   536   526   531   501   551   491   513   553   568

10. College Enrollment by High School Graduates In each of several recent and consecutive years, 1000 high school graduates were randomly selected and the numbers who enrolled in college were recorded (based on data from the *Statistical Abstract of the United States*). The data are the latest available as of this writing. Does the process appear to be proceeding as it should?

626   619   619   650   670   656   629   633   618

652   639   672   686   660   672   690   693   681

11. Cola Cans In each of several consecutive days of production of cola cans, 500 cans are tested and the numbers of defects each day are listed below. What action should be taken?

20   22   19   17   19   15   16   13   14   14

11   13   12   11   10   9   9   10   7   7

12. Smart Phone Batteries The SmartBatt company manufactures batteries for smart phones. Listed below are numbers of defects in batches of 200 randomly selected in each of 15 consecutive days of production. What action should be taken?

12   11   14   15   9   10   12   16   8   9   15   7   17   5   18

14-3 Beyond the Basics

13. np Chart A variation of the control chart for p is the **np chart** in which the *actual numbers* of defects are plotted instead of the *proportions* of defects. The np chart has a centerline value of $n\bar{p}$, and the control limits have values of $n\bar{p} + 3\sqrt{n\bar{p}\bar{q}}$ and $n\bar{p} - 3\sqrt{n\bar{p}\bar{q}}$. The p chart and the np chart differ only in the scale of values used for the vertical axis. Construct the np chart for Example 1 in this section. Compare the np chart to the control chart for p given in this section.

Chapter 14   Review

In Chapter 2 we noted that important characteristics of data include center, variation, distribution, outliers, and changing pattern of data over time. The focus of this chapter is the changing pattern of data over time, and we can monitor such changes using run charts and control charts. Control charts have a centerline, an upper control limit, and a lower control limit. A process is statistically stable (or within statistical control) if it has only natural variation, with no patterns, cycles, or unusual points. Decisions about statistical stability are based on how a process is actually behaving, not on how we might like it to behave because of such factors as manufacturer specifications. The following graphs were described:

- *Run chart:* a sequential plot of *individual* data values over time
- *R chart:* a control chart that uses ranges in an attempt to monitor the *variation* in a process
- *$\bar{x}$ chart:* a control chart used to determine whether the process *mean* is within statistical control
- *p chart:* a control chart used to monitor the proportion of some process *attribute*, such as whether items are defective

Chapter Quick Quiz

1. What are *process* data?

2. What is the difference between *random variation* and *assignable variation*?

3. Identify three specific criteria for determining when a process is out of statistical control.

4. What is the difference between an R chart and an $\bar{x}$ chart?

In Exercises 5–8, use the following two control charts that result from testing newly manu-factured aircraft altimeters. The original sample values are errors (in feet) obtained when the altimeters are tested in a pressure chamber that simulates an altitude of 1000 ft.

5. Is the process variation within statistical control? Why or why not?

6. What is the value of $\overline{R}$? In general, how is a value of $\overline{R}$ obtained?

7. Is the process mean within statistical control? Why or why not?

8. What is the value of $\overline{\overline{x}}$? In general, how is a value of $\overline{x}$ found?

9. What is a p chart?

10. Examine the following p chart for defective car batteries and briefly describe the action that should be taken.

Review Exercises

Energy Consumption.   *Exercises 1–5 refer to the amounts of energy consumed in the author's home. Each value represents energy consumed (kWh) in a two-month period. Let each subgroup consist of the six amounts within the same year.*

Year 1	3637	2888	2359	3704	3432	2446
Year 2	4463	2482	2762	2288	2423	2483
Year 3	3375	2661	2073	2579	2858	2296
Year 4	2812	2433	2266	3128	3286	2749
Year 5	3427	578	3792	3348	2937	2774
Year 6	3016	2458	2395	3249	3003	2118
Year 7	4261	1946	2063	4081	1919	2360
Year 8	2853	2174	2370	3480	2710	2327

1. Energy Consumption: Notation After finding the values of the mean and range for each year, find the values of $\bar{\bar{x}}$, and $\bar{R}$. Then find the values of LCL and UCL for an R chart and find the values of LCL and UCL for an $\bar{x}$ chart.

2. Energy Consumption: R Chart Let each subgroup consist of the 6 values within a year. Construct an R chart and determine whether the process variation is within statistical control. If it is not, identify which of the three out-of-control criteria lead to rejection of statistically stable variation.

3. Energy Consumption: $\bar{x}$ Chart Let each subgroup consist of the 6 values within a year. Construct an $\bar{x}$ chart and determine whether the process mean is within statistical control. If it is not, identify which of the three out-of-control criteria lead to rejection of a statistically stable mean.

4. Energy Consumption: Run Chart Construct a run chart for the 48 values. Does there appear to be a pattern suggesting that the process is not within statistical control?

5. Defective Aspirin Tablets The Acton Pharmaceutical Company manufactures aspirin tablets that are supposed to contain 325 mg of aspirin. Each day, 100 tablets are randomly selected and the amount of aspirin is measured. A tablet is considered defective if it has obvious physical deformities or the amount of aspirin is not between 315 mg and 335 mg. The numbers of defects are listed below for consecutive production days. Construct an appropriate control chart and determine whether the process is within statistical control. If not, identify which criteria lead to rejection of statistical stability.

2   3   3   2   4   6   3   7   8   6   9   7   6   8   10

Cumulative Review Exercises

Please be aware that some of the following problems may require knowledge of concepts presented in previous chapters.

1. Workplace Etiquette: Confidence Interval In a survey conducted by Opinion Research Corporation, randomly selected adults were asked what is inappropriate in the workplace. Among 1000 responses, 55% said that it is inappropriate to wear shorts. Use the sample results to construct a 95% confidence interval estimate of the proportion of the adult population believing that it is inappropriate to wear shorts at work. Based on the result, does it appear that the majority of adults believe that it is not appropriate to wear shorts at work?

2. Workplace Etiquette: Probability Based on the results in Exercise 1, assume that there is a 0.55 probability of randomly selecting an adult and getting someone who believes that it is inappropriate to wear shorts at work.

a. What is the probability of randomly selecting an adult and getting someone who does *not* believe that it is inappropriate to wear shorts at work.

b. If five different adults are randomly selected, what is the probability that they all believe that it is inappropriate to wear shorts at work?

c. If five different adults are randomly selected, what is the probability of getting at least one who does *not* believe that it is inappropriate to wear shorts at work?

3. Agriculture Experiment: Correlation In 1908, William Gosset published the article "The Probable Error of a Mean" under the pseudonym of "Student" (*Biometrika,* Vol. 6, No. 1). He included the data listed below for yields from two different types of seed (regular and kiln dried) that were used on adjacent plots of land. The listed values are the yields of straw in cwt per acre, where cwt represents 100 lb. Use a 0.05 significance level to test for a correlation between yields from regular seed and kiln-dried seed. Are the results useful for addressing the main purpose of the experiment?

Regular	19.25	22.75	23	23	22.5	19.75	24.5	15.5	18	14.25	17
Kiln-dried	25	24	24	28	22.5	19.5	22.25	16	17.25	15.75	17.25

4. Agriculture Experiment: Hypothesis Test Refer to the same sample data given in the preceding exercise. Assume that the experiment was conducted to determine whether the new method of using kiln-dried seed is better. Conduct an appropriate hypothesis test.

5. Agriculture Experiment: Descriptive Statistics Using the data given in Exercise 3, find the mean and standard deviation of each of the two samples, then informally compare the results.

6. Defective Child Restraint Systems The Tracolyte Manufacturing Company produces plastic frames used for child booster seats in cars. During each week of production, 50 frames are selected and tested for conformance to all regulations by the Department of Transportation. Frames are considered defective if they do not meet all requirements. Listed below are the numbers of defective frames among the 50 that are tested each week. Use a control chart for p to verify that the process is within statistical control. If it is not in control, explain why it is not.

4   5   5   3   6   5   7   7   9   10

7. Overtime Football Games: Graph The overtime rule for football became effective in 1974. Since then, 3.8% of overtime games have ended in a tie, 25.6% ended with a touchdown, 70.1% ended with a field goal, and 0.5% ended with a safety. Construct a graph that is effective in displaying these results.

8. Designing Motorcycle Helmets Engineers must consider the breadths of male heads when designing motorcycle helmets. Men have head breadths that are normally distributed with a mean of 15.2 cm and a standard deviation of 2.5 cm (based on anthropometric survey data from Gordon, Churchill, et al.).

a. What percentage of men have head breadths greater than 17 cm? If helmets are made to accommodate only males with head breadths less than 17 cm, would those helmets exclude too many males?

b. If, due to financial constraints, the helmets are designed to fit all men except those with head breadths that are in the smallest 5% or largest 5%, find the minimum and maximum head breadths that the helmets will fit.

9. Sampling What is the difference between a voluntary response sample and a simple random sample? Which is generally better for the use of statistical methods?

10. Statistics Which of the following is the single *most* important factor for obtaining good results from a statistical study?

a. Size of the sample

b. Importance of the topic being addressed

c. Sampling method

d. Using data at the ratio level of measurement

e. Using graphs that are not misleading

Technology Project

a. Simulate the following process for 20 days: Each day, 200 calculators are manufactured with a 5% rate of defects, and the proportion of defects is recorded for each of the 20 days. The calculators for one day are simulated by randomly generating 200 numbers, where each number is between 1 and 100. Consider an outcome of 1, 2, 3, 4, or 5 to be a defect, with 6 through 100 being acceptable. This corresponds to a 5% rate of defects. (See the technology instructions below.)

b. Construct a p chart for the proportion of defective calculators, and determine whether the process is within statistical control. Since we know the process is actually stable with $p = 0.05$, the conclusion that it is not stable would be a type I error; that is, we would have a false positive signal, causing us to believe that the process needed to be adjusted when in fact it should be left alone.

c. The result from part (a) is a simulation of 20 days. Now simulate another 10 days of manufacturing calculators, but modify these last 10 days so that the defect rate is 10% instead of 5%.

d. Combine the data generated from parts (a) and (c) to represent a total of 30 days of sample results. Construct a p chart for this combined data set. Is the process out of control? If we concluded that the process was not out of control, we would be making a type II error; that is, we would believe that the process was okay when in fact it should be repaired or adjusted to correct the shift to the 10% rate of defects.

Technology Instructions for Part (a):

STATDISK: Select **Data, Uniform Generator,** and generate 200 values with a minimum of 1 and a maximum of 100. Copy the data to the data window, then sort the values by clicking on **Data** and selecting the menu item of **Sort Data.** Repeat this procedure until results for 20 days have been simulated.

Minitab: Select **Calc, Random Data,** then **Integer.** Enter 200 for the number of rows of data, enter C1 as the column to be used for storing the data, enter 1 for the minimum value, and enter 100 for the maximum value. Repeat this procedure until results for 20 days have been simulated.

Excel: Click on the *fx* icon on the main menu bar, then select the function category **Math & Trig,** followed by **RANDBETWEEN.** In the dialog box, enter 1 for bottom and 100 for top. A random value should appear in the first row of column A. Use the mouse to click and drag the lower right corner of that cell, then pull down the cell to cover the first 200 rows of column A. When you release the mouse button, column A should contain 200 random numbers. You can also click/drag the lower right corner of the bottom cell by moving the mouse to the right so that you get 20 columns of 200 numbers each. The different columns represent the different days of manufacturing.

TI-83/84 Plus: Press the **MATH** key. Select **PRB,** then select the 5th menu item, **randInt(,** and enter 1, 100, 200; then press **ENTER**. Press **STO** and **L1** to store the data in list L1. After recording the number of defects, repeat this procedure until results for 20 days have been simulated.

StatCrunch: Open StatCrunch, click on **Data,** select the menu item of **Simulate data,** then select **Discrete Uniform.** In the dialog box, enter 200 for the number of rows, enter 20 for the number of columns, enter 1 for the minimum, and enter 100 for the maximum. Click on **Simulate** to obtain the results.

from data TO DECISION

Critical Thinking: Are the axial loads within statistical control? Is the process of manufacturing cans proceeding as it should?

Exercises 5–8 in Section 14-2 used process data from a New York company that manufactures 0.0109-in.-thick aluminum cans for a major beverage supplier. Refer to Data Set 22 in Appendix B and conduct an analysis of the process data for the cans that

are 0.0111 in. thick. The values in the data set are the measured axial loads of cans, and the top lids are pressed into place with pressures that vary between 158 lb and 165 lb.

Analyzing the Results

Based on the given process data, should the company take any corrective action? Write a report summarizing your

conclusions. Address not only the issue of statistical stability but also the ability of the cans to withstand the pressures applied when the top lids are pressed into place. Also compare the behavior of the 0.0111-in. cans to the behavior of the 0.0109-in. cans, and recommend which thickness should be used.

Cooperative Group Activities

1. Out-of-class activity Collect your own process data and analyze them using the methods of this chapter. It would be ideal to collect data from a real manufacturing process, but that may be difficult to accomplish. Instead, consider using a simulation or referring to published data, such as those found in an almanac. Obtain a printed copy of computer results and write a brief report summarizing your conclusions. Here are some suggestions:

• Shoot five basketball foul shots (or shoot five crumpled sheets of paper into a wastebasket) and record the number of shots made; then repeat this procedure 20 times. Use a p chart to test for statistical stability in the proportion of shots made.

• Measure your pulse rate by counting the number of times your heart beats in 1 min. Measure your pulse rate four times each hour for several hours, then construct appropriate control charts. What factors contribute to random variation? Assignable variation?

• Search newspapers or the Internet for the past 12 weeks and record the closing of the Dow Jones Industrial Average (DJIA) for each business day. Use run and control charts to explore the statistical stability of the DJIA. Identify at least one practical consequence of having this process statistically stable, and identify at least one practical consequence of having this process out of statistical control.

• Find the marriage rate per 10,000 population for several years. (See the *Information Please Almanac* or the *Statistical Abstract of the United States*.) Assume that in each year 10,000 people were randomly selected and surveyed to determine whether they were married. Use a p chart to test for statistical stability of the marriage rate. (Other possible rates: death, accident fatality, crime.)

2. In-class activity If the instructor can distribute the numbers of absences for each class meeting, groups of three or four students can analyze them for statistical stability and make recommendations based on the conclusions.

3. Out-of-class activity Conduct research to find a description of Deming's funnel experiment, then use a funnel and marbles to collect data for the different rules for adjusting the funnel location. Construct appropriate control charts for the different rules of funnel adjustment. What does the funnel experiment illustrate? What do you conclude?

Ethics, Projects, Procedures, and Perspectives

15

15-1 Ethics in Statistics

Key Concept Statistical methods give us tremendous power to better understand the world in which we live. This power, however, can be abused in ways that are fundamentally unethical. It is important for us to consider some ethical issues in statistics related to data collection, analysis, and reporting.

I. Data Collection

Obtaining Data

"The end does not justify the means" is a widely quoted phrase central to many ethical debates. Are actions that harm some individuals ever justifiable if the results of these actions benefit others? When, if ever, does the good of the many outweigh the good of the few? There are many research studies in which the health and safety of research subjects were compromised so that others might benefit.

Prisoner Studies In the early 1970s, it is estimated that 90% of pharmaceutical research in the United States was conducted using prisoners as human test subjects. In some cases, this research was conducted without the prisoner's knowledge or consent. These prisoners served as an easily accessible and controlled population for a wide range of research conducted by pharmaceutical companies, the U.S. Army, and others. The Common Rule (discussed later in this section) now protects human research subjects in the United States, and there is continuing debate about whether research should ever be allowed in prisons.

Milgram Experiment During the 1960s, Stanley Milgram conducted one of the most infamous psychological studies. Subjects were ordered to administer progressively stronger electrical shocks to actors who were in another room. These actors were not visible to the subject and were not actually receiving shocks. Prerecorded screams were played so the subject could hear them. The actor would bang on the wall and beg for the subject to stop.

Prior to the experiment, a poll of experts estimated that only 3% of subjects would continue giving shocks after hearing the screams and the pleas to stop, but 65% of the subjects increased shocks until the maximum of 375 volts was reached. This and subsequent follow-up studies provided valuable insight into the power of authority and the danger of obedience.

Milgram's experiment inflicted extreme emotional distress on its subjects and is now considered unethical and psychologically abusive by many. A similar psychological study would not be allowed today in most countries. The participants in this study, however, were later surveyed and 84% said they were "glad" or "very glad" to have participated while only 1% regretted their involvement.

Sampling Bias

Researchers can intentionally or unintentionally bias their study by the way in which subjects are selected. *Sampling bias* occurs when some individuals are more or less likely to be included in a study, and the result is a sample that is not random. Sampling bias can seriously distort the interpretation of study results and result in wrong or misleading conclusions. While most researchers take great care to avoid sampling bias, others have intentionally used biased samples to ensure that desired results were obtained.

Cherry Picking The report "Are Researchers Cherry Picking Participants for Studies of Antidepressants?" by the University of Pittsburgh Schools of the Health Sciences described findings from several clinical studies conducted for the purpose of gaining approval of antidepressants from the Food and Drug Administration. The report described how some common antidepressants do not help most patients with depression. Only a small percentage of depressed individuals met the criteria required for participation in the clinical trial, but the depressed individuals who qualified for the clinical trials had better outcomes from the drugs compared to other depressed individuals who did not qualify.

In this case, the criteria required to participate in the clinical trial created a sampling bias that favored the drug manufacturers who sponsored the research. (Changing the criteria to reduce sample bias could cause more patients to suffer serious side effects from the drugs. The lead author of the study recommended that the criteria not be changed. Instead, he suggested that medical care providers use their professional judgment in treating individual patients.)

Nonrespondent Bias Nonrespondent bias occurs when those who do not respond to a survey differ from those who do respond. Two aspects of a survey topic that affect responses are *salience* (whether or not the topic is of interest to the respondent) and *social desirability* (whether or not the topic is threatening or embarrassing to the respondent). One study found that when a topic has high interest to respondents, they were almost twice as likely to respond. Other studies have found that socially desirable behaviors like exercise and good nutrition are frequently overreported, while undesirable behaviors such as smoking are underreported.

Relative to alcohol research, several studies have shown that survey groups with higher proportions of heavy drinkers tend to have higher nonresponse rates. (See "Non-response Bias in a Sample Survey on Alcohol Consumption," by V. M. Lahaut et al., *Alcohol and Alcoholism*). Heavy drinkers are less likely to respond to a survey. For a survey related to alcohol consumption, heavy drinkers would likely be underrepresented and the results would be skewed. For a topic not related to alcohol consumption, however, underrepresentation of heavy drinkers might not distort results.

Interviewer Bias The manner in which a question is asked may affect the response. The author of this book recently received a survey in the mail asking the following questions:

• "Do you support the creation of a national health insurance policy that would be administered by bureaucrats in Washington, D.C.?"

Anonymity and Confidentiality

A survey is conducted with *anonymity* if the identities of the respondents are not known. A survey is conducted with *confidentiality* if the identities of the respondents are not disclosed. Ideally, surveys should be both anonymous and confidential, but that isn't always practical or good. Confidentiality might be ignored if it is found that some respondents are a danger to themselves or others. In such cases, respondents should be informed with a statement such as this: "All of the information that you provide will remain confidential, unless it involves risks of serious danger to yourself or others."

The *National Observer* newspaper was discontinued, but it once hired a firm to conduct a confidential mail survey. The survey was conducted with the promise that "each individual reply will be kept confidential." One clever subscriber used an ultraviolet light to detect a code printed on the survey in invisible ink. Here, confidentiality was promised and observed, but anonymity was not promised and it was not maintained. Instead of using invisible ink, respondents should have been informed that their information was not anonymous.

- "Are you in favor of creating a government-funded 'Citizen Volunteer Corps' that would pay young people to do work now being done by churches and charities, earning Corps Members the same pay and benefits given to military veterans?"

The questions above are worded in a way that is intended to bias the response by encouraging a negative response.

Volunteer Bias People who volunteer to participate constitute a voluntary response sample, and they typically have different characteristics when compared to participants who are selected by those conducting the survey. Volunteers typically have more interest in the topic being studied and are typically not representative of the population. Volunteer bias can be easily exploited to generate data that support a desired position.

The effects of volunteer bias have been extensively studied using the topic of human sexuality. "Volunteer Bias in Sexuality Research," by D. S. Strassberg et al., Department of Psychology, University of Utah, found that compared to nonvolunteers, volunteers reported a more positive attitude toward sexuality, less sexual guilt, and more sexual experience.

II. Analysis

Research study findings are often distorted by improper analysis. Even though the sample data may be inconclusive, insufficient, or supportive of an undesirable outcome, many researchers have succumbed to pressures and temptation to report significant or "conclusive" results through negligent and unethical analysis.

Falsified Data Several surveys have attempted to determine the incidence of data falsification or fabrication among scientists. "How Many Scientists Fabricate and Falsify Research? A Systematic Review and Meta-Analysis of Survey Data," by D. Fanelli, *PLoS ONE*, Vol. 4, No. 5, found that nearly 2% of scientists admitted to have fabricated, falsified, or modified data or results at least once. This is likely to be a conservative estimate, given the sensitivity of the topic and potential for sampling bias.

One notable example of data falsification is found in the original study suggesting a link between childhood vaccines and autism. Andrew Wakefield published a 1998 study claiming that the families of eight out of twelve children attending a routine hospital clinic had blamed the MMR vaccine for their autism and problems that appeared just two days after receiving the vaccine. This study was the catalyst for an international antivaccine movement. Following this study, United Kingdom inoculation rates fell from 92% to less than 80%, and in 2009 there were 1348 confirmed cases of measles in England and Wales, compared to just 56 such cases in 1998.

In 2010, the *British Medical Journal* provided evidence that Wakefield's study relied on falsified data. *The Lancet*, which published the original study in 1998, retracted the study. Wakefield's medical license was revoked. While some autism activists still defend his actions, the scientific community has condemned his research as unethical.

Inappropriate Statistical Methods The inappropriate use of statistical methods may lead to incorrect findings and distorted results even if the data are sound. Whether unintentional or intentional, studies on this topic have shown that errors in statistical analysis are widespread.

"Statistical Errors in Manuscripts Submitted to *Biochemia Medica* Journal," by Šimundić et al., *Biochemia Medica*, Volume 19, Number 2, examined 55 manuscripts that were submitted for publication and found that 48 (87%) contained at least one statistical error; 34 (62%) had an incorrect choice of the statistical test; 22% had incorrect interpretation of a *P*-value; and 75% included incorrect use of a statistical test for comparing three or more groups. Peer review is a primary defense against the use of inappropriate statistical methods, but it does not guarantee that such statistical errors will be identified and corrected.

III. Ethics and Reporting

Other opportunities for unethical practices occur with the interpretation of statistical results and the decision of how and where to report findings. Personal and self-serving interests may influence final conclusions and recommendations. The contribution of individual researchers may be misrepresented to enhance the credibility of the study, and the findings themselves may raise ethical questions.

Conflicts of Interest

Ghostwriting Medical ghostwriting is a practice that has recently raised serious ethical questions. A medical ghostwriter is someone who contributes to the writing of a research study or article but is not acknowledged in the published work. Litigation over the past several years has revealed that pharmaceutical companies have hired professional writers to draft papers regarding clinical trials and they have paid physicians to accept authorship of these articles. Neither the role of the ghostwriters nor the financial compensation for the acknowledged author was mentioned in the work. This was done to increase the credibility and visibility of the results. In some cases, those who accepted authorship made minimal contributions to the study.

Financial Support Pharmaceutical and medical device companies fund a substantial amount of medical research. There is concern that the financial relationship between researchers and sponsors can skew the work and distort findings so that the sponsor can benefit. For example, one study found that authors paid by manufacturers of diabetes medications were three times more likely to express favorable safety views than those not receiving payments. (See "Association between Industry Affiliation and Position on Cardiovascular Risk with Rosiglitazone: Cross-sectional Systematic Review," by Wang et al., *BMJ,* 340:c1344.)

The nonprofit organization Fair Warning reported that over the past several years, hospitals invested millions of dollars to purchase new automated heart defibrillators. A committee of the American Heart Association recommended the upgrade without the benefit of research or clinical trials showing that the new devices were better than the devices that were being used. According to Fair Warning, more than 25% of the committee members "had business ties with manufacturers of the devices" and "by one estimate, the shortcomings of the automated equipment mean that close to 1000 more hospital cardiac arrest patients die every year in the U.S."

Passage in 2010 of a federal law now requires companies to disclose payments or goods and services provided to physicians or teaching hospitals. While this law does not *prohibit* financial relationships between companies and physicians or teaching hospitals, it does require disclosure of these relationships.

Reporting Nonsignificant Results

A recent article appeared with the headline "In U.S., Support for Death Penalty Falls to 39 Year Low." A Gallup poll found that 61% of Americans were in favor of the death penalty and noted that this was a 3% drop from the previous year's rate. The "Survey Method" description at the end of the article indicated that "one can say with 95% confidence that the maximum margin of sampling error is $\pm 4\%$." With a sampling error of $\pm 4\%$, a 3% drop in respondents who indicated they were in favor of the death penalty is not significant. We don't really know whether there was a decrease, increase, or no change in opinions about the death penalty.

IV. Enforcing Ethics

To help prevent unethical statistical practices, many organizations have established ethical guidelines for their members or for authors whose works they publish. The American Statistical Association, for example, ratified their "Ethical Guidelines for Statistical Practice," which provides ethical guidelines in eight general topics including Responsibilities to Research Subjects, Responsibilities in Publications and Testimony, and Responsibilities to Other Statisticians. The complete text of the Ethical Guidelines can be can be found on the web site www.amstat.org.

The Common Rule has been established in the United States as the standard of ethics for biomedical and behavioral research involving human subjects. This is the baseline standard for any government-funded research and virtually all academic institutions. Central to the Common Rule are these requirements:

1. That people who participate as subjects in covered research are selected equitably and give their fully informed, fully voluntary written consent; and

2. That proposed research be reviewed by an independent oversight group referred to as an Institutional Review Board (IRB) and approved only if risks to subjects have been minimized and are reasonable in relation to anticipated benefits, if any, to the subjects, and the importance of the knowledge that may reasonably be expected to result.

The detailed text of the Common Rule can be found on the U.S. Department of Health & Human Services web site at www.hhs.gov.

Journals and granting agencies often require data sharing before studies are published or funded. This requirement allows for comprehensive peer review of the methodologies and results to minimize the chance that unintentional errors or unethical behavior is somehow influencing the study findings. A 2009 analysis by Thomson Reuters for *Times Higher Education* found that peer-reviewed science journal retractions have increased tenfold over the past two decades, indicating that the practice of researchers policing one another is becoming more effective.

As noted earlier, U.S. law now requires pharmaceutical and medical device manufacturers to disclose payments for goods and services provided to physicians and teaching hospitals to improve transparency between researchers and funding sources. Many journals also require disclosure of financial relationships for studies that are published. With greater transparency comes greater scrutiny to ensure that study findings are not being distorted because of financial relationships.

As consumers of data, each of us should hold researchers to high ethical standards. It is important to have a healthy skepticism when statistics are cited in support of a finding. We should ask questions such as these:

- Who is reporting about the study and do they have any financial or personal interest in the outcome?

- How were the sample data obtained? What is the potential for bias?

- Have these findings been reviewed or replicated by peers or anyone else?

- What specifics do they provide about the methods used? What is the margin of error, confidence interval, P-value, and so on?

Researchers must always adhere to the highest ethical standards in their work. We should all strive to behave ethically as follows:

- Be complete and honest about findings, even if the results are not what was expected or desired.

- Seek the advice of professionals when unsure about which statistical analyses are correct.

- Always disclose financial relationships or any other interests in the outcome of the research.
- Acknowledge only those who made a meaningful contribution to the study.
- Be ready and willing to share data, methods, analyses, and results.
- Clearly identify any assumptions, limitations, or outstanding questions in the research.

15-1 Discussion Points

Ethics and Data Collection

1. Is it ethical to use prisoners as subjects if they understand the potential risks and/or benefits and have given their consent?

- Is it ethical to offer an incentive for consent, such as additional privileges or a reduced sentence?

- Does the size and scope of the potential benefit of the study impact this assessment?

2. Do you think the Milgram experiment described in this section was unethical? Why or why not?

- Does the finding that only 1% of participants regretted their involvement affect your view?

3. Is potential psychological harm any different from potential physical harm?

4. Is it unethical to intentionally infect test subjects who are humans? What about animals?

5. Identify three survey topics that you think would have high or low response rates based on their salience and/or social desirability.

6. Volunteer bias is well documented on the topic of human sexuality. What are some other topics that might have high risk for this bias?

7. Have you ever been asked to volunteer in a survey or poll via the Internet, telephone, or mail? Do you think these studies were intentionally exploiting interviewer bias to generate a specific result?

8. Reducing sample bias may result in a less positive outcome overall, which may delay or stop the release of a drug that a subset of the population might benefit from. Is this an acceptable tradeoff?

Ethics and Analysis

1. Is peer review an effective mechanism to protect against data fabrication or use of inappropriate statistical methods? Why or why not?

2. One article on the topic of statistical errors in medical research listed 47 potential sources of error. Try to identify 5 potential sources of error.

Ethics and Reporting

1. What is medical ghostwriting? Is the practice of medical ghostwriting unethical?

2. Should common standards exist for claiming authorship of a study? What should be included in those standards?

3. Is the law requiring disclosure of payments sufficient to protect against financial support skewing study results? Do you have any other recommendations?

4. Find and identify a recent example where nonsignificant results were reported by the media. Do you consider such examples to be unethical?

5. Should there be any standards for reporting statistical results? What are some items that those standards should include?

6. How does the disclosure of financial support affect your perception of a study's legitimacy? Do the amount and/or source of funding affect this perception?

15-2   Projects

Key Concept Every statistics course can benefit greatly from a final capstone project. This activity is a fun, valuable, and rewarding experience for students as well as professors. A final project provides students with the opportunity to use principles of statistics in a real and interesting application. This section provides a suggested format for such a project.

Group Project vs. Individual Project

Although different topics could be assigned to individuals, group projects are more effective because they help develop the interpersonal skills that are so necessary in today's working environment. One study showed that the "inability to get along with others" is the main reason for firing employees, so a group project can be very helpful in preparing students for their future work environments. Groups of three, four, or five students work well. The professor should select groups with consideration given to relevant factors such as past class performance and attendance.

Oral Report A 10- to 15-minute class presentation should involve all group members in a coordinated effort to clearly describe the important results of the study. Students typically have some reluctance to speak in public, so a brief oral report can be very helpful in building confidence. The oral report is an activity that can better prepare students for future professional activities.

Written Report The goal of the final capstone project is not to produce a written document equivalent to a term paper. However, a brief written report should be submitted, and it should include the following components:

1. List of data collected along with a description of how the data were obtained.
2. Description of the method of analysis.
3. Relevant graphs and/or statistics, including displays from technology.
4. Statement of conclusions.
5. Reasons why the results might not be correct, along with a description of ways in which the study could be improved. (It may not be practical for students to use a sound sampling method. Practical considerations may require that they use a convenience sample, and stress that this is perfectly acceptable as long as they explain how their sampling method is flawed and how it could have been improved with sufficient resources of time, money, and effort.)

Large Classes or Online Classes: Posters or PowerPoint Some classes are too large for individual or group projects. Online classes are not able to meet as a group. For such classes, reports of individual or small group projects can be presented through posters similar to those found at conference poster sessions. Posters or PowerPoint presentations summarizing important elements of a project can be submitted to professors for evaluation.

Project Topics The "Cooperative Group Activities" listed near the end of each chapter include more than 100 suggestions for projects.

15-3 Procedures

Key Concept This section describes a general approach for the statistical analysis of data.

Prepare Instead of mindlessly plugging data into a statistical procedure, we should begin with a preparation that includes basic considerations, such as those included in Figure 1-2 from Section 1-2:

- Consider the *context* of the data
- Consider the *source* of the data
- Consider the *sampling method*

Analyze After completing the preliminary preparations, we should proceed with the following:

- Exploring the data by constructing appropriate graphs, visualizing the distribution of the data, identifying outliers, and computing values of relevant statistics
- Using technology to apply a suitable statistical method

Conclude Based on the results, consider the conclusions to be formed.

- Determine whether the results have *statistical significance.*
- Determine whether the results have *practical significance.*

Inferences: Estimating Parameters and Hypothesis Testing When trying to use sample data for making inferences about a population, it is often difficult to determine which particular procedure is best. Figure 15-1 on the following page includes the major methods included in this book, along with a scheme for determining which of those methods should be used. Figure 15-1 applies to a fixed population. If the data are from a process that may change over time, construct a control chart (see Chapter 14) to determine whether the process is statistically stable. Figure 15-1 applies to process data only if the process is statistically stable. In addition to the procedures identified in Figure 15-1, there are many other methods that might be more suitable for a particular statistical analysis. Consult your friendly professional statistician for help with other methods.

15-4 Perspectives

Key Concept It probably comes as no big surprise that successful completion of an introductory statistics course does not make anyone an expert statistician. But one of the great things about statistics is that the limited topics covered in the introductory course can enable you to understand the statistics presented in the media, professional journals, and your classes. And you will have improved job marketability.

Throughout this text we have emphasized the importance of good sampling methods. We should all know that a bad sample may be beyond repair by even the most expert statisticians using the most sophisticated techniques and the most expensive and extensive technology. There is a plethora of mail, magazine, Internet, and telephone call-in surveys that give respondents the option of whether to participate. The results of such voluntary response surveys are generally worthless when judged according to the criteria of sound statistical methodology. Conversely, we should all know that many surveys and polls obtain very good results, even though the sample

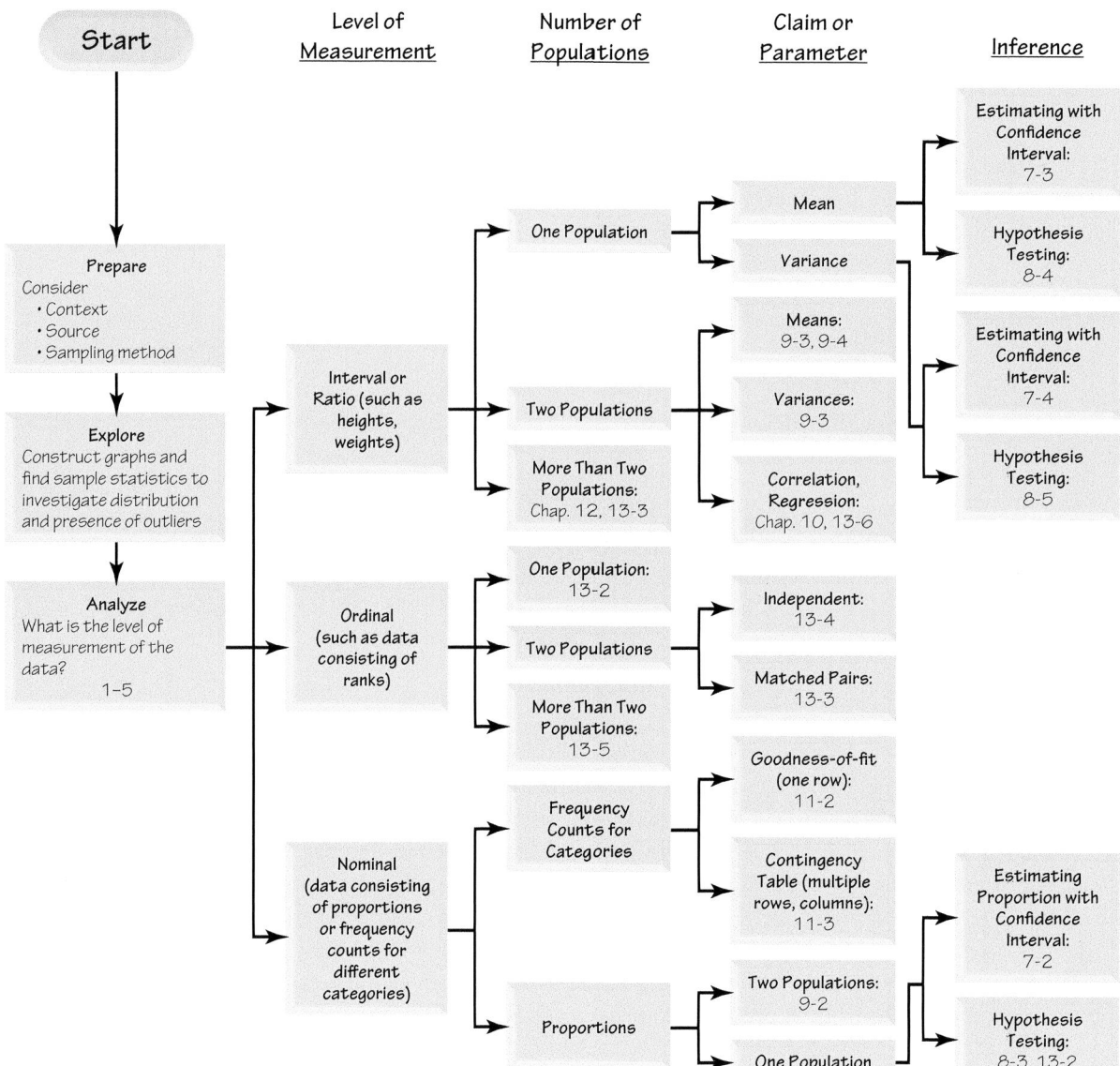

Figure 15-1   Selecting the Appropriate Procedure

sizes might seem to be relatively small. Although many people refuse to believe it, a nationwide survey of only 1200 voters can provide good results if the sampling is carefully planned and executed.

Throughout this text we have emphasized the *interpretation* of results. Computers and calculators are quite good at providing results, but such results require careful interpretation. We should know that a result is not automatically valid simply because it was computer-generated. Computers don't think, and they are quite capable of providing results that are quite ridiculous when considered in the context of the real world. We should always apply the most important and indispensable tool in all of statistics: *common sense!*

Appendix A   Tables

Table A-1 Binomial Probabilities

n	x	.01	.05	.10	.20	.30	.40	.50	.60	.70	.80	.90	.95	.99	x
2	0	.980	.902	.810	.640	.490	.360	.250	.160	.090	.040	.010	.002	0+	0
	1	.020	.095	.180	.320	.420	.480	.500	.480	.420	.320	.180	.095	.020	1
	2	0+	.002	.010	.040	.090	.160	.250	.360	.490	.640	.810	.902	.980	2
3	0	.970	.857	.729	.512	.343	.216	.125	.064	.027	.008	.001	0+	0+	0
	1	.029	.135	.243	.384	.441	.432	.375	.288	.189	.096	.027	.007	0+	1
	2	0+	.007	.027	.096	.189	.288	.375	.432	.441	.384	.243	.135	.029	2
	3	0+	0+	.001	.008	.027	.064	.125	.216	.343	.512	.729	.857	.970	3
4	0	.961	.815	.656	.410	.240	.130	.062	.026	.008	.002	0+	0+	0+	0
	1	.039	.171	.292	.410	.412	.346	.250	.154	.076	.026	.004	0+	0+	1
	2	.001	.014	.049	.154	.265	.346	.375	.346	.265	.154	.049	.014	.001	2
	3	0+	0+	.004	.026	.076	.154	.250	.346	.412	.410	.292	.171	.039	3
	4	0+	0+	0+	.002	.008	.026	.062	.130	.240	.410	.656	.815	.961	4
5	0	.951	.774	.590	.328	.168	.078	.031	.010	.002	0+	0+	0+	0+	0
	1	.048	.204	.328	.410	.360	.259	.156	.077	.028	.006	0+	0+	0+	1
	2	.001	.021	.073	.205	.309	.346	.312	.230	.132	.051	.008	.001	0+	2
	3	0+	.001	.008	.051	.132	.230	.312	.346	.309	.205	.073	.021	.001	3
	4	0+	0+	0+	.006	.028	.077	.156	.259	.360	.410	.328	.204	.048	4
	5	0+	0+	0+	0+	.002	.010	.031	.078	.168	.328	.590	.774	.951	5
6	0	.941	.735	.531	.262	.118	.047	.016	.004	.001	0+	0+	0+	0+	0
	1	.057	.232	.354	.393	.303	.187	.094	.037	.010	.002	0+	0+	0+	1
	2	.001	.031	.098	.246	.324	.311	.234	.138	.060	.015	.001	0+	0+	2
	3	0+	.002	.015	.082	.185	.276	.312	.276	.185	.082	.015	.002	0+	3
	4	0+	0+	.001	.015	.060	.138	.234	.311	.324	.246	.098	.031	.001	4
	5	0+	0+	0+	.002	.010	.037	.094	.187	.303	.393	.354	.232	.057	5
	6	0+	0+	0+	0+	.001	.004	.016	.047	.118	.262	.531	.735	.941	6
7	0	.932	.698	.478	.210	.082	.028	.008	.002	0+	0+	0+	0+	0+	0
	1	.066	.257	.372	.367	.247	.131	.055	.017	.004	0+	0+	0+	0+	1
	2	.002	.041	.124	.275	.318	.261	.164	.077	.025	.004	0+	0+	0+	2
	3	0+	.004	.023	.115	.227	.290	.273	.194	.097	.029	.003	0+	0+	3
	4	0+	0+	.003	.029	.097	.194	.273	.290	.227	.115	.023	.004	0+	4
	5	0+	0+	0+	.004	.025	.077	.164	.261	.318	.275	.124	.041	.002	5
	6	0+	0+	0+	0+	.004	.017	.055	.131	.247	.367	.372	.257	.066	6
	7	0+	0+	0+	0+	0+	.002	.008	.028	.082	.210	.478	.698	.932	7
8	0	.923	.663	.430	.168	.058	.017	.004	.001	0+	0+	0+	0+	0+	0
	1	.075	.279	.383	.336	.198	.090	.031	.008	.001	0+	0+	0+	0+	1
	2	.003	.051	.149	.294	.296	.209	.109	.041	.010	.001	0+	0+	0+	2
	3	0+	.005	.033	.147	.254	.279	.219	.124	.047	.009	0+	0+	0+	3
	4	0+	0+	.005	.046	.136	.232	.273	.232	.136	.046	.005	0+	0+	4
	5	0+	0+	0+	.009	.047	.124	.219	.279	.254	.147	.033	.005	0+	5
	6	0+	0+	0+	.001	.010	.041	.109	.209	.296	.294	.149	.051	.003	6
	7	0+	0+	0+	0+	.001	.008	.031	.090	.198	.336	.383	.279	.075	7
	8	0+	0+	0+	0+	0+	.001	.004	.017	.058	.168	.430	.663	.923	8

p is the column header spanning the probability columns.

NOTE: 0+ represents a positive probability less than 0.0005.

From Frederick C. Mosteller, Robert E. K. Rourke, and George B. Thomas, Jr., *Probability with Statistical Applications*, 2nd ed., © 1970. Reprinted and electronically reproduced by permission of Pearson Education, Inc., Upper Saddle River, New Jersey.

NEGATIVE z Scores

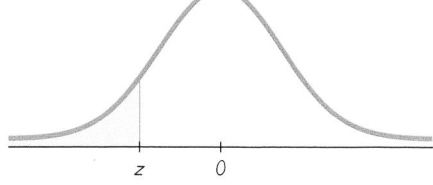

Table A-2 Standard Normal (z) Distribution: Cumulative Area from the LEFT

z	.00	.01	.02	.03	.04	.05	.06	.07	.08	.09
−3.50 and lower	.0001									
−3.4	.0003	.0003	.0003	.0003	.0003	.0003	.0003	.0003	.0003	.0002
−3.3	.0005	.0005	.0005	.0004	.0004	.0004	.0004	.0004	.0004	.0003
−3.2	.0007	.0007	.0006	.0006	.0006	.0006	.0006	.0005	.0005	.0005
−3.1	.0010	.0009	.0009	.0009	.0008	.0008	.0008	.0008	.0007	.0007
−3.0	.0013	.0013	.0013	.0012	.0012	.0011	.0011	.0011	.0010	.0010
−2.9	.0019	.0018	.0018	.0017	.0016	.0016	.0015	.0015	.0014	.0014
−2.8	.0026	.0025	.0024	.0023	.0023	.0022	.0021	.0021	.0020	.0019
−2.7	.0035	.0034	.0033	.0032	.0031	.0030	.0029	.0028	.0027	.0026
−2.6	.0047	.0045	.0044	.0043	.0041	.0040	.0039	.0038	.0037	.0036
−2.5	.0062	.0060	.0059	.0057	.0055	.0054	.0052	.0051 *	.0049	.0048
−2.4	.0082	.0080	.0078	.0075	.0073	.0071	.0069	.0068	.0066	.0064
−2.3	.0107	.0104	.0102	.0099	.0096	.0094	.0091	.0089	.0087	.0084
−2.2	.0139	.0136	.0132	.0129	.0125	.0122	.0119	.0116	.0113	.0110
−2.1	.0179	.0174	.0170	.0166	.0162	.0158	.0154	.0150	.0146	.0143
−2.0	.0228	.0222	.0217	.0212	.0207	.0202	.0197	.0192	.0188	.0183
−1.9	.0287	.0281	.0274	.0268	.0262	.0256	.0250	.0244	.0239	.0233
−1.8	.0359	.0351	.0344	.0336	.0329	.0322	.0314	.0307	.0301	.0294
−1.7	.0446	.0436	.0427	.0418	.0409	.0401	.0392	.0384	.0375	.0367
−1.6	.0548	.0537	.0526	.0516	.0505 *	.0495	.0485	.0475	.0465	.0455
−1.5	.0668	.0655	.0643	.0630	.0618	.0606	.0594	.0582	.0571	.0559
−1.4	.0808	.0793	.0778	.0764	.0749	.0735	.0721	.0708	.0694	.0681
−1.3	.0968	.0951	.0934	.0918	.0901	.0885	.0869	.0853	.0838	.0823
−1.2	.1151	.1131	.1112	.1093	.1075	.1056	.1038	.1020	.1003	.0985
−1.1	.1357	.1335	.1314	.1292	.1271	.1251	.1230	.1210	.1190	.1170
−1.0	.1587	.1562	.1539	.1515	.1492	.1469	.1446	.1423	.1401	.1379
−0.9	.1841	.1814	.1788	.1762	.1736	.1711	.1685	.1660	.1635	.1611
−0.8	.2119	.2090	.2061	.2033	.2005	.1977	.1949	.1922	.1894	.1867
−0.7	.2420	.2389	.2358	.2327	.2296	.2266	.2236	.2206	.2177	.2148
−0.6	.2743	.2709	.2676	.2643	.2611	.2578	.2546	.2514	.2483	.2451
−0.5	.3085	.3050	.3015	.2981	.2946	.2912	.2877	.2843	.2810	.2776
−0.4	.3446	.3409	.3372	.3336	.3300	.3264	.3228	.3192	.3156	.3121
−0.3	.3821	.3783	.3745	.3707	.3669	.3632	.3594	.3557	.3520	.3483
−0.2	.4207	.4168	.4129	.4090	.4052	.4013	.3974	.3936	.3897	.3859
−0.1	.4602	.4562	.4522	.4483	.4443	.4404	.4364	.4325	.4286	.4247
−0.0	.5000	.4960	.4920	.4880	.4840	.4801	.4761	.4721	.4681	.4641

NOTE: For values of z below 3.49, use 0.0001 for the area.   (continued)
* Use these common values that result from interpolation:

z Score	Area
−1.645	0.0500
−2.575	0.0050

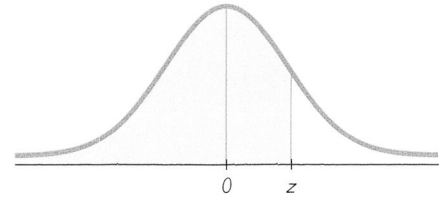

0   z

POSITIVE z Scores

Table A-2 *(continued)* Cumulative Area from the LEFT

z	.00	.01	.02	.03	.04	.05	.06	.07	.08	.09
0.0	.5000	.5040	.5080	.5120	.5160	.5199	.5239	.5279	.5319	.5359
0.1	.5398	.5438	.5478	.5517	.5557	.5596	.5636	.5675	.5714	.5753
0.2	.5793	.5832	.5871	.5910	.5948	.5987	.6026	.6064	.6103	.6141
0.3	.6179	.6217	.6255	.6293	.6331	.6368	.6406	.6443	.6480	.6517
0.4	.6554	.6591	.6628	.6664	.6700	.6736	.6772	.6808	.6844	.6879
0.5	.6915	.6950	.6985	.7019	.7054	.7088	.7123	.7157	.7190	.7224
0.6	.7257	.7291	.7324	.7357	.7389	.7422	.7454	.7486	.7517	.7549
0.7	.7580	.7611	.7642	.7673	.7704	.7734	.7764	.7794	.7823	.7852
0.8	.7881	.7910	.7939	.7967	.7995	.8023	.8051	.8078	.8106	.8133
0.9	.8159	.8186	.8212	.8238	.8264	.8289	.8315	.8340	.8365	.8389
1.0	.8413	.8438	.8461	.8485	.8508	.8531	.8554	.8577	.8599	.8621
1.1	.8643	.8665	.8686	.8708	.8729	.8749	.8770	.8790	.8810	.8830
1.2	.8849	.8869	.8888	.8907	.8925	.8944	.8962	.8980	.8997	.9015
1.3	.9032	.9049	.9066	.9082	.9099	.9115	.9131	.9147	.9162	.9177
1.4	.9192	.9207	.9222	.9236	.9251	.9265	.9279	.9292	.9306	.9319
1.5	.9332	.9345	.9357	.9370	.9382	.9394	.9406	.9418	.9429	.9441
1.6	.9452	.9463	.9474	.9484	.9495 *	.9505	.9515	.9525	.9535	.9545
1.7	.9554	.9564	.9573	.9582	.9591	.9599	.9608	.9616	.9625	.9633
1.8	.9641	.9649	.9656	.9664	.9671	.9678	.9686	.9693	.9699	.9706
1.9	.9713	.9719	.9726	.9732	.9738	.9744	.9750	.9756	.9761	.9767
2.0	.9772	.9778	.9783	.9788	.9793	.9798	.9803	.9808	.9812	.9817
2.1	.9821	.9826	.9830	.9834	.9838	.9842	.9846	.9850	.9854	.9857
2.2	.9861	.9864	.9868	.9871	.9875	.9878	.9881	.9884	.9887	.9890
2.3	.9893	.9896	.9898	.9901	.9904	.9906	.9909	.9911	.9913	.9916
2.4	.9918	.9920	.9922	.9925	.9927	.9929	.9931	.9932	.9934	.9936
2.5	.9938	.9940	.9941	.9943	.9945	.9946	.9948	.9949 *	.9951	.9952
2.6	.9953	.9955	.9956	.9957	.9959	.9960	.9961	.9962	.9963	.9964
2.7	.9965	.9966	.9967	.9968	.9969	.9970	.9971	.9972	.9973	.9974
2.8	.9974	.9975	.9976	.9977	.9977	.9978	.9979	.9979	.9980	.9981
2.9	.9981	.9982	.9982	.9983	.9984	.9984	.9985	.9985	.9986	.9986
3.0	.9987	.9987	.9987	.9988	.9988	.9989	.9989	.9989	.9990	.9990
3.1	.9990	.9991	.9991	.9991	.9992	.9992	.9992	.9992	.9993	.9993
3.2	.9993	.9993	.9994	.9994	.9994	.9994	.9994	.9995	.9995	.9995
3.3	.9995	.9995	.9995	.9996	.9996	.9996	.9996	.9996	.9996	.9997
3.4	.9997	.9997	.9997	.9997	.9997	.9997	.9997	.9997	.9997	.9998
3.50 and up	.9999									

NOTE: For values of *z* above 3.49, use 0.9999 for the area.
*Use these common values that result from interpolation:

z Score	Area
1.645	0.9500
2.575	0.9950

Common Critical Values

Confidence Level	Critical Value
0.90	1.645
0.95	1.96
0.99	2.575

Table A-3 *t* Distribution: Critical *t* Values

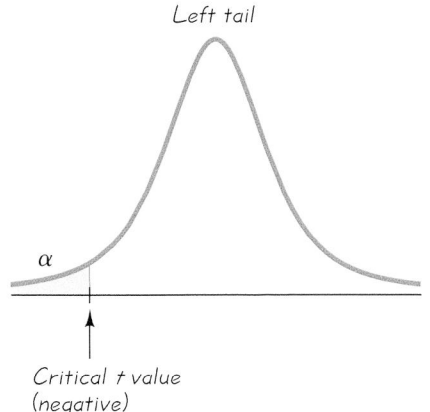

Left tail

α

Critical *t* value
(negative)

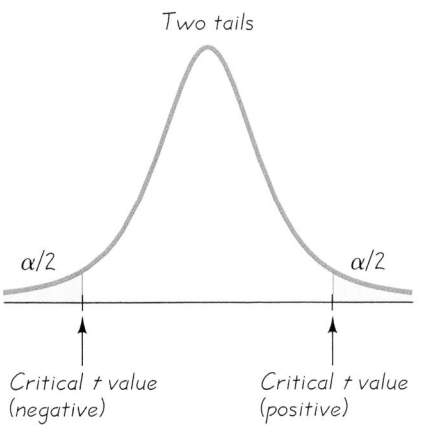

Right tail

α

Critical *t* value
(positive)

Two tails

$\alpha/2$ $\alpha/2$

Critical *t* value   Critical *t* value
(negative)   (positive)

			Area in One Tail		
	0.005	0.01	0.025	0.05	0.10
Degrees of			Area in Two Tails		
Freedom	0.01	0.02	0.05	0.10	0.20
1	63.657	31.821	12.706	6.314	3.078
2	9.925	6.965	4.303	2.920	1.886
3	5.841	4.541	3.182	2.353	1.638
4	4.604	3.747	2.776	2.132	1.533
5	4.032	3.365	2.571	2.015	1.476
6	3.707	3.143	2.447	1.943	1.440
7	3.499	2.998	2.365	1.895	1.415
8	3.355	2.896	2.306	1.860	1.397
9	3.250	2.821	2.262	1.833	1.383
10	3.169	2.764	2.228	1.812	1.372
11	3.106	2.718	2.201	1.796	1.363
12	3.055	2.681	2.179	1.782	1.356
13	3.012	2.650	2.160	1.771	1.350
14	2.977	2.624	2.145	1.761	1.345
15	2.947	2.602	2.131	1.753	1.341
16	2.921	2.583	2.120	1.746	1.337
17	2.898	2.567	2.110	1.740	1.333
18	2.878	2.552	2.101	1.734	1.330
19	2.861	2.539	2.093	1.729	1.328
20	2.845	2.528	2.086	1.725	1.325
21	2.831	2.518	2.080	1.721	1.323
22	2.819	2.508	2.074	1.717	1.321
23	2.807	2.500	2.069	1.714	1.319
24	2.797	2.492	2.064	1.711	1.318
25	2.787	2.485	2.060	1.708	1.316
26	2.779	2.479	2.056	1.706	1.315
27	2.771	2.473	2.052	1.703	1.314
28	2.763	2.467	2.048	1.701	1.313
29	2.756	2.462	2.045	1.699	1.311
30	2.750	2.457	2.042	1.697	1.310
31	2.744	2.453	2.040	1.696	1.309
32	2.738	2.449	2.037	1.694	1.309
33	2.733	2.445	2.035	1.692	1.308
34	2.728	2.441	2.032	1.691	1.307
35	2.724	2.438	2.030	1.690	1.306
36	2.719	2.434	2.028	1.688	1.306
37	2.715	2.431	2.026	1.687	1.305
38	2.712	2.429	2.024	1.686	1.304
39	2.708	2.426	2.023	1.685	1.304
40	2.704	2.423	2.021	1.684	1.303
45	2.690	2.412	2.014	1.679	1.301
50	2.678	2.403	2.009	1.676	1.299
60	2.660	2.390	2.000	1.671	1.296
70	2.648	2.381	1.994	1.667	1.294
80	2.639	2.374	1.990	1.664	1.292
90	2.632	2.368	1.987	1.662	1.291
100	2.626	2.364	1.984	1.660	1.290
200	2.601	2.345	1.972	1.653	1.286
300	2.592	2.339	1.968	1.650	1.284
400	2.588	2.336	1.966	1.649	1.284
500	2.586	2.334	1.965	1.648	1.283
1000	2.581	2.330	1.962	1.646	1.282
2000	2.578	2.328	1.961	1.646	1.282
Large	2.576	2.326	1.960	1.645	1.282

Table A-4 Chi-Square (χ^2) Distribution

Degrees of Freedom	Area to the Right of the Critical Value									
	0.995	0.99	0.975	0.95	0.90	0.10	0.05	0.025	0.01	0.005
1	—	—	0.001	0.004	0.016	2.706	3.841	5.024	6.635	7.879
2	0.010	0.020	0.051	0.103	0.211	4.605	5.991	7.378	9.210	10.597
3	0.072	0.115	0.216	0.352	0.584	6.251	7.815	9.348	11.345	12.838
4	0.207	0.297	0.484	0.711	1.064	7.779	9.488	11.143	13.277	14.860
5	0.412	0.554	0.831	1.145	1.610	9.236	11.071	12.833	15.086	16.750
6	0.676	0.872	1.237	1.635	2.204	10.645	12.592	14.449	16.812	18.548
7	0.989	1.239	1.690	2.167	2.833	12.017	14.067	16.013	18.475	20.278
8	1.344	1.646	2.180	2.733	3.490	13.362	15.507	17.535	20.090	21.955
9	1.735	2.088	2.700	3.325	4.168	14.684	16.919	19.023	21.666	23.589
10	2.156	2.558	3.247	3.940	4.865	15.987	18.307	20.483	23.209	25.188
11	2.603	3.053	3.816	4.575	5.578	17.275	19.675	21.920	24.725	26.757
12	3.074	3.571	4.404	5.226	6.304	18.549	21.026	23.337	26.217	28.299
13	3.565	4.107	5.009	5.892	7.042	19.812	22.362	24.736	27.688	29.819
14	4.075	4.660	5.629	6.571	7.790	21.064	23.685	26.119	29.141	31.319
15	4.601	5.229	6.262	7.261	8.547	22.307	24.996	27.488	30.578	32.801
16	5.142	5.812	6.908	7.962	9.312	23.542	26.296	28.845	32.000	34.267
17	5.697	6.408	7.564	8.672	10.085	24.769	27.587	30.191	33.409	35.718
18	6.265	7.015	8.231	9.390	10.865	25.989	28.869	31.526	34.805	37.156
19	6.844	7.633	8.907	10.117	11.651	27.204	30.144	32.852	36.191	38.582
20	7.434	8.260	9.591	10.851	12.443	28.412	31.410	34.170	37.566	39.997
21	8.034	8.897	10.283	11.591	13.240	29.615	32.671	35.479	38.932	41.401
22	8.643	9.542	10.982	12.338	14.042	30.813	33.924	36.781	40.289	42.796
23	9.260	10.196	11.689	13.091	14.848	32.007	35.172	38.076	41.638	44.181
24	9.886	10.856	12.401	13.848	15.659	33.196	36.415	39.364	42.980	45.559
25	10.520	11.524	13.120	14.611	16.473	34.382	37.652	40.646	44.314	46.928
26	11.160	12.198	13.844	15.379	17.292	35.563	38.885	41.923	45.642	48.290
27	11.808	12.879	14.573	16.151	18.114	36.741	40.113	43.194	46.963	49.645
28	12.461	13.565	15.308	16.928	18.939	37.916	41.337	44.461	48.278	50.993
29	13.121	14.257	16.047	17.708	19.768	39.087	42.557	45.722	49.588	52.336
30	13.787	14.954	16.791	18.493	20.599	40.256	43.773	46.979	50.892	53.672
40	20.707	22.164	24.433	26.509	29.051	51.805	55.758	59.342	63.691	66.766
50	27.991	29.707	32.357	34.764	37.689	63.167	67.505	71.420	76.154	79.490
60	35.534	37.485	40.482	43.188	46.459	74.397	79.082	83.298	88.379	91.952
70	43.275	45.442	48.758	51.739	55.329	85.527	90.531	95.023	100.425	104.215
80	51.172	53.540	57.153	60.391	64.278	96.578	101.879	106.629	112.329	116.321
90	59.196	61.754	65.647	69.126	73.291	107.565	113.145	118.136	124.116	128.299
100	67.328	70.065	74.222	77.929	82.358	118.498	124.342	129.561	135.807	140.169

Source: Donald B. Owen, Handbook of Statistical Tables.

Degrees of Freedom

$n - 1$	**Confidence interval or hypothesis test** for a standard deviation σ or variance σ^2
$k - 1$	**Goodness-of-fit** with k categories
$(r - 1)(c - 1)$	**Contingency table** with r rows and c columns
$k - 1$	**Kruskal-Wallis test** with k samples

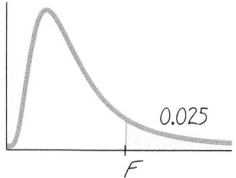

Table A-5 *F* Distribution ($\alpha = 0.025$ in the right tail)

				Numerator degrees of freedom (df$_1$)					
	1	2	3	4	5	6	7	8	9
1	647.79	799.50	864.16	899.58	921.85	937.11	948.22	956.66	963.28
2	38.506	39.000	39.165	39.248	39.298	39.331	39.335	39.373	39.387
3	17.443	16.044	15.439	15.101	14.885	14.735	14.624	14.540	14.473
4	12.218	10.649	9.9792	9.6045	9.3645	9.1973	9.0741	8.9796	8.9047
5	10.007	8.4336	7.7636	7.3879	7.1464	6.9777	6.8531	6.7572	6.6811
6	8.8131	7.2599	6.5988	6.2272	5.9876	5.8198	5.6955	5.5996	5.5234
7	8.0727	6.5415	5.8898	5.5226	5.2852	5.1186	4.9949	4.8993	4.8232
8	7.5709	6.0595	5.4160	5.0526	4.8173	4.6517	4.5286	4.4333	4.3572
9	7.2093	5.7147	5.0781	4.7181	4.4844	4.3197	4.1970	4.1020	4.0260
10	6.9367	5.4564	4.8256	4.4683	4.2361	4.0721	3.9498	3.8549	3.7790
11	6.7241	5.2559	4.6300	4.2751	4.0440	3.8807	3.7586	3.6638	3.5879
12	6.5538	5.0959	4.4742	4.1212	3.8911	3.7283	3.6065	3.5118	3.4358
13	6.4143	4.9653	4.3472	3.9959	3.7667	3.6043	3.4827	3.3880	3.3120
14	6.2979	4.8567	4.2417	3.8919	3.6634	3.5014	3.3799	3.2853	3.2093
15	6.1995	4.7650	4.1528	3.8043	3.5764	3.4147	3.2934	3.1987	3.1227
16	6.1151	4.6867	4.0768	3.7294	3.5021	3.3406	3.2194	3.1248	3.0488
17	6.0420	4.6189	4.0112	3.6648	3.4379	3.2767	3.1556	3.0610	2.9849
18	5.9781	4.5597	3.9539	3.6083	3.3820	3.2209	3.0999	3.0053	2.9291
19	5.9216	4.5075	3.9034	3.5587	3.3327	3.1718	3.0509	2.9563	2.8801
20	5.8715	4.4613	3.8587	3.5147	3.2891	3.1283	3.0074	2.9128	2.8365
21	5.8266	4.4199	3.8188	3.4754	3.2501	3.0895	2.9686	2.8740	2.7977
22	5.7863	4.3828	3.7829	3.4401	3.2151	3.0546	2.9338	2.8392	2.7628
23	5.7498	4.3492	3.7505	3.4083	3.1835	3.0232	2.9023	2.8077	2.7313
24	5.7166	4.3187	3.7211	3.3794	3.1548	2.9946	2.8738	2.7791	2.7027
25	5.6864	4.2909	3.6943	3.3530	3.1287	2.9685	2.8478	2.7531	2.6766
26	5.6586	4.2655	3.6697	3.3289	3.1048	2.9447	2.8240	2.7293	2.6528
27	5.6331	4.2421	3.6472	3.3067	3.0828	2.9228	2.8021	2.7074	2.6309
28	5.6096	4.2205	3.6264	3.2863	3.0626	2.9027	2.7820	2.6872	2.6106
29	5.5878	4.2006	3.6072	3.2674	3.0438	2.8840	2.7633	2.6686	2.5919
30	5.5675	4.1821	3.5894	3.2499	3.0265	2.8667	2.7460	2.6513	2.5746
40	5.4239	4.0510	3.4633	3.1261	2.9037	2.7444	2.6238	2.5289	2.4519
60	5.2856	3.9253	3.3425	3.0077	2.7863	2.6274	2.5068	2.4117	2.3344
120	5.1523	3.8046	3.2269	2.8943	2.6740	2.5154	2.3948	2.2994	2.2217
∞	5.0239	3.6889	3.1161	2.7858	2.5665	2.4082	2.2875	2.1918	2.1136

Denominator degrees of freedom (df$_2$)

(continued)

Table A-5 *(continued)* F Distribution ($\alpha = 0.025$ in the right tail)

		Numerator degrees of freedom (df_1)								
	10	12	15	20	24	30	40	60	120	∞
1	968.63	976.71	984.87	993.10	997.25	1001.4	1005.6	1009.8	1014.0	1018.3
2	39.398	39.415	39.431	39.448	39.456	39.465	39.473	39.481	39.490	39.498
3	14.419	14.337	14.253	14.167	14.124	14.081	14.037	13.992	13.947	13.902
4	8.8439	8.7512	8.6565	8.5599	8.5109	8.4613	8.4111	8.3604	8.3092	8.2573
5	6.6192	6.5245	6.4277	6.3286	6.2780	6.2269	6.1750	6.1225	6.0693	6.0153
6	5.4613	5.3662	5.2687	5.1684	5.1172	5.0652	5.0125	4.9589	4.9044	4.8491
7	4.7611	4.6658	4.5678	4.4667	4.4150	4.3624	4.3089	4.2544	4.1989	4.1423
8	4.2951	4.1997	4.1012	3.9995	3.9472	3.8940	3.8398	3.7844	3.7279	3.6702
9	3.9639	3.8682	3.7694	3.6669	3.6142	3.5604	3.5055	3.4493	3.3918	3.3329
10	3.7168	3.6209	3.5217	3.4185	3.3654	3.3110	3.2554	3.1984	3.1399	3.0798
11	3.5257	3.4296	3.3299	3.2261	3.1725	3.1176	3.0613	3.0035	2.9441	2.8828
12	3.3736	3.2773	3.1772	3.0728	3.0187	2.9633	2.9063	2.8478	2.7874	2.7249
13	3.2497	3.1532	3.0527	2.9477	2.8932	2.8372	2.7797	2.7204	2.6590	2.5955
14	3.1469	3.0502	2.9493	2.8437	2.7888	2.7324	2.6742	2.6142	2.5519	2.4872
15	3.0602	2.9633	2.8621	2.7559	2.7006	2.6437	2.5850	2.5242	2.4611	2.3953
16	2.9862	2.8890	2.7875	2.6808	2.6252	2.5678	2.5085	2.4471	2.3831	2.3163
17	2.9222	2.8249	2.7230	2.6158	2.5598	2.5020	2.4422	2.3801	2.3153	2.2474
18	2.8664	2.7689	2.6667	2.5590	2.5027	2.4445	2.3842	2.3214	2.2558	2.1869
19	2.8172	2.7196	2.6171	2.5089	2.4523	2.3937	2.3329	2.2696	2.2032	2.1333
20	2.7737	2.6758	2.5731	2.4645	2.4076	2.3486	2.2873	2.2234	2.1562	2.0853
21	2.7348	2.6368	2.5338	2.4247	2.3675	2.3082	2.2465	2.1819	2.1141	2.0422
22	2.6998	2.6017	2.4984	2.3890	2.3315	2.2718	2.2097	2.1446	2.0760	2.0032
23	2.6682	2.5699	2.4665	2.3567	2.2989	2.2389	2.1763	2.1107	2.0415	1.9677
24	2.6396	2.5411	2.4374	2.3273	2.2693	2.2090	2.1460	2.0799	2.0099	1.9353
25	2.6135	2.5149	2.4110	2.3005	2.2422	2.1816	2.1183	2.0516	1.9811	1.9055
26	2.5896	2.4908	2.3867	2.2759	2.2174	2.1565	2.0928	2.0257	1.9545	1.8781
27	2.5676	2.4688	2.3644	2.2533	2.1946	2.1334	2.0693	2.0018	1.9299	1.8527
28	2.5473	2.4484	2.3438	2.2324	2.1735	2.1121	2.0477	1.9797	1.9072	1.8291
29	2.5286	2.4295	2.3248	2.2131	2.1540	2.0923	2.0276	1.9591	1.8861	1.8072
30	2.5112	2.4120	2.3072	2.1952	2.1359	2.0739	2.0089	1.9400	1.8664	1.7867
40	2.3882	2.2882	2.1819	2.0677	2.0069	1.9429	1.8752	1.8028	1.7242	1.6371
60	2.2702	2.1692	2.0613	1.9445	1.8817	1.8152	1.7440	1.6668	1.5810	1.4821
120	2.1570	2.0548	1.9450	1.8249	1.7597	1.6899	1.6141	1.5299	1.4327	1.3104
∞	2.0483	1.9447	1.8326	1.7085	1.6402	1.5660	1.4835	1.3883	1.2684	1.0000

Denominator degrees of freedom (df_2)

Based on data from Maxine Merrington and Catherine M. Thompson, "Tables of Percentage Points of the Inverted Beta (*F*) Distribution," *Biometrika 33* (1943): 80–84.

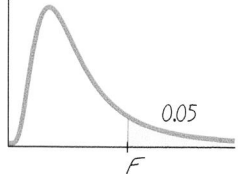

Table A-5 *(continued)* *F* Distribution ($\alpha = 0.05$ in the right tail)

		\multicolumn{9}{c}{Numerator degrees of freedom (df_1)}								
		1	2	3	4	5	6	7	8	9
	1	161.45	199.50	215.71	224.58	230.16	233.99	236.77	238.88	240.54
	2	18.513	19.000	19.164	19.247	19.296	19.330	19.353	19.371	19.385
	3	10.128	9.5521	9.2766	9.1172	9.0135	8.9406	8.8867	8.8452	8.8123
	4	7.7086	6.9443	6.5914	6.3882	6.2561	6.1631	6.0942	6.0410	6.9988
	5	6.6079	5.7861	5.4095	5.1922	5.0503	4.9503	4.8759	4.8183	4.7725
	6	5.9874	5.1433	4.7571	4.5337	4.3874	4.2839	4.2067	4.1468	4.0990
	7	5.5914	4.7374	4.3468	4.1203	3.9715	3.8660	3.7870	3.7257	3.6767
	8	5.3177	4.4590	4.0662	3.8379	3.6875	3.5806	3.5005	3.4381	3.3881
	9	5.1174	4.2565	3.8625	3.6331	3.4817	3.3738	3.2927	3.2296	3.1789
	10	4.9646	4.1028	3.7083	3.4780	3.3258	3.2172	3.1355	3.0717	3.0204
	11	4.8443	3.9823	3.5874	3.3567	3.2039	3.0946	3.0123	2.9480	2.8962
Denominator degrees of freedom (df_2)	12	4.7472	3.8853	3.4903	3.2592	3.1059	2.9961	2.9134	2.8486	2.7964
	13	4.6672	3.8056	3.4105	3.1791	3.0254	2.9153	2.8321	2.7669	2.7144
	14	4.6001	3.7389	3.3439	3.1122	2.9582	2.8477	2.7642	2.6987	2.6458
	15	4.5431	3.6823	3.2874	3.0556	2.9013	2.7905	2.7066	2.6408	2.5876
	16	4.4940	3.6337	3.2389	3.0069	2.8524	2.7413	2.6572	2.5911	2.5377
	17	4.4513	3.5915	3.1968	2.9647	2.8100	2.6987	2.6143	2.5480	2.4943
	18	4.4139	3.5546	3.1599	2.9277	2.7729	2.6613	2.5767	2.5102	2.4563
	19	4.3807	3.5219	3.1274	2.8951	2.7401	2.6283	2.5435	2.4768	2.4227
	20	4.3512	3.4928	3.0984	2.8661	2.7109	2.5990	2.5140	2.4471	2.3928
	21	4.3248	3.4668	3.0725	2.8401	2.6848	2.5727	2.4876	2.4205	2.3660
	22	4.3009	3.4434	3.0491	2.8167	2.6613	2.5491	2.4638	2.3965	2.3419
	23	4.2793	3.4221	3.0280	2.7955	2.6400	2.5277	2.4422	2.3748	2.3201
	24	4.2597	3.4028	3.0088	2.7763	2.6207	2.5082	2.4226	2.3551	2.3002
	25	4.2417	3.3852	2.9912	2.7587	2.6030	2.4904	2.4047	2.3371	2.2821
	26	4.2252	3.3690	2.9752	2.7426	2.5868	2.4741	2.3883	2.3205	2.2655
	27	4.2100	3.3541	2.9604	2.7278	2.5719	2.4591	2.3732	2.3053	2.2501
	28	4.1960	3.3404	2.9467	2.7141	2.5581	2.4453	2.3593	2.2913	2.2360
	29	4.1830	3.3277	2.9340	2.7014	2.5454	2.4324	2.3463	2.2783	2.2229
	30	4.1709	3.3158	2.9223	2.6896	2.5336	2.4205	2.3343	2.2662	2.2107
	40	4.0847	3.2317	2.8387	2.6060	2.4495	2.3359	2.2490	2.1802	2.1240
	60	4.0012	3.1504	2.7581	2.5252	2.3683	2.2541	2.1665	2.0970	2.0401
	120	3.9201	3.0718	2.6802	2.4472	2.2899	2.1750	2.0868	2.0164	1.9588
	∞	3.8415	2.9957	2.6049	2.3719	2.2141	2.0986	2.0096	1.9384	1.8799

(continued)

Table A-5 *(continued)* F Distribution ($\alpha = 0.05$ in the right tail)

					Numerator degrees of freedom (df$_1$)					
	10	12	15	20	24	30	40	60	120	∞
1	241.88	243.91	245.95	248.01	249.05	250.10	251.14	252.20	253.25	254.31
2	19.396	19.413	19.429	19.446	19.454	19.462	19.471	19.479	19.487	19.496
3	8.7855	8.7446	8.7029	8.6602	8.6385	8.6166	8.5944	8.5720	8.5494	8.5264
4	5.9644	5.9117	5.8578	5.8025	5.7744	5.7459	5.7170	5.6877	5.6581	5.6281
5	4.7351	4.6777	4.6188	4.5581	4.5272	4.4957	4.4638	4.4314	4.3985	4.3650
6	4.0600	3.9999	3.9381	3.8742	3.8415	3.8082	3.7743	3.7398	3.7047	3.6689
7	3.6365	3.5747	3.5107	3.4445	3.4105	3.3758	3.3404	3.3043	3.2674	3.2298
8	3.3472	3.2839	3.2184	3.1503	3.1152	3.0794	3.0428	3.0053	2.9669	2.9276
9	3.1373	3.0729	3.0061	2.9365	2.9005	2.8637	2.8259	2.7872	2.7475	2.7067
10	2.9782	2.9130	2.8450	2.7740	2.7372	2.6996	2.6609	2.6211	2.5801	2.5379
11	2.8536	2.7876	2.7186	2.6464	2.6090	2.5705	2.5309	2.4901	2.4480	2.4045
12	2.7534	2.6866	2.6169	2.5436	2.5055	2.4663	2.4259	2.3842	2.3410	2.2962
13	2.6710	2.6037	2.5331	2.4589	2.4202	2.3803	2.3392	2.2966	2.2524	2.2064
14	2.6022	2.5342	2.4630	2.3879	2.3487	2.3082	2.2664	2.2229	2.1778	2.1307
15	2.5437	2.4753	2.4034	2.3275	2.2878	2.2468	2.2043	2.1601	2.1141	2.0658
16	2.4935	2.4247	2.3522	2.2756	2.2354	2.1938	2.1507	2.1058	2.0589	2.0096
17	2.4499	2.3807	2.3077	2.2304	2.1898	2.1477	2.1040	2.0584	2.0107	1.9604
18	2.4117	2.3421	2.2686	2.1906	2.1497	2.1071	2.0629	2.0166	1.9681	1.9168
19	2.3779	2.3080	2.2341	2.1555	2.1141	2.0712	2.0264	1.9795	1.9302	1.8780
20	2.3479	2.2776	2.2033	2.1242	2.0825	2.0391	1.9938	1.9464	1.8963	1.8432
21	2.3210	2.2504	2.1757	2.0960	2.0540	2.0102	1.9645	1.9165	1.8657	1.8117
22	2.2967	2.2258	2.1508	2.0707	2.0283	1.9842	1.9380	1.8894	1.8380	1.7831
23	2.2747	2.2036	2.1282	2.0476	2.0050	1.9605	1.9139	1.8648	1.8128	1.7570
24	2.2547	2.1834	2.1077	2.0267	1.9838	1.9390	1.8920	1.8424	1.7896	1.7330
25	2.2365	2.1649	2.0889	2.0075	1.9643	1.9192	1.8718	1.8217	1.7684	1.7110
26	2.2197	2.1479	2.0716	1.9898	1.9464	1.9010	1.8533	1.8027	1.7488	1.6906
27	2.2043	2.1323	2.0558	1.9736	1.9299	1.8842	1.8361	1.7851	1.7306	1.6717
28	2.1900	2.1179	2.0411	1.9586	1.9147	1.8687	1.8203	1.7689	1.7138	1.6541
29	2.1768	2.1045	2.0275	1.9446	1.9005	1.8543	1.8055	1.7537	1.6981	1.6376
30	2.1646	2.0921	2.0148	1.9317	1.8874	1.8409	1.7918	1.7396	1.6835	1.6223
40	2.0772	2.0035	1.9245	1.8389	1.7929	1.7444	1.6928	1.6373	1.5766	1.5089
60	1.9926	1.9174	1.8364	1.7480	1.7001	1.6491	1.5943	1.5343	1.4673	1.3893
120	1.9105	1.8337	1.7505	1.6587	1.6084	1.5543	1.4952	1.4290	1.3519	1.2539
∞	1.8307	1.7522	1.6664	1.5705	1.5173	1.4591	1.3940	1.3180	1.2214	1.0000

Denominator degrees of freedom (df$_2$)

Based on data from Maxine Merrington and Catherine M. Thompson, "Tables of Percentage Points of the Inverted Beta (*F*) Distribution," *Biometrika* 33 (1943): 80–84.

Table A-6　Critical Values of the
Pearson Correlation
Coefficient r

n	$\alpha = .05$	$\alpha = .01$
4	.950	.990
5	.878	.959
6	.811	.917
7	.754	.875
8	.707	.834
9	.666	.798
10	.632	.765
11	.602	.735
12	.576	.708
13	.553	.684
14	.532	.661
15	.514	.641
16	.497	.623
17	.482	.606
18	.468	.590
19	.456	.575
20	.444	.561
25	.396	.505
30	.361	.463
35	.335	.430
40	.312	.402
45	.294	.378
50	.279	.361
60	.254	.330
70	.236	.305
80	.220	.286
90	.207	.269
100	.196	.256

NOTE: To test H_0: $\rho = 0$ against H_1: $\rho \neq 0$, reject H_0 if the absolute value of r is greater than the critical value in the table.

Table A-7 Critical Values for the Sign Test

	α			
	.005 (one tail)	.01 (one tail)	.025 (one tail)	.05 (one tail)
n	.01 (two tails)	.02 (two tails)	.05 (two tails)	.10 (two tails)
1	*	*	*	*
2	*	*	*	*
3	*	*	*	*
4	*	*	*	*
5	*	*	*	0
6	*	*	0	0
7	*	0	0	0
8	0	0	0	1
9	0	0	1	1
10	0	0	1	1
11	0	1	1	2
12	1	1	2	2
13	1	1	2	3
14	1	2	2	3
15	2	2	3	3
16	2	2	3	4
17	2	3	4	4
18	3	3	4	5
19	3	4	4	5
20	3	4	5	5
21	4	4	5	6
22	4	5	5	6
23	4	5	6	7
24	5	5	6	7
25	5	6	7	7

NOTES:
1. * indicates that it is not possible to get a value in the critical region, so fail to reject the null hypothesis.
2. Reject the null hypothesis if the number of the less frequent sign (x) is less than or equal to the value in the table.
3. For values of n greater than 25, a normal approximation is used with

$$z = \frac{(x + 0.5) - \left(\frac{n}{2}\right)}{\frac{\sqrt{n}}{2}}$$

Table A-8 Critical Values of T for the Wilcoxon Signed-Ranks Test

n	.005 (one tail) / .01 (two tails)	.01 (one tail) / .02 (two tails)	.025 (one tail) / .05 (two tails)	.05 (one tail) / .10 (two tails)
5	*	*	*	1
6	*	*	1	2
7	*	0	2	4
8	0	2	4	6
9	2	3	6	8
10	3	5	8	11
11	5	7	11	14
12	7	10	14	17
13	10	13	17	21
14	13	16	21	26
15	16	20	25	30
16	19	24	30	36
17	23	28	35	41
18	28	33	40	47
19	32	38	46	54
20	37	43	52	60
21	43	49	59	68
22	49	56	66	75
23	55	62	73	83
24	61	69	81	92
25	68	77	90	101
26	76	85	98	110
27	84	93	107	120
28	92	102	117	130
29	100	111	127	141
30	109	120	137	152

NOTES:
1. * indicates that it is not possible to get a value in the critical region, so fail to reject the null hypothesis.
2. Reject the null hypothesis if the test statistic T is less than or equal to the critical value found in this table. Fail to reject the null hypothesis if the test statistic T is greater than the critical value found in the table.

Based on data from *Some Rapid Approximate Statistical Procedures,* Copyright © 1949, 1964 Lederle Laboratories Division of American Cyanamid Company.

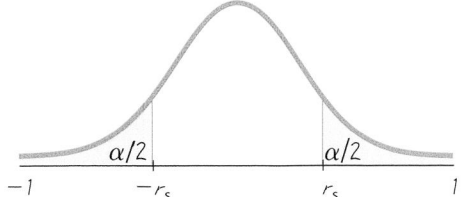

Table A-9 Critical Values of Spearman's Rank
Correlation Coefficient r_s

n	$\alpha = 0.10$	$\alpha = 0.05$	$\alpha = 0.02$	$\alpha = 0.01$
5	.900	—	—	—
6	.829	.886	.943	—
7	.714	.786	.893	.929
8	.643	.738	.833	.881
9	.600	.700	.783	.833
10	.564	.648	.745	.794
11	.536	.618	.709	.755
12	.503	.587	.678	.727
13	.484	.560	.648	.703
14	.464	.538	.626	.679
15	.446	.521	.604	.654
16	.429	.503	.582	.635
17	.414	.485	.566	.615
18	.401	.472	.550	.600
19	.391	.460	.535	.584
20	.380	.447	.520	.570
21	.370	.435	.508	.556
22	.361	.425	.496	.544
23	.353	.415	.486	.532
24	.344	.406	.476	.521
25	.337	.398	.466	.511
26	.331	.390	.457	.501
27	.324	.382	.448	.491
28	.317	.375	.440	.483
29	.312	.368	.433	.475
30	.306	.362	.425	.467

NOTES:
1. For $n > 30$ use $r_s = \pm z/\sqrt{n-1}$, where z corresponds to the level of significance. For example, if $\alpha = 0.05$, then $z = 1.96$.
2. If the absolute value of the test statistic r_s exceeds the positive critical value, then reject $H_0: \rho_s = 0$ and conclude that there is a correlation.

Based on data from *Biostatistical Analysis,* 4th edition © 1999, by Jerrold Zar, Prentice Hall, Inc., Upper Saddle River, New Jersey, and "Distribution of Sums of Squares of Rank Differences to Small Numbers with Individuals," *The Annals of Mathematical Statistics,* Vol. 9, No. 2.

Table A-10 Critical Values for Number of Runs G

Value of n_1	\	Value of n_2																		
		2	3	4	5	6	7	8	9	10	11	12	13	14	15	16	17	18	19	20
2		1	1	1	1	1	1	1	1	1	1	2	2	2	2	2	2	2	2	2
		6	6	6	6	6	6	6	6	6	6	6	6	6	6	6	6	6	6	6
3		1	1	1	1	2	2	2	2	2	2	2	2	2	3	3	3	3	3	3
		6	8	8	8	8	8	8	8	8	8	8	8	8	8	8	8	8	8	8
4		1	1	1	2	2	2	3	3	3	3	3	3	3	3	4	4	4	4	4
		6	8	9	9	9	10	10	10	10	10	10	10	10	10	10	10	10	10	10
5		1	1	2	2	3	3	3	3	3	4	4	4	4	4	4	4	5	5	5
		6	8	9	10	10	11	11	12	12	12	12	12	12	12	12	12	12	12	12
6		1	2	2	3	3	3	3	4	4	4	4	5	5	5	5	5	5	6	6
		6	8	9	10	11	12	12	13	13	13	13	14	14	14	14	14	14	14	14
7		1	2	2	3	3	3	4	4	5	5	5	5	5	6	6	6	6	6	6
		6	8	10	11	12	13	13	14	14	14	14	15	15	15	16	16	16	16	16
8		1	2	3	3	3	4	4	5	5	5	6	6	6	6	6	7	7	7	7
		6	8	10	11	12	13	14	14	15	15	16	16	16	16	17	17	17	17	17
9		1	2	3	3	4	4	5	5	5	6	6	6	7	7	7	7	8	8	8
		6	8	10	12	13	14	14	15	16	16	16	17	17	18	18	18	18	18	18
10		1	2	3	3	4	5	5	5	6	6	7	7	7	7	8	8	8	8	9
		6	8	10	12	13	14	15	16	16	17	17	18	18	18	19	19	19	20	20
11		1	2	3	4	4	5	5	6	6	7	7	7	8	8	8	9	9	9	9
		6	8	10	12	13	14	15	16	17	17	18	19	19	19	20	20	20	21	21
12		2	2	3	4	4	5	6	6	7	7	7	8	8	8	9	9	9	10	10
		6	8	10	12	13	14	16	16	17	18	19	19	20	20	21	21	21	22	22
13		2	2	3	4	5	5	6	6	7	7	8	8	9	9	9	10	10	10	10
		6	8	10	12	14	15	16	17	18	19	19	20	20	21	21	22	22	23	23
14		2	2	3	4	5	5	6	7	7	8	8	9	9	9	10	10	10	11	11
		6	8	10	12	14	15	16	17	18	19	20	20	21	22	22	23	23	23	24
15		2	3	3	4	5	6	6	7	7	8	8	9	9	10	10	11	11	11	12
		6	8	10	12	14	15	16	18	18	19	20	21	22	22	23	23	24	24	25
16		2	3	4	4	5	6	6	7	8	8	9	9	10	10	11	11	11	12	12
		6	8	10	12	14	16	17	18	19	20	21	21	22	23	23	24	25	25	25
17		2	3	4	4	5	6	7	7	8	9	9	10	10	11	11	11	12	12	13
		6	8	10	12	14	16	17	18	19	20	21	22	23	23	24	25	25	26	26
18		2	3	4	5	5	6	7	8	8	9	9	10	10	11	11	12	12	13	13
		6	8	10	12	14	16	17	18	19	20	21	22	23	24	25	25	26	26	27
19		2	3	4	5	6	6	7	8	8	9	10	10	11	11	12	12	13	13	13
		6	8	10	12	14	16	17	18	20	21	22	23	23	24	25	26	26	27	27
20		2	3	4	5	6	6	7	8	9	9	10	10	11	12	12	13	13	13	14
		6	8	10	12	14	16	17	18	20	21	22	23	24	25	25	26	27	27	28

NOTES:
1. The entries in this table are the critical G values, assuming a two-tailed test with a significance level of $\alpha = 0.05$.
2. The null hypothesis of randomness is rejected if the total number of runs G is less than or equal to the smaller entry or greater than than or equal to the larger entry.

From "Tables for Testing Randomness of Groupings in a Sequence of Alternatives," *The Annals of Mathematical Statistics*, Vol. 14, No. 1. Reprinted with permission of the Institute of Mathematical Statistics.

Appendix B   Data Sets

Data Set 1: Body Measurements

Data Set 2: Foot and Height Measurements

Data Set 3: Body Temperatures of Healthy Adults

Data Set 4: Freshman 15 Data

Data Set 5: IQ and Lead Exposure

Data Set 6: IQ and Brain Size

Data Set 7: Bear Measurements

Data Set 8: Alcohol and Tobacco Use in Animated Children's Movies

Data Set 9: Passive and Active Smoke

Data Set 10: Cigarette Tar, Nicotine, and Carbon Monoxide

Data Set 11: Ages of Oscar Winners

Data Set 12: POTUS

Data Set 13: Car Crash Tests

Data Set 14: Car Measurements

Data Set 15: Flight Data

Data Set 16: Earthquake Measurements

Data Set 17: Word Counts by Males and Females

Data Set 18: Voltage Measurements from a Home

Data Set 19: Cola Weights and Volumes

Data Set 20: M&M Plain Candy Weights

Data Set 21: Coin Weights

Data Set 22: Axial Loads of Aluminum Cans

Data Set 23: Weights of Discarded Garbage for One Week

Additional data sets are available at the Web site aw.com/Triola.

Data Set 1: Body Measurements

AGE is in years, PULSE is pulse rate (beats per minute), SYS is systolic blood pressure (mm Hg), DIAS is diastolic blood pressure (mm Hg), HDL is HDL cholesterol (mg/dL), LDL is LDL cholesterol (mg/dL), WHITE is white blood cell count (1000 cells/μL), RED is red blood cell count (million cells/μL), PLATE is platelet count (1000 cells/μL), WT is weight (kg), HT is height (cm), WAIST is circumference (cm), ARMC is arm circumference (cm), and BMI is body mass index (kg/m^2). Data are from the National Center for Health Statistics.

STATDISK:	Data set name for males is Body Measurements Male.
Minitab:	Worksheet name for males is MBODY.MTW.
Excel:	Workbook name for males is MBODY.XLS.
TI-83/84 Plus:	App name for male data is MBODY and the file names are the same as for text files.
Text file names for males:	MAGE, MPULS, MSYS, MDIAS, MHDL, MLDL, MWHT, MRED, MPLAT, MWT, MHT, MWAST, MARMC, MBMI.

Males

AGE	PULSE	SYS	DIAS	HDL	LDL	WHITE	RED	PLATE	WT	HT	WAIST	ARMC	BMI
18	60	132	68	44	213	8.7	4.91	409	64.4	178.8	81.4	28.4	20.14
20	74	120	68	41	88	5.9	5.59	187	61.8	177.5	74.8	26.8	19.62
43	86	106	84	71	174	7.3	4.44	250	78.5	187.8	84.1	32.3	22.26
39	54	104	60	41	121	6.2	4.80	273	86.3	172.4	95.5	39.0	29.04
60	90	122	80	57	124	5.9	5.17	278	73.1	181.7	90.1	29.4	22.14
18	80	122	62	50	99	6.4	5.24	279	58.5	169.0	69.8	28.7	20.48
57	66	126	78	60	114	3.9	4.51	237	134.3	186.9	137.8	42.8	38.45
27	68	118	60	47	122	6.4	4.77	200	79.8	183.1	94.4	32.0	23.80
20	68	110	40	44	112	9.8	5.02	209	64.8	176.4	74.2	29.2	20.82
18	56	96	56	33	67	4.0	5.10	203	58.1	183.4	69.9	26.2	17.27
63	80	114	76	48	108	3.8	4.45	206	76.1	169.6	95.2	32.0	26.46
20	62	128	78	46	94	5.6	5.41	174	118.4	185.4	117.5	39.9	34.45
24	74	108	76	62	69	6.6	5.45	219	56.2	166.1	77.0	26.2	20.37
46	60	126	78	45	77	4.9	4.27	302	73.4	169.3	90.5	33.1	25.61
29	52	116	82	43	120	9.6	4.90	285	126.9	193.5	122.0	37.9	33.89
63	60	138	76	39	84	8.6	4.60	254	84.4	173.1	104.0	32.2	28.17
21	66	110	50	41	86	5.2	4.93	195	97.8	171.6	104.1	37.9	33.21
45	64	144	84	47	77	9.2	4.28	290	66.5	180.8	76.4	29.9	20.34
40	64	112	70	46	201	6.6	4.74	240	90.5	175.3	98.6	37.0	29.45
50	46	130	74	56	196	3.2	4.98	270	83.7	178.3	89.7	36.0	26.33
48	68	136	82	38	179	6.9	5.20	264	88.7	172.8	102.1	33.7	29.71
64	58	146	70	37	140	7.1	5.17	208	80.4	165.2	104.6	32.6	29.46
18	68	106	62	61	117	6.9	4.85	271	64.0	176.6	77.6	26.1	20.52
50	70	136	76	41	117	7.0	5.77	386	65.7	174.2	87.5	30.2	21.65
20	56	122	86	56	87	8.4	5.09	203	58.9	181.7	69.1	25.1	17.84
20	66	112	80	59	78	5.9	5.24	223	82.4	176.0	83.4	36.0	26.60
47	78	128	90	40	159	5.1	5.18	261	85.1	173.7	96.1	33.2	28.21
19	68	114	56	54	113	10.0	5.34	282	87.7	177.1	97.2	35.3	27.96
55	62	100	68	40	155	4.4	4.89	184	111.9	174.5	122.4	36.5	36.75
23	70	106	78	75	85	7.1	5.59	204	70.9	180.4	81.5	31.0	21.79
21	72	134	78	55	90	7.9	5.94	287	101.8	177.3	97.5	38.8	32.38
19	74	128	68	48	104	8.1	5.39	219	99.0	172.5	106.7	36.4	33.27
64	64	108	80	50	154	5.6	5.24	257	100.5	180.2	109.6	36.9	30.95
30	50	106	68	57	114	4.1	4.72	206	78.9	172.7	91.8	33.2	26.45
43	70	112	68	38	156	9.5	5.34	342	79.2	168.6	96.7	34.0	27.86
23	58	120	68	78	103	4.9	5.23	319	86.1	178.3	86.6	38.2	27.08
64	60	140	62	45	145	8.9	4.98	251	100.8	176.7	118.1	36.0	32.28
40	88	98	56	82	135	11.0	5.06	178	76.4	174.8	81.5	34.7	25.00
23	84	126	68	44	123	8.6	5.64	220	77.4	172.1	92.1	31.9	26.13
44	76	154	86	51	170	6.9	5.47	268	89.7	173.4	103.3	37.5	29.83

(continued)

Data Set 1: Body Measurements (continued)

STATDISK: Data set name for females is Body Measurements Female.

Minitab: Worksheet name for females is FBODY.MTW.

Excel: Workbook name for females is FBODY.XLS.

TI-83/84 Plus: App name for female data is FBODY and the file names are the same as for text files.

Text file names for females: FAGE, FPULS, FSYS, FDIAS, FHDL, FLDL, FWHT, FRED, FPLAT, FWT, FHT, FWAST, FARMC, FBMI.

Females

AGE	PULSE	SYS	DIAS	HDL	LDL	WHITE	RED	PLATE	WT	HT	WAIST	ARMC	BMI
60	78	122	60	74	140	9.6	4.70	317	59.3	163.7	82.3	27.5	22.13
24	80	120	64	56	142	7.1	4.64	224	74.5	165.5	88.5	30.0	27.20
49	68	90	48	70	72	7.5	4.61	248	77.7	163.1	94.9	34.4	29.21
62	56	150	80	40	164	6.8	4.09	309	97.9	166.3	111.8	38.7	35.40
53	76	132	58	67	109	5.6	4.36	335	71.7	163.6	86.5	32.2	26.79
18	78	88	52	96	93	5.4	4.64	278	60.9	170.9	78.4	26.7	20.85
41	78	100	60	43	122	6.7	4.98	312	60.5	153.5	81.7	30.5	25.68
21	90	114	72	80	116	8.6	3.76	338	88.2	155.7	111.2	36.9	36.38
21	96	94	54	77	84	10.2	4.30	290	43.8	153.0	79.2	23.2	18.71
19	60	100	54	41	55	4.1	4.66	236	47.9	157.0	63.4	22.6	19.43
19	98	110	74	23	115	13.0	5.66	310	126.6	163.7	103.8	40.5	47.24
58	66	188	0	76	98	9.2	4.71	460	64.8	161.3	90.4	29.0	24.91
44	100	106	74	39	139	5.9	4.81	317	75.6	168.6	93.6	32.1	26.60
52	76	130	76	52	122	8.0	4.95	304	81.0	156.4	111.8	32.8	33.11
48	64	126	76	38	100	7.0	4.32	239	72.8	159.4	97.2	31.9	28.65
36	82	90	56	37	99	9.1	4.35	243	67.3	164.2	83.9	30.8	24.96
48	62	168	90	57	131	5.7	3.93	351	58.0	169.0	80.3	26.7	20.31
34	72	110	66	81	59	4.6	4.69	242	107.8	161.6	120.6	40.7	41.28
22	78	98	60	37	90	6.0	4.66	217	54.1	161.1	80.5	25.2	20.85
61	74	112	70	50	130	5.7	5.26	173	59.6	150.8	97.1	29.7	26.21
21	90	116	66	73	144	8.9	4.23	228	48.9	166.6	79.7	21.6	17.62
33	90	128	72	61	84	6.4	4.81	259	115.7	175.7	119.9	39.9	37.48
32	68	116	72	33	112	8.1	4.50	193	75.3	169.0	96.3	32.0	26.36
37	72	112	66	41	128	7.9	4.36	417	114.9	160.5	124.4	43.2	44.60
19	82	126	60	60	107	4.4	4.68	193	60.0	159.1	74.5	29.4	23.70
51	72	94	60	62	209	4.9	4.64	244	67.3	166.7	83.8	31.0	24.22
35	78	120	78	67	77	5.3	4.01	266	77.3	151.5	94.0	37.2	33.68
18	104	94	32	79	39	5.3	4.11	286	49.7	156.2	71.2	24.2	20.37
60	62	120	76	64	85	4.7	4.37	206	58.4	148.7	90.7	30.0	26.41
58	72	148	62	44	162	9.8	4.66	426	82.2	168.3	103.6	33.4	29.02
60	72	126	76	42	111	5.3	4.89	244	79.5	159.6	98.3	36.4	31.21
48	88	126	72	41	104	4.9	4.35	295	80.3	165.9	96.6	33.0	29.18
31	74	112	72	44	192	6.3	4.56	282	56.4	147.6	79.1	29.5	25.89
29	72	120	78	57	110	5.4	5.10	211	64.3	165.4	85.7	31.0	23.50
46	82	110	76	69	123	7.0	5.30	355	102.1	159.8	119.6	39.5	39.98
18	78	98	66	60	70	13.5	4.83	357	62.3	158.5	83.2	30.6	24.80
50	78	130	72	47	155	10.0	4.65	272	74.6	165.6	97.5	31.0	27.20
20	98	114	54	67	108	10.3	4.29	251	116.3	164.9	140.0	35.5	42.77
56	72	174	86	55	158	5.1	4.40	219	92.6	172.0	109.0	39.0	31.30
18	64	108	58	82	50	6.6	4.26	234	65.0	170.2	81.8	27.5	22.44

Data Set 2: Foot and Height Measurements

Sex is gender of subject, Age is age in years, Foot Length is foot length (cm), Shoe Print is length of shoe (cm), Shoe Size is reported shoe size, and Height is height (cm) of the subject.

Data from Rohren, Brenda, "Estimation of Stature from Foot and Shoe Length: Applications in Forensic Science." Copyright © 2006. Reprinted by permission of the author.

Brenda Rohren (M.A., MFS, LIMHP, LADC, MAC) was a graduate student at Nebraska Wesleyan University when she conducted the research and wrote the report.

STATDISK: Data set name is Foot and Height Measurements.
Minitab: Worksheet name for males is FOOT.MTW.
Excel: Workbook name for males is FOOT.XLS.
TI-83/84 Plus: App name is FOOT and the file names are the same as for text files.
Text file names: FTSEX, FTAGE, FTLN, SHOPT, SHOSZ, HT

Sex	Age	Foot Length	Shoe Print	Shoe Size	Height
M	67	27.8	31.3	11.0	180.3
M	47	25.7	29.7	9.0	175.3
M	41	26.7	31.3	11.0	184.8
M	42	25.9	31.8	10.0	177.8
M	48	26.4	31.4	10.0	182.3
M	34	29.2	31.9	13.0	185.4
M	26	26.8	31.8	11.0	180.3
M	29	28.1	31.0	10.5	175.3
M	60	25.4	29.7	9.5	177.8
M	48	27.9	31.4	11.0	185.4
M	30	27.5	31.4	11.0	190.5
M	43	28.8	31.6	12.0	195.0
M	54	26.7	31.8	10.0	175.3
M	31	26.7	32.4	10.5	180.3
M	42	25.1	27.6	9.0	172.7
M	21	28.7	31.8	12.5	182.9
M	59	29.2	31.3	11.0	189.2
M	58	27.9	31.3	11.5	185.4
M	42	28.6	34.5	14.0	193.7
F	47	23.2	24.8	7.0	165.1
F	19	24.3	28.6	9.0	166.4
F	20	26.0	25.4	10.0	177.8
F	27	23.8	26.7	8.0	167.6
F	19	25.1	26.7	9.0	168.3
F	21	25.4	27.9	8.5	165.7
F	32	21.9	27.9	8.0	165.1
F	19	26.2	28.9	11.0	165.1
F	27	23.8	27.9	8.0	165.1
F	18	22.2	25.9	9.5	152.4
F	26	24.6	25.4	8.5	162.6
F	36	24.6	28.1	9.0	179.1
F	28	23.7	27.6	9.0	175.9
F	29	25.6	26.5	8.5	166.4
F	58	24.1	26.5	7.0	167.6
F	30	23.8	28.4	9.0	162.6
F	23	23.3	26.5	8.0	167.6
F	26	23.5	26.0	8.0	165.1
F	47	25.1	27.0	10.0	172.7
F	36	24.1	25.1	7.5	157.5
F	19	23.8	27.9	10.0	167.6

Data Set 3: Body Temperatures (in degrees Fahrenheit) of Healthy Adults

Data provided by Dr. Steven Wasserman, Dr. Philip Mackowiak, and Dr. Myron Levine of the University of Maryland.

STATDISK: Data set name for the 12 A.M. temperatures on Day 2 is Body Temperatures of Healthy Adults.

Minitab: Worksheet name for the 12 A.M. temperatures on Day 2 is BODYTEMP.MTW.

Excel: Workbook name for the 12 A.M. temperatures on Day 2 is BODYTEMP.XLS.

TI-83/84 Plus: App name for 12 A.M. temperatures on Day 2 is BTEMP and the file name is BTEMP.

Text files: Text file name is BTEMP.

				Temperature Day 1		Temperature Day 2	
Subject	Age	Sex	Smoke	8 AM	12 AM	8 AM	12 AM
1	22	M	Y	98.0	98.0	98.0	98.6
2	23	M	Y	97.0	97.6	97.4	—
3	22	M	Y	98.6	98.8	97.8	98.6
4	19	M	N	97.4	98.0	97.0	98.0
5	18	M	N	98.2	98.8	97.0	98.0
6	20	M	Y	98.2	98.8	96.6	99.0
7	27	M	Y	98.2	97.6	97.0	98.4
8	19	M	Y	96.6	98.6	96.8	98.4
9	19	M	Y	97.4	98.6	96.6	98.4
10	24	M	N	97.4	98.8	96.6	98.4
11	35	M	Y	98.2	98.0	96.2	98.6
12	25	M	Y	97.4	98.2	97.6	98.6
13	25	M	N	97.8	98.0	98.6	98.8
14	35	M	Y	98.4	98.0	97.0	98.6
15	21	M	N	97.6	97.0	97.4	97.0
16	33	M	N	96.2	97.2	98.0	97.0
17	19	M	Y	98.0	98.2	97.6	98.8
18	24	M	Y	—	—	97.2	97.6
19	18	F	N	—	—	97.0	97.7
20	22	F	Y	—	—	98.0	98.8
21	20	M	Y	—	—	97.0	98.0
22	30	F	Y	—	—	96.4	98.0
23	29	M	N	—	—	96.1	98.3
24	18	M	Y	—	—	98.0	98.5
25	31	M	Y	—	98.1	96.8	97.3
26	28	F	Y	—	98.2	98.2	98.7
27	27	M	Y	—	98.5	97.8	97.4
28	21	M	Y	—	98.5	98.2	98.9
29	30	M	Y	—	99.0	97.8	98.6
30	27	M	N	—	98.0	99.0	99.5
31	32	M	Y	—	97.0	97.4	97.5
32	33	M	Y	—	97.3	97.4	97.3
33	23	M	Y	—	97.3	97.5	97.6
34	29	M	Y	—	98.1	97.8	98.2
35	25	M	Y	—	—	97.9	99.6
36	31	M	N	—	97.8	97.8	98.7
37	25	M	Y	—	99.0	98.3	99.4
38	28	M	N	—	97.6	98.0	98.2
39	30	M	Y	—	97.4	—	98.0
40	33	M	Y	—	98.0	—	98.6
41	28	M	Y	98.0	97.4	—	98.6
42	22	M	Y	98.8	98.0	—	97.2
43	21	F	Y	99.0	—	—	98.4
44	30	M	N	—	98.6	—	98.6
45	22	M	Y	—	98.6	—	98.2
46	22	F	N	98.0	98.4	—	98.0
47	20	M	Y	—	97.0	—	97.8
48	19	M	Y	—	—	—	98.0
49	33	M	N	—	98.4	—	98.4

(continued)

Data Set 3: Body Temperatures (in degrees Fahrenheit) of Healthy Adults *(continued)*

Subject	Age	Sex	Smoke	Temperature Day 1		Temperature Day 2	
				8 AM	12 AM	8 AM	12 AM
50	31	M	Y	99.0	99.0	—	98.6
51	26	M	N	—	98.0	—	98.6
52	18	M	N	—	—	—	97.8
53	23	M	N	—	99.4	—	99.0
54	28	M	Y	—	—	—	96.5
55	19	M	Y	—	97.8	—	97.6
56	21	M	N	—	—	—	98.0
57	27	M	Y	—	98.2	—	96.9
58	29	M	Y	—	99.2	—	97.6
59	38	M	N	—	99.0	—	97.1
60	29	F	Y	—	97.7	—	97.9
61	22	M	Y	—	98.2	—	98.4
62	22	M	Y	—	98.2	—	97.3
63	26	M	Y	—	98.8	—	98.0
64	32	M	N	—	98.1	—	97.5
65	25	M	Y	—	98.5	—	97.6
66	21	F	N	—	97.2	—	98.2
67	25	M	Y	—	98.5	—	98.5
68	24	M	Y	—	99.2	97.0	98.8
69	25	M	Y	—	98.3	97.6	98.7
70	35	M	Y	—	98.7	97.5	97.8
71	23	F	Y	—	98.8	98.8	98.0
72	31	M	Y	—	98.6	98.4	97.1
73	28	M	Y	—	98.0	98.2	97.4
74	29	M	Y	—	99.1	97.7	99.4
75	26	M	Y	—	97.2	97.3	98.4
76	32	M	N	—	97.6	97.5	98.6
77	32	M	Y	—	97.9	97.1	98.4
78	21	F	Y	—	98.8	98.6	98.5
79	20	M	Y	—	98.6	98.6	98.6
80	24	F	Y	—	98.6	97.8	98.3
81	21	F	Y	—	99.3	98.7	98.7
82	28	M	Y	—	97.8	97.9	98.8
83	27	F	N	98.8	98.7	97.8	99.1
84	28	M	N	99.4	99.3	97.8	98.6
85	29	M	Y	98.8	97.8	97.6	97.9
86	19	M	N	97.7	98.4	96.8	98.8
87	24	M	Y	99.0	97.7	96.0	98.0
88	29	M	N	98.1	98.3	98.0	98.7
89	25	M	Y	98.7	97.7	97.0	98.5
90	27	M	N	97.5	97.1	97.4	98.9
91	25	M	Y	98.9	98.4	97.6	98.4
92	21	M	Y	98.4	98.6	97.6	98.6
93	19	M	Y	97.2	97.4	96.2	97.1
94	27	M	Y	—	—	96.2	97.9
95	32	M	N	98.8	96.7	98.1	98.8
96	24	M	Y	97.3	96.9	97.1	98.7
97	32	M	Y	98.7	98.4	98.2	97.6
98	19	F	Y	98.9	98.2	96.4	98.2
99	18	F	Y	99.2	98.6	96.9	99.2
100	27	M	N	—	97.0	—	97.8
101	34	M	Y	—	97.4	—	98.0
102	25	M	N	—	98.4	—	98.4
103	18	M	N	—	97.4	—	97.8
104	32	M	Y	—	96.8	—	98.4
105	31	M	Y	—	98.2	—	97.4
106	26	M	N	—	97.4	—	98.0
107	23	M	N	—	98.0	—	97.0

Data Set 4: Freshman 15 Data

Weights are in kilograms, and BMI denotes measured body mass index. Measurements were made in September of freshman year and then later in April of freshman year. Results are published in Hoffman, D.J., Policastro, P., Quick, V., Lee, S.K.: "Changes in Body Weight and Fat Mass of Men and Women in the First Year of College: A Study of the 'Freshman 15.'" *Journal of American College Health*, July 1, 2006, vol. 55, no. 1, p. 41. Copyright © 2006. Reprinted by permission.

STATDISK: Data set name is Freshman 15 Study Data.
Minitab: Worksheet name is FRESH15.MTW.
Excel: Workbook name is FRESH15.XLS.
TI-83/84 Plus: App name is FRESH and the file names are the same as for text files.
Text file names: WTSEP, WTAPR, BMISP, BMIAP.

Sex	Weight in September	Weight in April	BMI in September	BMI in April
M	72	59	22.02	18.14
M	97	86	19.70	17.44
M	74	69	24.09	22.43
M	93	88	26.97	25.57
F	68	64	21.51	20.10
M	59	55	18.69	17.40
F	64	60	24.24	22.88
F	56	53	21.23	20.23
F	70	68	30.26	29.24
F	58	56	21.88	21.02
F	50	47	17.63	16.89
M	71	69	24.57	23.85
M	67	66	20.68	20.15
F	56	55	20.97	20.36
F	70	68	27.30	26.73
F	61	60	23.30	22.88
F	53	52	19.48	19.24
M	92	92	24.74	24.69
F	57	58	20.69	20.79
M	67	67	20.49	20.60
F	58	58	21.09	21.24
F	49	50	18.37	18.53
M	68	68	22.40	22.61
F	69	69	28.17	28.43
M	87	88	23.60	23.81
M	81	82	26.52	26.78
M	60	61	18.89	19.27
F	52	53	19.31	19.75
M	70	71	20.96	21.32
F	63	64	21.78	22.22
F	56	57	19.78	20.23
M	68	69	22.40	22.82
M	68	69	22.76	23.19
F	54	56	20.15	20.69
M	80	82	22.14	22.57
M	64	66	20.27	20.76
F	57	59	22.15	22.93
F	63	65	23.87	24.67
F	54	56	18.61	19.34
F	56	58	21.73	22.58
M	54	56	18.93	19.72
M	73	75	25.88	26.72
M	77	79	28.59	29.53
F	63	66	21.89	22.79
F	51	54	18.31	19.28
F	59	62	19.64	20.63
F	65	68	23.02	24.10
F	53	56	20.63	21.91
F	62	65	22.61	23.81
F	55	58	22.03	23.42
M	74	77	20.31	21.34
M	74	78	20.31	21.36
M	64	68	19.59	20.77
M	64	68	21.05	22.31
F	57	61	23.47	25.11
F	64	68	22.84	24.29
F	60	64	19.50	20.90
M	64	68	18.51	19.83
M	66	71	21.40	22.97
F	52	57	17.72	19.42
M	71	77	22.26	23.87
F	55	60	21.64	23.81
M	65	71	22.51	24.45
M	75	82	23.69	25.80
F	42	49	15.08	17.74
M	74	82	22.64	25.33
M	94	105	36.57	40.86

Data Set 5: IQ and Lead Exposure

Data are measured from children in two consecutive years, and the children were living close to a lead smelter. LEAD is blood lead level group [1 = *low lead level* (blood lead levels < 40 micrograms/100 mL in both years); 2 = *medium lead level* (blood lead levels ≥ 40 micrograms/100 mL in exactly one of two years); 3 = *high lead level* (blood lead level ≥ 40 micrograms/100 mL in both years)]. Age is age in years. Sex is sex of subject (1 = male; 2 = female). YEAR1 is blood lead level in first year, and YEAR2 is blood lead level in second year. IQV is measured verbal IQ score. IQP is measured performance IQ score. IQF is measured full IQ score.

Data are from "Neuropsychological Dysfunction in Children with Chronic Low-Level Lead Absorption," by P. J. Landrigan, R. H. Whitworth, R.W. Baloh, N. W. Staehling, W. F Barthel, and B. F. Rosenblum, *Lancet,* Vol. 1, Issue 7909.

STATDISK: Data set name is IQ and Lead Exposure.
Minitab: Worksheet name for males is IQLEAD.MTW.
Excel: Workbook name for males is IQLEAD.XLS.
TI-83/84 Plus: App name is IQLEAD and the file names are the same as for text files.
Text file names: LEAD, IQAGE, IQSEX, YEAR1, YEAR2, IQV, IQP, IQF

LEAD	AGE	SEX	YEAR1	YEAR2	IQV	IQP	IQF
1	11	1	25	18	61	85	70
1	9	1	31	28	82	90	85
1	11	1	30	29	70	107	86
1	6	1	29	30	72	85	76
1	11	1	2	34	72	100	84
1	6	1	29	25	95	97	96
1	6	1	25	24	89	101	94
1	15	2	24	15	57	64	56
1	7	2	24	16	116	111	115
1	7	1	31	24	95	100	97
1	13	2	21	19	82	76	77
1	10	2	29	27	116	136	128
1	12	1	32	29	99	100	99
1	12	1	36	32	74	90	80
1	15	1	30	25	100	135	118
1	10	1	29	23	72	104	86
1	15	1	28	28	126	149	141
1	9	2	28	19	80	99	88
1	8	1	34	22	86	107	96
1	11	1	21	22	94	99	96
1	7	1	35	27	100	113	107
1	11	2	39	38	72	104	86
1	6	1	36	31	63	101	80
1	6	1	19	25	101	111	107
1	9	1	29	24	85	118	101
1	13	2	1	24	85	99	91
1	9	2	22	20	124	122	125
1	6	1	23	18	105	87	96
1	13	1	21	18	81	118	99
1	6	1	32	26	87	113	99
1	12	2	26	27	100	128	115
1	8	2	20	24	91	121	106
1	9	1	2	22	99	111	105
1	7	2	36	31	89	104	96
1	12	1	24	34	57	51	50
1	6	2	38	37	99	100	99
1	9	2	14	25	58	113	85
1	14	2	18	20	97	82	88
1	15	1	24	16	94	146	120
1	14	1	20	21	82	107	93
1	9	2	33	34	92	83	87
1	7	2	36	27	89	108	98
1	12	2	18	22	69	93	78
1	8	1	31	26	87	114	100
1	7	1	33	30	97	113	105
1	15	2	27	33	82	94	87
1	6	2	28	26	85	106	94
1	14	2	24	23	89	92	89
1	7	1	30	23	85	79	80
1	13	1	24	23	92	129	111
1	12	1	29	24	95	114	104
1	6	1	38	31	76	99	85
1	7	1	31	39	80	110	94
1	9	1	28	32	66	90	75
1	12	2	22	23	67	85	73
1	15	1	22	16	63	94	76
1	10	1	27	28	87	127	107
1	9	1	24	33	79	101	88
1	13	2	36	34	82	99	89
1	12	2	10	38	82	113	96
1	6	2	30	21	70	80	72

(continued)

LEAD	AGE	SEX	YEAR1	YEAR2	IQV	IQP	IQF
1	11	2	27	31	81	115	97
1	15	2	34	33	72	85	76
1	4	1	35	34	101	112	107
1	4	2	27	27	95	112	104
1	3	1	23	26	81	92	85
1	4	1	27	20	61	97	76
1	4	1	2	27	94	97	95
1	3	1	32	28	85	91	86
1	4	1	33	31	76	105	89
1	4	1	32	28	72	84	76
1	4	2	35	37	97	95	96
1	5	1	35	34	95	108	101
1	4	2	30	34	97	118	108
1	4	2	34	23	87	118	102
1	5	2	18	25	74	86	77
1	4	1	38	25	66	89	74
1	6	2	36	23	86	100	92
2	14	1	42	38	72	78	72
2	7	2	40	34	85	97	90
2	7	1	40	34	80	107	92
2	13	2	41	33	67	80	71
2	6	1	41	32	85	90	86
2	15	1	41	30	79	83	79
2	12	1	43	32	70	101	83
2	9	1	66	25	105	121	114
2	9	2	51	39	92	108	100
2	8	1	44	31	89	100	93
2	14	2	64	38	74	110	91
2	9	1	43	32	86	111	98
2	11	2	43	24	87	97	91
2	7	1	40	37	51	51	46
2	9	2	40	35	80	94	85
2	4	1	47	22	87	80	82
2	3	2	44	34	94	101	97
2	5	2	45	29	91	92	91
2	4	1	41	34	92	100	92
2	5	2	51	30	81	77	77
2	3	1	42	32	111	108	111
2	3	1	50	36	75	85	78
3	10	1	68	53	75	93	82
3	10	2	53	49	87	100	93
3	9	1	48	40	76	97	85
3	6	1	41	40	76	79	75
3	5	1	45	47	76	97	85
3	12	2	62	45	92	71	80
3	6	1	49	43	91	111	101
3	7	2	52	58	82	99	89
3	12	2	61	48	80	85	80
3	8	1	41	50	91	99	94
3	6	1	59	40	81	97	88
3	6	1	57	58	97	111	104
3	8	1	58	57	76	104	88
3	11	2	40	51	85	93	88
3	9	1	57	48	80	90	83
3	8	1	48	43	100	107	104
3	4	1	57	43	86	108	96
3	4	1	51	49	79	78	76
3	4	1	59	47	70	95	80
3	3	1	44	45	84	78	79
3	3	2	42	45	69	86	75

Data Set 6: IQ and Brain Size

The data are obtained from monozygotic (identical) twins. PAIR identifies the set of twins, SEX is the gender of the subject (1 = male, 2 = female), ORDER is the birth order, IQ is full-scale IQ, VOL is total brain volume (cm^3), AREA is total brain surface area (cm^2), CCSA is corpus callosum (fissure connecting left and right cerebral hemispheres) surface area (cm^2), CIRC is head circumference (cm), and WT is body weight (kg).

Data provided by M. J. Tramo, W. C. Loftus, T. A. Stukel, J. B. Weaver, M. S. Gazziniga. See "Brain Size, Head Size, and IQ in Monozygotic Twins," *Neurology*, Vol. 50.

STATDISK:	Data set name is IQ and Brain Size.
Minitab:	Worksheet name is IQBRAIN.MTW.
Excel:	Workbook name is IQBRAIN.XLS.
TI-83/84 Plus:	App name is IQBRAIN and the individual column names are the same as for text files.
Text file names:	PAIR, SEX, ORDER, IQ, VOL, AREA, CCSA, CIRC, WT

PAIR	SEX	ORDER	IQ	VOL	AREA	CCSA	CIRC	WT
1	2	1	96	1005	1913.88	6.08	54.7	57.607
1	2	2	89	963	1684.89	5.73	54.2	58.968
2	2	1	87	1035	1902.36	6.22	53.0	64.184
2	2	2	87	1027	1860.24	5.80	52.9	58.514
3	2	1	101	1281	2264.25	7.99	57.8	63.958
3	2	2	103	1272	2216.40	8.42	56.9	61.690
4	2	1	103	1051	1866.99	7.44	56.6	133.358
4	2	2	96	1079	1850.64	6.84	55.3	107.503
5	2	1	127	1034	1743.04	6.48	53.1	62.143
5	2	2	126	1070	1709.30	6.43	54.8	83.009
6	1	2	101	1173	1689.60	7.99	57.2	61.236
6	1	1	96	1079	1806.31	8.76	57.2	61.236
7	1	2	93	1067	2136.37	6.32	57.2	83.916
7	1	1	88	1104	2018.92	6.32	57.2	79.380
8	1	2	94	1347	1966.81	7.60	55.8	97.524
8	1	1	85	1439	2154.67	7.62	57.2	99.792
9	1	1	97	1029	1767.56	6.03	57.2	81.648
9	1	2	114	1100	1827.92	6.59	56.5	88.452
10	1	2	113	1204	1773.83	7.52	59.2	79.380
10	1	1	124	1160	1971.63	7.67	58.5	72.576

Data Set 7: Bears (measurements from anesthetized wild bears)

AGE is in months, MONTH is the month of measurement (1 = January), SEX is coded with 1 = male and 2 = female, HEADLEN is head length (inches), HEADWTH is width of head (inches), NECK is distance around neck (in inches), LENGTH is length of body (inches), CHEST is distance around chest (inches), and WEIGHT is measured in pounds. Data are from Gary Alt and Minitab, Inc.

STATDISK: Data set name is Bears.
Minitab: Worksheet name is BEARS.MTW.
Excel: Workbook name is BEARS.XLS.
TI-83/84 Plus: App name is BEARS and the file names are the same as for text files.
Text file names: BAGE, BMNTH, BSEX, BHDLN, BHDWD, BNECK, BLEN, BCHST, BWGHT.

Age	Month	Sex	Headlen	Headwth	Neck	Length	Chest	Weight
19	7	1	11.0	5.5	16.0	53.0	26.0	80
55	7	1	16.5	9.0	28.0	67.5	45.0	344
81	9	1	15.5	8.0	31.0	72.0	54.0	416
115	7	1	17.0	10.0	31.5	72.0	49.0	348
104	8	2	15.5	6.5	22.0	62.0	35.0	166
100	4	2	13.0	7.0	21.0	70.0	41.0	220
56	7	1	15.0	7.5	26.5	73.5	41.0	262
51	4	1	13.5	8.0	27.0	68.5	49.0	360
57	9	2	13.5	7.0	20.0	64.0	38.0	204
53	5	2	12.5	6.0	18.0	58.0	31.0	144
68	8	1	16.0	9.0	29.0	73.0	44.0	332
8	8	1	9.0	4.5	13.0	37.0	19.0	34
44	8	2	12.5	4.5	10.5	63.0	32.0	140
32	8	1	14.0	5.0	21.5	67.0	37.0	180
20	8	2	11.5	5.0	17.5	52.0	29.0	105
32	8	1	13.0	8.0	21.5	59.0	33.0	166
45	9	1	13.5	7.0	24.0	64.0	39.0	204
9	9	2	9.0	4.5	12.0	36.0	19.0	26
21	9	1	13.0	6.0	19.0	59.0	30.0	120
177	9	1	16.0	9.5	30.0	72.0	48.0	436
57	9	2	12.5	5.0	19.0	57.5	32.0	125
81	9	2	13.0	5.0	20.0	61.0	33.0	132
21	9	1	13.0	5.0	17.0	54.0	28.0	90
9	9	1	10.0	4.0	13.0	40.0	23.0	40
45	9	1	16.0	6.0	24.0	63.0	42.0	220
9	9	1	10.0	4.0	13.5	43.0	23.0	46
33	9	1	13.5	6.0	22.0	66.5	34.0	154
57	9	2	13.0	5.5	17.5	60.5	31.0	116
45	9	2	13.0	6.5	21.0	60.0	34.5	182
21	9	1	14.5	5.5	20.0	61.0	34.0	150
10	10	1	9.5	4.5	16.0	40.0	26.0	65
82	10	2	13.5	6.5	28.0	64.0	48.0	356
70	10	2	14.5	6.5	26.0	65.0	48.0	316
10	10	1	11.0	5.0	17.0	49.0	29.0	94
10	10	1	11.5	5.0	17.0	47.0	29.5	86
34	10	1	13.0	7.0	21.0	59.0	35.0	150
34	10	1	16.5	6.5	27.0	72.0	44.5	270
34	10	1	14.0	5.5	24.0	65.0	39.0	202
58	10	2	13.5	6.5	21.5	63.0	40.0	202
58	10	1	15.5	7.0	28.0	70.5	50.0	365
11	11	1	11.5	6.0	16.5	48.0	31.0	79
23	11	1	12.0	6.5	19.0	50.0	38.0	148
70	10	1	15.5	7.0	28.0	76.5	55.0	446
11	11	2	9.0	5.0	15.0	46.0	27.0	62
83	11	2	14.5	7.0	23.0	61.5	44.0	236
35	11	1	13.5	8.5	23.0	63.5	44.0	212
16	4	1	10.0	4.0	15.5	48.0	26.0	60
16	4	1	10.0	5.0	15.0	41.0	26.0	64
17	5	1	11.5	5.0	17.0	53.0	30.5	114
17	5	2	11.5	5.0	15.0	52.5	28.0	76
17	5	2	11.0	4.5	13.0	46.0	23.0	48
8	8	2	10.0	4.5	10.0	43.5	24.0	29
83	11	1	15.5	8.0	30.5	75.0	54.0	514
18	6	1	12.5	8.5	18.0	57.3	32.8	140

Data Set 8: Alcohol and Tobacco Use in Animated Children's Movies

Movie lengths are in minutes, tobacco use times are in seconds, and alcohol use times are in seconds. The data are based on Goldstein, Adam O., Sobel, Rachel A., Newman, Glen R.; "Tobacco and Alcohol Use in G-Rated Children's Animated Films." *Journal of the American Medical Association,* March 24/31, 1999, vol. 281, no. 12, p. 1132. Copyright © 1999. All rights reserved.

STATDISK: Data set name is Alcohol and Tobacco in Movies.
Minitab: Worksheet name is CHMOVIE.MTW.
Excel: Workbook name is CHMOVIE.XLS.
TI-83/84 Plus: App name is CHMOVIE and the file names are the same as for text files.
Text file names: CHLEN, CHTOB, CHALC.

Movie	Company	Length (min)	Tobacco Use (sec)	Alcohol Use (sec)
Snow White	Disney	83	0	0
Pinocchio	Disney	88	223	80
Fantasia	Disney	120	0	0
Dumbo	Disney	64	176	88
Bambi	Disney	69	0	0
Three Caballeros	Disney	71	548	8
Fun and Fancy Free	Disney	76	0	4
Cinderella	Disney	74	37	0
Alice in Wonderland	Disney	75	158	0
Peter Pan	Disney	76	51	33
Lady and the Tramp	Disney	75	0	0
Sleeping Beauty	Disney	75	0	113
101 Dalmatians	Disney	79	299	51
Sword and the Stone	Disney	80	37	20
Jungle Book	Disney	78	0	0
Aristocats	Disney	78	11	142
Robin Hood	Disney	83	0	39
Rescuers	Disney	77	0	0
Winnie the Pooh	Disney	71	0	0
Fox and the Hound	Disney	83	0	0
Black Cauldron	Disney	80	0	34
Great Mouse Detective	Disney	73	165	414
Oliver and Company	Disney	72	74	0
Little Mermaid	Disney	82	9	0
Rescuers Down Under	Disney	74	0	76
Beauty and the Beast	Disney	84	0	123
Aladdin	Disney	90	2	3
Lion King	Disney	89	0	0
Pocahontas	Disney	81	6	7
Toy Story	Disney	81	0	0
Hunchback of Notre Dame	Disney	90	23	46
James and the Giant Peach	Disney	79	206	38
Hercules	Disney	92	9	13
Secret of NIMH	MGM	82	0	0
All Dogs Go to Heaven	MGM	89	205	73
All Dogs Go to Heaven 2	MGM	82	162	72
Babes in Toyland	MGM	74	0	0
Thumbelina	Warner Bros	86	6	5
Troll in Central Park	Warner Bros	76	1	0
Space Jam	Warner Bros	81	117	0
Pippi Longstocking	Warner Bros	75	5	0
Cats Don't Dance	Warner Bros	75	91	0
An American Tail	Universal	77	155	74
Land Before Time	Universal	70	0	0
Fievel Goes West	Universal	75	24	28
We're Back: Dinosaur Story	Universal	64	55	0
Land Before Time 2	Universal	73	0	0
Balto	Universal	74	0	0
Once Upon a Forest	20th Century Fox	71	0	0
Anastasia	20th Century Fox	94	17	39

Data Set 9: Passive and Active Smoke

All values are measured levels of serum cotinine (in ng/mL), a metabolite of nicotine. (When nicotine is absorbed by the body, cotinine is produced.) Data are from the U.S. Department of Health and Human Services, National Center for Health Statistics, Third National Health and Nutrition Examination Survey.

STATDISK: Data set name is Passive and Active Smoke.
Minitab: Worksheet name is COTININE.MTW.
Excel: Workbook name is COTININE.XLS.
TI-83/84 Plus: App name is COTININE and the file names are the same as for text files.
Text file names: SMKR, ETS, NOETS.

SMKR (smokers, or subjects reported tobacco use)

1	0	131	173	265	210	44	277	32	3
35	112	477	289	227	103	222	149	313	491
130	234	164	198	17	253	87	121	266	290
123	167	250	245	48	86	284	1	208	173

ETS (nonsmokers exposed to environmental tobacco smoke at home or work)

384	0	69	19	1	0	178	2	13	1
4	0	543	17	1	0	51	0	197	3
0	3	1	45	13	3	1	1	1	0
0	551	2	1	1	1	0	74	1	241

NOETS (nonsmokers with no exposure to environmental tobacco smoke at home or work)

0	0	0	0	0	0	0	0	0	0
0	9	0	0	0	0	0	0	244	0
1	0	0	0	90	1	0	309	0	0
0	0	0	0	0	0	0	0	0	0

Data Set 10: Cigarette Tar, Nicotine, and Carbon Monoxide

All measurements are in milligrams per cigarette. CO denotes carbon monoxide. The king-size cigarettes are nonfiltered, nonmenthol, and nonlight. The menthol cigarettes are 100 mm long, filtered, and nonlight. The cigarettes in the third group are 100 mm long, filtered, nonmenthol, and nonlight. Data are from the Federal Trade Commission.

STATDISK:	Data set name is Cigarette Tar, Nicotine, and Carbon Monoxide.
Minitab:	Worksheet name is CIGARET.MTW.
Excel:	Workbook name is CIGARET.XLS.
TI-83/84 Plus:	App name is CIGARET and the file names are the same as for text files.
Text file names:	KGTAR, KGNIC, KGCO, MNTAR, MNNIC, MNCO, FLTAR, FLNIC, FLCO (where KG denotes the king size cigarettes, MN denotes the menthol cigarettes, and FL denotes the filtered cigarettes that are not menthol types).

King Size

Brand	Tar	Nicotine	CO
Austin	20	1.1	16
Basic	27	1.7	16
Bristol	27	1.7	16
Cardinal	20	1.1	16
Cavalier	20	1.1	16
Chesterfield	24	1.4	17
Cimarron	20	1.1	16
Class A	23	1.4	15
Doral	20	1.0	16
GPC	22	1.2	14
Highway	20	1.1	16
Jacks	20	1.1	16
Marker	20	1.1	16
Monaco	20	1.1	16
Monarch	20	1.1	16
Old Gold	10	1.8	14
Pall Mall	24	1.6	16
Pilot	20	1.1	16
Prime	21	1.2	14
Pyramid	25	1.5	18
Raleigh Extra	23	1.3	15
Sebring	20	1.1	16
Summit	22	1.3	14
Sundance	20	1.1	16
Worth	20	1.1	16

Menthol

Brand	Tar	Nicotine	CO
Alpine	16	1.1	15
Austin	13	0.8	17
Basic	16	1.0	19
Belair	9	0.9	9
Best Value	14	0.8	17
Cavalier	13	0.8	17
Doral	12	0.8	15
Focus	14	0.8	17
GPC	14	0.9	15
Highway	13	0.8	17
Jacks	13	0.8	17
Kool	16	1.2	15
Legend	13	0.8	17
Marker	13	0.8	17
Maverick	18	1.3	18
Merit	9	0.7	11
Newport	19	1.4	18
Now	2	0.2	3
Pilot	13	0.8	17
Players	14	1.0	14
Prime	14	0.8	15
Pyramid	15	0.8	22
Salem	16	1.2	16
True	6	0.6	7
Vantage	8	0.7	9

Filtered 100-mm Nonmenthol

Brand	Tar	Nicotine	CO
Barclay	5	0.4	4
Basic	16	1.0	19
Camel	17	1.2	17
Highway	13	0.8	18
Jacks	13	0.8	18
Kent	14	1.0	13
Lark	15	1.1	17
Marlboro	15	1.1	15
Maverick	15	1.1	15
Merit	9	0.8	12
Monaco	13	0.8	18
Monarch	13	0.8	17
Mustang	13	0.8	18
Newport	15	1.0	16
Now	2	0.2	3
Old Gold	15	1.1	18
Pall Mall	15	1.0	15
Pilot	13	0.8	18
Players	14	1.0	15
Prime	15	0.9	17
Raleigh	16	1.1	15
Tareyton	15	1.1	15
True	7	0.6	7
Viceroy	17	1.3	16
Winston	15	1.1	14

Data Set 11: Ages of Oscar Winners

Ages (years) of actresses and actors at the times that they won Oscars for the categories of Best Actress and Best Actor. The ages are listed in chronological order by row, so that corresponding locations in the two tables are from the same year. (*Notes:* In 1968 there was a tie in the Best Actress category, and the mean of the two ages is used; in 1932 there was a tie in the Best Actor category, and the mean of the two ages is used. These data are suggested by the article "Ages of Oscar-winning Best Actors and Actresses" by Richard Brown and Gretchen Davis, *Mathematics Teacher* magazine. In that article, the year of birth of the award winner was subtracted from the year of

the awards ceremony, but the ages listed here are calculated from the birth date of the winner and the date of the awards ceremony.) The data are complete as of this writing.

STATDISK: Data set name is Ages of Oscar Winners.
Minitab: Worksheet name is OSCR.MTW.
Excel: Workbook name for males is OSCR.XLS.
TI-83/84 Plus: App name is OSCR and the file names are the same as for text files.
Text file names: OSCRF, OSCRM

Best Actresses

22	37	28	63	32	26	31	27	27	28
30	26	29	24	38	25	29	41	30	35
35	33	29	38	54	24	25	46	41	28
40	39	29	27	31	38	29	25	35	60
43	35	34	34	27	37	42	41	36	32
41	33	31	74	33	50	38	61	21	41
26	80	42	29	33	35	45	49	39	34
26	25	33	35	35	28	30	29	61	32
33	45								

Best Actors

44	41	62	52	41	34	34	52	41	37
38	34	32	40	43	56	41	39	49	57
41	38	42	52	51	35	30	39	41	44
49	35	47	31	47	37	57	42	45	42
44	62	43	42	48	49	56	38	60	30
40	42	36	76	39	53	45	36	62	43
51	32	42	54	52	37	38	32	45	60
46	40	36	47	29	43	37	38	45	50
48	60								

Data Set 12: POTUS
(Presidents of the United States)

AGE is age in years at time of inauguration. Days is the number of days served as president. Years is the number of years lived after the first inauguration. Ht is height (cm) of the president. HtOpp is the height (cm) of the major opponent for the presidency. *Note:* Presidents who took office as the result of an assassination or resignation are not included. Data are complete as of this writing.

STATDISK: Data set name is POTUS.
Minitab: Worksheet name for males is POTUS.MTW.
Excel: Workbook name for males is POTUS.XLS.
TI-83/84 Plus: App name is POTUS and the file names are the same as for text files.
               Caution: For TI-83/84 Plus calculators, missing values are entered as 9999.
Text file names: PRAGE, DAYS, YEARS, PRHT, HTOPP

	Age	Days	Years	Ht (cm)	HtOpp (cm)
Washington	57	2864	10	188	
J. Adams	61	1460	29	170	189
Jefferson	57	2921	26	189	170
Madison	57	2921	28	163	
Monroe	58	2921	15	183	
J. Q. Adams	57	1460	23	171	191
Jackson	61	2921	17	185	171
Van Buren	54	1460	25	168	180
W. H. Harrison	68	31	0	173	168
Polk	49	1460	4	173	185
Taylor	64	491	1	173	174
Pierce	48	1460	16	178	196
Buchanan	65	1460	12	183	175
Lincoln	52	1503	4	193	188
Grant	46	2921	17	173	
Hayes	54	1460	16	173	178
Garfield	49	199	0	183	187
Cleveland	47	2920	24	180	180
B. Harrison	55	1460	12	168	180
McKinley	54	1655	4	170	178
T. Roosevelt	42	2727	18	178	175
Taft	51	1460	21	182	178
Wilson	56	2921	11	180	182
Harding	55	881	2	183	178
Coolidge	51	2039	9	178	180
Hoover	54	1460	36	182	180
F. Roosevelt	51	4452	12	188	182
Truman	60	2810	28	175	173
Eisenhower	62	2922	16	179	178
J. Kennedy	43	1036	3	183	182
Johnson	55	1886	9	192	180
Nixon	56	2027	25	182	180
Carter	52	1461		177	183
Reagan	69	2922	23	185	177
G. H. W. Bush	64	1461		188	173
Clinton	46	2922		188	188
G. W. Bush	54	2920		183	185
Obama	47			188	175

Data Set 13: Car Crash Tests

The same cars are used in Data Set 14. The data are measurements from cars crashed into a fixed barrier at 35 mi/h with a crash test dummy in the driver's seat. HIC is a measurement of a standard "head injury criterion," CHEST is chest deceleration (in g, where g is a force of gravity), FEML is the measured load on the left femur (in lb), FEMR is the measured load on the right femur (in lb), TTI is a measurement of the side thoracic trauma index, and PLVS is pelvis deceleration (in g, where g is a force of gravity). Data are from the National Highway Traffic Safety Administration.

STATDISK: Data set name is Car Crash Tests.
Minitab: Worksheet name is CRASH.MTW.
Excel: Workbook name is CRASH.XLS.
TI-83/84 Plus: App name is CRASH and the individual column names are the same as for text files.
Text file names: HIC, CHEST, FEML, FEMR, TTI, PLVS.

CAR	SIZE	HIC	CHEST	FEML	FEMR	TTI	PLVS
Chev Aveo	Small	371	44	1188	1261	62	71
Honda Civic	Small	356	39	289	324	63	71
Mitsubishi Lancer	Small	275	37	329	446	35	45
VW Jetta	Small	544	54	707	1048	44	66
Hyundai Elantra	Small	326	39	602	1474	58	71
Kia Rio	Small	520	44	245	1046	64	84
Subaru Impreza	Small	443	42	334	455	50	53
Ford Fusion	Midsize	366	36	399	844	51	78
Nissan Altima	Midsize	287	53	317	713	53	53
Nissan Maxima	Midsize	255	43	301	133	44	59
Honda Accord	Midsize	249	42	297	236	59	55
Volvo S60	Midsize	502	52	810	687	49	67
VW Passat	Midsize	502	49	280	905	43	61
Toyota Camry	Midsize	505	41	411	547	42	57
Toyota Avalon	Large	342	32	215	752	36	55
Hyundai Azera	Large	698	45	1636	1202	48	75
Cadillac DTS	Large	346	41	738	772	61	75
Lincoln Town	Large	608	38	882	554	57	61
Dodge Charger	Large	216	37	937	669	63	53
Merc Gr Marq	Large	608	38	882	554	57	61
Buick Lucerne	Large	169	33	472	290	64	76

Data Set 14: Car Measurements

The same cars are used in Data Set 13. The data are measurements from cars that have automatic transmissions and were manufactured in the same recent year. WT is weight (lb), LN is length (inches), BRK is braking distance (feet) from 60 mi/h, CYL is the number of cylinders, DISP is the engine displacement (liters), CITY is the fuel consumption (mi/gal) for city driving conditions, HWY is the fuel consumption (mi/gal) for highway driving conditions, and GHG is a measure of greenhouse gas emissions (in tons/year, expressed as CO_2 equivalents).

STATDISK: Data set name is Car Measurements.
Minitab: Worksheet name is CARS.MTW.
Excel: Workbook name is CARS.XLS.
TI-83/84 Plus: App name is CARS and the individual column names are the same as for text files.
Text file names: CWT, CLN, CBRK, CCYL, CDISP, CCITY, CHWY, CGHG.

CAR	SIZE	WT	LN	BRK	CYL	DISP	CITY	HWY	GHG
Chev Aveo	Small	2560	154	133	4	1.6	25	34	6.6
Honda Civic	Small	2740	177	136	4	1.8	25	36	6.3
Mitsubishi Lancer	Small	3610	177	126	4	2.0	22	28	7.7
VW Jetta	Small	3225	179	137	4	2.0	29	40	6.4
Hyundai Elantra	Small	2895	177	138	4	2.0	25	33	6.6
Kia Rio	Small	2615	167	132	4	1.6	27	35	6.1
Subaru Impreza	Small	3110	180	135	4	2.5	20	26	8.3
Ford Fusion	Midsize	3320	191	136	4	2.3	20	28	8.0
Nissan Altima	Midsize	3215	190	136	4	2.5	23	31	7.1
Nissan Maxima	Midsize	3555	191	128	6	3.5	19	26	8.3
Honda Accord	Midsize	3270	194	140	4	2.4	21	30	7.7
Volvo S60	Midsize	3465	180	140	5	2.5	19	28	8.0
VW Passat	Midsize	3465	188	135	4	2.0	19	29	8.0
Toyota Camry	Midsize	3530	189	137	4	2.4	21	31	7.3
Toyota Avalon	Large	3600	197	139	6	3.5	19	28	8.0
Hyundai Azera	Large	3835	193	134	6	3.3	18	26	8.7
Cadillac DTS	Large	4085	208	145	8	4.6	15	23	10.2
Lincoln Town	Large	4415	215	143	8	4.6	16	24	9.6
Dodge Charger	Large	4170	200	131	6	2.7	18	26	8.7
Merc Gr Marq	Large	4180	212	140	8	4.6	16	24	9.6
Buick Lucerne	Large	4095	203	143	8	4.6	17	25	10.2

Data Set 15: Flight Data

All flights are American Airlines flights from New York (JFK) to Los Angeles (LAX), and all flights occurred in January of a recent year. ID is the identification number on the tail of the aircraft. Dep Delay is the departure delay time (minutes), and negative numbers correspond to flights that departed early. Taxi Out is the time (minutes) that the flight used to taxi from the terminal to the runway for departure. Taxi In is the time (minutes) that the flight used to taxi to the terminal after landing. Arr Delay is the arrival delay time (minutes), and negative numbers correspond to flights that arrived early (before the scheduled arrival time). Data are from the Bureau of Transportation.

STATDISK: Data set name is Flight Data.
Minitab: Worksheet name is FLIGHTS.MTW.
Excel: Workbook name is FLIGHTS.XLS.
TI-83/84 Plus: App name is FLIGHTS and the individual column names are the same as for text files.
Text file names: DPDLY, TXOUT, TXIN, ARDLY

Flight	ID	Dep Delay	Taxi Out	Taxi In	Arr Delay
1	N338AA	−2	30	12	−32
1	N329AA	−1	19	13	−25
1	N319AA	−2	12	8	−26
1	N319AA	2	19	21	−6
1	N329AA	−2	18	17	5
1	N320AA	0	22	11	−15
1	N321AA	−2	37	12	−17
1	N338AA	−3	13	12	−36
1	N327AA	−5	14	15	−29
1	N319AA	−4	15	26	−18
1	N320AA	2	31	9	−12
1	N320AA	−2	15	11	−35
3	N327AA	22	16	6	2
3	N332AA	−11	14	7	−33
3	N321AA	7	15	4	−5
3	N338AA	0	27	11	0
3	N328AA	−5	19	10	0
3	N319AA	3	22	7	−1
3	N338AA	−8	22	11	−33
3	N328AA	8	23	10	−5
3	N336AA	−2	16	3	−14
3	N320AA	−8	13	7	−39
3	N323AA	−3	16	7	−21
3	N338AA	−4	18	5	−32
19	N329AA	19	15	10	−5
19	N322AA	−4	12	10	−32
19	N328AA	−5	19	16	−13
19	N319AA	−1	18	13	−9
19	N335AA	−4	21	9	−19
19	N332AA	73	20	8	49
19	N329AA	0	13	4	−30
19	N338AA	1	15	3	−23
19	N328AA	13	43	8	14
19	N327AA	−1	18	16	−21
19	N322AA	−8	17	9	−32
19	N319AA	32	19	5	11
21	N336AA	18	13	13	−23
21	N336AA	60	20	4	28
21	N327AA	142	12	6	103
21	N336AA	−1	17	21	−19
21	N323AA	−11	35	29	−5
21	N324AA	−1	19	5	−46
21	N327AA	47	22	27	13
21	N320AA	13	43	9	−3
21	N322AA	12	49	12	13
21	N323AA	123	45	7	106
21	N335AA	1	13	36	−34
21	N332AA	4	23	12	−24

Data Set 16: Earthquake Measurements

Fifty matched pairs of magnitude/depth measurements randomly selected from 10,594 earthquakes recorded in one year from a location in southern California. MAG is magnitude measured on the Richter scale and DEPTH is depth in km. The magnitude and depth both describe the source of the earthquake. In the two tables below, magnitudes and depths are paired by their corresponding positions in the two tables. The data are from the Southern California Earthquake Data Center.

STATDISK:	Data set name is Earthquakes.
Minitab:	Worksheet name is QUAKE.MTW.
Excel:	Workbook name is QUAKE.XLS.
TI-83/84 Plus:	App name is QUAKE and the file names are the same as for text files.
Text file names:	MAG, DEPTH.

Mag

0.70	2.20	1.64	1.01	1.62	1.28	0.92	1.00	1.49	1.42
0.74	1.98	1.32	1.26	1.83	0.83	1.00	2.24	0.84	1.35
0.64	0.64	2.95	0.00	0.99	1.34	0.79	2.50	1.42	0.93
0.39	1.22	0.90	0.65	1.56	0.54	0.79	1.79	1.00	0.40
0.70	0.20	1.76	1.46	0.40	1.25	1.44	1.25	1.25	1.39

Depth

6.6	2.2	18.5	7.0	13.7	5.4	5.3	5.9	4.7	14.5
2.0	14.8	8.1	18.6	4.5	17.7	15.9	15.1	8.6	5.2
15.3	5.6	10.0	8.2	8.3	9.9	13.7	8.5	8.2	7.9
17.2	6.1	13.7	5.7	6.0	17.3	4.2	14.7	15.2	3.3
3.2	9.1	8.0	18.9	14.2	5.1	5.7	16.4	10.1	6.4

Data Set 17: Word Counts by Males and Females

The columns are counts of the numbers of words spoken in a day by male (M) and female (F) subjects in six different sample groups. Column M1 denotes the word counts for males in Sample 1, F1 is the count for females in Sample 1, and so on.

Sample 1:   Recruited couples ranging in age from 18 to 29

Sample 2:   Students recruited in introductory psychology classes, aged 17 to 23

Sample 3:   Students recruited in introductory psychology classes in Mexico, aged 17 to 25

Sample 4:   Students recruited in introductory psychology classes, aged 17 to 22

Sample 5:   Students recruited in introductory psychology classes, aged 18 to 26

Sample 6:   Students recruited in introductory psychology classes, aged 17 to 23

Results were published in "Are Women Really More Talkative Than Men?" by Mehl, Vazire, Ramirez-Esparza, Slatcher, Pennebaker, *Science,* Vol. 317, No. 5834.

STATDISK:	Data set name is Word Counts from Men and Women.
Minitab:	Worksheet name is WORDS.MTW.
Excel:	Workbook name is WORDS.XLS.
TI-83/84 Plus:	App name is WORDS, and the file names are the same as for text files.
Text file names:	Text file names correspond to the columns below: M1, F1, M2, F2, M3, F3, M4, F4, M5, F5 M6, F6.

M1	F1	M2	F2	M3	F3	M4	F4	M5	F5	M6	F6
27531	20737	23871	16109	21143	6705	47016	11849	39207	15962	28408	15357
15684	24625	5180	10592	17791	21613	27308	25317	20868	16610	10084	13618
5638	5198	9951	24608	36571	11935	42709	40055	18857	22497	15931	9783
27997	18712	12460	13739	6724	15790	20565	18797	17271	5004	21688	26451
25433	12002	17155	22376	15430	17865	21034	20104		10171	37786	12151
8077	15702	10344	9351	11552	13035	24150	17225		31327	10575	8391
21319	11661	9811	7694	11748	24834	24547	14356		8758	12880	19763
17572	19624	12387	16812	12169	7747	22712	20571			11071	25246
26429	13397	29920	21066	15581	3852	20858	12240			17799	8427
21966	18776	21791	32291	23858	11648	3189	10031			13182	6998
11680	15863	9789	12320	5269	25862	10379	13260			8918	24876
10818	12549	31127	19839	12384	17183	15750	22871			6495	6272
12650	17014	8572	22018	11576	11010	4288	26533			8153	10047
21683	23511	6942	16624	17707	11156	12398	26139			7015	15569
19153	6017	2539	5139	15229	11351	25120	15204			4429	39681
1411	18338	36345	17384	18160	25693	7415	18393			10054	23079
20242	23020	6858	17740	22482	13383	7642	16363			3998	24814
10117	18602	24024	7309	18626	19992	16459	21293			12639	19287
20206	16518	5488	14699	1118	14926	19928	12562			10974	10351
16874	13770	9960	21450	5319	14128	26615	15422			5255	8866
16135	29940	11118	14602		10345	21885	29011				10827
20734	8419	4970	18360		13516	10009	17085				12584
7771	17791	10710	12345		12831	35142	13932				12764
6792	5596	15011	17379		9671	3593	2220				19086
26194	11467	1569	14394		17011	15728	5909				26852
10671	18372	23794	11907		28575	19230	10623				17639
13462	13657	23689	8319		23557	17108	20388				16616
12474	21420	11769	16046		13656	23852	13052				
13560	21261	26846	5112		8231	11276	12098				
18876	12964	17386	8034		10601	14456	19643				
13825	33789	7987	7845		8124	11067	21747				
9274	8709	25638	7796			18527	26601				

(continued)

Data Set 17: Word Counts by Males and Females *(continued)*

M1	F1	M2	F2	M3	F3	M4	F4	M5	F5	M6	F6
20547	10508	695	20910			11478	17835				
17190	11909	2366	8756			6025	14030				
10578	29730	16075	5683			12975	7990				
14821	20981	16789	8372			14124	16667				
15477	16937	9308	17191			22942	5342				
10483	19049		8380			12985	12729				
19377	20224		16741			18360	18920				
11767	15872		16417			9643	24261				
13793	18717		2363			8788	8741				
5908	12685		24349			7755	14981				
18821	17646					9725	1674				
14069	16255					11033	20635				
16072	28838					10372	16154				
16414	38154					16869	4148				
19017	25510					16248	5322				
37649	34869					9202					
17427	24480					11395					
46978	31553										
25835	18667										
10302	7059										
15686	25168										
10072	16143										
6885	14730										
20848	28117										

Data Set 18: Voltage Measurements from a Home

All measurements are from the author's home. The voltage measurements are from the electricity supplied directly to the home, an independent Generac generator (model PP 5000), and an uninterruptible power supply (APC model CS 350) connected to the home power supply.

STATDISK: Data set name is Voltage Measurements from a Home.

Minitab: Worksheet name is VOLTAGE.MTW.

Excel: Workbook name is VOLTAGE.XLS.

TI-83/84 Plus: App name is VOLTAGE and the file names are the same as for text files.

Text file names: Text file names are VHOME, VGEN, VUPS.

Day	Home (volts)	Generator (volts)	UPS (volts)
1	123.8	124.8	123.1
2	123.9	124.3	123.1
3	123.9	125.2	123.6
4	123.3	124.5	123.6
5	123.4	125.1	123.6
6	123.3	124.8	123.7
7	123.3	125.1	123.7
8	123.6	125.0	123.6
9	123.5	124.8	123.6
10	123.5	124.7	123.8
11	123.5	124.5	123.7
12	123.7	125.2	123.8
13	123.6	124.4	123.5
14	123.7	124.7	123.7
15	123.9	124.9	123.0
16	124.0	124.5	123.8
17	124.2	124.8	123.8
18	123.9	124.8	123.1
19	123.8	124.5	123.7
20	123.8	124.6	123.7
21	124.0	125.0	123.8
22	123.9	124.7	123.8
23	123.6	124.9	123.7
24	123.5	124.9	123.8
25	123.4	124.7	123.7
26	123.4	124.2	123.8
27	123.4	124.7	123.8
28	123.4	124.8	123.8
29	123.3	124.4	123.9
30	123.3	124.6	123.8
31	123.5	124.4	123.9
32	123.6	124.0	123.9
33	123.8	124.7	123.9
34	123.9	124.4	123.9
35	123.9	124.6	123.6
36	123.8	124.6	123.2
37	123.9	124.6	123.1
38	123.7	124.8	123.0
39	123.8	124.3	122.9
40	123.8	124.0	123.0

Data Set 19: Cola Weights and Volumes

Weights are in pounds and volumes are in ounces.

STATDISK: Data set name is Weights and Volumes of Cola.
Minitab: Worksheet name is COLA.MTW.
Excel: Workbook name is COLA.XLS.
TI-83/84 Plus: App name is COLA, and the file names are the
                 same as for text files.
Text file names: CRGWT, CRGVL, CDTWT, CDTVL, PRGWT,
                 PRGVL, PDTWT, PDTVL.

Weight Regular Coke	Volume Regular Coke	Weight Diet Coke	Volume Diet Coke	Weight Regular Pepsi	Volume Regular Pepsi	Weight Diet Pepsi	Volume Diet Pepsi
0.8192	12.3	0.7773	12.1	0.8258	12.4	0.7925	12.3
0.8150	12.1	0.7758	12.1	0.8156	12.2	0.7868	12.2
0.8163	12.2	0.7896	12.3	0.8211	12.2	0.7846	12.2
0.8211	12.3	0.7868	12.3	0.8170	12.2	0.7938	12.3
0.8181	12.2	0.7844	12.2	0.8216	12.2	0.7861	12.2
0.8247	12.3	0.7861	12.3	0.8302	12.4	0.7844	12.2
0.8062	12.0	0.7806	12.2	0.8192	12.2	0.7795	12.2
0.8128	12.1	0.7830	12.2	0.8192	12.2	0.7883	12.3
0.8172	12.2	0.7852	12.2	0.8271	12.3	0.7879	12.2
0.8110	12.1	0.7879	12.3	0.8251	12.3	0.7850	12.3
0.8251	12.3	0.7881	12.3	0.8227	12.2	0.7899	12.3
0.8264	12.3	0.7826	12.3	0.8256	12.3	0.7877	12.2
0.7901	11.8	0.7923	12.3	0.8139	12.2	0.7852	12.2
0.8244	12.3	0.7852	12.3	0.8260	12.3	0.7756	12.1
0.8073	12.1	0.7872	12.3	0.8227	12.2	0.7837	12.2
0.8079	12.1	0.7813	12.2	0.8388	12.5	0.7879	12.2
0.8044	12.0	0.7885	12.3	0.8260	12.3	0.7839	12.2
0.8170	12.2	0.7760	12.1	0.8317	12.4	0.7817	12.2
0.8161	12.2	0.7822	12.2	0.8247	12.3	0.7822	12.2
0.8194	12.2	0.7874	12.3	0.8200	12.2	0.7742	12.1
0.8189	12.2	0.7822	12.2	0.8172	12.2	0.7833	12.2
0.8194	12.2	0.7839	12.2	0.8227	12.3	0.7835	12.2
0.8176	12.2	0.7802	12.1	0.8244	12.3	0.7855	12.2
0.8284	12.4	0.7892	12.3	0.8244	12.2	0.7859	12.2
0.8165	12.2	0.7874	12.2	0.8319	12.4	0.7775	12.1
0.8143	12.2	0.7907	12.3	0.8247	12.3	0.7833	12.2
0.8229	12.3	0.7771	12.1	0.8214	12.2	0.7835	12.2
0.8150	12.2	0.7870	12.2	0.8291	12.4	0.7826	12.2
0.8152	12.2	0.7833	12.3	0.8227	12.3	0.7815	12.2
0.8244	12.3	0.7822	12.2	0.8211	12.3	0.7791	12.1
0.8207	12.2	0.7837	12.3	0.8401	12.5	0.7866	12.3
0.8152	12.2	0.7910	12.4	0.8233	12.3	0.7855	12.2
0.8126	12.1	0.7879	12.3	0.8291	12.4	0.7848	12.2
0.8295	12.4	0.7923	12.4	0.8172	12.2	0.7806	12.2
0.8161	12.2	0.7859	12.3	0.8233	12.4	0.7773	12.1
0.8192	12.2	0.7811	12.2	0.8211	12.3	0.7775	12.1

Data Set 20: M&M Plain Candy Weights (grams)

STATDISK: Data set name is M&M Candy Weights.
Minitab: Worksheet name is M&M.MTW.
Excel: Workbook name is M&M.XLS.
TI-83/84 Plus: App name is MM, and the file names are the same
                 as for text files.
Text file names: Text file names are RED, ORNG, YLLW,
                 BROWN, BLUE, GREEN.

Red	Orange	Yellow	Brown	Blue	Green
0.751	0.735	0.883	0.696	0.881	0.925
0.841	0.895	0.769	0.876	0.863	0.914
0.856	0.865	0.859	0.855	0.775	0.881
0.799	0.864	0.784	0.806	0.854	0.865
0.966	0.852	0.824	0.840	0.810	0.865
0.859	0.866	0.858	0.868	0.858	1.015
0.857	0.859	0.848	0.859	0.818	0.876
0.942	0.838	0.851	0.982	0.868	0.809
0.873	0.863			0.803	0.865
0.809	0.888			0.932	0.848
0.890	0.925			0.842	0.940
0.878	0.793			0.832	0.833
0.905	0.977			0.807	0.845
	0.850			0.841	0.852
	0.830			0.932	0.778
	0.856			0.833	0.814
	0.842			0.881	0.791
	0.778			0.818	0.810
	0.786			0.864	0.881
	0.853			0.825	
	0.864			0.855	
	0.873			0.942	
	0.880			0.825	
	0.882			0.869	
	0.931			0.912	
				0.887	
				0.886	

Data Set 21: Coin Weights (grams)

The "pre-1983 pennies" were made after the Indian and wheat pennies, and they are 97% copper and 3% zinc. The "post-1983 pennies" are 3% copper and 97% zinc. The "pre-1964 silver quarters" are 90% silver and 10% copper. The "post-1964 quarters" are made with a copper-nickel alloy.

STATDISK: Data set name is Coin Weights.
Minitab: Worksheet name is COINS.MTW.
Excel: Workbook name is COINS.XLS.
TI-83/84 Plus: App name is COINS, and the file names are the same as for text files.
Text file names: Text file names are CPIND, CPWHT, CPPRE, CPPST, CPCAN, CQPRE, CQPST, CDOL.

Indian Pennies	Wheat Pennies	Pre-1983 Pennies	Post-1983 Pennies	Canadian Pennies	Pre-1964 Quarters	Post-1964 Quarters	Dollar Coins
3.0630	3.1366	3.1582	2.5113	3.2214	6.2771	5.7027	8.1008
3.0487	3.0755	3.0406	2.4907	3.2326	6.2371	5.7495	8.1072
2.9149	3.1692	3.0762	2.5024	2.4662	6.1501	5.7050	8.0271
3.1358	3.0476	3.0398	2.5298	2.8357	6.0002	5.5941	8.0813
2.9753	3.1029	3.1043	2.4950	3.3189	6.1275	5.7247	8.0241
	3.0377	3.1274	2.5127	3.2612	6.2151	5.6114	8.0510
	3.1083	3.0775	2.4998	3.2441	6.2866	5.6160	7.9817
	3.1141	3.1038	2.4848	2.4679	6.0760	5.5999	8.0954
	3.0976	3.1086	2.4823	2.7202	6.1426	5.7790	8.0658
	3.0862	3.0586	2.5163	2.5120	6.3415	5.6841	8.1238
	3.0570	3.0603	2.5222		6.1309	5.6234	8.1281
	3.0765	3.0502	2.5004		6.2412	5.5928	8.0307
	3.1114	3.1028	2.5248		6.1442	5.6486	8.0719
	3.0965	3.0522	2.5058		6.1073	5.6661	8.0345
	3.0816	3.0546	2.4900		6.1181	5.5361	8.0775
	3.0054	3.0185	2.5068		6.1352	5.5491	8.1384
	3.1934	3.0712	2.5016		6.2821	5.7239	8.1041
	3.1461	3.0717	2.4797		6.2647	5.6555	8.0894
	3.0185	3.0546	2.5067		6.2908	5.6063	8.0538
	3.1267	3.0817	2.5139		6.1661	5.5709	8.0342
	3.1524	3.0704	2.4762		6.2674	5.5591	
	3.0786	3.0797	2.5004		6.2718	5.5864	
	3.0131	3.0713	2.5170		6.1949	5.6872	
	3.1535	3.0631	2.4925		6.2465	5.6274	
	3.0480	3.0866	2.4876		6.3172	5.6157	
	3.0050	3.0763	2.4933		6.1487	5.6668	
	3.0290	3.1299	2.4806		6.0829	5.7198	
	3.1038	3.0846	2.4907		6.1423	5.6694	
	3.0357	3.0917	2.5017		6.1970	5.5454	
	3.0064	3.0877	2.4950		6.2441	5.6646	
	3.0936	2.9593	2.4973		6.3669	5.5636	
	3.1031	3.0966	2.5252		6.0775	5.6485	
	3.0408	2.9800	2.4978		6.1095	5.6703	
	3.0561	3.0934	2.5073		6.1787	5.6848	
	3.0994	3.1340	2.4658		6.2130	5.5609	
			2.4529		6.1947	5.7344	
			2.5085		6.1940	5.6449	
					6.0257	5.5804	
					6.1719	5.6010	
					6.3278	5.6022	

Data Set 22: Axial Loads of Aluminum Cans

Axial loads are measured in pounds. Axial loads are applied when the tops are pressed into place.

STATDISK: Data set name is Axial Loads of Cans.
Minitab: Worksheet name is CANS.MTW.
Excel: Workbook name is CANS.XLS.
TI-83/84 Plus: App name is CANS, and the file names are the same as for text files.
Text file names: CN109, CN111.

Sample	Aluminum cans 0.0109 in. thick Axial load (pounds)							Sample	Aluminum cans 0.0111 in. thick Axial load (pounds)						
1	270	273	258	204	254	228	282	1	287	216	260	291	210	272	260
2	278	201	264	265	223	274	230	2	294	253	292	280	262	295	230
3	250	275	281	271	263	277	275	3	283	255	295	271	268	225	246
4	278	260	262	273	274	286	236	4	297	302	282	310	305	306	262
5	290	286	278	283	262	277	295	5	222	276	270	280	288	296	281
6	274	272	265	275	263	251	289	6	300	290	284	304	291	277	317
7	242	284	241	276	200	278	283	7	292	215	287	280	311	283	293
8	269	282	267	282	272	277	261	8	285	276	301	285	277	270	275
9	257	278	295	270	268	286	262	9	290	288	287	282	275	279	300
10	272	268	283	256	206	277	252	10	293	290	313	299	300	265	285
11	265	263	281	268	280	289	283	11	294	262	297	272	284	291	306
12	263	273	209	259	287	269	277	12	263	304	288	256	290	284	307
13	234	282	276	272	257	267	204	13	273	283	250	244	231	266	504
14	270	285	273	269	284	276	286	14	284	227	269	282	292	286	281
15	273	289	263	270	279	206	270	15	296	287	285	281	298	289	283
16	270	268	218	251	252	284	278	16	247	279	276	288	284	301	309
17	277	208	271	208	280	269	270	17	284	284	286	303	308	288	303
18	294	292	289	290	215	284	283	18	306	285	289	292	295	283	315
19	279	275	223	220	281	268	272	19	290	247	268	283	305	279	287
20	268	279	217	259	291	291	281	20	285	298	279	274	205	302	296
21	230	276	225	282	276	289	288	21	282	300	284	281	279	255	210
22	268	242	283	277	285	293	248	22	279	286	293	285	288	289	281
23	278	285	292	282	287	277	266	23	297	314	295	257	298	211	275
24	268	273	270	256	297	280	256	24	247	279	303	286	287	287	275
25	262	268	262	293	290	274	292	25	243	274	299	291	281	303	269

Data Set 23: Weights of Discarded Garbage for One Week

Weights are in pounds. HHSIZE is the household size. Data provided by Masakuza Tani, the Garbage Project, University of Arizona.

STATDISK: Data set name is Weights of Garbage.
Minitab: Worksheet name is GARBAGE.MTW.
Excel: Workbook name is GARBAGE.XLS.
TI-83/84 Plus: App name is GARBAGE, and the file names are the same as for text files.
Text file names: HHSIZ, METAL, PAPER, PLAS, GLASS, FOOD, YARD, TEXT, OTHER, TOTAL.

Household	HHSize	Metal	Paper	Plas	Glass	Food	Yard	Text	Other	Total
1	2	1.09	2.41	0.27	0.86	1.04	0.38	0.05	4.66	10.76
2	3	1.04	7.57	1.41	3.46	3.68	0.00	0.46	2.34	19.96
3	3	2.57	9.55	2.19	4.52	4.43	0.24	0.50	3.60	27.60
4	6	3.02	8.82	2.83	4.92	2.98	0.63	2.26	12.65	38.11
5	4	1.50	8.72	2.19	6.31	6.30	0.15	0.55	2.18	27.90
6	2	2.10	6.96	1.81	2.49	1.46	4.58	0.36	2.14	21.90
7	1	1.93	6.83	0.85	0.51	8.82	0.07	0.60	2.22	21.83
8	5	3.57	11.42	3.05	5.81	9.62	4.76	0.21	10.83	49.27
9	6	2.32	16.08	3.42	1.96	4.41	0.13	0.81	4.14	33.27
10	4	1.89	6.38	2.10	17.67	2.73	3.86	0.66	0.25	35.54
11	4	3.26	13.05	2.93	3.21	9.31	0.70	0.37	11.61	44.44
12	7	3.99	11.36	2.44	4.94	3.59	13.45	4.25	1.15	45.17
13	3	2.04	15.09	2.17	3.10	5.36	0.74	0.42	4.15	33.07
14	5	0.99	2.80	1.41	1.39	1.47	0.82	0.44	1.03	10.35
15	6	2.96	6.44	2.00	5.21	7.06	6.14	0.20	14.43	44.44
16	2	1.50	5.86	0.93	2.03	2.52	1.37	0.27	9.65	24.13
17	4	2.43	11.08	2.97	1.74	1.75	14.70	0.39	2.54	37.60
18	4	2.97	12.43	2.04	3.99	5.64	0.22	2.47	9.20	38.96
19	3	1.42	6.05	0.65	6.26	1.93	0.00	0.86	0.00	17.17
20	3	3.60	13.61	2.13	3.52	6.46	0.00	0.96	1.32	31.60
21	2	4.48	6.98	0.63	2.01	6.72	2.00	0.11	0.18	23.11
22	2	1.36	14.33	1.53	2.21	5.76	0.58	0.17	1.62	27.56
23	4	2.11	13.31	4.69	0.25	9.72	0.02	0.46	0.40	30.96
24	1	0.41	3.27	0.15	0.09	0.16	0.00	0.00	0.00	4.08
25	4	2.02	6.67	1.45	6.85	5.52	0.00	0.68	0.03	23.22
26	6	3.27	17.65	2.68	2.33	11.92	0.83	0.28	4.03	42.99
27	11	4.95	12.73	3.53	5.45	4.68	0.00	0.67	19.89	51.90
28	3	1.00	9.83	1.49	2.04	4.76	0.42	0.54	0.12	20.20
29	4	1.55	16.39	2.31	4.98	7.85	2.04	0.20	1.48	36.80
30	3	1.41	6.33	0.92	3.54	2.90	3.85	0.03	0.04	19.02
31	2	1.05	9.19	0.89	1.06	2.87	0.33	0.01	0.03	15.43
32	2	1.31	9.41	0.80	2.70	5.09	0.64	0.05	0.71	20.71
33	2	2.50	9.45	0.72	1.14	3.17	0.00	0.02	0.01	17.01
34	4	2.35	12.32	2.66	12.24	2.40	7.87	4.73	0.78	45.35
35	6	3.69	20.12	4.37	5.67	13.20	0.00	1.15	1.17	49.37
36	2	3.61	7.72	0.92	2.43	2.07	0.68	0.63	0.00	18.06
37	2	1.49	6.16	1.40	4.02	4.00	0.30	0.04	0.00	17.41
38	2	1.36	7.98	1.45	6.45	4.27	0.02	0.12	2.02	23.67
39	2	1.73	9.64	1.68	1.89	1.87	0.01	1.73	0.58	19.13
40	2	0.94	8.08	1.53	1.78	8.13	0.36	0.12	0.05	20.99
41	3	1.33	10.99	1.44	2.93	3.51	0.00	0.39	0.59	21.18
42	3	2.62	13.11	1.44	1.82	4.21	4.73	0.64	0.49	29.06

(continued)

Household	HHSize	Metal	Paper	Plas	Glass	Food	Yard	Text	Other	Total
43	2	1.25	3.26	1.36	2.89	3.34	2.69	0.00	0.16	14.95
44	2	0.26	1.65	0.38	0.99	0.77	0.34	0.04	0.00	4.43
45	3	4.41	10.00	1.74	1.93	1.14	0.92	0.08	4.60	24.82
46	6	3.22	8.96	2.35	3.61	1.45	0.00	0.09	1.12	20.80
47	4	1.86	9.46	2.30	2.53	6.54	0.00	0.65	2.45	25.79
48	4	1.76	5.88	1.14	3.76	0.92	1.12	0.00	0.04	14.62
49	3	2.83	8.26	2.88	1.32	5.14	5.60	0.35	2.03	28.41
50	3	2.74	12.45	2.13	2.64	4.59	1.07	0.41	1.14	27.17
51	10	4.63	10.58	5.28	12.33	2.94	0.12	2.94	15.65	54.47
52	3	1.70	5.87	1.48	1.79	1.42	0.00	0.27	0.59	13.12
53	6	3.29	8.78	3.36	3.99	10.44	0.90	1.71	13.30	45.77
54	5	1.22	11.03	2.83	4.44	3.00	4.30	1.95	6.02	34.79
55	4	3.20	12.29	2.87	9.25	5.91	1.32	1.87	0.55	37.26
56	7	3.09	20.58	2.96	4.02	16.81	0.47	1.52	2.13	51.58
57	5	2.58	12.56	1.61	1.38	5.01	0.00	0.21	1.46	24.81
58	4	1.67	9.92	1.58	1.59	9.96	0.13	0.20	1.13	26.18
59	2	0.85	3.45	1.15	0.85	3.89	0.00	0.02	1.04	11.25
60	4	1.52	9.09	1.28	8.87	4.83	0.00	0.95	1.61	28.15
61	2	1.37	3.69	0.58	3.64	1.78	0.08	0.00	0.00	11.14
62	2	1.32	2.61	0.74	3.03	3.37	0.17	0.00	0.46	11.70

Appendix C

Bibliography of Books and Web Sites

Books

*An asterisk denotes a book recommended for reading. Other books are recommended as reference texts.

Bennett, D. 1998. *Randomness*. Cambridge, Mass.: Harvard University Press.

*Best, J. 2001. *Damned Lies and Statistics*. Berkeley: University of California Press.

*Best, J. 2004. *More Damned Lies and Statistics*. Berkeley: University of California Press.

*Butros, M. 2013. *Student Solutions Manual to Accompany Elementary Statistics*. 12th ed. Boston: Addison-Wesley.

*Campbell, S. 2004. *Flaws and Fallacies in Statistical Thinking*. Mineola, N.Y.: Dover Publications.

*Crossen, C. 1996. *Tainted Truth: The Manipulation of Fact in America*. New York: Simon & Schuster.

*Freedman, D., R. Pisani, R. Purves, and A. Adhikari. 2007. *Statistics*. 4th ed. New York: Norton.

*Gonick, L., and W. Smith. 1993. *The Cartoon Guide to Statistics*. New York: HarperCollins.

*Heyde, C., and E. Seneta, eds. 2001. *Statisticians of the Centuries*. New York: Springer-Verlag.

*Hollander, M., and F. Proschan. 1984. *The Statistical Exorcist: Dispelling Statistics Anxiety*. New York: Marcel Dekker.

*Holmes, C. 1990. *The Honest Truth About Lying with Statistics*. Springfield, Ill.: Charles C. Thomas.

*Hooke, R. 1983. *How to Tell the Liars from the Statisticians*. New York: Marcel Dekker.

*Huff, D. 1993. *How to Lie with Statistics*. New York: Norton.

*Jaffe, A., and H. Spirer. 1998. *Misused Statistics*. New York: Marcel Dekker.

Kotz, S., and D. Stroup. 1983. *Educated Guessing—How to Cope in an Uncertain World*. New York: Marcel Dekker.

*Moore, D., and W. Notz. 2009. *Statistics: Concepts and Controversies*. 6th ed. San Francisco: Freeman.

*Paulos, J. 2001. *Innumeracy: Mathematical Illiteracy and Its Consequences*. New York: Hill and Wang.

*Reichmann, W. 1981. *Use and Abuse of Statistics*. New York: Penguin.

*Rossman, A., and B. Chance. 2008. *Workshop Statistics: Discovery with Data*. Emeryville, Calif.: Key Curriculum Press.

*Salsburg, D. 2000. *The Lady Tasting Tea: How Statistics Revolutionized the Twentieth Century*. New York: W. H. Freeman.

Sheskin, D. 2011. *Handbook of Parametric and Nonparametric Statistical Procedures*. 5th ed. Boca Raton, Fla.: CRC Press.

Simon, J. 1997. *Resampling: The New Statistics*. 2nd ed. Arlington, Va.: Resampling Stats.

*Stigler, S. 1986. *The History of Statistics*. Cambridge, Mass.: Harvard University Press.

Triola, M. 2013. *Minitab Student Laboratory Manual and Workbook*. 12th ed. Boston: Addison-Wesley.

Triola, M. 2013. *STATDISK 12 Student Laboratory Manual and Workbook*. 12th ed. Boston: Addison-Wesley.

Triola, M., and L. Franklin. 1994. *Business Statistics*. Boston: Addison-Wesley.

Triola, M., and M. Triola. 2006. *Biostatistics for the Biological and Health Sciences*. Boston: Addison-Wesley.

*Tufte, E. 2001. *The Visual Display of Quantitative Information*. 2nd ed. Cheshire, Conn.: Graphics Press.

Tukey, J. 1977. *Exploratory Data Analysis*. Boston: Addison-Wesley.

Vickers, A. 2009. *What Is a P-Value Anyway?* Boston: Pearson.

Zwillinger, D., and S. Kokoska. 2000. *CRC Standard Probability and Statistics Tables and Formulae*. Boca Raton, Fla.: CRC Press.

Web Sites

Triola Statistics Series: www.aw.com/triola

STATDISK: www.statdisk.org

StatCrunch: www.statcrunch.com

Data and Story Library: http://lib.stat.cmu.edu/DASL/

Statistical Science Web Data Sets: http://www.statsci.org/datasets.html

***Journal of Statistics Education* Data Archive:** http://www.amstat.org/publications/jse/jse_data_archive.htm

UCLA Statistics Data Sets: http://www.stat.ucla.edu/data/

Appendix D

Chapter 1 Answers

Section 1-2

1. Statistical significance is indicated when methods of statistics are used to reach a conclusion that some treatment or finding is effective, but common sense might suggest that the treatment or finding does not make enough of a difference to justify its use or to be practical. Yes, it is possible for a study to have statistical significance but not practical significance.

3. A voluntary response sample is a sample in which the subjects themselves decide whether to be included in the study. A voluntary response sample is generally not suitable for a statistical study, because the sample may have a bias resulting from participation by those with a special interest in the topic being studied.

5. There does appear to be a potential to create a bias.

7. There does not appear to be a potential to create a bias.

9. The sample is a voluntary response sample and is therefore flawed.

11. The sampling method appears to be sound.

13. Because there is a 30% chance of getting such results with a diet that has no effect, it does not appear to have statistical significance, but the average loss of 45 pounds does appear to have practical significance.

15. Because there is a 23% chance of getting such results with a program that has no effect, the program does not appear to have statistical significance. Because the success rate of 23% is not much better than the 20% rate that is typically expected with random guessing, the program does not appear to have practical significance.

17. The male and female pulse rates in the same column are not matched in any meaningful way. It does not make sense to use the difference between any of the pulse rates that are in the same column.

19. The data can be used to address the issue of whether males and females have pulse rates with the same average (mean) value.

21. Yes, each IQ score is matched with the brain volume in the same column, because they are measurements obtained from the same person. It does not make sense to use the difference between each IQ score and the brain volume in the same column, because IQ scores and brain volumes use different units of measurement. It would make no sense to find the difference between an IQ score of 87 and a brain volume of 1035 cm^3.

23. Given that the researchers do not appear to benefit from the results, they are professionals at prestigious institutions, and funding is from a U.S. government agency, the source of the data appears to be unbiased.

25. It is questionable that the sponsor is the Idaho Potato Commission and the favorite vegetable is potatoes.

27. The correlation, or association, between two variables does not mean that one of the variables is the cause of the other. Correlation does not imply causation.

29. a. 397.02 adults
    b. No. Because the result is a count of people among the 1018 who were surveyed, the result must be a whole number.
    c. 397 adults   d. 25%

31. a. 322.28 adults
    b. No. Because the result is a count of adults among the 2302 who were surveyed, the result must be a whole number.
    c. 322 adults   d. 2%

33. Because a reduction of 100% would eliminate all of the size, it is not possible to reduce the size by 100% or more.

35. If foreign investment fell by 100%, it would be totally eliminated, so it is not possible for it to fall by more than 100%.

37. Without our knowing anything about the number of ATVs in use, or the number of ATV drivers, or the amount of ATV usage, the number of 740 fatal accidents has no context. Some information should be given so that the reader can understand the *rate* of ATV fatalities.

39. The wording of the question is biased and tends to encourage negative responses. The sample size of 20 is too small. Survey respondents are self-selected instead of being selected by the newspaper. If 20 readers respond, the percentages should be multiples of 5, so 87% and 13% are not possible results.

Section 1-3

1. A parameter is a numerical measurement describing some characteristic of a population, whereas a statistic is a numerical measurement describing some characteristic of a sample.

3. Parts a and c describe discrete data.

5. Statistic   7. Parameter   9. Parameter

11. Statistic   13. Continuous   15. Discrete

17. Discrete   19. Continuous   21. Nominal

23. Interval   25. Ratio   27. Ordinal

29. The numbers are not counts or measures of anything, so they are at the nominal level of measurement, and it makes no sense to compute the average (mean) of them.

31. The numbers are used as substitutes for the categories of low, medium, and high, so the numbers are at the ordinal level of measurement. It does not make sense to compute the average (mean) of such numbers.

33. a. Continuous, because the number of possible values is infinite and not countable
    b. Discrete, because the number of possible values is finite
    c. Discrete, because the number of possible values is finite
    d. Discrete, because the number of possible values is infinite and countable

35. With no natural starting point, temperatures are at the interval level of measurement, so ratios such as "twice" are meaningless.

Section 1-4

1. No. Not every sample of the same size has the same chance of being selected. For example, the sample with the first two names has no chance of being selected. A simple random sample of n items is selected in such a way that every sample of the same size has the same chance of being selected.

3. The population consists of the adult friends on the list. The simple random sample is selected from the population of adult friends on the list, so the results are not likely to be representative of the much larger general population of adults in the United States.

5. Because the subjects are subjected to anger and confrontation, they are given a form of treatment, so this is an experiment, not an observational study.

7. This is an observational study because the therapists were not given any treatment. Their responses were observed.

9. Cluster   11. Random   13. Convenience
15. Systematic   17. Random   19. Convenience

21. The sample is not a simple random sample. Because every 1000th pill is selected, some samples have no chance of being selected. For example, a sample consisting of two consecutive pills has no chance of being selected, and this violates the requirement of a simple random sample.

23. The sample is a simple random sample. Every sample of size 500 has the same chance of being selected.

25. The sample is not a simple random sample. Not every sample has the same chance of being selected. For example, a sample that includes people who do not appear to be approachable has no chance of being selected.

27. Prospective study   29. Cross-sectional study
31. Matched pairs design   33. Completely randomized design

35. Blinding is a method whereby a subject (or a person who evaluates results) in an experiment does not know whether the subject is treated with the DNA vaccine or the adenoviral vector vaccine. It is important to use blinding so that results are not somehow distorted by knowledge of the particular treatment used.

Chapter 1: Quick Quiz

1. No. The numbers do not measure or count anything.
2. Nominal   3. Continuous   4. Quantitative data
5. Ratio   6. False   7. No
8. Statistic   9. Observational study
10. False

Chapter 1: Review Exercises

1. a. Discrete   b. Ratio   c. Stratified   d. Cluster
   e. The mailed responses would be a voluntary response sample, so those with strong opinions are more likely to respond. It is very possible that the results do not reflect the true opinions of the population of all customers.

2. The survey was sponsored by the American Laser Centers, and 24% said that the favorite body part is the face, which happens to be a body part often chosen for some type of laser treatment. The source is therefore questionable.

3. The sample is a voluntary response sample, so the results are questionable.

4. a. It uses a voluntary response sample, and those with special interests are more likely to respond, so it is very possible that the sample is not representative of the population.
   b. Because the statement refers to 72% of all Americans, it is a parameter (but it is probably based on a 72% rate from the sample, and the sample percentage is a statistic).
   c. Observational study

5. a. If they have no fat at all, they have 100% less than any other amount with fat, so the 125% figure cannot be correct.
   b. 686   c. 28%

6. The Gallup poll used randomly selected respondents, but the AOL poll used a voluntary response sample. Respondents in the AOL poll are more likely to participate if they have strong feelings about the candidates, and this group is not necessarily representative of the population. The results from the Gallup poll are more likely to reflect the true opinions of American voters.

7. Because there is only a 4% chance of getting the results by chance, the method appears to have statistical significance. The result of 112 girls in 200 births is above the approximately 50% rate expected by chance, but it does not appear to be high enough to have practical significance. Not many couples would bother with a procedure that raises the likelihood of a girl from 50% to 56%.

8. a. Random   b. Stratified   c. Nominal
   d. Statistic, because it is based on a sample.
   e. The mailed responses would be a voluntary response sample. Those with strong opinions about the topic would be more likely to respond, so it is very possible that the results would not reflect the true opinions of the population of all adults.

9. a. Systematic   b. Random   c. Cluster
   d. Stratified   e. Convenience

10. a. 780 adults   b. 23%
    c. Men: 48.5%; women: 51.5%
    d. No, although this is a subjective judgment.
    e. No, although this is a subjective judgment.

Chapter 1: Cumulative Review Exercises

1. The mean is 11. Because the flight numbers are not measures or counts of anything, the result does not have meaning.

2. The mean is 101, and it is reasonably close to the population mean of 100.

3. 11.83 is an unusually high value.

4. 0.46   5. 1067   6. 0.0037
7. 28.0   8. 5.3   9. 0.00078364164
10. 68,719,476,736 (or about 68,719,476,000)
11. 678,223,072,849 (or about 678,223,070,000)
12. 0.0000059049

Chapter 2 Answers

Section 2-2

1. No. For each class, the frequency tells us how many values fall within the given range of values, but there is no way to determine the exact IQ scores represented in the class.

3. No. The sum of the percents is 199%, not 100%, so each respondent could answer "yes" to more than one category. The table does not show the distribution of a data set among all of several different categories. Instead, it shows responses to five separate questions.

5. Class width: 10. Class midpoints: 24.5, 34.5, 44.5, 54.5, 64.5, 74.5, 84.5. Class boundaries: 19.5, 29.5, 39.5, 49.5, 59.5, 69.5, 79.5, 89.5.

7. Class width: 10. Class midpoints: 54.5, 64.5, 74.5, 84.5, 94.5, 104.5, 114.5, 124.5. Class boundaries: 49.5, 59.5, 69.5, 79.5, 89.5, 99.5, 109.5, 119.5, 129.5.

9. Class width: 2.0. Class midpoints: 3.95, 5.95, 7.95, 9.95, 11.95. Class boundaries: 2.95, 4.95, 6.95, 8.95, 10.95, 12.95.

11. No. The frequencies do not satisfy the requirement of being roughly symmetric about the maximum frequency of 34.

13. 18, 7, 4

15. The actresses appear to be younger than the actors.

Age When Oscar Was Won	Relative Frequency (Actresses)	Relative Frequency (Actors)
20–29	32.9%	1.2%
30–39	41.5%	31.7%
40–49	15.9%	42.7%
50–59	2.4%	15.9%
60–69	4.9%	7.3%
70–79	1.2%	1.2%
80–89	1.2%	0.0%

17.

Age (years) of Best Actress When Oscar Was Won	Cumulative Frequency
Less than 30	27
Less than 40	61
Less than 50	74
Less than 60	76
Less than 70	80
Less than 80	81
Less than 90	82

19. Because there are disproportionately more 0s and 5s, it appears that the heights were reported instead of measured. Consequently, it is likely that the results are not very accurate.

x	Frequency
0	9
1	2
2	1
3	3
4	1
5	15
6	2
7	0
8	3
9	1

21. Yes, the distribution appears to be a normal distribution.

Pulse Rate (Male)	Frequency
40–49	1
50–59	7
60–69	17
70–79	9
80–89	5
90–99	1

23. No, the distribution does not appear to be a normal distribution.

Magnitude	Frequency
0.00–0.49	5
0.50–0.99	15
1.00–1.49	19
1.50–1.99	7
2.00–2.49	2
2.50–2.99	2

25. Yes, the distribution appears to be roughly a normal distribution.

Red Blood Cell Count	Frequency
4.00–4.39	2
4.40–4.79	7
4.80–5.19	15
5.20–5.59	13
5.60–5.99	3

27. Yes. Among the 48 flights, 36 arrived on time or early, and 45 of the 48 flights arrived no more than 30 minutes late.

Arrival Delay (min)	Frequency
(−60)–(−31)	11
(−30)–(−1)	25
0–29	9
30–59	1
60–89	0
90–119	2

29.

Category	Relative Frequency
Male Survivors	16.2%
Males Who Died	62.8%
Female Survivors	15.5%
Females Who Died	5.5%

31. Pilot error is the most serious threat to aviation safety. Better training and stricter pilot requirements can improve aviation safety.

Cause	Relative Frequency
Pilot Error	50.5%
Other Human Error	6.1%
Weather	12.1%
Mechanical	22.2%
Sabotage	9.1%

33. An outlier can dramatically affect the frequency table.

Weight (lb)	With Outlier	Without Outlier
200–219	6	6
220–239	5	5
240–259	12	12
260–279	36	36
280–299	87	87
300–319	28	28
320–339	0	
340–359	0	
360–379	0	
380–399	0	
400–419	0	
420–439	0	
440–459	0	
460–479	0	
480–499	0	
500–519	1	

Section 2-3

1. It is easier to see the distribution of the data by examining the graph of the histogram than by examining the numbers in a frequency distribution.

3. With a data set that is so small, the true nature of the distribution cannot be seen with a histogram. The data set has an outlier of 1 min. That duration time corresponds to the last flight, which ended in an explosion that killed the seven crew members.

5. Identifying the exact value is not easy, but answers not too far from 200 are good answers.

7. The tallest person is about 108 in., or about 9 ft, tall. That tallest height is depicted in the bar that is farthest to the right in the histogram. That height is an outlier because it is very far away from all of the other heights. That height of 9 ft must be an error, because nobody is that tall.

9. The digits 0 and 5 seem to occur much more often than the other digits, so it appears that the heights were reported and not

actually measured. This suggests that the results might not be very accurate.

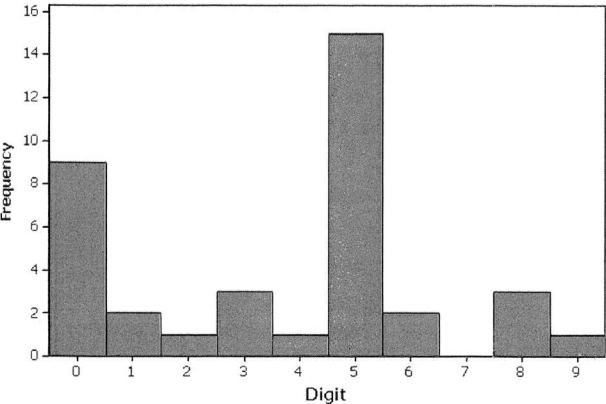

11. The histogram does appear to depict a normal distribution. The frequencies increase to a maximum and then decrease, and the histogram is symmetric with the left half being roughly a mirror image of the right half.

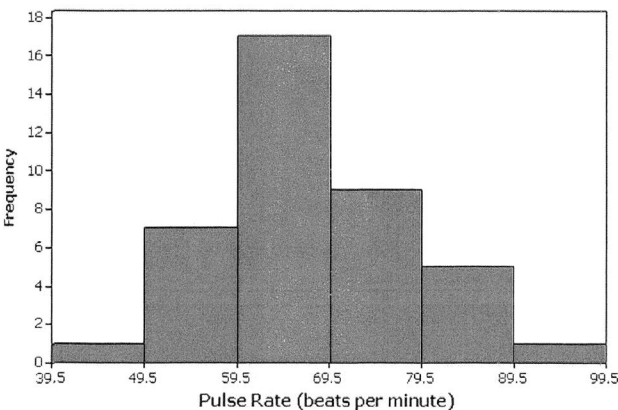

13. The histogram appears to roughly approximate a normal distribution. The frequencies increase to a maximum and then tend to decrease, and the histogram is symmetric with the left half being roughly a mirror image of the right half.

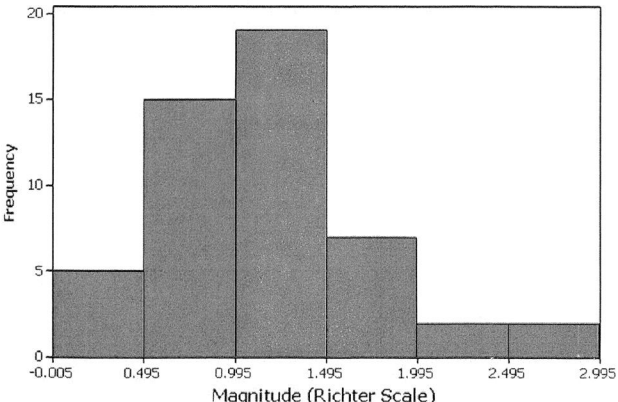

15. The histogram appears to roughly approximate a normal distribution. The frequencies increase to a maximum and then decrease, and the histogram is symmetric with the left half being roughly a mirror image of the right half.

17. The two leftmost bars depict flights that arrived early, and the other bars to the right depict flights that arrived late.

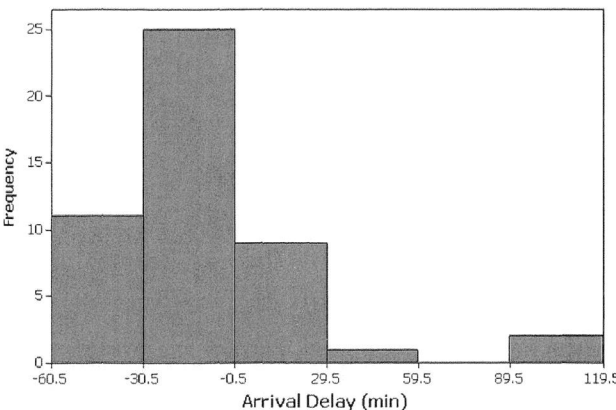

19. The ages of actresses are lower than those of actors.

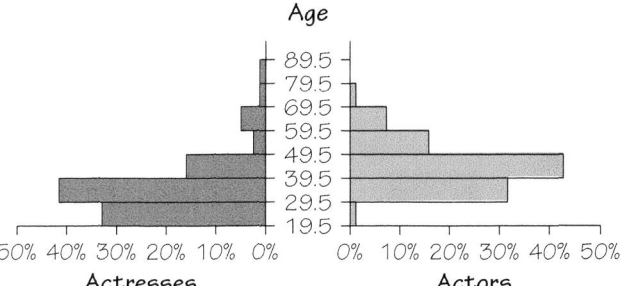

Section 2-4

1. In a Pareto chart, the bars are always arranged in descending order according to frequencies. The Pareto chart helps us understand data by drawing attention to the more important categories, which have the highest frequencies.

3. The data set is too small for a graph to reveal important characteristics of the data. With such a small data set, it would be better to simply list the data or place them in a table.

5. Because the points are scattered throughout with no obvious pattern, there does not appear to be a correlation.

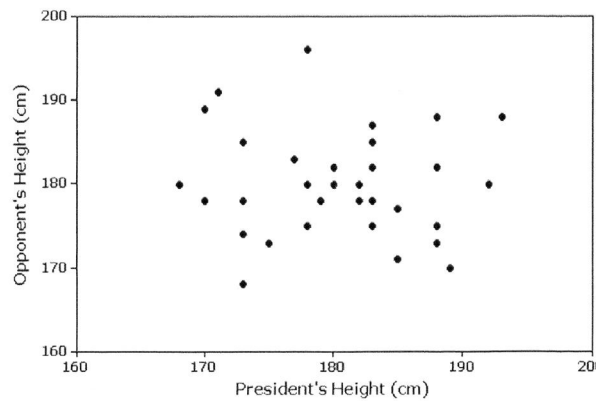

7. Yes. There is a very distinct pattern showing that bears with larger chest sizes tend to weigh more.

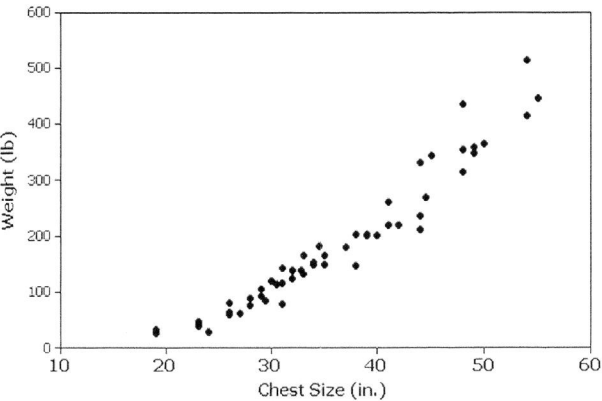

9. The first amount is highest for the opening day, when many Harry Potter fans are most eager to see the movie; the third and fourth values are from the first Friday and the first Saturday, which are the popular weekend days when movie attendance tends to spike.

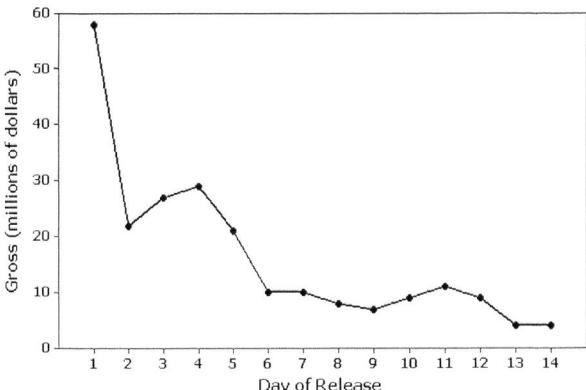

11. Yes, because the configuration of the points is roughly a bell shape, the volumes appear to be from a normally distributed population. The volume of 11.8 oz appears to be an outlier.

13. No. The distribution is not dramatically far from being a normal distribution with a bell shape, so there is not strong evidence against a normal distribution.

4	5
5	3335579
6	11167
7	1115568
8	4

15.

17.

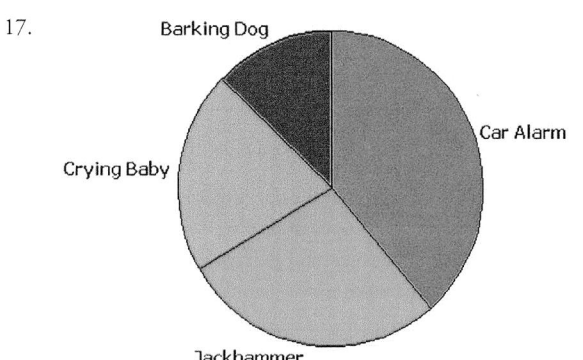

19. The frequency polygon appears to roughly approximate a normal distribution. The frequencies increase to a maximum and then tend to decrease, and the graph is symmetric with the left half being roughly a mirror image of the right half.

21. The vertical scale does not start at 0, so the difference is exaggerated. The graphs makes it appear that Obama got about twice as many votes as McCain, but Obama actually got about 69 million votes compared to 60 million for McCain.

23. China's oil consumption is 2.7 times (or roughly 3 times) that of the United States, but by using a larger barrel that is three times as wide and three times as tall (and also three times as deep) as the smaller barrel, the illustrator has made it appear that the larger barrel has a volume that is 27 times that of the smaller barrel. The actual ratio of U.S. consumption to China's consumption is roughly 3 to 1, but the illustration makes it appear to be 27 to 1.

25. The ages of actresses are lower than those of actors.

Chapter 2: Quick Quiz

1. 1.00   2. –0.005 and 0.995   3. No
4. 61 min, 62 min, 62 min, 62 min, 62 min, 67 min, 69 min
5. No   6. Bar graph   7. Scatterplot
8. Pareto chart   9. The distribution of the data
10. The bars of the histogram start relatively low, increase to some maximum, and then decrease. Also, the histogram is symmetric with the left half being roughly a mirror image of the right half.

Chapter 2: Review Exercises

1.

Volume (cm³)	Frequency
900–999	1
1000–1099	10
1100–1199	4
1200–1299	3
1300–1399	1
1400–1499	1

2. No, the distribution does not appear to be normal because the graph is not symmetric.

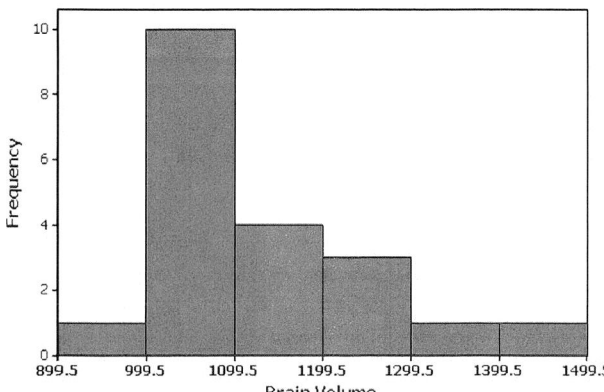

3. Although there are differences among the frequencies of the digits, the differences are not too extreme given the relatively small sample size, so the lottery appears to be fair.

4. The sample size is not large enough to reveal the true nature of the distribution of IQ scores for the population from which the sample is obtained.

```
  8 | 779
  9 | 66
 10 | 133
```

5. A time-series graph is best. It suggests that the amounts of carbon monoxide emissions in the United States are increasing.

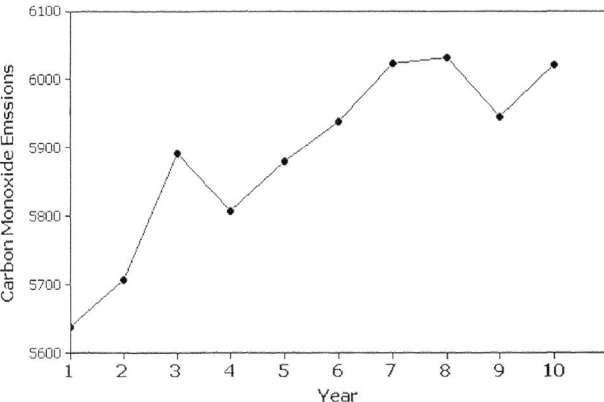

6. A scatterplot is best. The scatterplot does not suggest that there is a relationship.

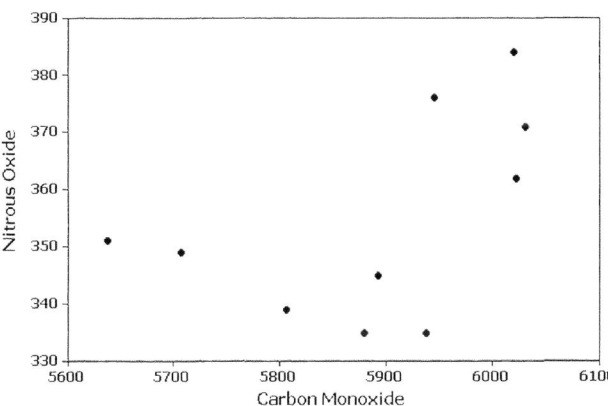

7. A Pareto chart is best.

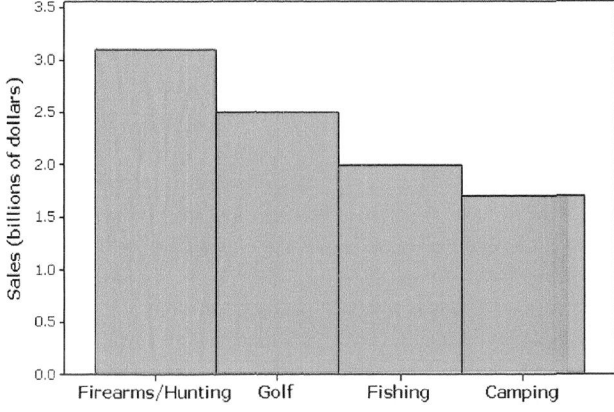

Chapter 2: Cumulative Review Exercises

1. Pareto chart

2. Nominal, because the responses consist of names only. The responses do not measure or count anything, and they cannot be arranged in order according to some quantitative scale.

3. Voluntary response sample (or self-selected sample). The voluntary response sample is not likely to be representative of the population, because those with special interests or strong feelings about the topic are more likely than others to respond, and their views might be very different from those of the general population.

4. By using a vertical scale that does not begin at 0, the graph exaggerates the differences in the numbers of responses. The graph could be modified by starting the vertical scale at 0 instead of 50.

5. 37.6% chose the category of boss. Because it is based on a sample (not on the population), that percentage is a statistic.

6.

Grooming Time (min)	Frequency
0–9	2
10–19	3
20–29	9
30–39	4
40–49	2

7. Because the frequencies increase to a maximum and then decrease, and the left half of the histogram is roughly a mirror image of the right half, the data do appear to be from a population with a normal distribution.

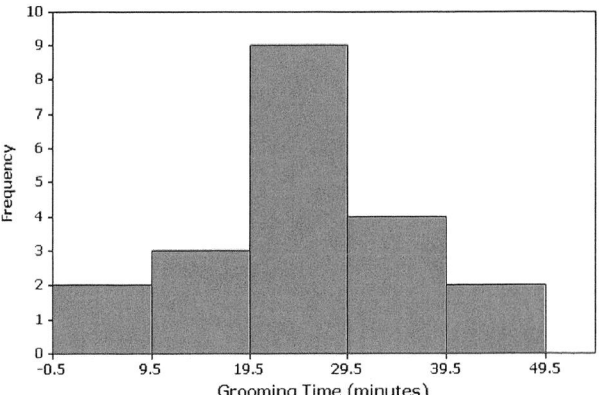

8.

```
 0 | 05
 1 | 255
 2 | 024555778
 3 | 0055
 4 | 05
```

Chapter 3: Answers

Section 3-2

1. No. The numbers do not measure or count anything, so the mean would be a meaningless statistic.

3. No. The price exactly in between the highest and lowest is the midrange, not the median.

5. $\bar{x} =$ \$159.8 million; median $=$ \$95.0 million; mode: none; midrange $=$ \$199.5 million. Apart from the obvious and trivial fact that the mean annual earnings of all celebrities is less than \$332 million, nothing meaningful can be known about the mean of the population.

7. $\bar{x} =$ 430.1 hic; median $=$ 393.0 hic; mode: none; midrange $=$ 435.0 hic. The safest of these cars appears to be the Hyundai Elantra. Because the measurements appear to vary substantially from a low of 326 hic to a high of 544 hic, it appears that some small cars are considerably safer than others.

9. $\bar{x} =$ \$16.4 million; median $=$ \$10.0 million; mode: \$4 million, \$9 million, and \$10 million; midrange $=$ \$31 million. The measures of center do not reveal anything about the pattern of the data over time, and that pattern is a key component of a movie's success. The first amount is highest for the opening day when many Harry Potter fans are most eager to see the movie; the third and fourth values are from the first Friday and the first Saturday, which are the popular weekend days when movie attendance tends to spike.

11. $\bar{x} =$ \$59.217; median $=$ \$57.835; mode: none; midrange $=$ \$60.345. None of the measures of center are most important here. The most relevant statistic in this case is the minimum value of \$48.92, because that is the lowest price for the software. Here, we generally care about the lowest price, not the mean price or median price.

13. $\bar{x} =$ 11.05 μg/g; median $=$ 9.50 μg/g; mode: 20.5 μg/g; midrange $=$ 11.75 μg/g. There is not enough information given here to assess the true danger of these drugs, but ingestion of any lead is generally detrimental to good health. All of the decimal values are either 0 or 5, so it appears that the lead concentrations were rounded to the nearest one-half unit of measurement (μg/g).

15. $\bar{x} =$ 6.5 years; median $=$ 4.5 years; mode: 4 and 4.5; midrange $=$ 9.5 years. It is common to earn a bachelor's degree in four years, but the typical college student requires more than four years.

17. $\bar{x} = -14.3$ min; median $= -16.5$ min; mode: -32 min; midrange $= -10.5$ min. Because the measures of center are all negative values, it appears that the flights tend to arrive early *before* the scheduled arrival times, so the on-time performance appears to be very good.

19. $\bar{x} =$ 50.4; median $=$ 73.0; mode: none; midrange $=$ 48.5. The numbers do not measure or count anything; they are simply replacements for names. The data are at the nominal level of measurement, and it makes no sense to compute the measures of center for these data.

21. White drivers: $\bar{x} =$ 73.0 mi/h; median $=$ 73.0 mi/h. African American drivers: $\bar{x} =$ 74.0 mi/h; median $=$ 74.0 mi/h. Although the African American drivers have a mean speed greater than the white drivers, the difference is very small, so it appears that drivers of both races appear to speed about the same amount.

23. Obama: $\bar{x} =$ \$653.9; median $=$ \$452.0. McCain: $\bar{x} =$ \$458.5; median $=$ \$350.0. The contributions appear to favor Obama because his mean and median are substantially higher. With 66 contributions to Obama and 20 contributions to McCain, Obama collected substantially more in total contributions.

25. $\bar{x} =$ 1.184; median $=$ 1.235. Yes, it is an outlier because it is a value that is very far away from all of the other sample values.

27. $\bar{x} =$ 15.0 years; median $=$ 16.0 years. Presidents receive Secret Service protection after they leave office, so the mean is helpful in planning for the cost and resources used for that protection.

29. $\bar{x} =$ 35.8 years. This result is quite close to the mean of 35.9 years found by using the original list of data values.

31. $\bar{x} =$ 84.7. This result is close to the mean of 84.4 found by using the original list of data values.

33. a. 0.6 parts per million   b. $n - 1$

35. $\bar{x} =$ 39.070; 10% trimmed mean: 27.677; 20% trimmed mean: 27.176. By deleting the outlier of 472.4, the trimmed means are substantially different from the untrimmed mean.

37. Geometric mean: 1.036711036, or 1.0367 when rounded. Single percentage growth rate: 3.67%. The result is not exactly the same as the mean, which is 3.68%.

39. 34.0 years (rounded from 33.970588 years); the value of 33.0 years is better because it is based on the original data and does not involve interpolation.

Section 3-3

1. The IQ scores of a class of statistics students should have less variation, because those students are a much more homogeneous group with IQ scores that are likely to be closer together.

3. Variation is a general descriptive term that refers to the amount of dispersion or spread among the data values, but the variance refers specifically to the square of the standard deviation.

5. Range $=$ \$265.0 million; $s^2 =$ 10,548.0 (the units are the square of "million dollars"); $s =$ \$102.7 million. Because the data values are the 10 highest from the population, nothing meaningful can be known about the standard deviation of the population.

7. Range $=$ 218.0 hic; $s^2 =$ 7879.8 hic^2; $s =$ 88.8 hic. Although all of the cars are small, the range from 326 hic to 544 hic appears to be relatively large, so the head injury measurements are not about the same.

9. Range $=$ \$54.0 million; $s^2 =$ 210.9 (the units are the square of "million dollars"); $s =$ \$14.5 million. An investor would care about the gross from opening day and the rate of decline after that, but the measures of center and variation are less important.

11. Range $=$ \$22.850; $s^2 =$ 99.141 dollars squared; $s =$ \$9.957. The measures of variation are not very helpful in trying to find the best deal.

13. Range $=$ 17.50 μg/g; $s^2 =$ 41.75 (μg/g)^2; $s =$ 6.46 μg/g. If the medicines contained no lead, all of the measures would be 0 μg/g, and the measures of variation would all be 0 as well.

15. Range $=$ 11.0 years; $s^2 =$ 12.3 year^2; $s =$ 3.5 years. No, because 12 years is within 2 standard deviations of the mean.

17. Range $=$ 43.0 min; $s^2 =$ 231.4 min^2; $s =$ 15.2 min. The standard deviation can never be negative.

19. Range $=$ 79.0; $s^2 =$ 1017.7; $s =$ 31.9. The data are at the nominal level of measurement and it makes no sense to compute the measures of variation for these data.

21. White drivers: 4.0%. African American drivers: 3.7%. The variation is about the same.

23. Obama: 80.0%. McCain: 91.3%. The variation among the Obama contributions is a little less than the variation among the McCain contributions.

25. Range = 2.950; s^2 = 0.345; s = 0.587.

27. Range = 36.0 years; s^2 = 94.5 years²; s = 9.7 years.

29. 0.738, which is not substantially different from s = 0.587.

31. 9.0 years, which is reasonably close to s = 9.7 years.

33. No. The pulse rate of 99 beats per minute is between the minimum usual value of 54.3 beats per minute and the maximum usual value of 100.7 beats per minute.

35. Yes. The volume of 11.9 oz is not between the minimum usual value of 11.97 oz and the maximum usual value of 12.41 oz.

37. s = 12.3 years. The result is not substantially different from the standard deviation of 11.1 years found from the original list of sample values.

39. s = 13.5. The result is very close to the standard deviation of 13.4 found from the original list of sample values.

41. a. 95%   b. 68%

43. At least 75% of women have platelet counts within 2 standard deviations of the mean. The minimum is 150 and the maximum is 410.

45. a. 6.9 min²   b. 6.9 min²   c. 3.4 min²
    d. Part (b), because repeated samples result in variances that target the same value (6.9 min²) as the population variance. Use division by $n - 1$.
    e. No. The mean of the sample variances (6.9 min²) equals the population variance (6.9 min²), but the mean of the sample standard deviations (1.9 min) does not equal the mean of the population standard deviation (2.6 min).

Section 3-4

1. Madison's height is below the mean. It is 2.28 standard deviations below the mean.

3. The lowest amount is $5 million, the first quartile Q_1 is $47 million, the second quartile Q_2 (or median) is $104 million, the third quartile Q_3 is $121 million, and the highest gross amount is $380 million.

5. a. $1,268,950   b. 0.16 standard deviations
   c. $z = -0.16$ d. Usual

7. a. $1,449,778   b. 2.75 standard deviations
   c. $z = -2.75$ d. Unusual

9. z scores: −2 and 2. IQ scores: 70 and 130.

11. 0.084 and 2.396

13. De-Fen Yao is relatively taller, because her z score is 12.33, which is greater than the z score of 10.29 for Sultan Kosen. De-Fen Yao is more standard deviations above the mean than Sultan Kosen.

15. The SAT score of 1490 has a z score of −0.09, and the ACT score of 17.0 has a z score −0.85. The z score of −0.09 is a larger number than the z score of −0.85, so the SAT score of 1490 is relatively better.

17. 13th percentile.

19. 50th percentile.

21. 251 sec (Tech: Excel: 250.8 sec).

23. 255 sec.

25. 247.5 sec.

27. 234.5 sec (Tech: Minitab: 234.25 sec; Excel: 234.75 sec).

29. 5-number summary: 1 sec, 8709 sec, 10,074.5 sec, 11,445 sec, 11,844 sec. (Tech: Minitab yields Q_1 = 8338 sec and Q_3 = 11,453 sec. Excel yields Q_1 = 8727.75 sec and Q_3 = 11,115 sec.)

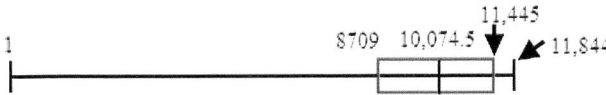

31. 5-number summary: 4 min, 14.0 min, 18.0 min, 32.0 min, 63 min. (Tech: Minitab yields Q_1 = 12.75 min and Q_3 = 34.25 min. Excel yields Q_1 = 14.25 min and Q_3 = 31.5 min.)

33. The top boxplot represents males. It appears that males have lower pulse rates than females.

35. The weights of regular Coke represented in the top boxplot appear to be generally greater than those of diet Coke, probably due to the sugar in cans of regular Coke.

37. Outliers for actresses: 60 years, 61 years, 61 years, 63 years, 74 years, 80 years. Outliers for actors: 76 years. The modified boxplots show that only one actress has an age that is greater than any actor.

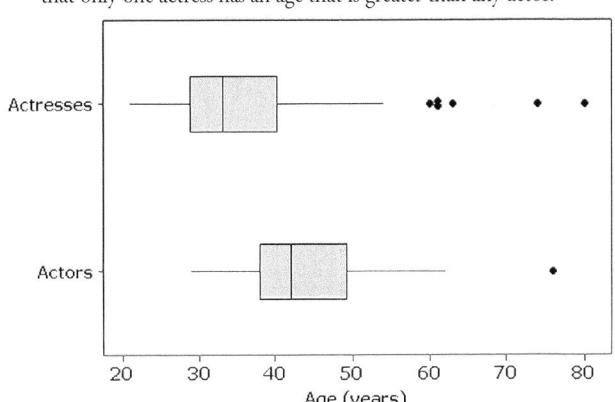

Chapter 3: Quick Quiz

1. 14.0 min.   2. 12.0 min.   3. 12 min.
4. 25.0 min².   5. −0.77.

6. Standard deviation; variance; range; mean absolute deviation
7. $\bar{x}$; μ.   8. s, σ, s^2, σ^2.   9. 75%.
10. Minimum, first quartile Q_1, second quartile Q_2 (or median), third quartile Q_3, maximum.

Chapter 3: Review Exercises

1. a. 1559.6 mm;   b. 1550.0 mm;   c. none;   d. 1569.5 mm; e. 145 mm;   f. 53.4 mm;   g. 2849.3 mm²;   h. 1538.0 mm; i. 1571.0 mm. (Tech: Minitab yields Q_1 = 1517.5 mm and Q_3 = 1606.5 mm.)
2. $z = 1.54$. The eye height is not unusual because its z score is between 2 and –2, so it is within 2 standard deviations of the mean.
3. Because the boxplot shows a distribution of data that is roughly symmetric, the data could be from a population with a normal distribution, but the data are not necessarily from a population with a normal distribution, because there is no way to determine whether a histogram is roughly bell-shaped.

4. 10053.7. The ZIP codes do not measure or count anything. They are at the nominal level of measurement, so the mean is a meaningless statistic.
5. The male has the larger relative BMI because his z score of 0.26 is larger than the z score of 0.08 for the female.
6. The answers vary, but a mean around $8 or $9 is reasonable, and a standard deviation around $1 or $2 is a reasonable estimate.
7. Answer varies, but $s \approx 12$ years, based on a minimum of 23 years and a maximum of 70 years.
8. Minimum: 842 mm; maximum: 986 mm. The maximum usual height of 986 mm is more relevant for designing overhead bin storage.
9. The minimum volume is 963 cm³, the first quartile Q_1 is 1034.5 cm³, the second quartile Q_2 (or median) is 1079 cm³, the third quartile Q_3 is 1188.5 cm³, and the maximum volume is 1439 cm³.

10. The median would be better because it is not affected much by the one very large income.

Chapter 3: Cumulative Review Exercises

1. a. Continuous.   b. Ratio.
2.

Hand Length (mm)	Frequency
150–159	1
160–169	0
170–179	2
180–189	0
190–199	3
200–209	1
210–219	1

3.

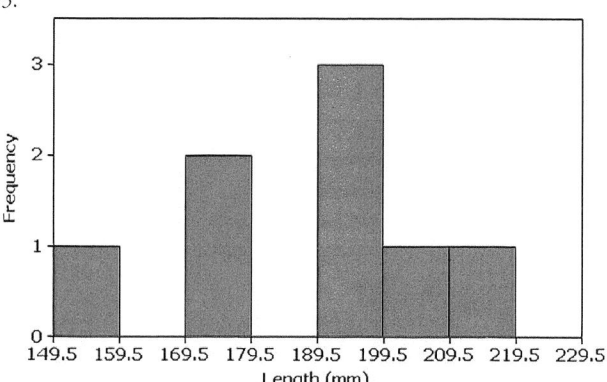

4. 15 | 8
    16 |
    17 | 39
    18 |
    19 | 569
    20 | 7
    21 | 4

5. a. 190.1 mm;   b. 195.5 mm;   c. 18.7 mm;   d. 348.7 mm² e. 56.0 mm.
6. Yes. The frequencies increase to a maximum; then they decrease. Also, the frequencies preceding the maximum are roughly a mirror image of those that follow the maximum.
7. No. Even though the sample is large, it is a voluntary response sample, so the responses cannot be considered to be representative of the population of the United States.
8. The vertical scale does not begin at 0, so the differences among the different outcomes are exaggerated.

Chapter 4 Answers

Section 4-2

1. $P(A) = 1/10,000$, or 0.0001. $P(\overline{A}) = 9999/10,000$, or 0.9999.
3. Part (c).
5. 5:2; 7/3; −0.9; 456/123
7. 1/5 or 0.2
9. Unlikely; neither unusually low nor unusually high.
11. Unlikely; unusually low.
13. 1/4, or 0.25
15. 1/2, or 0.5   17. 1/5, or 0.2   19. 0
21. 6/1000, or 0.006. The employer would suffer because it would be at risk by hiring someone who uses drugs.
23. 50/1000, or 0.05. This result is not close to the probability of 0.134 for a positive test result.
25. 879/945, or 0.930. Yes, the technique appears to be effective.
27. 0.00000101. No, the probability of being struck is much greater on an open golf course during a thunderstorm. The golfer should seek shelter.
29. a. 1/365   b. Yes   c. He already knew.   d. 0
31. 0.0767. No, a crash is not unlikely. Given that car crashes are so common, we should take precautions such as not driving after drinking and not using a cell phone or texting.

33. 0.00985. It is unlikely.

35. 0.00993. Yes, it is unlikely. The middle seat lacks an outside view, easy access to the aisle, and a passenger in the middle seat has passengers on both sides instead of on one side only.

37. 3/8, or 0.375

39. {bb, bg, gb, gg}; 1/2, or 0.5.

41. a. brown/brown, brown/blue, blue/brown, blue/blue
    b. 1/4   c. 3/4

43. a. 999:1   b. 499:1
    c. The description is not accurate. The odds against winning are 999:1 and the odds in favor are 1:999, not 1:1000.

45. a. $16   b. 8:1   c. About 9.75:1, which becomes 39:4
    d. $21.50

47. Relative risk: 0.939; odds ratio: 0.938; the probability of a headache with Nasonex (0.0124) is slightly less than the probability of a headache with the placebo (0.0132), so Nasonex does not appear to pose a risk of headaches.

49. 1/4

Section 4-3

1. Based on the rule of complements, the sum of $P(A)$ and $P(\overline{A})$ must always be 1, so that sum cannot be 0.5.

3. Because it is possible to select someone who is a male and a Republican, events M and R are not disjoint. Both events can occur at the same time when someone is randomly selected.

5. Disjoint.   7. Not disjoint.   9. Disjoint.

11. Not disjoint.   13. 0.53

15. $P(\overline{D}) = 0.450$, where $P(\overline{D})$ is the probability of randomly selecting someone who does not choose a direct in-person encounter as the most fun way to flirt.

17. 1   19. 0.956

21. 13/28, or 0.464. That probability is not as high as it should be.

23. 16/28 or 4/7 or 0.571

25. a. 0.786   b. 0.143
    c. The physicians given the labels with concentrations appear to have done much better. The results suggest that labels described as concentrations are much better than labels described as ratios.

27. 156/1205 = 0.129. Yes. A high refusal rate results in a sample that is not necessarily representative of the population, because those who refuse may well constitute a particular group with opinions different from others.

29. 1060/1205 = 0.880

31. 1102/1205 = 0.915

33. a. 300   b. 178   c. 178/300 = 0.593

35. 0.603

37. 27/300 = 0.090. With an error rate of 0.090 (or 9%), the test does not appear to be highly accurate.

39. 3/4, or 0.75

41. $P(A \text{ or } B) = P(A) + P(B) - 2P(A \text{ and } B)$

43. a. $1 - P(A) - P(B) + P(A \text{ and } B)$
    b. $1 - P(A \text{ and } B)$
    c. No

Section 4-4

1. The probability that the second selected senator is a Democrat given that the first selected senator was a Republican.

3. False. The events are dependent because the radio and air conditioner are both powered by the same electrical system. If you find that your car's radio does not work, there is a greater probability that the air conditioner will also not work.

5. a. Dependent   b. 1/132, or 0.00758

7. a. Independent   b. 1/12, or 0.0833

9. a. Independent   b. 0.000507

11. a. Dependent   b. 0.00586

13. a. 0.0081. Yes, it is unlikely.
    b. 0.00802. Yes, it is unlikely.

15. a. 0.739. No, it is not unlikely.
    b. 0.739. No, it is not unlikely.

17. 0.838. No, the entire batch consists of malfunctioning pacemakers.

19. a. 0.02   b. 0.0004   c. 0.000008
    d. By using one backup drive, the probability of failure is 0.02, and with three independent disk drives, the probability drops to 0.000008. By changing from one drive to three, the likelihood of failure drops from 1 chance in 50 to only 1 chance in 125,000, and that is a very substantial improvement in reliability. Back up your data!

21. a. 1/365, or 0.00274
    b. 0.00000751
    c. 1/365, or 0.00274

23. 0.828. No, it is not unlikely.

25. 0.000454. Yes, it is unlikely.

27. a. 0.900
    b. 0.00513 (using the 5% guideline for cumbersome calculations).

29. a. 0.143 (not 0.144)
    b. 0.00848 (using the 5% guideline for cumbersome calculations).

31. a. 0.9999   b. 0.9801
    c. The series arrangement provides better protection.

Section 4-5

1. a. Answer varies, but 0.98 is a reasonable estimate.
    b. Answer varies, but 0.999 is a reasonable estimate.

3. The probability that the polygraph indicates lying given that the subject is actually telling the truth.

5. At least one of the five children is a boy. 31/32, or 0.969.

7. None of the digits is 0; 0.656.

9. 0.893. The chance of passing is reasonably good.

11. 0.5   13. 0.965

15. 0.122. Given that the three cars are in the same family, they are not randomly selected and there is a good chance that the family members have similar driving habits, so the probability might not be accurate.

17. 0.988. It is very possible that the result is not valid because it is based on data from a voluntary response survey.

19. 90/950, or 0.0947. This is the probability of the test making it appear that the subject uses drugs when the subject is not a drug user.

21. 6/866, or 0.00693. This result is substantially different from the result found in Exercise 20. The probabilities $P(\text{subject uses drugs} \mid \text{negative test result})$ and $P(\text{negative test result} \mid \text{subject uses drugs})$ are not equal.

23. 44/134, or 0.328
25. a. 1/3, or 0.333
    b. 0.5
27. 0.5
29. a. 0.9996   b. 0.999992
31. 0.684. The probability is not low, so further testing of the individual samples will be necessary for about 68% of the combined samples.
33. a. 0.431   b. 0.569
35. a. 0.0748   b. 0.8
    c. The estimate of 75% is dramatically greater than the actual rate of 7.48%. They exhibited confusion of the inverse. A consequence is that they would unnecessarily alarm patients who are benign, and they might start treatments that are not necessary.

Section 4-6

1. The symbol ! is the factorial symbol that represents the product of decreasing whole numbers, as in $4! = 4 \cdot 3 \cdot 2 \cdot 1 = 24$. Four people can stand in line 24 different ways.
3. Because repetition is allowed, numbers are selected *with replacement*, so neither of the two permutation rules applies. The fundamental counting rule can be used to show that the number of possible outcomes is $10 \cdot 10 \cdot 10 \cdot 10 = 10,000$, so the probability of winning is 1/10,000.
5. 1/10,000
7. 1/362,880
9. 17,383,860. Because that number is so large, it is not practical to make a different CD for each possible combination.
11. 1/5,527,200. No, 5,527,200 is too many possibilities to list.
13. 34,650
15. 1/7,059,052
17. 1/24
19. a. 1/749,398   b. 1/10,000   c. $10,000
21. a. 11,880   b. 495   c. 1/495
23. 125,000. The fundamental counting rule can be used. The different possible codes are ordered sequences of numbers, not combinations, so the name of "combination lock" is not appropriate. Given that "fundamental counting rule lock" is a bit awkward, a better name would be something like "number lock."
25. 120; AMITY; 1/120
27. 26   29. 10   31. 64
33. 1/195,249,054
35. 2/252, or 1/128. Yes, if everyone treated is of one sex while everyone in the placebo group is of the opposite sex, you would not know if different reactions are due to the treatment or sex.
37. 2,095,681,645,538 (about 2 trillion)
39. 12

Chapter 4: Quick Quiz

1. 0   2. 0.7   3. 1   4. 0.04
5. Answer varies, but an answer such as 0.01 or lower is reasonable.
6. 512/839, or 0.610
7. 713/839, or 0.850
8. 126/839, or 0.150
9. 0.0224 (not 0.0226)
10. 126/350, or 0.360

Chapter 4: Review Exercises

1. 0.438   2. 0.410   3. 0.806
4. It appears that you have a substantially better chance of avoiding prison if you enter a guilty plea.
5. 0.986   6. 0.191   7. 0.00484
8. 0.619   9. 0.381   10. 0.0136
11. Answer varies, but DuPont data show that about 8% of cars are red, so any estimate between 0.01 and 0.2 would be reasonable.
12. a. 0.65
    b. 0.0150
    c. Yes, because the probability is so small (0.0150).
13. a. 1/365
    b. 31/365
    c. Answer varies, but it is probably small, such as 0.02.
    d. Yes
14. 0.0211. No.   15. 1/5,245,786
16. 1/575,757   17. 1/1000
18. 1320; 1/1320

Chapter 4: Cumulative Review Exercises

1. a. The mean of −8.9 years is not close to the value of 0 years that would be expected with no gender discrepancy.
   b. The median of −13.5 years is not close to the value of 0 years that would be expected with no gender discrepancy.
   c. $s = 10.6$ years
   d. $s^2 = 113.2$ years^2
   e. $Q_1 = -15.0$ years
   f. $Q_3 = -5.0$ years
   g. The boxplot suggests that the data have a distribution that is skewed.

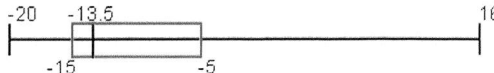

2. a. No. The pulse rate of 100 beats per minute is within 2 standard deviations of the mean, so it is not unusual.
   b. Yes. The pulse rate of 50 beats per minute is more than 2 standard deviations away from the mean, so it is unusual.
   c. Yes, because the probability of 1/256 (or 0.00391) is so small.
   d. No, because the probability of 1/8 (or 0.125) is not very small.
3. a. 46%   b. 0.460   c. Stratified sample
4. The graph is misleading because the vertical scale does not start at 0. The vertical scale starts at the frequency of 500 instead of 0, so the difference between the two response rates is exaggerated. The graph incorrectly makes it appear that "no" responses occurred about 60 times more often than the number of "yes" responses, but comparison of the actual frequencies shows that the "no" responses occurred about four times more often than the number of "yes" responses.
5. a. Convenience sample
   b. If the students at the college are mostly from a surrounding region that includes a large proportion of one ethnic group, the results will not reflect the general population of the United States.
   c. 0.75   d. 0.64

6. The straight-line pattern of the points suggests that there is a correlation between chest size and weight.

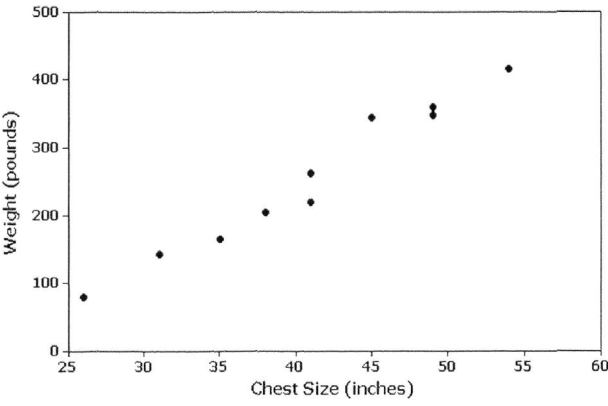

7. a. 1/575,757   b. 1/19   c. 1/10,939,383

Chapter 5: Answers

Section 5-2

1. The random variable is x, which is the number of girls in three births. The possible values of x are 0, 1, 2, and 3. The values of the random value x are numerical.

3. Table 5-7 does describe a probability distribution because the three requirements are satisfied. First, the variable x is a numerical random variable and its values are associated with probabilities. Second, $\Sigma P(x) = 0.125 + 0.375 + 0.375 + 0.125 = 1$ as required. Third, each of the probabilities is between 0 and 1 inclusive, as required.

5. a. Continuous random variable.   b. Discrete random variable.
   c. Not a random variable.   d. Discrete random variable.
   e. Continuous random variable.   f. Discrete random variable.

7. Probability distribution with $\mu = 2.0$, $\sigma = 1.0$.

9. Not a probability distribution because the sum of the probabilities is 0.601, which is not 1 as required. Also, Ted clearly needs a new approach.

11. Probability distribution with $\mu = 2.2$, $\sigma = 1.0$. (The sum of the probabilities is 0.999, but that is due to rounding errors.)

13. Not a probability distribution because the responses are not values of a numerical random variable. Also, the sum of the probabilities is 1.18 instead of being 1 as required.

15. $\mu = 5.0$, $\sigma = 1.6$.

17. a. 0.044   b. 0.055
    c. The probability from part (b).
    d. No, because the probability of 8 or more girls is 0.055, which is not very low (less than or equal to 0.05).

19. $\mu = 0.9$ car, $\sigma = 0.9$ car

21. a. 0.041   b. 0.046   c. The probability from part (b).
    d. Yes, because the probability of three or more failures is 0.046, which is very low (less than or equal to 0.05).

23. a. 1000   b. 1/1000   c. $499   d. −50¢
    e. The $1 bet on the pass line in craps is better because its expected value of −1.4¢ is much greater than the expected value of −50¢ for the Texas Pick 3 lottery.

25. a. −39¢
    b. The bet on the number 27 is better because its expected value of −26¢ is greater than the expected value of −39¢ for the other bet.

Section 5-3

1. The given calculation assumes that the first two adults include Wal-Mart and the last three adults do not include Wal-Mart, but there are other arrangements consisting of two adults who include Wal-Mart and three who do not. The probabilities corresponding to those other arrangements should also be included in the result.

3. Because the 30 selections are made without replacement, they are dependent, not independent. Based on the 5% guideline for cumbersome calculations, the 30 selections can be treated as being independent. (The 30 selections constitute 3% of the population of 1000 responses, and 3% is not more than 5% of the population.) The probability can be found by using the binomial probability formula.

5. Not binomial. Each of the weights has more than two possible outcomes.

7. Binomial.

9. Not binomial. Because the senators are selected without replacement, the selections are not independent. (The 5% guideline for cumbersome calculations cannot be applied because the 40 selected senators constitute 40% of the population of 100 senators, and 40% exceeds 5%.)

11. Binomial. Although the events are not independent, they can be treated as being independent by applying the 5% guideline. The sample size of 380 is no more than 5% of the population of all smartphone users.

13. a. 0.128
    b. WWC, WCW, CWW; 0.128 for each
    c. 0.384

15. 0.051   17. 0.057   19. 0.328

21. 0.257   23. 0.00125   25. 0.996; yes

27. 0.037; yes, because the probability of 2 or fewer peas with green pods is small (less than or equal to 0.05).

29. a. 0.002 (Tech: 0.00154)
    b. 0+ (Tech: 0.000064)
    c. 0.002 (Tech: 0.00160).
    d. Yes, the small probability from part (c) suggests that 5 is an unusually high number.

31. a. 0.328   b. 0.410   c. 0.738 (Tech: 0.737)
    d. No, the probability from part (c) is not small, so 1 is not an unusually low number.

33. 0.101. No, because the probability of exactly 12 is 0.101, the probability of 12 or more is greater than 0.101, so the probability of getting 12 or more is not very small, so 12 is not unusually high.

35. 0.287. No, because the flights all originate from New York, they are not randomly selected flights, so the 80.5% on-time rate might not apply.

37. a. 0.000766   b. 0.999   c. 0.00829
    d. Yes, the very low probability of 0.00829 would suggest that the 45 share value is wrong.

39. a. 0.000854   b. 0.0000610   c. 0.000916

   d. Yes. The probability of getting 13 girls or a result that is more extreme is 0.000916, so chance does not appear to be a reasonable explanation for the result of 13 girls. Because 13 is an unusually high number of girls, it appears that the probability of a girl is higher with the XSORT method, and it appears that the XSORT method is effective.

41. 0.134. It is not unlikely for such a combined sample to test positive.

43. 0.662. The probability shows that about 2/3 of all shipments will be accepted. With about 1/3 of the shipments rejected, the supplier would be wise to improve quality.

45. 0.0468

47. a. 0.000969   b. 0.0000000715   c. 0.436

Section 5-4

1. $n = 270$, $p = 0.07$, $q = 0.93$

3. 9.4 executives^2 (or 9.6 executives^2 if rounded standard deviation of 3.1 executives is used)

5. $\mu = 12.0$ correct guesses; $\sigma = 3.1$ correct guesses; minimum $= 5.8$ correct guesses; maximum $= 18.2$ correct guesses.

7. $\mu = 668.6$ worriers; $\sigma = 15.1$ worriers; minimum $= 638.4$ worriers; maximum $= 698.8$ worriers.

9. a. $\mu = 145.5$; $\sigma = 8.5$

   b. Yes. Using the range rule of thumb, the minimum usual value is 128.5 boys and the maximum usual value is 162.5 boys. Because 239 boys is above the range of usual values, it is unusually high. Because 239 boys is unusually high, it does appear that the YSORT method of gender selection is effective.

11. a. $\mu = 20.0$, $\sigma = 4.0$

   b. No, because 25 orange M&Ms is within the range of usual values (12 to 28). The claimed rate of 20% does not necessarily appear to be wrong, because that rate will usually result in 12 to 28 orange M&Ms (among 100), and the observed number of orange M&Ms is within that range.

13. a. $\mu = 142.8$, $\sigma = 11.9$

   b. No, 135 is not unusually low or high because it is within the range of usual values (119.0 to 166.6).

   c. Based on the given results, cell phones do not pose a health hazard that increases the likelihood of cancer of the brain or nervous system.

15. a. $\mu = 156.0$; $\sigma = 12.1$

   b. The minimum usual frequency is 131.8 and the maximum is 180.2. The occurrence of r 178 times is not unusually low or high because it is within the range of usual values (131.8 to 180.2).

17. a. $\mu = 74.0$; $\sigma = 7.7$

   b. The minimum usual number is 58.6 and the maximum usual value is 89.4. The value of 90 is unusually high because it is above the range of usual values (58.6 to 89.4).

19. a. $\mu = 0.0821918$; $\sigma = 0.2862981$

   b. The minimum usual number is -0.4904044 and the maximum usual number is 0.654788. The results of 2 students born on the 4th of July would be unusually high, because 2 is above of the range of usual values (from -0.4904044 to 0.654788).

21. $n = 150$; $p = 0.4$, so that 40% of the surveyed subjects could identify at least one member of the Supreme Court; $q = 0.6$, so that 60% of surveyed subjects could not identify at least one member of the Supreme Court.

23. $\mu = 3.0$ and $\sigma = 1.3$ (not 1.5)

Section 5-5

1. $\mu = 535/576 = 0.929$, which is the mean number of hits per region. $x = 2$, because we want the probability that a randomly selected region had exactly 2 hits, and $e \approx 2.71828$, which is a constant used in all applications of Formula 5-9.

3. With $n = 50$, the first requirement of $n \geq 100$ is not satisfied. With $n = 50$ and $p = 1/1000$, the second requirement of $np \leq 10$ is satisfied. Because both requirements are not satisfied, we should not use the Poisson distribution as an approximation to the binomial.

5. 0.000203; yes   7. 0.110; no

9. a. 6.5   b. 0.998 (Tech: 0.999)

   c. Yes. Based on the result in part (b), we are quite sure (with probability 0.998) that there is at least one earthquake measuring 6.0 or higher on the Richter scale, so there is a very low probability (0.002) that there will be no such earthquakes in a year.

11. a. 62.2

   b. 0.0155 (0.0156 using rounded mean)

13. a. 0.170

   b. The expected number is between 97.9 and and 98.2, depending on rounding.

   c. The expected number of regions with 2 hits is close to 93, which is the actual number of regions with 2 hits.

15. a. $P(26) = 0.0558$. Expected number: 1.9 cookies. The expected number of cookies is 1.9, and that is very close to the actual number of cookies with 26 chocolate chips, which is 2.

   b. $P(30) = 0.0724$. Expected number: 2.5 cookies. The expected number of cookies is 2.5, and that is very different from the actual number of cookies with 26 chocolate chips, which is 6.

17. a. No. With $n = 12$ and $p = 1/6$, the requirement of $n \geq 100$ is not satisfied, so the Poisson distribution is not a good approximation to the binomial distribution.

   b. No. The Poisson distribution approximation to the binomial distribution yields $P(3) = 0.180$, but the binomial distribution yields the correct result of $P(3) = 0.197$. The Poisson approximation of 0.180 is too far from the correct result of 0.197.

Chapter 5: Quick Quiz

1. Yes   2. 20.0   3. 4.0

4. Yes   5. No

6. Yes. (The sum of the probabilities is 0.999 and it can be considered to be 1 because of rounding errors.)

7. 0+ indicates that the probability is a very small positive number. It does not indicate that it is impossible for none of the five flights to arrive on time.

8. 0.945   9. Yes   10. No

Chapter 5: Review Exercises

1. 0.047 or 0.0467   2. 0.138

3. $\mu = 240.0$; $\sigma = 12.0$. Range of usual values: 216 to 264. The result of 200 with brown eyes is unusually low.

4. The probability of $P(239$ or fewer$) = 0.484$ is relevant for determining whether 239 is an unusually low number. Because that probability is not very small, it appears that 239 is not an unusually low number of people with brown eyes.

5. Yes, the three requirements are satisfied. There is a numerical random variable x and its values are associated with corresponding probabilities. $\sum P(x) = 1.001$, so the sum of the probabilities is 1 when we allow for a small discrepancy due to rounding. Also, each of the probability values is between 0 and 1 inclusive.

6. $\mu = 0.4$; $\sigma = 0.6$. Range of usual values: -0.8 to 1.6 (or 0 to 1.6). Yes, three is an unusually high number of males with tinnitus among four randomly selected males.

7. $\sum P(x) = 0.902$, so the sum of the probabilities is not 1 as required. Because the three requirements are not all satisfied, the given information does not describe a probability distribution.

8. $315,075. Because the offer is well below her expected value, she should continue the game (although the guaranteed prize of $193,000 had considerable appeal). (She accepted the offer of $193,000, but she would have won $500,000 if she continued the game and refused all further offers.)

9. a. 1.2¢   b. 1.2¢ minus cost of stamp.

10. a. $\mu = 0.6$
    b. $P(0) = 0.549$ c. 16.5 days
    d. The expected number of days is 16.5, and that is reasonably close to the actual number of days, which is 18.

Chapter 5: Cumulative Review Exercises

1. a. 24.4 hours   b. 24.2 hours   c. 4.7 hours
   d. 1.7 hours   e. 2.9 hours²
   f. Usual values: 21.0 hours to 27.8 hours.
   g. No, because none of the times are beyond the range of usual values.
   h. Ratio   i. Continuous
   j. The given times come from countries with very different population sizes, so it does not make sense to treat the given times equally. Calculations of statistics should take the different population sizes into account. Also, the sample is very small, and there is no indication that the sample is random.

2. a. 1/10,000 or 0.0001
   b.

x	P(x)
−$1	0.9999
$4999	0.0001

   c. 0.0365   d. 0.0352   e. −50¢

3. a. 0.282   b. 0.303   c. 0.242   d. 0.297
   e. 0.0792   f. 0.738   g. 0.703

4. Because the vertical scale begins at 60 instead of 0, the difference between the two amounts is exaggerated. The graph makes it appear that men's earnings are roughly twice those of women, but men earn roughly 1.2 times the earnings of women.

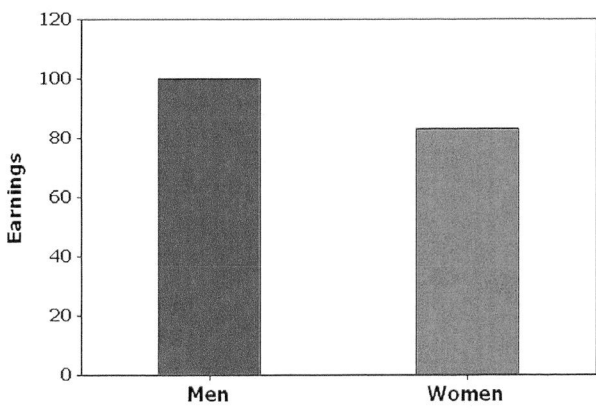

5. a. Frequency distribution or frequency table.
   b. Probability distribution.
   c. $\bar{x} = 4.7$. This value is a statistic.
   d. $\mu = 4.5$. This value is a parameter.
   e. The random generation of 1000 digits should have a mean close to $\mu = 4.5$ from part (d). The mean of 4.5 is the mean for the population of all random digits, so samples will have means that tend to center about 4.5.

6. a. 0.0514   b. 0.815
   c. This is a voluntary response (or self-selected) sample. This suggests that the results might not be valid, because those with a strong interest in the topic are more likely to respond.

Chapter 6 Answers

Section 6-2

1. The word "normal" has a special meaning in statistics. It refers to a specific bell-shaped distribution that can be described by Formula 6-1.

3. The mean and standard deviation have the values of $\mu = 0$ and $\sigma = 1$.

5. 0.75   7. 0.4   9. 0.6700
11. 0.6992 (Tech: 0.6993)
13. 1.23   15. −1.45   17. 0.0207
19. 0.9901   21. 0.2061   23. 0.9332
25. 0.2957 (Tech: 0.2956)
27. 0.0198   29. 0.9799   31. 0.9825
33. 0.9999   35. 0.5000   37. 1.28
39. −1.96, 1.96   41. 1.96   43. 1.645
45. 68.26% (Tech: 68.27%)
47. 99.74% (Tech: 99.73%)
49. a. 68.26% (Tech: 68.27%)
    b. 4.56%   c. 95.00%
    d. 95.44% (Tech: 95.45%)

Section 6-3

1. a. $\mu = 0$; $\sigma = 1$
   b. The z scores are numbers without units of measurement.

3. The standard normal distribution has a mean of 0 and a standard deviation of 1, but a nonstandard normal distribution has a different value for one or both of those parameters.

5. 0.8849   7. 0.9053   9. 136

11. 69   13. 0.1587

15. 0.4972 (Tech: 0.4950)

17. 119   19. 110

21. a. 75.48% (Tech: 75.56%). Yes, about 25% of women are not
    qualified because of their heights.

    b. 99.90% (Tech: 99.89%). No, only about 0.1% of men are
    not qualified because of their heights.

    c. 58.5 in. to 69.1 in.

    d. 63.9 in. to 75.1 in.

23. a. 99.86%

    b. 98.89% (Tech: 98.90%)

    c. 59.5 in. to 73.4 in.

25. a. 0.4129 (Tech: 0.4137)

    b. 25   c. 19

    d. The mean weight is increasing over time, so safety limits
    must be periodically updated to avoid an unsafe condition.

27. a. 0.0038; either a very rare event occurred or the husband is
    not the father.

    b. 240 days

29. a. 91.77% (Tech: 91.78%)

    b. 0.01% (Tech: 0.00%)

    c. 2.150. No.

31. P_1 = 17.9 chocolate chips (Tech: 18.0 chocolate chips); P_{99} =
    30.1 chocolate chips (Tech: 30.0 chocolate chips). The values
    can be used to identify cookies with an unusually low number
    of chocolate chips or an unusually high number of chocolate
    chips, so those numbers can be used to monitor the produc-
    tion process to ensure that the numbers of chocolate chips stay
    within reasonable limits.

33. a. The mean is 67.25 (67.3 rounded) beats per minute and the stan-
    dard deviation is 10.334781 (10.3 rounded) beats per minute. A
    histogram confirms that the distribution is roughly normal.

    b. 47.0 beats per minute; 87.5 beats per minute

35. a. 75; 10

    b. No, the conversion should also account for variation.

    c. B grade: 45.2 to 52.8

    d. Use a scheme like the one given in part (c), because variation
    is included in the curving process.

37. 0.0444 (Tech: 0.0430).

Section 6-4

1. a. The sample means will tend to center about the population
   parameter of 5.67 g.

   b. The sample means will tend to have a distribution that is
   approximately normal.

   c. The sample proportions will tend to have a distribution that
   is approximately normal.

3. Sample mean; sample variance; sample proportion

5. No. The sample is not a simple random sample from the population of all college statistics students. It is very possible that the
   students at Broward College do not accurately reflect the behavior of all college statistics students.

7. a. 4.7

   b.

Sample Variance s^2	Probability
0.0	3/9
0.5	2/9
8.0	2/9
12.5	2/9

   c. 4.7

   d. Yes. The mean of the sampling distribution of the sample
   variances (4.7) is equal to the value of the population variance
   (4.7), so the sample variances target the value of the population variance.

9. a. 5

   b.

Sample Median	Probability
4.0	1/9
4.5	2/9
5.0	1/9
6.5	2/9
7.0	2/9
9.0	1/9

   c. 6.0

   d. No. The mean of the sampling distribution of the sample
   medians is 6.0, and it is not equal to the value of the population median (5), so the sample medians do not target the
   value of the population median.

11. a.

$\bar{x}$	Probability
46	1/16
47.5	2/16
49	1/16
51	2/16
52	2/16
52.5	2/16
53.5	2/16
56	1/16
57	2/16
58	1/16

    b. The mean of the population is 52.25 and the mean of the
    sample means is also 52.25.

    c. The sample means target the population mean. Sample means
    make good estimators of population means because they tar-
    get the value of the population mean instead of systematically
    underestimating or overestimating it.

13. a.

Range	Probability
0	4/16
2	2/16
3	2/16
7	2/16
9	2/16
10	2/16
12	2/16

b. The range of the population is 12, but the mean of the sample ranges is 5.375. Those values are not equal.

c. The sample ranges do not target the population range of 12, so sample ranges do not make good estimators of population ranges.

15.

Proportion of Girls	Probability
0	0.25
0.5	0.50
1	0.25

Yes. The proportion of girls in 2 births is 0.5, and the mean of the sample proportions is 0.5. The result suggests that a sample proportion is an unbiased estimator of a population proportion.

17. a.

Proportion Correct	Probability
0	16/25
0.5	8/25
1	1/25

b. 0.2

c. Yes. The sampling distribution of the sample proportions has a mean of 0.2 and the population proportion is also 0.2 (because there is 1 correct answer among 5 choices). Yes, the mean of the sampling distribution of the sample proportions is always equal to the population proportion.

19. The formula yields $P(0) = 0.25$, $P(0.5) = 0.5$, and $P(1) = 0.25$, which does describe the sampling distribution of the sample proportions. The formula is just a different way of presenting the same information in the table that describes the sampling distribution.

Section 6-5

1. Because $n > 30$, the sampling distribution of the mean ages can be approximated by a normal distribution with mean μ and standard deviation $\sigma/\sqrt{40}$.

3. $\mu_{\bar{x}} = 60.5$ cm and it represents the mean of the population consisting of all sample means. $\sigma_{\bar{x}} = 1.1$ cm, and it represents the standard deviation of the population consisting of all sample means.

5. a. 0.9772
   b. 0.8888 (Tech: 0.8889)

7. a. 0.0668
   b. 0.6985 (Tech: 0.6996)
   c. Because the original population has a normal distribution, the distribution of sample means is normal for any sample size.

9. a. 0.9974 (Tech: 0.9973)
   b. 0.5086 (Tech: 0.5085)

11. 0.1112 (Tech: 0.1121). The elevator does not appear to be safe because there is a reasonable chance (0.1112) that it will be overloaded with 16 male passengers.

13. a. 0.9787 (Tech: 0.9788)
    b. 21.08 in. to 24.22 in.
    c. 0.9998. No, the hats must fit individual women, not the mean from 64 women. If all hats are made to fit head circumferences between 22.00 in. and 23.00 in., the hats won't fit about half of those women.

15. a. 140 lb
    b. 0.9999 (Tech: 0.99999993, or 1.0000 when rounded to four decimal places)
    c. 0.8078 (Tech: 0.8067)
    d. Given that there is a 0.8078 probability of exceeding the 3500 lb limit when the water taxi is loaded with 20 random men, the new capacity of 20 passengers does not appear to be safe enough because the probability of overloading is too high.

17. a. 0.6517 (Tech: 0.6516)
    b. 0.9115
    c. There is a high probability (0.9115) that the gondola will be overloaded if it is occupied by 12 men, so it appears that the number of allowed passengers should be reduced.

19. a. 0.5526 (Tech: 0.5517)
    b. 0.9994 (Tech: 0.9995)
    c. Part (a) because the ejection seats will be occupied by individual women, not groups of women.

21. a. 0.8508 (Tech: 0.8512)
    b. 0.9999 (Tech: 1.0000 when rounded to four decimal places)
    c. The probability from part (a) is more relevant because it shows that 85.08% of male passengers will not need to bend. The result from part (b) gives us information about the mean for a group of 100 men, but it doesn't give us useful information about the comfort and safety of individual male passengers.
    d. Because men are generally taller than women, a design that accommodates a suitable proportion of men will necessarily accommodate a greater proportion of women.

23. a. Yes. The sampling is without replacement and the sample size of $n = 50$ is greater than 5% of the finite population size of 275. $\sigma_{\bar{x}} = 2.0504584$.
    b. 0.5947 (Tech: 0.5963)

25. a. $\mu = 6.0$ and $\sigma = 2.1602469$
    b. 4.5, 4.5, 6.5, 6.5, 7.0, 7.0
    c. $\mu_{\bar{x}} = 6.0$ and $\sigma_{\bar{x}} = 1.0801235$
    d. $\mu_{\bar{x}} = \mu = 6.0$ and $\sigma_{\bar{x}} = \dfrac{2.1602469}{\sqrt{2}}\sqrt{\dfrac{3-2}{3-1}} = 1.0801235$, which is the same result from part (c).

Section 6-6

1. The histogram should be approximately bell-shaped, and the normal quantile plot should have points that approximate a straight-line pattern.

3. We must verify that the sample is from a population having a normal distribution. We can check for normality using a histogram, identifying the number of outliers, and constructing a normal quantile plot.

5. Not normal. The points show a systematic pattern that is not a straight-line pattern.

7. Normal. The points are reasonably close to a straight-line pattern, and there is no other pattern that is not a straight-line pattern.

9. Not normal

11. Normal

13. Not normal

15. Normal

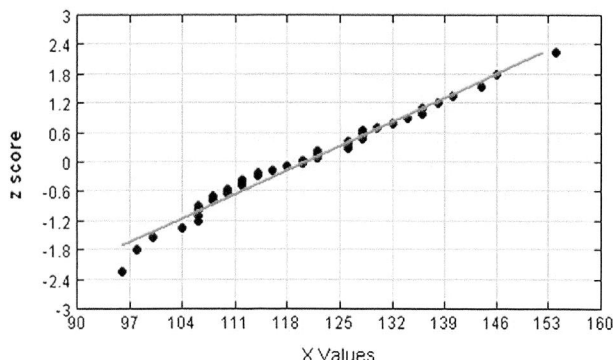

17. Normal. The points have coordinates $(131, -1.28)$, $(134, -0.52)$, $(139, 0)$, $(143, 0.52)$, $(145, 1.28)$.

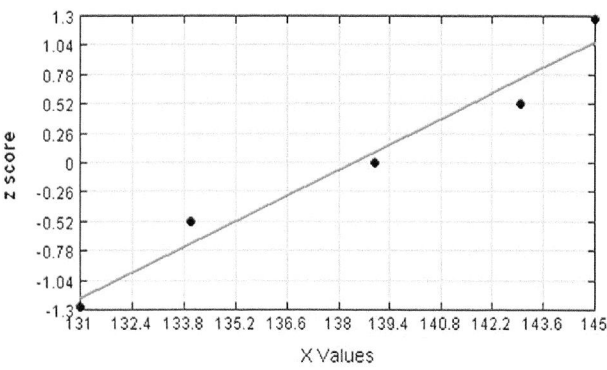

19. Not normal. The points have coordinates $(1034, -1.53)$, $(1051, -0.89)$, $(1067, -0.49)$ $(1070, -0.16)$, $(1079, 0.16)$, $(1079, 0.49)$, $(1173, 0.89)$, $(1272, 1.53)$.

21. a. Yes   b. Yes   c. No

23. The original values are not from a normally distributed population. After taking the logarithm of each value, the values appear to be from a normally distributed population. The original values are from a population with a lognormal distribution.

Section 6-7

1. The Minitab display shows that the region representing 235 wins is a rectangle. The result of 0.0068 is an approximation, but the result of 0.0066 is better because it is based on an exact calculation. The approximation differs from the exact result by a very small amount.

3. $p = 0.2$; $q = 0.8$; $\mu = 5$; $\sigma = 2$. The value of $\mu = 5$ shows that for many people who make random guesses for the 25 questions, the mean number of correct answers is 5. For many people who make random guesses, the standard deviation of $\sigma = 2$ is a measure of how much the numbers of correct responses vary.

5. 0.0630 (Tech: 0.0632)

7. Normal approximation should not be used.

9. 0.2743 (Tech: 0.2731)

11. 0.0928 (Tech: 0.0933)

13. a. 0.0219 (Tech using normal approximation: 0.0214; Tech using binomial: 0.0217)

    b. 0.1711 (Tech using normal approximation: 0.1702; Tech using binomial: 0.1703). The result of 172 overturned calls is not unusually low.

    c. The result from part (b) is useful. We want the probability of getting a result that is at least as extreme as the one obtained.

    d. If the 30% rate is correct, there is a good chance (0.1711) of getting 172 or fewer calls overturned, so there is not strong evidence against the 30% rate.

15. a. 0.0318 (Tech using normal approximation: 0.0305; Tech using binomial: 0.0301)

    b. 0.2676 (Tech using normal approximation: 0.2665; Tech using binomial: 0.2650). The result of 428 peas with green pods is not unusually low.

    c. The result from part (b) is useful. We want the probability of getting a result that is at least as extreme as the one obtained.

    d. No. Assuming that Mendel's probability of 3/4 is correct, there is a good chance (0.2676) of getting the results that were obtained. The obtained results do not provide strong evidence against the claim that the probability of a pea having a green pod is 3/4.

17. a. 0.0000 or 0+ (a very small positive probability that is extremely close to 0)

    b. 0.0001 (Tech: 0.0000 or 0+, which is a very small positive probability that is extremely close to 0). If boys and girls are equally likely, 879 girls in 945 births is unusually high.

    c. The result from part (b) is more relevant, because we want the probability of a result that is *at least as extreme* as the one obtained.

    d. Yes. It is very highly unlikely that we would get a result as extreme as 879 girls in 945 births by chance. Given that the 945 couples were treated with the XSORT method, it appears that this method is effective in increasing the likelihood that a baby will be a girl.

19. 0.0001 (Tech: 0.0000). The results suggest that the surveyed people did not respond accurately.

21. Probability of six or fewer: 0.1075 (Tech using normal approximation: 0.1080; Tech using binomial: 0.1034). Because that probability is not very small, the evidence against the rate of 20% is not very strong.

23. Probability of 170 or fewer: 0.0099 (Tech using normal approximation: 0.0098; Tech using binomial: 0.0089). Because the probability of 170 or fewer is so small with the assumed 20% rate, it appears that the rate is actually less than 20%.

25. a. 6; 0.4602 (Tech using normal approximation: 0.4583; tech using binomial: 0.4307)

   b. 101; 0.3936 (Tech using normal approximation: 0.3933; tech using binomial: 0.3932)

   c. The roulette game provides a better likelihood of making a profit.

Chapter 6: Quick Quiz

1. $\mu = 0$ and $\sigma = 1$

2.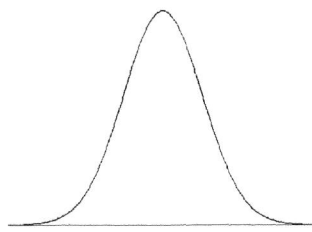

3. $z = 2.05$ (Tech: 2.05375)

4. 0.8413

5. 0.0775 (Tech: 0.0776)

6. 0.1611 (Tech: 0.1618)

7. 0.0158 (Tech: 0.0156)

8. 4.898   9. 0.0409

10. 82.31% (Tech: 82.26%)

Chapter 6: Review Exercises

1. a. 0.9983   b. 0.9370   c. 0.8385
   d. −0.52   e. 0.1401

2. a. 7.93% (Tech: 7.89%)
   b. 1369.2 mm (Tech: 1369.4 mm)

3. a. 97.88%   b. 1742.6 mm

4. a. Normal   b. 21.1   c. 0.57

5. a. An unbiased estimator is a statistic that targets the value of the population parameter in the sense that the sampling distribution of the statistic has a mean that is equal to the mean of the corresponding parameter.
   b. Mean; variance; proportion   c. True

6. a. 85.08% (Tech: 85.12%). With about 15% of all men needing to bend, the design does not appear to be adequate, but the Mark VI monorail appears to be working quite well in practice.

7. a. 0.5753 (Tech: 0.5766)
   b. 0.9976. Yes, if the plane is full of male passengers, it is highly likely that it is overweight.

8. a. No. A histogram is far from bell-shaped. A normal quantile plot reveals a pattern of points that is far from a straight-line pattern.

   b. No. The sample size of $n = 26$ does not satisfy the condition of $n > 30$, and the values do not appear to be from a population having a normal distribution.

9. 0.2296 (Tech using normal approximation: 0.2286; Tech using binomial: 0.2278). The occurrence of 787 offspring plants with long stems is not unusually low because its probability is not small. The results are consistent with Mendel's claimed proportion of 3/4.

10. a. 0.7019 (Tech using normal approximation: 0.7024; Tech using binomial: 0.7100)
    b. 0.1148 (Tech using normal approximation: 0.1158; Tech using binomial: 0.1190)

Chapter 6: Cumulative Review Exercises

1. a. $10,300,000
   b. $14,000,000
   c. $5,552,027
   d. 30,825,003,810,000 square dollars
   e. $z = 0.76$ f. Ratio   g. Discrete
   h. No, the starting players are likely to be the best players who receive the highest salaries.

2. a. $\overline{A}$ is the event of selecting someone who does not have the belief that college is not a good investment. (This is not the same as selecting someone who believes that college is a good investment.)
   b. 0.9   c. 0.001
   d. The sample is a voluntary response (or self-selected) sample. This suggests that the 10% rate might not be very accurate, because people with strong feelings or interest about the topic are more likely to respond.

3. a. 0.0630 (Tech: 0.0627)
   b. 2643 g (Tech: 2642 g)
   c. 0.0005
   d. 0.3936 (Tech: 0.3923)

4. a. The vertical scale does not start at 0, so differences are somewhat distorted. By using a scale ranging from 1 to 29 for frequencies that range from 2 to 14, the graph is flattened, so differences are not shown as they should be.
   b. The graph depicts a distribution that is not exactly normal, but it is approximately normal because it is roughly bell-shaped.
   c. Minimum: 42 years; maximum: 70 years. Using the range rule of thumb, the standard deviation is estimated to be $(70 − 42)/4 = 7$ years. The estimate of $s = 7$ years is very close to the actual standard deviation of $s = 6.6$ years, so the range rule of thumb works quite well here.

5. a. 0.001   b. 0.271
   c. The requirement that $np \geq 5$ is not satisfied, indicating that the normal approximation would result in errors that are too large.
   d. 5.0   e. 2.1
   f. No, 8 is within two standard deviations of the mean and is within the range of values that could easily occur by chance.

Chapter 7: Answers

Section 7-2

1. The confidence level (such as 95%) was not provided.

3. $\hat{p} = 0.26$ is the sample proportion; $\hat{q} = 0.74$ (found from evaluating $1 - \hat{p}$); $n = 1910$ is the sample size; $E = 0.03$ is the margin of error; p is the population proportion, which is unknown. The value of α is 0.05.

5. 1.28   7. 1.645   9. 0.125 ± 0.061

11. $0.0268 < p < 0.133$

13. a. 0.530   b. $E = 0.0309$ c. $0.499 < p < 0.561$
    d. We have 95% confidence that the interval from 0.499 to 0.561 actually does contain the true value of the population proportion.

15. a. 0.430   b. $E = 0.0162$ c. $0.414 < p < 0.446$
    d. We have 90% confidence that the interval from 0.414 to 0.446 actually does contain the true value of the population proportion.

17. a. 0.930   b. $0.914 < p < 0.946$
    c. Yes. The true proportion of girls with the XSORT method is substantially greater than the proportion of (about) 0.5 that is expected when no method of gender selection is used.

19. a. 0.5   b. 0.439   c. $0.363 < p < 0.516$
    d. If the touch therapists really had an ability to select the correct hand by sensing an energy field, their success rate would be significantly greater than 0.5, but the sample success rate of 0.439 and the confidence interval suggest that they do not have the ability to select the correct hand by sensing an energy field.

21. a. 124   b. $24.7\% < p < 33.3\%$
    c. Yes. Because all values of the confidence interval are less than 0.5, the confidence interval shows that the percentage of women who purchase books online is very likely less than 50%.
    d. No. The confidence interval shows that it is possible that the percentage of women who purchase books online could be less than 25%.
    e. Nothing.

23. a. 236
    b. $0.402 < p < 0.516$ (using $x = 236$: $0.403 < p < 0.516$).
    c. $0.431 < p < 0.487$
    d. The 95% confidence interval is wider than the 80% confidence interval. A confidence interval must be wider in order to be more confident that it captures the true value of the population proportion. (See Exercise 4.)

25. $0.0168 < p < 0.143$ (Tech: $0.0169 < p < 0.143$). No, the confidence interval limits contain the value of 0.13, so the claimed rate of 13% could be the true percentage for the population of brown M&Ms.

27. a. $0.0276\% < p < 0.0366\%$ (using $x = 135$: $0.0276\% < p < 0.0367\%$).
    b. No, because 0.0340% is included in the confidence interval.

29. 752   31. 339

33. a. 1537   b. 1449

35. a. 271   b. 139 (Tech: 138)

c. No. A sample of students at the nearest college is a convenience sample, not a simple random sample, so it is very possible that the results would not be representative of the population of adults.

37. $\hat{p} = 18/34$, or 0.529. CI: $36.2\% < p < 69.7\%$. Greater height does not appear to be an advantage for presidential candidates. If greater height is an advantage, then taller candidates should win substantially more than 50% of the elections, but the confidence interval shows that the percentage of elections won by taller candidates is likely to be anywhere between 36.2% and 69.7%.

39. a. 178   b. 176

41. $81.4\% < p < 101.9\%$. The upper confidence interval limit is greater than 100%. Given that the percentage cannot exceed 100%, change the upper limit to 100%.

43. $p > 0.831$ (Tech: $p > 0.832$). Because we have 95% confidence that p is greater than 0.831, we can safely conclude that more than 75% of adults know what Twitter is.

Section 7-3

1. a. 233.4 sec $< \mu < 256.65$ sec
   b. Best point estimate of μ is 245.025 sec. The margin of error is $E = 11.625$ sec.

3. We have 95% confidence that the limits of 233.4 sec and 256.65 sec contain the true value of the mean of the population of all duration times.

5. Neither the normal nor the t distribution applies.

7. $t_{\alpha/2} = 2.708$

9. 8.104 km $< \mu < 11.512$ km (Tech: 8.103 km $< \mu <$ 11.513 km). Because the sample size is greater than 30, the confidence interval yields a reasonable estimate of μ, even though the data appear to be from a population that is not normally distributed.

11. 3315.1 thousand dollars $< \mu < 22,480.9$ thousand dollars (Tech: 3313.5 thousand dollars $< \mu < 22,482.5$ thousand dollars). The $1 salary of Jobs is an outlier that is very far away from the other values, and that outlier has a dramatic effect on the confidence interval.

13. 98.08°F $< \mu < 98.32$°F. Because the confidence interval does not contain 98.6°F, it appears that the mean body temperature is not 98.6°F, as is commonly believed.

15. -6.8 mg/dL $< \mu < 7.6$ mg/dL. Because the confidence interval includes the value of 0, it is very possible that the mean of the changes in LDL cholesterol is equal to 0, suggesting that the garlic treatment did not affect LDL cholesterol levels. It does not appear that garlic is effective in reducing LDL cholesterol.

17. 4.7 million dollars $< \mu < 28.0$ million dollars. The data appear to have a distribution that is far from normal, so the confidence interval might not be a good estimate of the population mean. The population is likely to be the list of box office receipts for each day of the movie's release. Because the values are from the first 14 days of release, the sample values are not a simple random sample, and they are likely to be the largest of all such values, so the confidence interval is not a good estimate of the population mean.

19. The sample data meet the loose requirement of having a normal distribution. CI: 0.707 W/kg < μ < 1.169 W/kg. Because the confidence interval is entirely below the standard of 1.6 W/kg, it appears that the mean amount of cell phone radiation is less than the FCC standard, but there could be individual cell phones that exceed the standard.

21. The sample data meet the loose requirement of having a normal distribution. CI: 6.43 < μ < 15.67. We cannot conclude that the population mean is less than 7 μg/g, because the confidence interval shows that the mean might be greater than that level.

23. CI for ages of unsuccessful applicants: 43.8 years < μ < 50.1 years. CI for ages of successful applicants: 42.6 years < μ < 46.4 years. Although final conclusions about means of populations should not be based on the overlapping of confidence intervals, the confidence intervals do overlap, so it appears that both populations could have the same mean, and there is not clear evidence of discrimination based on age.

25. The sample size is 68, and it does appear to be very reasonable.

27. 405 (Tech: 403). It is not likely that you would find that many two-year-old used Corvettes in your region.

29. Use σ = 450 to get a sample size of 110. The margin of error of 100 points seems too high to provide a good estimate of the mean SAT score.

31. With the range rule of thumb, use σ = 11 to get a required sample size of 117. With σ = 10.3, the required sample size is 102. The better estimate of σ is the standard deviation of the sample, so the correct sample size is likely to be closer to 102 than 117.

33. 0.963 < μ < 1.407

35. 8.156 km < μ < 11.460 km (Tech: 8.159 km < μ < 11.457 km)

37. 6131.8 thousand dollars < μ < 19,663.4 thousand dollars (Tech: 6131.9 thousand dollars < μ < 19,663.3 thousand dollars)

39. The sample data do not appear to meet the loose requirement of having a normal distribution. CI: -24.54 < μ < 106.04 (Tech: -24.55 < μ < 106.05). The effect of the outlier on the confidence interval is very substantial. Outliers should be discarded if they are known to be errors. If an outlier is a correct value, it might be very helpful to see its effects by constructing the confidence interval with and without the outlier included.

41. -26.0 < μ < 32.0. The confidence interval based on the first sample value is much wider than the confidence interval based on all 10 sample values.

Section 7-4

1. 30.3 mg/dL < σ < 47.5 mg/dL. We have 95% confidence that the limits of 30.3 mg/dL and 47.5 mg/dL contain the true value of the standard deviation of the LDL cholesterol levels of all women.

3. The original sample values can be identified, but the dotplot shows that the sample appears to be from a population having a uniform distribution, not a normal distribution as required. Because the normality requirement is not satisfied, the confidence interval estimate of σ should not be constructed using the methods of this section.

5. df = 24. X_L^2 = 9.886 and X_R^2 = 45.559. CI: 0.17 mg < σ < 0.37 mg.

7. df = 39. X_L^2 = 24.433 (Tech: 23.654) and X_R^2 = 59.342 (Tech: 58.120). CI: 52.9 < σ < 82.4 (Tech: 53.4 < σ < 83.7).

9. 0.579°F < σ < 0.720°F (Tech: 0.557°F < σ < 0.700°F)

11. 30.9 mL < σ < 67.45 mL. The confidence interval shows that the standard deviation is not likely to be less than 30 mL, so the variation is too high instead of being at an acceptable level below 30 mL. (Such one-sided claims should be tested using the formal methods presented in Chapter 8.)

13. 0.252 ppm < σ < 0.701 ppm

15. CI for ages of unsuccessful applicants: 5.2 years < σ < 11.5 years. CI for ages of successful applicants: 3.7 years < σ < 7.5 years. Although final conclusions about means of populations should not be based on the overlapping of confidence intervals, the confidence intervals do overlap, so it appears that the two populations have standard deviations that are not dramatically different.

17. 0.01239 g < σ < 0.02100 g (Tech: 0.01291 g < σ < 0.02255 g)

19. 33,218 is too large. There aren't 33,218 statistics professors in the population, and even if there were, that sample size is too large to be practical.

21. The sample size is 768. Because the population does not have a normal distribution, the computed minimum sample size is not likely to be correct.

23. X_L^2 = 82.072 and X_R^2 = 129.635 (Tech using $z_{\alpha/2}$ = 1.644853626: X_L^2 = 82.073 and X_R^2 = 129.632). The approximate values are quite close to the actual critical values.

Chapter 7: Quick Quiz

1. 36.9% < p < 43.1%

2. 0.480

3. We have 95% confidence that the limits of 0.449 and 0.511 contain the true value of the proportion of females in the population of medical school students.

4. z = 1.645

5. 752

6. 373 (Tech: 374)

7. The sample must be a simple random sample and there is a loose requirement that the sample values appear to be from a normally distributed population.

8. The degrees of freedom is the number of sample values that can vary after restrictions have been imposed on all of the values. For the sample data in Exercise 7, df = 5.

9. t = 2.571

10. X_L^2 = 0.831 and X_R^2 = 12.833

Chapter 7: Review Exercises

1. a. 51.0%   b. 46.8% < p < 55.1%
   c. No, the confidence interval shows that the population percentage might be 50% or less, so we cannot safely conclude that the majority of adults say that they are underpaid.

2. 4145 (Tech: 4147)   3. 155 (Tech: 154)

4. a. Student t distribution   b. Normal distribution
   c. The distribution is not normal, Student t, or chi-square.
   d. X^2 (chi-square distribution)   e. Normal distribution

5. a. 543 (Tech: 542)   b. 247 (Tech: 246)   c. 543
6. $61.5\% < p < 66.5\%$. Because the entire confidence interval is above 50%, we can safely conclude that the majority of adults consume alcoholic beverages.
7. -22.1 sec $< \mu < 308.1$ sec
8. $6.54 < \mu < 7.76$. Because women and men have some notable physiological differences, the confidence interval does not necessarily serve as an estimate of the mean white blood cell count of men.
9. 37.5 g $< \mu < 47.9$ g. There is 95% confidence that the limits of 37.5 g and 47.9 g contain the true mean deceleration measurement for all small cars.
10. 3.6 g $< \sigma < 12.3$ g

Chapter 7: Cumulative Review Exercises

1. $\bar{x} = 5.5$; median $= 5.0$; $s = 3.8$
2. The range of usual values is from -2.1 to 13.1 (or from 0 to 13.1).
3. Ratio level of measurement; discrete data.
4. 33 campuses
5. $3.6 < \mu < 7.4$. The population should include only colleges of the same type as the sample, so the population consists of all large urban campuses with residence halls.
6. The graphs suggest that the population has a distribution that is skewed (to the right) instead of being normal. The histogram shows that some taxi-out times can be very long, and that can occur with heavy traffic, but little or no traffic cannot make the taxi-out time very low. There is a minimum time required, regardless of traffic conditions. Construction of a confidence interval estimate of a population standard deviation has a strict requirement that the sample data are from a normally distributed population, and the graphs show that this strict normality requirement is not satisfied.
7. a. $0.560 < p < 0.620$ (or $0.560 < p < 0.621$ if using $x = 592$)
   b. Because the survey was about shaking hands and because it was sponsored by a supplier of hand sanitizer products, the sponsor could potentially benefit from the results, so there might be some pressure to obtain results favorable to the sponsor.
   c. 1083
8. There does not appear to be a correlation between HDL and LDL cholesterol levels.

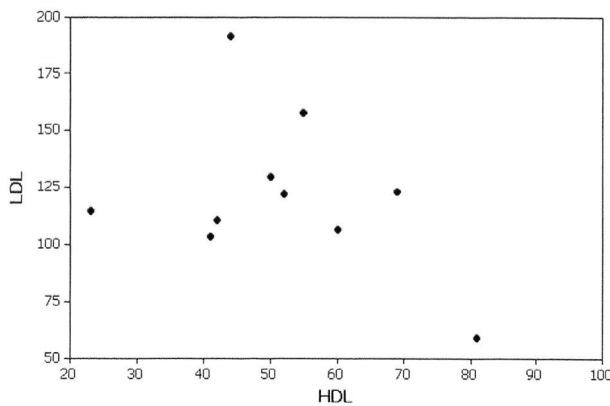

9. a. 13.35% (Tech: 13.32%). Yes, losing about 13% of the market would be a big loss.
   b. 160.2 mm; 189.8 mm
10. a. $1/1000$ b. $999/1000$ c. 0.990

Chapter 8

Section 8-2

1. Rejection of the aspirin claim is more serious because the aspirin is a drug treatment. The wrong aspirin dosage can cause adverse reactions. M&Ms do not have those same adverse reactions. It would be wise to use a smaller significance level for testing the aspirin claim.
3. a. H_0: $\mu = 98.6°F$ b. H_1: $\mu \neq 98.6°F$
   c. Reject the null hypothesis or fail to reject the null hypothesis.
   d. No. In this case, the original claim becomes the null hypothesis. For the claim that the mean body temperature is equal to 98.6°F, we can either reject that claim or fail to reject it, but we cannot state that there is sufficient evidence to *support* that claim.
5. a. $p = 0.2$ b. H_0: $p = 0.2$ and H_1: $p \neq 0.2$
7. a. $\mu \leq 76$ b. H_0: $\mu = 76$ and H_1: $\mu > 76$
9. There is not sufficient evidence to warrant rejection of the claim that 20% of adults smoke.
11. There is not sufficient evidence to warrant rejection of the claim that the mean pulse rate of adult females is 76 or lower.
13. $z = 10.33$ (or $z = 10.35$ if using $x = 909$)
15. $\chi^2 = 8.110$
17. P-value $= 0.0228$. Critical value: $z = 1.645$.
19. P-value $= 0.0802$ (Tech: 0.0801). Critical values: $z = -1.96$, $z = 1.96$.
21. P-value $= 0.2186$ (Tech: 0.2187). Critical values: $z = -1.96$, $z = 1.96$.
23. P-value $= 0.0013$. Critical value: $z = -1.645$.
25. a. Reject H_0.
    b. There is sufficient evidence to support the claim that the percentage of blue M&Ms is greater than 5%.
27. a. Fail to reject H_0.
    b. There is not sufficient evidence to warrant rejection of the claim that women have heights with a mean equal to 160.00 cm.
29. a. H_0: $p = 0.5$ and H_1: $p > 0.5$ b. $\alpha = 0.01$
    c. Normal distribution.   d. Right-tailed.
    e. $z = 1.00$ f. P-value: 0.1587   g. $z = 2.33$ h. 0.01
31. Type I error: In reality $p = 0.1$, but we reject the claim that $p = 0.1$. Type II error: In reality $p \neq 0.1$, but we fail to reject the claim that $p = 0.1$.
33. Type I error: In reality $p = 0.5$, but we support the claim that $p > 0.5$. Type II error: In reality $p > 0.5$, but we fail to support that conclusion.
35. The power of 0.96 shows that there is a 96% chance of rejecting the null hypothesis of $p = 0.08$ when the true proportion is actually 0.18. That is, if the proportion of Chantix users who experience abdominal pain is actually 0.18, then there is a 96% chance of supporting the claim that the proportion of Chantix users who experience abdominal pain is greater than 0.08.
37. 617

Section 8-3

1. The *P*-value method and the critical value method always yield the same conclusion. The confidence interval method might or might not yield the same conclusion obtained by using the other two methods.

3. *P*-value: 0.00000000550. Because the *P*-value is so low, we have sufficient evidence to support the claim that $p < 0.5$.

5. a. Left-tailed.   b. $z = -1.94$
   c. *P*-value: 0.0260 (rounded)
   d. H_0: $p = 0.1$. Reject the null hypothesis.
   e. There is sufficient evidence to support the claim that less than 10% of treated subjects experience headaches.

7. a. Two-tailed.   b. $z = -0.82$ c. *P*-value: 0.4106
   d. H_0: $p = 0.35$. Fail to reject the null hypothesis.
   e. There is not sufficient evidence to warrant rejection of the claim that 35% of adults have heard of the Sony Reader.

9. H_0: $p = 0.25$. H_1: $p \neq 0.25$. Test statistic: $z = 0.67$. Critical values: $z = \pm 2.575$ (Tech: ± 2.576). *P*-value: 0.5028 (Tech: 0.5021). Fail to reject H_0. There is not sufficient evidence to warrant rejection of the claim that 25% of offspring peas will be yellow.

11. H_0: $p = 0.5$. H_1: $p > 0.5$. Test statistic: $z = 1.90$. Critical value: $z = 1.645$. *P*-value: 0.0287 (Tech: 0.0290). Reject H_0. There is sufficient evidence to support the claim that the majority of adults feel vulnerable to identify theft.

13. H_0: $p = 0.5$. H_1: $p > 0.5$. Test statistic: $z = 26.45$. Critical value: $z = 2.33$. *P*-value: 0.0001 (Tech: 0.0000). Reject H_0. There is sufficient evidence to support the claim that the XSORT method is effective in increasing the likelihood that a baby will be a girl.

15. H_0: $p = 0.5$. H_1: $p \neq 0.5$. Test statistic: $z = -2.03$. Critical values: $z = \pm 1.645$. *P*-value: 0.0424 (Tech: 0.0422). Reject H_0. There is sufficient evidence to warrant rejection of the claim that touch therapists use a method equivalent to random guesses. However, their success rate of 123/280 (or 43.9%) indicates that they performed *worse* than random guesses, so they do not appear to be effective.

17. H_0: $p = 1/3$. H_1: $p < 1/3$. Test statistic: $z = -2.72$. Critical value: $z = -2.33$. *P*-value: 0.0033. Reject H_0. There is sufficient evidence to support the claim that fewer than 1/3 of the challenges are successful. Players don't appear to be very good at recognizing referee errors.

19. H_0: $p = 0.000340$. H_1: $p \neq 0.000340$. Test statistic: $z = -0.66$. Critical values: $z = \pm 2.81$. *P*-value: 0.5092 (Tech: 0.5122). Fail to reject H_0. There is not sufficient evidence to support the claim that the rate is different from 0.0340%. Cell phone users should not be concerned about cancer of the brain or nervous system.

21. H_0: $p = 0.5$. H_1: $p \neq 0.5$. Test statistic: $z = 2.75$. Critical values: $z = \pm 1.96$. *P*-value: 0.0060 (Tech: 0.0059). Reject H_0. There is sufficient evidence to warrant rejection of the claim that the coin toss is fair in the sense that neither team has an advantage by winning it. The coin toss rule does not appear to be fair.

23. H_0: $p = 0.5$. H_1: $p < 0.5$. Test statistic: $z = -3.90$. Critical value: $z = -2.33$. *P*-value: 0.0001 (Tech: 0.0000484). Reject H_0. There is sufficient evidence to support the claim that fewer than half of smartphone users identify the smartphone as the only thing they could not live without. Because only smartphone users were surveyed, the results do not apply to the general population.

25. H_0: $p = 0.25$. H_1: $p > 0.25$. Test statistic: $z = 1.91$ (using $\hat{p} = 0.29$) or $z = 1.93$ (using $x = 124$). Critical value: $z = 1.645$ (assuming a 0.05 significance level). *P*-value: 0.0281 (using $\hat{p} = 0.29$) or 0.0268 (using $x = 124$) (Tech *P*-value: 0.0269). Reject H_0. There is sufficient evidence to support the claim that more than 25% of women purchase books online.

27. H_0: $p = 3/4$. H_1: $p > 3/4$. Test statistic: $z = 7.85$ (using $\hat{p} = 0.9$) or $z = 7.89$ (using $x = 463$). Critical value: $z = 2.33$. *P*-value: 0.0001 (Tech: 0.0000). Reject H_0. There is sufficient evidence to support the claim that more than 3/4 of all human resource professionals say that the appearance of a job applicant is most important for a good first impression.

29. H_0: $p = 0.791$. H_1: $p < 0.791$. Test statistic: $z = -29.09$ (using $\hat{p} = 0.39$) or $z = -29.11$ (using $x = 339$). Critical value: $z = -2.33$. *P*-value: 0.0001 (Tech: 0.0000). Reject H_0. There is sufficient evidence to support the claim that the percentage of selected Americans of Mexican ancestry is less than 79.1%, so the jury selection process appears to be unfair.

31. H_0: $p = 0.75$. H_1: $p > 75$. Test statistic: $z = 7.30$. Critical value: $z = 2.33$. *P*-value: 0.0001 (Tech: 0.0000). Reject H_0. There is sufficient evidence to support the claim that more than 75% of of television sets in use were tuned to the Super Bowl.

33. Among 100 M&Ms, 19 are green. H_0: $p = 0.16$. H_1: $p \neq 0.16$. Test statistic: $z = 0.82$. Critical values: $z = \pm 1.96$. *P*-value: 0.4122 (Tech: 0.4132). Fail to reject H_0. There is not sufficient evidence to warrant rejection of the claim that 16% of plain M&M candies are green.

35. H_0: $p = 0.5$. H_1: $p > 0.5$. Using the binomial probability distribution with an assumed proportion of $p = 0.5$, the probability of 7 or more heads is 0.0352, so the *P*-value is 0.0352. Reject H_0. There is sufficient evidence to support the claim that the coin favors heads.

37. a. 0.7224 (Tech: 0.7219)
   b. 0.2776 (Tech: 0.2781)
   c. The power of 0.7224 shows that there is a reasonably good chance of making the correct decision of rejecting the false null hypothesis. It would be better if the power were even higher, such as greater than 0.8 or 0.9.

Section 8-4

1. The requirements are (1) the sample must be a simple random sample, and (2) either or both of these conditions must be satisfied: The population is normally distributed or $n > 30$. There is not enough information given to determine whether the sample is a simple random sample. Because the sample size is not greater than 30, we must check for normality, but the value of 583 sec appears to be an outlier, and a normal quantile plot or histogram suggests that the sample does not appear to be from a normally distributed population.

3. A *t* test is a hypothesis test that uses the Student *t* distribution, such as the method of testing a claim about a population mean as presented in this section. The *t* test methods are much more likely to be used than the *z* test methods because the *t* test does not require a known value of σ, and realistic hypothesis tests of claims about μ typically involve a population with an unknown value of σ.

5. *P*-value < 0.005 (Tech: 0.0013).

7. $0.02 <$ P-value < 0.05 (Tech: 0.0365).

9. H_0: $\mu = 24$. H_1: $\mu < 24$. Test statistic: $t = -7.323$. Critical value: $t = -1.685$. P-value < 0.005. (The display shows that the P-value is 0.00000000387325.) Reject H_0. There is sufficient evidence to support the claim that Chips Ahoy reduced-fat cookies have a mean number of chocolate chips that is less than 24 (but this does not provide conclusive evidence of reduced fat).

11. H_0: $\mu = 33$ years. H_1: $\mu \neq 33$ years. Test statistic: $t = 2.367$. Critical values: $t = \pm 2.639$ (approximately). P-value > 0.02 (Tech: 0.0204). Fail to reject H_0. There is not sufficient evidence to warrant rejection of the claim that the mean age of actresses when they win Oscars is 33 years.

13. H_0: $\mu = 0.8535$ g. H_1: $\mu \neq 0.8535$ g. Test statistic: $t = 0.765$. Critical values: $t = \pm 2.101$. P-value > 0.20 (Tech: 0.4543). Fail to reject H_0. There is not sufficient evidence to warrant rejection of the claim that the mean weight of all green M&Ms is equal to 0.8535 g. The green M&Ms do appear to have weights consistent with the package label.

15. H_0: $\mu = 0$ lb. H_1: $\mu > 0$ lb. Test statistic: $t = 3.872$. Critical value: $t = 2.426$. P-value < 0.005 (Tech: 0.0002). Reject H_0. There is sufficient evidence to support the claim that the mean weight loss is greater than 0. Although the diet appears to have statistical significance, it does not appear to have practical significance, because the mean weight loss of only 3.0 lb does not seem to be worth the effort and cost.

17. H_0: $\mu = 0$. H_1: $\mu > 0$. Test statistic: $t = 0.133$. Critical value: $t = 1.676$ (approximately, assuming a 0.05 significance level). P-value > 0.10 (Tech: 0.4472). Fail to reject H_0. There is not sufficient evidence to support the claim that with garlic treatment, the mean change in LDL cholesterol is greater than 0. The results suggest that the garlic treatment is not effective in reducing LDL cholesterol levels.

19. H_0: $\mu = 4$ years. H_1: $\mu > 4$ years. Test statistic: $t = 3.189$. Critical value: $t = 2.539$. P-value < 0.005 (Tech: 0.0024). Reject H_0. There is sufficient evidence to support the claim that the mean time required to earn a bachelor's degree is greater than 4.0 years. Because $n \leq 30$ and the data do not appear to be from a normally distributed population, the requirement that "the population is normally distributed or $n > 30$" is not satisfied, so the conclusion from the hypothesis test might not be valid. However, some of the sample values are equal to 4 years and others are greater than 4 years, so the claim does appear to be justified.

21. The sample data meet the loose requirement of having a normal distribution. H_0: $\mu = 14$ μg/g. H_1: $\mu < 14$ μg/g. Test statistic: $t = -1.444$. Critical value: $t = -1.833$. P-value > 0.05 (Tech: 0.0913). Fail to reject H_0. There is not sufficient evidence to support the claim that the mean lead concentration for all such medicines is less than 14 μg/g.

23. The sample data meet the loose requirement of having a normal distribution. H_0: $\mu = 63.8$ in. H_1: $\mu > 63.8$ in. Test statistic: $t = 23.824$. Critical value: $t = 2.821$. P-value < 0.005 (Tech: 0.0000). Reject H_0. There is sufficient evidence to support the claim that supermodels have heights with a mean that is greater than the mean height of 63.8 in. for women in the general population. We can conclude that supermodels are taller than typical women.

25. H_0: $\mu = 1.00$. H_1: $\mu > 1.00$. Test statistic: $t = 2.218$. Critical value: $t = 1.676$ (approximately). P-value < 0.025 (Tech: 0.0156). Reject H_0. There is sufficient evidence to support the claim that the population of earthquakes has a mean magnitude greater than 1.00.

27. H_0: $\mu = 83$ kg. H_1: $\mu < 83$ kg. Test statistic: $t = -5.524$. Critical value: $t = -2.453$. P-value < 0.005 (Tech: 0.0000). Reject H_0. There is sufficient evidence to support the claim that male college students have a mean weight that is less than the 83 kg mean weight of males in the general population.

29. H_0: $\mu = 24$. H_1: $\mu < 24$. Test statistic: $z = -7.32$. Critical value: $z = -1.645$. P-value: 0.0001 (Tech: 0.0000). Reject H_0. There is sufficient evidence to support the claim that Chips Ahoy reduced-fat cookies have a mean number of chocolate chips that is less than 24 (but this does not provide conclusive evidence of reduced fat).

31. H_0: $\mu = 33$ years. H_1: $\mu \neq 33$ years. Test statistic: $z = 2.37$. Critical values: $z = \pm 2.575$. P-value: 0.0178 (Tech: 0.0180). Fail to reject H_0. There is not sufficient evidence to warrant rejection of the claim that the mean age of actresses when they win Oscars is 33 years.

33. The approximation yields a critical value of $t = 1.655$, which is the same as the result from STATDISK or a TI-83/84 Plus calculator.

35. a. The power of 0.4274 shows that there is a 42.74% chance of supporting the claim that $\mu < 1.00$ W/kg when the true mean is actually 0.80 W/kg. This value of power is not very high, and it shows that the hypothesis test is not very effective in recognizing that the mean is less than 1.00 W/kg when the actual mean is 0.80 W/kg.

b. $\beta = 0.5726$. The probability of a type II error is 0.5726. That is, there is a 0.5726 probability of making the mistake of not supporting the claim that $\mu < 1.00$ W/kg when in reality the population mean is 0.80 W/kg.

Section 8-5

1. a. The mean waiting time remains the same.

b. The variation among waiting times is lowered.

c. Because customers all have waiting times that are roughly the same, they experience less stress and are generally more satisfied. Customer satisfaction is improved.

d. The single line is better because it results in lower variation among waiting times, so a hypothesis test of a claim of a lower standard deviation is a good way to verify that the variation is lower with a single waiting line.

3. Use a 90% confidence interval. The conclusion based on the 90% confidence interval will be the same as the conclusion from a hypothesis test using the P-value method or the critical value method.

5. H_0: $\sigma = 0.15$ oz. H_1: $\sigma < 0.15$ oz. Test statistic: $\chi^2 = 18.822$. Critical value of χ^2 is between 18.493 and 26.509, so it is estimated to be 22.501 (Tech: 22.465). P-value < 0.05 (Tech: 0.0116). Reject H_0. There is sufficient evidence to support the claim that the population of volumes has a standard deviation less than 0.15 oz.

7. H_0: $\sigma = 0.0230$ g. H_1: $\sigma < 0.0230$ g. Test statistic: $\chi^2 =$ 18.483. Critical value of χ^2 is between 18.493 and 26.509, so it is estimated to be 22.501 (Tech: 23.269). P-value < 0.05 (Tech: 0.0069). Reject H_0. There is sufficient evidence to support the claim that the population of weights has a standard deviation less than the specification of 0.0230 g.

9. The data appear to be from a normally distributed population. H_0: $\sigma = 10$. H_1: $\sigma \neq 10$. Test statistic: $\chi^2 = 41.375$. Critical values of χ^2 : 24.433 and 59.342 (approximately). P-value > 0.20 (Tech: 0.7347). Fail to reject H_0. There is not sufficient evidence to warrant rejection of the claim that pulse rates of men have a standard deviation equal to 10 beats per minute.

11. H_0: $\sigma = 3.2$ mg. H_1: $\sigma \neq 3.2$ mg. Test statistic: $\chi^2 = 32.086$. Critical values: $\chi^2 = 12.401$ and 39.364. P-value > 0.20 (Tech: 0.2498). Fail to reject H_0. There is not sufficient evidence to support the claim that filtered 100-mm cigarettes have tar amounts with a standard deviation different from 3.2 mg. There is not enough evidence to conclude that filters have an effect.

13. The data appear to be from a normally distributed population. H_0: $\sigma = 22.5$ years. H_1: $\sigma < 22.5$ years. Test statistic: $\chi^2 = 1.627$. Critical value: $\chi^2 = 4.660$. P-value < 0.005 (Tech: 0.0000). Reject H_0. There is sufficient evidence to support the claim that the standard deviation of ages of all race car drivers is less than 22.5 years.

15. H_0: $\sigma = 32.2$ ft. H_1: $\sigma > 32.2$ ft. Test statistic: $\chi^2 = 29.176$. Critical value: $\chi^2 = 19.675$. P-value: 0.0021. Reject H_0. There is sufficient evidence to support the claim that the new production method has errors with a standard deviation greater than 32.2 ft. The variation appears to be greater than in the past, so the new method appears to be worse, because there will be more altimeters that have larger errors. The company should take immediate action to reduce the variation.

17. H_0: $\sigma = 0.15$ oz. H_1: $\sigma < 0.15$ oz. Test statistic: $\chi^2 = 10.173$. Critical value of χ^2 is between 18.493 and 26.509, so it is estimated to be 22.501 (Tech: 22.465). P-value < 0.01 (Tech: 0.0000). Reject H_0. There is sufficient evidence to support the claim that the population of volumes has a standard deviation less than 0.15 oz.

19. Critical $\chi^2 = 22.189$, which is reasonably close to the value of 22.465 obtained from STATDISK and Minitab.

Chapter 8: Quick Quiz

1. H_0: $\mu = 0$ sec. H_1: $\mu \neq 0$ sec.
2. a. Two-tailed.   b. Student t.
3. a. Fail to reject H_0.
   b. There is not sufficient evidence to warrant rejection of the claim that the sample is from a population with a mean equal to 0 sec.
4. There is a loose requirement of a normally distributed population in the sense that the test works reasonably well if the departure from normality is not too extreme.
5. a. H_0: $p = 0.5$. H_1: $p > 0.5$.   b. $z = 6.33$
   c. P-value: 0.0000000001263996. There is sufficient evidence to support the claim that the majority of adults are in favor of the death penalty for a person convicted of murder.
6. 0.0456 (Tech: 0.0455)
7. The only true statement is the one given in part (a).
8. No. All critical values of χ^2 are greater than zero.
9. True.   10. False.

Chapter 8: Review Exercises

1. a. False.   b. True.   c. False.
   d. False.   e. False.
2. H_0: $p = 2/3$. H_1: $p \neq 2/3$. Test statistic: $z = -1.09$. Critical values: $z = \pm 2.575$ (Tech: ± 2.576). P-value: 0.2758 (Tech: 0.2756). Fail to reject H_0. There is not sufficient evidence to warrant rejection of the claim that 2/3 of adults are satisfied with the amount of leisure time that they have.
3. H_0: $p = 0.75$. H_1: $p > 0.75$. Test statistic: $z = 10.65$ (if using $x = 678$) or $z = 10.66$ (if using $\hat{p} = 0.92$). Critical value: $z = \pm 2.33$. P-value: 0.0001 (Tech: 0.0000). Reject H_0. There is sufficient evidence to support the claim that more than 75% of us do not open unfamiliar e-mail and instant-message links. Given that the results are based on a voluntary response sample, the results are not necessarily valid.
4. H_0: $\mu = 3369$ g. H_1: $\mu < 3369$ g. Test statistic: $t = -19.962$. Critical value: $t = -2.328$ (approximately). P-value < 0.005 (Tech: 0.0000). Reject H_0. There is sufficient evidence to support the claim that the mean birth weight of Chinese babies is less than the mean birth weight of 3369 g for Caucasian babies.
5. H_0: $\sigma = 567$ g. H_1: $\sigma \neq 567$ g. Test statistic: $\chi^2 = 54.038$. Critical values of χ^2 : 51.172 and 116.321. P-value is between 0.02 and 0.05 (Tech: 0.0229). Fail to reject H_0. There is not sufficient evidence to warrant rejection of the claim that the standard deviation of birth weights of Chinese babies is equal to 567 g.
6. H_0: $\mu = 1.5$ $\mu g/m^3$. H_1: $\mu > 1.5$ $\mu g/m^3$. Test statistic: $t = 0.049$. Critical value: $t = 2.015$. P-value > 0.10 (Tech: 0.4814). Fail to reject H_0. There is not sufficient evidence to support the claim that the sample is from a population with a mean greater than the EPA standard of 1.5 $\mu g/m^3$. Because the sample value of 5.40 $\mu g/m^3$ appears to be an outlier and because a normal quantile plot suggests that the sample data are not from a normally distributed population, the requirements of the hypothesis test are not satisfied, and the results of the hypothesis test are therefore questionable.
7. H_0: $\mu = 25$. H_1: $\neq 25$. Test statistic: $t = -0.567$. Critical values: $t = \pm 1.984$ (approximately). P-value > 0.20 (Tech: 0.5717). Fail to reject H_0. There is not sufficient evidence to warrant rejection of the claim that the sample is selected from a population with a mean equal to 25.
8. a. A type I error is the mistake of rejecting a null hypothesis when it is actually true. A type II error is the mistake of failing to reject a null hypothesis when in reality it is false.
   b. Type I error: Reject the null hypothesis that the mean of the population is equal to 25 when in reality, the mean is actually equal to 25. Type II error: Fail to reject the null hypothesis that the population mean is equal to 25 when in reality, the mean is actually different from 25.
9. The χ^2 test has a reasonably strict requirement that the sample data must be randomly selected from a population with a normal distribution, but the numbers are selected in such a way that they are all equally likely, so the population has a uniform distribution instead of the required normal distribution. Because the requirements are not all satisfied, the χ^2 test should not be used.

10. H_0: $\mu = 1000$ HIC. H_1: $\mu < 1000$ HIC. Test statistic: $t = -10.177$. Critical value: $t = -3.747$. P-value < 0.005 (Tech: 0.0003). Reject H_0. There is sufficient evidence to support the claim that the population mean is less than 1000 HIC. The results suggest that the population mean is less than 1000 HIC, so they appear to satisfy the specified requirement.

Chapter 8: Cumulative Review Exercises

1. a. 53.3 words   b. 52.0 words   c. 15.7 words
   d. 245.1 words^2 e. 45 words
2. a. Ratio.   b. Discrete.
   c. The sample is a simple random sample if it was selected in such a way that all possible samples of the same size have the same chance of being selected.
3. 42.1 words $< \mu <$ 64.5 words
4. H_0: $\mu = 48.0$ words. H_1: $\mu > 48.0$ words. Test statistic: $t = 1.070$. Critical value: $t = 1.833$. P-value > 0.10 (Tech: 0.1561). Fail to reject H_0. There is not sufficient evidence to support the claim that the mean number of words on a page is greater than 48.0. There is not enough evidence to support the claim that there are more than 70,000 words in the dictionary.
5. a. 2.28%   b. 38.9 in.   c. 0.9236 (Tech: 0.9234)
6. a. 0.00195. It is unlikely because the probability of the event occurring is so small.
   b. 0.0121   c. 0.487
7. No. The distribution is very skewed. A normal distribution would be approximately bell-shaped, but the displayed distribution is very far from being bell-shaped.
8. Because the vertical scale starts at 7000 and not at 0, the difference between the number of males and the number of females is exaggerated, so the graph is deceptive by creating the wrong impression that there are many more male graduates than female graduates.
9. a. 373   b. 34.2% $< p <$ 40.2%
   c. Yes. With test statistic $z = -8.11$ and with a P-value close to 0, there is sufficient evidence to support the claim that less than 50% of adults answer "yes."
   d. The required sample size depends on the confidence level and the sample proportion, not the population size.
10. H_0: $p = 0.5$. H_1: $p < 0.5$. Test statistic: $z = -8.11$. Critical value: $z = -2.33$. P-value: 0.0001 (Tech: 0.0000). Reject H_0. There is sufficient evidence to support the claim that fewer than 50% of Americans say that they have a gun in their home.

Chapter 9 Answers

Section 9-2

1. The samples are simple random samples that are independent. For each of the two groups, the number of successes is at least 5 and the number of failures is at least 5. (Depending on what we call a success, the four numbers are 33, 115, 201,229 and 200,745 and all of those numbers are at least 5.) The requirements are satisfied.
3. a. H_0: $p_1 = p_2$. H_1: $p_1 < p_2$.
   b. If the P-value is less than 0.001 we should reject the null hypothesis and conclude that there is sufficient evidence to support the claim that the rate of polio is less for children given the Salk vaccine than it is for children given a placebo.

5. Test statistic: $z = -12.39$ (rounded). The P-value of $3.137085E^{-}35$ is 0.0000 when rounded to four decimal places. There is sufficient evidence to warrant rejection of the claim that the vaccine has no effect.
7. a. H_0: $p_1 = p_2$. H_1: $p_1 > p_2$. Test statistic: $z = 6.44$. Critical value: $z = 2.33$. P-value: 0.0001 (Tech: 0.0000). Reject H_0. There is sufficient evidence to support the claim that the proportion of people over 55 who dream in black and white is greater than the proportion for those under 25.
   b. 98% CI: $0.117 < p_1 - p_2 < 0.240$. Because the confidence interval limits do not include 0, it appears that the two proportions are not equal. Because the confidence interval limits include only positive values, it appears that the proportion of people over 55 who dream in black and white is greater than the proportion for those under 25.
   c. The results suggest that the proportion of people over 55 who dream in black and white is greater than the proportion for those under 25, but the results cannot be used to verify the cause of that difference.
9. a. H_0: $p_1 = p_2$. H_1: $p_1 > p_2$. Test statistic: $z = 6.11$. Critical value: $z = 1.645$. P-value: 0.0001 (Tech: 0.0000). Reject H_0. There is sufficient evidence to support the claim that the fatality rate is higher for those not wearing seat belts.
   b. 90% CI: $0.00556 < p_1 - p_2 < 0.0122$. Because the confidence interval limits do not include 0, it appears that the two fatality rates are not equal. Because the confidence interval limits include only positive values, it appears that the fatality rate is higher for those not wearing seat belts.
   c. The results suggest that the use of seat belts is associated with lower fatality rates than not using seat belts.
11. a. H_0: $p_1 = p_2$. H_1: $p_1 \neq p_2$. Test statistic: $z = 0.57$. Critical values: $z = \pm 1.96$. P-value: 0.5686 (Tech: 0.5720). Fail to reject H_0. There is not sufficient evidence to support the claim that echinacea treatment has an effect.
   b. 95% CI: $-0.0798 < p_1 - p_2 < 0.149$. Because the confidence interval limits do contain 0, there is not a significant difference between the two proportions. There is not sufficient evidence to support the claim that echinacea treatment has an effect.
   c. Echinacea does not appear to have a significant effect on the infection rate. Because it does not appear to have an effect, it should not be recommended.
13. a. H_0: $p_1 = p_2$. H_1: $p_1 \neq p_2$. Test statistic: $z = 0.40$. Critical values: $z = \pm 1.96$. P-value: 0.6892 (Tech: 0.6859). Fail to reject H_0. There is not sufficient evidence to warrant rejection of the claim that men and women have equal success in challenging calls.
   b. 95% CI: $-0.0318 < p_1 - p_2 < 0.0484$. Because the confidence interval limits contain 0, there is not a significant difference between the two proportions. There is not sufficient evidence to warrant rejection of the claim that men and women have equal success in challenging calls.
   c. It appears that men and women have equal success in challenging calls.

15. a. H_0: $p_1 = p_2$. H_1: $p_1 > p_2$. Test statistic: $z = 9.97$. Critical value: $z = 2.33$. P-value: 0.0001 (Tech: 0.0000). Reject H_0. There is sufficient evidence to support the claim that the cure rate with oxygen treatment is higher than the cure rate for those given a placebo. It appears that the oxygen treatment is effective.

    b. 98% CI: $0.467 < p_1 - p_2 < 0.687$. Because the confidence interval limits do not include 0, it appears that the two cure rates are not equal. Because the confidence interval limits include only positive values, it appears that the cure rate with oxygen treatment is higher than the cure rate for those given a placebo. It appears that the oxygen treatment is effective.

    c. The results suggest that the oxygen treatment is effective in curing cluster headaches.

17. a. H_0: $p_1 = p_2$. H_1: $p_1 < p_2$. Test statistic: $z = -1.17$. Critical value: $z = -2.33$. P-value: 0.1210 (Tech: 0.1214). Fail to reject H_0. There is not sufficient evidence to support the claim that the rate of left-handedness among males is less than that among females.

    b. 98% CI: $-0.0849 < p_1 - p_2 < 0.0265$ (Tech: $-0.0848 < p_1 - p_2 < 0.0264$). Because the confidence interval limits include 0, there does not appear to be a significant difference between the rate of left-handedness among males and the rate among females. There is not sufficient evidence to support the claim that the rate of left-handedness among males is less than that among females.

    c. The rate of left-handedness among males does not appear to be less than the rate of left-handedness among females.

19. a. $0.0227 < p_1 - p_2 < 0.217$; because the confidence interval limits do not contain 0, it appears that $p_1 = p_2$ can be rejected.

    b. $0.491 < p_1 < 0.629$; $0.371 < p_2 < 0.509$; because the confidence intervals do overlap, it appears that $p_1 = p_2$ cannot be rejected.

    c. H_0: $p_1 = p_2$. H_1: $p_1 \neq p_2$. Test statistic: $z = 2.40$. P-value: 0.0164. Critical values: $z = \pm 1.96$. Reject H_0. There is sufficient evidence to reject $p_1 = p_2$.

    d. Reject $p_1 = p_2$. Least effective: Using the overlap between the individual confidence intervals.

21. 3383 (Tech: 3382)

Section 9-3

1. Independent: b, d, e

3. Because the confidence interval does not contain 0, it appears that there is a significant difference between the mean height of women and the mean height of men. Based on the confidence interval, it appears that the mean height of men is greater than the mean height of women.

5. a. H_0: $\mu_1 = \mu_2$. H_1: $\mu_1 \neq \mu_2$. Test statistic: $t = -2.979$. Critical values: $t = \pm 2.032$ (Tech: ± 2.002). P-value < 0.01 (Tech: 0.0042). Reject H_0. There is sufficient evidence to warrant rejection of the claim that the samples are from populations with the same mean. Color does appear to have an effect on creativity scores. Blue appears to be associated with higher creativity scores.

    b. 95% CI: $-0.98 < \mu_1 - \mu_2 < -0.18$ (Tech: $-0.97 < \mu_1 - \mu_2 < -0.19$)

7. a. H_0: $\mu_1 = \mu_2$. H_1: $\mu_1 > \mu_2$. Test statistic: $t = 0.132$. Critical value: $t = 1.729$. P-value > 0.10 (Tech: 0.4480). Fail to reject H_0. There is not sufficient evidence to support the claim that the magnets are effective in reducing pain. It is valid to argue that the magnets might appear to be effective if the sample sizes are larger.

    b. 90% CI: $-0.61 < \mu_1 - \mu_2 < 0.71$ (Tech: $-0.59 < \mu_1 - \mu_2 < 0.69$)

9. a. The sample data meet the loose requirement of having a normal distribution. H_0: $\mu_1 = \mu_2$. H_1: $\mu_1 > \mu_2$. Test statistic: $t = 0.852$. Critical value: $t = 2.426$ (Tech: 2.676). P-value > 0.10 (Tech: 0.2054). Fail to reject H_0. There is not sufficient evidence to support the claim that men have a higher mean body temperature than women.

    b. 98% CI: $-0.54°F < (\mu_1 - \mu_2) < 1.02°F$ (Tech: $-0.51°F < (\mu_1 - \mu_2) < 0.99°F$)

11. a. H_0: $\mu_1 = \mu_2$. H_1: $\mu_1 < \mu_2$. Test statistic: $t = -3.547$. Critical value: $t = -2.462$ (Tech: -2.392). P-value < 0.005 (Tech: 0.0004). Reject H_0. There is sufficient evidence to support the claim that the mean maximal skull breadth in 4000 B.C. is less than the mean in A.D. 150.

    b. 98% CI: -8.13 mm $< \mu_1 - \mu_2 < -1.47$ mm (Tech: -8.04 mm $< (\mu_1 - \mu_2) < -1.56$ mm)

13. a. H_0: $\mu_1 = \mu_2$. H_1: $\mu_1 < \mu_2$. Test statistic: $t = -3.142$. Critical value: $t = -2.462$ (Tech: -2.403). P-value < 0.005 (Tech: 0.0014). Reject H_0. There is sufficient evidence to support the claim that students taking the nonproctored test get a higher mean than those taking the proctored test.

    b. 98% CI: $-25.54 < \mu_1 - \mu_2 < -3.10$ (Tech: $-25.27 < (\mu_1 - \mu_2) < -3.37$)

15. a. H_0: $\mu_1 = \mu_2$. H_1: $\mu_1 \neq \mu_2$. Test statistic: $t = 1.274$. Critical values: $t = \pm 2.023$ (Tech: ± 1.994). P-value > 0.20 (Tech: 0.2066). Fail to reject H_0. There is not sufficient evidence to warrant rejection of the claim that males and females have the same mean BMI.

    b. 95% CI: $-1.08 < \mu_1 - \mu_2 < 4.76$ (Tech: $-1.04 < \mu_1 - \mu_2 < 4.72$)

17. a. H_0: $\mu_1 = \mu_2$. H_1: $\mu_1 > \mu_2$. Test statistic: $t = 0.089$. Critical value: $t = 1.725$ (Tech: 2.029). P-value > 0.10 (Tech: 0.4648.) Fail to reject H_0. There is not sufficient evidence to support the claim that the mean IQ score of people with medium lead levels is higher than the mean IQ score of people with high lead levels.

    b. 90% CI: $-5.9 < \mu_1 - \mu_2 < 6.6$ (Tech: $-5.8 < (\mu_1 - \mu_2) < 6.4$)

19. a. H_0: $\mu_1 = \mu_2$. H_1: $\mu_1 < \mu_2$. Test statistic: $t = -1.810$. Critical value: $t = -2.650$ (Tech: -2.574). P-value > 0.025 (Tech: 0.0442). Fail to reject H_0. There is not sufficient evidence to support the claim that the mean longevity for popes is less than the mean for British monarchs after coronation.

    b. 98% CI: -23.6 years $< (\mu_1 - \mu_2) < 4.4$ years (Tech: -23.2 years $< (\mu_1 - \mu_2) < 4.0$ years)

21. $H_0: \mu_1 = \mu_2$. $H_1: \mu_1 \neq \mu_2$. Test statistic: $t = 32.773$. Critical values: $t = \pm 2.023$ (Tech: ± 1.994). P-value < 0.01 (Tech: 0.0000). Reject H_0. There is sufficient evidence to warrant rejection of the claim that the two populations have equal means. The difference is highly significant, even though the samples are relatively small.

23. 0.03795 lb $< (\mu_1 - \mu_2) < 0.04254$ lb (Tech: 0.03786 lb $< (\mu_1 - \mu_2) < 0.04263$ lb). Because the confidence interval does not include 0, there appears to be a significant difference between the two population means. It appears that the cola in cans of regular Pepsi weighs more than the cola in cans of Diet Pepsi, and that is probably due to the sugar in regular Pepsi that is not in Diet Pepsi.

25. a. The sample data meet the loose requirement of having a normal distribution. $H_0: \mu_1 = \mu_2$. $H_1: \mu_1 > \mu_2$. Test statistic: $t = 1.046$. Critical value: $t = 2.381$ (Tech: 2.382). P-value > 0.10 (Tech: 0.1496). Fail to reject H_0. There is not sufficient evidence to support the claim that men have a higher mean body temperature than women.

    b. $-0.31°F < (\mu_1 - \mu_2) < 0.79°F$. The test statistic became larger, the P-value became smaller, and the confidence interval became narrower, so pooling had the effect of attributing more significance to the results.

27. $H_0: \mu_1 = \mu_2$. $H_1: \mu_1 \neq \mu_2$. Test statistic: $t = 15.322$. Critical values: $t = \pm 2.080$. P-value < 0.01 (Tech: 0.0000). Reject H_0. There is sufficient evidence to warrant rejection of the claim that the two populations have the same mean.

29. a. $H_0: \mu_1 = \mu_2$. $H_1: \mu_1 < \mu_2$. Test statistic: $t = -3.002$. Critical value based on 68.9927614 degrees of freedom: $t = -2.381$ (Tech: -2.382). P-value < 0.005 (Tech: 0.0019). Reject H_0. There is sufficient evidence to support the claim that students taking the nonproctored test get a higher mean than those taking the proctored test.

    b. $-25.68 < \mu_1 - \mu_2 < -2.96$ (Tech: $-25.69 < \mu_1 - \mu_2 < -2.95$)

Section 9-4

1. Parts (c) and (e) are true.

3. The test statistic will remain the same. The confidence interval limits will be expressed in the equivalent values of km/L.

5. $H_0: \mu_d = 0$ cm. $H_1: \mu_d > 0$ cm. Test statistic: $t = 0.036$ (rounded). Critical value: $t = 1.692$. P-value > 0.10 (Tech: 0.4859). Fail to reject H_0. There is not sufficient evidence to support the claim that for the population of heights of presidents and their main opponents; the differences have a mean greater than 0 cm (with presidents tending to be taller than their opponents).

7. a. $\bar{d} = -11.6$ years   b. $s_d = 17.2$ years
   c. $t = -1.507$ d. $t = \pm 2.776$

9. $H_0: \mu_d = 0$. $H_1: \mu_d \neq 0$. Test statistic: $t = -1.507$. Critical values: $t = \pm 2.776$. P-value > 0.20 (Tech: 0.2063). Fail to reject H_0. There is not sufficient evidence to support the claim that there is a difference between the ages of actresses and actors when they win Oscars.

11. 1.0 min $< \mu_d < 12.0$ min. Because the confidence interval includes only positive values and does not include 0 min, it

appears that the taxi-out times are greater than the corresponding taxi-in times, so there is sufficient evidence to support the claim of the flight operations manager that for flight delays, more of the blame is attributable to taxi-out times at JFK than taxi-in times at LAX.

13. $H_0: \mu_d = 0$. $H_1: \mu_d > 0$. Test statistic: $t = 2.579$. Critical value: $t = 2.015$. P-value < 0.025 (Tech: 0.0247). Reject H_0. There is sufficient evidence to support the claim that among couples, males speak more words in a day than females.

15. $-6.5 < \mu_d < -0.2$. Because the confidence interval does not include 0, it appears that there is sufficient evidence to warrant rejection of the claim that when the 13th day of a month falls on a Friday, the numbers of hospital admissions from motor vehicle crashes are not affected. Hospital admissions do appear to be affected.

17. $H_0: \mu_d = 0$. $H_1: \mu_d < 0$. Test statistic: $t = -1.080$. Critical value: $t = -1.833$. P-value > 0.10 (Tech: 0.1540). Fail to reject H_0. There is not sufficient evidence to support the claim that *Harry Potter and the Half-Blood Prince* did better at the box office. After a few years, the gross amounts from both movies can be identified, and the conclusion can then be judged objectively without using a hypothesis test.

19. $0.69 < \mu_d < 5.56$. Because the confidence interval limits do not contain 0 and they consist of positive values only, it appears that the "before" measurements are greater than the "after" measurements, so hypnotism does appear to be effective in reducing pain.

21. $H_0: \mu_d = 0$. $H_1: \mu_d \neq 0$. Test statistic: $t = -5.553$. Critical values: $t = \pm 1.990$. P-value < 0.01 (Tech: 0.0000). Reject H_0. There is sufficient evidence to support the claim that there is a difference between the ages of actresses and actors when they win Oscars.

23. $H_0: \mu_d = 0$. $H_1: \mu_d < 0$. Test statistic: $t = -1.560$. Critical value of t is between -1.671 and -1.676 (Tech: -1.673). P-value > 0.05 (Tech: 0.0622). Fail to reject H_0. There is not sufficient evidence to support the claim that among couples, males speak fewer words in a day than females.

25. $H_0: \mu_d = 6.8$ kg. $H_1: \mu_d \neq 6.8$ kg. Test statistic: $t = -11.833$. Critical values: $t = \pm 1.994$ (Tech: ± 1.997). P-value < 0.01 (Tech: 0.0000). Reject H_0. There is sufficient evidence to warrant rejection of the claim that $\mu_d = 6.8$ kg. It appears that the "Freshman 15" is a myth, and college freshman might gain some weight, but they do not gain as much as 15 pounds.

Section 9-5

1. a. No.
   b. No.
   c. The two samples have the same standard deviation (or variance).

3. The F test is very sensitive to departures from normality, which means that it works poorly by leading to wrong conclusions when either or both of the populations has a distribution that is not normal. The F test is not robust against sampling methods that do not produce simple random samples. For example, conclusions based on voluntary response samples could easily be wrong.

5. $H_0: \sigma_1 = \sigma_2$. $H_1: \sigma_1 \neq \sigma_2$. Test statistic: $F = 1.7341$. Upper critical F value is between 1.8752 and 2.0739 (Tech: 1.9611). P-value: 0.1081. Fail to reject H_0. There is not sufficient evidence to support the claim that weights of regular Coke and weights of regular Pepsi have different standard deviations.

7. $H_0: \sigma_1 = \sigma_2$. $H_1: \sigma_1 \neq \sigma_2$. Test statistic: $F = 1.1592$. Upper critical F value is between 1.8752 and 2.0739 (Tech: 1.9678). P-value: 0.6656. Fail to reject H_0. There is not sufficient evidence to warrant rejection of the claim that the samples are from populations with the same standard deviation. The background color does not appear to have an effect on the variation of word recall scores.

9. $H_0: \sigma_1 = \sigma_2$. $H_1: \sigma_1 > \sigma_2$. Test statistic: $F = 9.3364$. Critical F value is between 12.0540 and 2.0960 (Tech: 2.0842). P-value: 0.0000. Reject H_0. There is sufficient evidence to support the claim that the treatment group has errors that vary more than the errors of the placebo group.

11. $H_0: \sigma_1 = \sigma_2$. $H_1: \sigma_1 > \sigma_2$. Test statistic: $F = 2.1267$. Critical F value is between 2.1555 and 2.2341 (Tech: 2.1682). P-value: 0.0543. Fail to reject H_0. There is not sufficient evidence to support the claim that those given a sham treatment (similar to a placebo) have pain reductions that vary more than the pain reductions for those treated with magnets.

13. $H_0: \sigma_1 = \sigma_2$. $H_1: \sigma_1 > \sigma_2$. Test statistic: $F = 4.1648$. Critical F value is between 2.7876 and 2.8536 (Tech: 2.8179). P-value: 0.0130. Reject H_0. There is sufficient evidence to support the claim that amounts of strontium-90 from Pennsylvania residents vary more than amounts from New York residents.

15. $H_0: \sigma_1 = \sigma_2$. $H_1: \sigma_1 \neq \sigma_2$. Test statistic: $F = 1.0073$. Upper critical F value is 4.0260. P-value: 0.9915. Fail to reject H_0. There is not sufficient evidence to warrant rejection of the claim that females and males have heights with the same amount of variation.

17. $H_0: \sigma_1 = \sigma_2$. $H_1: \sigma_1 > \sigma_2$. Test statistic: $F = 1.2397$. Critical F value is between 1.6928 and 1.8409 (Tech: 1.7045). P-value: 0.2527. Fail to reject H_0. There is not sufficient evidence to support the claim that males have weights with more variation than females.

19. $c_1 = 4$, $c_2 = 0$, critical value is 5. Fail to reject $\sigma_1^2 = \sigma_2^2$.

21. 0.2727, 2.8365

Chapter 9: Quick Quiz

1. $H_0: p_1 = p_2$. $H_1: p_1 \neq p_2$.
2. 0.875
3. 0.0414
4. $0.00172 < p_1 - p_2 < 0.0970$
5. Because the data consist of matched pairs, they are dependent.
6. $H_0: \mu_d = 0$. $H_1: \mu_d > 0$.
7. There is not sufficient evidence to support the claim that front repair costs are greater than the corresponding rear repair costs.
8. F distribution
9. False.
10. True.

Chapter 9: Review Exercises

1. $H_0: p_1 = p_2$. $H_1: p_1 > p_2$. Test statistic: $z = 3.12$. Critical value: $z = 2.33$. P-value: 0.0009. Reject H_0. There is sufficient evidence to support a claim that the proportion of successes with surgery is greater than the proportion of successes with splinting. When treating carpal tunnel syndrome, surgery should generally be recommended instead of splinting.

2. 98% CI: $0.0581 < p_1 - p_2 < 0.332$ (Tech: $0.0583 < p_1 - p_2 < 0.331$). The confidence interval limits do not contain 0; the interval consists of positive values only. This suggests that the success rate with surgery is greater than the success rate with splints.

3. $H_0: p_1 = p_2$. $H_1: p_1 < p_2$. Test statistic: $z = -1.91$. Critical value: $z = -1.645$. P-value: 0.0281 (Tech: 0.0280). Reject H_0. There is sufficient evidence to support the claim that the fatality rate of occupants is lower for those in cars equipped with airbags.

4. $H_0: \mu_d = 0$. $H_1: \mu_d > 0$. Test statistic: $t = 4.712$. Critical value: $t = 3.143$. P-value < 0.005 (Tech: 0.0016). Reject H_0. There is sufficient evidence to support the claim that flights scheduled 1 day in advance cost more than flights scheduled 30 days in advance. Save money by scheduling flights 30 days in advance.

5. $H_0: \mu_d = 0$. $H_1: \mu_d \neq 0$. Test statistic: $t = -0.574$. Critical values: $t = \pm 2.365$. P-value > 0.20 (Tech: 0.5840). Fail to reject H_0. There is not sufficient evidence to support the claim that there is a difference between self-reported heights and measured heights of females aged 12–16.

6. $H_0: \mu_1 = \mu_2$. $H_1: \mu_1 > \mu_2$. Test statistic: $t = 2.879$. Critical value: $t = 2.429$ (Tech: 2.376). P-value < 0.005 (Tech: 0.0026). Reject H_0. There is sufficient evidence to support the claim that "stress decreases the amount recalled."

7. 98% CI: $1.3 < (\mu_1 - \mu_2) < 14.7$ (Tech: $1.4 < (\mu_1 - \mu_2) < 14.6$). The confidence interval limits do not contain 0; the interval consists of positive values only. This suggests that the numbers of details recalled are lower for those in the stress population.

8. $H_0: p_1 = p_2$. $H_1: p_1 \neq p_2$. Test statistic: $z = -4.20$. Critical values: $z = \pm 2.575$. P-value: 0.0002 (Tech: 0.0000). Reject H_0. There is sufficient evidence to warrant rejection of the claim that the acceptance rate is the same with or without blinding. Without blinding, reviewers know the names and institutions of the abstract authors, and they might be influenced by that knowledge.

9. $H_0: \mu_1 = \mu_2$. $H_1: \mu_1 \neq \mu_2$. Test statistic: $t = 0.679$. Critical values: $t = \pm 2.014$ approximately (Tech: ± 1.985). P-value > 0.20 (Tech: 0.4988). Fail to reject H_0. There is not sufficient evidence to warrant rejection of the claim of no difference between the mean LDL cholesterol levels of subjects treated with raw garlic and subjects given placebos. Both groups appear to be about the same.

10. $H_0: \sigma_1 = \sigma_2$. $H_1: \sigma_1 \neq \sigma_2$. Test statistic: $F = 1.1480$. Upper critical F value is between 1.6668 and 1.8752 (Tech: 1.7799). P-value: 0.6372. Fail to reject H_0. There is not sufficient evidence to warrant rejection of the claim that the two populations have LDL levels with the same standard deviation.

Chapter 9: Cumulative Review Exercises

1. a. Because the sample data are matched with each column consisting of heights from the same family, the data are dependent.
   b. Mean: 63.81 in.; median: 63.70 in.; mode: 62.2 in.; range: 8.80 in.; standard deviation: 2.73 in.; variance: 7.43 in^2
   c. Ratio

2. There does not appear to be a correlation or association between the heights of mothers and the heights of their daughters.

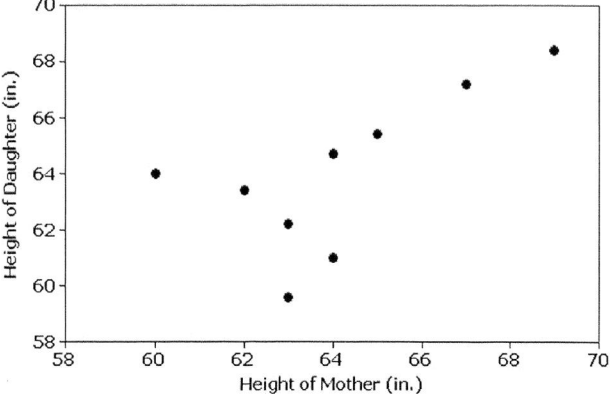

3. 61.86 in. $< \mu <$ 65.76 in. We have 95% confidence that the limits of 61.86 in. and 65.76 in. actually contain the true value of the mean height of all adult daughters.

4. H_0: $\mu_d = 0$. H_1: $\mu_d \neq 0$. Test statistic: $t = 0.283$. Critical values: $t = \pm 2.262$. P-value > 0.20 (Tech: 0.7834). Fail to reject H_0. There is not sufficient evidence to warrant rejection of the claim of no significant difference between the heights of mothers and the heights of their daughters.

5. Because the points lie reasonably close to a straight-line pattern and there is no other pattern that is not a straight-line pattern and there are no outliers, the sample data appear to be from a population with a normal distribution.

6. 0.109 $< p <$ 0.150. Because the entire range of values in the confidence interval lies below 0.20, the results do justify the statement that "fewer than 20% of Americans choose their computer and/or Internet access when identifying what they miss most when electrical power is lost."

7. No. Because the Internet users chose to respond, we have a voluntary response sample, so the results are not necessarily valid.

8. 2944. The survey should not be conducted using only local phone numbers. Such a convenience sample could easily lead to results that are dramatically different from results that would be obtained by randomly selecting respondents from the entire population, not just those having local phone numbers.

9. a. 0.9332   b. 0.9987
   c. 167.5 cm (Tech: 167.6 cm)

10. No. Because the states have different population sizes, the mean cannot be found by adding the 50 state means and dividing the total by 50. The mean income for the U.S. population can be found by using a weighted mean that incorporates the population size of each state.

Chapter 10

Section 10-2

1. r represents the value of the linear correlation computed by using the paired sample data. ρ represents the value of the linear correlation coefficient that would be computed by using all of the paired data in the population. The value of r is estimated to be 0 (because there is no correlation between sunspot numbers and the Dow Jones Industrial Average).

3. The headline is not justified because it states that increased salt consumption is the *cause* of higher blood pressure levels, but the presence of a correlation between two variables does not necessarily imply that one is the *cause* of the other. Correlation does not imply causality. A correct headline would be this: "Study Shows That Increased Salt Consumption Is Associated with Higher Blood Pressure."

5. Yes. With $r = 0.687$ and critical values of ± 0.312, there is sufficient evidence to support the claim that there is a linear correlation between the durations of eruptions and the time intervals to the next eruptions.

7. No. With $r = 0.149$ and a P-value of 0.681 (or critical values of ± 0.632), there is not sufficient evidence to support the claim that there is a linear correlation between the heights of fathers and the heights of their sons.

9. a.

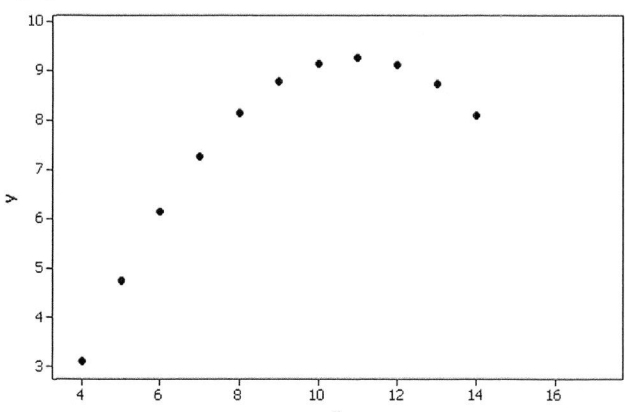

   b. $r = 0.816$. Critical values: $r = \pm 0.602$. P-value = 0.002. There is sufficient evidence to support the claim of a linear correlation between the two variables.
   c. The scatterplot reveals a distinct pattern that is not a straight-line pattern.

11. a. There appears to be a linear correlation.
   b. $r = 0.906$. Critical values: $r = \pm 0.632$ (for a 0.05 significance level). There is a linear correlation.
   c. $r = 0$. Critical values: $r = \pm 0.666$ (for a 0.05 significance level). There does not appear to be a linear correlation.
   d. The effect from a single pair of values can be very substantial, and it can change the conclusion.

13. $r = -0.959$. Critical values: $r = \pm 0.878$. P-value = 0.010. There is sufficient evidence to support the claim that there is a linear correlation between weights of lemon imports from Mexico and U.S. car fatality rates. The results do not suggest any cause-effect relationship between the two variables.

15. $r = 0.561$. Critical values: $r = \pm 0.632$. P-value $= 0.091$. There is not sufficient evidence to support the claim that there is a linear correlation between enrollment and burglaries. The results do not change if the actual enrollments are listed as 32,000, 31,000, 53,000, and so on.

17. $r = 0.864$. Critical values: $r = \pm 0.666$. P-value $= 0.003$. There is sufficient evidence to support the claim that there is a linear correlation between court incomes and justice salaries. The correlation does not imply that court incomes directly affect justice s alaries, but it does appear that justices might profit by levying larger fines, or perhaps justices with higher salaries impose larger fines.

19. $r = 1.000$. Critical values: $r = \pm 0.811$. P-value $= 0.000$. There is sufficient evidence to support the claim that there is a linear correlation between amounts of redshift and distances to clusters of galaxies. Because the linear correlation coefficient is 1.000, it appears that the distances can be directly computed from the amounts of redshift.

21. $r = 0.948$. Critical values: $r = \pm 0.811$. P-value $= 0.004$. There is sufficient evidence to support the claim of a linear correlation between the overhead width of a seal in a photograph and the weight of a seal.

23. $r = 0.867$. Critical values: $r = \pm 0.878$. P-value $= 0.057$. There is not sufficient evidence to support the claim of a linear correlation between the systolic blood pressure measurements of the right and left arm.

25. $r = 0.197$. Critical values: $r = \pm 0.707$. P-value $= 0.640$. There is not sufficient evidence to support the claim that there is a linear correlation between prices of regular gas and prices of premium gas. Because there does not appear to be a linear correlation between prices of regular and premium gas, knowing the price of regular gas is not very helpful in getting a good sense for the price of premium gas.

27. $r = 1.000$. Critical values: $r = \pm 0.707$. P-value $= 0.000$. There is sufficient evidence to support the claim that there is a linear correlation between diameters and circumferences. A scatterplot confirms that there is a *linear* association between diameters and volumes.

29. $r = -0.063$. Critical values: $r = \pm 0.444$. P-value $= 0.791$. There is not sufficient evidence to support the claim of a linear correlation between IQ and brain volume.

31. $r = 0.319$. Critical values: $r = \pm 0.254$ (approximately) (Tech: ± 0.263). P-value $= 0.017$. There is sufficient evidence to support the claim of a linear correlation between the numbers of words spoken by men and women who are in couple relationships.

33. a. 0.911   b. 0.787
    c. 0.9999 (largest)   d. 0.976
    e. -0.948

Section 10-3

1. The symbol $\hat{y}$ represents the predicted pulse rate. The predictor variable represents height. The response variable represents pulse rate.

3. If r is positive, the regression line has a positive slope and rises from left to right. If r is negative, the slope of the regression line is negative and it falls from left to right.

5. The best predicted time for an interval after the eruption is 69.0 min.

7. The best predicted height is $\bar{y} = 68.0$ in.

9. $\hat{y} = 3.00 + 0.500x$. The data have a pattern that is not a straight line.

11. a. $\hat{y} = 0.264 + 0.906x$
    b. $\hat{y} = 2 + 0x$ (or $\hat{y} = 2$)
    c. The results are very different, indicating that one point can dramatically affect the regression equation.

13. $\hat{y} = 16.5 - 0.00282x$; best predicted value is 15.1 fatalities per 100,000 population.

15. $\hat{y} = -36.8 + 3.47x$; best predicted value is $\bar{y} = 87.7$ burglaries. The predicted value is not close to the actual value of 329 burglaries.

17. $\hat{y} = 27.7 + 0.0373x$; best predicted value is $30,800. The predicted value is not very close to the actual salary of $26,088.

19. $\hat{y} = -0.00440 + 14.0x$; best predicted value is 0.172 billion light-years. The predicted value is very close to the actual distance of 0.18 light-years.

21. $\hat{y} = -157 + 40.2x$; best predicted weight is -76.6 kg (Tech: -76.5 kg). That prediction is a negative weight that cannot be correct. The overhead width of 2 cm is well beyond the scope of the available sample widths, so the extrapolation might be off by a considerable amount.

23. $\hat{y} = 43.6 + 1.31x$; best predicted value is $\bar{y} = 163.2$ mm Hg.

25. $\hat{y} = 2.57 + 0.172x$; best predicted value is $\bar{y} = $3.05. The predicted price is not very close to the actual price of $2.93.

27. $\hat{y} = -0.00396 + 3.14x$; best predicted value is 4.7 cm. Even though the diameter of 1.50 cm is beyond the scope of the sample diameters, the predicted value yields the actual circumference.

29. $\hat{y} = 109 - 0.00670x$; best predicted IQ score is $\bar{y} = 101$.

31. $\hat{y} = 13,400 + 0.302x$; best predicted value is 16,400 (Tech: 16,458).

33. With $\beta_1 = 0$, the regression line is horizontal so that different values of x result in the same y value, and there is no correlation between x and y.

Section 10-4

1. The value of $s_e = 17.5436$ cm is the standard error of estimate, which is a measure of the differences between the observed weights and the weights predicted from the regression equation. It is a measure of the variation of the sample points about the regression line.

3. The coefficient of determination is $r^2 = 0.127$. We know that 12.7% of the variation in weight is explained by the linear correlation between height and weight, and 87.3% of the variation in weight is explained by other factors and/or random variation.

5. $r^2 = 0.870$. 87.0% of the variation in waist size is explained by the linear correlation between weight and waist size, and 13.0% of the variation in waist size is explained by other factors and/or random variation.

7. $r^2 = 0.629$. 62.9% of the variation in highway fuel consumption is explained by the linear correlation between weight and highway fuel consumption, and 37.1% of the variation in highway fuel consumption is explained by other factors and/or random variation.

9. $r = 0.842$. Critical values: $r = \pm 0.312$ (assuming a 0.05 significance level). P-value $= 0.000$. There is sufficient evidence to support a claim of a linear correlation between foot length and height.

11. 189 cm

13. 160 cm $< y <$ 183 cm

15. 149 cm $< y <$ 168 cm

17. a. 10,626.59   b. 68.83577   c. 38.0°F $< y <$ 60.4°F

19. a. 0.466276   b. 0.000007359976
    c. 0.168 billion light-years $< y <$ 0.176 billion light-years

21. $58.9 < \beta_0 < 103$; $2.46 < \beta_1 < 3.98$

Section 10-5

1. The response variable is weight and the predictor variables are length and chest size.

3. The unadjusted R^2 increases (or remains the same) as more variables are included, but the adjusted R^2 is adjusted for the number of variables and sample size. The unadjusted R^2 incorrectly suggests that the best multiple regression equation is obtained by including all of the available variables, but by taking into account the sample size and number of predictor variables, the adjusted R^2 is much more helpful in weeding out variables that should not be included.

5. LDL $= 47.4 + 0.085$ WT $+ 0.497$ SYS

7. No. The P-value of 0.149 is not very low, and the values of R^2 (0.098) and adjusted R^2 (0.049) are not high. Although the multiple regression equation fits the sample data best, it is not a good fit.

9. HWY (highway fuel consumption) because it has the best combination of small P-value (0.000) and highest adjusted R^2 (0.920).

11. CITY $= -3.15 + 0.819$ HWY. That equation has a low P-value of 0.000 and its adjusted R^2 value of 0.920 isn't very much less than the values of 0.928 and 0.935 that use two predictor variables, so in this case it is better to use the one predictor variable instead of two.

13. The best regression equation is $\hat{y} = 0.127 + 0.0878x_1 - 0.0250x_2$, where x_1 represents tar and x_2 represents carbon monoxide. It is best because it has the highest adjusted R^2 value of 0.927 and the lowest P-value of 0.000. It is a good regression equation for predicting nicotine content because it has a high value of adjusted R^2 and a low P-value.

15. The best regression equation is $\hat{y} = 109 - 0.00670x_1$, where x_1 represents volume. It is best because it has the highest adjusted R^2 value of -0.0513 and the lowest P-value of 0.791. The three regression equations all have adjusted values of R^2 that are very close to 0, so none of them are good for predicting IQ. It does not appear that people with larger brains have higher IQ scores.

17. For H_0: $\beta_1 = 0$, the test statistic is $t = 5.486$, the P-value is 0.000, and the critical values are $t = \pm 2.110$, so reject H_0 and conclude that the regression coefficient of $b_1 = 0.707$ should be kept. For H_0: $\beta_2 = 0$, the test statistic is $t = 1.292$, the P-value is 0.213, and the critical values are $t = \pm 2.110$, so

fail to reject H_0 and conclude that the regression coefficient of $b_2 = 0.164$ should be omitted. It appears that the regression equation should include the height of the mother as a predictor variable, but the height of the father should be omitted.

19. $\hat{y} = 3.06 + 82.4x_1 + 2.91x_2$, where x_1 represents sex and x_2 represents age. Female: 61 lb; male: 144 lb. The sex of the bear does appear to have an effect on its weight. The regression equation indicates that the predicted weight of a male bear is about 82 lb more than the predicted weight of a female bear with other characteristics being the same.

Section 10-6

1. $y = x^2$; quadratic; $R^2 = 1$

3. 10.3% of the variation in Super Bowl points can be explained by the quadratic model that relates the variable of year and the variable of points scored. Because such a small percentage of the variation is explained by the model, the model is not very useful.

5. Quadratic: $d = -4.88t^2 + 0.0214t + 300$

7. Exponential: $y = 100(1.03^x)$

9. Power: $y = 65.7x^{-0.945}$. Prediction for the 22nd day: $3.5 million, which isn't very close to the actual amount of $2.2 million. The model does not take into account the fact that movies do better on weekend days.

11. Logarithmic: $y = 3.22 + 0.293 \ln x$

13. Exponential: $y = 10(2^x)$

15. Quadratic: $y = 125x^2 - 439x + 3438$. The projected value for 2010 is 49,344 (Tech: 49,312), which is dramatically greater than the actual value of 11,655.

17. a. Exponential: $y = 2^{\frac{2}{3}(x-1)}$ [or $y = (0.629961)(1.587401)^x$ for an initial value of 1 that doubles every 1.5 years].
    b. Exponential: $y = (1.36558)(1.42774)^x$, where 1971 is coded as 1.
    c. Moore's law does appear to be working reasonably well. With $R^2 = 0.990$, the model appears to be very good.

Chapter 10: Quick Quiz

1. ± 0.878

2. Based on the critical values of ± 0.878 (assuming a 0.05 significance level), conclude that there is not sufficient evidence to support the claim of a linear correlation between systolic and diastolic readings.

3. The best predicted diastolic reading is 90.6, which is the mean of the five sample diastolic readings.

4. The best predicted diastolic reading is 85.3, which is found by substituting 125 for x in the regression equation.

5. $r^2 = 0.342$

6. False.   7. False.   8. $r = 1$

9. Because r must be between -1 and 1 inclusive, the value of 3.335 is the result of an error in the calculations.

10. $r = -1$

Chapter 10: Review Exercises

1. a. $r = 0.926$. Critical values: $r = \pm 0.707$ (assuming a 0.05 significance level). P-value $= 0.001$. There is sufficient evidence to support the claim that there is a linear correlation between duration and interval-after time.
    b. 85.7%   c. $\hat{y} = 34.8 + 0.234x$ d. 81.6 min

2. a. The scatterplot suggests that there is not sufficient sample evidence to support the claim of a linear correlation between heights of eruptions and interval-after times.

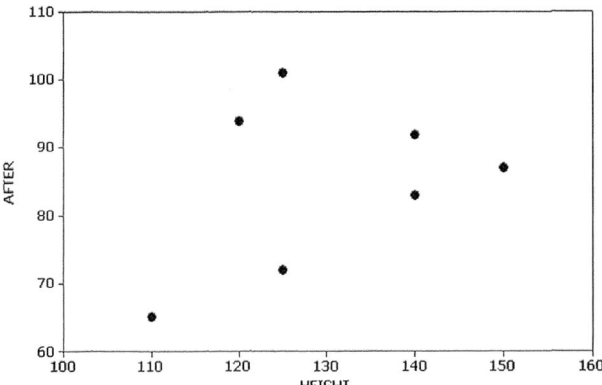

   b. $r = 0.259$. Critical values: $r = \pm 0.707$ (assuming a 0.05 significance level). P-value $= 0.519$. There is not sufficient evidence to support the claim that there is a linear correlation between height and interval-after time.
   c. $\hat{y} = 54.3 + 0.246x$
   d. 86.0 min

3. a. The scatterplot suggests that there is not sufficient sample evidence to support the claim of a linear correlation between duration and height.

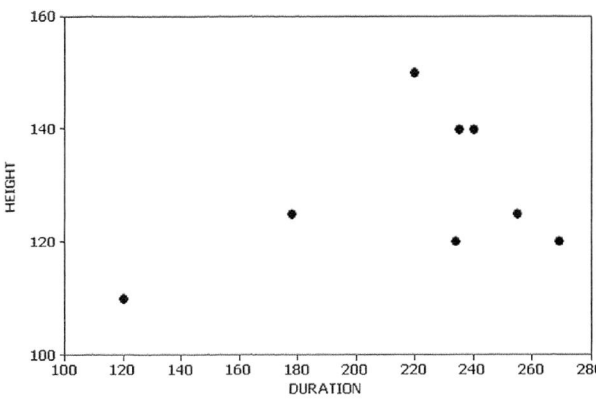

   b. $r = 0.389$. Critical values: $r = \pm 0.707$ (assuming a 0.05 significance level). P-value $= 0.340$. There is not sufficient evidence to support the claim that there is a linear correlation between duration and height.
   c. $\hat{y} = 105 + 0.108x$
   d. 128.8 ft

4. $r = 0.450$. Critical values: $r = \pm 0.632$ (assuming a 0.05 significance level). P-value $= 0.192$. There is not sufficient evidence to support the claim that there is a linear correlation between time and height. Although there is no *linear* correlation between time and height, the scatterplot shows a very distinct pattern revealing that time and height are associated by some function that is not linear.

5. AFTER $= 50.1 + 0.242$ Duration $- 0.178$ BEFORE, or $\hat{y} = 50.1 + 0.242x_1 - 0.178x_2$.

$R^2 = 0.872$; adjusted $R^2 = 0.820$; P-value $= 0.006$. With high values of R^2 and adjusted R^2 and a small P-value of 0.006, it appears that the regression equation can be used to predict the time interval after an eruption given the duration of the eruption and the time interval before that eruption.

Chapter 10: Cumulative Review Exercises

1. $\bar{x} = 3.3$ lb, $s = 5.7$ lb
2. The highest weight before the diet is 212 lb, which converts to $z = 1.55$. The highest weight is not unusual because its z score of 1.55 shows that it is within 2 standard deviations of the mean.
3. $H_0: \mu_d = 0$. $H_1: \mu_d > 0$. Test statistic: $t = 1.613$. Critical value: $t = 1.895$. P-value > 0.05 (Tech: 0.075). Fail to reject H_0. There is not sufficient evidence to support the claim that the diet is effective.
4. 161.8 lb $< \mu <$ 197.0 lb. We have 95% confidence that the interval limits of 161.8 lb and 197.0 lb contain the true value of the mean of the population of all subjects before the diet.
5. a. $r = 0.965$. Critical values: $r = \pm 0.707$ (assuming a 0.05 significance level). P-value $= 0.000$. There is sufficient evidence to support the claim that there is a linear correlation between before and after weights.
   b. $r = 1$ c. $r = 1$
   d. The effectiveness of the diet is determined by the amounts of weight lost, but the linear correlation coefficient is not sensitive to different amounts of weight loss. Correlation is not a suitable tool for testing the effectiveness of the diet.
6. a. 43.64% (Tech: 43.58%)
   b. 2786.4 g (Tech: 2785.6 g)
   c. 5.00%. Yes, many of the babies do require special treatment.
7. a. $H_0: p = 0.5$. $H_1: p > 0.5$. Test statistic: $z = 3.84$. Critical value: $z = 1.645$. P-value: 0.0001. Reject H_0. There is sufficient evidence to support the claim that the majority of us say that honesty is always the best policy.
   b. The sample is a voluntary response (or self-selected) sample. This type of sample suggests that the results given in part (a) are not necessarily valid.
8. a. Nominal.   b. Ratio.
   c. Discrete.   d. 0.575
   e. Parameter.
9. a. 0.330   b. 0.870   c. 0.972   d. 7.37%
10.

Chapter 11

Section 11-2

1. The test is to determine whether the observed frequency counts agree with the claimed uniform distribution so that frequencies for the different days are equally likely.

3. Because the given frequencies differ substantially from frequencies that are all about the same, the X^2 test statistic should be large and the P-value should be small.

5. Test statistic: $X^2 = 1934.979$. Critical value: $X^2 = 12.592$. P-value $= 0.000$. There is sufficient evidence to warrant rejection of the claim that the days of the week are selected with a uniform distribution with all days having the same chance of being selected.

7. Critical value: $X^2 = 16.919$. P-value > 0.10 (Tech: 0.516). There is not sufficient evidence to warrant rejection of the claim that the observed outcomes agree with the expected frequencies. The slot machine appears to be functioning as expected.

9. Test statistic: $X^2 = 10.375$. Critical value: $X^2 = 19.675$. P-value > 0.10 (Tech: 0.497). There is not sufficient evidence to warrant rejection of the claim that homicides in New York City are equally likely for each of the 12 months. There is not sufficient evidence to support the police commissioner's claim that homicides occur more often in the summer when the weather is better.

11. Test statistic: $X^2 = 5.860$. Critical value: $X^2 = 11.071$. P-value > 0.10 (Tech: P-value $= 0.320$). There is not sufficient evidence to support the claim that the outcomes are not equally likely. The outcomes appear to be equally likely, so the loaded die does not appear to behave differently from a fair die.

13. Test statistic: $X^2 = 13.483$. Critical value: $X^2 = 16.919$. P-value > 0.10 (Tech: 0.142). There is not sufficient evidence to warrant rejection of the claim that the likelihood of winning is the same for the different post positions. Based on these results, post position should not be considered when betting on the Kentucky Derby race.

15. Test statistic: $X^2 = 29.814$. Critical value: $X^2 = 16.812$. P-value < 0.005 (Tech: 0.000). There is sufficient evidence to warrant rejection of the claim that the different days of the week have the same frequencies of police calls. The highest numbers of calls appear to fall on Friday and Saturday, and these are weekend days with disproportionately more partying and drinking.

17. Test statistic: $X^2 = 7.579$. Critical value: $X^2 = 7.815$. P-value > 0.05 (Tech: 0.056). There is not sufficient evidence to warrant rejection of the claim that the actual numbers of games fit the distribution indicated by the proportions listed in the given table.

19. Test statistic: $X^2 = 6.682$. Critical value: $X^2 = 11.071$ (assuming a 0.05 significance level). P-value > 0.10 (Tech: 0.245). There is not sufficient evidence to warrant rejection of the claim that the color distribution is as claimed.

21. Test statistic: $X^2 = 3650.251$. Critical value: $X^2 = 20.090$. P-value < 0.005 (Tech: 0.000). There is sufficient evidence to warrant rejection of the claim that the leading digits are from a population with a distribution that conforms to Benford's law. It does appear that the checks are the result of fraud

(although the results cannot confirm that fraud is the cause of the discrepancy between the observed results and the expected results).

23. Test statistic: $X^2 = 1.762$. Critical value: $X^2 = 15.507$. P-value > 0.10 (Tech: 0.988). There is not sufficient evidence to warrant rejection of the claim that the leading digits are from a population with a distribution that conforms to Benford's law. The tax entries do appear to be legitimate.

25. a. 6, 13, 15, 6
    b. 0.1587, 0.3413, 0.3413, 0.1587 (Tech: 0.1587, 0.3413, 0.3414, 0.1586)
    c. 6.348, 13.652, 13.652, 6.348 (Tech: 6.348, 13.652, 13.656, 6.344)
    d. Test statistic: $X^2 = 0.202$ (Tech: 0.201). Critical value: $X^2 = 11.345$. P-value > 0.10 (Tech: 0.977). There is not sufficient evidence to warrant rejection of the claim that heights were randomly selected from a normally distributed population. The test suggests that the data are from a normally distributed population.

Section 11-3

1. Because the P-value of 0.216 is not small (such as 0.05 or lower), fail to reject the null hypothesis of independence between the treatment and whether the subject stops smoking. This suggests that the choice of treatment doesn't appear to make much of a difference.

3. $df = 2$ and the critical value is $X^2 = 5.991$.

5. Test statistic: $X^2 = 3.409$. Critical value: $X^2 = 3.841$. P-value > 0.05 (Tech: 0.0648). There is not sufficient evidence to warrant rejection of the claim that the form of the 100-Yuan gift is independent of whether the money was spent. There is not sufficient evidence to support the claim of a denomination effect.

7. Test statistic: $X^2 = 25.571$. Critical value: $X^2 = 3.841$. P-value < 0.005 (Tech: 0.000). There is sufficient evidence to warrant rejection of the claim that whether a subject lies is independent of the polygraph test indication. The results suggest that polygraphs are effective in distinguishing between truths and lies, but there are many false positives and false negatives, so they are not highly reliable.

9. Test statistic: $X^2 = 42.557$. Critical value: $X^2 = 3.841$. P-value < 0.005 (Tech: 0.000). There is sufficient evidence to warrant rejection of the claim that the sentence is independent of the plea. The results encourage pleas for guilty defendants.

11. Test statistic: $X^2 = 0.164$. Critical value: $X^2 = 3.841$. P-value > 0.10 (Tech: 0.686). There is not sufficient evidence to warrant rejection of the claim that the gender of the tennis player is independent of whether the call is overturned.

13. Test statistic: $X^2 = 14.589$. Critical value: $X^2 = 9.488$. P-value < 0.01 (Tech: 0.0056). There is sufficient evidence to warrant rejection of the claim that the direction of the kick is independent of the direction of the goalkeeper jump. The results do not support the theory that because the kicks are so fast, goalkeepers have no time to react, so the directions of their jumps are independent of the directions of the kicks.

15. Test statistic: $X^2 = 2.925$. Critical value: $X^2 = 5.991$. P-value > 0.10 (Tech: 0.232). There is not sufficient evidence to warrant rejection of the claim that getting a cold is independent of the treatment group. The results suggest that echinacea is not effective for preventing colds.

17. Test statistic: $X^2 = 20.271$. Critical value: $X^2 = 15.086$. P-value < 0.005 (Tech: 0.0011). There is sufficient evidence to warrant rejection of the claim that cooperation of the subject is independent of the age category. The age group of 60 and over appears to be particularly uncooperative.

19. Test statistic: $X^2 = 0.773$. Critical value: $X^2 = 11.345$. P-value > 0.10 (Tech: 0.856). There is not sufficient evidence to warrant rejection of the claim that getting an infection is independent of the treatment. The atorvastatin treatment does not appear to have an effect on infections.

21. Test statistics: $X^2 = 12.1619258$ and $z = 3.487395274$, so that $z^2 = X^2$. Critical values: $X^2 = 3.841$ and $z = \pm 1.96$, so $z^2 = X^2$ (approximately).

Chapter 11: Quick Quiz

1. H_0: $p_1 = p_2 = p_3 = p_4 = p_5$. H_1: At least one of the probabilities is different from the others.
2. $O = 23$ and $E = 21.4$.
3. Right-tailed.
4. $df = 4$ and the critical value is $X^2 = 9.488$.
5. There is not sufficient evidence to warrant rejection of the claim that occupation injuries occur with equal frequency on the different days of the week.
6. H_0: Response to the question is independent of gender. H_1: Response to the question and gender are dependent.
7. Chi-square distribution.
8. Right-tailed.
9. $df = 2$ and the critical value is $X^2 = 5.991$.
10. There is not sufficient evidence to warrant rejection of the claim that response is independent of gender.

Chapter 11: Review Exercises

1. Test statistic: $X^2 = 931.347$. Critical value: $X^2 = 16.812$. P-value: 0.000. There is sufficient evidence to warrant rejection of the claim that auto fatalities occur on the different days of the week with the same frequency. Because people generally have more free time on weekends and more drinking occurs on weekends, the days of Friday, Saturday, and Sunday appear to have disproportionately more fatalities.

2. Test statistic: $X^2 = 6.500$. Critical value: $X^2 = 16.919$. P-value > 0.10 (Tech: 0.689). There is not sufficient evidence to warrant rejection of the claim that the last digits of 0, 1, 2, . . . , 9 occur with the same frequency. It does appear that the weights were obtained through measurements.

3. Test statistic: $X^2 = 288.448$. Critical value: $X^2 = 24.725$. P-value < 0.005 (Tech: 0.000). There is sufficient evidence to warrant rejection of the claim that weather-related deaths occur in the different months with the same frequency. The summer months appear to have disproportionately more weather-related deaths, and that is probably due to the fact that vacations and outdoor activities are much greater during those months.

4. Test statistic: $X^2 = 10.708$. Critical value: $X^2 = 3.841$. P-value: 0.00107. There is sufficient evidence to warrant rejection of the claim that wearing a helmet has no effect on whether facial injuries are received. It does appear that a helmet is helpful in preventing facial injuries in a crash.

5. Test statistic: $X^2 = 4.955$. Critical value: $X^2 = 3.841$. P-value < 0.05 (Tech: 0.0260). There is sufficient evidence to warrant rejection of the claim that when flipping or spinning a penny, the outcome is independent of whether the penny was flipped or spun. It appears that the outcome is affected by whether the penny is flipped or spun. If the significance level is changed to 0.01, the critical value changes to 6.635, and we fail to reject the given claim, so the conclusion does change.

6. Test statistic: $X^2 = 4.737$. Critical value: $X^2 = 7.815$. P-value > 0.10 (Tech: 0.192). There is not sufficient evidence to warrant rejection of the claim that home/visitor wins are independent of the sport.

Chapter 11: Cumulative Review Exercises

1. H_0: $p = 0.5$. H_1: $p \neq 0.5$. Test statistic: $z = 7.28$. Critical values: $z = \pm 1.96$. P-value: 0.0002 (Tech: 0.0000). Reject H_0. There is sufficient evidence to warrant rejection of the claim that among those who die in weather-related deaths, the percentage of males is equal to 50%.

2. $59.0\% < p < 65.0\%$. Because the confidence interval does not include 50% (or "half"), we should reject the stated claim.

3. $\bar{x} = 53.7$ years, median $= 60.0$ years, $s = 16.1$ years. Because an age of 16 differs from the mean by more than 2 standard deviations, it is an unusual age.

4. 42.2 years $< \mu < 65.2$ years. Yes, the confidence interval limits do contain the value of 65.0 years that was found from a sample of 9269 ICU patients.

5. a. $r = -0.0458$. Critical values: $r = \pm 0.632$. P-value $= 0.900$. There is not sufficient evidence to support the claim that there is a linear correlation between the numbers of boats and the numbers of manatee deaths.
   b. $\hat{y} = 96.1 - 0.137x$
   c. 83.2 manatee deaths (the value of $\bar{y}$). The predicted value is not very accurate because it is not very close to the actual value of 78 manatee deaths.

6. a. 630 mm
   b. 14.46% (Tech: 14.48%). That percentage is too high, because too many women would not be accommodated.
   c. 0.7611 (Tech: 0.7599). Groups of 16 women do not occupy a cockpit; because individual women occupy the cockpit, this result has no effect on the design.

7. a. Statistic.
   b. Quantitative.
   c. Discrete.
   d. The sampling is conducted so that all samples of the same size have the same chance of being selected.
   e. The sample is a voluntary response sample (or self-selected sample), and those with strong feelings about the topic are more likely to respond, so it is not a valid sampling plan.

8. a. 0.130   b. 0.4

Chapter 13

Section 13-2

1. The only requirement for the matched pairs is that they constitute a simple random sample. There is no requirement of a normal distribution or any other specific distribution. The sign test is "distribution free" in the sense that it does not require a normal distribution or any other specific distribution.

3. H_0: There is no difference between the populations of September weights and April weights. H_1: There is a difference between the populations of September weights and April weights. The sample data do not contradict H_1 because the numbers of positive signs (2) and negative signs (7) are not exactly the same.

5. The test statistic of $x = 1$ is less than or equal to the critical value of 2 (from Table A-7). There is sufficient evidence to warrant rejection of the claim of no difference. There does appear to be a difference.

7. The test statistic of $z = -22.18$ falls in the critical region bounded by $z = -1.96$ and 1.96. There is sufficient evidence to warrant rejection of the claim of no difference. There does appear to be a difference.

9. The test statistic of $x = 1$ is less than or equal to the critical value of 1 (from Table A-7). There is sufficient evidence to warrant rejection of the claim of no difference. There does appear to be a difference.

11. The test statistic of $z = -0.53$ does not fall in the critical region bounded by $z = -1.96$ and 1.96. There is not sufficient evidence to warrant rejection of the claim of no difference. There does not appear to be a difference.

13. The test statistic of $z = -10.90$ is in the critical region bounded by $z = -2.575$ and 2.575. There is sufficient evidence to warrant rejection of the claim of no difference. The YSORT method appears to have an effect on the gender of the child. (Because so many more boys were born than would be expected with no effect, it appears that the YSORT method is effective in increasing the likelihood that a baby will be a boy.)

15. The test statistic of $z = -1.97$ is not in the critical region bounded by $z = -2.575$ and 2.575. There is not sufficient evidence to warrant rejection of the claim that the touch therapists make their selections with a method equivalent to random guesses. The touch therapists do not appear to be effective in selecting the correct hand.

17. The test statistic of $z = -2.37$ is not in the critical region bounded by $z = -2.575$ and 2.575. There is not sufficient evidence to warrant rejection of the claim that the median is equal to 5.670 g. The quarters appear to be minted according to specifications.

19. The test statistic of $z = -5.32$ is in the critical region bounded by $z = -1.96$ and 1.96. There is sufficient evidence to warrant rejection of the claim that the median amount of Coke is equal to 12 oz. Consumers are not being cheated because they are generally getting more than 12 oz of Coke, not less.

21. Second approach: The test statistic of $z = -4.29$ is in the critical region bounded by $z = -1.645$, so the conclusions are the same as in Example 4. Third approach: The test statistic of

$z = -2.82$ is in the critical region bounded by $z = -1.645$, so the conclusions are the same as in Example 4. The different approaches can lead to very different results; see the test statistics of -4.21, -4.29, and -2.82. The conclusions are the same in this case, but they could be different in other cases.

Section 13-3

1. The only requirements are that the matched pairs be a simple random sample and the population of differences be approximately symmetric. There is no requirement of a normal distribution or any other specific distribution. The Wilcoxon signed-ranks test is "distribution free" in the sense that it does not require a normal distribution or any other specific distribution.

3. The sign test uses only the signs of the differences, but the Wilcoxon signed-ranks test uses ranks that are affected by the magnitudes of the differences.

5. Test statistic: $T = 6$. Critical value: $T = 8$. Reject the null hypothesis that the population of differences has a median of 0. There is sufficient evidence to warrant rejection of the claim of no difference. There does appear to be a difference.

7. Convert $T = 247$ to the test statistic $z = -0.32$. Critical values: $z = \pm 1.96$. (Tech: P-value $= 0.751$.) Fail to reject the null hypothesis that the population of differences has a median of 0. There is not sufficient evidence to warrant rejection of the claim of no difference. There does not appear to be a difference.

9. Convert $T = 196$ to the test statistic $z = -2.88$. Critical values: $z = \pm 2.575$. (Tech: P-value $= 0.004$.) There is sufficient evidence to warrant rejection of the claim that the median is equal to 5.670 g. The quarters do not appear to be minted according to specifications.

11. Convert $T = 15.5$ to the test statistic $z = -4.82$. Critical values: $z = \pm 1.96$. (Tech: P-value $= 0.000$.) There is sufficient evidence to warrant rejection of the claim that the median amount of Coke is equal to 12 oz. Consumers are not being cheated because they are generally getting more than 12 oz of Coke, not less.

13. a. 0 and 2850
    b. 1425   c. 2000
    d. $\dfrac{n(n + 1)}{2} - k$

Section 13-4

1. Yes. The two samples are independent because the flight data are not matched. The samples are simple random samples. Each sample has more than 10 values.

3. H_0: Arrival delay times from Flights 19 and 21 have the same median. There are three different possible alternative hypotheses: H_1: Arrival delay times from Flights 19 and 21 have different medians.
H_1: Arrival delay times from Flight 19 have a median greater than the median of arrival delay times from Flight 21.
H_1: Arrival delay times from Flight 19 have a median less than the median of arrival delay times from Flight 21.

5. $R_1 = 137.5$, $R_2 = 162.5$, $\mu_R = 150$, $\sigma_R = 17.321$, test statistic: $z = -0.72$. Critical values: $z = \pm 1.96$. (Tech: P-value $= 0.4705$.) Fail to reject the null hypothesis that the populations have the same median. There is not sufficient evidence to warrant rejection of the claim that Flights 19 and 21 have the same median arrival delay time.

7. $R_1 = 253.5$, $R_2 = 124.5$, $\mu_R = 182$, $\sigma_R = 20.607$, test statistic: $z = 3.47$. Critical values: $z = \pm 1.96$. (Tech: P-value $= 0.0005$.) Reject the null hypothesis that the populations have the same median. There is sufficient evidence to reject the claim that for those treated with 20 mg of atorvastatin and those treated with 80 mg of atorvastatin, changes in LDL cholesterol have the same median. It appears that the dosage amount does have an effect on the change in LDL cholesterol.

9. $R_1 = 501$, $R_2 = 445$, $\mu_R = 484$, $\sigma_R = 41.158$, test statistic: $z = 0.41$. Critical value: $z = 1.645$. (Tech: P-value $= 0.3398$.) Fail to reject the null hypothesis that the populations have the same median. There is not sufficient evidence to support the claim that subjects with medium lead levels have full IQ scores with a higher median than the median full IQ score for subjects with high lead levels. It does not appear that lead level affects full IQ scores.

11. $R_1 = 2420$, $R_2 = 820$, $\mu_R = 1620$, $\sigma_R = 103.923$, test statistic: $z = 7.70$. Critical values: $z = \pm 1.96$. (Tech: P-value $= 0.0000$.) Reject the null hypothesis that the populations have the same median. It appears that the design of quarters changed in 1964.

13. Using $U = 86.5$, we get $z = -1.26$. The test statistic is the same value with opposite sign.

Section 13-5

1. $R_1 = 36.5$, $R_2 = 52.5$, $R_3 = 47$
3. $n_1 = 5$, $n_2 = 6$, $n_3 = 5$, and $N = 16$.
5. Test statistic: $H = 9.9800$. Critical value: $\chi^2 = 5.991$. (Tech: P-value $= 0.0068$.) Reject the null hypothesis of equal medians. The data suggest that the different miles present different levels of difficulty.
7. Test statistic: $H = 4.9054$. Critical value: $\chi^2 = 5.991$. (Tech: P-value $= 0.0861$.) Fail to reject the null hypothesis of equal medians. The data do not suggest that larger cars are safer.
9. Test statistic: $H = 8.0115$. Critical value: $\chi^2 = 9.210$. (Tech: P-value $= 0.0182$.) Fail to reject the null hypothesis of equal medians. The data do not suggest that lead exposure has an adverse effect.
11. Test statistic: $H = 27.9098$. Critical value: $\chi^2 = 5.991$. (Tech: P-value: 0.0000.) Reject the null hypothesis of equal medians. There is sufficient evidence to warrant rejection of the claim that the three different types of cigarettes have the same median amount of nicotine. It appears that the filters do make a difference.
13. Using $\Sigma T = 16,836$ and $N = 75$, the corrected value of H is 29.0701, which is not substantially different from the value found in Exercise 11. In this case, the large numbers of ties do not appear to have a dramatic effect on the test statistic H.

Section 13-6

1. The methods of Section 10-3 should not be used for predictions. The regression equation is based on a linear correlation between the two variables, but the methods of this section do not require a linear relationship. The methods of this section could suggest that there is a correlation with paired data associated by some nonlinear relationship, so the regression equation would not be a suitable model for making predictions.

3. r represents the linear correlation coefficient computed from sample paired data; ρ represents the parameter of the linear correlation coefficient computed from a population of paired data; r_s denotes the rank correlation coefficient computed from sample paired data; ρ_s represents the rank correlation coefficient computed from a population of paired data. The subscript s is used so that the rank correlation coefficient can be distinguished from the linear correlation coefficient r. The subscript does not represent the standard deviation s. It is used in recognition of Charles Spearman, who introduced the rank correlation method.

5. $r_s = 1$. Critical values are -0.886 and 0.886. Reject the null hypothesis of $\rho_s = 0$. There is sufficient evidence to support a claim of a correlation between distance and time.

7. $r_s = 0.821$. Critical values: -0.786, 0.786. Reject the null hypothesis of $\rho_s = 0$. There is sufficient evidence to support the claim of a correlation between the quality scores and prices. These results do suggest that you get better quality by spending more.

9. $r_s = -0.929$. Critical values: -0.786, 0.786. Reject the null hypothesis of $\rho_s = 0$. There is sufficient evidence to support the claim of a correlation between the two judges. Examination of the results shows that the first and third judges appear to have opposite rankings.

11. $r_s = 1$. Critical values: -0.886, 0.886. Reject the null hypothesis of $\rho_s = 0$. There is sufficient evidence to conclude that there is a correlation between overhead widths of seals from photographs and the weights of the seals.

13. $r_s = 0.394$. Critical values: -0.314, 0.314. Reject the null hypothesis of $\rho_s = 0$. There is sufficient evidence to conclude that there is a correlation between the systolic and diastolic blood pressure levels in males.

15. $r_s = 0.651$. Critical values: -0.286, 0.286. Reject the null hypothesis of $\rho_s = 0$. There is sufficient evidence to conclude that there is a correlation between departure delay times and arrival delay times.

17. a. ± 0.707 is not very close to the values of ± 0.738 found in Table A-9.
    b. ± 0.463 is quite close to the values of ± 0.467 found in Table A-9.

Section 13-7

1. No. The runs test can be used to determine whether the sequence of World Series wins by American League teams and National League teams is not random, but the runs test does not

show whether the proportion of wins by the American League is significantly greater than 0.5.

3. a. Answers vary, but here is a sequence that leads to rejection of randomness because the number of runs is 2, which is very low:
W W W W W W W W W W W E E E E E E E E

b. Answers vary, but here is a sequence that leads to rejection of randomness because the number of runs is 17, which is very high:
W E W E W E W E W E W E W E W E W W W W

5. $n_1 = 19$, $n_2 = 15$, $G = 16$, critical values: 11, 24. Fail to reject randomness. There is not sufficient evidence to support the claim that we elect Democrats and Republicans in a sequence that is not random. Randomness seems plausible here.

7. $n_1 = 20$, $n_2 = 10$, $G = 16$, critical values: 9, 20. Fail to reject randomness. There is not sufficient evidence to reject the claim that the dates before and after July 1 are randomly selected.

9. $n_1 = 24$, $n_2 = 21$, $G = 17$, $\mu_G = 23.4$, $\sigma_G = 3.3007$. Test statistic: $z = -1.94$. Critical values: $z = \pm 1.96$. (Tech: P-value $= 0.05252$.) Fail to reject randomness. There is not sufficient evidence to reject randomness. The runs test does not test for disproportionately more occurrences of one of the two categories, so the runs test does not suggest that either conference is superior.

11. The median is 2453, $n_1 = 23$, $n_2 = 23$, $G = 4$, $\mu_G = 24$, $\sigma_G = 3.3553$. Test statistic: $z = -5.96$. Critical values: $z = \pm 1.96$. (Tech: P-value $= 0.0000$.) Reject randomness. The sequence does not appear to be random when considering values above and below the median. There appears to be an upward trend, so the stock market appears to be a profitable investment for the long term, but it has been more volatile in recent years.

13. b. The 84 sequences yield these results: 2 sequences have 2 runs, 7 sequences have 3 runs, 20 sequences have 4 runs, 25 sequences have 5 runs, 20 sequences have 6 runs, and 10 sequences have 7 runs.

c. With $P(2 \text{ runs}) = 2/84$, $P(3 \text{ runs}) = 7/84$, $P(4 \text{ runs}) = 20/84$, $P(5 \text{ runs}) = 25/84$, $P(6 \text{ runs}) = 20/84$, and $P(7 \text{ runs}) = 10/84$, each of the G values of 3, 4, 5, 6, 7 can easily occur by chance, whereas $G = 2$ is unlikely because $P(2 \text{ runs})$ is less than 0.025. The lower critical value of G is therefore 2, and there is no upper critical value that can be equaled or exceeded.

d. Critical value of $G = 2$ agrees with Table A-10. The table lists 8 as the upper critical value, but it is impossible to get 8 runs using the given elements.

Chapter 13: Quick Quiz

1. Distribution-free test
2. 2, 5, 2, 2, 4
3. The efficiency rating of 0.91 indicates that with all other factors being the same, rank correlation requires 100 pairs of sample observations to achieve the same results as 91 pairs of observations with the parametric test for linear correlation, assuming that the stricter requirements for using linear correlation are met.
4. The Wilcoxon rank-sum test does not require that the samples be from populations having a normal distribution or any other specific distribution.

5. $G = 4$
6. Because there are only two runs, all of the values below the mean occur at the beginning and all of the values above the mean occur at the end, or vice versa. This indicates an upward (or downward) trend.
7. Sign test and Wilcoxon signed-ranks test
8. Rank correlation
9. Kruskal-Wallis test
10. Test claims involving matched pairs of data; test claims involving nominal data; test claims about the median of a single population

Chapter 13: Review Exercises

1. The test statistic of $z = -1.65$ is not less than or equal to the critical value of $z = -1.96$. Fail to reject the null hypothesis of $p = 0.5$. There is not sufficient evidence to warrant rejection of the claim that in each World Series, the American League team has a 0.5 probability of winning.

2. The test statistic of $x = 0$ is less than or equal to the critical value of 0. There is sufficient evidence to reject the claim of no difference. It appears that there is a difference in cost between flights scheduled 1 day in advance and those scheduled 30 days in advance. Because all of the flights scheduled 30 days in advance cost less than those scheduled 1 day in advance, it is wise to schedule flights 30 days in advance.

3. The test statistic of $T = 0$ is less than or equal to the critical value of 0. There is sufficient evidence to reject the claim that differences between fares for flights scheduled 1 day in advance and those scheduled 30 days in advance have a median equal to 0. Because all of the flights scheduled 1 day in advance have higher fares than those scheduled 30 days in advance, it appears that it is generally less expensive to schedule flights 30 days in advance instead of 1 day in advance.

4. The sample mean is 54.8 years. $n_1 = 19$, $n_2 = 19$, and the number of runs is $G = 18$. The critical values are 13 and 27. Fail to reject the null hypothesis of randomness. There is not sufficient evidence to warrant rejection of the claim that the sequence of ages is random relative to values above and below the mean. The results do not suggest that there is an upward trend or a downward trend.

5. $r_s = 0.714$. Critical values: ± 0.738. Fail to reject the null hypothesis of $\rho_s = 0$. There is not sufficient evidence to support the claim that there is a correlation between the student ranks and the magazine ranks. When ranking colleges, students and the magazine do not appear to agree.

6. The test statistic of $z = -0.88$ is not in the critical region bounded by $z = -1.96$ and 1.96. There is not sufficient evidence to warrant rejection of the claim that the population of differences has a median of zero. Based on the sample data, it appears that the predictions are reasonably accurate, because there does not appear to be a difference between the actual high temperatures and the predicted high temperatures.

7. Convert $T = 230.5$ to the test statistic $z = -0.62$. Critical values: $z = \pm 1.96$. (Tech: P-value $= 0.531$.) There is not sufficient evidence to warrant rejection of the claim that the population of differences has a median of zero. Based on the

sample data, it appears that the predictions are reasonably accurate, because there does not appear to be a difference between the actual high temperatures and the predicted high temperatures.

8. Test statistic: $H = 6.6305$. Critical value: $\chi^2 = 5.991$. (Tech: P-value $= 0.0363$.) Reject the null hypothesis of equal medians. Interbreeding of cultures is suggested by the data.

9. $R_1 = 60$, $R_2 = 111$, $\mu_R = 85.5$, $\sigma_R = 11.3248$, test statistic: $z = -2.25$. Critical values: $z = \pm1.96$. (Tech: P-value $= 0.0243$.) Reject the null hypothesis that the populations have the same median. Skull breadths from 4000 B.C. appear to have a different median than those from A.D. 150.

10. $r_s = 0.473$. Critical values: ±0.587. Fail to reject the null hypothesis of $\rho_s = 0$. There is not sufficient evidence to support the claim that there is a correlation between weights of plastic and weights of food.

Chapter 13: Cumulative Review Exercises

1. $\bar{x} = 14.6$ hours, median $= 15.0$ hours, $s = 1.7$ hours, $s^2 = 2.9$ hour^2, range $= 6.0$ hours

2. a. Convenience sample
   b. Because the sample is from one class of statistics students, it is not likely to be representative of the population of all full-time college students.
   c. Discrete
   d. Ratio

3. H_0: $\mu = 14$ hours. H_1: $\mu > 14$ hours. Test statistic: $t = 1.446$. Critical value: $t = 1.729$ (assuming a 0.05 significance level). P-value > 0.05 (Tech: 0.0822). Fail to reject H_0. There is not sufficient evidence to support the claim that the mean is greater than 14 hours.

4. The test statistic of $x = 5$ is not less than or equal to the critical value of 4. There is not sufficient evidence to support the claim that the sample is from a population with a median greater than 14 hours.

5. 13.8 hours $< \mu <$ 15.3 hours. We have 95% confidence that the limits of 13.8 hours and 15.3 hours contain the true value of the population mean.

6. $r = 0.205$. Critical values: $r = \pm0.811$. P-value $= 0.697$. There is not sufficient evidence to support the claim of a linear correlation between price and quality score. It appears that you don't get better quality by paying more.

7. $r_s = -0.543$. Critical values: ±0.886. Fail to reject the null hypothesis of $\rho_s = 0$. There is not sufficient evidence to support the claim that there is a correlation between price and rank.

8. $0.276 < p < 0.343$. Because the value of 0.25 is not included in the range of values in the confidence interval, the result suggests that the percentage of all such telephones that are not functioning is different from 25%.

9. 1692 (Tech: 1691)

10. There must be an error, because the rates of 13.7% and 10.6% are not possible with samples of size 100.

Chapter 14

Section 14-2

1. No. If we know that the manufacture of quarters is within statistical control, we know that the three out-of-control criteria are not violated, but we know nothing about whether the *specification* of 5.670 g is being met. It is possible to be within statistical control by manufacturing quarters with weights that are very far from the desired target of 5.670 g.

3. To use an $\bar{x}$ chart without an R chart is to ignore variation, and amounts of variation that are too large will result in too many defective goods or services, even though the mean might appear to be acceptable. To use an R chart without an $\bar{x}$ chart is to ignore the central tendency, so the goods or services might not vary much, but the process could be drifting so that daily process data do not vary much, but the daily means are steadily increasing or decreasing.

5. $\bar{\bar{x}} = 267.11$ lb, $\bar{R} = 54.96$ lb. For R chart: LCL $= 4.18$ lb and UCL $= 105.74$ lb. For $\bar{x}$ chart: LCL $= 244.08$ lb and UCL $= 290.14$ lb.

7. The R chart does not violate any of the out-of-control criteria, so the variation of the process appears to be within statistical control.

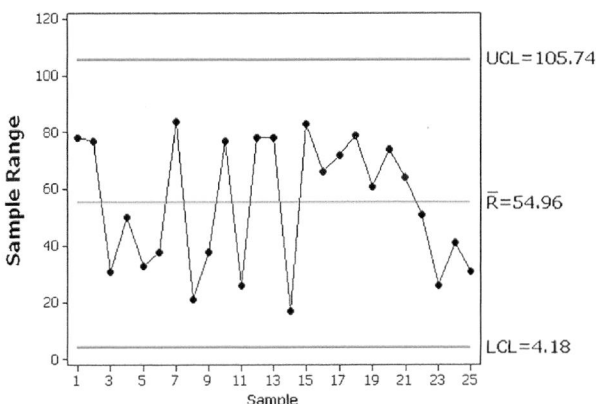

9. $\bar{\bar{x}} = 14.250°C$, $\bar{R} = 0.414°C$. For R chart: LCL $= 0.092°C$ and UCL $= 0.736°C$. For $\bar{x}$ chart: LCL $= 14.122°C$ and UCL $= 14.377°C$.

11. Because there is a pattern of an upward trend and there are points lying beyond the control limits, the $\bar{x}$ chart shows that the process is out of statistical control.

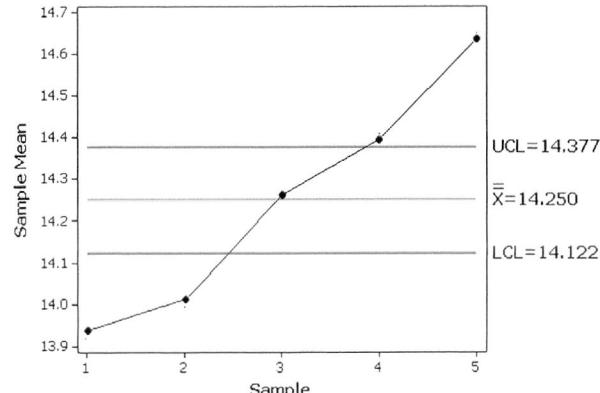

13. The *R* chart and the *s* chart are very similar.

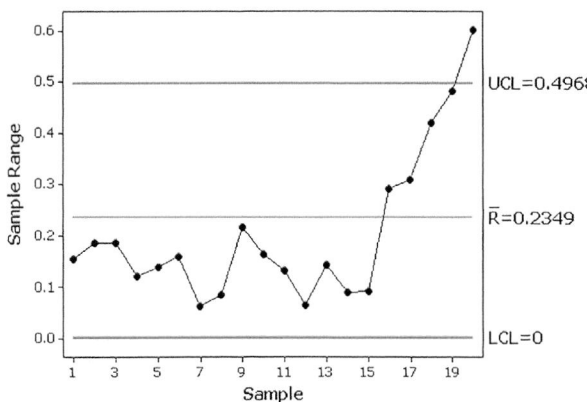

Section 14-3

1. No, the process does not appear to be within statistical control. There is a downward trend, there are at least 8 consecutive points all lying above the centerline, and there are at least 8 consecutive points all lying below the centerline. Because the proportions of defects are decreasing, the manufacturing process is not deteriorating; it is improving.

3. LCL denotes the lower control limit. Because the value of −0.000025 is negative and the actual proportion of defects cannot be less than 0, we should replace that value by 0.

5. The process appears to be within statistical control.

7. Because there appears to be a pattern of a downward shift and there are at least 8 consecutive points all lying above the center-line, the process is not within statistical control.

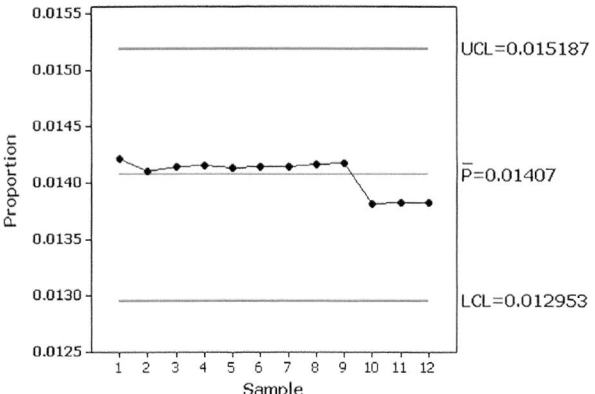

9. The process is out of control because there are points lying beyond the control limits and there are at least 8 points all lying below the centerline. The percentage of voters started to increase in recent years, and it should be much higher than any of the rates shown.

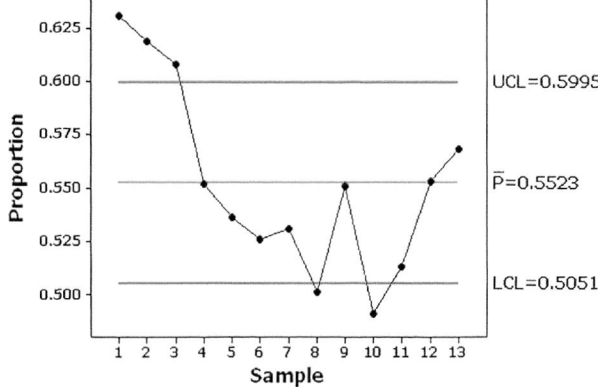

11. There is a pattern of a downward trend and there are at least 8 consecutive points all below the centerline, so the process does not appear to be within statistical control. Because the rate of defects is decreasing, the process is actually improving and we should investigate the cause of that improvement so that it can be continued.

13. Except for the vertical scale, the control chart is identical to the one obtained for Example 1.

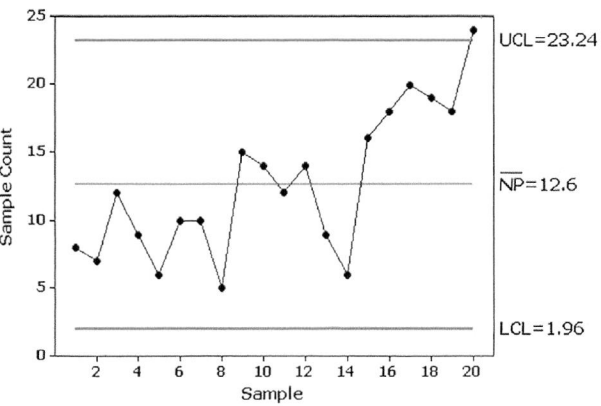

Chapter 14: Quick Quiz

1. Process data are data arranged according to some time sequence. They are measurements of a characteristic of goods or services that result from some combination of equipment, people, materials, methods, and conditions.

2. Random variation is due to chance, but assignable variation results from causes that can be identified, such as defective machinery or untrained employees.

3. There is a pattern, trend, or cycle that is obviously not random. There is a point lying outside of the region between the upper and lower control limits. There are at least 8 consecutive points all above or all below the centerline.

4. An R chart uses ranges to monitor variation, but an $\bar{x}$ chart uses sample means to monitor the center (mean) of a process.

5. No. The R chart has at least 8 consecutive points all lying below the centerline and there are points lying beyond the upper control limit. Also, there is a pattern showing that the ranges have jumped in value for the most recent samples.

6. $\bar{R} = 52.8$ ft. In general, a value of $\bar{R}$ is found by first finding the range for the values within each individual subgroup; the mean of those ranges is the value of $\bar{R}$.

7. No. The $\bar{x}$ chart has a point lying below the lower control limit.

8. $\bar{\bar{x}} = 3.95$ ft. In general, a value of $\bar{\bar{x}}$ is found by first finding the mean of the values within each individual subgroup; the mean of those subgroup means is the value of $\bar{\bar{x}}$.

9. A p chart is a control chart of the proportions of some attribute, such as defective items.

10. Because there is a downward trend, the process is not within statistical control, but the rate of defects is decreasing, so we should investigate and identify the cause of that trend so that it can be continued.

Chapter 14: Review Exercises

1. $\bar{\bar{x}} = 2781.71$, $\bar{R} = 1729.38$. R chart: LCL $= 0$, UCL $= 3465.67$. $\bar{x}$ chart: LCL $= 1946.42$, UCL $= 3617.00$.

2. The process variation is within statistical control.

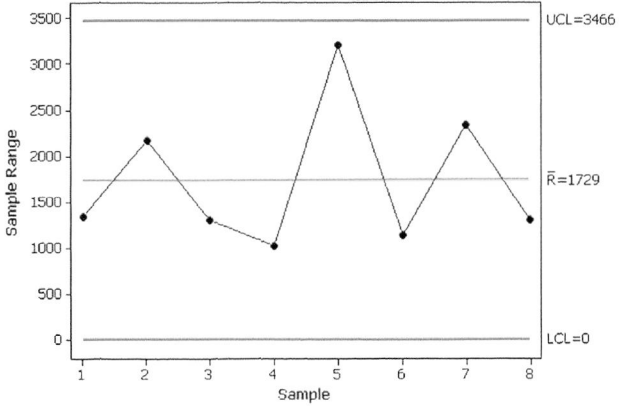

3. The process mean is within statistical control.

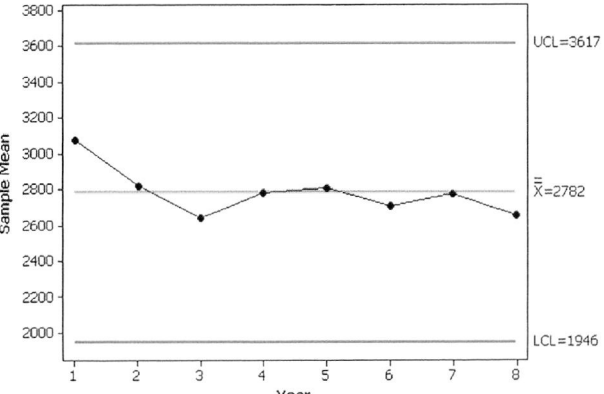

4. There does not appear to be a pattern suggesting that the process is not within statistical control. There is 1 point that appears to be exceptionally low. (The author's power company made an error in recording and reporting the energy consumption for that time period.)

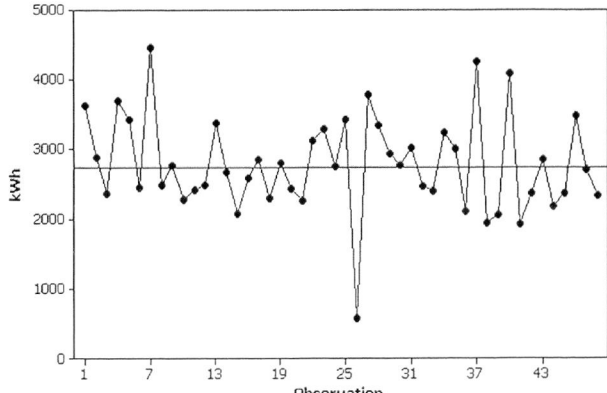

5. Because there are 8 consecutive points above the centerline and there is an upward trend, the process does not appear to be within statistical control.

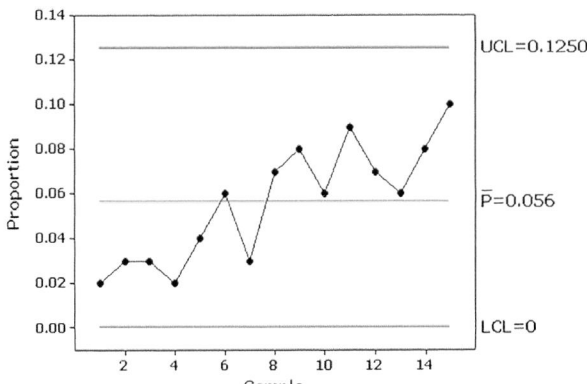

Chapter 14: Cumulative Review Exercises

1. $0.519 < p < 0.581$. Because all of the values in the confidence interval estimate of the population proportion are greater than 0.5, it does appear that the majority of adults believe that it is not appropriate to wear shorts at work.

2. a. 0.45   b. 0.0503   c. 0.950

3. $r = 0.820$. Critical values: $r = \pm 0.602$. P-value = 0.00202. There is sufficient evidence to support the claim that there is a linear correlation between yields from regular seed and kiln-dried seed. The purpose of the experiment was to determine whether there is a difference in yield from regular seed and kiln-dried seed (or whether kiln-dried seed produces a higher yield), but results from a test of correlation do not provide us with the information we need to address that issue.

4. $H_0: \mu_d = 0$. $H_1: \mu_d < 0$. Test statistic: $t = -1.532$. Critical value: $t = -1.812$ (assuming a 0.05 significance level). P-value > 0.05 (Tech: 0.0783). Fail to reject $H0$. There is not sufficient evidence to support the claim that kiln-dried seed is better in the sense that it produces a higher mean yield than regular seed. (The sign test can be used to arrive at the same conclusion; the test statistic is $x = 3$ and the critical value is 1. Also, the Wilcoxon signed-ranks test can be used; the test statistic is $T = 13.5$ and the critical value is 8.)

5. For the sample of yields from regular seed, $\bar{x} = 20.0$ and for the sample of yields from kiln-dried seed, $\bar{x} = 21.0$, so there does not appear to be a significant difference. For the sample of yields from regular seed, $s = 3.4$ and for the sample of yields from kiln-dried seed, $s = 4.1$, so there does not appear to be a significant difference.

6. There appears to be a pattern of an upward trend, so the process is not within statistical control.

7.

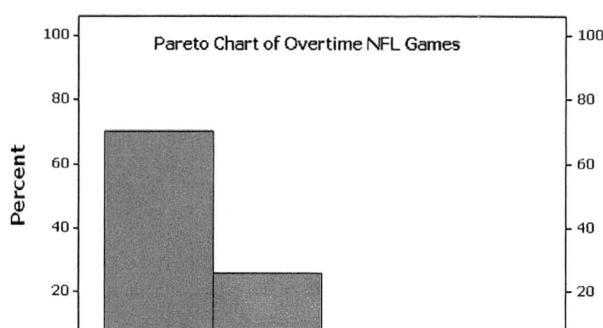

8. a. With 23.58% of males with head breadths greater than 17 cm, too many males would be excluded.

   b. 11.1 cm and 19.3 cm

9. With a voluntary response sample, the subjects decide themselves whether to be included. With a simple random sample, subjects are selected through some random process in such a way that all samples of the same size have the same chance of being selected. A simple random sample is generally better for use with statistical methods.

10. Sampling method (part c)

Credits

Photographs

Title page: top left, Stephen Bonk/Fotolia; top right, Blend Images/Alamy; bottom left, Domine/Shutterstock; bottom right, AISPIX by Image Source/Shutterstock. The pencil graphic shown on the title page and chapter openers is from Dinnyd/iStockphoto.

Chapter 1

Pages 2–3, Lightpost/Shutterstock
Page 5, Jacek Chabraszewski/Fotolia
Page 7, Sergey Kelin/Shutterstock
Page 8, Ryan McVay/Photodisc/Getty Images
Page 9, Jozsef Szasz-Fabian/Shuterstock
Page 10, William Perugini/Shutterstock
Page 16, Allstar Picture Library/Alamy
Page 17, Andriy Solovyov/Fotolia
Page 18, PVMil/Fotolia
Page 19, Olly/Shutterstock
Page 24, Andersen Ross/Stockbyte/Getty Images
Page 26, Karramba Production/Shutterstock
Page 27, Digital Vision/Getty Vision
Page 28, Tatyana Gladskih/Fotolia
Page 29, Yuri Arcurs/Shutterstock
Page 31, Mearicon/Shutterstock

Chapter 2

Pages 42–43, Guryanov Andrey Vladimirovich/Shutterstock
Page 44, Scott David Patterson/Shutterstock
Page 46, United States Mint Headquarters
Page 47, David Castillo Dominici/Shutterstock
Page 48, Lightpoet/Shutterstock
Page 50, Corbis
Page 61, Stockbyte/Getty Images
Page 62, North Wind Picture Archives/Alamy

Chapter 3

Pages 78–79, Stephen Bonk/Fotolia
Page 81, Anne Kitzman/Shutterstock
Page 82, Lightpoet/Fotolia
Page 96, Fabian Petzold/Fotolia
Page 97, Yuri Arcurs/Fotolia

Page 98, Sergej Razvodovskij/Shutterstock
Page 99, Scott Martin/AP Images
Page 101, Photodisc/Getty Images
Page 113, Andrew Wakeford/Photodisc/Getty Images
Page 114, Jozsef Szasz-Fabian/Shutterstock
Page 115, Shutterstock
Page 118, Shutterstock

Chapter 4

Pages 132–133, Kenon/Shutterstock
Page 135, Studiovespa/Fotolia
Page 136, (a) Pakhnyushchyy/Fotolia; (b) Thumb/Shutterstock; (c) Andrejs Zavadskis/Shutterstock
Page 137, Binkski/Shutterstock
Page 138, Fotolia
Page 139, Shutterstock
Page 140, Olga Lyubkina/Shutterstock
Page 141, Serg Shalimoff/Shutterstock
Page 142, Oleg Svyatoslavsky/Life File/Getty Images
Page 143, S. Meltzer/PhotoLink/Getty Images
Page 144, Photodisc/Getty Images
Page 149, Michael Pettigrew/Fotolia
Page 150, Everett Collection
Page 158, Dejan Milinkovic/Shutterstock
Page 159, L. Barnwell/Shutterstock
Page 160, Dorling Kindersley, Ltd
Page 161, Mayonaise/Fotolia
Page 162, Chepe Nicoli/Shutterstock
Page 169, Corbis
Page 171, Scott Rothstein/Shutterstock
Page 176, Don Farrall/PhotoDisc/Getty Images
Page 177, Ene/Shutterstock
Page 178, Don Farrall/PhotoDisc/Getty Images

Chapter 5

Pages 194–195, Serhiy Kobyakov/Fotolia
Page 200, Ene/Shutterstock
Page 211, Barbara Penoyar/Photodisc/Getty Images

Chapter 6

Pages 242–243, Andres Rodriguez/Fotolia
Page 273, Jacob Hamblin/Shutterstock

Page 289, Image Source/Getty Images
Page 291, Chieh Cheng/iStockphoto

Chapter 7

Pages 322–323, Lucky Business/Shutterstock
Page 326, Ryan McVay/Digital Vision/Getty Images
Page 327, Jason Stitt/Fotolia
Page 345, Paul Hakimata/Alamy
Page 346, Lebrecht/The Image Works
Page 347, Eric Isselée/Fotolia.
Page 348, Anna Kaminska/Shutterstock
Page 349, Gary Blakeley/Shutterstock
Page 354, Jürgen Fälchle/Fotolia
Page 363, Yuri Arcurs/Fotolia

Chapter 8

Pages 380–381, Blend Images/Alamy
Page 383, Bruce Rolff/Shutterstock
Page 392, Photodisc/Getty Images
Page 393, Charlie Hutton/Shutterstock
Page 394, Chad McDermott/Shutterstock
Page 401, Digital Vision/Photodisc/Getty Images
Page 403, Pete Saloutos/Shutterstock
Page 405, Photodisc/Getty Images
Page 416, Ken Hurst/Fotolia
Page 426, Pearson Education, Inc
Page 427, Mark Burnett/Alamy

Chapter 9

Pages 440–441, Helder Almeida/Shutterstock
Page 444, S. Meltzer/Photodisc/Getty Images
Page 445, Rafa Irusta/Fotolia
Page 446, Topham/The Image Works
Page 447, Beboy/Fotolia
Page 454, Keith Brofsky/Stockbyte/Getty Images
Page 457, James Steidl/Shutterstock
Page 458, AVAVA/Fotolia
Page 461, JupiterImages/Arts Corporation/Brand X
Page 469, Milos Luzanin/Shutterstock
Page 470, Barbara Penoyar/Photodisc/Getty Images
Page 471, Monkey Business Images/Shutterstock

Credits

Chapter 10

Pages 494–495, Domine/Shutterstock
Page 497, Juan Fuertes/Shutterstock
Page 500, Anneka/Shutterstock
Page 501, Alexander Raths/Fotolia
Page 517, NetPics/Alamy
Page 520, Ryan McVay/Photodisc/Getty
  Images
Page 521, Digital Vision/Getty Images
Page 533, Photodisc/Getty Images
Page 542, Comstock Images/JupiterImages
Page 543, Iofoto/Fotolia
Page 544, Stephen Coburn/Shutterstock
Page 545, Nick Koudis/Photodisc/Getty
  Images
Page 546, Digital Vision/Getty Images

Chapter 11

Pages 564–565, Haveseen/Fotolia
Page 570, Shutterstock
Page 571, Chad McDermott/Shutterstock
Page 572, Serhiy Shullye/Shutterstock
Page 579, Jack Star/PhotoLink/Photodisc/
  Getty Images

Chapter 13

Pages 634–635, Tyler Olson/Shutterstock
Page 652, Morgan Lane Photography/
  Shutterstock
Page 669, Michael Matisse/Photodisc/
  Getty Images
Page 675, Synto/Fotolia
Page 678, Rubberball/Getty Images

Chapter 14

Pages 690–691, Electrochris/Fotolia
Page 692, Icholakov/Fotolia
Page 693, Dave Willman/Fotolia
Page 696, Nataliya Hora/Fotolia
Page 697, NASA Headquarters
Page 698, Moreno Soppelsa/Fotolia
Page 699, AGE Fotostock/SuperStock
Page 702, Leonid Smirnov/Fotolia
Page 704, Lisa F. Young/Fotolia

Chapter 15

Page 715, Umberto Shtanzman/
  Shutterstock

Technology

Portions of information contained in this publication/book are printed with permission of Minitab Inc. All such material remains the exclusive property and copyright of Minitab Inc. All rights reserved.

All images showing usage of TI83/84 Plus calculator are copyright © Texas Instruments Inc. Reproduced by permission.

Charts generated using SPSS software have been reprinted courtesy of International Business Machines Corporation, © SPSS, Inc., and IBM Company. The figures shown in this product were created using PASW Statistics Student Version 18.0.

Charts created using JMP® software (in this product, Student Edition 8) are copyright © SAS Institute Inc. SAS and all other SAS Institute Inc. product or service names are registered trademarks or trademarks of SAS Institute Inc., Cary, NC, USA.

StatCrunch screenshots appearing in this book are copyright 2007–2012 by Integrated Analytics LLC. Reproduced by permission of Pearson Education.

Statdisk software developed by Marc Triola, MD, and Mario Triola. Statdisk figures shown in this product were created using versions 11 and 12.

MICROSOFT® WINDOWS®, and MICROSOFT OFFICE® ARE REGISTERED TRADEMARKS OF THE MICROSOFT CORPORATION IN THE U.S.A. AND OTHER COUNTRIES. THIS BOOK IS NOT SPONSORED OR ENDORSED BY OR AFFILIATED WITH THE MICROSOFT CORPORATION. Examples in this text have been taken from Microsoft Excel 2010, Professional Office version. The concepts and theory being taught are applicable in other, similar versions of software.

MICROSOFT AND/OR ITS RESPECTIVE SUPPLIERS MAKE NO REPRESENTATIONS ABOUT THE SUITABILITY OF THE INFORMATION CONTAINED IN THE DOCUMENTS AND RELATED GRAPHICS PUBLISHED AS PART OF THE SERVICES FOR ANY PURPOSE. ALL SUCH DOCUMENTS AND RELATED GRAPHICS ARE PROVIDED "AS IS" WITHOUT WARRANTY OF ANY KIND. MICROSOFT AND/OR ITS RESPECTIVE SUPPLIERS HEREBY DISCLAIM ALL WARRANTIES AND CONDITIONS WITH REGARD TO THIS INFORMATION, INCLUDING ALL WARRANTIES AND CONDITIONS OF MERCHANTABILITY, WHETHER EXPRESS, IMPLIED OR STATUTORY, FITNESS FOR A PARTICULAR PURPOSE, TITLE AND NON-INFRINGEMENT. IN NO EVENT SHALL MICROSOFT AND/OR ITS RESPECTIVE SUPPLIERS BE LIABLE FOR ANY SPECIAL, INDIRECT OR CONSEQUENTIAL DAMAGES OR ANY DAMAGES WHATSOEVER RESULTING FROM LOSS OF USE, DATA OR PROFITS, WHETHER IN AN ACTION OF CONTRACT, NEGLIGENCE OR OTHER TORTIOUS ACTION, ARISING OUT OF OR IN CONNECTION WITH THE USE OR PERFORMANCE OF INFORMATION AVAILABLE FROM THE SERVICES. THE DOCUMENTS AND RELATED GRAPHICS CONTAINED HEREIN COULD INCLUDE TECHNICAL INACCURACIES OR TYPOGRAPHICAL ERRORS. CHANGES ARE PERIODICALLY ADDED TO THE INFORMATION HEREIN. MICROSOFT AND/OR ITS RESPECTIVE SUPPLIERS MAY MAKE IMPROVEMENTS AND/OR CHANGES IN THE PRODUCT(S) AND/OR THE PROGRAM(S) DESCRIBED HEREIN AT ANY TIME. PARTIAL SCREEN SHOTS MAY BE VIEWED IN FULL WITHIN THE SOFTWARE VERSION SPECIFIED.

Index

The following is taken from
Statistics: The Art and Science of Learning from Data
Third Edition
by Alan Agresti and Christine Franklin

11 Analyzing the Association Between Categorical Variables

Example 1

Happiness

Picture the Scenario

What contributes to your overall happiness? Is it love? Your health? Your friendships? The amount of money you make?

To investigate which variables are associated with happiness, we can use data from the General Social Survey (GSS). In each survey, the GSS asks, "Taken all together, would you say that you are very happy, pretty happy, or not too happy?" Table 11.1 uses the 2008 survey to cross-tabulate happiness with family income, here measured as the response to the question, "Compared with American families in general, would you say that your family income is below average, average, or above average?"

Table 11.1 Happiness and Family Income, from 2008 General Social Survey

	Happiness			
Income	Not Too Happy	Pretty Happy	Very Happy	Total
Above average	26	233	164	423
Average	117	473	293	883
Below average	172	383	132	687

Questions to Explore

- How can you determine if there is an association between happiness and family income in the population of all adult Americans?

- If there is an association, what is its nature? For example, do people with above-average family income tend to be happier than people with below-average family income?

- Can you think of a variable that might have a stronger association with happiness than family income?

Thinking Ahead

Both variables in Table 11.1 are categorical. The focus of this chapter is learning how to describe associations between categorical variables. To do this, we'll continue to apply the basic tools of statistical inference. These inferential methods help us answer questions such as, "Do people with higher family incomes tend to be happier?" and "Are married people happier than unmarried people?" We'll analyze Table 11.1 in Examples 3 and 4 and other data on happiness in Example 8 and in the exercises.

Recall

In the Chapter 3 introduction, we stated that two variables have an **association** if a particular value for one variable is more likely to occur with certain values of the other variable—for example, if being very happy is more likely to happen if a person has an above average income. Section 3.1 introduced the analysis of association for categorical variables. ◀

Association Between Variables

Let's recap where we are at this stage of our study. Chapter 7 introduced the fundamental concept of a *sampling distribution.* Chapter 8 showed how the sampling distribution is the basis of estimation, using *confidence intervals,* and Chapter 9 showed how it is the basis of *significance testing.* Those chapters focused on inference for a single proportion or a single mean.

Chapter 10 introduced methods for two variables—a response variable and a binary explanatory variable for which the two categories define two groups to compare (such as females and males). For a binary response variable, we compared two proportions, and for a quantitative response variable, we compared two means. Other methods apply when (a) both variables are quantitative or (b) both variables are categorical with possibly several categories. We'll study these cases in this chapter and in Chapter 12.

This chapter presents methods for investigating associations between two categorical variables. We'll refine what we mean by an association or lack of association, in the context of contingency tables such as Table 11.1 in Example 1.

11.1 Independence and Dependence (Association)

First, let's identify the response variable and the explanatory variable. In Table 11.1 it's more natural to study how happiness depends on income than how income depends on happiness. We'll treat happiness as the response variable and income as the explanatory variable.

Comparing Percentages

Table 11.1 is easier to digest if we convert the frequencies to percentages for the response categories. Within each category of income, Table 11.2 shows the percentages for the three categories of happiness. For example, of the 423 subjects who reported their family income as above average, 164 identified themselves as very happy. This is a proportion of $164/423 = 0.388$ or 39%. By contrast, 132 out of the 687 below-average income subjects said they were very happy, a percentage of 19%. The row totals in Table 11.1 are the basis of these percentage calculations. Within each row, the percentages sum to 100%.

Table 11.2 Conditional Percentages for Happiness Categories, Given Each Category of Family Income

The percentages are computed by dividing the counts in Table 11.1 by their row totals, and then multiplying by 100.

	Happiness			
Income	Not Too Happy	Pretty Happy	Very Happy	Total
Above average	6%	55%	39%	423 (100%)
Average	13%	54%	33%	883 (100%)
Below average	25%	56%	19%	687 (100%)

Recall

Section 3.1 introduced **conditional proportions,** which are proportions for the categories of a categorical response variable that are calculated **conditional** upon (i.e., "given") the value of another variable. ◄

The three percentages in a particular row are called **conditional percentages**. They refer to a sample data distribution of happiness, *conditional* on the category for family income. They form the **conditional distribution** for happiness, given a particular income level. For those who reported above-average family income, the conditional distribution of happiness is the set of percentages (6%, 55%, 39%) for the responses (not too happy, pretty happy, very happy). The proportions (0.06, 0.55, 0.39) are the estimated **conditional probabilities** of happiness, given above-average family income. For instance, given that a subject reported above-average family income, the estimated probability of being very happy is 0.39.

Let's compare the happiness percentages for the subjects who reported above-average income to those who reported below-average income. From Table 11.2, the higher-income subjects were more likely to be very happy (39% versus 19%) and less likely to be not too happy (6% versus 25%). Figure 11.1 uses a bar graph to portray the three conditional distributions.

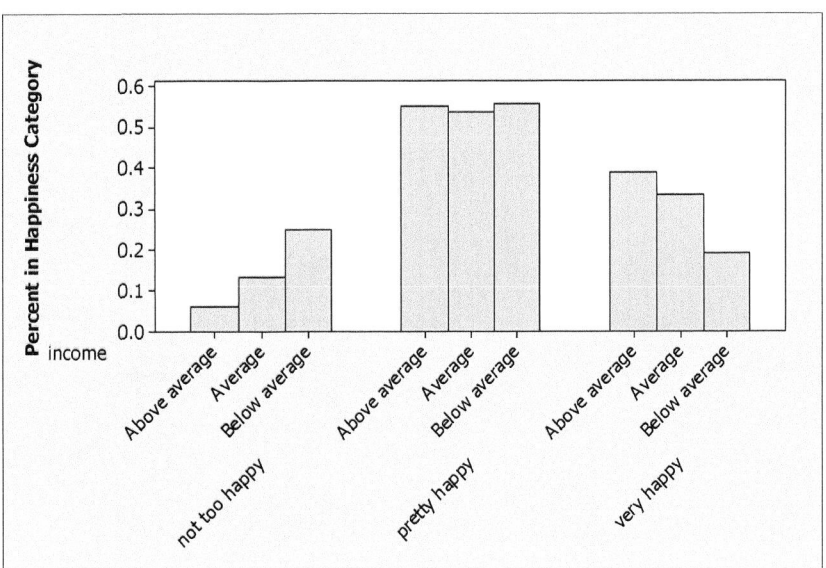

▲ **Figure 11.1** MINITAB Bar Graph of Conditional Distributions of Happiness, Given Income, from Table 11.2. For each happiness category, you can compare the three categories of income on the percent in that happiness category. Question Based on this graph, how would you say that happiness depends on income?

We'll use the following guidelines when constructing tables with conditional distributions:

■ Make the response variable the column variable. The response categories are shown across the top of the table.

■ Compute conditional proportions for the response variable within each row by dividing each cell frequency by the row total. Those proportions multiplied by 100 are the conditional percentages.

■ Include the total sample sizes on which the percentages are based. That way, readers who want to can reconstruct the cell counts.

Independence Versus Dependence (Association)

Table 11.2 shows conditional distributions for a sample. We'll use sample conditional distributions to make inferences about the corresponding population conditional distributions.

For instance, to investigate how happiness compares for females and males, we'd make inferences about the population conditional distributions of happiness for females and for males. Suppose that those population distributions are as shown in Table 11.3. (In fact, the percentages in Table 11.3 are consistent with data from the GSS. See Exercise 11.4.) We see that the percentage classified as very happy is the same for females and males, 30%. Similarly, the percentage classified as pretty happy (54%) and the percentage classified as not too happy (16%) is the same for females and for males. The probability that a person is classified in a particular happiness category is the same for females and males. The categorical variables happiness and gender are then said to be **independent.**

Table 11.3 Population Conditional Distributions Showing Independence

The conditional distribution of happiness is the same for each gender, namely (16%, 54%, 30%).

	Happiness			
Gender	**Not Too Happy**	**Pretty Happy**	**Very Happy**	**Total**
Female	16%	54%	30%	100%
Male	16%	54%	30%	100%
Overall	16%	54%	30%	100%

Source: Data from CSM, UC Berkeley.

In Words

Happiness and gender are **independent** if (as in Table 11.3) the probability of a particular response on happiness is the same for females and males.

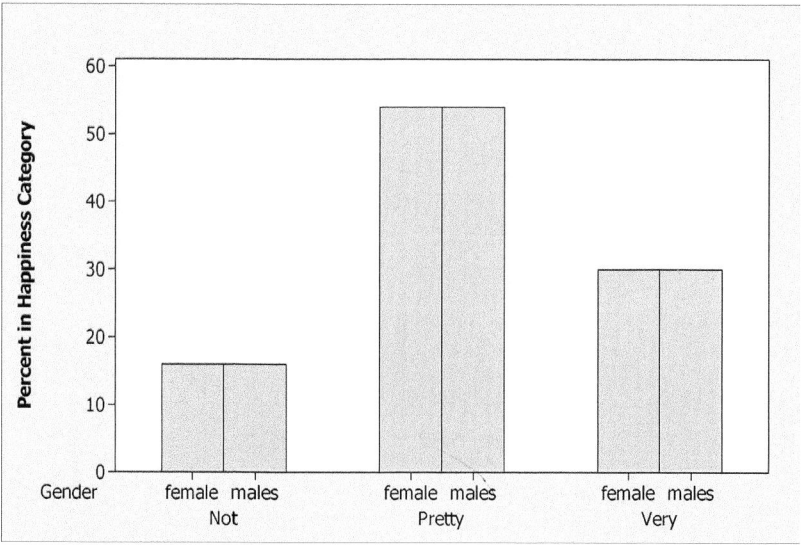

▲ **Figure 11.2** MINITAB Output of Population Conditional Distributions Showing Independence. Question What feature of the bar graph reflects the independence?

Independence and Dependence (Association)

Two categorical variables are **independent** if the population conditional distributions for one of them are identical at each category of the other. The variables are **dependent** (or **associated**) if the conditional distributions are not identical.

Recall

Section 5.3 in Chapter 5 defined A and B to be **independent events** if

$P(A \mid B) = P(A)$.

Chapter 10 used **independent samples** to mean that observations in one sample are independent of those in the other sample. ◄

For two variables to be independent, the population percentage in any category of one variable is the same for all categories of the other variable, as in Table 11.3. Figure 11.2 portrays this for Table 11.3.

This definition extends independence of **events** to independence of **variables.** Recall that two *events* A and B are independent if P(A) is the same as the conditional probability of A, given B, denoted by $P(A \mid B)$. When two *variables* are independent, any event about one variable is independent of any event about the other variable. In Table 11.3, $P(A \mid B) = P(A)$ if A is an event about happiness and B is an event about gender. For example if A = very happy and B = female, then $P(A \mid B) = 0.30$. Notice in Table 11.3, this also equals P(A).

Independence and dependence

Example 2

Belief in Life After Death and Race

Picture the Scenario

Table 11.4 cross-tabulates belief in life after death with race, using data from the 2008 GSS. The table also shows sample conditional distributions for life after death, given race, and the overall percentages for the life after death categories.

Table 11.4 Sample Conditional Distributions for Belief in Life After Death, Given Race

Race	Postlife		
	Yes	No	Total
White	1132 (82.1%)	247 (17.9%)	1379 (100%)
Black	203 (82.2%)	44 (17.8%)	247 (100%)
Other	120 (74.5%)	41 (25.5%)	161 (100%)
Overall	1455 (81.4%)	332 (18.6%)	1787 (100%)

Source: Data from CSM, UC Berkeley.

Question to Explore

Are race and belief in life after death independent or dependent?

Think It Through

The conditional distributions in Table 11.4 are similar but not exactly identical. So it is tempting to conclude that the variables are dependent. For example, if A = yes for belief in life after death, we estimate P(A | white) = 1132/1379 = 0.821, P(A | black) = 0.822, P(A | other) = 0.745, whereas we estimate that P(A) = 1455/1787 = 0.814. However, the definition of independence between variables refers to the *population*. Since Table 11.4 refers to a *sample* rather than a population, it provides evidence but does not definitively tell us whether these variables are independent or dependent.

Even if the variables *were* independent, we would not expect the *sample* conditional distributions to be identical. Because of sampling variability, each sample percentage typically differs somewhat from the true population percentage. We would expect to observe *some* differences between sample conditional distributions such as we see in Table 11.4 even if *no* differences exist in the population.

Insight

If the observations in Table 11.4 were the entire population, the variables would be dependent. But the association would not necessarily be practically important, because the percentages are similar from one category to another of race. The next section presents a significance test of the hypothesis that the variables are independent.

Try Exercise 11.2

11.1   Practicing the Basics

11.1 Gender gap in politics?   In the United States, is there a gender gap in political beliefs? That is, do women and men tend to differ in their political thinking and voting behavior? The table taken from the 2008 GSS relates gender and political party identification. Subjects indicated whether they identified more strongly with the Democratic or Republican party or as Independents.

	Political Party Identification			
Gender	**Democrat**	**Independent**	**Republican**	**Total**
Female	422	381	273	1076
Male	299	365	232	896

Source: Data from CSM, UC Berkeley.

a. Identify the response variable and the explanatory variable.
b. Construct a table that shows the conditional distributions of the response variable. Interpret.
c. Give a hypothetical example of population conditional distributions for which these variables would be independent.
d. Sketch bar graphs to portray the distributions in part b and in part c.

11.2 Beliefs of college freshmen   Every year, a large-scale poll of college freshmen conducted by the Higher Education Research Institute at UCLA asks their opinions about a variety of issues. In 2004, although women were more likely to rate their time management skills as "above average," they were also twice as likely as men to indicate that they frequently feel overwhelmed by all they have to do (36.4% versus 16.3%).

a. If results for the population of college freshmen were similar to these, would gender and feelings of being overwhelmed be independent or dependent?
b. Give an example of hypothetical population percentages for which these variables would be independent.

11.3 UGA enrollment statistics   Data posted at the University of Georgia Web site indicated that of all female students in 2011, 78% were undergraduates, and of male students in 2011, 16% were graduate students. Let x denote gender of student and y denote type of student.

a. Which conditional distributions do these statistics refer to, those of y at given categories of x, or those of x at given categories of y? Set up a table with type of student as columns and gender of student as rows, showing the two conditional distributions.
b. Are x and y independent or dependent? Explain. (*Hint:* These results refer to the population.)

11.4 Happiness and gender   The contingency table shown relates happiness and gender for the 2008 GSS.

	Happiness			
Gender	Not Too Happy	Pretty Happy	Very Happy	Total
Female	174	587	328	1089
Male	142	513	271	926

Source: Data from CSM, UC Berkeley.

a. Identify the response variable and the explanatory variable.

b. Construct a table or graph showing the conditional distributions. Interpret.

c. Give an example of population conditional distributions that would seem to be consistent with this sample and for which happiness and gender would be independent.

11.5 Marital happiness and income   In the GSS, subjects who were married were asked about the happiness of their marriage, the variable coded as HAPMAR.

a. Go to the GSS Web site sda.berkeley.edu/GSS/ and construct a contingency table for 2008 relating HAPMAR (the column variable) to family income as measured in this section, by entering FINRELA (r: 1-2; 3; 4-5) as the row variable and YEAR(2008) in the selection filter, selecting No Weight from the weight menu.

b. Construct a table or graph that shows the conditional distributions of marital happiness, given family income. How would you describe the association?

c. Compare the conditional distributions to those in Table 11.2. For a given family income, what tends to be higher, general happiness or marital happiness for those who are married? Explain.

11.6 What is independent of happiness?   Which one of the following variables would you think most likely to be independent of happiness: belief in an afterlife, family income, quality of health, region of the country in which you live, satisfaction with job? Explain the basis of your reasoning.

11.7 Sample evidence about independence   Refer to the previous exercise. Go to the GSS Web site and construct a table relating happiness (HAPPY) to the variable you chose (AFTERLIF, FINRELA, HEALTH, REGION, or JOBSAT). Inspect the conditional distributions and indicate whether independence seems plausible, with the sample conditional distributions all being quite similar.

11.2 Testing Categorical Variables for Independence

How can we judge whether two categorical variables are independent or dependent? The definition of independence refers to the *population*. Could the observed *sample* association be due to sampling variation? Or would the observed results be unusual if the variables were truly independent?

A significance test can answer these questions. The hypotheses for the test are

H_0: The two variables are independent.

H_a: The two variables are dependent (associated).

The test assumes randomization and a large sample size. The test compares the cell counts in the contingency table with counts we would expect to see if the null hypothesis of independence were true.

Expected Cell Counts If the Variables Are Independent

The count in any particular cell is a random variable: Different samples have different values for the count. The mean of its distribution is called an **expected cell count.** This is found under the presumption that H_0 is true. That is, the expected cell counts are values that satisfy the null hypothesis of independence.

Table 11.5 shows the observed cell counts from Table 11.1, with the expected cell counts below them. How do we find the expected cell counts? Recall that when two variables are independent, any event about one variable is independent of any event about the other variable. Consider the events A = not too happy and B = above-average income. From the Total column and Total row (table margins) of Table 11.5 we estimate P(A) by 315/1993 and P(B) by 423/1993. The event

A and B (not too happy *and* above-average income) corresponds to the first cell in the table, with cell count of 26. Under the presumption of independence,

$$P(A \text{ and } B) = P(A) \times P(B),$$

which we estimate by $(315/1993)(423/1993)$. For the $n = 1993$ subjects, the *number* of them we expect in this cell is 1993 times the cell's probability. So we estimate the **expected cell count** (presuming H_0 to be true) by

$$1993\left(\frac{315}{1993}\right)\left(\frac{423}{1993}\right) = \frac{315 \times 423}{1993} = 66.86.$$

If happiness were independent of income, we would expect about 67 subjects in that first cell. Since the observed cell count is 26, fewer people had above-average income and were not too happy than we would expect if the variables were independent.

Table 11.5 Happiness by Family Income, Showing Observed and Expected Cell Counts
We use the highlighted totals to get the expected count of $66.86 = (315 \times 423)/1993$ in the first cell.

Income	Happiness			Total
	Not Too Happy	**Pretty Happy**	**Very Happy**	
Above average	26	233	164	423
	66.86	231.13	125.01	
Average	117	473	293	883
	139.56	482.48	260.96	
Below average	172	383	132	687
	108.58	375.39	203.03	
Total	315 (15.8%)	1089 (54.6%)	589 (29.6%)	1993 (100%)

This discussion illustrates the general rule for calculating expected cell counts.

Expected Cell Count

For a particular cell, the **expected cell count** equals

$$\text{Expected cell count} = \frac{(\text{Row total}) \times (\text{Column total})}{\text{Total sample size}}.$$

For instance, the first cell in Table 11.5 has expected cell count = $(315 \times 423)/1993 = 66.86$, the product of the row total (423) for that cell by the column total (315) for that cell, divided by the overall sample size (1993).

Let's see more about why this rule makes sense. For A = not too happy we estimated $P(A)$ by $315/1993 = 0.158$. If the variables were independent, we would expect this probability to be the same if we condition on any event about income. For instance, for B = above-average income, we expect $P(A \mid B) = P(A)$. Thus, 15.8% of the 423 who report above average income should be classified in the not too happy category. The expected cell count is then $0.158(423) = (315/1993)(423) = 0.6686$. But this is the column total of 315 times the row total of 423 divided by the overall sample size of 1993.

Table 11.5 shows that for the overall sample, the percentages in the three happiness categories are (15.8%, 54.6%, 29.6%). You can check that the expected cell counts have these percentages in each of the three rows. For instance, for the first cell in row 1, $66.86/423 = 0.158$. In fact, the expected frequencies are values that have the same row and column totals as the observed counts, but for which the conditional distributions are identical.

Recall

From Section 5.2, two events A and B can also be defined as **independent** if

$$P(A \text{ and } B) = P(A) \times P(B). \blacktriangleleft$$

Chi-Squared Test Statistic

The test statistic for the test of independence summarizes how close the observed cell counts fall to the expected cell counts. Symbolized by X^2, it is called the **chi-squared statistic,** taking the name of its (approximate) sampling distribution. It is the oldest test statistic in use today. Introduced by the British statistician Karl Pearson in 1900, it is sometimes also called Pearson's chi-squared statistic.

Chi-Squared Statistic

The **chi-squared statistic** summarizes how far the observed cell counts in a contingency table fall from the expected cell counts for a null hypothesis. Its formula is

$$X^2 = \Sum \frac{(\text{observed count} - \text{expected count})^2}{\text{expected count}}.$$

For each cell, square the difference between the observed count and expected count, and then divide that square by the expected count. After calculating this term for every cell, sum the terms to find X^2.

When H_0: independence is true, the observed and expected cell counts tend to be close for each cell. Then X^2 has a relatively small value. If H_0 is false, at least some observed counts and expected counts tend to be far apart. For a cell where this happens, its value of [(observed count − expected count)^2/expected count] tends to be large. Then, X^2 has a relatively large value.

Example 3

Chi-squared statistic

Happiness and Family Income

Picture the Scenario

Table 11.5 showed the observed and expected cell counts for the data on family income and happiness. Table 11.6 shows MINITAB output for the chi-squared test. The margin on the next page shows screen shots from the TI-83+/84. The matrix [B] referred to with the word **Expected** in the second screen shot contains the expected cell counts.

Table 11.6 Chi-Squared Test of Independence of Happiness and Family Income

This table shows how MINITAB reports, for each cell, the observed and expected cell counts and the contribution [(observed − expected)^2/expected] to X^2, as well as the overall X^2 value and its P-value for testing H_0: independence.

```
Rows: income        Columns: happy
                not    pretty      very
above            26       233       164    423   ←   Observed cell count

              66.86    231.13    125.01           ←   Expected cell count

             24.968     0.015    12.160           ←   Contribution to X²
average         117       473       293    883
             139.56    482.48    260.96
              3.647     0.186     3.935
below           172       383       132    687
             108.58    375.39    203.03
             37.039     0.154    24.851
Total           315      1089       589   1993
Cell contents:            Count
                          Expected count
                          Contribution to Chi-square
Pearson Chi-Square = 106.955, DF = 4, P-Value = 0.000
```

```
MATRIX[A] 3█×3
[ 26.000  233.00  164.00 ]
[ 117.00  473.00  293.00 ]
[ 172.00  383.00  132.00 ]
```

```
X²-Test
 Observed:[A]
 Expected:[B]
 Calculate Draw
```

```
X²-Test
 X²=106.9553
 P=3.2447ᴇ-22
 df=4.0000
```

```
X²-Test
 X²=106.9553
 P=3.2447ᴇ-22
 df=4.0000
```

TI-83+/84 output

▶ Activity 1

When using software, try to re-create a table like Table 11.6. First create a data file with nine rows, such as shown below, and then choose an option to create a contingency table and find appropriate statistics.

Income	Happy	Count
above	not	26
above	pretty	233
above	very	164
average	not	117
average	pretty	473
average	very	293
below	not	172
below	pretty	383
below	very	132

Questions to Explore

a. State the null and alternative hypotheses for this test.

b. Report the X^2 statistic and explain how it was calculated.

Think It Through

a. The hypotheses for the chi-squared test are

H_0: Happiness and family income are independent.

H_a: Happiness and family income are dependent (associated).

The alternative hypothesis is that there's an association between happiness and family income.

b. Finding X^2 involves a fair amount of computation, and it's best to let software do the work for us. Beneath the observed and expected cell counts in a cell, MINITAB reports the contribution of that cell to the X^2 statistic. For the first cell (above average income and not too happy), for instance,

(observed count − expected count)^2 /expected count =
$(26 − 66.86)^2$ /66.86 = 25.0.

For all nine cells,

$$X^2 = \frac{(26 - 66.86)^2}{66.86} + \frac{(233 - 231.13)^2}{231.13} +$$
$$\frac{(164 - 125.01)^2}{125.01} + \frac{(117 - 139.56)^2}{139.56} + \frac{(473 - 482.48)^2}{482.48}$$
$$+ \frac{(293 - 260.96)^2}{260.96} + \frac{(172 - 108.56)^2}{108.56} + \frac{(383 - 375.39)^2}{375.39}$$
$$+ \frac{(132 - 203.03)^2}{203.03}$$

$$= 24.968 + 0.015 + 12.160 + 3.647 + 0.186 + 3.935 + 37.039$$
$$+ 0.154 + 24.851 = 106.955.$$

Insight

Table 11.6 has some large differences between observed and expected cell counts, so X^2 is large. The larger the X^2 value, the greater the evidence against H_0: independence and in support of the alternative hypothesis that happiness and income are associated. We next learn how to interpret the magnitude of the X^2 test statistic, so we know what is small and what is large and how to find the P-value.

Try Exercise 11.11

Chi-Squared Distribution

To find the P-value for the X^2 test statistic, we use the sampling distribution of the X^2 statistic. For large sample sizes, this sampling distribution is well approximated by the **chi-squared probability distribution.** Figure 11.3 shows several chi-squared distributions.

The main properties of the chi-squared distribution are as follows:

■ **Always positive.** The chi-squared distribution falls on the positive part of the real number line. The X^2 test statistic cannot be negative since it sums squared

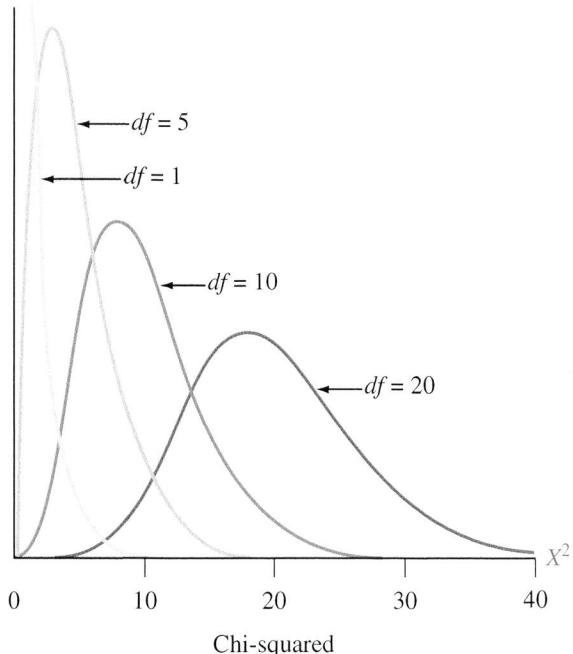

▲ **Figure 11.3** The Chi-Squared Distribution. The curve has larger mean and standard deviation as the degrees of freedom increase. Question Why can't the chi-squared statistic be negative?

differences divided by positive expected frequencies. The minimum possible value, $X^2 = 0$, would occur if observed count = expected count in each cell.

■ **Degrees of freedom from row and column.** The precise shape of the distribution depends on the **degrees of freedom** (df). For testing independence in a table with r rows and c columns (called an $r \times c$ table), the formula for the degrees of freedom is

$$df = (r - 1) \times (c - 1).$$

For example, Table 11.5 has $r = 3$ and $c = 3$, so $df = (3 - 1) \times (3 - 1) = 2 \times 2 = 4$. We'll see the reason behind this formula later in the section.

■ **Mean equals *df*.** The mean of the distribution equals the df value. Since $df = (r - 1) \times (c - 1)$, larger numbers of rows and columns produce larger df values. Since larger tables have more terms in the summation for the X^2 statistic, the X^2 values also tend to be larger.

■ **As *df* increases distribution goes to bell shaped.** The chi-squared distribution is skewed to the right. As df increases, the skew lessens and the chi-squared curve becomes more bell-shaped.

■ **Large chi-square evidence against independence.** The larger the X^2 value, the greater the evidence against H_0: independence. Thus, the P-value equals the right-tail probability. It measures the probability that the X^2 statistic for a random sample would be larger than the observed value, if the variables are truly independent. Figure 11.4 depicts the P-value.

Table C at the back of the text lists values from the chi-squared distribution for various right-tail probabilities. These are X^2 test statistic values that have P-values equal to those probabilities. Table 11.7 shows an excerpt from Table C for small df values. For example, a 3×3 table has $df = 4$, for which Table 11.7 reports that an X^2 value of 9.49 has P-value = 0.05. In practice, software provides the P-value.

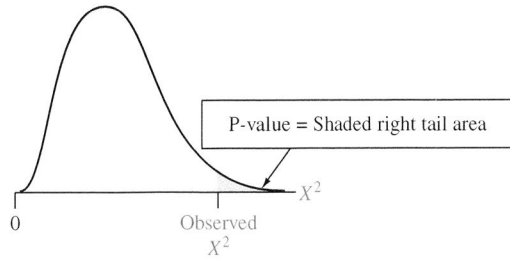

▲ **Figure 11.4** The P-value for the Chi-Squared Test of Independence. This is the right-tail probability, above the observed value of the X^2 test statistic. Question Why do we not also use the left tail in finding the P-value?

Table 11.7 Rows of Table C Displaying Chi-Squared Values

The values have right-tail probabilities between 0.250 and 0.001. For a table with $r = 3$ rows and $c = 3$ columns, $df = (r - 1) \times (c - 1) = 4$, and 9.49 is the chi-squared value with a right-tail probability of 0.05.

	Right-Tail Probability						
df	**.250**	**.100**	**.050**	**.025**	**.010**	**.005**	**.001**
1	1.32	2.71	3.84	5.02	6.63	7.88	10.83
2	2.77	4.61	5.99	7.38	9.21	10.60	13.82
3	4.11	6.25	7.81	9.35	11.34	12.84	16.27
4	5.39	7.78	9.49	11.14	13.28	14.86	18.47

Chi-squared distribution

Example 4

Happiness and Income

Picture the Scenario

For testing the null hypothesis of independence of happiness and family income, Table 11.6 in Example 3 reported a test statistic value of $X^2 = 106.955$.

Questions to Explore

a. What is the P-value for the chi-squared test of independence for these data?

b. State your decision for a significance level of 0.05 and interpret in context.

Think It Through

a. Since the table has $r = 3$ rows and $c = 3$ columns, $df = (r - 1) \times (c - 1) = 4$. In Table 11.7, for $df = 4$ the largest chi-squared value shown is 18.47. It has tail probability $= 0.001$ (see the margin figure). Since $X^2 = 106.955$ falls well above this, it has a smaller right-tail probability. Thus, the P-value is < 0.001. The actual P-value would be 0 to many decimal places. MINITAB reports P-value $= 0.000$, as Table 11.6 showed.

b. Since the P-value is below 0.05, we can reject H_0. Based on this sample, we have evidence to support that an association exists between happiness and family income in the population.

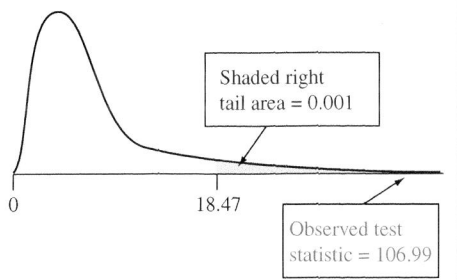

> **Insight**
>
> The extremely small P-value provides very strong evidence against H_0: independence. If the variables were independent, it would be highly unusual for a random sample to have this large a chi-squared statistic.
>
> *Try Exercise 11.10*

Sample Size and the Chi-Squared Test

Presuming H_0 is true, the sampling distribution of the X^2 test statistic gets closer to the chi-squared distribution as the sample size increases. The approximation is good when each expected cell count exceeds about 5. Section 11.5 discusses the sample size issue further and presents a small-sample test.

The box summarizes the steps of the chi-squared test of independence.

SUMMARY: The Five Steps of the Chi-Squared Test of Independence

1. **Assumptions:** Two categorical variables
   Randomization, such as random sampling or a randomized experiment
   Expected count ≥ 5 in all cells (otherwise, use small-sample test in Section 11.5)

2. **Hypotheses:**
   H_0: The two variables are independent.
   H_a: The two variables are dependent (associated).

3. **Test statistic:**

$$X^2 = \sum \frac{(observed\ count - expected\ count)^2}{expected\ count},$$

   where expected count = (row total $\times$ column total)/total sample size

4. **P-value:** Right-tail probability above observed X^2 value, for the chi-squared distribution with $df = (r - 1) \times (c - 1)$

5. **Conclusion:** Report P-value and interpret in context. If a decision is needed, reject H_0 when P-value $\leq$ significance level (such as 0.05).

As with other inferential methods, the chi-squared test assumes randomization, such as the simple random sampling that many surveys use. As explained in Section 4.4, the General Social Survey uses a rather complex multistage random sampling design. Its characteristics are similar, however, to those of a simple random sample. Inferences that assume simple random sampling, such as the chi-squared test, are routinely used with GSS data. The chi-squared test is also valid with randomized experiments. In that case, subjects are randomly assigned to different treatments, and the contingency table summarizes the subjects' responses on a categorical response variable. If the table compares groups, the random samples from those groups must be independent random samples. The test works best with large sample sizes.

In Practice Chi-Squared Is Also Used as a "Test of Homogeneity"

The **chi-squared test** does not depend on which is the response variable and which is the explanatory variable (if either). The steps of the test and the results are identical either way. When a response variable *is* identified and the population conditional distributions are identical, they are said to be **homogeneous.** The chi-squared test is then referred to as a **test of homogeneity.** The examples using the chi-squared test statistic considered thus far in the chapter have tested the notion of independence between two categorical variables. A test of independence is based on data on two categorical variables from a single random sample. In a test of homogeneity, data are observed on a single categorical variable from random samples selected independently from two or more populations or from an experiment where subjects are assigned at random to different treatment groups with a categorical response. The chi-squared statistic for a test of homogeneity has the same form as the chi-squared statistic for a test of independence. The differences in the two tests are in the nature of the hypotheses being tested and the study design employed for collecting data. Computationally, the chi-square test statistic and P-value are identical for the two tests. For simplicity, we will refer to the test statistic as a chi-squared test of independence for both study designs.

Chi-Squared and the Test Comparing Proportions in 2 × 2 Tables

In practice, contingency tables of size 2×2 are very common. These occur in summarizing responses of two groups on a binary response variable, such as belief in life after death (yes, no). For convenience, here, as in the discussion of the binomial distribution in Section 6.3, we label the two possible outcomes by the generic labels *success* and *failure.*

Denote the population proportion of success by p_1 in group 1 and p_2 in group 2. Then $(1 - p_1)$ and $(1 - p_2)$ are the population proportions of failures. Table 11.8 displays the notation. The rows are the groups to be compared and the columns are the response categories.

Table 11.8 A 2 × 2 Table Compares Two Groups on a Binary Response Variable

The proportions in a row form a population conditional distribution.

| | **Population Proportion** | | |
Group	**Success**	**Failure**	**Total**
1	p_1	$1 - p_1$	1.0
2	p_2	$1 - p_2$	1.0

If the response variable is independent of the group, then $p_1 = p_2$, so the conditional distributions are identical. H_0: independence is, equivalently, the *homogeneity* hypothesis H_0: $p_1 = p_2$ of equality of population proportions.

Section 10.1 presented a z test of H_0: $p_1 = p_2$. The test statistic is the difference between the sample proportions divided by its standard error, that is,

$$z = (\hat{p}_1 - \hat{p}_2)/se_0,$$

where se_0 is the standard error estimated under the presumption that H_0 is true. In fact, using algebra, it can be shown that the chi-squared statistic for 2×2 tables is related to this z statistic by

$$X^2 = z^2.$$

In other words, square the z statistic, and you get the X^2 statistic. For H_a: $p_1 \neq p_2$, the z test has exactly the same P-value as the chi-squared test.

Chi-squared test and 2 × 2 contingency tables

Example 5

Aspirin and Cancer Death Rates Revisited

Picture the Scenario

Examples 2–4 in Chapter 10 discussed a meta-study on the effects of aspirin on cancer death rates, in which subjects were randomly assigned to take aspirin or placebo regularly. That example analyzed a 2×2 contingency table that compared the proportions of cancer deaths during a five-year period for those who took placebo and for those who took aspirin. Table 11.9 shows the data again with the expected cell counts, as part of MINITAB output for a chi-squared test of independence (or homogeneity).

Table 11.9 Annotated MINITAB Output for Chi-Squared Test of Independence of Group (Placebo, Aspirin) and Whether or Not Subject Died of Cancer

The same P-value results as with a two-sided Z test comparing the two population proportions.

```
Rows:  group  Columns:  heart

              yes         no        Total

placebo       347       11188       11535       ←   Cell counts

              304       11230                   ←   Expected cell counts

aspirin       327       13708       14035

              370       13665

Cell Contents:            Count

                          Expected count

Pearson  Chi-Square = 11.35,  DF = 1,  P-Value = 0.001
```

Denote the population proportion of cancer deaths by p_1 for the placebo treatment and by p_2 for the aspirin treatment. For H_0: $p_1 = p_2$, the z test of Section 10.1 has a test statistic value of $z \approx 3.45$ (Exercise 10.8). Its P-value is 0.001 for H_a: $p_1 \neq p_2$.

Questions to Explore

a. What are the hypotheses for the chi-squared test for these data?

b. Report the test statistic and P-value for the chi-squared test. How do these relate to results from the z test comparing the proportions?

Think It Through

a. The null hypothesis is that whether or not a someone dies of certain cancers is not associated with whether he or she takes placebo or aspirin. This is equivalent to H_0: $p_1 = p_2$, the population proportion of cancer deaths being the same for each group. The alternative hypothesis is that there's an association. This is equivalent to H_a: $p_1 \neq p_2$.

b. From Table 11.9, more subjects taking placebo died of cancer than we would expect if the variables were not associated (347 observed versus 304 expected). Fewer subjects taking aspirin died of cancer than we would expect if the variables were not associated (327 observed versus 370 expected). Table 11.9 reports $X^2 = 11.35$. This approximates the square of the z test statistic, $X^2 = z^2 = (3.45)^2 = 11.9$, which is close to the 11.35 value. (Note that the numerical values are not exact due to rounding error.) Table 11.9 reports a chi-squared P-value of 0.001. This is very strong evidence that the population proportions of cancer deaths differed for those taking aspirin and for those taking placebo. The sample proportions suggest that the aspirin group had a lower rate of cancer deaths than the placebo group.

Insight

For 2×2 tables, $df = (r - 1) \times (c - 1) = (2 - 1) \times (2 - 1) = 1$. Whenever a statistic has a standard normal distribution, the square of that statistic has a chi-squared distribution with $df = 1$. The chi-squared test and the two-sided z test necessarily have the same P-value and the same conclusion. Here, both the z and X^2 statistics show extremely strong evidence against the null hypothesis of equal population proportions. An advantage of the z test over X^2 is that it also can be used with one-sided alternative hypotheses. The direction of the effect is lost in squaring z and using X^2.

Try Exercise 11.18

For 2×2 tables, we don't really need the chi-squared test because we can use the z test. Why can't we use a z statistic to test independence for larger tables, for which $df > 1$? The reason is that a z statistic can be used only to compare a *single* estimate to a *single* null hypothesis value. Examples are a z statistic for comparing a sample proportion to a null hypothesis proportion, or a difference of sample proportions to a null hypothesis value of 0 for $p_1 - p_2$.

When a table is larger than 2×2 and thus $df > 1$, we need more than one difference parameter to describe the association. For instance, suppose Table 11.9 had three groups: placebo, regular-dose aspirin, and low-dose (children's) aspirin. Then the null hypothesis of no association corresponds to $p_1 = p_2 = p_3$, where p_3 is the population proportion of cancer death rates for the low-dose aspirin group. (See margin for 3×2 table.) The comparison parameters are $(p_1 - p_2)$, $(p_1 - p_3)$, and $(p_2 - p_3)$. We could use a z statistic for each comparison, but not a single z statistic for the overall test of independence (or homogeneity).

	Cancer Death	
Group	**Yes**	**No**
Placebo	p_1	$1 - p_1$
Regular dose	p_2	$1 - p_2$
Low dose	p_3	$1 - p_3$

Interpretation of Degrees of Freedom

The *df* value in a chi-squared test indicates how many parameters are needed to determine all the comparisons for describing the contingency table. For instance, we've just seen that a 3×2 table for comparing three treatments (placebo, regular aspirin, low-dose aspirin) on whether a subject died of cancer would have three parameters for making comparisons: $(p_1 - p_2)$, $(p_1 - p_3)$, and $(p_2 - p_3)$. We need to know only two of these to figure out the third. For instance, if we know $(p_1 - p_2)$ and $(p_2 - p_3)$, then

$$(p_1 - p_3) = (p_1 - p_2) + (p_2 - p_3).$$

A 3×2 table can use two parameters to determine all the comparisons, so its $df = 2$.

The *df* term also has the following interpretation: Given the row and column marginal totals in an $r \times c$ contingency table, the cell counts in a rectangular block of size $(r - 1) \times (c - 1)$ determine all the other cell counts. We illustrate using Table 11.10 from the GSS, which cross-tabulates political views by whether the subject would ever vote for a female for president. The table shows results for those subjects who called themselves extremely liberal, moderate, or extremely conservative.[1] For this 3×2 table, suppose we know the two counts in the upper left-hand $(3 - 1) \times (2 - 1) = 2 \times 1$ part of the table. Table 11.10 shows the cell counts in this block. Given these and the row and column totals, we can determine all the other cell counts.

Table 11.10 Illustration of Degrees of Freedom

A block of $(r - 1) \times (c - 1)$ cell counts determine the others, given the marginal totals. Here, a $(3 - 1) \times (2 - 1) = 2 \times 1$ block of cell counts in the first two rows and first column determines the others.

	Vote for Female President		
Political Views	**Yes**	**No**	**Total**
Extremely liberal	39	—	41
Moderate	435	—	469
Extremely conservative	—	—	45
Total	516	39	555

Source: Data from CSM, UC Berkeley.

---

[1] The 1998 GSS was the most recent one to ask the question about a female president.

	Vote Female?		
Political	**Yes**	**No**	**Total**
Liberal	39	2	41
Moderate	435	34	469
Conserv.	42	3	45
Total	516	39	555

Recall

From Section 9.5, a small P-value does not imply an important result in practical terms. Statistical significance is not the same as *practical* significance. ◄

For instance, the marginal total in row 1 is 41 and the first cell count is 39, so the second cell has $41 - 39 = 2$ subjects. Likewise, there are

$$469 - 435 = 34 \text{ subjects in the second cell in the second row, and}$$

$$516 - (39 + 435) = 42 \text{ subjects in the third cell in the first column.}$$

From these counts and the fact that the third row has 45 observations, there must be $45 - 42 = 3$ in the final cell in the third row and second column. To check that you understand, try reconstructing the table if you know only the cell counts in the two cells that are in the second and third rows and second column.

Once the marginal totals are fixed in a contingency table, a block of only $(r - 1) \times (c - 1)$ cell counts is free to vary, since these cell counts determine the remaining ones. The degrees of freedom value equals the number of cells in this block, or $df = (r - 1) \times (c - 1)$. (See margin for full table.)

Limitations of the Chi-Squared Test

The chi-squared test of independence, like other significance tests, provides limited information. If the P-value is very small, strong evidence exists against the null hypothesis of independence. We can infer that the variables are associated. The chi-squared statistic and the P-value tell us nothing, however, about the nature or the strength of the association. We know there is statistical significance, but the test alone does not indicate whether there is practical significance as well. A large X^2 means strong evidence of association, but not necessarily a strong association. We'll see how to investigate the strength of association in the next section.

SUMMARY: Misuses of the Chi-Squared Test

The chi-squared test is often misused. Some common misuses are applying it

■ When some of the expected frequencies are too small.
■ When separate rows or columns are dependent samples,[2] such as when each row of the table has the same subjects.
■ To data that do not result from a random sample or randomized experiment.
■ To data by classifying quantitative variables into categories. This results in a loss of information. It is usually more appropriate to analyze the data with methods for quantitative variables, like those the next chapter presents.

"Goodness of Fit" Chi-Squared Tests

So far we've used the chi-squared statistic to test the null hypothesis that two categorical variables are independent. In practice, the chi-squared statistic is used for a variety of hypotheses about categorical variables. For example, for three variables, the chi-squared statistic can test the hypothesis that two variables are independent at each fixed category of the third variable, such as happiness and income being independent both for women and for men (the two categories of the categorical variable, sex). What all of the various chi-squared tests have in common is that they all have a formula for finding the expected frequencies that satisfy that hypothesis and a formula for the df value for the test statistic.

The chi-squared statistic can be used even for a hypothesis involving a *single* categorical variable. For example, in one of his experiments, the geneticist Gregor Mendel crossed pea plants of pure yellow strain with plants of pure green strain. He predicted that a second-generation hybrid seed would have probability 0.75

---

[2]With dependent samples, McNemar's test (Section 10.4) is the appropriate test with binary variables, and extensions of it handle categorical variables with more than two categories.

of being yellow and 0.25 of being green (yellow being the dominant strain). The experiment produced 8023 seeds. If Mendel's theory is correct, we would expect to see 75% yellow seeds and 25% green seeds, that is, $8023(0.75) = 6017.25$ yellow seeds and $8023(0.25) = 2005.75$ green seeds. In the actual experiment, of the 8023 hybrid seeds, 6022 were yellow and 2001 were green. Are these results far enough from Mendel's predictions to give evidence against his theory? Applying the chi-squared statistics to test Mendel's hypothesis, we obtain

$$X^2 = \sum \frac{(\text{observed count} - \text{expected count})^2}{\text{expected count}} =$$

$$\frac{(6022 - 6017.25)^2}{6017.25} + \frac{(2001 - 2005.75)^2}{2005.75} = 0.015$$

When a hypothesis predicts a population proportion value for each category of a variable that has c categories, the chi-squared statistic has $df = c - 1$. For this example with $c = 2$ categories (green and yellow for the color of a hybrid seed), $df = 2 - 1 = 1$. The chi-squared statistic value of 0.015 has a P-value = 0.90. The data in Mendel's experiment did not contradict his hypothesis.

When testing particular proportion values for a categorical variable, the chi-squared statistic is referred to as a **goodness-of-fit statistic.** The statistic summarizes how well the hypothesized values predict what happens with the observed data. With $c = 2$ categories, the chi-squared statistic equals the square of the z statistic used in Chapter 9 to test a hypothesis about the proportion value for one of the two categories. For example, to test Mendel's hypothesis $H_0: p = 0.75$ that the probability is 0.75 that a second-generation hybrid seed is yellow, we find $\hat{p} = 6022/8023 = 0.7506$, $se_0 = \sqrt{p_0(1 - p_0)/n} = \sqrt{0.75(0.25)/8023} = 0.00483$, and

$$z = \frac{\hat{p} - p_0}{se_0} = \frac{0.7506 - 0.75}{0.00483} = 0.124. \text{ Note that } z^2 = 0.015.$$

The P-value using the chi-squared distribution with test statistic X^2 is identical to the two-sided P-value using the standard normal distribution with test statistic z. An advantage of the X^2 test is that it applies even when there are more than two categories. See Exercise 11.22 for an example.

A limitation of the goodness-of-fit test, like other significance tests, is that it does not tell you the ranges of plausible values for the proportion parameters. To do this, you can find confidence intervals for the individual population proportions (Section 8.2). For Mendel's experiment, a 95% confidence interval for the probability of a yellow hybrid seed is

$$0.7506 \pm 1.96(0.0048), \text{ which is } (0.74, 0.76).$$

Activity 2

Analyzing Contingency Tables of GSS Data

It's easy to analyze associations between categorical variables measured by the General Social Survey. Let's see how.

- Go to the GSS Web site, sda.berkeley.edu/GSS/. Click on GSS, with *No Weight* as the default weight selection.
- The GSS names for Table 11.1 are HAPPY (for general happiness) and FINRELA (for family income in relative terms). Enter HAPPY in the column space and FINRELA in the

row space to construct a table with these as the column and row variables. Entering YEAR (2004) in the selection filter restricts the search to GSS data from the survey in 2004. Select *No Weight* from the Weight menu. You can rerun the analysis with the YEAR (2010) and compare results with the year 2004.

- Put a check in the row box . . . for the Percentaging option and in the Summary Statistics box for Table Options, and click on *Run the Table.*

You'll now get a contingency table relating happiness to family income for the 2003 survey. The table shows the cell counts and sample conditional distributions. It treats as the response variable the one you check for the Percentaging option. The output also shows some statistics (such as Chisq-P) for the Pearson chi-squared statistic) that we're using in this chapter to analyze contingency tables.

The family income variable has five categories (far below average, below average, average, above average, far above average). Table 11.1 combined categories 1 and 2 into a single category (for below average) and categories 4 and 5 into a single category (for above average). To create this collapsed table, type the family income variable as FINRELA(r:1-2;3; 4-5) instead of FINRELA.

Now, create a table relating another variable to happiness. At the page on which you enter the variable names, click on *Standard Codebook* under the codebooks menu and you will see indexes for the variables. Look up a subject that interests you and find the GSS code name for a variable. For the table you create,

■ Find the chi-squared statistic and *df* value.
■ Report the P-value and interpret the results in context.

11.2   Practicing the Basics

11.8   What gives P-value = 0.05?   How large a X^2 test statistic value provides a P-value of 0.05 for testing independence for the following table dimensions?
  a. 2 × 2
  b. 2 × 3
  c. 2 × 5
  d. 5 × 5
  e. 3 × 9

11.9   Happiness and gender   For the 2 × 3 table on gender and happiness in Exercise 11.4 (shown again following), software tells us that $X^2 = 0.46$ and the P-value = 0.79.
  a. State the null and alternative hypothesis, in context, to which these results apply.
  b. Interpret the P-value.

Gender	Happiness		
	Not	Pretty	Very
Female	174	587	328
Male	142	513	271

11.10   Marital happiness and income   In Exercise 11.5 when you used the GSS to download a 3 × 3 table for marital happiness and family income in 2008, you should have obtained results similar to the table shown below.

Income	Marital Happiness		
	Not	Pretty	Very
Above	123	105	7
Average	291	151	17
Below	172	83	6

  a. State the null and alternative hypotheses for the test.
  b. How large a X^2 value would give a P-value of exactly 0.05?
  c. The chi-squared statistic for the table equals 12.837. Find and interpret the P-value.
  d. State your decision for a significance level of 0.05, and interpret in context.

11.11   Life after death and gender   In the 2008 GSS, 620 of 809 males and 835 of 978 females indicated a belief in life after death. (*Source*: Data from CSM, UC Berkeley.)
  a. Construct a 2 × 2 contingency table relating gender of respondent (SEX, categories male and female) as the rows to belief about life after death (POSTLIFE, categories yes and no) as the columns.
  b. Find the four expected cell counts for the chi-squared test. Compare them to the observed cell counts, identifying cells having more observations than expected.
  c. The data have $X^2 = 22.36$. Set up its calculation by showing how to substitute the observed and expected cell counts you found into its formula.

11.12   Basketball shots independent?   In pro basketball games during 1980–1982, when Larry Bird of the Boston Celtics missed his first free throw, 48 out of 53 times he made the second one, and when he made his first free throw, 251 out of 285 times he made the second one.
  a. Form a 2 × 2 contingency table that cross-tabulates the outcome of the first free throw (with categories made and missed) and the outcome of the second free throw (made and missed).
  b. When we use MINITAB to analyze the contingency table, we get the result

```
Pearson Chi-Square = 0.273, DF = 1,
          P-Value = 0.602
```

Does it seem as if his success on the second shot depends on whether he made the first? Explain how to interpret the result of the chi-squared test.

11.13   Cigarettes and marijuana   The table on the following page refers to a survey[3] in which senior high school students in Dayton, Ohio, were randomly sampled. It cross-tabulates whether a student had ever smoked cigarettes and whether a student had ever used marijuana. Analyze these data by

[3]*Source*: Data from personal communication from Harry Khamis, Wright State University.

(a) finding and interpreting conditional distributions with marijuana use as the response variable and (b) reporting all five steps of the chi-squared test of independence.

Cigarettes	Marijuana	
	Yes	No
Yes	914	581
No	46	735

11.14 Smoking and alcohol Refer to the previous exercise. A similar table relates cigarette use to alcohol use. The MINITAB output for the chi-squared test follows.

a. True or false: If we use cigarette use as the column variable instead of alcohol use, then we will get different values for the chi-squared statistic and the P-value shown in the table.

b. Explain what value you would get for the z statistic and P-value if you conducted a significance test of $H_0: p_1 = p_2$ against $H_a: p_1 \neq p_2$, where p_1 is the population proportion of non cigarette users who have drunk alcohol and p_2 is the population proportion of cigarette users who have drunk alcohol.

Dayton student survey

```
Row: cigarette Columns: alcohol
        no      yes
no      281     500
yes     46      1449
Pearson Chi-Square = 451.404,
DF = 1,  P-Value = 0.000
```

11.15 Help the environment In 2000 the GSS asked whether a subject is willing to accept cuts in the standard of living to help the environment (GRNSOL), with categories (vw = very willing, fw = fairly willing, nwu = neither willing nor unwilling, nvw = not very willing, nw = not at all willing). When this was cross-tabulated with gender (SEX), as shown below, $X^2 = 8.0$.

a. What are the hypotheses for the test to which X^2 refers?

b. Report r and c and the df value on which X^2 is based.

c. Is the P-value less than (i) 0.05? (ii) 0.10? Explain.

d. What conclusion would you make, using a significance level of (i) 0.05 and (ii) 0.10? State your conclusion in the context of this study.

Help the Environment					
Sex	vw	fw	nwu	nvw	nw
F	34	149	160	142	168
M	30	131	152	98	106

11.16 What predicts being green? Refer to the previous exercise. What is associated with environmental opinion? Go to the GSS Web site sda.berkeley.edu/GSS/.

a. Find a variable that is significantly associated with GRNSOL, using the 0.05 significance level. (*Hint:* You could first try some demographic variables, such as gender (variable SEX) or race (RACE).)

b. For the variable you found, in which cells are there considerably (i) more and (ii) fewer, subjects than you would expect if the variables were independent?

11.17 Aspirin and heart attacks A Swedish study used 1360 patients who had suffered a stroke. The study randomly assigned each subject to an aspirin treatment or a placebo treatment. In this study heart attacks were suffered by 28 of the 684 subjects taking placebo and 18 of the 676 subjects taking aspirin.

a. Report the data in the form of a 2×2 contingency table.

b. Show how to carry out all five steps of the null hypothesis that having a heart attack is not associated with whether one takes placebo or aspirin. (You should get a chi-squared statistic equal to 2.1.) Interpret.

11.18 z test for heart attack study Refer to the previous exercise. The printout from MINITAB reports

```
Test for difference = 0 (vs not = 0):
        Z = 1.46 P-Value = 0.144
```

a. Define population proportions p_1 and p_2 and state the hypotheses for that test.

b. Explain how the result of the chi-squared test in (b) in the previous exercise corresponds to this z test result.

11.19 Happiness and life after death Are people who believe in life after death happier?

a. Go to the GSS Web site sda.berkeley.edu/GSS and download the contingency table for the 2008 survey relating happiness and whether you believe in life after death (variables denoted HAPPY and POSTLIFE). Construct the conditional distributions, using happiness as the response variable, and interpret.

b. Check the Summary Statistics box in GSS to show that $X^2 = 7.7$. What is the P-value? Interpret.

c. Based on the test in part b, what can you conclude?

11.20 What is independent of happiness? Refer to Exercises 11.6 and 11.7. For the variables that you thought might be independent,

a. At the GSS Web site, conduct all five steps of the chi-squared test.

b. Based on part a, which inference is most appropriate? (i) We accept the hypothesis that the variables are independent; (ii) the variables may be independent; (iii) the variables are associated.

11.21 Testing a genetic theory In an experiment on chlorophyll inheritance in corn, for 1103 seedlings of self-fertilized heterozygous green plants, 854 seedlings were green and 249 were yellow. Theory predicts that 75% of the seedlings would be green.

a. Specify a null hypothesis for testing the theory.

b. Find the value of the chi-squared goodness-of-fit statistic and report its df.

c. Report the P-value, and interpret.

11.22 Checking a roulette wheel Karl Pearson devised the chi-squared goodness-of-fit test partly to analyze data from an experiment to analyze whether a particular roulette wheel in Monte Carlo was fair, in the sense that each outcome was equally likely in a spin of the wheel. For a given European roulette wheel with 37 pockets (with numbers $0, 1, 2, \ldots, 36$), consider the null hypothesis that the wheel is fair.

a. For the null hypothesis, what is the probability for each pocket?

b. For an experiment with 3700 spins of the roulette wheel, find the expected number of times each pocket is selected.

c. In the experiment, the 0 pocket occurred 110 times. Show the contribution to the X^2 statistic of the results for this pocket.

d. Comparing the observed and expected counts for all 37 pockets, we get $X^2 = 34.4$ Specify the df value, and indicate whether there is strong evidence that the roulette wheel is not balanced. (*Hint:* Recall that the df value is the mean of the distribution.)

11.3 Determining the Strength of the Association

Three questions are normally addressed in analyzing contingency tables:

- **Is there an association?** The chi-squared test of independence addresses this. When the P-value is small, we infer that the variables are associated.
- **How do the cell counts differ from what independence predicts?** To answer this question, we compare each observed cell count to the corresponding expected cell count. We'll say more about this in Section 11.4.
- **How strong is the association?** Analyzing the *strength* of the association reveals whether the association is an important one, or if it is statistically significant but weak and unimportant in practical terms. We now focus on this third question.

Measures of Association

For recent GSS data, Table 11.11 shows associations between opinion about the death penalty and two explanatory variables—gender and race. Both sides of Table 11.11 have large chi-squared statistics and small P-values for the test of independence. We can conclude that both gender and race are associated with the death penalty opinion.

Table 11.11 GSS Data Showing Race and Gender as Explanatory Variables for Opinion About the Death Penalty

	Opinion				Opinion		
Race	Favor	Oppose	n	Gender	Favor	Oppose	n
White	71%	29%	1473	Male	71%	29%	885
Black	46%	54%	259	Female	62%	38%	1017
Chi-squared = 65.55				Chi-squared = 17.78			
$df = 1$, P-value = 0.00				$df = 1$, P-value = 0.00			

Source: Data from CSM, UC Berkeley.

The X^2 test statistic is larger for the first table. Does this mean that opinion is more strongly associated with race than with gender? How can we quantify the strength of the association in a contingency table?

Measure of Association

A **measure of association** is a statistic or a parameter that summarizes the strength of the dependence between two variables.

A measure of association takes a range of values from one extreme to another as data range from the weakest to the strongest association. It is useful for comparing associations to determine which is stronger. Later in this section we'll see that although the chi-squared test tells us how strong the evidence is that an association truly exists in the population, it does not describe the strength of that association.

Difference of Proportions

An easily interpretable measure of association is the difference between the proportions making a particular response. The population difference of proportions is 0 whenever the conditional distributions are identical, that is, when the variables are independent. The difference of proportions falls between −1 and +1, where 1 and −1 represent the strongest possible association. Whether you get a negative or a positive value merely reflects how the rows are ordered. Section 10.1 showed how to use a sample difference of proportions value to conduct inference (such as a confidence interval) about a population value.

Table 11.12 shows two hypothetical contingency tables relating a subject's income and whether the subject responds to a promotional mailing from a bank offering a special credit card. Case A exhibits the weakest possible association—no association. Both the high-income and the low-income subjects have 60% rejecting the credit card. The difference of proportions is $0.60 - 0.60 = 0$. By contrast, case B exhibits the strongest possible association. All those with high income accept the card, whereas all those with low income decline it. The difference of proportions is $0 - 1.0 = -1$.

Table 11.12 Decision About Accepting a Credit Card Cross-Tabulated by Income

In Case A, the conditional distributions are the same in each row, so the difference of proportions is 0. In Case B the acceptance decision is completely dependent on income level, and the difference of proportions is −1.

	Case A Accept Credit Card			Case B Accept Credit Card		
Income	No	Yes	Total	No	Yes	Total
High	240 (60%)	160 (40%)	400 (100%)	0 (0%)	400 (100%)	400 (100%)
Low	360 (60%)	240 (40%)	600 (100%)	600 (100%)	0 (0%)	600 (100%)

	Opinion	
Race	Favor	Oppose
White	71%	29%
Black	46%	54%
Gender		
Male	71%	29%
Female	62%	38%

In practice, we don't expect data to follow either of these extremes, but the stronger the association, the larger the absolute value of the difference of proportions. For Table 11.11, shown again in the margin, the difference of proportions is $0.71 - 0.46 = 0.25$ for whites and blacks, and the difference of proportions is $0.71 - 0.62 = 0.09$ for males and females. The difference of 0.25 for whites and blacks is much larger than the difference of 0.09 for males and females.

Strength of an association

Example 6

Student Stress, Depression, and Gender

Picture the Scenario

Every year, the Higher Education Research Institute at UCLA conducts a large-scale survey of college freshmen on a variety of issues. From the survey of 283,000 freshmen in 2002, Table 11.13 compares females and males on the percent who reported feeling frequently stressed (overwhelmed by all they have to do) and the percent who reported feeling frequently depressed during the past year. P-values for chi-squared tests of independence were 0.000 (rounded) for each data set.

Table 11.13 Conditional Distributions of Stress and Depression, by Gender

	Stress				Depression		
Gender	Yes	No	Total	Gender	Yes	No	Total
Female	35%	65%	100%	Female	8%	92%	100%
Male	16%	84%	100%	Male	6%	94%	100%

Question to Explore

Which response variable, stress or depression, has the stronger sample association with gender?

Think It Through

The difference of proportions between females and males was $0.35 - 0.16 = 0.19$ for feeling stressed. It was $0.08 - 0.06 = 0.02$ for feeling depressed. Since 0.19 is much larger than 0.02, there is evidence of a greater difference between reports of females and males on their feeling stress than on depression. In the sample, stress has the stronger association with gender.

Insight

Although the difference of proportions can be as large as 1 or -1, in practice in comparisons of groups, it is rare to find differences near these limits.

Try Exercise 11.24

Recall

Section 10.3 introduced **relative risk.** It showed that software can report a confidence interval for a population relative risk. ◄

The Ratio of Proportions: Relative Risk

Another measure of association, introduced in Section 10.3, is the ratio of two proportions, p_1/p_2. In medical applications in which the proportion refers to an adverse outcome, it is called the **relative risk.**

Relative risk

Example 7

Seat Belt Use and Outcome of Auto Accidents

Picture the Scenario

Based on records of automobile accidents in a recent year, the Department of Highway Safety and Motor Vehicles in Florida reported Table 11.14 on the counts of nonfatalities and fatalities. The data have $X^2 = 2338$, with P-value $= 0.00000. \ldots$

Table 11.14 Outcome of Auto Accident by Whether or Not Subject Wore Seat Belt

	Outcome		
Wore Seat Belt	Survived	Died	Total
Yes	412,368	510	412,878
No	162,527	1601	164,128

Source: Department of Highway Safety and Motor Vehicles, Florida.

Question to Explore

Treating the auto accident outcome as the response variable, find and interpret the relative risk.

Think It Through

In Table 11.14, the adverse outcome is death, rather than survival. The relative risk is formed for that outcome. For those who wore a seat belt, the proportion who died equaled 510/412,878 = 0.00124. For those who did not wear a seat belt, the proportion who died was 1601/164,128 = 0.00975. The relative risk is the ratio, 0.00124/0.00975 = 0.127. The proportion of subjects wearing a seat belt who died was 0.127 times the proportion of subjects not wearing a seat belt who died.

Equivalently, since 0.00975/0.00124 = 1/0.127 = 7.9, the proportion of subjects *not wearing* a seat belt who died was nearly eight times the proportion of subjects *wearing* seat belts who died. This reciprocal value is the relative risk when the rows are interchanged, with no for seat-belt use in row 1.

Insight

The ordering of rows is arbitrary. Many people find it easier to interpret the relative risk for the ordering for which its value is *above* 1.0. A relative risk of 7.9 represents a strong association. This is far from the value of 1.0 that would occur if the proportion of deaths were the same for each group. Wearing a seat belt has a practically significant effect in enhancing the chance of surviving an auto accident.

> *Try Exercises 11.27, part c, and 11.30*

In Example 7 the proportion of interest was close to 0 for each group, but the relative risk was far from 1. When this happens, an association may be practically important even though the difference of proportions is near 0 (it was 0.0085 in Example 7). If the chance of death is only a bit higher when one does not wear a seat belt, but that chance is nearly eight times the chance of death when wearing a seat belt, the association is practically significant. The relative risk is often more informative than the difference of proportions for comparing proportions that are both close to 0.

Properties of the Relative Risk

■ The relative risk can equal any nonnegative number.

■ When $p_1 = p_2$, the variables are independent and relative risk = 1.0.

■ Values farther from 1.0 (in either direction) represent stronger associations. Two values for the relative risk represent the same strength of association, but in opposite directions, when one value is the reciprocal of the other. See Figure 11.5.

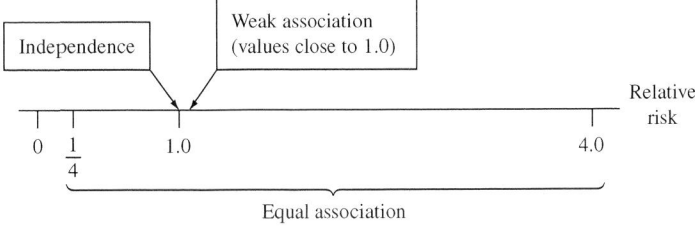

▲ **Figure 11.5** Values of the Relative Risk Farther from 1.0 Represent Stronger Association. Question Why do relative risks that take reciprocal values, such as 4 and $\frac{1}{4}$, represent the same strength of association?

A relative risk of 8 is farther from independence and represents a stronger association than a relative risk of 4, and a relative risk of $\frac{1}{8}$ is farther from independence than a relative risk of $\frac{1}{4}$. But relative risk = 4.0 and relative risk = 1/4.0 = 0.25

represent the same strength of association. When relative risk $p_1/p_2 = 0.25$, then p_1 is 0.25 times p_2. Equivalently, p_2 is $1/0.25 = 4.0$ times p_1. Whether we get 4.0 or 0.25 for the relative risk depends merely on which group we call group 1 and which we call group 2.

Association in $r \times c$ Tables

The difference of proportions and the relative risk are defined for 2×2 tables. For $r \times c$ (r = # of rows, c = # of columns) tables, they can compare proportions in a particular response category for various pairs of rows.

Association in r × c tables

Example 8

General Happiness and Marital Happiness

Picture the Scenario

Earlier in the chapter we studied the association between happiness and family income. For married subjects, a possible predictor of happiness is their reported happiness with their marriage. Table 11.15 cross-tabulates these variables, using data from the 2008 GSS. It also reports conditional distributions with happiness as the response variable. The data have chi-squared statistic $X^2 = 263.9$, with $df = 4$ and a P-value of 0.0000....

Table 11.15 Happiness and Marital Happiness

The percentages are the conditional distributions of happiness in each row. When percentages are compared in rows 1 and 3, the highlighted cells reveal a strong association.

	Happiness			
Marital Happiness	**Not Too Happy**	**Pretty Happy**	**Very Happy**	**Total**
Not Too Happy	13 (43.3%)	15 (50.0%)	2 (6.7%)	30 (100%)
Pretty Happy	44 (12.8%)	259 (75.5%)	40 (11.7%)	343 (100%)
Very Happy	24 (4.0%)	215 (36.1%)	356 (59.8%)	595 (100%)

Source: Data from CSM, UC Berkeley.

Question to Explore

Describe the association between marital happiness and general happiness, using the not too happy and very happy categories.

Think It Through

Let's consider the Very Happy category of happiness. The difference between the proportions in this category for the Not Too Happy and Very Happy categories of marital happiness (that is, rows 1 and 3) is $0.067 - 0.598 = -0.531$. Those who are not too happy with their marriage are much less likely to be very happy overall. Consider next the Not Too Happy category of happiness. The difference between the proportions in this category for the Not Too Happy and Very Happy categories of marital happiness is $0.433 - 0.04 = 0.393$. This is also a substantial difference.

Likewise, we could use the *ratio* of proportions. For instance, consider the Not Too Happy category of happiness as an undesirable outcome. The relative risk of this outcome, comparing the Not Too Happy and Very Happy categories of marital happiness, is $0.433/0.04 = 10.825$. The estimated proportion who are not too happy is nearly 11 times larger for those who have not too happy marriages than for those who have very happy marriages.

This ratio of 10.825 is very far from 1.0, indicating that this part of the table reveals an extremely strong association.

Insight

It is unusual to find such strong associations. For instance, family income also has a substantial association with happiness, but it is not as strong. Using Table 11.1 (partly shown in the margin), you can check that the relative risk of being not too happy equals 4.07 when you compare the below-average and above-average levels of income. This is much less than the relative risk of 10.825 and is a weaker association.

> *Try Exercises 11.26 and 11.27*

Recall

From Table 11.1,

Income	Not Too Happy	Total
Below average	172	687
Above average	26	423

◄

Chi-Squared and Association

You may be tempted to regard a large value of the X^2 statistic in the test of independence as indicating a strong association. This is a misuse of the statistic.

In Practice Large X^2 Does Not Mean There's a Strong Association

A large value for X^2 provides strong evidence that the variables are associated. It does not imply, however, that the variables have a strong association. This statistic merely indicates (through its P-value) how certain we can be that the variables are associated, not how strong that association is. For a given strength of association, larger X^2 values occur for larger sample sizes. Large X^2 values can occur with weak associations, if the sample size is sufficiently large.

Caution

If the sample size is sufficiently large, a X^2 value large enough to be considered statistically significant can occur even if the association between the two categorical variables is weak. ◄

For example, Cases A, B, and C in Table 11.16 are hypothetical tables relating gender and whether or not one attends religious services weekly. The association in each case is weak—the conditional distribution for females (51% yes, 49% no) is nearly identical to the conditional distribution for males (49% yes, 51% no). All three cases show the same weak strength of association: The difference between the proportions of females and males who say yes is $0.51 - 0.49 = 0.02$ in each.

Table 11.16 Response on Attending Religious Services Weekly by Gender, Showing Weak but Identical Associations

In each case the difference between proportions is small, only 0.02.

	Case A			Case B			Case C		
	Yes	No	*n*	Yes	No	*n*	Yes	No	*n*
Female	51%	49%	100	51%	49%	200	51%	49%	10,000
Male	49%	51%	100	49%	51%	200	49%	51%	10,000
Chi-squared = 0.08				Chi-squared = 0.16				Chi-squared = 8.0		
P-value = 0.78				P-value = 0.69				P-value = 0.005		

For the sample of size 200 in Case A, $X^2 = 0.08$, which has a P-value of 0.78. Case B has twice as large a sample size, with the cell counts doubling. For its sample of size 400, $X^2 = 0.16$, for which the P-value = 0.69. So, when the cell counts double, X^2 doubles. Similarly, for the sample size of 20,000 (100 times as large as $n = 200$) in Case C, $X^2 = 8.0$ (100 times as large as $X^2 = 0.08$). Then the P-value = 0.005.

In summary, for fixed conditional distributions, the value of X^2 is directly proportional to the sample size—larger values occur with larger sample sizes. Like other test statistics, the larger the X^2 statistic, the smaller the P-value and the stronger the evidence against the null hypothesis. However, a small P-value results from even a weak association when the sample size is large, as Case C shows.

11.3 Practicing the Basics

11.23 Party ID and race The table shows 2008 GSS data on race and political party identification.

| Race | Party Identification | | | n |
	Democrat	Independent	Republican	
Black	192	75	8	275
White	459	586	471	1516

Source: Data from CSM, UC Berkeley.

a. The chi-squared test of independence has $X^2 = 177.312$. Carry out the five steps of the test, and interpret the result in the context of these variables.

b. Estimate the difference between black subjects and white subjects in the proportion who identify themselves as Democrats. Interpret. Does this seem to be a weak (practically insignificant), or a strong (practically significant), association? Explain.

11.24 Party ID, race and gender Refer to the previous exercise and to the data in the table below from Exercise 11.1. Which has a stronger association with whether one identifies as a Democrat—race or gender? Justify your answer by comparing the difference between blacks and whites in the proportion identifying as Democrat to the difference between females and males in the proportion identifying as Democrat.

Data from Exercise 11.1

Gender	Democrat	n
Female	422	1076
Male	299	896

11.25 Happiness and highest degree The table shows 2008 GSS data on happiness and the highest degree attained.

| Highest Degree | Happiness | | |
	Not Too Happy	Pretty Happy	Very Happy
< High school	87	137	72
HS, junior college	181	654	337
College, grad school	48	308	190

Source: Data from CSM, UC Berkeley.

a. The chi-squared test of independence has $X^2 = 64.41$. What conclusion would you make using a significance level of 0.05? Interpret.

b. Does this large chi-squared value mean there is a strong association between happiness and highest degree? Explain.

c. Estimate the difference between the lowest and highest education groups in the proportion who report being not too happy. Interpret.

d. Find and interpret the relative risk of being not too happy, comparing the lowest and highest education groups. Interpret.

11.26 Income and highest degree The table shows 2008 GSS data on family income and the subject's highest degree attained, for which $X^2 = 315.98$ (P-value = 0.000).

| Highest Degree | Family Income | | |
	Below Average	Average	Above Average
< High school	176	98	18
HS, junior college	429	573	165
College, grad school	85	426	242

a. Estimate the difference between the lowest and highest education groups in the proportion who report (i) below average income and (ii) above average income. Interpret. Does this seem to be a practically significant, or practically insignificant, association?

b. Find and interpret the relative risk of a below-average income, comparing the lowest and highest education groups. Interpret.

11.27 Smoking and alcohol The table refers to a survey[4] of senior high school students in Dayton, Ohio. It cross-tabulates whether a student had ever smoked cigarettes and whether a student had ever drunk alcohol. The table also shows MINITAB output of conditional distributions.

a. Describe the strength of association using the difference between users and nonusers of cigarettes in the proportions who have used alcohol. Interpret.

b. Describe the strength of association using the difference between users and nonusers of alcohol in the proportions who have used cigarettes. Interpret.

c. Describe the strength of association using the relative risk of using cigarettes, comparing those who have used or not used alcohol. interpret.

Data from Dayton Student Survey

Rows:	cigarette	Columns:	alcohol
		no	yes
no		281	500
		35.98	64.02	← For row conditional distribution
		85.93	25.65	← For column conditional distribution
yes		46	1449
		3.08	96.92
		14.07	74.35
Cell Contents:		Count	
		% of Row	
		% of Column	

---

[4]*Source*: Data from survey from Harry Khamis, Wright State University.

11.28 Sex of victim and offender For murders in the United States in 2009, the table cross-tabulates the sex of the victim by the sex of the offender. Find and interpret a measure of association, treating sex of victim as the response variable.

	Sex of Victim	
Sex of Offender	**Female**	**Male**
Female	182	484
Male	1719	4078

Source: Data from www.fbi.gov.

11.29 Prison and gender According to the U.S. Department of Justice, in 2009 the incarceration rate in the nation's prisons was 949 per 100,000 male residents, and 67 per 100,000 female residents.

   a. Find the relative risk of being incarcerated, comparing males to females. Interpret.

   b. Find the difference of proportions of being incarcerated. Interpret.

   c. Which measure do you think is more appropriate for these data? Why?

11.30 Risk of dying for teenagers According to summarized data from 1999 to 2006 accessed from the Centers of Disease Control and Prevention, the annual probability that a male teenager at age 19 is likely to die is about 0.00135 and 0.00046 for females age 19. (www.cdc.gov)

   a. Compare these rates using the difference of proportions, and interpret.

   b. Compare these rates using the relative risk, and interpret.

   c. Which of the two measures seems more useful when both proportions are very close to 0? Explain.

11.31 Death penalty associations Table 11.11, summarized again here, showed the associations between death penalty opinion and gender and race.

	Opinion	
Race	**Favor**	**Oppose**
White	71%	29%
Black	46%	54%
Gender		
Male	71%	29%
Female	62%	38%

   a. True or false: The table with the larger X^2 statistic necessarily has the stronger association. Explain.

   b. To make an inference about the strength of association in the population, you can construct confidence intervals around the sample differences of proportions. The 95% confidence intervals are (0.19, 0.32) comparing whites and blacks and (0.05, 0.13) comparing males and females in the proportions favoring the death penalty. In the *population,* can you make a conclusion about which variable is more strongly associated with the death penalty opinion? Explain.

11.32 Chi-squared versus measuring association For Table 11.15 on general happiness and marital happiness, the chi-squared statistic equals 263.9 ($df = 4$, P-value = 0.000). Explain the difference between the purpose of the chi-squared test and the descriptive analysis in Example 8 comparing conditional distributions using measures of association. (*Hint:* Is a chi-squared test a descriptive or inferential analysis?)

11.4 Using Residuals to Reveal the Pattern of Association

The chi-squared test and measures of association such as $p_1 - p_2$ and p_1/p_2 are fundamental methods for analyzing contingency tables. The P-value for X^2 summarizes the strength of evidence against H_0: independence. If the P-value is small, then we conclude that somewhere in the contingency table the population cell proportions differ from independence. The chi-squared test does not indicate, however, whether all cells deviate greatly from independence or perhaps only some of them do so.

Recall

Section 3.3 introduced a **residual** for quantitative variables as the difference between an observed response and a predicted response for a regression equation. For categorical variables, a residual compares an observed count to an expected count that represents what H_0 predicts. ◄

Residual Analysis

A cell-by-cell comparison of the observed counts with the counts that are expected when H_0 is true reveals the nature of the evidence. The difference between an observed and expected count in a particular cell is called a **residual.**

For example, Table 11.5 reported observed and expected cell counts for happiness and family income. The first column of this table is summarized in the margin on the next page, with the expected cell counts in parentheses. The first cell reports 26 subjects with above-average income who are not too happy.

Income	Not Too Happy
Above average	26 (66.86)
Average	117 (139.56)
Below average	172 (108.58)

The expected count is 66.86. The residual is $26 - 66.86 = -40.86$. The residual is negative when, as in this cell, fewer subjects are in the cell than expected under H_0. The residual is positive when more subjects are in the cell than expected, as in the cell having observed count = 172 (below-average income subjects who are not too happy) and residual $172 - 108.58 = 63.42$.

How do we know whether a residual is large enough to indicate strong evidence of a deviation from independence in that cell? To answer this question, we use an adjusted form of the residual that behaves like a z-score. It is called the **standardized residual.**

> ## Standardized Residual
>
> The **standardized residual** for a cell equals
>
> $$(\text{observed count} - \text{expected count})/se.$$
>
> Here, se denotes a standard error for the sampling distribution of (observed count − expected count), when the variables are independent.

A standardized residual reports the number of standard errors that an observed count falls from its expected count. The se describes how much the (observed − expected) difference would tend to vary in repeated random sampling if the variables were independent. Its formula is complex, and we'll not give it here. Software can easily find standardized residuals for us.

When H_0: independence is true, the standardized residuals have approximately a standard normal distribution: They fluctuate around a mean of 0, with a standard deviation of 1. There is about a 5% chance that any particular standardized residual exceeds 2 in absolute value, and less than a 1% chance that it exceeds 3 in absolute value. See the margin figure. A large standardized residual provides evidence against independence in that cell. A value exceeding about 3 in absolute value provides strong evidence against independence. A value above +3 suggests that the population proportion for that cell is higher than what independence predicts. A value below −3 indicates that the population proportion for that cell is lower than what independence predicts.

When we inspect many cells in a table, some standardized residuals could be large just by random variation. Values below −3 or above +3, however, are quite convincing evidence of a true effect in that cell.

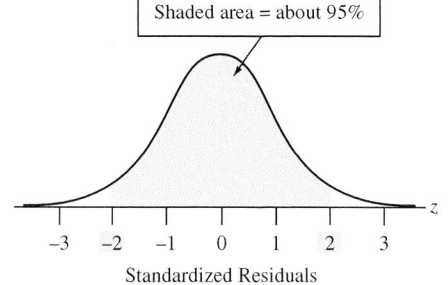

Shaded area = about 95%

Standardized Residuals

Standardized residuals

Example 9

Religiosity and Gender

Picture the Scenario

Table 11.16 shows some artificial tables comparing females and males on their religious attendance. Let's look at some actual data on religiosity. Table 11.17 displays observed and expected cell counts and the standardized residuals for the association between gender and response to the question, "To what extent do you consider yourself a religious person?" The possible responses were (very religious, moderately religious, slightly religious, not religious at all). The data are from the 2008 GSS. The table is in the form provided by MINITAB (which actually calls the standardized residuals "adjusted residuals").

Table 11.17 Religiosity by Gender, With Expected Counts and Standardized Residuals

Large positive standardized residuals (in green) indicate strong evidence of a higher population cell proportion than expected under independence. Large negative standardized residuals (in red) indicate strong evidence of a lower population proportion than expected.

Rows: gender   Columns: religiosity

	Very	Moderately	Slightly	Not	All	
Female	241	499	208	131	1079	← Counts
	201.8	454.8	251.4	171.0	1079.0	← Expected counts
	4.513	4.016	−4.606	−4.916		← Standardized residuals
Male	133	344	258	186	921	
	172.2	388.2	214.6	146.0	921.0	
	−4.513	−4.016	4.606	4.916		
All	374	843	466	317	2000	

Cell Contents: Count

Expected count

Adjusted residual   ← This is the name MINITAB uses for standardized residuals.

Source: Data from CSM, UC Berkeley.

Questions to Explore

a. How would you interpret the standardized residual of 4.513 in the first cell?

b. Interpret the standardized residuals in the entire table.

Think It Through

a. The cell for females who are very religious has observed count = 241, expected count = 201.8, and the standardized residual = 4.513. The difference between the observed and expected counts is more than 3 standard errors. In fact it exceeds 4 in absolute value, which tells us this cell shows a much greater discrepancy than we'd expect if the variables were truly independent. There's strong evidence that the population proportion for that cell (female and very religious) is higher than independence predicts.

b. Table 11.17 exhibits large positive residuals above 4 in four out of eight cells. These are the cells in which the observed count is much larger than the expected count. Those cells had strong evidence of more frequent occurrence than if religiosity and gender were independent. The table exhibits large negative residuals in the other four cells. In these cells, the observed count is much smaller than the expected count. There's strong evidence that the population has fewer subjects in these cells than if the variables were independent.

Insight

The standardized residuals help to describe the pattern of this association: Compared to what we'd expect if religiosity and gender were independent it appears based on this sample, there are more females who are very religious or moderately religious and more males who are slightly religious or not at all religious.

Try Exercise 11.33

In Practice Software Can Find Standardized Residuals

Most software has the option of reporting **standardized residuals.** For instance, they are available in MINITAB (where they are called *adjusted residuals*), in SPSS (where they are called *adjusted standardized residuals*), and at the GSS Web site (by checking Show Z-statistic).

11.4 Practicing the Basics

11.33 Standardized residuals for happiness and income The
table displays the observed and expected cell counts and
the standardized residuals for testing independence of
happiness and family income, for GSS data.

```
Rows:   income    Columns:   happiness
            not     pretty     very    All
above        26        233      164    423
           66.9      231.1    125.0  423.0
         -6.136      0.206    4.681
average     117        473      293    883
          139.6      482.5    261.0  883.0
         -2.789     -0.859    3.167
below       172        383      132    687
          108.6      375.4    203.0  687.0
          8.193      0.721   -7.337
All         315       1089      589   1993
```

a. How would you interpret the standardized residual of
4.681?

b. Interpret the standardized residuals highlighted in
green.

c. Interpret the standardized residuals highlighted in red.

11.34 Happiness and religious attendance The table shows
MINITAB output for data from the 2008 GSS on happiness and frequency of attending religious services (1 = at
most several times a year, 2 = once a month to nearly
every week, 3 = every week to several times a week).

```
Rows: religion   Columns:    happiness
Not too happy    Pretty happy    Very happy
1     201             609            268
     4.057           1.731         -5.107
2      46             224            132
    -2.566           0.456          1.541
3      66             265            196
    -2.263          -2.376          4.385
Cell Contents:   Count
                 Adjusted residual
Pearson Chi-Square = 36.445, DF = 4,
P-Value = 0.000
```

a. Based on the chi-squared statistic and P-value, give
a conclusion about the association between the
variables.

b. The numbers below the counts in the table are standardized residuals. Which cells have strong evidence
that in the population there are more subjects than if
the variables were independent?

c. Which cells have strong evidence that in the population there are fewer subjects than if the variables were
independent?

11.35 Marital happiness and general happiness Table 11.15
showed the association between general happiness and
marital happiness. The table shown here gives the standardized residuals for those data, in parentheses.

a. Explain what a relatively small standardized residual
such as −0.1 in the second cell represents.

b. Identify the cells in which you'd infer that the population has more cases than would occur if happiness and
marital happiness were independent.

Marital	Happiness		
Happiness	Not Too Happy	Pretty Happy	Very Happy
Not too happy	13 (7.0)	15 (−0.1)	2 (−3.9)
Pretty happy	44 (3.7)	259 (11.5)	40 (−13.8)
Very happy	24 (−6.2)	215 (−11.3)	356 (14.9)

11.36 Happiness and marital status For the 2008 GSS, the table
shows cell counts and standardized residuals (in parentheses)
for happiness and marital status. Summarize the association
by indicating which marital statuses have strong evidence of
(i) more and (ii) fewer people in the population in the Very
Happy category than if the variables were independent.

	Happiness		
Marital Status	Very Happy	Pretty Happy	Not Too Happy
Married	398 (10.8)	490 (−3.6)	81 (−8.7)
Widowed	31 (−3.1)	95 (1.0)	37 (2.6)
Divorced	56 (−3.8)	169 (2.1)	55 (2.0)
Separated	11 (−2.6)	41 (0.7)	18 (2.4)
Never married	101 (−6.2)	304 (1.6)	123 (5.7)

Source: Data from CSM, UC Berkeley.

11.37 Gender gap? The table in Exercise 11.1 on gender and
party identification is shown again. The largest standardized residuals in absolute value were 2.69 for females
who identified as Democrats and −2.69 for males who
identified as Democrats. Interpret.

Sex	Political Party		
---	Dem	Indep	Repub
F	422	381	273
M	299	365	232

Source: Data from CSM, UC Berkeley.

11.38 Ideology and political party   Go to the GSS Web site sda.berkeley.edu/GSS/. For the 2008 survey, construct the 7 × 8 contingency table relating political ideology (POLVIEWS) and party identification (PARTYID).

a. Summarize the results of carrying out the chi-squared test.

b. Find the standardized residuals (by checking Show *z* Statistic). What do you learn from these residuals that you did not learn from the chi-squared test?

11.5 Small Sample Sizes: Fisher's Exact Test

The chi-squared test of independence, like one- and two-sample *z* tests for proportions, is a large-sample test. When the expected frequencies are small, any of them being less than about 5, small-sample tests are more appropriate than the chi-squared test. For 2 × 2 contingency tables, **Fisher's exact test** is a small-sample test of independence.

Fisher's exact test of the null hypothesis that two variables are independent was proposed by the British statistician and geneticist, Sir Ronald Fisher. The test is called *exact* because it uses a sampling distribution that gives exact probability calculations rather than the approximate ones that use the chi-squared distribution.

The calculations for Fisher's exact test are complex and beyond the scope of this text. The principle behind the test is straightforward (see Exercise 11.75), however, and statistical software provides its P-value. The smaller the P-value, the stronger is the evidence that the variables are associated.

Example 10

Fisher's exact test

A Tea-Tasting Experiment

Picture the Scenario

In introducing his small-sample test of independence in 1935, Fisher described the following experiment: Fisher enjoyed taking a break in the afternoon for tea. One day, his colleague Dr. Muriel Bristol claimed that when drinking tea she could tell whether the milk or the tea had been added to the cup first (she preferred milk first). To test her claim, Fisher asked her to taste eight cups of tea, four of which had the milk added first and four of which had the tea added first. She was told there were four cups of each type and was asked to indicate which four had the milk added first. The order of presenting the cups to her was randomized.

Table 11.18 shows the result of the experiment. Dr. Bristol predicted three of the four cups correctly that had milk poured first.

Table 11.18 Result of Tea-Tasting Experiment

The table cross-tabulates what was actually poured first (milk or tea) by what Dr. Bristol predicted was poured first. She had to indicate which four of the eight cups had the milk poured first.

Actual	Prediction		Total
---	Milk	Tea	
Milk	3	1	4
Tea	1	3	4
Total	4	4	8

For those cases where milk was poured first (row 1), denote p_1 as the probability of guessing that milk was added first. For those cases where tea was poured first, denote p_2 as the probability of guessing that milk was added first. If she really could predict when milk was poured first better than with random guessing, then $p_1 > p_2$. So we shall test $H_0: p_1 = p_2$ (prediction independent of actual pouring order) against $H_a: p_1 > p_2$.

Questions to Explore

a. Show the sample space of the five possible contingency table outcomes that could have occurred for this experiment.

b. Table 11.19 shows the result of using SPSS software to conduct the chi-squared test of the null hypothesis that her predictions were independent of the actual order of pouring. Is this test and its P-value appropriate for these data? Why or why not?

Table 11.19 Result of Fisher's Exact Test for Tea-Tasting Experiment

The chi-squared P-value is listed under Asymp. Sig. and the Fisher's exact test P-values are listed under Exact Sig. "Sig" is short for *significance* and "asymp." is short for *asymptotic*.

	Value	df	Asymp. Sig. (2-sided)	Exact Sig. (2-sided)	Exact Sig. (1-sided)
Pearson Chi-Square	2.000	1	.157		
Fisher's Exact Test				.486	.243

4 cells (100.0%) have expected count less than 5.

c. Table 11.19 also shows the result for Fisher's exact test of the same null hypothesis. The one-sided version of the test pertains to the alternative that her predictions are better than random guessing. How does the one-sided P-value relate to the probabilities for the five tables in part a? Does this P-value suggest that she had the ability to predict better than random guessing?

Think It Through

a. The possible sample tables have four observations in each row, because there were four cups with milk poured first and four cups with tea poured first. The tables also have four observations in each column, because Dr. Bristol was told there were four cups of each type and was asked to predict which four had the milk added first. Of the four cups where milk was poured first (row 1 of the table), the number she could predict correctly is 4, 3, 2, 1, or 0. These outcomes correspond to the sample tables:

	Guess Poured First									
Poured First	**Milk**	**Tea**	**Milk**	**Tea**	**Milk**	**Tea**	**Milk**	**Tea**	**Milk**	**Tea**
Milk	4	0	3	1	2	2	1	3	0	4
Tea	0	4	1	3	2	2	3	1	4	0

These are the five possible tables with totals of 4 in each row and 4 in each column.

b. The cell counts in Table 11.18 are small. Each cell has expected count $(4 \times 4)/8 = 2$. Since they are less than 5, the chi-squared test is not appropriate. In fact, Table 11.19 warns us that all four cells have expected counts less than 5. The table reports $X^2 = 2.0$ with

Recall

Expected cell count = (row total ×
column total) divided by total sample size. ◄

P-value = 0.157, but software provides results whether or not they are valid, and it's up to us to know when we can use a method.

c. The one-sided P-value reported by SPSS is for the alternative $H_a: p_1 > p_2$. It equals 0.243. This is the probability, presuming H_0 to be true, of the observed table (Table 11.18) and the more extreme table giving even more evidence in favor of $p_1 > p_2$. That more extreme table is the one with counts (4, 0) in the first row and (0, 4) in the second row, corresponding to guessing all four cups correctly. The P-value of 0.243 does not give much evidence against the null hypothesis.

Insight

This experiment did not establish an association between the actual order of pouring and Dr. Bristol's predictions. If she had predicted all four cups correctly, the one-sided P-value would have been 0.014. We might then believe her claim. With a larger sample, we would not need such extreme results to get a small P-value.

Try Exercise 11.41

Actual	Guess Milk	Guess Tea	Total
Milk	3	—	4
Tea	—	—	4
Total	4	4	8

In part a of Example 10, notice that for the given row and column marginal totals of four each, the count in the first cell determines the other three cell counts. For example, for the actual data (Table 11.18), knowing she guessed three of the four cups correctly that had milk poured first determines the other three cells (see the margin). Because the count in the first cell determines the others, that cell count is regarded as the test statistic for Fisher's exact test. The P-value finds the probability of that count and of the other possible counts for that cell that provide even more evidence in support of H_a. Table 11.19 indicates that the P-value is 0.486 for the two-alternative, $H_a: p_1 \neq p_2$. This alternative hypothesis investigates whether her predictions are better or worse than with random guessing. The P-value of 0.486 also does not give much evidence against the null hypothesis that her predictions are independent of the actual pouring order.

SUMMARY: Fisher's Exact Test of Independence for 2 × 2 Tables

1. **Assumptions:**
   Two binary categorical variables
   Randomization, such as random sampling or a randomized experiment

2. **Hypotheses:**
   H_0: The two variables are independent ($H_0: p_1 = p_2$)
   H_a: The two variables are associated
   $$\text{(Choose } H_a: p_1 \neq p_2 \text{ or } H_a: p_1 > p_2 \text{ or } H_a: p_1 < p_2).$$

3. **Test statistic:** First cell count (this determines the others, given the margin totals).

4. **P-value:** Probability that the first cell count equals the observed value or a value even more extreme than observed in the direction predicted by H_a.

5. **Conclusion:** Report P-value and interpret in context. If a decision is needed, reject H_0 when P-value ≤ significance level (such as 0.05).

The main use of Fisher's exact test is for small sample sizes, when the chi-squared test is not valid. However, Fisher's exact test can be used with *any* sample sizes. It also extends to tables of arbitrary size $r \times c$. The computations are complex, and unfortunately most software currently can perform it only for 2 × 2 tables.

Using the Ordering of Categories

Some categorical variables have a natural ordering of the categories. There is a low end and a high end of the categorical scale. Examples are education attained (less than high school, high school, some college, college degree, advanced degree), appraisal of a company's inventory level (too low, about right, too high), and the happiness and income variables used in this chapter. Such variables are called **ordinal** variables. The chi-squared test of independence treats the categories as unordered. It takes the same value regardless of the order the categories are listed in the table. This is because with any reordering of the categories, the set of row and column totals does not change, and so the expected frequency that goes with a particular observed cell count does not change.

When there is only a weak association, tests that use the ordering information are often more powerful than the chi-squared, giving smaller P-values and stronger evidence against H_0. One way to do this treats the two categorical variables as quantitative: Assign scores to the rows and to the columns, and then use the correlation to describe the strength of the association. A significance test can be based on the size of the correlation. This is beyond our scope here, but the next chapter presents inference methods for two quantitative variables.

11.5 Practicing the Basics

11.39 Keeping old dogs mentally sharp In an experiment with beagles ages 7–11, the dogs attempted to learn how to find a treat under a certain black-colored block and then relearn that task with a white-colored block. The control group of dogs received standard care and diet. The diet and exercise group were given dog food fortified with vegetables and citrus pulp and vitamin E and C supplements plus extra exercise and social play. All 12 dogs in the diet and exercise group were able to solve the entire task, but only 2 of the 8 dogs in the control group could do so. (Background material from N. W. Milgram et al., *Neurobiology of Aging,* vol. 26, 2005, pp. 77–90.)

a. Show how to summarize the results in a contingency table.

b. Conduct all steps of Fisher's exact test of the hypothesis that whether a dog can solve the task is independent of the treatment group. Use the two-sided alternative hypothesis. Interpret.

c. Why is it improper to conduct the chi-squared test for these data?

11.40 Tea-tasting results Consider the tea-tasting experiment of Example 10 and Table 11.18. Consider the possible sample table in which all four of her predictions about the cups that had milk poured first are correct. Using software, find the P-value for the one-sided alternative. Interpret the P-value.

11.41 Claritin and nervousness An advertisement by Schering Corporation for the allergy drug Claritin mentioned that in a pediatric randomized clinical trial, symptoms of nervousness were shown by 4 of 188 patients on Claritin and 2 of 262 patients taking placebo.

Denote the population proportion who would show such symptoms by p_1 for Claritin and by p_2 for placebo. The computer printout shows results of significance tests for H_0: $p_1 = p_2$.

a. Report the P-value for the small-sample test, with H_a: $p_1 \neq p_2$. Interpret in the context of this study.

b. Is it appropriate to conduct the chi-squared test for these data? Why or why not?

Analyses of Claritin data

```
Rows: treatment Columns: nervousness

              yes       no

Claritin     4        184
Placebo      2        260

Statistic                      P-Value
Fisher's Exact Test (2-Tail)    0.24
Chi-squared = 1.55              0.21
```

11.42 AIDS and condom use Chatterjee et al. (1995, p. 132) described a study about the effect of condoms in reducing the spread of AIDS. This two-year Italian study followed heterosexual couples where one partner was infected with the HIV virus. Of 171 couples who always used condoms, 3 partners became infected with HIV, while of 55 couples who did not always use condoms, 8 partners became infected. Test whether the rates are significantly different.

a. Define p_1 and p_2 in this context, and specify the null and two-sided alternative hypotheses.

b. For these data, software reports

```
Pearson Chi-Square = 14.704, DF = 1,
P-Value = 0.0001
*Note* 1 cell with expected count less than 5
Fisher's exact test: P-Value = 0.0007
```

Report the result of the test that you feel is most appropriate for these data. For the test you chose, report the P-value and interpret in the context of this study.

Chapter Review

ANSWERS TO THE CHAPTER FIGURE QUESTIONS

Figure 11.1 The higher-income subjects were more likely to be very happy and less likely to be not too happy.

Figure 11.2 The height of the bars is the same for males and females at each level of happiness.

Figure 11.3 The chi-squared statistic can't be negative because it sums squared differences divided by positive expected frequencies.

Figure 11.4 We use only the right tail because larger chi-squared values provide greater evidence against H_0. Chi-squared values in the left tail represent small differences between observed and expected frequencies and do not provide evidence against H_0.

Figure 11.5 Whether we get $\frac{1}{4}$ or 4 for the relative risk depends merely on which group we call group 1 and which we call group 2.

CHAPTER SUMMARY

This chapter showed how to analyze the association between two categorical variables:

- By *describing the counts* in contingency tables using the **conditional distributions** across the categories of the response variable. If the population conditional distributions are identical, the two variables are **independent.**

- By using the **chi-squared** statistic to **test the null hypothesis of independence.**

- By *describing the strength of association with a* **measure of association** such as the **difference of proportions** and the **ratio of proportions** (the **relative risk**). When there is independence, a population difference of proportions equals 0 and a population relative risk equals 1. The stronger the association, the farther the measures fall from these baseline values.

- By *describing the pattern of association* by comparing observed and expected cell counts using **standardized residuals.** A standardized residual reports the number of standard errors that an observed count falls from an expected count. A value larger than about 3 in absolute value indicates that the cell provides strong evidence of association.

The **expected cell counts** are values with the same margins as the observed cell counts but that satisfy the null hypothesis

of independence. The **chi-squared test statistic** compares the observed cell counts to the expected cell counts, using

$$X^2 = \sum \frac{(\text{observed count} - \text{expected count})^2}{\text{expected count}}.$$

Under the null hypothesis, the X^2 test statistic has a large-sample **chi-squared distribution.** The **degrees of freedom** depend on the number of rows r and the number of columns c through $df = (r - 1) \times (c - 1)$. The P-value is the right-tail probability above the observed value of X^2.

The expected cell counts for the chi-squared test should be at least 5. **Fisher's exact test** does not have a sample size restriction. It is used to test independence with samples that are too small for the chi-squared test.

The chi-squared statistic can also be used for a hypothesis involving a single categorical variable. For testing a hypothesis that predicts particular population proportion values for each category of the variable, the chi-squared statistic is referred to as a **goodness-of-fit** statistic.

The next chapter introduces methods for describing and making inferences about the association between two *quantitative* variables. We'll learn more about the correlation and regression methods that Chapter 3 introduced.

SUMMARY OF NOTATION

$X^2 = $ chi-squared statistic for testing independence of two categorical variables

CHAPTER PROBLEMS

Practicing the Basics

11.43 Female for president? When recent General Social Surveys have asked, "If your party nominated a woman for president, would you vote for her if she were qualified for the job?" about 94% of females and 94% of males

answered yes, the rest answered no. (*Source*: Data from CSM, UC Berkeley.)

a. For males and for females, report the conditional distributions on this response variable in a 2 × 2 table, using outcome categories (yes, no).

b. If results for the entire population are similar to these, does it seem possible that gender and opinion about having a woman president are independent? Explain.

11.44 Down syndrome diagnostic test The table shown, from Example 8 in Chapter 5, cross-tabulates whether a fetus has Down syndrome by whether or not the triple blood diagnostic test for Down syndrome is positive (that is, indicates that the fetus has Down syndrome).

a. Tabulate the conditional distributions for the blood test result, given the true Down syndrome status.

b. For the Down cases, what percentage was diagnosed as positive by the diagnostic test? For the unaffected cases, what percentage got a negative test result? Does the diagnostic test appear to be a good one?

c. Construct the conditional distribution on Down syndrome status, for those who have a positive test result. (*Hint:* You condition on the first column total and find proportions in that column.) Of those cases, what percentage truly have Down syndrome? Is the result surprising? Explain why this probability is small.

Down Syndrome Status	Blood Test Result		
	Positive	**Negative**	**Total**
D (Down)	48	6	54
D^c (unaffected)	1307	3921	5228
Total	1355	3927	5282

11.45 Down and chi-squared For the data in the previous exercise, $X^2 = 114.4$. Show all steps of the chi-squared test of independence.

11.46 What is *df*? The contingency table that follows has $df = 4$. Show this, by filling in the missing cell counts.

	A	B	C	D	E	Total
	24	21	12	10	—	100
	—	—	—	—	—	100
Total	40	40	40	40	40	200

11.47 Herbs and the common cold A recent randomized experiment of a multiherbal formula (Immumax) containing echinacea, garlic, ginseng, zinc and vitamin C, was found to improve cold symptoms in adults over a placebo group. "At the end of the study, eight (39%) of the placebo recipients and 18 (60%) of the Immumax recipients reported that the study medication had helped improve their cold symptoms (chi-squared P-value = 0.01)." (M. Yakoot et al., *International Journal of General Medicine*, vol. 4, 2011, pp. 45–51).

a. Identify the response variable and the explanatory variable and their categories for the 2 × 2 contingency table that provided this particular analysis.

b. How would you explain to someone who has never studied statistics how to interpret the parenthetical part of the quoted sentence?

11.48 Happiness and number of friends The table shows GSS data on happiness and the number of close friends, with expected cell counts given underneath the observed counts.

Number of Close Friends	Happiness			Total
	Not Too Happy	**Pretty Happy**	**Very Happy**	
0–1	34	92	43	169
	19.2	95.1	54.7	
2–5	83	418	200	701
	79.5	394.6	226.9	
6 or more	47	304	225	576
	65.3	324.3	186.4	
Total	164	814	468	1446

a. Suppose the variables were independent. Explain what this means in this context.

b. Explain what is meant by an expected cell count. Show how to get the expected cell count for the first cell, for which the observed count is 34.

c. Compare the expected cell frequencies to the observed counts. Based on this, what is a profile of subjects who tend to be (i) more happy than independence predicts and (ii) less happy than independence predicts.

11.49 Gender gap? Exercise 11.1 showed a 2 × 3 table relating gender and political party identification, shown again here. The chi-squared statistic for these data equals 8.294. Conduct all five steps of the chi-squared test.

Sex	Political Party		
	Dem	**Indep**	**Repub**
F	422	381	273
M	299	365	232

11.50 Job satisfaction and income A recent GSS was used to cross-tabulate income (<$15 thousand, $15–25 thousand, $25–40 thousand, >$40 thousand) in dollars with job satisfaction (very dissatisfied, little dissatisfied, moderately satisfied, very satisfied) for 96 subjects.

a. For these data, $X^2 = 6.0$. What is its *df* value, and what is its approximate sampling distribution, if H_0 is true?

b. For this test, the P-value is 0.74. Interpret in the context of these variables.

c. What decision would you make with a 0.05 significance level? Can you accept H_0 and conclude that job satisfaction is independent of income?

11.51 Aspirin and heart attacks for women A study in the *New England Journal of Medicine* compared cardiovascular events for treatments of low-dose aspirin or placebo among 39, 876 healthy female health care providers for an average duration of about 10 years. Results indicated that women receiving aspirin and those receiving placebo did not differ for rates of a first major cardiovascular event, death from cardiovascular causes, or fatal or non-fatal heart attacks. However, women receiving aspirin had lower rates of stroke than those receiving placebo (Data from *N. Engl. J. Med.*, vol. 352, 2005, pp. 1293–1304).

Women's Aspirin Study Data

Group	Cardiovascular Events		
	Mini-Stroke	**Stroke**	**No Strokes**
Placebo	240	259	19443
Aspirin	185	219	19530

a. Use software to test independence. Show (i) assumptions, (ii) hypotheses, (iii) test statistic, (iv) P-value, (v) conclusion in the context of this study.

b. Describe the association by finding and interpreting the relative risk for the stroke category.

11.52 Women's role A recent GSS presented the statement, "Women should take care of running their homes and leave running the country up to men," and 14.8% of the male respondents agreed. Of the female respondents, 15.9% agreed. Of respondents having less than a high school education, 39.0% agreed. Of respondents having at least a high school education, 11.7% agreed.

a. Report the difference between the proportion of males and the proportion of females who agree.

b. Report the difference between the proportion at the low education level and the proportion at the high education level who agree.

c. Which variable, gender or educational level, seems to have the stronger association with opinion? Explain your reasoning.

11.53 Seat belt helps? The table refers to passengers in autos and light trucks involved in accidents in the state of Maine in a recent year.

a. Use the difference of proportions to describe the strength of association. Interpret.

b. Use the relative risk to describe the strength of association. Interpret.

Maine Accident Data

Seat Belt	Injury	
	Yes	**No**
No	3865	27,037
Yes	2409	35,383

Source: Dr. Cristanna Cook, Medical Care Development, Augusta, Maine.

11.54 Race and party ID The table shows data from an SPSS printout for some analyses of 2008 GSS data on race and party ID.

a. Interpret the expected count for the first cell.

b. Interpret the standardized residual of 12.5 for the first cell (SPSS calls it an adjusted residual).

c. How would you summarize to someone who has never studied statistics what you learn from the standardized residuals given in the four corner cells on this printout?

race* party_ID Crosstabulation

			party ID			
			democrat	independent	republican	Total
race	black	Count	192	75	8	275
		Expected Count	100.0	101.5	73.5	275.0
		Adjusted Residual	12.5	−3.6	−9.7	
	white	Count	459	586	471	1516
		Expected Count	551.0	559.5	405.5	1516.0
		Adjusted Residual	−12.5	3.6	9.7	
Total		Count	651	661	479	1791
		Expected Count	651.0	661.0	479.0	1791.0

Source: Data from CSM, UC Berkeley.

11.55 Happiness and sex A contingency table from the 2008 GSS relating happiness to number of sex partners in the previous year (0, 1, at least 2) had standardized residuals as shown in the table. Interpret the highlighted standardized residuals.

Results on Happiness and Sex

```
Rows:   partners  Columns: happy
              not        pretty        very
0              84          235          95
             (3.1)        (0.7)       (-3.3)
1             130          578         381
            (-5.2)       (-2.3)        (6.6)
2              58          160          41
             (3.4)        (2.3)       (-5.2)
```

Source: Data from CSM, UC Berkeley.

11.56 Education and religious beliefs When data from a recent GSS were used to form a 3 × 3 table that cross-tabulates highest degree (1 = less than high school, 2 = high school or junior college, 3 = bachelor or graduate) with religious beliefs (F = fundamentalist, M = moderate, L = liberal), the three largest standardized residuals were: 6.8 for the cell (3, F), 6.3 for the cell (3, L), and 4.5 for the cell (1, F). Summarize how to interpret these three standardized residuals.

11.57 TV and aggression From a study described in Example 5 in the previous chapter, the proportion of males committing aggressive acts was 4 out of 45 for those who watched less than 1 hour of TV a day, and 117 out of 315 for those who watched at least 1 hour per day. MINITAB reports the printout shown for conducting Fisher's exact test (two-sided) for these data.

a. State hypotheses for the test, defining the notation.

b. Report the P-value that software reports, and interpret in the context of this study.

Data on TV watching and aggression

```
Rows: TV  Columns: aggression
           no        yes
high      198        117
low        41          4
Fisher's exact test:
P-Value = 0.0000751
```

11.58 Botox side effects An advertisement for Botox Cosmetic by Allergan, Inc. for treating wrinkles appeared in several magazines. The back page of the ad showed the results of a randomized clinical trial to compare 405 people receiving Botox injections to 130 people receiving placebo in terms of the frequency of various side effects. The side effect of pain in the face was reported by 9 people receiving Botox and 0 people receiving placebo. Use software to conduct a two-sided test of the hypothesis that the probability of this side effect is the same for each group. Report all steps of the test, and interpret results.

Concepts and Applications

11.59 Student data Refer to the FL Student Survey data file on the text CD. Using software, create and analyze descriptively and inferentially the contingency table relating religiosity and belief in life after death. Summarize your analyses in a short report.

11.60 Marital happiness decreasing? At sda.berkeley.edu /GSS, cross-tabulate HAPMAR with YEAR, so you can see how conditional distributions on marital happiness in the GSS have changed since 1973. Using conditional distributions and standardized residuals, explain how these results show a very slight trend over time for fewer people to report being very happy. (You can get the standardized residuals by checking Show z-statistic at the Web site.)

11.61 Another predictor of happiness? Go to sda.berkeley .edu/GSS and find a variable that is associated with happiness, other than variables used in this chapter. Use methods from this chapter to describe and make inferences about the association, in a one-page report.

11.62 Pregnancy associated with contraceptive use? Whether or not a young married woman becomes pregnant in the next year is a categorical variable with categories (yes, no). Another categorical variable to consider is whether she and her partner use contraceptives with categories (yes, no). Would you expect these variables to be independent, or associated? Explain.

11.63 Babies and gray hair A young child wonders what causes women to have babies. For each woman who lives on her block, she observes whether her hair is gray and whether she has young children, with the results shown in the table that follows.

a. Construct the 2×2 contingency table that cross-tabulates gray hair (yes, no) with has young children (yes, no) for these nine women.

b. Treating has young children as the response variable, obtain the conditional distributions for those women who have gray hair and for those who do not. Does there seem to be an association?

c. Noticing this association, the child concludes that not having gray hair is what causes women to have children. Use this example to explain why association does not necessarily imply causation.

Woman	Gray Hair	Young Children
Andrea	No	Yes
Mary	Yes	No
Linda	No	Yes
Jane	No	Yes
Maureen	Yes	No
Judy	Yes	No
Margo	No	Yes
Carol	Yes	No
Donna	No	Yes

11.64 When is chi-squared not valid? Give an example of a contingency table for which the chi-squared test of independence should not be used.

11.65 Gun homicide in United States and Britain According to recent United Nations figures, the annual gun homicide rate is 62.4 per one million residents in the United States and 1.3 per one million residents in Britain.

a. Show how to compare the proportion of residents of the two countries killed annually by guns using the difference of proportions. Show how the results differ according to whether the United States or Britain is identified as Group 1.

b. Show how to compare the proportion of residents of the two countries using the relative risk. Show how the results differ according to whether the United States or Britain is identified as Group 1.

c. When both proportions are very close to 0, as in this example, which measure do you think is more useful for describing the strength of association? Why?

11.66 Colon cancer and race The State Center for Health Statistics for the North Carolina Division of Public Health released a report in 2010 that indicates that there are racial disparities in colorectal cancer incidence and mortality rates. The report states, "African Americans are less likely to receive appropriate screenings that reduce the risk of developing or dying from colorectal cancer." During 2002–2006, the rate of incidence for African Americans was 57.3 per 100,000 versus 46.5 per 100,000 for White residents (www.schs.state.nc.us/SCHS). African Americans were 19% more likely to have been diagnosed with colon cancer. Explain how to get this estimate.

11.67 True or false: $X^2 = 0$ The null hypothesis for the test of independence between two categorical variables is H_0: $X^2 = 0$, for the sample chi-squared statistic X^2. (*Hint:* Do hypotheses refer to a sample or the population?)

11.68 True or false: Group 1 becomes Group 2 Interchanging two rows or interchanging two columns in a contingency table has no effect on the value of the X^2 statistic.

11.69 True or false: Statistical but not practical significance Even when the sample conditional distributions in a contingency table are only slightly different, when the sample size is very large it is possible to have a large X^2 statistic and a very small P-value for testing H_0: independence.

11.70 Statistical versus practical significance In any significance test, when the sample size is very large, we have not necessarily established an important result when we obtain statistical significance. Explain what this means in the context of analyzing contingency tables with a chi-squared test.

11.71 Normal and chi-squared with $df = 1$ When $df = 1$, the P-value from the chi-squared test of independence is the same as the P-value for the two-sided test comparing two proportions with the z test statistic. This is because of a direct connection between the standard normal distribution and the chi-squared distribution with $df = 1$: Squaring a z-score yields a chi-squared value with $df = 1$ having chi-squared right-tail probability equal to the two-tail normal probability for the z-score.

a. Illustrate this with $z = 1.96$, the z-score with a two-tail probability of 0.05. Using the chi-squared table or software, show that the square of 1.96 is the chi-squared score for $df = 1$ with a P-value of 0.05.

b. Show the connection between the normal and chi-squared values with P-value $= 0.01$.

11.72 Multiple response variables ◆◆ Each subject in a sample of 100 men and 100 women is asked to indicate which of the following factors (one or more) are responsible for increases in crime committed by teenagers: A—the increasing gap in income between the rich and poor, B—the increase in the percentage of single-parent families, C—insufficient time that parents spend with their children. To analyze whether responses differ by gender of respondent, we cross-classify the responses by gender, as the table shows.

a. Is it valid to apply the chi-squared test of independence to these data? Explain.

b. Explain how this table actually provides information needed to cross-classify gender with each of three variables. Construct the contingency table relating gender to opinion about whether factor A is responsible for increases in teenage crime.

Three Factors for Explaining Teenage Crime

Gender	A	B	C
Men	60	81	75
Women	75	87	86

11.73 Standardized residuals for 2×2 tables ◆◆ The table that follows shows the standardized residuals in parentheses for GSS data about the statement, "Women should take care of running their homes and leave running the country up to men." The absolute value of the standardized residual is 13.2 in every cell. For chi-squared tests with 2×2 tables, since $df = 1$, only one nonredundant piece of information exists about whether an association exists. If observed count > expected count in one cell, observed count < expected count in the other cell in that row or column. Explain why this is true, using the fact that observed and expected counts have the same row and column totals. (In fact, in 2×2 tables, all four standardized residuals have absolute value equal to the square root of the X^2 test statistic.)

Year	Agree	Disagree
1974	509 (13.2)	924 (−13.2)
1998	280 (−13.2)	1534 (13.2)

11.74 Variability of chi-squared For the chi-squared distribution, the mean equals df and the standard deviation equals $\sqrt{2(df)}$.

a. Explain why, as a rough approximation, for a large df value, 95% of the chi-squared distribution falls within $df \pm 2\sqrt{2(df)}$.

b. With $df = 8$, show that $df \pm 2\sqrt{2(df)}$ gives the interval $(0, 16)$ for *approximately* containing 95% of the distribution. Using the chi-squared table, show that *exactly* 95% of the distribution actually falls between 0 and 15.5.

11.75 Explaining Fisher's exact test ◆◆ A pool of six candidates for three managerial positions includes three females and three males. Denote the three females by F1, F2, F3 and the three males by M1, M2, M3. The result of choosing three individuals for the managerial positions is (F2, M1, M3).

a. Identify the 20 possible samples that could have been selected. Explain why the contingency table relating gender to whether chosen for the observed sample is

Chosen For Position

Gender	Yes	No
Male	2	1
Female	1	2

b. Let $\hat{p}_1$ denote the sample proportion of males selected and $\hat{p}_2$ the sample proportion of females. For the observed table, $\hat{p}_1 - \hat{p}_2 = (2/3) - (1/3) = 1/3$. Of the 20 possible samples, show that 10 have $\hat{p}_1 - \hat{p}_2 \geq 1/3$. (Note that, if the three managers were randomly selected, the probability would equal $10/20 = 0.50$ of obtaining $\hat{p}_1 - \hat{p}_2 \geq 1/3$. This is the reasoning that provides the one-sided P-value for Fisher's exact test with $H_a: p_1 > p_2$.)

11.76 Likelihood-ratio chi-squared ◆◆ For testing independence, most software also reports another chi-squared statistic, called **likelihood-ratio chi-squared.** It equals

$$G^2 = 2\sum \left[\text{observed count} \times \log\left(\frac{\text{observed count}}{\text{expected count}} \right) \right].$$

It has similar properties as the X^2 statistic, such as $df = (r - 1) \times (c - 1)$.

a. Show that $G^2 = X^2 = 0$ when each observed count = expected count.

b. Explain why in practice you would not expect to get *exactly* $G^2 = X^2 = 0$, even if the variables are truly independent.

Student Activities

11.77 Conduct a research study using the GSS Go to the GSS codebook at sda.berkeley.edu/GSS. Your instructor will assign a categorical response variable. Conduct a research study in which you find at least two other categorical variables that have both a statistically significant and a practically significant association with that response variable, using data for the most recent year in which the response variable was surveyed. Analyze each association using the methods of this chapter. Write a two-page report, describing your analyses and summarizing the results of your research study. Be prepared to discuss your results in a class discussion, because the class will discuss which variables seemed to be especially relevant.

BIBLIOGRAPHY

Alan Agresti (2007). *An Introduction to Categorical Data Analysis,* 2nd edition. Hoboken, New Jersey: Wiley.

Samprit Chatterjee, Mark S. Handcock, and Jeffrey S. Simonoff (1995). A Case Book for *A First Course in Statistics and Data Analysis.* Hoboken, New Jersey: Wiley.

13

Multiple Regression

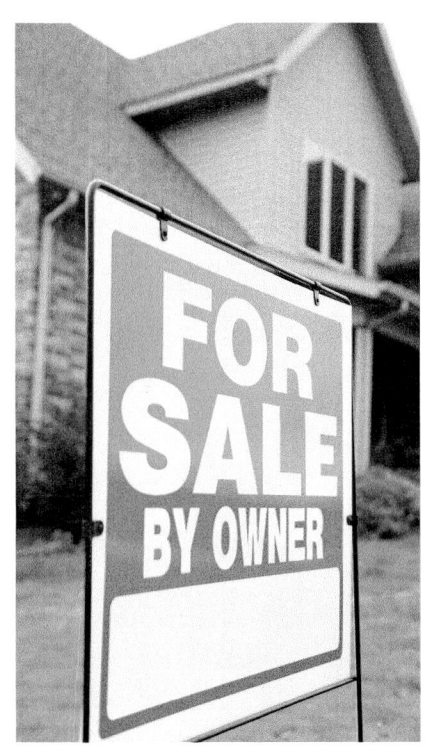

Example 1

Predicting the Selling Price of a House

Picture the Scenario

You are saving to buy a home, and you wonder how much it will cost. The House Selling Prices OR data file on the text CD has observations on 200 recent home sales in Corvallis, Oregon. Table 13.1 shows data for two homes.

Table 13.1 Selling Prices and Related Factors for a Sample of Home Sales

House	Selling Price	House Size (sq. ft)	Number of Bedrooms	Number of Bathrooms	Lot Size (sq. ft)	Year Built	Garage (Y/N)
1	$232,500	1679	3	1.5	10,019	1976	Y
2	$158,000	1292	1	1	217,800	1958	N

Variables listed are the selling price (in dollars), house size (in square feet), number of bedrooms, number of bathrooms, the lot size (in square feet), and whether or not the house has a garage. Table 13.2 reports the mean and standard deviation of these variables for all 200 home sales.

Table 13.2 Descriptive Statistics for Sales of 200 Homes

	Selling Price	House Size (sq. ft)	Number of Bedrooms	Number of Bathrooms	Lot Size (sq. ft)	Age
Mean	$267,466	2551	3.08	2.03	23,217	34.75
Standard deviation	$115,808	1238	1.10	0.77	47,637	24.44

Questions to Explore

In your community, if you know the values of such variables,

- How can you predict a home's selling price?
- How can you describe the association between selling price and the other variables?
- How can you make inferences about the population based on the sample data?

Thinking Ahead

You can find a regression equation to predict selling price by treating one of the other variables as the explanatory variable. However, since there are *several* explanatory variables, you might make better predictions by using *all* of them at once. That's the idea behind **multiple regression**. It uses *more than one* explanatory variable to predict a response variable. We'll learn how to apply multiple regression to a variety of analyses in Examples 2, 3, 8, 9, and 10 of this chapter.

Recall

Review the concept of *lurking variables* in Section 3.4. ◄

Besides helping you to better predict a response variable, multiple regression can help you analyze the association between two variables while controlling (keeping fixed) values of other variables. Such adjustment is important because the effect of an explanatory variable can change considerably after you account for potential lurking variables. A multiple regression analysis provides information not available from simple regression analyses involving only two variables at a time.

Section 13.1 presents the basics of multiple regression. Section 13.2 extends the concepts of correlation and r^2 for describing strength of association to multiple predictors (explanatory variables). Section 13.3 presents inference methods, and Section 13.4 shows how to check the model. Section 13.5 extends the model further to incorporate categorical explanatory variables. The final section presents a regression model for a categorical response variable.

Recall

This chapter builds strongly on the content in Chapter 12 on **regression** and **correlation** methods. You may want to review Sections 12.1 and 12.2 as you read Sections 13.1 and 13.2. ◄

13.1 Using Several Variables to Predict a Response

Chapter 12 modeled the mean μ_y of a quantitative response variable y and a quantitative explanatory variable x by the straight-line equation $\mu_y = \alpha + \beta x$. We refer to this model with a *single* predictor as **bivariate** (two-variable) **regression**, since it contains only two variables (x and y).

Now, suppose there are two predictors, denoted by x_1 and x_2. The bivariate regression equation generalizes to the **multiple regression** equation,

$$\mu_y = \alpha + \beta_1 x_1 + \beta_2 x_2.$$

In this equation, α, β_1, and β_2 are parameters. When we substitute values for x_1 and x_2, the equation specifies the population mean of y for all subjects with those values of x_1 and x_2. When there are additional predictors, each has a βx term.

Multiple Regression Model

The **multiple regression model** relates the mean μ_y of a quantitative response variable y to a set of explanatory variables $x_1, x_2, \ldots$ For three explanatory variables, for example, the multiple regression equation is

$$\mu_y = \alpha + \beta_1 x_1 + \beta_2 x_2 + \beta_3 x_3,$$

and the sample prediction equation is

$$\hat{y} = a + b_1 x_1 + b_2 x_2 + b_3 x_3.$$

With sample data, software estimates the multiple regression equation. It uses the method of least squares to find the best prediction equation (the one with the smallest possible sum of squared residuals).

Multiple regression

Example 2

Predicting Selling Price Using House Size and Number of Bedrooms

Picture the Scenario

For the house selling price data described in Example 1, MINITAB reports the results in Table 13.3 for a multiple regression analysis with selling price as the response variable and with house size and number of bedrooms as explanatory variables.

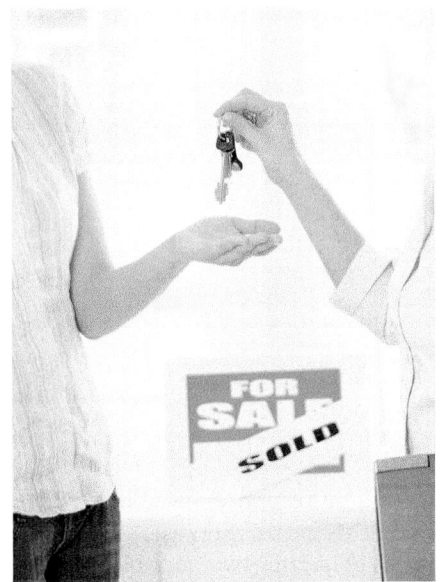

In Words

As in **bivariate regression**, we use the Greek letter β (beta) for parameters describing effects of explanatory variables, with β_1 and β_2 read as "beta one" and "beta two."

Table 13.3 Regression of Selling Price on House Size and Bedrooms

The regression equation is price = 60,102 + 63.0 house_size + 15,170 bedrooms

Predictor	Coef	SE Coef	T	P
Constant	60102	18623	3.23	0.001
House_size	62.983	4.753	13.25	0.000
Bedrooms	15170	5330	2.85	0.005

Questions to Explore

a. State the prediction equation.
b. The first home listed in Table 13.1 has house size = 1679 square feet, three bedrooms, and selling price $232,500. Find its predicted selling price and the residual (prediction error). Interpret the residual.

Think It Through

a. The response variable is y = selling price. Let x_1 = house size and x_2 = the number of bedrooms. From Table 13.3, the prediction equation is

$$\hat{y} = 60,102 + 63.0x_1 + 15,170x_2.$$

b. For $x_1 = 1679$ and $x_2 = 3$, the predicted selling price is

$$\hat{y} = 60,102 + 63.0(1679) + 15,170(3) = 211,389, \text{ that is, } \$211,389.$$

The residual is the prediction error,

$$y - \hat{y} = \$232,500 - \$211,389 = \$21,111.$$

This result tells us that the actual selling price was $21,111 higher than predicted.

Insight

The coefficients of house size and number of bedrooms are positive. As these variables increase, the predicted selling price increases, as we would expect.

Try Exercise 13.1

In Practice The Number of Explanatory Variables You Can Use Depends on the Amount of Data

In practice, you should not use many explanatory variables in a multiple regression model unless you have lots of data. A rough guideline is that *the sample size n should be at least 10 times the number of explanatory variables.* For example, to use two explanatory variables, you should have at least $n = 20$ observations.

Plotting Relationships

Always look at the data before doing a multiple regression analysis. Most software has the option of constructing scatterplots on a single graph for each pair of variables. This type of plot is called a **scatterplot matrix**.

Figure 13.1 shows a MINITAB scatterplot matrix for selling price, house size, and number of bedrooms. It shows each pair of variables twice. For a given pair, in one plot a variable is on the y-axis and in another it is on the x-axis. For instance, selling price of house is on the y-axis for the plots in the first row, whereas it is on the x-axis for the plots in the first column. Since selling price is the response variable for this example, the plots in the first row (where selling price is on the *y*-axis) are the ones of primary interest. These graphs show strong positive linear relationships between selling price and both house size and number of bedrooms. Because a scatterplot matrix shows each pair of variables twice, you only need to look at the plots in the upper-right triangle.

Selling price of houses is on the x-axis in the plots in this column

Selling price of houses is on the y-axis in the plots in this row

This plot is the scatterplot comparing price as the y-axis and bedrooms as the x-axis

Matrix Plot of House Price, House Size, Bedrooms

▲ **Figure 13.1** Scatterplot Matrix for Selling Price, House Size, and Number of Bedrooms. The middle plot in the top row has house size on the *x*-axis and selling price on the *y*-axis. The first plot in the second row reverses this, with selling price on the *x*-axis and house size on the *y*-axis. Question Why are the plots of main interest the ones in the top row?

Each scatterplot portrays only *two* variables. It's a two-dimensional picture. A multiple regression equation, which has *several* variables, is more difficult to portray graphically. Note also that the scatterplot involving the variable number of bedrooms as an explanatory variable has an appearance of columns of points. This is due to the highly discrete nature of this quantitative variable.

Interpretation of Multiple Regression Coefficients

The simplest way to interpret a multiple regression equation is to look at it in *two dimensions* as a function of a *single* explanatory variable. We can do this by fixing values for the other explanatory variable(s). For instance, let's fix x_1 = house size at the value 2000 square feet. Then the prediction equation simplifies to one with x_2 = number of bedrooms alone as the predictor,

$$\hat{y} = 60{,}102 + 63.0(2000) + 15{,}170x_2 = 186{,}102 + 15{,}170x_2.$$

For 2000-square-foot houses, the predicted selling price relates to number of bedrooms by $\hat{y} = 186{,}102 + 15{,}170x_2$. Since the slope coefficient of x_2 is 15,170, the predicted selling price increases by $15,170 for every bedroom added.

Likewise, we could fix the number of bedrooms, and then describe how the predicted selling price depends on the house size. Let's consider houses with number of bedrooms x_2 = three bedrooms. The prediction equation becomes

$$\hat{y} = 60{,}102 + 63.0x_1 + 15{,}170(3) = 105{,}612 + 63.0x_1.$$

For houses with this number of bedrooms, the predicted selling price increases by $63 for every additional square foot in house size or $6300 for every 100 square foot in size increase.

Can we say an increase of one bedroom has a larger impact on the selling price ($15,170) than an increase of a square foot in house size ($63 per square foot)?

No, we cannot compare these slopes for these explanatory variables because their units of measurement are not the same. Slopes can't be compared when the units differ. We could compare house size and lot size directly if they had the same units of square feet.

Recall

Section 10.5 showed that in multivariate analyses, we can **control** a variable statistically by keeping its value constant while we study the association between other variables. ◄

Summarizing the Effect While Controlling for a Variable

The multiple regression model states that *each* explanatory variable has a straight line relationship with the mean of y, given fixed values of the other explanatory variables. Specifically, *the model assumes that the slope for a particular explanatory variable is identical for all fixed values of the other explanatory variables.* For instance, the coefficient of x_1 in the prediction equation $\hat{y} = 60,102 + 63.0x_1 + 15,170x_2$ is 63.0 regardless of whether we plug in $x_2 = 1$ or $x_2 = 2$ or $x_2 = 3$ for the number of bedrooms. When you fix x_2 at these three levels, you can check that:

x_2	$\hat{y} = 60,102 + 63.0x_1 + 15,170x_2$
1	$\hat{y} = 75,272 + 63.0x_1$
2	$\hat{y} = 90,442 + 63.0x_1$
3	$\hat{y} = 105,612 + 63.0x_1$

The slope effect of house size is 63.0 for each equation. Setting x_2 at a variety of values yields a collection of parallel lines, each having slope 63.0. See Figure 13.2.

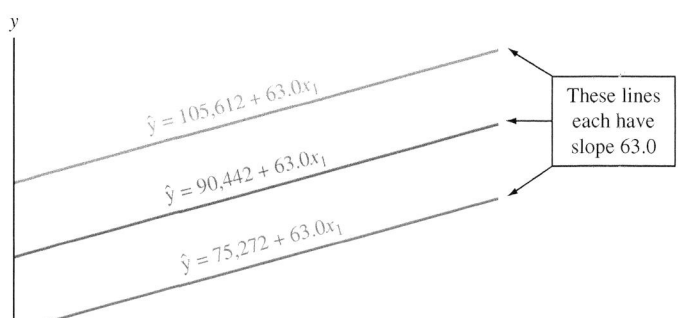

▲ **Figure 13.2** The Relationship Between $\hat{y}$ and x_1 for the Multiple Regression Equation $\hat{y} = 60,102 + 63.0x_1 + 15,170x_2$. This shows how the equation simplifies when number of bedrooms $x_2 = 1$, or $x_2 = 2$, or $x_2 = 3$. Question The lines move upward (to higher $\hat{y}$-values) as x_2 increases. How would you interpret this fact?

When we fix the value of x_2 we are holding it constant: We are *controlling* for x_2. That's the basis of the major difference between the interpretation of slopes in multiple regression and in bivariate regression:

- In multiple regression, a slope describes the effect of an explanatory variable while *controlling* effects of the other explanatory variables in the model.
- Bivariate regression has only a single explanatory variable. So a slope in bivariate regression describes the effect of that variable while *ignoring* all other possible explanatory variables.

For example, the bivariate regression between $y =$ selling price and $x_1 =$ house size is $\hat{y} = 97,997 + 66.4x_1$. In this equation, $x_2 =$ number of bedrooms and other possible predictors are ignored, not controlled. The equation describes the relationship for *all* the house sales in the data set. On the other hand, the equation $\hat{y} = 90,442 + 63.0x_1$ we obtained above by substituting $x_2 = 2$ into the multiple regression equation applies only for houses that have that number of bedrooms. In this case, number of bedrooms is controlled. This is why the slopes are different, 66.4 for bivariate regression and 63.0 for multiple regression.

One of the main uses of multiple regression is to identify potential lurking variables and control for them by including them as explanatory variables in the model. Doing so can have a major impact on a variable's effect. When we control a variable, we keep that variable from influencing the associations among the other variables in the study. As we've seen before, the direction of the effect can change after we control for a variable. Exercise 13.5 illustrates this for multiple regression modeling.

13.1 Practicing the Basics

13.1 Predicting weight For a study of University of Georgia female athletes, the prediction equation relating y = total body weight (in pounds) to x_1 = height (in inches) and x_2 = percent body fat is $\hat{y} = -121 + 3.50x_1 + 1.35x_2$.

  a. Find the predicted total body weight for a female athlete at the mean values of 66 and 18 for x_1 and x_2.

  b. An athlete with $x_1 = 66$ and $x_2 = 18$ has actual weight $y = 115$ pounds. Find the residual, and interpret it.

13.2 Does study help GPA? For the Georgia Student Survey file on the text CD, the prediction equation relating y = college GPA to x_1 = high school GPA and x_2 = study time (hours per day), is $\hat{y} = 1.13 + 0.643x_1 + 0.0078x_2$.

  a. Find the predicted college GPA of a student who has a high school GPA of 3.5 and who studies three hours a day.

  b. For students with fixed study time, what is the change in predicted college GPA when high school GPA increases from 3.0 to 4.0?

13.3 Predicting college GPA For all students at Walden University, the prediction equation for y = college GPA (range 0–4.0) and x_1 = high school GPA (range 0–4.0) and x_2 = college board score (range 200–800) is $\hat{y} = 0.20 + 0.50x_1 + 0.002x_2$.

  a. Find the predicted college GPA for students having (i) high school GPA = 4.0 and college board score = 800 and (ii) $x_1 = 2.0$ and $x_2 = 200$.

  b. For those students with $x_2 = 500$, show that $\hat{y} = 1.20 + 0.50x_1$.

  c. For those students with $x_2 = 600$, show that $\hat{y} = 1.40 + 0.50x_1$. Thus, compared to part b, the slope for x_1 is still 0.50, and increasing x_2 by 100 (from 500 to 600) shifts the intercept upward by $100 \times$ (slope for x_2) = $100(0.002) = 0.20$ units.

13.4 Interpreting slopes on GPA Refer to the previous exercise.

  a. Explain why setting x_2 at a variety of values yields a collection of parallel lines relating $\hat{y}$ to x_1. What is the value of the slope for those parallel lines?

  b. Since the slope 0.50 for x_1 is larger than the slope 0.002 for x_2, does this imply that x_1 has a larger effect than x_2 on y in this sample? Explain.

13.5 Does more education cause more crime? The FL Crime data file on the text CD has data for the 67 counties in Florida on

y = crime rate: Annual number of crimes in county per 1000 population

x_1 = education: Percentage of adults in county with at least a high school education

x_2 = urbanization: Percentage in county living in an urban environment.

The figure shows a scatterplot matrix. The correlations are 0.47 between crime rate and education, 0.68 between crime rate and urbanization, and 0.79 between education and urbanization. MINITAB multiple regression results are also displayed.

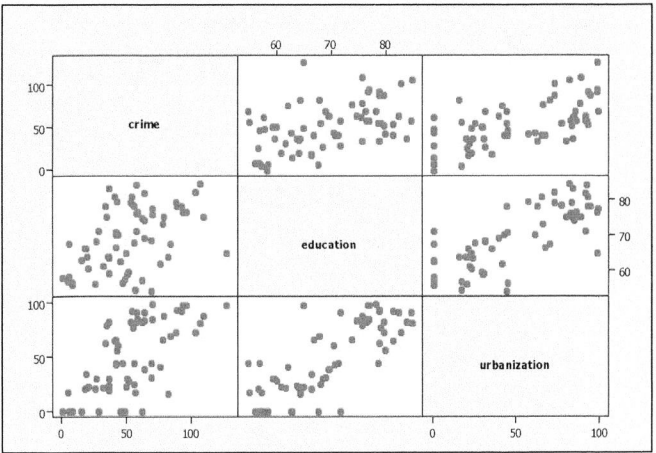

Scatterplot matrix for crime rate, education, and urbanization.

Multiple regression for y = crime rate, x_1 = education, and x_2 = urbanization.

Predictor	Coef	SE Coef	T	P
Constant	59.12	28.37	2.08	0.041
education	-0.5834	0.4725	-1.23	0.221
urbanization	0.6825	0.1232	5.54	0.000

  a. Find the predicted crime rate for a county that has 0% in an urban environment and (i) 70% high school graduation rate and (ii) 80% high school graduation rate.

b. Use results from part a to explain how education affects the crime rate, controlling for urbanization, interpreting the slope coefficient −0.58 of education.

c. Using the prediction equation, show that the equation relating crime rate and education when urbanization is fixed at (i) 0, (ii) 50, and (iii) 100, is as follows:

x_2	$\hat{y} = 59.1 - 0.58x_1 + 0.68x_2$
0	$\hat{y} = 59.1 - 0.58x_1$
50	$\hat{y} = 93.2 - 0.58x_1$
100	$\hat{y} = 127.4 - 0.58x_1$

Sketch a plot with these lines and use it to interpret the effect of education on crime rate, controlling for urbanization.

d. The scatterplot matrix shows that education has a *positive* association with crime rate, but the multiple regression equation shows that the association is *negative* when we keep x_2 = urbanization fixed. The reversal in the association is an example of **Simpson's paradox** (See Example 16 in Sec. 3.4 and Example 17 in Sec. 10.5). Consider the hypothetical figure that follows. Sketch lines that represent (i) the bivariate relationship, ignoring the information on urbanization and (ii) the relationship for counties having urbanization = 50. Use this figure and the correlations provided to explain how Simpson's paradox can happen.

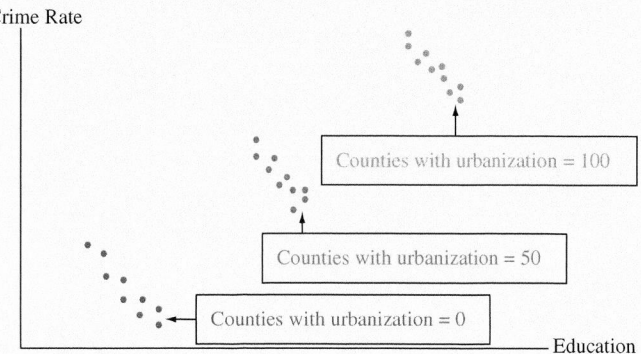

Hypothetical scatterplot for crime rate and education, labeling by urbanization.

13.6 **Crime rate and income** Refer to the previous exercise. MINITAB reports the results below for the multiple regression of y = crime rate on x_1 = median income (in thousands of dollars) and x_2 = urbanization.

Results of regression analysis

Predictor	Coef	SE Coef	T	P
Constant	39.97	16.35	2.44	0.017
income	−0.7906	0.8049	−0.98	0.330
urbanization	0.6418	0.1110	5.78	0.000

Correlations: crime, income, urbanization

	crime	urbanization
urbanization	0.677	
income	0.434	0.731

a. Report the prediction equations relating crime rate to income at urbanization levels of (i) 0 and (ii) 100. Interpret.

b. For the bivariate model relating y = crime rate to x = income, MINITAB reports

```
crime = -11.6 + 2.61 income
```

Interpret the effect of income, according to the sign of its slope. How does this effect differ from the effect of income in the multiple regression equation?

c. The correlation matrix for these three variables is shown in the table. Use these correlations to explain why the income effect seems so different in the models in part a and part b.

d. Do these variables satisfy Simpson's paradox? Explain.

13.7 **The economics of golf** The earnings of a PGA Tour golfer are determined by performance in tournaments. A study analyzed tour data to determine the financial return for certain skills of professional golfers. The sample consisted of 393 golfers competing in one or both of the 2002 and 2008 seasons. The most significant factors that contribute to earnings were the percent of attempts a player was able to hit the green in regulation (GIR), the number of times that a golfer made par or better after hitting a bunker divided by the number of bunkers hit (SS), the average of putts after reaching the green (AvePutt), and the number of PGA events entered (Events). The resulting coefficients from multiple regression to predict 2008 earnings are:

Predictor	Coefficient
Constant	$26,417,000
GIR	$168,300
SS	$33,859
AvePutt	−$19,784,000
Events	−$44,725

Source: Some data from K. Rinehart, *Major Themes in Economics*, 2009.

a. State the regression formula for a PGA Tour golfer's earnings for 2008.

b. Explain how to interpret the coefficients for AvePutt and Events.

c. Find the predicted total score for a golfer who had a GIR score of 60, SS score of 50, AvePutt is 1.5, for 20 Events.

13.8 **Comparable number of bedrooms and house size effects** In Example 2, the prediction equation between y = selling price and x_1 = house size and x_2 = number of bedrooms was $\hat{y} = 60{,}102 + 63.0x_1 + 15{,}170x_2$.

a. For fixed number of bedrooms, how much is the house selling price predicted to increase for each square foot increase in house size? Why?

b. For a fixed house size of 2000 square feet, how does the predicted selling price change for two, three, and four bedrooms?

13.9 **Controlling can have no effect** Suppose that the correlation between x_1 and x_2 equals 0. Then, for multiple regression with those predictors, it can be shown that the slope for x_1 is the same as in bivariate regression when x_1 is the only predictor. Explain why you would expect this to be true. (*Hint:* If you don't control x_2, would you expect it to have an impact on how x_1 affects y, if x_1 and x_2 have correlation of 0?)

13.10 House selling prices Using software with the House Selling Prices OR data file on the text CD, analyze y = selling price, x_1 = house size, and x_2 = lot size.

  a. Construct box plots for each variable and a scatterplot matrix or scatter plots between y and each of x_1 and x_2. Interpret.

  b. Find the multiple regression prediction equation.

  c. If house size remains constant, what, if any, is the effect of an increase in lot size? Why do you think this is?

13.2 Extending the Correlation and R^2 for Multiple Regression

The correlation r and its square r^2 describe strength of association in a straight-line regression analysis. These measures can also describe association between y and a set of explanatory variables that predict y in a multiple regression model.

Multiple Correlation

To summarize how well a multiple regression model predicts y, we analyze how well the observed y values correlate with the predicted $\hat{y}$ values. As a set, the explanatory variables are strongly associated with y if the correlation between the y and $\hat{y}$ values is strong. Treating the $\hat{y}$ as a variable gives us a way of summarizing several explanatory variables by *one* variable, for which we can use its ordinary correlation with the y values. The correlation between the observed y values and the predicted $\hat{y}$ values from the multiple regression model is called the **multiple correlation**.

In Words

From Sections 3.2 and 12.2, the **correlation** describes the association between the response variable y and a single explanatory variable x. It is denoted by r (lowercase). The **multiple correlation** describes the association between y and a set of explanatory variables in a multiple regression model. It is denoted by R (uppercase).

Multiple Correlation, R

For a multiple regression model, the **multiple correlation** is the correlation between the observed y values and the predicted $\hat{y}$ values. It is denoted by R.

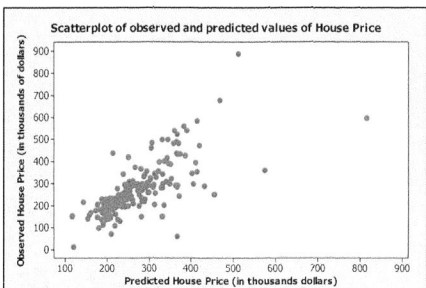

Scatterplot of observed and predicted values of House Price

For each subject, the regression equation provides a predicted value $\hat{y}$. So, each subject has a y value and a $\hat{y}$ value. For the two houses listed in Table 13.1, Table 13.4 shows the actual selling price y and the predicted selling price $\hat{y}$ from the equation $\hat{y} = 60{,}102 + 63.0x_1 + 15{,}170x_2$ with house size and number of bedrooms as predictors. The correlation computed between all 200 pairs of y and $\hat{y}$ values is the multiple correlation, R. Software tells us that this equals 0.72. The scatterplot in the margin displays these pairs of y and $\hat{y}$ values.

Table 13.4 Selling Prices and Their Predicted Values

These values refer to the two home sales listed in Table 13.1. The predictors are x_1 = house size and x_2 = number of bedrooms.

Home	Selling Price	Predicted Selling Price
1	232,500	$\hat{y} = 60{,}102 + 63.0(1679) + 15{,}170(3) = 211{,}389$
2	158,000	$\hat{y} = 60{,}102 + 63.0(1292) + 15{,}170(1) = 156{,}668$

Recall

For the first home sale listed in Table 13.1, $y = 232{,}500$, $x_1 = 1679$ and $x_2 = 3$. ◄

The larger the multiple correlation, the better are the predictions of y by the set of explanatory variables. For the housing data, $R = 0.72$ indicates a moderately strong association.

The predicted values $\hat{y}$ cannot correlate negatively with y. Otherwise, the predictions would be worse than merely using $\bar{y}$ to predict y. Therefore, *R falls between 0 and 1.* In this way, the multiple correlation R differs from the bivariate correlation r between y and a single variable x, which falls between -1 and $+1$.

R^2

Recall

Section 12.2 introduced r^2 (*r*-squared) as measuring the proportional reduction in prediction error from using $\hat{y}$ to predict y compared to using $\bar{y}$ to predict y. It falls between 0 and 1, with larger values representing stronger association. ◄

For predicting y, the statistic of R^2 describes the relative improvement from using the prediction equation instead of using the sample mean $\bar{y}$. The error in using the prediction equation to predict y is summarized by the *residual sum of squares*, $\Sigma(y - \hat{y})^2$. The error in using $\bar{y}$ to predict y is summarized by the *total sum of squares*, $\Sigma(y - \bar{y})^2$. The *proportional reduction in error* is

$$R^2 = \frac{\Sigma(y - \bar{y})^2 - \Sigma(y - \hat{y})^2}{\Sigma(y - \bar{y})^2}.$$

The better the predictions are using the regression equation, the larger R^2 is. The bivariate measure r^2 is the special case of R^2 applied to regression with one explanatory variable. As the notation suggests, for multiple regression R^2 is the square of the multiple correlation. Regression software reports R^2, and you can take the positive square root of it to get the multiple correlation, R.

Example 3

Multiple correlation and R^2

Predicting House Selling Prices

Picture the Scenario

For the 200 observations on y = selling price in thousands of dollars, using, x_1 = house size in thousands of square feet and x_2 = number of bedrooms, Table 13.5 shows the ANOVA (analysis of variance) table that MINITAB reports for the multiple regression model.

Table 13.5 ANOVA Table and R^2 for Predicting House Selling Price (in thousands of dollars) Using House Size (in thousands of square feet) and Number of Bedrooms

```
R-Sq = 52.4%

Analysis of Variance

Source                    DF              SS

Regression                 2         1399524

Residual Error           197         1269345

Total                    199         2668870
```

Questions to Explore

a. Show how to use the sums of squares in the ANOVA table to find R^2 for this multiple regression model. Interpret.

b. Find and interpret the multiple correlation.

Think It Through

a. From the sum of squares (SS) column, the total sum of squares is $\Sigma(y - \bar{y})^2 = 2{,}668{,}870$. The residual sum of squares from using the multiple regression equation to predict y is $\Sigma(y - \hat{y})^2 = 1{,}269{,}345$. The value of R^2 is

$$R^2 = \frac{\Sigma(y - \bar{y})^2 - \Sigma(y - \hat{y})^2}{\Sigma(y - \bar{y})^2} = \frac{2,668,870 - 1,269,345}{2,668,870} = 0.524.$$

Using house size and number of bedrooms together to predict selling price reduces the prediction error by 52%, relative to using $\bar{y}$ alone to predict selling price. The R^2 statistic appears (in percentage form) in Table 13.5 under the heading "R-sq."

b. The multiple correlation between selling price and the two explanatory variables is $R = \sqrt{R^2} = \sqrt{0.524} = 0.72$. This equals the correlation for the 200 homes between the observed selling prices and the predicted selling prices from multiple regression. There's a moderately strong association between the observed and the predicted selling prices. In summary, house size and number of bedrooms are very helpful in predicting selling prices.

Insight

The bivariate r^2 value for predicting selling price is 0.51 with house size as the predictor. The multiple regression model has $R^2 = 0.52$, only a marginally larger value to using only house size as a predictor. We appear to be just as well off with the bivariate model using house size as the predictor as compared to using the multiple model. An advantage of using only the bivariate model is easier interpretation of the coefficients.

Try Exercise 13.11

Properties of R^2

The example showed that R^2 for the multiple regression model was larger than r^2 for a bivariate model using only one of the explanatory variables. In fact, *a key property of R^2 is that it cannot decrease when predictors are added to a model.*

The difference $\Sigma(y - \bar{y})^2 - \Sigma(y - \hat{y})^2$ that forms the numerator of R^2 also appears in the ANOVA table. It is called the *regression sum of squares.* A simpler formula for it is

$$\text{Regression SS} = \Sigma(\hat{y} - \bar{y})^2.$$

If each $\hat{y} = \bar{y}$, then the regression equation predicts no better than $\bar{y}$. Then regression SS $= 0$, and $R^2 = 0$.

The numerical values of the sums of squares reported in Table 13.5 result when y is measured in *thousands* of dollars (for instance, the first house y is 232.5 rather than 232,500, and $\hat{y}$ is 211.4 rather than 211,389). We truncated the numbers for convenience, because the sums of squares would otherwise be enormous with each one having six more zeros on the end! It makes no difference to the result. Another property of R and R^2 is that, like the correlation, *their values don't depend on the units of measurement.*

In summary, the properties of R^2 are similar to those of r^2 for bivariate models. Here's a list of the main properties:

SUMMARY: Properties of R^2

■ R^2 falls between 0 and 1. The larger the value, the better the explanatory variables collectively predict y.

- $R^2 = 1$ only when all residuals are 0, that is, when all regression predictions are perfect (each $y = \hat{y}$), so residual SS $= \Sigma(y - \hat{y})^2 = 0$.
- $R^2 = 0$ when each $\hat{y} = \bar{y}$. In that case, the estimated slopes all equal 0, and the correlation between y and each explanatory variable equals 0.
- R^2 gets larger, or at worst stays the same, whenever an explanatory variable is added to the multiple regression model.
- The value of R^2 does not depend on the units of measurement.

Explanatory variable	r^2
House Size	0.505
Bedrooms	0.100
Lot Size	0.053
Baths	0.331
Garage	0.009
Age	0.029

Table 13.6 shows how R^2 increases as we add explanatory variables to a multiple regression model to predict $y =$ house selling price. The single predictor in the data set that is most strongly associated with y is the house size ($r^2 = 0.505$). See the margin table. When we add number of bedrooms as a second predictor, R^2 goes up from 0.505 to 0.524. As other predictors are added, R^2 continues to go up, but not by much. Predictive power is not much worse with only house size as a predictor than with all six predictors in the regression model.

Table 13.6 R^2 Value for Multiple Regression Models for $y =$ House Selling Price

Explanatory Variables in Model	R^2
House size	0.505
House size, Number of bedrooms	0.524
House size, Number of bedrooms, Lot size	0.524
House size, Number of bedrooms, Lot size, Number of bathrooms	0.604
House size, Number of bedrooms, Lot size, Number of bathrooms, Garage	0.608
House size, Number of bedrooms, Lot size, Number of bathrooms, Garage, Age	0.612

Although R^2 goes up by only small amounts when we add other variables after house size is already in the model, this does not mean that the other predictors are only weakly correlated with selling price. Because the predictors are themselves highly correlated, once one or two of them are in the model, the remaining ones don't help much in adding to the predictive power. For instance, lot size is highly positively correlated with number of bedrooms and with size of house. So, once number of bedrooms and size of house are included as predictors in the model, there's not much benefit to including lot size as an additional predictor.

In Practice R^2 Often Does Not Increase Much After a Few Predictors Are in the Model

When there are many explanatory variables but the correlations among them are strong, once you have included a few of them in the model, R^2 usually doesn't increase much more when you add additional ones. This does not mean that the additional variables are uncorrelated with the response variable but merely that they don't add much new power for predicting y, given the values of the predictors already in the model.

As in the bivariate case, a disadvantage of R^2 (compared to the multiple correlation R) is that its units are the *square* of the units of measurement. The R^2 of 0.524 in Example 3 implies that the estimated *variance* of y at fixed values of the predictors is 52.4% less than the overall variance of y.

13.2   Practicing the Basics

13.11 Predicting sports attendance   Keeneland Racetrack
(TRY) in Lexington, Kentucky, has been a social gathering
place since 1935. Every spring and fall thousands of
people come to the racetrack to socialize, gamble,
and enjoy the horse races that have become so popular
in Kentucky. A study investigated the different factors that affect the attendance at Keeneland. To many
people, the social aspect of Keeneland is equally as
important as watching the races, if not more. The study
investigates which factors significantly contribute to
attendance by Keeneland visitors. (*Source*: Data from
Gatton School of Business and Economics publication,
Gatton College, 2009.)

ANOVA table for y = attendance at Keeneland

```
Source      DF       SS           MS         F      Significance F
Regression  6.00     2360879925   393479988  21.71  0.00
Residual    110.00   1993805006   18125500
Total       116.00   4354684931
```

a. Show how R^2 is calculated from the SS values, and
   report its value.
b. Interpret the R^2 value. Does the multiple regression
   equation help us predict the attendance much better
   than we could without knowing that equation?
c. Find the multiple correlation. Interpret.

13.12 Predicting weight   Let's use multiple regression to predict total body weight (in pounds) using data from a study
of University of Georgia female athletes. Possible predictors are HGT = height (in inches), %BF = percent body
fat, and age. The display shows correlations among these
explanatory variables.

```
        TBW       HGT       %BF
HGT     0.745
%BF     0.390     0.096
AGE     -0.187    -0.120    0.024
```

a. Which explanatory variable gives by itself the best predictions of weight? Explain.
b. With height as the sole predictor, $\hat{y} = -106 + 3.65$
   (HGT) and $r^2 = 0.55$. If you add %BF as a predictor,
   you know that R^2 will be at least 0.55. Explain why.
c. When you add % body fat to the model,
   $\hat{y} = -121 + 3.50(\text{HGT}) + 1.35(\%\text{BF})$ and
   $R^2 = 0.66$. When you add age to the model,
   $\hat{y} = -97.7 + 3.43(\text{HGT}) + 1.36(\%\text{BF}) - 0.960(\text{AGE})$
   and $R^2 = 0.67$. Once you know height and % body
   fat, does age seem to help you in predicting weight?
   Explain, based on comparing the R^2 values.

13.13 When does controlling have little effect?   Refer to the
previous exercise. Height has a similar estimated slope
for each of the three models. Why do you think that controlling for % body fat and then age does not change the
effect of height much? (*Hint:* How strongly is height correlated with the other two variables?)

13.14 Internet use   For countries listed in the Twelve
Countries data file on the text CD, y = Internet use
(percent) is predicted by x_1 = per capita GDP
(gross domestic product, in thousands of dollars) with
$r^2 = 0.88$. Adding x_2 = carbon dioxide emissions
per capita to the model yields the results in the
following display.

**Regression of Internet use on GDP and carbon dioxide
emissions per capita**

```
Predictor    Coef        SE Coef      T       P
Constant     2.843       5.473        0.52    0.616
GDP          0.0021875   0.0002779    7.87    0.000
CDE          -1.3849     0.7270       -1.90   0.089
S = 9.23490      R-Sq = 91.4%
Analysis of Variance
Source           DF        SS
Regression       2         8176.7
Residual Error   9         767.6
Total            11        8944.2
```

a. Report R^2 and show how it is determined by SS values
   in the ANOVA table.
b. Interpret its value as a proportional reduction in prediction error.

13.15 More Internet use   In the previous exercise,
$r^2 = 0.88$ when x_1 is the predictor and $R^2 = 0.914$
when both x_1 and x_2 are predictors. Why do you think
that the predictions of y don't improve much when x_2
is added to the model? (The association of x_2 with y is
$r = 0.5692$.)

13.16 Softball data   For the Softball data set on the text
CD, for each game the variables are a team's
number of runs scored (RUNS), number of hits
(HIT), number of errors (ERR), and the difference
(DIFF) between the number of runs scored by that team
and by the other team, which is the response variable.
MINITAB reports

```
Difference = - 4.03 + 0.0260 Hits
+ 1.04 Run - 1.22 Errors
```

a. If you know the team's number of runs and number of
   errors in a game, explain why it does not help much to
   know how many hits the team has.
b. Explain why the result in part a is also suggested by
   knowing that $R^2 = 0.7594$ for this model, whereas
   $R^2 = 0.7593$ when only runs and errors are the explanatory variables in the model.

13.17 Slopes, correlations, and units   In Example 2
on y = house selling price, x_1 = house
size, and x_2 = number of bedrooms,
$\hat{y} = 60,102 + 63.0x_1 + 15,170x_2$, and $R = 0.72$.

a. Interpret the value of the multiple correlation.

b. Suppose house selling prices are changed from dollars to *thousands* of dollars. Explain why if each house price in Table 13.1 is divided by 1000, then the prediction equation changes to $\hat{y} = 60.102 + 0.063x_1 + 15.170x_2$.

c. In part b, does the multiple correlation change to 0.00072? Justify your answer.

13.18 Predicting college GPA Using software with the Georgia Student Survey data file from the text CD, find and interpret the multiple correlation and R^2 for the relationship between y = college GPA, x_1 = high school GPA, and x_2 = study time.

13.3 Using Multiple Regression to Make Inferences

We've seen that multiple regression uses more than one explanatory variable to predict a response variable y. With it, we can study an explanatory variable's effect on y while controlling other variables that could affect the results. Now, let's turn our attention to using multiple regression to make inferences about the population.

Inferences require the same assumptions as in bivariate regression:

- The regression equation truly holds for the population means.
- The data were gathered using randomization.
- The response variable y has a normal distribution at each combination of values of the explanatory variables, with the same standard deviation.

The first assumption implies that there is a straight-line relationship between the mean of y and each explanatory variable, with the same slope at each value of the other predictors. We will see how to check this assumption and the third assumption in Section 13.4.

Estimating Variability Around the Regression Equation

A check for normality is needed to validate the third assumption; this is discussed in the next section. In addition to normality, a constant standard deviation for each combination of explanatory variables is assumed. This standard deviation is similar to the standard error for the explanatory variable in bivariate data. (Recall Section 12.4.) As in bivariate regression, a standard deviation parameter σ describes variability of the observations around the regression equation. Its sample estimate is

$$s = \sqrt{\frac{\text{Residual SS}}{df}} = \sqrt{\frac{\Sigma(y - \hat{y})^2}{n - (\text{number of parameters in regression equation})}}.$$

This *residual standard deviation* describes the typical size of the residuals. Its degrees of freedom are df = sample size n - number of parameters in the regression equation. Software reports s and its square, the **mean square error**.

Example 4

Estimating residual standard deviation

Female Athletes' Weight

Picture the Scenario

The College Athletes data set on the text CD comes from a study of 64 University of Georgia female athletes who participated in Division I sports. The study measured several physical characteristics, including total body weight in pounds (TBW), height in inches (HGT), the percent of body fat (%BF), and age. Table 13.7 shows the ANOVA table for the regression of weight on height, % body fat, and age.

Table 13.7 ANOVA Table for Multiple Regression Analysis of Athlete Weights

```
Analysis of Variance

Source            DF       SS       MS       F       P

Regression         3   12407.9   4136.0   40.48   0.000

Residual Error    60    6131.0    102.2

Total             63   18539.0

S = 10.1086      R-Sq = 66.9%
```

Question to Explore

For female athletes at particular values of height, percent of body fat, and age, estimate the standard deviation of their weights.

Think It Through

The SS column tells us that the residual sum of squares is 6131.0. There were $n = 64$ observations and 4 parameters in the regression model, so the DF column reports $df = n - 4 = 60$ opposite the residual SS. The mean square error is

$$s^2 = (\text{residual SS})/df = 6131.0/60 = 102.2.$$

It appears in the mean square (MS) column, in the row labeled "Residual Error." The residual standard deviation is $s = \sqrt{102.2} = 10.1$, identified as S. For athletes with certain fixed values of height, percent body fat, and age, the weights vary with a standard deviation of about 10 pounds.

Insight

If the conditional distributions of weight are approximately bell shaped, about 95% of the weight values fall within about $2s = 20$ pounds of the true regression equation. More precisely, software can report *prediction intervals* within which a response outcome has a certain chance of falling. For instance, at $x_1 = 66$, $x_2 = 18$, and $x_3 = 20$, which are close to the mean predictor values, software reports $\hat{y} = 133.9$ and a 95% prediction interval of 133.9 ± 20.4.

> *Try Exercise 13.21*

Recall

Recall that the prediction equation was $\hat{y} = -97.7 + 3.43x_1 + 1.36x_2 - 0.96x_3$, so there were four parameters in the regression model. ◄

Recall

For bivariate regression, Example 16 in Section 12.4 discussed confidence intervals for the mean and prediction intervals for *y* at a particular setting of *x*. These intervals can be formed with multiple regression as well. ◄

In the sample, weight has standard deviation = 17 pounds, describing variability around mean weight = 133 pounds (see Table 13.9). How is it that the *residual* standard deviation could be only 10 pounds? The residual standard deviation is smaller because it refers to variability at *fixed* values of the predictors. Weight varies less at given values of the predictors than it does overall. If we could predict weight perfectly knowing height, percent body fat, and age, the residual standard deviation would be 0.

The ANOVA table also reports another mean square, called a *mean square for regression,* or *regression mean square* for short. We'll next see how to use the mean squares to conduct a significance test about all the slope parameters together.

The Collective Effect of Explanatory Variables

Do the explanatory variables collectively have a statistically significant effect on the response variable y? With three predictors in a model, we can check this by testing

$$H_0: \beta_1 = \beta_2 = \beta_3 = 0.$$

This hypothesis states that the mean of y does not depend on *any* of the predictors in the model. That is, *y is statistically independent of all the explanatory variables*. The alternative hypothesis is

$$H_a: \text{At least one } \beta \text{ parameter is not equal to } 0.$$

This states that *at least one* explanatory variable is associated with y.

The null hypothesis that all the slope parameters equal 0 is equivalent to the hypothesis that the population values of the multiple correlation and R^2 equal 0. The equivalence occurs because the population values of R and R^2 equal 0 only in those situations in which all the β parameters equal 0.

The test statistic for H_0 is denoted by F. It equals the ratio of the mean squares from the ANOVA table,

$$F = \frac{\text{Mean square for regression}}{\text{Mean square error}}.$$

We won't need the formulas for the mean squares here, but the value of F is proportional to $R^2/(1 - R^2)$. As R^2 increases, the F test statistic increases.

When H_0 is true, the expected value of the F test statistic is approximately 1. When H_0 is false, F tends to be larger than 1. The larger the F test statistic, the stronger the evidence against H_0. The P-value is the right-tail probability from the sampling distribution of the F test statistic.

From the ANOVA table in Table 13.7 (shown again in the margin) for the regression model predicting weight, the mean square for regression = 4136.0 and the mean square error = 102.2. Then the test statistic

$$F = 4136.0/102.2 = 40.5.$$

Before conclusions can be made about this test, we must first understand the F distribution better.

ANOVA Table from Table 13.7

Source	DF	SS	MS	F	P
Reg.	3	12407.9	4136.0	40.5	.000
Error	60	6131.0	102.2		
Total	63	18539.0			

The *F* Distribution and Its Properties

The sampling distribution of the F test statistic is called the **F distribution**. The symbol for the F statistic and its distribution honors the eminent British statistician R. A. Fisher, who discovered the F distribution in 1922. Like the chi-squared distribution, the F distribution can assume only nonnegative values and is skewed to the right. See Figure 13.3. The mean is approximately 1.

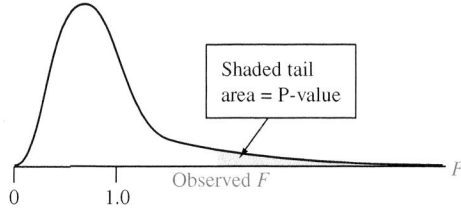

▲ **Figure 13.3** The *F* Distribution and the P-Value for *F* Tests. **Question** Why does the P-value use the right tail but not the left tail?

The precise shape of the F distribution is determined by two degrees of freedom terms, denoted by df_1 and df_2. These are the df values in the ANOVA table for the two mean squares whose ratio equals F. The first one is

$$df_1 = \text{number of explanatory variables in the model.}$$

The second,

$$df_2 = n - \text{number of parameters in regression equation,}$$

is the df for the t tests about the individual regression parameters. Sometimes df_1 is called the **numerator df**, because it is listed in the ANOVA table next to the mean square for regression, which goes in the numerator of the F test statistic. Likewise, df_2 is called the **denominator df**, because it is listed in the ANOVA table next to the mean square error, which goes in the denominator of the F test statistic.

Table D at the end of the text lists the F values that have P-value $= 0.05$, for various df_1 and df_2 values. Table 13.8 shows a small excerpt. For instance, when $df_1 = 3$ and $df_2 = 40$, $F = 2.84$ has P-value $= 0.05$. When $F > 2.84$, the test statistic is farther out in the tail and the P-value < 0.05. (See margin figure.) Regression software reports the actual P-value. The F value for our example is extremely large ($F = 40.5$). See Table 13.7. With this large value of F the ANOVA table reports P-value $= 0.000$.

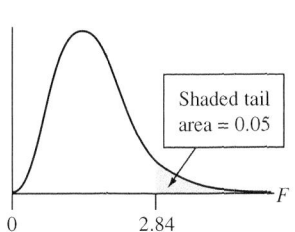

Shaded tail area = 0.05

Table 13.8 An Excerpt of Table D Displaying F Values

These are the values that have right-tail probability equal to 0.05.

	df_1				
df_2	1	2	3	4	5
30	4.17	3.32	2.92	2.69	2.69
40	4.10	3.23	2.84	2.61	2.45
60	4.00	3.15	2.76	2.52	2.37

SUMMARY: F Test That All the Multiple Regression β Parameters $= 0$

1. **Assumptions:**
   - Multiple regression equation holds
   - Data gathered using randomization
   - Normal distribution for y with same standard deviation at each combination of predictors.

2. **Hypotheses:**

   H_0: $\beta_1 = \beta_2 = \ldots = 0$ (all the beta parameters in the model $= 0$)

   H_a: At least one β parameter differs from 0.

3. **Test statistic:** $F = $ (mean square for regression)/(mean square error)

4. **P-value:** Right-tail probability above observed F test statistic value from F distribution with

   $$df_1 = \text{number of explanatory variables,}$$

   $$df_2 = n - (\text{number of parameters in regression equation}).$$

5. **Conclusion:** The smaller the P-value, the stronger the evidence that at least one explanatory variable has an effect on y. If a decision is needed, reject H_0 if P-value $\leq$ significance level, such as 0.05. Interpret in context.

F test for predictors

Athletes' Weight

Picture the Scenario

For the 64 female college athletes, the ANOVA table for the multiple regression predicting y = weight using x_1 = height, x_2 = percent body fat, and x_3 = age shows:

Source	DF	SS	MS	F	P
Regression	3	12407.9	4136.0	40.48	0.000
Residual Error	60	6131.0	102.2		

Questions to Explore

a. State and interpret the null hypothesis tested in this table.
b. From the F table, which F value would have a P-value of 0.05 for these data?
c. Report the observed test statistic and P-value. Interpret the P-value, and make a decision for a 0.05 significance level.

Think It Through

a. Since there are three explanatory variables, the null hypothesis is $H_0: \beta_1 = \beta_2 = \beta_3 = 0$. It states that weight is independent of height, percent body fat, and age.
b. In the DF column, the ANOVA table shows $df_1 = 3$ and $df_2 = 60$. The F table or software indicates that the F value with right-tail probability of 0.05 is 2.76. (See also Table 13.8.)
c. From the ANOVA table, the observed F test statistic value is 40.5. Since this is well above 2.76, the P-value is less than 0.05. The ANOVA table reports P-value = 0.000. If H_0 were true, it would be extremely unusual to get such a large F test statistic. We can reject H_0 at the 0.05 significance level. In summary, we conclude that at least one predictor has an effect on weight.

Insight

The F test tells us that *at least one* explanatory variable has an effect. The following section discusses how to follow up from the F test to investigate which explanatory variables have a statistically significant effect on predicting y.

Try Exercise 13.25

Inferences About Individual Regression Parameters

Recall

Section 12.3 showed that the *t* test statistic for $H_0: \beta = 0$ in the bivariate model is

$$t = \frac{\text{(sample slope} - 0)}{\text{std. error of sample slope}}$$
$$= (b - 0)/se,$$

with $df = n - 2$. ◄

For the bivariate model, $\mu_y = \alpha + \beta x$, there's a t test for the null hypothesis $H_0: \beta = 0$ that x and y are statistically independent. Likewise, a t test applies to any slope parameter in multiple regression. Let's consider a particular parameter, say β_1.

If $\beta_1 = 0$, the mean of y is identical for all values of x_1, at fixed values for the other explanatory variables. So, $H_0: \beta_1 = 0$ states that *y and x_1 are statistically independent, controlling for the other variables.* This means that once the other explanatory variables are in the model, it doesn't help to have x_1 in the model. The alternative hypothesis usually is two sided, H_a: $\beta_1 \neq 0$, but one-sided alternative hypotheses are also possible.

The test statistic for H_0: $\beta_1 = 0$ is

$$t = (b_1 - 0)/se,$$

where se is the standard error of the slope estimate b_1 of β_1. Software provides the se value, the t test statistic, and the P-value. If H_0 is true and the inference assumptions hold, the t test statistic has the t distribution. The degrees of freedom are

$$df = \text{sample size } n - \text{number of parameters in the regression equation.}$$

The degrees of freedom are also equal to those used to calculate residual standard deviation. The bivariate model $\mu_y = \alpha + \beta x$ has two parameters (α and β), so $df = n - 2$, as Section 12.3 used. The model with two predictors, $\mu_y = \alpha + \beta_1 x_1 + \beta_2 x_2$, has three parameters, so $df = n - 3$. Likewise, with three predictors, $df = n - 4$, and so on.

SUMMARY: Significance Test About a Multiple Regression Parameter (such as β_1)

1. **Assumptions:**
   - Each explanatory variable has a straight-line relation with μ_y, with the same slope for all combinations of values of other predictors in model
   - Data gathered with randomization (such as a random sample or a randomized experiment)
   - Normal distribution for y with same standard deviation at each combination of values of other predictors in model

2. **Hypotheses:**

$$H_0: \beta_1 = 0$$

$$H_a: \beta_1 \neq 0$$

When H_0 is true, y is independent of x_1, controlling for the other predictors.

3. **Test statistic:** $t = (b_1 - 0)/se$. Software supplies the slope estimate b_1, its se, and the value of t.

4. **P-value:** Two-tail probability from t distribution of values larger than observed t test statistic (in absolute value). The t distribution has

$$df = n - \text{number of parameters in regression equation}$$

   (such as $df = n - 3$ when $\mu_y = \alpha + \beta_1 x_1 + \beta_2 x_2$, which has three parameters).

5. **Conclusion:** Interpret P-value in context; compare to significance level if decision needed.

Hypothesis test for multiple regression parameter β

Example 6

What Helps Predict a Female Athlete's Weight?

Picture the Scenario

The College Athletes data set (Examples 4 and 5) measured several physical characteristics, including total body weight in pounds (TBW), height in inches (HGT), the percent of body fat (%BF), and age. Table 13.9 shows summary statistics for these variables.

Table 13.9 Summary Statistics for Study of Female College Athletes

Variables are TBW = total body weight, HGT = height, %BF = percent body fat, and AGE.

Variable	Mean	StDev	Minimum	Q1	Median	Q3	Maximum
TBW	133.0	17.2	96.0	119.2	131.5	143.8	185.0
HGT	65.5	3.5	56.0	63.0	65.0	68.2	75.0
%BF	18.4	4.1	11.2	15.2	18.5	21.5	27.6
AGE	20.0	1.98	17.0	18.0	20.0	22.0	23.0

Table 13.10 shows results of fitting a multiple regression model for predicting weight using the other variables. The predictive power is good, with $R^2 = 0.669$.

Table 13.10 Multiple Regression Analysis for Predicting Weight

Predictors are HGT = height, %BF = body fat, and age of subject.

Predictor	Coef	SE Coef	T	P
Constant	−97.69	28.79	−3.39	0.001
HGT	3.4285	0.3679	9.32	0.000
%BF	1.3643	0.3126	4.36	0.000
AGE	−0.9601	0.6483	−1.48	0.144

R-Sq = 66.9%

Questions to Explore

a. Interpret the effect of age on weight in the multiple regression equation.

b. In the population, does age help you to predict weight if you already know height and percent body fat? Show all steps of a significance test, and interpret.

Think It Through

a. Let $\hat{y}$ = predicted weight, x_1 = height, x_2 = %body fat, and x_3 = age. Then

$$\hat{y} = -97.7 + 3.43x_1 + 1.36x_2 - 0.96x_3.$$

The slope coefficient of age is −0.96. The sample effect of age on weight is negative, which may seem surprising, but in practical terms it is small: For athletes having fixed values of x_1 and x_2, the predicted weight decreases by only 0.96 pounds for a one-year increase in age, and the ages vary only from 17 to 23.

b. If $\beta_3 = 0$, then x_3 = age has *no* effect on weight in the population, controlling for height and body fat. The hypothesis that age does *not* help us better predict weight, if we already know height and body fat, is $H_0: \beta_3 = 0$. Here are the steps:

1. **Assumptions:** The 64 female athletes were a convenience sample, not a random sample. Although the goal was to make inferences about all female college athletes, inferences are tentative. We'll discuss the other assumptions and learn how to check them in Section 13.4.

2. **Hypotheses:** The null hypothesis is $H_0: \beta_3 = 0$. Since there's no prior prediction about whether the effect of age is positive or negative (for fixed values of x_1 and x_2), we use the two-sided $H_a: \beta_3 \neq 0$.

3. **Test statistic:** Table 13.10 reports a slope estimate of -0.960 for age and a standard error of $se = 0.648$. It also reports the t test statistic of

$$t = (b_3 - 0)/se = -0.960/0.648 = -1.48.$$

Since the sample size equals $n = 64$ and the regression equation has four parameters, the degrees of freedom are $df = n - 4 = 60$.

4. **P-value:** Table 13.10 reports P-value $= 0.14$. This is the two-tailed probability of a t statistic below -1.48 or above 1.48, if H_0 were true.

5. **Conclusion:** The P-value of 0.14 does not give much evidence against the null hypothesis that $\beta_3 = 0$. At common significance levels, such as 0.05, we cannot reject H_0. Age does not significantly predict weight if we already know height and percentage of body fat. These conclusions are tentative because the sample of 64 female athletes was selected using a convenience sample rather than a random sample.

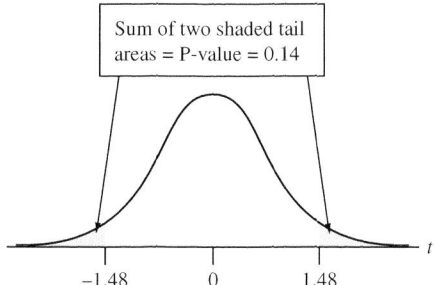

Sum of two shaded tail areas = P-value = 0.14

Insight

By contrast, Table 13.10 shows that $t = 9.3$ for testing the effect of height (H_0: $\beta_1 = 0$) and $t = 4.4$ for testing the effect of %BF (H_0: $\beta_2 = 0$). Both P-values are 0.000. It *does* help to have each of these variables in the model, given the other two.

Try Exercise 13.19

As usual, a test merely tells us whether the null hypothesis is plausible. In Example 6 we saw that β_3 may equal 0, but what are its other plausible values? A confidence interval answers this question.

Confidence Interval for a Multiple Regression β Parameter

A 95% confidence interval for a β slope parameter in multiple regression equals

$$\text{Estimated slope} \pm t_{.025}(se).$$

The t-score has $df = n -$ number of parameters in regression equation, as in the t test. The assumptions are also the same as for the t test.

Example 7

Confidence interval for β

What's Plausible for the Effect of Age on Weight?

Picture the Scenario

For the college athletes data, consider the multiple regression analysis of $y =$ weight and predictors $x_1 =$ height, $x_2 =$ %body fat, and $x_3 =$ age.

Question to Explore

Find and interpret a 95% confidence interval for β_3, the effect of age while controlling for height and percent of body fat.

Recall

From Table 13.10,

Predictor	Coef	SE
Constant	-97.7	28.8
HGT	3.43	0.368
%BF	1.36	0.313
AGE	-0.96	0.648 ◄

Think It Through

From the previous example, $df = 60$. For $df = 60$, $t_{.025} = 2.00$. From Table 13.10 (shown partly in the margin), the estimate of β_3 is -0.96, with $se = 0.648$. The 95% confidence interval equals

$$b_3 \pm t_{.025}(se) = -0.96 \pm 2.00(0.648),$$

or -0.96 ± 1.30, roughly $(-2.3, 0.3)$.

At fixed values of x_1 and x_2, we infer that the population mean of weight changes very little (and may not change at all) for a one-year increase in age.

Insight

The confidence interval contains 0. Age may have *no* effect on weight, once we control for height and percent body fat. This is in agreement with not rejecting H_0: $\beta_3 = 0$ in favor of H_a: $\beta_3 \neq 0$ at the $\alpha = 0.05$ level in the significance test.

> *Try Exercise 13.20*

Model Building

Unless the sample size is small and the correlation is weak between y and each explanatory variable, the F test usually has a small P-value. If the explanatory variables are chosen sensibly, at least one should have *some* predictive power. When the P-value is small, we can conclude merely that *at least* one explanatory variable affects y. The more narrowly focused t inferences about individual slopes judge *which* effects are nonzero and estimate their sizes.

In Practice The Overall F Test is Done Before the Individual t Inferences

As illustrated in the previous examples, the F test is typically performed *first* before looking at the individual t inferences. The F test result tells us if there is sufficient evidence to make it worthwhile to consider the individual effects. When there are many explanatory variables, doing the F test first provides protection from doing lots of t tests and having one of them be significant merely by random variation when, in fact, there truly are no effects in the population.

After finding the highly significant F test result of Example 5, we would study the individual effects, as we did in Examples 6 and 7. When we look at an individual t inference, suppose we find that the plausible values for a parameter are all relatively near 0. This was the case for the effect of age on weight (controlling for the other variables) as shown by the confidence interval in Example 7. Then, to simplify the model, you can remove that predictor, refitting the model with the other predictors. When we do this for y = weight, x_1 = height, and x_2 = percent body fat, we get

$$\hat{y} = -121.0 + 3.50x_1 + 1.35x_2.$$

Recall

The multiple regression equation using all three predictors was

$\hat{y} = -97.7 + 3.43x_1 + 1.36x_2 - 0.96x_3$.

The effects of height and percent body fat are similar in the equation without x_3 = age. ◄

For the simpler model, $R^2 = 0.66$. This is nearly as large as the value of $R^2 = 0.67$ with age also in the model. The predictions of weight are essentially as good without age in the model.

When you have several potential explanatory variables for a multiple regression model, how do you decide which ones to include? As just mentioned, the lack of statistical and practical significance is one criterion for deleting a term from the model. Many other possible criteria can also be considered. Most regression software has automatic procedures that successively add or delete predictor variables from models according to criteria such as statistical significance. Three of the most common procedures are **backward elimination, forward selection,** and **stepwise regression.** It is possible that all three procedures result in identical models; however, this is not always the case. In a situation where you must choose between models it is best to look at R^2 values and sensibility of model.

Caution

Procedures for regression model selection must be used with care. Consultation with a trained statistician is recommended. ◄

These procedures must be used with great caution. There is no guarantee that the final model chosen is sensible. Model selection requires quite a bit of statistical sophistication, and for applications with many potential explanatory variables we recommend that you seek guidance from a statistician.

13.3   Practicing the Basics

13.19 Predicting GPA   For the 59 observations in the Georgia
Student Survey data file on the text CD, the result of
regressing college GPA on high school GPA and study
time follows.

College GPA, high school GPA, and study time

```
The regression equation is
CGPA = 1.13 + 0.643 HSGPA + 0.0078 Studytime
Predictor    Coef    SE Coef    T       P
Constant     1.1262  0.5690    1.98    0.053
HSGPA        0.6434  0.1458    4.41    0.000
Studytime    0.00776 0.01614   0.48    0.633
S = 0.3188    R-Sq = 25.8%
```

a. Explain in nontechnical terms what it means if the
population slope coefficient for high school GPA
equals 0.

b. Show all steps for testing the hypothesis that this slope
equals 0.

13.20 Study time help GPA?   Refer to the previous exercise.

a. Report and interpret the P-value for testing the
hypothesis that the population slope coefficient for
study time equals 0.

b. Find a 95% confidence interval for the true slope for
study time. Explain how the result is in accord with the
result of the test in part a.

c. Does the result in part a imply that in the corresponding population, study time has no association with college GPA? Explain. (*Hint:* What is the impact of also
having HSGPA in the model?)

13.21 Variability in college GPA   Refer to the previous two
exercises.

a. Report the residual standard deviation. What does this
describe?

b. Interpret the residual standard deviation by predicting where approximately 95% of the Georgia college GPAs fall when high school GPA = 3.80 and
study time = 5.0 hours per day, which are the sample
means.

13.22 Does leg press help predict body strength?   Chapter 12
analyzed strength data for 57 female high school athletes.
Upper body strength was summarized by the maximum
number of pounds the athlete could bench press (denoted
BP below, 1RM Bench in file). This was predicted well by
the number of times she could do a 60-pound bench press
(denoted BP_60 in output, BRTF(60) in file). Can we
predict BP even better if we also know how many times
an athlete can perform a 200-pound leg press? The table
shows results after adding this second predictor (denoted
LP_200 in output, LP RTF(200) in file) to the model.

Multiple regression analysis of strength data

```
Predictor    Coef    SE Coef    T       P
Constant     60.596  2.872     21.10   0.000
BP_60        1.3318  0.1876    7.10    0.000
LP_200       0.2110  0.1519    1.39    0.171
```

```
Analysis of Variance
Source        DF    SS       MS       F       P
Regression     2    6473.3   3236.6   51.39   0.000
Res. Error    54    3401.3   63.0
Total         56    9874.6
S = 7.93640   R-Sq = 65.6%
```

a. Does LP_200 have a significant effect on BP, if BP_60
is also in the model? Show all steps of a significance
test to answer this.

b. Show that the 95% confidence interval for the slope
for LP_200 equals 0.21 ± 0.30, roughly $(-0.1, 0.5)$.
Based on this interval, does LP_200 seem to have a
strong impact, or a weak impact, on predicting BP, if
BP_60 is also in the model?

c. Given that LP_200 is in the model, provide evidence
from a significance test that shows why it *does* help to
add BP_60 to the model.

13.23 Leg press uncorrelated with strength?   The P-value
of 0.17 in part a of the previous exercise suggests that
LP_200 plausibly had no effect on BP, once BP_60 is in
the model. Yet when LP_200 is the sole predictor of BP,
the correlation is 0.58 and the significance test for its
effect has a P-value of 0.000, suggesting very strong evidence of an effect. Explain why this is not a contradiction.

13.24 Interpret strength variability   Refer to the previous two
exercises. The sample standard deviation of BP was 13.3.
The residual standard deviation of BP when BP_60 and
LP_200 are predictors in a multiple regression model is 7.9.

a. Explain the difference between the interpretations of
these two standard deviations.

b. If the conditional distributions of BP are approximately bell shaped, explain why most maximum bench
press values fall within about 16 pounds of the regression equation, when the predictors BP_60 and LP_200
are near their sample mean values.

c. At $x_1 = 11$ and $x_2 = 22$, which are close to the sample
mean values, software reports $\hat{y} = 80$ and a 95% prediction interval of 80 ± 16, or $(64, 96)$. Is this interval
an inference about where the population BP values fall
or where the population *mean* of the BP values fall (for
subjects having $x_1 = 11$ and $x_2 = 22$)? Explain.

d. Refer to part c. Would it be unusual for a female athlete with these predictor values to be able to bench
press more than 100 pounds? Why?

13.25 Any predictive power?   Refer to the previous three
exercises.

a. State and interpret the null hypothesis tested with the
F statistic in the ANOVA table given in Exercise 13.22.

b. From the *F* table (Table D), which *F* statistic value
would have a P-value of 0.05 for these data?

c. Report the observed *F* test statistic and its P-value.
Interpret the P-value, and make a decision for a 0.05
significance level. Explain in nontechnical terms what
the result of the test means.

13.26 Predicting pizza revenue Aunt Erma's Pizza restaurant keeps monthly records of total revenue, amount spent on TV advertising, and amount spent on newspaper advertising.

 a. Specify notation and formulate a multiple regression equation for predicting the monthly revenue. Explain how to interpret the parameters in the equation.

 b. State the null hypothesis that you would test if you want to analyze whether TV advertising is helpful, for a given amount of newspaper advertising.

 c. State the null hypothesis that you would test if you want to analyze whether *at least one* of the sources of advertising has some effect on monthly revenue.

13.27 Regression for mental health A study in Alachua County, Florida, investigated an index of mental health impairment, which had $\bar{y} = 27.3$ and $s = 5.5$. Two explanatory variables were x_1 = life events score (mean = 44.4, $s = 22.6$) and x_2 = SES (socioeconomic status, mean = 56.6, $s = 25.3$). Life events is a composite measure of the number and severity of major life events, such as death in the family, that the subject experienced within the past three years. SES is a composite index based on occupation, income, and education. The table shows data for 6 subjects. The complete data[1] for a random sample of 40 adults in the county is in the Mental Health data file on the text CD. Some regression results are also shown.

 a. Find the 95% confidence interval for β_1.

 b. Explain why the interval in part a means that an increase of 100 units in life events corresponds to anywhere from a 4- to 17-unit increase in mean mental impairment, controlling for SES. (This lack of precision reflects the small sample size.)

y = **mental impairment**, x_1 = **life events index**, and x_2 = **socioeconomic status**

y	x_1	x_2	y	x_1	x_2	y	x_1	x_2
17	46	84	26	50	40	30	44	53
19	39	97	26	48	52	31	35	38

```
Predictor      Coef     SE Coef        T        P
Constant     28.230     2.174      12.98    0.000
life          0.10326   0.03250     3.18    0.003
ses          -0.09748   0.02908    -3.35    0.002
S = 4.55644   R-Sq = 33.9%
```

[1]Based on a larger survey reported in a Ph.D. thesis by C. E. Holzer III at University of Florida.

```
Analysis of Variance
Source        DF    SS       MS      F      P
Regression     2   394.24  197.12   9.49  0.000
Res. Error    37   768.16   20.76
Total         39  1162.40
```

13.28 Mental health again Refer to the previous exercise.

 a. Report the test statistic and P-value for testing H_0: $\beta_1 = \beta_2 = 0$.

 b. State the alternative hypothesis that is supported by the result in part a.

 c. Does the result in part a imply that necessarily *both* life events and SES are needed in the model? Explain.

13.29 More predictors for house price The MINITAB results are shown for predicting selling price using x_1 = size of home, x_2 = number of bedrooms, and x_3 = age.

Regression of selling price on house size, number of bedrooms, and age

```
The regression equation is
HP in thousands = 80.5 + 0.0626 House Size + 13.5 Bedrooms
  - 0.418 Age
Predictor        Coef      SE Coef      T       P
Constant        80.49      21.81      3.69    0.000
House Size       0.062646   0.004732  13.24   0.000
Bedrooms        13.543      5.380      2.52    0.013
Age             -0.4177     0.2359    -1.77    0.078
```

 a. State the null hypothesis for an *F* test, in the context of these variables.

 b. The *F* statistic equals 74.23, with P-value = 0.000. Interpret.

 c. Explain in nontechnical terms what you learn from the results of the *t* tests reported in the table for the three explanatory variables.

13.30 House prices Use software to do further analyses with the multiple regression model of y = selling price of home in thousands, x_1 = size of home, and x_2 = number of bedrooms, considered in Section 13.1. The data file House Selling Prices OR is on the text CD.

 a. Report the *F* statistic and state the hypotheses to which it refers. Report its P-value, and interpret. Why is it not surprising to get a small P-value for this test?

 b. Report and interpret the *t* statistic and P-value for testing H_0: $\beta_2 = 0$ against H_a: $\beta_2 > 0$.

 c. Construct a 95% confidence interval for β_2, and interpret. This inference is more informative than the test in part b. Explain why.

13.4 Checking a Regression Model Using Residual Plots

In capsule form, recall that the three assumptions for inference with a multiple regression model are that (1) the regression equation approximates the true relationship between the predictors and the mean of y (that is, straight-line relationships between the mean of y and each explanatory variable, at fixed values of the other explanatory variables), (2) the data were gathered randomly, and (3) y has a normal distribution with the same standard deviation at each combination of predictors. Now, let's see how to check the assumptions about the regression equation and the distribution of y.

For bivariate regression, the scatterplot provides a simple visual check of whether the straight-line model is appropriate. For multiple regression, a plot of all the variables at once would require many dimensions. So instead, we study how the predicted values $\hat{y}$ compare to the observed values y. This is done using the residuals, $y - \hat{y}$.

Checking Shape and Detecting Unusual Observations

Recall

As discussed in Section 12.4, software can plot a histogram of the residuals or the *standardized residuals*, which are the residuals divided by their standard errors. ◄

Consider first the assumption that the conditional distribution of y is normal, at any fixed values of the explanatory variables. If this is true, the residuals should have approximately a bell-shaped histogram. Nearly all the standardized residuals should fall between about -3 and $+3$. A standardized residual below -3 or above $+3$ indicates a potential regression outlier.

When some observations have large standardized residuals, you should think about whether or not there is an explanation. Often this merely reflects skew in the conditional distribution of y, with a long tail in one direction. Other times the observations differ from the others on a variable that was not included in the model. Once that variable is added, those observations cease to be so unusual. For instance, suppose the data file from the weight study of Examples 4–7 also contained observations for a few males. Then we might have observed a few y values considerably above the others and with very large positive standardized residuals. These residuals would probably diminish considerably once the model also included gender as a predictor.

Residuals

Example 8

House Selling Price

Picture the Scenario

For the House Selling Price OR data set (Examples 1–3), Figure 13.4 is a MINITAB histogram of the standardized residuals for the multiple regression model predicting selling price by the house size and the number of bedrooms.

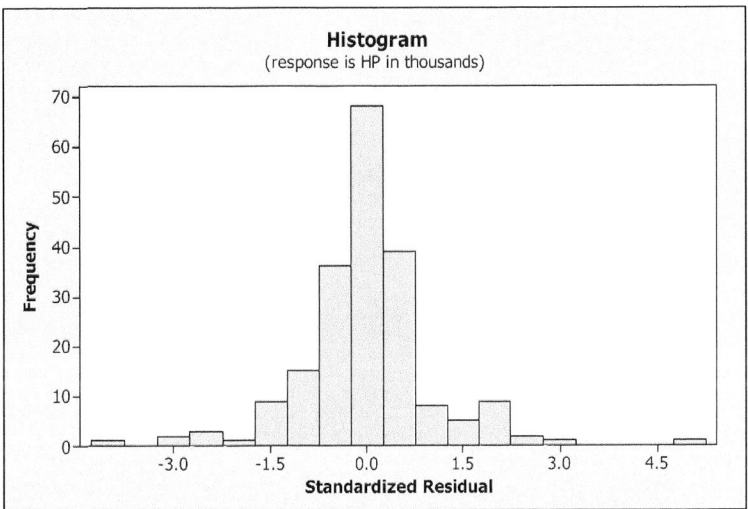

▲ **Figure 13.4** Histogram of Standardized Residuals for Multiple Regression Model Predicting Selling Price. Question Give an example of a shape for this histogram that would indicate that a few observations are highly unusual.

Question to Explore

What does Figure 13.4 tell you? Interpret.

Think It Through

The residuals are roughly bell shaped about 0. They fall mostly between about −3 and +3. The shape suggests that the conditional distribution of the response variable may have a bit of skew, but no severe nonnormality is indicated.

Insight

When n is small, don't make the mistake of reading too much into such plots. We're mainly looking for dramatic departures from the assumptions and highly unusual observations that stand apart from the others.

Try Exercise 13.31

Two-sided inferences about slope parameters are *robust*. The normality assumption is not as important as the assumption that the regression equation approximates the true relationship between the predictors and the mean of y. We consider that assumption next.

Plotting Residuals Against Each Explanatory Variable

Plots of the residuals against each explanatory variable help us check for potential problems with the regression model. We discuss this in terms of x_1, but you should view a plot for each predictor. Ideally, the residuals should fluctuate randomly about the horizontal line at 0, as in Figure 13.5a. There should be no obvious change in trend or change in variation as the values of x_1 increase.

By contrast, a scattering of the residuals as in Figure 13.5b suggests that y is actually *nonlinearly* related to x_1. It suggests that y tends to be *below* $\hat{y}$ for very small and very large x_1 values (giving negative residuals) and *above* $\hat{y}$ for medium-sized x_1 values (giving positive residuals).

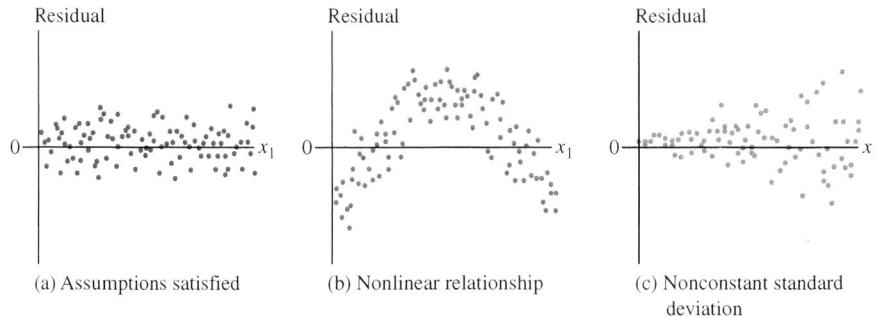

▲ **Figure 13.5** Possible Patterns for Residuals, Plotted Against an Explanatory Variable. Question Why does the pattern in (b) suggest that the effect of x_1 is not linear?

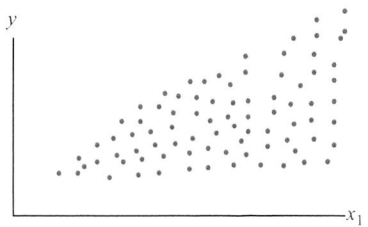

Scatterplot of data with nonconstant variance

A common occurrence is that residuals have increased variation as x_1 increases, as seen in Figure 13.5c. A pattern like this indicates that the residual standard deviation of y is not constant—the data display more variability at larger values of x_1 (see the margin figure). Two-sided inferences about slope parameters still perform well. However, ordinary prediction intervals are invalid. The width of such intervals is similar at relatively high and relatively low x_1 values, but in reality, observations on y are displaying more variability at high x_1 values than at low x_1 values. Figure 13.5a suggests that y is linearly related to x_1. It also suggests there is a constant variation as x_1 increases. Therefore, Assumption 1 and part of Assumption 3 are met.

In Practice Use Caution in Interpreting Residual Patterns

Residual patterns are often not as neat as the ones in Figure 13.5. Be careful not to let a single outlier or ordinary sampling variability overly influence your reading of a pattern from the plot.

Example 9

Plotting residuals

House Selling Price

Picture the Scenario

For the House Selling Price OR data set, Figure 13.6 is a residual plot for the multiple regression model relating selling price to house size and to number of bedrooms. It plots the standardized residuals against house size.

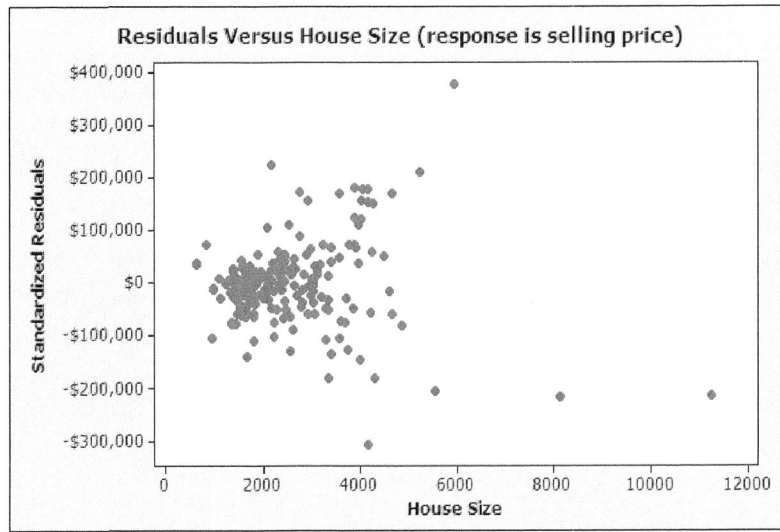

▲ **Figure 13.6** Standardized Residuals of Selling Price Plotted Against House Size, for Model With House Size and Number of Bedrooms as Predictors. Questions How does this plot suggest that selling price has more variability at higher house size values, for given number of bedrooms? You don't see number of bedrooms on the plot, so how do its values affect the analysis?

Question to Explore

Does this plot suggest any irregularities with the model?

Think It Through

As house size increases, the variability of the standardized residuals seems to increase. This suggests more variability in selling prices when house size is larger, for a given number of bedrooms. We must be cautious, though, because the few points with large negative residuals for the largest houses and the one point with a large positive residual may catch our eyes more than the others. Generally, it's not a good idea to allow a few points to overly influence your judgment about the shape of a residual pattern. However, there is definite evidence that the variability increases as house size increases. A larger data set would provide more evidence about this.

Insight

Nonconstant variability does not invalidate the use of multiple regression. It would, however, make us cautious about using prediction intervals. We would expect predictions about selling price to have smaller prediction errors when house size is small than when house size is large.

> *Try Exercise 13.32*

We have seen several examples illustrating the components of multiple regression analysis. A summary of the entire process of multiple regression follows.

SUMMARY: The Process of Multiple Regression

Steps should include:

1. Identify response and potential explanatory variables
2. Create a multiple regression model; perform appropriate tests (F and t) to see if and which explanatory variables have a statistically significant effect in predicting y
3. Plot y versus $\hat{y}$ for resulting models and find R and R^2 values
4. Check assumptions (residual plot, randomization, residuals histogram)
5. Choose appropriate model
6. Create confidence intervals for slope
7. Make predictions at specified levels of explanatory variables
8. Create prediction intervals

13.4 Practicing the Basics

13.31 Body weight residuals Examples 4–7 used multiple regression to predict total body weight of college athletes. The figure shows the standardized residuals for another multiple regression model for predicting weight.

a. About which distribution do these give you information—the overall distribution of weight or the conditional distribution of weight at fixed values of the predictors?

b. What does the histogram suggest about the likely shape of this distribution? Why?

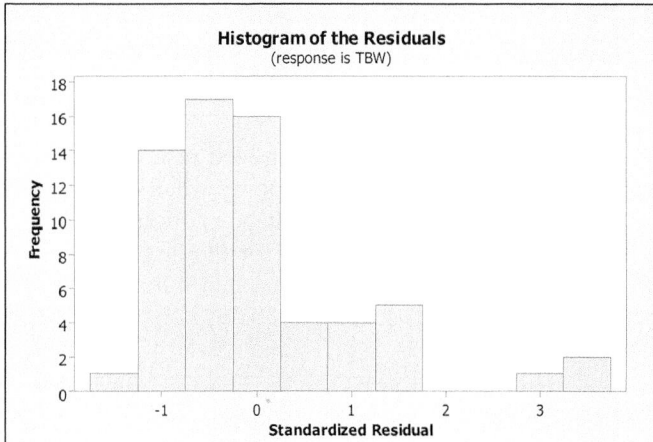

model relating the maximum number of pounds the athlete could bench press (BP) to the number of 60-pound bench presses (BP_60) and the number of 200-pound leg presses (LP_200). It plots the standardized residuals against the values of LP_200.

a. You don't see BP_60 on the plot, so how do its values affect the analysis?

b. Explain how the plot might suggest less variability at the lower values of LP_200.

c. Suppose you remove the three points with standardized residuals around −2. Then is the evidence about variability in part b so clear? What does this suggest about cautions in looking at residual plots?

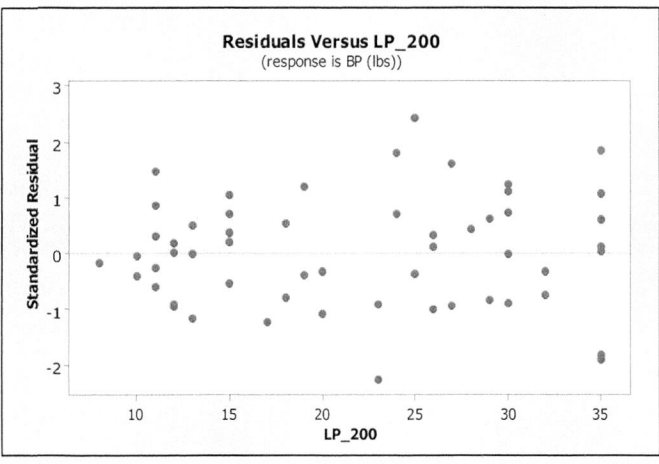

13.32 Strength residuals In Chapter 12, we analyzed strength data for a sample of female high school athletes. The following figure is a residual plot for the multiple regression

13.33 More residuals for strength Refer to the previous exercise. The following figure is a residual plot for the model relating maximum bench press to LP_200 and BP_60. It plots the standardized residuals against the values of BP_60. Does this plot suggest any irregularities with the model? Explain.

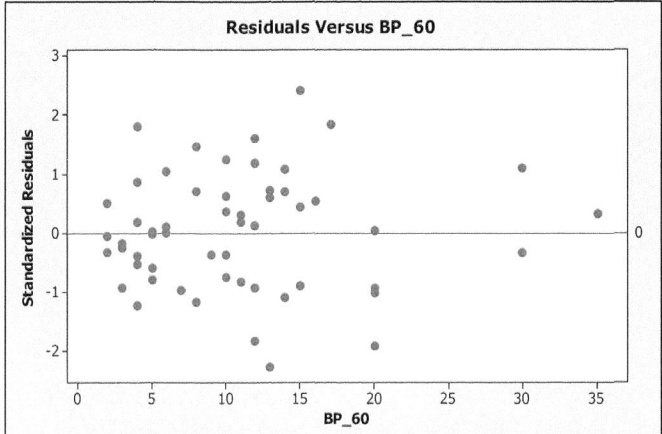

13.34 Nonlinear effects of age Suppose you fit a straight-line regression model to y = amount of time sleeping per day and x = age of subject. Values of y in the sample tend to be quite large for young children and for elderly people, and they tend to be lower for other people. Sketch what you would expect to observe for (a) the scatterplot of x and y and (b) a plot of the residuals against the values of age.

13.35 Driving accidents Suppose you fit a straight-line regression model to x = age of subjects and y = driving accident rate. Sketch what you would expect to observe for (a) the scatterplot of x and y and (b) a plot of the residuals against the values of age.

13.36 Why inspect residuals? When we use multiple regression, what's the purpose of doing a residual analysis? Why can't we just construct a single plot of the data for all the variables at once in order to tell whether the model is reasonable?

13.37 College athletes The College Athletes data set on the text CD comes from a study of University of Georgia female athletes. The response variable BP = maximum bench press (1RM in data set) has explanatory variables LBM = lean body mass (which is weight times 1 minus the proportion of body fat) and REP_BP = number of repetitions before fatigue with a 70-pound bench press (REPS70 in data set). Let's look at all the steps of a regression analysis for these data.

a. The first figure shows a scatterplot matrix. Which two plots in the figure describe the associations with BP as a response variable? Describe those associations.

b. Results of a multiple regression analysis are shown in the next column. Write down the prediction equation, and interpret the coefficient of REP_BP.

c. Report R^2, and interpret its value in the context of these variables.

d. Based on the value of R^2, report and interpret the multiple correlation.

e. Interpret results of the F test that BP is independent of these two predictors. Show how to obtain the F statistic from the mean squares in the ANOVA table.

f. Once REP_BP is in the model, does it help to have LBM as a second predictor? Answer by showing all steps of a significance test for a regression parameter.

g. Examine the histogram shown of the residuals for the multiple regression model. What does this describe, and what does it suggest?

h. Examine the plot shown of the residuals plotted against values of REP_BP. What does this describe, and what does it suggest?

i. From the plot in part h, can you identify a subject whose BP value was considerably lower than expected based on the predictor values? Identify by indicating the approximate values of REP_BP and the standardized residual for that subject.

Regression of maximum bench press on LBM and REP_BP

```
Predictor        Coef      SE Coef     T       P
Constant        55.012     7.740      7.11    0.000
LBM              0.16676   0.07522    2.22    0.030
REP_BP           1.6575    0.1090    15.21    0.000
S = 7.11957   R-Sq = 83.2%
Analysis of Variance
Source        DF      SS       MS       F      P
Regression     2   15283.0   7641.5  150.75  0.000
Res.          61    3092.0     50.7
Total         63   18375.0
```

Scatterplot matrix for Exercise 13.37.

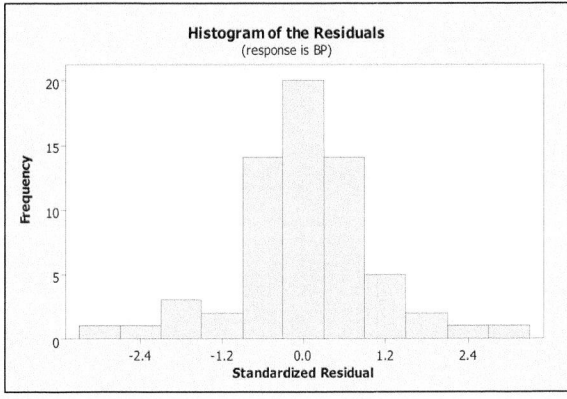

Residual plot for Exercise 13.37, part g.

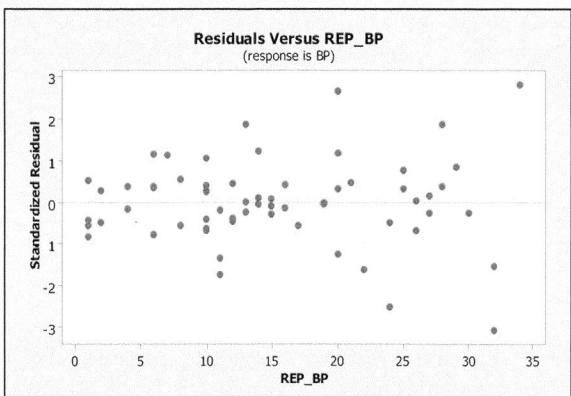

Residuals Versus REP_BP
(response is BP)

Residual plot for Exercise 13.37, part h.

multiple regression model for y = house selling price (in thousands), x_1 = lot size, and x_2 = number of bathrooms.

a. Find a histogram of the standardized residuals. What assumption does this check? What do you conclude from the plot?

b. Plot the standardized residuals against the lot size. What does this check? What do you conclude from the plot?

13.39 Selling prices level off In the previous exercise, suppose house selling price tends to increase with a straight-line trend for small to medium size lots, but then levels off as lot size gets large, for a fixed value of number of bathrooms. Sketch the pattern you'd expect to get if you plotted the residuals against lot size.

13.38 House prices Use software with the House Selling Prices OR data file on the text CD to do residual analyses with the

13.5 Regression and Categorical Predictors

So far, we've studied regression models for quantitative variables. Next, we'll learn how to include a *categorical explanatory* variable. The final section shows how to perform regression for a *categorical response* variable.

Indicator Variables

Regression models specify categories of a categorical explanatory variable using artificial variables, called **indicator variables**. The indicator variable for a particular category is binary. It equals 1 if the observation falls into that category and it equals 0 otherwise.

In the house selling prices (Oregon) data set, the condition of the house is a categorical variable. It was measured with categories (good, not good), The indicator variable x for condition is

$$x = 1 \text{ if house in good condition}$$
$$x = 0 \text{ otherwise.}$$

This indicator variable indicates whether or not a home is in good condition. Let's see how an indicator variable works in a regression equation. To start, suppose condition is the only predictor of selling price. The regression model is then $\mu_y = \alpha + \beta x$, with x as just defined. Substituting the possible values 1 and 0 for x,

$$\mu_y = \alpha + \beta(1) = \alpha + \beta, \text{ if house is in good condition (so } x = 1)$$
$$\mu_y = \alpha + \beta(0) = \alpha, \qquad \text{if house is not in good condition (so } x = 0).$$

The difference between the mean selling price for houses in good condition and other conditions is

$$(\mu_y \text{ for good condition}) - (\mu_y \text{ for other}) = (\alpha + \beta) - \alpha = \beta.$$

The coefficient β of the indicator variable x is the difference between the mean selling prices for homes in good condition and for homes not in good condition.

Example 10

Including Condition in Regression for House Selling Price

Picture the Scenario

Let's now fit a regression model for y = selling price of home using x_1 = house size and x_2 = condition of the house. Table 13.11 shows MINITAB output.

Table 13.11 Regression Analysis of y = Selling Price Using x_1 = House Size and x_2 = Indicator Variable for Condition (Good, Not Good)

```
The regression equation is

House Price = 96271 + 66.5 House Size + 12927 Condition

Predictor      Coef      SE Coef      T       P

Constant       96271     13465       7.15    0.000

House Size     66.463    4.682       14.20   0.000

Condition      12927     17197       0.75    0.453

S = 81787.4 R-Sq = 50.6%
```

Questions to Explore

a. Find and plot the lines showing how predicted selling price varies as a function of house size, for homes in good condition or not in good condition.

b. Interpret the coefficient of the indicator variable for condition.

Think It Through

a. Table 13.11 reports the prediction equation,

$$\hat{y} = 96{,}271 + 66.5x_1 + 12{,}927x_2.$$

For homes not in good condition, $x_2 = 0$. The prediction equation for y = selling price using x_1 = house size then simplifies to

$$\hat{y} = 96{,}271 + 66.5x_1 + 12{,}927(0) = 96{,}271 + 66.5x_1.$$

For homes in good condition, $x_2 = 1$. The prediction equation then simplifies to

$$\hat{y} = 96{,}271 + 66.5x_1 + 12{,}927(1) = 109{,}198 + 66.5x_1.$$

Both lines have the same slope, 66.5. For homes in good condition or not in good condition, the predicted selling price increases by \$66.5 for each square-foot increase in house size. Figure 13.7 plots the two prediction equations. The quantitative explanatory variable, house size, is on the x-axis. The figure portrays a separate line for each category of condition (good, other).

b. At a fixed value of x_1 = house size, the difference between the predicted selling prices for homes in good (1) versus not good (0) condition is

$$(109{,}198 + 66.5x_1) - (96{,}271 + 66.5x_1) = 12{,}927.$$

This is precisely the coefficient of the indicator variable, x_2. For any fixed value of house size, we predict that the selling price is \$12,927 higher for homes that are good versus not in good condition.

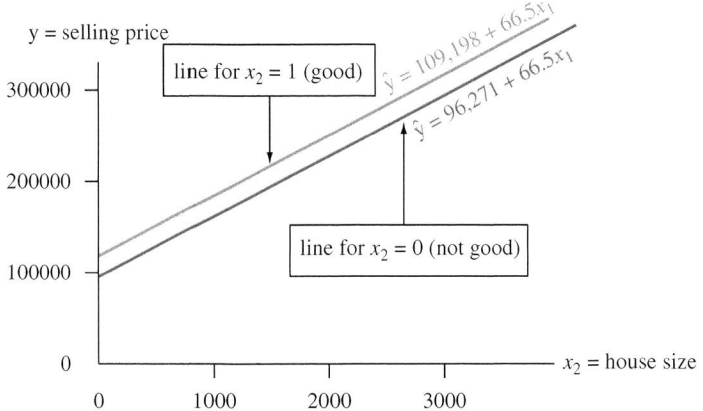

▲ **Figure 13.7** Plot of Equation Relating $\hat{y}$ = Predicted Selling Price to x_1 = House Size, According to x_2 = Condition (1 = Good, 0 = Not Good). Question Why are the lines parallel?

Insight

Since the two lines have the same slope, they are parallel. The line for homes in good condition is above the other line because its y-intercept is larger. This means that for any fixed value of house size, the predicted selling price is higher for homes in good condition. The P-value of 0.453 for the test for the coefficient of the indicator variable suggests that this difference is not statistically significant.

> *Try Exercise 13.40*

A categorical variable having more than two categories uses an additional indicator variable for each category. For instance, if we want to use all three categories good, average, fair in the model, we could use two indicator variables:

$$x_1 = 1 \text{ for houses in good condition, and } x_1 = 0 \text{ otherwise,}$$
$$x_2 = 1 \text{ for houses in average condition, and } x_2 = 0 \text{ otherwise,}$$

If $x_1 = x_2 = 0$, the house is in fair condition. We don't need a separate indicator variable for fair, as it would be redundant. We can tell whether a house is in the fair condition merely from seeing the values of x_1 and x_2. Generally, *a categorical explanatory variable in a regression model uses one fewer indicator variable than the number of categories.* For instance, with the two categories (good condition, other), we needed only a single indicator variable.

Why can't we specify the three categories merely by setting up a variable x that equals 1 for homes in good condition, 0 for homes in average condition, and −1 for fair condition? Because this would treat condition as *quantitative* rather than *categorical*. It would treat condition as if different categories corresponded to different *amounts* of the variable. But the variable measures *which* condition, not *how much* condition. Treating it as quantitative is inappropriate.

Determining if Interaction Exists

In Example 10, the regression equation simplified to two straight lines:

$$\hat{y} = 109{,}198 + 66.5x_1 \text{ for homes in good condition,}$$
$$\hat{y} = 96{,}271 + 66.5x_1 \text{ for homes in other conditions.}$$

Both equations have the same slope. The model forces the effect of x_1 = house size on selling price to be the same for both conditions.

Likewise, in a multiple regression model, *the slope of the relationship between the population mean of y and each explanatory variable is identical for all values of the other explanatory variables.* Such models are sometimes too simple. The effect of an explanatory variable may change considerably as the value of another explanatory variable in the model changes. The multiple regression model we've studied assumes this does not happen. When it does happen, there is **interaction.**

Interaction

For two explanatory variables, **interaction** exists between them if their effects on the response variable when the slope of the relationship between μ_y and one of them changes as the value of the other changes.

Suppose the *actual* population relationship between x_1 = house size and the mean selling price is

$$\mu_y = 100{,}000 + 50x_1 \text{ for homes in good condition,}$$

and

$$\mu_y = 80{,}000 + 35x_1 \text{ for homes in other conditions.}$$

The slope for the effect of x_1 differs (50 versus 35) for the two conditions. There is then interaction between house size and condition in their effects on selling price. See Figure 13.8.

How can you allow for interaction when you do a regression analysis? With two explanatory variables, one quantitative and one categorical (as in Example 10), you can fit a separate line with a different slope between the two quantitative variables for each category of the categorical variable.

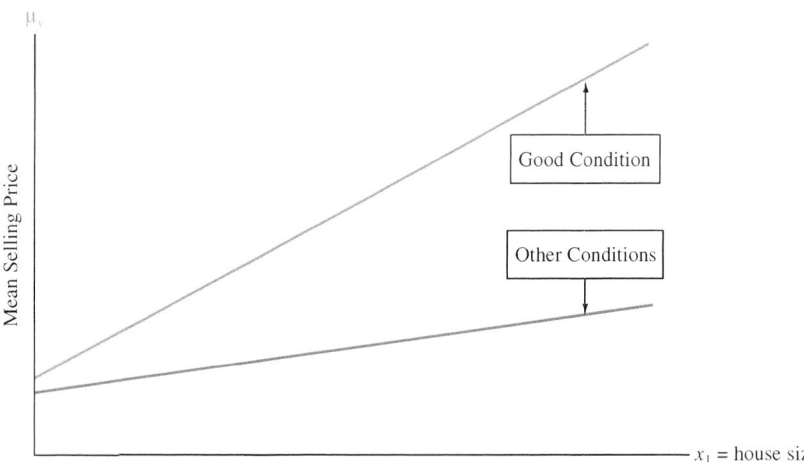

▲ **Figure 13.8** An Example of Interaction. There's a larger slope between selling price and house size for homes in good condition than in other conditions.

Interaction

Example 11

Comparing Winning High Jumps for Men and Women

Picture the Scenario

Men have competed in the high jump in the Olympics since 1896 and women since 1928. Figure 13.9 shows how the winning high jump in the Olympics has changed over time for men and women. The High Jump data file on

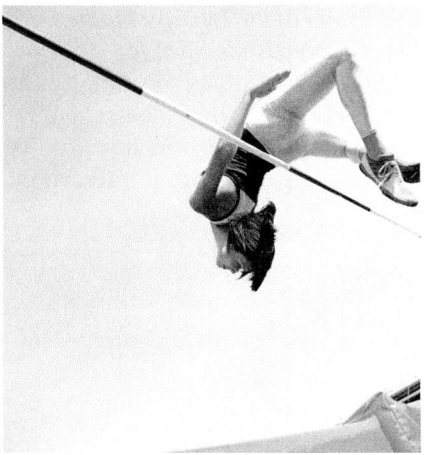

the text CD contains the winning heights for each year. A multiple regression analysis of y = winning height (in meters) as a function of x_1 = number of years since 1928 (when women first participated in the high jump) and x_2 = gender (1 = male, 0 = female) gives $\hat{y} = 1.63 + 0.0057x_1 + 0.35x_2$.

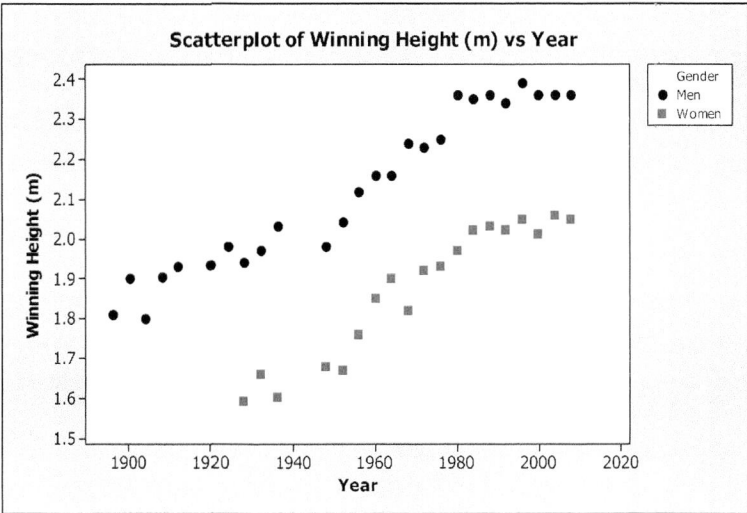

▲ **Figure 13.9** Scatterplot for the Winning High Jumps (in Meters) in the Olympic Games from 1896–2008.

Recall

These data were first analyzed in Example 11 in Chapter 3. ◄

Questions to Explore

a. Interpret the coefficient of year and the coefficient of gender in the equation.

b. To allow interaction, we can fit equations separately to the data for males and the data for females. We then get $\hat{y} = 1.98 + 0.0055x_1$ for males and $\hat{y} = 1.60 + 0.0065x_1$ for females. Describe the interaction by comparing slopes.

c. Describe the interaction allowed in part b by comparing predicted winning high jumps for males and females in 1928 and in 2008.

Think It Through

a. For the prediction equation $\hat{y} = 1.63 + 0.0057x_1 + 0.35x_2$, the coefficient of year is 0.0057. For each gender, the predicted winning high jump increases by 0.0057 meters per year. This seems small, but over a hundred years it projects to an increase of $100(0.0057) = 0.57$ meters, about 27 inches. The model does not allow interaction, as it assumes that the slope of 0.0057 is the same for each gender. The coefficient of gender is 0.35. In a given year, the predicted winning high jump for men is 0.35 meters higher than for women. Because this model does not allow interaction, the predicted difference between men and women is the same each year.

b. The slope of 0.0065 for females is higher than the slope of 0.0055 for males. So the predicted winning high jump increases a bit more for females than for males over this time period.

c. In 1928, $x_1 = 0$, and the predicted winning high jump was $\hat{y} = 1.98 + 0.0055(0) = 1.98$ for males and $\hat{y} = 1.60 + 0.0065(0) = 1.60$ for females, a difference of 0.38 meters. In 2008, $x_1 = 2008 - 1928 = 80$ and the predicted winning high jump was $1.98 +$

$0.0055(80) = 2.42$ for males and $1.60 + 0.0065(80) = 2.12$ for females, a difference of 0.30 meters. The predicted difference between the winning high jumps of males and females decreased a bit between 1928 and 2008.

Insight

When we allow interaction, the estimated slope is a bit higher for females than for males. This is what caused the difference in predicted winning high jumps to be less in 2008 than in 1928. However, the slopes were not dramatically different, as Figure 13.9 shows that the points go up at similar rates for the two genders. The sample degree of interaction was not strong.

Try Exercises 13.46 and 13.47

How do we know whether the interaction shown by the sample is sufficiently large to indicate that there is interaction in the population? There is a significance test for checking this, but it is beyond the scope of this book. In practice, it's usually adequate to investigate interaction informally using graphics. For example, suppose there are two predictors, one quantitative and one categorical. Then you can plot y against the quantitative predictor, identifying the data points by the category of the categorical variable, as we did in Example 11. Do the points seem to go up or go down at quite different rates, taking into account sampling error? If so, it's safer to fit a separate regression line for each category, which then allows different slopes.

13.5 Practicing the Basics

13.40 Winning high jump Refer to Example 11 on winning
(TRY) Olympic high jumps. The prediction equation relating y = winning height (in meters) as a function of x_1 = number of years since 1928 and x_2 = gender (1 = male, 0 = female) is $\hat{y} = 1.63 + 0.0057x_1 + 0.348x_2$.

  a. Using this equation, find the prediction equations relating winning height to year, separately for males and for females.

  b. Find the predicted winning height in 2012 for (i) females, (ii) males, and show how the difference between them relates to a parameter estimate for the model.

13.41 Mountain bike prices The Mountain Bike data file on the text CD shows selling prices for mountains bikes. When y = mountain bike price ($) is regressed on x_1 = weight of bike (lbs) and x_2 = the type of suspension (0 = full, 1 = front end), $\hat{y} = 2741.62 - 53.752x_1 - 643.595x_2$.

  a. Interpret the estimated effect of the weight of the bike.

  b. Interpret the estimated effect of the type of suspension on the mountain bike.

13.42 Predict using house size and condition For the House Selling Prices OR data set, when we regress y = selling price (in thousands) on x_1 = house size and x_2 = condition (1 = Good, 0 = Not Good), we get the results shown.

Regression of selling price of house in thousands versus house size and condition

Predictor	Coef	SE Coef	T	P
Constant	96.27	13.46	7.15	0.000
House Size	0.066463	0.004682	14.20	0.000
Condition	12.93	17.20	0.75	0.453

S = 81.7874 R-Sq = 50.6% R-Sq(adj) = 50.1%

  a. Report the regression equation. Find and interpret the separate lines relating predicted selling price to house size for good condition homes and for homes in not good condition.

  b. Sketch how selling price varies as a function of house size, for homes in good condition and for homes in not good condition.

  c. Estimate the difference between the mean selling price of homes in good and in not good condition, controlling for house size.

13.43 Quality and productivity The table shows data from 27 automotive plants on y = number of assembly defects per 100 cars and x = time (in hours) to assemble each vehicle. The data are in the Quality and Productivity file on the text CD.

Number of defects in assembling 100 cars and time to assemble each vehicle

Plant	Defects	Time	Plant	Defects	Time	Plant	Defects	Time
1	39	27	10	89	17	19	69	54
2	38	23	11	48	20	20	79	18
3	42	15	12	38	26	21	29	31
4	50	17	13	68	21	22	84	28
5	55	12	14	67	26	23	87	44
6	56	16	15	69	30	24	98	23
7	57	18	16	69	32	25	100	25
8	56	26	17	70	31	26	140	21
9	61	20	18	68	37	27	170	28

Source: Data from S. Chatterjee, M. Handcock, and J. Simonoff, *A Casebook for a First Course in Statistics and Data Analysis* (Wiley, 1995); based on graph in *The Machine that Changed the World*, by J. Womack, D. Jones, and D. Roos (Macmillan, 1990).

a. The prediction equation is $\hat{y} = 61.3 + 0.35x$. Find the predicted number of defects for a car having assembly time (i) 12 hours (the minimum) and (ii) 54 hours (the maximum).

b. The first 11 plants were Japanese facilities and the rest were not. Let x_1 = time to assemble vehicle and x_2 = whether facility is Japanese $(1 = \text{yes}, 0 = \text{no})$. The fit of the multiple regression model is $\hat{y} = 105.0 - 0.78x_1 - 36.0x_2$. Interpret the coefficients that estimate the effect of x_1 and the effect of x_2.

c. Explain why part a and part b indicate that Simpson's paradox has occurred.

d. Explain *how* Simpson's paradox occurred. To do this, construct a scatterplot between y and x_1 in which points are identified by whether the facility is Japanese. Note that the Japanese facilities tended to have low values for both x_1 and x_2.

13.44 Predicting hamburger sales A chain restaurant that specializes in selling hamburgers wants to analyze how y = sales for a customer (the total amount spent by a customer on food and drinks, in dollars) depends on the location of the restaurant, which is classified as inner city, suburbia, or at an interstate exit.

a. Construct indicator variables x_1 for inner city and x_2 for suburbia so you can include location in a regression equation for predicting the sales.

b. For part a, suppose $\hat{y} = 5.8 - 0.7x_1 + 1.2x_2$. Find the difference between the estimated mean sales in suburbia and at interstate exits.

13.45 Houses, size, and garage Use the House Selling Prices OR data file on the text CD to regress selling price in thousands on house size and whether the house has a garage.

a. Report the prediction equation. Find and interpret the equations predicting selling price using house size, for homes with and without a garage.

b. How do you interpret the coefficient of the indicator variable for whether the home has a garage?

13.46 House size and garage interact? Refer to the previous exercise.

a. Explain what the no interaction assumption means for this model.

b. Sketch a hypothetical scatter diagram, showing points identified by garage or no garage, suggesting that there is actually a substantial degree of interaction.

13.47 Equal high jump for men and women Refer to Example 11 and Exercise 13.40, with $\hat{y}$ = predicted winning high jump and x_1 = number of years since 1928. When equations are fitted *separately* for males and for females, we get $\hat{y} = 1.98 + 0.0055x_1$ for males and $\hat{y} = 1.60 + 0.0065x_1$ for females.

a. In allowing the lines to have different slopes, the overall model allows for _____ between gender and year in their effects on the winning high jump. (Fill in the correct word.)

b. Show that both equations yield the same predicted winning high jump when $x_1 = 380$ (that is, 380 years after 1928, or in 2308).

c. Is it sensible to use this model to predict that in the year 2308 men and women will have about the same winning high jump? Why or why not?

13.48 Comparing sales You own a gift shop that has a campus location and a shopping mall location. You want to compare the regressions of y = daily total sales on x = number of people who enter the shop, for total sales listed by day at the campus location and at the mall location. Explain how you can do this using regression modeling

a. With a single model, having an indicator variable for location, that assumes the slopes are the same for each location.

b. With separate models for each location, permitting the slopes to be different.

13.6 Modeling a Categorical Response

The regression models studied so far are designed for a quantitative response variable y. When y is categorical, a different regression model applies, called **logistic regression**. Logistic regression can model

- A voter's choice in an election (Democrat or Republican), with explanatory variables of annual income, political ideology, religious affiliation, and race.

- Whether a credit card holder pays his or her bill on time (yes or no), with explanatory variables of family income and the number of months in the past year that the customer paid the bill on time.

We'll study logistic regression in this section for the special case of **binary** y.

The Logistic Regression Model

Recall

Section 2.3 (Example 12) showed that **a proportion for a category is a mean calculated for a binary variable** that has score 1 for that category and score 0 otherwise. ◄

Denote the possible outcomes for y by 0 and 1. We'll use the generic terms *failure* and *success* for these outcomes. The population mean of the 0 and 1 scores equals the population *proportion* of 1 outcomes (successes) for the response variable. That is, $\mu_y = p$, where p denotes the population proportion of successes. This proportion also represents the *probability* that a randomly selected subject has a success outcome. The model describes how p depends on the values of the explanatory variables.

For a single explanatory variable, x, the straight-line regression model is

$$p = \alpha + \beta x.$$

As Figure 13.10 shows, this model implies that p falls below 0 or above 1 for sufficiently small or large x-values. However, a proportion must fall between 0 and 1. Although the straight-line model may be valid over a restricted range of x-values, it is usually inadequate when there are multiple explanatory variables.

Figure 13.10 also shows a more realistic model. It has a curved, S-shape instead of a straight-line trend. The regression equation that best models this S-shaped curve is known as the **logistic regression equation**.

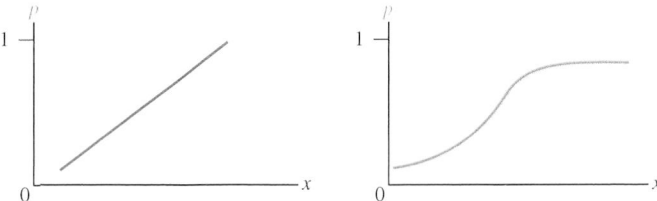

▲ **Figure 13.10** Two Possible Regressions for a Probability p of a Binary Response Variable. A straight line is usually less appropriate than an S-shaped curve. Question Why is the straight-line regression model for a binary response variable often poor?

Logistic Regression

A regression equation for an S-shaped curve for the probability of success p is

$$p = \frac{e^{\alpha + \beta x}}{1 + e^{\alpha + \beta x}}.$$

This equation for p is called the **logistic regression** equation. Logistic regression is used when the response variable has only two possible outcomes (it's binary.)

Here, e raised to a power represents the *exponential function* evaluated at that number. Most calculators have an e^x key that provides values of e raised to a power. The model has two parameters, α and β. Since the numerator of the formula for p is smaller than the denominator, the model forces p to fall between 0 and 1. With a regression model having this S-shape, the probability p falls between 0 and 1 for all possible x values.

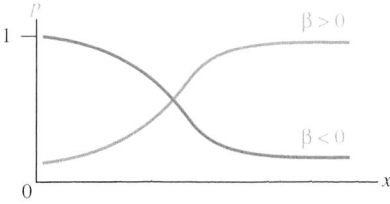

Like the slope of a straight line, the parameter β in this model refers to whether the mean of y increases or decreases as x increases. When $\beta > 0$, the probability p increases as x increases. When $\beta < 0$, the probability p decreases as x increases. See the margin figure. If $\beta = 0$, p does not change as x changes, so the curve flattens to a horizontal straight line. The steepness of the curve increases as the absolute value of β increases. However, unlike in the straight-line model, β is *not* a slope—the change in the mean per one-unit change in x. For this S-shaped curve, the rate at which the curve climbs or descends *changes* according to the value of x.

Software can estimate the parameters α and β in the logistic regression model. Calculators or software can find estimated probabilities $\hat{p}$ based on the model fit.

Example 12

Logistic regression model

Travel Credit Cards

Picture the Scenario

An Italian study with 100 randomly selected Italian adults considered factors associated with whether a person has at least one travel credit card. Table 13.12 shows results for the first 15 people on this response variable and on the person's annual income, in thousands of euros.[2] The complete data set is in the Credit Card and Income data file on the text CD. Let x = annual income and let y = whether the person has a travel credit card (1 = yes, 0 = no).

Table 13.12 Annual Income (in thousands of euros) and Whether Person Has a Travel Credit Card

The response y equals 1 if a person has a travel credit card and equals 0 otherwise. The complete data set is on the text CD.

Income	y	Income	y	Income	y
12	0	14	1	15	0
13	0	14	0	15	1
14	1	14	0	15	0
14	0	14	0	15	0
14	0	14	0	15	0

Source: Data from R. Piccarreta, Bocconi University, Milan (personal communication).

Questions to Explore

Table 13.13 shows what software provides for conducting a logistic regression analysis.

Table 13.13 Results of Logistic Regression for Italian Credit Card Data

Predictor	Coef	SE Coef	Z	P
Constant	−3.5180	0.71034	−4.95	0.000
income	0.1054	0.02616	4.03	0.000

a. State the prediction equation for the probability of owning a travel credit card, and explain whether annual income has a positive or a negative effect.

b. Find the estimated probability of having a travel credit card at the lowest and highest annual income levels in the sample, which were $x = 12$ and $x = 65$.

---

[2]The data were originally recorded in Italian lira but have been changed to euros and adjusted for inflation.

Think It Through

a. Substituting the α and β estimates from Table 13.13 into the logistic regression model formula, $p = e^{\alpha+\beta x}/(1 + e^{\alpha+\beta x})$, we get the equation for the estimated probability $\hat{p}$ of having a travel credit card,

$$\hat{p} = \frac{e^{-3.52+0.105x}}{1 + e^{-3.52+0.105x}}.$$

Because the estimate 0.105 of β (the coefficient of x) is positive, this sample suggests that annual income has a positive effect: The estimated probability of having a travel credit card is higher at higher levels of annual income.

b. For subjects with income $x = 12$ thousand euros, the estimated probability of having a travel credit card equals

$$\hat{p} = \frac{e^{-3.52+0.105(12)}}{1 + e^{-3.52+0.105(12)}} = \frac{e^{-2.26}}{1 + e^{-2.26}} = \frac{0.104}{1.104} = 0.09.$$

For $x = 65$, the highest income level in this sample, you can check that the estimated probability equals 0.97.

Insight

There is a strong effect. The estimated probability of having a travel credit card changes from 0.09 to 0.97 (nearly 1.0) as annual income changes over its range.

Using software, we could also fit the straight-line regression model. Its prediction equation is $\hat{p} = -0.159 + 0.0188x$. However, its $\hat{p}$ predictions are quite different at the low end and at the high end of the annual income scale. At $x = 65$, for instance, it provides the prediction $\hat{p} = 1.06$. This is a poor prediction because we know that a proportion must fall between 0 and 1.

Try Exercise 13.50

Ways to Interpret the Logistic Regression Model

The sign of β in the logistic regression model tells us whether the probability p increases or decreases as x increases. How else can we interpret the model parameters and their estimates? Here, we'll describe three ways.

1. To describe the effect of x, you can compare estimates of p at two different values of x. One possibility is to compare $\hat{p}$ found at the minimum and maximum values of x, as we did in Example 12. There we saw that the estimated probability changed from 0.09 to 0.97, a considerable change. An alternative is to instead use values of x to evaluate this probability that are not as affected by outliers, such as the first and third quartiles.

2. It's good to know the value of x at which $p = 0.50$, that is, that value of x for which each outcome is equally likely. This depends on the logistic regression parameters α and β. It can be shown that $x = -\alpha/\beta$ when $p = 0.50$. (Exercise 13.92).

3. The simplest way to use the logistic regression parameter β to interpret the *steepness* of the curve uses a straight-line approximation. Because the logistic regression formula is a curve rather than a straight line, β itself is no longer the ordinary slope. At the x-value where $p = 0.50$, the line drawn tangent to the logistic regression curve has slope $\beta/4$. See Figure 13.11. The value $\beta/4$ represents the approximate change in the probability p for a one-unit increase in x, when x is close to the value at which $p = 0.50$. Tangent lines at other points have weaker slopes (Exercise 13.91), close to 0 when p is near 0 or 1.

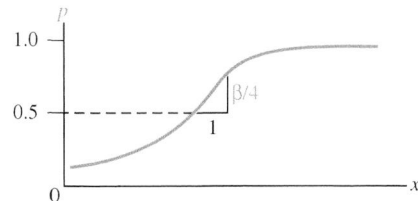

▲ **Figure 13.11** When the Probability $p = 0.50$, for a One-unit Change in x, p Changes by About $\beta/4$. Here, β is the coefficient of x from the logistic regression model.

Example 13

Interpreting a logistic regression model

Effect of Income on Credit Card Use

Picture the Scenario

For the Italian travel credit card study, Example 12 found that the equation

$$\hat{p} = \frac{e^{-3.52+0.105x}}{1 + e^{-3.52+0.105x}}$$

estimates the probability p of having such a credit card as a function of annual income x.

Questions to Explore

Interpret this equation by (a) finding the income value at which the estimated probability of having a credit card equals 0.50 and (b) finding the approximate rate of change in the probability at that income value.

Think It Through

a. The estimate of α is -3.52 and the estimate of β is 0.105. Substituting the estimates into the expression $-\alpha/\beta$ for the value of x at $p = 0.50$, we get $x = (3.52)/(0.105) = 33.5$. The estimated probability of having a travel credit card equals 0.50 when annual income equals €33,500.

b. A line drawn tangent to the logistic regression curve at the point where $p = 0.50$ has slope equal to $\beta/4$. The estimate of this slope is $0.105/4 = 0.026$. For each increase of €1000 in annual income near the income value of €33,500, the estimated probability of having a travel credit card increases by approximately 0.026.

Insight

Figure 13.12 shows the estimated logistic regression curve, highlighting what we've learned in Examples 12 and 13: The estimated probability increases from 0.09 to 0.97 between the minimum and maximum income values, and it equals 0.50 at an annual income of €33,500.

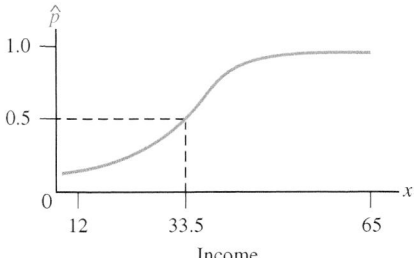

▲ **Figure 13.12** Logistic Regression Curve Relating Estimated Probability $\hat{p}$ of Having a Travel Credit Card to Annual Income x.

Try Exercise 13.54

Inference for Logistic Regression

Software also reports a z test statistic for the hypothesis H_0: $\beta = 0$. When $\beta = 0$, the probability of possessing a travel credit card is the same at all income levels. The test statistic equals the ratio of the estimate b of β divided by its standard error. Sections 8.2 and 9.2 showed that **inference about proportions uses z test statistics** rather than t test statistics. From Table 13.13 (shown again in the margin), the z test statistic equals

$$z = (b - 0)/se = (0.105 - 0)/0.0262 = 4.0.$$

This has a P-value of 0.000 for H_a: $\beta \neq 0$. Since the sample slope is positive, for the population of adult Italians, there is strong evidence of a positive association between annual income and having a travel credit card.

The result of this test is no surprise. We would expect people with higher annual incomes to be more likely to have travel credit cards. Some software can construct a confidence interval for the probability p at various x levels. A 95% confidence interval for the probability of having a credit card equals (0.04, 0.19) at the lowest sample income level of €12,000, and (0.78, 0.996) at the highest sample income level of €65,000.

Table 13.13 was

Predictor	Coef	SE	Z	P
Constant	-3.518	0.710	-4.95	0.000
income	0.105	0.0262	4.03	0.000

Multiple Logistic Regression

Just as ordinary regression extends to handle several explanatory variables, so does logistic regression. Also, logistic regression can include categorical explanatory variables using indicator variables.

Multiple logistic regression

Example 14

Estimating Proportion of Students Who've Used Marijuana

Picture the Scenario

Table 13.14 is a three-variable contingency table from a Wright State University survey asking senior high-school students near Dayton, Ohio, whether they had ever used alcohol, cigarettes, or marijuana. We'll treat marijuana use as the response variable and cigarette use and alcohol use as explanatory variables.

Table 13.14 Alcohol, Cigarette, and Marijuana Use for High School Seniors

Alcohol Use	Cigarette Use	Marijuana Use Yes	No
Yes	Yes	911	538
	No	44	456
No	Yes	3	43
	No	2	279

Source: Data from Professor Harry Khamis, Wright State University (personal communication).

Questions to Explore

Let y indicate marijuana use, coded $1 = $ yes, $0 = $ no. Let x_1 be an indicator variable for alcohol use ($1 = $ yes, $0 = $ no), and let x_2 be an indicator variable for cigarette use ($1 = $ yes, $0 = $ no). Table 13.15 shows MINITAB output for a logistic regression model.

Table 13.15 MINITAB Output for Estimating the Probability of Marijuana Use Based on Alcohol Use and Cigarette Use

Predictor	Coef	SE Coef	Z	P
Constant	−5.30904	0.475190	−11.17	0.000
alcohol	2.98601	0.464671	6.43	0.000
cigarettes	2.84789	0.163839	17.38	0.000

a. Report the prediction equation, and interpret.
b. Find the estimated probability $\hat{p}$ of having used marijuana (i) for students who have not used alcohol or cigarettes and (ii) for students who have used both alcohol and cigarettes.

Think It Through

a. From Table 13.15, the logistic regression prediction equation is

$$\hat{p} = \frac{e^{-5.31+2.99x_1+2.85x_2}}{1 + e^{-5.31+2.99x_1+2.85x_2}}.$$

The coefficient of alcohol use (x_1) is positive (2.99). The indicator variable x_1 equals 1 for those who've used alcohol. Thus, the alcohol users have a higher estimated probability of using marijuana, controlling for whether they used cigarettes. Likewise, the coefficient of cigarette use (x_2) is positive (2.85), so the cigarette users have a higher estimated probability of using marijuana, controlling for whether they used alcohol. Table 13.15 tells us that for each predictor, the test statistic is large. In other words, the estimated effect is a large number of standard errors from 0. The P-values are both 0.000, so there is strong evidence that the corresponding population effects are positive also.

b. For those who have not used alcohol or cigarettes, $x_1 = x_2 = 0$. For them, the estimated probability of marijuana use is

$$\hat{p} = \frac{e^{-5.31+2.99(0)+2.85(0)}}{1 + e^{-5.31+2.99(0)+2.85(0)}} = \frac{e^{-5.31}}{1 + e^{-5.31}} = \frac{0.0049}{1.0049} = 0.005.$$

For those who have used alcohol and cigarettes, $x_1 = x_2 = 1$. For them, the estimated probability of marijuana use is

$$\hat{p} = \frac{e^{-5.31+2.99(1)+2.85(1)}}{1 + e^{-5.31+2.99(1)+2.85(1)}} = 0.629.$$

In summary, the probability that students have tried marijuana seems highly related on whether they've used alcohol and cigarettes.

Insight

Likewise, you can find the estimated probability of using marijuana for those who have used alcohol but not cigarettes (let $x_1 = 1$ and $x_2 = 0$) and for those who have not used alcohol but have used cigarettes. Table 13.16 summarizes results. We see that marijuana use is unlikely unless a student has used both alcohol and cigarettes.

Table 13.16 Estimated Probability of Marijuana Use, by Alcohol Use and Cigarette Use, Based on Logistic Regression Model

The sample proportions of marijuana use are shown in parentheses for the four cases.

	Cigarette Use	
Alcohol Use	**Yes**	**No**
Yes	0.629 (0.629)	0.089 (0.088)
No	0.079 (0.065)	0.005 (0.007)

Try Exercises 13.56 and 13.57

Checking the Logistic Regression Model

		Marijuana	
Alcohol	**Cigarette**	**Yes**	**No**
Yes	Yes	911	538
	No	44	456
No	Yes	3	43
	No	2	279

How can you check whether a logistic regression model fits the data well? When the explanatory variables are categorical, you can find the sample proportions for the outcome of interest. Table 13.16 also shows these for the marijuana use example. For instance, for those who had used alcohol and cigarettes, from Table 13.14 (shown again in the margin) the sample proportion who had used marijuana is $911/(911 + 538) = 0.629$. Table 13.16 shows that the sample proportions are close to the estimated proportions generated by the model. The model seems to fit well.

Table 13.16 may suggest the question, why bother to fit the model? Why not merely inspect a table of sample proportions? One important reason is that the model enables us to easily conduct inferences about the effects of explanatory variables, while controlling for other variables. For instance, if we want to test the effect of alcohol use on marijuana use, controlling for cigarette use, we can test $H_0: \beta_1 = 0$ in the model with alcohol use and cigarette use as predictors.

13.6 Practicing the Basics

13.49 Income and credit cards Example 12 used logistic regression to estimate the probability of having a travel credit card when x = annual income (in thousands of euros). At the mean income of €25,000, show that the estimated probability of having a travel credit card equals 0.29.

13.50 Hall of Fame induction Baseball's highest honor is election to the Hall of Fame. The history of the election process, however, has been filled with controversy and accusations of favoritism. Most recently, there is also the discussion about players who used performance enhancement drugs. The Hall of Fame has failed to define what the criteria for entry should be. Several statistical models have attempted to describe the probability of a player being offered entry into the Hall of Fame. How does hitting 400 or 500 home runs affect a player's chances of being enshrined? What about having a .300 average or 1500 RBI? One factor, the number of home runs, is examined by using logistic regression as the probability of being elected:

$$P(\text{HOF}) = \frac{e^{-6.7+0.0175\text{HR}}}{1 + e^{-6.7+0.0175\text{HR}}}.$$

a. Compare the probability of election for two players who are 10 home runs apart—say, 369 home runs versus 359 home runs.

b. Compare the probability of election for a player with 475 home runs versus the probability for a player with 465 home runs. (These happen to be the figures for Willie Stargell and Dave Winfield.)

13.51 Horseshoe crabs A study of horseshoe crabs by zoologist Dr. Jane Brockmann at the University of Florida used logistic regression to predict the probability that a female crab had a male partner nesting nearby. One explanatory variable was x = weight of the female crab (in kilograms). The results were

```
Predictor        Coef
Constant        -3.695
Weight           1.815
```

The quartiles for weight were Q1 = 2.00, Q2 = 2.35, and Q3 = 2.85.

a. Find the estimated probability of a male partner at Q1 and at Q3.

b. Interpret the effect of weight by estimating how much the probability increases over the middle half of the sampled weights, between Q1 and Q3.

13.52 More crabs Refer to the previous exercise. For what weight values do you estimate that a female crab has probability (a) 0.50, (b) greater than 0.50, and (c) less than 0.50, of having a male partner nesting nearby?

13.53 Voting and income A logistic regression model describes how the probability of voting for the Republican candidate in a presidential election depends on x, the voter's total family income (in thousands of dollars) in the previous year. The prediction equation for a particular sample is

$$\hat{p} = \frac{e^{-1.00+0.02x}}{1 + e^{-1.00+0.02x}}.$$

Find the estimated probability of voting for the Republican candidate when (a) income = $10,000, (b) income = $100,000. Describe how the probability seems to depend on income.

13.54 Equally popular candidates Refer to the previous exercise.

a. At which income level is the estimated probability of voting for the Republican candidate equal to 0.50?

b. Over what region of income values is the estimated probability of voting for the Republican candidate (i) greater than 0.50 and (ii) less than 0.50?

c. At the income level for which $\hat{p} = 0.50$, give a linear approximation for the change in the probability for each $1000 increase in income.

13.55 Many predictors of voting Refer to the previous two exercises. When the explanatory variables are x_1 = family income, x_2 = number of years of education, and x_3 = gender (1 = male, 0 = female), suppose a logistic regression reports

```
Predictor      Coef        SE Coef
Constant      -2.40         0.12
income         0.02         0.01
education      0.08         0.05
gender         0.20         0.06
```

For this sample, x_1 ranges from 6 to 157 with a standard deviation of 25, and x_2 ranges from 7 to 20 with a standard deviation of 3.

a. Interpret the effects using the sign of the coefficient for each predictor.

b. Illustrate the gender effect by finding and comparing the estimated probability of voting Republican for (i) a man with 16 years of education and income $40,000 and (ii) a woman with 16 years of education and income $40,000.

13.56 Graduation, gender, and race The U.S. Census Bureau lists college graduation numbers by race and gender. The table shows the data for graduating 25-year-olds.

College graduation

Group	Sample Size	Graduates
White females	31,249	10,781
White males	39,583	10,727
Black females	13,194	2,309
Black males	17,707	2,054

Source: J. J. McArdle and F. Hamagami, *J. Amer. Statist. Assoc.*, vol. 89 (1994), pp. 1107–1123. Data from U.S. Census Bureau, American Community Survey 2005–2007.

a. Identify the response variable.

b. Express the data in the form of a three-variable contingency table that cross-classifies whether graduated (yes, no), race, and gender.

c. When we use indicator variables for race (1 = white, 0 = black) and for gender (1 = female, 0 = male), the coefficients of those predictors in the logistic regression model are 0.975 for race and 0.375 for gender. Based on these estimates, which race and gender combination has the highest estimated probability of graduation? Why?

13.57 Death penalty and race The three-dimensional contingency table shown is from a study of the effects of racial characteristics on whether or not individuals convicted of homicide receive the death penalty. The subjects classified were defendants in indictments involving cases with multiple murders in Florida between 1976 and 1987.

Death penalty verdict by defendant's race and victims' race

Defendant's Race	Victims' Race	Death Penalty Yes	Death Penalty No	Percent Yes
White	White	53	414	11.3
	Black	0	16	0.0
Black	White	11	37	22.9
	Black	4	139	2.8

Source: Data from M. L. Radelet and G. L. Pierce, *Florida Law Rev.*, vol. 43, 1991, pp. 1–34.

a. Based on the percentages shown, controlling for victims' race, for which defendant's race was the death penalty more likely?

b. Let y = death penalty verdict (1 = yes, 0 = no), let d be an indicator variable for defendant's race (1 = white, 0 = black), and let v be an indicator variable for victims' race (1 = white, 0 = black). The logistic regression prediction equation is

$$\hat{p} = \frac{e^{-3.596-0.868d+2.404v}}{1 + e^{-3.596-0.868d+2.404v}}.$$

According to this equation, for which of the four groups is the death penalty most likely? Explain your answer.

13.58 Death penalty probabilities Refer to the previous exercise.

a. Based on the prediction equation, when the defendant is black and the victims were white, show that the estimated death penalty probability is 0.233.

b. The model-estimated probabilities are 0.011 when the defendant is white and victims were black, 0.113 when the defendant and the victims were white, and 0.027 when the defendant and the victims were black. Construct a table cross-classifying defendant's race by victims' race and show the estimated probability of the death penalty for each cell. Use this to interpret the effect of defendant's race.

c. Collapse the contingency table over victims' race, and show that (ignoring victims' race) white defendants were more likely than black defendants to get the death penalty. Comparing this with what happens when you control for victims' race, explain how Simpson's paradox occurs.

Chapter Review

ANSWERS TO THE CHAPTER FIGURE QUESTIONS

Figure 13.1 Selling price is the response variable, and the graphs that show it as the response variable are in the first row.

Figure 13.2 The coefficient (15,170) of x_2 = number of bedrooms is positive, so increasing it has the effect of increasing the predicted selling price (for fixed house size).

Figure 13.3 We use only the right tail because larger F values provide greater evidence against H_0.

Figure 13.4 A histogram that shows a few observations that have extremely large or extremely small standardized residuals, well removed from the others.

Figure 13.5 The pattern suggests that y tends to be below $\hat{y}$ for very small and large x_1-values and above $\hat{y}$ for medium-sized x_1-values. The

effect of x_1 appears to be better modeled by a mathematical function that has a parabolic shape.

Figure 13.6 As house size increases, the variability of the standardized residuals appears to increase, suggesting more variability in selling prices when house size is larger, for a given number of bedrooms. The number of bedrooms affect the analysis because they have an effect on the predicted values for the model, on which the residuals are based.

Figure 13.7 Each line has the same slope.

Figure 13.10 A straight line implies that p falls below 0 or above 1 for sufficiently small or large x-values. This is a problem, because a proportion must fall between 0 and 1.

CHAPTER SUMMARY

This chapter generalized regression to include more than one explanatory variable in the model. The **multiple regression model** relates the mean μ_y of a response variable y to several explanatory variables, for instance,

$$\mu_y = \alpha + \beta_1 x_1 + \beta_2 x_2$$

for two predictors. Advantages over bivariate regression include better predictions of y and being able to study the effect of an explanatory variable on y while *controlling* (keeping fixed) values of other explanatory variables in the model.

- The **regression parameters** (the betas) are slopes that represent effects of the explanatory variables while controlling for the other variables in the model. For instance, β_1 represents the change in the mean of y for a one-unit increase in x_1, at fixed values of the other explanatory variables.

- The **multiple correlation** R and its square (R^2) describe the predictability of the response variable y by the set of explanatory variables. The multiple correlation R equals the correlation between the observed and predicted y values. Its square, R^2, is the proportional reduction in error from predicting y using the prediction equation instead of using $\bar{y}$ (and ignoring x). Both R and R^2 fall between 0 and 1, with larger values representing stronger association.

- An **F statistic** tests $H_0: \beta_1 = \beta_2 = \ldots = 0$, which states that y is independent of all the explanatory variables in the model. The F test statistic equals a ratio of mean squares. A small P-value suggests that at least one explanatory variable affects the response.

- Individual **t tests** and **confidence intervals** for each β parameter analyze separate population effects of each explanatory variable, controlling for the other variables in the model.

- Categorical explanatory variables can be included in a regression model using **indicator variables.** With two categories, the

indicator variable equals 1 when the observation is in the first category and 0 when it is in the second.

- For binary response variables, the **logistic regression model** describes how the probability of a particular category depends on the values of explanatory variables. An S-shaped curve describes how the probability changes as the value of a quantitative explanatory variable increases.

Table 13.17 summarizes the basic properties and inference methods for multiple regression and those that Chapter 12 introduced for bivariate regression, with quantitative variables.

Table 13.17 Summary of Bivariate and Multiple Regression

	Bivariate Regression Model formula $\mu_y = \alpha + \beta x$	Multiple Regression $\mu_y = \alpha + \beta_1 x_1 + \beta_2 x_2 + \ldots$	
		Simultaneous Effect	**Separate Effects**
Properties of measures	β = slope r = sample correlation $-1 \le r \le 1$	R = multiple correlation $0 \le R \le 1$	$\beta_1, \beta_2, \ldots$ are slopes for each predictor at fixed values of others
	r^2 is proportional reduction in error (PRE)	R^2 is PRE	
Hypotheses of no effect	$H_0: \beta = 0$	$H_0: \beta_1 = \beta_2 = \ldots = 0$	$H_0: \beta_1 = 0,$ $H_0: \beta_2 = 0, \ldots$
Test statistic	$t = (b - 0)/se$	$F = $ (MS for regression)/MSE	$t = (b_1 - 0)/se, \ldots$
	$df = n - 2$	$df_1 = $ no. predictors $df_2 = n - $ no. regression para.	$df = n - $ no. regression para.

SUMMARY OF NOTATION

$x_1, x_2, \ldots$ = explanatory variables in multiple regression model

R = multiple correlation = correlation between observed y and predicted y values

R^2 = proportional reduction in prediction error, for multiple regression

F = test statistic for testing that all β parameters = 0 in regression model

$e^{\alpha+\beta x}$ = exponential function used in numerator and denominator of logistic regression equation, which models the probability p of a binary outcome by

$$p = e^{\alpha+\beta x}/(1 + e^{\alpha+\beta x}).$$

CHAPTER PROBLEMS

Practicing the Basics

13.59 House prices This chapter has considered many aspects of regression analysis. Let's consider several of them at once by using software with the House Selling Prices OR data file on the text CD to conduct a multiple regression analysis of y = selling price of home, x_1 = size of home, x_2 = number of bedrooms, x_3 = number of bathrooms.

   a. Construct a scatterplot matrix. Identify the plots that pertain to selling price as a response variable. Interpret, and explain how the highly discrete nature of x_2 and x_3 affects the plots.

   b. Fit the model. Write down the prediction equation, and interpret the coefficient of size of home by its effect when x_2 and x_3 are fixed.

   c. Show how to calculate R^2 from SS values in the ANOVA table. Interpret its value in the context of these variables.

   d. Find and interpret the multiple correlation.

   e. Show all steps of the F test that selling price is independent of these predictors. Explain how to obtain the F statistic from the mean squares in the ANOVA table.

   f. Report the t statistic for testing $H_0: \beta_2 = 0$. Report the P-value for $H_a: \beta_2 < 0$, and interpret. Why do you think this effect is not significant? Does this imply that the number of bedrooms is not associated with selling price?

   g. Construct and examine the histogram of the residuals for the multiple regression model. What does this describe, and what does it suggest?

   h. Construct and examine the plot of the residuals plotted against size of home. What does this describe, and what does it suggest?

13.60 Predicting body strength In Chapter 12, we analyzed strength data for a sample of female high school athletes. When we predict the maximum number of pounds the athlete can bench press using the number of times she can do a 60-pound bench press (BP_60), we get $r^2 = 0.643$. When we add the number of times an athlete can perform a 200-pound leg press (LP_200) to the model, we get $\hat{y} = 60.6 + 1.33(\text{BP\_60}) + 0.21(\text{LP\_200})$ and $R^2 = 0.656$.

   a. Find the predicted value and residual for an athlete who has BP = 85, $\text{BP}_{60} = 10$, and $\text{LP}_{200} = 20$.

   b. Find the prediction equation for athletes who have $\text{LP}_{200} = 20$, and explain how to interpret the slope for BP_60.

   c. Note that $R^2 = 0.656$ for the multiple regression model is not much larger than $r^2 = 0.643$ for the bivariate model with LP_{200} as the only explanatory variable. What does this suggest?

13.61 Softball data Refer to the Softball data set on the text CD. Regress the difference (DIFF) between the number of runs scored by that team and by the other team on the number of hits (HIT) and the number of errors (ERR).

   a. Report the prediction equation, and interpret the slopes.

   b. From part a, approximately how many hits does the team need so that the predicted value of DIFF is positive (corresponding to a predicted win), if they can play error-free ball (ERR = 0)?

13.62 Violent crime A MINITAB printout is provided from fitting the multiple regression model to U.S. crime data for the 50 states (excluding Washington, D.C.), on y = violent crime rate, x_1 = poverty rate, and x_2 = percent living in urban areas.

   a. Predict the violent crime rate for Massachusetts, which has violent crime rate = 476, poverty rate = 10.2%, and urbanization = 92.1%. Find the residual, and interpret.

   b. Interpret the effects of the predictors by showing the prediction equation relating y and x_1 for states with (i) $x_2 = 0$ and (ii) $x_2 = 100$. Interpret.

Regression of violent crime rate on poverty rate and urbanization

Predictor	Coef	SE Coef	T	P
Constant	−270.7	121.1	−2.23	0.030
poverty	28.334	7.249	3.91	0.000
urbanization	5.416	1.035	5.23	0.000

13.63 Effect of poverty on crime Refer to the previous exercise. Now we add x_3 = percentage of single-parent families to the model. The SPSS table on the next page shows results. Without x_3 in the model, poverty has slope 28.33, and when x_3 is added, poverty has slope 14.95. Explain the differences in the interpretations of these two slopes.

Violent crime predicted by poverty rate, urbanization, and single-parent family

	Coefficients[a]			
	Unstandardized Coefficients			
Model	B	Std. Error	t	Sig.
1 (Constant)	−631.700	149.604	−4.222	.000
poverty	14.953	7.540	1.983	.053
urbanization	4.406	.973	4.528	.000
singleparent	25.362	7.220	3.513	.001

[a] Dependent Variable: violent crime rate.

13.64 Modeling fertility For the World Data for Fertility and Literacy data file on the text CD, a MINITAB printout follows that shows fitting a multiple regression model for y = fertility, x_1 = adult literacy rate (both sexes), x_2 = combined educational enrollment (both sexes). Report the value of each of the following:

   a. r between y and x_1

   b. R^2

   c. Total sum of squares

   d. Residual sum of squares

   e. Standard deviation of y

   f. Residual standard deviation of y

   g. Test statistic value for H_0: $\beta_1 = 0$

   h. P-value for H_0: $\beta_1 = \beta_2 = 0$

```
Analysis of fertility, literacy, and combined
educational enrollment:
Variable              N    Mean  SE Mean  StDev  Median
Adolescent fertility 142  60.42  3.73    44.50   49.55
Adult literacy rate
(both sexes)         142  80.80  1.64    19.56   88.40
Combined educ enrol
(both sexes)         142  68.59  1.32    15.79   71.20

Predictor              Coef   SE Coef      T      P
Constant             187.95   12.92     14.55  0.000
Adult literacy rate
(both sexes)         -1.2590  0.2416    -5.21  0.000
Combined educ
enrollment(both sexes) -0.3762 0.2994  -1.26  0.211

S = 33.4554  R-Sq = 44.3%
Analysis of Variance
Source         DF      SS      MS      F      P
Regression      2   123582   61791  55.21  0.000
Residual Error 139  155577   1119
Total          141  279160
Correlations:
                  Fertility  Adult literacy
Adult literacy      -0.661
Combined educ enroll -0.578        0.803
```

13.65 Significant fertility prediction? Refer to the previous exercise.

   a. Show how to construct the F statistic for testing H_0: $\beta_1 = \beta_2 = 0$ from the reported mean squares, report its P-value, and interpret.

   b. If these are the only nations of interest to us for this study, rather than a random sample of such nations, is this significance test relevant? Explain.

13.66 Motivation to study medicine What motivates someone to pursue the study of medicine? A student's interest and motivation to study medicine can depend on the strength of motivation and career-related values and approaches to learning. Validated and reliable questionnaires were used to obtain data from 116 first-year medical students. This study found no differences in strength of motivation based on sex, nationality, or age. It did find that the motivation to enter medical school was based on interpersonal factors such as wanting to help people, being respected and successful, and fulfilling a sense of achievement. Students motivated to perform better were driven either by positive self-esteem or by perceiving medicine as a means of enhancing their social status. Students who set their own goals and work toward these goals are more likely to succeed. A regression analysis for predicting motivation score is shown below.

	Coefficients	Std Error	P-value
Constant	44.677	6.749	0.000
Strategic approach to learning	0.252	0.065	0.000
Avoidance of role strain	−0.340	0.135	0.013
Prestige	0.451	0.117	0.000
Lack of purpose	−0.755	0.230	0.001
Income	−0.243	0.114	0.035

   a. Find the equation relating predicted motivation score to the explanatory factors listed.

   b. Interpret the signs of the coefficients in the equation for each of the explanatory variables as the explanatory variable relates to motivation.

13.67 Education and gender in modeling income Consider the relationship between $\hat{y}$ = annual income (in thousands of dollars) and x_1 = number of years of education, by x_2 = gender. Many studies in the United States have found that the slope for a regression equation relating y to x_1 is larger for men than for women. Suppose that in the population, the regression equations are $\mu_y = -10 + 4x_1$ for men and $\mu_y = -5 + 2x_1$ for women. Explain why these equations imply that there is *interaction* between education and gender in their effects on income.

13.68 Horseshoe crabs and width A study of horseshoe crabs found a logistic regression equation for predicting the probability that a female crab had a male partner nesting nearby using x = width of the carapace shell of the female crab (in centimeters). The results were

```
Predictor  Coef
Constant   -12.351
Width       0.497
```

   a. For width, Q1 = 24.9 and Q3 = 27.7. Find the estimated probability of a male partner at Q1 and at Q3. Interpret the effect of width by estimating the increase in the probability over the middle half of the sampled widths.

   b. At which carapace shell width level is the estimated probability of a male partner (i) equal to 0.50, (ii) greater than 0.50, and (iii) less than 0.50?

13.69 **AIDS and AZT** In a study (reported in *New York Times,* February 15, 1991) on the effects of AZT in slowing the development of AIDS symptoms, 338 veterans whose immune systems were beginning to falter after infection with the AIDS virus were randomly assigned either to receive AZT immediately or to wait until their T cells showed severe immune weakness. The study classified the veterans' race, whether they received AZT immediately, and whether they developed AIDS symptoms during the three-year study. Let x_1 denote whether used AZT ($1 = $ yes, $0 = $ no) and let x_2 denote race ($1 = $ white, $0 = $ black). A logistic regression analysis for the probability of developing AIDS symptoms gave the prediction equation

$$\hat{p} = \frac{e^{-1.074 - 0.720x_1 + 0.056x_2}}{1 + e^{-1.074 - 0.720x_1 + 0.056x_2}}.$$

   a. Interpret the sign of the effect of AZT.

   b. Show how to interpret the AZT effect for a particular race by comparing the estimated probability of AIDS symptoms for black veterans with and without immediate AZT use.

   c. The *se* value was 0.279 for the AZT use effect. Does AZT use have a significant effect, at the 0.05 significance level? Show all steps of a test to justify your answer.

13.70 **Factors affecting first home purchase** The table summarizes results of a logistic regression model for predictions about first home purchase by young married households. The response variable is whether the subject owns a home ($1 = $ yes, $0 = $ no). The explanatory variables are husband's income, wife's income (each in ten-thousands of dollars), the number of years the respondent has been married, the number of children aged 0–17 in the household, and an indicator variable that equals 1 if the subject's parents owned a home in the last year the subject lived in the parental home.

   a. Explain why, other things being fixed, the probability of home ownership increases with husband's earnings, wife's earnings, the number of children, and parents' home ownership.

   b. From the table, explain why the number of years married seems to show little evidence of an effect, given the other variables in the model.

Results of logistic regression for probability of home ownership

Variable	Estimate	Std. Error
Husband earnings	0.569	0.088
Wife earnings	0.306	0.140
No. years married	−0.039	0.042
No. children	0.220	0.101
Parents' home ownership	0.387	0.176

Source: Data from J. Henretta, "Family Transitions, Housing Market Context, and First Home Purchase," *Social Forces,* vol. 66, 1987, pp. 520–536.

Concepts and Investigations

13.71 **Student data** Refer to the FL Student Survey data file on the text CD. Using software, conduct a regression analysis using $y = $ college GPA and predictors high school GPA and sports (number of weekly hours of physical exercise).

Prepare a report, summarizing your graphical analyses, bivariate models and interpretations, multiple regression models and interpretations, inferences, checks of effects of outliers, and overall summary of the relationships.

13.72 **Why regression?** In 100–200 words, explain to someone who has never studied statistics the purpose of multiple regression and when you would use it to analyze a data set or investigate an issue. Give an example of at least one application of multiple regression. Describe how multiple regression can be useful in analyzing complex relationships.

13.73 **Modeling salaries** The table shows results of fitting a regression model to data on Oklahoma State University salaries (in dollars) of 675 full-time college professors of different disciplines with at least two years of instructional employment. All of the predictors are categorical (binary), except for years as professor, merit ranking, and market influence. The market factor represents the ratio of the average salary at comparable institutions for the corresponding academic field and rank to the actual salary at OSU. Prepare a summary of the results in a couple of paragraphs, interpreting the effects of the predictors. The levels of ranking for professors are assistant, associate, and full professor from low to high. An instructor ranking is nontenure track. Gender and race predictors were not significant in this study.

Modeling professor salaries

Variable	Estimate	Std. Error
Intercept	17.870	0.272
Nontenure track	−0.010	0.011
Instructor	−0.284	0.018
Associate professor	0.170	0.013
Full professor	0.407	0.018
Years as professor	0.004	0.001
Average merit rating	0.044	0.005
Business	0.395	0.015
Education	0.053	0.015
Engineering	0.241	0.014
Fine arts	0.000	0.018
Social science	0.077	0.013
Market influence	−7.046	0.268

Note: Dependent variable is the logarithm of annual salary. Model summary: Adjusted $R_2 = 0.94$; *F*-ration $= 411.76$; $N = 675$; P-value $= 0.001$.
Source: Some data from *New Directions for Institutional Research,* no. 140, Winter 2008 (www.interscience.wiley.com).

13.74 **Multiple choice: Interpret parameter** If $\hat{y} = 2 + 3x_1 + 5x_2 - 8x_3$, then controlling for x_2 and x_3, the change in the estimated mean of y when x_1 is increased from 10 to 20

   a. equals 30.

   b. equals 0.3.

   c. Cannot be given — depends on specific values of x_2 and x_3.

   d. Must be the same as when we ignore x_2 and x_3.

13.75 **Multiple choice: Interpret indicator** In the model $\mu_y = \alpha + \beta_1 x_1 + \beta_2 x_2$, suppose that x_2 is an indicator variable for gender, equaling 1 for females and 0 for males.

   a. We set $x_2 = 0$ if we want a predicted mean without knowing gender.

b. The slope effect of x_1 is β_1 for males and β_2 for females.

c. β_2 is the difference between the population mean of y for females and for males.

d. β_2 is the difference between the population mean of y for females and males, for all those subjects having x_1 fixed, such as $x_1 = 10$.

13.76 Multiple choice: Regression effects Multiple regression is used to model $y =$ annual income using $x_1 =$ number of years of education and $x_2 =$ number of years employed in current job.

a. It is possible that the coefficient of x_2 is positive in a bivariate regression but negative in multiple regression.

b. It is possible that the correlation between y and x_1 is 0.30 and the multiple correlation between y and x_1 and x_2 is 0.26.

c. If the F statistic for $H_0: \beta_1 = \beta_2 = 0$ has a P-value $= 0.001$, then we can conclude that *both* predictors have an effect on annual income.

d. If $\beta_2 = 0$, then annual income is independent of x_2 in bivariate regression.

13.77 True or false: R and R^2 For each of the following statements, indicate whether it is true or false. If false, explain why it is false.

a. The multiple correlation is always the same as the ordinary correlation computed between the values of the response variable and the values $\hat{y}$ predicted by the regression model.

b. The multiple correlation is like the ordinary correlation in that it falls between -1 and 1.

c. R^2 describes how well you can predict y using x_1 when you control for the other variables in the multiple regression model.

d. It's impossible for R^2 to go down when you add explanatory variables to a regression model.

13.78 True or false: Regression For each of the following statements, indicate whether it is true or false. If false, explain why it is false. In regression analysis:

a. The estimated coefficient of x_1 can be positive in the bivariate model but negative in a multiple regression model.

b. When a model is refitted after $y =$ income is changed from dollars to euros, R^2, the correlation between y and x_1, the F statistics and t statistics will not change.

c. If $r^2 = 0.6$ between y and x_1 and if $r^2 = 0.6$ between y and x_2, then for the multiple regression model with both predictors $R^2 = 1.2$.

d. The multiple correlation between y and $\hat{y}$ can equal -0.40.

13.79 True or false: Slopes For data on $y =$ college GPA, $x_1 =$ high school GPA, and $x_2 =$ average of mathematics and verbal entrance exam score, we get $\hat{y} = 2.70 + 0.45x_1$ for bivariate regression and $\hat{y} = 0.3 + 0.40x_1 + 0.003x_2$ for multiple regression. For each of the following statements, indicate whether it is true or false. Give a reason for your answer.

a. The correlation between y and x_1 is positive.

b. A one-unit increase in x_1 corresponds to a change of 0.45 in the predicted value of y, controlling for x_2.

c. Controlling for x_1, a 100-unit increase in x_2 corresponds to a predicted increase of 0.30 in college GPA.

13.80 Scores for religion You want to include religious affiliation as a predictor in a regression model, using the categories Protestant, Catholic, Jewish, Other. You set up a variable x_1 that equals 1 for Protestants, 2 for Catholics, 3 for Jewish, and 4 for Other, using the model $\mu_y = \alpha + \beta x_1$. Explain why this is inappropriate.

13.81 Lurking variable Give an example of three variables for which you expect $\beta \neq 0$ in the model $\mu_y = \alpha + \beta x_1$ but $\beta_1 = 0$ in the model $\mu_y = \alpha + \beta_1 x_1 + \beta_2 x_2$. (*Hint*: The bivariate effect of x_1 could be completely due to a lurking variable, x_2.)

13.82 Properties of R^2 Using its definition in terms of SS values, explain why $R^2 = 1$ only when all the residuals are 0, and $R^2 = 0$ when each $\hat{y} = \bar{y}$. Explain what this means in practical terms.

13.83 Why an F test? When a model has a very large number of predictors, even when none of them truly have an effect in the population, one or two may look significant in t tests merely by random variation. Explain why performing the F test first can safeguard against getting such false information from t tests.

13.84 Multicollinearity For the high school female athletes data file, regress the maximum bench press on weight and percent body fat.

a. Show that the F test is statistically significant at the 0.05 significance level.

b. Show that the P-values are both larger than 0.35 for testing the individual effects with t tests. (It seems like a contradiction when the F test tells us that at least one predictor has an effect but the t tests indicate that neither predictor has a significant effect. This can happen when the predictor variables are highly correlated, so a predictor has little impact when the other predictors are in the model. Such a condition is referred to as **multicollinearity.** In this example, the correlation is 0.871 between weight and percent body fat.)

13.85 Logistic versus linear For binary response variables, one reason that logistic regression is usually preferred over straight-line regression is that a fixed change in x often has a smaller impact on a probability p when p is near 0 or near 1 than when p is near the middle of its range. Let y refer to the decision to rent or to buy a home, with $p =$ the probability of buying, and let $x =$ weekly family income. In which case do you think an increase of $100 in x has greater effect: when $x = 50,000$ (for which p is near 1), when $x = 0$ (for which p is near 0), or when $x = 500$? Explain how your answer relates to the choice of a linear versus logistic regression model.

13.86 **Adjusted R^2** When we use R^2 for a random sample to
◆◆   estimate a population R^2, it's a bit biased. It tends to be
a bit too large, especially when n is small. Some software
also reports

$$\text{Adjusted } R^2 = R^2 - \{p/[n - (p + 1)]\}(1 - R^2),$$

where p = number of predictor variables in the model.
This is slightly smaller than R^2 and is less biased. Suppose
$R^2 = 0.500$ for a model with $p = 2$ predictors. Calculate
adjusted R^2 for the following sample sizes: 10, 100, 1000.
Show that the difference between adjusted R^2 and R^2
diminishes as n increases.

13.87 **R can't go down** The least squares prediction equation
◆◆   provides predicted values $\hat{y}$ with the strongest possible
correlation with y, out of all possible prediction equations
of that form. Based on this property, explain why the
multiple correlation R cannot decrease when you add a
variable to a multiple regression model. (*Hint*: The prediction equation for the simpler model is a special case
of a prediction equation for the full model that has coefficient 0 for the added variable.)

13.88 **Indicator for comparing two groups** Chapter 10 pre-
◆◆   sented methods for comparing means for two groups.
Explain how it's possible to perform a significance test
of equality of two population means as a special case of
a regression analysis. (*Hint*: The regression model then
has a single explanatory variable—an indicator variable
for the two groups being compared. What does $\mu_1 = \mu_2$
correspond to in terms of a value of a parameter in this
model?)

13.89 **Simpson's paradox** Let y = death rate and
◆◆ x = average age of residents, measured for each county
in Louisiana and in Florida. Draw a hypothetical scatterplot, identifying points for each state, such that the mean
death rate is higher in Florida than in Louisiana when x
is ignored, but lower when it is controlled. (*Hint*: When
you fit a line for each state, the line should be higher for
Louisiana, but the y-values for Florida should have an
overall higher mean.)

13.90 **Parabolic regression** A regression formula that gives a
◆◆   parabolic shape instead of a straight line for the relationship between two variables is

$$\mu_y = \alpha + \beta_1 x + \beta_2 x^2.$$

a. Explain why this is a multiple regression model, with
x playing the role of x_1 and x^2 (the square of x) playing the role of x_2.

b. For x between 0 and 5, sketch the prediction equation (i) $\hat{y} = 10 + 2x + 0.5x^2$ and (ii)
$\hat{y} = 10 + 2x - 0.5x^2$. This shows how the parabola
is bowl-shaped or mound-shaped, depending on
whether the coefficient x^2 is positive or negative.

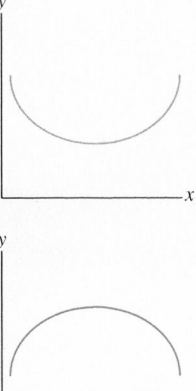

13.91 **Logistic slope** At the x value where the probability of
◆◆   success is some value p, the line drawn tangent to the
logistic regression curve has slope $\beta p(1 - p)$.

a. Explain why the slope is $\beta/4$ when $p = 0.5$.

b. Show that the slope is weaker at other p values by
evaluating this at $p = 0.1, 0.3, 0.7$, and 0.9. What does
the slope approach as p gets closer and closer to 0 or 1?
Sketch a curve to illustrate.

13.92 **When is $p = 0.50$?** When $\alpha + \beta x = 0$, so that
◆◆ $x = -\alpha/\beta$, show that the logistic regression equation
$p = e^{\alpha + \beta x}/(1 + e^{\alpha + \beta x})$ gives $p = 0.50$.

Student Activities

13.93 **Class data** Refer to the data file your class created in
   Activity 3 in Chapter 1. For variables chosen by your
instructor, fit a multiple regression model and conduct
descriptive and inferential statistical analyses. Interpret
and summarize your findings, and prepare to discuss
these in class.

Comparing Groups: Analysis of Variance Methods

14

Example 1

Investigating Customer Satisfaction

Picture the Scenario

In recent years, many companies have increased the attention paid to measuring and analyzing customer satisfaction. Here are examples of two recent studies of customer satisfaction:

- A company that makes personal computers has provided a toll-free telephone number for owners of their PCs to call and seek technical support. For years the company had two service centers for these calls: San Jose, California, and Toronto, Canada. Recently the company outsourced many of the customer service jobs to a new center in Bangalore, India, because employee salaries are much lower there. The company wanted to compare customer satisfaction at the three centers.

- An airline has a toll-free telephone number that potential customers can call to make flight reservations. Usually the call volume is heavy and callers are placed on hold until an agent is free to answer. Researchers working for the airline recently conducted a randomized experiment to analyze whether callers would remain on hold longer if they heard (a) an advertisement about the airline and its current promotions, (b) recorded Muzak ("elevator music"), or (c) recorded classical music. Currently, messages are five minutes long and then repeated; the researchers also wanted to find out if it would make a difference if messages were instead 10 minutes long before repeating.

Questions to Explore

In the second study, the company's CEO had some familiarity with statistical methods, based on a course he took in college. He asked the researchers:

- In this experiment, are the sample mean times that callers stayed on hold before hanging up significantly different for the three recorded message types?

- What conclusions can you make if you take into account both the type of recorded message and whether it was repeated every five minutes or every ten minutes?

Thinking Ahead

Chapter 10 showed how to compare two means. In practice, there may be *several* means to compare, such as in the second example. This chapter shows how to use statistical inference to compare several means. We'll see how to determine whether a set of sample means is significantly different and how to estimate the differences among corresponding population means. To illustrate, we'll analyze data from the second study in Examples 2–4 and 7.

The methods introduced in this chapter apply when a quantitative response variable has a categorical explanatory variable. The categories of the explanatory variable identify the groups to be compared in terms of their means on the response variable. For example, the first study in Example 1 compared mean customer satisfaction for three groups—customers who call the service centers at the three locations. The response variable is customer satisfaction (on a scale of 0 to 10), and the explanatory variable is the service center location.

The inferential method for comparing means of several groups is called **analysis of variance**, denoted **ANOVA**. Section 14.1 shows that the name "analysis of variance" refers to the significance test's focus on two types of variability in the data. Section 14.2 shows how to construct confidence intervals comparing the means. It also shows that ANOVA methods are special cases of a multiple regression analysis.

Categorical explanatory variables in multiple regression and in ANOVA are often referred to as **factors**. ANOVA with a single factor, such as service center location, is called **one-way ANOVA**. Section 14.3 introduces ANOVA for two factors, called **two-way ANOVA**. The second study in Example 1 requires the use of two-way ANOVA to analyze how the mean telephone holding time varies across categories of recorded message type and categories defined by the length of time before repeating the message.

14.1 One-Way ANOVA: Comparing Several Means

The analysis of variance method compares means of *several* groups. Let g denote the number of groups. Each group has a corresponding population of subjects. The means of the response variable for the g populations are denoted by $\mu_1, \mu_2, \ldots, \mu_g$.

Hypotheses and Assumptions for the ANOVA Test Comparing Means

The analysis of variance is a significance test of the null hypothesis of equal population means,

$$H_0: \mu_1 = \mu_2 = \cdots = \mu_g.$$

An example is $H_0: \mu_1 = \mu_2 = \mu_3$ for testing population mean satisfaction at $g = 3$ service center locations. The alternative hypothesis is

$$H_a: \text{at least two of the population means are unequal.}$$

If H_0 is false, perhaps all the population means differ, but perhaps merely one mean differs from the others. The test analyzes whether the differences observed among the *sample* means could have reasonably occurred by chance, if the null hypothesis of equal *population* means were true.

The assumptions for the ANOVA test comparing population means are as follows:

- The population distributions of the response variable for the g groups are normal, with the same standard deviation for each group.
- Randomization (depends on data collection method): In a survey sample, independent random samples are selected from each of the g populations. For an experiment, subjects are randomly assigned separately to the g groups.

Under the first assumption, when the population means are equal, the population distribution of the response variable is the same for each group. The population distribution does not depend on the group to which a subject belongs. The ANOVA test is a test of independence between the quantitative response variable and the group factor.

ANOVA hypotheses

Example 2

Tolerance of Being on Hold?

Picture the Scenario

Let's refer back to the second scenario in Example 1. An airline has a toll-free telephone number for reservations. Often the call volume is heavy, and callers are placed on hold until a reservation agent is free to answer. The airline hopes a caller remains on hold until the call is answered, so as not to lose a potential customer.

The airline recently conducted a randomized experiment to analyze whether callers would remain on hold longer, on average, if they heard (a) an advertisement about the airline and its current promotions, (b) Muzak, or (c) classical music (Vivaldi's *Four Seasons*). The company randomly selected one out of every 1000 calls in a particular week. For each call, they randomly selected one of the three recorded messages to play and then measured the number of minutes that the caller remained on hold before hanging up (these calls were purposely not answered). The total sample size was 15. The company kept the study small, hoping it could make conclusions without alienating too many potential customers! Table 14.1 shows the data. It also shows the mean and standard deviation for each recorded message type.

Table 14.1 Telephone Holding Times by Type of Recorded Message

Each observation is the number of minutes a caller remained on hold before hanging up, rounded to the nearest minute.

Recorded Message	Holding Time Observations	Sample Size	Mean	Standard Deviation
Advertisement	5, 1, 11, 2, 8	5	5.4	4.2
Muzak	0, 1, 4, 6, 3	5	2.8	2.4
Classical	13, 9, 8, 15, 7	5	10.4	3.4

Questions to Explore

a. What are the hypotheses for the ANOVA test?

b. Figure 14.1 displays the sample means. Since these means are quite different, is there sufficient evidence to conclude that the population means differ?

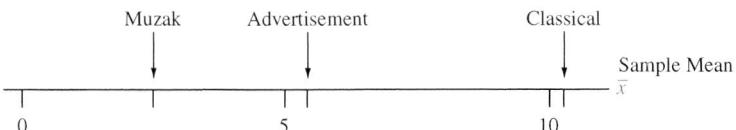

▲ **Figure 14.1** Sample Means of Telephone Holding Times for Callers Who Hear One of Three Recorded Messages. Question Since the sample means are quite different, can we conclude that the population means differ?

Think It Through

a. Denote the holding time means for the population that these three random samples represent by μ_1 for the advertisement, μ_2 for Muzak, and μ_3 for classical music. ANOVA tests whether these are equal. The null hypothesis is $H_0: \mu_1 = \mu_2 = \mu_3$. The alternative hypothesis is that at least two of the population means are different.

b. The sample means are quite different. But even if the population means are equal, we expect the sample means to differ because of sampling variability. So these differences alone are not sufficient evidence to enable us to reject H_0.

Insight

The strength of evidence against H_0 will also depend on the sample sizes and the variability of the data. We'll next study how to test these hypotheses.

> *Try Exercise 14.1, parts a and b*

Variability Between Groups and Within Groups Is the Key to Significance

The ANOVA method is used to compare population means. So, why is it called analysis of *variance*? The reason is that the test statistic uses evidence about two types of variability. Rather than presenting a formula now for this test statistic, which is rather complex, we'll discuss the reasoning behind it, which is quite simple.

Table 14.1 on the previous page listed data for three groups. Figure 14.2a shows the same data with dot plots. Suppose the sample data were different, as shown in Figure 14.2b. The data in Figure 14.2b have the same means as the data in Figure 14.2a but have smaller standard deviations within each group. Which case do you think gives stronger evidence against $H_0: \mu_1 = \mu_2 = \mu_3$?

What's the difference between the data in these two cases? The variability *between* pairs of sample means is the same in each case because the sample means are the same. However, the variability *within* each sample is much smaller in Figure 14.2b than in Figure 14.2a. The sample standard deviation is about 1.0 for each sample in Figure 14.2b whereas it is between 2.4 and 4.2 for the samples in Figure 14.2a. We'll see that the evidence against $H_0: \mu_1 = \mu_2 = \mu_3$ is stronger when the variability *within* each sample is smaller. Figure 14.2b has less variability within each sample than Figure 14.2a. Therefore, it gives stronger evidence against H_0. The evidence against H_0 is also stronger when the variability *between* sample

(a)

(b)

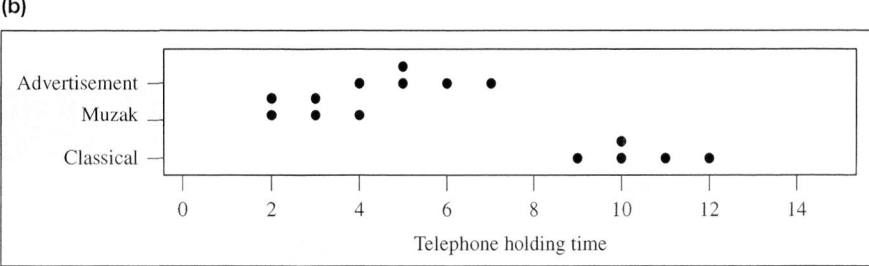

▲ **Figure 14.2** Data from Table 14.1 in Figure 14.2a and Hypothetical Data in Figure 14.2b That Have the Same Means but Less Variability Within Groups. Question Do the data in Figure 14.2b give stronger or weaker evidence against $H_0: \mu_1 = \mu_2 = \mu_3$ than the data in Figure 14.2a. Why?

means increases (that is, when the sample means are farther apart) and as the sample sizes increase.

ANOVA *F* Test Statistic

The **analysis of variance (ANOVA) *F* test statistic** summarizes

$$F = \frac{\text{Between-groups variability}}{\text{Within-groups variability}}.$$

The larger the variability *between* groups relative to the variability *within* groups, the larger the *F* test statistic tends to be. For instance, $F = 6.4$ for the data in Figure 14.2a, whereas $F = 67.8$ for the data in Figure 14.2b. The between-groups variability is the same in each figure, but Figure 14.2b has much less within-groups variability and thus a larger test statistic value. Later in the section, we'll see the two types of variability described in the *F* test statistic are measured by estimates of *variances.*

The Test Statistic for Comparing Means Has the *F* Distribution

When H_0 is true, the *F* test statistic has the *F* sampling distribution. The formula for the *F* test statistic is such that when H_0 is true, the *F* distribution has a mean of approximately 1. When H_0 is false, the *F* test statistic tends to be larger than 1, more so as the sample sizes increase. The larger the *F* test statistic value, the stronger the evidence against H_0.

Recall that we used the *F* distribution in the *F* test that the slope parameters of a multiple regression model are all zero (Section 13.3). As in that test, the P-value here is the probability (presuming that H_0 is true) that the *F* test statistic is larger than the observed *F* value. That is, it is the right-hand tail probability, as shown in the margin figure, representing results even more extreme than observed. The larger the *F* test statistic, the smaller the P-value.

In Section 13.3, we learned that the *F* distribution has two *df* values. For ANOVA with *g* groups and total sample size for all groups combined of $N = n_1 + n_2 + \cdots + n_g$,

$$df_1 = g - 1 \text{ and } df_2 = N - g.$$

Table D in the appendix reports *F* values having P-value of 0.05, for various df_1 and df_2 values. For any given *F* value and *df* values, software provides the P-value. The following summarizes the steps of an ANOVA *F* test.

SUMMARY: Steps of ANOVA *F* Test for Comparing Population Means of Several Groups

1. **Assumptions:** Independent random samples (either from random sampling or a randomized experiment), normal population distributions with equal standard deviations

2. **Hypotheses:** $H_0: \mu_1 = \mu_2 = \cdots = \mu_g$ (Equal population means for *g* groups), H_a: at least two of the population means are unequal.

3. **Test statistic:** $F = \dfrac{\text{Between-groups variability}}{\text{Within-groups variability}}.$

   F sampling distribution has $df_1 = g - 1$, $df_2 = N - g$ = total sample size − number of groups

4. **P-value:** Right-tail probability of above observed *F* value

5. **Conclusion:** Interpret in context. If decision needed, reject H_0 if P-value ≤ significance level (such as 0.05).

In Words

The P-value for an ANOVA *F* test statistic is the right-tail probability from the *F* distribution.

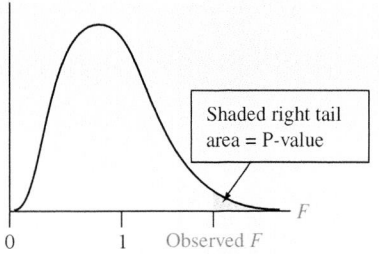

Shaded right tail area = P-value

Recall

The **F distribution** was introduced in Section 13.3. It's used for tests about several parameters (rather than a single parameter or a difference between two parameters, for which we can use a *t* test). ◄

F values with

	df_1		
df_2	1	2	3
6	5.99	5.14	4.76
12	4.75	3.88	3.49
18	4.41	3.55	3.16
24	4.26	3.40	3.01
30	4.17	3.32	2.92
120	3.92	3.07	2.68

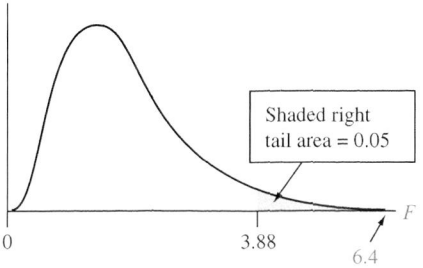

Example 3

One-way ANOVA

Telephone Holding Times

Picture the Scenario

Examples 1 and 2 discussed a study of the length of time that 15 callers to an airline's toll-free telephone number remain on hold before hanging up. The study compared three recorded messages: an advertisement about the airline, Muzak, and classical music. Let μ_1, μ_2, and μ_3 denote the population mean telephone holding times for the three messages.

Questions to Explore

a. For testing H_0: $\mu_1 = \mu_2 = \mu_3$ based on this experiment, what value of the F test statistic would have a P-value of 0.05?

b. For the data in Table 14.1 on page 682, we'll see that software reports $F = 6.4$. Based on the answer to part a, will the P-value be larger, or smaller, than 0.05?

c. Can you reject H_0, using a significance level of 0.05? What can you conclude from this?

Think It Through

a. With $g = 3$ groups and a total sample size of $N = 15$ (5 in each group), the test statistic has

$$df_1 = g - 1 = 2 \text{ and } df_2 = N - g = 15 - 3 = 12.$$

From Table D (see the excerpt in the margin), with these df values an F test statistic value of 3.88 has a P-value of 0.05.

b. Since the F test statistic of 6.4 is farther out in the tail than 3.88 (see figure in margin), the right-tail probability above 6.4 is less than 0.05. So, the P-value is less than 0.05.

c. Since P-value < 0.05, there is sufficient evidence to reject H_0: $\mu_1 = \mu_2 = \mu_3$. We conclude that a difference exists among the three types of messages in the population mean amount of time that customers are willing to remain on hold.

Insight

We'll see that software reports a P-value = 0.013. This is quite strong evidence against H_0. If H_0 were true, there'd be only about a 1% chance of getting an F test statistic value larger than the observed F value of 6.4.

Try Exercise 14.2, parts a–c

The Variance Estimates and the ANOVA Table

Now let's take a closer look at the F test statistic. Denote the group sample means by $\bar{y}_1, \bar{y}_2, \ldots, \bar{y}_g$. (We use y rather than x because the quantitative variable is the response variable when used in a corresponding regression analysis.) We'll see that the F test statistic depends on these sample means, the sample standard deviations—$s_1, s_2, \ldots, s_g$—for the g groups, and the sample sizes.

One assumption for the ANOVA F test is that each population has the same standard deviation. Let σ denote the standard deviation for each of the g population distributions. The F test statistic for $H_0: \mu_1 = \mu_2 = \cdots = \mu_g$ is the ratio of two estimates of σ^2, the population *variance* for each group. Since we won't usually do computations by hand, we'll show formulas merely to give a better sense of what the F test statistic represents. The formulas are simplest when the group sample sizes are equal (as in Example 3), the case we'll show.

The estimate of σ^2 in the *denominator* of the F test statistic uses the variability *within* each group. The sample standard deviations $s_1, s_2, \ldots, s_g$ summarize the variation of the observations within the groups around their means.

- With equal sample sizes, the **within-groups estimate** of the variance σ^2 is the mean of the g sample variances for the g groups,

$$\text{Within-groups variance estimate } s^2 = \frac{s_1^2 + s_2^2 + \cdots + s_g^2}{g}.$$

When the sample sizes are not equal, the within-groups estimate is a *weighted average* of the sample variances, with greater weight given to samples with larger sample sizes. In either case, this estimate is unbiased: Its sampling distribution has σ^2 as its mean, regardless of whether H_0 is true.

The estimate of σ^2 in the *numerator* of the F test statistic uses the variability *between* each sample mean and the overall sample mean $\bar{y}$ for all the data.

- With equal sample sizes, n in each group, the **between-groups estimate** of the variance σ^2 is

$$\frac{\text{Between-groups}}{\text{variance estimate}} = \frac{n[(\bar{y}_1 - \bar{y})^2 + (\bar{y}_2 - \bar{y})^2 + \cdots + (\bar{y}_g - \bar{y})^2]}{g - 1}.$$

If H_0 is true, this estimate is also unbiased. We expect this estimate to take a similar value as the within-groups estimate, apart from sampling error. If H_0 is false, however, the population means differ and the sample means tend to differ more greatly. Then, the between-groups estimate tends to overestimate σ^2.

The F test statistic is the ratio of these two estimates of the population variance,

$$F = \frac{\text{Between-groups estimate of } \sigma^2}{\text{Within-groups estimate of } \sigma^2}.$$

Computer software displays the two estimates in an ANOVA table similar to tables displayed in regression. Table 14.2 shows the basic format, illustrating the test in Example 3:

- The MS column contains the two estimates, which are called *mean squares*.
- The ratio of the two mean squares is the F test statistic, $F = 74.6/11.6 = 6.4$.

This F test statistic has P-value $= 0.013$, also shown in Table 14.2.

Table 14.2 ANOVA Table for F Test Using Data From Table 14.1

Source	DF	SS	MS	F	P
Group	2	149.2	74.6	6.43	0.013
Error	12	139.2	11.6		
Total	14	288.4			

Between groups → Group. Within groups → Error. F test statistic = ratio of the MS values.

Did You Know?

Without n in the formula, the between-groups estimate is the sample variance of the g sample means. That sample variance of $\{\bar{y}_1, \bar{y}_2, \ldots, \bar{y}_g\}$ estimates the variance of the sampling distribution of each sample mean, which is σ^2/n. Multiplying by n then gives an estimate of σ^2 itself. See Exercise 14.66.

Recall

In Sections 12.4 and 13.3, we saw that a **mean square** (MS) is a ratio of a sum of squares (SS) to its df value.

The mean square in the group row of the ANOVA table is based on variability *between* the groups. It is the *between-groups* estimate of the population variance σ^2. This is 74.6 in Table 14.2, listed under MS. The mean square error is the *within-groups* estimate s^2 of σ^2. This is 11.6 in Table 14.2. The "Error" label for this MS refers to the fact that it summarizes the error from not being able to predict subjects' responses exactly if we know only the group to which they belong.

Each mean square equals a sum of squares (in the SS column) divided by a degrees of freedom value (in the DF column). The *df* values for Group and Error in Table 14.2 are the *df* values for the *F* distribution, $df_1 = g - 1 = 3 - 1 = 2$ and $df_2 = N - g = 15 - 3 = 12$.

The sum of the between-groups sum of squares and the within-groups (Error) sum of squares is the **total sum of squares**. This is the sum of squares of the combined sample of *N* observations around the overall sample mean. The analysis of variance partitions the total sum of squares into two independent parts, the between-groups SS and the within-groups SS. It can be shown that the total sum of squares equals

$$\text{Total SS} = \Sigma(y - \bar{y})^2 = \text{between-groups SS} + \text{within-groups SS}.$$

In Table 14.2, for example,

$$\text{Total SS} = 288.4 = 149.2 + 139.2.$$

The total SS divided by $N - 1$ (the *df* for the total SS) is the sample variance when the data for the *g* groups are combined and treated as a single sample. The margin shows the TI-83+/84 output for this one-way ANOVA.

```
One-way ANOVA
 F=6.431
 p=.013
 Factor
  df=2.000
  SS=149.200
↓ MS=74.600
■
```

```
One-way ANOVA
↑ MS=74.600
 Error
  df=12.000
  SS=139.200
  MS=11.600
 Sxp=3.406
■
```

TI-83+/84 output

Assumptions and the Effects of Violating Them

The assumptions for the ANOVA *F* test comparing population means are:

(1) The population distributions of the response variable for the *g* groups are normal,

(2) Those distributions have the same standard deviation σ, and

(3) The data resulted from randomization.

Figure 14.3 portrays the population distribution assumptions.

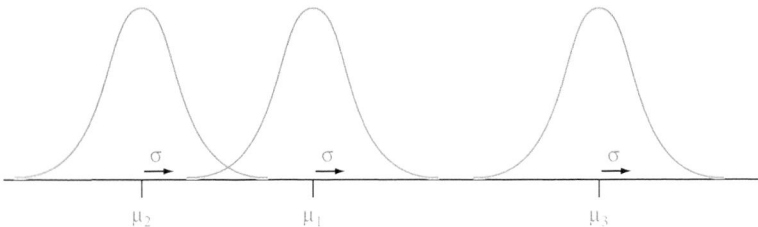

▲ **Figure 14.3** The Assumptions About the Population Distributions: Normal With Equal Standard Deviations. Question In practice, what types of evidence would suggest that these assumptions are badly violated?

The assumptions that the population distributions are normal with identical standard deviations seem stringent. They are never satisfied exactly in practice. Moderate violations of the normality assumption are not serious. The *F* sampling distribution still provides a reasonably good approximation to the actual sampling distribution of the *F* test statistic. This becomes even more the case as the sample sizes increase, because the sampling distribution then has weaker dependence on the form of the population distributions.

Moderate violations of the equal population standard deviation assumption are also not serious. When the sample sizes are identical for the groups, the *F* test still works well even with severe violations of this assumption. When the sample sizes are not equal, the F test works quite well as long as the largest group standard deviation is no more than about twice the smallest group standard deviation.

You can construct box plots or dot plots for the sample data distributions to check for extreme violations of normality. Misleading results may occur with the F test if the distributions are highly skewed and the sample size N is small, or if there are relatively large differences among the standard deviations (the largest sample standard deviation being more than double the smallest one) and the sample sizes are unequal. When the distributions are highly skewed, the mean may not even be a relevant summary measure.[1]

In Practice   Robustness of ANOVA F test

Since the ANOVA F test is robust to moderate breakdowns in the population normality and equal standard deviation assumptions, in practice it is used unless (1) graphical methods show extreme skew for the response variable or (2) the largest group standard deviation is more than about double the smallest group standard deviation and the sample sizes are unequal.

Example 4

ANOVA assumptions

Telephone Holding Time Study

Picture the Scenario

Let's check the assumptions for the F test on telephone holding times (Example 3).

Question to Explore

Is it appropriate to apply ANOVA to the data in Table 14.1 to compare mean telephone holding times for three message types?

Think It Through

Subjects were selected randomly for the experiment and assigned randomly to the three recorded messages. From Table 14.1 (summarized in the margin), the largest sample standard deviation of 4.2 is less than twice the smallest standard deviation of 2.4 (In any case, the sample sizes are equal, so this assumption is not crucial). The sample sizes in Table 14.1 are small, so it is difficult to make judgments about shapes of population distributions. However, the dot plots in Figure 14.2a on page 683 did not show evidence of severe nonnormality. Thus, ANOVA is suitable for these data.

Insight

As in other statistical inferences, the method used to gather the data is the most crucial factor. Inferences have greater validity when the data are from an experimental study that randomly assigned subjects to groups or from a sample survey that used random sampling.

> *Try Exercise 14.11, part c*

Recall

Table 14.1 showed the following:

Recorded Message	Sample Size	Mean	Std. Dev.
Advert.	5	5.4	4.2
Muzak	5	2.8	2.4
Classical	5	10.4	3.4

◄

Recall

See the beginning of Chapter 10 to review the distinction between **independent samples** and **dependent samples**. ◄

The ANOVA methods in this chapter are designed for *independent* samples. Recall that for independent samples, the subjects in one sample are distinct from those in other samples. Separate methods, beyond the scope of this text, handle *dependent* samples.

---

[1]Chapter 15 discusses methods that apply when these assumptions are badly violated.

Recall

To compare two means while assuming equal population standard deviations, Section 10.3 showed the test statistic is

$$t = \frac{\bar{y}_1 - \bar{y}_2}{s\sqrt{\dfrac{1}{n_1} + \dfrac{1}{n_2}}},$$

where the standard deviation s pools information from within both samples. It has $df = n_1 + n_2 - 2 = N - g$ for $N = n_1 + n_2$ and $g = 2$. ◄

Using One F Test or Several t Tests to Compare the Means

With two groups, Section 10.3 showed how a t test can compare the means under the assumption of equal population standard deviations. That test also uses between-groups and within-groups variation. The t test statistic has the difference *between* the two group means in the numerator and a denominator based on pooling variability *within* the two groups. See the formula in the margin. In fact, if we apply the ANOVA F test to data from $g = 2$ groups, it can be shown that the F test statistic equals the square of this t test statistic. The P-value for the F test is exactly the same as the two-sided P-value for the t test. We can use either test to conduct the analysis.

When there are several groups, instead of using the F test why not use a t test to compare each pair of means? One reason for doing the F test is that using a *single* test rather than multiple tests enables us to control the probability of a Type I error. With a significance level of 0.05 in the F test, for instance, the probability of incorrectly rejecting a true H_0 is fixed at 0.05. When we do a separate t test for each pair of means, by contrast, a Type I error probability applies for *each* comparison. In that case, we are not controlling the *overall* Type I error rate for all the comparisons.

But the F test has its own disadvantages. With a small P-value, we can conclude that the population means are not identical. However, the result of the F test does not tell us *which* groups are different or *how* different they are. In Example 3, we have not concluded whether one recorded message works significantly better than the other two at keeping potential customers on the phone. We can address these issues using confidence intervals, as the next section shows.

14.1 Practicing the Basics

14.1 **Hotel satisfaction** The CEO of a company that owns (TRY) five resort hotels wants to evaluate and compare satisfaction with the five hotels. The company's research department randomly sampled 125 people who had stayed at any of the hotels during the past month and asked them to rate their expectations of the hotel before their stay and to rate the quality of the actual stay at the hotel. Both observations used a rating scale of 0–10, with 0 = very poor and 10 = excellent. The researchers compared the hotels on the gap between prior expectation and actual quality, using the difference score, $y = $ performance gap = (prior expectation score − actual quality score).

  a. Identify the response variable, the factor, and the categories that form the groups.

  b. State the null and alternative hypotheses for conducting an ANOVA.

  c. Explain why the df values for this ANOVA are $df_1 = 4$ and $df_2 = 120$.

  d. How large an F test statistic is needed to get a P-value = 0.05 in this ANOVA?

14.2 **Satisfaction with banking** A bank conducts a survey (TRY) in which it randomly samples 400 of its customers. The survey asks the customers which way they use the bank the most: (1) interacting with a teller at the bank,

(2) using ATMs, or (3) using the bank's Internet banking service. It also asks their level of satisfaction with the service they most often use (on a scale of 0 to 10 with 0 = very poor and 10 = excellent). Does mean satisfaction differ according to how they most use the bank?

  a. Identifying notation, state the null and alternative hypotheses for conducting an ANOVA with data from the survey.

  b. Report the df values for this ANOVA. Above what F test statistic values give a P-value below 0.05?

  c. For the data, $F = 0.46$ and the P-value equals 0.63. What can you conclude?

  d. What were the assumptions on which the ANOVA was based? Which assumption is the most important?

14.3 **What's the best way to learn French?** The following table shows scores on the first quiz (maximum score 10 points) for eighth-grade students in an introductory level French course. The instructor grouped the students in the course as follows:

Group 1: Never studied foreign language before but have good English skills

Group 2: Never studied foreign language before and have poor English skills

Group 3: Studied at least one other foreign language

French scores on the quiz

	Group 1	Group 2	Group 3
	4	1	9
	6	5	10
	8		5
Mean	6.0	3.0	8.0
Std. Dev.	2.000	2.828	2.646

Source	DF	SS	MS	F	P
Group	2	30.00	15.00	2.50	0.177
Error	5	30.00	6.00		
Total	7	60.00			

a. Defining notation and using results obtained with software, also shown in the table, report the five steps of the ANOVA test.

b. The sample means are quite different, but the P-value is not small. Name one important reason for this. (*Hint*: For given sample means, how do the results of the test depend on the sample sizes?)

c. Was this an experimental study, or an observational study? Explain how a lurking variable could be responsible for Group 3 having a larger mean than the others. (Thus, even if the P-value were small, it is inappropriate to assume that having studied at least one foreign language causes one to perform better on this quiz.)

14.4 What affects the F value? Refer to the previous exercise.

a. Suppose that the first observation in the second group was actually 9, not 1. Then the standard deviations are the same as reported in the table, but the sample means are 6, 7, and 8 rather than 6, 3, and 8. Do you think the F test statistic would be larger, the same, or smaller? Explain your reasoning, without doing any calculations.

b. Suppose you had the same means as shown in the table but the sample standard deviations were 1.0, 1.8, and 1.6, instead of 2.0, 2.8, and 2.6. Do you think the F test statistic would be larger, the same, or smaller? Explain your reasoning.

c. Suppose you had the same means and standard deviations as shown in the table but the sample sizes were 30, 20, and 30, instead of 3, 2, and 3. Do you think the F test statistic would be larger, the same, or smaller? Explain your reasoning.

d. In parts a, b, and c, would the P-value be larger, the same, or smaller? Why?

14.5 Outsourcing Example 1 at the beginning of this chapter mentioned a study to compare customer satisfaction at service centers in San Jose, California; Toronto, Canada; and Bangalore, India. Each center randomly sampled 100 people who called during a two-week period. Callers rated their satisfaction on a scale of 0 to 10, with higher scores representing greater satisfaction. The sample means were 7.6 for San Jose, 7.8 for Toronto, and 7.1 for Bangalore. The table shows the results of conducting an ANOVA.

a. Define notation and specify the null hypothesis tested in this table.

b. Explain how to obtain the F test statistic value reported in the table from the MS values shown, and report the values of df_1 and df_2 for the F distribution.

c. Interpret the P-value reported for this test. What conclusion would you make using a 0.05 significance level?

Customer satisfaction with outsourcing

Source	DF	SS	MS	F	P
Group	2	26.00	13.00	27.6	0.000
Error	297	140.00	0.47		
Total	299	60.00			

14.6 Good friends and astrological sign A recent General Social Survey asked subjects how many good friends they have. Is number of friends associated with the respondent's astrological sign (the 12 symbols of the Zodiac)? The ANOVA table for the GSS data reports $F = 0.61$ based on $df_1 = 11$, $df_2 = 813$.

a. Introduce notation, and specify the null hypothesis and alternative hypothesis for the ANOVA.

b. Based on what you know about the F distribution, would you guess that the test statistic value of 0.61 provides strong evidence against the null hypothesis? Explain.

c. Software reports a P-value of 0.82. Explain how to interpret this.

14.7 How many kids to have? A recent General Social Survey asked subjects, "What is the ideal number of kids for a family?" Do responses tend to depend on the subjects' religious affiliation? Results of an ANOVA are shown in the printout, for religion categories (Protestant, Catholic, Jewish, or Other).

a. Define notation and specify the null hypothesis tested in this printout.

b. Summarize the assumptions made to conduct this test.

c. Report the F test statistic value and the P-value for this test. Interpret the P-value.

d. Based on part c, can you conclude that *every* pair of religious affiliations has different population means for ideal family size? Explain.

Ideal number of kids in a family by religious affiliation

Source	DF	SS	MS	F	P
Religion	3	11.72	3.91	5.48	0.001
Error	1295	922.82	0.71		
Total	1298	934.54			

14.8 Smoking and personality A study about smoking and personality (by A. Terracciano and P. Costa, *Addiction*, vol. 99, 2004, pp. 472–481) used a sample of 1638 adults in the Baltimore Longitudinal Study on Aging. The subjects formed three groups according to smoking status (never, former, current). Each subject completed a personality questionnaire that provided scores on various personality scales designed to have overall means of about 50 and standard deviations of about 10. The table shows some results for three traits, giving the means with standard deviations in parentheses.

	Never smokers (n = 828)	Former smokers (n = 694)	Current smokers (n = 116)	F
Neuroticism	46.7 (9.6)	48.5 (9.2)	51.9 (9.9)	17.77
Extraversion	50.4 (10.3)	50.2 (10.0)	50.9 (9.4)	0.24
Conscientiousness	51.8 (10.1)	48.9 (9.7)	45.6 (10.3)	29.42

a. For the F test for the extraversion scale, using the 0.05 significance level, what conclusion would you make?

b. Refer to part a. Does this mean that the population means are necessarily equal?

14.9 **Florida student data** Refer to the Florida Student
Survey data file on the text CD. For the response variable,
use the number of weekly hours engaged in sports and
other physical exercise. For the explanatory variable, use
gender.

 a. Using software, for each gender construct box plots
and find the mean and standard deviation of the
response variable.

 b. Conduct an ANOVA. Report the hypotheses, F test
statistic value, P-value, and interpret results.

 c. To compare the means, suppose you instead used the
two-sided t test from Section 10.3, which assumes equal
population standard deviations. How would the t test
statistic and P-value for that test relate to the F test statistic and P-value for ANOVA?

14.10 **Software and French ANOVA** Refer to Exercise 14.3.
Using software,

 a. Create the data file and find the sample means and
standard deviations.

 b. Find and report the ANOVA table. Interpret the
P-value.

 c. Change an observation in Group 2 so that the P-value
will be smaller. Specify the value you changed, and
report the resulting F test statistic and the P-value.
Explain why the value you changed would have this
effect.

14.11 **Comparing therapies for anorexia** The Anorexia data
file on the text CD shows weight change for 72 anorexic
teenage girls who were randomly assigned to one of three
psychological treatments. Use software to analyze these
data. (The change scores are given in the file for the
control and cognitive therapy groups. You can create the
change scores for the family therapy group.)

 a. Construct box plots for the three groups. Use these
and sample summary means and standard deviations to
describe the three samples.

 b. For the one-way ANOVA comparing the three mean
weight changes, report the test statistic and P-value.
Explain how to interpret.

 c. State and check the assumptions for the test in part b.

14.2 Estimating Differences in Groups for a Single Factor

When an analysis of variance F test has a small P-value, the test does not specify *which* means are different or *how* different they are. In practice, we can estimate differences between population means with confidence intervals.

Confidence Intervals Comparing Pairs of Means

Recall

s^2 is an unbiased estimator of σ^2, regardless of whether H_0 is true in the ANOVA F test. ◄

Let s denote the estimate of the residual standard deviation. This is the square root of the within-groups variance estimate s^2 of σ^2 that is the denominator of the F test statistic in ANOVA. It is also the square root of the mean square error that software reports (the MS in the row for "Error" of any ANOVA table).

SUMMARY: Confidence Interval Comparing Means

For two groups i and j, with sample means $\bar{y}_i$ and $\bar{y}_j$ having sample sizes n_i and n_j, the 95% confidence interval for $\mu_i - \mu_j$ is

$$\bar{y}_i - \bar{y}_j \pm t_{.025}\, s \sqrt{\frac{1}{n_i} + \frac{1}{n_j}}.$$

The t-score from the t table has $df = N - g$ = total sample size $-$ # groups.

The df value of $N - g$ for the t-score is also df_2 for the F test. This is the df for the MS error. For $g = 2$ groups, $N = n_1 + n_2$ and $df = N - g = (n_1 + n_2 - 2)$. This confidence interval is then identical to the one introduced in Section 10.3 for $(\mu_1 - \mu_2)$ based on a pooled standard deviation. In the context of follow-up analyses after the ANOVA F test where we form this confidence interval to compare a pair of means, some software (such as MINITAB) refers to this method of comparing means as the **Fisher method**.

When the confidence interval does not contain 0, we can infer that the population means are different. The interval shows just how different they may be.

Example 5

Number of Good Friends and Happiness

Picture the Scenario

Chapter 11 investigated the association between happiness and several categorical variables, using data from the General Social Survey. The respondents indicated whether they were very happy, pretty happy, or not too happy. Is happiness associated with having lots of friends? A recent GSS asked, "About how many good friends do you have?" Here, we could treat either happiness (variable HAPPY in GSS) or number of good friends (NUMFREND in GSS) as the response variable. If we choose number of good friends, then we are in the ANOVA setting, having a quantitative response variable and a categorical explanatory variable (happiness).

For each happiness category, Table 14.3 shows the sample mean, standard deviation, and sample size for the number of good friends. It also shows the ANOVA table for the F test comparing the population means. The small P-value of 0.03 suggests that at least two of the three population means are different.

Table 14.3 Summary of ANOVA for Comparing Mean Number of Good Friends for Three Happiness Categories

The analysis is based on GSS data.

	Very happy	Pretty happy	Not too happy
Mean	10.4	7.4	8.3
Standard deviation	17.8	13.6	15.6
Sample size	276	468	87

Source	DF	SS	MS	F	P
Group	2	1626.8	813.4	3.47	0.032
Error	828	193900.9	234.2		
Total	830	195527.7			

Question to Explore

Use 95% confidence intervals to compare the population mean number of good friends for the three pairs of happiness categories—very happy with pretty happy, very happy with not too happy, and pretty happy with not too happy.

Think It Through

From Table 14.3, the MS error is 234.2. The residual standard deviation is $s = \sqrt{234.2} = 15.3$, with $df = 828$ (listed in the row for the MS error). For a 95% confidence interval with $df = 828$, software reports $t_{.025} = 1.963$. For comparing the very happy and pretty happy categories, the confidence interval for $\mu_1 - \mu_2$ is

$$(\bar{y}_1 - \bar{y}_2) \pm t_{.025}\, s \sqrt{\frac{1}{n_1} + \frac{1}{n_2}} = (10.4 - 7.4) \pm 1.963(15.3)\sqrt{\frac{1}{276} + \frac{1}{468}}$$

which is 3.0 ± 2.3, or $(0.7, 5.3)$.

We infer that the population mean number of good friends is between about 1 and 5 higher for those who are very happy than for those who are pretty happy. Since the confidence interval contains only positive numbers, this suggests that $\mu_1 - \mu_2 > 0$; that is, μ_1 exceeds μ_2. On the average, people who are very happy have more good friends than people who are pretty happy.

For the other comparisons, you can find

Very happy, not too happy: 95% CI for $\mu_1 - \mu_3$ is
$(10.4 - 8.3) \pm 3.7$, or $(-1.6, 5.8)$.

Pretty happy, not too happy: 95% CI for $\mu_2 - \mu_3$ is
$(7.4 - 8.3) \pm 3.5$, or $(-4.4, 2.6)$.

These two confidence intervals contain 0. So there's not enough evidence to conclude that a difference exists between μ_1 and μ_3 or between μ_2 and μ_3.

Insight

The confidence intervals are quite wide, even though the sample sizes are fairly large. This is because the sample standard deviations (and hence s) are large. Table 14.3 reports that the sample standard deviations are larger than the sample means, suggesting that the three distributions are skewed to the right. The margin figure shows a box plot of the overall sample data distribution of number of good friends, except for many large outliers. It would also be sensible to compare the median responses, but these are not available at the GSS website. Do non-normal population distributions invalidate this inferential analysis? We'll discuss this next.

Try Exercise 14.12

Number of Good Friends

Recall

From Section 10.2, a 95% confidence interval for $\mu_2 - \mu_1$ using separate standard deviations s_1 and s_2 is

$$\bar{y}_1 - \bar{y}_2 \pm t_{.025}\sqrt{\frac{s_1^2}{n_1} + \frac{s_2^2}{n_2}}.$$

Software supplies the *df* value and the confidence interval. ◄

The Effects of Violating Assumptions

The t confidence intervals have the same assumptions as the ANOVA F test: (1) normal population distributions, (2) identical standard deviations, and (3) data that resulted from randomization. These inferences also are not highly dependent on the normality assumption, especially when the sample sizes are large, such as in Example 5. When the standard deviations are quite different, with the ratio of the largest to smallest exceeding about 2, it is preferable to use the confidence interval formula from Section 10.2 (see the margin Recall) that uses *separate* standard deviations for the groups rather than a single pooled value s. That approach does not assume equal standard deviations.

In Example 5, the sample standard deviations are not very different (ranging from 13.6 to 17.8), and the GSS is a multistage random sample with properties similar to a simple random sample. Thus, Assumptions 2 and 3 are reasonably well satisfied. The sample sizes are fairly large, so Assumption 1 of normality is not crucial. It's justifiable to use ANOVA and follow-up confidence intervals with these data.

Controlling Overall Confidence With Many Confidence Intervals

With g groups, there are $g(g-1)/2$ pairs of groups to compare. With $g = 3$, for instance, there are $g(g-1)/2 = 3(2)/2 = 3$ comparisons: Group 1 with Group 2, Group 1 with Group 3, and Group 2 with Group 3.

The confidence interval method just discussed is mainly used when g is small or when only a few comparisons are of main interest. When there are many groups, the number of comparisons can be large. For example, when $g = 10$, there are $g(g - 1)/2 = 45$ pairs of means to compare. If we plan to construct 95% confidence intervals for these comparisons, an error probability of 0.05 applies to *each* comparison. On average, $45(0.05) = 2.25$ of the confidence intervals would *not* contain the true differences of means.

For 95% confidence intervals, the confidence level of 0.95 is the probability that *any particular* confidence interval that we plan to construct will contain the parameter. The probability that *all* the confidence intervals will contain the parameters is considerably smaller than the confidence level for any particular interval. How can we construct the intervals so that the 95% confidence extends to the *entire set* of intervals rather than to *each single* interval? Methods that control the probability that *all* confidence intervals will contain the true differences in means are called **multiple comparison methods**. For these methods, *all* intervals are designed to contain the true parameters *simultaneously* with an overall fixed probability.

Multiple Comparisons for Comparing All Pairs of Means

Multiple comparison methods compare pairs of means with a confidence level that applies simultaneously to the entire set of comparisons rather than to each separate comparison.

The simplest multiple comparison method uses the confidence interval formula from the beginning of this section. However, for each interval it uses a t-score for a more stringent confidence level. This ensures that the overall confidence level is acceptably high. The desired overall error probability is split into equal parts for each comparison. Suppose we want a confidence level of 0.95 that *all* confidence intervals will be simultaneously correct. If we plan five confidence intervals comparing means, then the method uses error probability $0.05/5 = 0.01$ for each one; that is, a 99% confidence level for each separate interval. This approach ensures that the overall confidence level is *at least* 0.95. (It is actually slightly larger.) Called the **Bonferroni** method, it is based on a special case of a probability theorem shown by Italian probabilist, Carlo Bonferroni, in 1936 (Exercise 14.67).

We shall instead use the **Tukey method**. It is designed to give an overall confidence level *very close* to the desired value (such as 0.95), and it has the advantage that its confidence intervals are slightly narrower than the Bonferroni intervals. The Tukey method is more complex, using a sampling distribution pertaining to the difference between the largest and smallest of the g sample means. We do not present its formula, but it is easy to obtain with software.

Recall

John Tukey was responsible for many statistical innovations, including box plots and other methods of exploratory data analysis (EDA). See On the Shoulders of ... John Tukey in Section 2.6 to read more about Tukey and EDA. ◄

Tukey method

Example 6

Number of Good Friends

Picture the Scenario

Example 5 compared the population mean numbers of good friends, for three levels of reported happiness. There, we constructed a *separate* 95% confidence interval for the difference between each pair of means. Table 14.4 displays these three intervals. It also displays the confidence intervals that software reports for the Tukey multiple comparison method.

Table 14.4 Multiple Comparisons of Mean Good Friends for Three Happiness Categories

An asterisk * indicates a significant difference, with the confidence interval not containing 0.

Groups	Difference of means	Separate 95% CIs	Tukey 95% Multiple Comparison CIs
(Very happy, Pretty happy)	$\mu_1 - \mu_2$	$(0.7, 5.3)^*$	$(0.3, 5.7)^*$
(Very happy, Not too happy)	$\mu_1 - \mu_3$	$(-1.6, 5.8)$	$(-2.6, 6.5)$
(Pretty happy, Not too happy)	$\mu_2 - \mu_3$	$(-4.4, 2.6)$	$(-5.1, 3.3)$

Question to Explore

a. Explain how the Tukey multiple comparison confidence intervals differ from the separate confidence intervals in Table 14.4.

b. Summarize results shown for the Tukey multiple comparisons.

Think It Through

a. The Tukey confidence intervals hold with an *overall* confidence level of about 95%. This confidence applies to the entire set of three intervals. The Tukey confidence intervals are wider than the separate 95% confidence intervals because the multiple comparison approach uses a higher confidence level for each separate interval to ensure achieving the overall confidence level of 95% for the entire set of intervals.

b. The Tukey confidence interval for $\mu_1 - \mu_2$ contains only positive values, so we infer that $\mu_1 > \mu_2$. The mean number of good friends is higher, although perhaps barely so, for those who are very happy than for those who are pretty happy. The other two Tukey intervals contain 0, so we cannot infer that those pairs of means differ.

Insight

Figure 14.4 summarizes the three Tukey comparisons from Table 14.4. The intervals have different lengths because the group sample sizes are different.

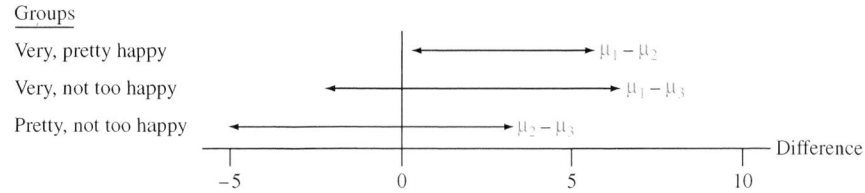

▲ **Figure 14.4** Summary of Tukey Comparisons of Pairs of Means.

Try Exercise 14.15

ANOVA and Regression

ANOVA can be presented as a special case of multiple regression. The factor enters the regression model using *indicator variables*. Each indicator variable takes only two values, 0 and 1, and indicates whether an observation falls in a particular group.

With three groups, we need two indicator variables to indicate the group membership. The first indicator variable is

$$x_1 = 1 \text{ for observations from the first group}$$
$$= 0 \text{ otherwise.}$$

Recall

You can review **indicator variables** in Section 13.5. We used them there to include a categorical explanatory variable in a regression model. ◄

The second indicator variable is

$$x_2 = 1 \text{ for observations from the second group}$$
$$= 0 \text{ otherwise.}$$

The indicator variables identify the group to which an observation belongs as follows:

$$\text{Group 1: } x_1 = 1 \text{ and } x_2 = 0$$
$$\text{Group 2: } x_1 = 0 \text{ and } x_2 = 1$$
$$\text{Group 3: } x_1 = 0 \text{ and } x_2 = 0.$$

We don't need a separate indicator variable for the third group. We know an observation is in that group if $x_1 = 0$ and $x_2 = 0$.

With these indicator variables, the multiple regression equation for the mean of y is

$$\mu_y = \alpha + \beta_1 x_1 + \beta_2 x_2.$$

For observations from the third group, $x_1 = x_2 = 0$, and the equation reduces to

$$\mu_y = \alpha + \beta_1(0) + \beta_2(0) = \alpha.$$

So the parameter α represents the population mean of the response variable y for the last group. For observations from the first group, $x_1 = 1$ and $x_2 = 0$, so

$$\mu_y = \alpha + \beta_1(1) + \beta_2(0) = \alpha + \beta_1$$

equals the population mean μ_1 for that group. Similarly, $\alpha + \beta_2$ equals the population mean μ_2 for the second group (let $x_1 = 0$ and $x_2 = 1$).

Since $\alpha + \beta_1 = \mu_1$ and $\alpha = \mu_3$, the difference between the means

$$\mu_1 - \mu_3 = (\alpha + \beta_1) - \alpha = \beta_1.$$

That is, the coefficient β_1 of the first indicator variable represents the difference between the first mean and the last mean. Likewise, $\beta_2 = \mu_2 - \mu_3$. The beta coefficients of the indicator variables represent differences between the mean of each group and the mean of the last group. Table 14.5 summarizes the parameters of the regression model and their correspondence with the three population means.

Table 14.5 Interpretation of Coefficients of Indicator Variables in Regression Model

The indicator variables represent a categorical predictor with three categories specifying three groups.

Group	Indicator x_1	Indicator x_2	Mean of y	Interpretation of β
1	1	0	$\mu_1 = \alpha + \beta_1$	$\beta_1 = \mu_1 - \mu_3$
2	0	1	$\mu_2 = \alpha + \beta_2$	$\beta_2 = \mu_2 - \mu_3$
3	0	0	$\mu_3 = \alpha$	

Using Regression for the ANOVA Comparison of Means

Recall

Section 13.3 introduced the **F test** that all the beta parameters in a multiple regression model equal 0. ◀

For three groups, the null hypothesis for the ANOVA F test is $H_0: \mu_1 = \mu_2 = \mu_3$. If H_0 is true, then $\mu_1 - \mu_3 = 0$ and $\mu_2 - \mu_3 = 0$. In the multiple regression model

$$\mu_y = \alpha + \beta_1 x_1 + \beta_2 x_2$$

with indicator variables, recall that $\mu_1 - \mu_3 = \beta_1$ and $\mu_2 - \mu_3 = \beta_2$. Therefore, the ANOVA null hypothesis $H_0: \mu_1 = \mu_2 = \mu_3$ is equivalent to $H_0: \beta_1 = \beta_2 = 0$ in the regression model. If the beta parameters in the regression model all equal 0, then the mean of the response variable equals α for each group. We can perform the ANOVA test comparing means using the F test of $H_0: \beta_1 = \beta_2 = 0$ for this regression model.

Example 7

Regression analysis

Telephone Holding Times

Picture the Scenario

Let's return to the data we analyzed in Examples 1–4 on telephone holding times for callers to an airline for which the recorded message is an advertisement, Muzak, or classical music.

Questions to Explore

a. Set up indicator variables to use regression to model the mean holding times with the type of recorded message as explanatory variable.

b. Table 14.6 shows a portion of a MINITAB printout for fitting this model. Use it to find the estimated mean holding time for the advertisement recorded message.

c. Use Table 14.6 to conduct the ANOVA F test (which Example 3 had shown).

Table 14.6 Printout for Regression Model $\mu_y = \alpha + \beta_1 x_1 + \beta_2 x_2$ for Telephone Holding Times and Type of Recorded Message

The indicator variables are x_1 for the advertisement and x_2 for Muzak.

Predictor	Coef	SE Coef	T	P
Constant	10.400	1.523	6.83	0.000
x1	−5.000	2.154	−2.32	0.039
x2	−7.600	2.154	−3.53	0.004

Analysis of Variance					
Source	DF	SS	MS	F	P
Regression	2	149.20	74.60	6.43	0.013
Residual Error	12	139.20	11.60		
Total	14	288.40			

Think It Through

a. The factor (type of recorded message) has three categories—advertisement, Muzak, and classical music. We set up indicator variables x_1 and x_2 with

$$x_1 = 1 \text{ for the advertisement (and 0 otherwise)},$$
$$x_2 = 1 \text{ for Muzak (and 0 otherwise)},$$

so $x_1 = x_2 = 0$ for classical music.

The regression model for the mean of $y =$ telephone holding time is then

$$\mu_y = \alpha + \beta_1 x_1 + \beta_2 x_2.$$

b. From Table 14.6, the prediction equation is

$$\hat{y} = 10.4 - 5.0x_1 - 7.6x_2.$$

For the advertisement, $x_1 = 1$ and $x_2 = 0$, so the estimated mean is $\hat{y} = 10.4 - 5.0(1) - 7.6(0) = 5.4$. This is the sample mean for the five subjects in that group.

c. From Table 14.6, the F test statistic for testing

$$H_0: \beta_1 = \beta_2 = 0$$

is $F = 6.43$, with $df_1 = 2$ and $df_2 = 12$. This null hypothesis is equivalent to

$$H_0: \mu_1 = \mu_2 = \mu_3.$$

Table 14.6 reports a P-value of 0.013. The regression approach provides the same F test statistic and P-value as the ANOVA did in Table 14.2 on page 686.

Insight

Testing that the beta coefficients equal zero is a way of testing that the population means are equal. Likewise, confidence intervals for those coefficients give us confidence intervals for differences between means. For instance, since $\beta_1 = \mu_1 - \mu_3$, a confidence interval for β_1 is also a confidence interval comparing μ_1 and μ_3. From Table 14.6, the estimate -5.0 of β_1 has $se = 2.154$. Since $df = 12$ for that interval, $t_{.025} = 2.179$, and a 95% confidence interval for $\mu_1 - \mu_3$ is

$$-5.0 \pm 2.179(2.154), \text{ or } -5.0 \pm 4.7, \text{ which is } (-9.7, -0.3).$$

This agrees with the 95% confidence interval you would obtain using the difference between the sample means and its standard error.

Try Exercise 14.17

Table 14.2: ANOVA Table for Comparing Means

Source	DF	SS	MS	F	P
Group	2	149.2	74.6	6.4	0.013
Error	12	139.2	11.6		
Total	14	288.4			

Table 14.6: ANOVA Table for Regression Model

Source	DF	SS	MS	F	P
Regression	2	149.2	74.6	6.4	.013
Residual	12	139.2	11.6		
Total	14	288.4			

Notice the similarity between the ANOVA table for comparing means (Table 14.2) and the ANOVA table for regression (Table 14.6), both shown again in the margin. The "between-groups sum of squares" for ordinary ANOVA is the "regression sum of squares" for the regression model. This is the variability explained by the indicator variables for the groups. The "error sum of squares" for ordinary ANOVA is the residual error sum of squares for the regression model. This represents the variability within the groups. This sum of squares divided by its degrees of freedom is the mean square error = 11.6 (MS in the error row), which is also the within-groups estimate of the variance of the observations within the groups. The regression mean square is the between-groups estimate = 74.6. The ratio of the regression mean square to the mean square error is the F test statistic ($F = 6.4$).

So far, this chapter has shown how to compare groups for a single factor. This is **one-way ANOVA**. Sometimes the groups to compare are the cells of a cross-classification of two or more factors. For example, the four groups (employed men, employed women, unemployed men, unemployed women) result from cross classifying employment status and gender. The next section presents **two-way ANOVA**, the procedure for comparing the mean of a quantitative response variable across categories of each of two factors.

14.2 Practicing the Basics

14.12 House prices and age For the House Selling Prices OR data file on the text CD, the output shows the result of conducting an ANOVA comparing mean house selling prices (in $1000) by Age Category (New = 0 to 24 years old, Medium = 25 to 50 years old, Old = 51 to 74 years old, Very Old = 75 + years old). It also shows a summary table of means and standard deviations of the selling prices, by condition. Consider the New and Medium ages, where 150 of the 200 observations fall.

a. Using information given in the tables, show how to construct a 95% confidence interval comparing the corresponding population means.

b. Interpret the confidence interval.

Age	N	Mean	StDev
Medium	71	243.6	79.5
New	78	305.8	125.9
Old	37	215.7	85.3
Very Old	14	311.6	188.5

Source	DF	SS	MS	F	P
Age Condition	3	281272	93757	7.70	0.000
Error	196	2387598	12182		
Total	199	2668870			

14.13 Religious importance and educational level An extensive survey by the Pew Forum on Religion & Public Life, conducted in 2007, details views on religion in the United States. Based on interviews with a representative sample of more than 35,000 Americans age 18 and older, the U.S. Religious Landscape Survey found that religious affiliation in the United States is both diverse and dependent on a lot of factors. The table shows results of ANOVA for comparing feelings about the importance of religion in life and the subject's level of education (scale increasing with education: 3 = HS Graduate, 5 = Some College or Associate Degree, 6 = College Graduate, 7 = Post-Graduate Training). It appears that as educational level increases, the importance of religion in daily life decreases. Construct a 95% confidence interval to compare the population mean educational level for the Very Important and Not at All Important religious attitude groups. Interpret the interval.

Summary of ANOVA for mean education level of subjects and the level of importance of religion in daily life

	Very important	Somewhat important	Not too important	Not at all important
Mean	4.55	4.61	4.87	5.12
N	1959	776	309	341

Source	DF	SS	MS	F	P
Educ	8	69.17	8.65	6.65	0.000
Error	3403	4425.25	1.30		
Total	3411	4494.43			

14.14 Comparing telephone holding times Examples 2 and 3 analyzed whether telephone callers to an airline would stay on hold different lengths of time, on average, if they heard (a) an advertisement about the airline, (b) Muzak, or (c) classical music. The sample means were 5.4, 2.8, and 10.4, with $n_1 = n_2 = n_3 = 5$. The ANOVA test had $F = 74.6/11.6 = 6.4$ and a P-value of 0.013.

a. A 95% confidence interval comparing the population mean times that callers are willing to remain on hold for classical music and Muzak is (2.9, 12.3). Interpret this interval.

b. The margin of error was 4.7 for this comparison. Without doing a calculation, explain why the margin of error is 4.7 for comparing *each* pair of means.

c. The 95% confidence intervals are (0.3, 9.7) for $\mu_3 - \mu_1$ and (−2.1, 7.3) for $\mu_1 - \mu_2$. Interpret these two confidence intervals. Using these two intervals and the interval from part a, summarize what the airline company learned from this study.

d. The confidence intervals are wide. In the design of this experiment, what could you change to estimate the differences in means more precisely?

14.15 Tukey holding time comparisons Refer to the previous exercise. We could instead use the Tukey method to construct multiple comparison confidence intervals. The Tukey confidence intervals having *overall* confidence level 95% have margins of error of 5.7, compared to 4.7 for the separate 95% confidence intervals in the previous exercise.

a. According to this method, which groups are significantly different?

b. Why are the margins of error larger than with the separate 95% intervals?

14.16 REM sleep A psychologist compares the mean amount of time of rapid-eye movement (REM) sleep for subjects under three conditions. She randomly assigns 12 subjects to the three groups, four per group. The sample means for the three groups were 18, 15, and 12. The table shows the ANOVA table from SPSS.

REM sleep

Source	DF	SS	MS	F	P
Group	2	72.00	36.00	0.79	0.481
Error	9	408.00	45.33		
Total	11	480.00			

a. Report and interpret the P-value for the ANOVA F test.

b. For the Tukey 95% multiple comparison confidence intervals comparing each pair of means, the margin of error for each interval is 13.3. Is it true or false that since all the confidence intervals contain 0, it is plausible that all three population means equal 0.

c. Would the margin of error for each separate 95% confidence interval be less than 13.3, equal to 13.3, or larger than 13.3? Explain why.

14.17 REM regression Refer to the previous exercise.

a. Set up indicator variables for a regression model so that an F test for the regression parameters is equivalent to the ANOVA test comparing the three means.

b. Express the null hypothesis both in terms of population means and in terms of regression parameters for the model in part a.

c. The sample means were 18, 15, and 12. Explain why the prediction equation is $\hat{y} = 12 + 6x_1 + 3x_2$. Interpret the three parameter estimates in this equation.

14.18 Outsourcing satisfaction Exercise 14.5 showed an ANOVA for comparing mean customer satisfaction scores for three service centers. The sample means on a scale of 0 to 10 were 7.60 in San Jose, 7.80 in Toronto, and 7.10 in Bangalore. Each sample size $= 100$, MS error $= 0.47$, and the F test statistic $= 27.6$ has P-value < 0.001.

a. Explain why the margin of error for separate 95% confidence intervals is the same for comparing the population means for each pair of cities. Show that this margin of error is 0.19.

b. Find the 95% confidence interval for the difference in population means for each pair of service centers. Interpret.

c. The margin of error for Tukey 95% multiple comparison confidence intervals for comparing the service centers is 0.23. Construct the intervals. Interpret.

d. Why are the confidence intervals different in part b and in part c? What is an advantage of using the Tukey intervals?

14.19 Regression for outsourcing Refer to the previous exercise.

a. Set up indicator variables to represent the three service centers.

b. The prediction equation is $\hat{y} = 7.1 + 0.5x_1 + 0.7x_2$. Show how the terms in this equation relate to the sample means of 7.6 for San Jose, 7.8 for Toronto, and 7.1 for Bangalore.

14.20 Advertising effect on sales Each of 100 restaurants in a fast-food chain is randomly assigned one of four media for an advertising campaign: A = radio, B = TV, C = newspaper, D = mailing. For each restaurant, the observation is the change in sales, defined as the difference between the sales for the month during which the advertising campaign took place and the sales in the same month a year ago (in thousands of dollars).

a. By creating indicator variables, write a regression equation for the analysis to compare mean change in sales for the four media.

b. Explain how you could use the regression model to test the null hypothesis of equal population mean change in sales for the four media.

c. The prediction equation is $\hat{y} = 35 + 5x_1 - 10x_2 + 2x_3$. Estimate the difference in mean change in sales for media (i) A and D, (ii) A and B.

14.21 French ANOVA Refer to Exercise 14.3 about studying French, with data shown again below. Using software,

a. Compare the three pairs of means with separate 95% confidence intervals. Interpret.

b. Compare the three pairs of means with Tukey 95% multiple comparison confidence intervals. Interpret, and explain why the intervals are different than in part a.

Group 1	Group 2	Group 3
4	1	9
6	5	10
8		5

14.3 Two-Way ANOVA

Recall

A **factor** is a categorical explanatory variable. **One-way ANOVA** has a single factor. ◄

One-way ANOVA is a *bivariate* (two-variable) method. It analyzes the relationship between the mean of a quantitative response variable and the groups that are categories of a factor. ANOVA extends to handle two or more factors. With multiple factors, the analysis is *multivariate*. We'll illustrate for the case of two factors. This extension is a **two-way ANOVA**. It enables us to study the effect of one factor at a fixed level of a second factor.

The great British statistician R. A. Fisher (see *On the Shoulders of R. A. Fisher* at the end of Section 8.5) developed ANOVA methods in the 1920s. Agricultural experiments were the source of many of the early ANOVA applications. For instance, ANOVA has often been used to compare the mean yield of a crop for different fertilizers.

Two factors

Did You Know?

A **metric ton** is 1000 kilograms, which is about 2200 pounds. A **hectare** is 10,000 square meters (e.g., 100 meters by 100 meters), which is about 2.5 acres. ◀

Example 8

Amounts of Fertilizer and Manure

Picture the Scenario

This example presents a typical ANOVA application, based on a study at Iowa State University.[2] A large field was portioned into 20 equal-size plots. Each plot was planted with the same amount of corn seed, using a fixed spacing pattern between the seeds. The goal was to study how the yield of corn later harvested from the plots (in metric tons) depended on the levels of use of nitrogen-based fertilizer and manure. Each factor was measured in a binary manner. The fertilizer level was low = 45-kg per hectare or high = 135 kg per hectare. The manure level was low = 84 kg per hectare or high = 168 kg per hectare.

Questions to Explore

a. What are four treatments you can compare with this experiment?

b. What comparisons are relevant when you control for (keep fixed) manure level?

Think It Through

a. Four treatments result from cross-classifying the two binary factors: fertilizer level and manure level. Table 14.7 shows the four treatments, defined for the $2 \times 2 = 4$ combinations of categories of the two factors (fertilizer level and manure level).

Table 14.7 Four Groups for Comparing Mean Corn Yield

These result from the two-way cross classification of fertilizer level with manure level.

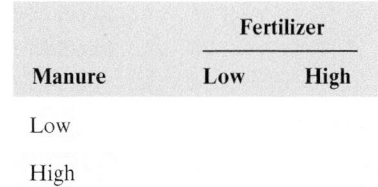

	Fertilizer	
Manure	**Low**	**High**
Low		
High		

b. We can compare the mean corn yield for the two levels of fertilizer, controlling for manure level (that is, at a fixed level of manure use). For fields in which manure level was *low*, we can compare the mean yields for the two levels of fertilizer use. These refer to the first row of Table 14.7. Likewise, for fields in which manure level was *high*, we can compare the mean yields for the two levels of fertilizer use. These refer to the second row of Table 14.7.

Insight

Among the questions we'll learn how to answer in this section are: Does the mean corn yield depend significantly on the fertilizer level? Does it depend on the manure level? Does the effect of fertilizer depend on the manure level?

Try Exercise 14.22

---

[2]Thanks to Dan Nettleton, Iowa State University, for data on which this example is based.

Inference About Effects in Two-Way ANOVA

In two-way ANOVA, a null hypothesis states that the population means are the same in each category of one factor, at each fixed level of the other factor. For example, we could test

H_0: Mean corn yield is equal for plots at the low and high levels of fertilizer, for each fixed level of manure.

Table 14.8a displays a set of population means satisfying this null hypothesis of "no effect of fertilizer level."

Table 14.8 Population Mean Corn Yield Satisfying Null Hypotheses: (a) No Effect of Fertilizer Level, (b) No Effect of Manure Level

		Fertilizer				Fertilizer	
	Manure	Low	High		**Manure**	Low	High
(a)	Low	10	10	**(b)**	Low	10	20
	High	20	20		High	10	20

We could also test

H_0: Mean corn yield is equal for plots at the low and high levels of manure, for each fixed level of fertilizer.

Table 14.8b displays a set of population means satisfying this null hypothesis of "no effect of manure level." The effects of individual factors tested with these two null hypotheses are called **main effects**. We'll discuss a third null hypothesis later in the section.

As in one-way ANOVA, the F tests of hypotheses in two-way ANOVA assume that

- The population distribution for each group is normal.
- The population standard deviations are identical.
- The data result from random sampling or a randomized experiment.

Here, each group refers to a cell in the two-way classification of the two factors. ANOVA procedures still usually work quite well if the population distributions are not normal with identical standard deviations. As in other ANOVA inferences, the quality of the sample is the most important assumption.

The test statistics have complex formulas. We'll rely on software. As in one-way ANOVA, the test for a factor uses two estimates of the variance for each group. These estimates appear in the mean square (MS) column of the ANOVA table.

SUMMARY: *F* Test Statistics in Two-Way ANOVA

For testing the main effect for a factor, the test statistic is the ratio of mean squares,

$$F = \frac{\text{MS for the factor}}{\text{MS error}}.$$

The MS for the factor is a variance estimate based on between-groups variation for that factor. The MS error is a within-groups variance estimate that is always unbiased.

When the null hypothesis of equal population means for the factor is true, the F test statistic values tend to fluctuate around 1. When it is false, they tend to be larger. The P-value is the right-tail probability above the observed F value. That is, it is the probability (presuming H_0 is true) of even more extreme results than we observed in the sample.

Testing the
main effects

Example 9

Corn Yield

Picture the Scenario

Let's analyze the relationship between corn yield and the two factors, fertilizer level and manure level. Table 14.9 shows the data and the sample mean and standard deviation for each group.

Table 14.9 Corn Yield by Fertilizer Level and Manure Level

Fertilizer Level	Manure Level	Plot 1	2	3	4	5	Sample Size	Mean	Std. Dev.
High	High	13.7	15.8	13.9	16.6	15.5	5	15.1	1.3
High	Low	16.4	12.5	14.1	14.4	12.2	5	13.9	1.7
Low	High	15.0	15.1	12.0	15.7	12.2	5	14.0	1.8
Low	Low	12.4	10.6	13.7	8.7	10.9	5	11.3	1.9

Questions to Explore

a. Summarize the factor effects as shown by the sample means.

b. Table 14.10 is an ANOVA table for two-way ANOVA. Specify the two hypotheses tested, give the test statistics and P-values, and interpret.

Table 14.10 Two-Way ANOVA for Corn Yield Data in Table 14.9

MS values for numerator of F statistics

Source	DF	SS	MS	F	P
Fertilizer	1	17.67	17.67	6.33	0.022
Manure	1	19.21	19.21	6.88	0.018
Error	17	47.44	2.79		
Total	19	84.32			

MS error is denominator of each F statistic

Think It Through

a. Table 14.9 (with means summarized in the margin) shows that for each manure level, the sample mean yield is higher for the plots using more fertilizer. For each fertilizer level, the sample mean yield is higher for the plots using more manure.

b. First, consider the hypothesis

H_0: Mean corn yield is equal for plots at the low and high levels of fertilizer, for each fixed level of manure.

For the fertilizer main effect, Table 14.10 reports that the between-groups estimate of the variance is 17.67. This is the mean square (MS)

Means from Table 14.9

Manure	Fertilizer Low	High
Low	11.3	13.9
High	14.0	15.1

for fertilizer in Table 14.10. The within-groups estimate is the MS error, or 2.79. The F test statistic is the ratio,

$$F = 17.67 / 2.79 = 6.33.$$

From Table 14.10, the df values are 1 and 17 for the two estimates. From the F distribution with $df_1 = 1$ and $df_2 = 17$, the P-value is 0.022, also reported in Table 14.10. If the population means were equal at the two levels of fertilizer, the probability of an F test statistic value larger than 6.33 would be only 0.022. There is strong evidence that the mean corn yield depends on fertilizer level.

Next, consider the hypothesis

H_0: Mean corn yield is equal for plots at the low and high levels of manure, for each fixed level of fertilizer.

For the manure main effect, the F test statistic is $F = 19.21 / 2.79 = 6.88$. From Table 14.10, $df_1 = 1$ and $df_2 = 17$, and the P-value is 0.018. There is strong evidence that the mean corn yield also depends on the manure level.

Insight

As with any significance test, the information gain is limited. We do not learn *how large* the fertilizer and manure effects are on the corn yield. We can use confidence intervals to investigate the sizes of the main effects. We'll now learn how to do this by using regression modeling with indicator variables.

Try Exercise 14.27

Regression Model with Indicator Variables for Two-Way ANOVA

Let f denote an indicator variable for fertilizer level and let m denote an indicator variable for manure level. Specifically,

$$f = 1 \text{ for plots with high fertilizer level}$$
$$= 0 \text{ for plots with low fertilizer level}$$
$$m = 1 \text{ for plots with high manure level}$$
$$= 0 \text{ for plots with low manure level.}$$

The multiple regression model for the mean corn yield with these two indicator variables is

$$\mu_y = \alpha + \beta_1 f + \beta_2 m.$$

To find the population means for the four groups, we substitute the possible combinations of values for the indicator variables. For example, for plots that have high fertilizer level ($f = 1$) and low manure level ($m = 0$), the mean corn yield is

$$\mu_y = \alpha + \beta_1(1) + \beta_2(0) = \alpha + \beta_1.$$

Table 14.11 shows the four means. The difference between the means at the high and low levels of fertilizer equals β_1 for each manure level. That is, the coefficient β_1 of the indicator variable f for fertilizer level equals the difference between the means at its high and low levels, controlling for manure level. The null hypothesis of no fertilizer effect is H_0: $\beta_1 = 0$. Likewise, β_2 is the difference between the means at the high and low levels of manure, for each fertilizer level.

Table 14.11 Population Mean Corn Yield for Fertilizer and Manure Levels

		Indicator Variables		
Fertilizer	**Manure**	f	m	**Mean of y**
High	High	1	1	$\alpha + \beta_1 + \beta_2$
High	Low	1	0	$\alpha + \beta_1$
Low	High	0	1	$\alpha + \beta_2$
Low	Low	0	0	α

We do not need to use regression modeling to conduct the ANOVA F tests. They're easy to do using software. But the modeling approach helps us to focus on estimating the means and the differences among them. We can compare means using an ordinary confidence interval for the regression parameter that equals the difference between those means. The 95% confidence interval has the usual form of

$$\text{parameter estimate } \pm\ t_{0.025}(se).$$

The df for the t-score is the df value for the MS error.

Regression modeling

Example 10

Estimate and Compare Mean Corn Yields

Picture the Scenario

Table 14.12 shows the result of fitting the regression model for predicting corn yield with indicator variables for fertilizer level and manure level.

Table 14.12 Estimates of Regression Parameters for Two-Way ANOVA of the Mean Corn Yield by Fertilizer Level and Manure Level

```
Predictor       Coef      SE Coef      T        P

Constant       11.6500     0.6470     18.01    0.000

fertilizer      1.8800     0.7471      2.52    0.022

manure          1.9600     0.7471      2.62    0.018
```

Questions to Explore

a. Find and use the prediction equation to estimate the mean corn yield for each group.

b. Use a parameter estimate from the prediction equation to compare mean corn yields for the high and low levels of fertilizer, at each manure level.

c. Find a 95% confidence interval comparing the mean corn yield at the high and low levels of fertilizer, controlling for manure level. Interpret it.

Think It Through

a. From Table 14.12, the prediction equation is (rounding to one decimal place)

$$\hat{y} = 11.6 + 1.9f + 2.0m.$$

The y-intercept equals 11.6. This is the estimated mean yield (in metric tons per hectare) when both indicator variables equal 0, that is, with fertilizer and manure at the low levels. The estimated means for the other cases result from substituting values for the indicator variables. For instance, at fertilizer level = high and manure level = low, $f = 1$ and $m = 0$, so the estimated mean yield is $\hat{y} = 11.6 + 1.9(1) + 2.0(0) = 13.5$. Doing this for all four groups, we get

| | Fertilizer | |
Manure	Low	High
Low	11.6	$11.6 + 1.9 = 13.5$
High	$11.6 + 2.0 = 13.6$	$11.6 + 1.9 + 2.0 = 15.5$

b. The coefficient of the fertilizer indicator variable f is 1.9. This is the estimated difference in mean corn yield between the high and low levels of fertilizer, for each level of manure (for instance, $13.5 - 11.6 = 1.9$ when manure level = low).

c. Again, The estimate of the fertilizer effect is 1.9. Its standard error, reported in Table 14.12, is 0.747. From Table 14.10 (see page 703), the df for the MS error is 17. From Table B, $t_{.025} = 2.11$ when $df = 17$. The 95% confidence interval is

$$1.9 \pm 2.11(0.747), \text{ which is } (0.3, 3.5).$$

At each manure level, we estimate that the mean corn yield is between 0.3 and 3.5 metric tons per hectare higher at the high fertilizer level than at the low fertilizer level. The confidence interval contains only positive values (does not contain 0), reflecting the conclusion that the mean yield is significantly higher at the higher level of fertilizer. This agrees with the P-value falling below 0.05 in the test for the fertilizer effect.

Insight

The *estimated* means are not the same as the *sample* means in Table 14.9. (Both sets are shown again in the margin.) The model *smooths* the sample means so that the difference between the estimated means for two categories of a factor is *exactly* the same at each category of the other factor. For example, from the estimated group means found previously, the fertilizer effect of $1.9 = 13.5 - 11.6 = 15.5 - 13.6$.

Try Exercise 14.28

Estimated Means

| | Fertilizer | |
Manure	Low	High
Low	11.6	13.5
High	13.6	15.5

Table 14.9: Sample Means

| | Fertilizer | |
Manure	Low	High
Low	11.3	13.9
High	14.0	15.1

The regression model assumes that the difference between means for the two categories for one factor is the same in each category of the other factor. The next section shows how to check this assumption. When it is reasonable, we can use a single comparison, rather than a separate one at each category of the other variable. In Example 10, we estimated the difference in mean corn yield between the pair of fertilizer levels, a single comparison (with estimate 1.9) holding at each level of manure.

Recall

Section 13.5 introduced the concept of **interaction** between two explanatory variables in their effects on a response variable. In a regression context, **no interaction** implied parallel lines (common slopes). ◄

Exploring Interaction Between Factors in Two-Way ANOVA

Investigating whether **interaction** occurs is important whenever we analyze multivariate relationships. *No interaction* between two factors means that the effect of either factor on the response variable is the same at each category of the other factor. The regression model in Example 10 and the ANOVA tests of main

	Fertilizer	
Manure	**Low**	**High**
Low	11.6	13.5
High	13.6	15.5

effects assume there is no interaction between the factors. What does this mean in this context?

From Example 10, the estimated mean corn yields for the regression model having an indicator variable for fertilizer level and an indicator variable for manure level are shown in the table in the margin.

What pattern do these show? Let's plot the means for the two fertilizer levels, within each level of manure. Figure 14.5 shows a plot in which the *y*-axis gives estimated mean corn yields, and points are shown for the four fertilizer–manure combinations. The horizontal axis is not a numerical scale but merely lists the two fertilizer levels. The drawn lines connect the means for the two fertilizer levels, for a given manure level. The absence of interaction is indicated by the *parallel lines.*

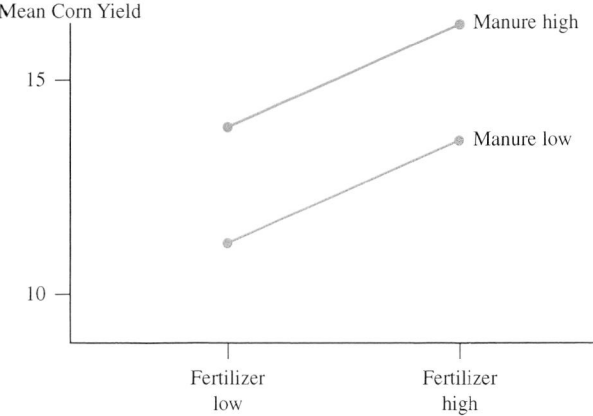

▲ **Figure 14.5** Mean Corn Yield, by Fertilizer and Manure Levels, Showing No Interaction. The parallel lines reflect an absence of interaction. This implies that the difference in estimated means between the two fertilizer levels is the same for each manure level. Question Is it also true that the difference in estimated means between the two manure levels is the same for each fertilizer level?

The parallelism of lines occurs because the difference in the estimated mean corn yield between the high and low levels of fertilizer is the same for each manure level. The difference equals 1.9. Also, the difference between the high and low levels of manure in the estimated mean corn yield is 2.0 for each fertilizer level.

By contrast, Table 14.13 and Figure 14.6 show a set of means for which there is interaction. The difference between the high and low levels of fertilizer in the mean corn yield is $14 - 10 = 4$ for low manure and $12 - 16 = -4$ for high manure. Here, the difference in means depends on the manure level: According to these means, it's better to use a high level of fertilizer when the manure level is low but it's better to use a low level of fertilizer when the manure level is high. Similarly, the manure effect differs at the two fertilizer levels; for the low level, it is $16 - 10 = 6$ whereas at the high level, it is $12 - 14 = -2$. The lines in Figure 14.6 are not parallel.

Table 14.13 Means that Show Interaction Between the Factors in Their Effects on the Response

The effect of fertilizer differs according to whether manure level is low or high. See Figure 14.6.

	Fertilizer	
Manure	**Low**	**High**
Low	10	14
High	16	12

In Table 14.13, suppose the numbers of observations are the same for each group. Then the overall mean corn yield, ignoring manure level, is 13 for each fertilizer level (the average of 10 and 16, and the average of 14 and 12). The overall

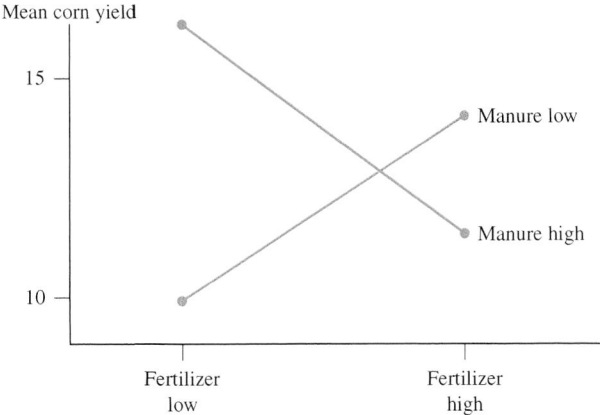

▲ **Figure 14.6** Mean Corn Yield, by Fertilizer and Manure Levels, Displaying Interaction. Question What aspect of the plot reflects the interaction?

difference in means between the two fertilizer levels then equals 0. A one-way analysis of mean corn yield by fertilizer level would conclude that fertilizer level has no effect. However, a two-way analysis that allows for interaction would detect that fertilizer has an effect, but that effect differs according to the manure level.

Testing for Interaction

In conducting a two-way ANOVA, before testing the main effects, it is customary to test a third null hypothesis stating that there is no interaction between the factors in their effects on the response. The test statistic providing the sample evidence of interaction is

$$F = \frac{\text{MS for interaction}}{\text{MS error}}.$$

When H_0 is false, the F statistic tends to be large. Therefore, as usual, the P-value is the right-tail probability.

Testing for interaction

Example 11

Corn Yield Data

Picture the Scenario

Let's return to our analysis of the corn yield data, summarized in the margin table. In Example 10 we analyzed these data assuming no interaction. Let's see if that analysis is valid. Table 14.14 is an ANOVA table for a model that allows interaction in assessing the effects of fertilizer level and manure level on the mean corn yield.

Table 14.14 Two-Way ANOVA of Mean Corn Yield by Fertilizer Level and Manure Level, Allowing Interaction

Source	DF	SS	MS	F	P
Fertilizer	1	17.67	17.67	6.37	0.023
Manure	1	19.21	19.21	6.92	0.018
Interaction	1	3.04	3.04	1.10	0.311
Error	16	44.40	2.78		
Total	19	84.32			

F statistic for test of no interaction

Corn Yields

Fertilizer Level	Manure Level	Mean	Std. Dev.
High	High	15.1	1.3
High	Low	13.9	1.7
Low	High	14.0	1.8
Low	Low	11.3	1.9

Question to Explore

Give the result of the test of H_0: no interaction, and interpret.

Think It Through

The test statistic for H_0: no interaction is

$$F = (\text{MS for interaction})/(\text{MS error}) = 3.04 / 2.78 = 1.10.$$

Based on the F distribution with $df_1 = 1$ and $df_2 = 16$ for these two mean squares, the ANOVA table reports P-value = 0.31. This is not much evidence of interaction. We would not reject H_0 at the usual significance levels, such as 0.05.

Insight

Because there is not much evidence of interaction, we are justified in conducting the simpler two-way ANOVA about main effects. The tests presented previously in Table 14.10 for effects of fertilizer and manure on mean corn yield are valid.

Try Exercise 14.29

It is not meaningful to test the main effects hypotheses when there is interaction. A small P-value in the test of H_0: no interaction suggests that each factor has an effect, but the size of effect for one factor varies according to the category of the other factor. Then, you should investigate the nature of the interaction by plotting the sample cell means, using a plot like Figure 14.6. You should compare categories of one factor separately at different levels of the other factor.

Recall

From the box at the beginning of Section 14.2, the 95% confidence interval comparing two means is

$(\bar{y}_i - \bar{y}_j) \pm t_{.025}\, se$, where $se = s\sqrt{\dfrac{1}{n_i} + \dfrac{1}{n_j}}$,

s is the square root of the MS error, and df for the t distribution is df for MS error. ◄

In Practice Check Interaction Before Main Effects

In practice, in two-way ANOVA you should *first test the hypothesis of no interaction*. If the evidence of interaction is not strong (that is, if the P-value is not small), then test the main effects hypotheses and/or construct confidence intervals for those effects. But if important evidence of interaction exists, plot and compare the cell means for a factor separately at each category of the other factor.

For comparing means in two cells using a confidence interval, use the formula from the box at the beginning of Section 14.2, shown again in the margin. Substitute the cell sample sizes for n_i and n_j and use the MS error for the two-way ANOVA that allows interaction.

Interactions and confidence interval

Example 12

Political Ideology by Gender and Race

Picture the Scenario

In most years, the General Social Survey asks subjects to report their political ideology, measured with seven categories in which 1 = extremely liberal, 4 = moderate, 7 = extremely conservative. Table 14.15 shows results from the 2008 General Social Survey on mean political ideology classified by gender and by race.

Table 14.15 Mean Political Ideology by Gender and by Race

Gender	Race Black	White
Female	4.164 ($n = 165$)	4.268 ($n = 840$)
Male	3.819 ($n = 116$)	4.444 ($n = 719$)

For the test of H_0: no interaction, software reports an F test statistic of 6.19 with $df_1 = 1$ and $df_2 = 1836$, for a P-value of 0.013. So, in comparing females and males on their mean political ideology, we should do it separately by race. The MS error for the model allowing interaction equals 2.534, so the residual standard deviation is $s = \sqrt{2.534} = 1.592$.

```
Analysis of Variance for POLVIEWS, using Adjusted SS for Tests

Source        DF      Seq SS    Adj SS    Adj MS    F       P

SEX           1        5.138     1.652     1.652    0.65    0.420

RACE          1       24.786    30.780    30.780   12.15   0.001

SEX*RACE      1       15.693    15.693    15.693    6.19    0.013

Error      1836     4651.981  4651.981    2.534

Total      1839     4697.598
```

Questions to Explore

a. Interpret the significant interaction by comparing sample mean political ideology of females and males for each race descriptively and using 95% confidence intervals.

b. Interpret the confidence intervals derived in part a.

Think It Through

a. The sample means show that for black subjects, females are more conservative (have the higher mean). By contrast, for white subjects, males are more conservative. For a confidence interval comparing mean political ideology for females and males who are black, the standard error (using the sample sizes reported in the table) is

$$se = s\sqrt{\frac{1}{n \text{ for black females}} + \frac{1}{n \text{ for black males}}} =$$

$$1.592\sqrt{\frac{1}{165} + \frac{1}{116}} = 0.193.$$

The 95% confidence interval is

$$(4.164 - 3.819) \pm 1.96(0.193), \text{ which is } 0.345 \pm 0.378, \text{ or}$$
$$(-0.03, 0.72).$$

Likewise, you can find that the 95% confidence interval comparing mean political ideology for females and males who are white is -0.1768 ± 0.159, or $(-0.33, -0.02)$.

b. Since the confidence interval for black subjects contains zero we cannot infer that there is a difference in the populations. For white subjects, however, all values in the interval are negative. We infer that white females are *less* conservative than white males in the population.

Insight

The confidence interval for white subjects has an endpoint that is close to 0. So, the true gender effect in the population could be small.

> *Try Exercise 14.33*

Why Not Instead Perform Two Separate One-Way ANOVAs?

When you have two factors, rather than performing a two-way ANOVA, why not instead perform two separate one-way ANOVAs? For instance, in Example 12 you could compare the mean political ideology for females and males using a one-way ANOVA, ignoring the information about race. Likewise, you could perform a separate one-way ANOVA to compare the means for blacks and whites, ignoring the information about gender.

The main reason is that you learn more from two-way ANOVA. The two-way ANOVA indicates whether there is interaction. When there is, as in Example 12, it is more informative to compare levels of one factor *separately* at each level of the other factor. This enables us to investigate how the effect depends on that other factor. For instance, a one-way ANOVA of mean political ideology by gender might show *no* gender effect, whereas the two-way ANOVA has shown that there *is* a gender effect but it varies by race.

Similarly, in experimental studies, rather than carrying out one experiment to investigate the effect of one factor and a separate experiment to investigate the effect of a second factor, it is better to carry out a *single* experiment and study both factors at the same time. Besides the advantage of being able to check for interaction, this is more cost effective. If we have funds to experiment with 100 subjects, we can use a sample size of 100 for studying each factor with a two-way ANOVA, rather than use 50 subjects in one experiment about one factor and 50 subjects in a separate experiment about the other factor.

Yet another benefit of a two-way ANOVA is that the residual variability, which affects the MS error and the denominators of the F test statistics, tends to decrease. When we use two factors to predict a response variable, we usually tend to get better predictions (that is, less residual variability) than when we use one factor. With less residual (within-groups) variability, we get larger test statistics, and hence greater power for rejecting false null hypotheses.

Factorial ANOVA

The methods of two-way ANOVA extend to the analysis of several factors. A multifactor ANOVA with observations from all combinations of the factors is called **factorial ANOVA**. For example, with three factors, **three-way ANOVA** considers main effects for those factors as well as possible interactions.

In Practice Use Regression With Categorical and Quantitative Predictors

With several explanatory variables, usually some are categorical and some are quantitative. Then, it is sensible to build a multiple regression model containing both types of predictors. That's what we did in Example 10 in the previous chapter when we modeled house selling prices in terms of house size and condition of the house.

14.3   Practicing the Basics

14.22 Reducing cholesterol   An experiment randomly assigns 100 subjects suffering from high cholesterol to one of four groups: low-dose Lipitor, high-dose Lipitor, low-dose Zocor, high-dose Zocor. After three months of treatment, the change in cholesterol level is measured.
  a. Identify the response variable and the two factors.
  b. What are four treatments that can be compared with this experiment?
  c. What comparisons are relevant when we control for dose level?

14.23 Drug main effects   For the previous exercise, show a hypothetical set of population means for the four groups that would have
  a. A dose effect but no drug effect.
  b. A drug effect but no dose effect.
  c. A drug effect and a dose effect.
  d. No drug effect and no dose effect.

14.24 Reasons for divorce   The 26 students in a statistics class at the University of Florida were surveyed about their attitudes toward divorce. Each received a response score according to how many from a list of 10 possible reasons were regarded as legitimate for a woman to seek a divorce. The higher the score, the more willing the subject is to accept divorce as an option in a variety of circumstances. The students were also asked whether they were fundamentalist or nonfundamentalist in their religious beliefs and whether their church attendance frequency was frequent (more than once a month) or infrequent. The table displays the data and the results of a two-way ANOVA.
  a. State the null hypothesis to which the F test statistic in the religion row refers.
  b. Show how to use mean squares to construct the F test statistic for the religion main effect, report its P-value, and interpret.

		Religion	
		Fundamentalist	**Non fundamentalist**
Church	**Frequent**	0, 3, 4, 0, 3, 2, 0, 1, 1, 3	2, 5, 1, 2, 3, 3
Attendance	**Infrequent**	4, 3, 4	6, 8, 6, 4, 6, 3, 7, 4

Source	DF	SS	MS	F	P
Religion	1	11.07	11.07	5.20	0.032
Church_attend	1	36.84	36.84	17.32	0.000
Error	23	48.93	2.13		
Total	25	117.12			

14.25 House prices, age, and bedrooms   For the House Selling Prices OR data file on the text CD, the output shows the result of conducting a two-way ANOVA of house selling prices (in thousands) by the number of bedrooms in the house and the age (New, Medium, Old, Very Old—see exercise 14.12) of the houses in Corvallis, Oregon.
  a. For testing the main effect of age, report the F test statistic value, and show how it was formed from other values reported in the ANOVA table.
  b. Report the P-value for the main effect test for age, and interpret.

Source	DF	SS	MS	F	P
Bedrooms	7	517868	68523	6.79	0.000
Age Condition	3	243063	81021	8.03	0.000
Error	189	1907939	10095		
Total	199	2668870			

14.26 Corn and manure   In Example 10, the coefficient of the manure-level indicator variable m is 1.96.
  a. Explain why this coefficient is the estimated difference in mean corn yield between the high and low levels of manure, for each level of fertilizer.
  b. Explain why the 95% confidence interval for the difference in mean corn yield between the high and low levels of manure is $1.96 \pm 2.11(0.747)$.

14.27 Hang up if message repeated?   Example 2 described an experiment in which telephone callers to an airline were put on hold with an advertisement, Muzak, or classical music in the background. Each caller who was chosen was also randomly assigned to a category of a second factor: Whether the message played was five minutes long or ten minutes long. (In each case, it was repeated at the end.) The table shows the data classified by both factors and the results of a two-way ANOVA.

Telephone holding times by type of recorded message and repeat time

	Repeat Time	
Message	**Ten Minutes**	**Five Minutes**
Advertisement	**8, 11, 2**	**5, 1**
Muzak	**1, 4, 3**	**0, 6**
Classical	**13, 8, 15**	**7, 9**

Source	DF	SS	MS	F	P
Message	2	149.20	74.60	7.09	0.011
Repeat	1	23.51	23.51	2.24	0.163
Error	11	115.69	10.52		
Total	14	288.40			

  a. State the null hypothesis to which the F test statistic in the Message row refers.
  b. Show how to use mean squares to construct the F test statistic for the Message main effect, report its P-value, and interpret.
  c. On what assumptions is this analysis based?

14.28 Regression for telephone holding times   Refer to the previous exercise. Let $x_1 = 1$ for the advertisement and 0 otherwise, $x_2 = 1$ for Muzak and 0 otherwise, and $x_1 = x_2 = 0$ for classical music. Likewise, let $x_3 = 1$ for repeating in 10-minute cycles and $x_3 = 0$ for repeating in 5-minute cycles. The display shows results of a regression of the telephone holding times on these indicator variables.

Regression for telephone holding times

Predictor	Coef	SE Coef	T	P
Constant	8.867	1.776	4.99	0.000
x1	−5.000	2.051	−2.44	0.033
x2	−7.600	2.051	−3.71	0.003
x3	2.556	1.709	1.50	0.163

a. State the prediction equation. Interpret the parameter estimates.

b. Find the estimated means for the six groups in the two-way cross-classification of message type and repeat time.

c. Find the estimated difference between the mean holding times for 10-minute repeats and 5-minute repeats, for a fixed message type. How can you get this estimate from a coefficient of an indicator variable in the prediction equation?

14.29 Interaction between message and repeat time? Refer to the previous two exercises. When we allow interaction, two of the rows in the new ANOVA table are

```
Source          DF    SS      MS      F      P
Group*Repeat    2     15.02   7.51    0.67   0.535
Error           9     100.67  11.19
```

where Group*Repeat denotes the interaction effect.

a. Show the hypotheses, test statistic, and P-value for the test of H_0: no interaction.

b. What is the implication of the result of this test? For instance, the analyses in previous exercises assumed a lack of interaction. Was it valid to do so?

14.30 Income by gender and job type In 2000, the population mean hourly wage for males was $22 for white-collar jobs, $11 for service jobs, and $14 for blue-collar jobs. For females the means were $15 for white-collar jobs, $8 for service jobs, and $10 for blue-collar jobs.[3]

a. Identify the response variable and the two factors.

b. Show these means in a two-way classification of the two factors.

c. Compare the differences between males and females for (i) white-collar jobs and (ii) blue-collar jobs. Explain why there is interaction, and describe it.

d. Show a set of six population mean incomes that would satisfy H_0: no interaction.

14.31 Ideology by gender and race Refer to Example 12, the sample means from which are shown again below.

Mean political Ideology

Gender	Race	
	Black	White
Female	4.164	4.2675
Male	3.819	4.4443

a. Explain how to obtain the following interpretation for the interaction from the sample means: "For females there is no race effect on ideology. For males, whites are more conservative by about half an ideology category, on the average."

b. Suppose that instead of the two-way ANOVA, you performed a one-way ANOVA with gender as the predictor and a separate one-way ANOVA with race as the predictor. Suppose the ANOVA for gender does not show a significant effect. Explain how this could happen, even though the two-way ANOVA showed a gender effect for each race. (*Hint:* Will the overall sample means for females and males be more similar than they are for each race?)

c. Refer to part b. Summarize what you would learn about the gender effect from a two-way ANOVA that you would fail to learn from a one-way ANOVA.

14.32 Attractiveness and getting dates The results in the table are from a study of physical attractiveness and subjective well-being (E. Diener et al., *Journal of Personality and Social Psychology*, vol. 69, 1995, pp. 120–129). A panel rated a sample of college students on their physical attractiveness. The table presents the number of dates in the past three months for students rated in the top or bottom quartile of attractiveness.

a. Identify the response variable and the factors.

b. Do these data appear to show interaction? Explain.

c. Based on the results in the table, specify one of the ANOVA assumptions that these data violate. Is this the most important assumption?

Dates and attractiveness

	Number of DATES, MEN			Number of DATES, WOMEN		
ATTRACTIVENESS	Mean	Std. Dev	n	Mean	Std. Dev	n
More	9.7	10.0	35	17.8	14.2	33
Less	9.9	12.6	36	10.4	16.6	27

14.33 Diet and weight gain A randomized experiment[4] measured weight gain (in grams) of male rats under six diets varying by source of protein (beef, cereal, pork) and level of protein (high, low). Ten rats were assigned to each diet. The data are shown in the table that follows and are also available in the Protein and Weight Gain data file on the book's CD.

a. Conduct a two-way ANOVA that assumes a lack of interaction. Report the F test statistic and the P-value for testing the effect of the protein level. Interpret.

b. Now conduct a two-way ANOVA that also considers potential interaction. Report the hypotheses, test statistic and P-value for a test of no interaction. What do you conclude at the 0.05 significance level? Explain.

c. Refer to part b. Allowing interaction, construct a 95% confidence interval to compare the mean weight gain for the two protein levels, for the beef source of protein.

Weight gain by source of protein and by level of protein

	High Protein	Low Protein
Beef	73, 102, 118, 104, 81, 107, 100, 87, 117, 111	90, 76, 90, 64, 86, 51, 72, 90, 95, 78
Cereal	98, 74, 56, 111, 95, 88, 82, 77, 86, 92	107, 95, 97, 80, 98, 74, 74, 67, 89, 58
Pork	94, 79, 96, 98, 102, 102, 108, 91, 120, 105	49, 82, 73, 86, 81, 97, 106, 70, 61, 82

14.34 Regression of weight gain on diet Refer to the previous exercise.

a. Set up indicator variables for protein source and for protein level, and specify a regression model with the effects both of protein level and protein source on weight gain.

---

[3]*Source*: Data from *The State of Working America 2000–2001*, Economic Policy Institute.

[4]*Source*: Data from G. Snedecor and W. Cochran, *Statistical Methods*, 6th ed. (Iowa State University Press, 1967), p. 347.

b. Fit the model in part a, and explain how to interpret the parameter estimate for the protein level indicator variable.

c. Show how you could test a hypothesis about beta parameters in the model in part a to analyze the effect of protein source on weight gain.

d. Using the fit of the model, find the estimated mean for each of the six diets. Explain what it means when we say that these estimated means do not allow for interaction between protein level and source in their effects on weight loss.

Chapter Review

ANSWERS TO THE CHAPTER FIGURE QUESTIONS

Figure 14.1 No, even if the population means are equal we would expect the sample means to vary due to sample to sample variability. Differences among the sample means is not sufficient evidence to conclude that the population means differ.

Figure 14.2 The data in Figure 14.2b give stronger evidence against H_0 because Figure 14.2b has less variability within each sample than Figure 14.2a.

Figure 14.3 Evidence suggesting the normal with equal standard deviation assumptions are violated would be (1) graphical methods showing extreme skew for the response variable, or (2) the largest group standard deviation is more than about double the smallest group standard deviation when the sample sizes are unequal.

Figure 14.5 Yes. The parallelism of lines implies that no interaction holds no matter which factor we choose for making comparisons of means.

Figure 14.6 The lines are not parallel.

CHAPTER SUMMARY

Analysis of variance (ANOVA) methods compare several groups according to their means on a quantitative response variable. The groups are categories of categorical explanatory variables. A categorical explanatory variable is also called a **factor**.

■ The **one-way ANOVA** F test compares means for a single factor. The groups are specified by categories of a single categorical explanatory variable.

■ **Two-way ANOVA** methods compare means across categories of each of two factors, at fixed levels of the other factor. When there is **interaction** between the factors in their effects, differences between response means for categories of one factor change according to the category of the other factor.

■ **Multiple comparison methods** such as the **Tukey method** compare means for each pair of groups while controlling the overall confidence level.

■ Analysis of variance methods can be conducted by using multiple regression models. The regression model uses **indicator variables** as explanatory variables to represent the factors. Each indicator variable equals 1 for observations from a particular category and 0 otherwise.

■ The ANOVA methods assume randomization and that the population distribution for each group is normal, with the same standard deviation for each group. In practice, *the randomness assumption is the most important*, and ANOVA methods are *robust* to moderate violations of the other assumptions.

CHAPTER PROBLEMS

Practicing the Basics

14.35 **Good friends and marital status**   Is the number of good friends associated with marital status? For GSS data with marital status measured with the categories (married, widowed, divorced, separated, never married), an ANOVA table reports $F = 0.80$ based on $df_1 = 4$, $df_2 = 612$.

a. Introduce notation, and specify the null hypothesis and the alternative hypothesis for the ANOVA F test.

b. Based on what you know about the F distribution, would you guess that the test statistic value of 0.80 provides strong evidence against the null hypothesis? Explain.

c. Software reports a P-value of 0.53. Explain how to interpret it.

14.36 **Going to bars and having friends**   Do people who go to bars and pubs a lot tend to have more friends? A recent GSS asked, "How often do you go to a bar or tavern?" The table shows results of ANOVA for comparing the mean number of good friends at three levels of this variable. The very often group reported going to a bar at least several times a week. The occasional group reported going occasionally, but not as often as several times a week.

Summary of ANOVA for mean number of good friends and going to bars

```
                 Very often    Occasional      Never
Mean               12.1            6.4           6.2
Standard dev.      21.3           10.2          14.0
Sample size          41            166           215

Source        DF       SS       MS       F       P
Group          2     1116.8    558.4    3.03    0.049
Error        419    77171.8    184.2
Total        421    78288.5
```

a. State the (i) hypotheses, (ii) test statistic value, and (iii) P-value for the significance test displayed in this table. Interpret the P-value.

b. Based on the assumptions needed to use the method in part a, is there any aspect of the data summarized here that suggests that the ANOVA test and follow-up confidence intervals may not be appropriate? Explain.

14.37 TV watching The 2008 General Social Survey asked 1324 subjects how many hours per day they watched TV, on the average. Are there differences in population means according to the race of the subject (white, black, other)? The sample means were 2.76 for whites ($n = 1014$), 4.38 for blacks ($n = 188$), and 2.70 for other ($n = 122$). In a one-way ANOVA, the between-groups estimate ofthe variance is 215.26 and the within-groups estimate is 6.76.

a. Conduct the ANOVA test and make a decision using 0.05 significance level.

b. The 95% confidence interval comparing the population means is (1.1, 2.2) for blacks and whites, (−0.4, 0.5) for whites and the other category, and (1.0, 2.4) for blacks and the other category. Based on the three confidence intervals, indicate which pairs of means are significantly different. Interpret.

c. Based on the information given, show how to construct the confidence interval that compares the population mean TV watching for blacks and whites.

d. Refer to part c. Would the corresponding interval formed with the Tukey method be wider, or narrower? Explain why.

14.38 Comparing auto bumpers A consumer organization compares the sturdiness of three types of front bumpers. In the study, a particular brand of car is driven into a concrete wall at 15 miles per hour. The response is the amount of damage, as measured by the repair costs, in hundreds of dollars. Due to the potentially large costs, the study conducts only two tests with each bumper type, using six cars. The table shows the data and some ANOVA results. Show the (a) assumptions, (b) hypotheses, (c) test statistic and *df* values, (d) P-value, and (e) interpretation for testing the hypothesis that the true mean repair costs are the same for the three bumper types.

Bumper A	Bumper B	Bumper C
1	2	11
3	4	15

```
Source    DF      SS      MS       F       P
Bumper     2   148.00   74.00    18.50   0.021
Error      3    12.00    4.00
Total      5   160.00
```

14.39 Compare bumpers Refer to the previous exercise.

a. Find the margin of error for constructing a 95% confidence interval for the difference between any pair of the true means. Interpret by showing which pairs of bumpers (if any) are significantly different in their true mean repair costs.

b. For Tukey 95% multiple comparison confidence intervals, the margin of error is 8.4. Explain the difference between confidence intervals formed with this method and separate confidence intervals formed with the method in part a.

c. Set up indicator variables for a multiple regression model including bumper type.

d. The prediction equation for part c is $\hat{y} = 13 - 11x_1 - 10x_2$. Explain how to interpret the three parameter estimates in this model, and show how these estimates relate to the sample means for the three bumpers.

14.40 Segregation by region Studies of the degree of residential racial segregation often use the *segregation index*. This is the percentage of nonwhites who would have to change the block on which they live to produce a fully nonsegregated city—one in which the percentage of nonwhites living in each block is the same for all blocks in the city. This index can assume values ranging from 0 to 100, with higher values indicating greater segregation. (The national average for large U.S. metropolitan areas in 2009 was 27, down from 33 in 2000.) The table shows the index for a sample of cities for 2005–2009, classified by region.

Segregation index

Northeast	North Central	South	West
Boston: 67	Minneapolis-St. Paul: 56	New Orleans: 64	San Francisco-Oakland: 64
NY, Long Island, Northern NJ: 79	Detroit: 80	Tampa: 58	Dallas-Ft Worth: 57
Philadelphia: 69	Chicago: 78	Miami: 66	Los Angeles: 70
Pittsburgh: 68	Milwaukee: 81	Atlanta: 60	Seattle: 54

Source: Racial and Ethnic Residential Segregation in the United States, 1980–2000, U.S. Census Bureau Series CENSR-3, 2002. www.psc.isr.umich.edu/dis/census/segregation.html.

a. Report the mean and standard deviation for each of the four regions.

b. Define notation, and state the hypotheses for one-way ANOVA.

c. Report the *F* test statistic and its P-value. What do you conclude about the mean segregation indices for the four regions?

d. Suppose we took these data from the Census Bureau report by choosing only the cities in which we know people. Is the ANOVA valid? Explain.

14.41 Compare segregation means Refer to the previous exercise.

a. Using software, find the margin of error that pertains to each comparison using the Tukey method for 95% multiple comparison confidence intervals.

b. Using part a, determine which pairs of means, if any, are significantly different.

14.42 **Georgia political ideology** The Georgia Student Survey file on the text CD asked students their political party affiliation (1 = Democrat, 2 = Republican, 3 = Independent) and their political ideology (on a scale from 1 = very liberal to 7 = very conservative). The table shows results of an ANOVA, with political ideology as the response variable.

Georgia political ideology and party affiliation

		Political ideology	
Affiliation	**N**	**Mean**	**StDev**
Democrat	8	2.6250	1.0607
Republican	36	5.5000	1.0000
Independent	15	3.4667	0.9155

```
Source        DF    SS       MS      F      P
PoliticalAff  2     79.629   39.814  40.83  0.000
Error         56    54.608   0.975
Total         58    134.237
```

a. Does the ANOVA assumption of equal population standard deviations seem plausible, or is it so badly violated that ANOVA is inappropriate?

b. Are the population distributions normal? Why or why not? Which is more important, the normality assumption or the assumption that the groups are random samples from the population of interest?

c. The next table shows 95% confidence intervals comparing pairs of means. Interpret the confidence interval comparing Republicans and Democrats.

Affiliations

	95% CI		
	Lower	**Center**	**Upper**
Republican–Democrat	2.10	2.87	3.65
Independent–Democrat	−0.02	0.84	1.71
Republican–Independent	1.43	2.03	2.64

d. Explain how you would summarize the results of the ANOVA F test and the confidence intervals to someone who has not studied statistics.

14.43 **Comparing therapies for anorexia** The Anorexia data file on the text CD shows weight change for 72 anorexic teenage girls who were randomly assigned to one of three psychological treatments.

a. Show how to construct 95% confidence intervals to investigate how the population means differ. Interpret them.

b. Report the Tukey 95% multiple comparison confidence intervals. Interpret, and explain why they are wider than the confidence intervals in part a.

14.44 **Lot size varies by region?** A geographer compares residential lot sizes in four quadrants of a city. To do this, she randomly samples 300 records from a city file on home residences and records the lot sizes (in thousands of square feet) by quadrant. The ANOVA table, shown in the table that follows, refers to a comparison of mean lot sizes for the northeast (NE), northwest (NW), southwest (SW), and southeast (SE) quadrants of the city. Fill in all the blanks in the table.

Lot sizes by quadrant of city

Source	DF	SS	MS	F	P-value
Quadrant	____	____	____	____	0.000
Error	296	1480	____		
Total	____	4180			

14.45 **House with garage** Refer to the House Selling Price OR data file on the text CD.

a. Set up an indicator variable for whether a house has a garage or not. Using software, put this as the sole predictor of house selling price (in thousands) in a regression model. Report the prediction equation, and interpret the intercept and slope estimates.

b. For the model fitted in part a, conduct the t test for the effect of the indicator variable in the regression analysis (that is, test $H_0: \beta = 0$). Interpret.

c. Use software to conduct the F test for the analysis of variance comparing the mean selling prices of homes with and without a garage. Interpret.

d. Explain the connection between the value of t in part b and the value of F in part c.

14.46 **Ideal number of kids by gender and race** The GSS asks, "What is the ideal number of kids for a family?" When we use a recent GSS to evaluate how the mean response depends on gender and race (black or white), we get the results shown in the ANOVA table.

a. Identify the response variable and the factors.

b. Explain what it would mean if there were no interaction between gender and race in their effects. Show a hypothetical set of population means that would show a strong race effect and a weak gender effect and no interaction.

c. Using the table, specify the null and alternative hypotheses, test statistic, and P-value for the test of no interaction. Interpret the result.

ANOVA of ideal number of kids by gender and race

```
Source        DF    SS       MS      F      P
Gender        1     0.25     0.25    0.36   0.546
Race          1     16.98    16.98   24.36  0.000
Interaction   1     0.95     0.95    1.36   0.244
Error         1245  867.72   0.70
Total         1248  886.12
```

14.47 **Regress kids on gender and race** Refer to the previous exercise. Let $f = 1$ for females and 0 for males, and let $r = 1$ for blacks and 0 for whites. The regression model for predicting y = ideal number of kids is $\hat{y} = 2.42 + 0.04f + 0.37r$.

a. Interpret the coefficient of f. What is the practical implication of this estimate being so close to 0?

b. Find the estimated mean for each of the four combinations of gender and race.

c. Summarize what you learn about the effects based on the analyses in this and the previous exercise.

14.48 **Florida student data** For the FL Student Survey data file on the text CD, we use as the response variable sports (the number of weekly hours engaged in sports and other physical exercise). For the explanatory variables, we use gender and whether the student is a vegetarian. The output shows results of a two-way ANOVA.

a. State the hypotheses for the vegetarian main effect.

b. Show how the F test statistic for part a was obtained from mean squares reported in the ANOVA table.

c. Report and interpret the P-value of the test for the vegetarian main effect.

```
Source      DF    SS      MS      F      P
vegetarian   1    7.89    7.89  0.56    0.457
gender       1   64.35   64.35  4.59    0.037
Error       57  799.80   14.03
Total       59  878.98
```

14.49 **Regress TV watching on gender and religion** When we use a recent GSS and regress $y =$ number of hours per day watching TV on $g =$ gender ($1 =$ male, $0 =$ female) and religious affiliation ($r_1 = 1$ for Protestant, $r_2 = 1$ for Catholic, $r_3 = 1$ for Jewish, $r_1 = r_2 = r_3 = 0$ for none or other), we get the prediction equation TVHOURS $= 2.65 - 0.186g + 0.666r_1 + 0.373r_2 - 0.270r_3$

a. Interpret the gender effect.

b. Interpret the coefficient of r_1.

c. State a corresponding model for the population, and indicate which parameters would need to equal zero for the response variable to be independent of religious affiliation, for each gender.

14.50 **Income, gender, and education** According to the U.S. Census Bureau, as of March 2009, the average earnings of full-time workers was estimated to be $31,666 for females with high school education, $43,493 for males with high school education, $60,293 for white females with a bachelor's degree, and $94,206 for males with a bachelor's degree.

a. Identify the response variable and the two factors.

b. Show these means in a two-way classification of the factors.

c. Compare the differences between males and females for (i) high school graduates and (ii) college graduates. If these are close estimates of the population means, explain why there is interaction. Describe its nature.

14.51 **Birth weight, age of mother, and smoking** A study on the effects of prenatal exposure to smoke (by J. Nigg and N. Breslau, *Journal of the American Academy of Child & Adolescent Psychiatry*, vol. 46, 2009, pp. 362–369) indicated that mean birth weight was significantly lower for babies born to mothers who smoked during pregnancy. It also suggested that increasing age of the mother resulted in increased effects. Explain how this suggests interaction between smoking status and age of mother in their effects on birth weight of the child.

14.52 **TV watching by gender and race** When we use the 2008 GSS to evaluate how the mean number of hours a day watching TV depends on gender and race, we get the results shown in the ANOVA table that follows.

a. Identify the response variable and the factors.

b. From the table, specify the test statistic and P-value for the test of no interaction. Interpret the result.

c. Is there a significant (i) gender effect and (ii) race effect? Explain.

d. The sample means were 2.82 for white females, 2.68 for white males, 4.52 for black females, and 4.19 for black males. Explain how these results are compatible with the results of the tests discussed in part c.

Analysis of Variance for TVHOURS, using Adjusted SS for Tests

```
Source     DF   Seq SS   Adj SS   Adj MS    F      P
RACE        1   419.60   399.12   399.12  58.32  0.000
SEX         1     8.74     8.74     8.74   1.28  0.259
RACE*SEX    1     1.42     1.42     1.42   0.21  0.649
Error    1198  8199.10  8199.10     6.84
Total    1201  8628.86
S = 2.61610  R-Sq = 4.98%  R-Sq(adj) = 4.74%
```

14.53 **Salary and gender** The American Association of University Professors (AAUP) reports yearly on faculty salaries for all types of higher education institutions across the United States. Regard *Salary* as the response variable, *Gender* as the explanatory variable, and *Academic Rank* as the control variable. A regression analysis using these data could include an indicator variable for *Gender* and an indicator variable for *Rank*. The estimated coefficients are -13 (thousands of dollars) for *Gender* ($x_1 = 1$ for female and $x_1 = 0$ for male) and -40 (thousands of dollars) for a lesser assistant *Rank* ($x_2 = 1$ for assistant professor and $x_2 = 0$ for professor).

a. Interpret the coefficient for gender.

b. At particular settings of the other predictors, the estimated mean salary for female professors was 96.2 thousand dollars. Using the estimated coefficients, find the estimated means for (i) male professors and (ii) female assistant professors.

14.54 **Political ideology by religion and gender** The table shown summarizes responses on political ideology (where $1 =$ extremely liberal and $7 =$ extremely conservative) in a General Social Survey by religion and gender. The P-value is 0.414 for testing the null hypothesis of no interaction. Explain what this means in the context of this example. (*Hint*: Is the difference between males and females in sample mean ideology about the same for each religion?)

Political ideology by religion and gender

Religion		Political Ideology				
		Mean	Std Dev.		Mean	Std. Dev.
Protestant	Female	4.35	1.44	Male	4.50	1.39
Catholic	Female	3.97	1.29	Male	4.04	1.34
Jewish	Female	2.86	1.49	Male	3.50	1.16
None	Female	3.25	1.31	Male	3.60	1.42

Concepts and Applications

14.55 **Number of friends and degree** Using the GSS Web site sda.berkeley.edu/GSS, analyze whether the number of good friends (the variable NUMFRIEND) depends on the subject's highest degree (the variable DEGREE). To do so, at this web address look under the Analysis tab to pick comparison of means and then enter the variable names and check the ANOVA stats box. Prepare a short report summarizing your analysis and its interpretation.

14.56 Sketch within- and between-groups variability Sketch a dot plot of data for 10 observations in each of three groups such that

a. You believe the P-value would be very small for a one-way ANOVA. (You do not need to do the ANOVA; merely show points for which you think this would happen.)

b. The P-value in one-way ANOVA would not be especially small.

14.57 A = B and B = C, but A ≠ C? In multiple comparisons following a one-way ANOVA with equal sample sizes, the margin of error with a 95% confidence interval for comparing each pair of means equals 10. Give three sample means illustrating that it is possible that Group A is not significantly different from Group B and Group B is not significantly different from Group C, yet Group A is significantly different from Group C.

14.58 Multiple comparison confidence For four groups, explain carefully the difference between a confidence level of 0.95 for a single comparison of two means and a confidence level of 0.95 for a multiple comparison of all six pairs of means.

14.59 Another Simpson paradox The 25 women faculty members in the humanities division of a college have a mean salary of $65,000, whereas the five women faculty in the science division have a mean salary of $72,000. The 20 men in the humanities division have a mean salary of $64,000, and the 30 men in the science division have a mean salary of $71,000.

a. Construct a 2 × 2 table of sample mean incomes for the table of gender and division of college. Use weighted averages to find the overall means for men and women.

b. Discuss how the results of a one-way comparison of mean incomes by gender would differ from the results of a two-way comparison of mean incomes by gender, controlling for division of college. (*Note*: This reversal of which gender has the higher mean salary, according to whether one controls division of college, illustrates *Simpson's paradox*.)

14.60 Multiple choice: ANOVA/regression similarities Analysis of variance and multiple regression have many similarities. Which of the following is *not* true?

a. The response variable is quantitative for each.

b. They both have F tests for testing that the response variable is statistically independent of the explanatory variable(s).

c. For inferential purposes, they both assume that the response variable y is normally distributed with the same standard deviation at all combinations of levels of the explanatory variable(s).

d. They are both appropriate when the main focus is on describing straight-line effects of quantitative explanatory variables.

14.61 Multiple choice: ANOVA variability One-way ANOVA provides relatively more evidence that H_0: $\mu_1 = \cdots = \mu_g$ is false:

a. The smaller the between-groups variation and the larger the within-groups variation.

b. The smaller the between-groups variation and the smaller the within-groups variation.

c. The larger the between-groups variation and the smaller the within-groups variation.

d. The larger the between-groups variation and the larger the within-groups variation.

14.62 Multiple choice: Multiple comparisons For four means, it is planned to construct Tukey 95% multiple comparison confidence intervals for the differences between the six pairs.

a. For each confidence interval, there is a 0.95 chance that the interval will contain the true difference.

b. The probability that all six confidence intervals will contain the true differences is 0.70.

c. The probability that all six confidence intervals will contain the true differences is about 0.95.

d. The probability that all six confidence intervals will contain the true differences is $(0.95)^6$.

14.63 Multiple choice: Interaction There is interaction in a two-way ANOVA model when

a. The two factors are associated.

b. Both factors have significant effects in the model without interaction terms.

c. The difference in true means between two categories of one factor varies among the categories of the other factor.

d. The mean square for interaction is about the same size as the mean square error.

14.64 True or false: Interaction For subjects aged under 50, there is little difference in mean annual medical expenses for smokers and nonsmokers. For subjects aged over 50, there is a large difference. Is it true or false that there is interaction between smoking status and age in their effects on annual medical expenses.

14.65 What causes large or small F? An experiment used four ◆◆ groups of five individuals each. The overall sample mean was 60.

a. What did the sample means look like if the one-way ANOVA for comparing the means had test statistic $F = 0$? (*Hint:* What would have to happen in order for the between-groups variability to be 0?)

b. What did the data look like in each group if $F =$ infinity? (*Hint:* What would have to happen in order for the within-groups variability to be 0?)

14.66 Between-subjects estimate This exercise motivates the ◆◆ formula for the between-subjects estimate of the variance in one-way ANOVA. Suppose each population mean equals μ (that is, H_0 is true) and each sample size equals n. Then the sampling distribution of each $\bar{y}_i$ has mean μ and variance σ^2/n, and the sample mean of the $\bar{y}_i$ values is the overall sample mean, $\{\bar{y}\}$.

a. Treating the g sample means as g observations having sample mean $\bar{y}$, explain why $\Sigma(\bar{y}_i - \bar{y})^2/(g-1)$

estimates the variance σ^2/n of the distribution of the $\{\bar{y}_i\}$ values.

b. Using part a, explain why the between-groups estimate $\sum n(\bar{y}_i - \bar{y})^2/(g - 1)$ estimates σ^2. (For the unequal sample size case, the formula replaces n by n_i.)

14.67 Bonferroni multiple comparisons The Bonferroni theo-
◆◆ rem states that the probability that *at least* one of a set of events occurs can be no greater than the sum of the sepa-rate probabilities of the events. For instance, if the prob-ability of an error for each of five separate confidence intervals equals 0.01, then the probability that *at least* one confidence interval will be in error is no greater than $(0.01 + 0.01 + 0.01 + 0.01 + 0.01) = 0.05$.

a. Following Example 10, construct a confidence inter-val for each factor and guarantee that they both hold with overall confidence level at least 95%. [*Hint*: Each interval should use $t_{.0125} = 2.46$.]

b. Exercise 14.8 referred to a study comparing three groups (smoking status never, former, or current) on various personality scales. The study measured 35 per-sonality scales and reported an F test comparing the three smoking groups for each scale. The researchers mentioned doing a Bonferroni correction for the 35 F tests. If the nominal *overall* probability of Type I error was 0.05 for the 35 tests, how small did the P-value have to be for a particular test to be significant? (*Hint*: What should the Type I error probability be for each of 35 tests in order for the overall Type I error probability to be no more than 0.05?)

14.68 Independent confidence intervals You plan to construct
◆◆ a 95% confidence interval in five different situations with independent data sets.

a. Assuming that the results of the confidence intervals are statistically independent, find the probability that *all* five confidence intervals will contain the param-eters they are designed to estimate. (*Hint*: Use the binomial distribution.)

b. Which confidence level should you use for each confi-dence interval so that the probability that all five inter-vals contain the parameters equals *exactly* 0.95?

14.69 Regression or ANOVA? You want to analyze $y =$
◆◆ house selling price and $x =$ number of bathrooms (1, 2, or 3) by testing whether x and y are independent.

a. You could conduct a test of independence using (i) the ANOVA F test for a multiple regression model with two indicator variables or (ii) a regression t test for the coefficient of the number of bathrooms when it is treated as a quantitative predictor in a straight-line regression model. Explain the difference between these two ways of treating the number of bathrooms in the analysis.

b. What do you think are the advantages and disadvan-tages of the straight-line regression approach to con-ducting the test?

c. Give an example of three population means for which the straight-line regression model would be less appro-priate than the model with indicator variables.

14.70 Three factors An experiment analyzed how the mean
◆◆ corn yield varied according to three factors: nitrogen-based fertilizer, phosphate-based fertilizer, and potash (potassium chloride)-based fertilizer, each applied at low and at high levels.

a. How many groups result from the different combina-tions of the three factors?

b. Defining indicator variables, state the regression model that corresponds to an ANOVA assuming a lack of interaction.

c. Give possible estimates of the model parameters in part b for which the estimated corn yield would be highest at the high level of nitrogen fertilizer and phosphate fertilizer and the low level of potash.

Student Activities

14.71 Student survey data Refer to the student survey data file that your class created with Activity 3 in Chapter 1. For variables chosen by your instructor, use ANOVA methods and related inferential statistical analyses. Interpret and summarize your findings in a short report, and prepare to discuss your findings in class.

Answers

Chapter 11

11.1 **(a)** Response: political party identification; explanatory: gender.
(b)

Political Party Identification

Gender	Democrat	Independent	Republican	Total	*n*
Female	39.2%	35.4%	25.4%	100%	1076
Male	33.4%	40.7%	25.9%	100%	896

Women are more likely than are men to be Democrats, whereas men are more likely than are women to be Independents. **(c)** Distributions should show percentages in the party categories that are the same for men and women, such as (36%, 38%, 26%). **11.3** **(a)** These distributions refer to those of *y* at given categories of *x*.

	Type of Student	
Gender of Student	Undergraduate	Graduate
Female	78%	22%
Male	84%	16%

(b) x and y are dependent because the probability of a randomly chosen student being an undergraduate or graduate changes according to gender.
11.5 **(a)**

Happiness Of Marriage

Income	Very Happy	Pretty Happy	Not Too Happy	*n*
Below	123	105	7	235
Average	291	151	17	459
Above	172	83	6	261

(b)

Happiness Of Marriage

Income	Very Happy	Pretty Happy	Not Too Happy	*n*
Below	52.3%	44.7%	3.0%	235
Average	63.4%	32.9%	3.7%	459
Above	65.9%	31.8%	2.3%	261

Average-income people tend to have slightly less happy marriages than those in the other two brackets; high-income people tend to have slightly happier marriages. **(c)** Regardless of income brackets, marital happiness tends to be higher than general happiness for the Very Happy and the Not Too Happy categories. **11.7** Answers will vary depending on the column variable selected. **11.9** **(a)** H_0: Gender and happiness are independent. H_a: Gender and happiness are dependent. **(b)** The P-value is not especially small. If the null hypothesis were true, the probability would be 0.79 of getting a test statistic at least as extreme as the value observed. So, there is not strong evidence against the null hypothesis, and it is plausible that gender and happiness are independent.

11.11 **(a)**

Gender	Believe	Don't Believe	Total
Male	620	189	808
Female	835	143	979

(b)

Gender	Believe	Don't Believe	Total
Male	658.7	150.3	808
Female	796.3	181.7	979

There are more women who believe than expected and more men who do not believe than expected. **(c)** $X^2 = (620 - 658.7)^2/658.7 + \cdots + (143 - 181.7)^2/181.7 = 22.362$. **11.13** **(a)** (61.1%, 38.9%) and (5.9%, 94.1%); suggests marijuana use much more common for those who have smoked cigarettes than for those who have not. **(b)** **(1)** Assumptions: two categorical variables (cigarette use and marijuana use), randomization, expected count at least five in all cells. **(2)** H_0: marijuana use independent of cigarette use; H_a: dependence. **(3)** $X^2 = 642.0$. **(4)** P-value: 0.000. **(5)** Extremely strong evidence that marijuana use and cigarette use are associated. **11.15** **(a)** H_0: opinion about the environment independent of sex; H_a: dependence. **(b)** $r = 2$; $c = 5$; $df = 4$. **(c)** The P-value is 0.09. **(i)** No; **(ii)** Yes. **(d)** **(i)** Fail to reject the null hypothesis, and conclude that variables may be independent; **(ii)** Reject the null hypothesis, there is evidence to suggest that opinion depends on gender.

11.17 **(a)**

	H_a	No H_a
placebo	28	656
aspirin	18	658

(b) **(1)** 2 categorical variables, randomization, expected count at least 5 in all cells. **(2)** H_0: whether have heart attack independent of treatment; H_a: dependence. **(3)** $X^2 = 2.1$. **(4)** P-value: 0.14. **(5)** It is plausible that treatment and heart attack incidence are independent. **11.19** **(a)** Data show a strong association between happiness and belief in life after death. **(b)** 0.03 (as reported by GSS); results would be unusual if variables were independent. **(c)** There is strong evidence that happiness depends on opinion about the afterlife. **11.21** **(a)** H_0: $p = 0.75$. **(b)** $X^2 = 3.46$; $df = 1$. **(c)** P-value $= 0.06$. The probability of obtaining a test statistic at least as extreme as that observed, assuming the null hypothesis is true, is 0.06. Some evidence against the null, but not very strong. **11.23** **(a)** **(1)** 2 categorical variables, randomization, expected count at least 5 in all cells. **(2)** H_0: party identification independent of race; H_a: dependence. **(3)** $X^2 = 177.312$. **(4)** P-value: 0.000. **(5)** Very strong evidence that party identification and race are associated. **(b)** 0.395; strong; it is quite far from 0.00, the difference corresponding to no association. **11.25** **(a)** Reject the null hypothesis of independence, because P-value is less than 0.05. The data suggests happiness depends of independence on highest degree. **(b)** No; with a large sample size, even a weak association could be statistically significant. **(c)** 0.21; in the sample, happiness is higher among those who completed college than among those who did not complete high school. **(d)** 3.3; college graduates are 3.3 times as likely to be happy as students who did not complete high school. **11.27** **(a)** The proportion who had used alcohol is 0.33 higher for cigarette users versus non-cigarette users. **(b)** The proportion who had used cigarettes is 0.60 higher for alcohol users than for those who had not used alcohol. **(c)** Alcohol users are 5.3 times as likely to have smoked as are non-alcohol users. **11.29** **(a)** $949/100,000 = 0.00949$ of men were incarcerated, whereas $67/100,000 = 0.00067$ for women. The relative risk of being incarcerated is $0.00949/0.00067 = 14.2$. Men were 14.2 times as likely as women were to be incarcerated. **(b)** The difference of proportions being incarcerated is $0.00949 - 0.00067 = 0.009$. The proportion of men who are incarcerated is 0.009 higher than the proportion of women who are incarcerated. **(c)** The response in part a is more appropriate because it shows there is a substantial gender effect, which the difference does not show when both proportions are close to 0. **11.31** **(a)**

False; larger chi-squared might be due to a larger sample size rather than a stronger association. **(b)** Yes; evidence suggests race is more strongly associated. **11.33 (a)** The observed count falls 4.681 standard errors above the expected count. **(b)** They designate conditions in which the observed counts are much higher than the expected counts, relative to what we'd expect due to sampling variability. **(c)** They designate conditions in which the observed counts are much lower than the expected counts, relative to what we'd expect due to sampling variability. **11.35 (a)** Observed count for this cell is only 0.1 standard errors below the expected count. **(b)** People who are not happy in their marriage are more likely to be not happy in general than would be expected if the variables were independent. People who are pretty happy in their marriage are more likely to be pretty happy overall than would be expected if the variables were independent. Lastly, people who are very happy in their marriage are more likely to be very happy overall than would be expected if the variables were independent. **11.37** Females tend to be Democrat more often and males tend to be Democrat less often than one would expect if party ID were independent of gender.

11.39 (a)

	S	F	Total
control	2	6	8
treatment	12	0	12

(b) (1) There are two binary categorical variables, and randomization was used. **(2)** $H_0: p_1 = p_2; H_a: p_1 \neq p_2$. **(3)** Test statistic: 2. **(4)** P-value: 0.001. **(5)** Strong evidence that care and diet are associated with ability to solve a task. **(c)** Because the expected cell counts are less than 5 for at least some cells. **11.41 (a)** 0.24; it is plausible that nervousness and treatment are independent. **(b)** No, because two cells have an expected count of less than five. **11.43 (a)**

	Y	N
male	0.94	0.06
female	0.94	0.06

(b) Yes; percentages of men and women who would vote for a qualified woman may be the same. **11.45 (1)** Two categorical variables, randomization, expected count at least 5 in all cells. **(2)** H_0: blood test result independent of Down syndrome status; H_a: dependence. **(3)** $X^2 = 114.4$, $df = 1$. **(4)** P-value $= 0.000$. **(5)** Very strong evidence of an association between test result and actual status. **11.47 (a)** The response variable is level of common cold symptoms and the explanatory variable is treatment (placebo versus Immumax). **(b)** I would explain that if the decrease of common cold symptoms did not depend on whether one took Immumax or placebo, then it would be quite unusual to observe the results actually obtained. This provides relatively strong evidence of decreased cold symptoms for those taking Immumax. **11.49 (1)** Two categorical variables, randomization, expected count at least 5 in all cells. **(2)** H_0: political party independent of sex; H_a: dependence. **(3)** $X^2 = 8.294; df = 2$. **(4)** P-value $= 0.016$. **(5)** strong evidence that party identification and gender are associated. **11.51 (a) (i)** The assumptions are that there are two categorical variables (group and cardiovascular event), that randomization was used to obtain the data, and that the expected count was at least five in all cells; **(ii)** H_0: Group and cardiovascular event are independent. H_a: Group and cardiovascular event are dependent; **(iii)** $X^2 = 10.7; df = 2$; **(iv)** P-value: 0.005; **(v)** The P-value is very small. If the null hypothesis were true, the probability would be close to 0 of getting a test statistic at least as extreme as the value observed. We have very strong evidence that there is an association between cardiovascular event and group. **(b)** The proportion of those on placebo who had a stroke is 0.013. The proportion of those on aspirin who had a stroke is 0.011. Thus, the relative risk is $0.013/0.011 = 1.2$. Those on placebo are 1.2 times as likely as those on aspirin to have stroke. **11.53 (a)** The proportion who were injured is 0.06 higher for those who did not wear a seat belt than for those who wore a seat belt. **(b)** People were 1.95 times as likely to be injured if they were not wearing a seat belt than if they were wearing a seat belt. **11.55** Those with no partners or two or more partners are less likely to be very happy, and those with one partner are more likely to be very happy, than would be expected if these variables were independent. **11.57 (a)** H_0: $p_1 = p_2; H_a: p_1 \neq p_2; p_1$: population proportion of those who are aggres-

sive in the group that watches less than one hour of TV per day; p_2: population proportion of those who are aggressive in the group that watches more than one hour of TV per day. **(b)** 0.0001; very strong evidence that TV watching and aggression are associated. **11.59** Report could include: Contingency table of summary counts and Pearson chi-squared $= 21.4$, $df = 6$, P-Value $= 0.002$. **11.61** Answers will vary.

11.63 (a)

	Has Young Children	
Gray Hair	**Yes**	**No**
Yes	0	4
No	5	0

(b) Yes. **(c)** There often are third factors, such as age in this case, that influence an association. **11.65 (a)** Difference of proportions with U.S. as Group 1: 0.000061; Britain as Group 1: -0.000061. **(b)** U.S. as Group 1: 48; Britain as Group 1: 0.021. **(c)** Relative risk; the difference between proportions might be very small, even when one is many times larger than the other. **11.67** False. **11.69** True. **11.71 (a)** The chi-squared value for a right-tail probability of 0.05 and $df = 1$s 3.84, which is the z value for a two-tail probability of 0.05 squared: $(1.96)(1.96) = 3.84$. **(b)** The chi-squared value for P-value of 0.01 and $df = 1$ is 6.64. This is the square of the z value for a two-tail P-value of 0.01, which is 2.58. **11.73** The two observed values in a given row (or column) must add up to the same total as the two expected values in that same row (or column). **11.75 (a)**

F1, F2, F3	F1, F2, M1	F1, F2, M2	F1, F2, M3
F1, F3, M1	F1, F3, M2	F1, F3, M3	F1, M1, M2
F1, M1, M3	F1, M2, M3	F2, F3, M1	F2, F3, M2
F2, F3, M3	F2, M1, M2	F2, M1, M3	F2, M2, M3
F3, M1, M2	F3, M1, M3	F3, M2, M3	M1, M2, M3

This contingency table shows that two males were chosen (M1 and M3) and one was not (M2). It also shows that one female was chosen (F2) and two were not (F1 and F3). **(b)** Ten samples have a difference greater than or equal to 1/3. A difference greater than or equal to 1/3 indicates more men than women in the sample.

Chapter 13

13.1 (a) $\hat{y} = 134.3$. **(b)** -19.3. The actual total body weight is 19.3 pounds lower than predicted. **13.3 (a) (i)** 3.80; **(ii)** 1.60; **(b)** $\hat{y} = 0.20 + 0.50 x_1 + 0.002(500) = 0.20 + 0.50 x_1 + 1 = 1.20 + 0.50 x_1$. **(c)** $\hat{y} = 0.20 + 0.50 x_1 + 0.002(600) = 0.20 + 0.50 x_1 + 1.2 = 1.40 + 0.50 x_1$. **13.5 (a) (i)** 18.3; **(ii)** 12.5; **(b)** When education goes up $10 = 80 - 70$, predicted crime rate changes by 10 multiplied by the slope, $10(-0.58) = -5.8$. **(c) (i)** $\hat{y} = 59.12 - 0.5834 x_1 + 0.6825(0) = 59.12 - 0.5834 x_1$; **(ii)** $\hat{y} = 59.12 - 0.5834 x_1 + 0.6825(50) = 93.2 - 0.5834 x_1$; **(iii)** $\hat{y} = 59.12 - 0.5834 x_1 + 0.6825(100) = 127.4 - 0.5834 x_1$; **(d)** The line passing through the points having urbanization $= 50$ has a negative slope. The line passing through all the data points has a positive slope. Simpson's paradox occurs because the association between crime rate and education is positive overall but is negative at each fixed value of urbanization. It happens because urbanization is positively associated with crime rate and with education. As urbanization increases, crime rate and education tend to increase, giving an overall positive association between crime rate and education. **13.7 (a)** $\hat{y} = \$26,417,000 + \$168,300(\text{GIR}) + \$33,859(\text{SS}) - \$19,784,000(\text{AvePutt}) - \$44,725(\text{Events})$. **(b)** The average of putts after reaching the green (AvePutt) will increase a golfer's score and therefore decrease his or her earnings. The number of PGA events entered (Events) is a bit harder to explain. One would think that the more events a golfer participated in, the more money he or she would earn. However, the negative sign implies the opposite. An excellent golfer may enter only select events on the tour. If he or she is able to win enough by August, the golfer would be hesitant to participate in more events instead of resting or participating in other promotions. A worse golfer has to play in more events to make a living. **(c)** $\hat{y} = \$26,417,000 + \$168,300(60) + \$33,859(50) - \$19,784,000(1.5) -$

$44,725(20) = \$7,637,450$. **13.9** We don't need to control x_2 if it's not associated with x_1. Changes in x_2 will not have an impact on the effect of x_1 on y. **13.11 (a)**

$$R^2 = \frac{\Sigma(y - \bar{y})^2 - \Sigma(y - \hat{y})^2}{\Sigma(y - \bar{y})^2} = (4354684931 - 1993805006)/4354684931$$

$= 0.542$. **(b)** Using these variables together to predict attendance reduces the prediction error by 54%, relative to using $\bar{y}$ alone to predict attendance. Yes, the prediction is at least somewhat better. **(c)** $R = \sqrt{R^2} = \sqrt{0.542} = 0.736$; there is a moderately strong association between the observed attendance and the predicted attendance. **13.13** Height is not strongly correlated with either body fat or age. **13.15** Because x_1 and x_2 are themselves highly correlated, once one of them is in the model, the remaining one does not help much in adding to the predictive power. **13.17 (a)** The correlation between predicted house selling price and actual house selling price is 0.72. **(b)** If selling price is measured in thousands of dollars, each y value would be divided by 1000. For example, \$145,000 would become 145 thousands of dollars. Each slope also would be divided by 1000 (e.g., a slope of 63 for house size on selling price in dollars corresponds to 0.063 in thousands of dollars for $\hat{y}$). **(c)** The multiple correlation would not change because it is not dependent on units. **13.19 (a)** It means that, in the population of all students, high school GPA doesn't predict college GPA for students having any given value for study time. **(b) (1)** Assumptions: We assume a random sample and that the model holds (each explanatory variable has a straight-line relation with μ_y, controlling for the other predictors, with the same slope for all combinations of values of other predictors in model, and there is a normal distribution for y with the same standard deviation at each combination of values of the predictors). Here, the 59 students were a convenience sample, not a random sample, so inferences are highly tentative. **(2)** Hypotheses: H_0: $\beta_1 = 0$; H_a: $\beta_1 \neq 0$. **(3)** Test statistic: $t = (b_1 - 0)/se = 0.6434/0.1458 = 4.41$. **(4)** P-value: 0.000. **(5)** Conclusion: The P-value of 0.000 gives strong evidence against the null hypothesis that $\beta_1 = 0$. At common significance levels, such as 0.05, we can reject H_0. **13.21 (a)** 0.32 describes the typical size of the residuals and also estimates the standard deviation of y at fixed values of the predictors. **(b)** Between 2.97 and 4.25. **13.23** The first test analyzes the effect of LP_200 at any given fixed value of BP_60, whereas the second test describes the overall effect of LP_200 ignoring other variables. These are different effects, so one can exist when the other does not. In this case, it is likely that LP_200 and BP_60 are strongly associated with one another, and the effect of LP_200 is weaker once we control for BP_60. **13.25 (a)** H_0: $\beta_1 = \beta_2 = 0$; the null hypothesis states that neither of the two explanatory variables have an effect on the response variable y. **(b)** 3.17. **(c)** 51.39 with a P-value of 0.000. Extremely strong evidence against the null, and we can reject H_0. At least one of the two explanatory variables has an effect on BP. **13.27 (a)** (0.04, 0.17). **(b)** The confidence interval gives plausible values for the slope, the amount that mean mental impairment will increase when life events score increases by one, when controlling for SES. For an increase of 100 units in life events, we multiply each endpoint of the confidence interval by 100, giving (4, 17). **13.29 (a)** H_0: $\beta_1 = \beta_2 = \beta_3 = 0$ means that house selling price is independent of size of home, number of bedrooms, and age. **(b)** The large F-value and small P-value provide strong evidence that at least one of the three explanatory variables has an effect on selling price. **(c)** The results of the t tests at the 5% significance level tell us that house size and number of bedrooms are statistically significant predictors when controlling for the other explanatory variables. Age is not statistically significant. **13.31 (a)** Conditional distribution. **(b)** That the distribution may be skewed to the right rather than normal. **13.33** One might think this suggests less variability at low levels and even less at high levels of BP_60, but this may merely reflect fewer points in those regions. Overall, it seems OK. **13.35 (a)** U-shaped scatterplot. **(b)** U-shaped pattern, with residuals above 0 for small age and large age and residuals below 0 for medium-size age values. **13.37 (a)** Bottom left and bottom middle plots; strong, positive associations. **(b)** $\hat{y} = 55.012 + 0.16676\text{LBM} + 1.6575\text{REP\_BP}$; 1.66 is the amount that maximum bench press changes for a one-unit increase in number of repetitions, controlling for lean body

mass. **(c)** 0.832; using these variables together to predict BP reduces the prediction error by 83%, relative to using $\bar{y}$ alone to predict BP. **(d)** 0.91; there is a strong association between the observed BPs and the predicted BPs. **(e)** $F = (7641.5/50.7) = 150.75$; P-value is 0.000; strong evidence that BP is not independent of these two predictors. **(f) (1)** Assumptions: The 64 athletes were a random sample (actually a convenience sample, so inferences are highly tentative). We must assume that the model holds. **(2)** Hypotheses: H_0: $\beta_1 = 0$; H_a: $\beta_1 \neq 0$. **(3)** Test statistic: $t = 2.22$. **(4)** P-value: 0.030. **(5)** Conclusion: The P-value of 0.030 gives relatively strong evidence against the null hypothesis that $\beta_1 = 0$. **(g)** The histogram suggests that the residuals are roughly bell-shaped about 0. They fall between about -3 and $+3$. The shape suggests that the conditional distribution of the response variable is roughly normal. **(h)** The plot of residuals against values of REP_BP describes the degree to which the response variable is linearly related to this particular explanatory variable. It suggests that the residuals are less variable at smaller values of REP_BP than at larger values of REP_BP. **(i)** The individual with REP_BP around 32 and standardized residual around -3 had a BP value considerably lower than expected. **13.39** For large values of lot size, residuals would be negative and have decreasing trend. **13.41 (a)** For each increase in one pound, predicted price of bike decreased by \$53.75. **(b)** When suspension type is front end the predicted price is \$643.60 cheaper. **13.43 (a) (i)** Minimum: $61.3 + 0.35(12) = 65.5$; **(ii)** Maximum: $61.2 + 0.35(54) = 80.2$. **(b)** When controlling for region, an increase of one hour leads to a decrease in predicted defects of 0.78 per 100 cars. Japanese facilities had 36 fewer predicted defects, on average, than did other facilities when controlling for time. **(c)** Because the direction of the association between time and defects changed with the variable of whether facility is Japanese was added. **(d)** Because, overall, Japanese facilities have fewer defects and take less time; other facilities have more defects and take more time. When the data are looked at together, this leads to an overall positive association between defects and time. (Student's answer will include a scatterplot.) **13.45 (a)** From software: price in thousands $= 64.7 + 0.0674$ House_Size $+ 40.3$ Garage. For homes with a garage, price in thousands $= 105 + 0.0674$ House_Size. For homes without a garage, price in thousands $= 64.7 + 0.0674$ House_Size. **(b)** The coefficient, 40.3, indicates that the predicted selling price for houses with a garage is \$40,300 higher than for houses without.

Predictor	Coef	SE Coef	T	P
Constant	64.66	17.07	3.79	0.000
House Size	0.067431	0.004596	14.67	0.000
Garage	40.29	13.39	3.01	0.003

13.47 (a) Interaction. **(b)** Males: $\hat{y} = 1.98 + 0.0055(380) = 4.07$; Females: $\hat{y} = 1.60 + 0.0065(380) = 4.07$. **(c)** No; it is dangerous to extrapolate beyond our existing data. We do not know whether trends will change in the future.

13.49 $\hat{p} = \dfrac{e^{-3.52+0.105x}}{1 + e^{-3.52+0.105x}} = \dfrac{e^{-3.52+0.105(25)}}{1 + e^{-3.52+0.105(25)}} = (0.41/1.41) = 0.29$.

13.51 (a) Q1: 0.48; Q3: 0.81. **(b)** $0.81 - 0.48 = 0.33$. **13.53 (a)** 0.31. **(b)** 0.73; probability of voting Republican increases as income increases. **13.55 (a)** As family income increases, people are more likely to vote Republican. As number of years of education increases, people are more likely to vote Republican. Men are more likely to vote Republican than are women. **(b) (i)** $\hat{p} = 0.47$; **(ii)** $\hat{p} = 0.42$. **13.57 (a)** White. **(b)** Black defendants who had white victims.

13.59 (a) The plots that pertain to selling price as a response variable are those across the top row. The highly discrete nature of x_2 and x_3 limits the number of values these variables can take on. This is reflected in the plots, particularly the plot for bedrooms by baths. **(b)** From software: Pred Price $= 39001 + 53.21$ House Size $- 7885$ Bedrooms $+ 57796$ Bath. When number of bedrooms and number of bathrooms are fixed, an increase of one in size of home leads to an increase of 53.2 in predicted selling price. **(c)** $R^2 = 0.603$; this indicates that predictions are about 60% better when using the prediction equation instead of using the sample mean $\bar{y}$ to predict y. **(d)** The multiple correlation, 0.77, is the square root of R^2. It is the correlation between the observed y values and the predicted $\hat{y}$ values. **(e) (i)** Assumptions: multiple regression equation holds, data gathered randomly, normal distribution for y with same standard deviation at each combination of predictors; **(ii)** Hypotheses: H_0: $\beta_1 = \beta_2 = \beta_3 = 0$; H_a: At least one β parameter differs from 0; **(iii)** Test statistic: $F = 99.14$; **(iv)** P-value: for df (3,196); 0.000; **(v)** Conclusion: If the null hypothesis were true, the probability would be close to 0 of getting a test statistic at least as extreme as the value observed. We have very strong evidence that at least one explanatory variable has an effect on y; **(f)** The t statistic is -1.29 with a one-sided P-value of $0.200/2 = 0.100$. If the null hypothesis were true, the probability would be 0.100 of getting a test statistic at least as extreme as the value observed. At a significance level of 0.05, we cannot reject the null. It is plausible that the number of bedrooms does not have an effect on selling price. This is likely not significant because it is correlated with the other explanatory variables in this model. It might be associated with selling price on its own, but might not provide additional predictive information over and above the other explanatory variables. **(g)** This histogram describes the shape of the conditional distribution of y at given values of the explanatory variables. It suggests that the distribution may be slightly skewed to the right. **(h)** This plot depicts the size of the residuals for the different house sizes observed in this sample. It indicates possibly greater residual variability (and hence, greater variability in selling price) as house size increases. **13.61 (a)** $Difference = -5.00 + 0.934$ Hits $- 1.61$ Errors; for each increase of one hit, the predicted difference increases by 0.93, and for each increase of one error, the predicted difference decreases by 1.61. **(b)** Six. **13.63** Slope with x_3 in the model: effect of poverty when controlling for percentage of single-parent families, as well as percent living in urban areas; slope without x_3 in the model: effect of poverty when controlling only for percent living in urban areas. **13.65 (a)** $F = 61791/1119 = 55.2$; P-value: 0.000; if the null hypothesis were true, the probability would be close to 0 of getting a test statistic at least as extreme as the value observed. We have very strong evidence that at least one of these explanatory variables predicts y better than the sample mean does. **(b)** The significance test would not be relevant if we were not interested in nations beyond those in the study; if this were the case, the group of nations that we studied would be a population and not a sample. **13.67** Since the effect of education on income changes depending on gender, the explanatory variables, education and gender, are said to interact. **13.69 (a)** Negative; if an individual used AZT, the probability of developing symptoms was lower. **b)** Black/yes:$\hat{p}$ $= 0.14$; black/no:$\hat{p} = 0.26$ **(c) (1)** Assumptions: The data were generated randomly. The response variable is binary. **(2)** Hypotheses: H_0: $\beta_1 = 0$; H_a: $\beta_1 \neq 0$; **(3)** Test statistic: -2.58 **(4)** P-value: 0.010 **(5)** Conclusion: The P-value of 0.010 gives sufficient evidence against the null hypothesis that $\beta_1 = 0$. We can reject H_0. **13.71** The reports can include information such as regression equation: college_GPA $= 2.83 + 0.203$ high_sch_GPA $- 0.0092$ sports. **13.73** The two-paragraph summary report will be different for each student. It should indicate that two of the noncategorical explanatory variables—years of experience and merit rating—are both positively associated with salary. The rankings of a nontenure track instructor is negatively associated with salary. In addition, the influence of the increased factors have a greater affect on increasing salary. One other noncategorical explanatory variable of market influence is negatively associated indicating that OSU salaries are better than comparable salaries at other institutions. For the categorical variables, predicted salary is higher among those with a full professor ranking and in the business discipline; professors in nontenure track positions are also negatively associated with salary. **13.75** (d). **13.77 (a)** False; the multiple correlation is at least as large as the ordinary correlations. **(b)** False; it falls between 0 and 1. **(c)** False; R^2 describes how well you can predict y using a set of explanatory variables together in a multiple regression model. **(d)**True. **13.79 (a)** True; the slope for this variable is positive in the bivariate equation. **(b)** False; such a change occurs only when we ignore x_2. **(c)** True; the slope for x_2 is 0.003 when controlling for x_1. 0.003. multiplied by 100 is 0.30. **13.81** y = math achievement score, x_1 = height, x_2 =age for a sample of children from all the different grades in a school system. **13.83** When there are many explanatory variables, doing the F test first provides protection from doing lots of t tests and having one of them be significant merely by random variation when, in fact, there truly are no effects in the

population. **13.85** When $x = 0$, you likely can't afford a home no matter what. Similarly, when $x = 50,000$, you likely can afford a home no matter what. But at $x = 500$ the extra income may have an effect on whether you feel you can afford a home. This suggests an S-shaped curve for the relationship and thus a logistic regression model. **13.87** When you add a predictor, if it has no effect its coefficient is 0. Then the prediction equation is exactly the same as with the simpler model without that variable and R will be exactly the same as before. If having a nonzero coefficient results in better predictions overall, then R will increase. **13.89** Answer is scatterplot showing two lines with positive slopes, the one for Florida falling below the one for Louisiana. The points for Florida should scatter about its line but tend to have higher age values than the points for Louisiana. **13.91 (a)** When $p = 0.5$, $p(1 - p) = 0.5(1 - 0.5) = 0.25$; 0.25 multiplied by β is the same as $\beta/4$. **(b)** $0.1(1 - 0.1) = 0.09; 0.3(1 - 0.3) = 0.21;$ $0.7(1 - 0.7) = 0.21; 0.9(1 - 0.9) = 0.09$; as p gets closer and closer to 1, the slope approaches 0. (Student's answer will include a sketched curve.) **13.93** The responses will be different for each class.

Chapter 14

14.1 (a) Response variable: performance gap; factor: which hotel the guest stayed in; categories: five hotels. **(b)** H_0: $\mu_1 = \mu_2 = \mu_3 = \mu_4 = \mu_5$; H_a: at least two of the population means are unequal. **(c)** $df_1 = g-1 = 5-1 = 4$; $df_2 = N-g = 125-5 = 120$. **(d)** From a table or software, $F = 2.45$. **14.3 (a) (i)** Assumptions: Independent random samples, normal population distributions with equal standard deviations; **(ii)** Hypotheses: H_0: $\mu_1 = \mu_2 = \mu_3$; H_a: at least two population means are unequal; **(iii)** Test statistic: $F = 2.50$ $(df_1 = 2, df_2 = 5)$; **(iv)** P-value = 0.18; **(v)** Conclusion: It is plausible that H_0 is true. **(b)** The sample sizes are very small. **(c)** Observational; a lurking variable might be school GPA. Perhaps higher GPA students are more likely to have previously studied a language and higher GPA students also tend to do better on quizzes than other students. **14.5 (a)** H_0: $\mu_1 = \mu_2 = \mu_3$; μ_1 represents the population mean satisfaction rating for San Jose, μ_2 for Toronto, and μ_3 for Bangalore. **(b)** 27.6 = 13.00/0.47; $df_1 = 2$ and $f_2 = 297$. **(c)** Very small P-value of 0.000 gives strong evidence against the null; we would reject the null and conclude at least two population means differ. **14.7 (a)** μ_1 represents the population mean ideal number of kids for Protestant; μ_2 represents the population mean for Catholic; μ_3 for Jewish; μ_4 for those of Another Religion; H_0: $\mu_1 = \mu_2 = \mu_3 = \mu_4$. **(b)** Independent random samples; normal population distributions with equal standard deviations. **(c)** $F = 5.48$; P-value = 0.001. Very strong evidence that at least two of the population means differ. **(d)** No; ANOVA tests only whether at least two population means are different.

14.9 (a)

Variable	gender	N	Mean	StDev
sports	f	31	4.129	3.640
	m	29	6.310	3.828

(b) Hypotheses: H_0:$\mu_1 = \mu_2$; H_a: $\mu_1 \neq \mu_2$. $F = 5.12$; P-value = 0.027. Strong evidence that the population means differ. **(c)** The t statistic would be the square root of the F statistic, and the P-values would be identical.

14.11 (a)

Level	N	Mean	StDev
famchange	17	7.265	7.157
cogchange	29	3.007	7.309
conchange	26	−0.450	7.989

The means of these groups are somewhat different. The standard deviations are similar. **(b)** $F = 5.42$; P-value = 0.006; strong evidence that at least two population means are different. **(c)** The assumptions are that there are independent random samples and normal population distributions with equal standard deviations. There is evidence of skew, but the test is robust with respect to this assumption. The subjects were randomly assigned to treatments. Note that since this was not a random sample of subjects suffering from anorexia, the scope of inference to the population may be limited. **14.13** $(\bar{y}_1 - \bar{y}_2)$

$$t_{0.25}\, s\sqrt{\frac{1}{n_1} + \frac{1}{n_2}} = (4.55 - 5.12) \pm 1.960(1.140)\sqrt{\frac{1}{1959} + \frac{1}{341}} = -0.57 \pm$$

0.13; which is $(-0.70, - 0.44)$. Because 0 does not fall in this confidence interval, we can infer at the 95% confidence level that the population means are different (higher for the not important group than for the very important group). **14.15 (a)** Classical music and Muzak. **(b)** Because the Tukey method uses an overall confidence level of 95% for the entire set of intervals. **14.17 (a)** $x_1 = 1$ for observations from the first group and $=0$ otherwise; $x_2 = 1$ for observations from the second group and $= 0$ otherwise. **(b)** H_0: $\mu_1 = \mu_2 = \mu_3$; H_0: $\beta_1 = \beta_2 = 0$. **(c)** The intercept estimate is the mean for the third group, which is 12. The first estimated regression coefficient is the difference between the means for the first and third groups, or $18 - 12 = 6$, and the second is the difference between the means for the second and third groups, or $15 - 12 = 3$. **14.19 (a)** $x_1 = 1$ for observations from San Jose and $= 0$ otherwise; $x_2 = 1$ for observations from Toronto and $= 0$ otherwise. **(b)** 7.1 is the sample mean for Bangalore, 0.5 is the difference between the sample means for San Jose and Bangalore, and 0.7 is the difference between the sample means for Toronto and Bangalore. **14.21 (a)** Group 2 – Group 1: $(-8.7, 2.7)$, Group 3 – Group 1: $(-3.1, 7.1)$ Group 3 – Group 2: $(-0.7, 10.7)$ Because 0 falls in all three confidence intervals, we cannot infer that any of the pairs of population means are different. **(b)** Note: Statistical software such as MINITAB is needed to complete this solution. Group 2 – Group 1: $(-10.3, 4.3)$ Group 3 – Group 1: $(-4.5, 8.5)$, Group 3 – Group 2: $(-2.3, 12.3)$. Again, we cannot infer that any of the pairs of population means are different. The intervals are wider because we are now using a 95% confidence level for the overall set of intervals.

14.23 (a)

	Lipitor	Zocor
Low	10	10
High	20	20

(b)

	Lipitor	Zocor
Low	10	20
High	10	20

(c)

	Lipitor	Zocor
Low	10	20
High	20	30

(d)

	Lipitor	Zocor
Low	10	10
High	10	10

14.25 (a) $F = 81021/10095 = 8.03$. **(b)** The small P-value of 0.000 provides strong evidence that the population mean house selling price depends on the age of the house. If the null hypothesis were true, the probability would be 0.000 of getting a test statistic at least as extreme as the value observed. **14.27 (a)** H_0: Population mean holding time is equal for the three types of messages, for each fixed level of repeat time. **(b)** $F = 74.60/10.52 = 7.09$; the small P-value of 0.011 provides strong evidence that the population mean holding time depends on the type of message. **(c)** Population distribution for each group is normal, the population standard deviations are identical, and the data result from a random sample or randomized experiment. **14.29 (a)** H_0: no interaction; $F = 0.67$; P-value $= 0.535$. **(b)** Large P-value; it is plausible that there is no interaction. This lends validity to the previous analyses that assumed a lack of interaction. **14.31 (a)** The means for women of each race are almost the same, whereas the mean for white males is about 0.6 higher than the mean for black males. **(b)** The gender effect was such that women had the higher mean for blacks but men had the higher mean for whites. Overall, ignoring race, the means may be quite similar for men and for women, and the one-way ANOVA for testing the gender effect may not be significant. **(c)** From a two-way ANOVA, we learn that the effect of gender differs based on race (as described previously), but we do not learn this from the one-way ANOVA. **14.33 (a)** $F = 13.90$; P-value $=0.000$; very strong evidence that the mean weight gain depends on the protein level. **(b)** H_0: no interaction; $F = 2.75$; P-value: 0.07, so we cannot reject the null hypothesis. No interaction is plausible. **(c)** $(7.7, 33.9)$. **14.35 (a)** Population means, μ_1 for married, μ_2 for widowed, μ_3 for divorced,

μ_4 for separated, and μ_5 for never married. H_0: $\mu_1 = \mu_2 = \mu_3 = \mu_4 = \mu_5$. H_a: at least two of the population means are different. **(b)** No; large values of F contradict the null, and when the null is true the expected value of the F statistic is approximately 1. **(c)** The null hypothesis is plausible. **14.37 (a)** $F = 215.26/6.76 = 31.84$; this test statistic has a P-value far smaller than 0.05; we can reject the null hypothesis. **(b)** The mean differences between blacks and whites and between blacks and other we can conclude are statistically significant; it appears that blacks watch more hours of TV per day than either whites or those in the category other. **(c)**

$$(4.38 - 2.76) \pm (1.962)(2.6)\sqrt{\frac{1}{188} + \frac{1}{1014}} = 1.62 \pm 0.4051 = (1.22, 2.03).$$

(d) Wider; it uses a 95% confidence level for the overall set of intervals.

14.39 (a) $3.182(2.00)\sqrt{\frac{1}{2} + \frac{1}{2}} = 6.4$. **(b)** The confidence interval formed using the Tukey 95% multiple comparison uses a 95% confidence level for the overall set of intervals. **(c)** Let $x_1 = 1$ for Bumper A and 0 otherwise, $x_2 = 1$ for Bumper B and 0 otherwise, and $x_1 = x_2 = 0$ for Bumper C. **(d)** 13 is the estimated mean damage cost for Bumper C, -11 is the difference between the estimated mean damage costs between Bumpers A and C, and -10 is the difference between the estimated mean damage costs between Bumpers B and C. **14.41 (a)** From software: 16.2. **(b)** All intervals contain 0; therefore, no pair is significantly different. **14.43 (a)** Software gives the following 95% confidence intervals: control and cog: $(-7.5, 0.6)$, family and cog: $(-8.8, 0.3)$, family and control: $(-12.4, -3.0)$. Only the interval for family and control does not include 0. We can infer that the population mean weight change is greater among those who receive family therapy than among those in the control group. **(b)** Software gives the following Tukey 95% multiple comparison confidence intervals: Difference between control and cognitive: $(-8.3, 1.4)$. Difference between family and cognitive: $(-9.8, 1.3)$. Difference between family and control: $(-13.3, -2.1)$. The interpretations are the same as for the intervals in part a. The intervals are wider because the 95% confidence level is for the entire set of intervals rather than for each interval separately. **14.45 (a)** Let $x_1 = 1$ for having a garage and 0 otherwise. From software: House price in thousands $= 247 + 26.3x_1$. The intercept, 247, is the estimated mean selling price (in thousands) when a house does not have a garage, and 26.3 (in thousands) is the difference in the estimated mean selling price between a house with and without a garage. **(b)** From software:

```
Predictor   Coef    SE Coef   T       P
Garage      26.28   19.27     1.36    0.174
```

If the null hypothesis were true, the probability would be 0.174 of getting a test statistic at least as extreme as the value observed. We do not have sufficient evidence that the population mean house selling price is significantly higher with a garage than without a garage. **(c)** From software:

```
Analysis of Variance
Source          DF    SS        MS      F     P
Regression      1     24830     24830   1.86  0.174
Residual Error  198   2644040   13354
Total           199   2668870
```

As with the regression model, the P-value is 0.174; this is the same result. **(d)** The value of t in part b is the square root of the value of F in part c. **14.47 (a)** The coefficient of f (0.04) is the difference between the estimated population means for men and women for each level of race. The fact that it is close to 0 indicates that there is a small estimated difference between the population means for men and women, given race. **(b)** Black female: 2.83, white female: 2.46; black male: 2.79; white male: 2.42. **(c)** From the P-value of 0.000 for race, we can conclude that on the average blacks report a higher ideal number of children than whites do (by 0.37). **14.49 (a)** The mean estimate for men is 0.19 lower than the mean estimate for women at each fixed level of religion. **(b)** The mean estimate for Protestants is 0.67 higher than the mean estimate for other religions at each fixed level of gender. **(c)** $\mu_y = \alpha + \beta_1 g + \beta_2 r_1 + \beta_3 r_2 + \beta_4 r_3$; for the response variable to be independent of religion, for each gender, β_2, β_3, and β_4 would need to equal 0. **14.51** This suggests an interaction since smoking status has a different impact at different levels of age. There is a bigger mean difference between smokers and non-smokers among older women than among younger women. **14.53 (a)** The coefficient for gender, −13 (thousands of dollars), indicates that at fixed levels of race, men have higher estimated mean salaries than women. Women salaries are reduced by 13 (thousands of dollars). **(b) (i)** 109.2 (calculation: 96.2 + 13); **(ii)** 56.2 (calculation: 96.2 − 40). **14.55** The short report will be different for each student, but can include and interpret the F test statistic of 0.81 and the P-value of 0.52 for number of friends and degree of education. **14.57** Means 10, 17, 24 for A, B, C. **14.59 (a)**

	Female	Male
Humanities	65,000	64,000
Science	72,000	71,000

The overall mean for women is [25(65,000) + 5(72,000)]/30 = 66,167. The overall mean for men is [20(64,000) + 30(71,000)]/50 = 68,200. **(b)** A one-way comparison of mean income by gender would reveal that men have a higher mean income than women do. A two-way comparison

of mean incomes by gender, however, would show that at fixed levels of university divisions, women have the higher mean. **14.61** (c). **14.63** (c). **14.65 (a)** Identical sample means. **(b)** No variability (standard deviation of 0) within each sample. **14.67 (a)** f: 1.88 ± 2.46(0.7471), which is (0.04, 3.7), m: 1.96 ± 2.46(0.7471), which is (0.1, 3.8). **(b)** 0.05/35 = 0.0014. **14.69 (a) (i)** number of bathrooms would be treated as a categorical variable; **(ii)** number of bathrooms would be a treated as a quantitative variable and we'd be assuming a linear trend. **(b)** The straight-line regression approach would allow us to know whether increasing numbers of bathrooms led to an increasing mean house selling price. The ANOVA would only let us know that the mean house price was different at each of the three categories. Moreover, we could not use the ANOVA as a prediction tool for other numbers of bathrooms. **(c)** Mean selling price $150,000 for one bathroom, $100,000 for two bathrooms, $200,000 for three bathrooms. (There is not an increasing or decreasing overall trend.) **14.71** The short reports will be different for each class.

The following is taken from
Stats: Data and Models
Third Edition
by Richard D. De Veaux, Paul F. Velleman,
and David E. Bock

Experiments and Observational Studies

Where are we going?

Experiments are the "Gold Standard" of data collection. No drug comes to market without at least one FDA-approved experiment to demonstrate its safety and effectiveness. Much of what we know in science and social science comes from carefully designed experiments.

The Four Principles of Experimental Design (Control what you can, Randomize for the rest, Replicate the trials, and, when appropriate, Block to remove identifiable variation) describe what makes a sound experiment and how to understand the results.

Who gets good grades? And, more important, why? Is there something schools and parents could do to help weaker students improve their grades? Some people think they have an answer: music! No, not your iPod, but an instrument. In a study conducted at Mission Viejo High School, in California, researchers compared the scholastic performance of music students with that of non-music students. Guess what? The music students had a much higher overall grade point average than the non-music students, 3.59 to 2.91. Not only that: A whopping 16% of the music students had all A's compared with only 5% of the non-music students.

As a result of this study and others, many parent groups and educators pressed for expanded music programs in the nation's schools. They argued that the work ethic, discipline, and feeling of accomplishment fostered by learning to play an instrument also enhance a person's ability to succeed in school. They thought that involving more students in music would raise academic performance. What do you think? Does this study provide solid evidence? Or are there other possible explanations for the difference in grades? Is there any way to really prove such a conjecture?

Observational Studies

This research tried to show an association between music education and grades. But it wasn't a survey. Nor did it assign students to get music education. Instead, it simply observed students "in the wild," recording the choices they made and the outcome. Such studies are called **observational studies**. In observational studies, researchers don't *assign* choices; they simply observe them.

In addition, this was a **retrospective study**, because researchers first identified subjects who studied music and then collected data on their past grades.

What's wrong with concluding that music education causes good grades? One high school during one academic year may not be representative of the whole United States. That's true, but the real problem is that the claim that music study *caused* higher grades depends on there being *no other differences* between the groups that could account for the differences in grades, and studying music was not the *only* difference between the two groups of students.

We can think of lots of lurking variables that might cause the groups to perform differently. Students who study music may have better work habits to start with, and this makes them successful in both music and course work. Music students may have more parental support (someone had to pay for all those lessons), and that support may have enhanced their academic performance, too. Maybe they came from wealthier homes and had other advantages. Or it could be that smarter kids just like to play musical instruments.

Observational studies are valuable for discovering trends and possible relationships. They are used widely in public health and marketing. Observational studies that try to discover variables related to rare outcomes, such as specific diseases, are often retrospective. They first identify people with the disease and then look into their history and heritage in search of things that may be related to their condition. But retrospective studies have a restricted view of the world because they are usually restricted to a small part of the entire population. And because retrospective records are based on historical data, they can have errors. (Do you recall *exactly* what you ate even yesterday? How about last Wednesday?)

A somewhat better approach is to observe individuals over time, recording the variables of interest and ultimately seeing how things turn out. For example, we might start by selecting young students who have not begun music lessons. We could then track their academic performance over several years, comparing those who later choose to study music with those who do not. Identifying subjects in advance and collecting data as events unfold would make this a **prospective study**.

Although an observational study may identify important variables related to the outcome we are interested in, there is no guarantee that we have found the right or the most important related variables. Students who choose to study an instrument might still differ from the others in some important way that we failed to observe. It may be this difference—whether we know what it is or not—rather than music itself that leads to better grades. It's just not possible for observational studies, whether prospective or retrospective, to demonstrate a causal relationship.

> For rare illnesses, it's not practical to draw a large enough sample to see many ill respondents, so the only option remaining is to develop retrospective data. For example, researchers can interview those who have become ill. The likely causes of both Legionnaires' disease and HIV were initially identified from such retrospective studies of the small populations who were initially infected. But to confirm the causes, researchers needed laboratory-based experiments.

//// FOR EXAMPLE   Designing an Observational Study

In early 2007, a larger-than-usual number of cats and dogs developed kidney failure; many died. Initially, researchers didn't know why, so they used an observational study to investigate.

QUESTION: Suppose you were called on to plan a study seeking the cause of this problem. Would your design be retrospective or prospective? Explain why.

I would use a retrospective observational study. Even though the incidence of disease was higher than usual, it was still rare. Surveying all pets would have been impractical. Instead, it makes sense to locate some who were sick and ask about their diets, exposure to toxins, and other possible causes.

Randomized, Comparative Experiments

Is it *ever* possible to get convincing evidence of a cause-and-effect relationship? Well, yes it is, but we would have to take a different approach. We could take a group of third graders, randomly assign half to take music lessons, and forbid the other half to do so. Then we could compare their grades several years later. This kind of study design is called an **experiment**.

An experiment requires a **random assignment** of subjects to treatments. Only an experiment can justify a claim like "Music lessons cause higher grades." Questions such as "Does taking vitamin C reduce the chance of getting a cold?" and "Does working with computers improve performance in Statistics class?" and "Is this drug a safe and effective treatment for that disease?" require a designed experiment to establish cause and effect.

Experiments study the relationship between two or more variables. An experimenter must identify at least one explanatory variable, called a **factor**, to manipulate and at least one **response variable** to measure. What distinguishes an experiment from other types of investigation is that the experimenter actively and deliberately manipulates the factors to control the details of the possible treatments, and assigns the subjects to those treatments *at random*. The experimenter then observes the response variable and *compares* responses for different groups of subjects who have been treated differently. For example, we might design an experiment to see whether the amount of sleep and exercise you get affects your performance.

The individuals on whom or which we experiment are known by a variety of terms. Humans who are experimented on are commonly called **subjects** or **participants**. Other individuals (rats, days, petri dishes of bacteria) are commonly referred to by the more generic term **experimental unit**. When we recruit subjects for our sleep deprivation experiment by advertising in Statistics class, we'll probably have better luck if we invite them to be participants than if we advertise that we need experimental units.

The specific values that the experimenter chooses for a factor are called the **levels** of the factor. We might assign our participants to sleep for 4, 6, or 8 hours. Often there are several factors at a variety of levels. (Our subjects will also be assigned to a treadmill for 0 or 30 minutes.) The combination of specific levels from all the factors that an experimental unit receives is known as its **treatment**. (Our subjects could have any one of six different treatments—three sleep levels, each at two exercise levels.)

How should we assign our participants to these treatments? Some students prefer 4 hours of sleep, while others need 8. Some exercise regularly; others are couch potatoes. Should we let the students choose the treatments they'd prefer? No. That would not be a good idea. To have any hope of drawing a fair conclusion, we must assign our participants to their treatments *at random*.

It may be obvious to you that we shouldn't let the students choose the treatment they'd prefer, but the need for random assignment is a lesson that was once hard for some to accept. For example, physicians might naturally prefer to assign patients to the therapy that they think best rather than have a random element such as a coin flip determine the treatment. But we've known for more than a century that for the results of an experiment to be valid, we must use deliberate randomization.

Experimental design was advanced in the 19th century by work in psychophysics by Gustav Fechner (1801-1887), the founder of experimental psychology. Fechner designed ingenious experiments that exhibited many of the features of modern designed experiments. Fechner was careful to control for the effects of factors that might affect his results. For example, in his 1860 book *Elemente der Psychophysik* he cautioned readers to group experiment trials together to minimize the possible effects of time of day and fatigue.

AN EXPERIMENT:

Manipulates the factor levels to create treatments. *Randomly assigns* subjects to these treatment levels. *Compares* the responses of the subject groups across treatment levels.

"He that leaves nothing to chance will do few things ill, but he will do very few things."

—Lord Halifax
(1633-1695)

The Women's Health Initiative is a major 15-year research program funded by the National Institutes of Health to address the most common causes of death, disability, and poor quality of life in older women. It consists of both an observational study with more than 93,000 participants and several randomized comparative experiments. The goals of this study include

(continued)

No drug can be sold in the United States without first showing, in a suitably designed experiment approved by the Food and Drug Administration (FDA), that it's safe and effective. The small print on the booklet that comes with many prescription drugs usually describes the outcomes of that experiment.

▶ giving reliable estimates of the extent to which known risk factors predict heart disease, cancers, and fractures;

▶ identifying "new" risk factors for these and other diseases in women;

▶ comparing risk factors, presence of disease at the start of the study, and new occurrences of disease during the study across all study components; and

▶ creating a future resource to identify biological indicators of disease, especially substances and factors found in blood.

That is, the study seeks to identify possible risk factors and assess how serious they might be. It seeks to build up data that might be checked retrospectively as the women in the study continue to be followed. There would be no way to find out these things with an experiment because the task includes identifying new risk factors. If we don't know those risk factors, we could never control them as factors in an experiment.

By contrast, one of the clinical trials (randomized experiments) that received much press attention randomly assigned postmenopausal women to take either hormone replacement therapy or an inactive pill. The results published in 2002 and 2004 concluded that hormone replacement with estrogen carried increased risks of stroke.

FOR EXAMPLE   Determining the Treatments and Response Variable

RECAP: In 2007, deaths of a large number of pet dogs and cats were ultimately traced to contamination of some brands of pet food. The manufacturer now claims that the food is safe, but before it can be released, it must be tested.

QUESTION: In an experiment to test whether the food is now safe for dogs to eat,[1] what would be the treatments and what would be the response variable?

The treatments would be ordinary-size portions of two dog foods: the new one from the company (the test food) and one that I was certain was safe (perhaps prepared in my kitchen or laboratory). The response would be a veterinarian's assessment of the health of the test animals.

The Four Principles of Experimental Design

A S

Video: **An Industrial Experiment.** Manufacturers often use designed experiments to help them perfect new products. Watch this video about one such experiment.

1. **Control.** We control sources of variation other than the factors we are testing by making conditions as similar as possible for all treatment groups. For human subjects, we try to treat them alike. However, there is always a question of degree and practicality. Controlling extraneous sources of variation reduces the variability of the responses, making it easier to detect differences among the treatment groups.

   Making generalizations from the experiment to other levels of the controlled factor can be risky. For example, suppose we test two laundry detergents and carefully control the water temperature at 180°F. This would reduce the variation in our results due to water temperature, but what could we say about the detergents' performance in cold water? Not much. It would be hard to justify extrapolating the results to other temperatures.

   Although we control both experimental factors and other sources of variation, we think of them very differently. We control a factor by assigning subjects to different factor levels because we want to see how the

---

[1] It may disturb you (as it does us) to think of deliberately putting dogs at risk in this experiment, but in fact that is what is done. The risk is borne by a small number of dogs so that the far larger population of dogs can be kept safe.

The deep insight that experiments should use random assignment is quite an old one. It can be attributed to the American philosopher and scientist C. S. Peirce in his experiments with J. Jastrow, published in 1885.

A S *Activity:* **The Three Rules of Experimental Design.** Watch an animated discussion of three rules of design.

A S *Activity:* **Perform an Experiment.** How well can you read pie charts and bar charts? Find out as you serve as the subject in your own experiment.

response will change at those different levels. We control other sources of variation to *prevent* them from changing and affecting the response variable.

2. **Randomize.** As in sample surveys, **randomization** allows us to equalize the effects of unknown or uncontrollable sources of variation. It does not eliminate the effects of these sources, but it should spread them out across the treatment levels so that we can see past them. If experimental units were not assigned to treatments at random, we would not be able to use the powerful methods of Statistics to draw conclusions from an experiment. Assigning subjects to treatments at random reduces bias due to uncontrolled sources of variation. Randomization protects us even from effects we didn't know about. There's an adage that says "control what you can, and randomize the rest."

3. **Replicate.** Two kinds of replication show up in comparative experiments. First, we should apply each treatment to a number of subjects. Only with such replication can we estimate the variability of responses. If we have not assessed the variation, the experiment is not complete. The outcome of an experiment on a single subject is an anecdote, not data.

A second kind of replication shows up when the experimental units are not a representative sample from the population of interest. We may believe that what is true of the students in Psych 101 who volunteered for the sleep experiment is true of all humans, but we'll feel more confident if our results for the experiment are *replicated* in another part of the country, with people of different ages, and at different times of the year. **Replication** of an entire experiment with the controlled sources of variation at different levels is an essential step in science.

4. **Block.** The ability of randomizing to equalize variation across treatment groups works best in the long run. For example, if we're allocating players to two 6-player soccer teams from a pool of 12 children, we might do so at random to equalize the talent. But what if there were two 12-year-olds and ten 6-year-olds in the group? Randomizing may place both 12-year-olds on the same team. In the long run, if we did this over and over, it would all equalize. But wouldn't it be better to assign one 12-year-old to each group (at random) and five 6-year-olds to each team (at random)? By doing this, we would improve fairness in the short run. This approach makes the division more fair by recognizing the variation in *age* and allocating the players at random *within* each age level. When we do this, we call the variable *age* a **blocking variable.** The levels of *age* are called blocks.

Sometimes, attributes of the experimental units that we are not studying and that we can't control may nevertheless affect the outcomes of an experiment. If we group similar individuals together and then randomize within each of these **blocks,** we can remove much of the variability due to the difference among the blocks. Blocking is an important compromise between randomization and control. However, unlike the first three principles, blocking is not *required* in an experimental design.

FOR EXAMPLE   Control, Randomize, and Replicate

RECAP: We're planning an experiment to see whether the new pet food is safe for dogs to eat. We'll feed some animals the new food and others a food known to be safe, comparing their health after a period of time.

QUESTION: In this experiment, how will you implement the principles of control, randomization, and replication?

I'd control the portion sizes eaten by the dogs. To reduce possible variability from factors other than the food, I'd standardize other aspects of their environments—housing the dogs in similar pens and ensuring that each got the same amount of water, exercise, play, and sleep time, for example. I might restrict the experiment to a single breed of dog and to adult dogs to further minimize variation.

To equalize traits, pre-existing conditions, and other unknown influences, I would assign dogs to the two feed treatments randomly.

I would replicate by assigning more than one dog to each treatment to allow for variability among individual dogs. If I had the time and funding, I might replicate the entire experiment using, for example, a different breed of dog.

Diagrams

An experiment is carried out over time with specific actions occurring in a specified order. A diagram of the procedure can help in thinking about experiments.[2]

The diagram emphasizes the random allocation of subjects to treatment groups, the separate treatments applied to these groups, and the ultimate comparison of results. It's best to specify the responses that will be compared. A good way to start comparing results for the treatment groups is with boxplots.

STEP-BY-STEP EXAMPLE   Designing an Experiment

An ad for OptiGro plant fertilizer claims that with this product you will grow "juicier, tastier" tomatoes. You'd like to test this claim, and wonder whether you might be able to get by with half the specified dose. How can you set up an experiment to check out the claim?

Of course, you'll have to get some tomatoes, try growing some plants with the product and some without, and see what happens. But you'll need a clearer plan than that. How should you design your experiment?

---

[2] Diagrams of this sort were introduced by David Moore in his textbooks and are widely used.

A **completely randomized experiment** is the ideal simple design, just as a *simple random sample* is the ideal simple sample—and for many of the same reasons.

Let's work through the design, step by step. We'll design the simplest kind of experiment, a **completely randomized experiment in one factor**. Since this is a *design* for an experiment, most of the steps are part of the *Think* stage. The statements in the right column are the kinds of things you would need to say in *proposing* an experiment. You'd need to include them in the "methods" section of a report once the experiment is run.

Question: How would you design an experiment to test OptiGro fertilizer?

 THINK

Plan State what you want to know.

I want to know whether tomato plants grown with OptiGro yield juicier, tastier tomatoes than plants raised in otherwise similar circumstances but without the fertilizer.

Response Specify the response variable.

I'll evaluate the juiciness and taste of the tomatoes by asking a panel of judges to rate them on a scale from 1 to 7 in juiciness and in taste.

Treatments Specify the factor levels and the treatments.

The factor is fertilizer, specifically OptiGro fertilizer. I'll grow tomatoes at three different factor levels: some with no fertilizer, some with half the specified amount of OptiGro, and some with the full dose of OptiGro. These are the three treatments.

Experimental Units Specify the experimental units.

I'll obtain 24 tomato plants of the same variety from a local garden store.

Experimental Design Observe the principles of design:

Control any sources of variability you know of and can control.

I'll locate the farm plots near each other so that the plants get similar amounts of sun and rain and experience similar temperatures. I will weed the plots equally and otherwise treat the plants alike.

Replicate results by placing more than one plant in each treatment group.

I'll use 8 plants in each treatment group.

Randomly assign experimental units to treatments, to equalize the effects of unknown or uncontrollable sources of variation.

Describe how the randomization will be accomplished.

To randomly divide the plants into three groups, first I'll label the plants with numbers 00–23. I'll look at pairs of digits across a random number table. The first 8 plants identified (ignoring numbers 24–99 and any repeats) will go in Group 1, the next 8 in Group 2, and the remaining plants in Group 3.

Make a Picture A diagram of your design can help you think about it clearly.

Specify any other experiment details. You must give enough details so that another experimenter could exactly replicate your experiment. It's generally better to include details that might seem irrelevant than to leave out matters that could turn out to make a difference.

> I will grow the plants until the tomatoes are mature, as judged by reaching a standard color.
>
> I'll harvest the tomatoes when ripe and store them for evaluation.

Specify how to measure the response.

> I'll set up a numerical scale of juiciness and one of tastiness for the taste testers. Several people will taste slices of tomato and rate them.

SHOW Once you collect the data, you'll need to display them and compare the results for the three treatment groups.

> I will display the results with side-by-side boxplots to compare the three treatment groups.
>
> I will compare the means of the groups.

TELL To answer the initial question, we ask whether the differences we observe in the means of the three groups are meaningful.

Because this is a randomized experiment, we can attribute significant differences to the treatments. To do this properly, we'll need methods from what is called "statistical inference," the subject of the rest of this book.

> If the differences in taste and juiciness among the groups are greater than I would expect by knowing the usual variation among tomatoes, I may be able to conclude that these differences can be attributed to treatment with the fertilizer.

Does the Difference Make a Difference?

If the differences among the treatment groups are big enough, we'll attribute the differences to the treatments, but how can we decide whether the differences are big enough?

Would we expect the group means to be identical? Not really. Even if the treatment made no difference whatever, there would still be some variation. We assigned the tomato plants to treatments at random. But a different random assignment would have led to different results. Even a repeat of the *same* treatment on a different randomly assigned set of plants would lead to a different mean. The real question is whether the differences we observed are about as big as we might get just from the randomization alone, or whether they're bigger than that. If we decide that they're bigger, we'll attribute the differences to the treatments. In that case we say the differences are **statistically significant**.

How will we decide if something is different enough to be considered statistically significant? Later chapters will offer methods to help answer that question, but to get some intuition, think about deciding whether a coin is fair. If we flip a fair coin 100 times, we expect, *on average*, to get 50 heads. Suppose we get 54 heads out of 100. That doesn't seem very surprising. It's well within the bounds of ordinary random fluctuations. What if we'd seen 94 heads? That's clearly outside the bounds. We'd be pretty sure that the coin flips were not random. But what about 74 heads? Is that far enough from 50% to arouse our suspicions? That's the sort of question we need to ask of our experiment results.

In Statistics terminology, 94 heads would be a statistically significant difference from 50, and 54 heads would not. Whether 74 is *statistically significant* or not would depend on the chance of getting 74 heads in 100 flips of a fair coin and on our tolerance for believing that rare events can happen to us.

Back at the tomato patch, we ask whether the differences we see among the treatment groups are the kind of differences we'd expect from randomization. A good way to get a feeling for that is to look at how much our results vary among plants that get the *same* treatment. Boxplots of our results by treatment group can give us a general idea.

For example, Figure 13.1 shows two pairs of boxplots whose centers differ by exactly the same amount. In the upper set, that difference appears to be larger than we'd expect just by chance. Why? Because the variation is quite small *within* treatment groups, so the larger difference *between* the groups is unlikely to be just from the randomization. In the bottom pair, that same difference between the centers looks less impressive. There the variation *within* each group swamps the difference *between* the two medians. We'd say the difference is statistically significant in the upper pair and not statistically significant in the lower pair.

In later chapters we'll see statistical tests that quantify this intuition. For now, the important point is that a difference is statistically significant if we don't believe that it's likely to have occurred only by chance.

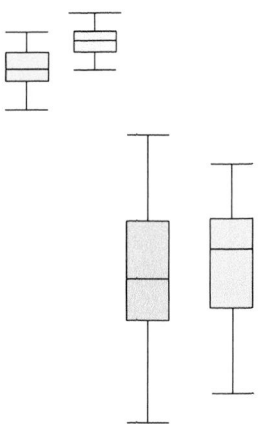

FIGURE 13.1
The boxplots in both pairs have centers the same distance apart, but when the spreads are large, the observed difference may be just from random fluctuation.

JUST CHECKING

1. At one time, a method called "gastric freezing" was used to treat people with peptic ulcers. An inflatable bladder was inserted down the esophagus and into the stomach, and then a cold liquid was pumped into the bladder. Now you can find the following notice on the Internet site of a major insurance company:

[Our company] does not cover gastric freezing (intragastric hypothermia) for chronic peptic ulcer disease. . . .

Gastric freezing for chronic peptic ulcer disease is a non-surgical treatment which was popular about 20 years ago but now is seldom performed. It has been abandoned due to a high complication rate, only temporary improvement experienced by patients, and a lack of effectiveness when tested by double-blind, controlled clinical trials.

What did that "controlled clinical trial" (experiment) probably look like? (Don't worry about "double-blind"; we'll get to that soon.)

a) What was the factor in this experiment?
b) What was the response variable?
c) What were the treatments?

d) How did researchers decide which subjects received which treatment?
e) Were the results statistically significant?

Experiments and Samples

Both experiments and sample surveys use randomization to get unbiased data. But they do so in different ways and for different purposes. Sample surveys try to estimate population parameters, so the sample needs to be as representative of the population as possible. By contrast, experiments try to assess the effects of treatments. Experimental units are not always drawn randomly from the population. For example, a medical experiment may deal only with local patients who have the disease under study. The randomization is in the assignment of their therapy. We want a sample to exhibit the diversity and variability of the population, but for an experiment the more homogeneous the subjects the more easily we'll spot differences in the effects of the treatments.

Unless the experimental units are chosen from the population at random, you should be cautious about generalizing experiment results to larger populations until the experiment has been repeated under different circumstances. Results become more persuasive if they remain the same in completely different settings, such as in a different season, in a different country, or for a different species, to name a few.

Even without choosing experimental units from a population at random, experiments can draw stronger conclusions than surveys. By looking only at the differences across treatment groups, experiments cancel out many sources of bias. For example, the entire pool of subjects may be biased and not representative of the population. (College students may need more sleep, on average, than the general population.) When we assign subjects randomly to treatment groups, all the groups are still biased, but *in the same way*. When we consider the differences in their responses, these biases cancel out, allowing us to see the *differences* due to treatment effects more clearly.

Experiments are rarely performed on random samples from a population. Don't describe the subjects in an experiment as a random sample unless they really are. More likely, the randomization was in assigning subjects to treatments.

Control Treatments

Suppose you wanted to test a $300 piece of software designed to shorten download times. You could just try it on several files and record the download times, but you probably want to *compare* the speed with what would happen *without* the software installed. Such a baseline measurement is called a **control** treatment, and the experimental units to whom it is applied are called a **control group**.

This is a use of the word "control" in an entirely different context. Previously, we controlled extraneous sources of variation by keeping them constant. Here, we use a control treatment as another *level* of the factor in order to compare the treatment results to a situation in which "nothing happens." That's what we did in the tomato experiment when we used no fertilizer on the 8 tomato plants in Group 1.

Blinding

Humans are notoriously susceptible to errors in judgment.[3] All of us. When we know what treatment was assigned, it's difficult not to let that knowledge influence our assessment of the response, even when we try to be careful.

Suppose you were trying to advise your school on which brand of cola to stock in the school's vending machines. You set up an experiment to see which of the three competing brands students prefer (or whether they can tell the difference at all). But people have brand loyalties. You probably prefer one brand already. So if you knew which brand you were tasting, it might influence your rating. To avoid this problem, it would be better to disguise the brands as much as possible. This strategy is called **blinding** the participants to the treatment.[4]

But it isn't just the subjects who should be blind. Experimenters themselves often subconsciously behave in ways that favor what they believe. Even technicians may treat plants or test animals differently if, for example, they

A S   *Activity:* **Control Groups in Experiments.** Is a control group really necessary?

---

[3] For example, here we are in Chapter 13 and you're still reading the footnotes.
[4] C. S. Peirce, in the same 1885 work in which he introduced randomization, also recommended blinding.

Social science experiments can sometimes blind subjects by misleading them about the purpose of a study. One of the authors participated as an undergraduate in a (now infamous) psychology experiment using such a blinding method. The subjects were told that the experiment was about three-dimensional spatial perception and were assigned to draw a horse. While they were drawing, they heard a loud noise and groaning from the next room. The *real* purpose of the experiment was to see whether the social pressure of being in groups made people react to disaster differently. Subjects had been randomly assigned to draw either in groups or alone; that was the treatment. The experimenter was not interested in the drawings, but the subjects were blinded to the treatment because they were misled.

expect them to die. An animal that starts doing a little better than others by showing an increased appetite may get fed a bit more than the experimental protocol specifies.

People are so good at picking up subtle cues about treatments that the best (in fact, the *only*) defense against such biases in experiments on human subjects is to keep *anyone* who could affect the outcome or the measurement of the response from knowing which subjects have been assigned to which treatments. So, not only should your cola-tasting subjects be blinded, but also *you,* as the experimenter, shouldn't know which drink is which, either—at least until you're ready to analyze the results.

There are two main classes of individuals who can affect the outcome of the experiment:

- those who could influence the results (the subjects, treatment administrators, or technicians)
- those who evaluate the results (judges, treating physicians, etc.)

When all the individuals in either one of these classes are blinded, an experiment is said to be **single-blind**. When everyone in *both* classes is blinded, we call the experiment **double-blind**. Even if several individuals in one class are blinded—for example, both the patients and the technicians who administer the treatment—the study would still be just single-blind. If only some of the individuals in a class are blind—for example, if subjects are not told of their treatment, but the administering technician is not blind—there is a substantial risk that subjects can discern their treatment from subtle cues in the technician's behavior or that the technician might inadvertently treat subjects differently. Such experiments cannot be considered truly blind.

In our tomato experiment, we certainly don't want the people judging the taste to know which tomatoes got the fertilizer. That makes the experiment single-blind. We might also not want the people caring for the tomatoes to know which ones were being fertilized, in case they might treat them differently in other ways, too. We can accomplish this double-blinding by having some fake fertilizer for them to put on the other plants. Read on.

FOR EXAMPLE   Blinding

RECAP: In our experiment to see if the new pet food is now safe, we're feeding one group of dogs the new food and another group a food we know to be safe. Our response variable is the health of the animals as assessed by a veterinarian.

QUESTIONS: Should the vet be blinded? Why or why not? How would you do this? (Extra credit: Can this experiment be double-blind? Would that mean that the test animals wouldn't know what they were eating?)

Whenever the response variable involves judgment, it is a good idea to blind the evaluator to the treatments. The veterinarian should not be told which dogs ate which foods.

Extra credit: There is a need for double-blinding. In this case, the workers who care for and feed the animals should not be aware of which dogs are receiving which food. We'll need to make the "safe" food look as much like the "test" food as possible.

A S

Activity: Blinded Experiments. This narrated account of blinding isn't a placebo!

Placebos

Often, simply applying *any* treatment can induce an improvement. Every parent knows the medicinal value of a kiss to make a toddler's scrape or bump stop hurting. Some of the improvement seen with a treatment—even an effective treatment—can be due simply to the act of treating. To separate these two effects, we can use a control treatment that mimics the treatment itself.

The placebo effect is stronger when placebo treatments are administered with authority or by a figure who appears to be an authority. "Doctors" in white coats generate a stronger effect than salespeople in polyester suits. But the placebo effect is not reduced much even when subjects know that the effect exists. People often suspect that they've gotten the placebo if nothing at all happens. So, recently, drug manufacturers have gone so far in making placebos realistic that they cause the same side effects as the drug being tested! Such "active placebos" usually induce a stronger placebo effect. When those side effects include loss of appetite or hair, the practice may raise ethical questions.

A "fake" treatment that looks just like the treatments being tested is called a **placebo**. Placebos are the best way to blind subjects from knowing whether they are receiving the treatment or not. One common version of a placebo in drug testing is a "sugar pill." Especially when psychological attitude can affect the results, control group subjects treated with a placebo may show an improvement.

The fact is that subjects treated with a placebo sometimes improve. It's not unusual for 20% or more of subjects given a placebo to report reduction in pain, improved movement, or greater alertness, or even to demonstrate improved health or performance. This **placebo effect** highlights both the importance of effective blinding and the importance of comparing treatments with a control. Placebo controls are so effective that you should use them as an essential tool for blinding whenever possible.

The best experiments are usually

- randomized.
- comparative.
- double-blind.
- placebo-controlled.

Does ginkgo biloba improve memory? Researchers investigated the purported memory-enhancing effect of ginkgo biloba tree extract (P. R. Solomon, F. Adams, A. Silver, J. Zimmer, R. De Veaux, "Ginkgo for Memory Enhancement. A Randomized Controlled Trial." *JAMA* 288 [2002]: 835-840). In a randomized, comparative, double-blind, placebo-controlled study, they administered treatments to 230 elderly community members. One group received Ginkoba™ according to the manufacturer's instructions. The other received a similar-looking placebo. Thirteen different tests of memory were administered before and after treatment. The placebo group showed greater improvement on 7 of the tests, the treatment group on the other 6. None showed any significant differences. In the margin are boxplots of one measure.

By permission of John L. Hart FLP and Creators Syndicate, Inc.

Blocking

We might want to use 18 tomato plants of the same variety for our experiment, but suppose the garden store had only 12 plants left. So we drove down to the nursery and bought 6 more plants of that variety. We worry that the tomato plants from the two stores are different somehow, and, in fact, they don't really look the same.

How can we design the experiment so that the differences between the stores don't mess up our attempts to see differences among fertilizer levels? We can't measure the effect of a store the same way as we can the fertilizer because we can't assign it as we would a factor in the experiment. You can't tell a tomato plant what store to come from.

Because stores may vary in the care they give plants or in the sources of their seeds, the plants from either store are likely to be more like each other than they are like the plants from the other store. When groups of experimental units are similar, it's often a good idea to gather them together into blocks. By blocking, we isolate the variability attributable to the differences between the blocks, so that we can see the differences caused by the treatments more clearly. Here, we would define the plants from each store to be a block. The randomization is introduced when we randomly assign treatments within each block.

In a completely randomized design, each of the 18 plants would have an equal chance to land in each of the three treatment groups. But we realize that the store may have an effect. To isolate the store effect, we block one store by assigning the plants from each store to treatments at random. So we now have six treatment groups, three for each block. Within each block, we'll randomly assign the same number of plants to each of the three treatments. The experiment is still fair because each treatment is still applied (at random) to the same number of plants and to the same proportion from each store: 4 from store A and 2 from store B. Because the randomization occurs only within the blocks (plants from one store cannot be assigned to treatment groups for the other), we call this a **randomized block design**.

In effect, we conduct two parallel experiments, one for tomato plants from each store, and then combine the results. The picture tells the story:

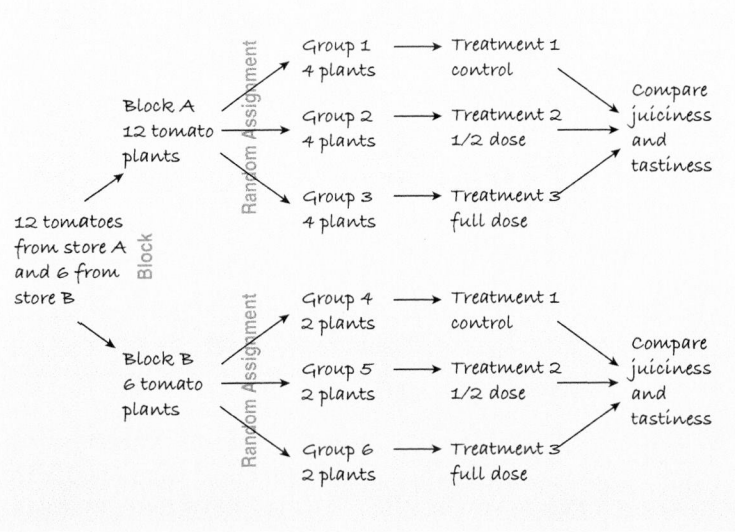

In a retrospective or prospective study, subjects are sometimes paired because they are similar in ways *not* under study. **Matching** subjects in this way can reduce variation in much the same way as blocking. For example, a retrospective study of music education and grades might match each student who studies an instrument with someone of the same sex who is similar in family income but didn't study an instrument. When we compare grades of music students with those of non-music students, the matching would reduce the variation due to income and sex differences.

Blocking is the same idea for experiments as stratifying is for sampling. Both methods group together subjects that are similar and randomize within those groups as a way to remove unwanted variation. (But be careful to keep the terms straight. Don't say that we "stratify" an experiment or "block" a sample.) We use blocks to reduce variability so we can see the effects of the factors; we're not usually interested in studying the effects of the blocks themselves.

FOR EXAMPLE   Blocking

RECAP: In 2007, pet food contamination put cats at risk, as well as dogs. Our experiment should probably test the safety of the new food on both animals.

QUESTIONS: Why shouldn't we randomly assign a mix of cats and dogs to the two treatment groups? What would you recommend instead?

Dogs and cats might respond differently to the foods, and that variability could obscure my results. Blocking by species can remove that superfluous variation. I'd randomize cats to the two treatments (test food and safe food) separately from the dogs. I'd measure their responses separately and look at the results afterward.

2. Recall the experiment about gastric freezing, an old method for treating peptic ulcers that you read about in the first Just Checking. Doctors would insert an inflatable bladder down the patient's esophagus and into the stomach and then pump in a cold liquid. A major insurance company now states that it doesn't cover this treatment because "double-blind, controlled clinical trials" failed to demonstrate that gastric freezing was effective.

a) What does it mean that the experiment was double-blind?

b) Why would you recommend a placebo control?

c) Suppose that researchers suspected that the effectiveness of the gastric freezing treatment might depend on whether a patient had recently developed the peptic ulcer or had been suffering from the condition for a long time. How might the researchers have designed the experiment?

Adding More Factors

There are two kinds of gardeners. Some water frequently, making sure that the plants are never dry. Others let Mother Nature take her course and leave the watering to her. The makers of OptiGro want to ensure that their product will work under a wide variety of watering conditions. Maybe we should include the amount of watering as part of our experiment. Can we study a second factor at the same time and still learn as much about fertilizer?

We now have two factors (fertilizer at three levels and irrigation at two levels). We combine them in all possible ways to yield six treatments:

	No Fertilizer	Half Fertilizer	Full Fertilizer
No Added Water	1	2	3
Daily Watering	4	5	6

THINK LIKE A STATISTICIAN

With two factors, we can account for more of the variation. That lets us see the underlying patterns more clearly.

If we allocate the original 24 plants, 4 plants to each of these six treatments at random. This experiment is a **completely randomized two-factor experiment** because any plant could end up assigned at random to any of the six treatments (and we have two factors).

It's often important to include several factors in the same experiment in order to see what happens when the factor levels are applied in different *combinations*. A common misconception is that applying several factors at once makes it difficult to separate the effects of the individual factors. You may hear

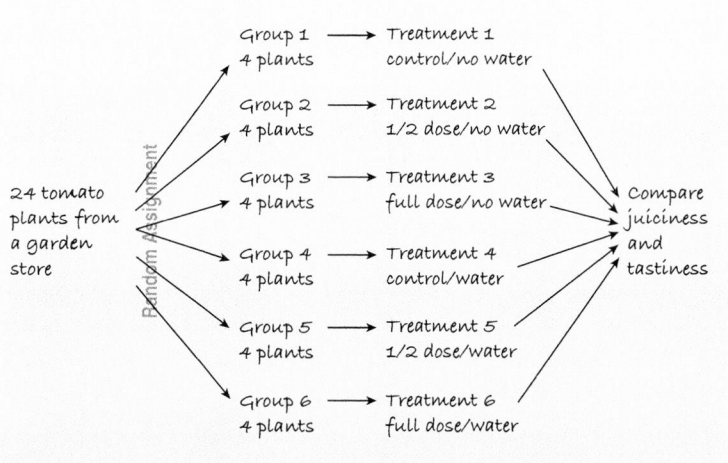

people say that experiments should always be run "one factor at a time." In fact, just the opposite is true: Experiments with more than one factor are both more efficient and provide more information than one-at-a-time experiments. There are many ways to design efficient multifactor experiments. You can take a whole course on the design and analysis of such experiments.

Confounding

Professor Stephen Ceci of Cornell University performed an experiment to investigate the effect of a teacher's classroom style on student evaluations. He taught a class in developmental psychology during two successive terms to a total of 472 students in two very similar classes. He kept everything about his teaching identical (same text, same syllabus, same office hours, etc.) and modified only his style in class. During the fall term, he maintained a subdued demeanor. During the spring term, he used expansive gestures and lectured with more enthusiasm, varying his vocal pitch and using more hand gestures. He administered a standard student evaluation form at the end of each term.

The students in the fall term class rated him only an average teacher. Those in the spring term class rated him an excellent teacher, praising his knowledge and accessibility, and even the quality of the textbook. On the question "How much did you learn in the course?" the average response changed from 2.93 to 4.05 on a 5-point scale.[5]

How much of the difference he observed was due to his difference in manner, and how much might have been due to the season of the year? Fall term in Ithaca, NY (home of Cornell University), starts out colorful and pleasantly warm but ends cold and bleak. Spring term starts out bitter and snowy and ends with blooming flowers and singing birds. Might students' overall happiness have been affected by the season and reflected in their evaluations?

Unfortunately, there's no way to tell. Nothing in the data enables us to tease apart these two effects, because all the students who experienced the subdued manner did so during the fall term and all who experienced the expansive manner did so during the spring. When the levels of one factor are associated with the levels of another factor, we say that these two factors are **confounded**.

In some experiments, such as this one, it's just not possible to avoid some confounding. Professor Ceci could have randomly assigned students to one of two classes during the same term, but then we might question whether

---

[5] But the two classes performed almost identically well on the final exam.

mornings or afternoons were better, or whether he really delivered the same class the second time (after practicing on the first class). Or he could have had another professor deliver the second class, but that would have raised more serious issues about differences in the two professors and concern over more serious confounding.

//// FOR EXAMPLE   Confounding

RECAP: After many dogs and cats suffered health problems caused by contaminated foods, we're trying to find out whether a newly formulated pet food is safe. Our experiment will feed some animals the new food and others a food known to be safe, and a veterinarian will check the response.

QUESTION: Why would it be a bad design to feed the test food to some dogs and the safe food to cats?

This would create confounding. We would not be able to tell whether any differences in animals' health were attributable to the food they had eaten or to differences in how the two species responded.

> **A two-factor example**   Confounding can also arise from a badly designed multifactor experiment. Here's a classic. A credit card bank wanted to test the sensitivity of the market to two factors: the annual fee charged for a card and the annual percentage rate charged. Not wanting to scrimp on sample size, the bank selected 100,000 people at random from a mailing list. It sent out 50,000 offers with a low rate and no fee and 50,000 offers with a higher rate and a $50 annual fee. Guess what happened? That's right—people preferred the low-rate, no-fee card. No surprise. In fact, they signed up for that card at over twice the rate as the other offer. And because of the large sample size, the bank was able to estimate the difference precisely. But the question the bank really wanted to answer was "how much of the change was due to the rate, and how much was due to the fee?" Unfortunately, there's simply no way to separate out the two effects. If the bank had sent out all four possible different treatments—low rate with no fee, low rate with $50 fee, high rate with no fee, and high rate with $50 fee—each to 25,000 people, it could have learned about both factors and could have also seen what happens when the two factors occur in combination.

Lurking or Confounding?

Confounding may remind you of the problem of lurking variables we discussed back in Chapters 7 and 9. Confounding variables and lurking variables are alike in that they interfere with our ability to interpret our analyses simply. Each can mislead us, but there are important differences in both how and where the confusion may arise.

A lurking variable creates an association between two other variables that tempts us to think that one may cause the other. This can happen in a regression analysis or an observational study when a lurking variable influences both the explanatory and response variables. Recall that countries with more TV sets per capita tend to have longer life expectancies. We shouldn't conclude it's the TVs "causing" longer life. We suspect instead that a generally higher standard of living may mean that people can afford more TVs and get better health care, too. Our data revealed an association between TVs and life expectancy, but economic conditions were a likely lurking variable. A lurking variable, then, is usually thought of as a variable associated with both y and x that makes it appear that x may be causing y.

Confounding can arise in experiments when some other variable associated with a factor has an effect on the response variable. However, in a designed experiment, the experimenter *assigns* treatments (at random) to subjects rather than just observing them. A confounding variable can't be thought of as causing that assignment. Professor Ceci's choice of teaching styles was not caused by the weather, but because he used one style in the fall and the other in the spring, he was unable to tell how much of his students' reactions were attributable to his teaching and how much to the weather. A confounding variable, then, is associated in a noncausal way with a factor and affects the response. Because of the confounding, we find that we can't tell whether any effect we see was caused by our factor or by the confounding variable—or even by both working together.

Both confounding and lurking variables are outside influences that make it harder to understand the relationship we are modeling. However, the nature of the causation is different in the two situations. In regression and observational studies, we can only observe associations between variables. Although we can't demonstrate a causal relationship, we often imagine whether x could cause y. We can be misled by a lurking variable that influences both. In a designed experiment, we often hope to show that the factor causes a response. Here we can be misled by a confounding variable that's associated with the factor and causes or contributes to the differences we observe in the response.

It's worth noting that the role of blinding in an experiment is to combat a possible source of confounding. There's a risk that knowledge about the treatments could lead the subjects or those interacting with them to behave differently or could influence judgments made by the people evaluating the responses. That means we won't know whether the treatments really do produce different results or if we're being fooled by these confounding influences.

What Can Go Wrong?

- **Don't give up just because you can't run an experiment.** Sometimes we can't run an experiment because we can't identify or control the factors. Sometimes it would simply be unethical to run the experiment. (Consider randomly assigning students to take—and be graded in—a Statistics course deliberately taught to be boring and difficult or one that had an unlimited budget to use multimedia, real-world examples, and field trips to make the subject more interesting.) If we can't perform an experiment, often an observational study is a good choice.

- **Beware of confounding.** Use randomization whenever possible to ensure that the factors not in your experiment are not confounded with your treatment levels. Be alert to confounding that cannot be avoided, and report it along with your results.

- **Bad things can happen even to good experiments.** Protect yourself by recording additional information. An experiment in which the air conditioning failed for 2 weeks, affecting the results, was saved by recording the temperature (although that was not originally one of the factors) and estimating the effect the higher temperature had on the response.[6]

  It's generally good practice to collect as much information as possible about your experimental units and the circumstances of the experiment. For example, in the tomato experiment, it would be wise to record details of the weather (temperature, rainfall, sunlight) that might affect the plants

---

[6] R. D. DeVeaux and M. Szelewski, "Optimizing Automatic Splitless Injection Parameters for Gas Chromatographic Environmental Analysis." *Journal of Chromatographic Science* 27, no. 9 (1989): 513–518.

and any facts available about their growing situation. (Is one side of the field in shade sooner than the other as the day proceeds? Is one area lower and a bit wetter?) Sometimes we can use this extra information during the analysis to reduce biases.

- **Don't spend your entire budget on the first run.** Just as it's a good idea to pretest a survey, it's always wise to try a small pilot experiment before running the full-scale experiment. You may learn, for example, how to choose factor levels more effectively, about effects you forgot to control, and about unanticipated confoundings.

CONNECTIONS

The fundamental role of randomization in experiments clearly points back to our discussions of randomization, to our experiments with simulations, and to our use of randomization in sampling. The similarities and differences between experiments and samples are important to keep in mind and can make each concept clearer.

If you think that blocking in an experiment resembles stratifying in a sample, you're quite right. Both are ways of removing variation we can identify to help us see past the variation in the data.

Experiments compare groups of subjects that have been treated differently. Graphics such as boxplots that help us compare groups are closely related to these ideas. Think about what we look for in a boxplot to tell whether two groups look really different, and you'll be thinking about the same issues as experiment designers.

Generally, we're going to consider how different the mean responses are for different treatment groups. And we're going to judge whether those differences are large by using standard deviations as rulers. (That's why we needed to replicate results for each treatment; we need to be able to estimate those standard deviations.) The discussion in Chapter 6 introduced this fundamental statistical thought, and it's going to keep coming back over and over again. Statistics is about variation.

We'll see a number of ways to analyze results from experiments in subsequent chapters.

WHAT HAVE WE LEARNED?

We've learned to recognize sample surveys, observational studies, and randomized comparative experiments. We know that these methods collect data in different ways and lead us to different conclusions.

We've learned to identify retrospective and prospective observational studies and understand the advantages and disadvantages of each.

We've learned that only well-designed experiments can allow us to reach cause-and-effect conclusions. We manipulate levels of treatments to see if the factor we have identified produces changes in our response variable.

We've learned the principles of experimental design:

▶ We want to be sure that variation in the response variable can be attributed to our factor, so we identify and control as many other sources of variability as possible.

▶ Because there are many possible sources of variability that we cannot identify, we try to equalize those by randomly assigning experimental units to treatments.

▶ We replicate the experiment on as many subjects as possible.

▶ We consider blocking to reduce variability from sources we recognize but cannot control.

We've learned the value of having a control group and of using blinding and placebo controls.

Finally, we've learned to recognize the problems posed by confounding variables in experiments and lurking variables in observational studies.

Terms

Observational study	A study based on data in which no manipulation of factors has been employed (p. 305).
Retrospective study	An observational study in which subjects are selected and then their previous conditions or behaviors are determined. Retrospective studies need not be based on random samples and they usually focus on estimating differences between groups or associations between variables (p. 306).
Prospective study	An observational study in which subjects are followed to observe future outcomes. Because no treatments are deliberately applied, a prospective study is not an experiment. Nevertheless, prospective studies typically focus on estimating differences among groups that might appear as the groups are followed during the course of the study (p. 306).
Experiment	An experiment *manipulates* factor levels to create treatments, *randomly assigns* subjects to these treatment levels, and then *compares* the responses of the subject groups across treatment levels (p. 307).
Random assignment	To be valid, an experiment must assign experimental units to treatment groups at random (p. 307).
Factor	A variable whose levels are manipulated by the experimenter. Experiments attempt to discover the effects that differences in factor levels may have on the responses of the experimental units (p. 307).
Response	A variable whose values are compared across different treatments. In a randomized experiment, large response differences can be attributed to the effect of differences in treatment level (p. 307).
Subjects or Participants	The individuals who participate in an experiment, especially when they are human. A more general term is experimental unit (p. 307).
Experimental units	Individuals on whom an experiment is performed. Usually called **subjects** or **participants** when they are human (p. 307).
Level	The specific values that the experimenter chooses for a factor are called the levels of the factor (p. 307).
Treatment	The process, intervention, or other controlled circumstance applied to randomly assigned experimental units. Treatments are the different levels of a single factor or are made up of combinations of levels of two or more factors (p. 307).
Principles of experimental design	▶ **Control** aspects of the experiment that we know may have an effect on the response, but that are not the factors being studied (p. 308). ▶ **Randomize** subjects to treatments to even out effects that we cannot control (p. 309). ▶ **Replicate** over as many subjects as possible. Results for a single subject are just anecdotes. If, as often happens, the subjects of the experiment are not a representative sample from the population of interest, replicate the entire study with a different group of subjects, preferably from a different part of the population (p. 309). ▶ **Block** to reduce the effects of identifiable attributes of the subjects that cannot be controlled (p. 309).
Statistically significant	When an observed difference is too large for us to believe that it is likely to have occurred naturally, we consider the difference to be statistically significant. Subsequent chapters will show specific calculations and give rules, but the principle remains the same (p. 312).
Control group	The experimental units assigned to a baseline treatment level, typically either the default treatment, which is well understood, or a null, placebo treatment. Their responses provide a basis for comparison (p. 314).
Blinding	Any individual associated with an experiment who is not aware of how subjects have been allocated to treatment groups is said to be blinded (p. 314).
Single-blind Double-blind	There are two main classes of individuals who can affect the outcome of an experiment: ▶ those who could *influence the results* (the subjects, treatment administrators, or technicians). ▶ those who *evaluate the results* (judges, treating physicians, etc.). When every individual in *either* of these classes is blinded, an experiment is said to be single-blind. When everyone in *both* classes is blinded, we call the experiment double-blind (p. 315).

Placebo	A treatment known to have no effect, administered so that all groups experience the same conditions. Many subjects respond to such a treatment (a response known as a placebo effect). Only by comparing with a placebo can we be sure that the observed effect of a treatment is not due simply to the placebo effect (p. 316).
Placebo effect	The tendency of many human subjects (often 20% or more of experiment subjects) to show a response even when administered a placebo (p. 316).
Blocking	When groups of experimental units are similar, it is often a good idea to gather them together into blocks. By blocking, we isolate the variability attributable to the differences between the blocks so that we can see the differences caused by the treatments more clearly (p. 316).
Matching	In a retrospective or prospective study, subjects who are similar in ways not under study may be matched and then compared with each other on the variables of interest. Matching, like blocking, reduces unwanted variation (p. 317).
Designs	In **a completely randomized design,** all experimental units have an equal chance of receiving any treatment (p. 318). In **a randomized block design,** the randomization occurs only within blocks (p. 317).
Confounding	When the levels of one factor are associated with the levels of another factor in such a way that their effects cannot be separated, we say that these two factors are confounded (p. 319).

Skills

▶ Recognize when an observational study would be appropriate.

▶ Be able to identify observational studies as retrospective or prospective, and understand the strengths and weaknesses of each method.

▶ Know the four basic principles of sound experimental design—control, randomize, replicate, and block—and be able to explain each.

▶ Be able to recognize the factors, the treatments, and the response variable in a description of a designed experiment.

▶ Understand the essential importance of randomization in assigning treatments to experimental units.

▶ Understand the importance of replication to move from anecdotes to general conclusions.

▶ Understand the value of blocking so that variability due to differences in attributes of the subjects can be removed.

▶ Understand the importance of a control group and the need for a placebo treatment in some studies.

▶ Understand the importance of blinding and double-blinding in studies on human subjects, and be able to identify blinding and the need for blinding in experiments.

▶ Understand the value of a placebo in experiments with human participants.

▶ Be able to design a completely randomized experiment to test the effect of a single factor.

▶ Be able to design an experiment in which blocking is used to reduce variation.

▶ Know how to use graphical displays to compare responses for different treatment groups. Understand that you should *never* proceed with any other analysis of a designed experiment without first looking at boxplots or other graphical displays.

▶ Know how to report the results of an observational study. Identify the subjects, how the data were gathered, and any potential biases or flaws you may be aware of. Identify the factors known and those that might have been revealed by the study.

▶ Know how to compare the responses in different treatment groups to assess whether the differences are larger than could be reasonably expected from ordinary sampling variability.

▶ Know how to report the results of an experiment. Tell who the subjects are and how their assignment to treatments was determined. Report how and in what measurement units the response variable was measured.

▶ Understand that your description of an experiment should be sufficient for another researcher to replicate the study with the same methods.

▶ Be able to report on the statistical significance of the result in terms of whether the observed group-to-group differences are larger than could be expected from ordinary sampling variation.

EXPERIMENTS ON THE COMPUTER

Most experiments are analyzed with a statistics package. You should almost always display the results of a comparative experiment with side-by-side boxplots. You may also want to display the means and standard deviations of the treatment groups in a table.

The analyses offered by statistics packages for comparative randomized experiments fall under the general heading of Analysis of Variance, usually abbreviated ANOVA. We'll see this method in Chapters 28 and 29.

EXERCISES

1. **Standardized test scores.** For his Statistics class experiment, researcher J. Gilbert decided to study how parents' income affects children's performance on standardized tests like the SAT. He proposed to collect information from a random sample of test takers and examine the relationship between parental income and SAT score.
   a) Is this an experiment? If not, what kind of study is it?
   b) If there is a relationship between parental income and SAT score, why can't we conclude that differences in score are caused by differences in parental income?

2. **Heart attacks and height.** Researchers who examined health records of thousands of males found that men who died of myocardial infarction (heart attack) tended to be shorter than men who did not.
   a) Is this an experiment? If not, what kind of study is it?
   b) Is it correct to conclude that shorter men are at higher risk for heart attack? Explain.

3. **MS and vitamin D.** Multiple sclerosis (MS) is an autoimmune disease that strikes more often the farther people live from the equator. Could vitamin D—which most people get from the sun's ultraviolet rays—be a factor? Researchers compared vitamin D levels in blood samples from 150 U.S. military personnel who have developed MS with blood samples of nearly 300 who have not. The samples were taken, on average, five years before the disease was diagnosed. Those with the highest blood vitamin D levels had a 62% lower risk of MS than those with the lowest levels. (The link was only in whites, not in blacks or Hispanics.)
   a) What kind of study was this?
   b) Is that an appropriate choice for investigating this problem? Explain.
   c) Who were the subjects?
   d) What were the variables?

4. **Super Bowl commercials.** When spending large amounts to purchase advertising time, companies want to know what audience they'll reach. In January 2007, a poll asked 1008 American adults whether they planned to watch the upcoming Super Bowl. Men and women were asked separately whether they were looking forward more to the football game or to watching the commercials. Among the men, 16% were planning to watch and were looking forward primarily to the commercials. Among women, 30% were looking forward primarily to the commercials.
   a) Was this a stratified sample or a blocked experiment? Explain.
   b) Was the design of the study appropriate for the advertisers' questions?

5. **Menopause.** Researchers studied the herb black cohosh as a treatment for hot flashes caused by menopause. They randomly assigned 351 women aged 45 to 55 who reported at least two hot flashes a day to one of five groups: (1) black cohosh, (2) a multiherb supplement with black cohosh, (3) the multiherb supplement plus advice to consume more soy foods, (4) estrogen replacement therapy, or (5) a placebo. After a year, only the women given estrogen replacement therapy had symptoms different from those of the placebo group. [*Annals of Internal Medicine* 145:12, 869–897]
   a) What kind of study was this?
   b) Is that an appropriate choice for this problem?
   c) Who were the subjects?
   d) Identify the treatment and response variables.

6. **Honesty.** Coffee stations in offices often just ask users to leave money in a tray to pay for their coffee, but many people cheat. Researchers at Newcastle University replaced the picture of flowers on the wall behind the

coffee station with a picture of staring eyes. They found that the average contribution increased significantly above the well-established standard when people felt they were being watched, even though the eyes were patently not real. (New York *Times* 12/10/06)

a) Was this a survey, an observational study, or an experiment? How can we tell?

b) Identify the variables.

c) What does "increased significantly" mean in a statistical sense?

7–20. *What's the design?* *Read each brief report of statistical research, and identify*

a) whether it was an observational study or an experiment.

If it was an observational study, identify (if possible)

b) whether it was retrospective or prospective.

c) the subjects studied and how they were selected.

d) the parameter of interest.

e) the nature and scope of the conclusion the study can reach.

If it was an experiment, identify (if possible)

b) the subjects studied.

c) the factor(s) in the experiment and the number of levels for each.

d) the number of treatments.

e) the response variable measured.

f) the design (completely randomized, blocked, or matched).

g) whether it was blind (or double-blind).

h) the nature and scope of the conclusion the experiment can reach.

7. Over a 4-month period, among 30 people with bipolar disorder, patients who were given a high dose (10 g/day) of omega-3 fats from fish oil improved more than those given a placebo. (*Archives of General Psychiatry* 56 [1999]: 407)

8. Among a group of disabled women aged 65 and older who were tracked for several years, those who had a vitamin B$_{12}$ deficiency were twice as likely to suffer severe depression as those who did not. (*American Journal of Psychiatry* 157 [2000]: 715)

9. In a test of roughly 200 men and women, those with moderately high blood pressure (averaging 164/89 mm Hg) did worse on tests of memory and reaction time than those with normal blood pressure. (*Hypertension* 36 [2000]: 1079)

10. Is diet or exercise effective in combating insomnia? Some believe that cutting out desserts can help alleviate the problem, while others recommend exercise. Forty volunteers suffering from insomnia agreed to participate in a month-long test. Half were randomly assigned to a special no-desserts diet; the others continued desserts as usual. Half of the people in each of these groups were randomly assigned to an exercise program, while the others did not exercise. Those who ate no desserts and engaged in exercise showed the most improvement.

11. After menopause, some women take supplemental estrogen. There is some concern that if these women also drink alcohol, their estrogen levels will rise too high. Twelve volunteers who were receiving supplemental estrogen were randomly divided into two groups, as

were 12 other volunteers not on estrogen. In each case, one group drank an alcoholic beverage, the other a nonalcoholic beverage. An hour later, everyone's estrogen level was checked. Only those on supplemental estrogen who drank alcohol showed a marked increase.

12. Researchers have linked an increase in the incidence of breast cancer in Italy to dioxin released by an industrial accident in 1976. The study identified 981 women who lived near the site of the accident and were under age 40 at the time. Fifteen of the women had developed breast cancer at an unusually young average age of 45. Medical records showed that they had heightened concentrations of dioxin in their blood and that each tenfold increase in dioxin level was associated with a doubling of the risk of breast cancer. (*Science News*, Aug. 3, 2002)

13. In 2002 the journal *Science* reported that a study of women in Finland indicated that having sons shortened the lifespans of mothers by about 34 weeks per son, but that daughters helped to lengthen the mothers' lives. The data came from church records from the period 1640 to 1870.

14. Scientists at a major pharmaceutical firm investigated the effectiveness of an herbal compound to treat the common cold. They exposed each subject to a cold virus, then gave him or her either the herbal compound or a sugar solution known to have no effect on colds. Several days later they assessed the patient's condition, using a cold severity scale ranging from 0 to 5. They found no evidence of benefits associated with the compound.

15. The May 4, 2000, issue of *Science News* reported that, contrary to popular belief, depressed individuals cry no more often in response to sad situations than nondepressed people. Researchers studied 23 men and 48 women with major depression and 9 men and 24 women with no depression. They showed the subjects a sad film about a boy whose father has died, noting whether or not the subjects cried. Women cried more often than men, but there were no significant differences between the depressed and nondepressed groups.

16. Some people who race greyhounds give the dogs large doses of vitamin C in the belief that the dogs will run faster. Investigators at the University of Florida tried three different diets in random order on each of five racing greyhounds. They were surprised to find that when the dogs ate high amounts of vitamin C they ran more slowly. (*Science News*, July 20, 2002)

17. Some people claim they can get relief from migraine headache pain by drinking a large glass of ice water. Researchers plan to enlist several people who suffer from migraines in a test. When a participant experiences a migraine headache, he or she will take a pill that may be a standard pain reliever or a placebo. Half of each group will also drink ice water. Participants will then report the level of pain relief they experience.

18. A dog food company wants to compare a new lower-calorie food with their standard dog food to see if it's effective in helping inactive dogs maintain a healthy weight. They have found several dog owners willing to participate in the trial. The dogs have been classified as small, medium, or large breeds, and the company will

supply some owners of each size of dog with one of the two foods. The owners have agreed not to feed their dogs anything else for a period of 6 months, after which the dogs' weights will be checked.

19. Athletes who had suffered hamstring injuries were randomly assigned to one of two exercise programs. Those who engaged in static stretching returned to sports activity in a mean of 15.2 days faster than those assigned to a program of agility and trunk stabilization exercises. (*Journal of Orthopaedic & Sports Physical Therapy* 34 [March 2004]: **3**)

20. Pew Research compared respondents to an ordinary 5-day telephone survey with respondents to a 4-month-long rigorous survey designed to generate the highest possible response rate. They were especially interested in identifying any variables for which those who responded to the ordinary survey were different from those who could be reached only by the rigorous survey.

21. **Omega-3.** Exercise 7 describes an experiment that showed that high doses of omega-3 fats might be of benefit to people with bipolar disorder. The experiment involved a control group of subjects who received a placebo. Why didn't the experimenters just give everyone the omega-3 fats to see if they improved?

22. **Insomnia.** Exercise 10 describes an experiment showing that exercise helped people sleep better. The experiment involved other groups of subjects who didn't exercise. Why didn't the experimenters just have everyone exercise and see if their ability to sleep improved?

23. **Omega-3, revisited.** Exercises 7 and 21 describe an experiment investigating a dietary approach to treating bipolar disorder. Researchers randomly assigned 30 subjects to two treatment groups, one group taking a high dose of omega-3 fats and the other a placebo.
    a) Why was it important to randomize in assigning the subjects to the two groups?
    b) What would be the advantages and disadvantages of using 100 subjects instead of 30?

24. **Insomnia, again.** Exercises 10 and 22 describe an experiment investigating the effectiveness of exercise in combating insomnia. Researchers randomly assigned half of the 40 volunteers to an exercise program.
    a) Why was it important to randomize in deciding who would exercise?
    b) What would be the advantages and disadvantages of using 100 subjects instead of 40?

25. **Omega-3, finis.** Exercises 7, 21, and 23 describe an experiment investigating the effectiveness of omega-3 fats in treating bipolar disorder. Suppose some of the 30 subjects were very active people who walked a lot or got vigorous exercise several times a week, while others tended to be more sedentary, working office jobs and watching a lot of TV. Why might researchers choose to block the subjects by activity level before randomly assigning them to the omega-3 and placebo groups?

26. **Insomnia, at last.** Exercises 10, 22, and 24 describe an experiment investigating the effectiveness of exercise in combating insomnia. Suppose some of the 40 subjects had maintained a healthy weight, but others were quite overweight. Why might researchers choose to block the subjects by weight level before randomly assigning some of each group to the exercise program?

27. **Tomatoes.** Describe a strategy to randomly split the 24 tomato plants into the three groups for the chapter's completely randomized single factor test of OptiGro fertilizer.

28. **Tomatoes II.** The chapter also described a completely randomized two-factor experiment testing OptiGro fertilizer in conjunction with two different routines for watering the plants. Describe a strategy to randomly assign the 24 tomato plants to the six treatments.

29. **Shoes.** A running-shoe manufacturer wants to test the effect of its new sprinting shoe on 100-meter dash times. The company sponsors 5 athletes who are running the 100-meter dash in the 2004 Summer Olympic games. To test the shoe, it has all 5 runners run the 100-meter dash with a competitor's shoe and then again with their new shoe. The company uses the difference in times as the response variable.
    a) Suggest some improvements to the design.
    b) Why might the shoe manufacturer not be able to generalize the results they find to all runners?

30. **Swimsuits.** A swimsuit manufacturer wants to test the speed of its newly designed suit. The company designs an experiment by having 6 randomly selected Olympic swimmers swim as fast as they can with their old swimsuit first and then swim the same event again with the new, expensive swimsuit. The company will use the difference in times as the response variable. Criticize the experiment and point out some of the problems with generalizing the results.

31. **Hamstrings.** Exercise 19 discussed an experiment to see if the time it took athletes with hamstring injuries to be able to return to sports was different depending on which of two exercise programs they engaged in.
    a) Explain why it was important to assign the athletes to the two different treatments randomly.
    b) There was no control group consisting of athletes who did not participate in a special exercise program. Explain the advantage of including such a group.
    c) How might blinding have been used?
    d) One group returned to sports activity in a mean of 37.4 days (*SD* = 27.6 days) and the other in a mean of 22.2 days (*SD* = 8.3 days). Do you think this difference is statistically significant? Explain.

32. **Diet and blood pressure.** An experiment showed that subjects fed the DASH diet were able to lower their blood pressure by an average of 6.7 points compared to a group fed a "control diet." All meals were prepared by dieticians.
    a) Why were the subjects randomly assigned to the diets instead of letting people pick what they wanted to eat?
    b) Why were the meals prepared by dieticians?
    c) Why did the researchers need the control group? If the DASH diet group's blood pressure was lower at the end of the experiment than at the beginning, wouldn't that prove the effectiveness of that diet?
    d) What additional information would you want to know in order to decide whether an average reduction in blood pressure of 6.7 points was statistically significant?

33. **Mozart.** Will listening to a Mozart piano sonata make you smarter? In a 1995 study published in the journal *Psychological Science,* Rauscher, Shaw, and Ky reported that when students were given a spatial reasoning section of a standard IQ test, those who listened to Mozart for 10 minutes improved their scores more than those who simply sat quietly.

    a) These researchers said the differences were statistically significant. Explain what that means in context.
    b) Steele, Bass, and Crook tried to replicate the original study. In their study, also published in *Psychological Science* (1999), the subjects were 125 college students who participated in the experiment for course credit. Subjects first took the test. Then they were assigned to one of three groups: listening to a Mozart piano sonata, listening to music by Philip Glass, and sitting for 10 minutes in silence. Three days after the treatments, they were retested. Draw a diagram displaying the design of this experiment.
    c) These boxplots show the differences in score before and after treatment for the three groups. Did the Mozart group show improvement?

    d) Do you think the results prove that listening to Mozart is beneficial? Explain.

34. Contrast bath treatments use the immersion of an injured limb alternately in water of two contrasting temperatures. Those who use the method claim that it can reduce swelling. Researchers compared three treatments: (1) contrast baths and exercise, (2) contrast baths alone, and (3) exercise alone. (R. G. Janssen, D. A. Schwartz, and P.F. Velleman "A Randomized Controlled Study of Contrast Baths on Patients with Carpal Tunnel Syndrome." *Journal of Hand Therapy,* 2009). They report the following boxplots comparing the change in hand volume after treatment:

    a) The researchers conclude that the differences were not statistically significant. Explain what that means in context.
    b) The title says that the study was randomized and controlled. Explain what that probably means for this study.
    c) The study did not use a placebo treatment. What was done instead? Do you think that was an appropriate choice? Explain.

35. **Wine.** A 2001 Danish study published in the *Archives of Internal Medicine* casts significant doubt on suggestions that adults who drink wine have higher levels of "good" cholesterol and fewer heart attacks. These researchers followed a group of individuals born at a Copenhagen hospital between 1959 and 1961 for 40 years. Their study found that in this group the adults who drank wine were richer and better educated than those who did not.

    a) What kind of study was this?
    b) It is generally true that people with high levels of education and high socioeconomic status are healthier than others. How does this call into question the supposed health benefits of wine?
    c) Can studies such as these prove causation (that wine helps prevent heart attacks, that drinking wine makes one richer, that being rich helps prevent heart attacks, etc.)? Explain.

36. **Swimming.** Recently, a group of adults who swim regularly for exercise were evaluated for depression. It turned out that these swimmers were less likely to be depressed than the general population. The researchers said the difference was statistically significant.

    a) What does "statistically significant" mean in this context?
    b) Is this an experiment or an observational study? Explain.
    c) News reports claimed this study proved that swimming can prevent depression. Explain why this conclusion is not justified by the study. Include an example of a possible lurking variable.
    d) But perhaps it is true. We wonder if exercise can ward off depression, and whether anaerobic exercise (like weight training) is as effective as aerobic exercise (like swimming). We find 120 volunteers not currently engaged in a regular program of exercise. Design an appropriate experiment.

37. **Dowsing.** Before drilling for water, many rural homeowners hire a dowser (a person who claims to be able to sense the presence of underground water using a forked stick.) Suppose we wish to set up an experiment to test one dowser's ability. We get 20 identical containers, fill some with water, and ask him to tell which ones they are.

    a) How will we randomize this procedure?
    b) The dowser correctly identifies the contents of 12 out of 20 containers. Do you think this level of success is statistically significant? Explain.
    c) How many correct identifications (out of 20) would the dowser have to make to convince you that the forked-stick trick works? Explain.

38. **Healing.** A medical researcher suspects that giving post-surgical patients large doses of vitamin E will speed their recovery times by helping their incisions heal more quickly. Design an experiment to test this conjecture. Be sure to identify the factors, levels, treatments, response variable, and the role of randomization.

39. **Reading.** Some schools teach reading using phonics (the sounds made by letters) and others using whole language (word recognition). Suppose a school district wants to know which method works better. Suggest a design for an appropriate experiment.

40. **Gas mileage.** Do cars get better gas mileage with premium instead of regular unleaded gasoline? It might be possible to test some engines in a laboratory, but we'd rather use real cars and real drivers in real day-to-day driving, so we get 20 volunteers. Design the experiment.

41. **Weekend deaths.** A study published in the *New England Journal of Medicine* (Aug. 2001) suggests that it's dangerous to enter a hospital on a weekend. During a 10-year period, researchers tracked over 4 million emergency admissions to hospitals in Ontario, Canada. Their findings revealed that patients admitted on weekends had a much higher risk of death than those who went on weekdays.
    a) The researchers said the difference in death rates was "statistically significant." Explain in this context what that means.
    b) What kind of study was this? Explain.
    c) If you think you're quite ill on a Saturday, should you wait until Monday to seek medical help? Explain.
    d) Suggest some possible explanations for this troubling finding.

42. **Shingles.** A research doctor has discovered a new ointment that she believes will be more effective than the current medication in the treatment of shingles (a painful skin rash). Eight patients have volunteered to participate in the initial trials of this ointment. You are the statistician hired as a consultant to help design a completely randomized experiment.
    a) Describe how you will conduct this experiment.
    b) Suppose the eight patients' last names start with the letters A to H. Using the random numbers listed below, show which patients you will assign to each treatment. Explain your randomization procedure clearly.

    41098   18329   78458   31685   55259

    c) Can you make this experiment double-blind? How?
    d) The initial experiment revealed that males and females may respond differently to the ointment. Further testing of the drug's effectiveness is now planned, and many patients have volunteered. What changes in your first design, if any, would you make for this second stage of testing?

43. **Beetles.** Hoping to learn how to control crop damage by a certain species of beetle, a researcher plans to test two different pesticides in small plots of corn. A few days after application of the chemicals, he'll check the number of beetle larvae found on each plant. The researcher wants to know whether either pesticide works and whether there is a significant difference in effectiveness between them. Design an appropriate experiment.

44. **SAT prep.** Can special study courses actually help raise SAT scores? One organization says that the 30 students they tutored achieved an average gain of 60 points when they retook the test.
    a) Explain why this does not necessarily prove that the special course caused the scores to go up.
    b) Propose a design for an experiment that could test the effectiveness of the tutorial course.
    c) Suppose you suspect that the tutorial course might be more helpful for students whose initial scores were particularly low. How would this affect your proposed design?

45. **Safety switch.** An industrial machine requires an emergency shutoff switch that must be designed so that it can be easily operated with either hand. Design an experiment to find out whether workers will be able to deactivate the machine as quickly with their left hands as with their right hands. Be sure to explain the role of randomization in your design.

46. **Washing clothes.** A consumer group wants to test the effectiveness of a new "organic" laundry detergent and make recommendations to customers about how to best use the product. They intentionally get grass stains on 30 white T-shirts in order to see how well the detergent will clean them. They want to try the detergent in cold water and in hot water on both the "regular" and "delicates" wash cycles. Design an appropriate experiment, indicating the number of factors, levels, and treatments. Explain the role of randomization in your experiment.

47. **Skydiving, anyone?** A humor piece published in the *British Medical Journal* ("Parachute use to prevent death and major trauma related to gravitational challenge: Systematic review of randomized control trials," Gordon, Smith, and Pell, *BMJ*, 2003:327) notes that we can't tell for sure whether parachutes are safe and effective because there has never been a properly randomized, double-blind, placebo-controlled study of parachute effectiveness in skydiving. (Yes, this is the sort of thing statisticians find funny. . . .) Suppose you were designing such a study:
    a) What is the factor in this experiment?
    b) What experimental units would you propose?[7]
    c) What would serve as a placebo for this study?
    d) What would the treatments be?
    e) What would the response variable be?
    f) What sources of variability would you control?
    g) How would you randomize this "experiment"?
    h) How would you make the experiment double-blind?

_____
[7] Don't include your Statistics instructor!

ANSWERS

1. **a)** The factor was type of treatment for peptic ulcer.
    b) The response variable could be a measure of relief from gastric ulcer pain or an evaluation by a physician of the state of the disease.
    c) Treatments would be gastric freezing and some alternative control treatment.
    d) Treatments should be assigned randomly.
    e) No. The website reports "lack of effectiveness," indicating that no large differences in patient healing were noted.

2. **a)** Neither the patients who received the treatment nor the doctor who evaluated them afterward knew what treatment they had received.
    b) The placebo is needed to accomplish blinding. The best alternative would be using body-temperature liquid rather than the freezing liquid.
    c) The researchers should block the subjects by the length of time they had had the ulcer, then randomly assign subjects in each block to the freezing and placebo groups.

PART

III

PART REVIEW

Gathering Data

Quick Review

Before you can make a boxplot, calculate a mean, describe a distribution, or fit a line, you must have meaningful data to work with. Getting good data is essential to any investigation. No amount of clever analysis can make up for badly collected data. Here's a brief summary of the key concepts and skills:

▸ The way you gather data depends both on what you want to discover and on what is practical.

▸ To get some insight into what might happen in a real situation, model it with a **simulation** using random numbers.

▸ To answer questions about a target population, collect information from a sample with a **survey** or poll.
  • Choose the sample randomly. Random sampling designs include simple, stratified, systematic, cluster, and multistage.
  • A simple random sample draws without restriction from the entire target population.
  • When there are subgroups within the population that may respond differently, use a stratified sample.
  • Avoid bias, a systematic distortion of the results. Sample designs that allow undercoverage or response bias and designs such as voluntary response or convenience samples don't faithfully represent the population.
  • Samples will naturally vary one from another. This sample-to-sample variation is called sampling error. Each sample only approximates the target population.

▸ **Observational studies** collect information from a sample drawn from a target population.
  • Retrospective studies examine existing data. Prospective studies identify subjects in advance, then follow them to collect data as the data are created, perhaps over many years.
  • Observational studies can spot associations between variables but cannot establish cause and effect. It's impossible to eliminate the possibility of lurking or confounding variables.

▸ To see how different treatments influence a response variable, design an **experiment**.
  • Assign subjects to treatments randomly. If you don't assign treatments randomly, your experiment is not likely to yield valid results.

- Control known sources of variation as much as possible. Reduce variation that cannot be controlled by using blocking, if possible.
- Replicate the experiment, assigning several subjects to each treatment level.
- If possible, replicate the entire experiment with an entirely different collection of subjects.

- A well-designed experiment can provide evidence that changes in the factors cause changes in the response variable.

Now for more opportunities to review these concepts and skills . . .

REVIEW EXERCISES

1–18. *What design? Analyze the design of each research example reported. Is it a sample survey, an observational study, or an experiment? If a sample, what are the population, the parameter of interest, and the sampling procedure? If an observational study, was it retrospective or prospective? If an experiment, describe the factors, treatments, randomization, response variable, and any blocking, matching, or blinding that may be present. In each, what kind of conclusions can be reached?*

1. Researchers identified 242 children in the Cleveland area who had been born prematurely (at about 29 weeks). They examined these children at age 8 and again at age 20, comparing them to another group of 233 children not born prematurely. Their report, published in the *New England Journal of Medicine*, said the "preemies" engaged in significantly less risky behavior than the others. Differences showed up in the use of alcohol and marijuana, conviction of crimes, and teenage pregnancy.

2. The journal *Circulation* reported that among 1900 people who had heart attacks, those who drank an average of 19 cups of tea a week were 44% more likely than nondrinkers to survive at least 3 years after the attack.

3. Researchers at the Purina Pet Institute studied Labrador retrievers for evidence of a relationship between diet and longevity. At 8 weeks of age, 2 puppies of the same sex and weight were randomly assigned to one of two groups—a total of 48 dogs in all. One group was allowed to eat all they wanted, while the other group was fed a diet about 25% lower in calories. The median lifespan of dogs fed the restricted diet was 22 months longer than that of other dogs. (*Science News* 161, no. 19)

4. The radioactive gas radon, found in some homes, poses a health risk to residents. To assess the level of contamination in their area, a county health department wants to test a few homes. If the risk seems high, they will publicize the results to emphasize the need for home testing. Officials plan to use the local property tax list to randomly choose 25 homes from various areas of the county.

5. Almost 90,000 women participated in a 16-year study of the role of the vitamin folate in preventing colon cancer. Some of the women had family histories of colon cancer in close relatives. In this at-risk group, the incidence of colon cancer was cut in half among those who maintained a high folate intake. No such difference was observed in those with no family-based risk. (*Science News*, Feb. 9, 2002)

6. In the journal *Science*, a research team reported that plants in southern England are flowering earlier in the spring. Records of the first flowering dates for 385 species over a period of 47 years indicate that flowering has advanced an average of 15 days per decade, an indication of climate warming, according to the authors.

7. Fireworks manufacturers face a dilemma. They must be sure that the rockets work properly, but test-firing a rocket essentially destroys it. On the other hand, not testing the product leaves open the danger that they sell a bunch of duds, leading to unhappy customers and loss of future sales. The solution, of course, is to test a few of the rockets produced each day, assuming that if those tested work properly, the others are ready for sale.

8. Can makeup damage fetal development? Many cosmetics contain a class of chemicals called phthalates. Studies that exposed some laboratory animals to these chemicals found a heightened incidence of damage to male reproductive systems. Since traces of phthalates are found in the urine of women who use beauty products, there is growing concern that they may present a risk to male fetuses. (*Science News*, July 20, 2002)

9. Can long-term exposure to strong electromagnetic fields cause cancer? Researchers in Italy tracked down 13 years of medical records for people living near Vatican Radio's powerful broadcast antennas. A disproportionate share of the leukemia cases occurred among men and children who lived within 6 kilometers of the antennas. (*Science News*, July 20, 2002)

10. Some doctors have expressed concern that men who have vasectomies seemed more likely to develop prostate cancer. Medical researchers used a national cancer registry to identify 923 men who had had prostate cancer and 1224 men of similar ages who had not. Roughly one quarter of the men in each group had undergone a vasectomy, many more than 25 years before the study. The study's authors concluded that there is strong evidence that having the operation presents no long-term risk for developing prostate cancer. (*Science News*, July 20, 2002)

11. Researchers investigating appetite control as a means of losing weight found that female rats ate less and lost weight after injections of the hormone leptin, while male rats responded better to insulin. (*Science News*, July 20, 2002)

12. An artisan wants to create pottery that has the appearance of age. He prepares several samples of clay with four different glazes and test fires them in a kiln at three different temperature settings.

13. Tests of gene therapy on laboratory rats have raised hopes of stopping the degeneration of tissue that characterizes chronic heart failure. Researchers at the University of California, San Diego, used hamsters with cardiac disease, randomly assigning 30 to receive the gene therapy and leaving the other 28 untreated. Five weeks after treatment the gene therapy group's heart muscles stabilized, while those of the untreated hamsters continued to weaken. (*Science News*, July 27, 2002)

14. Researchers at the University of Bristol (England) investigated reasons why different species of birds begin to sing at different times in the morning. They captured and examined birds of 57 species at seven different sites. They measured the diameter of the birds' eyes and also recorded the time of day at which each species began to sing. These researchers reported a strong relationship between eye diameter and time of singing, saying that birds with bigger eyes tended to sing earlier. (*Science News*, 161, no. 16 [2002])

15. An orange-juice processing plant will accept a shipment of fruit only after several hundred oranges selected from various locations within the truck are carefully inspected. If too many show signs of unsuitability for juice (bruised, rotten, unripe, etc.), the whole truckload is rejected.

16. A soft-drink manufacturer must be sure the bottle caps on the soda are fully sealed and will not come off easily. Inspectors pull a few bottles off the production line at regular intervals and test the caps. If they detect any problems, they will stop the bottling process to adjust or repair the machine that caps the bottles.

17. Physically fit people seem less likely to die of cancer. A report in the May 2002 issue of *Medicine and Science in Sports and Exercise* followed 25,892 men aged 30 to 87 for 10 years. The most physically fit men had a 55% lower risk of death from cancer than the least fit group.

18. Does the use of computer software in Introductory Statistics classes lead to better understanding of the concepts? A professor teaching two sections of Statistics decides to investigate. She teaches both sections using the same lectures and assignments, but gives one class statistics software to help them with their homework. The classes take the same final exam, and graders do not know which students used computers during the semester. The professor is also concerned that students who have had calculus may perform differently from those who have not, so she plans to compare software vs. no-software scores separately for these two groups of students.

19. **Point spread.** When taking bets on sporting events, bookmakers often include a "point spread" that awards the weaker team extra points. In theory this makes the outcome of the bet a toss-up. Suppose a gambler places a $10 bet and picks the winners of five games. If he's right about fewer than three of the games, he loses. If he gets three, four, or all five correct, he's paid $10, $20, and $50,

respectively. Estimate the amount such a bettor might expect to lose over many weeks of gambling.

20. **The lottery.** Many people spend a lot of money trying to win huge jackpots in state lotteries. Let's play a simplified version using only the numbers from 1 to 20. You bet on three numbers. The state picks five winning numbers. If your three are all among the winners, you are rich!
    a) Simulate repeated plays. How long did it take you to win?
    b) In real lotteries, there are many more choices (often 54) and you must match all five winning numbers. Explain how these changes affect your chances of hitting the jackpot.

21. **Everyday randomness.** Aside from casinos, lotteries, and games, there are other situations you encounter in which something is described as "random" in some way. Give three different examples. Describe how randomness is (or is not) achieved in each.

22. **Cell phone risks.** Researchers at the Washington University School of Medicine randomly placed 480 rats into one of three chambers containing radio antennas. One group was exposed to digital cell phone radio waves, the second to analog cell phone waves, and the third group to no radio waves. Two years later the rats were examined for signs of brain tumors. In June 2002 the scientists said that differences among the three groups were not statistically significant.
    a) Is this a study or an experiment? Explain.
    b) Explain in this context what "not statistically significant" means.
    c) Comment on the fact that this research was funded by Motorola, a manufacturer of cell phones.

23. **Tips.** In restaurants, servers rely on tips as a major source of income. Does serving candy after the meal produce larger tips? To find out, two waiters determined randomly whether or not to give candy to 92 dining parties. They recorded the sizes of the tips and reported that guests getting candy tipped an average of 17.8% of the bill, compared with an average tip of only 15.1% from those who got no candy. ("Sweetening the Till: The Use of Candy to Increase Restaurant Tipping." *Journal of Applied Social Psychology* 32, no. 2 [2002]: 300–309)
    a) Was this an experiment or an observational study? Explain.
    b) Is it reasonable to conclude that the candy caused guests to tip more? Explain.
    c) The researchers said the difference was statistically significant. Explain in this context what that means.

24. **Tips, take 2.** In another experiment to see if getting candy after a meal would induce customers to leave a bigger tip, a waitress randomly decided what to do with 80 dining parties. Some parties received no candy, some just one piece, and some two pieces. Others initially got just one piece of candy, and then the waitress suggested that they take another piece. She recorded the tips received, finding that, in general, the more candy, the higher the tip, but the highest tips (23%) came from the parties who got one piece and then were offered more. ("Sweetening the Till: The Use of Candy to Increase

Restaurant Tipping." *Journal of Applied Social Psychology* 32, no. 2 [2002]: 300–309)

a) Diagram this experiment.
b) How many factors are there? How many levels?
c) How many treatments are there?
d) What is the response variable?
e) Did this experiment involve blinding? Double-blinding?
f) In what way might the waitress, perhaps unintentionally, have biased the results?

25. **Cloning.** In September 1998, *USA Weekend* magazine asked, "Should humans be cloned?" Readers were invited to vote "Yes" or "No" by calling one of two different 900 numbers. Based on 38,023 responses, the magazine reported that "9 out of 10 readers oppose cloning."

a) Explain why you think the conclusion is not justified. Describe the types of bias that may be present.
b) Reword the question in a way that you think might create a more positive response.

26. **Laundry.** An experiment to test a new laundry detergent, SparkleKleen, is being conducted by a consumer advocate group. They would like to compare its performance with that of a laboratory standard detergent they have used in previous experiments. They can stain 16 swatches of cloth with 2 tsp of a common staining compound and then use a well-calibrated optical scanner to detect the amount of the stain left after washing. To save time in the experiment, several suggestions have been made. Comment on the possible merits and drawbacks of each one.

a) Since data for the laboratory standard detergent are already available from previous experiments, for this experiment wash all 16 swatches with SparkleKleen, and compare the results with the previous data.
b) Use both detergents with eight separate runs each, but to save time, use only a 10-second wash time with very hot water.
c) To ease bookkeeping, first run all of the standard detergent washes on eight swatches, then run all of the SparkleKleen washes on the other eight swatches.
d) Rather than run the experiment, use data from the company that produced SparkleKleen, and compare them with past data from the standard detergent.

27. **When to stop?** You play a game that involves rolling a die. You can roll as many times as you want, and your score is the total for all the rolls. But . . . if you roll a 6 your score is 0 and your turn is over. What might be a good strategy for a game like this?

a) One of your opponents decides to roll 4 times, then stop (hoping not to get the dreaded 6 before then). Use a simulation to estimate his average score.
b) Another opponent decides to roll until she gets at least 12 points, then stop. Use a simulation to estimate her average score.
c) Propose another strategy that you would use to play this game. Using your strategy, simulate several turns. Do you think you would beat the two opponents?

28. **Rivets.** A company that manufactures rivets believes the shear strength of the rivets they manufacture follows a Normal model with a mean breaking strength of 950 pounds and a standard deviation of 40 pounds.

a) What percentage of rivets selected at random will break when tested under a 900-pound load?
b) You're trying to improve the rivets and want to examine some that fail. Use a simulation to estimate how many rivets you might need to test in order to find three that fail at 900 pounds (or below).

29. **Homecoming.** A college Statistics class conducted a survey concerning community attitudes about the college's large homecoming celebration. That survey drew its sample in the following manner: Telephone numbers were generated at random by selecting one of the local telephone exchanges (first three digits) at random and then generating a random four-digit number to follow the exchange. If a person answered the phone and the call was to a residence, then that person was taken to be the subject for interview. (Undergraduate students and those under voting age were excluded, as was anyone who could not speak English.) Calls were placed until a sample of 200 eligible respondents had been reached.

a) Did every telephone number that could occur in that community have an equal chance of being generated?
b) Did this method of generating telephone numbers result in a simple random sample (SRS) of local residences? Explain.
c) Did this method generate an SRS of local voters? Explain.
d) Is this method unbiased in generating samples of households? Explain.

30. **Youthful appearance.** *Readers' Digest* reported results of several surveys that asked graduate students to examine photographs of men and women and try to guess their ages. Researchers compared these guesses with the number of times the people in the pictures reported having sexual intercourse. It turned out that those who had been more sexually active were judged as looking younger, and that the difference was described as "statistically significant." Psychologist David Weeks, who compiled the research, speculated that lovemaking boosts hormones that "reduce fatty tissue and increase lean muscle, giving a more youthful appearance."

a) What does "statistically significant" mean in this context?
b) Explain in statistical terms why you might be skeptical about Dr. Weeks's conclusion. Propose an alternative explanation for these results.

31. **Smoking and Alzheimer's.** Medical studies indicate that smokers are less likely to develop Alzheimer's disease than people who never smoked.

a) Does this prove that smoking may offer some protection against Alzheimer's? Explain.
b) Offer an alternative explanation for this association.
c) How would you conduct a study to investigate this?

32. **Antacids.** A researcher wants to compare the performance of three types of antacid in volunteers suffering from acid reflux disease. Because men and women may react differently to this medication, the subjects are split into two groups, by sex. Subjects in each group are randomly assigned to take one of the antacids or to take

a sugar pill made to look the same. The subjects will rate their level of discomfort 30 minutes after eating.

a) What kind of design is this?

b) The experiment uses volunteers rather than a random sample of all people suffering from acid reflux disease. Does this make the results invalid? Explain.

c) How may the use of the placebo confound this experiment? Explain.

33. **Sex and violence.** Does the content of a television program affect viewers' memory of the products advertised in commercials? Design an experiment to compare the ability of viewers to recall brand names of items featured in commercials during programs with violent content, sexual content, or neutral content.

34. **Pubs.** In England, a Leeds University researcher said that the local watering hole's welcoming atmosphere helps men get rid of the stresses of modern life and is vital for their psychological well-being. Author of the report, Dr. Colin Gill, said rather than complain, women should encourage men to "pop out for a swift half." "Pub-time allows men to bond with friends and colleagues," he said. "Men need break-out time as much as women and are mentally healthier for it." Gill added that men might feel unfulfilled or empty if they had not been to the pub for a week. The report, commissioned by alcohol-free beer brand Kaliber, surveyed 900 men on their reasons for going to the pub. More than 40% said they went for the conversation, with relaxation and a friendly atmosphere being the other most common reasons. Only 1 in 10 listed alcohol as the overriding reason.

Let's examine this news story from a statistical perspective.

a) What are the W's: *Who, What, When, Where, Why, How?*

b) What population does the researcher think the study applies to?

c) What is the most important thing about the selection process that the article does *not* tell us?

d) How do *you* think the 900 respondents were selected? (Name a method of drawing a sample that is likely to have been used.)

e) Do you think the report that only 10% of respondents listed alcohol as an important reason for going to the pub might be a biased result? Why?

35. **Age and party.** The Gallup Poll conducted a representative telephone survey during the first quarter of 1999. Among its reported results was the following table concerning the preferred political party affiliation of respondents and their ages:

		Party		
		Republican	Democrat	Independent	Total
Age	18–29	241	351	409	1001
	30–49	299	330	370	999
	50–64	282	341	375	998
	65+	279	382	343	1004
	Total	1101	1404	1497	4002

a) What sampling strategy do you think the pollsters used? Explain.

b) What percentage of the people surveyed were Democrats?

c) Do you think this is a good estimate of the percentage of voters in the United States who are registered Democrats? Why or why not?

d) In creating this sample design, what question do you think the pollsters were trying to answer?

36. **Bias?** Political analyst Michael Barone has written that "conservatives are more likely than others to refuse to respond to polls, particularly those polls taken by media outlets that conservatives consider biased" (*The Weekly Standard*, March 10, 1997). The Pew Research Foundation tested this assertion by asking the same questions in a national survey run by standard methods and in a more rigorous survey that was a true SRS with careful follow-up to encourage participation. The response rate in the "standard survey" was 42%. The response rate in the "rigorous survey" was 71%.

a) What kind of bias does Barone claim may exist in polls?

b) What is the population for these surveys?

c) On the question of political position, the Pew researchers report the following table:

	Standard Survey	Rigorous Survey
Conservative	37%	35%
Moderate	40%	41%
Liberal	19%	20%

What makes you think these results are incomplete?

d) The Pew researchers report that differences between opinions expressed on the two surveys were not statistically significant. Explain what "not statistically significant" means in this context.

37. **Save the grapes.** Vineyard owners have problems with birds that like to eat the ripening grapes. Some vineyards use scarecrows to try to keep birds away. Others use netting that covers the plants. Owners really would like to know if either method works and, if so, which one is better. One owner has offered to let you use his vineyard this year for an experiment. Propose a design. Carefully indicate how you would set up the experiment, specifying the factor(s) and response variable.

38. **Bats.** It's generally believed that baseball players can hit the ball farther with aluminum bats than with the traditional wooden ones. Is that true? And, if so, how much farther? Players on your local high school baseball team have agreed to help you find out. Design an appropriate experiment.

39. **Knees.** Research reported in the spring of 2002 cast doubt on the effectiveness of arthroscopic knee surgery for patients with arthritis. Patients suffering from arthritis pain who volunteered to participate in the study were randomly divided into groups. One group received

arthroscopic knee surgery. The other group underwent "placebo surgery" during which incisions were made in their knees, but no surgery was actually performed. Follow-up evaluations over a period of 2 years found that differences in the amount of pain relief experienced by the two groups were not statistically significant. (*NEJM* 347:81–88, July 11, 2002)

a) Why did the researchers feel it was necessary to have some of the patients undergo "placebo surgery"?

b) Because patients had to consent to participate in this experiment, the subjects were essentially self-selected—a kind of voluntary response group. Explain why that does not invalidate the findings of the experiment.

c) What does "statistically significant" mean in this context?

40. NBA draft lottery. Professional basketball teams hold a "draft" each year in which they get to pick the best available college and high school players. In an effort to promote competition, teams with the worst records get to pick first, theoretically allowing them to add better players. To combat the fear that teams with no chance to make the playoffs might try to get better draft picks by intentionally losing late-season games, the NBA's Board of Governors adopted a weighted lottery system in 1990. Under this system, the 11 teams that did not make the playoffs were eligible for the lottery. The NBA prepared 66 cards, each naming one of the teams. The team with the worst win-loss record was named on 11 of the cards, the second-worst team on 10 cards, and so on, with the team having the best record among the nonplayoff clubs getting only one chance at having the first pick. The cards were mixed, then drawn randomly to determine the order in which the teams could draft players. (Since 1995, 13 teams have been involved in the lottery, using a complicated system with 14 numbered Ping-Pong balls drawn in groups of four.) Suppose there are two exceptional players available in this year's draft and your favorite team had the third-worst record. Use a simulation to find out how likely it is that your team gets to pick first or second. Describe your simulation carefully.

41. Security. There are 20 first-class passengers and 120 coach passengers scheduled on a flight. In addition to the usual security screening, 10% of the passengers will be subjected to a more complete search.

a) Describe a sampling strategy to randomly select those to be searched.

b) Here is the first-class passenger list and a set of random digits. Select two passengers to be searched, carefully demonstrating your process.

65436 71127 04879 41516 20451 02227 94769 23593

Bergman	Cox	Fontana	Perl
Bowman	DeLara	Forester	Rabkin
Burkhauser	Delli-Bovi	Frongillo	Roufaiel
Castillo	Dugan	Furnas	Swafford
Clancy	Febo	LePage	Testut

c) Explain how you would use a random number table to select the coach passengers to be searched.

42. Profiling? Among the 20 first-class passengers on the flight described in Exercise 41, there were four businessmen from the Middle East. Two of them were the two passengers selected to be searched. They complained of profiling, but the airline claims that the selection was random. What do you think? Support your conclusion with a simulation.

43. Par 4. In theory, a golfer playing a par-4 hole tees off, hitting the ball in the fairway, then hits an approach shot onto the green. The first putt (usually long) probably won't go in, but the second putt (usually much shorter) should. Sounds simple enough, but how many strokes might it really take? Use a simulation to estimate a pretty good golfer's score based on these assumptions:

• The tee shot hits the fairway 70% of the time.
• A first approach shot lands on the green 80% of the time from the fairway, but only 40% of the time otherwise.
• Subsequent approach shots land on the green 90% of the time.
• The first putt goes in 20% of the time, and subsequent putts go in 90% of the time.

44. The back nine. Use simulations to estimate more golf scores, similar to the procedure in Exercise 43.

a) On a par 3, the golfer hopes the tee shot lands on the green. Assume that the tee shot behaves like the first approach shot described in Exercise 43.

b) On a par 5, the second shot will reach the green 10% of the time and hit the fairway 60% of the time. If it does not hit the green, the golfer must play an approach shot as described in Exercise 43.

c) Create a list of assumptions that describe your golfing ability, and then simulate your score on a few holes. Explain your simulation clearly.

APPENDIX A

Answers

Chapter 13

1. a) No. There are no manipulated factors. Observational study.
   b) There may be lurking variables that are associated with both parental income and performance on the SAT.

3. a) This is a retrospective observational study.
   b) That's appropriate because MS is a relatively rare disease.
   c) The subjects were U.S. military personnel, some of whom had developed MS.
   d) The variables were the vitamin D blood levels and whether or not the subject developed MS.

5. a) This was a randomized, placebo-controlled experiment.
   b) Yes, such an experiment is the right way to determine whether black cohosh has an effect.
   c) 351 women aged 45 to 55 who reported at least two hot flashes a day.
   d) The treatments were black cohosh, a multiherb supplement, a multiherb supplement plus advice, estrogen, and a placebo. The response was the women's symptoms (presumably frequency of hot flashes).

7. a) Experiment.
   b) Bipolar disorder patients.
   c) Omega-3 fats from fish oil, two levels.
   d) 2 treatments.
   e) Improvement (fewer symptoms?).
   f) Design not specified.
   g) Blind (due to placebo), unknown if double-blind.
   h) Individuals with bipolar disease improve with high-dose omega-3 fats from fish oil.

9. a) Observational study.
   b) Prospective.
   c) Men and women with moderately high blood pressure and normal blood pressure, unknown selection process.
   d) Memory and reaction time.
   e) As there is no random assignment, there is no way to know that high blood pressure *caused* subjects to do worse on memory and reaction-time tests. A lurking variable may also be the cause.

11. a) Experiment.
    b) Postmenopausal women.
    c) Alcohol—2 levels; blocking variable—estrogen supplements (2 levels).
    d) 1 factor (alcohol) at 2 levels = 2 treatments.
    e) Increase in estrogen levels.
    f) Blocked.
    g) Not blind.
    h) Indicates that alcohol consumption *for those taking estrogen supplements* may increase estrogen levels.

13. a) Observational study.
    b) Retrospective.
    c) Women in Finland, unknown selection process with data from church records.
    d) Women's lifespans.
    e) As there is no random assignment, there is no way to know that having sons or daughters shortens or lengthens the life span of mothers.

15. a) Observational study.
    b) Prospective.
    c) People with or without depression, unknown selection process.
    d) Frequency of crying in response to sad situations.
    e) There is no apparent difference in crying response (to sad movies) for depressed and nondepressed groups.

17. a) Experiment.
    b) People experiencing migraines.
    c) 2 factors (pain reliever and water temperature), 2 levels each.
    d) 4 treatments.
    e) Level of pain relief.
    f) Completely randomized over 2 factors.
    g) Blind, as subjects did not know if they received the pain medication or the placebo, but not blind, as the subjects will know if they are drinking regular or ice water.
    h) It may indicate whether pain reliever alone or in combination with ice water gives pain relief, but patients are not blinded to ice water, so placebo effect may also be the cause of any relief seen caused by ice water.

19. a) Experiment.
    b) Athletes with hamstring injuries.

c) 1 factor: type of exercise program (2 levels).
d) 2 treatments.
e) Time to return to sports.
f) Completely randomized.
g) No blinding—subjects must know what kind of exercise they do.
h) Can determine which of the two exercise programs is more effective.

21. They need to compare omega-3 results to something. Perhaps bipolarity is seasonal and would have improved during the experiment anyway.

23. a) Subjects' responses might be related to many other factors (diet, exercise, genetics, etc). Randomization should equalize the two groups with respect to unknown factors.
b) More subjects would minimize the impact of individual variability in the responses, but the experiment would become more costly and time consuming.

25. People who engage in regular exercise might differ from others with respect to bipolar disorder, and that additional variability could obscure the effectiveness of this treatment.

27. Answers may vary. Use a random-number generator to randomly select 24 numbers from 01 to 24 without replication. Assign the first 8 numbers to the first group, the second 8 numbers to the second group, and the third 8 numbers to the third group.

29. a) First, they are using athletes who have a vested interest in the success of the shoe by virtue of their sponsorship. They should choose other athletes. Second, they should randomize the order of the runs, not run all the races with their shoes second. They should blind the athletes by disguising the shoes if possible, so they don't know which is which. The timers shouldn't know which athletes are running with which shoes, either. Finally, they should replicate several times, since times will vary under both shoe conditions.
b) Because of the problems in part a, the results they obtain may favor their shoes. In addition, the results obtained for Olympic athletes may not be the same as for the general runner.

31. a) Allowing athletes to self-select treatments could confound the results. Other issues such as severity of injury, diet, age, etc., could also affect time to heal; randomization should equalize the treatment groups with respect to any such variables.
b) A control group could have revealed whether either exercise program was better (or worse) than just letting the injury heal.
c) Doctors who evaluated the athletes to approve their return to sports should not know which treatment the subject had.
d) It's hard to tell. The difference of 15 days seems large, but the standard deviations indicate that there was a great deal of variability in the times.

33. a) The differences among the Mozart and quiet groups were more than would have been expected from sampling variation.

b)
Pretest → Music by Glass → Post-test
Pretest → Mozart Piano sonata → Post-test
Pretest → Silence → Post-test
c) The Mozart group seems to have the smallest median difference and thus the *least* improvement, but there does not appear to be a significant difference.
d) No, if anything, there is less improvement, but the difference does not seem significant compared with the usual variation.

35. a) Observational, prospective study.
b) The supposed relation between health and wine consumption might be explained by the confounding variables of income and education.
c) None of these. While the variables have a relation, there is no causality indicated for the relation.

37. a) Arrange the 20 containers in 20 separate locations. Use a random-number generator to identify the 10 containers that should be filled with water.
b) Guessing, the dowser should be correct about 50% of the time. A record of 60% (12 out of 20) does not appear to be significantly different.
c) Answers may vary. You would need to see a high level of success—say, 90% to 100%, that is, 18 to 20 correct.

39. Randomly assign half the reading teachers in the district to use each method. Students should be randomly assigned to teachers as well. Make sure to block both by school and grade (or control grade by using only one grade). Construct an appropriate reading test to be used at the end of the year, and compare scores.

41. a) They mean that the difference is higher than they would expect from normal sampling variability.
b) An observational study.
c) No. Perhaps the differences are attributable to some confounding variable (e.g., people are more likely to engage in riskier behaviors on the weekend) rather than the day of admission.
d) Perhaps people have more serious accidents and traumas on weekends and are thus more likely to die as a result.

43. Answers may vary. This experiment has 1 factor (pesticide), at 3 levels (pesticide A, pesticide B, no pesticide), resulting in 3 treatments. The response variable is the number of beetle larvae found on each plant. Randomly select a third of the plots to be sprayed with pesticide A, a third with pesticide B, and a third with no pesticide (since the researcher also wants to know whether the pesticides even work at all). To control the experiment, the plots of land should be as similar as possible with regard to amount of sunlight, water, proximity to other plants, etc. If not, plots with similar characteristics should be blocked together. If possible, use some inert substance as a placebo pesticide on the control group, and do not tell the counters of the beetle larvae which plants have been treated with pesticides. After a given period of

time, count the number of beetle larvae on each plant and compare the results.

45. Answers may vary. Find a group of volunteers. Each volunteer will be required to shut off the machine with his or her left hand and right hand. Randomly assign the left or right hand to be used first. Complete the first attempt for the whole group. Now repeat the experiment with the alternate hand. Check the differences in time for the left and right hands.

47. a) Jumping with or without a parachute.
    b) Volunteer skydivers (the dimwitted ones).
    c) A parachute that looks real but doesn't work.
    d) A good parachute and a placebo parachute.
    e) Whether parachutist survives the jump (or extent of injuries).
    f) All should jump from the same altitude in similar weather conditions and land on similar surfaces.
    g) Randomly assign people the parachutes.
    h) The skydivers (and the people involved in distributing the parachute packs) shouldn't know who got a working chute. And the people evaluating the subjects after the jumps should not be told who had a real parachute either!

Part III Review

1. Observational prospective study. Indications of behavior differences can be seen in the two groups. May show a link between premature birth and behavior, but there may be lurking variables involved.

3. Experiment, matched by gender and weight, randomization within blocks of two pups of same gender and weight. Factor: type of diet. Treatments: low-calorie diet and allowing the dog to eat all it wants. Response variable: length of life. Can conclude that, on average, dogs with a lower-calorie diet live longer.

5. Observational prospective study. Indicates folate *may* help in reducing colon cancer for those with family histories of the disease.

7. Sampling. Probably a simple random sample, although may be stratified by type of firework. Population is all fireworks produced each day. Parameter is proportion of duds. Can determine if the day's production is ready for sale.

9. Observational retrospective study. Living near strong electromagnetic fields may be associated with more leukemia than normal. May be lurking variables, such as socioeconomic level.

11. Experiment. Blocked by sex of rat. Randomization is not specified. Factor is type of hormone given. Treatments are leptin and insulin. Response variable is lost weight. Can conclude that hormones can help suppress appetites in rats, and the type of hormone varies by gender.

13. Experiment. Factor is gene therapy. Hamsters were randomized to treatments. Treatments were gene therapy or not.

Response variable is heart muscle condition. Can conclude that gene therapy is beneficial (at least in hamsters).

15. Sampling. Population is all oranges on the truck. Parameter is proportion of unsuitable oranges. Procedure is probably simple random sampling. Can conclude whether or not to accept the truckload.

17. Observational prospective study. Physically fit men may have a lower risk of death from cancer.

19. Answers will vary. This is a simulation problem. Using a random digits table or software, call 0–4 a loss and 5–9 a win for the gambler on a game. Use blocks of 5 digits to simulate a week's pick.

21. Answers will vary.

23. a) Experiment. Actively manipulated candy giving, diners were randomly assigned treatments, control group was those with no candy, lots of dining parties.
    b) It depends on when the decision was made. If early in the meal, the server may give better treatment to those who will receive candy—biasing the results.
    c) A difference in response so large it cannot be attributed to natural sampling variability.

25. a) Voluntary response. Only those who feel strongly will pay for the 900 phone call.
    b) "If it would help future generations live a longer, healthier life, would you be in favor of human cloning?"

27. a) Simulation results will vary. Average will be around 5.8 points.
    b) Simulation results will vary. Average will also be around 5.8 points.
    c) Answers will vary.

29. a) Yes.
    b) No. Residences without phones are excluded. Residences with more than one phone number had a higher chance.
    c) No. People who respond to the survey may be of age but not registered voters.
    d) No. Households who answered the phone may be more likely to have someone at home when the phone call was generated. These may not be representative of all households.

31. a) Does not prove it. There may be other confounding variables. Only way to prove this would be to do a controlled experiment.
    b) Alzheimer's usually shows up late in life. Perhaps smokers have died of other causes before Alzheimer's is evident.
    c) An experiment would be unethical. One could design a prospective study in which groups of smokers and nonsmokers are followed for many years and the incidence of Alzheimer's is tracked.

33.

Numerous subjects will be randomly assigned to see shows with violent, sexual, or neutral content. They will see the same commercials. After the show, they will be interviewed for their recall of brand names in the commercials.

35. a) May have been a simple random sample, but given the relative equality in age groups, may have been stratified.
    b) 35.1%.
    c) We don't know. Perhaps cell phones or unlisted numbers were excluded, and Democrats have more (or fewer) of those. Probably OK, though.
    d) Do party affiliations differ for different age groups?

37. The factor in the experiment will be type of bird control. I will have three treatments: scarecrow, netting, and no control. I will randomly assign several different areas in the vineyard to one of the treatments, taking care that there is sufficient separation that the possible effect of the scarecrow will not be confounded. At the end of the season, the response variable will be the proportion of bird-damaged grapes.

39. a) We want all subjects treated as alike as possible. If there were no "placebo surgery," subjects would know this and perhaps behave differently.
    b) The experiment looked for a difference in the effectiveness of the two treatments. (If we wanted to generalize, we would need to assume that the results for these volunteers are the same as on all patients who might need this operation.)
    c) "Not statistically significant" means the difference in results were small enough that it could be explained by natural sampling variability.

41. a) Use stratified sampling to select 2 first-class passengers and 12 from coach.
    b) Number passengers alphabetically, 01 = Bergman to 20 = Testut. Read in blocks of two, ignoring any numbers more than 20. This gives 65, 43, 67, 11 (selects Fontana), 27, 04 (selects Castillo).
    c) Number passengers alphabetically from 001 to 120. Use the random-number table to find three-digit numbers in this range until 12 different values have been selected.

43. Simulation results will vary. (Use integers 00 to 99 as a basis. Use integers 00 to 69 to represent a tee shot on the fairway. If on the fairway, use digits 00 to 79 to represent on the green. If off the fairway, use 00 to 39 to represent getting on the green. If not on the green, use digits 00 to 89 to represent landing on the green. For the first putt, use digits 00 to 19 to represent making the shot. For subsequent putts, use digits 00 to 89 to represent making the shot.)

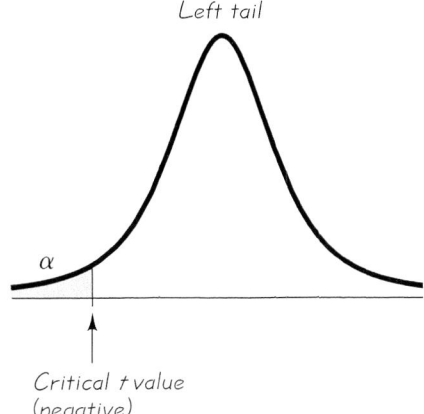

Left tail

α

Critical t value
(negative)

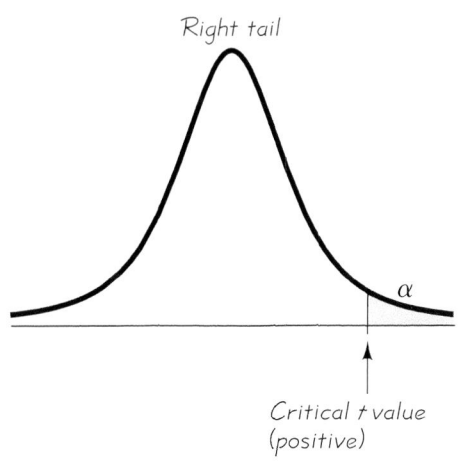

Right tail

α

Critical t value
(positive)

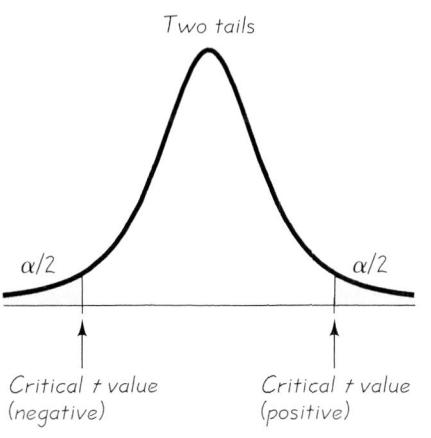

Two tails

α/2   α/2

Critical t value   Critical t value
(negative)   (positive)

Table A-3 *t* Distribution: Critical *t* Values

Degrees of Freedom	Area in One Tail				
	0.005	0.01	0.025	0.05	0.10
	Area in Two Tails				
	0.01	0.02	0.05	0.10	0.20
1	63.657	31.821	12.706	6.314	3.078
2	9.925	6.965	4.303	2.920	1.886
3	5.841	4.541	3.182	2.353	1.638
4	4.604	3.747	2.776	2.132	1.533
5	4.032	3.365	2.571	2.015	1.476
6	3.707	3.143	2.447	1.943	1.440
7	3.499	2.998	2.365	1.895	1.415
8	3.355	2.896	2.306	1.860	1.397
9	3.250	2.821	2.262	1.833	1.383
10	3.169	2.764	2.228	1.812	1.372
11	3.106	2.718	2.201	1.796	1.363
12	3.055	2.681	2.179	1.782	1.356
13	3.012	2.650	2.160	1.771	1.350
14	2.977	2.624	2.145	1.761	1.345
15	2.947	2.602	2.131	1.753	1.341
16	2.921	2.583	2.120	1.746	1.337
17	2.898	2.567	2.110	1.740	1.333
18	2.878	2.552	2.101	1.734	1.330
19	2.861	2.539	2.093	1.729	1.328
20	2.845	2.528	2.086	1.725	1.325
21	2.831	2.518	2.080	1.721	1.323
22	2.819	2.508	2.074	1.717	1.321
23	2.807	2.500	2.069	1.714	1.319
24	2.797	2.492	2.064	1.711	1.318
25	2.787	2.485	2.060	1.708	1.316
26	2.779	2.479	2.056	1.706	1.315
27	2.771	2.473	2.052	1.703	1.314
28	2.763	2.467	2.048	1.701	1.313
29	2.756	2.462	2.045	1.699	1.311
30	2.750	2.457	2.042	1.697	1.310
31	2.744	2.453	2.040	1.696	1.309
32	2.738	2.449	2.037	1.694	1.309
33	2.733	2.445	2.035	1.692	1.308
34	2.728	2.441	2.032	1.691	1.307
35	2.724	2.438	2.030	1.690	1.306
36	2.719	2.434	2.028	1.688	1.306
37	2.715	2.431	2.026	1.687	1.305
38	2.712	2.429	2.024	1.686	1.304
39	2.708	2.426	2.023	1.685	1.304
40	2.704	2.423	2.021	1.684	1.303
45	2.690	2.412	2.014	1.679	1.301
50	2.678	2.403	2.009	1.676	1.299
60	2.660	2.390	2.000	1.671	1.296
70	2.648	2.381	1.994	1.667	1.294
80	2.639	2.374	1.990	1.664	1.292
90	2.632	2.368	1.987	1.662	1.291
100	2.626	2.364	1.984	1.660	1.290
200	2.601	2.345	1.972	1.653	1.286
300	2.592	2.339	1.968	1.650	1.284
400	2.588	2.336	1.966	1.649	1.284
500	2.586	2.334	1.965	1.648	1.283
1000	2.581	2.330	1.962	1.646	1.282
2000	2.578	2.328	1.961	1.646	1.282
Large	2.576	2.326	1.960	1.645	1.282

NEGATIVE z Scores

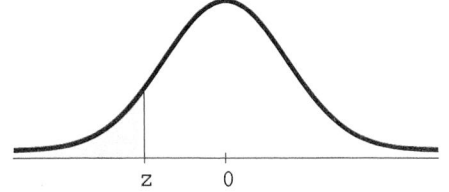

z   0

Table A-2 Standard Normal (*z*) Distribution: Cumulative Area from the LEFT

z	.00	.01	.02	.03	.04	.05	.06	.07	.08	.09
−3.50 and lower	.0001									
−3.4	.0003	.0003	.0003	.0003	.0003	.0003	.0003	.0003	.0003	.0002
−3.3	.0005	.0005	.0005	.0004	.0004	.0004	.0004	.0004	.0004	.0003
−3.2	.0007	.0007	.0006	.0006	.0006	.0006	.0006	.0005	.0005	.0005
−3.1	.0010	.0009	.0009	.0009	.0008	.0008	.0008	.0008	.0007	.0007
−3.0	.0013	.0013	.0013	.0012	.0012	.0011	.0011	.0011	.0010	.0010
−2.9	.0019	.0018	.0018	.0017	.0016	.0016	.0015	.0015	.0014	.0014
−2.8	.0026	.0025	.0024	.0023	.0023	.0022	.0021	.0021	.0020	.0019
−2.7	.0035	.0034	.0033	.0032	.0031	.0030	.0029	.0028	.0027	.0026
−2.6	.0047	.0045	.0044	.0043	.0041	.0040	.0039	.0038	.0037	.0036
−2.5	.0062	.0060	.0059	.0057	.0055	.0054	.0052	.0051 *	.0049	.0048
−2.4	.0082	.0080	.0078	.0075	.0073	.0071	.0069	.0068	.0066	.0064
−2.3	.0107	.0104	.0102	.0099	.0096	.0094	.0091	.0089	.0087	.0084
−2.2	.0139	.0136	.0132	.0129	.0125	.0122	.0119	.0116	.0113	.0110
−2.1	.0179	.0174	.0170	.0166	.0162	.0158	.0154	.0150	.0146	.0143
−2.0	.0228	.0222	.0217	.0212	.0207	.0202	.0197	.0192	.0188	.0183
−1.9	.0287	.0281	.0274	.0268	.0262	.0256	.0250	.0244	.0239	.0233
−1.8	.0359	.0351	.0344	.0336	.0329	.0322	.0314	.0307	.0301	.0294
−1.7	.0446	.0436	.0427	.0418	.0409	.0401	.0392	.0384	.0375	.0367
−1.6	.0548	.0537	.0526	.0516	.0505 *	.0495	.0485	.0475	.0465	.0455
−1.5	.0668	.0655	.0643	.0630	.0618	.0606	.0594	.0582	.0571	.0559
−1.4	.0808	.0793	.0778	.0764	.0749	.0735	.0721	.0708	.0694	.0681
−1.3	.0968	.0951	.0934	.0918	.0901	.0885	.0869	.0853	.0838	.0823
−1.2	.1151	.1131	.1112	.1093	.1075	.1056	.1038	.1020	.1003	.0985
−1.1	.1357	.1335	.1314	.1292	.1271	.1251	.1230	.1210	.1190	.1170
−1.0	.1587	.1562	.1539	.1515	.1492	.1469	.1446	.1423	.1401	.1379
−0.9	.1841	.1814	.1788	.1762	.1736	.1711	.1685	.1660	.1635	.1611
−0.8	.2119	.2090	.2061	.2033	.2005	.1977	.1949	.1922	.1894	.1867
−0.7	.2420	.2389	.2358	.2327	.2296	.2266	.2236	.2206	.2177	.2148
−0.6	.2743	.2709	.2676	.2643	.2611	.2578	.2546	.2514	.2483	.2451
−0.5	.3085	.3050	.3015	.2981	.2946	.2912	.2877	.2843	.2810	.2776
−0.4	.3446	.3409	.3372	.3336	.3300	.3264	.3228	.3192	.3156	.3121
−0.3	.3821	.3783	.3745	.3707	.3669	.3632	.3594	.3557	.3520	.3483
−0.2	.4207	.4168	.4129	.4090	.4052	.4013	.3974	.3936	.3897	.3859
−0.1	.4602	.4562	.4522	.4483	.4443	.4404	.4364	.4325	.4286	.4247
−0.0	.5000	.4960	.4920	.4880	.4840	.4801	.4761	.4721	.4681	.4641

NOTE: For values of *z* below 3.49, use 0.0001 for the area.

*Use these common values that result from interpolation:

z Score	Area
−1.645	0.0500
−2.575	0.0050

(*continued*)

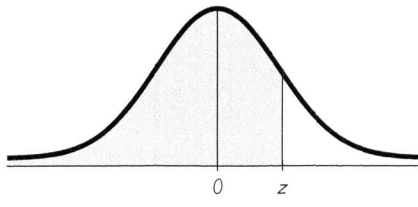

POSITIVE z Scores

Table A-2 *(continued)* Cumulative Area from the LEFT

z	.00	.01	.02	.03	.04	.05	.06	.07	.08	.09
0.0	.5000	.5040	.5080	.5120	.5160	.5199	.5239	.5279	.5319	.5359
0.1	.5398	.5438	.5478	.5517	.5557	.5596	.5636	.5675	.5714	.5753
0.2	.5793	.5832	.5871	.5910	.5948	.5987	.6026	.6064	.6103	.6141
0.3	.6179	.6217	.6255	.6293	.6331	.6368	.6406	.6443	.6480	.6517
0.4	.6554	.6591	.6628	.6664	.6700	.6736	.6772	.6808	.6844	.6879
0.5	.6915	.6950	.6985	.7019	.7054	.7088	.7123	.7157	.7190	.7224
0.6	.7257	.7291	.7324	.7357	.7389	.7422	.7454	.7486	.7517	.7549
0.7	.7580	.7611	.7642	.7673	.7704	.7734	.7764	.7794	.7823	.7852
0.8	.7881	.7910	.7939	.7967	.7995	.8023	.8051	.8078	.8106	.8133
0.9	.8159	.8186	.8212	.8238	.8264	.8289	.8315	.8340	.8365	.8389
1.0	.8413	.8438	.8461	.8485	.8508	.8531	.8554	.8577	.8599	.8621
1.1	.8643	.8665	.8686	.8708	.8729	.8749	.8770	.8790	.8810	.8830
1.2	.8849	.8869	.8888	.8907	.8925	.8944	.8962	.8980	.8997	.9015
1.3	.9032	.9049	.9066	.9082	.9099	.9115	.9131	.9147	.9162	.9177
1.4	.9192	.9207	.9222	.9236	.9251	.9265	.9279	.9292	.9306	.9319
1.5	.9332	.9345	.9357	.9370	.9382	.9394	.9406	.9418	.9429	.9441
1.6	.9452	.9463	.9474	.9484	.9495 *	.9505	.9515	.9525	.9535	.9545
1.7	.9554	.9564	.9573	.9582	.9591	.9599	.9608	.9616	.9625	.9633
1.8	.9641	.9649	.9656	.9664	.9671	.9678	.9686	.9693	.9699	.9706
1.9	.9713	.9719	.9726	.9732	.9738	.9744	.9750	.9756	.9761	.9767
2.0	.9772	.9778	.9783	.9788	.9793	.9798	.9803	.9808	.9812	.9817
2.1	.9821	.9826	.9830	.9834	.9838	.9842	.9846	.9850	.9854	.9857
2.2	.9861	.9864	.9868	.9871	.9875	.9878	.9881	.9884	.9887	.9890
2.3	.9893	.9896	.9898	.9901	.9904	.9906	.9909	.9911	.9913	.9916
2.4	.9918	.9920	.9922	.9925	.9927	.9929	.9931	.9932	.9934	.9936
2.5	.9938	.9940	.9941	.9943	.9945	.9946	.9948	.9949 *	.9951	.9952
2.6	.9953	.9955	.9956	.9957	.9959	.9960	.9961	.9962	.9963	.9964
2.7	.9965	.9966	.9967	.9968	.9969	.9970	.9971	.9972	.9973	.9974
2.8	.9974	.9975	.9976	.9977	.9977	.9978	.9979	.9979	.9980	.9981
2.9	.9981	.9982	.9982	.9983	.9984	.9984	.9985	.9985	.9986	.9986
3.0	.9987	.9987	.9987	.9988	.9988	.9989	.9989	.9989	.9990	.9990
3.1	.9990	.9991	.9991	.9991	.9992	.9992	.9992	.9992	.9993	.9993
3.2	.9993	.9993	.9994	.9994	.9994	.9994	.9994	.9995	.9995	.9995
3.3	.9995	.9995	.9995	.9996	.9996	.9996	.9996	.9996	.9996	.9997
3.4	.9997	.9997	.9997	.9997	.9997	.9997	.9997	.9997	.9997	.9998
3.50 and up	.9999									

NOTE: For values of z above 3.49, use 0.9999 for the area.
*Use these common values that result from interpolation:

z Score	Area
1.645	0.9500
2.575	0.9950

Common Critical Values

Confidence Level	Critical Value
0.90	1.645
0.95	1.96
0.99	2.575